THE OXFORD HANDBOOK OF
ANCIENT IRAN

THE OXFORD HANDBOOK OF
ANCIENT IRAN

Edited by
D. T. POTTS

OXFORD
UNIVERSITY PRESS

OXFORD
UNIVERSITY PRESS

Oxford University Press is a department of the University of Oxford.
It furthers the University's objective of excellence in research, scholarship,
and education by publishing worldwide.

Oxford   New York
Auckland   Cape Town   Dar es Salaam   Hong Kong   Karachi
Kuala Lumpur   Madrid   Melbourne   Mexico City   Nairobi
New Delhi   Shanghai   Taipei   Toronto

With offices in
Argentina   Austria   Brazil   Chile   Czech Republic   France   Greece
Guatemala   Hungary   Italy   Japan   Poland   Portugal   Singapore
South Korea   Switzerland   Thailand   Turkey   Ukraine   Vietnam

Oxford is a registered trademark of Oxford University Press in the UK and certain other
countries.

Published in the United States of America by
Oxford University Press
198 Madison Avenue, New York, NY 10016

© Oxford University Press 2013

First issued as an Oxford University Press Paperback 2017

All rights reserved. No part of this publication may be reproduced, stored in a
retrieval system, or transmitted, in any form or by any means, without the prior
permission in writing of Oxford University Press, or as expressly permitted by law,
by license, or under terms agreed with the appropriate reproduction rights organization.
Inquiries concerning reproduction outside the scope of the above should be sent to the Rights
Department, Oxford University Press, at the address above.

You must not circulate this work in any other form
and you must impose this same condition on any acquirer.

Library of Congress Cataloging-in-Publication Data

The Oxford handbook of ancient Iran / edited by D. T. Potts.
p. cm.
Includes bibliographical references and index.
ISBN 978-0-19-973330-9 (alk. paper); 978-0-19-066866-2 (Pbk.)
1. Iran–Civilization–To 640.   I. Potts, Daniel T.   II. Title: The Oxford Handbook of Ancient Iran.
DS266.O94 2013
935'.7–dc23
2012034686

Contents

List of Maps	*x*
Contributors	*xi*
Acknowledgments	*xv*
Abbreviations	*xvii*
Introduction	*xxvii*

PART I BACKGROUND AND BEGINNINGS

1. The history of archaeological research in Iran: A brief survey   3
   ALI MOUSAVI

2. Key questions regarding the paleoenvironment of Iran   17
   MATTHEW D. JONES

3. The Paleolithic of Iran   29
   NICHOLAS J. CONARD, ELHAM GHASIDIAN, AND SAMAN HEYDARI-GURAN

4. The development and expansion of a Neolithic way of life   49
   LLOYD R. WEEKS

PART II THE CHALCOLITHIC PERIOD

5. The Chalcolithic of northern Iran   79
   BARBARA HELWING

6. The Chalcolithic in the Central Zagros   93
   ABBAS MOGHADDAM AND ARDASHIR JAVANMARDZADEH

7. The Later Village (Chalcolithic) period in Khuzestan   105
   ABBAS MOGHADDAM

8. The Chalcolithic in southern Iran   120
   CAMERON A. PETRIE

PART III THE BRONZE AGE

9. The Early Bronze Age in northwestern Iran — 161
   GEOFFREY D. SUMMERS

10. The Bronze Age in northeastern Iran — 179
    CHRISTOPHER P. THORNTON

11. Luristan and the central Zagros in the Bronze Age — 203
    D. T. POTTS

12. Khuzestan in the Bronze Age — 217
    JAVIER ÁLVAREZ-MON

13. Early writing in Iran — 233
    JACOB L. DAHL

14. The use of Akkadian in Iran — 263
    KATRIEN DE GRAEF

15. Bronze Age Fars — 283
    BERNADETTE McCALL

16. Eastern Iran in the Early Bronze Age — 304
    HOLLY PITTMAN

PART IV THE IRON AGE

17. The Late Bronze and Early Iron Age in northwestern Iran — 327
    MICHAEL D. DANTI

18. Luristan during the Iron Age — 377
    BRUNO OVERLAET

19. The central Alborz region in the Iron Age — 392
    ALI MOUSAVI

20. Linguistic groups in Iran — 407
    RAN ZADOK

21. Iranian migration — 423
    MICHAEL WITZEL

22. Assyria and the Medes 442
    KAREN RADNER

23. Elam in the Iron Age 457
    JAVIER ÁLVAREZ-MON

24. Elam, Assyria, and Babylonia in the early first
    millennium BC 478
    MATTHEW WATERS

25. Iron Age southeastern Iran 493
    PETER MAGEE

PART V THE ACHAEMENID PERIOD

26. Southwestern Iran in the Achaemenid period 503
    RÉMY BOUCHARLAT

27. Administrative realities: The Persepolis
    Archives and the archaeology of the
    Achaemenid heartland 528
    WOUTER F. M. HENKELMAN

28. *Avesta* and Zoroastrianism under the Achaemenids
    and early Sasanians 547
    PRODS OKTOR SKJÆRVØ

29. Royal Achaemenid iconography 566
    MARK B. GARRISON

30. Color and gilding in Achaemenid architecture
    and sculpture 596
    ALEXANDER NAGEL

31. Eastern Iran in the Achaemenid period 622
    BRUNO GENITO

32. Old Persian 638
    JAN TAVERNIER

33. Greek sources on Achaemenid Iran 658
    MARIA BROSIUS

PART VI SELEUCID, POST-ACHAEMENID, AND ARSACID ARCHAEOLOGY AND HISTORY

34. Alexander the Great and the Seleucids in Iran 671
    PAUL J. KOSMIN

35. Media, Khuzestan, and Fars between the end of the Achaemenids and the rise of the Sasanians 690
    PIERFRANCESCO CALLIERI AND ALIREZA ASKARI CHAVERDI

36. *Fratarakā* and Seleucids 718
    JOSEF WIESEHÖFER

37. The Arsacids (Parthians) 728
    STEFAN R. HAUSER

38. Parthian and Elymaean rock reliefs 751
    TRUDY S. KAWAMI

39. Arsacid, Elymaean, and Persid coinage 766
    KHODADAD REZAKHANI

40. Aramaic, Parthian, and Middle Persian 779
    SEIRO HARUTA

41. The use of Greek in pre-Sasanian Iran 795
    GEORGES ROUGEMONT

PART VII THE SASANIAN PERIOD

42. Sasanian political ideology 805
    M. RAHIM SHAYEGAN

43. Sasanian coinage 814
    NIKOLAUS SCHINDEL

44. Sasanian interactions with Rome and Byzantium 840
    PETER EDWELL

45. Sasanian rock reliefs 856
    MATTHEW P. CANEPA

46. Kuh-e Khwaja and the religious architecture of Sasanian Iran   878
    SOROOR GHANIMATI

47. Sasanian administation and sealing practices   909
    NEGIN MIRI

48. Luxury silver vessels of the Sasanian period   920
    KATE MASIA-RADFORD

49. Sasanian textiles   943
    CAROL BIER

50. Pre-Islamic Iranian calendrical systems in the
    context of Iranian religious and scientific history   953
    ANTONIO C. D. PANAINO

51. The Islamic conquest of Sasanian Iran   975
    MICHAEL G. MORONY

Index   987

List of Maps

MAP 1 Map of Iran, showing principal modern towns and physical features mentioned in the text — xxxi

MAP 2 Map of western Iran showing early sites mentioned in the text (prehistoric–Iron Age) — xxxii

MAP 3 Map of eastern Iran showing early sites mentioned in the text (prehistoric–Iron Age) — xxxiii

MAP 4 Map of western Iran showing late sites mentioned in the text (Achaemenid–Sasanian) — xxxiv

MAP 5 Map of eastern Iran showing late sites mentioned in the text (Achaemenid–Sasanian) — xxxv

MAP 6 Map of Luristan and Khuzestan showing early sites mentioned in the text (prehistoric–Iron Age) — xxxvi

MAP 7 Map of Fars showing early sites mentioned in the text (prehistoric–Iron Age) — xxxvii

MAP 8 Map of Fars showing late sites mentioned in the text (Achaemenid–Sasanian) — xxxviii

MAP 9 Map of Khuzestan showing late sites mentioned in the text (Achaemenid–Sasanian) — xxxix

Contributors

Javier Álvarez-Mon is an Associate Professor at Macquarie University (Australia).

Alireza Askari Chaverdi is an Assistant Professor at Shiraz University (Iran).

Carol Bier is a Research Associate at the Textile Museum (USA).

Rémy Boucharlat is an Emeritus Senior Researcher in the Centre National de la Recherche Scientifique (CNRS) at the University of Lyon (France).

Maria Brosius is an Associate Professor at the University of Toronto (Canada).

Pierfrancesco Callieri is the Professor of the Archaeology of Ancient Iran at the University of Bologna (Italy).

Matthew P. Canepa is an Associate Professor of Art and Archaeology at the University of Minnesota (USA).

Nicholas J. Conard is the Professor of Early Prehistory at the Eberhard-Karls University in Tübingen (Germany).

Jacob L. Dahl is the University Lecturer in Assyriology at the University of Oxford (UK).

Michael D. Danti is Academic Director of the American Schools of Oriental Research Cultural Heritage Initiative and Consulting Scholar at the University of Pennsylvania Museum of Archaeology and Anthropology.

Katrien De Graef is a Lecturer in Assyriology and History of the Ancient Near East at Ghent University (Belgium).

Peter Edwell is a Lecturer in Ancient History at Macquarie University (Australia).

Mark B. Garrison is the Alice Pratt Brown Distinguished Professor in Art History at Trinity University (USA).

Bruno Genito is the Professor of the Archaeology and Art of the Ancient Near East at the University of Naples "L'Orientale" (Italy).

Soroor Ghanimati is a Research Fellow at the University of California at Berkeley, lecturer at the University of California at Merced (USA), and cultural consultant for the UNESCO Cluster Offices in Tehran (Iran).

Elham Ghasidian is a Post-Doctoral Research Fellow at the Eberhard-Karls University of Tübingen (Germany).

Seiro Haruta is Professor at Tokai University (Japan).

Stefan R. Hauser is Professor of the Archaeology of ancient Mediterranean cultures and their relations to the Ancient Near East and Egypt at the University of Konstanz (Germany).

Barbara Helwing is Edwin Cuthbert Hall Professor in Middle Eastern Archaeology at the University of Sydney (Australia).

Wouter F. M. Henkelman is 'Maître de conférences at the École Pratique des Hautes Études (France).

Saman Heydari-Guran is Wissenschaftlicher Mitarbeiter at the Eberhard-Karls University of Tübingen (Germany).

Ardashir Javanmardzadeh is Assistant Professor of Archaeology at the University of Mohaghegh Ardabili (Iran).

Matthew D. Jones is an Associate Professor in Quaternary Science at the University of Nottingham (UK).

Trudy S. Kawami is Director of Research at the Arthur M. Sackler Foundation in New York (USA).

Paul J. Kosmin is Assistant Professor of Ancient History at Harvard University (USA).

Peter Magee is Professor of Archaeology at Bryn Mawr College (USA).

Bernadette McCall is Classics and Ancient History Research Administrator at the University of Sydney (Australia).

Negin Miri is an Assistant Professor at Shahid Beheshti University (Iran).

Abbas Moghaddam works for the Iranian Center for Archaeological Research in Tehran (Iran).

Michael G. Morony is a Professor of History at UCLA (USA).

Ali Mousavi is Lecturer in Iranian Archaeology at UCLA (USA).

Alexander Nagel is the Assistant Curator of the Ancient Near East in the Freer|Sackler Galleries (USA).

Bruno Overlaet is the Curator of the Iranian collection of the Royal Museums of Art and History, Brussels (Belgium).

Antonio C. D. Panaino is a Professor of Iranian Studies at the University of Bologna (Italy).

Cameron A. Petrie is Senior Lecturer in South Asian and Iranian archaeology at the University of Cambridge (UK).

Holly Pittman is the Bok Family Professor in the Humanities at the University of Pennsylvania (USA).

D. T. Potts is the Professor of Ancient Near Eastern Archaeology and History at the Institute for the Study of the Ancient World, New York University (USA).

Kate Masia-Radford is an independent scholar in Sydney (Australia).

Karen Radner is the Alexander von Humboldt Professor of Ancient History at the Ludwig-Maximilians-University (Germany).

Khodadad Rezakhani is a post-doctoral researcher at the Max Planck Institute for the History of Science and a Humboldt Fellow at the Free University of Berlin (Germany).

Georges Rougemont is Emeritus Professor of History and Greek Epigraphy at the University of Lyon II (France).

Nikolaus Schindel is a Researcher at the Numismatic Commission of the Austrian Academy of Sciences in Vienna (Austria).

M. Rahim Shayegan is a Jahangir and Eleanor Amuzegar Chair of Iranian at UCLA (USA).

Prods Oktor Skjærvø is Aga Khan Professor of Iranian Emeritus at Harvard (USA).

Geoffrey D. Summers is a Research Associate at the Oriental Institute, University of Chicago (USA).

Jan Tavernier is a Professor of Assyriology at the Catholic University of Louvain (Belgium).

Christopher P. Thornton is Lead Program Officer at the National Geographic Society (USA).

Matthew Waters is a Professor of Classics and Ancient History at the University of Wisconsin–Eau Claire (USA).

Lloyd R. Weeks is Professor and Head of School at the University of New England (Australia).

Josef Wiesehöfer is a Professor of Ancient History at the Christian-Albrechts University in Kiel (Germany).

Michael Witzel is the Wales Professor of Sanskrit at Harvard University (USA).

Ran Zadok is the Professor of Mesopotamian, Iranian, and Judaic Studies Emeritus at Tel Aviv University (Israel).

Acknowledgments

On the editorial side, I would like to thank Stefan Vranka at Oxford University Press (New York) for taking on this project; Sarah Pirovitz, the assistant editor, for her help with innumerable queries; Michael Durnin, for his meticulous copyediting; and of course the authors, who have given a great deal of their time and effort to produce what I hope will prove to be a useful volume for those who already know something about Iranian archaeology and history, and an even more useful volume for those who don't. For the second time I have been able to collaborate with Dr. Thomas Urban of Dr. Th. Urban & Partner Denkmaldokumentation und Archäologie (Germany), who is responsible for the introductory set of nine maps showing the locations of the sites mentioned in the text, and I would like to thank him warmly for his outstanding work to a tight deadline. Dr. Kate Masia-Radford, a former student of mine and author of the chapter on Sasanian silver vessels (Chapter 48), assisted me with the initial copyediting of some of the chapters published here, for which I would like to express my sincere thanks. Prof. Rahim Shayegan (UCLA) deserves my sincerest thanks for kindly advising me on the orthography to use for the names of Sasanian royalty.

Finally, it may seem like a small gesture, but I would like to dedicate this book to my family—Hildy, Hallam, Morgan, and Rowena—who bore with me throughout its gestation.

Abbreviations

AA	*Archäologischer Anzeiger*
AAASH	*Acta Antiqua Academiae Scientiarum Hungaricae*
AACA	*After Alexander: Central Asia before Islam*, ed. J. Cribb and G. Herrmann. Oxford and New York: Proceedings of the British Academy 133, 2007.
AAE	*Arabian Archaeology and Epigraphy*
AAIAC	*Aryas, Aryens, et Iraniens en Asie Centrale*, G. Fussman, J. Kellens, H.-P. Francfort, and X. Tremblay. Paris: de Boccard, 2005.
AASFC	*Ancient Art from the Shumei Family Collection*, ed. D. Arnold. New York: Metropolitan Museum of Art, 1996.
AchHist	Achaemenid History (Leiden)
ACSS	*Ancient Civilizations from Scythia to Siberia*
AEA	*L'archéologie de l'Empire achéménide, nouvelles recherches*, ed. P. Briant and R. Boucharlat. Paris: Persika 6, 2005.
AfO	*Archiv für Orientforschung*
AFP	*L'Archive des Fortifications de Persépolis: État des questions et perspectives de recherches*, ed. P. Briant, W. F. M. Henkelman, and M. W. Stolper. Paris: Persika 12, 2008.
AIN	*Ancient Iran and its neighbors: Local developments and long-range interactions in the 4th millennium BC*, ed. C. A. Petrie. Oxford: British Institute of Persian Studies Archaeological Monographs Series, 2013.
AINX	*Archaeological investigations in northeastern Xuzestan*, ed. H. T. Wright. Ann Arbor: Technical Reports 10, Research Reports in Archaeology 5, 1979.
AIO	*Archaeologia Iranica et Orientalis: Miscellanea in honorem Louis Vanden Berghe*, ed. L. De Meyer and E. Haerinck. Gent: Peeters, 1989.
AIT	Archäologie in Iran und Turan (Berlin)
AION	*Annali dell'Istituto Universitario Orientale di Napoli*
AJ	*Antiquaries Journal*
AJA	*American Journal of Archaeology*
AJSL	*American Journal of Semitic Languages and Literature*
AMI(T)	*Archäologische Mitteilungen aus Iran (und Turan)*
AMMD	*The archaeological map of the Murghab Delta: Preliminary reports 1990–95*, ed. A. Gubaev, G. Koshelenko, and M. Tosi. Rome: IsIAO Reports and Memoirs Series Minor 3, 1998.
ANES	*Ancient Near Eastern Studies*
AnSt	*Anatolian Studies*

AOASH	*Acta Orientalia Academiae Scientiarum Hungaricae*
AOAT	Alter Orient und Altes Testament (Münster)
AoF	*Altorientalische Forschungen*
AOS	American Oriental Series
APP	*A Persian Perspective: Essays in Memory of Heleen Sancisi-Weerdenburg*, ed. W. H. M. Henkelman and A. Kuhrt. Leiden: Nederlands Instituut voor het Nabije Oosten, 2003.
ARTA	*Achaemenid Research on Texts and Archaeology*
A²S	Artaxerxes II, inscription at Susa
AS	Assyriological Studies
ASJ	*Acta Sumerologica* (Japan)
ASPR	American School of Prehistoric Research
Av.	Avestan
AVH	*A view from the highlands: Studies in honor of Charles Burney*, ed. Antonio Sagona. Leuven: Peeters, 2004.
AWE	*Ancient West & East*
AWI	*The archaeology of western Iran: Settlement and society from prehistory to the Islamic conquest*, ed. F. Hole. Washington, DC: Smithsonian Series in Archaeological Inquiry, 1987.
BAI	*Bulletin of the Asia Institute*
BaM	*Baghdader Mitteilungen*
BAMI	Belgian Archaeological Mission to Iran
BAR Int Ser	British Archaeological Reports, International Series
BASOR	*Bulletin of the American Schools of Oriental Research*
BAuA	*Bastam: Ausgrabungen in den urartäischen Anlagen*, ed. W. Kleiss. Berlin: Tehraner Forschungen 4–5, 1979.
BBVO	Berliner Beiträge zum Vorderen Orient
BCHP	Babylonian Chronicles of the Hellenistic Period, http://www.livius.org/babylonia.html
BCMA	*Bulletin of the Cleveland Museum of Art*
BIAAM	British Institute of Archaeology at Ankara Monograph
BICS	*Bulletin of the Institute of Classical Studies*
BiOr	*Bibliotheca Orientalis*
BIWA	*Beiträge zur Inschriftenwerk Assurbanipals: Die Prismenklassen A, B, C = K, D, E, F, G, H, J und T sowie andere Inschriften*, ed. R. Borger. Wiesbaden: Harrassowitz, 1996.
BSO[A]S	*Bulletin of the School of Oriental (and African) Studies*
BTU	*Beyond the Ubaid: Transformation and integration in the late prehistoric societies of the Middle East*, ed. R. A. Carter and G. Philip. Chicago: SAOC 63, 2010.
BU	*Biainili-Urartu*, ed. S. Kroll, C. Gruber, U. Hellwag, M. Roaf, and P. Zimansky. Leuven: Acta Iranica 51, 2011.
CA	*Current Anthropology*

CAD	*The Assyrian Dictionary of the Oriental Institute of the University of Chicago*
CAH	*Cambridge Ancient History*
CAJ	*Cambridge Archaeological Journal*
CDAFI	*Cahiers de la Délégation archéologique française en Iran*
CDLB	*Cuneiform Digital Library Bulletin* (online)
CDLJ	*Cuneiform Digital Library Journal* (online)
CDLN	*Cuneiform Digital Library Notes* (online)
CDR	*Cinquante-deux reflexions sur le Proche-Orient ancien offertes en homage à Léon De Meyer*, ed. H. Gasche, M. Tanret, C. Jansen, and A. Degraeve. Gent: Peeters, 1994.
CE	*Continuity of empire (?): Assyria, Media, Persia*, ed. G. B. Lanfranchi, M. Roaf, and R. Rollinger. Padua: HANEM 5, 2003.
CHI	*Cambridge History of Iran*
CII	Corpus Inscriptionum Iranicarum
CKA	*Concepts of Kingship in Antiquity. Proceedings of the European Science Foundation Exploratory Workshop Held in Padova, November 28–December 1, 2007*, ed. G. B. Lanfranchi and R. Rollinger. Padua: HANEM 11, 2010.
CLeO	Classica et Orientalia
CNIP	Carsten Niebuhr Institute Publications
CO	*Collectanea Orientalia: Histoire, arts de l'espace et industrie de la terre. Études offertes en hommage à Agnès Spycket*, ed. H. Gasche and B. Hrouda. Neuchâtel/Paris: Civilisations du Proche-Orient Série 1, Archéologie et environnement 3, 1996.
CP	*Classical Philology*
CRAIBL	*Comptes-rendus de l'Académie des inscriptions et belles-lettres*
CTN	Cuneiform texts from Nimrud
CTU	M. Salvini, *Corpus dei Testi Urartei*, vol. 1. Roma: Documenta Asiana 8/1, 2008.
DA	*Dossiers d'Archéologie*
DB	Darius, inscription at Bisotun
DN	Darius, inscription at Naqsh-e Rustam
DOP	*Dumbarton Oaks Papers*
DP	Darius, inscription at Persepolis
DS	Darius, inscription at Susa
EAC	*Extraction and control: Studies in honor of Matthew W. Stolper*, ed. M. Kozuh, W.F.M. Henkelman, C.E. Jones and C. Woods. Chicago: SAOC 68, 2014.
EAH	Entretiens d'Archéologie et d'Histoire
EASDLP	*Elamite and Achaemenid settlement on the Deh Luran Plain*, ed. H. T. Wright and J. A. Neely. Ann Arbor: Memoirs of the Museum of Anthropology 47, 2010.

EKI	F. W. König, *Die elamischen Königsinschriften*. Graz: *AfO* Beiheft, 1965.
EMM	*Early mining and metallurgy on the western central Iranian plateau: Report on the first five years of research of the Joint Iranian-German research project*, ed. A. Vatandoust, H. Parzinger, and B. Helwing. Mainz: AIT 9, 2011.
EnIr	*Encyclopaedia Iranica*
EP	*Elam and Persia*, ed. J. Álvarez-Mon and M. B. Garrison. Winona Lake: Eisenbrauns, 2011.
ETDLP	*An early town on the Deh Luran plain: Excavations at Tepe Farukhabad*, ed. H. T. Wright. Ann Arbor: Memoirs of the Museum of Anthropology 13, 1981.
EW	*East and West*
FAOS	Freiburger Altorientalischen Studien
FGrH	*Die Fragmente der griechischen Historiker*, ed. F. Jacoby. Leiden: Brill, 2005.
FHE	*Fragmenta historiae elamicae: Mélanges offertes à M.-J. Steve*, ed. L. De Meyer, H. Gasche and F. Vallat. Paris: Éditions Recherche sur les Civilisations, 1986.
FHK	*From handaxe to khan: Essays presented to Peder Mortensen on the occasion of his 70th birthday*, ed. K. Folsach, H. Thrane, and I. Thuesen. Aarhus: Aarhus University Press, 2004.
GB	*Gozāreshhāy-e Bāstānshenāsi/Archaeological Reports*
GJ	*Geographical Journal*
HANEM	History of the Ancient Near East Monographs
HCCA 1	*History of civilizations of Central Asia. Vol. 1. The dawn of civilization: earliest times to 700 B.C.*, A. H. Dani and V. M. Masson. Paris: UNESCO, 1992.
HdO	Handbuch der Orientalistik
HEL	*The Holmes Expeditions to Luristan*, 2 vols., ed. E. F. Schmidt, M. N. van Loon, and H. H. Curvers. Chicago: OIP 108, 1989.
HSAO	Heidelberger Studien zum Alten Orient
ICAR	Iranian Center for Archaeological Research
ICH(T)O	Iranian Cultural Heritage (and Tourism) Organization
IEJ	*Israel Exploration Journal*
IEO	*Iscrizioni dello Estremo Oriente greco*, F. Canali di Rossi. Bonn: Inschriften griechischer Städte aus Kleinasien 65, 2004.
IGIAC	*Inscriptions grecques d'Iran et d'Asie centrale*, G. Rougemont, with contributions by P. Bernard. London: CII 2/1/1, 2012.
IILP	*Indo-Iranian Languages and Peoples*, ed. N. Sims-Williams. Oxford: Oxford University Press, 2002.
IJAH	*Iranian Journal of Archaeology and History*
ILN	*Illustrated London News*
IP	*Iran Palaeolithic/Le Paléolithique d'Iran: Proceedings of the XV World Congress UISSP, Lisbon, September 4–9, 2006*, ed. M. Otte, F. Biglari, and J. Jaubert. Oxford: BAR Int Ser 1968, 2009.

IrAnt	*Iranica Antiqua*
Ir.Bd.	Iranian or Great(er) *Bundahišn*
IRSA	*Inscriptions Royales sumériennes et akkadiennes*, E. Sollberger and J.-R. Kupper. Paris: Éditions du Cerf, 1971.
IrSt	*Iranian Studies*
IsIAO	Istituto Italiano per l'Africa e l'Oriente
IsMEO	Istituto per il Medio ed Estremo Oriente
IW	*The Iranian world: Essays on Iranian art and archaeology presented to Ezat O. Negahban*, ed. A Alizadeh, Y. Majidzadeh, and S. M. Shahmirzadi. Tehran: Iran University Press, 1999.
JA	*Journal Asiatique*
JAOS	*Journal of the American Oriental Society*
JAS	*Journal of Archaeological Science*
JCS	*Journal of Cuneiform Studies*
JEOL	*Jaarbericht "Ex Oriente Lux"*
JESHO	*Journal of the Economic and Social History of the Orient*
JFA	*Journal of Field Archaeology*
JHS	*Journal of Hellenic Studies*
JIAAA	*Journal of Inner Asian Art and Archaeology*
JNES	*Journal of Near Eastern Studies*
JRAS	*Journal of the Royal Asiatic Society*
JRGS	*Journal of the Royal Geographical Society*
JSAI	*Jerusalem Studies in Arabic and Islam*
JWP	*Journal of World Prehistory*
ka	kiloannum (1000 years before present)
KKZ	trilingual inscription of Kartir (Kerdir) on the Ka'ba-ye Zardosht at Naqsh-e Rustam
KMKG-MRAH	Musées royaux d'art et d'histoire (Brussels)
LED	Luristan Excavation Documents
LNV	*Litterae Numismaticae Vindobonenses*
LPII	*The literature of pre-Islamic Iran*, ed. R. E. Emmerick and M. Macuch. London: I. B. Tauris, 2009.
MAPSO	*The Mamasani Archaeological Project Stage One: A report on the first two seasons of the ICAR—University of Sydney Expedition to the Mamasani District, Fars Province, Iran*, ed. D. T. Potts, K. Roustaei, C. A. Petrie, and L. R. Weeks. Oxford: BAR Int Ser 2044, 2009.
masl	meters above sea level
MASP	*Materialien zur Archäologie der Seleukiden- und Partherzeit im südlichen Babylonien und im Golfgebiet*, ed. U. Finkbeiner. Tübingen: Wasmuth, 1993.
MDAFA	Mémoires de la Délégation archéologique Française en Afghanistan
MDAI	Mémoires de la Délégation archéologique en Iran
MDP	Mémoires de la Délégation en Perse

ME	*Mésopotamie et Elam,* ed. L. De Meyer and H. Gasche. Gent: MHE Occasional Publications 1, 1991.
ME	Middle Elamite
MHE	Mesopotamian History and Environment
MJP	*Contribution à l'histoire de l'Iran ancien, mélanges offerts à Jean Perrot,* ed. F. Vallat. Paris: Éditions Recherche sur les Civilisations, 1990.
ML	*Mountains and lowlands: Essays in the archaeology of greater Mesopotamia,* ed. L. D. Levine and T. C. Young Jr. Malibu: Bibliotheca Mesopotamica 7, 1977.
MLSR	*'My life is like a summer rose': Maurizio Tosi e l'Archeologia come modo di vivere. Papers in honour of Maurizio Tosi for his 70th birthday,* ed. C.C. Lamberg-Karlovsky and B Genito. Oxford: BAR Int Ser 2690, 2014.
MMAI	Mémoires de la Mission archéologique en Iran
MMJ	*Metropolitan Museum Journal*
MP	Middle Persian
NABU	*Nouvelles Assyriologiques Brèves et Utilitaires*
N-AG	*Neo-Assyrian Geography,* ed. M. Liverani. Rome: Istituto di studi del Vicino Oriente, 1995.
NC	*Numismatic Chronicle*
NE	Neo-Elamite
NEA	*Near Eastern Archaeology*
NES	*Near Eastern Studies*
NP	New Persian
NTOA	Novum Testamentum et Orbis Antiquus/Studien zur Umwelt des Neuen Testaments
OBO	Orbis Biblicus et Orientalis
OE	Old Elamite
OEANE	*The Oxford encyclopedia of archaeology in the Near East*
OGIS	W. Dittenberger, *Orientis Graecae Inscriptiones Selectae.* Leipzig: S. Hirzel, 1903–5.
OHR	*On the high road: The history of Godin Tepe, Iran,* ed. H. Gopnik and M. S. Rothman. Costa Mesa: Mazda Publishers, 2011.
OIC	Oriental Institute Communications
OIP	Oriental Institute Publications
OLA	Orientalia Lovaniensia Analecta
OLZ	*Orientalistische Literaturzeitung*
OP	Old Persian
OPBF	Occasional Publications of the Babylonian Fund
Or	*Orientalia*
Pahl.	Pahlavi
PAP	*Persiens Antike Pracht: Bergbau, Handwerk, Archäologie,* ed. T. Stöllner, R. Slotta and A. Vatandoust. Bochum: Deutsches Bergbau Museum, 2004.
PAPS	*Proceedings of the American Philosophical Society*

Parth.	Parthian
PASARI	*Proceedings of the Annual Symposium on Archaeological Research in Iran*, ed. F. Bagherzadeh. Tehran: ICAR.
PBf	Prähistorische Bronzefunde
PCPIVB	*Peoples and crafts in Period IVB at Hasanlu Tepe, Iran*, ed. M. De Schauensee. Philadelphia: UMM 132 [= Hasanlu Special Studies 4], 2011.
PDS	*Le palais de Darius à Suse. Une résidence royale sur la route de Persépolis à Babylone*, ed. J. Perrot. Paris: Presses universitaires de Paris, 2010.
PF	siglum of Persepolis Fortification Tablets (1–2078) published in Hallock 1969
PFa	siglum of Persepolis Fortification Tablets (1–33) published in Hallock 1978
PFA	Persepolis Fortification archive
PFAT	Persepolis Fortification Aramaic tablets
PISIANR	*Proceedings of the International Symposium on Iranian Archaeology: Northwestern region*, ed. M. Azarnoush. Tehran: ICAR, 2004.
PM	*Préhistoire de la Mésopotamie*, ed. J.-L. Huot. Paris: Éditions du CNRS, 1987.
PNAS	*Proceedings of the National Academy of Sciences*
PPP	*Palaeogeography, Palaeoclimatology, Palaeoecology*
PPS	*Proceedings of the Prehistoric Society*
PPZT	*The Paleolithic prehistory of the Zagros-Taurus*, ed. D. Olszewski and H. Dibble. Philadelphia: University Museum Symposium Series 5, 1993.
PR	*Persian Responses: Political and Cultural Interaction with(in) the Achaemenid Empire*, ed. C. Tuplin. Swansea: Classical Press of Wales, 2007.
PSZ	*Das Partherreich und seine Zeugnisse*, ed. J. Wiesehöfer. Stuttgart: Historia-Einzelschriften 122, 1998.
PT	Persepolis Treasury Tablet
QGP	*Quellen zur Geschichte des Partherreiches*, 3 vols., ed. U. Hackl, B. Jacobs, and D. Weber. Göttingen: NTOA, 2010.
QR	*Quaternary Research*
QSR	*Quaternary Science Reviews*
RA	*Revue d'Assyriologie et d'Archéologie orientale*
RAE	Royal Achaemenid Elamite
RCS	*The royal city of Susa, Ancient Near Eastern treasures in the Louvre*, ed. P. O. Harper, J. Aruz, and F. Tallon. New York: Metropolitan Museum of Art, 1992.
RGTC	Répertoire géographique des textes cunéiformes
RIMA	Royal Inscriptions of Mesopotamia, Assyrian Periods
RIME	Royal Inscriptions of Mesopotamia, Early Periods
RINAP	Royal Inscriptions of the Neo-Assyrian Period

RlA	*Reallexikon der Assyriologie*
RN	royal name
RO	Res Orientales
ROMAAOP	Royal Ontario Museum Art and Archaeology Occasional Paper
SA	*Sovetskaja Arheologija*
SAA	State Archives of Assyria
SAAB	*State Archives of Assyria Bulletin*
SAAS	State Archives of Assyria Studies
SAOC	Studies in Ancient Oriental Civilization
SDB	*Supplément au Dictionnaire de la Bible*
SE	*Susa and Elam. Archaeological, Philological, Historical and Geographical Perspectives: Proceedings of the International Congress held at Ghent University, 14–17 Dec. 2009*, ed. K. De Graef and J. Tavernier. Leiden/Boston: Brill, 2013.
SEL	*Studi Epigrafici e Linguistici sul Vicino Oriente*
ŠKZ	trilingual inscription of Shapur I on the Kaʿba-ye Zardosht at Naqsh-e Rustam
SMEA	*Studi Micenei ed Egeo-Anatolici*
SNS	*Sylloge nummorum sasanidorum*
SPA	*A Survey of Persian Art*, ed. A. U. Pope. New York: Oxford University Press, 1938 (and later reprinted editions, with P. Ackerman).
SPH	*Studies in Persian history: Essays in memory of David M. Lewis*, ed. M. Brosius and A. Kuhrt. Leiden: AchHist 11, 1998.
SPO	Studi di Preistoria Orientale
SRAA	*Silk Road Art & Archaeology*
SRPR	Sialk Reconsideration Project Report
StIr	*Studia Iranica*
StOr/*StOr*	Studia Orientalia (unitalicized: monograph; italicized: multiauthor journal issue)
TAVO	Tübinger Atlas des Vorderen Orients
TCS	Texts from Cuneiform Sources
THRRP	*Tappeh Hesar: Reports of the restudy project, 1976*, ed. R. H. Dyson Jr. and S. M. Howard. Florence: Monografie di *Mesopotamia* 2, 1989.
TMO	Travaux de la Maison de l'Orient
TÜBA-AR	*Turkish Academy of Sciences Journal of Archaeology*
UMM	University Museum Monograph
UNHAII	Uitgaven van het Nederlands Historisch-Archaeologisch Instituut te Istanbul
VD	*Variatio Delectat: Iran und der Westen Gedenkschrift für Peter Calmeyer*, ed. R. Dittmann, B. Hrouda, U. Löw, P. Matthiae, R. Mayer-Opificius, and S. Thürwächter. Münster: AOAT 272, 2000.
VDI	*Vestnik Drevnej Istorii*
VHA	*Vegetation History and Archaeobotany*

WA	*World Archaeology*
WAP	*The world of Achaemenid Persia: History, art and society in Iran and the Ancient Near East*, ed. J. Curtis, and St. J. Simpson. London: I. B. Tauris, 2010.
XP	Xerxes, inscription at Persepolis
YBYN	*Yeki Bud, Yeki Nabud: Essays on the archaeology of Iran in honor of William M. Sumner*, ed. N. F. Miller and K. Abdi. Los Angeles: Cotsen Institute of Archaeology, 2003.
ZA	*Zeitschrift für Assyriologie*
ZDMG	*Zeitschrift der Deutschen Morgenländischen Gesellschaft*
ZOA	*Zeitschrift für Orient-Archäologie*

Introduction

Iran represents a cultural *massif* that, while never isolated from its neighbors, demands attention in its own right. The country's history and monuments have been objects of wonder throughout the ages, exuding an aura that can be as difficult to explain to the uninitiated as it is palpable to all who have fallen under their spell. Western students of Iranian history and archaeology are apt to trace the origins of this strong attachment to the sixteenth and seventeenth centuries, when many European travelers, merchants, clerics, and diplomats journeyed to Iran, visited Persepolis, and published etchings and descriptions of the site and its monuments that fired the imaginations of thousands of readers (Sancisi-Weerdenburg 1989). Yet it would be naïve to think that this fascination with Iran's antiquity was a construct of European antiquarianism stretching back in time to Herodotus. Long before any European set foot in the ruins of Persepolis or gazed in wonder at the rock reliefs and tombs of Naqsh-e Rustam, Sasanian, Buyid, and Timurid princes, as well as more than one provincial governor of Fars, had left visible signs of their visits to and regard for Persepolis. Moreover, nineteenth-century accounts of European visitors to Iran are replete with anecdotes showing an awareness by tribesmen, government officials, and other subjects of the Qajar Empire of the antiquity of many of the monuments that dotted the landscape, long before their documentation and study by Western archaeologists and historians.

This volume aims to expose readers to some of the diversity and complexity of the cultural, archaeological, and linguistic record of pre-Islamic Iran. Whereas the *Oxford handbook of Iranian history* (2012) is very explicitly aimed at presenting readers with concise overviews of major periods in Iranian history, the present *Handbook* seeks to complement narrative history with a different set of studies. These commence (Part I) with chapters dedicated to the history of archaeological research in Iran (Mousavi); its ancient climate and environment (Jones); and its early occupation during the Pleistocene (Conard, Ghasidian, and Heydari-Guran) and early Holocene era, when the basic building blocks of a herding and farming way of life were established (Weeks).

From there we move on to a series of chapters devoted to the beginnings of more complex social formations in Iran (Part II). Often referred to as the "Chalcolithic" or "Copper-Stone Age," the period between the era of early farming communities (Neolithic) and the emergence of true cities and social complexity (Bronze Age) is one in which many of the trends that we can follow in later prehistory find their first expression. Because of Iran's size and topographic diversity, different traditions of material culture—house forms, burial patterns, pottery styles, and so on—arose in different parts of the Iranian landmass. For this reason, it is traditional in archaeological scholarship to consider these regions individually, hence the division of this section into chapters on northern (Helwing), western (Moghaddam and Javanmardzadeh), southwestern (Moghaddam), and southern (Petrie) Iran. The same sort of geographical specificity marks the section on the Bronze Age (Part III), which includes chapters on northwestern (Summers), northeastern (Thornton), western (Potts), southwestern (Álvarez-Mon, McCall), and eastern (Pittman) Iran. The late Chalcolithic and Bronze Age witnessed the first extensive use of writing in Iran, and chapters are devoted to the earliest forms of writing, documented at Susa and half a dozen other sites across the Iranian plateau (Dahl), as well as the use of Akkadian, a Semitic language introduced from Mesopotamia that was extensively used at Susa (De Graef).

By the late second and early first millennia BC the quality and quantity of data available, both archaeological and epigraphic or linguistic, mean that additional issues invite consideration. The archaeological evidence from the different regions of Iran is still extremely important, and chapters devoted to the northwest (Danti), west (Overlaet), north (Mousavi), southwest (Álvarez-Mon), and southeast (Magee) reflect the availability of data from those regions, unlike the northeast which is poorly known (but better covered in this time period across the border in Turkmenistan). On the other hand, the involvement of western Iran in wider political and military conflicts during the early and mid-first millennium, particularly with the Assyrians (Radner, Waters), are topics of great complexity that yield insights of the sort unimaginable in studies of the earlier periods that simply lack a comparable number of sources. One by-product of the confrontation between the polities of western Iran and Assyria is the attestation of a great number of peoples and place names in cuneiform sources that can be attributed to Azerbaijan, Kurdistan, and Luristan, even if these can rarely be located with precision. The analysis of these names offers a window on the linguistic and, to some extent, ethnic make-up of the indigenous populations of those areas (Zadok). The same sources, moreover, contain etymologically Iranian names, raising the issue of when and whence the earliest Iranians reached the Iranian plateau (Witzel).

Quintessentially Iranian, the Achaemenid Persian dynasty that arose in the late sixth century BC is so rich in content that it demands a section of its own (Part V). Many studies of the Persian Empire review the political and military history in great detail but the emphasis here is on archaeological, iconographic, linguistic, and religious issues. The major sites of the Achaemenid heartland—Pasargadae, Persepolis, and Susa—are reviewed in detail (Boucharlat, Henkelman), as are the intricacies of royal Achaemenid iconography (Garrison). The evidence from the east Iranian satrapies (Genito) constitutes another large body of data that complements the traditional western focus in Achaemenid studies. The use of color on Achaemenid monuments has long been noted anecdotally but only recently has it been the object of intensive investigation (Nagel). The economic administration of the Persian heartland, as evidenced by the Persepolis Fortification archive, is highlighted (Henkelman), providing an important corpus of data that is entirely different than what we see in contemporary and later Greek sources (Brosius). The knotty problem of religion in the Achaemenid period, particularly Zoroastrianism, is another important topic (Skjærvø), while the cuneiform system devised for the Old Persian language spoken by the Achaemenid elite is also treated (Tavernier).

Alexander's conquest famously ushered in many important changes in the lands of the former Achaemenid Empire. For Iran itself much of the available archaeological and epigraphic evidence comes from the western and southwestern parts of the country (Callieri and Askari Chaverdi). The fate of Iran under Alexander's Seleucid successors was variable and is dealt with in two chapters (Kosmin, Wiesehöfer). But the loss of Seleucid control over Iran and the arrival of the Arsacids from Parthia, to the east of the Caspian, brought about even more changes for the population of Iran. The Arsacids are known from a variety of monuments and sites (Hauser), both inside and outside the modern boundaries of Iran. The Arsacids and their contemporaries in southwestern Iran left a number of important rock reliefs (Kawami) and minted a large number of coins (Rezakhani) that constitute an important field in numismatic research. Greek speakers and the Greek language continued to play an important role in the region, particularly in western Iran (Rougemont), but Parthian, Middle Persian, and Aramaic were used as well and a variety of epigraphic sources on coins, parchments, stone stelae, and rock reliefs have survived (Haruta).

For many observers of Iranian antiquity, the Sasanian Empire of late antiquity represents another high point, every bit as complex and important as the earlier Achaemenid Empire. Sasanian Iran is examined here through a number of different lenses. These include political ideology (Shayegan) and administration (Miri); calendrical systems (Panaino); and ongoing relations with Rome and Byzantium to the west (Edwell). The material culture of Sasanian Iran is varied and chapters included here treat rock reliefs (Canepa), coinage (Schindel), textiles (Bier), architecture (Ghanimati), and luxury silver vessels (Masia-Radford). The volume concludes with an analysis of the Islamic conquest of Sasanian Iran (Morony). Many more topics could have been included in this volume but the texts published here, and their extensive bibliographies, should serve most readers as a solid foundation from which to expand their reading and investigation of ancient Iran.

One of the perils of working in a field like Iranology is the difficult problem of orthography. There are multiple systems of transliteration and one could waste an inordinate amount of time trying to harmonize the spellings of all the toponyms, ethnonyms, and anthroponyms that appear in a book of this sort. I confess here that my approach has been inconsistent and probably unsatisfactory for those of a more philological bent. Archaeologists, in particular, become fond of spelling the names of sites in a certain way, and that way is normally not philologically correct. On the other hand, historians who are not Iranologists are often just as happy to write "Shapur" as "Šābuhr" when referring to Sasanian kings by that name. And some scholars who might take pains to insert all of the correct diacritics on personal names, such as those of rulers, are quite happy to abandon these and use conventional spellings for familiar toponyms. All of this adds up to a simple admission that there is inconsistency across the chapters in this volume, which, however, a few words of explanation may ameliorate. In those chapters concerning manly archaeological topics, I have not scrupulously replaced Tappeh with Tepe or vice versa, in the names of archaeological sites, but any multiplication of forms is flagged in the index to avoid confusion. Exceptions concern toponyms in some of the more historical chapters (e.g., Chapter 27) in which names are spelled more "correctly" with their diacritics. Similarly, in the chapters concerned with the Sasanian period (Chapters 42–51), the more correct forms of the names of the Sasanian kings are used—thus Ardašīr (not Ardashir), Šābuhr (not Shapur), Ōhrmazd (not Hormizd), Warahrān (not Bahram), Narseh, Pērōz, Kawād, Xosrow (not Khusro, Chosroes), Yazdgerd, Walāxš, Jāmāsp, Bōrānduxt, and Ādarmīgduxt—but the same rigor has not been applied to toponyms. It is hoped that this inconsistency will not prove a distraction for those who care. Imposing long vowel markers on all names and achieving orthographic consistency would have probably taken more time than the writing and editing of this book.

Sydney
June 2012

Reference

Sancisi-Weerdenburg, H. 1989. *Persepolis en Pasargadae in wisselend perspectief: Iraanse oudheden beschreven en getekend door Europese reizigers*. Leiden/Groningen: Vooraziatisch-Egyptisch genootschap "Ex Oriente Lux" and Universiteitsbibliotheek.

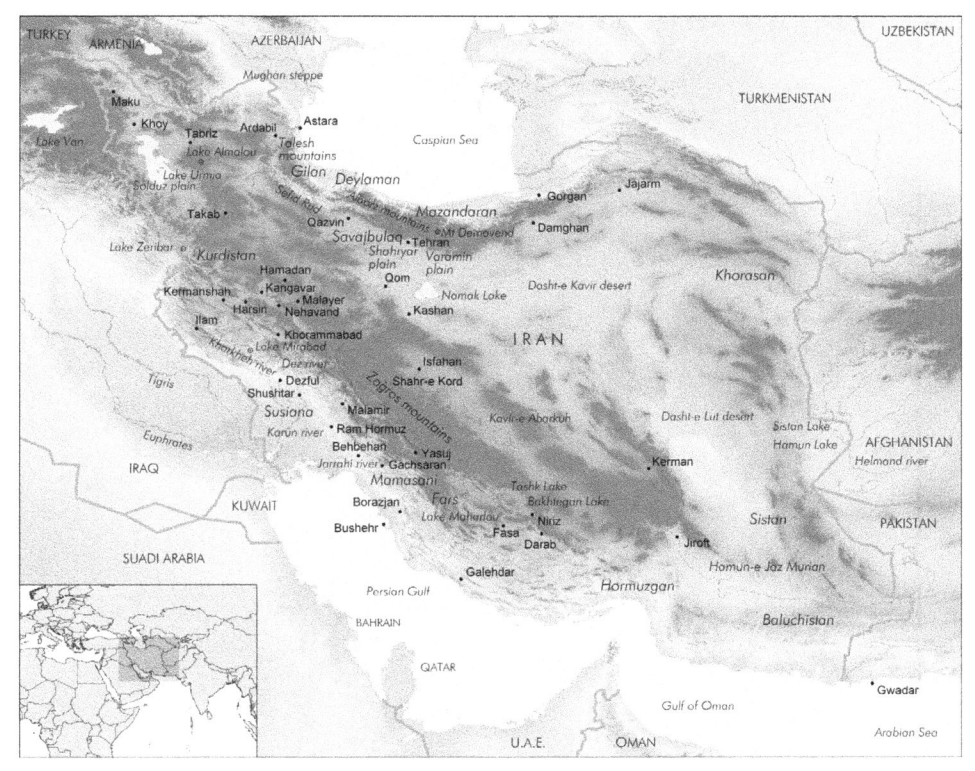

MAP 1 Map of Iran, showing principal modern towns and physical features mentioned in the text.

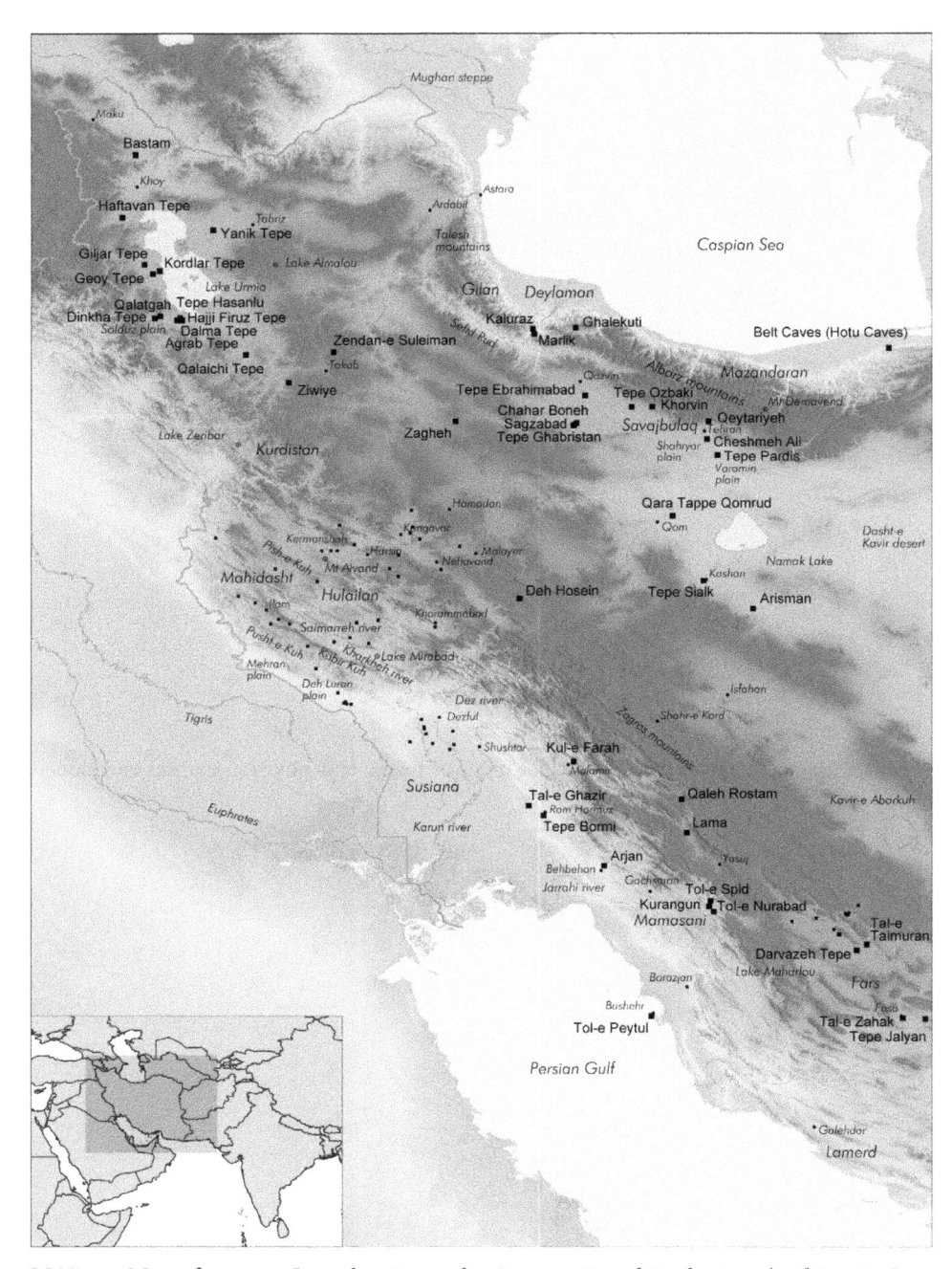

MAP 2 Map of western Iran showing early sites mentioned in the text (prehistoric–Iron Age).

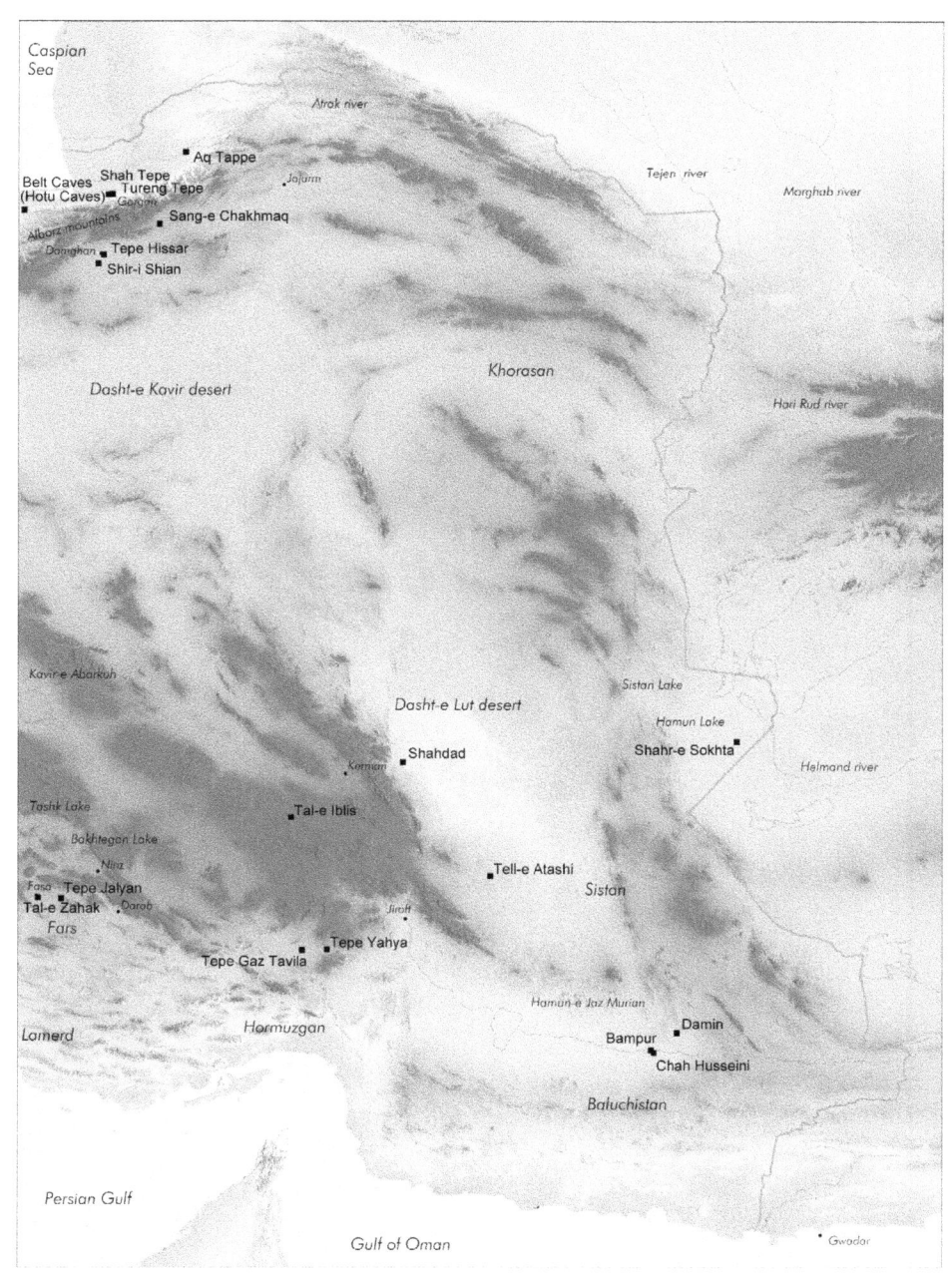

MAP 3 Map of eastern Iran showing early sites mentioned in the text (prehistoric–Iron Age).

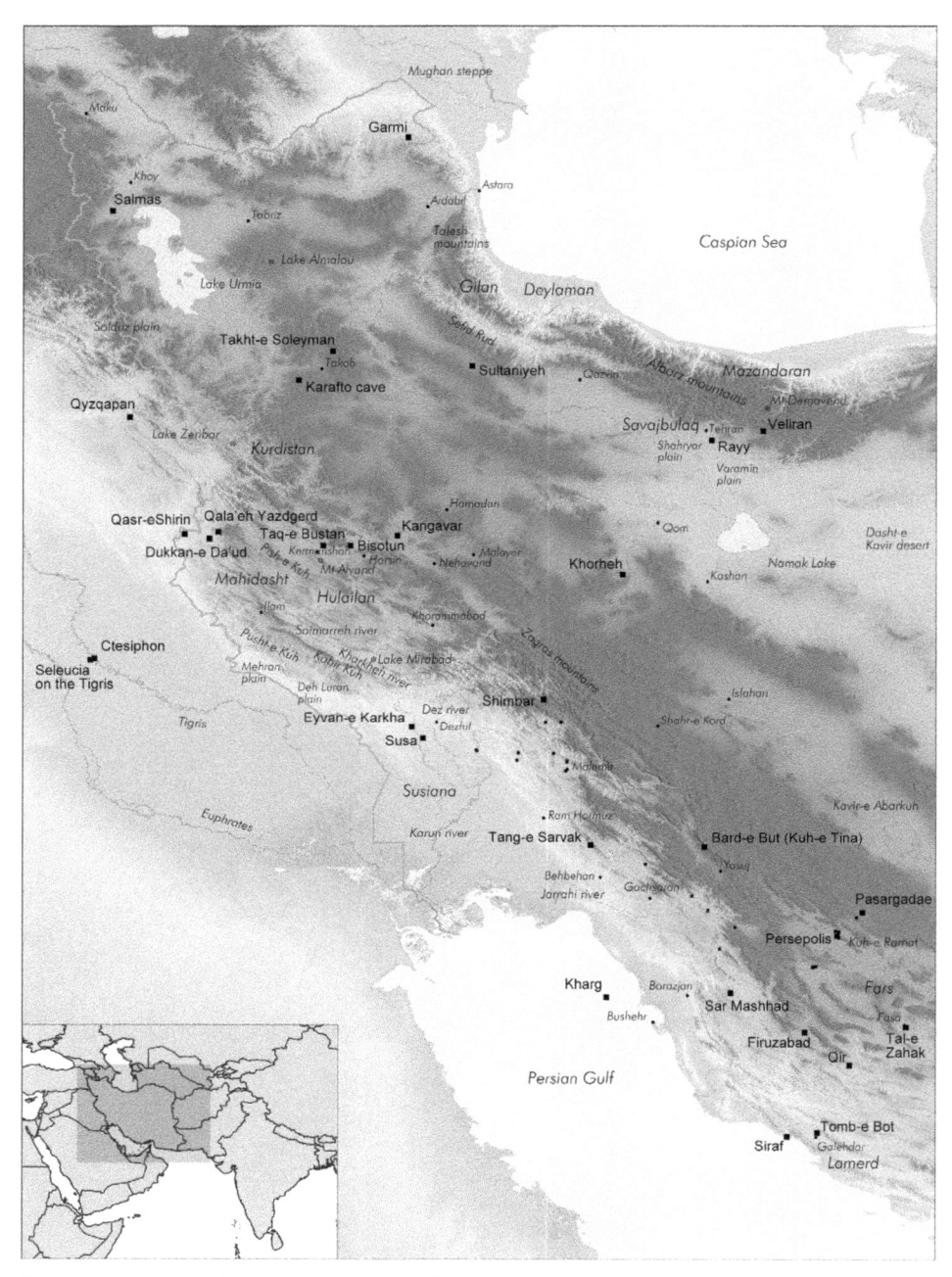

MAP 4 Map of western Iran showing late sites mentioned in the text (Achaemenid–Sasanian).

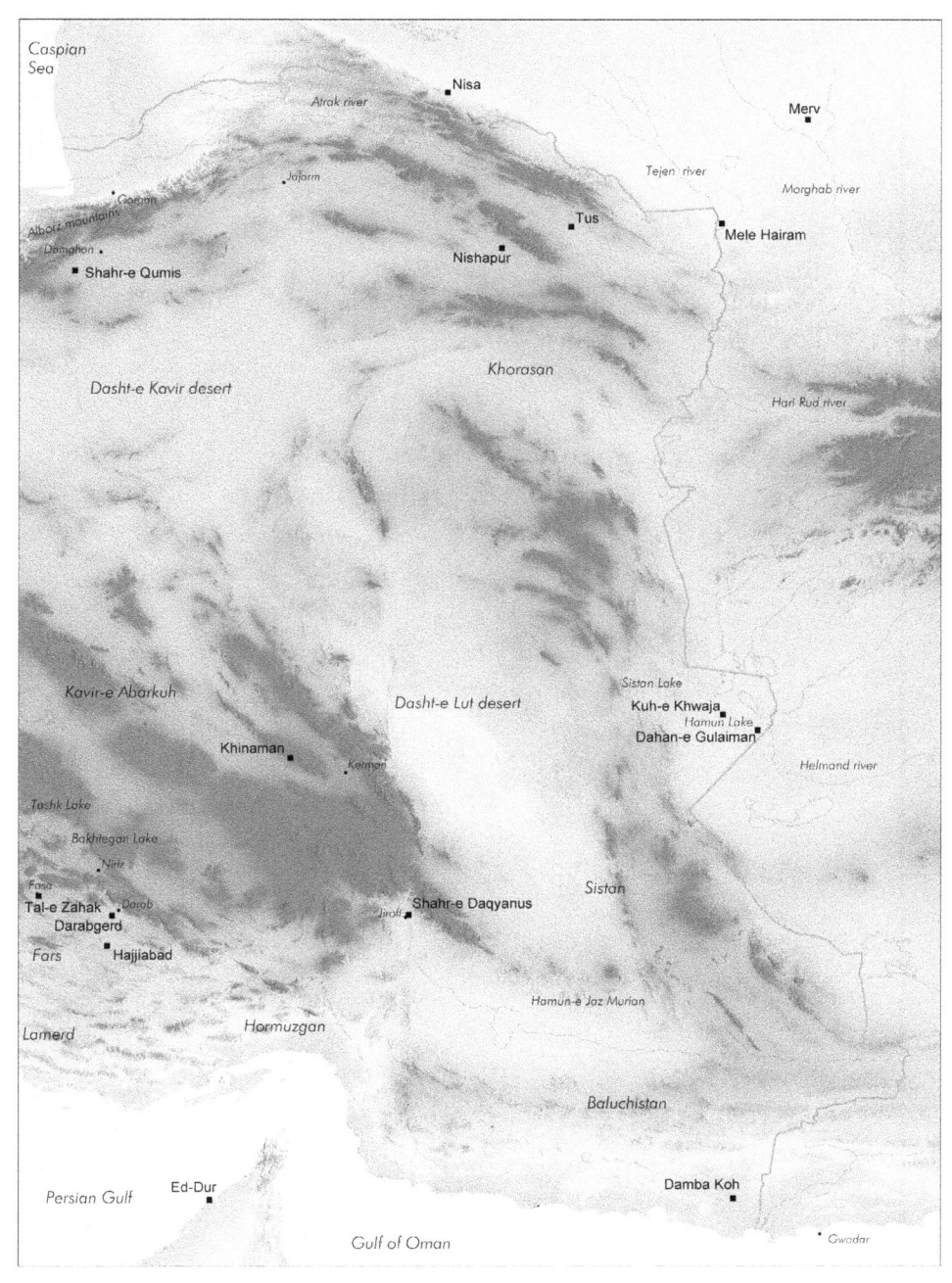

MAP 5 Map of eastern Iran showing late sites mentioned in the text (Achaemenid–Sasanian).

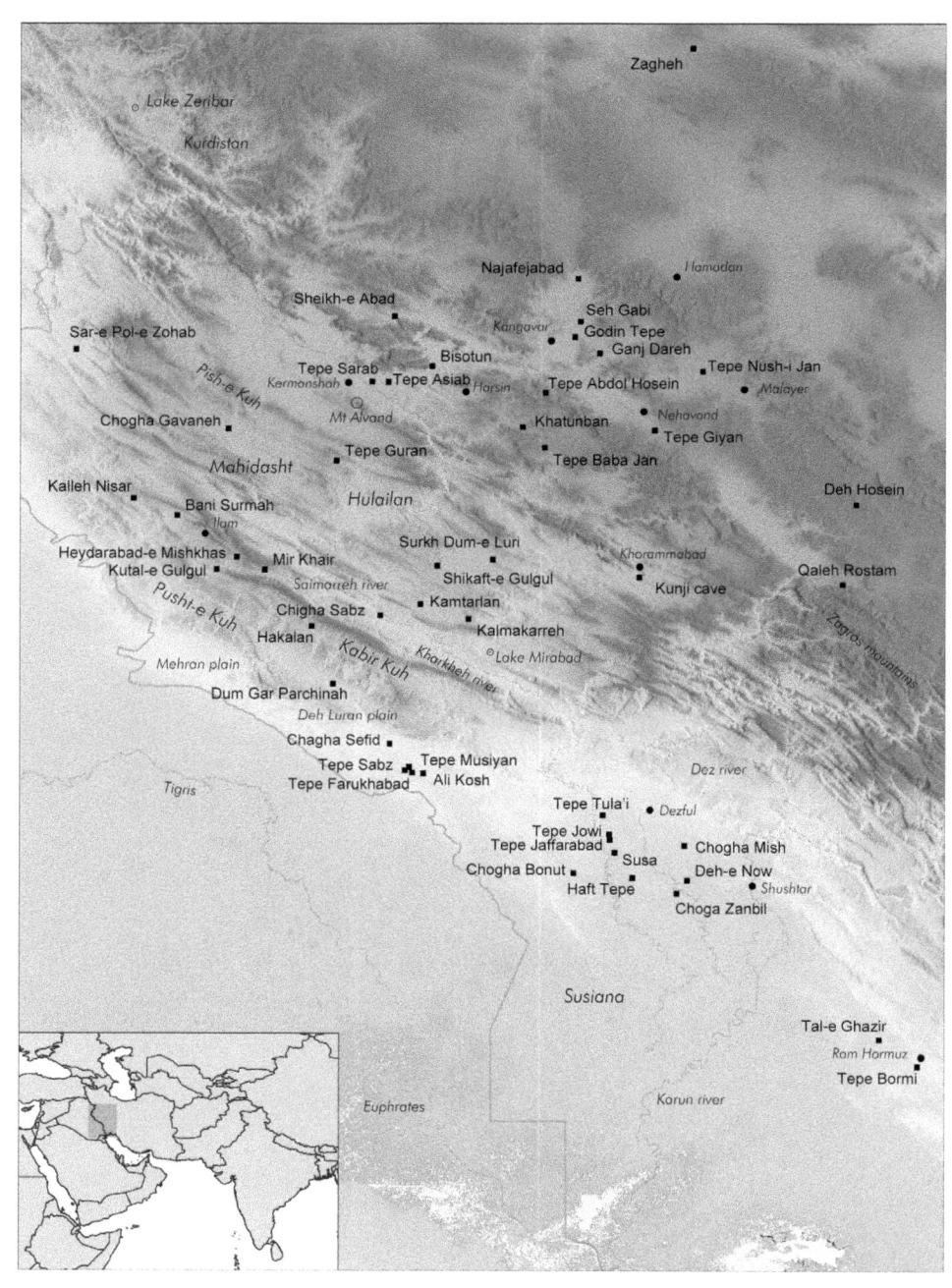

MAP 6 Map of Luristan and Khuzestan showing early sites mentioned in the text (prehistoric–Iron Age).

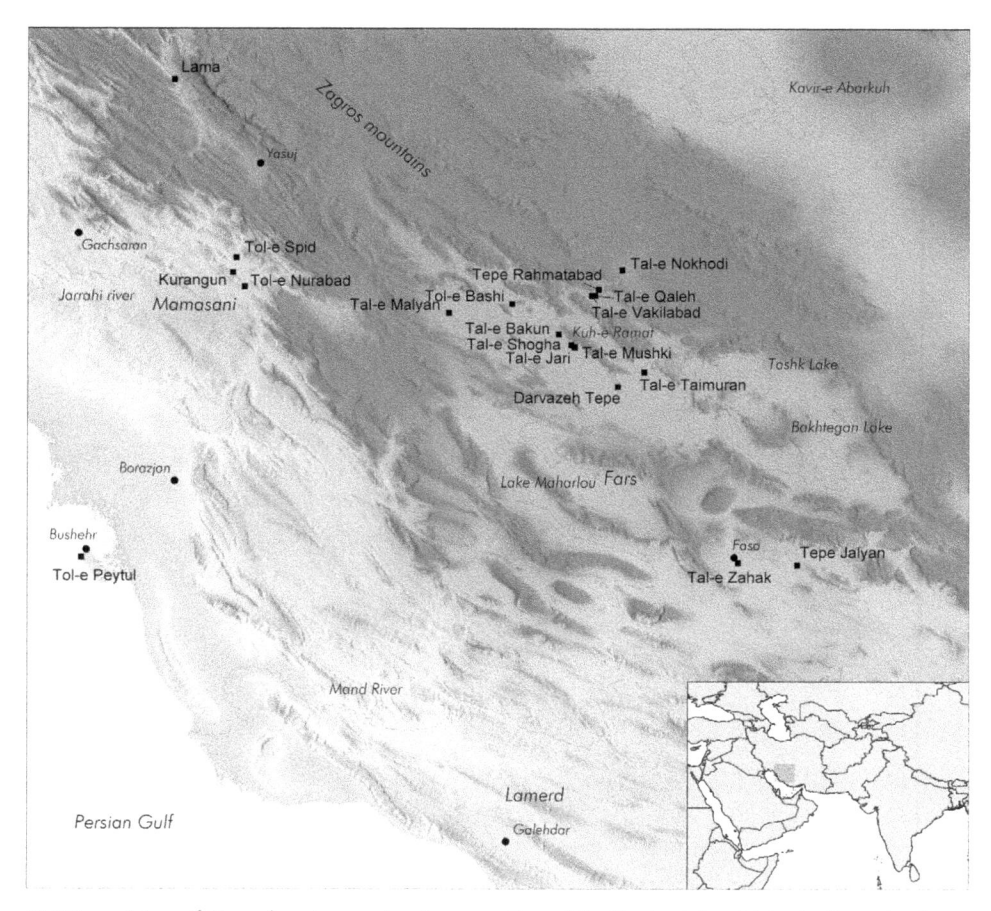

MAP 7   Map of Fars showing early sites mentioned in the text (prehistoric–Iron Age).

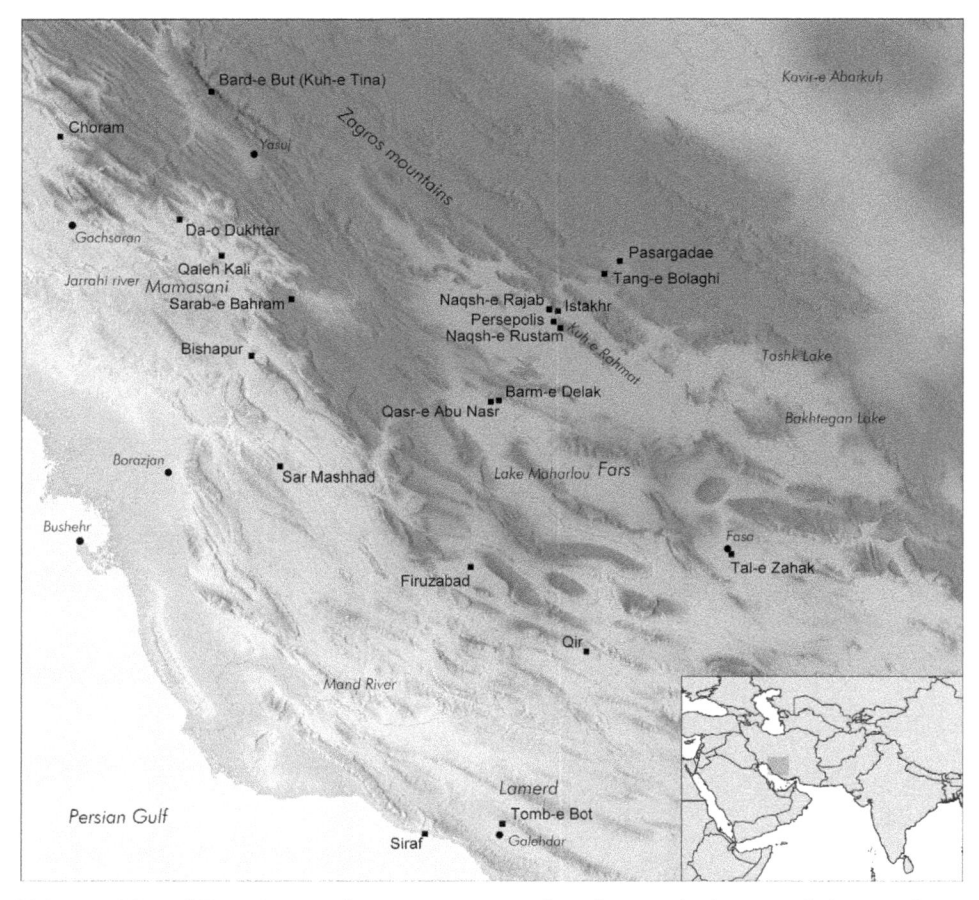

MAP 8 Map of Fars showing late sites mentioned in the text (Achaemenid–Sasanian).

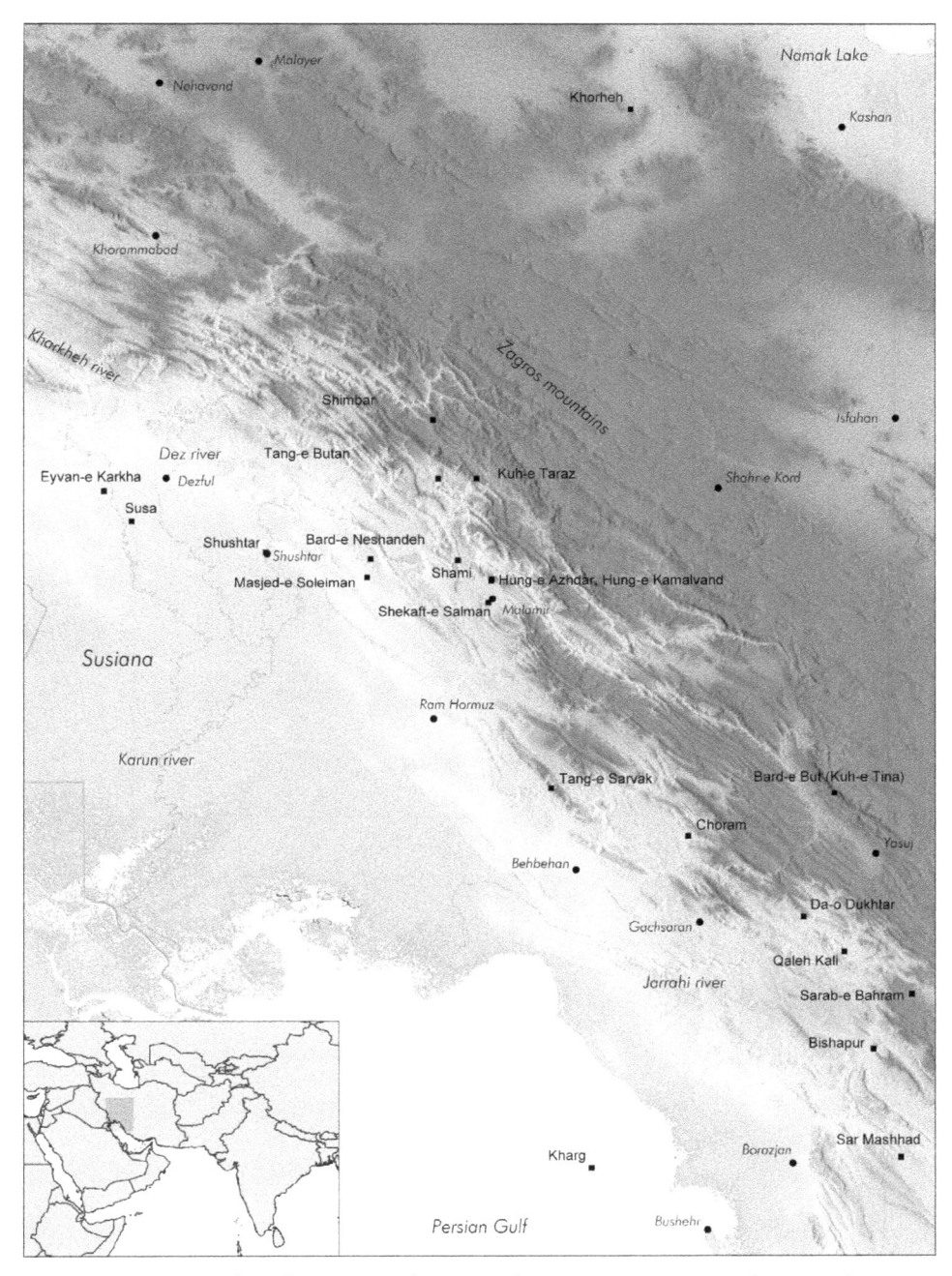

MAP 9 Map of Khuzestan showing late sites mentioned in the text (Achaemenid–Sasanian).

PART I
BACKGROUND AND BEGINNINGS

CHAPTER 1

THE HISTORY OF ARCHAEOLOGICAL RESEARCH IN IRAN
A brief survey

ALI MOUSAVI

Introduction

The history of Iranian archaeology can be divided into four principal periods: the period of early exploration (1600–1800), the nineteenth century, and emerging archaeology; the period of the French excavations at Susa (1884–1927); 1931 to 1979; and the period from the Islamic Revolution of 1979 to the present. T. Cuyler Young Jr. divided the history of Iranian archaeology into two periods: before and after World War II (Young 1986: 281–4). His article does not take into consideration activities before the French excavations at Susa or those after 1979. On the other hand, Mahmoud Mousavi's article takes up the history of Iranian archaeology from 1979 onward, revising some of Young's subdivisions and tables (Mousavi 1994: 501–3). Sadegh Malek Shahmirzadi's articles provide the most comprehensive survey of archaeological exploration in Iran (Shahmirzadi 1987, 2004). Both Robert H. Dyson Jr. and David Stronach contributed to the study of the history of archaeology in Iran (Dyson 1997; Stronach 1999).

The idea of the past has always marked the memory of successive generations throughout the history of Iran. The earliest manifestation of such a conscious engagement with the past goes back to Sasanian times (Shahbazi 2001; Daryaee 2001). The vestiges of Achaemenid monuments in Fars, the homeland of the Sasanians, stimulated the Sasanians' own memorial and monumental practices, in particular at Persepolis and Naqsh-e Rustam (Mousavi 2002: 213–14; 2012; Canepa 2010: 564–5). The way the

Sasanians engaged with their ancestors' monuments can be understood as an interesting reflection of a pervasive situation that runs like a thread through most of Iranian history. The dialogues between the present and the past were created by generations of rulers inscribing their name or leaving their mark in the ruins of Persepolis or Naqsh-e Rustam. This notion has been at the heart of the resonance of the ruins with Iranian tradition. It reflects a very different approach to monuments and history than that exercised by Western travelers.

Early explorations

Many Europeans who visited Iran from the fourteenth century onward have left us their narratives. Travels before the seventeenth century were usually occasioned by political circumstances of the time. The advent of the Safavids in the early sixteenth century brought back political stability and security to Persia. The search for new markets and trade routes in the East was probably the origin of the intensification of European travels to the Safavid kingdom. Shah Abbas encouraged political and economic relations with the West, and foreign envoys found a welcome at his court (Gabriel 1952: 60–61). The most visited region was Fars, situated halfway between the Persian Gulf and the capital cities of the kingdom, Qazvin and Isfahan. The Achaemenid ruins at Persepolis, Naqsh-e Rustam, and Pasargadae attracted most of the European visitors (Sancisi-Weerdenburg 1990), such as the Spaniard Don Garcia da Silva Figueroa (1550–1624), the Italian Pietro Della Valle (1586–1652), the Frenchmen Jean Chardin (1643–1713) and Jean Thevenot (1633–1667), and the German Engelbert Kaempfer (1651–1716). In the eighteenth century the Dutchman Cornelis de Bruin (1652–1726) produced excellent engravings of the ruins (Sancisi-Weerdenburg 1991: 18–22) and in 1765 the German Carsten Niebuhr (1733–1815) brought back to Europe accurate copies of cuneiform inscriptions (Booth 1902: 76–8; Budge 1925: 39). In his report on the Arabia expedition, Niebuhr published copies of eleven cuneiform inscriptions from Persepolis (Booth 1902: 77; Wiesehöfer 1994: 232; Mousavi 2012). Niebuhr's copies were later used by Georg Friedrich Grotefend (1775–1853) in his work on the decipherment of cuneiform, presented to the Göttingen Academy in 1802 (Wiesehöfer 1994: 231–3). The successful reading of the Old Persian cuneiform text at Bisotun by Sir Henry C. Rawlinson (1810–1895), published in 1847 (Rawlinson 1846–7), had a tremendous impact on the future of archaeological exploration in the entire Near East.

With the creation of national museums in Europe from the second half of the eighteenth century onward and the resulting increased demand for art objects, travelers attempted to do further investigation through excavation for portable artifacts and architectural elements. Unfortunately, very few of them left records describing their work. There is no mention of excavation prior to the early years of the nineteenth century, when European travels to Persia intensified because of the Napoleonic wars in Europe and the Russo-Persian conflicts between 1804 and 1828. A series of British and French diplomatic missions were sent to Persia with the aim of seeking an alliance for an ultimate intervention by Persia in case of any threat to India. Of these missions, one should particularly note the embassy of Sir Gore Ouseley, which included his brother Sir William Ouseley (1767–1842), a noted orientalist, whose explorations in southern Iran in 1810–12 produced a valuable set of observations on archaeological sites and monuments in Fars (Ouseley 1823). Two members of his mission, James Morier (1780–1849) and Robert Gordon (1791–1847), excavated at Persepolis with the aim of finding sculptures (Curtis 1998: 48–9; Mousavi 2012). Morier was also the first to draw attention to the fact that the so-called "tomb of the Mother of Solomon" corresponds to the monument described as the tomb of Cyrus the Great by classical authors like Arrian and Strabo (Stronach 1978: 2–3). In 1817–18, Sir Robert Ker Porter, a British painter, traveler, and adventurer, visited Persia and gave a full account of the Achaemenid ruins in Fars. He had the trained eye of a skilled draughtsman and painter. This visual ability gave his reports a significant level of accuracy. He had a good knowledge of the ancient history of Iran, particularly its mythological and legendary aspects (Barnett 1972: 20–21). His merit lies in the careful investigations he made on the ground, most notably the painstaking and accurate measurements he took of each monument he visited (Ker Porter 1821). Ker Porter's account was superseded only by the publication of the elaborate work of Eugène Flandin (1809–1876) and Pascal Coste (1787–1879), who visited Iran on a diplomatic mission sent by Louis Philippe to Persia under Count de Sercey between 1839 and 1841 (Flandin and Coste 1843–54).

The brief excavations carried out at Susa by Williams and Loftus between 1849 and 1851 did not produce many valuable objects, but they resulted in the first plan of the site and the identification of Susa as the Biblical Shushan. Moreover, Henry Churchill's drawings represented the first pictures of the intact mounds (Loftus 1857: 418–22). Like his contemporaries, Layard, Botta, and Place, Loftus opened large areas in search of objects but soon became disappointed because he did not find bas-reliefs at Susa comparable to those that had been discovered by Botta at Khorsabad and by Layard at Nimrud. The excavations were terminated by the Trustees of the British Museum and Rawlinson who believed the mounds of Susa to be exhausted. "Had he stayed at Susa the whole pattern of archaeological research in the Near East may have been different, but such are the accidents of history" (Curtis 1993: 15).

In 1898, Luigi Pesce, an Italian officer of infantry in the service of the Qajars, took the first photographs of the ruins at Persepolis and offered them in an album to Naser al-Din Shah who was himself a passionate amateur photographer (Adle and Zoka 1983: 256; Mousavi 2002: 218). It is noteworthy that Naser al-Din Shah had already demonstrated his interest in photography in the service of archaeology by supporting the first Iranian excavation at Khorheh, where the work was documented photographically (Adle 2000: 231). The archaeological expedition at Khorheh in 1859 is probably the earliest excavation in which photography was used to record the finds. It thus preceded the use of this technology in archaeology by the Austrians at Samothrace in 1875.

The French Era: 1884–1927

This period was marked by the beginning of French excavations at Susa, following a royal decree granting the engineer Marcel-Auguste Dieulafoy (1844–1920) and his wife, Jane Dieulafoy (1851–1916), permission to excavate there. The work at Susa was the subject of two adventure books by Mme. Dieulafoy, written in the Victorian romantic style of the late nineteenth century (Dieulafoy 1887, 1888). Dieulafoy described Susa as a site with four distinct mounds: the Apadana (the northern mound); the Acropole or citadel (the highest mound); the Ville Royale, where he supposed the ruins of the Achaemenid town to be; and the Ville des Artisans (the eastern part of the site) (Dieulafoy 1893). During two seasons of excavation at Susa, Dieulafoy discovered an invaluable mass of glazed bricks, column bases, and capitals from the palace of the Achaemenid kings. As an architect, he was able to correctly trace the plan of the Achaemenid palace and to investigate some of the technical problems related to its abandonment and destruction. However, like his successor, Jacques de Morgan, Dieulafoy was unable to identify mud-brick walls, which were consequently destroyed in the course of excavation.

In 1894, René de Balloy, minister of France in Tehran, obtained the approval of a treaty granting France exclusive rights to excavate in Persia. Five years later, with the creation of the Délégation en Perse, the French obtained a total concession for all archaeological excavations in Iran for an indefinite period (Chevalier 2002: 512, 515–16; Nasiri-Moghaddam 2004: 347–9, 357–62). In the remarkably creative period of the Third Republic (1870–1914), the French resumed their activities in Iran but this time with a long-term program directed by Jacques Jean-Marie de Morgan (1857–1924), a renowned archaeologist and prehistorian who had visited Iran in the 1890s. De Morgan built a castle on the highest point of the Acropole to serve as the expedition house. In the winter of 1898, he began to excavate the Acropole in trenches that took the form of tunnels dug into the high, vertical face of the mound. De Morgan's most important work at Susa was the excavation of the "Grande Tranchée" in the south-central part of the Acropole. The Grande Tranchée ran across the middle of the mound from the north/northwest to the south/southeast and served as the main axis of his excavations (Mousavi 1996: 8–9; Perrot 1997: 183). The finds were remarkable: the stele of Naram-Sin; a collection of Babylonian *kudurrus* (boundary stones); an ornamented bronze table of snakes; the stele bearing the law code of Hammurabi; the bronze statue of Queen Napir-Asu; and thousands of inscribed bricks. All of this revealed the richness of the site and showed it to be the most important center of Elamite civilization, a civilization effectively discovered by the French mission. At the base of the trench and beyond the mass of earth, de Morgan had found the necropolis of the "first Susian agglomeration" with its celebrated painted pottery vessels of the fifth millennium BC (Perrot 1997: 183). French excavations at Susa continued until 1979.

The first third of the twentieth century was a time of important sociopolitical change that greatly affected the future of archaeology in Iran. The Constitutional Revolution of

1906 in Iran engendered and promoted new ideas, including a greater consciousness of Iran's cultural heritage and economic resources, as well as stimulating nationalistic feelings in defense of the historical heritage of the country (Abdi 2001: 52). In 1910 San'i al-Molk, the Minister of Culture, took the initiative to create the first antiquities service, the direction of which was entrusted to Iraj Mirza, a famous poet and cultural personality of his time. In 1916, Momtaz al-Molk, the Minister of Public Instruction, opened the first antiquities museum in Tehran with 270 objects (Afshar and Mousavi 1976: 40–45). Both of these institutions continued to function until the early 1930s.

The international era of Iranian archaeology (1927–1979)

In 1923, a group of Iranian elites and intellectuals founded the Society for National Heritage (Anjoman-e Āthār-e Melli) in Tehran, in order to "promote public interest in ancient knowledge and crafts, and to preserve antiquities and handicrafts." One of the primary goals of the society was to "build a museum and library, and to employ knowledgeable specialists for their maintenance, and the proper recording of all the remains, the protection of which as national heritage would be necessary." The society organized conferences and invited Ernst Herzfeld (1870–1948) to give lectures on the prehistory and history of Iran (Mousavi 2005: 449–50).

The abolition of the French monopoly in 1927 was followed by the promulgation of the Antiquities Law of 1930, which paved the way for international teams to carry out archaeological research in Iran (Shahmirzadi 2004: 23; Mousavi 2005: 457). The Iranian government agreed to entrust the direction of the newly created Antiquities Service to the French architect and art historian André Godard (Mousavi 1994: 488). One of Godard's first tasks was the construction of an archaeological museum (the Iran Bastan Museum) which opened in 1937.

In April 1928, a year after the French monopoly was abolished, Herzfeld made plans to excavate at Pasargadae under the auspices of the Notgemeinschaft der Deutschen Wissenschaft. With limited funds, he set out for Fars with Friedrich Krefter, a talented young architect from Berlin, and a cook. He unearthed major palatial buildings and took a complete set of photographs of the monumental buildings at the site (Stronach 1978: plates 47, 58, 61; 2005: 113–20, 124–33, figs. 2–11). The work lasted twenty-eight days, after which Herzfeld and Krefter went to Persepolis, where Krefter was in charge of verifying Herzfeld's earlier plan of the site. The expedition to Pasargadae was the only archaeological exploration that was carried out before the passage of the new Antiquities Law of 1930 (Mousavi 2005: 459).

Herzfeld's excavations at Persepolis, which began in 1931, opened a new chapter in the history of archaeological research in Iran. From 1931 to 1939, a team from the Oriental Institute (University of Chicago) uncovered a number of major buildings on and outside the Terrace, including the monumental staircases of the Apadana and the Tripylon. In 1931, Herzfeld and Krefter excavated and reconstructed the northern part of the palace known as the Harem to serve as the expedition house. In 1933, Krefter discovered the gold and silver foundation plaques of the Apadana (Schmidt 1953: 79, and 99, fig. 43; Mousavi 2012). The discovery of thousands of cuneiform tablets in the northeastern fortification tower revealed the most substantial body of texts ever found at an Achaemenid site (see Chapter 27; Hallock 1969; Cameron 1948). More tablets were found during Erich F. Schmidt's excavation of the Treasury between 1935 and 1939 (Cameron 1948). Schmidt's aerial survey of Persepolis and other historical sites and cities in Iran pioneered the use of aerial photography in archaeological research (Schmidt 1940). Simultaneously, excavations at Naqsh-e Rustam and Istakhr revealed a mudbrick enclosure in front of the Achaemenid royal tombs and a continuous, post-Achaemenid sequence at Istakhr. One of the significant accomplishments of Schmidt's work was the excavation at Naqsh-e Rustam where the clearing of the mounds and deposits around the lower part of the Ka'ba-ye Zardošt resulted in the discovery of the monumental trilingual inscription of Šābuhr I (Sprengling 1940: 341). Schmidt's three Persepolis volumes provide full documentation on sites and monuments in Fars from the Achaemenid to the early Islamic period (Schmidt 1953, 1957, 1970). The Oriental Institute team also excavated Tal-e Bakun, a prehistoric site of the fifth to fourth millennium BC a few kilometers to the southwest of Persepolis. The site consists of two mounds labeled A and B. Tal-e Bakun A was first sounded by Herzfeld in 1928 and later excavated by Alexander Langsdorff and Donald McCown in 1932 and 1937 on behalf of the Oriental Institute (Langsdorff and McCown 1942; Alizadeh 2006: 39–40). The site was again excavated by a Japanese team in 1956 and by a joint Iranian-American team in 2004 under the direction of Abbas Alizadeh (Alizadeh 2006: 40). Excavations at Tal-e Bakun B and Tal-e Jari (another prehistoric mound in Marv Dasht) provided evidence for the early prehistoric sequence in Fars (Alizadeh 2008).

The 1930s witnessed the introduction of a new generation of archaeologists to Iranian archaeology, the youngest of whom was Roman Ghirshman, a scholar whose theories and excavations had a great impact on the development of archaeological research in Iran. Ghirshman had trained at the École du Louvre and obtained field experience at Telloh in southern Mesopotamia; his first Iranian excavation was at Tepe Giyan, under the direction of his former mentor, Georges Contenau. Regardless of the lack of precision in the excavation method and final report, Tepe Giyan proved to be an important Bronze Age and Iron Age site in the region of Nehavand (Contenau and Ghirshman 1935). Ghirshman's excavations at Tepe Sialk, near Kashan, revealed the earliest occupation levels ever found in this particular part of the Iranian plateau, dating back to at least 6000 BC, and an almost continuous sequence of more than three thousand years. The early periods at Tepe Sialk (I–IV) were a time of important technological innovation. A carved bone knife handle representing a man wearing a cap and a loincloth found in a Sialk I context is one of the earliest known anthropomorphic representations from Iran (Ghirshman 1939: plate 54). Prehistoric Sialk is also known for its fine, black-on-buff painted pottery decorated with naturalistic animals and geometric motifs. Sialk was also noteworthy for its exploitation of metal sources on the central Iranian plateau. At the southernmost area of the Southern Mound, where the summit had been leveled to increase the area available for building, Ghirshman unearthed a massive, polygonal terrace in mudbrick, which he interpreted as the residence of a chieftain whose subjects resided on the plain below (Ghirshman 1939: 106, plates 34; 1954: 76–7). The dead at Sialk were buried outside the settlement in two successive cemeteries, labeled A and B, that stood on the south and west sides of the Southern Mound (Ghirshman 1939: 3ff., 23 ff.; 1954: 77). The B cemetery marked a major change in burial practice and provided the basis for Ghirshman's theory of the coming of the Indo-Europeans onto the Iranian plateau, a thesis that he later developed (1954, 1977). With his broad vision of historical and archaeological sites in Iran, Ghirshman was among the rare archaeologists of his generation to have paid attention to the historic periods. His excavations on behalf of the Louvre Museum at Bishapur (1934–41), the great Sasanian capital of the later third century AD, and at Susa (1946–67), where he explored the Parthian and Sasanian remains, bespeak his keen interest in the later periods of Iranian history.

The exploration of medieval sites was also pursued in this period with three major excavations at Rayy (Schmidt 1936), Istakhr (Schmidt 1937), and Nishapur (Hauser and Wilkinson 1942). From 1931 to 1932 Schmidt also excavated Tepe Hissar, one of the large Bronze Age settlements near Damghan, where excavations revealed one of the most important prehistoric settlements in Iran (Schmidt 1937). Tepe Hissar was the object of a reexamination project involving new soundings by Robert H. Dyson Jr. and Maurizio Tosi in the 1970s (Dyson and Howard 1981). In the same region lies the imposing, multiperiod site of Tureng Tepe, 18 km to the northeast of Gorgan. The site consists of three archaeological mounds representing a more or less continuous sequence from the late fifth millennium BC to the fifth century AD when the summit of the *grand tépé* was occupied by an imposing mudbrick Sasanian fort. The most important Bronze Age settlement in the region, Tureng Tepe also yielded archaeological evidence of the introduction of a new type of pottery, the gray ware of the northeast, often associated with the appearance of Indo-Europeans on the Iranian plateau (Deshayes 1969a). Tureng Tepe was twice the object of archaeological excavations, once in 1931 by Frederick Wulsin on behalf of the University Museum of the University of Pennsylvania (Wulsin 1932), and again between 1960 and 1977 by a team under the direction of J. Deshayes of the University of Lyon (Boucharlat and Lecomte 1987). The excavations at Tureng Tepe reflect a pattern of continuous development from the sixth millennium BC to the Sasanian period. The results obtained at Tureng Tepe correspond to those from another site in the Gorgan plain of northeastern Iran, Shah Tepe, which was excavated by a Swedish team in 1933 (Arne 1945). In 1932–33, Sir Aurel Stein traveled from Sistan to the region of Lake Urmia, crossing most of the southern half of the Iranian plateau in the process. He briefly explored the prehistoric site of Bampur (Stein 1934: 122–3) and reported on other sites such as Khinaman, Shahr-e Daqyanus, and Siraf. In Fars he sounded a small prehistoric tepe named Do-Tolan in the Murghab plain near Pasargadae (Stein 1935: 496–7). In the west, Stein's work at Shami in highland

Khuzestan was noteworthy. In the northwest, he explored a number of sites, including Hasanlu (Stein 1940).

None of the large excavations that were terminated with the outbreak of World War II were resumed after the war, apart from Susa, where Ghirshman's tenure witnessed a new trend aimed at the exploration of urbanism and the excavation of historic periods. The postwar period also saw a progressive increase in the involvement of Iranian archaeologists. In 1941, Fereydoun Tavalli, the first graduate in archaeology from the University of Tehran, carried out soundings at prehistoric sites in the Marv Dasht plain (Fars), including Tal-e Malyan (Shahmirzadi 1987: 70). Other Iranian archaeologists of the time had a different training and background: Muhammad Taqi Mustafavi, who later became Director General of the Department of Archaeology under Godard's supervision, had a degree in law; Ali Sami had studied art and literature in Shiraz before beginning his excavations at Pasargadae and Persepolis in 1949, which lasted for another two decades; Ali Hakemi, the excavator of Khorvin, Kaluraz, and Shahdad, was an architect. With enthusiasm and determination, these erudite pioneers kept up archaeological activity in Iran during the postwar years.

The late 1940s witnessed the fortuitous discovery and subsequent plundering of the Ziwiye treasure and the brief excavation of Hasanlu by A. Hakemi and M. Rad in 1947. The beginning of the 1950s was marked by the publication of Ghirshman's *L'Iran des origines à l'Islam* (1951, English ed. 1954), a book that, along with Herzfeld's *Iran in the Ancient East* (1941), has become a great classic in Iranian archaeology. Louis Vanden Berghe's *L'Archéologie de l'Iran ancien* (1959) was long considered the "Bible of Iranian archaeology." The 1950s were also important for research on the early human occupation of Iran. In 1951, Carleton Coon of the University Museum in Philadelphia explored the prehistoric caves of Bisotun in the west and Hotu and Kamarband on the Caspian shore (Coon 1952; 1957: 86–127, 128–73, 174–216). The discovery and excavation of a Neanderthal occupation at Shanidar (Iraq) in the western Zagros Mountains (1957–61) by Ralph Solecki showed that the entire region was inhabited as early as the Middle Palaeolithic period (Solecki 1971). Robert J. Braidwood's excavation of the small Neolithic sites of Tepe Sarab and Tepe Asiab near Kermanshah in western Iran (Braidwood 1961) and Frank Hole's excavation of Neolithic sites in the plain of Deh Luran considerably enriched the study of the early human occupation of Iran (Hole, Flannery, and Neely 1969). In Fars, Vanden Berghe's soundings at several sites, most notably Tal-e Shogha and Tal-e Teimuran in Marv Dasht, provided a preliminary ceramic sequence for the region that could be linked with Sialk, Giyan, and Susa (Vanden Berghe 1952; 1957: 41–5).

The primary aim of archaeologists in this era was to establish a chronology of the prehistoric periods using typological studies of artifacts, particularly pottery. Donald McCown had established a typological division of Iran into two cultural areas, the "red ware" and "buff ware" cultures (McCown 1942). This typology was accepted until the 1950s, when its validity was questioned by a new group of scholars who began to develop a new set of objectives for the investigation and analysis of existing data (Shahmirzadi 2004). Increasingly the research of American archaeologists who went to Iran in the

1950s and 1960s was focused on problem-oriented studies concerned with the beginnings of agriculture and food production, the use of domesticated plants and animals, the rise of cities and complex societies, and state formation in southwestern Iran.

In 1954, Ezattollah Negahban graduated from the University of Chicago. Negahban is often considered the patriarch of Iranian archaeologists. He began to teach a modern program of archaeology at the University of Tehran and later founded the Archaeological Institute there. Negahban is well known for his excavations at Marlik in Gilan (1961–62); Haft Tepe in Khuzestan; and Sagzabad, in the Qazvin plain. Two of his students became major figures and took over the task of teaching and training of students: Yussef Majidzadeh, who received his PhD from the University of Chicago and is well known for his excavations in Jiroft, and Sadegh Malek Shahmirzadi, who obtained his doctorate from the University of Pennsylvania and excavated the prehistoric sites of Zagheh, near Qazvin, and Tepe Sialk (2000–2007). In the 1960s and 1970s, a whole generation of archaeologists was trained at the University of Tehran, including M. Azarnoush, M.-A. Kaboli, M. Mousavi, M. Rahbar and E. Yaghmai. All were soon hired by the Iranian Archaeological Department and became prominent figures in the development of archaeological research in the country.

A large number of archaeologists were trained in the Hasanlu Project launched in 1959 by Robert H. Dyson Jr. of the University of Pennsylvania. Those who worked at Hasanlu soon opened their own excavations in different parts of Iran. The Hasanlu Project had a long-lasting impact on Iranian archaeology. The increase in archaeological activity in Iran which followed the Hasanlu Project is remarkable. A glance at the sheer number of surveys and excavations in this period shows an intellectual and scholarly explosion in Iran during the 1960s and 1970s (Young 1986: 282–3).

Changes within the Iranian institutions also contributed to the development of archaeological research in Iran. The Department of Archaeology was attached to the Ministry of Culture and Arts, created in 1964. Later, the foundation in 1972 of the Iranian Center for Archaeological Research (ICAR) by Firouz Bagherzadeh brought all archaeological fieldwork into a well-organized center. The ICAR gave an unprecedented boost to the number and quality of archaeological investigations in Iran, the results of which were presented at five annual symposia in Tehran (*PASARI* 2–4). By the end of the 1970s, there were fifty Iranian and international archaeological missions working in different parts of the country. One of the memorable initiatives of Bagerzadeh was his decision to end the division of excavated finds (Bagherzadeh 1990: xvii–xviii). The 1970s also witnessed a great period of restoration of historical monuments, such as those at Persepolis, Isfahan, and Sultaniyeh.

AFTER 1979

The Islamic Revolution of 1979 put an end to the cooperation of international teams in Iran, and the outbreak of the eight-year Iran-Iraq war in 1981 interrupted most archaeological activities in the country. A number of sites and monuments along the western border suffered war damage, including the Sasanian sites of Eyvan-e Karkha and Qasr-e Shirin, which were largely destroyed by Iraqi artillery. Five years after the dissolution of the former Ministry of Culture and Arts by the Revolutionary Council, the Iranian Cultural Heritage Organization (ICHO), including the ICAR, was founded in 1985. This new organization took charge of public museums, archaeological research, and the restoration of historic monuments. It continues in this capacity today.

Despite the tumult of the Islamic Revolution and the Iran-Iraq war, archaeological research in Iran never completely halted. A few Iranian teams took up the task of excavating and preserving archaeological sites and monuments during the difficult years of war. The ICHO maintained the minimum standards of maintenance and protection at sites and sponsored a number of excavations at Nishapur, Tus, Shahdad, Susa, Shushtar, Bisotun, and Rayy. One should also mention the fortuitous discovery and excavation of a Neo-Elamite burial at Arjan in the plain of Behbahan, on the border of Fars and Khuzestan (Towhidi and Khalilian 1982; Alizadeh 1985; Álaverez-Mon 2010). Later, following the end of the Iran-Iraq war, the number of archaeological activities in Iran increased and the 1990s witnessed a considerable reinvigoration of archaeological research in the country.

International cooperation was resumed in 1994 and in 2003 the ICAR was refounded by its new director, Massoud Azarnoush. His six-year tenure as the head of the ICAR witnessed remarkable progress and development in different fields of archaeological research in Iran. This included the creation of well-planned national projects, in which all the relevant parties—the ICAR and developers—were involved. In 2004, there were sixty such projects. Azarnoush was well aware that the country's archaeologists might not be prepared for the challenges posed by the demands of a rapidly evolving economy and industrial expansion. This is why he welcomed constructive cooperation with international teams of archaeologists. When in 2003, the construction of the Sivand dam in the region of Pasargadae in Fars raised international concerns about potential damage to archaeological sites in the area, the ICAR urged the international community of archaeologists to join it in carrying out rescue excavations in the area that was to be flooded. This international call was well received, and a number of archaeological teams from Germany, France, Italy, and Poland participated in what became the Sivand Dam Archaeological Project. The archaeological work postponed the construction schedule of the dam for four years. The success of this international enterprise led to the exploration of the entire valley and resulted in the discovery of important sites near Pasargadae. Moreover, some of the joint expeditions, the work of which had been interrupted in 1979, were able to resume their fieldwork in order to complete the final publication of their results. Parallel, independent projects were also undertaken in southwestern Fars by a joint Australian-Iranian team from the University of Sydney (*MAPSO*) and in the area of Persepolis by joint teams from France, Italy, and Iran. Two major projects, one at Jiroft (Majidzadeh 2003) and the other at Sialk (Shahmirzadi 2006), were undertaken during the early years of the present century.

In the summer of 2011, following the government's decision to relocate administrative bodies outside the capital, the ICAR was effectively dissolved, and some of the departments within the Iranian Cultural Heritage, Tourism, and Handicrafts Organization were transferred to Isfahan and Shiraz. The administrative and research offices of the Archaeological Research Center were moved to Persepolis. It is still hard to assess the impact of this reorganization on archaeological activity in Iran.

A fair assessment of archaeological activities in Iran over the past three decades cannot be made for a number of reasons. A large number of operations, such as restoration work, excavations, and surveys, remain unpublished. There is no substantial report for most of the work carried out in the 1980s or even early 1990s. Another issue is the lack of access to the unpublished materials and reports. There is also the problem of immediacy, which affects the writing of the contemporary history of archaeology. The passage of time will certainly reveal unknown facts, untold stories, deeds and misdeeds with regard to the recent archaeological history of Iran.

References

Abdi, K. 2001. Nationalism, politics and the development of archaeology in Iran. *AJA* 105: 51–76.
Adle, C. 2000. Khorheh, the dawn of Iranian scientific archaeological excavation. *Tavoos Quarterly* 3–4: 4–31 (in English), 226–239 (in Persian).
Adle, C., and Y. Zoka. 1983. Notes et documents sur la photographie iranienne et son histoire. *StIr* 12/2: 249–80.
Afshar, K., and S.A. Mousavi. 1976. *Pāsdāri az Asār-e Bāstān dar Asr-e Pahlavi*. Tehran.
Alizadeh, A. 1985. A tomb of the Neo-Elamite period at Arjan, near Behbahān. *AMI* 18: 49–73.
———. 2003. Some observations based on the nomadic character of Fars prehistoric cultural development. *YBYN*: 83–97.
———. 2006. *The origins of state organizations in prehistoric highland Fars, southern Iran. Excavations at Tall-e Bakun*. Chicago: OIP 128.
———. 2008. Fars ix. Prehistoric sequence. *EnIr* online edition.
Álvarez-Mon, J. 2010. *The Arjan tomb, at the crossroads of the Elamite and the Persian Empires*. Leuven: Acta Iranica 49.
Arne, T. J. 1945. *Excavations at Shah Tepe*. Stockholm: Reports from the Scientific Expedition to the North-Western Provinces of China under the leadership of Dr. Sven Hedin Publication 27.
Bagherzadeh, F. 1990. Jean Perrot ami de l'Iran. *MJP*: xv–xxi.
Barnett, R. D. 1972. Sir Robert Ker Porter: Regency artist and traveller. *Iran* 10: 19–24.
Booth, A. J. 1902. *The discovery and decipherment of the trilingual cuneiform inscriptions*. London: Longmans Green.
Boucharlat, R., and O. Lecomte. 1987. *Fouilles de Tureng Tepe 1: Les périodes sassanides et islamiques*. Paris: Éditions Recherche sur les Civilisations.
Braidwood, R. J. 1961. The Iranian prehistoric project, 1959–1960. *IrAnt* 1: 3–7.
Budge, E. A. W. 1925. *The rise and progress of Assyriology*. London: Martin Hopkinson.
Cameron, G. G. 1948. *Persepolis Treasury Tablets*. Chicago: OIP 65.
Canepa, M. 2010. Technologies of memory in early Sasanian Iran: Achaemenid sites and Sasanian identity. *AJA* 114: 563–96.

Chevalier, N. 2002. *La recherche archéologique française au Moyen-Orient, 1842–1947*. Paris: Éditions Recherche sur les Civilisations.

Contenau, G., and R. Ghirshman. 1935. *Fouilles de Tépé Giyan, près de Néhavend, 1931–32*. Paris: Geuthner.

Coon, C. S. 1952. Excavations in Hotu Cave, Iran, 1951: A preliminary report. *PAPS* 96/3: 231–49.

——. 1957. *The seven caves: Archaeological explorations in the Middle East*. New York: Alfred Knopf.

Curtis, J. 1993. William Kennett Loftus and his excavations at Susa. *IrAnt* 28: 1–55.

——. 1998. A chariot scene from Persepolis. *Iran* 36: 45–51.

Daryaee, T. 2001. Memory and history: The construction of the past in Late Antique Persia. *Nāme-ye Irān-e Bāstān* 1/2: 1–14.

Deshayes, J. 1969. New evidence for the Indo-Europeans from Tureng Tepe, Iran. *Archaeology* 22/1: 10–17.

Dieulafoy, J. 1887. *La Perse, la Chaldée et la Susiane, Relation de voyage*. Paris: Hachette.

——. 1888. *A Suse: Journal des fouilles, 1884–1886*. Paris: Hachette.

Dieulafoy, M. A. 1893. *L'Acropole de Suse, d'après les fouilles exécutées en 1884, 1885, 1886 sous les auspices du Musée du Louvre*. Paris: Hachette.

Dyson, R. H., Jr. 1997. History of the field: Archaeology in Persia. *OEANE* 3: 60–63.

Dyson, R. H., Jr. and Howard, S. M. 1989. *Tappeh Hesār: Reports of the restudy project, 1976*. Florence: Monografi di Mesopotamia 2.

Flandin, E. and Coste, P. 1843–54. *Voyage en Perse, entrepris par ordre de M. le Ministre des Affaires Etrangères, d'après les instructions dressées par l'Institut*. 6 vols. Paris: Gide et J. Baudry.

Gabriel, A. 1952. *Die Erforschung Persiens*. Vienna: Adolf Holzhausen.

Ghirshman, R. 1939. *Fouilles de Sialk, près de Kashan, 1933, 1934, 1937*, vol. 2. Paris: Geuthner.

——. 1954. *Iran from the earliest times to the Islamic conquest*. Harmondsworth: Penguin.

——. 1977. *L'Iran et la migration des Indo-aryens et des Iraniens*. Leiden: Brill.

Hallock, R. T. 1969. *Persepolis Fortification Tablets*. Chicago: OIP 92.

Hauser, W., and C. K. Wilkinson. 1942. The Museum's excavations at Nishapur. *Bulletin of the Metropolitan Museum of Art* 37/4: 83–119.

Herzfeld, E. 1929. Rapport sur l'état actuel des ruines de Persépolis et propositions pour leur conservation. *AMI* 1: 17–38.

——. 1941. *Iran in the Ancient East*. Oxford: Oxford University Press.

Hole, F., K. V. Flannery, and J. A. Neely. 1969. *Prehistory and human ecology of the Deh Luran Plain: An early village sequence from Khuzistan, Iran*. Ann Arbor: Memoirs of the Museum of Anthropology 1.

Ker Porter, R. 1821. *Travels in Georgia, Persia, Armenia, Ancient Babylonia &c. &c. during the years 1817, 1818, 1819, and 1820*. London: Longman, Hurst, Rees, Orme and Brown.

Langsdorff, A., and D. E. McCown. 1942. *Tall-i Bakun A: Season of 1932*. Chicago: OIP 59.

Loftus, W. K. 1857. *Travels and researches in Chaldea and Susiana with an Account of Excavations at Warka, the "Erech" of Nimrod, and Shush, "Shushan the Palace" of Esther, in 1849–52*. London: Nisbet.

Majidzadeh, Y. 2003. La découverte de Jiroft. *Dossiers d'Archéologie* 287: 19–26.

McCown, D. E. 1942. *The comparative stratigraphy of early Iran*. Chicago: SAOC 23.

Mousavi, A. 1994. Bastanshenasiy-e jahan-e eslam. *The Persian encyclopaedia of Islam* 4: 486–510 (in Persian).

——. 1996. Early archaeological adventures and methodological problems in Iranian archaeology: The evidence from Susa. *IrAnt* 31: 1–17.

———. 2002. Persepolis in retrospect: Histories of discoveries and archaeological exploration at the ruins of ancient Parseh. *Ars Orientalis* 32: 209–251.

———. 2005. Ernst Herzfeld, politics, and antiquities legislation in Iran. In *Ernst Herzfeld and the development of Near Eastern studies, 1900–1950*, ed. A. C. Gunter and S. R. Hauser, 445–75. Leiden: Brill.

———. 2012. *Persepolis: Discovery and afterlife of a world wonder*. Boston: De Gruyter.

Nasiri-Moghaddam, N. 2004. *L'archéologie française en Perse et les antiquités nationales (1884–1914)*. Paris: Éditions Connaissances et Savoirs.

Ouseley, W. 1821–3. *Travels in various countries of the East*. London: Rodwell and Martin.

Perrot, J. 1997. Les recherches de 1968 à 1979. In *Une mission en Perse 1892–1912*, ed. N. Chevalier, 180–92. Paris: Réunion des Musées nationaux.

Rawlinson, H. C. 1846–7. The Persian Cuneiform Inscription at Behistun, deciphered and translated; with a memoir on Persian cuneiform inscriptions in general, and on that of Behistun in particular. *JRAS* 10: 1–349.

Sancisi-Weerdenburg, H. 1991. Through travellers' eyes: The Persian monuments as seen by European visitors. In *Through travellers' eyes: European travellers on the Iranian monuments*, ed. H. Sancisi-Weerdenburg and J. Drijvers, 1–35. Leiden: AchHist 7.

Schmidt, E. F. 1936. The excavation of the Citadel Hill. *University Museum Bulletin* 1–2: 79–87, 133–35.

———. 1937. *Excavations at Tepe Hissar, Damghan*. Philadelphia: University of Pennsylvania Press.

———. 1940. *Flights over ancient cities of Iran*. Chicago: University of Chicago Press.

———. 1953. *Persepolis I. Structures, reliefs, inscriptions*. Chicago: OIP 68.

———. 1957. *Persepolis II. Contents of the Treasury and other discoveries*. Chicago: OIP 69.

Shahbazi, A. S. 2001. Early Sasanians' claim to Achaemenid heritage. *Nāme-ye Irān Bāstān* 1 (1): 61–73.

Shahmirzadi, S. M. 1987. History of the archaeological studies in Iran. *IJAH* 2: 57–73 (in Persian).

———. 2004. A short history of archaeological research in Iran. *PAP*: 22–7.

———. 2006. *Sialk, the oldest fortified village of Iran*. Tehran: ICAR.

Solecki, R. S. 1971. *Shanidar, the first flower people*. New York: Alfred Knopf.

Sprengling, M. 1940. Shahpuhr I, the Great, on the Kaabah of Zoroaster (KZ). *AJSL* 57/4: 341–429.

Stein, M. A. 1934. Archaeological reconnaissances in southern Persia. *GJ* 83/2: 119–34.

———. 1935. An archaeological tour in the Ancient Persis. *GJ* 86/6: 489–97.

———. 1940. *Old routes of Western Irān: Narrative of an archaeological journey*. London: Macmillan.

Stronach, D. 1978. *Pasargadae: A report on the excavations conducted by the British Institute of Persian Studies from 1961 to 1963*. Oxford: Clarendon Press.

———. 1999. Excavations i. In Persia. *EnIr* 9: 88–94.

———. 2005. Ernst Herzfeld and Pasargadae. In *Ernst Herzfeld and the Development of Near Eastern Studies, 1900–1950*, ed. A. C. Gunter and S. R. Hauser, 103–35. Leiden: Brill.

Stronach, D., and M. Roaf. 2007. *Nush-i Jan I: The major buildings of the Median settlement*. Leuven, Paris, Dudley: British Institute of Persian Studies and Peeters.

Towhidi, F., and A. Khalilian. 1982. A report on the study of the objects from the Arjan tomb, Behbahan. *Athar* 7–9: 232–6 (in Persian).

Vanden Berghe, L. 1952. Archaeologische opzoekingen in de Marv Dasht vlakte. *JEOL* 12: 211–20.

———. 1959. *L'archéologie de l'Iran ancien*. Leiden: Brill.
Wiesehöfer, J. 1994. *Ancient Persia*. London: I. B. Tauris.
Wulsin, F. R. 1932. *Excavations at Tureng Tepe near Asterabad*. New York: Supplement to the Bulletin of the American Institute for Persian Art and Archaeology 2/1 bis.
Young, T. C., Jr. 1986. Archaeology i. Pre-Median. *EnIr* 2: 281–8.

CHAPTER 2

KEY QUESTIONS REGARDING THE PALEOENVIRONMENT OF IRAN

MATTHEW D. JONES

Introduction

Irrespective of the validity of environmental deterministic approaches to explain past social change (e.g., Wright 1993; Staubwasser and Weiss 2006; Rosen 2007), understanding the environments in which past peoples have lived is vital to coming to a full comprehension of their particular place in time and space. This chapter reviews evidence of how the environment of Iran has changed, particularly over the last 20,000 years, and looks at the key questions driving paleoenvironmental work in the region. These questions are also valid in regions outside of Iran, but given Iran's size and geographical and geological location many of these issues come together in Iran leading to a complex, but fascinating, paleoenvironmental picture which has the potential to teach us much about change in Iran itself but also further afield. This chapter will look at issues of variability in space and time and the many controls on paleoenvironment; it is important throughout to distinguish the final environment that is reconstructed from the many potential drivers that control it, such as climate, land use, and tectonics. Specifically the chapter will be divided into subsections looking at the following key questions:

- What is the temporal variability of paleoenvironmental change in Iran? As well as interannual or intermillennial change, Iran has a strongly seasonal climate, and changes on all scales therefore have important implications for those people living through them.

- What is the spatial variability of paleoenvironmental change in Iran? Environments within a short lateral extent can vary significantly, with topography for example, and Iran has various climatic zones, with change driven by climatic phenomena which will have varied with time. Care needs to be taken when using a paleoenvironmental record from one zone to inform discussion of change in another.
- What is the relationship between people and the(ir) environment? Given the long history of human occupation in Iran there has been an equally long interaction between the environment and the people living in it. This has been, and always will be, a two-way relationship and, increasingly through time, care must be taken as to whether we are reconstructing environmental change with implications for people, or change in people with implications for the environment.

What is the temporal variability of paleoenvironmental change in Iran?

The longest, uninterrupted records of past climatic and environmental variability in Iran come from lake records in the north and west (Fig. 2.1). The long record from Urmia (Djamali et al. 2008), which spans the last 200,000 years, shows changes in vegetation through glacial-interglacial time scales, with glacials characterized by an upland steppe dominated by *Artemisia* and Poaceae and interglacial vegetation dominated by increased tree cover, including oak and juniper. Pollen evidence also suggests the last, Sahand, interglacial (equivalent to marine isotope stage 5e) was different in nature to the Holocene, possibly with milder winters and increased spring or summer rainfall (Djamali et al. 2006). There is also significant evidence of glacial activity in the Zagros although the exact age of this is unknown (Wright 1962; Brookes 1982).

Lake deposits in large basins in the south and east of the country, for example, in the Sistan Basin (Fig. 2.1) (Smith 1974), may also be Pleistocene in age, as with other Near Eastern Pleistocene mega lakes, such as Konya (Roberts 1983) and Van (Landmann et al. 1996) in Turkey, however robust dating of these records is still required to place these sites correctly into the regional chronological framework.

There is, therefore, evidence that environmental conditions in Iran changed on glacial-interglacial timescales (see also Kehl 2009), although the chronological evidence to look at leads and lags in Iran compared to regional or global records is not currently available and detailed evidence of the environmental conditions during these changes comes only from the northwest of the country. The more detailed record of vegetation and palaeolimnological change from Lake Zeribar (e.g., Wasylikowa and Witkowski 2008) also suggests that there were climatic shifts in Iran at times similar to the northern

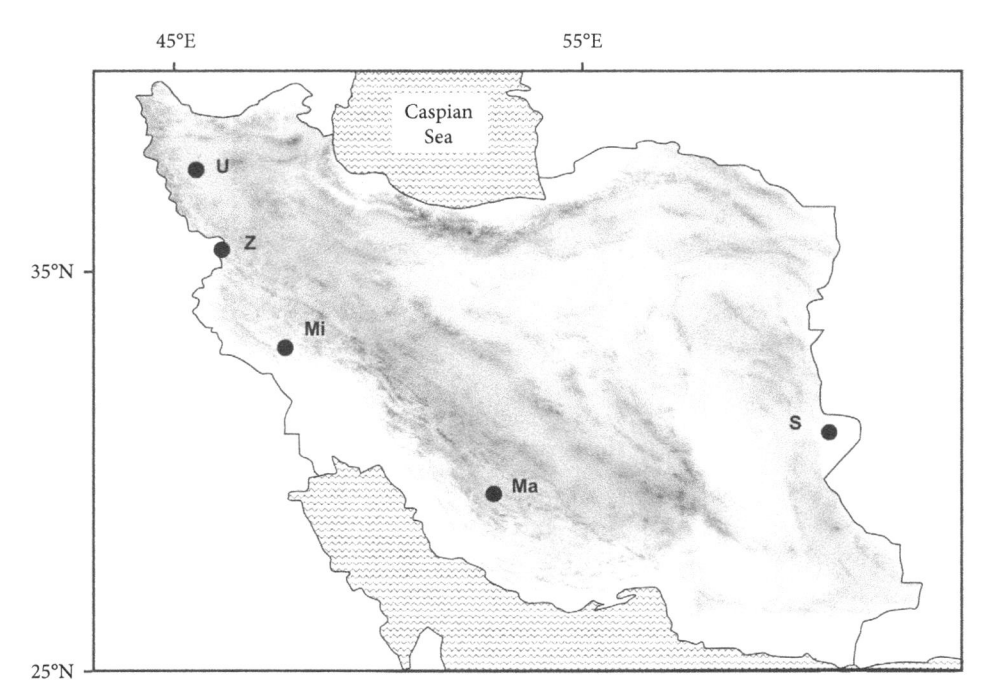

FIGURE 2.1 Location of key sites discussed in the text. U = Urmia; Z = Zeribar; Mi = Mirabad; S = Sistan; and Ma = Maharlou. Map background is topographic (white, low elevations, black high elevations); from the GTOPO30 digital elevation model (available from the US Geological Survey).

European Younger Dryas event (Fig. 2.2), although the nature, timing and duration of this event in Iran remains unclear.

Changes in oak pollen recorded in Zeribar and Mirabad (Figs. 2.1–2.2) through the Holocene have been interpreted as reflecting change in available moisture, although the similarities and differences between the coupled pollen and lake isotope records from these sites, compared to others in the Near East, have led to much debate about the exact nature of climatic change in the region through the Holocene (e.g., Jones and Roberts 2008; Djamali et al. 2010; Schmidt et al. 2011; Roberts et al. 2011) due to what Stevens et al. (2006) termed the "early-Holocene precipitation paradox." This "paradox" results from interpretations of the amount of oak seen in the pollen records, an increase in which would normally signify increased moisture, as seen in Zeribar and Mirabad c.6.5 ka, alongside other palaeolimnological indicators of early Holocene low lake levels (Griffiths et al. 2001), compared to standard interpretations of Near East lake isotope records from evaporated lake systems, where moves to more positive values, as also seen in Zeribar and Mirabad c.6.5 ka, would be interpreted as shifts to drier conditions. Stevens et al. (2001, 2006) suggest a change in rainfall seasonality, rather than the amount of rainfall, could explain this shift in isotope values.

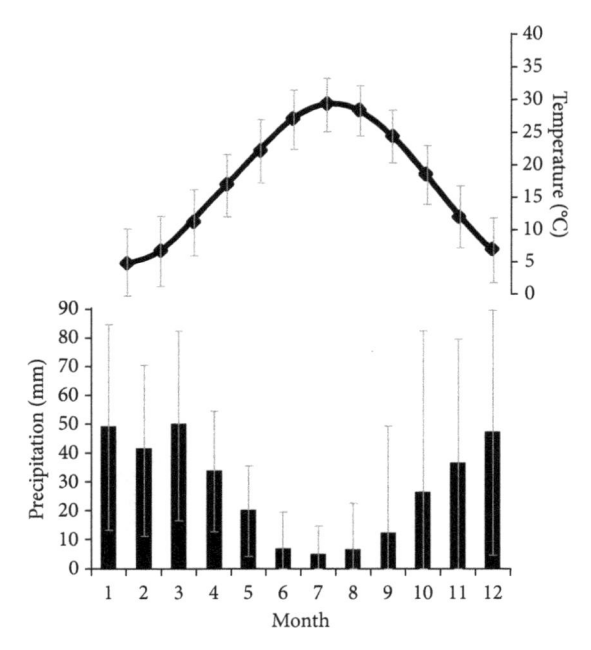

FIGURE 2.2 Percentage of oak (Van Zeist and Bottema 1977) and δ¹⁸O data (Stevens et al. 2001; Stevens et al. 2006) from Lakes Zeribar and Mirabad. Age models constructed from published radiocarbon dates calibrated using Calib 6.0 (Stuiver and Reimer 1993) and INTCAL09 (Reimer et al. 2009), using a third-order polynomial model for Zeribar and a linear model for Mirabad, removing samples above 90 cm in the Mirabad sequence due to uncertainties in the age model at these depths.

Irrespective of the correct interpretation, the resolution of these records only allows multicentennial climate events to be resolved at best, the average time between each data point is ~200 and 250 years for the data from Zeribar and Mirabad respectively (Fig. 2.2). Regional, submillennial-scale droughts have been recorded through the Holocene, which have been used to explain significant societal shifts in the region (e.g., Staubwasser and Weiss 2006). There is a single point in the Mirabad pollen and isotope curves which suggests conditions may have been significantly dry during the 5.2 ka event (Stevens et al. 2006; Fig. 2.2), but it is impossible to prove given the sampling resolution and the chronological control on the core.

Much of the debate surrounding the early Holocene precipitation paradox is centered on the possibility of changing climate seasonality with time. The climate of Iran today is very seasonal (Fig. 2.3; Table 2.1), with winter- and spring-dominated precipitation (see further discussion below) and warm summers and cold winters, with an average annual range of around 25°C. Given this clear seasonality, interpretations of proxy records are further complicated as changes in water availability can be due to changes in annual or seasonal conditions and due to the duration and/or intensity of winter- and spring-dominated precipitation and/or summer-dominated evaporation. Multiproxy

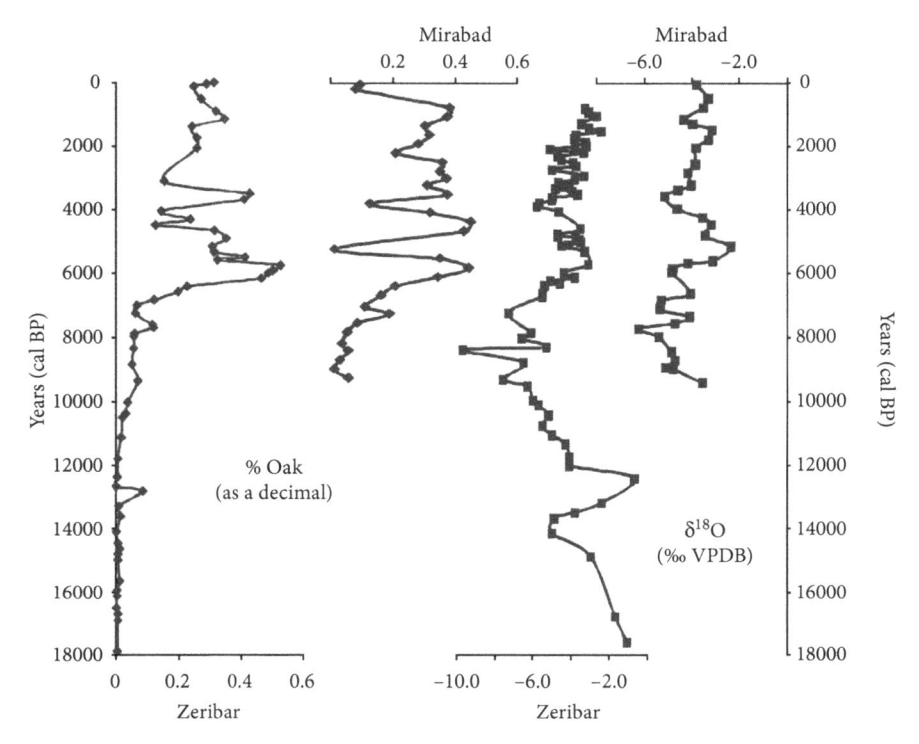

FIGURE 2.3 Average monthly temperatures and rainfall for the forty-one sites in Table 2.1, with one standard deviation error bars highlighting the seasonal differences between cold wet winters and warm dry summers in Iran.

reconstructions, preferably from different archives, are therefore key to fully understanding the detail of past change.

WHAT IS THE SPATIAL VARIABILITY OF PALAEOENVIRONMENTAL CHANGE IN IRAN?

Iran's climate is controlled by its geographical location relative to rain-bearing air masses and its topography. Today nearly 90 percent of the average temperature variability across the country (Table 2.1) can be explained by latitude and altitude (Fig. 2.4B). Variation in precipitation is slightly more complex, and many studies (e.g., Alijani and Harman 1985; Modarres and Sarhadi 2011) have discussed the spatial distribution of rainfall. Total annual precipitation varies from over 1000 mm a year in the north, particularly around the shores of the Caspian Sea, to less than 100 mm a year in the south and east (Table 2.1; Fig. 2.4C). The majority of precipitation across the country (83 percent on average) falls

Table 2.1 Climate summaries for forty-one synoptic stations across Iran (shown in Fig. 2.4). Precipitation data (averaged from the start date of each station until 2003) shows balance for summer (June–July–Aug–Sept), winter and spring (Nov–Dec–Jan–Feb–Mar–Apr) and the transition months (May–Oct) as well as the balance of winter precipitation compared to spring (Nov–Dec–Jan/Feb–Mar–Apr). Temperature data are average values from station start date until 2005 (Iran Meteorological Organization, 2010).

Site		Location			Precipitation					Temperature	
No.	Name	Long. (Decimal degrees)	Lat.	Altitude (masl)	Annual total (mm)	JJAS (%)	NDJFMA (%)	MO (%)	NDJ/FMA	Annual average (°C)	Seasonality (Jul–Jan; °C)
1	Ardebil	48.28	38.25	1332	303.9	13.6	60.7	25.7	0.9	9.0	21.6
2	Tabriz	46.28	38.08	1361	288.9	11.6	66.1	22.3	0.6	12.0	27.9
3	Orumieh	45.08	37.53	1312	341.0	7.7	72.6	19.8	0.7	11.2	26.4
4	Bojnurd	57.32	37.47	1091	272.4	12.2	69.9	17.9	0.7	13.1	24.7
5	Rasht	49.60	37.25	37	1359.0	23.2	56.9	19.8	1.6	16.2	19.0
6	Ramsar	50.66	36.90	20	1217.8	26.8	47.1	26.1	1.7	16.0	17.9
7	Gorgan	54.46	36.81	13	601.0	20.3	61.4	18.3	1.0	17.8	20.0
8	Babulsar	52.65	36.71	21	894.4	21.7	59.1	19.2	2.1	16.6	18.7
9	Zanjan	48.48	36.68	1663	313.1	7.9	71.7	20.4	0.7	11.5	27.0
10	Shahrud	55.03	36.41	1345	154.4	7.3	75.6	17.1	0.6	14.5	25.5
11	Mashhad	59.63	36.26	999	255.2	3.1	82.8	14.2	0.5	14.0	26.0
12	Ghazvin	50.00	36.25	1278	316.0	3.0	80.3	16.6	0.8	14.3	26.9
13	Sabzevar	57.66	36.21	977	188.6	2.6	87.1	10.3	0.7	17.6	27.9
14	Tehran	51.35	35.68	1191	232.8	3.5	85.2	11.3	0.9	17.2	27.3
15	Semnan	53.38	35.55	1171	140.8	7.5	78.2	14.3	0.8	18.3	28.2
16	Sanandaj	47.00	35.33	1373	458.4	1.0	85.4	13.6	0.8	14.2	28.9
17	Torbat Heydarieh	59.21	35.26	1333	274.8	2.2	88.7	9.1	0.7	14.8	26.6
18	Hamedan	48.53	34.85	1749	316.6	2.3	81.2	16.5	0.9	11.8	28.2
19	Qom	50.85	34.70	877	151.1	2.1	85.9	12.0	0.9	18.1	28.3
20	Kermanshah	47.11	34.26	1322	445.1	0.8	87.0	12.2	0.9	14.5	26.9
21	Arak	49.70	34.10	1720	341.7	1.6	84.6	13.8	0.8	13.7	28.7
22	Kashan	51.45	33.98	982	138.4	1.6	85.7	12.7	0.9	19.8	29.0
23	Ilam	46.42	33.63	1363	616.0	0.2	93.2	6.6	1.1	17.1	25.9

24	Tabas	56.92	33.60	711	83.2	0.2	92.9	6.9	0.7	22.4	28.5
25	Khoram Abad	48.30	33.50	1125	509.0	0.5	90.0	9.5	1.0	17.3	25.6
26	Birjand	59.20	32.86	1491	170.8	0.6	93.2	6.2	0.6	16.7	24.6
27	Isfahan	51.66	32.61	1590	122.8	2.7	87.1	10.3	1.0	16.2	26.4
28	Shahre-Kord	50.85	32.31	2078	321.5	1.0	92.5	6.5	1.0	12.5	27.5
29	Yazd	54.40	31.90	1230	60.8	1.3	90.3	8.4	0.9	19.3	27.0
30	Ahwaz	48.66	31.33	22	213.4	0.3	94.4	5.3	1.8	26.2	26.1
31	Zabol	61.48	31.33	489	61.0	0.0	96.1	3.9	0.7	22.7	26.3
32	Yasouj	51.58	30.67	1837	864.9	0.5	96.6	3.0	1.2	15.0	24.5
33	Abadan	48.25	30.36	11	156.0	0.1	95.1	4.8	1.7	25.4	24.4
34	Kerman	56.96	30.25	1754	152.9	2.4	89.1	8.6	0.7	17.0	23.9
35	Shiraz	52.58	29.53	1491	346.0	0.6	96.2	3.2	1.5	17.9	24.3
36	Zahedan	60.88	29.46	1370	90.6	2.6	89.7	7.6	0.8	18.6	22.7
37	Bam	58.40	29.10	1067	61.3	3.8	84.8	11.4	0.6	23.1	23.6
38	Fasa	53.68	28.96	1383	301.7	1.2	97.5	1.4	1.3	20.3	24.4
39	Bushehr	50.85	28.95	20	279.1	0.1	96.7	3.1	3.1	24.6	18.6
40	Bandar Abbas	56.36	27.31	10	182.5	1.6	94.4	3.9	1.0	27.3	16.4
41	Chahbahar	60.62	25.28	1193	111.0	7.5	88.6	3.9	1.2	26.5	10.2

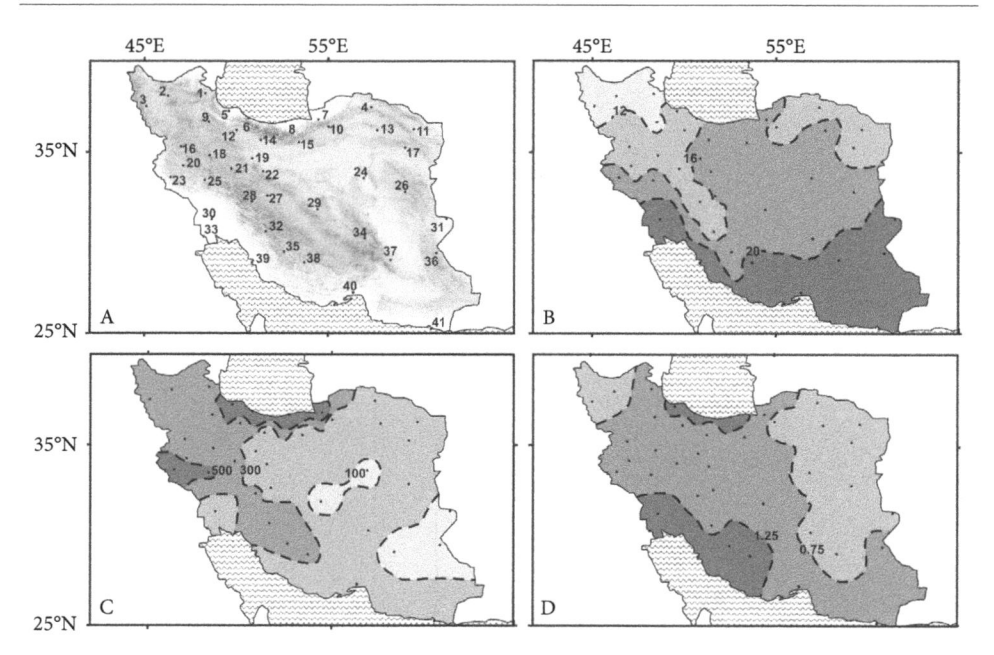

FIGURE 2.4 Spatial variability of average annual temperature (B) and average annual precipitation (C) across Iran. (D) shows the variability in the balance of winter (NDJ) to spring (FMA) rainfall; > 1.25 winter dominated, < 0.75 spring dominated. Maps drawn from data collected at the forty-one stations in Table 2.1 (A).

in winter and spring (November through April) with spatial differences in the timing of precipitation maxima (Fig. 2.4D; Table 2.1). An average of only 5.1 percent of precipitation falls in the summer months (June to September; Fig. 2.3). Precipitation values are low across the central desert basin due to the lee effect from the Zagros and the Alborz Mountains in the west and north respectively. Most of Iran's winter rain has a cyclonic source from the west which tracks down the Zagros or can pick up additional moisture from the Caspian Sea before falling in the north. Spring rains fall in the northwest in particular, where northeasterly moving depressions are blocked by high pressure over the Caspian (Domroes et al. 1998). It is possible that in the past there were other rainfall source areas for Iran. The south of the country may have received monsoonal rainfall during the early Holocene in particular, when monsoonal rains were pushed north as far as Hoti Cave in Northern Oman until 6.3 ka (Fleitmann et al. 2007), however there is no evidence currently from Iran with which to discuss this hypothesis.

Given this spatial variability numerous and well-spaced records are required to distinguish localized landscape change from regional patterns. In eastern Iran, Walker and Fattahi (2011) propose a pattern of change, through the time periods similar to those represented by the Zeribar and Mirabad lake sequences, from the dating of alluvial fan and basin deposits in what is today the arid interior. They propose that large alluvial fans were deposited at mountain fronts between ~30 and 13 ka during cold and arid conditions, during which time there was high sediment supply. Between 13 and 9 ka there is evidence of lakes beginning to form on the basin floors and fan deposition continued. A reduction in sediment supply in the early Holocene (~9–7 ka) and possibly higher precipitation leads to incision of the large fans, basinward migration of fan deposition, and lake highstands at this time. The current landscape, with dry lakes and ephemeral rivers, is preserved following arid conditions that have persisted since the mid-Holocene. This pattern of a wet Holocene between 9 and 7 ka is concurrent with the most negative isotope values in Zeribar and Mirabad (Fig. 2.3) but predates the oak maxima.

The topographic highs that influence the spatial differences in climate are a result of the regional tectonic setting linked to the collision of the Eurasian plate with the Arabian and Indian plates to the south. Earthquakes and longer-term changes in base level have, therefore, been a persistent control on the paleoenvironment of Iran, certainly over the last 20,000 years. Prior to AD 1800, after which time more information became available, there had been an "earthquake worthy of notice" somewhere in the region every four to nine years since AD 622 (Ambraseys and Melville 1982). Most of the earthquakes recorded since AD 622 are associated with fault systems through the Zagros in the west and the Khorasan–Baluchistan–Sistan massifs in the east or with the faults running east-west through the Alborz Mountains in the north of the country, therefore the spatial distribution of earthquakes follows that of the high ground evident in Fig. 2.1. This topographic and tectonic pattern, along with climatic variability, also has a direct influence on the geomorphological zones of Iran (Brookes 1982) with the most significant and rapid geomorphic changes driven by winter rains and spring snow melts in the mountain zones. The stability of the landscape is also controlled by change in vegetation, hence its importance in paleoenvironmental reconstructions, not only as a climate proxy.

WHAT IS THE RELATIONSHIP BETWEEN PEOPLE AND THE(IR) ENVIRONMENT?

People have a two-way relationship with the environment and are therefore an agent of environmental change present and past. The balance of this relationship has changed with time and space, and identifying a tipping point between the dominant partner is difficult. It has been argued that people have been significantly altering the environment throughout the Holocene, including retarding early Holocene trees in the Near East (Roberts 2002), which may have impacted our interpretations of past environments (see discussion of the early Holocene precipitation paradox above), as well as the environments themselves. It seems apparent that by the late Holocene pollen records in the Near East are controlled more by people than climate (e.g., England et al. 2008). Djamali et al. (2009b) describe changes in vegetation around Lake Maharlou (Fig. 2.1) which reflect occupation changes through the last 5000 years with cultivated species such as olives and vines appearing in the pollen record from around 4.3 ka. The pollen record from Lake Almalou in northwestern Iran (Djamali et al. 2009a) also shows significant changes in vegetation associated with historical events.

People's ability to develop technology to overcome obstacles resulting from climatic and/or environmental change complicates the human–environment relationship and the use of people themselves as a paleoenvironmental proxy. For example *qanat* systems, gently sloping tunnels carrying water from beneath the water table to a surface outflow, are found across Iran (e.g., Beaumont 1971) and may date from as early as 800 BC (Magee 2005). People are also increasingly resilient to environmental change. People in Iran have been dealing with the direct (e.g., destructions of infrastructure) and indirect results (e.g., change in hydroenvironment) (e.g., Walker and Fattahi 2011) of earthquakes throughout time, as until now the benefits of living near high ground, with associated water resources, outweigh any earthquake risk (Jackson 2006).

Conclusions

Understanding the past environment and climate in Iran is important for ongoing archaeological and palaeoclimatic narratives. Reconstructing the palaeoenvironment of Iran involves picking apart the influence of climate, people, tectonics, and vegetation on the records under investigation (e.g., Heyvaert and Baeteman 2007; Schmidt et al. 2011) and an understanding of the feedbacks between these controls. Whilst acknowledging that we can work only with what we have, care must be taken when drawing interpretations from the paleoenvironmental information currently available. This chapter has shown that change can differ on all temporal and spatial scales, and paleoenvironmental information should be used only with an understanding of its limitations. Many of the outstanding issues regarding filling in the paleoenvironmental holes in Iran, such as the development of age models and the use of high-resolution analysis, have been dealt with elsewhere and new work in Iran therefore has a body of experience to draw on to ensure new paleoenvironmental archives are analyzed to their full potential and resulting interpretations are robust.

Acknowledgments

I would like to thank Lloyd Weeks for inviting me to join the Mamasani Archaeological Project and for introducing me to Iran alongside Dan Potts, Cameron Petrie, and the Iranian Center for Archaeological Research. Most of all I would like to thank my Iranian colleagues, who have made my own work in Iran possible, in particular Dariush Noorollahi, Hajar Askari, Alireza Askari Chaverdi, Alireza Sardari, Arash Lashkari, and Kourosh Alamdari; this chapter is for them. I also wish to acknowledge the significant Iranian geomorphology literature, which I have not drawn on here due to my own inadequacies with the language, and Richard Walker for his comments on an earlier version of the chapter.

Further reading

The benchmark studies of van Zeist, Bottema, and Wright and the follow-up work of Stevens and colleagues, cited in the references below, have long provided the most reliable data on the ancient climate of the Zagros region. In the last decade much new work has been undertaken in the Zagros and beyond, although much of this has not yet been published at the time of writing. There is still no overarching study of this topic, however, and readers are advised to consult the specialist literature cited below.

References

Alijani, B., and J. R. Harman. 1985. Synoptic climatology of precipitation in Iran. *Annals of the Association of American Geographers* 75: 404–416.

Ambraseys, N. N., and C. P. Melville. 1982. *A history of Persian earthquakes*. Cambridge: Cambridge University Press.

Beaumont, P. 1971. Qanat systems in Iran. *Bulletin of the International Association of Scientific Hydrology* 16: 39–50.

Brookes, I. A. 1982. Geomorphological evidence for climatic change in Iran during the last 20,000 years. In *Palaeoclimates, palaeoenvironments and human communities in the eastern Mediterranean region in later prehistory*, ed. J. L. Bintliff and W. van Zeist, 191–229. Oxford: BAR Int Ser 133.

Djamali, M., H. Akhani, V. Andrieu-Ponel, P. Bracconnot, S. Brewer, J.-L. de Beaulieu, D. Fleitmann et al. 2010. Indian summer monsoon variations could have affected the early-Holocene woodland expansion in the Near East. *The Holocene* 20: 813–20.

Djamali, M., J.-L. de Beaulieu, N. F. Miller, V. Andrieu-Ponel, M. Berberian, E. Gandouin, H. Lahijani et al. 2009a. A late Holocene pollen record from Lake Almalou in NW Iran: Evidence for changing land-use in relation to some historical events during the last 3700 years. *JAS* 36: 1346–75.

Djamali, M., J.-L. de Beaulieu, N. F. Miller, V. Andrieu-Ponel, R. Lak, P. Ponel, M. Sadeddin et al. 2009b. Vegetation history of the SE section of the Zagros Mountains during the last five millennia: A pollen record from the Maharlou Lake, Fars province, Iran. *VHA* 18: 123–36.

Djamali, M., J. L. de Beaulieu, M. Shah-Hosseini, V. Andrieu-Ponel, P. Ponel, A. Amini, H. Akhani et al. 2008. An Upper Pleistocene long pollen record from the Near East, the 100 m-long sequence of Lake Urmia, NW Iran. *QR* 69: 413–20.

Domroes, M., M. Kaviani, and D. Schaefer. 1998. An analysis of regional and intra-annual precipitation variability over Iran using multivariate statistical methods. *Theoretical and Applied Climatology* 61: 151–9.

England, A., W. J. Eastwood, C. N. Roberts, R. Turner, and J. F. Haldon. 2008. Historical landscape change in Cappadocia (central Turkey): A palaeoecological investigation of annually laminated sediments from Nar lake. *The Holocene* 18: 1229–45.

Fleitmann, D., S. J. Burns, A. Mangini, M. Mudelsee, J. Kramers, I. Villa, U. Neff et al. 2007. Holocene ITCZ and Indian monsoon dynamics recorded in stalagmites from Oman and Yemen (Socotra). *QSR* 26: 170–88.

Griffiths, H. I., A. Schwalb, and L. R. Stevens. 2001. Environmental change in south-western Iran: the Holocene ostracod fauna of Lake Mirabad. *The Holocene* 11: 757–64.

Heyvaert, V. M. A., and C. Baeteman. 2007. Holocene sedimentary evolution and palaeocoastlines of the lower Khuzestan plain (southwest Iran). *Marine Geology* 242/1: 83–108.

Iran Meteorological Organisation. 2010. *Climatic statistics 2010*. http://www.irimo.ir/english/statistics/index.asp. June 16, 2011.

Jackson, J. 2006. Fatal attraction: Living with earthquakes, the growth of villages into megacities, and earthquake vulnerability in the modern world. *Philosophical Transactions of the Royal Society A: Mathematical, Physical and Engineering Sciences* 364/1845: 1911–25.

Jones, M. D., and C. N. Roberts. 2008. Interpreting lake isotope records of Holocene environmental change in the Eastern Mediterranean. *Quaternary International* 181: 32–8.

Kehl, M. 2009. Quaternary climate change in Iran—the state of knowledge. *Erdkunde* 63: 1–17.

Landmann, G., A. Reimer, and S. Kempe. 1996. Climatically induced lake level changes at Lake Van, Turkey, during the Pleistocene/Holocene transition. *Global Biogeochemical Cycles* 10: 797–808.

Magee, P. 2005. The chronology and environmental background of Iron Age settlement in southeastern Iran and the question of the origin of the qanat irrigation system. *IrAnt* 40: 217–31.

Modarres, R., and A. Sarhadi. 2011. Statistically-based regionalization of rainfall climates of Iran. *Global and Planetary Change* 75: 67–75.

Roberts, N. 1983. Age, paleoenvironments, and climatic significance of late Pleistocene Konya Lake, Turkey. *QR* 19: 154–71.

———. 2002. Did prehistoric landscape management retard the post-glacial spread of woodland in Southwest Asia? *Antiquity* 76: 1002–10.

Roberts, N., W. J. Eastwood, C. Kuzucuoğlu, G. Fiorentino, and V. Caracuta. 2011. Climatic, vegetation and cultural change in the eastern Mediterranean during the mid-Holocene environmental transition. *The Holocene* 21: 147–62.

Rosen, A. 2007. *Civilizing climate: Social responses to climate change in the Ancient Near East*. Lanham: AltaMira Press.

Schmidt, A., M. Quigley, M. Fattahi, G. Azizi, M. Maghsoudi, and H. Fazeli. 2011. Holocene settlement shifts and palaeoenvironments on the Central Iranian Plateau: Investigating linked systems. *The Holocene* 21/4: 583–95.

Smith, G. I. 1974. Quaternary deposits in south-western Afghanistan. *QR* 4: 39–52.

Staubwasser, M., and H. Weiss. 2006. Holocene climate and cultural evolution in late prehistoric-early historic West Asia—Introduction. *QR* 66: 372–87.

Stevens, L. R., E. Ito, A. Schwalb, and H. E. Wright. 2006. Timing of atmospheric precipitation in the Zagros Mountains inferred from a multi-proxy record from Lake Mirabad, Iran. *QR* 66: 494–500.

Stevens, L. R., H. E. Wright, and E. Ito. 2001. Proposed changes in seasonality of climate during the Late glacial and Holocene at Lake Zeribar, Iran. *The Holocene* 11: 747–55.

Walker, R. T., and M. Fattahi. 2011. A framework of Holocene and Late Pleistocene environmental change in eastern Iran inferred from the dating of periods of alluvial fan abandonment, river terracing, and lake deposition. *QSR* 30: 1256–71.

Wasylikowa, K., and A. Witkowski, eds. 2008. *The palaeoecology of Lake Zeribar and surrounding areas, Western Iran, during the last 48,000 years*. Ruggell: Diaton Monographs 8.

Wright, H. E. 1962. Pleistocene glaciation in Kurdistan. *Eiszeitalter und Gegenwart* 12: 131–64.

———. 1993. Environmental determinism in Near Eastern prehistory. *CA* 34: 458–69.

CHAPTER 3

THE PALEOLITHIC OF IRAN

NICHOLAS J. CONARD, ELHAM GHASIDIAN,
AND SAMAN HEYDARI-GURAN

INTRODUCTION AND HISTORY OF RESEARCH

With its geographic position between the Levant and Mesopotamia and the great expanses of Asia, Iran is of critical importance for many questions related to human evolution and the development and spread of Paleolithic cultural innovations. In this context, one issue that arises repeatedly is whether researchers are better served by viewing Iran as a corridor between east and west and north and south, or rather as a large region of autochthonous cultural development. In this review, both these approaches have their strengths as well as their limitations, and in the end we are probably best served by establishing the Paleolithic record of Iran (Fig. 3.1) in its own right before we view it as a donor, receiver, or corridor for human dispersals and cultural innovations.

Research into the Paleolithic archaeology of Iran has a long and punctuated history. This history can be organized in: (1) an unstructured period of antiquarian activities; (2) a poorly developed pioneering stage that corresponds roughly to the period between the two world wars; (3) a classic phase between the end of the second world war and the Islamic Revolution; (4) a period beginning in 1979 and corresponding to the early years of the existence of the Islamic Republic of Iran; and (5) a recent phase of more intense research, with many Iranian and international teams conducting fieldwork across nearly the whole country (Smith 1986; Otte et al. 2007; Heydari-Guran 2010; Vahdati Nasab 2011). In 1989, Philip Smith synthesized the state of Paleolithic research in Iran up to the Islamic Revolution in a short monograph which serves as a convenient benchmark for the research community. This publication summarized the state of discourse until the late 1970s, when for all practical purposes Paleolithic fieldwork in Iran stopped for two decades. Most recently Hamed Vahdati Nasab (2011) has addressed the current state of research and summarized the history of research.

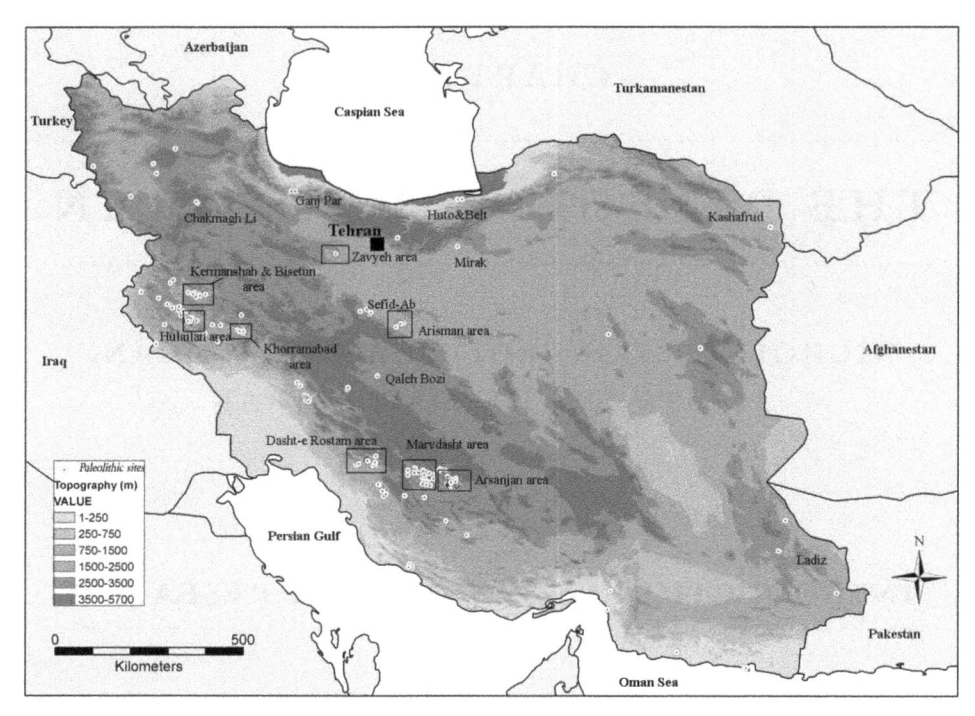

FIGURE 3.1 Map of Iran, showing the most important Paleolithic sites and areas cited in the text.

Jacques de Morgan (1907) conducted survey alongside the river terraces of Pardameh in Mazandaran province in the early twentieth century and identified Paleolithic artifacts, but recently Vahdati Nasab has concluded that these finds are more likely ecofacts. Across the border in Iraqi Kurdistan, D. Garrod (1930) had already excavated Zarzi Cave in the late 1920s and documented an important sequence of late Upper Paleolithic and Epipaleolithic deposits. Zarzi today is the type site of the Zarzian, and Garrod's important work documented the first well-stratified Paleolithic material from the Zagros and demonstrated the great research potential of the karst landscape of the Zagros for Paleolithic research (Wahida 1975). In the 1930s, Henry Field, accompanied by geologists, led a Paleolithic survey in the Zagros Mountains (Piperno 1972) and excavated a small test trench in Kunji Cave (Fig. 3.2) on the outskirts of Khorramabad in Luristan (Field 1951).

The period between the end of the World War II and the Islamic Revolution can be considered the classic phase of Paleolithic research in Iran. Starting in the 1940s, Carleton Coon led excavations at a number of key sites including Hunters' Cave at the base of Bisotun Mountain in the west central Zagros Mountains and Hotu and Belt Caves in the Mazandaran region, northern Iran and Khunik Cave in Khorasan province, northeastern Iran (Coon 1951, 1952). Coon's publication of *The Seven Caves* in 1957 captured the ambitious spirit and enthusiasm reflected in this early fieldwork. Starting in the early 1950s, Ralph and Rose Solecki conducted survey and a series of important

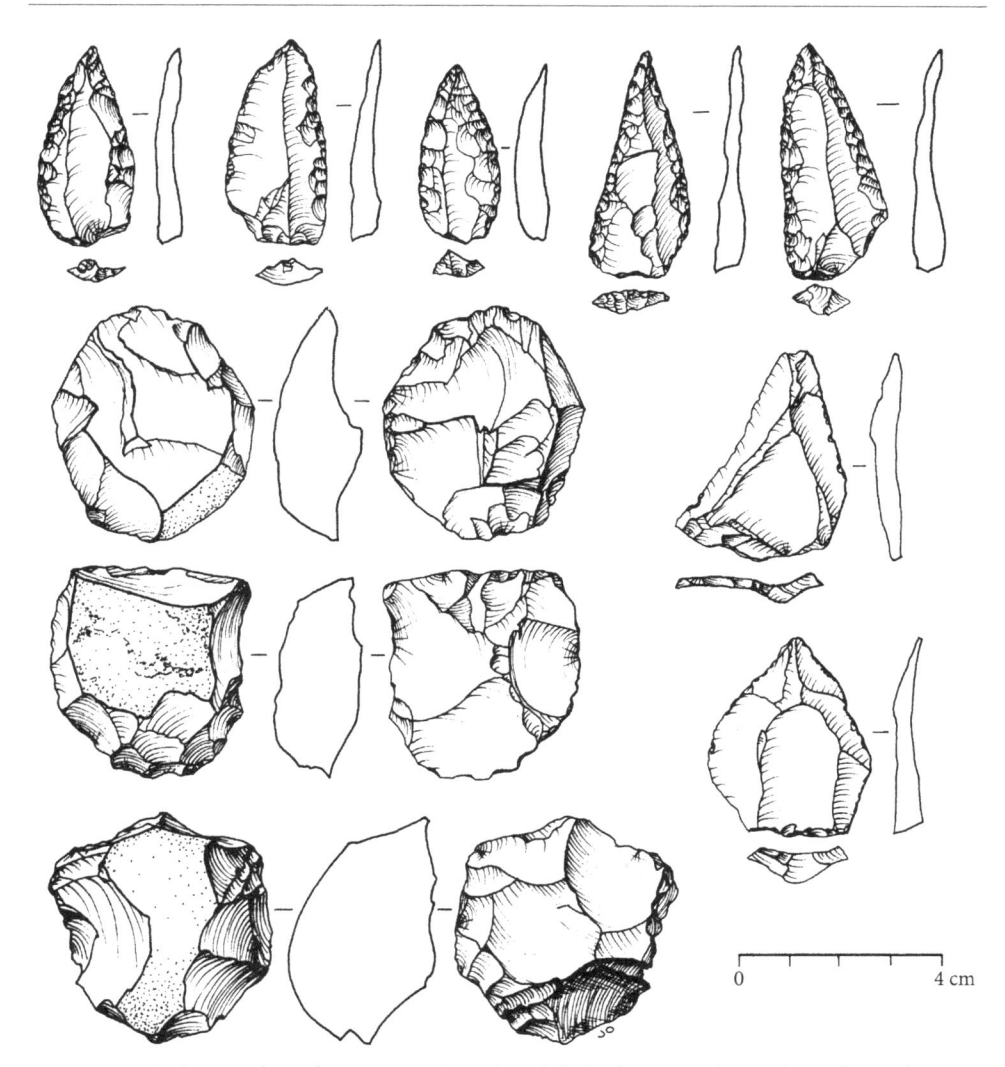

FIGURE 3.2 Lithic artifacts from Kunji Cave (modified after Baumler and Speth 1993).

excavations at Shanidar in Iraqi Kurdistan. Like the earlier work by Garrod in the Zagros, the Soleckis' work at Shanidar had major ramifications for research in Iran and, as happened a generation earlier with Garrod, Solecki's definition of the Baradostian culture of the early Upper Paleolithic was quickly adopted for similar assemblages from the Zagros Mountains of Iran. At this time Charles McBurney (1950, 1968, 1969) began fieldwork in Iran that led to excavations at Ali Tappeh and Keyaram Caves in the northeastern Alborz Mountains and the two rock-shelter sites of Houmian and Bard Spid in the Kuh-e Dasht region.

As an offshoot of Braidwood's interdisciplinary research on the origins of Neolithic societies, researchers from the University of Chicago, including Hole, Howe, Flannery, and others led large-scale, systematic surveys and excavations. The work of Hole and

Flannery (1967) in particular represents one of the best examples of problem-driven Paleolithic research during the heyday of the "new archaeology." Much of this research served as a highly visible example of how archaeological methods could be applied to collect reliable data and formulate models explaining long-term patterns of cultural evolution from the earliest occupation of Iran until the rise of the region's great civilizations. Even today this research remains highly relevant. Other scholars, including Mortensen, Piperno, Smith, Rosenberg, Speth, and Ikeda, made major contributions to Paleolithic research in Iran, and made Iran as a whole and the Zagros Mountains in particular a key region of Paleolithic research.

This unusually productive period of research came to a sudden end with the Islamic Revolution in 1979 and the ousting of the leading political figures, who had been very open to allowing Western scientists to conduct research in Iran. During the decades immediately following the revolution, publications continued to appear on the collections recovered during fieldwork in the 1950s, 1960s, and 1970s, but new field projects by non-Iranian researchers did not begin until around the start of the new millennium.

Since around 2000, Paleolithic research in Iran has gradually intensified. Although the last few years have seen a decline in fieldwork in connection with restrictive policies regarding permits and political tensions in the region, the first decade of the twenty-first century will no doubt be considered something of a renaissance for Paleolithic archaeology, and many international collaborative projects and Iranian excavations and surveys have taken place. At the same time a generation of young archaeologists in their twenties and thirties left Iran to receive training abroad and earned graduate degrees on Paleolithic topics, and thereby became the first Iranian experts on the Paleolithic. Similar developments occurred in the allied fields of biological anthropology and human evolution. During the last decade researchers from Belgium, France, Germany, Japan, the United States, and other countries joined Iranian colleagues to conduct important fieldwork in many parts of the country (Otte et al. 2007). This work has highlighted the traditional research areas of the Zagros, but also covered in varying degrees of intensity nearly all parts of the country.

This chapter is organized chronologically, and as we move through the major periods of the Paleolithic, we shall try to highlight important work that took place during all of the phases of research as well as accenting the current state of knowledge and current research questions. In this chapter we use new environmental classifications of the Iranian plateau in order to better characterize the geo-ecological framework of early human settlement systems (Heydari-Guran 2010).

Lower Paleolithic

While much of southwestern Asia, including most notably Israel, Jordan, and Syria, have a rich record of research on the Lower Paleolithic and many important stratified sites from this period, to date not a single, well-documented, stratified Lower Paleolithic site is known in Iran. Without exception, all of the sites with typologically Lower Paleolithic finds are surface sites lacking organic preservation and reliable means of dating the lithic artifacts recovered there. The sites are invariably reworked and unable to provide the meaningful spatial information needed for a contextual analysis of past human behavior. Thus, most work until now has mainly addressed the basic question of whether or not an assemblage can be attributed to the Lower Paleolithic. While this kind of simple question is fairly straightforward in regions with a rich Lower Paleolithic record—where the presence of clear Acheulean handaxes or archaic flake assemblages can reliably be attributed to the Lower Paleolithic—in Iran, where such comparative material from reliable contexts in stratified sites is absent, most attributions to the Lower Paleolithic are based on assumptions about the Paleolithic cultural sequence in Iran and on geological observations.

In 1986, when Smith published his review of the Paleolithic in Iran, the only sites he could attribute to the Lower Paleolithic were in the alluvial deposits of the Kashafrud Basin in northeastern Iran, where Ariai and Thibault found "pebble tools" at about sixty sites (Smith 1986: 15). There are at least two other surface lithic collections in southeastern Iran that Hume reported as Lower Paleolithic, naming the local industry "Ladizian" (Hume 1976). Subsequent research has led to the discovery of several more sites with Lower Paleolithic artifacts. The river terrace site of Ganj Par, reported by Biglari and Shidrang in 2006, is one of those promising Lower Paleolithic localities. It yielded about 140 lithic artifacts including core scrapers, bifaces, large flakes, and hammer stones. Based on the use of volcanic rocks as raw material, the high frequency of core-choppers, the presence of discoid and anvil flaking, along with other methods, Biglari and Shidrang argued that the assemblages from Ganj Par resemble Early and Middle Acheulian assemblages elsewhere in western Asia (Biglari and Shidrang 2006: 166). This region also boasts the only cave with Lower Paleolithic evidence in the form of a flake-based industry (Biglari and Shidrang 2006: 166). In western Azerbaijan traces of Lower Paleolithic occupation have been discovered on the river terraces of the Mahabad River. The Lower Paleolithic artifacts at Shiwatoo include Acheulean chopper-cores, along with bipolar on anvil flaking technique, large flakes, and pebble tools (Jaubert et al. 2006).

The only indication of Lower Paleolithic in the southern Zagros Mountains is the open air site of Baba Guri. This site was discovered by the joint Tübingen-Iranian Stone Age research project during its Paleolithic survey in the southern Zagros Mountains. The lithic assemblage with archaic technological features consists of inclined and platform cores, blades, flakes, and a core tablet.

A series of isolated Lower Paleolithic finds have also been reported from different parts of the country including Gakia (Braidwood et al. 1961); Quri Gol in the northwest ecozone of Iran (Singer and Wymer 1978); and Pal Barik in the west-central Zagros Mountains (Mortensen 1993). The latter yielded one handaxe and thirty-one choppers and chopping tools. Mortensen assigned the assemblage to the Zagros Acheulian. In dating the assemblage on the basis of the geomorphological setting of the site, Mortensen concluded that it might be younger than 130,000 BP. He also drew a typological comparison between the lithic tools at Pal Barik and those from Barda Balka, located in the northern Zagros of Iraq, and based on the typological parallels he estimated the site was between 100,000 and 80,000 years old (Mortensen 1993), which would be an unexpectedly young age for Lower Paleolithic artifacts.

Middle Paleolithic

The first Middle Paleolithic sites on the Iranian Plateau were discovered in the rock shelter sites of the Kermanshah and Khorramabad valleys of the west-central Zagros. In 1951, Carleton Coon excavated the Hunter's Cave in the Bisotun region of Kermanshah where he recovered a large number of lithic artifacts assigned to the Zagros Mousterian (Coon 1951, 1957; Dibble 1984). He also excavated the Middle Paleolithic cave site of Tamtameh close to Lake Urmia in northwestern Iran (Coon 1951). Bruce Howe conducted an excavation in 1959 at Kobeh Cave in the Kermanshah valley, which also yielded Middle Paleolithic artifacts (Smith 1986).

In the 1960s, Frank Hole and Kent Flannery began a series of Paleolithic investigations in the Khorramabad valley c.200 km south of Kermanshah (Hole and Flannery 1967). They conducted test excavation at Kunji and Ghamari Caves and Gar Arjeneh rock shelter and addressed the nature of the transition from the Middle to the Upper Paleolithic.

In the Hulailan region in the west-central Zagros P. Mortensen conducted one of the few prehistoric investigations on the Iranian plateau through systematic surface survey (Mortensen 1974, 1975). The Hulailan Paleolithic survey resulted in the discovery of twenty-four sites from the Lower through Epipaleolithic periods. The Middle Paleolithic of the Hulailan valley reflected denser occupation than that of the Lower Paleolithic. Mortensen recorded eight sites with Middle Paleolithic finds, including the five open-air sites (Cheshmeh Kahreh, Sar Sarab, site no. 7, Saimarreh E, and Saimarreh F) and three rock shelters (Ghar Huchi, Ghar Villa, and Ghar Sefid). The Middle Paleolithic industries of these sites have much in common with those of Bisotun, Kunji, and Warwasi Caves in the west-central Zagros, which places them in the Zagros Mousterian. The Hulailan assemblages include Levallois points, flakes, and cores, as well as discoidal cores. Diverse side scrapers, end scrapers, and Mousterian points are abundant. As at Kunji Cave, backed knives and notched and denticulated flakes occur in Hulailan, while blade production is infrequent, as is the case at Bisotun Cave. The Mousterian artifacts of the Hulailan valley were mostly discovered near rivers or in the western part of the valley in an area with many rock shelters close to springs and streams (Mortensen 1993).

In 1966, P. E. L. Smith conducted a test excavation in the cave site of Ghar-e Khar, in the Bisotun region of Kermanshah province, that yielded material dating from the Middle Paleolithic through the Islamic period. The base level of the excavated area produced typical Mousterian artifacts such as asymmetrical side scrapers and thick retouched blades. The Middle Paleolithic artifacts from this cave resemble the ones recovered from the neighboring site of Bisotun Cave (Smith 1967).

In the southern Zagros, the first evidence of Middle Paleolithic occupation was discovered by W. M. Sumner near Jahrom. This site, along with the Eshkaft-e Ghad-e Barm-e

Shur Cave on the edge of Lake Neyriz, near Shiraz, yielded a Levallois Middle Paleolithic industry (Piperno 1972). Rosenberg (1988) surveyed the Marv Dasht area and documented six Middle Paleolithic sites associated with Levallois Zagros Mousterian material among the thirty-one sites recorded. There are several more Paleolithic sites in the southern Zagros but they are isolated, like the one discovered by Vita-Finzi on the Persian Gulf coast (Vita-Finzi and Copeland 1980).

In early 2000, Iranian archaeologists conducted a Paleolithic survey in the Khorramabad valley, revisiting the Paleolithic sites discovered by Hole and Flannery and identifying several more sites as well (Roustaei et al. 2004). Biglari (2001) has reported three more Middle Paleolithic rock shelter sites in Bisotun Mountain, one of which, Mar Tarik (Fig. 3.3), has been excavated by a joint Iranian-French team. The lithic industry there is very similar to the industries previously documented at excavated sites in the west-central Zagros and is characterized by the use of raw materials from the nearby vicinity, Levallois flaking technique, and a high proportion of retouched tools dominated by points, elongated points, convergent scrapers, and *déjetés* or double scrapers with frequently sharpened edges (Jaubert et al. 2006).

In 2009, Roustaei (2010) conducted a survey in the Bakhtiyari region of the south-central Zagros Mountains, identifying more than 160 localities associated with lithic artifacts, predominantly of Middle Paleolithic origin. Among the Middle Paleolithic localities are at least five large knapping areas with thousands of artifacts scattered on the surface. The lithic assemblages there are characterized by Levallois technology associated with different kinds of scrapers and points.

Elsewhere in the Zagros, scattered Paleolithic investigations have resulted in the discovery of Paleolithic sites such as Jam-o-Riz (Dashtizadeh 2008) and six rock-shelter sites in Dasht-e Rostam in western Fars (Heydari-Guran 2010). In northern Iran, the joint French-Iranian Paleoanthropological Programme (FIPP) conducted survey and excavation in the central Alborz Mountains. Their investigations documented two Middle Paleolithic open-air sites at Moghak and Otchounak in the southern foothills of the Alborz. These are characterized by a Mousterian industry but one that was less elaborated than the Mousterian industry of Keyaram Cave and the Zagros Mountain sites (Berillon et al. 2007).

In addition, new archaeological investigations in the central desert basin of Iran have refuted the old view that Middle Paleolithic occupation was found only in the Zagros Mountains. Recent discoveries in new regions such as Takht-e Solayman, Arisman, Mirak, Qaleh Bozi, and Kashan, all of which lie outside the Zagros Mountains, are changing our image of Middle Paleolithic settlement. These sites are located in a variety of lacustrine, dune field, and travertine spring-fed Quaternary sedimentary environments (Heydari-Guran et al. forthcoming). The Takht-e Solayman area, where two surface Middle Paleolithic localities have been reported, has one of the greatest concentrations of travertine spring-fed deposits in Iran. Chakhmaq Li is a large, homogenous chert outcrop, associated with travertine terraces. At 2300 masl, this is one of the highest Middle Paleolithic localities in Iran (Heydari-Guran et al. 2009). In general, the assemblage of Chakhmaq Li was based on the flake production. Most of the cores are inclined

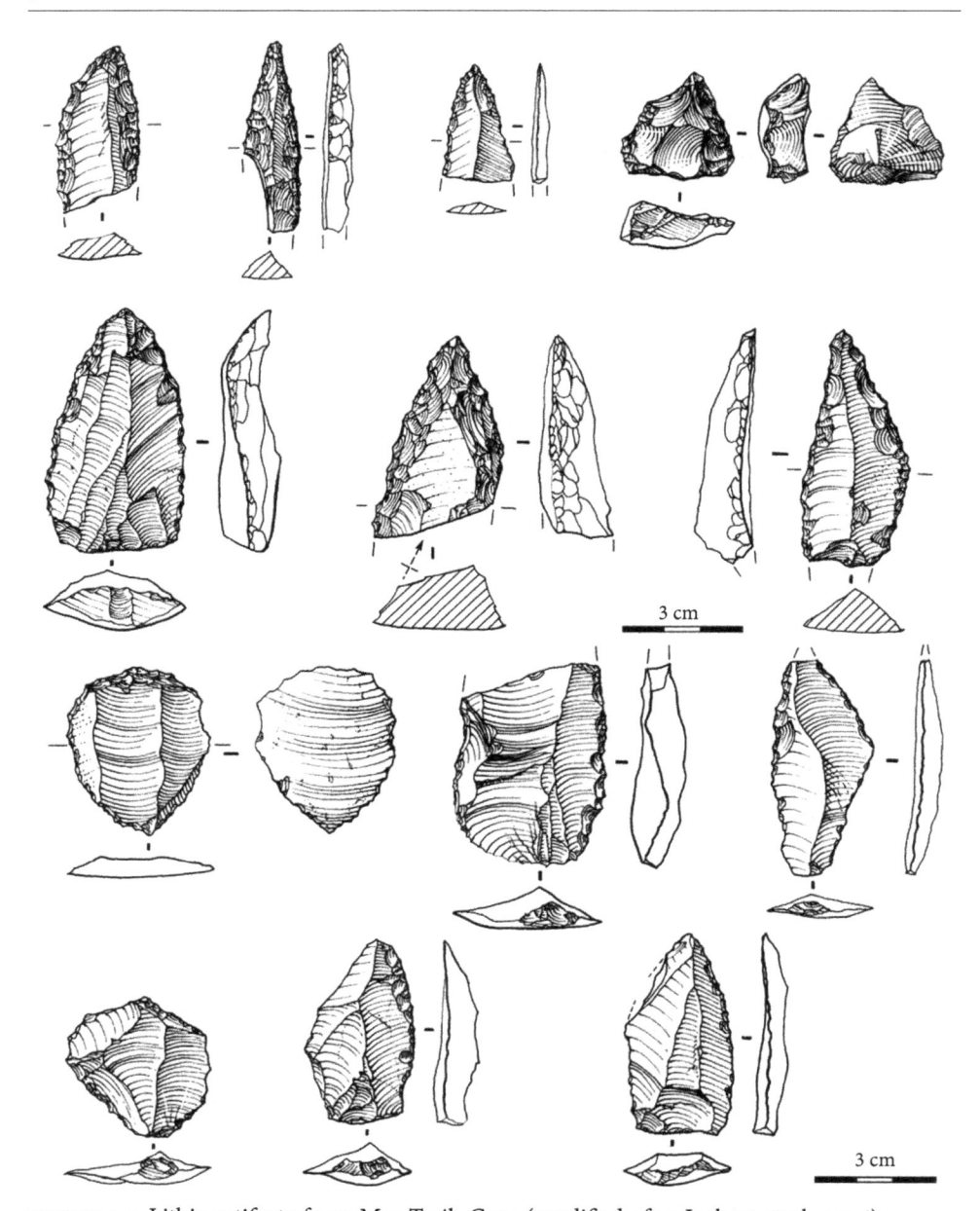

FIGURE 3.3 Lithic artifacts from Mar Tarik Cave (modified after Jaubert et al. 2006).

Levallois flake, blade, and point cores. Flakes also form a large component of the assemblage and include Levallois and non-Levallois debitage. The average sizes of the flakes and their technological features conform to the cores, confirming their contemporaneity (Heydari-Guran et al. 2009: 113).

Mirak is the largest Middle Paleolithic open-air site on the central plateau of Iran. Archaeological survey there has yielded a large lithic assemblage dominated by Levallois technology associated with different kinds of scrapers, Mousterian points, and discoidal cores. The presence of blades may indicate occupation in the later phases of the Paleolithic as well (Rezvani and Vahdati Nasab 2010). A recently discovered cluster of shelter sites includes Qaleh Bozi, 25 km south-southwest of Isfahan, one of the few shelter sites on the central plateau with Middle Paleolithic artifacts (Biglari et al. 2009). In contrast to the Middle Paleolithic industries of the open-air sites on the central plateau, which are dominated by Levallois technology, the lithic industry of Qaleh Bozi yielded only a small number of Levallois pieces. Unifacial and bifacial points, including foliate points, comprised a large portion of these assemblages, distinguishing them from contemporary sites on the Iranian plateau. Side scrapers; heavily retouched, notched and denticulated pieces; and small-sized artifacts show close resemblances to the Zagros Mousterian industry (Biglari et al. 2009).

A number of Paleolithic localities have been discovered in a formerly lacustrine environment on the north-central plateau (Djamali et al. 2006, Conard et al. 2007). Typologically the Middle Paleolithic artifacts of Zavyeh (Fig. 3.4) are characterized by

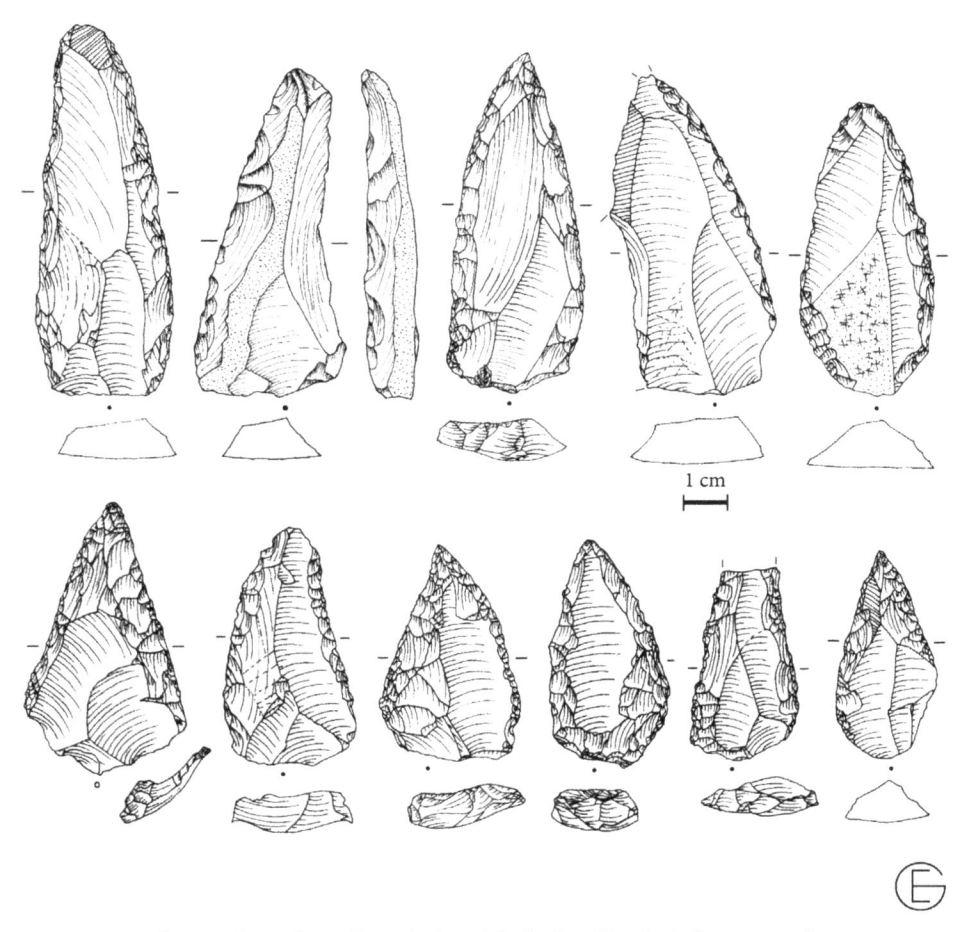

FIGURE 3.4 Lithic artifacts from Zavyeh (modified after Heydari-Guran 2010).

points and scrapers. The points are mostly retouched Levallois points. There are also some Levallois flakes that have been made into points through heavy retouch. The number of retouched pieces, including scrapers, is high (Heydari-Guran et al. forthcoming).

There are at least two areas alongside the eastern Karkas Mountains in the interior desert basin where Middle Paleolithic stone artifacts have been found. The first includes several travertine formations close to Kashan (Biglari 2004) and the second comprises the dune field sites of Qaleh Gusheh and Holabad, and a travertine deposit near Arisman. Over the course of two seasons of survey in the Qaleh Gusheh area in 2004 and 2005, eight localities with Middle Paleolithic artifacts were recognized amongst sixteen Paleolithic sites (Conard et al. 2009; Heydari-Guran 2010; Heydari-Guran and Ghasidian 2011). Of these, the Holabad travertine sites yielded the most homogenous Middle Paleolithic assemblages. These are characterized by large number of Levallois and discoidal cores, Levallois flakes, blades and points, and different kinds of scrapers (Heydari-Guran et al. forthcoming). The Middle Paleolithic industry from dune field sites in Ghaleh Gusheh, like nearby Holabad, is dominated by Levallois technology. Retouched Levallois flakes and points are abundant among the assemblages there (Heydari-Guran et al. forthcoming; Heydari-Guran and Ghasidian 2011).

Middle Paleolithic sites have also been reported around Minab, near the Straits of Hormuz (Dashtizadeh forthcoming). There, lithic artifacts from the open-air sites of Hasanlangi and Gourband 2 are characterized by Levallois technology.

In general, the "Zagros Mousterian" remains the main Middle Paleolithic cultural group so far defined, but clearly, as Zavyeh and other sites show, the Middle Paleolithic of Iran is much more complex and interesting than was thought until recently (Heydari-Guran et al. forthcoming).

Upper Paleolithic

During the Upper and Epipaleoltihic periods the Iranian plateau underwent important changes with respect to both the number of sites occupied and the variety of the lithic industry. The Soleckis named the early Upper Paleolithic assemblage of the northern Zagros the "Baradostian" and the Epipaleolithic "Zarzian" (Hole and Flannery 1967, Olszewski 1993a, 1993b). However, to date no sites have been identified with a continuous Paleolithic sequence that covers the transition from the Middle to the Upper and the Upper to the Epipaleolithic.

The first late Paleolithic industries in Iran were recovered by C. Coon in Hotu and Belt Caves on the Caspian Sea shore (Coon 1951). The lithic artifacts from these caves were dated typologically to the late Epipaleolithic period. During their mission to Khorramabad in 1960, Hole and Flannery conducted several excavations that revealed Upper and Epipaleolithic artifacts. In Gar Arjeneh, Pa Sangar rock shelter, and Yafteh Cave (Fig. 3.5) they recovered Baradostian and Zarzian industries (Hole and Flannery 1967). The Baradostian lithic industry is dominated by blade production. Characteristic

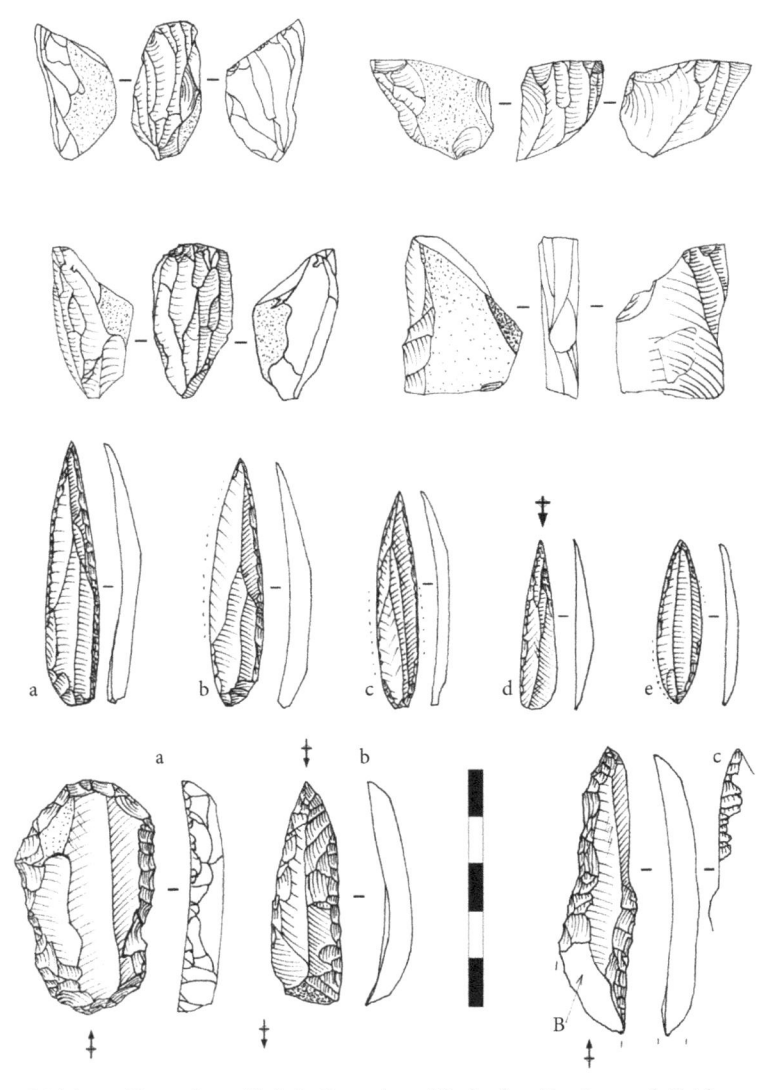

FIGURE 3.5 Lithic artifacts from Yafteh Cave (modified after Bordes and Shidrang 2009).

tools include slender points, backed blades and bladelets, twisted bladelets with various kinds of light retouch, end scrapers, discoidal scrapers, side scrapers, and burins (Hole 1970). Yafteh Cave was later reexcavated by M. Otte, who recovered the same industry as Hole and Flannery (Otte et al. 2007; Bordes and Shidrang 2009). Emphasizing its purported Aurignacian lithic elements and perforated marine shell beads, Otte and colleagues identified the industry of Yafteh Cave as belonging to the Zagros Aurignacian, with dates as far back as c.40,000 cal. BP.

A Baradostian industry was also identified by D. I. Olszewski in the rock-shelter site of Warwasi (Fig. 3.6) in the Kermanshah region (Olszewski 1993a). Later, because of the presence of what she considered Aurignacian elements, Olszewski and Dibble classified

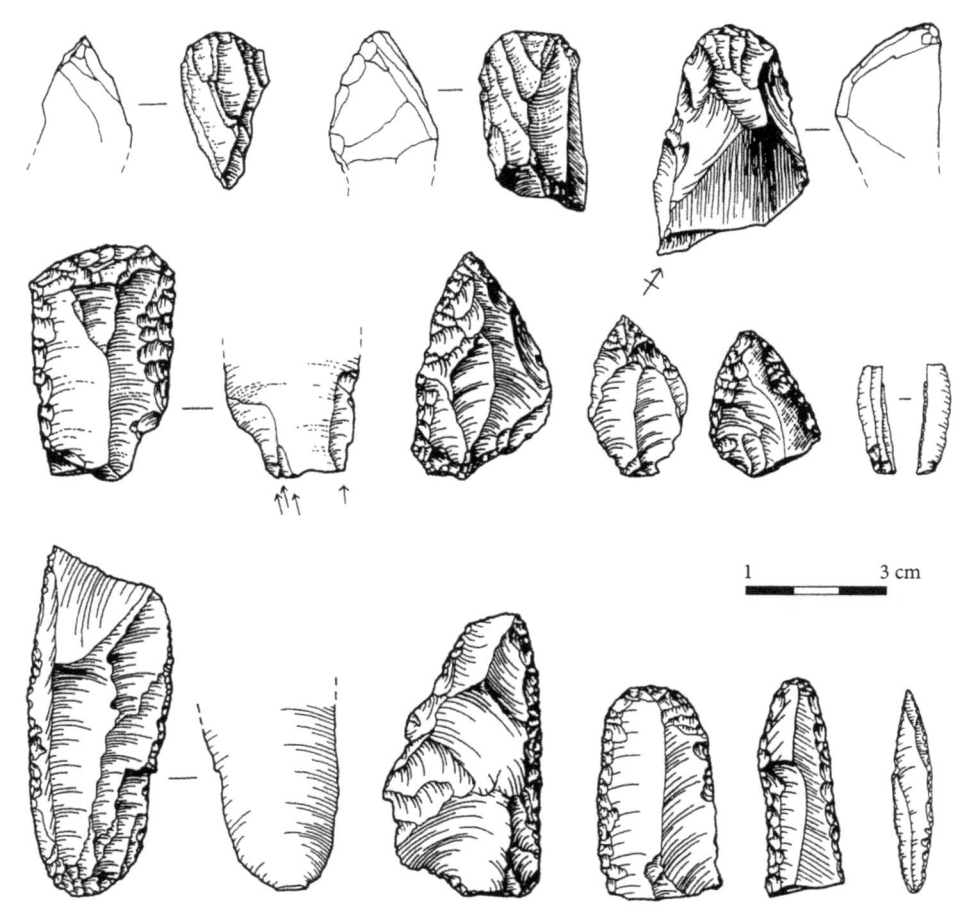

FIGURE 3.6 Baradostian artifacts from Warwasi Rockshelter (modified after Olszewski and Dibble 1994).

these assemblages as Zagros Aurignacian instead of Baradostian (Olszewski and Dibble 1994, 2006).

In the Hulailan valley, Mortensen documented fifteen sites with Late Paleolithic artifacts (mixed Upper and Epipaleolithic) (Mortensen 1993, 1974, 1975) but the assemblages at these sites made it impossible to link the earlier Mousterian to the Upper Paleolithic sequence. Baradostian elements were possibly present among the Hulailan assemblages but they were difficult to distinguish from the mixed Mousterian and Zarzian elements (Mortensen 1993: 165). The assemblages contained retouched flakes and blades, notches, borers, and burins. The cores were mainly blade and bladelet cores. While flakes were dominant, blades and bladelets were common as well.

In 1972, Piperno revisited the sites that Field had recorded around Lake Maharlu near Shiraz (Piperno 1974). Eshkaft-e Ghad-e Barm-e Shur was the largest cave site in this group, but apart from a description of the lithics found there, Piperno gave no further information on the other sites. At Eshkaft-e Ghad-e Barm-e Shur Piperno collected

287 lithic artifacts. The general characteristic of the assemblage is the small size of the tools, which were probably struck from small flint pebbles. Retouched blades and bladelets, burins, end scrapers and notches, and denticulates predominate. Piperno related the industry to the middle or final phases of the Baradostian although, given the presence of several bladelets, backed bladelets, and inversely retouched bladelets, he did not reject of the possibility of a Zarzian attribution and suggested a chronological span from the Baradostian into the Zarzian period. He interpreted the assemblage as evidence of the geographical expansion of the Baradostian industry into the southern Zagros Mountains.

A mission from Kyoto University to the Arsanjan area has documented several Paleolithic sites in the southern Zagros Mountains as well (Ikeda 1979; Tsuneki and Nishida 2007). Although illustrations of some of the lithics have been published, no descriptions are yet available.

The main source of data on the later Paleolithic in Fars comes from the Kur River Basin (KRB) thanks to the surveys of W. M. Sumner (Sumner 1972) and M. Rosenberg. Rosenberg documented thirty-one rock-shelter sites with Middle to Epipaleolithic artifacts (Rosenberg 1988, 2003). In order to establish the chronostratigraphy of the Paleolithic sites in the KRB, he excavated one of the most promising cave sites, Eshkaft-e Gavi (Fig. 3.7), which is dated to the Upper Paleolithic (Rosenberg 1979). He classified the material as Baradostian, while in another promising cave site called KMC, he found Zarzian material, though in both cases the assemblages lacked some of the characteristic elements of both the Baradostian and the Zarzian as defined in the west-central Zagros. Most of the laminar assemblage in the upper the strata of Eshkaft-e Gavi showed Upper Paleolithic affinities and included backed blades, notched blades, burins, end scrapers, carinated scraper, and some fragmentary Baradostian points. Unfortunately Rosenberg's investigations were cut short in 1979 by the Islamic Revolution.

In recent years, many Paleolithic sites and finds have been recorded in Fars. A. Dashtizadeh conducted an intensive survey in the Kazerun area and to the southwest of Shiraz and resurveyed the Marv Dasht as well. In 2003, he revisited the KRB, identifying twenty-one sites dating mainly to the Epipaleolithic, with a few Upper Paleolithic as well (Dashtizadeh forthcoming). He also observed some diagnostic Middle Paleolithic artifacts. His work largely confirmed what Rosenberg had demonstrated.

On the intermontane plain of Kazerun, Dashtizadeh documented twenty-seven sites, the most promising of which are caves. The analysis of the lithics is still at a preliminary stage but the assemblage is mainly characterized by blade and bladelet-based debitage and cores. The tools included thumbnail scrapers, borers, end scrapers, carinated scrapers and burins. Dashtizadeh compared them to the Late Baradostian and Zarzian traditions of the western Zagros (Dashtizadeh 2006).

One of the most intensive Paleolithic missions in recent years in the southern Zagros has been conducted by the Tübingen Iranian Stone Age Research Project (TISARP) in the Dasht-e Rostam-Basht region, where numerous Paleolithic sites with lithic artifacts have been recorded (Conard et al. 2006, 2007; Heydari-Guran 2010). This team

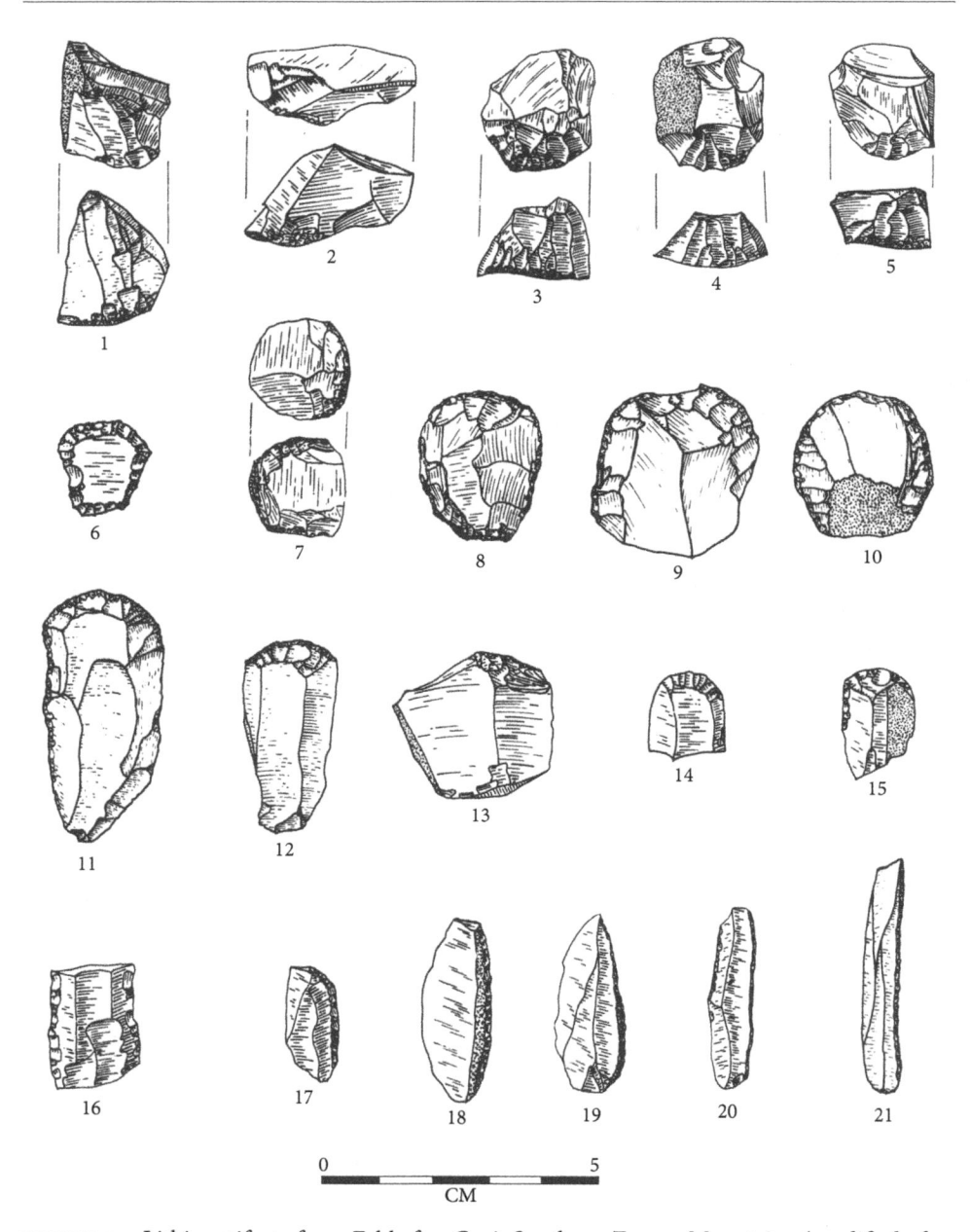

FIGURE 3.7 Lithic artifacts from Eshkaft-e Gavi; Southern Zagros Mountains (modified after Rosenberg 1985).

has documented numerous Upper Paleolithic sites, including Ghar-e Boof (Ghasidian 2010; Conard and Ghasidian 2011; Ghasidian et al. 2009). The radiocarbon dates from Ghar-e Boof Cave (Fig. 3.8) make it one of the oldest Upper Paleolithic sites of Iran, dating back to c.40,000 cal. BP (Ghasidian 2010; Conard and Ghasidian 2011). The flints used were mainly cobbles of red raw material from the Fahliyan River (Conard et al.

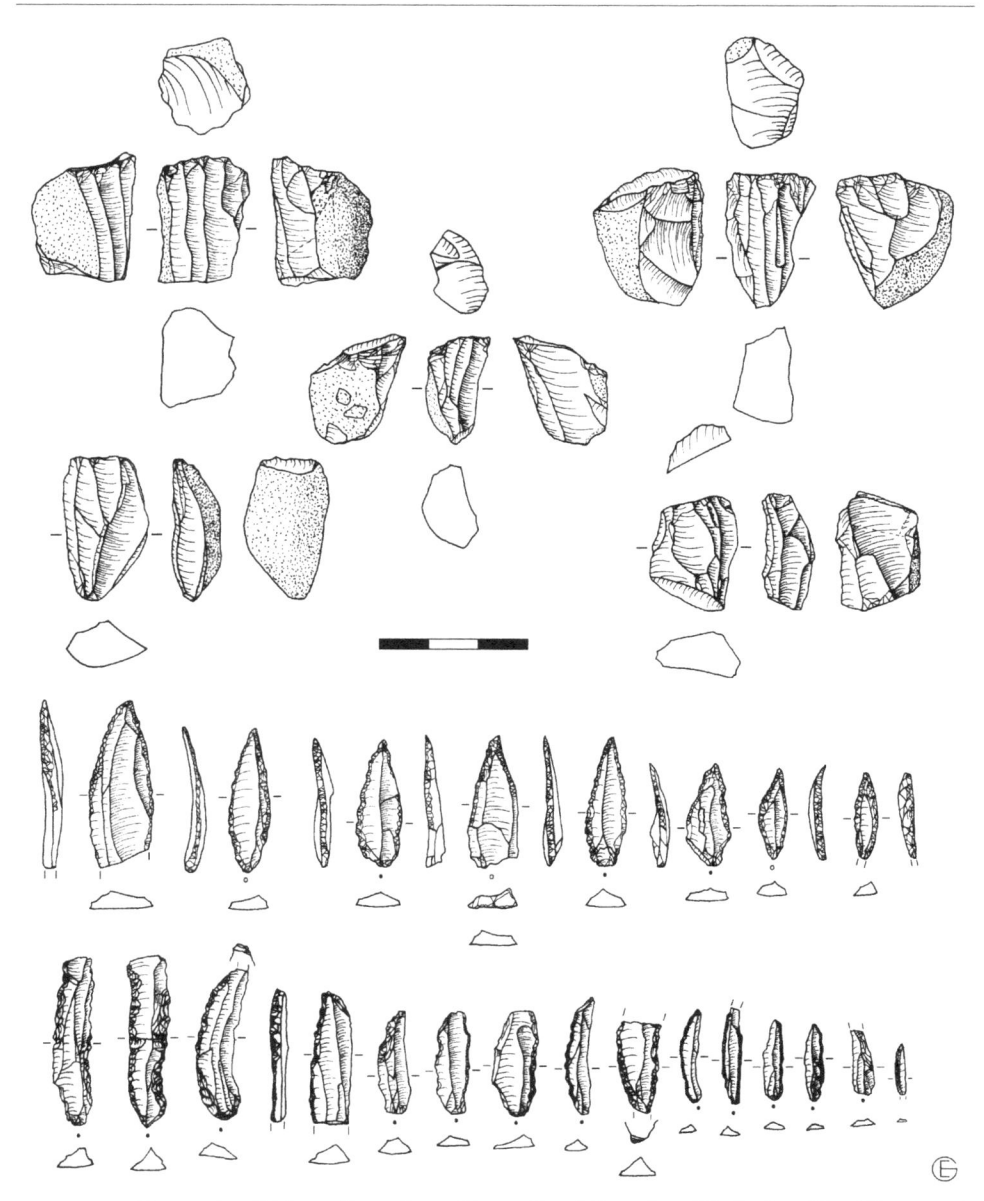

FIGURE 3.8 Rostamian lithic artifacts from Ghar-e Boof Cave (modified after Ghasidian 2010).

2007; Heydari-Guran 2010; Ghasidian 2010). The lithic assemblages of Ghar-e Boof are characterized by bladelets and many unidirectional, single-platform bladelet cores. The tools are dominated by different kinds of retouched bladelets with twisted profile. We refer to these larger retouched bladelets of diverse types as "Rostamian bladelets" (Ghasidian 2010). Rostamian bladelets are the most abundant tool type at Ghar-e Boof. These tools, although somewhat variable, are characterized by their distinctive blank morphology and abrupt and semiabrupt retouch. Their presence in large numbers helps

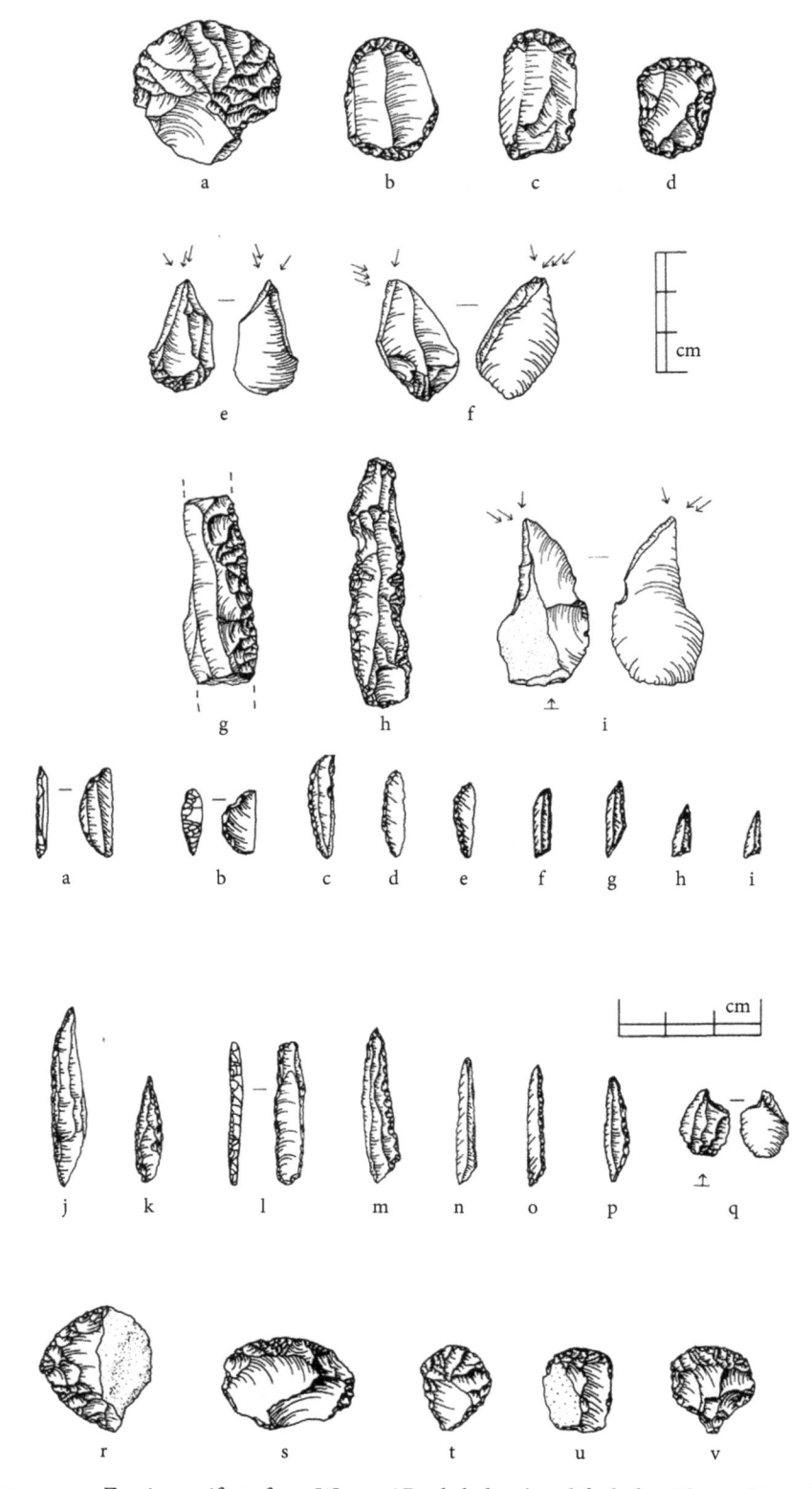

FIGURE. 3.9 Zarzian artifacts from Warwasi Rockshelter (modified after Olszewski 1993b).

to define the lithic assemblage at Ghar-e Boof Cave, which we classify as belonging to the Rostamian. This site also produced forty-one examples of personal ornaments made from five species of shells originating from the early Upper Paleolithic deposits (Conard and Ghasidian 2011).

Recently scholars including Olszewski and Dibble (2006) and Otte and Kozłowski (2007) have equated the Baradostian with the Aurignacian. Olszewski's work on the rich lithic assemblages from Howe's excavations at Warwasi near Kermanshah has fundamentally questioned the earlier taxonomic system by arguing for strong links between the assemblages from Warwasi and the European Aurignacian. Otte in particular has not only argued that Upper Paleolithic assemblages from Yafteh should be classified as Aurignacian, but that the Aurignacian originated in Iran (Otte and Kozłowski 2007; Otte et al. 2007: 94). We, however, remain skeptical of such claims for intercontinental cultural contact and instead advocate that researchers first establish reliable local cultural chronological sequences before engaging in broad comparative studies with such radical implications. In our view, the fieldwork in recent years has demonstrated that the Iranian Upper Paleolithic cannot be limited to the Baradostian, Zagros Aurignacian, and Zarzian (Fig. 3.9). Instead this period documents a variety of local assemblage types such as those from the Dasht-e Rostam and Ghaleh Gusheh that indicate much more spatial and temporal diversity within the Upper Paleolithic than researchers previously thought.

Further reading

So much recent research has occurred in the Paleolithic archaeology of Iran that older syntheses like Smith (1986) are now very outdated. The edited volume *IP* from 2009 provides more recent data but readers should note the many journal articles cited below for the most recent advances in Paleolithic studies in Iran.

References

Baumler, M., and J. D. Speth. 1993. A Middle Paleolithic assemblage from Kunji Cave, Iran. In *The Paleolithic prehistory of the Zagros-Taurus*, ed. D. I. Olszewski and H. L. Dibble, 1–74. Philadelphia: The University Museum.
Berillon, J., A. Asgari Khanghah, P. Antoine, J.-J. Bahain, B. Chevrier, V. Zeitoun, N. Aminzadeh et al. 2007. Discovery of new open-air Paleolithic localities in Central Alborz, Northern Iran. *Journal of Human Evolution* 52/4: 380–87.
Biglari, F. 2001. Report on newly discovered Paleolithic sites at Bisitun, central-western Iran. *IJAH* 28: 50–60 (in Persian).
——. 2004. The preliminary report on the Paleolithic sites in Kashan Region. In *The silversmiths of Sialk*, ed. S. M. Shahmirzadi, 151–68. Tehran: SRPR 2.
Biglari, F., and S. Shidrang. 2006. The Lower Paleolithic occupation of Iran. *NEA* 69/3–4: 160–8.

Biglari, F, M. Javeri, M. Mashkour, Y. Yazdi, S. Shidrang, M. Tengberg, K. Taheri et al. 2009. Test excavations at the Middle Paleolithic sites of Qaleh Bozi, southwest of central Iran: A preliminary report. *IP*: 29–38.

Bordes, J. G., and S. Shidrang. 2009. La Séquence baradostienne de Yafteh (Khorramabad, Lorestan, Iran). *IP*: 85–100.

Braidwood, R. J., B. Howe, and C. A. Reed. 1961. The Iranian Prehistoric Project. *Science* 133: 2008–10.

Conard, N. J., E. Ghasidian, S. Heydari, and M. Zeidi. 2006. Report on the 2005 survey of the Tübingen-Iranian Stone Age Research Project in the Provinces of Esfahan, Fars and Kohgiluyeh-Boyerahmad. In *Archaeological Reports*, vol. 5, ed. M. Azarnoush, 9–34. Tehran: ICAR.

Conard, N. J., E. Ghasidian, S. Heydari, R. Naderi, and M. Zaidee. 2007. The 2006 Season of the Tübingen-Iranian Stone Age Research Project in the provinces of Fars and Markazi. In *9th Annual report of Archaeological Organisation*, ed. H. Fazeli, 43–67. Tehran: ICAR.

Conard, N. J., E. Ghasidian, and S. Heydari-Guran. 2009. The open-air Late Paleolithic site of Bardia and the Paleolithic occupation of the Qaleh Gusheh Sand Dunes, Esfahan Province, Iran. *IP*: 141–54.

Conard, N. J., and E. Ghasidian. 2011. The Rostamian Cultural Group and the taxonomy of the Iranian Upper Paleolithic. In *Between sand and sea: The archaeology and human ecology of southwestern Asia, Festschrift in honor of Hans-Peter Uerpmann*, ed. N. J. Conard, P. Drechsler, and A. Morales, 33–52. Tübingen: Kerns Verlag.

Coon, C. S. 1951. *Cave explorations in Iran 1949*. Philadelphia: University of Pennsylvania Press.

———. 1952. Excavations in Hotu Cave, Iran, 1951: A preliminary report. *PAPS* 96/3: 231–49.

———. 1957. *The seven caves: Archaeological explorations in the Middle East*. New York: Alfred Knopf.

Djamali, M., I. Soulié-Märsche, D. Esu, E. Gliozzi, and R. Okhravi. 2006. Palaeoenvironment of a Late Quaternary lacustrine-palustrine carbonate complex: Zarand Basin, Saveh, central Iran. *Palaeogeography, Palaeoclimatology, Palaeoecology* 237: 315–34.

Dashtizadeh, A. 2006. Survey and reconnaissance of the Paleolithic settlements of Saadatshahr, Fars. In *Third conference of the young archaeologists and reviewing the archaeology of Khorasan and Bam*, ed. S. Zare, 17. Tehran: ICHTO (In Farsi).

———. 2008. Paleolithic remains from the north coast of the Persian Gulf: Preliminary results from the Jam-o-Riz plain, Busher Province, Iran. *Antiquity* 83/319: Project Gallery.

———. Forthcoming. Report on the Paleolithic archaeological survey at Marvdasht.

Dibble, H. L. 1984. The Mousterian Industry from Bisitun Cave (Iran). *Paléorient* 10/2: 23–34.

Field, H. 1951. Reconnaissance in Southwestern Asia. *Southwestern Journal of Anthropology* 7: 86–102.

Garrod, D. A. E. 1930. The Paleolithic of southern Kurdistan: Excavations in the caves of Zarzi and Hazar Merd. *BASOR* 6: 8–43.

Ghasidian, E., A. Azadi, S. Heydari, and N. J. Conard. 2009. Late Paleolithic cultural traditions in the Basht region of the southern Zagros of Iran. *IP*: 125–40.

Ghasidian, E. 2010. Early Upper Paleolithic occupation at Ghar-e Boof Cave: A reconstruction of cultural traditions in southern Zagros mountains of Iran. Unpublished PhD diss., Eberhard Karls University of Tübingen.

Heydari-Guran, S. 2010. Paleolithic landscapes of Iran. Unpubl. Ph.D. diss., Eberhard Karls University of Tübingen.

Heydari-Guran, S., and E. Ghasidian 2011. Paleolithic survey in the Arisman region, western central Iranian plateau. *EMM*: 484–98.

Heydari-Guran, S., E. Ghasidian, and N. J. Conard. 2009. Paleolithic sites on travertine and tufa formations in Iran. *IP*: 109–24.

———. Forthcoming. The desert behind the Zagros mountains. *Quaternary International*.

Hole, F., and K. V. Flannery 1967. The prehistory of southwestern Iran: A preliminary report. *PPS* 22: 147–206.

Hole, F. 1970. The Paleolithic culture sequence in western Iran. In *Actes du VII Congrès international des Sciences préhistoriques et protohistoriques*, ed. J. Filip, 286–92. Prague: Institut d'Archéologie de l'Académie.

Hume, G. W. 1976. *The Ladizian: An industry of the Asian chopper-chopping tool complex in Iranian Baluchistan*. Philadelphia: Dorrance.

Ikeda, J. 1979. *Preliminary report of an archaeological survey in Arsanjan area, Fars Province, Iran, 1977*. Kyoto: Kyoto University.

Jaubert, J., F. Biglari, J.-G. Bordes, L. Bruxelles, V. Mourre, S. Shidrang, R. Naderi, and S. Alipour. 2006. New research on Paleolithic of Iran: Preliminary report of 2004 Iranian-French Joint Mission. In *Archaeological Reports*, vol. 4, ed. M. Azarnoush, 17–26. Tehran: ICAR.

McBurney, C. B. M. 1950. The geographical study of the older Palaeolithic stages in Europe. *PPS* 16: 163–83.

———. 1964. Preliminary report on Stone Age reconnaissance in north-eastern Iran. *PPS* 30: 382–99.

———. 1968. The cave of Ali Tappeh and the Epi-Paleolithic in N.E. Iran. *PPS* 34: 385–413.

———. 1969. Report on further excavations in the caves of the Kuh-i Dasht area, during August 1969. *Bastan Chenassi va Honar-e Iran* 3: 8–9.

Morgan, J. de. 1907. Le Plateau iranien pendant l'époque Pléistocène. *Revue de l'École d'Anthropologie de Paris* 17: 213–16.

Mortensen, P. 1974. A survey of early prehistoric sites in the Holailān Valley in Lorestān. *PASARI* 2: 34–52.

———. 1975. Survey and soundings in the Holailān Valley in Lorestān. *PASARI* 3: 1–12. Tehran: ICAR.

———. 1993. Paleolithic and Epipaleolithic sites in the Hulailan valley, northern Luristan. *PPZT*: 158–86.

Olszewski, D. I. 1993a. The Late Baradostian occupation at Warwasi rockshelter, Iran. *PPZT*: 186–206.

———. 1993b. The Zarzian occupation at Warwasi rockshelter, Iran. *PPZT*: 207–36.

Olszewski, D. I., and H. L. Dibble. 1994. The Zagros Aurignacian. *CA* 35/1: 68–75.

———. 2006. To be or not to be Aurignacian: The Zagros Upper Paleolithic. In *Towards a definition of the Aurignacian*, ed. O. Bar-Yosef and J. Zilhão, 355–73. Lisbon: Instituto Português de Arqueologia.

Otte, M., F. Biglari, D. Flas, S. Shidrang, N. Zwyns, M. Mashkour, R. Naderi et al. 2007. The Aurignacian in the Zagros region: New research at Yafteh Cave, Lorestan, Iran. *Antiquity* 81: 82–96.

Otte, M., and J. Kozłowski. 2007. *L'Aurignacien du Zagros*. Liège: ERAUL.

Piperno, M. 1972. Jahrom, a Middle Paleolithic Site in Fars, Iran. *EW* 22: 183–97.

———. 1974. Upper Paleolithic caves in southern Iran, preliminary report. *EW* 24: 9–13.

Rezvani, H., and H. Vahdati Nasab. 2010. A major Middle Palaeolithic open-air site at Mirak, Semnan Province, Iran. *Antiquity* 84/323: Project Gallery.

Rosenberg, M. S. 1979. Eshkaft-e Gavi (The Malyan Project). *Iran* 17: 148–9.

———. 1985. Report on the sondage at Eshakft-e Gavi. *Iran* 23: 51–62.

———. 1988. *Paleolithic settlement pattern in the Marv Dasht, Fars Province, Iran*. Unpublished PhD diss., University of Pennsylvania.

———. 2003. The Epipaleolithic in the Marvdasht. *YBYN*: 98–108.

Roustaei, K., H. Vahdati Nasab, F. Biglari, S. Heydari, G. A. Clark, and J. M. Lindly. 2004. Recent Paleolithic surveys in Lurestan. *CA* 45: 692–707.

Roustaei, K. 2010. Discovery of Middle Palaeolithic occupation at high altitude in the Zagros Mountains, Iran. *Antiquity* 84/325: Project Gallery.

Singer, R., and J. Wymer. 1978. A hand-ax from northwest Iran: the questions of human movement between Africa and Asia in the Lower Paleolithic periods. In *Views of the past*, ed. L. G. Freeman, 13–27. The Hague: Mouton.

Smith, P. E. L. 1967. Ghar-i-Khar and Ganj-i-Dareh. *Iran* 5: 138–39.

———. 1986. *Paleolithic Archaeology in Iran*. Philadelphia: University Museum of Archaeology and Anthropology.

Sumner, W. M. 1972. Cultural development in the Kur River Basin, Iran: An archaeological analysis of settlement patterns. Unpublished PhD diss., University of Pennsylvania.

Tsuneki, A., and M. Nishida. 2007. *Stone tools from Arsanjan area, Fars province, Iran*. Ibaraki: University of Tsukuba.

Vahdati Nasab, H., 2011. Paleolithic archaeology in Iran. *The International Journal of Humanities of the Islamic Republic of Iran* 18/2: 63–87.

Vita-Finzi, C., and L. Copeland. 1980. Surface finds from Iranian Makran. *Iran* 18: 149–55.

Wahida, G. E. 1975. A reconsideration of the Upper Paleolithic in the Zagros Mountains. Unpublished PhD diss., University of Cambridge.

CHAPTER 4

THE DEVELOPMENT AND EXPANSION OF A NEOLITHIC WAY OF LIFE

LLOYD R. WEEKS

Introduction

The Neolithic was a critical period in cultural and technological development, witnessing the transition from a way of life based upon hunting and foraging to one based primarily upon farming. Alongside these changes in basic subsistence strategies, there were also changes in the nature of settlement, especially the move toward longer-term or permanent residence in one location, the development of durable housing structures of packed mud or mudbrick, and the first use of pottery. In addition to these material changes, the Neolithic is regarded by some scholars as a period of dramatic change in human beliefs and ideologies, during which individuals and societies restructured their relationships with one another and with the natural world. Many of the material and cultural foundations of developments in later prehistoric and early historic Iran were laid in the Neolithic period.

The transition to farming

Some of the best information regarding the transition from mobile hunting and foraging groups to sedentary farming communities comes from the central Zagros Mountains, in Luristan and Kermanshah (Hole 1987: fig. 5). Critically, this region is within the natural distribution of the wild ancestors of sheep, goats, cattle, and pigs, and also of wild cereal crops including wheat and barley, and had sufficient rainfall to support agriculture without the need for irrigation (Clutton-Brock 1999; Uerpmann 1987; Harlan and Zohary 1966; Zohary and Hopf 2000). The sites of Ganj Dareh, Tepe Guran, and Sheikh-e Abad stand as particularly important witnesses to this transition in subsistence and settlement.

Recent excavations at Sheikh-e Abad, near Kermanshah, have shown that the earliest levels at the site, radiocarbon dated to $c.10{,}000{-}8000$ cal BC, are characterized by ashy midden layers with no observable architecture (Matthews et al. 2010). These deposits attest to a subsistence based upon foraging for local wild plant resources such as almonds, pistachios, and lentils and the hunting of wild sheep and goats. In contrast, the upper levels at Sheikh-e Abad, radiocarbon dated to $c.7600$ cal BC, are characterized by rectilinear structures of *chineh*/mudbrick, one of which has been labeled as a "shrine" due to the presence of pairs of large wild goat and sheep skulls with applied ocher that were built into the structure. The management of morphologically wild sheep and goat may be indicated by micromorphological analyses from the site, which have identified "widespread traces of herbivore dung pre- and post-dating $c.8000$ cal BC" (Matthews et al. 2010).

The discoveries from the upper levels at Sheikh-e Abad closely parallel those from the site of Ganj Dareh, currently the most important site for understanding the earliest Neolithic communities of Iran. Ganj Dareh is a small settlement of substantially less than 1 ha, located in a small valley southeast of Kermanshah at about 1400 masl. Field surveys and excavations in the region have documented contemporary sites with similar occupational sequences at Tepe Ghenil and Tepe Qazemi, forming a cluster of sites within a few hours' walk of one another (Smith and Mortensen 1980). Excavations at Ganj Dareh have documented a series of five superimposed phases of occupation from Level A (uppermost) to E (lowermost). Whilst Level E has no solid architectural remains, comprising only firepits dug into virgin soil, a group of mudbrick and *chineh* buildings, some with two stories, was present at Ganj Dareh by Level D (Smith 1990; Van Zeist et al. 1984: 201). Radiocarbon dates place Levels E, D, and C at $c.8000$ cal BC, and Levels B and A at $c.7800$ cal BC (Zeder and Hesse 2000: table 1). The houses display a substantial degree of practical knowledge of working with *chineh* and mudbrick (Smith 1990), as well as the possible ritual use of structures indicated by the incorporation of goat horns and skulls into architectural niches (Smith 1976: fig. 5; 1990: fig. 1; Zeder 2001). A very similar process of architectural elaboration, from simple pits to rectilinear *chineh* and mudbrick houses, has been recorded at the roughly contemporary aceramic Neolithic site of Tepe Abdul Hosein, located at $c.1860$ masl in the Kangavar region (Pullar 1990).

Aceramic Neolithic sites at lower elevations in the central Zagros include Jani on the Islamabad plain (Matthews et al. 2010; Abdi 2003: 414), radiocarbon dated to $c.8000$ cal BC, and Tepe Guran and related sites such as Tepe Faiz'ollah, Tappeh Chena, and Sar Asiaban in the Hulailan Valley (Meldgaard et al. 1963; Mortensen 1974: 36-7, figs. 6-9). The best known of these is Tepe Guran, which upon excavation produced twenty-one main occupational levels, labeled A (uppermost) to V (Meldgaard et al. 1963). The lowest three levels of the site (T-V) are aceramic, with Level U radiocarbon dated to $c.7600{-}7200$ cal BC. Levels D-S date to the ceramic Neolithic period, with Level H producing a radiocarbon date of c.6800–6400 cal BC. Like Ganj Dareh and Tepe Abdul Hosein, Tepe Guran demonstrates significant architectural change during the early Neolithic period, in particular the "transition from hut to house" (Meldgaard et al. 1963: 104). The lowest 1.5 m of occupation at the site were characterized by settlement in wooden huts, remains of which are represented archaeologically only by dark stains in excavated deposits of Levels V–M (Meldgaard et al. 1963: fig. 10; Mortensen 1972). Well-built *chineh* houses appear from Level P, alongside wooden huts, and from Level M onward rectilinear mud or mudbrick houses are used exclusively. These later house walls, sometimes built onto a stone socle, were faced with straw-tempered mud plaster sometimes decorated with a thin coating of white or red gypsum plaster. Some houses also exhibited elaborate floors, in which small pieces of white feldspar were placed in a matrix of fine clay colored with red ocher (Meldgaard et al. 1963: figs. 11–12), and installations including domed ovens that preserved carbonized cereal grains.

The faunal and botanical material from these sites has been critical in documenting processes of Neolithization in the central Zagros region. At Ganj Dareh, pioneering studies by Zeder and Hesse (Zeder 2001; Zeder and Hesse 2000) have demonstrated the selective harvesting of subadult male goats by the Ganj Dareh inhabitants. Such animal management strategies were a key component of the early stages of domestication and are suggested by Zeder (2001) to significantly predate morphological changes in faunal assemblages previously regarded as indices of domestication, such as horn core morphology, that were a by-product of the movement of goats outside their natural highland habitats and into hot, arid lowland Iran (Zeder 2008: 11598). Domesticated goats were also recorded from the aceramic levels of Tepe Guran, representing the great majority of the studied ungulate remains from the earliest occupation of the site.

Hunted animal species were also important to the early Neolithic subsistence economy at Ganj Dareh, where wild sheep, cattle, pigs, red and fallow deer, and gazelle were recorded, as well as smaller creatures including hares, foxes, reptiles, and waterfowl (Smith 1978: 539). In contrast, the remains of wild animals were relatively scarce at aceramic Tepe Guran, with the exception of migratory waterfowl whose remains were concentrated in the nine earliest levels of the site, suggesting a limited winter-time occupation. Later levels at Tepe Guran incorporated a much broader range of wild species, including gazelle, aurochs, wild boar, and red deer as well as edible land snails, reflecting a more intensive exploitation of the varied environs surrounding the site (Mortensen 1972: 295–6; Balossi-Restelli 2001: table 6).

With regard to botanical remains, the inhabitants of Ganj Dareh also exploited domesticated two-row hulled barley (*Hordeum distichum*), whose importance increased over time from the Level E to Level A (van Zeist et al. 1984). Archaeobotanical studies at Tepe Abdul Hosein likewise indicate the common use of two-row hulled barley, alongside emmer wheat (*Triticum dicoccum*) and (rarely) lentils (*Lens culinaris*), and it has been suggested that this array of plants was brought to the site already domesticated (Hubbard 1990: 220). At Tepe Guran, domed ovens preserved carbonized grains of domesticated two-row hulled barley and (rarely) two-row wild barley. Such crops would have been grown at these sites using rain-fed agriculture.

Other plant species exploited at early Neolithic sites in the central Zagros included wild barley (*Hordeum spontaneum*), wild or domestic lentils and peas, and other wild legumes, as well as almonds and pistachios (Van Zeist et al. 1984; Hubbard 1990). Studies of charcoal from Tepe Abdul Hosein indicate the use of pistachio, almond, and tamarisk wood, most probably for fires and also construction, as well as willow, which was used mainly for construction, as at Ganj Dareh (Willcox 1990). In addition to the archaeobotanical remains, pounding and grinding stones and chipped stone blades with sickle polish attest to the collection and processing of plant foods at these early Neolithic sites (Pullar 1990).

The chipped stone tools from the central Zagros aceramic Neolithic sites form a largely coherent group. Typical artifacts include borers, backed points, and backed blades, blades and bladelets, end scrapers, sickles, retouched flakes, and "bullet cores" (Pullar 1990: fig. 50; Meldgaard et al. 1963: 119). Obsidian of eastern Anatolian origin appears at all but the earliest aceramic Neolithic sites in the central Zagros. Thus, it is not present at Ganj Dareh, but appears at Tepe Abdul Hosein from Period II, where it accounts for a small percentage of the chipped stone assemblage, and at Tepe Guran, where 5–10 percent of chipped stone artifacts are of obsidian (Meldgaard et al. 1963: 119; Pullar 1990: 27; Renfrew 1977). Numerous tools of animal bone are known from these sites, including points, gouges, and scrapers, indicating the exploitation of sheep/goat, hare, fox, boar (wild boar teeth are also recorded; Flannery 1983: 175), red deer (antler tips), and wolf/leopard (Pullar 1990; Meldgaard et al. 1963). Other small finds common to the earliest Neolithic sites of the central Zagros include clay figurines of humans and animals (boar, deer, and possibly caprids and cattle) as well as other clay tokens, predominantly of the conical type, and a variety of beads of shell and stone (Pullar 1990; Meldgaard et al. 1963).

These sites also share a general tradition of intramural human burial. The largest number of burials comes from Ganj Dareh, where dozens of individuals were interred under the house floors of Phases D–A, and child burials seem to have been preferentially placed under wall niches (Balossi Restelli 2001: 35). At Tepe Abdul Hosein, several human burials were found in the upper aceramic Neolithic levels (Pullar 1990), most of which had been buried under or into existing living structures, and intramural human burials have been also recorded in the upper levels at Sheikh-e Abad (Matthews et al. 2010). The very lowest levels of Tepe Guran produced a pit, dug into virgin soil, with the secondary interment of the bones of at least four individuals. Other burials at the site were concentrated below house floors, usually in a contracted position, in a pattern typical for the early Neolithic sites of the region. The burials at these sites generally held little in the way of material remains other than small personal ornaments such as beads. Occasionally, individuals were interred with larger artifacts, such as the carved stone bowl associated with an intramural burial at Tepe Abdul Hosein (Pullar 1990: pl. 3) that is similar to examples from domestic contexts at Tepe Guran (Meldgaard et al. 1963: fig. 19). Interestingly, many early Neolithic burials exhibit evidence for artificial cranial modification during infancy, including examples from Ganj Dareh and Tepe Ghenil as well as early lowland Neolithic sites like Ali Kosh and Chagha Sefid (see below). This intentional modification of appearance resulted in dramatically elongated head shapes in adults and was most probably undertaken to denote differences in identity, whether arising from ethnicity, gender, status or other factors (Daems and Croucher 2008).

In summary, the currently available archaeological evidence suggests that the earliest aceramic Neolithic communities in Iran developed in the central Zagros Mountains in the period from c.8500 to 7500 cal BC. There is additional if limited evidence to suggest that early aceramic Neolithic sites also existed in neighboring Iranian Kurdistan (Mohammadifar and Motarjem 2008), which is perhaps unsurprising given the presence of such sites in Iraqi Kurdistan (Braidwood and Howe 1960). Archaeological evidence from the central Zagros sites is critical for understanding the move from a system of mobile seasonal settlement to one of semi- or fully sedentary village life. The elaboration of dwellings observed throughout the occupational sequences at Sheikh-e Abad, Ganj Dareh, Tepe Abdul Hosein, and Tepe Guran can be regarded as an index of increased sedentism, and such architectural evidence is in accord with bioarchaeological data from these sites. Both Tepe Abdul Hosein and Ganj Dareh, for example, have early occupational levels that consist predominantly of the remains of pits dug into virgin soil, and both witness a transition to more elaborate *chineh* and mudbrick architecture that can show many stages of maintenance, such as the repeated replastering of floors and hearths (Pullar 1990: 9; Smith 1990). Although the bioarchaeological data from Ganj Dareh cannot be used to conclusively indicate permanent or seasonal occupation, Smith (1990: 324) has suggested that "Level E was occupied during the period from spring to fall, but probably not in winter, and represents a phase of limited sedentism and food production, while in the later phase the site was occupied at all seasons by groups somewhat more committed to food production although we cannot be sure that people were present in every month of the year." Elsewhere, the diversification of subsistence observed in the later levels at Tepe Guran (see above) is regarded by Mortensen (1972) as indicating a transition from a semipermanent seasonal camp of transhumant herders to a permanent village of farmers. Mortensen (1972: fig. 1) has proposed a general model to explain the transition to village life in the central Zagros, arguing for the following developmental sequence:

Stage I: a pattern of circulating annual movement between short-term seasonal camps, regarded as characteristic of Epipaleolithic hunter-forager groups

Stage II: a pattern of circulating annual movement focused on longer-term occupation of semipermanent seasonal base camps, regarded as characteristic of the earliest stages of the move toward Neolithic subsistence when hunting-foraging has been supplemented by herding and/or cultivation (as seen, for example, in the lowest levels of Ganj Dareh and Tepe Guran)

Stage III: a pattern of radiating movement from permanent villages that is characteristic of more developed Neolithic settlements (such as the later levels at Tepe Guran).

Based upon anthropological case studies of swidden agriculturalists, Pullar (1977: fig. 4) proposed a more elaborate version of this general model that allowed for the development of a range of mobility strategies, including transhumant nomadism, in the prehistoric Zagros.

The expansion of Neolithic lifeways: Pre-pottery Neolithic sites in southern and eastern Iran

Beginning in the second half of the eighth millennium BC, aceramic Neolithic sites began to appear in areas outside of the central Zagros, occurring in many, but not all, regions of Iran. The best and earliest evidence comes from lowland southwest Iran (Khuzestan and Ilam), particularly from the excavated sites of Ali Kosh and Chagha Sefid in Deh Luran (Hole et al. 1969; Hole 1977) and Chogha Bonut in the Susiana plain (Alizadeh 2003). Additionally, surface surveys and soundings have revealed aceramic Neolithic occupation at Chogha Khulaman and Fasil in the Mehran plain to the north of Deh Luran (Darabi and Fazeli 2009). Such discoveries are significant, as these lowland sites are outside the natural distributions of the wild ancestors of domesticated sheep, goat, and cereals, and may represent the expansion of established Neolithic communities from the Zagros highlands.

Two phases of aceramic Neolithic occupation have been excavated at Ali Kosh, the earlier Bus Mordeh phase and the later Ali Kosh phase. Recent radiocarbon dates indicate that these phases span the period from *c*.7600 to 7200 cal BC, whilst the earliest ceramic-bearing deposits of the subsequent Mohammad Jaffar phase date to *c*.7200–7000 cal BC (Hole 2000; Zeder and Hesse 2000: table 1). The lowest levels in the Bus Mordeh phase are characterized by rectilinear mudbrick buildings and midden areas of gray/black ashy material, which produced large numbers of carbonized seeds including wild legumes (*Astragalus* and *Trigonella*), emmer wheat, and two-row hulled barley (Hole et al. 1969: 35–6). The Bus Mordeh levels also produced grinding and pounding stones alongside bones of domesticated goats, as well as hunted wild species including gazelle, onager, aurochs, and boar and substantial evidence for the exploitation of aquatic resources such as fish, clams, turtles, and swamp vegetation. The subsequent Ali Kosh Phase produced mudbrick rectilinear houses with hearths, ovens, and roasting pits, examples of which were filled with goat bones. The houses appear to have had packed-earth floors on which reed mats were laid. By the Mohammad Jaffar Phase at Ali Kosh, some walls show a foundation level of river cobbles, a feature seen also at Chagha Sefid in the Sefid and Surkh Phases (Hole 1977).

In the Ali Kosh Phase, adults and children wrapped in reed mats were buried beneath the house floors, accompanied by small items including turquoise beads, and one instance of the secondary collective burial of the ocher-coated bones of multiple individuals is also known (Hole et al. 1969: 36–40). The skulls of three females show intentional premortem cranial deformation (Hole et al. 1969: 42, pl. 12b). There seems to be some change through time in burial practice, as in the Mohammad Jaffar Phase, five adult burials were found in an area immediately outside houses, accompanied by small items such as turquoise and stone beads and labrets.

The small aceramic Neolithic site of Chogha Bonut, in eastern Susiana, appears to be roughly contemporary with Ali Kosh, based upon a series of five radiocarbon dates that span the range c.7500–6800 cal BC (Alizadeh 2003: table 15). The aceramic phases at Chogha Bonut are characterized by beaten earth floors and associated fire pits, although the presence of a few fragmentary mudbricks suggests that more substantial architecture may have existed on other parts of the site at this time. Later ceramic Neolithic deposits (labeled Formative Susiana and Archaic Susiana 0) have produced the remains of rectilinear houses of mudbrick (Alizadeh 2003: fig. 11), whilst the presence of a shallow niche and numerous fire pits with cracked rocks in the floor of one building has led to the suggestion that it may have had a nondomestic function (Alizadeh 2003: 40). The uppermost levels at the site are characterized by rectilinear buildings made of long cigar-shaped mudbricks (Alizadeh 2003: fig. 10).

Studies of the faunal remains from Chogha Bonut indicate that its occupants herded goats and sheep, with goats numerically dominant, as well as keeping domestic cattle and hunting gazelles and wild cattle and pigs. Other faunal indicators, especially birds, suggest that the site was occupied at least during the winter months (Redding 2003). Phytoliths from Chogha Bonut indicate the exploitation of reeds (*Phragmites* sp.), probably for making fences and mats, or as fodder, which are evidence for a near-site environment characterized by high water-tables and/or slow-moving streams. Phytolith analyses also indicate the presence of wheat and barley, and the possibility that deposits at the site are middens or threshing floors (Rosen 2003). Archaeobotanical specimens from the site indicate the common exploitation of barley (two-rowed and/or six-rowed variants) and emmer wheat, with lesser amounts of einkorn (*T. monococcum*, possibly a weedy contaminant rather than a domesticate) and hard wheat (*T. durum*) and rare, possibly wild lentils (Miller 2003). Like Ali Kosh, the site produced no wood charcoal, indicating that reeds and dung were probably the main sources of fuel.

The chipped stone industries of the lowland aceramic Neolithic sites are relatively uniform, being characterized by blades and microblades and the common occurrence of bullet cores (Alizadeh 2003: figs. 38–41; Hole 1977; Hole et al. 1969). Some obsidian tools are known from Chogha Bonut, but no obsidian cores, paralleling the situation in Deh Luran, where obsidian of eastern Anatolian origin was present at generally low frequencies in the aceramic Neolithic levels of Ali Kosh and Chagha Sefid (Renfrew 1969, 1977). The lowland aceramic Neolithic sites are also linked artifactually by the presence of clay human and animal figurines, including T-shaped figurines, as well as a range of small finds including bone awls and needles (Hole et al. 1969: figs. 97–8; Hole 1977: figs. 90–91; Alizadeh 2003: figs. 30–31).

As for the central Zagros, archaeological evidence from the early Neolithic sites of lowland Khuzestan has been regarded as indicating seasonal occupation and the mobility of some or all members of early Neolithic communities. Alizadeh (2003: 40), for example, has suggested that the ephemeral architectural remains from the earliest levels at Chogha Bonut indicate that the site may have been occupied only seasonally during the winter months, in contrast to permanent occupation in later levels that produced substantial mudbrick structures. The continuation or development of Neolithic subsistence adaptations involving mobility is also raised by archaeological remains from the later ceramic Neolithic site of Tepe Tula'i in northwestern Susiana (Hole 1974, 2004), which have been interpreted as footings for the tents of a mobile pastoralist campsite, on analogy with the remains left by modern pastoral nomad groups from western Iran. Hole (1974: 71) used this evidence to suggest that "some pastoral peoples were detached from farming villages rather earlier than most archaeologists had expected," although alternative interpretations derived from study of the abundant faunal remains suggest that Tepe Tula'i may be a village-based fallow herding site (Pires-Ferreira 1977; Hole 2004: 80). Such sites, although open to interpretation, highlight the fact that sedentary agricultural villages should not necessarily be regarded as the only settlement adaptation that characterized the Neolithic transition in western Iran, nor indeed as an end-point in such developments. Rather, permanent villages represent only one component of a series of potential adaptations by early herders and cultivators.

Outside of the central Zagros and Khuzestan, the earliest aceramic Neolithic occupation of Iran remains relatively poorly known, partly reflecting the much lower intensity of archaeological fieldwork in eastern Iran. However, early Neolithic settlements have proven difficult to document even in intensively surveyed regions. In northern Fars province, for example, more than fifty years of archaeological research had failed to conclusively identify aceramic Neolithic settlements (Weeks et al. 2006) until recent excavations at the site of Tepe Rahmatabad near Pasargadae revealed a sequence of ceramic Neolithic deposits overlaying more than two meters of aceramic remains. These deposits are characterized by ephemeral surfaces and ash layers that have been radiocarbon dated to $c.7100–6700$ cal BC (Bernbeck et al. 2008). The recent discovery of aceramic Neolithic occupation at several sites near Darestan in Kerman province, most notably the relatively large ($c.3–5$ ha) site of Tell-e Ataşhi (Garazhian 2009), may provide further evidence for the spread of aceramic Neolithic settlement east of the Zagros, although the site has not been radiocarbon dated. Tell-e Ataşhi exhibits substantial rectilinear mudbrick architecture with internal hearth installations and a range of lithic remains (e.g., bullet cores) and small finds such as clay cone tokens, a possible human figurine, and a large marble bowl that are well paralleled in Neolithic sites further to the west. Although the bioarchaeological assemblages from Tepe Rahmatabad and Tell-e Ataşhi are still being studied, these sites are likely to be critical for understanding the spread of the Neolithic east of the Zagros and may provide important context for understanding early Neolithic occupation at Mehrgarh in Pakistani Baluchistan (Jarrige and Jarrige 2006; Meadow 1996), nearly 1000 km further to the east.

In northeastern Iran, aceramic Neolithic occupation has long been known at the site of Sang-e Chakhmaq near Shahrud in Semnan province (Masuda 1974; Thornton 2010), although the evidence has only been published in preliminary form. Excavations on the west mound at Sang-e Chakhmaq indicate that it is aceramic in its lower levels, with the remains of rectilinear architecture, rooms with fireplaces, and some buildings containing plastered floors (Masuda 1974: fig. 7). A raw radiocarbon date of 7800 BP is reported from Layer 2 of the west mound (Masuda 1974: 25), which when calibrated would fall in the range $c.7000–6500$ cal BC. Although the bioarchaeological remains from the site have not been published, Thornton (2010) notes that "the abundance of stone querns and grindstones in these levels points to a Neolithic subsistence." As with the aceramic sites of western Iran, the west mound at Sang-e Chakhmaq is characterized by a tradition of intramural burials, especially of infants, and has also produced other items typical for the early Neolithic including flint bullet cores and obsidian blades, as well as T-shaped human figurines and animal figurines (Masuda 1974: fig. 3). Further to the north, on the Caspian littoral, Belt (aka Kamarband) and Hotu caves were used in the terminal Pleistocene and early Holocene by "Mesolithic" hunter-gatherer groups. Subsequent occupations at these caves containing domesticated animal bones and, eventually, pottery, provide broadly dated and, at present, poorly understood depositional sequences that appear to chart the earliest Neolithic occupation of the region in the period from *c*.8000 to 5000 cal BC (Coon 1951, 1957). The possibility of aceramic Neolithic sites even further to the northeast is raised by fieldwork at the site DG 19 in the Darreh Gaz plain on the border with Turkmenistan. In addition to surface assemblages incorporating Neolithic and Chalcolithic pottery, Kohl and Heskel (1980: 163) note that "efforts at scraping down its badly eroded eastern section yielded neither ceramics nor architecture in the lowest two metres of cultural deposit" at the site. Aceramic Neolithic sites have not yet been recorded in northwestern Iran, despite intensive surveys in the Ushnu-Solduz valley (Voigt 1983) and regional surveys on the eastern and western sides of Lake Urmia. Likewise, the central Iranian Plateau (i.e., the Tehran and Qazvin plains and Kashan) has yet to produce evidence of aceramic Neolithic occupation, although there are possible hints of such settlements in the hinterland of Arisman (Chegini and Helwing 2011).

The Pottery Neolithic period and the "soft-ware horizon"

The invention and widespread adoption of pottery represents a major transition in the material culture of the Neolithic societies of the Near East. Neolithic sites displaying coarse, chaff-tempered, burnished, and often painted ceramics have been found in virtually every region of Iran, to the extent that Dyson (1965) has reasonably regarded these sites as representing a "soft-ware horizon."

The Central Zagros and Khuzestan

As for the earliest development of Neolithic subsistence in Iran, the origins of ceramics can best be documented in the west, particularly in the central Zagros and Khuzestan. The earliest evidence for the use of clay to make vessels comes from the "aceramic" site of Ganj Dareh, Levels D–A, where burning has fortuitously preserved the remains of vessels that may well have been originally used in an unfired state or only secondarily hardened near hearths (Smith 1976: 16). A considerable variety of vessel sizes is evident, from very large containers more than 1 m tall (and up to 200 liter capacity; Smith 1990: 332) sometimes built into architectural structures, to much smaller, hand-made vessels (Smith and Crépeau 1983). It is suggested that the smaller vessels may actually have been fired at low temperatures, c.300–700°C, in open campfires. These early "experimental" vessels from Ganj Dareh range in color from gray-brown to black, are made from fine, untempered clay, and occasionally display lightly burnished surfaces or impressed decoration (Mortensen 1992). It is clear that these items were produced as part of much wider developments in working with clay that included the construction of walls and houses from mudbrick and *chineh*, the manufacture of large, thin clay slabs to construct storage bins in the settlement, and the production of figurines, tokens and other small clay items (Smith 1990; Mortensen 1992).

The later site of Tepe Guran spans the aceramic and ceramic Neolithic periods, and provides further evidence of the adoption and development of ceramic production in the seventh millennium BC, particularly for the development of characteristic Neolithic chaff-tempered soft-wares. The first ceramics at the site—undecorated, grayish-brown coarse vessels, often smoothed or burnished and lightly fired—appear in limited quantities from Level S. More elaborate chaff-tempered, buff-colored wares with slipped and sometimes burnished surfaces appear from Level R, mostly in the form of simple bowls or carinated bowls with an outflaring upper body. Alongside the plain wares occur very small amounts of the earliest painted pottery, characterized by an orange-buff surface with fugitive decoration in red ocher. From Levels O and higher, the site is characterized by "Standard Painted Ware" or "Zagros Standard Ware," which is chaff tempered, slipped, and sometimes burnished, buff to orange-buff or reddish in color, and painted with a range of geometric patterns (e.g., Meldgaard et al. 1963: figs. 15–18) that appear over a considerable area of the central Zagros including sites such as Jarmo and Sarab (Braidwood and Howe 1960; Kozlowski and Aurenche 2005: fig. 13.1). The top of the Neolithic sequence at Tepe Guran (Levels H–D) is characterized by red-burnished wares.

In the southwestern lowlands, Chogha Bonut provides an important archaeological sequence attesting to the local development of ceramics. Following the aceramic Neolithic occupation of the site, the excavated material indicates the following developmental sequence: an initial use of coarse, largely undecorated, chaff-tempered wares, followed stratigraphically by "smeared-painted" wares (together comprising what Alizadeh terms the Formative Susiana period); a subsequent distinct phase with maroon-on-cream painted chaff-tempered wares and early painted-burnished wares (Archaic Susiana 0); followed by the standard painted burnished wares of the Archaic Susiana 1 phase known very well from nearby Chogha Mish (Delougaz and Kantor 1996). A number of other sites in lowland southwest Iran display both aceramic and early ceramic Neolithic deposits, including Ali Kosh and Chagha Sefid in the Deh Luran plain. However, at these sites the earliest ceramics (Mohammad Jaffar phase at Ali Kosh and Sefid Phase at Chagha Sefid) show a greater degree of development and elaboration than witnessed in the earliest ceramics from Chogha Bonut. Based on such considerations, Alizadeh (2003: 45) has stated that "it is tempting to consider Susiana as the primary locus for the invention of pottery in southwestern Iran."

The ceramic Neolithic period in lowland Khuzestan is generally termed the Archaic Susiana phase, and is best documented at Chogha Bonut, Chogha Mish and Tepe Tula'i (Hole 1974) in Susiana and Ali Kosh and Chagha Sefid in Deh Luran. In Susiana, Chogha Mish provides evidence of a sequence of village occupation spanning the Archaic Susiana 0–3 periods, c.6700–5700 BC (Delougaz and Kantor 1996; Alizadeh 2008). The settlement is a small hamlet of less than 1 ha in its earliest phase of occupation, but expands to cover perhaps 2–3 ha by the late Archaic period (Alizadeh 2008: 7, although see Delougaz and Kantor 1996: figs. 39–40 for a lower estimate). It is characterized by rectilinear, multiroomed houses made from long cigar-shaped mudbricks with finger impressions, with fire pits in open areas between structures (e.g. Delougaz and Kantor 1996: pls. 53–4, 272). By the Archaic Susiana 2 phase, some mudbrick walls have stone foundations, as seen also at Chagha Sefid, for example. The dead at Chogha Mish were buried, in typical Neolithic fashion, under floors of houses and in adjacent open areas, mostly in elongated position, and although associated with few or no grave goods they are sometimes covered with ocher.

The subsistence economy of Chogha Mish was based around hunting of gazelle, aurochs, and onager and the exploitation of domesticated goats and sheep, supplemented in the later Archaic phase by domesticated cattle and pigs. Domestic dogs were also kept (Alizadeh 2008: 6, table 14). The site's plant remains contain an abundance of wild and domestic legumes, including small seeded legumes such as milk vetch, clover, and vetch, as well as domesticated pea and lentil (Woosley 1996). Seeds of wild cereals and grasses (oats, goat face grass, rye, canary grass, fescue) were also common and much more abundant than those of domesticated cereals, which are represented by barley (six-row hulled and naked varieties) and one grain of wheat (*T. aestivum*). Wheat is, in fact, barely represented at Chogha Mish before the fourth millennium BC. Small fragments of pistachio nutlets were also recovered, along with a range of species that could have been weeds in fields of cultivated crops (*Lolium*, *Aegilops*, *Plantago*) and other species from the nearby site environment such as rushes. Woosley (1996: 316) summarizes the archaeobotanical evidence thus: "Though barley was probably cultivated on a small scale, the first several thousand years of agriculture seem to have been characterized by an emphasis on legume crops, including *Pisum*, *Lens*, and *Vicia*, over cereals." The site also produced a large variety of grinding and pounding stones which were used for preparing pigments as well as processing plant and animal remains, chipped stone tools including blades, scrapers, and bullet cores, and bone tools including awls/reamers and sickle hafts. Other small finds include round, hemispherical, and conical "tokens," a variety of small items interpreted as labrets, and a range of human and animal figurines, including T-shaped figurines as known from Chogha Bonut, Ali Kosh, Chagha Sefid, and elsewhere. The extensive Archaic pottery assemblage is characteristic for Neolithic Iran in its incorporation of a variety of chaff-tempered, burnished, painted wares, made using sequential slab construction (Delougaz and Kantor 1996; Vandiver 1986). More variety is seen in the later Archaic phases, with the appearance of a dense sandy ware with finely chopped chaff inclusions in the Archaic Susiana 2 phase and grit-tempered "close-line ware" in the Archaic Susiana 3 phase, which the excavators compare to Ubaid 0 material from southern Mesopotamia, and Chogha Mami Transitional ware from Ali Kosh and Chagha Sefid in Deh Luran and Chogha Mami in Iraq. In Deh Luran, the Chogha Mami Transitional phase is tentatively regarded as a period of population migration into the region, undertaken by irrigation agriculturalists whose origins probably lay in or near central Iraq (Hole 1977: 12–17).

Northwestern Iran

In northwestern Iran, ceramic Neolithic villages represent the first evidence for Holocene human occupation in the region. Surveys have identified small numbers of ceramic Neolithic sites in most areas of the region (Voigt 1983: fig. 120; Burney 1964; Kearton 1969) and a detailed understanding of local Neolithic adaptations has been gained from excavations at Yanik Tepe in eastern Azerbaijan (Burney 1964) and especially from Hajji Firuz Tepe in the Ushnu-Solduz Valley. Radiocarbon dates from these sites, which share a very similar material culture, span the late seventh and early sixth millennia cal BC (Voigt 1983: 348–50, recalibrated with Calib 5.01). Yanik Tepe (Burney 1964) has nearly 5 m of Neolithic occupation, characterized by rectilinear houses with hard gypsum floors (some colored with red ocher), and a tradition of intramural burials in shallow pits, one of which displays artificial cranial deformation. The material assemblage from the site incorporates soft, straw-tempered, low-fired ceramics, commonly painted and burnished, whose decoration is very similar to that from Hajji Firuz Tepe. The site has also produced typical Neolithic chipped stone tools of flint and obsidian, bone tools, and a range of other small finds including alabaster bracelets and bowls and two small human heads of stone covered with red pigment (Burney 1964: pl. 15).

A much greater degree of information is available from the broad excavations at Hajji Firuz Tepe, a mounded site south of Lake Urmia situated at about 1300 masl in an area with ample rainfall for dry farming. Excavations at the site produced a deep sequence of superimposed occupation layers characterized predominantly by rectilinear mud and mudbrick structures divided by internal walls into two rooms, with hearths and storage vessels dug into the floor. Interior walls were plastered with a lime and mud mixture, and show traces of black and red pigments. The Hajji Firuz houses were likely roofed with organic material, including wooden beams, reeds or reed mats, and mud/straw, although buildings often had an unroofed enclosure at the eastern end. Roofed dwelling areas of individual houses ranged from $c.27$–37 m². Hearths and ovens were found also in open areas of the site, attesting to cooking activities and the need for warmth during cooler periods. Hajji Firuz Tepe is characterized by numerous "ossuary burials," that is, graves with a number of burials, usually partly or completely disarticulated. Intramural burial was the dominant mode during the Neolithic at the site and the human remains were placed in "bins" or platforms (in one instance in a storage jar) on or beneath the living room floors of the houses. The ossuary burials were deposited over a considerable time during the use of the buildings and perhaps also in the phase immediately after their abandonment. The burials seem to represent a mix of primary (rare) and secondary (common) interments and included ocher. Analysis of the skeletal remains suggests a "short statured, muscular, active" and generally healthy population at Hajji Firuz Tepe, "with little evidence for pathologies other than arthritis, fractures, and dental pathologies" (Turnquist 1983: 341).

The Hajji Firuz pottery is chaff-tempered (occasionally exhibiting the use of limestone as a temper) and fired at relatively low temperatures. Vessels are most commonly pale brown, pink, or reddish yellow and display a gray core, indicating incomplete oxidization during firing. Vessels were finished by wet-smoothing or, more commonly, burnishing. Decoration consisted of either thin, colored red-brown washes, geometric incision, or application of red-brown iron-oxide paint in geometric designs, predominantly nested chevrons and triangles. Some sherds were decorated in a creamy-white paint (applied over a red wash), and a black carbon paint may also have been used. The pottery included a range of forms, notably miniature vessels, simple open bowls of various sizes (some with carinations), trays and husking trays, and closed forms including collared jars of various sizes and large pithoi. Vessels were generally made by slab construction, incorporating reed mats and baskets to support the clay during the manufacturing process. Whilst the Hajji Firuz pottery shows some technological links with the central Zagros Neolithic sites, Voigt argues that it is technically most similar to pottery from early Hassuna settlements in northern Mesopotamia, including Umm Dabaghiyah, Tell es-Sotto and Telul eth-Thalathat. She suggests, therefore, that the initial Neolithic occupation at Hajji Firuz Tepe represented migration into the Ushnu-Solduz valley by groups from a region where they were in close contact with Hassuna pottery-using communities (Voigt 1983: 166). The site also produced spindle whorls (often found in burials), human figurines, clay cones or tokens, and bone artifacts such as awls (Voigt 1983: 168ff.). A very small number of chipped stone pieces were recovered during excavations. They are manufactured of obsidian and flint or chert in roughly equal amounts, and include blades with edge sheen most probably from harvesting cereal crops. Pounding and grinding stones for the processing of pigments and of cereals and other foodstuffs occur at the site, and there is also evidence for the use of plaited and coiled basketry.

Botanical remains from Hajji Firuz indicate the exploitation of domesticated crops including barley (unknown species), wheat (emmer and bread wheat), and lentils, as well as a range of wild plants included pulses, rye grass, and sea club-rushes. Although very small, the assemblage of animal bone includes a range of bird species comprising heron and mallard as well as migratory species including cormorant, goose, teal, pintail, and bustard that would have been present in the region in late winter and spring. Domesticated mammals included most commonly sheep and goat but also dogs and pigs, whilst wild aurochs, red deer, and boar were hunted. Critically, most of the necked jars at Hajji Firuz Tepe are regarded by Voigt (1983: 279) as having been used for milk storage and processing. This hypothesis receives support from the more recent pottery residue analyses undertaken by Evershed et al. (2008) at other ceramic Neolithic sites in the Near East, which demonstrate milk production by the seventh millennium BC.

The Iranian Plateau and northeastern Iran

Sites of the ceramic Neolithic period are also well attested on the northern Iranian Plateau, in the Tehran and Qazvin Plains and in the vicinity of modern-day Kashan. Outside these major plains, sites with characteristic Neolithic chaff-tempered soft-ware pottery have been recorded in Zanjan province (Alibaigi and Khosravi 2009), to the northwest of the Qazvin plain at the site of Arg-e Dasht B in southern Gilan (Nokandeh 2005), and in the hinterland of Arisman, *c*.60 km southeast of Kashan (Chegini and Helwing 2011). The first Neolithic material recovered by archaeologists on the plateau came from Ghirshman's excavations at the site of Tepe Sialk near Kashan, where the lowest Sialk I levels of the north mound produced a series of deposits characterized by several regionally distinct varieties of chaff-tempered Neolithic soft-ware (Ghirshman 1938; Mellaart 1975: 187–94, fig. 116), most commonly buff-colored wares with dark painted geometric decoration very reminiscent of basketry. The earliest levels of Tepe Sialk are characterized by layers of ash and the remains of (presumably) light structures made of organic materials such as reeds and branches covered with mud. Later Neolithic deposits show the development of structures made from *chineh* and, as typical for the Neolithic in Iran, human burials with red ocher were located beneath house floors. Bioarchaeological evidence indicates the exploitation of domesticated two-row hulled barley and goats at Neolithic Sialk, as well as the hunting of gazelle, wild sheep, and aurochs. Artifactual indicators of farming at the site include chipped stone hoes, sickle blades, and grinding stones, as well as a bone sickle handle with elaborate carving. Although Tepe Sialk was the first plateau Neolithic site excavated on a substantial scale, it is clear that Sialk I does not represent the earliest Neolithic in the region. Recently, an earlier chaff-tempered and painted soft-ware pottery tradition has been recovered from Tepe Shurabeh, located 5 km to the southwest of Tepe Sialk (Shahmirzadi 2004: pl. 13), although little more is known of this site or its ceramics.

On the Qazvin Plain, the Neolithic sequence was originally defined by excavations at the site of Tepe Zagheh, investigated in a series of campaigns since the 1970s. However, recent reexcavation and redating has suggested that the site was only founded in the "transitional Chalcolithic" period, in the last third of the sixth millennium cal BC (Fazeli et al. 2005: 46, fig. 12). The evidence for ceramic Neolithic occupation in the Qazvin plain is therefore limited to several sites known from recent surface surveys and excavations, including Chahar Boneh and Tepe Ebrahimabad, which have been radiocarbon dated to the period from *c*.6000–5200 cal BC (Fazeli Nashli et al. 2009: tables 1–3; Fazeli et al. 2005: 75). Excavations at Chahar Boneh revealed no evidence for substantial structures, with ephemeral ashy occupation deposits interspersed with natural accumulations of water-borne sediment, suggesting that the site was relatively short lived and occupied only seasonally (Fazeli Nashli et al. 2009: 3). At Tepe Ebrahimabad, pottery sherds of Sialk I type were recorded and there was limited evidence for *chineh* and mudbrick architecture as well as a single human burial (Fazeli Nashli et al. 2009: 3–6). Chahar Boneh produced a range of plain and geometrically painted buff-colored soft-ware ceramics in its earliest period of occupation (*c*.6000–5600 cal BC), whilst ceramic variability was greater in the deposits from Ebrahimabad (*c*.5600–5200 cal BC), which included examples of local plain and painted wares as well as types of decoration best known from the Sialk I period (Fazeli Nashli et al. 2009: 10–13). Chahar Boneh produced a wide range of botanical remains, including some domestic species such as emmer wheat, free-threshing wheat, six-row barley, and small legumes, alongside a very broad spectrum of wild plants. A broader range of domestic plants was recorded at Ebrahimabad, including emmer, free-threshing wheat, hulled two-row barley, lentils, vetch, peas, and other small legumes, alongside a variety of wild plants. The archaeobotanical evidence for agriculture is supported by discoveries of grinding stones and sickle blades at both sites (Fazeli Nashli et al. 2009: 14–17). The faunal collections from Ebrahimabad show a developed pastoral economy: domesticated sheep/goats are dominant, making up about three-quarters of all identified bone, followed by domestic cattle (12 percent) and wild equids (10 percent). The earlier and much smaller faunal assemblage from Chahar Boneh also shows a dominance of domestic sheep/goat, but with other species (including cattle, equid, gazelle, pig, and wild goat) making up more than one-third of the identified bones.

In the Tehran plain to the east, the known Neolithic settlements include the sites of Cheshmeh Ali, Sadeghabadi, Tepe Pardis, and Tepe Arastu (Fazeli Nashli et al. 2009: 3; Fazeli et al. 2004, 2005: table 25). Recent reexcavation of Cheshmeh Ali, first sounded in the early twentieth century, has documented an early occupational phase characterized by chaff-tempered Neolithic soft-ware ceramics decorated with painted geometric designs that have parallels to the Sialk I material from Kashan (Fazeli Nashli et al. 2009: 3; Fazeli et al. 2004: fig. 8), although these levels have not been radiocarbon dated.

Very little is known of the Neolithic period in northeastern Iran. The earliest ceramics reported from Belt and Hotu caves in Mazandaran are relatively plain chaff-tempered soft-wares, often burnished and in some cases decorated with red paint or a chocolate-brown slip (Voigt and Dyson 1992: 172). Sang-e Chakhmaq in Semnan Province, initially exhibiting aceramic Neolithic occupation, also showed a transition to the use of plain chaff-tempered soft-ware ceramics in the upper levels of the west mound (Thornton 2010). In the east mound sequence, the Sang-e Chakhmaq ceramics resemble those from early Neolithic sites in Central Asia, particularly Djeitun (Thornton 2010; Masuda 1974; Harris 2010). Similar ceramics have been recorded from the surface surveys and soundings at other sites in Semnan province, including Kalate Khan and Deh Kheir Tepe, also in the Shahrud area (Harris and Coolidge 2010b). Djeitun-like ceramics are, in fact, very widely distributed in northeastern Iran, being found stratified above early chaff-tempered wares at Hotu cave (Voigt and Dyson 1992: 172), in the lowest levels at Yarim Tepe in the Gorgan Plain (Crawford 1963: 272–3), in post-Neolithic mudbricks at the site of Tureng Tepe (where Neolithic levels are inaccessible below the modern water table; Deshayes 1967: 123–5, pl. 1a–c), and at sites in the Atrek Valley and the Darreh Gaz plain near the Turkmenistan border (Kohl et al. 1982; Kohl and Heskel 1980; Harris and Coolidge 2010a: 51, 2010b: 62–4). Alongside these wares, surface surveys indicate various regional ceramic traditions, as for example at Tepe Pahlavan in the Jajarm Plain, Khorasan, as well as typical Neolithic chipped-stone tools including bullet cores, sickle blades, and other microlithic types (Vahdati 2010).

The Southern Zagros and Kerman

Surveys in the Bakhtiyari region of the Zagros Mountains have isolated several Neolithic sites in the high Khana Mirza and Shahr-e Kord Plains (Nissen and Zagarell 1976; Zagarell 1982). In addition, excavations at the site of Qaleh Rostam, at $c.$1900 masl in the southern Khana Mirza plain, exposed a $c.$4 m. deep sequence of deposits subdivided into three major phases by changes in ceramics. All the ceramics are chaff tempered, beginning with the plain, poorly fired wares of Phase III (lowest), developing into wares with red paint on a highly burnished red slip in Phase II, and finally the elaborately decorated wares of Phase I, with black and red paint in geometric and anthropomorphic designs (Nissen and Zagarell 1976; Zagarell 1982: 20–22; Bernbeck 1989). The ceramics are mostly open forms of bowls and beakers, often with a strong carination. The deposits at Qaleh Rostam were rich in bone, chipped stone, and other artifacts, but analyses of these assemblages have not yet been fully published. In general, the Neolithic sites of the Bakhtiyari display similar chipped-stone assemblages to contemporary sites in the Zagros, incorporating bullet- and tongue-shaped cores, blades, truncated blades and backed blades, some with silica sheen, and rare obsidian pieces (Zagarell 1982).

The most comprehensive information on the southern Zagros in the ceramic Neolithic period comes from northern Fars, where a now well-understood sequence of deposits at sites in the Kur River Basin attests to increasing settlement from $c.$6300 to 5000/4800 cal BC. The major sites include Tal-e Mushki, the type site for the Mushki Period ($c.$6300–6100 cal BC); Tol-e Bashi, the type site for the Bashi period ($c.$6100–6000 cal BC); and Tal-e Jari A and B, the type sites for the Jari Period ($c.$6000–5600 cal BC) and the Shamsabad period ($c.$5600–5000/4800 cal BC). A number of other sites known from surface survey suggest the possibility of even more chronological and subregional variability in the early ceramic Neolithic assemblages of the region (e.g., Alden et al. 2004).

The occupation at Tal-e Mushki is characterized by limited evidence for *chineh* and mudbrick architecture, which nevertheless appears at the site from the earliest deposits. The pottery itself is typical for early Neolithic pottery across most of Iran, being made of relatively coarse, chaff-tempered paste that is often underfired, and displaying a thick, burnished surface slip decorated with distinctive geometric patterns in black paint. The deposits of Tal-e Mushki are characterized by an unusual set of bioarchaeological remains: whilst the limited number of flotation samples analyzed attest to the exploitation of domesticated two-row and six-row barley and emmer and einkorn wheat (Miller and Kimiaie 2006), faunal assemblages indicate a focus upon hunted species, including predominantly Persian onager, gazelle, and aurochs, with a limited reliance upon (possibly wild) goats (Mashkour 2006). Later ceramic Neolithic period occupations at Tol-e Bashi and Tal-e Jari document a decline in the relative importance of hunting and an increasing reliance on domesticated animals including especially goats, but also cattle and sheep by the late seventh or early sixth millennium BC, alongside the continued exploitation of domesticated wheat (emmer, einkorn, bread wheat) and barley (two-row, six-row) and the gathering of wild plant resources such as pistachios and almonds. Houses in this period were rectilinear, multiroomed, and made of mudbrick and/or *chineh*, with the best examples coming from the extensive Japanese excavations at the site of Tal-e Jari B (Nishiaki 2010b: figs. 3–8), although it is clear that outside activity areas were also important for a range of daily activities at these villages (Pollock et al. 2010). Important studies of ceramic Neolithic occupation in other areas of Fars include the excavations and surveys in the Mamasani district *c.*100 km. to the west of the Kur River Basin (Weeks et al. 2006, 2009; Zeidi et al. 2009), which have outlined a series of regionally distinctive Neolithic ceramic assemblages contemporary with the Bashi-Jari-Shamsabad periods in the Marv Dasht, with villages characterized by rectilinear mudbrick and *chineh* houses and an overwhelming subsistence focus on the exploitation of domesticated goats and sheep (Mashkour 2009). In addition, surface surveys undertaken in more southerly parts of Fars, especially the valleys of Fasa and Darab, have demonstrated extensive occupation in the ceramic Neolithic period, characterized, typically, by distinctively painted chaff-tempered soft-ware ceramics (Miroschedji 1972). These technological links in ceramic production, as well as a variety of other exotic goods including obsidian (in limited amounts at Tal-e Mushki), sea shells, native copper and bitumen attest to widespread contacts between Neolithic communities over vast areas of Iran, incorporating lowland Khuzestan, the Persian Gulf littoral and the Iranian Plateau, already by the late seventh millennium BC.

Further to the south and east, ceramic Neolithic occupation is known from excavations and surveys in the Soghun and Shah Maran-Daulatabad valleys of Kerman, undertaken as part of the Tepe Yahya project (Prickett 1986a, 1986b) as well as at Tal-e Iblis in the Bard Sir valley (Caldwell 1967). Neolithic ceramics from Kerman are typically coarse, chaff-tempered, and burnished, but they are only rarely decorated with paint (Prickett 1986b: 1379–1386; Beale 1986: 39–47). Based on radiocarbon dates and ceramic typologies, the earliest Neolithic deposits in the area are those of Tepe Gaz Tavila (R37) to the west of Daulatabad, which date to the mid-sixth millennium BC (Beale 1986: table 2.1). The lowest occupational levels at Tepe Yahya comprise Period VII, which has been radiocarbon dated to the late sixth millennium cal BC (Beale 1986: table 2.1) and which is characterized by the presence of rectilinear mudbrick structures, with pits and lenses containing burnt materials, as well as several human burials associated with ashy eroded deposits in peripheral areas of the site not used for houses. The small-roomed structures that characterize the Period VIIB settlement at Tepe Yahya may have been for the storage of agricultural produce or for the penning of animals (Beale 1986: 109). The rooms were flat roofed with wooden beams overlaid with brush and reeds, covered with chaff-tempered mud (Beale 1986: 111), and walls and floors were often plastered and replastered several times. These levels produced a large female figurine carved from chlorite, standing more than 26 cm high. Tepe Yahya is the only known settlement site in the Soghun Valley during the Neolithic period, although a possible seventh to sixth millennium cal BC campsite has also been recorded (Prickett 1986b: 218–19) which is thought to be associated with exploitation of the region in the early Holocene climatic optimum, when there was a standing lake in the valley. Much more substantial Neolithic settlement, both contemporary with and earlier than Yahya Period VII, is documented in the Shah Maran-Daulatabad valley system immediately to the west of the Soghun valley, in particular at the site of Tepe Gaz Tavila (or R37) (Prickett 1986a: fig. 9.4). Altogether, there is perhaps 20–30 ha of Neolithic occupation in the Shah Maran-Daulatabad valley system spread over a total of fourteen known mounded settlements and twelve surface scatter sites, with the sites of R35, R36, R36A and R37 possibly representing a single site of $c.10$ ha in area now subdivided by erosion—although it is likely that occupation there expanded laterally and that not all of the site was occupied in any one phase of the Neolithic (Prickett 1986b: 545, table 5.1). Faunal remains from Tepe Gaz Tavila and Yahya period VII reveal an overwhelming reliance on domesticated goats, sheep and cattle, with less than 2 percent of remains coming from other animals including birds, land tortoise and gazelles, wild boar and onager (Meadow 1986: 32–7, table 3.4). Archaeobotanical analyses indicate that the earliest farmers of the region cultivated einkorn and emmer wheat alongside a range of barley types. Date seeds are also attested from Tepe Gaz Tavila, possibly dating to the sixth millennium BC (Meadow 1986: 27–30).

The spread of farming: Invention, migration, transmission

The processes by which Neolithic communities were established in early Holocene Iran remain far from clear. The concentration of much recent archaeological research on Neolithic origins in the western and central parts of the Fertile Crescent has meant that the Zagros Mountains have tended to be regarded as witnessing a relatively late transition to agriculture resulting from the spread of Neolithic subsistence practices rather than their local, independent development. However, the recent zooarchaeological work of Zeder and colleagues has reopened the debate about the origins of domesticated goats, and the evidence from Ganj Dareh marks it as one of the earliest loci of herd management known from the Ancient Near East (Zeder 2008). The earliest Neolithic sites of central western Iran, particularly Ganj Dareh, Tepe Abdul Hosein, and Sheikh-e Abad, therefore offer tremendous potential for understanding internal developments toward Neolithic subsistence practices and sedentary settlement, as outlined above. Future work on the bioarchaeological assemblages from these sites will be critical in developing the archaeological understanding of these issues.

In most other areas of Iran, however, the earliest known Neolithic communities display an apparently well-established and integrated economy of plant and animal husbandry. Such sites seem more likely to represent agricultural dispersals rather than independent agricultural origins. In these instances, the cultural context of the spread of agriculture is of critical interest, that is, whether food production spread by "demic diffusion," through the movement of migrants who settled in new areas with their domesticated plants and animals, or by "cultural diffusion," whereby foraging groups began to herd animals and cultivate crops as a result of cultural contact with food producers.

Further east, in Central Asia and Baluchistan, the "Near Eastern" associations of the earliest Neolithic adaptations (Fuller 2011; Harris 2010) suggest a strong influence from the West and support the idea of an eastward Neolithic dispersal across Iran. In such cases, the likelihood of the spread of farming with the actual movement of farmers is high (e.g., Harris 2010: 233; Harris and Gosden 1996: 383). Colonizing farming groups have been implicated in the spread of agriculture to various parts of Iran, including the Urmia Basin, where ceramic parallels have led Voigt (1983) to suggest that farming colonists came from northern Mesopotamia. Likewise, in southern Fars the first Neolithic settlements are thought to represent "a diffusion of population" from the north (Hole 1987: 83). This Neolithic dispersal across Iran is in many ways analogous to the westward expansion of farming across Europe, the most recent synthesis of which focuses upon diffusion of farmers as the major mechanism of spread (Rowley-Conwy 2011), supported strongly by studies of ancient DNA in early European farming populations (Haak et al. 2010). Although no ancient human DNA studies exist for Iran, analyses of modern Y-chromosome DNA by Quintana-Murci et al. (2001: 541) "support a model of demic diffusion of early farmers from southwestern Iran...bringing the spread of genes and culture (including language) to southwestern Asia," and are strongly supported by studies of modern human mitochondrial DNA from the region (Quintana-Murci et al. 2004: 838).

The reasons for these possible farming migrations remain unclear. Some scholars have focused upon environments and environmental change during the early to mid-Holocene. Hole (1998: 88–9), for example, has suggested that Neolithic groups responsible for the earliest animal management in the central Zagros "exploited the grazing potential of the upland regions in the summer and retreated back into the oak/pistachio/almond zones during the winter where gathered tree fruits could sustain the carbohydrate needs of the people. In time, this tree zone moved farther and farther south along the front of the Zagros, thus providing new opportunities for winter camps of herders."

Similarly, Harris (1998) has suggested that the apparently rapid eastward movement of farmers to Central Asia was facilitated by an east-west-oriented "corridor" of Mediterranean climate across northern Iran, running from the northern Zagros south of the Caspian Sea to as far east as modern-day Mashhad in northeastern Iran, that was favorable to a mixed Neolithic economy dependent upon dry farming and caprine pastoralism. Other scholars have suggested more specific links, with Nishiaki (2010a) and Weeks et al. (2006) allowing for the possibility that the earliest ceramic Neolithic occupation of Fars was linked to the movement of groups affected by a century-long period of climatic deterioration at *c*.8200 cal BP (Staubwasser and Weiss 2006).

In addition to these environmental factors, demographic changes associated with the move to food production may have been important for Neolithic dispersals. As outlined by Bocquet-Appel (2011) in his model of the "agricultural demographic transition," increased mortality rates in agricultural communities are more than matched by highly increased fertility/birth rates, leading to population expansion in comparison to foraging groups (see also Bellwood 2011). Nevertheless, the numbers of early Neolithic sites discovered during archaeological survey in different parts of Iran are generally very small, suggesting low population densities (e.g., Miroschedji 1972; Voigt 1983; Prickett 1986b; Sumner 1994; Fazeli et al. 2009; Harris 2010; Vahdati 2010). If population growth was indeed a factor in the Neolithic dispersal, it seems much more likely to have operated in the later Neolithic period rather than the aceramic Neolithic, when the number of known sites is extremely small.

In this case, recent arguments regarding the specific and geographically limited locations preferred for early Neolithic settlement may be critical. Petrie and Thomas (2015) have argued that, in parts of Iran and South Asia, Neolithic settlements were preferentially located adjacent to the distal ends of alluvial fans that were characterized by predictable sheet run-off and low-energy water flows that could be redirected to fields of crops (see also Prickett 1986b: 761). Such environments, although commonplace, comprise only a very small proportion of the area of the generally large, flat valleys that now support widespread agriculture in the Zagros and other parts of Iran. It may be that small numbers of Neolithic settlements *did* fill up these preferred environmental niches, necessitating fissioning of demographically expanding farming groups and their migration to discover and colonize new tracts of suitable land in neighboring (or distant) valley systems.

The possible role of indigenous foraging groups in the spread of agriculture is very difficult to determine, particularly as most areas of Iran lack archaeological evidence for early Holocene hunter-gatherers. The same situation persisted in Fars province, despite decades of archaeological survey (Rosenberg 2003), until the recent discovery and excavation of two early Holocene rock shelter sites in the Tang-e Bolaghi, to the north of the Kur River Basin. These sites attest to hunter-gatherer occupation in the period from *c*.18,000 to 7500 cal BC, with the latest "Proto-Neolithic" levels tentatively indicating intensified exploitation of local wild goat populations (Tsuneki and Zeidi 2008). The lack of archaeological evidence for early Holocene foragers in other parts of Iran and neighboring areas has been regarded more as an accident of discovery than a real indication of the absence of such groups (Prickett 1986b: 416; Harris 2010: 233). Given the likely existence of such groups, there are a multitude of interactions that may have taken place between incoming farming groups and indigenous foragers across Iran, including competition and conflict, transfer of materials and ideas, and intermarriage.

At Tal-e Mushki in Fars province, for example, the overwhelming reliance on hunted equids and gazelle for subsistence has suggested to Mashkour (2009: 138) "a kind of 'Mesolithic' society in contact with Neolithic communities," albeit one that existed centuries after the earliest apparent aceramic Neolithic occupation in the region at Tepe Rahmatabad. It may be that this site demonstrates the flexibility of early subsistence adaptations incorporating food production, whereby populations could move from reliance upon food production to hunting and gathering, depending on specific environmental and social conditions and the permanence of settlement. Pollock and Bernbeck (2010; also Bernbeck 2001) have further suggested that hunter-gatherer ideologies of community-wide sharing might have characterized early Neolithic societies in Iran, in contrast to prevailing reconstructions of Neolithic society that focus upon the development of separate and distinct household economies.

It is interesting in this situation to consider the implications of DNA studies of modern plant and animal domesticates from the region, which allow for a more complex picture than simply the movement of colonizing farmers with their herds and crops. Saisho and Purugganan (2007: 1765), for example, have suggested that wild barley was brought under domestication east of the Fertile Crescent, "possibly at the eastern edge of the Iranian Plateau." They consequently propose that "knowledge transfer or independent innovation, rather than the spread of domestic species, may have driven the initial expansion of agriculture" eastwards across Iran (Saisho and Purugganan 2007: 1774–5). Morrell and Clegg (2007: 3291–2) support this view, emphasizing the likelihood of a second independent domestication of barley (over one domestication event followed by introgression of eastern barley species), but allow a much broader region within which this process could have occurred, stretching from the western Zagros to the Kopet Dagh piedmont and western Pakistan.

Similarly, the study of modern goat mtDNA by Naderi et al. (2008) indicates a possible independent locus of domestication for goats in Fars province or the central Iranian plateau during the early Holocene. According to these authors, the genetic data suggest bezoar management in the Southern Zagros earlier than c.9900–9700 BP, although this second domesticated population "probably collapsed when domestic goats from the Anatolian center [of domestication] spread in this region" (Naderi et al. 2008: 17663). Fuller (2011: S539) likewise emphasizes that domesticates "were not a single package entirely from one area of origin but were shuffled together along the trajectory to Baluchistan," agreeing with the more general consensus that Neolithic dispersals incorporated a substantial amount of subsistence variation (e.g., Evershed et al. 2008: 531).

It seems likely that the variability seen in early Iranian Neolithic culture and economy reflects not only adaptations by farmers to the new environments they were experiencing, but also interactions with foraging groups in many regions across the broad area of Iran, although we are at present in no position to assess the scale and nature of such interactions. Wild plant and animal populations in Iran appear to have been brought under control as part of the process of Neolithic dispersal, but whether this was by migrating and colonizing farming groups, by native hunter-foragers influenced by contact with farmers, or entirely independently, remains open to debate. The social, economic, and ideological transitions that characterized the arrival of the Neolithic in Iran are likely to have been as complex and varied as they are, at present, elusive.

FURTHER READING

Good summaries of Neolithic research in Iran are provided by Hole (1987, 1998). Fundamental reviews of the origins of animal domestication in Iran and the wider Near East are given by Zeder (2001, 2008) and Zeder and Hesse (2000). A broader context for understanding Neolithic origins in Iran and the Near East is provided by Watkins (2010), Harris (2010), and various papers in the supplement to *CA* 52 (2011) entitled "The origins of agriculture: New data, new ideas."

REFERENCES

Abdi, K. 2003. The early development of pastoralism in the central Zagros Mountains. *JWP* 17/4: 395–448.

Alden, J. R., K. Abdi, A. Azadi, F. Biglari, and S. Heydari. 2004. Kushk-e Hezar: A Mushki/Jari period site in the Kur River Basin, Fars, Iran. *Iran* 42: 25–45.

Alibaigi, S., and S. Khosravi. 2009. Tepeh Khaleseh: A new Neolithic and Palaeolithic site in the Abharrud basin in north-western Iran. *Antiquity* 83/319: Project Gallery.

Alizadeh, A. 2003. *Excavations at the prehistoric mound of Chogha Bonut, Khuzestan, Iran: Seasons 1976/77, 1977/78, and 1996.* Chicago: OIP 120.

———. 2008. *Chogha Mish II: The development of a prehistoric regional center in lowland Susiana, southwestern Iran: Final report on the last six seasons of excavations, 1972–1978.* Chicago: OIP 130.

Balossi Restelli, F. 2001. *Formation processes of the first developed Neolithic societies in the Zagros and the northern Mesopotamian plain.* Rome: SPO 1.

Beale, T. W. 1986. *Excavations at Tepe Yahya, Iran, 1967–1976: The early periods.* Cambridge: ASPR Bulletin 38.

Bellwood, P. 2011. Holocene population history in the Pacific region as a model for worldwide food producer dispersals. *CA* 52/S4: S363–78.

Bernbeck, R. 1989. *Die neolithische Keramik aus Qale Rostam, Bakhtiyari-Gebiet (Iran): Klassifikation, Produktionsanalyse und Datierungspotential.* Berlin: Altertumswissenschaften 9.

———. 2001. Forschungsperspektiven für das iranische Neolithikum. *AMIT* 33: 1–18.

Bernbeck, R., S. Pollock, and H. Fazeli Nashli. 2008. Rahmatabad: Dating the aceramic Neolithic in Fars province, Iran. *Neo-Lithics* 1/08: 37–9.

Bocquet-Appel, J.-P. 2011. The agricultural demographic transition during and after the agriculture inventions. *CA* 52/S4: S497–510.

Braidwood, R. J., and B. Howe. 1960. *Prehistoric investigations in Iraqi Kurdistan.* Chicago: SAOC 31.

Burney, C. A. 1964. Excavations at Yanik Tepe, Azerbaijan, 1962: Third preliminary report. *Iraq* 26/1: 54–61.

Caldwell, J. R. 1967. *Investigations at Tal-i Iblis.* Springfield: Illinois State Museum Preliminary Reports 9.

Chegini, N. N., and B. Helwing. 2011. Archaeological survey in the hinterland of Arismān and Kāšān. *EMM*: 421–83.

Clutton-Brock, J. 1999. *A natural history of domesticated mammals.* Cambridge: Cambridge University Press.

Coon, C. S. 1951. *Cave explorations in Iran 1949.* Philadelphia: University of Pennsylvania Press.

———. 1957. *The seven caves: Archaeological explorations in the Middle East.* London: Jonathan Cape.

Crawford, V. E. 1963. Beside the Kara Su. *Metropolitan Museum of Art Bulletin* 21/8: 263–73.

Daems, A., and K. Croucher. 2008. Prehistory of Iran: artificial cranial modifications. *EnIr* online edition.

Darabi, H., and H. Fazeli. 2009. The Neolithic of the Mehran plain: An introduction. *Antiquity* 83/322: Project Gallery.

Delougaz, P., and H. J. Kantor, eds. 1996. *Chogha Mish*, vol. 1, *The first five seasons of excavations, 1961–1971.* Chicago: OIP 101.

Deshayes, J. 1967. Céramiques peintes de Tureng Tépé. *Iran* 5: 123–31.

Dyson, R. H., Jr. 1965. Problems in the relative chronology of Iran, 6000–2000 BC. In *Chronologies in Old World archaeology*, 2nd ed., ed. R. W. Ehrich, 215–56. Chicago: University of Chicago Press.

———. 1991. Ceramics i. The Neolithic period through the Bronze Age in northeastern and north-central Persia. *EnIr* online edition.

Evershed, R. P., S. Payne, A. G. Sherratt, M. S. Copley, J. Coolidge, D. Urem-Kotsu, K. Kotsakis et al. 2008. Earliest date for milk use in the Near East and southeastern Europe linked to cattle herding. *Nature* 455/7212: 528–31.

Fazeli, H., R. A. E. Coningham, and C. M. Batt. 2004. Cheshmeh-Ali revisited: Towards an absolute dating of the Late Neolithic and Chalcolithic of Iran's Tehran plain. *Iran* 42: 13–23.

Fazeli, H., E. H. Wong, and D. T. Potts. 2005. The Qazvin Plain revisited: A reappraisal of the chronology of the northwestern Central Plateau, Iran, in the 6th to the 4th millennium BC. *ANES* 42: 3–82.

Fazeli Nashli, H., A. Beshkani, A. Markosian, H. Ilkani, R. Abbasnejad Sereshti, and R. L. Young. 2009. The Neolithic to Chalcolithic transition in the Qazvin Plain, Iran: Chronology and subsistence strategies. *AMIT* 41: 1–21.

Flannery, K. V. 1983. Early pig domestication in the Fertile Crescent: A retrospective look. In *The hilly flanks: Essays on the prehistory of Southwestern Asia presented to Robert J. Braidwood*, eds. T. C. Young Jr., P. E. L. Smith, and P. Mortensen, 163–88. Chicago: SAOC 36.

Fuller, D. Q. 2011. Finding plant domestication in the Indian subcontinent. *CA* 52/S4: S347–62.

Garazhian, O. 2009. Darestan: A group of Pre-Pottery Neolithic (PPN) sites in south-eastern Iran. *Antiquity* 83/319: Project Gallery.

Ghirshman, R. 1938. *Fouilles de Sialk, près de Kashan, 1933, 1934, 1937*, vol. 1. Paris: Geuthner.

Haak, W., O. Balanovsky, J. J. Sanchez, S. Koshel, V. Zaporozhchenko, C. J. Adler, C. S. I. Der Sarkissian et al. 2010. Ancient DNA from European early Neolithic farmers reveals their Near Eastern affinities. *PLoS Biology* 8/11: 1–16.

Harlan, J. R., and D. Zohary. 1966. Distribution of wild wheats and barley. *Science* 153: 1074–80.

Harris, D. R. 1998. The spread of Neolithic agriculture from the Levant to western Central Asia. In *The origins of agriculture and crop domestication: Proceedings of the Harlan Symposium, 10–14 May 1997, Aleppo, Syria*, eds. A. B. Damania, J. Valkoun, G. Willcox, and C. O. Qualset, 65–82. Aleppo: International Center for Agricultural Research in the Dry Areas.

———. 2010. *Origins of agriculture in western Central Asia: An environmental-archaeological study.* Philadelphia: University of Pennsylvania Museum of Archaeology and Anthropology.

Harris, D. R., and J. Coolidge. 2010a. History of archaeological research. In *Origins of agriculture in western Central Asia: An environmental-archaeological study*, ed. D. R. Harris, 43–52. Philadelphia: University of Pennsylvania Museum of Archaeology and Anthropology.

———. 2010b. The Mesolithic and Neolithic periods: Sites, sequences, and subsistence. In *Origins of agriculture in western Central Asia: An environmental-archaeological study*, ed. D. R. Harris, 53–69. Philadelphia: University of Pennsylvania Press.

Harris, D. R., and C. Gosden. 1996. The beginnings of agriculture in Central Asia. In *The origins and spread of agriculture and pastoralism in Eurasia*, ed. D. R. Harris, 370–89. London: UCL Press.

Hole, F. 1974. Tepe Tūlā'ī: An early campsite in Khuzistan, Iran. *Paléorient* 2/2: 219–42.

———. 1977. *Studies in the archaeological history of the Deh Luran Plain: The excavation of Chagha Sefid*. Ann Arbor: Memoirs of the Museum of Anthropology 9.

———. 1987. Archaeology of the Village Period. *AWI*: 29–78.

———. 1998. The spread of agriculture to the eastern arc of the Fertile Crescent: Food for the herders. In *The origins of agriculture and crop domestication: Proceedings of the Harlan Symposium, 10–14 May 1997, Aleppo, Syria*, ed. A. B. Damania, J. Valkoun, G. Willcox, and C. O. Qualset, 83–92. Aleppo: International Center for Agricultural Research in the Dry Areas.

———. 2000. New radiocarbon dates for Ali Kosh, Iran. *Neo-Lithics* 1: 13.

———. 2004. Campsites of the seasonally mobile in western Iran. *FHK*: 67–85.

Hole, F., K. V. Flannery, and J. A. Neely. 1969. *Prehistory and human ecology of the Deh Luran plain: An early village sequence from Khuzistan, Iran*. Ann Arbor: Memoirs of the Museum of Anthropology 1.

Hubbard, R. N. L. B. 1990. The carbonized seeds from Tepe Abdul Hosein: results of preliminary analyses. In *Tepe Abdul Hosein: A Neolithic Site in Western Iran, Excavations 1978*, ed. J. Pullar, 217–22. Oxford: BAR Int Ser 563.

Jarrige, J.-F., and C. Jarrige, 2006. Premiers pasteurs et agriculteurs dans les sous-continent Indo-Pakistanais. *Comptes Rendus Palevol* 5: 463–72.

Kearton, R. R. B. 1969. Survey in Azerbaijan. *Iran* 7: 186–7.

Kohl, P. L., R. L. Biscione, and M. L. Ingraham. 1982. Implications of recent evidence for the prehistory of northeastern Iran and southwestern Turkmenistan. *IrAnt* 17: 1–20.

Kohl, P. L., and D. L. Heskel 1980. Archaeological reconnaissance in the Darreh Gaz Plain: A short report. *Iran* 18: 160–72.

Kozlowski, S. K., and O. Aurenche. 2005. *Territories, boundaries and cultures in the Neolithic Near East*. Oxford: BAR Int Ser 1362.

Mashkour, M. 2006. Towards a specialized subsistence economy in the Marv Dasht plain: preliminary zooarchaeological analysis of the faunal assemblages from Tall-e Mushki, Tall-e Jari A and B and Tall-e Bakun A and B. In *The origins of state organizations in prehistoric highland Fars, southern Iran: Excavations at Tall-e Bakun*, ed. A. Alizadeh, 101–6. Chicago: OIP 128.

———. 2009. Faunal remains from Tol-e Nurabad and Tol-e Spid. *MAPSO*: 135–46.

Masuda, S. 1974. Excavations at Tappeh Sang-e Caxmaq. *PASARI* 2: 23–33.

Matthews, R., Y. Mohammadifar, W. Matthews, and A. Motarjem. 2010. Investigating the Early Neolithic of western Iran: The Central Zagros Archaeological Project (CZAP). *Antiquity* 84/323: Project Gallery.

Meadow, R. H. 1986. The geographical and palaeoenvironmental setting of Tepe Yahya. In *Excavations at Tepe Yahya, Iran 1967–1976: The Early Periods*, ed. T. W. Beale, 21–38. Cambridge: ASPR Bulletin 38.

———. 1996. The origins and spread of agriculture and pastoralism in northwestern South Asia. In *The origins and spread of agriculture and pastoralism in Eurasia*, ed. D. Harris, 390–412. London: UCL Press.
Meldgaard, J., P. Mortensen, and H. Thrane. 1963. Excavations at Tepe Guran, Luristan: Preliminary report of the Danish Archaeological Expedition to Iran 1963. *Acta Archaeologica* 34: 97–133.
Mellaart, J. 1975. *The Neolithic of the Near East*. London: Thames and Hudson.
Miller, N. F. 2003. Plant remains from the 1996 excavation. In *Excavations at the prehistoric mound of Chogha Bonut, Khuzestan, Iran: Seasons 1976/77, 1977/78, and 1996*, ed. A. Alizadeh, 123–8. Chicago: OIP 120.
Miller, N. F., and M. Kimiaie. 2006. Some plant remains from the 2004 excavations at Tall-e Mushki, Tall-e Jari A and B, and Tall-e Bakun A and B. In *The origins of state organizations in prehistoric highland Fars, southern Iran: Excavations at Tall-e Bakun*, ed. A. Alizadeh, 107–118. Chicago: OIP 128.
Miroschedji, P. de. 1973. Prospections archéologiques dans les vallées de Fasa et de Darab (rapport préliminaire). *PASARI* 1: 1–7.
Mohammadifar, Y., and A. Motarjem. 2008. Settlement continuity in Kurdistan. *Antiquity* 82/317: Project Gallery.
Morrell, P. L., and M. T. Clegg. 2007. Genetic evidence for a second domestication of barley (Hordeum vulgare) east of the Fertile Crescent. *PNAS* 104/9: 3289–94.
Mortensen, P. 1972. Seasonal camps and early villages in the Zagros. In *Man, Settlement and Urbanism*, ed. P. J. Ucko, R. Tringham, and G. W. Dimbleby, 293–7. London: Duckworth.
———. 1974. A survey of early prehistoric sites in the Holailān Valley in Lorestān. *PASARI* 2: 34–52.
———. 1992. Ceramics iii. The Neolithic period in central and western Persia. *EnIr* 5: 276–8.
Naderi, S., H.-R. Rezaei, F. Pompanon, M. G. B. Blum, R. Negrini, H.-R. Naghash, O. Balkız et al. 2008. The goat domestication process inferred from large-scale mitochondrial DNA analysis of wild and domestic individuals. *PNAS* 105/46: 17659–64.
Nishiaki, Y. 2010a. A radiocarbon chronology for the Neolithic settlement of Tall-i Mushki, Marv Dasht plain, Fars. *Iran* 48: 1–10.
———. 2010b. The development of architecture and pottery at the Neolithic settlement of Tall-i Jari B, Marv Dasht, southwest Iran. *AMIT* 42: 113–28.
Nissen, H. J., and A. Zagarell. 1976. Expedition to the Zagros Mountains. *PASARI* 4: 159–89.
Nokandeh, J. 2005. Arg-e Dasht, the first Neolithic discovered region in Gilan Province. In *Preliminary report of the Iran Japan Joint Archaeological Expedition to Gilan, fourth season*, ed. O. Tadahiko, J. Nokandeh, and Y. Kazuya, 50–56. Tehran: ICHTO.
Petrie, C. A., and K. D. Thomas. 2015. The topographic and environmental context of the earliest village sites in western South Asia. *Antiquity* 86: 1055–67.
Pires-Ferreira, J. W. 1977. Tepe Tula'i: Faunal remains from an early campsite in Khuzistan, Iran. *Paléorient* 3: 275–80.
Pollock, S., and R. Bernbeck. 2010. Neolithic worlds at Tol-e Baši. In *The 2003 excavations at Tol-e Baši, Iran: Social life in a Neolithic village*, ed. S. Pollock, R. Bernbeck, and K. Abdi, 274–87. Berlin: AIT 10.
Pollock, S., R. Bernbeck, and K. Abdi. 2010. *The 2003 excavations at Tol-e Baši, Iran: Social life in a Neolithic village*. Berlin: AIT 10.
Prickett, M. 1986a. Settlement during the early periods. In *Excavations at Tepe Yahya, Iran, 1967–1976: The early periods*, ed. T. W. Beale, 215–46. Cambridge: ASPR Bulletin 38.

———. 1986b. Man, land, and water: Settlement distribution and the development of irrigation agriculture in the Upper Rud-i Gushk drainage, southeastern Iran. Unpublished PhD diss., Harvard University.

Pullar, J. 1977. Early cultivation in the Zagros. *Iran* 15: 15–37.

———. 1990. *Tepe Abdul Hosein: A Neolithic site in western Iran, excavations 1978*. Oxford: BAR Int Ser 563.

Quintana-Murci, L., R. Chaix, R. S. Wells, et al. 2004. Where west meets east: the complex mtDNA landscape of the southwest and Central Asian corridor. *American Journal of Human Genetics* 74: 827–45.

Quintana-Murci, L., C. Krausz, T. Zerjal, S. H. Sayar, M. F. Hammer, S. Q. Mehdi, Q. Ayub et al. 2001. Y-chromosome lineages trace diffusion of people and languages in southwestern Asia. *American Journal of Human Genetics* 68: 537–42.

Redding, R. W. 2003. First report on faunal remains. In *Excavations at the prehistoric mound of Chogha Bonut, Khuzestan, Iran: Seasons 1976/77, 1977/78, and 1996*, ed. A. Alizadeh, 137–48. Chicago: OIP 120.

Renfrew, C. 1969. The obsidian from Ali Kosh and Tepe Sabz. In *Prehistory and human ecology of the Deh Luran Plain: An early village sequence from Khuzistan, Iran*, ed. F. Hole, K. V. Flannery, and J. A. Neely, 429–34. Ann Arbor: Memoirs of the Museum of Anthropology Number 1.

———. 1977. The later obsidian of Deh Luran: The evidence from Chagha Sefid. In *Studies in the Archaeological History of the Deh Luran Plain: the Excavation of Chagha Sefid*, ed. F. Hole, 289–311. Ann Arbor: Memoirs of the Museum of Anthropology 9.

Rosen, A. M. 2003. Preliminary phytolith analyses. In *Excavations at the prehistoric mound of Chogha Bonut, Khuzestan, Iran: Seasons 1976/77, 1977/78, and 1996*, ed. A. Alizadeh, 129–36. Chicago: OIP 120.

Rosenberg, M. 2003. The Epipaleolithic in the Marvdasht. *YBYN*: 98–108.

Rowley-Conwy, P. 2011. Westward ho! The spread of agriculture from central Europe to the Atlantic. *CA* 52/S4: S431–51.

Saisho, D., and M. D. Purugganan. 2007. Molecular phylogeography of domesticated barley traces expansion of agriculture in the Old World. *Genetics* 177: 1765–76.

Shahmirzadi, S. M. 2004. *The potters of Sialk*. Tehran: SRPR 3.

Smith, P. E. L. 1976. Reflections on four seasons of excavations at Tappeh Ganj Dareh. *PASARI* 4: 11–22.

———. 1978. An interim report on Ganj Dareh Tepe, Iran. *AJA* 82: 538–40.

———. 1990. Architectural innovation and experimentation at Ganj Dareh, Iran. *WA* 21/3: 323–35.

Smith, P. E. L., and R. Crépeau. 1983. Fabrication expérimentale de répliques d'un vase néolithique du site de Ganj Dareh, Iran: Recherche technologique. *Paléorient* 9/2: 55–62.

Smith, P. E. L., and P. Mortensen. 1980. Three new Early Neolithic sites in western Iran. *CA* 21/4: 511–12.

Staubwasser, M., and H. Weiss. 2006. Holocene climate and cultural evolution in late prehistoric-early historic West Asia. *QR* 66: 372–87.

Sumner, W. M. 1994. The evolution of tribal society in the southern Zagros Mountains, Iran. In *Chiefdoms and early states in the Near East: The organizational dynamics of complexity*, ed. G. J. Stein and M. S. Rothman, 47–66. Madison: Monographs in World Archaeology 18.

Thornton, C. P. 2010. Sang-e Chakhmaq. *EnIr* online edition.

Tsuneki, A., and M. Zeidi. 2008. *Tang-e Bolaghi: The Iran-Japan Archaeological Project for the Sivand Dam Salvage Area.* Tsukuba: AL-SHARK 3 (University of Tsukuba, Studies for West Asian Archaeology).

Turnquist, J. 1983. The Neolithic skeletal population from Hajji Firuz Tepe. In *Hajji Firuz Tepe, Iran: The Neolithic settlement*, ed. M. M. Voigt, 340–43. Philadelphia: UMM 50.

Uerpmann, H.-P. 1987. *The ancient distribution of ungulate mammals in the Middle East.* Wiesbaden: TAVO Beiheft A 27.

Vahdati, A. A. 2010. Tepe Pahlavan: A Neolithic-Chalcolithic site in the Jajarm Plain, north-eastern Iran. *IrAnt* 45: 7–30.

Vandiver, P. 1986. Sequential slab construction; a conservative southwest Asiatic ceramic tradition, ca. 7000–3000 B.C. *Paléorient* 13/2: 9–35.

Van Zeist, W., P. E. L Smith, R. M. Palfenier-Wegter, M. Suwijn, and W. A. Casparie. 1984. An archaeobotanical study of Ganj Dareh Tepe, Iran. *Palaeohistoria* 26: 201–224.

Voigt, M. M. 1983. *Hajji Firuz Tepe, Iran: The Neolithic settlement.* Philadelphia: UMM 50.

Voigt, M. M., and R. H. Dyson. 1992. The chronology of Iran, ca. 8000–2000 B.C. In *Chronologies of Old World archaeology*, 3rd ed., ed. R. W. Ehrich, vol. 1, 122–78, vol. 2, 125–53. Chicago: University of Chicago Press.

Watkins, T. 2010. New light on the Neolithic revolution in south-west Asia. *Antiquity* 84: 621–34.

Weeks, L. R., K. Alizadeh, L. Niakan, K. Alamdari, A. Khosrowzadeh, B. McCall, and M. Zeidi. 2006. The Neolithic settlement of highland SW Iran: New evidence from the Mamasani district. *Iran* 44: 1–31.

Weeks, L. R., K. Alizadeh, L. Niakan, K. Alamdari, M. Zeidi, and A. Khosrowzadeh. 2009. Excavations at Tol-e Nurabad. *MAPSO*: 31–88.

Willcox, G. 1990. Charcoal remains from Tepe Abdul Hosein. In *Tepe Abdul Hosein: A Neolithic site in Western Iran, excavations 1978*, ed. J. Pullar, 223–8. Oxford: BAR Int Ser 563.

Woosley, A. I. 1996. Early agriculture at Chogha Mish. In *Chogha Mish volume 1: The first five seasons of excavations 1961–1971*, ed. P. Delougaz and H. J. Kantor, 307–318. Chicago: OIP 101

Zagarell, A. 1982. *The prehistory of the northeast Bahtiyari Mountains, Iran: The rise of a highland way of life.* Wiesbaden: TAVO Beiheft 42.

Zeder, M. A. 2001. A metrical analysis of a collection of modern goats (*Capra hircus aegargus* and *C. h. hircus*) from Iran and Iraq: implications for the study of caprine domestication. *JAS* 28: 61–79.

———. 2008. Domestication and early agriculture in the Mediterranean Basin: origins, diffusion, and impact. *PNAS* 105/33: 11597–604.

Zeder, M. A., and B. Hesse. 2000. The initial domestication of goats (*Capra hircus*) in the Zagros Mountains 10,000 years ago. *Science* 287: 2254–57.

Zeidi, M., B. McCall, and A. Khosrowzadeh. 2009. Survey of Dasht-e Rostam-e Yek and Dasht-e Rostam-e Do. *MAPSO*: 147–68.

Zohary, D., and M. Hopf. 2000. *Domestication of plants in the Old World.* Oxford: Oxford University Press.

PART II
THE CHALCOLITHIC PERIOD

CHAPTER 5

THE CHALCOLITHIC OF NORTHERN IRAN

BARBARA HELWING

INTRODUCTION

From the final centuries of the sixth millennium BC until the second third of the fourth millennium BC, communities in the Iranian highlands set out on a track of increasingly accelerating innovation. These changes concern the introduction of new technologies to work on materials, but also, and even more, the development of complex forms of social and economic organization. The most obvious innovation is the introduction of metal as a new material, reflected in the term "Chalcolithic"—Copper-Stone-Age—used for this period. But most importantly, we can observe profound reorganizations of the social fabric that are reflected in the architectural record and can be reconstructed from archaeological evidence: a rise in population; an increasing differentiation of agricultural and craft production and the introduction of new materials; the exploitation of "secondary products"; and a growing network of long-distance contacts. These processes reached an apogee around 3400 BC and were soon after followed first by a collapse of these early complex polities and subsequently by the rise of early urban societies in the proto-Elamite or Early Bronze Age, beginning in the late fourth millennium BC.

REGIONAL SETTING

The region covered within this chapter comprises the highlands of central and northern Iran, that is, the fertile stretches of land surrounding the western end of the central desert, known as the Dasht-e Kavir, from the area of Kashan in the southwest (systematic archaeological research along the desert fringe east of Kashan is still lacking at this moment) to the Damghan plain in the northeast; a series of smaller plains extending toward the environs of Lake Urmia in northwestern Iran; and encompassing the area beyond the Alborz Mountains, including the Caspian littoral and the Gorgan plain. Except for the northern slopes of the Alborz Mountains and the Caspian littoral with its subtropical climate, the central highlands are today characterized by a semiarid to arid environment with only limited natural niches for human settlement. This has meant that reliable agriculture is possible only with the aid of large-scale landscape engineering. Conditions during the Chalcolithic period were probably less harsh than today, since the fifth and fourth millennia BC coincided with the so-called climatic optimum (Chapter 2; cf. Jones et al. 2013), when the Iranian highlands generally received higher rainfall and hence stable agricultural yields could be achieved. The end of the Chalcolithic falls into a period of increased aridity in at least some locations (Schmidt et al. 2011: 587).

Archaeological sources

The sources on which the reconstruction of the Chalcolithic period in northern Iran can be based remain patchy. In comparison to other areas, like southwestern Iran, which have been intensively surveyed since the 1960s (*AWI*), the Iranian highlands have received considerably less attention. As a rule, archaeological research has concentrated on the exploration of a few large, highly visible settlement mounds like Tepe Sialk (Ghirshman 1938) and Tepe Hissar (Schmidt 1937). This emphasis on settlement mounds often renders other categories, like graveyards, flat settlements, and cave sites, archaeologically invisible, and places of important functional specialization, like mines and open-air workshops, were often discovered only by chance. Only recently have systematic surveys begun in some areas, providing the first insights into the development of the archaeological landscapes there, most notably in the Qazvin and Tehran plains (Coningham et al. 2004, 2006; Fazeli Nashli et al. 2009). Furthermore, surveys of the surrounding landscape have been launched as a complement to new excavations, for example, around Arisman in Natanz (Chegini and Helwing 2011), Tepe Sialk in Kashan (Danti 2006), and Qara Tepe in Qomrud (Kaboli 2000).

Chronology

Early investigations in the Iranian highlands that began with large-scale excavation at major settlement mounds like Tepe Hissar (Schmidt 1937), Tepe Sialk (Ghirshman 1938), and Cheshmeh Ali (Matney 1995; Schmidt 1935a) aimed first and foremost at establishing a chronological framework for the prehistoric cultures of highland Iran. Despite flaws in excavation technique and interpretation rooted in the archaeological methodology of the time, the stratigraphic sequences developed then still remain the cornerstone of chronological sequences at sites on the Iranian plateau today, and the respective stratigraphic levels have remained enshrined in the periodization of the region. In this terminology, Sialk II–III and Hissar I describe the Chalcolithic. These phases formed the basis of the first synthetic study of the development of prehistoric cultures in Iran (McCown 1942) and since the 1970s they have been reworked and refined on the basis of newly excavated evidence (Majidzadeh 1976, 1978, 1981; Shahmirzadi 1995). A new terminology that took a supralocal perspective, modeled on the Khuzestan sequence (Le Breton 1957; Delougaz and Kantor 1972), uses the sequence Archaic, Early, Middle, and Late Plateau. Thanks to systematic surveying and dating projects in the Tehran and Qazvin plains (Fazeli Nashli et al. 2009; Fazeli Nashli and Sereshti 2005; Fazeli, Wong and Potts 2005) our knowledge has advanced considerably over the past decade.

Soundings in select locations within the survey areas and in some of the key sites explored in the 1960 to 1970s have been used to build a radiocarbon-based chronology for the prehistoric cultural sequences of the Iranian plateau. These efforts allow us to give greater precision to the existing sequences. Moreover, they open up new possibilities of exploring major developments in settlement patterns, demographic trends, and social development. Of major importance for the period discussed here are reconsiderations of old excavation data through soundings and excavation at Cheshmeh Ali, Tepe Ghabrestan, Tepe Zagheh, Tepe Sialk, and Tepe Sagzabad, and soundings in some newly recorded sites such as Ebrahimabad and Chahar Boneh. According to this new and constantly refined sequence (Fazeli Nashli et al. 2009, 2013), three major phases can now be distinguished. At c.5200 BC a 900-year long phase of smooth transition from the Late Neolithic to the Chalcolithic began (Early Transitional Chalcolithic: 5200–4600 BC; Late Transitional Chalcolithic: 4600–4300 BC). Subsequently, the fully developed Chalcolithic extended over the subsequent millennium with three major phases: Early (4300–4000 BC), Middle (4000–3700 BC), and Late Chalcolithic (3700–3300 BC). Within this system, the Early and Middle Chalcolithic present a sort of run-up to complex societies that became fully established only in the Late Chalcolithic. For the purpose of the following account, this chronological sequence serves as the cornerstone against which all other evidence will be interpreted. The systematic redating of the highland Iranian Neolithic to Chalcolithic in absolute terms has important consequences for our understanding of some key assemblages, the dating of which needs to be lowered: Tepe Zagheh can now be considered typical of the beginning of the Transitional Chalcolithic period around 5200 BC; and Middle Chalcolithic Tepe Ghabrestan, with its well-known metallurgical workshop, belongs to the early centuries of the fourth millennium BC.

Other regions adjacent to central Iran provide less reliable dating evidence. Northwestern Iran is still dependent on the Hasanlu sequence established in the 1960s that combined evidence from various complementary sites (Dyson and Muscarella 1989). Within that sequence, Hasanlu IX (Dalma phase; 5350–4700 BC) and VIII (Pisdeli phase; 4700–3950 BC; both date ranges are based on a recalibration of old radiocarbon dates by Tonoike 2009: 27) cover the time span discussed here.

Even less accessible is the sequence of fifth to fourth millennium BC occupation for northeastern Iran (Dyson 1991), although surveys indicate considerable occupation throughout these millennia (Chapter 10; Rezvani 1999; Roustaie 2012). The important data from Sang-e Chakhmaq East, where the two uppermost levels correspond to the Transitional Chalcolithic, remain inadequately published (Masuda 1976). Rescue excavations at Aq Tappeh in the Gorgan plain (Shahmirzadi and Nokandeh 2001) have not provided radiocarbon evidence, and the reconstruction of the chronological sequence in this area remains difficult, despite important contributions like the publication of the mid-fifth millennium BC Shir-e Shian assemblage (Dyson and Thornton 2009). The situation improves in the fourth millennium BC, when Chalcolithic layers covered by later occupation are at least recorded, if not uncovered at larger scale, for example, in Tepe Hissar I (Thornton et al. 2013).

Incipient complexity: the Transitional Chalcolithic (5200–4300 BC)

In some regions, occupation appears interrupted in key sequences: in northwestern Iran, the transition from Late Neolithic Hajji Firuz (Hasanlu X) to the Transitional Chalcolithic Dalma period (Hasanlu IX) is obscured by a gap in the combined Hasanlu sequence (Tonoike 2009: 27) and in central Iran, occupation at Tepe Sialk seems suspended for several centuries in the early fifth millennium BC when the settlement shifted from the north mound to the south mound (Fazeli Nashli et al. 2009: 10, fig. 7). But this impression of occupational gaps can be rooted in the traditional focus of archaeological investigations on individual site sequences and the lack of full-coverage research with regard to landscapes at large, which renders conclusive statements on the regional validity of these gaps premature and makes the transition from the Late Neolithic to the Transitional Chalcolithic period difficult to tackle. It is therefore largely defined through changes in ceramic styles (Fazeli Nashli et al. 2009: 10), most markedly through the introduction of a reddish ware with burnished surface and simple dark painted geometric decoration, commonly known as black-on-red or Cheshmeh Ali Ware (Fazeli Nashli et al. 2009: 14), which occurs together with regionally more restricted wares, like Zagheh crusted ware in the Qazvin plain, or Dalma surface manipulated ware in northwestern Iran.

Although individual sequences seem to expose gaps in the occupation from the Late Neolithic to the Transitional Chalcolithic, it seems that overall settlement density and pattern remained constant. Surveys in the Tehran and Qazvin plains identified a considerable number of sites attributable to the Transitional Chalcolithic that surpasses the number of sites from both the preceding Late Neolithic and the subsequent Chalcolithic period (Fazeli Nashli et al. 2013: figs. 1–2). But when these numbers are recalculated with regard to the comparatively long duration of almost one millennium for the

Transitional Chalcolithic versus the 400 years of the Late Neolithic and the 300 years of the Early Chalcolithic, settled occupation appears more balanced and almost constant.

There are, nevertheless, changes, smooth and almost invisible at first, that become significant in accumulation and over time: most importantly, and this is the reason why the Transitional Chalcolithic is set apart from the Late Neolithic at all, there are increasing signs of specialization in subsistence and craft production. These changes are intrinsically related to social changes reflected in the accumulation of exotic materials and their display in burials, and in the construction of special buildings related to communal events, possibly feasts.

Two sites on the central plateau provide excavated evidence for the beginning of the Transitional Chalcolithic on a larger scale. One is Tepe Zagheh in the Qazvin plain (Shahmirzadi 1977, 1990), dated at the time of excavation to the Neolithic and only recently reattributed to $c.5200$ BC (Fazeli et al. 2005). Zagheh is a good example of the introduction of important new features in the Chalcolithic period that all point to increased degrees of specialization, be it in construction techniques and building layout (Shahmirzadi 1979, 1990) or in craft production. Houses at Zagheh were arranged in a dense pattern of irregular plan but all consisted of a combination of roofed and unroofed, subrectangular spaces with hearths and benches. Walls were not shared but two parallel walls sometimes formed the exterior of two neighboring houses, giving the impression hence on schematic plans of one coherent unit. The construction materials used were *pisé* and mudbrick, the later hand-formed into an oblong shape and marked with finger impressions. As a special building, the so-called Painted Building stands out as a house of communal function central to the site (Negahban 1979): it is a rectangular building measuring 11×7 m with a large central room surrounded by a wall. This wall was supported on the exterior by long, narrow buttresses. The space between the buttresses was later closed by adding another wall from the outside to create small cists that could be filled with construction material, probably a necessary construction measure when the roof statics of the unusually large central room gave in. The central room was equipped with hearths, benches, and containers, and its walls were painted with a geometric meander design in white and black on a red ocher ground. Reminiscent of older Neolithic traditions, eighteen skulls of wild mountain goats were integrated into the wall decoration.

At Zagheh the burials of both adults and children were usually located within the house area. These were equipped with personal ornaments such as beads and sprinkled with red ocher, but eight burials with rich bead adornment and sprinkled ocher seem to have been oriented toward the Painted Building (Tala'i 1999).

Few other sites have been exposed to such an extent that complete architectural plans have been uncovered. Examples of multiple-room architecture seem to have come to light in E. F. Schmidt's excavations at Cheshmeh Ali (Schmidt 1935b). In phase II the North Mound at Tepe Sialk revealed a solid, rectangular, "casemate"-like construction made from and filled with hand-shaped mudbricks (Ghirshman 1938: pl. 58), possibly a foundation on which to erect *pisé* walls. The massive use of mudbrick for floors or possibly substructure is also attested at Yan Tepe in the Qazvin plain (Majidzadeh 2010:

pl. 3). In northwestern Iran, Dalma Tepe represents the type site for the Transitional Chalcolithic (Hamlin 1975). Emphasis there was on small, individual houses, comparable to those found already in the Neolithic layers at Hajji Firuz Tepe (Voigt 1983).

In northeastern Iran, Transitional Chalcolithic occupation is attested in the uppermost layers (2–1) of Sang-e Chakhmaq East and displays significant changes in subsistence, architecture, and burial traditions when compared to the preceding Late Neolithic period. Sang-e Chakhmaq East houses were constructed from rectangular mudbricks with finger impressions. They consisted of rectangular rooms arranged around a central room equipped with a hearth. Burial customs shifted from flexed to extended burials, and a visible increase in the use of cattle bones for bone tools has been interpreted as reflecting a shift in faunal preferences (Thornton 2010).

The Transitional Chalcolithic was set apart from the Late Neolithic because of the evidence of increased specialization in subsistence economy and in craft production. An intensification of agricultural practice is indicated by the introduction of simple irrigation techniques, such as at Tepe Pardis (Gillmore et al. 2009). Increased agricultural yields required new methods of storage, leading to the introduction of giant storage vessels at several sites. The herding of sheep and goat was now the basis of animal husbandry (Young and Fazeli 2008), and it is highly likely that in addition to milking, which seems to have been established since the Neolithic, the use of wool as a secondary product became widespread, as is indicated by the appearance of spindle whorls at most major sites in this period, such as Hajji Firuz (Voigt 1983: 169–72, figs. 99–100), Jeyran Tepe (Majidzadeh 2010: fig. 99), Tepe Sialk (Ghirshman 1938: pl. 52.1.4.9; for a general assessment of wool exploitation in the fifth millennium BC, with a focus on northern Ubaid sites, see Sudo 2010).

In craft production the Transitional Chalcolithic witnessed for the first time a deliberate separation of residential and workshop areas. Ceramic workshops are attested at Zagheh and Tepe Pardis (Fazeli Nashli and Djamali 2003; Fazeli Nash[a]li et al. 2010), and lithic workshops were now located outside of settlements, probably to specialized knapping places close to the flint sources. No such workshops proper have been recorded in northern Iran, but the lack of debitage in the lithic inventories of settlements indicates that some operations, like core preparation and the roughing-out of blanks, must have been carried out before the implements reached the settlements (Thomalsky 2010). Most probably, the same is true of the production of metal artifacts that now began in earnest with the cold and hot working of copper to produce decorative items and small implements (Thornton 2009).

An increased rate of specialization is furthermore evident from a close study of the ceramic record. In the Transitional Chalcolithic at Tepe Pardis potters began to use an increasingly fine raw material and to abandon the previously used coarse organic temper, probably in order to use this fine clay to throw vessels on a fast wheel. Pottery kilns documented at Tepe Pardis were large, rectangular, room-like structures that could accommodate a large number of vessels, including the giant storage vessels that were also an innovation in this period. A firing temperature of 750°C could regularly be achieved in these kilns (Fazeli Nash[a]li et al. 2010).

These trends toward increased specialization correlate with the emergence of long-distance contacts, attested since the Neolithic and responsible for the wide distribution of certain raw materials such as turquoise and obsidian. In the Transitional Chalcolithic, more materials entered this circulation system: exotic shells, lapis lazuli, and especially copper reached many sites. Since archaeologists usually consider objects made of these rare materials to have been prestige items, their appearance in burials may reflect an increasing emphasis on social rank. Such a tendency is also visible in internal settlement patterns and the spatially separate organization of craft production. The Transitional Chalcolithic was thus a period lasting almost one millennium during which communities in the Iranian highlands display increasing complexity.

Established complexity: The Chalcolithic (4300–3400 BC)

The rate of change and innovation that marked the Transitional Chalcolithic accelerated in the second half of the fifth millennium, the mature Chalcolithic. This period comprises another 900 years, but changes in the ceramic record follow now more rapidly upon each other. As a hallmark of the period, black-on-red pottery was replaced by a black-on-buff ware. This pottery was first discovered in Level III of the South Mound at Tepe Sialk (Ghirshman 1938) and is therefore called Sialk III pottery throughout central and northern Iran. The obvious change in color is related to the introduction of a new type of kiln, one of which was uncovered in Tepe Sialk III_1 (Ghirshman 1938): these are single- or double-chambered, semisubterranean kilns with pierced grates that allowed the firing of pottery at temperatures up to 1000°C (for an overview of the various types of kilns, see Streily 2000; Alizadeh 1985). Only northwestern Iran stayed with a different ceramic tradition of Chaff Faced Ware (CFW), a pottery production widely distributed between northwestern Iran, the southern Caucasus, eastern Turkey, and northern Syria (for an overview, see Marro 2010) that is characterized by the addition of organic temper to the clay as a means of lowering firing temperatures.

There are still too few data from central and northern Iran to say much about changes in demography or settlement density, since previous surveys concentrated mainly on the visible mounded sites and systematic survey data are only available from select, small areas. Nevertheless, in comparing the three subphases of the Chalcolithic, an increase in the number of settlements since the Middle Chalcolithic can be detected. The functional and hierarchical differentiation between sites also increased. Some settlements grew to a large size and seem to have functioned as central places. Tepe Sialk was probably the center of the Kashan plain; Tepe Ghabrestan and Ebrahimabad may have been centers on the Qazvin plain (Fazeli Nashli et al. 2009); and Qara Tepe on the Qomrud plain (Kaboli 1997, 2000), already a large site during the Transitional Chalcolithic, continued to function as a local center. Among the functionally specialized sites are small copper-smelting sites that have been recorded on the edge of the desert in the Natanz area near Arisman (Chegini and Helwing 2011).

The architectural record provides little evidence of an increase in ranking or social differentiation. From period III_2 onward, houses at Tepe Sialk were rectangular with oblong rooms (Ghirshman 1938), although no clear architectural system is recognizable. In Sialk III_4 the exterior of houses began to be reinforced with rectangular buttresses. Finally, in III_{6-7}, a singular, multiroomed building replaced the previous independent rooms. The intensity of occupation was undoubtedly high: frequent rebuilding led to the accumulation of almost 10 m of settlement debris at Sialk in less than a millennium (Nokandeh 2002). Attributable to the Middle Chalcolithic, Tepe Ghabrestan was exposed on a larger scale and consisted of a densely arranged cluster of small, one-room buildings and larger, multiroomed buildings (Majidzadeh 2008). Several smaller house units joined together formed residential blocks of differing orientation. One block, the so-called Main Building, was larger than the others and was unusual by virtue of its extremely wide walls, suggesting an internal differentiation according to rank or function. Some of the smaller rooms in the Ghabrestan houses were used as workshops (Majidzadeh 1979). Copper artifacts were produced in two small chambers which were equipped with small pit furnaces, benches, and sets of metallurgical tools, including molds. Finished artifacts were found here as well.

Tepe Hissar I was a spread-out settlement site with separate quarters having different functions. Architecture exposed on the so-called Main Mound (Howard 1989) comprises almost quadrangular, one-room buildings with markedly niched exterior walls, while the apparently more domestic North Flat area (Dyson and Remsen 1989) appears less regular. Spatial separation of crafts is evident, with separate areas for the processing of copper, lapiz lazuli and steatite (Tosi 1989).

Copper processing was one of the most obvious technical innovations of the Chalcolithic (Thornton 2009). But since the period is a true phase of experimentation, people also tried to work with many previously unexploited materials, such as silver and gold (Pernicka 2004). As for copper, although it is not exactly clear when the smelting of copper ore began (possibly as early as the late sixth millennium BC), its use was well established throughout Iran by the later fifth millennium BC, and centers of copper working blossomed in the western part of north-central Iran. Besides Tepe Ghabrestan, the best evidence comes from the recent investigations at Arisman (Pernicka et al. 2011; Helwing 2011a) and Tepe Sialk (Nezafati and Pernicka 2006). Both sites yielded large amounts of metallurgical debris that attest to the smelting of copper ores and the production of arsenical copper in small pit furnaces by crucible smelting in freestanding crucibles with a pierced foot of so-called Ghabrestan type. Raw materials for smelting were obtained from various localities: at least four different sources are attested for Arisman. As smelting allowed the metal to be shaped in a liquid state, the casting of artifacts became a new technique that allowed for the production of larger, more complex objects. For the first time long blades and heavy double axes of arsenical copper are attested. Their production relied on new techniques like casting and smithing. Furthermore, these innovations reflect a social need to signal rank and status through ostentatious weaponry.

This new emphasis on the visibility of social rank can be observed at the same time as long-distance contacts further intensified. The circulation of exotic goods had long been established in the Chalcolithic, but in the fourth millennium BC, beasts of burden—domesticated donkeys—became available and could be used for overland transport of goods (Benecke 2011; Potts 2011). Furthermore, the creation of a completely new industry, metal production, seems to have fueled intensified exchange between production centers and distant consumers. The metal objects found in the enigmatic Susa I cemetery were probably produced in the highlands of central Iran where the corresponding casting molds have been found at Tepe Ghabrestan and Arisman (Helwing 2011a). The circulation of characteristic Late Chalcolithic double axes not only to the south, but also toward the Caucasus, also suggests that a larger regional network was responsible for this distribution pattern (Boroffka 2009; Helwing 2012). Stamp seals are attested at some sites, such as Tepe Ghabrestan (Majidzadeh 2008: 41, fig. 55), Tepe Sialk (Ghirshman 1938: pl. 23.2) and Tepe Hissar (Schmidt 1937: pl. 15), certainly reflecting a usage widespread in Western Asia at that time. Hence, not only materials but sets of artifacts that relate to specific traditions of usage as social markers or, as in the case of the double axes, as weapons, can be interpreted as evidence of shared social practices and social rules that seem to apply across a larger network of settlements extending beyond the Iranian plateau.

In the Late Chalcolithic, these long-distance contacts found their material expression in the introduction of occasional objects grounded in the cultural system of the Mesopotamian and Susa lowlands: the spread of lowland food consumption habits is visible through the adoption of a select few ceramic types like spouted jars and bevel-rim bowls (Potts 2009). Occasionally administrative devices, such as cylinder seals and tokens, appear, for example at Tepe Sialk (Ghirshman 1938) and Arisman (Helwing 2011b). Imitations of cylinder seals made of clay and locally made cylinder seals appear as well. One indicator of the early beginning of such contacts is a marble figurine from Ghabrestan (Majidzadeh 2008: 43, fig. 56.5–6) that closely resembles theriomorphic stamp seals of a type widely known in the Syrian Jazirah during the early fourth millennium BC at Uruk-related sites (Pittman 2001: fig. 11.20). These finds illustrate the gradually growing familiarity of the highland centers with these exotic lowland traditions. It was in the subsequent proto-Elamite phase that these cultural borrowings came to full fruition in their specific highland form.

Outlook: Early Bronze Age—early proto-Elamite

As contact between the Iranian highlands and the lowland communities intensified and more goods came into circulation, social differences within the highland communities seem to have grown as well. Increasing social stratification seems to have been a consequence and was fully established in the urban-type settlements of the subsequent proto-Elamite period. Many sites have gaps in their occupational sequence at the moment of transition (Voigt and Dyson 1992; Dyson 1987; Helwing 2004), and it remains to be understood how this transition unfolded. The proto-Elamite period brought about numerous innovations in architecture, ceramic production, and social techniques, including the short-term adoption of a writing system (Chapter 13). Since these changes were so profound and appeared after a disruptive moment, they are often attributed to colonization by settlers from the lowlands (Alden 1982; Lamberg-Karlovsky 1978); however, on closer examination, there are many continuities in daily practice and craft production with the Late Chalcolithic (Helwing 2013). Thus, the Late Chalcolithic period seems to have ended in a scenario of collapse around 3400 BC, following several centuries of rapid growth. This collapse allowed new elites to take control, and singular urban-type centers attracted the population from the hinterlands as well. A period of growth and prosperity followed, and for several centuries into the third millennium BC, the proto-Elamite towns with their large-scale manufacture of copper and silver, stone vessels, and jewelry flourished in the highlands.

Further reading

For a general overview of periodization in the various subregions of Iran, Voigt and Dyson (1992) remains a standard and is useful when updated with recent data on absolute chronology, especially Fazeli Nashli et al. (2009). An update on fieldwork in Iran from 1979 to 2005 can be found in Azarnoush und Helwing (2005). For conceptual aspects of centralization and labor specialization, see Matthews und Fazeli (2004). The development of metallurgy as a central theme of the Chalcolithic is summarized in Thornton (2009).

References

Alden, J. R. 1982. Trade and politics in Proto-Elamite Iran. *CA* 23: 613–40.
Alizadeh, A. 1985. A Protoliterate pottery kiln from Choga Mish. *Iran* 23: 39–50.
Azarnoush, M., and B. Helwing. 2005. Recent archaeological research in Iran: Prehistory to Iron Age. *AMIT* 37: 189–246.
Benecke, N. 2011. Faunal remains of Arisman. *EMM*: 376–82.
Boroffka, N. 2009. Simple technology: Casting moulds for axe-adzes. In *Metals and society: Studies in honour of Barbara S. Ottaway*, ed. T. L. Kienlin and B. W. Roberts, 246–57. Bonn: Universitätsforschungen Zur Prähistorischen Archäologie 169.
Chegini, N. N., and B. Helwing. 2011. Archaeological survey in the hinterland of Arismān and Kāšān. *EMM*: 421–83.
Coningham, R. A. E., H. Fazeli, R. L. Young, and R. E. Donahue. 2004. Location, location, location: A pilot survey of the Tehran plain in 2003. *Iran* 42: 1–12.

Coningham, R. A. E., H. Fazeli, R. L. Young, G. K. Gillmore, H. Karimian, M. Maghsoudi, R. E. Donahue et al. 2006. Socio-economic transformations: Settlement survey in the Tehran plain and excavations at Tepe Pardis. *Iran* 44: 33–62.

Danti, M. D. 2006. The Sialk Regional Archaeological Survey 2005. In *The Fishermen of Sialk*. ed. S. M. Shahmirzadi, 67–78. Tehran: SRPR 4.

Delougaz, P., and H. J. Kantor. 1972. New evidence for the prehistoric & Protoliterate culture development of Khuzestan. In *The Memorial Volume of the Vth International Congress of Iranian Art and Archaeology. Tehran-Isfahan-Shiraz, 11th–18th April 1968*, 14–33. Tehran: Ministry of Culture and Arts.

Dyson, R. H., Jr. 1987. The relative and absolute chronology of Hissar II and the Proto-Elamite horizon of northern Iran. In *Chronologies in the Near East: Relative chronologies and absolute chronology, 16,000–4,000 B.P.*, ed. O. Aurenche, J. Evin, and F. Hours, 647–78. Oxford: BAR Int Ser 379.

———. 1991. Ceramics i. The Neolithic period through the Bronze Age in northeastern and north-central Persia. *EnIr* 5/3: 266–75.

Dyson, R. H., Jr., and O. W. Muscarella. 1989. Constructing the chronology and historical implications of Hasanlu IV. *Iran* 27: 1–27.

Dyson, R.H., Jr., and W. C. S. Remsen. 1989. Observations on architecture and stratigraphy. *THRRP*: 69–109.

Dyson, R.H., Jr., and C. P. Thornton. 2009. Shir-i Shian and the fifth millennium sequence of northern Iran. *Iran* 47: 1–22.

Fazeli, H., E. H. Wong, and D. T. Potts. 2005. The Qazvin Plain revisited: A reappraisal of the chronology of the northwestern central plateau, Iran, in the 6th to the 4th millennium BC. *ANES* 42: 3–82.

Fazeli Nashali, H., M. Vidale, P. Bianchetti, G. Guida, and R.A.E. Coningham. 2010. The evolution of ceramic manufacturing technology during the Late Neolithic and Transitional Chalcolithic periods at Tepe Pardis, Iran. *AMIT* 42: 87–112.

Fazeli Nashli, H., and R. Abbasnezhad Sereshti. 2005. Social transformation and interregional interaction in the Qazvin Plain during the 5th, 4th, and 3rd millennia B. C. *AMIT* 37: 7–26.

Fazeli Nashli, H., A. Beshkani, A. Markosian, H. Ilkani, R. Abbasnejad Sereshti, and R. L. Young. 2009. The Neolithic to Chalcolithic transition in the Qazvin plain, Iran: Chronology and subsistence strategies. *AMIT* 41: 1–21.

Fazeli Nashli, H., and M. Djamali. 2003. Specialized pottery production in Zagheh. In *The first symposium of archaeometry in Iran: The role of sciences in archaeology. Summary of articles*, ed. M. Azarnoush, 203–24. Tehran: ICAR (in Persian).

Fazeli Nashli, H., H. R. Valipour, and M. H. A. Kharanaghi. 2013. The Late Chalcolithic and Bronze Age in the Qazvin and Tehran plains: Chronological perspective. *AIN*: 107–29.

Ghirshman, R. 1938. *Fouilles de Sialk, près de Kashan, 1933, 1934, 1937*, vol. 1. Paris: Geuthner.

Gillmore, G. K., R. A. E. Coningham, H. Fazeli Nashli, R. L. Young, M. Magsoudi, C. M. Batt, and G. Rishworth. 2009. Irrigation on the Tehran plain Iran: Tepe Pardis: The site of a possible Neolithic irrigation feature? *Catena* 78: 285–300.

Hamlin, C. 1975. Dalma Tepe. *Iran* 13: 111–28.

Helwing, B. 2004. Tracking the proto-Elamite on the central Iranian plateau. In *The potters of Sialk*, ed. S. M. Shahmirzadi, 45–58. Tehran: SRPR 3.

———. 2011a. Conclusions: The Arisman copper production in a wider context. *EMM*: 523–31.

———. 2011b. The small finds from Arisman. *EMM*: 254–327.

———. 2012. Late Chalcolithic craft traditions at the north-eastern "periphery" of Mesopotamia: Potters vs. smiths in the southern Caucausus. *Origini* 34: 201–20.

———. 2013. Some thoughts on the mode of culture change in the 4th millennium BC Iranian highlands. *AIN*: 93–105.

Howard, S.M. 1989. Sequence of the Main Mound. *THRRP*: 55–68.

Jones, M., M. Djamali, L. Stevens, V. Heyvaert, H. Askari, D. Norolahie, and L. R. Weeks. 2013. Mid-Holocene environmental and climatic change in Iran. *AIN*: 25–34.

Kaboli, M. A. 1997. Dar Baraye Dovomin Fasl-ye Kavush Dar Ghar-e Tappeh Qomrud. *Gozareshhaye Bastan Shenasi* 1: 299–300.

———. 2000. *Archaeological survey at Qomrud*. Tehran: Iranian Cultural Heritage Organization (in Persian).

Lamberg-Karlovsky, C. C. 1978. The Proto-Elamites on the Iranian plateau. *Antiquity* 52: 114–20.

Le Breton, L. 1957. The early periods at Susa: Mesopotamian relations. *Iraq* 19: 79–124.

Majidzadeh, Y. 1976. Early prehistoric cultures of the central Plateau of Iran: An archaeological history of its development during the fifth and fourth millennia B.C. Unpublished PhD diss., University of Chicago.

———. 1978. Correction of the internal chronology for the Sialk III period on the basis of the pottery sequence at Tepe Ghabristan. *Iran* 16: 93–101.

———. 1979. An early prehistoric coppersmith workshop at Tepe Ghabristan. In *Akten des VII. Internationalen Kongresses für iranische Kunst und Archäologie, München, 7.–10. September 1976*, ed. W. Kleiss, 82–92. Berlin: AMI Ergänzungsband 6.

———. 1981. Sialk III and the pottery sequence at Tepe Ghabristan: The coherence of the cultures of the Iranian plateau. *Iran* 19: 141–6.

———. 2008. *Excavations at Tepe Ghabristan, Iran*. Rome: IsIAO Reports and Memoirs 7.

———. 2010. *Kawoshha-ye mohavate-ye bastani-ye Ozbaki. Jeld-e awal: honar va me'mari (Excavations at Tepe Ozbaki, Iran*. vol. 1: *Art and architecture)*. Tehran: Cultural Heritage, Handicrafts and Tourism General Office of Tehran Province.

Marro, C. 2010. Where did Late Chalcolithic chaff-faced ware originate? Cultural dynamics in Anatolia and Transcaucasia at the dawn of urban Civilization (ca 4500–3500 BC). *Paléorient* 36/2: 35–55.

Masuda, S. 1976. Report of archaeological investigations at Shahr, 1975. *PASARI* 4: 63–70.

Matney, T. 1995. Re-excavating Cheshmeh Ali. *Expedition* 37: 26–38.

Matthews, R. J., und H. Fazeli. 2004. Copper and complexity: Iran and Mesopotamia in the fourth millennium B.C. *Iran* 42: 61–75.

McCown, D. E. 1942. *The comparative stratigraphy of early Iran*. Chicago: SAOC 23.

Negahban, E.O. 1979. A brief report on the painted building of Zaghe (late 7th–early 6th millennium B.C.). *Paléorient* 5: 239–50.

Nezafati, N., and E. Pernicka. 2006. The smelters of Sialk: Outcomes of the first stage of archaeometallurgical researches at Tappeh Sialk. In *The fishermen of Sialk*. ed. S.M. Shahmirzadi, 79–102. Tehran: SRPR 4.

Nokandeh, J. 2002. Gozaresh-e layeh negari-e boresh-e alef dar Tappeh-e Jonoubi-ye Sialk. In *The ziggurat of Sialk*, ed. S. M. Shahmirzadi, 55–84. Tehran: SRPR 1 (in Persian).

Pernicka, E. 2004. Kupfer und Silber in Arisman und Tappeh Sialk und die frühe Metallurgie in Iran. *PAP*: 232–9.

Pernicka, E., M. Momenzadeh, A. Vatandoust, K. Adam, M. Böhme, Z. Hezarkhani, N. Nezafati et al. 2011. Archaeometallurgical research on the western central Iranian plateau. *EMM*: 633–87.

Pittman, H. 2001. Mesopotamian intraregional relations reflected through glyptic evidence in the Late Chalcolithic 1–5 periods. In *Uruk Mesopotamia and its neighbors: Cross-cultural interaction and its consequences in the era of state tormation*, ed. M. S. Rothman, 403–43. Santa Fe: School of American Research Press.

Potts, D. T. 2009. Bevel-rim bowls and bakeries: Evidence and explanations from Iran and the Indo-Iranian borderlands. *JCS* 61/2: 1–23.

———. 2011. Equus Asinus in highland Iran: Evidence old and new. In *Between sand and sea: The archaeology and human ecology of southwestern Asia, Festschrift in honor of Hans-Peter Uerpmann*, ed. N. J. Conard, P. Drechsler, and A. Morales, 167–76. Tübingen: Kerns Verlag.

Rezvani, H. 1999. Prehistoric settlement patterns and cultures in Semnan Province, Central Plateau, Iran. *IW*: 220–21.

Roustaei, K. 2012. Archaeological survey of the Šāhrud area, northeast Iran: A landscape approach. *AMIT* 44: 191–219.

Schmidt, A., M. Quigley, M. Fattahi, G. Azizi, M. Maghsoudi, and H. Fazeli. 2011. Holocene settlement shifts and palaeoenvironments on the Central Iranian Plateau: Investigating linked systems. *The Holocene* 21/4: 583–95.

Schmidt, E. F. 1935a. The Persian Expedition. *Bulletin of the University Museum* 4/5: 41–49.

———. 1935b. Excavations at Rayy. *Bulletin of the University Museum* 5/4: 25–27.

———. 1937. *Excavations at Tepe Hissar, Damghan*. Philadelphia: University of Pennsylvania Press.

Shahmirzadi, S. M. 1977. Tepe Zagheh: A sixth millennium B.C. village in the Qazvin plain of the central Iranian plateau. Unpublished PhD diss., University of Pennsylvania.

———. 1979. A specialized housebuilder in an Iranian village of the VIth millennium B.C. *Paléorient* 5: 183–92.

———. 1990. Private houses at Zagheh: A sixth millennium B.C. village in Iran. *Bulletin of the Ancient Oriental Museum* 11: 1–23.

———. 1995. Gahnjegari-e pish az tarikh falat-e markazi-ye Iran: Doran nosangi ta aghaz-e shar neshini [The chronology of the central Iranian plateau in the Neolithic period]. *Majale-ye Bastanshenasi va Tarikh* 9: 2–18 (in Persian).

Shahmirzadi, S. M., and J. Nokandeh. 2001. *Agh Tepe, Miras-e farhangi, Ostan-e Golestan* Tehran: ICAR.

Streily, A. H. 2000. Early pottery kilns in the Middle East. *Paléorient* 26/2: 69–82.

Sudo, H. 2010. The development of wool exploitation in Ubaid period settlements in north Mesopotamia. *BTU*: 169–80.

Tala'i, H. 1999. Funeral rites at Zagheh: A Neolithic site in the Qazvin plain, Iran. *Documenta Praehistorica* 26: 15–20.

Thomalsky, J. 2010. Lithische Industrien im vorderasiatischen und ägyptischen Raum: Untersuchungen zur Organisation lithischer Produktion vom späten 6. bis zum ausgehenden 4. Jahrtausend v. Chr. Unpublished PhD diss., Eberhard-Karls University of Tübingen.

Thornton, C. P. 2009. The emergence of complex metallurgy on the Iranian plateau: Escaping the Levantine paradigm. *JWP* 22/3: 301–27.

———. 2010. Sang-e Chakhmaq. *EnIr* online edition.

Thornton, C. P., A. Gürsan-Salzman, and R. H. Dyson Jr. 2013. Tepe Hissar and the fourth millennium of northeastern Iran. *AIN*: 131–44.

Tonoike, Y. 2009. Beyond style: Petrographic analysis of Dalma ceramics in two regions of Iran. Unpublished PhD diss., Yale University.

Tosi, M. 1989. The distribution of industrial debris on the surface of Tappeh Hesar as an indication of activity areas. *THRRP*: 13–24.

Voigt, M. M. 1983. *Hajji Firuz Tepe, Iran: The Neolithic settlement*. Philadelphia: UMM 50.

Voigt, M. M., and R. H. Dyson Jr. 1992. The chronology of Iran, 8000 to 2000 B.C. In *Chronologies in Old World archaeology*, 3rd ed., vol. 1, ed. R. W. Ehrich, 122–78. Chicago/London: University of Chicago Press.

Young, R., and H. Fazeli. 2008. Interpreting animal bones in Iran: Considering new animal bone assemblages from three sites in the Qazvin plain within a broader geographical and chronological perspective. *Paléorient* 34/2: 153–72.

CHAPTER 6

THE CHALCOLITHIC IN THE CENTRAL ZAGROS

ABBAS MOGHADDAM AND
ARDASHIR JAVANMARDZADEH

Introduction

The term "Central Zagros" refers to the lands falling between Hamadan in the northeast and Saimarrah in the south (Fig. 6.1). It is of great importance as regards one of the major episodes of transformation in human history toward the end of the last Ice Age, namely the shifting from a mobile hunting and gathering to a sedentary economy based on agriculture and animal husbandry. This is one of the key areas where wild plants and animals were domesticated. The evidence of early villages in the region comes from Tappeh Ganj Dareh (Smith 1968, 1970), Tappeh Asiab and Tappeh Sarab (Braidwood 1960b, 1961), Tappeh Guran (Meldgaard et al. 1963), and Tappeh Abdulhosein (Pullar 1975).

The Central Zagros region has been divided in three main areas: (1) Mahidasht in the west; (2) the Kangavar plain in the east; and (3) the Khorramabad valleys to the south (Hole 1987). The Mahidasht region includes several intermontane plains and valleys, such as Shah Abad, Zobeiri, Mahidasht, and Kermanshah; to the south of these areas lies the Hulailan valley (Fig. 6.1). The major characteristics of the geographical traits of the region have often been discussed (Fisher 1968; Harrison 1946, 1968). The most prominent landforms are parallel mountain chains, trending northwest to southeast. The highest peaks (e.g., the Kuh-e Sefid, Kuh-e Garin, and Kabir Kuh) reach 3000–4000 masl (Henrickson 1985a: 2–4; Märker and Heydari-Guran 2009:2). This natural landscape shaped the contact routes between valley systems through time, whether nomadic pastoralists on migration, traders, travelers, or invaders. The most important route system across the region is known as the Great Khorasan Road, which served as a bridge linking Mesopotamia with Central Asia via central and northern Iran (Henrickson

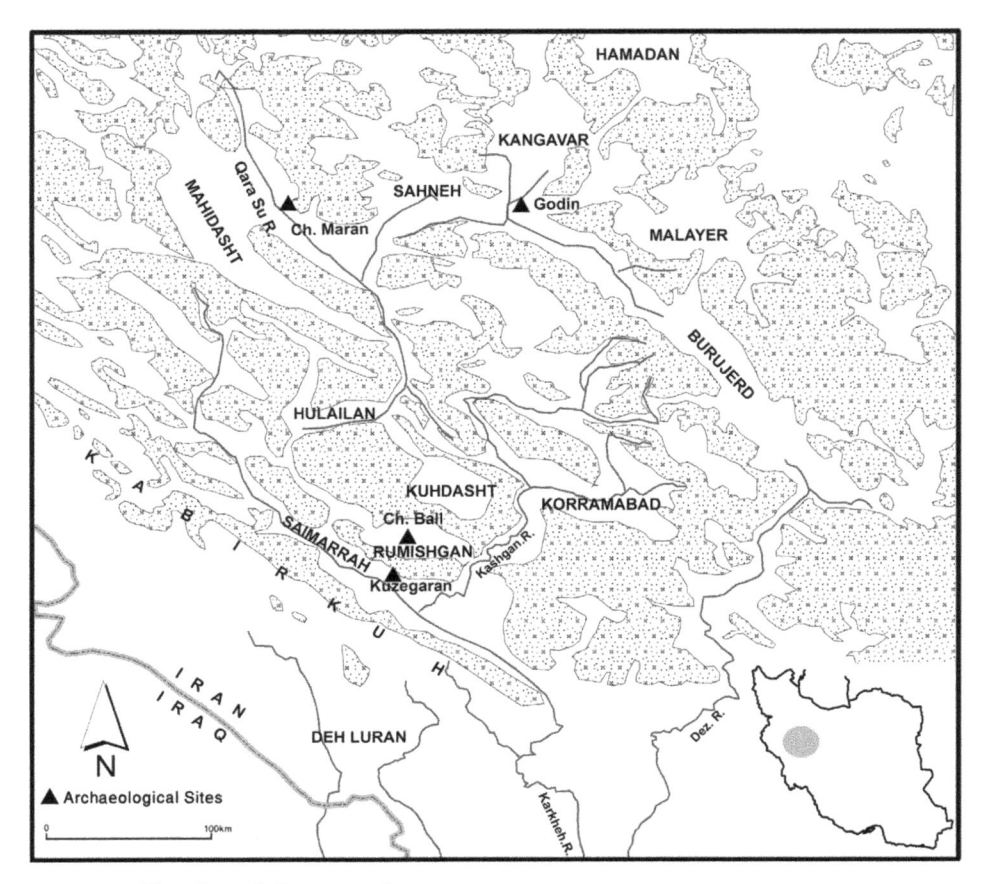

FIGURE 6.1 The Central Zagros region.

1983: 33). The climate of the Central Zagros is characterized generally by cold winters, with rainfall averaging 400 mm per year and hot summers (Henrickson 1985a: 10). The more southerly and westerly valleys experienced a warmer, wetter regime than the higher, more easterly valleys.

THE ARCHAEOLOGICAL HISTORY OF THE AREA

The Central Zagros valleys have been the focus of archaeological research since the mid-nineteenth century, but even before that time many travelers passing through the region recorded their observations on its geography and historical remains (Abdi 2002: 102). The first archaeological survey of the Central Zagros was carried out by Jacques de Morgan (Morgan 1895); the first serious excavations were those undertaken at Tepe Giyan by Georges Contenau and Roman Ghirshman. Over the course of two seasons

(1931–2), materials from the late sixth to the late second millennium BC were recovered (Contenau and Ghirshman 1935). Soon afterward, Sir Aurel Stein started his long journey through southern and western Iran, from the extreme southeast corner of Persian Baluchistan to the frontiers of Iraq and Turkey. Stein visited Saimarreh, Harsin, and Kermanshah and conducted brief excavations at a number of sites in Saimarreh (Kuzeh Garan), Kuhdasht (Chigha Pahn) Rumishgan, Tarhan, Alishtar, Khaweh, and Hulailan (Kazabad Mounds), which led to the discovery of important Chalcolithic remains (Stein 1938, 1940). During October–November 1935, Erich Schmidt excavated in the primarily Chalcolithic and Bronze Age sites of Kamtarlan I and II and Chigha Sabz as part of the Holmes Expedition (*HEL*). He also surveyed, both on the ground and in the air, taking aerial photos of Mahidasht and Pish-e Kuh, and landing to inspect ancient remains in the Mahidasht and Kuhdasht (Schmidt 1940). More systematic survey and excavation were undertaken by the Iranian Prehistoric Project, directed by Robert Braidwood in 1959–60 as part of his broader investigation of the early Neolithic (Braidwood 1960a, 1960b, 1961). Archaeological investigations in this area were continued by L. D. Levine and M. McDonald from the Royal Ontario Museum (ROM) (Levine and McDonald 1977). These studies were an extension of those conducted by T. C. Young Jr. for the ROM, especially at Godin Tepe in the Kangavar region and in the Burujird plain, both of which were surveyed (Young 1966; *OHR*). Clare Goff (1971) conducted a widespread general survey along the southern regions of Central Zagros (Pish-e Kuh) and visited a large number of Chalcolithic sites, many of which had already been surveyed by Stein and Schmidt. Her survey was important because it recorded the main archaeological sites in the buffer zone between Khuzestan and southern Luristan. Goff visited the Saimarreh valley, the northern half of Bala Giriveh between Khorramabad and Pol-e Dokhtar, a migration route running through it as well as the Nur 'Ali migration route and the intermontane valleys in this area. In 1977, P. E. L. Smith and P. Mortensen surveyed the Harsin area (where Smith had been excavating Ganj Dareh) and recorded several newly discovered sites (Smith and Mortensen 1980). A Belgian team under the directorship of L. Vanden Berghe carried out extensive surveys and excavations in the most western part of the Central Zagros or Pusht-e Kuh from 1964 to 1979. This research was primarily concerned with the later Bronze and Iron Age graveyards, but also revealed Middle Chalcolithic material (Haerinck and Overlaet 1996).

Archaeological data on the Central Zagros Chalcolithic

The Central Zagros region remains one of the least-known regions in Iran with respect to Chalcolithic or Village Period archaeology. Most of the available evidence comes from surface survey and a few limited soundings (Henrickson 1983: 77). The term Chalcolithic as used here commonly refers to generally similar ceramic assemblages attested in Susiana (Susa A), Fars (Bakun A), and Mesopotamia (Ubaid), although some scholars tried to coin the term "Zagros Chalcolithic" (Henrickson 1983: 78) to refer to those formative and developmental aspects that span the period between Neolithic village life and state-level society proposed by Childe (1942: 77–83).

The topography of the Zagros valleys has tended to isolate prehistoric cultures. This is reflected in the great variety of pottery assemblages, each typically extending over only a few adjacent valleys. The Zagros Chalcolithic has been divided into three subphases: Early, Middle, and Late Chalcolithic (Vanden Berghe 1959: 206–7; Mortensen 1974, 1976; Zagarell 1977). However, the periodization of the ceramics of the Central Zagros is based on the ROM projects in Mahidasht and Godin Tepe in the Kangavar valley (Levine 1974; Levine and McDonald 1977; Levine and Young 1987; *OHR*). The same periodization has been used in the Hamadan region of the eastern Central Zagros (Young 1969).

Early Chalcolithic (5500–5000 BC)

The Early Chalcolithic of the Central Zagros is almost completely unknown outside of the Mahidasht and the Kangavar, Nehavand, and Malayer valleys. Two different ceramic assemblages are known (Abdi 2002: 133–5). The distinctive Shahnabad assemblage is found only in Kangavar and Malayer (Hole 1987: 49). The Mahidasht and adjacent valleys are distinguished by an assemblage characterized by J Ware, a fine, thin ware with a reddish and/or black slip. Many vessels are painted with various combinations of black, red, and white horizontal lines and other simple linear motifs. Exterior and interior surfaces often bear strikingly different combinations of slips, paints, and motifs. Common forms include open hemispherical bowls and small, high-collared jars (Levine and McDonald 1977). J ware is generally similar to, and may have been derived from, contemporary Mesopotamian, late Halaf painted ware, though it is simpler in terms of both technology and style (Levine and McDonald 1977; Levine and Young 1987). The existence or presence of Halaf sherds in Mahidasht is the key element in the terminal Neolithic and Early Chalcolithic. Over sixty J ware–related sites are found in Mahidasht, some of which exceed 4 ha and may reflect an emergent settlement hierarchy (Levine and McDonald 1977). The appearance of Halaf material in the Central Zagros has been attributed to either the immigration of people with Halafian culture or a gradual mixture of such people, rather than exchange (Oates 1983). Petrographic analysis of sherds from Mandali has demonstrated their Iranian origin, especially with those that resemble examples from Hulailan published by Mortensen (Oates 1983: 259).

Early Chalcolithic pottery known from surface survey is generally made of a fine, grit-tempered ware decorated with geometric and seminaturalistic motifs. These sherds find parallels in Giyan VA and can be paralleled with Samarran material in Mesopotamia, in terms of both texture and decoration (Goff 1971: 137). In the Pish-e Kuh, the Early Chalcolithic is attested by surface sherds at sites like Chia Zargaran and Tepe Siah in Kuhdasht (Goff 1971: 134). Other early Chalcolithic sites in the Pish-e Kuh are known at Khargoar-e Robat near Khorramabad, at sites on the Khorramabad plain, at Baba Mohammad on the Khaweh Plain, and at Chia Sabz in Rumishgan (Darabi et al. 2011). In the Hulailan valley, eleven sites of Early Chalcolithic date have been identified. The earliest materials come from Tepe Chena A, an oval mound located close to the confluence of the Saimarreh and Jezman Rud Rivers. The Early Chalcolithic in the Hulailan valley is characterized by sherds tempered with both chaff and sand, slipped in buff and red, and decorated with black to tawny paint with close, linear, geometric patterns. As Mortensen observed, there are no exact parallels for the black-on-buff sherds from Hulailan, but they can be generally related to Sabz and Khazineh pottery in the Deh Luran sequence. In addition, many decorated sherds bear a general resemblance to Archaic 2 examples from Chogha Mish in Susiana (Mortensen 1975: 43).

Middle Chalcolithic (5000–3800 BC)

The Middle Chalcolithic is better known than the Early Chalcolithic and appears more complex and diverse. Henrickson divided this period into three subphases: Middle Chalcolithic I (c.5000–4800 BC), II (c.4800–4200 BC), and III (c.4200–3800 BC) (Henrickson 1991: 278), characterized by different material evidence, principally ceramics.

Middle Chalcolithic I

The dominant pottery tradition of Middle Chalcolithic I (or the Dalma Phase) is so-called Dalma ware, named after its place of initial discovery, Dalma Tappeh in the Solduz Valley (Hamlin 1975). This is a regional pottery tradition distributed from southern Azerbaijan to the southern Central Zagros (Henrickson 1983; Henrickson and Vidali 1987; Moghaddam et al. 2010), including the Hamrin region in eastern Mesopotamia (Oates 1983). In the Central Zagros, Dalma ware appears in three variants: Dalma Impressed, Dalma Painted or Dalma-Ubaid, and Dalma Red-slipped (Abdi 2002: 136; Young 1963).

Dalma Impressed is characterized by a streaky, pinched, and manipulated outer surface. The fabric of Dalma Impressed ware is the same as that from Dalma Monochrome (see below), but instead of being painted the outer surface has been modified with finger impressions, pinching (by an instrument like a nail), incision, excision, and irregular finger manipulation. Dalma Streaky (Henrickson 1983, 1985a, 1987), known throughout the Central Zagros sites, tends to have a harder, denser fabric and is covered with a streaky slip. The most common vessel form is a globular, holemouthed pot with a low, pinched neck above a grooved ledge as well as a narrow, flat "shelf" between the body and neck, indented and smoothed in the neck-formation process.

Dalma Painted or *Dalma-Ubaid* is a finer, redder fabric attested in small quantities at Seh Gabi and Godin Tepe (Levine and Young 1987; Goff 1971). Highly fired, unslipped, dark-painted buff and black-on-buff are two painted varieties of this tradition and can be found in various colors, including red, purple, brown, and black. Geometric and stylistic animal motives cover exterior surfaces. Common Dalma painted vessel forms include holemouth pots and hemispherical bowls (Levine and Young 1987: 21–9). Dalma monochrome is the most common and widespread variant. It was fired at relatively low temperatures and shows smoothed, single-slipped or double-slipped surfaces. Goff called the examples from Chia Sabz at Rumishgan the earliest Ubaid-related material in southern Luristan and paralleled it with Giyan VB finds from Nehavand to the north (Goff 1971: 139). The main shapes are bowls with slightly flaring rims, holemouthed bowls and jars with out-turned rims. Clubbed rims decorated with semicircular blobs of paint are highly characteristic. The ware occurs all over the Pish-e Kuh, notably at Baba Mohammed in Khaweh, Robat, the Khorramabad plain, and Rumishgan. Comparable material is known in the upper levels of Tepe Jowi and in Susiana C (cf. Ubaid 3) assemblages in Susiana (Goff 1971: 137).

Dalma Red-slipped and *Dalma Bichrome* wares are soft, chaff-tempered wares slipped in dark red to brown. Sometimes the surface carries a double slip, with the dark one on top. Common forms of Dalma Red-slipped ware include holemouth pots, cylindrical vessels, and open hemispherical bowls (Henrickson 1983, 1985a; Levine and Young 1987; Abdi 2002: 138). Rare variants of monochrome, known only from Kangavar, are decorated with red and black motifs on a cream-slipped surface (Henrickson 1985a, 1985b). The assemblage as described by Goff (1971: 139) for the southern Central Zagros seems to parallel material from Kangavar. Both assemblages are painted with linear geometric motifs, in black or brown, showing lowland Mesopotamian Ubaid influence (Henrickson 1985b).

All of the Dalma Painted and Impressed types are fairly common in the east and west of the Pish-e Kuh, the area surveyed by Goff from 1963 to 1967. As she noted, all of the Dalma Impressed types found in Mahidasht and Kangavar were attested in her survey regions (1971: 137). One of the puzzling points about the Dalma-related materials is their absence in the Hulailan valley (Mortensen 1975), although they appear to the south, east, and north of it (Goff 1971; Henrickson and Vidali 1987). At Godin Tepe both Dalma Painted and Dalma Impressed appear in Period X levels (Levine and Young 1987).

As Henrickson and Vidali have shown (1987), the Dalma tradition is one of the earliest examples of the transfer of technology over a fairly widespread area, extending from Dalma in Azerbaijan through eastern Kurdistan, all the way to the Saimarreh region in southern Luristan (Moghaddam 2010). Recently, the Saimarreh Archaeological Project has recorded a whole complex of different types of Dalma ware in the southernmost part of the Pish-e Kuh (Moghaddam et al. 2009, 2010), which find clear parallels in eastern Mesopotamia on the Mandali plain and in Jabal Hamrin (Oates 1983: 258).

Middle Chalcolithic II

One of the characteristics of Middle Chalcolithic II in the Central Zagros is strong ceramic regionalization, along with clear interaction with lowland Khuzestan and Mesopotamia. In the northeastern part of the Central Zagros, the Seh Gabi phase (Period IX at Godin Tepe) follows the preceding Dalma phase and marks a sudden change in the material culture. The new decorated ware, Seh Gabi Painted, is a highly fired, unslipped, tan-to-greenish, fine or medium-fine buff ware decorated on the upper (exterior) third of the vessel with linear geometric and occasionally zoomorphic motifs, often in form of stylized goats, in a distinctive thick, shiny, vitrified black paint. Common vessel forms include small, holemouth pots and hemispherical, round-based bowls. Another group of wares with a thick red slip, often burnished and sometimes finger-impressed, is also known (Henrickson 1983, 1985a; Levine and Young 1987: 29).

In the Lake Urmia Basin of southern Azerbaijan, the characteristic Middle Chalcolithic II or Pisdeli assemblage is a highly varied group of wares that lasted into Middle Chalcolithic III time (Dyson and Young 1960). It included several types of plain, painted, and impressed groups that cannot be classified easily into discrete categories or "wares." Both fine chaff and fine-to-coarse grit-tempered varieties are present. Firing was less uniform than in the case of Dalma wares. The color of the fabric is typically light orange to buff and the surface is smoothed, matte, red-slipped, white-slipped, burnished, or a combination thereof. Impressed, decorated vessels are also sometimes covered with a red slip. The painted variety belongs "within the Ubaid tradition" (Voigt 1987: 621) and is decorated with simple linear and occasional zoomorphic motives in matte black-brown paint. Common forms include deep, hemispherical bowls and cups; simple, wide-mouth pots; and necked jars. Numerous parallels in shape and decoration link the Pisdeli assemblage with Gawra XIII (Ubaid 4) and XII–XIIA (terminal Ubaid) in northern Iraq, and with the early part of the long Chalcolithic sequence at Yanik Tepe in the eastern Urmia Basin (Voigt and Dyson 1992).

In Pusht-e Kuh to the south, nomadic pastoralism may have already been established before the Middle Chalcolithic. Material from this period has been found at two isolated cemeteries, Hakalan and Dum Gar-e Parchineh (Vanden Berghe 1974; Henrickson 1983: 436–43; Haerinck and Overlaet 1996). Nearly 200 stone-lined tombs were documented at these two cemeteries, most of which belonged to adults. Grave goods were limited to mostly coarse and occasional fine pottery. Other grave goods included stone tools, stamp seals, and items of personal jewelry that may indicate the emergence of differences in social status. Two different types of pottery were recovered in the graves: black-on-red ware in small quantities and a painted ware similar to Maran red, white, and black ware (see below), although the painting style is not closely related to any contemporary highland or lowland assemblages (Henrickson 1983, 1985b, 1991). During Late Middle and Early Late Chalcolithic times, isolated examples of Susa A pottery appeared in the Central Zagros, but the Susiana ceramic tradition of southwestern Iran appears to have had little direct influence on highland assemblages (Abdi 2002). Surveys in Hulailan (Mortensen 1975, 1976) and other valleys in Luristan (Goff 1971; Stein 1938, 1940) have yielded a wide variety of additional black-on-buff and red-slipped wares that probably date to the Middle Chalcolithic period but their exact affinities and chronology are unclear (Henrickson 1983, 1985b, 1991).

Middle Chalcolithic III

The poorly known Ṭaherabad phase (Godin VIII) follows the Seh Gabi phase in Kangavar and is characterized by black-on-buff ware similar to that of Middle Chalcolithic I and II. In the Mahidasht, the Maran phase, which is only known only from Cogha Maran, is characterized by red, white, and black (RWB) ware, and a thin, well-made, hard-fired, fine to medium-fine, chaff-tempered red ware with a thin, streaky, white wash on the exterior and sparse linear motifs in black near the rim. Deep hemispherical bowls are the most common form. Occurring in much smaller quantities is black-on-red (BOR) ware, a fine reddish-buff ware with a distinctive, thick, dark plum-red slip decorated with simple motifs in black on the exterior and upper interior surfaces (Henrickson 1983, 1985a). BOR is widely but sparsely distributed in the western and southwestern Central Zagros and adjacent central Mesopotamian lowlands. It serves as a useful horizon marker linking Middle Chalcolithic III with the late Ubaid and Susa A assemblages (Henrickson 1985b).

Late Chalcolithic (3800–3300 BC)

Two pottery assemblages are attributed to period VII and VI at Godin Tepe. These are considered contemporary with the Ḥoseinabad and Češmeh Nuš phases at Seh Gabi. There is considerable evidence of continuity between the two periods and it is assumed that Godin VII had probably started in Middle Chalcolithic III (Young 1969; Henrickson 1991: 281).

Godin VII

Godin VII is marked by two major and two minor groups of buff and red-slipped wares, and unsmoothed coarse and S-wares. The fabrics of the buff-ware group range from plain or fine white-slipped to more common medium-fine wares. Forms include everted and straight-sided, hemispherical bowls of various depths and S-walled jars. Red-slipped vessels are larger, coarser, and thicker than those of the buff-ware group and are finished with a thick, powdery, brick-red slip. Common red-slipped forms include deep, S-walled jars, trays, and deep vertical-walled pots with diagnostic wavy or zigzag motifs modeled on the exterior of the rim. Unsmoothed coarse ware is a poorly fired, straw-tempered fabric with unfinished, typically smoke-blackened surfaces. Almost all vessels are "perforated pots." S-ware is carefully smoothed, slipped, and burnished on the interior surface; most vessels are heavy-rimmed trays. The Godin VII assemblage is attested in northeastern Luristan and from survey in Kurdistan; it is paralleled on the plateau at Tepe Ghabristan I (Majidzadeh, 1976, 1978, 2008).

Godin VI

This period at Godin Tepe can be regarded as an indigenous culture that interacted with resident Urukian agents from lowland Mesopotamia (Young 1969) or "merchants" from Susa (Weiss and Young 1975; see now *OHR*). There was no gap between periods VII and VI at Godin (Young 1969: 3). The pottery of Godin VI includes unsmoothed coarse and red-slipped wares, as in Godin VII, but in greatly reduced quantities. The most common wares in Godin VI are medium and fine buff wares. Typical forms include vertical and inverted rimmed hemispherical bowls of shallow to medium depth, some with pedestal bases; open, carinated bowls; and globular, steep-shouldered pots, often with pedestal bases. Some buff-ware vessels were finished, and perhaps even formed, on a slow wheel. Period VI buff ware has been found in Central Zagros valleys to the west and south of northeastern Luristan. Typically Mesopotamian forms include bevel-rim bowls and low-sided trays (Badler 2004).

Conclusion

The settlement patterns of the Early Chalcolithic period suggest that some important changes took place at this time in the Central Zagros. In contrast to the Neolithic period, settlements were mainly villages rather than caves or rock shelters, and some sort of hierarchy is suggested by variation in site size, particularly in the Mahidasht plain, where Halaf-related material appeared as well (Hole 1987: 47–8). Settlements were mainly situated close to rivers and streams, presumably to facilitate irrigation agriculture. A reduction in the number of flint tools recovered that could be related to hunting and butchering activities has reinforced the assumption that agriculture and herding were now dominant in the economy, and a diminution in the number of pastoralist campsites, together with the appearance of more permanent village sites near water resources in the Central Zagros from Middle Neolithic to Early Chalcolithic periods, may indicate a shift toward less herding and more agriculture (Abdi 2002; Mortensen 1975; Levine and Young 1987; Hole 1987).

By the Middle Chalcolithic period almost every valley with sufficient water resources and cultivable land had a small center surrounded by several smaller villages. On the larger plains such as Mahidasht-Kermanshah an even more hierarchical settlement pattern is visible, with centers covering c.10 ha, several villages of 2–5 ha, and numerous small hamlets of 1 ha or less (Abdi 2002: 123). Interestingly, Dalma-related settlements in the Mahidasht are less numerous than Ubaid-related ones. Whether this indicates a genuine scarcity of Dalma-related sites in the Mahidasht or the better survival of Ubaid-related sites is unknown (Hole 1987: 48).

By the Middle to Late Chalcolithic period, the local cultures in the Central Zagros had not achieved the same level of sociopolitical complexity as seen in Susiana and Fars (Abdi 2002: 125). While the societies in these regions were on the path to state formation, nomadic pastoralism was being developed in the Central Zagros. The sharp decline in the number of sedentary sites from the Middle to Late Chalcolithic period in the Zagros suggests that a fair proportion of the population may have adopted a nomadic way of life (Abdi 2002: 126).

In the Late Chalcolithic Central Zagros we see the appearance of complex, Uruk-related assemblages at Chogha Gavaneh in Islamabad and Godin Tepe in Kangavar (Abdi 2002: 144). Based on surveyed data, it seems that the sociopolitical organization of the societies in the Central Zagros remained relatively simple during the late fourth millennium BC. This period is contemporary with the Late Uruk era in southern Mesopotamia and Susiana. Most of the cultural manifestations of the Late Chalcolithic culture of the Central Zagros may be attributed to the indigenous population. These show parallels with Level IV at Tappeh Ghabristan (Majidzadeh 2008) and Sialk III_{6-7} (Ghirshman 1938) on the central plateau. The number of Late Chalcolithic sites in the Central Zagros surpassed that of the Middle Chalcolithic. In the region adjacent to the Kuh-e Sefid and to the south of this valley, less painted ware is attested, while some new types appear, evidently from lowland Mesopotamia (bevel-rim bowls, low-sided trays). At this time, valleys such as the Mahidasht and Hulailan experienced a significant decrease in the number and permanence of their settlements. In Hulailan, four out of six Late Chalcolithic sites are transient open-air or cave sites rather than permanent villages, suggesting a shift to a more mobile, pastoral way of life (Mortensen 1975: 47–8).

Further reading

Apart from the chapter on chronology in the last edition of *Chronologies in Old World archaeology* (Voigt and Dyson 1992), now over twenty years old, there is no synthetic treatment of the sites discussed here. The interested reader, therefore, must consult a wide array of individual site reports, many of which are cited below. Haerinck and Overlaet (1996) provide a good overview of ceramics and metal weaponry in Luristan, and Levine and Young (1987) is also still very valuable as an overview.

References

Abdi, K. 2002. Strategies of herding: Pastoralism in the Middle Chalcolithic period of the west central Zagros Mountains, Unpublished PhD diss., University of Michigan.

Badler, V. 2004. A chronology of Uruk artifacts from Godin Tepe in central western Iran and its implications for the interrelationships between the local and foreign cultures. In *Artefacts of complexity: Tracking the Uruk in the Near East*, ed. J. N. Postgate, 79–110. Warminster: Aris and Phillips.

Braidwood, R. J. 1960a. Preliminary investigations concerning the origins of food production in Iranian Kurdistan. *British Association for the Advancement of Science* 17: 214–18.

——. 1960b. Seeking the world's first farmers in Persian Kurdistan. *ILN* October 22: 695–7.

——. 1961. The Iranian Prehistoric Project, 1959–1960. *IrAnt* 1: 3–7.

Childe, V. G. 1942. *What happened in history*. Harmondsworth: Penguin.

Contenau, G., and R. Ghirshman. 1935. *Fouilles de Tépé Giyan, près de Néhavend, 1931–32*. Paris: Geuthner.

Darabi, H., R. Naseri, R. Young, and H. Fazeli Nashli. 2011. The absolute chronology of East Chia Sabz: A Pre-Pottery Neolithic site in western Iran. *Documenta Praehistorica* 38: 255–66.

Dyson, R. H., Jr., and T. C. Young Jr. 1960. The Solduz valley, Iran: Pisdeli Tepe. *Antiquity* 34: 19–27.

Fisher, W. B. 1968. Physical geography. *CHI* 1: 3–110.

Ghirshman, R. 1938. *Fouilles de Sialk, près de Kashan, 1933, 1934, 1937*, vol. 1. Paris: Geuthner.

Goff, C. 1971. Luristan before the Iron Age. *Iran* 9: 131–52.

Haerinck, E., and B. Overlaet. 1996. *The Chalcolithic period, Parchinah and Hakalan*. Brussels: LED 1.

Hamlin, C. 1975. Dalma Tepe. *Iran* 13: 111–28.

Harrison, J. V. 1946. South-West Persia: A survey of Pish-i-Kuh in Luristan. *GJ* 108: 55–70.

———. 1968. Geology. *CHI* 1: 111–85.

Henrickson, E. F. 1983. Ceramic styles and cultural interaction in the Early and Middle Chalcolithic of the central Zagros, Iran. Unpublished PhD diss, University of Toronto.

———. 1985a. The early development of pastoralism in the central Zagros highlands (Luristan). *IrAnt* 20: 1–42.

———. 1985b. An updated chronology of the Early and Middle Chalcolithic of the central Zagros highlands, western Iran. *Iran* 23: 63–108.

———. 1991. The Chalcolithic period in the Zagros highlands. *EnIr* 5: 278–82.

Henrickson, E. F., and V. Vidali. 1987. Dalma tradition: Prehistoric inter-regional cultural in highland western Iran. *Paléorient* 13: 37–45.

Hole, F. 1987. Archaeology of the Village Period. *AWI*: 29–78.

Levine, L. D. 1974. Archaeological investigations in the Mahidasht, western Iran. *Paléorient* 2: 487–90.

Levine, L. D., and M. A. McDonald. 1977. The Neolithic and Chalcolithic periods in the Mahidasht. *Iran* 15: 39–50.

Levine, L. D., and T. C. Young Jr. 1987. A summary of pottery assemblages of the central western Zagros from the middle Neolithic to the late third millennium B.C. *PM*: 15–53.

Majidzadeh, Y. 1976. Early prehistoric cultures of the central Plateau of Iran: An archaeological history of its development during the fifth and fourth millennia B.C. Unpublished PhD diss., University of Chicago.

———. 1978. Correction of the internal chronology for the Sialk III period on the basis of the pottery sequence at Tepe Ghabristan. *Iran* 16: 93–101.

———. 2008. *Excavations at Tepe Ghabristan, Iran*. Rome: IsIAO Reports and Memoirs 7.

Märker, M., and S. Heydari-Guran. 2009. Application of datamining technologies to predict Paleolithic site locations in the Zagros Mountains of Iran. In *Computer applications in archaeology 2009, Williamsburg*, ed. B. Frischer and G. Guidi. http://www.caa2009.org/articles/Maerker_298.pdf [accessed June 4, 2012].

Meldgaard, J., P. Mortensen, and H. Thrane. 1963. Excavations at Tepe Guran, Luristan: Preliminary report of the Danish Archaeological Expedition to Iran 1963. *Acta Archaeologica* 34: 97–133.

Moghaddam, A., A. Javanmardzadeh, N. Soraqi, S. Abdolvand, and J. Hosyn Nejhad. 2009. *Kavoshhay Nejatbakhshi dar Mohavateye Cham Qulah, Fasle Aval (Salvage excavations at Tappe Cham Qulah)*. Tehran: ICAR (in Persian).

Moghaddam, A., A. Maleki, S. Abdolvand, E. Vosuq, P. Arabi, J. Hosey Zadeh, and J. Hosyn Nejhad. 2010. *Kavoshhay Nejatbakhshi dar Mohavateye Cham Qulah, Fasle dovvom (Salvage excavations at Tappe Cham Qulah)*. Tehran: ICAR (in Persian).

Morgan, J. de. 1895. *Mission scientifique en Perse: Cartes des rives méridionales de la Mer caspienne du Kurdistan, du Moukri et Elam*. Paris: E. Leroux.

Mortensen, P. 1974. A survey of prehistoric settlements in northern Luristan. *Acta Archaeologica* 45: 1–47.

———. 1975. Survey and soundings in the Holailan Valley. *PASARI* 3: 1–12.

———. 1976. Chalcolithic settlements in the Holailan Valley. *PASARI* 4: 42–62.

Oates, J. 1983. Ubaid Mesopotamia reconsidered. In *The hilly flanks and beyond: Essays in the prehistory of Southwestern Asia presented to Robert J. Braidwood*, ed. T. C. Young Jr., P. E. L. Smith, and P. Mortensen, 251–81. Chicago: SAOC 36.

Pullar, J. 1975. The Neolithic of the Iranian Zagros. Unpublished PhD diss., University of London.

Schmidt, E. F. 1940. *Flights over ancient Iranian*. Chicago: University of Chicago Press.

Smith, P. E. L. 1968. Ganj Darreh Tepe. *Iran* 6: 158–60.

———. 1970. Ganj Darreh Tepe. *Iran* 8: 174–6.

Smith, P. E. L., and P. Mortensen. 1980. Three new Early Neolithic sites in western Iran. *CA* 21/4: 511–12.

Stein, M. A. 1938. An archaeological journey in western Iran. *GJ* 92/4: 313–42.

———. 1940. *Old routes of Western Īrān: Narrative of an archaeological journey*. London: Macmillan.

Vanden Berghe, L. 1959. *Archéologie de l'Iran ancien*. Leiden: Brill.

———. 1974. *La nécropole de Dum Gar Parchinah: Rapport préliminaire*. Ghent: Mission archeologique de le Pusht-e Kuh, Luristan.

Voigt, M. M. 1987. Relative and absolute chronologies for Iran between 6500 and 3500 cal. B.C. In *Chronologies in the Near East: Relative chronologies and absolute chronology, 16,000–4,000 B.P.*, ed. O. Aurenche, J. Evin, and F. Hours, 615–46. Oxford BAR Int Ser 379.

Voigt, M. M., and R. H. Dyson Jr. 1992. The chronology of Iran, ca. 8000–2000 B.C. In *Chronologies in Old World archaeology*, 3rd ed., vol. 1, ed. R. W. Ehrich, 122–78. Chicago: University of Chicago Press.

Weiss, H. and T. C. Young Jr. 1975. The merchants of Susa: Godin V and plateau-lowland relations in the late fourth millennium BC. *Iran* 13: 1–17.

Young, T. C., Jr. 1963. Dalma Painted Ware. *Expedition* 5: 38–39.

———. 1966. Survey in western Iran. *JNES* 25: 228–39.

———. 1969. *Excavations at Godin Tepe: First progress report*. Toronto: ROMAAOP 17.

Zagarell, A. 1977. The role of highland pastoralism in the development of Iranian civilization. Unpublished PhD diss., Free University of Berlin.

CHAPTER 7

THE LATER VILLAGE (CHALCOLITHIC) PERIOD IN KHUZESTAN

ABBAS MOGHADDAM

Introduction

Thanks to pioneering work at Ali Kosh, Tepe Tula'i, and Chagha Sefid in Deh Luran (Hole et al. 1969; 1974, 1977), as well as excavations at Chogha Bonut (Alizadeh 2003) and Chogha Mish (Delugaz and Kantor 1996; Alizadeh 2008) further south, the early phases of human occupation in Khuzestan are reasonably well known. Moreover, recent archaeological surveys have revealed vast Lower and Upper Paleolithic evidence near the Karkheh River (Sheykh 2010). However, in this chapter we start our journey with the first phase of the Later Village (Chalcolithic) period.

Khuzestan, in which we include the Deh Luran plain, is that part of southwestern Iran with probably the largest number of sites dating to the Later Village (Chalcolithic) period (c.5500–3900 BC). This intensive settlement record is unique in this part of the country and not until the Parthian period, thousands of years later, was Khuzestan again settled as intensively. The most diagnostic criterion of this period is the well-made, highly fired, buff-colored, painted pottery, variants of which have been found across the Near East region from Syria to Iran (Hole 1987a: 31). The Chalcolithic sites of Khuzestan allow us to explore subsistence economy, social organization, and settlement patterns. Several scholars have suggested that the Chalcolithic of Khuzestan reflects a chiefdom-level society with centers that coordinated social, economic, and religious activities within clearly defined territorial boundaries and attributes such as craft specialization, dense population, religion, and communal labor (Johnson 1973; Wright and Johnson 1975; Pollock 1983; Hole 1987; Wright 1994).

Natural setting

The marked geographic, environmental, and economic contrast between the steppes of the central plains of southwestern Iran, described as a "single developing ecosystem" (Hole and Flannery 1968: 198), and the immediately adjacent regions—the inner valleys of the Zagros in the north and east (Luristan and Fars) and the lowlands regions of southern Mesopotamia and low-lying plains of the Persian Gulf—has long been recognized. The entire area has been considered a suitable area in which to study human exploitation of the environment since the early periods (Hole and Flannery 1968: 148–9). Broadly speaking, the southwestern lowlands are demarcated by the first folds of the Zagros Mountains to the north and several low, outlying folds in the south including Jebel Hamrin and the Dezful, Haft Tepe, Shaur, Ahwaz, Kupal, and Gachsaran anticlines. Toward the south and southeast, the region is hemmed in by the Persian Gulf. The Zagros and aforementioned anticlines run in a parallel, northwest-southeast direction. Both small and large plains were created here as a result of tectonic uplift and alluviation (cf. Hamzehpour et al. 1999: 180). These boundaries have created a distinct, and to some extent unique, region in southwest Asia that provides access to three distinct environmental zones—the highland Zagros, lowland Mesopotamia, and the Persian Gulf.

The prevailing view in most studies on southwestern Iran is that the Khuzestan plain is an extension of the lower Mesopotamian plain. However, this is not entirely correct. Geographically, it is a distinct and markedly unique interface zone that lies between lowland Mesopotamia and the highland Zagros. It is an "ecotone," which is a transitional area between two adjacent ecosystems bisected by several rivers, foothills, and plains. Climatically, it is capable of sustaining both dry-farming and irrigation agriculture. Strategically, it has easy access to lowland Mesopotamia, the southern plains of the Persian Gulf region, and the foothills and highland pastures or the north and east with their vast resources of wool, stone, wood, bitumen, tree fruits, metal ores, gypsum, and so on (Pollock 1999: 40, box 4). The proximity of the Khuzestan plain to the marshlands in the south and southwest with their rich ecosystem of flora and fauna is often neglected (cf. Hole et al. 1969: 10–22; Neely 1974: 22; Baeteman et al. 2004–5: 156; for a comprehensive study of the lower Khuzestan plains see Heyvaert and Baeteman 2007; Walstra et al. 2010). In summer the temperature can reach 50°C and in winter 16°C. During the wetter months (December to February) cold nights with frost occur. These are typically followed by heavy mist close to the surface on the following morning. The hot, dry season extends from May to October, while the wet season begins in November and ends in April. Most precipitation is generated by intense storms occurring from January to March (Veenenbos 1958: 49). Average rainfall of 250 mm per year varies from area to area and is greatest close to the Zagros foothills.

Halophytic plants (e.g., *Alhagi maurorum* and *Tamarix* sp.), provide dense cover in saline areas, as well as in areas cut by gullies, and in lagoons beside the Karun, Dez, and Karkheh Rivers, the major perennial streams of Khuzestan. Sporadic salt-cedar trees, known locally as *konar*, with deep root systems, are found along ephemeral stream terraces and in some gullies. The most common plant forms in the region are low grasses that begin to grow immediately after the rainy season. At the beginning of spring, in late February, the plain exhibits a dense cover of such ephemeral plants. By the end of March the green surface of the plain has been transformed into a largely barren land where only sporadic plant growth is visible in gullies and relict stream channels. In cultivated areas close to the major rivers, where irrigation is practiced, different weed species grow in abundance.

The marshes and lagoons formed by the major rivers in Khuzestan are among the most important regions in the Middle East for hosting different species of water birds on their migration in the wet season. Because of their proximity, the Khuzestan plain, Zagros highlands, lowland Iraq, and northern Arabia exhibit close affinities in faunal populations (Firouz 2005: 41).

Adams divided the Khuzestan plain into three zones. The first is the lower plain or old shore line, which extends from the Persian Gulf to the south of Ahwaz. This has limited evidence of human occupation, at least before the Christian era. The intermediate zone is a neglected plain of "widespread salinity, poor drainage, and extensive dune formation" with "nothing to attest a significant occupation prior to Alexander's conquests." Finally, a third zone consists of the Upper Plains to the north of the intermediate zone, where the surface gradients constitute a region with remarkable drainage capability and agricultural potential (Adams 1962: 110). In Adams' opinion, "gross descriptive categories like 'semiarid steppeland' and 'dependence on large-scale irrigation agriculture' may be as inadequate for a deeper historical understanding as they are for the contemporary planner" (Adams 1962: 109). Dyson (Dyson 1965: 6) proposed a more detailed description of southwestern Iran which was further amplified by Carter (Carter 1971: 8–12), whose approach provides a more meaningful basis for studying the plains of Khuzestan by facilitating a framework for analyzing intervalley cultural interaction during the Elamite era. She divided the Khuzestan plains into three groups: the Lower Plains between the Tigris marshes and coastal plains and the outer chain of Jabal Hamrin in the west to Behbahan; the Middle Plains, from Deh Luran to Ram Hormuz and including the Deh Luran, central Khuzestan and Ram Hormuz plains, situated mostly within the Assyrian Steppe; and lastly the Upper Plains, to the north of the inner chains, from Shushtar to the east of Ram Hormuz plain and the high valleys between Malamir and Qaleh Tul (Carter 1971: 326–9, figs. 1–2).

Searching for the Later Village (Chalcolithic) period in Khuzestan

The long history of archaeological studies in Khuzestan has made this one of the most archaeologically studied and best-known regions in Iran. From the late nineteenth to the early twentieth century archaeological investigation in Khuzestan by English and French missions (Loftus 1857; Dieulafoy 1893; Morgan 1895, 1900, 1902, 1912; Gautier and Lampre 1905) was concerned mainly with revealing ancient monuments and excavating large, mounded sites, the most important of which was Susa (Shahmirzadi 1986, 1987, 1990; Chevalier 1997; Abdi 2001). Unearthing elaborate objects to enrich the Louvre was one of the main goals of the French delegation, who had a monopoly over archeological investigations in Iran at that time (Mousavi 1996: 6; Abdi 2001: 54). Eventually more scientific, rather than object-oriented, investigations at Susa and neighboring sites took place from the mid-twentieth century onward (Ghirshman 1952, 1953, 1954, 1964; Le Breton 1957; Steve and Gasche 1971, 1990; Perrot 1978; Dollfus 1978, 1983a, 1983b, 1985).

In the 1950s, new research was undertaken, based primarily on a study of ceramic typology, to better understand the material recovered during the early excavations in Khuzestan (Vanden Berghe 1959; McCown 1954; Le Breton 1957). In particular, Le Breton's work resulted in a refinement of the local chronological sequence, which was enriched and modified by later, more accurate excavations at Susa (Le Brun 1978) and other major sites including Chogha Mish (Kantor 1976a, 1976b; Delugaz and Kantor 1996), Jaffarabad, Jowi, and Bandebal (Dollfus 1978; cf. Hole 1987a: 57, table 2).

Beginning in the early 1960s the Khuzestan plains became the object of systematic, problem-oriented, archaeological, and ecological surveys. Many attempts were made to understand the cultural and natural contexts and circumstances under which various developments and human-nature interactions took place (Kouchoukos 1998: 75–89). Pioneering work in the late 1960s and early 1970s in the Deh Luran and Khuzestan plains improved our understanding of the occupational history of this important region from the eighth millennium BC onward (Johnson 1987: 283–91).

In light of previous studies, much can already be inferred about the social organization of the Village Period in southwestern Iran (cf. Hole 1987a, 1987b). These studies have provided the fundamental basis for further inquiry into the human history of this part of the Near East, particularly how prehistoric societies organized themselves and modified the environment to suit their needs; how interactions between humans and nature resulted in the known spatial distribution of settlements across the landscape; how population fluctuated throughout time and space; what the nature of relationships between and within settlements was; what the degree of integration between different modes of livelihood may have been, including the relative contributions of agriculture, herding, mining, and other land-use strategies; and how fundamental concepts like the organization of power and status, symbols, production specialization, colonization, exchange, and social organization (in chiefdoms, complex chiefdoms, and early states) can be investigated using archaeological evidence in Khuzestan. We turn now to an examination of the three successive phases of the Village Period.

Susiana a (Early Susiana) period

Susiana a or Early Susiana is contemporary with the Sabz phase in the Deh Luran sequence and has been called the "crucial transition phase toward population expansion and urban life" in the region (Hole 1969: 354). In Deh Luran settlement size in this phase continued to be small, c.0.05–1.00 ha (Neely and Wright 1994: 166, table 5.2), while Chogha Mish on the Susiana plain is the largest settlement known, at c.5 ha. Smaller settlements include Tepe Jaffarabad, which is thought to represent the initial colonization of the western Khuzestan plain (Alizadeh 2008: 9–10).

Adams reasoned that because thirty-four small villages of this phase in Khuzestan were almost all located in the northern part of the plain in close proximity to the Zagros foothills, where rainfall is highest, agriculture in this phase was mainly rain fed (Adams 1962: 112). The evidence from Deh Luran, however, indicates that small canals were dug to control floodwater for small-scale irrigation agriculture at a number of Sabz phase settlements (Neely and Wright 1994: 166). A detailed study by Hans Helbaek also maintains that in the Sabz phase at Tape Sabz crops were irrigated (Hole et al 1969: 412–24). Along with cultivated crops, cattle, sheep, and goat were herded in this early phase.

The chief characteristics of Early Susiana ceramics are its friable, grit- and chaff-tempered paste. Purely chaff-tempered vessels also occur. It is difficult to evaluate ceramic production in this period as no pottery kilns datable to this period are known in Khuzestan proper. The frequency of potter's marks, particularly on "flanged vessels" (see Delougaz and Kantor 1996: pl. 200; Alizadeh 2008: fig. 64), suggests that households may have fired their pots in communal kilns. In terms of decoration and production technology, the Early Susiana ceramic tradition shows a clear link to the Ubaid 0 and 1 wares of southern Mesopotamia and, in particular, Tell el-'Oueili (Delougaz and Kantor 1996: 297; Alizadeh 2008: 10).

Whereas T-shaped stone hoes (9 to 13 cm wide, with a shaft of 3 to 5 cm) were found in the Ali Kosh and Mohammad Jaffar phases (eighth to seventh millennium BC) in Deh Luran (Hole et al 1969: 189), these appeared in Khuzestan only during the Early Susiana period (Alizadeh 2008: 10). Such hoes were hafted to wooden handles with naturally occurring asphalt (Hole et al. 1969: fig. 81; Kantor 1976a: fig. 21; Delougaz and Kantor 1996: fig. 38). Moreover, the "polished celt" appeared for the first time in Deh Luran during the Sabz phase (Hole et al. 1969: 355–6). It has been suggested that this tool was used mostly for irrigation agriculture as well (Hole et al 1969: 356).

The most coherent architectural plan of the Early Susiana period comes from Chogha Mish (Delougaz and Kantor 1996:162–3; Alizadeh 2008: 10, fig. 14) where a large, multiroom building with courtyard built of mudbrick was excavated (Delugaz and Kantor 1996: 162–3). The builders of this period continued the Archaic-period tradition of paving the entrance and the open spaces in front of rooms with cobblestones (Alizadeh 2008: 11).

Susiana b and c (Middle Susiana) period

The Middle Susiana period was a pivotal period in the socioeconomic evolution of southwestern Iran. Previously, this period has been divided into three subphases known as Middle Susiana 1–3 (Kantor 1976a). After a detailed analysis of pottery and stratigraphy, Alizadeh suggested that it was better divided into an Early Middle and Late Middle Susiana (Alizadeh 1996: xxiii; 2008: 11). This period is also known as the Chogha Mish phase (Hole 1987: 57, table 2), largely because of the dominance of the flourishing settlement at Chogha Mish during the Chalcolithic period.

Settlement in Khuzestan expanded rapidly throughout this period and reached its maximum in the Late Middle Susiana phase. A landscape of tells is evident in this period. All of the plains of southwestern Iran—Mehran, Deh Luran, Susiana, Eastern Corridor, Ram Hormuz, Behbahan, and Zohreh—show the emergence of specific settlements as major centers. In the central Khuzestan plain, Chogha Mish covered about 15 ha (Delougaz and Kantor 1996: 184) whereas in Deh Luran, where a reduction in settlement appears to have occurred from the Khazineh through the Bayat phase, Tepe Musiyan gradually became the largest settlement in the region during the Mehmeh and Bayat phases (Neely and Wright 1994: 166–70) alongside Tepe Sabz and Tepe Farukhabad (Hole 1987: 84). Some settlements are considered subcenters, like Chogha Do Sar in central Khuzestan. The rest of the settlements ranged from 1 to 3 ha in size. The growth of Chogha Mish was coincident with other developments at the site, marked by extensive architectural complexes, functional architectural units such as kilns and storage bins, monumental buildings, and residential segregation (Delougaz and Kantor 1996: 161). The existence of an offsite cemetery at this time is assumed (Hole 1987: 88) as no graves have yet been found.

Most of Khuzestan probably received the minimum of 250 mm of rainfall necessary for dry farming (Brichambaut and Wallen 1963: 10; Oates and Oates 1976: 111). Excellent natural drainage due to underlying gravels favored agricultural productivity during the Village Period and salinization was a minor concern (Hole et al. 1969: 366). Dry farming, supplemented by herding and hunting, is likely to have been dominant. Later, there appears to have been a gradual shift from a wheat, goat, dry farming complex to a barley, sheep, small-scale irrigation complex (Hole et al. 1969: 368–9; Miller 1977: 51; Pollock 1983: 367–8). In the Deh Luran plain, Hole and Flannery postulated "two basic and temporally distinct patterns of subsistence," which they referred to as "The era of dry farming and caprine domestication," and "The era of early irrigation and cattle domestication" (Hole and Flannery 1968: 166–83). The latter stage was, without doubt, the period that saw the fusion of increasing material production and social differentiation. Hole and Flannery stressed variables such as irrigation and cattle domestication in the rapid emergence of social complexity, population expansion, and urban life (Hole and Flannery 1968: 181).

During the Mehmeh phase in Deh Luran, settlements clustered on alluvial fans. Neely and Wright argued that this was due to the ease of channeling for irrigation over longer distances from fans (Neely and Wright 1994: 167–8). Subsistence at this time was based on the cultivation of barley, wheat, lentils, vetch, vetchling, grass peas, and flax; the herding of sheep, goat, and some cattle; and hunting. Based on the size of the flax seeds recovered, Hole, Flannery, and Neely suggested that irrigation agriculture was practiced at this time (Hole et al. 1969: 361). The most favored cereal was barley. This may have been due to barley's greater tolerance of low rainfall and high salinity (Hole et al. 1969: 363). Hole and his colleagues suggested that human modifications to the landscape around villages with a long history of occupation, such as Tepe Sabz, increased salinity, causing the abandonment of such sites and the search by settlers for new locations with unspoiled soil and water resources (Hole et al. 1969: 364). Later, Kirkby elaborated on Hole's observation, highlighting the idea of changing efficiency of land use for food production through time (Kirkby 1973: 145). Sheep became the dominant herd animal in this phase although goat, cattle, and pig were also kept. Hunting and seasonal transhumance were also practiced.

Tepe Jaffarabad appears to have been a ceramic workshop site rather than a proper village (Hole 1987: 84). Ceramic production showed strong ties with both Mesopotamia and highland Iran. In particular, the black-on-buff ceramics of the Mehmeh phase show that links to the Iranian plateau had never been stronger. Some of the ceramics show evidence of standardization in production. "Sherds of ... salmon colored pottery from Tepe Sabz were literally indistinguishable from those at Chogha Mish, more than 100 km. away. They could easily have come from the same kiln in the same pottery making town" (Hole et al. 1969: 365). The similarity of the ceramics of the Bayat phase in Deh Luran, Susiana c in central Khuzestan, Eridu VIII and IX-related communities in southern Iraq, and Gawra XVII–related communities in northern Iraq is obvious (Le Breton 1957: figs. 4, 6; Wright 1981: 68–9). As Wright emphasized, this may reflect increased interaction throughout the lowlands at this time (Wright 1981: 69). Nevertheless, some scholars consider the Deh Luran plain marginal in terms of scale and centrality in relation to the larger plains of southern Mesopotamia and Susiana during this phase (Hole et al. 1969: 362–3).

In the Deh Luran plain, the evidence of flint knapping and sickles, drills, limestone celts, and heavy grooved mauls shows that craft production was actively pursued. Flint blades were common in this phase as well as hafted sickle blades. Limestone celts were not as common as before.

Social differences were apparent during the Bayat phase (Neely and Wright 1994: 170). The limited exposure at Tape Sabz was not sufficient to evaluate the architectural characteristics of this phase. Nevertheless, it provided limited evidence of status differentiation in burials (Hole et al. 1969: 363). Jar sealings and cylindrical bead seals in this phase suggested "property marking" for the first time in the Deh Luran prehistoric sequence (Hole et al. 1969: 365).

Recent studies suggest that some sites functioned as production centers specializing in, for example, pottery production, stone tool manufacture, and bitumen extraction during the Late Middle Susiana period. In the Eastern Corridor, Tall-e Abu Chizan, which covers almost 8 ha, is a clear example of such a site (Moghaddam 2012; Moghaddam and Miri 2007; Connan et al. 2008).

Susiana d–e (Late Susiana) period

The last major period of our study is Susiana d–e or Late Susiana. Le Breton identified Susiana d as a single phase spanning the period between Susiana c (Late Middle Susiana) and Susa A or Susa I (Late Susiana) period. However, later research suggests that Le Breton's Susiana d phase should be considered the first subphase of the Late Susiana period (Wright 1981; Weiss 1977; Dollfus 1983b: 133). Alizadeh has identified Susiana d as Late Susiana 1 and Susiana e as Late Susiana II (Alizadeh 1992: 21–6). Further study has made it possible to distinguish the latest phase of Late Susiana, also known as Terminal Susa A (Johnson 1973: 87–8).

Based on the available evidence, it is clear that Susa was founded in this period, a development many scholars believe was linked to the abandonment of Chogha Mish. Late Susiana remains have been identified in two soundings at Susa (Acropole I levels 27–23 and Acropole II levels 11–7) and the site is thought to have originally covered c. 15 ha (Hole 1987b: 63, table 9). Late Susiana features have also been identified at Jaffarabad and Chogha Mish, although further excavation is needed to clarify the Late Susiana levels at these sites.

With a monumental mudbrick platform on the Acropole, Susa dominated the plain. The platform rose in two tiers with each stage displaying buried corners, creating a cruciform design; atop the platform was a complex of buildings, including temples, storage rooms, a residential building, and a charnel house (Steve and Gasche 1971; Hole 1992, 2010). Adjacent to the platform was a large cemetery. Many of the burials were fractional, perhaps due to delayed interment after the flesh had decomposed (Canal 1978), and many appear to have been interred simultaneously (Hole 1992). Supplementary to each grave was an assemblage of ceramic vessels comprising three types—a highly decorated drinking beaker, a serving dish, and a small jar.

In some areas, particularly in the western portion of the Susiana plain (around Susa and Abu Fanduweh), the natural position of the Karkheh River levee above the level of the plain facilitated irrigation agriculture in the later phases (Johnson 1973: 100). This may have been one of the reasons for the growth of settlement on the western Susiana plain from Late Susiana times onward, contrary to some scholars' view that the migration of the river westward, coupled with social problems, were responsible for the westward shift of settlement (Veenenbos 1958: 34–9; Hole 1987b: 85; Kouchoukos 1998: 110). It is also possible that the westward shift of Susiana settlement was a consequence of high-risk cultivation in areas that were adversely affected by deep plowing, which was responsible for destroying the natural vegetation communities and causing serious erosion closer to Susa (Kouchoukos et al. 1998: 481; cf. Hole 1994).

As regards the sociopolitical organization of Susiana society, Pollock suggested that different parts of the plain had different settlement systems (Pollock 1983: 371). Her observations elaborated previous views (Wright and Johnson 1975; Weiss 1976) and shed new light on the processes of political and economic centralization in prehistoric Susiana. Her study emphasized the role of "Chogha Mish as a center" several centuries before Susa became the undisputed center on the plain. On the other hand, some scholars see no reason to attribute any political or economical status to such a center (Hole 1987c: 96), preferring to characterize Susiana's settlement system as "a series of independent, shifting communities occupying a large territory in common, with little or no hostile competition" (Hole 1987c: 96). This consisted of Susa, its dominance guaranteed by its religious status in the Late Susiana period, along with the "village and herding camp as economic units" and specialist communities: Khan's houses, craft manufactories, and possibly trading posts (Hole 1987: 92).

As regards material culture, Pollock's stylistic analysis of Late Susiana painted pottery suggests the elaborately decorated ceramics found in the Susa cemetery were prestige goods (Pollock 1983: 383). Neutron activation analysis (Berman 1987, 1994) has demonstrated that Susa's funerary ceramics were made at several different nearby sites. This analysis pinpoints an important feature in the economic organization of the Susiana plain at the time when paramount rulers (if any existed) at Susa had no direct control over the highly elaborated ceramics being deposited in the graves there.

In contrast, the ceramics of the Farukh phase in Deh Luran, while unlike any material in Iraq, are very similar to Susiana d material and that of Tal-e Bakun AIII in the highlands of Fars (Wright 1981: 69). Discussing Kouchoukos' (1998: 20–27) study of population growth during the Middle Susiana period, Alizadeh has stated that the "attention shift" from lowland Mesopotamia to highland Iran began in the Late Middle Susiana period and continued into the early Protoliterate period due to "new socioeconomic and political developments that eventually resulted in the formation of state societies there in the late fourth millennium B.C." (Alizadeh 2006: 97).

Studies at Tape Farukhabad have revealed more details of economic and political processes in this, the second-largest settlement of the region during the Farukh phase (Susiana d or Late Susiana 1). Higher-status people at Farukhabad controlled "the large storage structures, consumed more beverages, and had preferential access to exotic chipped stone raw materials" (Wright et al. 1999: 72 Wright 1981: 65–6). Wright pointed to socially differentiated houses at Tepe Farukhabad (Wright 1981: 12–22, 65–6), emphasizing chiefly symbolism on stamp seals, such as the "master of animals" figure (Amiet 1966: 32–49), and painted ceramics as indicators of the type of social distinction found in the cemetery at Susa (Wright 1984: 58).

Besides routine activities at Farukhabad, a notable activity in this phase was the extraction of bitumen from sources about 12 km away. As little bitumen seems to have been used at the site itself, the bitumen extraction was primarily for export (Wright et al. 1999: 72). Although it is evident that Mesopotamia had its own bitumen sources available at Hit, Ramadi, and Abu Jir in the southwest and Qalat Shergat and Kirkuk in the northeast, Tell el-Oueili's bitumens were mainly imported from nearby Iranian sources during the Ubaid 0 to Ubaid 2 periods (5800–4550 BC) (Huot 1994; Connan 1999: 41). The direction of supply gradually shifted during the following period (Ubaid 3, c.4550–4000 BC), while new south-north links emerged and the southerners perhaps obtained their bitumen from Kirkuk in the north, resulting in the discontinuation of the former Iranian supply to Tell el-Oueili (Connan 1999: 41). Such changes may have had many cultural, economical and political reasons. It is interesting to compare the available bitumen analyses with those of the above-mentioned ceramics because at roughly the same time a major shift in ceramic production occurred in Greater Susiana (Le Breton 1957: 88–9; Alizadeh 1992: 20–26; 2006: 97), and links with Mesopotamia grew weaker, while those with the Zagros grew stronger.

The Late Susiana period in Deh Luran appears to have been a phase of dramatic decline. Some scholars see this as a justification for speaking of system collapse in the region (Johnson 1987: 286), while others see the decline in Susiana society as an inevitable development in the "context of competitive emulation" that was introduced into Susiana during the Uruk Period (Hole 1987c: 96). Susa is thought to have shrunk to 5 ha. in the Terminal Susa A phase (Dollfus in Pollock 1989: 289; Steve and Gasche 1990: 25; Hole 2010: 229). Settlement dropped from twelve Farukh/Late Susiana 1 phase settlements to just three in this phase, suggesting to Neely and Wright that a threat from the west may have emerged at this time (Neely and Wright 1994: 7172). The decline in settlement is also seen in the shrinkage of Tepe Musiyan from 9 ha. in the Farukh phase to 5 ha. thereafter (Neely and Wright 1994: tables V.6–7). Moreover, a drastic change in settlement organization, due to both political and environmental reasons, is indicated by the abandonment of the long-settled alluvial plain along the Mehmeh River at this time (Neely and Wright 1994: 172).

Deh Luran also had very close ties to the Zagros Mountains from an early date. This is illustrated at two of the earliest "nomadic" cemeteries with highly furnished graves dating to the Later Village Period—Dum Gar Parchineh and Hakalan, about 50.5 km and 57.5 km, respectively, to the northwest of Musiyan (Vanden Berghe 1987; Haerinck and Overlaet 1996). Their contents (ceramics, metals, etc.) would indicate some form of symbiosis between "nomads or villagers" of the highlands and the settlers of the Deh Luran plain, especially with the long-lived settlement of Musiyan (Vanden Berghe 1973, 1975; Alizadeh 1992: 57). Kouchoukos suggested that the appearance of such cemeteries during the Late Susiana period was a response to "The increasing importance of sheep and goat in the Village Period economy" and was "consistent with trends documented elsewhere in western Iran" (Kouchoukos 1998: 68). Unfortunately, there is not enough evidence to confirm this theory.

Of the settlement in southwestern Iran, Susa, in the center of this region, was able to successfully coordinate labor for ritual and economic purposes, playing both a political and a religious role as it did in later periods as well (Hole 1990; Pollock 1983; Potts 1999). There are many other tells in the region that were, most likely, centers where the intensive production of goods, the mobilization of labor, the collection of tribute, and interregional trade occurred (Rothman 1987: 88; Wright 2000: 209).

Conclusion

Through the examination of several hundred mounded sites in the Susiana plain, scholars have detected a general hierarchical trend from the Susiana a to the Susa A period, to use Le Breton's 1957 terminology). This began with a small, centralized polity during the Susiana a phase, leading to a pattern of autonomous units in the Susiana d phase, and finally a more dynamic pattern of centralization in the Susa A phase (Johnson 1973: 89; Wright et al. 1975: 130; Wright 1977: 387; Pollock 1983: 375; Kouchoukos 1998: 69–72).

Between Susiana c and Susa A times, Chogha Mish, Chogha Do Sar (KS 0004), and Susa were extensive sites, as were Tepe Musiyan and Tepe Farukhabad in the Deh Luran plain. At the very end of this period (Terminal Susa A phase), a drastic decline in settlement size and number seems to have occurred, which remains obscure at best. Many of the Chalcolithic traditions of Khuzestan were interrupted in the following Uruk period. However, the long Chalcolithic tradition of the region seems to have been somehow revived during the later proto-Elamite period.

References

Abdi, K. 2001. Nationalism, politics, and the development of archaeology in Iran. *AJA* 105: 51–76.
Adams, R. McC. 1962. Agriculture and urban life in early southwestern Iran. *Science* 136: 109–22.
Alizadeh, A. 1992 *Prehistoric settlement patterns and cultures in Susiana, southwestern Iran*. Ann Arbor: Technical Report of the Museum of Anthropology, University of Michigan, 24.
———. 1996. Editor's preface. In *Chogha Mish*, vol. 1, *The first five seasons of excavations, 1961–1971*, ed. P. Delougaz and H. J. Kantor, xxiii–xxv. Chicago: OIP 101.
———. 2003. *Excavations at the prehistoric mound of Chogha Bonut, Khuzestan, Iran: Seasons, 1976/77, 1977/78, and 1996*. Chicago: OIP 120.
———. 2006. *The origins of state organizations in prehistoric highland Fars, southern Iran: Excavations at Tall-e Bakun*. Chicago: OIP 128.
———. 2008. *Chogha Mish*, vol. 2, *The development of a prehistoric regional center in lowland Susiana, southwestern Iran: Final report on the last six seasons of excavations, 1972–1978*. Chicago: OIP 130.
Amiet, P. 1966. *Elam*. Auvers-sur-Oise: Archée Éditeur.
Baeteman, C., V. M. A. Heyvaert, and L. Dupin. 2004–5. Geo-environmental Investigation. *Akkadica* 125/126: 5–13, 151–215.
Berman, J. 1987. Ceramic production and its implications for the sociopolitical organization of the Suse Phase Susiana. *Paléorient* 18: 77–88.
———. 1994. The ceramic evidence for sociopolitical organization in Ubaid southwestern Iran. In *Chiefdoms and early states in Near East: The organizational dynamics of complexity*, ed. G. J. Stein and M. S. Rothman, 23–34. Madison: Monographs in World Archaeology 18.
Brichambaut, P. G. de, and C. C. Wallen. 1963. *A study of agro-climatology in semi-arid and arid zones of the Near East*. Geneva: World Meteorological Organization Technical Note 56.
Canal, D. 1978. La haute terrasse de l'Acropole de Suse. *Paléorient* 4: 169–76.
Carter, E. 1971. Elam in the second millennium B.C.: The archaeological evidence. Unpublished PhD diss., University of Chicago.
Chevalier, N. 1997. *Une mission en Perse: 1897–1912*. Paris: Réunion des Musées nationaux.
Connan, J. 1999. Use and trade of bitumen in antiquity and prehistory: Molecular archaeology reveals secrets of past civilizations. *Philosophical Transactions of the Royal Society, London* B354: 33–50.
Connan, J., J. Zumberge, K. Imbus, and A. Moghaddam. 2008. The bituminous mixtures of Tall-e Abu Chizan: A Vth millennium BC settlement in southwestern Iran. *Organic Geochemistry* 39: 1772–89.

Delougaz P., and H. J. Kantor, eds. 1996 *Chogha Mish*, vol. 1, *The first five seasons of excavations, 1961-1971*. Chicago: OIP 101.

Dieulafoy, M. A. 1893. *L'Acropole de Suse, d'après les fouilles exécutées en 1884, 1885, 1886 sous les auspices du Musée du Louvre*. Paris: Hachette.

Dollfus, G. 1978. Djaffarabad, Djowi, Bendebal: Contributions à l'étude de la Susiane au Ve millénaire et au début du IVe millénaire. *Paléorient* 4: 141-67.

———. 1983a. Tépé Bendebal, travaux 1977, 1978. *CDAFI* 13: 133-275.

———. 1983b. Tépé Djowi: Contrôle stratigraphique, 1975. *CDAFI* 13: 17-131.

———. 1985. L'occupation de la Susiane au Ve millénaire et au début IVe millénaire: Réflexions et comparaisons. *Paléorient* 11: 11-20.

Dyson, R. H., Jr. 1965. Problems in the relative chronology of Iran, 6000-2000 BC. In *Chronologies in Old World archaeology*, 2nd ed., ed. R. W. Ehrich, 215-56. Chicago: University of Chicago Press.

Firouz, E. 2005. *The complete fauna of Iran*. New York: I. B. Tauris.

Gautier, J. E., and G. Lampre. 1905. Fouilles de Moussian. In *Recherches archéologiques, troisième série*, ed. G. Jéquier, J. de Morgan, J. E. Gautier, G. Lampre, A. Jouannin, A. de la Füye, and H. de Morgan, 59-149. Paris: MDP 8.

Ghirshman, R. 1952. Cinq campagnes de fouilles à Suse, 1946-1951. *RA* 46: 1-18.

———. 1953. Mission archéologique en Susiane en hiver, 1952-1953. *Syria* 30: 222-33.

———. 1954. *Village perse-achéménide*. Paris: MDP 34.

———. 1964. Suse, campagne de fouilles, 1962-1963: Rapport préliminaire. *Arts Asiatiques* 10: 3-10.

Haerinck, E., and B. Overlaet. 1996. *The Chalcolithic period, Parchinah and Hakalan*. Brussels: LED 1.

Hamzehpour, B., D. Paul, and E. Wiesner. 1999. Views on the structural development of the Zagros Simply Folded Belt in Khuzestan Province, Iran. *Zeitschrift der Deutschen Geologischen Gesellschaft* 150: 167-88.

Heyvaert, V. M. A., and C. Baeteman. 2007. Holocene sedimentary evolution and palaeocoastlines of the lower Khuzestan plain (southwest Iran). *Marine Geology* 242/1: 83-108.

Hole, F. 1969 *Preliminary reports of the Rice University Project in Iran 1968-1969*. Houston: Rice University, Department of Anthropology (mimeograph).

———. 1974. Tepe Tūlā'ī: An early campsite in Khuzistan, Iran. *Paléorient* 2/2: 219-42.

———. 1977. *Studies in the archaeological history of the Deh Luran Plain: The excavation of Chagha Sefid*. Ann Arbor: Memoirs of the Museum of Anthropology 9.

———. 1987a. Archaeology of the Village Period. *AWI*: 29-78.

———. 1987b. Settlement and society in the Village Period. *AWI*: 79-105.

———. 1990. Cemetery or mass grave?: Reflections on Susa I. *MJP*: 1-14.

———. 1992. The cemetery of Susa: An interpretation. *RCS*: 26-31.

———. 1994. Environmental instabilities and urban origins. In *Chiefdoms and early states in the Near East*, ed. G. J. Stein and M. S. Rothman, 121-51. Madison: Monographs in World Archaeology 18.

———. 2010. A monumental failure: The collapse of Susa. *BTU*: 227-43.

Hole, F., and K. V. Flannery. 1968. The prehistory of southwestern Iran: A preliminary report. *PPS* 22: 147-206.

Hole, F., K. V. Flannery, and J. A. Neely. 1969. *Prehistory and human ecology of the Deh Luran Plain: An early village sequence from Khuzistan, Iran*. Ann Arbor: Memoirs of the Museum of Anthropology 1.

Huot, J.-L. 1994. *Les premiers villageois de la Méspotamie.* Paris: Armand Colin.

Johnson, G. A. 1973 *Local exchange and early state development in southwestern Iran.* Ann Arbor: Anthropological Papers of the Museum of Anthropology 51.

———. 1987. Nine thousand years of social change in western Iran. *AWI*: 283–91.

Kantor, H. J. 1976a. The excavations at Chogha Mish, 1974–1975. *PASARI* 4: 23–41.

———. 1976b. The prehistoric cultures of Chogha Mish and Bone Fazili. In *The Memorial Volume of the Sixth International Congress of Iranian Art and Archaeology, Oxford, September 11–16, 1972*, ed. M. Y. Kiani, 177–93. Tehran: ICAR.

———. 1976-7. Excavations at Chogha Mish and Chogha Bonut. *Oriental Institute Annual Report* 1976/77: 15–24.

Kirkby, A. V. T. 1973 *The use of land and water resources in the past and present in the Valley of Oaxaca, Mexico.* Ann Arbor: Memoirs of the Museum of Anthropology 5.

Kouchoukos, N. 1998. Landscape and social change in late prehistoric Mesopotamia. Unpublished PhD diss., Yale University.

Kouchoukos, N., R. Smith, A. Gleason, P. Thenkabail, F. Hole, Y. Barkoudah, J. Albert et al.. 1998. Monitoring the distribution, use, and regeneration of natural resources in semi-arid southwest Asia. In *Transformations of Middle Eastern natural environments: Legacies and lessons*, ed. J. Albert, M. Bernardsson, and R. Kenna, 467–91. New Haven: Yale School of Forestry and Environmental Studies Bulletin 103.

Le Breton, L. 1957. The early periods at Susa: Mesopotamian relations. *Iraq* 19: 79–124.

Le Brun, A. 1978. La glyptique du Niveau 17B de l'Acropole (campagne de 1972). *CDAFI* 8: 61–79.

Loftus, W. K. 1857. *Travels and researches in Chaldea and Susiana with an Account of Excavations at Warka, the "Erech" of Nimrod, and Shush, "Shushan the Palace" of Esther, in 1849–52.* London: Nisbet.

McCown, D. E. 1942. *The comparative stratigraphy of early Iran.* Chicago: SAOC 23.

———. 1954. The relative stratigraphy and chronology of Iran. In *Relative chronologies in Old World archaeology*, ed. R. W. Ehrich, 56–68. Chicago: University of Chicago Press.

Miller, N. 1977. Preliminary report on the botanical remains from Tepe Jaffarabad, 1969–1974 campaigns. *CDAFI* 7: 49–53.

Moghaddam, A. 2012. *Later Village Period settlement development in the Karun River Basin, greater Susiana, southwestern Iran.* Oxford: BAR Int Ser 2347.

Moghaddam A., and N. Miri. 2007. Archaeological surveys in the Eastern Corridor, southwestern Iran. *Iran* 44: 23–55.

Morgan, J. de 1895. *Mission scientifique en Perse*, Paris: Leroux

———. 1900. *Recherches archéologiques, première série: Fouilles à Suse en 1897–1898 et 1898–1899.* Paris: MDP 1.

———. 1902. *La Délégation en Perse du Ministère de l'Instruction publique, 1897 à 1902.* Paris: E. Leroux.

———. 1912. Observations sur les couches profondes de l'Acropole de Suse. In *Recherches archéologiques, cinquième série: Céramique peinte de Suse et petits monuments de l'Époque archaïque*, ed. E. Pottier, J. de Morgan, and R. de Mecquenem, 1–25. Paris: MDP 13.

Mousavi, A. 1996. Early archaeological adventures and methodological problems in Iranian archaeology: The evidence from Susa. *IrAnt* 31: 1–17.

Neely, J. A. 1974. Sassanian and early Islamic water-control and irrigation systems on the Deh Luran plain, Iran. In *Irrigation's impact on society*, ed. T. E. Downing and M. Gibson, 21–42. Tucson: Anthropological Papers of the University of Arizona 25.

Neely, J. A., and H. T. Wright. 1994. *Early settlement and irrigation on the Deh Luran plain, Iran: Technical Report 26*. Ann Arbor: University of Michigan Museum of Anthropology.

Oates, D., and J. Oates. 1976. Early irrigation agriculture in Mesopotamia. In *Problems in economic and social archaeology*, ed. G. de G. Sieveking, I. H. Longworth, and K. E. Wilson, 109–35. London: Duckworth.

Perrot, J. 1978. Introduction. *Paléorient* 4: 133–40.

Pollock, S. 1983. Style and information: An analysis of Susiana ceramics. *Journal of Anthropological Archaeology* 2: 354–90.

———. 1989. Power politics in the Susa A period. In *Upon this foundation: The Ubaid reconsidered*, ed. E. Henrickson and I. Thuesen, 281–92. Copenhagen: CNIP 10.

———. 1999. *Ancient Mesopotamia: The Eden that never was*. Cambridge: Cambridge University Press.

Potts, D. T. 1999. *The archaeology of Elam: Formation and transformation of an ancient Iranian state*. Cambridge: Cambridge University Press.

Rothman, M. S. 1987. Graph theory and the interpretation of regional survey data. *Paléorient* 13/2: 73–91.

Shahmirzadi, S. M. 1986. A review of the development of archaeology in Iran. *Asar* 12–14: 133–60 (in Persian).

———. 1987. History of the archaeological research in Iran. *IJAH* 2: 57–73 (in Persian).

———. 1990. Development of archaeological research in Iran. In *Proceedings of the 1st Symposium of Iranian Studies*, ed. A. Mousavi Garmarudi, 373–447. Tehran: Institute of Political and International Students of the Ministry of Foreign Affairs (in Persian).

Sheykh, M. 2010. *Barresi Parineh Sangi ye Dasht-e Sush, Huze ye Rud-e Karkheh (Palaeolithic Expedition in Susa plain, the Karkheh River basin)*. Ahwaz: Khuzestan Cultural Heritage, Handicraft and Tourism Organization.

Steve, M.-J., and H. Gasche. 1971. *L'Acropole de Suse*. Paris: MDAI 46.

———. 1990. Le Tell de l'Apadana avant les Achéménides. *MJP*: 15–60.

Vanden Berghe, L. 1959. *Archéologie de l'Iran ancien*. Leiden: Brill.

———. 1973. Le nécropole de Hakalan. *Archeologia* 57: 49–58.

———. 1975. Fouilles au Lorestan: La nécropole de Dum Gar Parchinah. *PASARI* 3: 45–62.

———. 1987. Luristan, Pusht-e Kuh au chalcolithique moyen (les nécropoles de Parchinah et Hakalan). In *Préhistorie de la Mésopotamie*, ed. J.-L. Huot, 91–106. Paris: Éditions du CNRS.

Veenenbos, J. 1958 *Unified report on the soil and land classification survey of Dezful Project, Khuzestan Iran*. Tehran: Khuzestan Development Service.

Walstra, J., V. M. A. Heyvaert, and P. Verkinderen. 2010. Assessing human impact on alluvial fan development: A multidisciplinary case-study from Lower Khuzestan (SW Iran). *Geodinamica Acta* 23/5–6: 267–85.

Weiss, H. 1976. Ceramics for chronology: Discrimination and cluster analysis of fifth millennium ceramic assemblages from Qabr Sheykheyn, Khuzestan. Unpublished PhD diss., University of Pennsylvania.

———. 1977. Periodization, population and early state formation in Khuzestan. *ML*: 347–69.

Wright, H. T. 1977. Recent research on the origin of the state. *Annual Review of Anthropology* 6: 379–97.

———. 1981. *An early town in the Deh Luran plain: Excavations at Tepe Farukhabad*. Ann Arbor: Memoirs of the Museum of Anthropology 13.

———. 1984. Prestate political formations. In *On the evolution of complex societies: Essays in*

Honor of Harry Hoijer, ed. T. Earle, 41–77. Malibu: Undena.

———. 1994. Pre-state political formations. In *Chiefdoms and early states in the Near East*, ed. G. J. Stein and M. S. Rothman, 67–84. Madison: Monographs in World Archaeology 18.

———. 2000. Modeling tributary economies and hierarchical polities. In *Cultural evolution: Contemporary viewpoints*, ed. G. M. Feinman and L. Manzanilla, 197–213. New York: Kluwer Academic/Plenum Publishers.

Wright, H. T., and G. A. Johnson. 1975. Population, exchange, and early state formation in southwestern Iran. *American Anthropologist* 77: 267–89.

Wright, H. T., N. Miller, J. A. Neely, and R. W. Redding. 1999. A Late Susiana society in southwestern Iran. *IW*: 64–79.

Wright H. T., J. A. Neely, G. A. Johnson, and J. D. Speth. 1975. Early fourth millennium developments in southwestern Iran. *Iran* 13: 129–47.

CHAPTER 8

THE CHALCOLITHIC IN SOUTHERN IRAN

CAMERON A. PETRIE

INTRODUCTION

This chapter covers what could be termed the Chalcolithic and beginning of the Early Bronze Age in southern Iran, as the archaeology of the late fourth millennium BC in other parts of the Ancient Near East is often referred to as being part of the earliest phases of the Early Bronze Age. However, in what follows here the Late Uruk and proto-Elamite periods are considered the culmination of a long-term developmental sequence that witnessed the rise of the first urban centers in highland Iran during the late fourth millennium BC. As copper artifacts are not common, this period can quite justifiably be called Chalcolithic.

Throughout most of the fifth and fourth millennia BC the societies of southern Iran underwent a number of major social, economic, and political transformations. Although the Neolithic village-based societies of these regions at this time (see Chapter 4) primarily practiced small-scale agriculture and engaged in limited, long-distance, down-the-line trade, those of the subsequent two millennia experienced progressive increases in population and the development of settlement hierarchies, increasing sophistication in craft activities and technologies, the development of elaborate iconography, and the adoption of sealing technology and incipient administrative practices. This protracted phase of transformation culminated in the rise of the first city-sized settlements in highland Iran, limited literacy, and long-range interactions with neighboring populations.

The dominant geographical feature in southern Iran is the Zagros mountain range, which forms the western and southern edges of the Iranian plateau and abuts the plains of Mesopotamia to the west and the Persian Gulf to the southwest, south, and southeast (Map 0.1). The eastern parts of modern Iran also include the Dasht-e Lut and the arid

Sistan Basin, which continues across the modern border into Afghanistan. The topography of the Zagros Mountains and the desertic regions to the east is such that the broad geographical expanse of southern Iran is broken up into several distinctive geographical and cultural zones (Prickett 1986a, 1986b; Petrie 2011).

Today, the environment and climate of southwestern Iran are characterized by considerable variation according to altitude, with the northern and western parts comprising a number of specific environmental and climatic zones marked by seasonal variation in temperature and vegetation cover (Ganji 1968; Bobek 1968). It has been argued that this variation promoted specific patterns of human exploitation in the past, particularly nomadic pastoralism (e.g., Alizadeh 2006, 2010), although this has been contested (e.g., Askari Chaverdi et al. 2008; Petrie et al. 2009b; Weeks et al. 2010; Potts 2008, 2011). The southern and southeastern areas are largely dry and hot, receive little annual rainfall, and have tree and shrub-steppe vegetation (Ganji 1968; Bobek 1968). The climate and vegetation of the inland areas of the plateau are either steppic or desertic and receive very little rainfall (Bobek 1968; Ganji 1968).

Sedentary settlement throughout south Iran is limited to those plains and valleys that have both adequate water resources and sufficient arable land, and only certain areas were intensively settled in the past (Prickett 1986a, 1986b; Carter 1994: 75; Miroschedji 2003; Roustaei et al. 2009; Askari Chaverdi et al. 2008; Petrie 2011). These valleys and plains (Fig. 8.1) were and are connected to each other by paths, tracks, and passes, which form a network of routes of interaction and communication traversing the Zagros. These were used by people to move between lowland and highland areas and the interior of the plateau and also between areas within each of these zones. It is very likely that the distinctive topography of southern Iran imposed specific constraints on prehistoric human behavior, particularly on the nature of communication and interaction between the inhabitants of the different valleys and plains, and also on the way that innovations were transmitted and received (Petrie 2011).

This chapter endeavors to situate the archaeology of the fifth and fourth millennia BC in southern Iran in its specific geographical context. Assessing the processes of cultural development over a span of 2000 years across such an enormous area is an ambitious task, particularly as the archaeological evidence from this region as a whole is relatively limited. Some intermontane valleys and plains have been the focus of systematic archaeological research, while others have seen little or no archaeological exploration at all. As a result, our knowledge of the prehistoric occupation of southern Iran is patchy. Although ceramics constitute just one aspect of a larger cultural milieu, archaeologists have traditionally delineated the major chronological periods in southern Iran on the basis of developments in ceramic technology and style. These developments reflect broad patterns of human behavior, material culture, and technological practices and inform discussions of the types of interaction that occurred between populations in different regions. This chapter identifies key themes in the development of socioeconomic complexity in southern Iran as far as it can be reconstructed based on current evidence. It also reflects upon the approaches that have been used to reconstruct the dynamics and processes in operation during this period with a view to highlighting which aspects

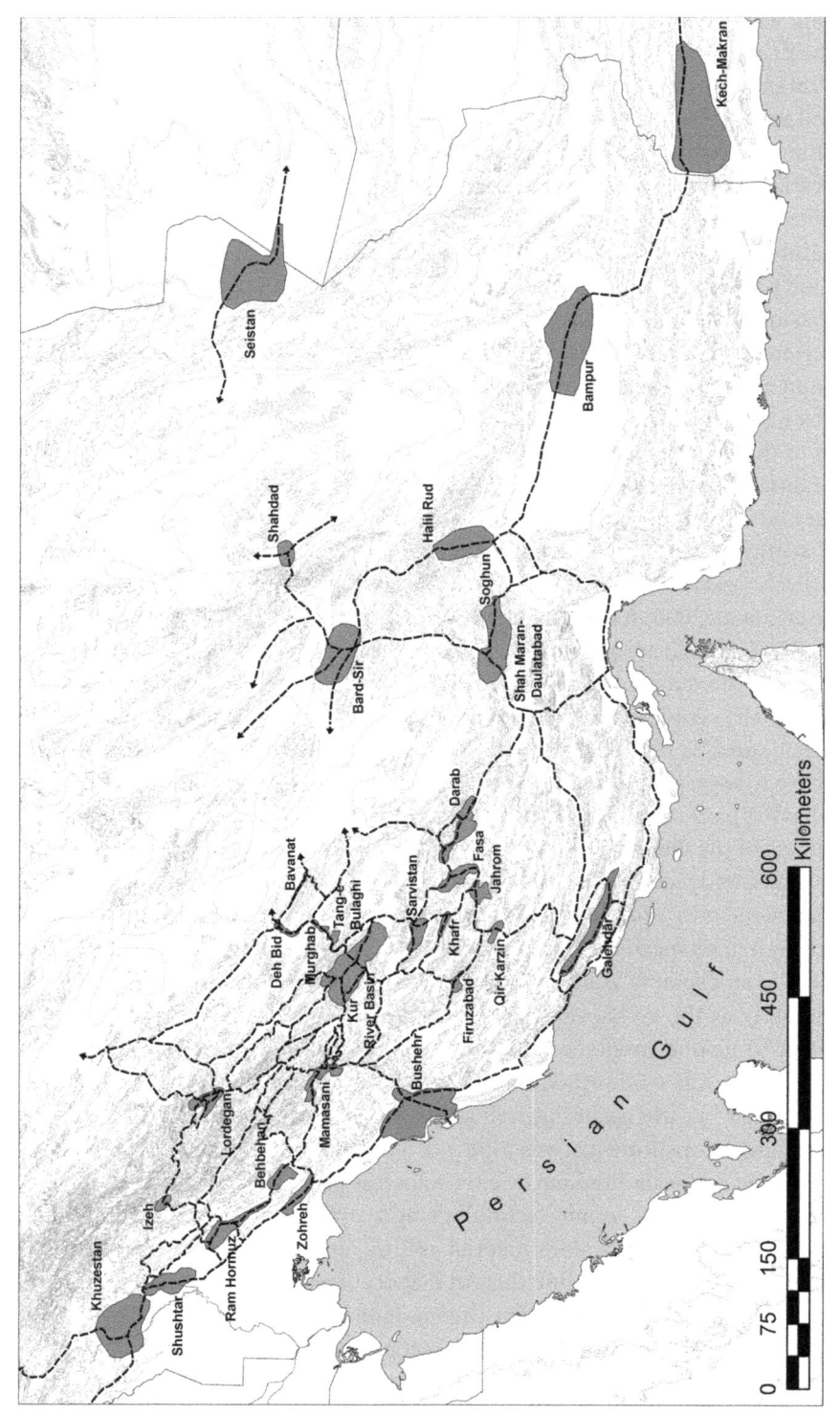

FIGURE 8.1. Topographic map of southern Iran, showing regions that have been investigated archaeologically and some of the routes that would have connected them in the fifth and fourth millennia BC.

are in need of further investigation. The review that follows will be presented chronologically and will differentiate developments in the fifth millennium BC from those of the fourth, though these boundaries are not hard and fast, because the boundaries of chronological phases do not always fall neatly at the beginning or end of a millennium. Within this framework, southwestern and southeastern Iran will be discussed separately and, where appropriate, the evidence for connections between these two zones will be highlighted.

THE FIFTH MILLENNIUM BC

Southwestern Iran

The Neolithic of southwestern Iran has received considerable attention, and our understanding of cultural dynamics and human behavior in this period continues to develop as a result of several ongoing research projects. In contrast, there are many questions about the fifth millennium BC of southwestern Iran that remain to be answered. Throughout Fars, the fifth millennium BC is referred to as the Bakun period, traditionally divided into three phases (Early, Middle, and Late Bakun) (Voigt and Dyson 1992; Alizadeh 2006 identifies only Middle and Late Bakun phases). The most overt marker of the Bakun period is a range of buff ware ceramic vessel types that show indications of having been manufactured using basic turning devices; they display a range of geometric, zoomorphic, and anthropomorphic motifs in monochrome black pigment, and they were fired at a high temperature (Weeks et al. 2010; see below).

Basis of knowledge

Our knowledge of the Bakun period in Fars comes primarily from excavations and surveys in the Kur River Basin (hereafter KRB), which is arguably the most intensively investigated region in all of southern Iran. In the KRB, Bakun black-on-buff painted ceramics have been recovered through excavation at Tal-e Bakun A and B, Tal-e Jari A, Tal-e Gap, and Tol-e Bashi (Voigt and Dyson 1992: 137–140; cf. Alizadeh 2006; Abdi et al. 2003; Bernbeck et al. 2004, 2010), and a number of extensive surveys (Vanden Berghe 1952, 1954; Gotch 1968, 1969; Sumner 1972, 1994). Outside the KRB, contemporaneous black-on-buff ceramics have been found at settlements throughout Fars and some adjacent areas (Alizadeh 2006: 49–55, fig. 5b; Weeks et al. 2010). These include two unexcavated (the nomenclature for excavated and unexcavated sites used here deliberately differentiates sites that have seen formal excavation from those that have been discovered through survey and subjected to quick soundings, the latter of which were largely carried out by Sir M. Aurel Stein [1935, 1937] and Louis Vanden Berghe [1952, 1954]) at sites adjacent to the Persian Gulf coast in Bushehr (BH56 and H200) (Carter et al. 2006); at least five unexcavated sites adjacent to the Persian Gulf coast in Galehdar (including Tol-e Pir) (Stein 1937; Askari Chaverdi et al. 2008); two excavated (Tol-e Nurabad and

Tol-e Spid) and fourteen unexcavated sites in Mamasani (Weeks et al. 2009; Petrie et al. 2009a, 2009b; Zeidi et al. 2009; McCall 2009); one excavated (Tal-e Nokhodi) and numerous unexcavated sites in Sarvestan, Firuzabad, Qir-Karzin, Fasa, Darab, Bavanat, and Khorrambid (Stein 1935; Sami 1956; Goff 1963, 1964; Miroschedji 1973; Dittmann 1986; Kerner 1993; Taylor 2007); five excavated sites in or close to the Tang-e Bolaghi (Tol-e Rahmatabad, DB73, DB91, DB119, and DB 131) (Bernbeck et al. 2005; Helwing and Seyedin 2010; Azizi and Taylor forthcoming); and one excavated (Tappeh Mehr Ali; Sardari 2012) and a small number of unexcavated sites in some of the smaller valleys to the northwest of the KRB (Alizadeh 2003, 2006: 51–55; Sardari 2012) (Fig. 8.1). Although this appears to be a considerable amount of archaeological evidence for one period, the coverage is relatively thin for what is a sizable region. It should be noted that there is considerable disagreement over the attribution of specific stratigraphic phases at individual sites and the associated cultural material at various sites to the Early, Middle, and Late Bakun phases, and this impedes interpretation and comprehension of socioeconomic developments and cultural relationships (see below).

By and large, the Bakun period as a whole represents a continuation of the ceramic Neolithic pattern of sedentary populations living in small villages within mudbrick and/or *chineh* buildings, whose subsistence system was largely based on the exploitation of domesticated goat, sheep, cattle, and pig, as well as wheat, barley, and lentils (Mashkour 2009). Although there are changes in the proportion of species exploited at different sites and in different periods, it is clear that caprids significantly dominated the faunal assemblages of highland Fars from the mid-ceramic Neolithic (Jari period) up until the end of the fourth millennium BC and beyond (Mashkour 2009). There is some evidence for the development of a settlement hierarchy during this phase (see below), and copper-base tools, weapons, and jewelry appeared in increasing numbers, indicating that it was a true Chalcolithic phase.

Chronology

The absolute chronology of the beginning and end of the Bakun period, and the individual subphases that comprise it, are imprecise. Our understanding is hampered by the fact that none of the sites thus far excavated and published have evidence of continuous occupation throughout the fifth millennium BC. This means that there are a number of specific chronological and interpretative issues that remain unresolved. For example, the nature and timing of the transition from the Neolithic to the Early Bakun period are unclear, due in part to a lack of focused research directed at this problem. Early Bakun occupation has been identified only at two excavated sites, Tal-e Jari A (I) and Tal-e Bakun B (II) (Voigt and Dyson 1992: 138; Weeks et al. 2006). Similarly, there is some debate over the dating of the different phases of occupation at Tal-e Gap, such that different scholars have attributed occupation at the site variously to the Middle Bakun (Alizadeh 2006; Potts et al. 2009; Pollock et al. 2010), Early and Middle Bakun (Taylor 2007) and Early, Middle, and Late Bakun phases (Voigt and Dyson 1992). Evidence of Early, Middle, and Late Bakun occupation has been exposed in two separate trenches at Tol-e Nurabad (Trench A, Weeks et al. 2009; and Trench C, Petrie and Taylor forthcoming; Taylor forthcoming), but a continuous sequence has not been found in either area, so questions that might be answered through the investigation of a continuous sequence of occupation remain unresolved. According to Sardari (2012), Tappeh Mehr Ali has a fifth millennium BC sequence spanning the Early to Late Bakun, but these levels have not yet been published in any detail.

There are radiocarbon determinations from the KRB and the Mamasani district that provide some indication of the absolute dating of the Bakun period and its subphases. Excavations at several sites in the KRB by the ICAR and the Oriental Institute and reanalysis of museum-curated dating material have resulted in the publication of a number of relevant radiocarbon dates (Alizadeh 2006: tables 9–11; Nishiaki 2010). These dates generally show good agreement with those from excavations at Tol-e Nurabad and Tol-e Spid in the Mamasani district. Calibrated radiocarbon dates on samples from levels preceding the use of black-on-buff ceramics (the Shamsabad or Bakun B1 period) at Tal-e Jari A and Tal-e Bakun B span the period $c.$5360–4700 cal BC (Alizadeh 2006: tables 9–11; Mashkour et al. 2006; Nishiaki 2010; Weeks et al. 2010) and are in agreement with the early fifth millennium BC dates from the final Neolithic or transitional Bakun deposits at Tol-e Nurabad Phase A19 ($c.$4940–4550 cal BC; Weeks et al. 2009: 68; 2010: 254–5). Given the ranges of the calibrated dates, a very early fifth millennium BC date for the beginning of the Bakun period in the KRB seems likely (Weeks et al. 2006, 2010).

The best *terminus ante quem* for the end of the Bakun period in Fars is provided by a series of radiocarbon dates from the post-Bakun period deposits at Tol-e Spid, the earliest of which falls at $c.$4050–3910 cal BC, and indicates that the Late Bakun period must predate this span (Petrie et al. 2007, 2009, 2013). Of course, the radiocarbon dating evidence for the end of the Bakun period in Mamasani cannot be automatically assumed to apply to the KRB, let alone all the other subregions of Fars, but for the moment there are no reliable radiocarbon dates for the end of the Bakun period in the KRB. Three dates from the lower levels of Tal-e Bakun A, which ceramic comparanda indicate belong to the Middle/Late Bakun transition (contra Alizadeh 2006: 46–7), consistently date to the period $c.$4500–4250 cal BC. These dates suggest that the end of the Bakun period in the KRB should fall in the last quarter of the fifth millennium BC, and this proposal in no way contradicts the very late fifth/early fourth millennium BC dates obtained from the early Lapui deposits at Tol-e Spid.

Settlement distribution

The KRB provides the largest data set on prehistoric settlement distribution in southwestern Iran (Sumner 1972, 1988b, 1994). Sumner (1972, 1994) argued that the Bakun period was the most intensive phase of prehistoric settlement in the KRB, and his full-coverage regional survey indicated that the settled population steadily grew during the course of the Neolithic (Mushki phase: eight sites; Jari phase: fifty sites; Shamsabad phase: 102 sites), reaching a peak in the Bakun period (156 sites) (Sumner 1994: table 1). While the earliest ceramic Neolithic settlements appear to have been located close to natural springs (Sumner 1990: 97, 1994: 52) or on alluvial fans, where they would have benefited from annual soil replenishment caused by sheet wash (Petrie and Thomas

2015), subsequent Neolithic and Bakun settlements in the KRB were much more widely distributed, implying changes to the agrarian system and some degree of agricultural intensification (Sumner 1994: 52; see below). Sumner was unable to allocate sites to the individual subphases of the Bakun period based on ceramic criteria, but he attempted to reconstruct intraperiod dynamics using a statistical model that attributed sites to subphases on the basis of whether there was earlier or later occupation (Sumner 1990, 1994: 63, table 3; Weeks et al. 2010: 268). Sumner's (1994: 63, table 3) modeling led him to suggest that there was an increase of settlement and population between the Early Shamsabad (forty-seven sites), and Early Bakun phases (seventy-three sites); more intensive settlement in the Middle Bakun (eighty-five sites); and a marked decrease in settlement during the Late Bakun (sixty-five sites). Alizadeh (2006: 49) subsequently assessed the ceramics from a subset of thirty-six of Sumner's sites to differentiate individual subphases on the basis of the decorative motifs seen on the ceramics. This led him to suggest that there was a gradual increase in settlement numbers throughout the Bakun period and a sharp increase in the subsequent Lapui period (Alizadeh 2006: 49), though the numbers that he cited do not clearly support this contention (see below).

The survey and excavation data indicate that Bakun settlements in the KRB were generally small, less than 1 ha in size, although three larger sites (6–7.8 ha) were also recorded (Sumner 1972: 256, 1994: table 2; Kole 1980: 85). The largest of these, Tol-e Bashi, was briefly excavated, but the Bakun period deposits were not investigated in any detail (Abdi et al. 2003: 339; Bernbeck et al. 2004, Pollock et al. 2010). The Bakun ceramics from the surface of Tol-e Bashi suggest that it was a large settlement during the Early and Middle Bakun periods, before being abandoned and then reoccupied on a smaller scale at the end of the Late Bakun phase (Pollock et al. 2010: 161). This evidence, combined with the existence of two other large sites, implies the existence of a two-tier site settlement hierarchy in the KRB during the Early and Middle Bakun and potentially also in the Late Bakun phases (Sumner 1994: figs. 2–4; Alizadeh 2006: 19; contra Alizadeh 2003: 89–90), though the latter remains to be demonstrated. The Bakun settlement system thus appears to contrast markedly with that of the preceding Neolithic periods and potentially also that of the subsequent Lapui period, when no such hierarchy was observed (Sumner 1988b, 1990; see below).

Settlement structure

Horizontal excavations at Tal-e Bakun A and, to a lesser extent, Tal-e Gap showed that Middle and Late Bakun period settlements comprised multiroomed, rectilinear structures made of mudbrick or *chineh* (Langsdorff and McCown 1942; Egami and Sono 1962). There is little evidence of significant distinctions in building size or architectural elaboration at either site. Tal-e Bakun A does, however, yield extensive evidence of metallurgy, interregional trade, specialized craft production (particularly ceramic), planned architecture, segregation of activities, and the use of stamp seals and clay sealings (Langsdorff and McCown 1942; Alizadeh 2006). Alizadeh (2006: 58, 64) has argued that there is evidence of functional differences in building use within individual sites, and proposed that Building VIII at Tal-e Bakun A was the primary elite residence at that settlement. No incontrovertible evidence for any Bakun temples or ritual structures has yet been recovered, but Fraser (2008: 12–13, 16) has suggested that although Building VIII lacked the evidence of seals and sealings seen in other buildings, it may have served a religious/cultic function, as it is the largest, most prominent, and, with its niches on the exterior walls, most architecturally distinctive building at Tal-e Bakun A.

Ceramics

The most obvious indicator of cultural change at the end of the Neolithic and the beginning of the Early Bakun phase (*c.*4800 cal BC) in Fars was the adoption of calcareous buff ware fabrics for the production of ceramics. Once adopted, variants of these buff wares continued in use until the end of the Late Bakun phase (*c.*4100 cal BC).

The shift to calcareous clays is one of several technological innovations in ceramic production that characterize the Bakun period. Others include the adoption of basic turning devices, the use of monochrome black in preference to bi- or polychrome decoration, and higher firing temperatures (Petrie 2011). Alizadeh (2006: 11, 67, 97; cf. Alden 1982) attributed the appearance of Bakun period buff ware ceramics in the KRB to the immigration of either foreign groups or specialized potters, possibly from Khuzestan, where buff wares appeared earlier (Johnson 1973; Voigt and Dyson 1992; Delougaz and Kantor 1996; Alizadeh 2008). Although the black-on-buff tradition is new in a stylistic and technological sense, there are many indicators of cultural continuity between the Neolithic and Bakun periods in highland Fars. Sumner's (1990: 99) survey evidence demonstrated considerable settlement continuity between the Shamsabad and Bakun periods, with up to 108 sites being occupied in both periods. Secondly, as noted above, there are similarities in building construction techniques and subsistence practices. Thirdly, although calcareous buff wares largely replaced the vegetal-tempered soft-ware fabrics that characterized the Neolithic, there is evidence that soft-wares and calcareous buff wares were used contemporaneously at Tal-e Bakun B and Tal-e Jari A in the KRB (Voigt and Dyson 1992 1: 138; Alizadeh 2006: 68) and Tol-e Nurabad in Mamasani (Weeks et al. 2006, 2009). There are signs that some of the artistic and technological traditions leading to the production of Bakun black-on-buff painted wares developed in the later Neolithic, possibly through contact with or inspiration from contemporary black-on-buff ceramic-using groups in neighboring regions (Weeks et al. 2010: 264). Furthermore, the replacement of Neolithic soft-wares by black-on-buff wares in Mamasani and the KRB is part of a geographically and chronologically protracted process that was occurring across western and southern Iran (Petrie et al. 2009: 172; Weeks et al. 2010: 246–7; see below). It is thus clear that the developments that took place during the Bakun period are unlikely to have been solely a result of migration.

The Early Bakun calcareous buff ware is buff slipped and has black painted decoration and there is evidence of a burnished or a brush-marked surface (Voigt and Dyson 1992: 138) with parallels in the Middle Susiana ceramic tradition in Khuzestan (Alizadeh 2006: 11). Early Bakun decoration includes the use of solid and/or thick bands of paint; elaborate interior decoration; dense, cross-hatched geometric decoration; and anthropomorphic and zoomorphic designs (Voigt and Dyson 1992; Weeks et al. 2009, 2010). During the Middle Bakun phase, there is less interior decoration but clear use of horizontal registers on the exterior to enclose geometric motifs, including crosses, dashes, zigzags, and dots and/or stylized anthropomorphic, zoomorphic, and vegetal elements (Voigt and Dyson 1992: 138–9). The Late Bakun phase is primarily attested at Tal-e Bakun A and saw the appearance of more variety in vessel forms, including tall conical cups with pointed or rounded bases (Voigt and Dyson 1992: 139). There was a degree of continuity in some decorative motifs but also a dramatic floruit of elaborate geometric and representational decorative motifs that often cover the entire exterior of the vessel and make use of negative space (Voigt and Dyson 1992: 139; Langsdorff and McCown 1942; Alizadeh 2006). There is no evidence for the use of a wheel to produce Bakun ceramics, and there are clear signs that many vessels were hand formed. Nevertheless, Late Bakun vessel forms are particularly thin walled and often have relatively consistent rim forms, suggesting that some form of slow rotation, for example in baskets or round-bottomed vessels, was employed in their production.

Sumner (1994: 59) recovered evidence of ceramic production at thirteen of the 175 Bakun sites that he identified, suggesting that pottery production was undertaken at multiple sites in the KRB. The Late Bakun levels at Tal-e Bakun A (Period III) yielded evidence of kilns, production debris, and massive ash deposits in various locations across the site (Langsdorff and McCown 1942: 6, 70–71; Alizadeh 1988, 2006). Outside of the KRB, excavations at the Middle Bakun site of Tappeh Rahmatabad revealed the possible use of small round turntables and kilns within a settled area (Bernbeck et al. 2005: 102–3), and in the Darre-ye Bolaghi, Middle Bakun period kilns were exposed at DB91 and DB131, and a Late Bakun kiln was excavated at DB73 (Helwing and Seyedin 2010). Pottery wasters were also recovered at BH56 near Bushire (R. Carter et al. 2006: 78) and Tol-e Spid (Petrie et al. 2007).

The presence of kilns in the KRB and the Tang-e Bolaghi raises the possibility of specialized Bakun-period settlements where pottery for exchange was produced as one aspect of the local economy (e.g., Tal-e Bakun A and Tappeh Rahmatabad) and where ceramic production may have been the principal activity (e.g., DB91, DB131). Nevertheless, it is still unclear whether the potters at Tal-e Bakun A and Tappeh Rahmatabad were full-time craftsmen and/or produced pottery for other sites. The absence of evidence of ceramic production at the vast majority of Bakun sites suggests that pottery manufacture was not undertaken universally (Sumner 1994: 59). There does not appear to be any evidence of specific vessel types having been manufactured at one site; rather, the evidence from the Tang-e Bolaghi sites suggests that a single site produced a very wide range of shapes and motifs (Helwing and Seyedin 2010). Based primarily upon the quality of Bakun pottery and the limited evidence of localized production, Sumner (1994: 59) suggested that ceramic production was a "specialized craft industry" throughout the Bakun period.

Socioeconomy

The differing opinions on the interpretation of Bakun-period settlement distibution and internal organization are reflected in the two prevailing models of socioeconomy and subsistence practices of the Bakun period. Sumner (1994: 60–62) argued that the evidence of increased population, productive specialization, administrative control, and socioeconomic integration in the Bakun period points to the existence of hierarchically ranked kinship units that competed for power. He also argued that linear distributions of Bakun-period settlements indicate that Bakun agricultural production was irrigation based (Sumner 1990: 99–101, 1994: 51–9). Alizadeh (1988, 2003: 88–90, 2006: 83–90) also regards the Bakun period as a critical stage in the development of social complexity in highland southwestern Iran, but he has emphasized the role of mobile pastoralism in the rise of complex prestate formations in this period in highland Iran, rather than the political role of kinship relations (Alizadeh 1988, 1994–5; 2003: 88–90; 2006: 83–90). Drawing heavily on the Tal-e Bakun A evidence of administration (stamp seals and sealings), specialized ceramic production, and to a lesser extent plant and animal remains (Mashkour et al. 2006; Miller and Kimiaie 2006), Alizadeh proposed that the Bakun period witnessed the rise of full-fledged nomadic pastoralism and that sites such as Tal-e Bakun A were unable to generate an agricultural surplus from cereal cultivation to support specialized manufacturing (Alizadeh 2003: 89–90; 2006: 94–6; 1988). In Alizadeh's (1988; 1994; 2003: 88–90; 2006: 94–6) reconstruction, surpluses from nomadic pastoralist groups were used to maintain the administrative and manufacturing community at Tal-e Bakun A, and he cited this as evidence of complex, prestate formations based on mobile pastoralism during the fifth millennium BC.

Limitations on currently available evidence mean that neither of these models can be regarded as conclusive. Weeks et al. (2010) have argued that much of the evidence summoned by Alizadeh does not permit the discrimination of a generalized agro-pastoral economy from one that had specialized farmers and herders. Also, provided rainfall was sufficient, it would have been possible to achieve agricultural surpluses without irrigation (Weiss 1986), thus removing the need for other sources of Bakun surplus. While there is evidence of an increase in the exploitation of caprids during the Late Bakun phase at Tal-e Bakun A (Mashkour et al. 2006: 105), Miller and Kimiaie (2006: 107, 113) have argued that bioarchaeological samples from settled communities are unlikely to speak directly to the question of nomadic pastoralism. The discovery of ceramic spindle whorls at Tal-e Bakun A (Langsdorff and McCown 1942: 69, pl. 82; Alizadeh 2006: 77–8), Tal-e Bakun B (Egami and Masuda 1962: pl. 4), and Tal-e Gap (Egami and Sono 1962: pl. 40) suggests that settled agricultural groups had access to wool and may indicate that they practiced caprid pastoralism (Sumner 1994: 59). While this invariably involved some seasonal transhumance, it need not require a nomadic pastoralist mode of subsistence. On balance, the extant evidence is more supportive of Sumner's more conservative claims for the existence of settled Bakun communities characterized by a mixed agro-pastoral subsistence base (Askari Chaverdi et al. 2008; Weeks et al. 2010; Potts 2008, 2011).

Perhaps the most problematic element of our understanding of Bakun socioeconomics is the fact that the Bakun levels at the three largest Bakun period sites in the KRB remain largely uninvestigated (Sumner 1994; Abdi et al. 2003; Pollock et al. 2010), and it has been noted that some uninvestigated sites have deep Bakun period deposits (Kole

1980; Voigt and Dyson 1992: 137). Interpretations of Bakun political, economic, and cultural interaction and integration will undoubtedly be enhanced once such large sites are investigated in detail.

Southeastern Iran

Our understanding of the archaeology of the fifth millennium BC in southeastern Iran is relatively limited, for while a significant number of ancient settlements have been discovered through survey, only a small number of these have been excavated. Most of what is known of the archaeology of the fifth millennium BC in the southeast comes from Kerman, and at present there is little survey evidence of occupation in Sistan and Baluchistan and Hormuzgan provinces before the later fourth millennium BC (see below). There are contemporary settlements in the eastern reaches of Pakistani Baluchistan but very little archaeological evidence from the intervening area, and excavations at Miri Qalat and Shahi-Tump indicate that the inhabitants of those settlements made use of flint tools but not ceramics (Besenval 2005; Besenval et al. 2005; Mutin 2012).

As in southwestern Iran, the fifth millennium BC in southeastern Iran was a period of transformation, and this region also saw the adoption of the technology for making black-on-buff ware ceramics. However, this process occurred later than it did in the southwest and was just one element of a diverse southeastern ceramic assemblage and production repertoire that reflects the area's location at the intersection of a diverse range of cultural influences (Beale 1986: 39ff., fig. 4.1). It is also significant that evidence of precocious metalworking innovations during this period was found at Tal-e Iblis and Tepe Yahya, and these were arguably the most important technological developments in southeastern Iran during this entire period (see below; Weeks 2012). Although the pyrotechnologies required for firing hard buff wares and metals are very different (Frame 2004), both demand control of high temperatures in controlled environments.

Basis of knowledge

Our understanding of the archaeology of the fifth millennium BC in southeastern Iran is primarily derived from two distinct but related stratified sequences at Tepe Yahya (Beale 1986) and Tal-e Iblis (e.g., Caldwell 1967; Chase, Caldwell, and Fehérvári 1967) in Kerman, combined with evidence from the extensive surveys carried out in the Shah Maran-Daulatabad region (Prickett 1986a, 1986b) and Bard Sir (Caldwell 1967; Chase, Caldwell, and Fehérvári 1967; Khosrowzadeh 2005; Fig. 8.1). Surveys have been carried out in other parts of the southeast, and excavations have been conducted at sites in the Sistan, Shahdad, and Halil Rud regions (Stein 1937; Tosi 1968, 1970; Hakemi 1997; Sajjadi 2004, Sajjadi et al. 2008; Madjidzadeh 2008), but although these investigations have revealed evidence of fourth millennium BC occupation, particularly at Mahtoutabad in the Halil Rud (Vidale and Desset 2013), evidence of fifth millennium BC occupation is largely lacking. Although Prickett (1986a: 759–74; 1986b:

237) argued that there are sites in southern Kerman and the Bampur valley with fifth millennium BC occupation, a reanalysis of this material has shown that none of these sites have clear occupation earlier than the fourth millennium BC (Mutin 2012). Exceptions to this might be a possible fifth millennium BC settlement mound at Shahdad (Tepe II; Vidale et al. 2012) and the claimed but undemonstrated identification of fifth millennium BC settlements in the Halil Rud Basin (Madjidzadeh 2008: 73).

Chronology

The excavations at Tepe Yahya produced a coherent sequence of occupation in the fifth millennium BC, particularly in the trenches on the south side of the mound (Beale 1986: 11ff.). The entire sequence of occupation at Tepe Yahya was divided into seven periods by the excavators (Yahya Periods VII–I, earliest to latest), but there has been some inconsistency in the interpretation of the absolute dates of individual chronological phases, and this has relevance when considering which of the Yahya phases relate to the fifth millennium BC. Beale (1986: 11–12, table 2.1) initially proposed that what are ostensibly the ceramic Neolithic phases at the site (periods VIID, VIIC, VIIB, and VIIA) span the fifth millennium BC (i.e., 4900–3900 BC). However, Voigt and Dyson (1992: 148) cogently argued that Yahya VII is more likely to have been contemporaneous with the ceramic Neolithic in Fars (i.e., the sixth or early fifth millennium BC), and this is borne out by a recalibration of the available radiocarbon dates (Petrie 2011: table 1; forthcoming a). Voigt and Dyson's (1992) relative chronology for the remainder of the fifth millennium BC sequence at Tepe Yahya (c.4900–3800 BC) has also been largely confirmed by a recalibration of the radiocarbon dates and supersedes that outlined by Beale (1986: 11–12). Some of the problems surrounding the absolute dating of Tepe Yahya stem from the fact that most of the dates from the site have very broad standard deviations, which means that there is a greater than usual imprecision in the calibrated dates. Recently, however, there have been dramatic improvements to the radiocarbon calibration curve and the statistical processing involved in the radiocarbon calibration procedure, so that old absolute dates can be recalibrated with considerable success (Petrie forthcoming a, 2015).

Parallels with the Early Bakun ceramics from Fars indicate that Yahya VI dates to the early or mid-fifth millennium BC (Voigt and Dyson 1992: 148–9; Petrie 2011: table 1). Yahya VC correlates with the Early-Middle Bakun (mid-fifth millennium BC); Yahya VB with the Middle Bakun (mid- to late fifth millennium BC); and Yahya VA with the Late Bakun and Lapui periods (late fifth to early fourth millennium BC) (Voigt and Dyson 1992: 148–9; Petrie 2011: table 1). The phases of occupation at Yahya that date to the fifth millennium BC therefore include Yahya VI, VC, VB, and part of VA. After the Yahya VA phase, there was a hiatus in occupation at Tepe Yahya (see below).

The fifth millennium BC stratigraphic sequence at Tal-e Iblis largely overlaps with that from Tepe Yahya, and while there are clear parallels between the two sequences, occupation at Tal-e Iblis started later. As at Tepe Yahya, the sequence of occupation at Tal-e Iblis was divided into site-specific periods (Iblis 0/I being earliest and VII being latest).

However, this is not a sequence obtained from one set of interconnected trenches but rather from trenches dug into different mounds at the site (Areas A–G; Chase, Caldwell, and Fehérvári 1967; Voigt and Dyson 1992: 143–6). As with Tepe Yahya, there is a lack of consensus about the absolute dates of the individual chronological phases, partially as a result of imprecise dates that are in need of recalibration. As with Beale's Yahya dates, by and large the Tal-e Iblis radiocarbon ranges, as presented by Caldwell (1967: 24), are too late, but this has largely been resolved by the comprehensive relative chronological scheme outlined by Voigt and Dyson (1992) and confirmed by recalibrating the existing radiocarbon dates (Petrie 2011, forthcoming a).

Voigt and Dyson (1992: 143) argued that Iblis 0 should be combined with Iblis I. The resultant Iblis 0/I period has clear parallels with Yahya VII and VI and the Shamsabad and Early Bakun periods in Fars, indicating that it dates to the late sixth and early fifth millennia BC. The Iblis II period appears to be related to Yahya VC, VB, and VA, and to the Middle and Late Bakun phases in Fars, indicating that it probably ran from the early or mid- to the late fifth millennium BC (Voigt and Dyson 1992: 144–5).

Settlement distribution

Excavations at both Tal-e Iblis and Tepe Yahya were accompanied by surveys of the surrounding regions. To date, the Bard Sir plain has been surveyed multiple times (e.g., Chase, Fehérvári, and Caldwell 1967; Khosrowzadeh 2005), while the Soghun plain and the neighboring Shah Maran and Daulatabad Basin were the object of a protracted program of intensive and extensive survey (Prickett 1986a, 1986b).

Prickett's survey of the Shah Maran and Daulatabad Basin and her detailed work in the upper Rud-e Gushk drainage showed that early settlement in the region was largely concentrated on or around a series of large fans formed by the Rud-e Gushk as it flowed from the uplands to the northeast of the basin (Prickett 1986a, 1986b: 223, figs. 9.2, 9.3, and 9.5). In Yahya VII (Muradabad Phase), settlements were primarily located at the distal ends of alluvial fans, though some sites are located in the center of the basin, beyond the edge of the fan (Prickett 1986a: 555ff., 1986b: 233). In the neighboring Soghun valley Tepe Yahya was the only site with evidence of continuous occupation from Yahya VII to VI (Prickett 1986a). Between Yahya VI and VB (Soghun/Yahya Phase) there was a dramatic discontinuity in settlement location and density, as settled occupation moved away from the basin edge to locations further to the north on the distal fan and also onto the proximal fan. Prickett (1986a: 583ff, 1986b: 234) suggested that this was because of either increased flooding or decreased water flow. The northernmost area of settlement on the fan has clear evidence of a terrace field system, suggesting that this move was accompanied by agricultural intensification (Prickett 1986a: 656ff, 696ff, 1986b: 234–5).

Surveys of the Bard Sir have shown that there were few sites in Iblis 0/I and II, and in the early fourth millennium BC Iblis III period (fewer than four in each), before a dramatic change occurred in the later fourth millennium BC Iblis IV period (see below). Prickett (1986a: 767, 1986b: 237) observed that the known settlements with early (Iblis 0/I–II, Yahya VI–VB Soghun/Yahya Phase) occupation in southeastern Iran outside of the Shah Maran and Daulatabad Basin were scattered across Kerman, Sistan, and Baluchistan and were typically more than 10 km apart, the only exception being the pair of mounds at Chah Hussaini in the Bampur Basin (Prickett 1986a: 767, figs. 7.3–7.4; after Stein 1937: 128–130). Mutin (2012) has, however, suggested that most of these settlements were occupied only in the fourth millennium BC (i.e., Iblis III/IV and Yahya VA).

Settlement structure

Several building complexes dating to the fifth millennium BC were exposed at Tepe Yahya. A Period VIB building showed significant changes in construction techniques and architectural style compared with those of the ceramic Neolithic Period VII deposits, including the appearance of a new house type with walls made of thumb-impressed bricks, with external corner buttressing and raised interior corner hearths (Beale 1986: 127; Voigt and Dyson 1992: 148). Period VC had a large residential complex built above a platform supported by retaining walls constructed in Period VIA (Beale 1986: 140). Both of these building complexes appear to have been domestic (Beale 1986: 164; see below). Broadly contemporary buildings were exposed in Areas D, F, and G at Tal-e Iblis, all three of which date to the Iblis 0/I period (Evett 1967: 202ff.), spanning the late sixth to early fifth millennium BC. Based on an exhaustive analysis of room content and function, Evett (1967: 202, 219, 248–51; see below) proposed that these were domestic houses. Beale (1986: 164; also Voigt and Dyson 1992: 148) observed that the Iblis 0/I buildings were similar to those seen at Tepe Yahya, but noted that the rooms at Iblis were approximately 30 percent larger than their counterparts in Yahya VC, though the significance of this is unclear.

Ceramic and metal production

The earliest ceramics used in Kerman (Muradabad phase at Tappeh Gaz Tavila) were a local variety of undecorated soft-ware with a dense fabric akin to the unpainted Shamsabad ware from Fars (Prickett 1986a: 416–7, 1379–86, 1986b: 233; Voigt and Dyson 1992: 148; Petrie 2011). Similar material appeared slightly later in the earliest levels at Tepe Yahya (Period VII) (Beale 1986: 39–47) and later still at Tal-e Iblis (Iblis 0/I—paralleling Yahya Period VIB; Chase, Caldwell, and Fehérvári 1967: 149–50; Beale 1986: 39–42, 85–7, fig. 4.1; Voigt and Dyson 1992: 143, 148). Although it first appeared in the ceramic Neolithic, "soft-ware" continued to be used throughout the fifth millennium BC in Kerman, with a distinctive porous fabric being characteristic (Beale 1986: 39–43, fig. 4.1; Prickett 1986a: 417, 1387–91; Petrie 2011). Vandiver (1986, 1987) has proposed that these early vessels were made by a technique known as "sequential slab construction."

In Yahya VI this porous "soft-ware" appeared with small quantities of various fine wares that have been collectively referred to as Soghun ware (Beale 1986: 47ff., fig. 4.1; Voigt and Dyson 1992: 148). A Soghun Plain ware was attested during the ceramic Neolithic (Yahya VII), but during the early fifth millennium BC (Yahya VI), Soghun Mottled Purple, Soghun Red-painted, and Soghun Bichrome varieties of this ware all appeared (Beale 1986: 47–55). These are comparable to Bard Sir fine wares seen at Tal-i Iblis (Prickett 1986a; Voigt and Dyson 1992: 143; also Caldwell and Sarraf 1967: 306). They are hard and well fired, and are either wet smoothed or coated with a thick, buff slip (Beale 1986: 49–52). Some decorative motifs are comparable to designs found in the Early Bakun phase in Fars (Voigt and Dyson 1992: 148), but the technological innovations required to produce these wares appear to have developed independently in Kerman (Beale and Lamberg-Karlovsky 1986: 256; Vandiver 1986; Petrie 2011).

In the mid-fifth millennium BC, the distinctive, harder-fired, black-on-buff ware, which appeared in the Early Bakun phase in Fars at the beginning of the fifth millennium BC, first appeared at Tepe Yahya (Period VC). Analysis of some of this material revealed that it was imported from the west, probably from Fars (Kamilli and Lamberg-Karlovsky 1979; Beale 1986: 87; Voigt and Dyson 1992: 149). Many motifs characteristic of Bard Sir Painted ware from Early Iblis II appear also on Early and Middle Bakun ceramics in Fars (Beale 1986: 86–87, 1992: 284; Voigt and Dyson 1992: 149). It is notable that limited but significant quantities of vessels made from what has been labeled Lapui-related ware (5 percent of the assemblage), were also recovered in Yahya Period VC and Iblis II deposits, where they are called Bard Sir Red-slipped ware (Beale 1986: 55–8, 85–6). These wares appear to be related to a distinctive type of burnished and/or slipped red-ware that was first identified in Fars and used there in the very late fifth to early fourth millennium BC (see below). Prickett (1986a: 1391–6) implied that the Lapui-related wares from southeastern Iran did not have a consistent red fabric or slip but appeared in different colors (e.g., purple-and-brown-polished, tan to light orange fabric), suggesting stylistic differences between Lapui-related wares in Kerman and classic Lapui ware in Fars (see below). Beale (1986: 87) suggested that interaction between Fars and Kerman stopped after Yahya Period VC. The Lapui-related wares increased in quantity in Period VB and appeared together with locally produced Black-on-Buff Ware, Coarse Ware, and Red-painted Coarse Ware (Beale 1986: 87, fig. 4.1, 1992: 284; Voigt and Dyson 1992: 149). These wares appear to be contemporaneous with the Early and Late Iblis II phases and also the Middle and Late Bakun phases in Fars (Voigt and Dyson 1992: 149; Petrie 2011).

The fifth millennium BC in Kerman saw increasing sophistication in the organization of ceramic production (Vandiver 1986: 99, fig. 5.3), but there is no primary evidence of ceramic production other than the fired vessels and sherds themselves. The evidence for the importation of black-on-buff ware vessels from Fars to Kerman in the mid-fifth millennium BC (Yahya V/Iblis II; Beale 1986: 86–7) potentially explains the adoption and elaboration of related production technologies in the later fifth millennium BC for the local production of black-on-buff ware (Beale 1986: 67–82, 257, fig. 4.1), but it is important not to overemphasize the impact of influence from the southwest. The dating of the first appearance of Lapui-related red ware vessel forms suggests that Lapui-related wares and the associated technological traditions and innovations appeared earlier in Kerman than in Fars and likely had an eastern origin (Beale 1986: 87; Voigt and Dyson 1992: 145, 149; see below).

More and more copper-based artifacts were recovered from Tepe Yahya Period VI to VA deposits, showing increasing sophistication in production technology involving casting, hammering, and annealing (Heskel and Lamberg-Karlovsky 1986; Thornton and Lamberg-Karlovsky 2004), though there is no direct evidence that production was taking place at Tepe Yahya itself. There is, however, a range of evidence for copper smelting at Tal-e Iblis during the early fifth millennium BC, including crucible sherds in Iblis I and II deposits (Dougherty and Caldwell 1967; Smith et al. 1967). Crucible fragments were also found in Iblis II and III period deposits in Areas A, C, and E, apparently amongst domestic refuse (Evett 1967: 254). A shallow firepit containing a crucible fragment and fragments of oxidized copper was also found in Area G in levels dating to the Iblis II (Bard Sir) period, indicating that some smelting took place within the settlement itself (Evett 1967: 252). Similar firepits, but without copper ore, were found in other parts of Area G, and Evett (1967: 254) argued that this might imply "backyard," nonspecialist copper production, which may be better termed small-scale, household production.

Analyses of crucible fragments have shown that copper carbonates, sulfides, arsenates, and chlorides were smelted in elongated, bowl-shaped crucibles, in simple charcoal-filled pits, to produce copper with variable arsenical content (Pigott and Lechtman 2003: 294–5; Weeks 2012: 301). Frame (2004: fig. 5.46) has shown that temperatures of around 1200°C were achieved through the use of forced drafts produced by blowpipes and bellows (Weeks 2012: 301).

Socioeconomy

We can only speculate on the socioeconomy of southeastern Iran during the fifth millennium BC. Beale and Lamberg-Karlovsky (1986: 252) pointed out that while the presence of four- and five-roomed houses at Tepe Yahya and Tal-i Iblis implies that the core economic unit was the nuclear or extended family, these structures also have courtyards with surrounding walls, and even more space appears to be taken up by some individual household units. The Yahya VC building, in particular, indicates that individual living units existed within a larger complex and that each of these managed its own subsistence, prompting Beale and Lamberg-Karlovsky (1986: 253) to suggest that nuclear and extended families were related. In Yahya VB, the multigroup structures were replaced by single-family complexes with their own walls and courtyard, which conforms to a pattern of larger-scale, communal economic units based on extended families, and this continued into Yahya VA (Beale and Lamberg-Karlovsky 1986: 254, 262). The reasons for this shift are unclear but may have included environmental pressure, including hydrological change, and population pressure (Beale and Lamberg-Karlovsky 1986: 262). The other major shift that occurred was the abandonment of Tepe Yahya after Period VA and the abandonment of the Shah Maran and Daulatabad Basin after the Iblis IV/V transition (Prickett 1986a: 599ff., 1986b: 236–7; see below).

The appearance at Tepe Yahya of ceramic imports from Fars indicates the broadening of the world of the site's inhabitants toward the west, but expanded contact with areas to the east is also attested (Beale and Lamberg-Karlovsky 1986: 256; Mutin 2013). Perhaps more importantly, the fifth millennium BC saw increasing sophistication in ceramic and metallurgical technology locally in Kerman, demonstrating that significant socioeconomic developmental processes were underway in southeastern Iran during the fifth millennium BC.

The fourth millennium BC

Southwestern Iran

In the fourth millennium BC southwestern Iran experienced a number of dramatic social, economic, and political changes that are reflected in technological and stylistic changes in the production and use of material culture, the development of new forms of social organization, and new patterns of trade and influence. Overt technological changes in ceramic production during the fourth millennium BC included a progressive increase in the speed of rotation used in vessel forming until the fast wheel was adopted and the incorporation of a number of what appear to be "disposable" vessel forms, including the distinctive bevel-rim bowl (Blackman 1989; Petrie 2011). In addition, there were changes to settlement systems and subsistence practices, the most dramatic of which saw the development of the first highland urban center at Tal-e Malyan. The major cultural phases of the fourth millennium BC in Fars are referred to as the Lapui and Banesh periods, the latter being divided into Early, Middle, and Late Banesh phases (Sumner 1986: 199; 1988a: 317; 2003), though Alden (1979: 47–52; 2003b; Sumner 2003: 53) earlier subdivided the Banesh period into Initial, Early, Early Middle, Late Middle, and Late Banesh subphases. Tal-e Malyan became urban in scale during the Middle Banesh period and although a fortification wall was built around it during the Late Banesh period, the occupied area reduced in size. The Late Banesh phase largely falls within the third millennium BC and is covered in Chapter 15 of this volume.

Basis of knowledge

Our initial knowledge of the Lapui period came from surface surveys in the KRB (Sumner 1972, 1988b), though Lapui sites have now also been discovered in other valleys and plains, including areas to the north of the KRB (Alizadeh 2003, 2006; Sardari and Rezaei 2007; Sardari 2012) and the Mamasani region of northwestern Fars (Zeidi et al. 2009; McCall 2009). What is called Lapui ware was first found at Tal-e Bakun A and initially labeled Bakun AV ware as it was found in the disturbed upper levels above the Period IV structures at Tal-e Bakun A (McCown 1942: 48; Langsdorff and McCown 1942: 32–3, pls. 20–21; Sumner 1988b: 24, 28). For many years the stratigraphic relationship between the Late Bakun and Lapui periods was unclear, and it was not until excavations at Tol-e Spid in the Mamasani region in 2003 and 2007 that clearly stratified evidence from the Lapui period was revealed (Petrie et al. 2007, 2009). A 2 × 1 m deep sounding excavated at Tol-e Spid exposed 7 m of occupation deposit dating to the fourth millennium BC, 6 m of which dates to the Lapui period (Phases 32–20; Petrie et al. 2007,

2009, et al. 2013). Lapui period deposits have also been exposed at Tol-e Nurabad (Phases A13–A12: Weeks et al. 2009). Knowledge of the Lapui period was dramatically expanded in 2006 with the excavation of Tappeh Mehr Ali, on the Sedeh plain in northern Fars, where a sequence of fifth millennium BC Bakun occupation (see above) overlain by 6 m of Lapui-period occupation was revealed (Sardari 2012). This is the first sequence of its kind in southwestern Iran and is potentially the most important fifth and early fourth millennium BC sequence in Fars.

The Lapui period saw distinct changes in ceramic technology and style from those used in the Bakun period, as well as shifts in settlement location, and it has also been suggested that there were changes in approaches to subsistence. The new ceramic tradition that first appeared in Fars near the end of the fifth millennium BC comprised two distinctive red wares, one coarse and one fine (Sumner 1988b; Petrie et al. 2009, 2012; see below). Lapui settlements were almost exclusively small villages (Sumner 1988b), and although larger Bakun period settlements (up to 7.8 ha) have been found in the KRB (Sumner 1994; see above), no large Lapui period settlements have yet been recorded (Sumner 1988b). The excavations at Tol-e Spid and Tappeh Mir Ali show that Lapui period populations lived in mudbrick and/or *chineh* buildings and had a subsistence economy based on the exploitation of domesticated goat, sheep, cattle, and pig, along with wheat, barley, and lentils (Mashkour 2009; Shaikhi 2008; Petrie et al. 2013; Sardari 2012; see below).

In the KRB, the Lapui period was succeeded by the Banesh period, which spans the mid- to late fourth millennium BC and was marked by the adoption of a range of vegetal and grit-tempered fabrics (Sumner 1972, 1986, 1988a). Most of our knowledge of the Banesh period comes from surveys and limited excavations conducted in the KRB. Banesh period deposits have been revealed in a 2 × 1 m sounding at Tal-e Kureh (Initial and Early Banesh; Alden 1979: 48–50, fig. 52; 2003a: 187–98, D1–D8) and in Operations ABC, TUV, GHI, and By8 at Tal-e Malyan (Middle and Late Banesh; Sumner 1988a; 2003; Alden 1979; 2003c; Nicholas 1990; Miller and Sumner 2004; Alden et al. 2005). Beyond these excavations, the primary information about the separate Banesh subphases of the mid- to late fourth millennium BC comes from surveys (Sumner 1972; Alden 1979, 2003b). Outside of the KRB, knowledge of mid- to late fourth millennium BC occupation is limited, and primarily comes from excavations at Tol-e Spid (Phase 18; Petrie et al. 2009) and Tol-e Nurabad (Phases A11–A6; Weeks et al. 2009), and the regional survey carried out in Mamasani (Zeidi et al. 2009; McCall 2009).

Chronology

Tappeh Mir Ali is currently the only site in Fars that potentially has excavated evidence covering the transition between the Late Bakun and Lapui phases, but the only radiocarbon dates available from the site come from the Lapui period deposits (Sardari 2012). As noted above, the clearest *terminus ante quem* for the end of the Bakun period in Fars is the earliest radiocarbon date from the Lapui levels at Tol-e Spid (Phase 30), which has a range of 4050–3910 cal BC (Petrie 2015). There is no evidence for the continuation of the Bakun black-on-buff ceramic tradition into the early fourth millennium BC at the site (Petrie et al. 2007, 2009, 2013), although Sumner suggested that there was a phase during which both Bakun and Lapui ceramic wares were used (Sumner 1988b: 28–31). While the Tol-e Spid radiocarbon date indicates that the Late Bakun period ended in the late fifth millennium BC, it also indicates that the Lapui period may have begun as early as the very late fifth millennium BC (Petrie et al. 2007, 2013).

There are thirteen radiocarbon dates for the remainder of the Lapui sequence at Tol-e Spid (Phases 29 to 20), and their internal consistency and overlapping ranges show that the settlement was occupied more or less continuously throughout the first half of the fourth millennium BC, until 3510 BC and possibly as late as 3380 BC (Wk13979: 3710–3510 cal BC [94.1 percent], 3400–3380 cal BC [1.4 percent]; Petrie et al. 2007, 2009, 2013). Although there are radiocarbon dates from Terminal Lapui and Initial Banesh levels at Tal-e Kureh (Voigt and Dyson 1992; Sumner 2003), these have standard deviations of 230–290 years, which means that, after calibration, they have date ranges of up to 2000 years, making them essentially unusable (Petrie forthcoming a). The excavations at Tol-e Spid also provide some insight into the nature and chronology of the transition between the Lapui and Banesh periods. Tol-e Spid Phase 19 witnessed the first appearance of bevel-rim bowl fragments, and the radiocarbon determination from this phase (Wk13981: 3760–3520 cal BC) is statistically identical to the latest Lapui period date, indicating that the Transitional Lapui/Banesh phase at the site dates to the mid-fourth millennium BC.

Lapui ceramics have also been found stratified above Bakun black-on-buff ceramics at Tol-e Nurabad, although it is likely that there was a gap between the two phases (Weeks et al. 2009; Petrie et al. 2009b). Radiocarbon dates show that fourth millennium BC occupation at Tol-e Nurabad began during the Late Lapui period (Phase A13–A12b; OZI134: 3640–3490 cal BC [76.2 percent], 3440–3370 cal BC [19.2 percent]) and continued throughout the Initial, Early, Middle, and Late Banesh periods (Phases A12a/A11–A6). This is the only excavated sequence of continuous, late fourth millennium BC occupation in southwestern Iran (Weeks et al. 2009: 68–70). Precise dates from Late Lapui/Initial Banesh (Phase A12a/A11; 3650–3300 cal BC [84 percent], 3250–3100 cal BC [11.4 percent]) and Initial/Early Banesh deposits (Phase A10; WK13998: 3640–3360 BC) at Tol-e Nurabad containing bevel-rim bowl fragments correspond well with the date of the Lapui–Banesh transition at Tol-e Spid.

There are no radiocarbon dates for the Early Banesh or Early Middle Banesh periods in the KRB, though the presence of bevel-rim bowl fragments together with a range of local forms led Alden (2003b) to propose that the Early Banesh phase there was contemporary with the latest Susa II levels (Acropole I.17 and I.17x; Sumner 2003: 52–3). This correlation implies that Alden's Terminal Lapui and the Initial Banesh phases are partially contemporaneous with the earlier Susa II period in Susiana (presumably Acropole I Levels 22–18; Potts et al. 2009; Petrie et al. 2009a). Drooping tube spouts and jars with nose lugs were recovered from the surface of Tal-e Qarib and two other sites in the KRB (Alden 1979: figs. 45.3; 47.10, 15, 20, 22), and this feature led Alden to propose that all three were occupied in the Early Middle Banesh phase, which is also contemporary with late Susa II (Acropole I.17 and I.17x; Alden 1979: 198–200, 353, table 48). This relative chronology is congruent with the radiocarbon dates from the Mamasani sites.

Tal-e Malyan had extensive and well-dated evidence for occupation dating to the Middle Banesh period, which is contemporary with Susa III (i.e., the proto-Elamite period proper) (Sumner 2003: table 12; Voigt and Dyson 1992: 141; Potts 1999: 71ff.; Petrie 2015). The major Middle Banesh phase occupation at Tal-e Malyan (Phase III in Operation ABC) comprised a monumental building and its associated tablets, seals, and wall paintings (Sumner 1988a: 308; 2003). Additional architecture was exposed in TUV (Nicholas 1990). There are also two earlier phases of occupation (Phases IV and V) in ABC (Sumner 1988a; 2003). Although there are no radiocarbon dates from the ABC Phase V levels, Pittman (2013) observed that the seals and sealings recovered there have strong parallels to the material from Susa Acropole I.17, implying that this phase may be Early Banesh or Early Middle Banesh in date (Sumner 2003: 52–3). ABC Phase IV and III both have radiocarbon dates but by and large these span the period between 3350 and 3000 BC (Voigt and Dyson 1992 2: 131, table 2; Sumner 2003) and are statistically identical to the Middle Banesh dates from Tol-e Nurabad and Tol-e Spid, which both span the period from 3350–3000 BC (Weeks et al. 2009; Petrie et al. 2009b; Petrie 2015). The dating of the Middle Banesh phase to such a broad time span means that it overlaps with the projected date ranges for the Late Uruk and Jamdat Nasr periods in Mesopotamia, the Susa II/Late Uruk (I.22–18), Susa II/III Transition (I.17–17X) and Susa III/proto-Elamite (I.16–14B) occupations at Susa, as well as Godin VI:1, Sialk IV_{1-2}, Jebel Aruda and Habuba Kabira (Petrie 2015; Dahl et al. 2013). This dating thus has significant implications for our understanding of cultural dynamics and interaction during this period, but it is potentially irrevocably hampered by the presence of a significant plateau in the radiocarbon calibration curve between c.3350–2900 BC (Petrie 2015; Dahl et al. 2013; cf. Wright 1985: 96–7).

Settlement distribution

The KRB provides the largest set of settlement distribution data for the fourth millennium BC in highland southwestern Iran (Sumner 1972, 1988b, 1990). Prior to the recent excavations at Tol-e Spid, Tol-e Nurabad, and Tappeh Mir Ali, virtually all that was known about the Lapui and Banesh periods in Fars came from the surveys in the KRB (Sumner 1988b, 1990; Alden 1979; 2003b) and the excavations at Tal-e Malyan (Sumner 1988a; 2003) and Tal-e Kureh (Alden 2003a, 2003b).

The distinctive red-slipped and coarse-burnished Lapui red wares were found on the surface of as many as 108 sites in the KRB (Sumner 1990). Following a similar interpretative approach to that applied to the Bakun period survey data, Sumner differentiated Lapui/Bakun, Middle Lapui, and Banesh/Lapui stages of occupation (Sumner 1988b: 29, tables 3–4). A significant number of sites presented evidence of both Bakun and Lapui period occupation (75 of 156; Sumner 1988b: table 1; 1989: table 2), and from this Sumner (1988b: 29–30) inferred cultural continuity between the two periods. This interpretation of the survey data from the KRB suggested that the Lapui period marked a progressive drop in the settled population, from 65 settlements in the Bakun/Lapui to 58 in the Middle Lapui and 18/28 in the Lapui/Banesh (Sumner 1988b: 31, table 3).

There is no unequivocal evidence for settlement hierarchy in the Lapui period in Fars (Sumner 1988b). Most Lapui period settlements in the KRB were under 2 ha, and only four sites were 2–3.5 ha (Sumner 1988b: 32–3, fig. 4). It has not yet been possible to establish the size of the Lapui period occupation at either Tol-e Nurabad or Tol-e Spid in Mamasani, though the former may have been approximately 3–4 ha and the latter up to 2 ha in size. The largest of the other known sites with Lapui period occupation in Mamasani, Tappeh Mishband, is only 1.5 ha in size (Zeidi et al. 2009; McCall 2009). It thus seems likely that the population of Fars in the early to mid-fourth millennium BC lived in both small and large villages.

Two different surveys, using distinct approaches to document and interpret, have investigated Banesh period settlement in the KRB. On the basis of his survey evidence, Sumner (1972; 1988b: 30, table 3) proposed that there was a degree of settlement continuity between the Lapui and the subsequent Banesh periods, as there is evidence for Lapui period occupation at twenty-eight of his forty-six Banesh sites (Sumner 1988b; 1990: table 2). Relying on ceramic indicators, Alden (2012) has suggested that only ten of these sites have clearly transitional occupation, while twenty-three Banesh period sites could not be assigned to a subphase, though they were incorporated in Sumner's calculations. In general, the pattern of progressive decline in the density of sedentary settlement does appear to have continued into the Banesh period. Other than occupation at Tal-e Malyan and Tal-e Qarib, Sumner (1986: 202, 206) suggested that there were twenty-one villages in the KRB during the Early Banesh, seventeen during the Middle Banesh, and fifteen villages during the Late Banesh, implying a gradual decline of the village-based population.

There are clear signs of change in settlement structure and distribution in the Early Banesh period, continuing into the Middle Banesh. Sumner (1986: 200) and Alden (2012) identified the beginnings of settlement clustering in particularly well-watered locations in the KRB during the Early Banesh period, including clusters of mounds at Tal-e Qarib and Dorudzan and a possible third cluster that is potentially buried under later occupation at Tal-e Malyan. All of this suggests the existence of two-stage, hierarchy-dominated, town-sized centers during the Early Banesh. During the Middle Banesh phase, the Tal-e Qarib and Dorudzan clusters were abandoned and Tal-e Malyan grew into a city-sized settlement ($c.$50 ha), apparently continuing the two-tier hierarchy but that is slightly different than Sumner's (1986: 202) interpretation, which included occupation at Tal-e Qarib in this phase. With the abandonment of Tal-e Qarib, ceramic production appears to have shifted to Tal-e Malyan (Blackman 1981). The growth of Tal-e Malyan as a regional center appears to have coincided with an overall decline in the number of settlements (Sumner 1986), perhaps as a result of the nucleation of the KRB population (see below).

Ceramics

Perhaps the most overt indicator of cultural change in southwestern Iran in the late fifth to early fourth millennium BC was the appearance of the distinctive Lapui red ware ceramics. The Lapui ceramic tradition comprises two red wares: a coarse ware, which typically has grit inclusions and an irregularly burnished surface, and a fine ware, which has either a red or a buff fabric and a polished red slip (Sumner 1988b; Blackman 1989; Petrie et al. 2009a). In contrast to the elaborately decorated, calcareous black-on-buff Bakun pottery, the Lapui period ceramics typically lack decoration. The approaches to ceramic paste preparation, techniques of vessel production, and surface-finishing processes that were used to produce these distinctive Lapui red wares represent a marked shift from the *châine opératoire* used to produce the black-on-buff wares of the Bakun period, particularly in the selection of raw materials (Blackman 1989: 104). Lapui coarse ware appears to have been produced from clay with naturally occurring coarse inclusions, while the fine ware was made from either fine low-calcium clay, or fine high-calcium clay and a low-calcium red slip (Blackman 1989: 104–5; Petrie 2011). Although very rare, painted ceramics dating to the Lapui period have been identified. An unusual painted ware with a fine buff paste, called Asupas Ware, has been found on the surface of as many as six sites in the KRB (Alden 2012: table 2; contra Sumner 1972: 41–2). Painted Lapui wares have also been excavated in Early and Middle Lapui contexts at Tol-e Spid (Phases 27 and 23; Petrie et al. 2009a: fig. 4.51; Petrie et al. 2013).

These Lapui wares were used to produce a limited range of vessel forms, including open bowls, beakers with upright or flared rims, holemouth jars, and jars with out-turned rims. Most of these appear to have been turned on a slow wheel or tournette (Sumner 1972: 40–2; 1988b: 25–7; Blackman 1989; Petrie et al. 2009a; Petrie 2011). The uniformity of many of the vessel forms shows that steps were being taken toward standardizing the assemblage (Petrie 2011). These changes suggest that there were moves toward efficiency and increased product specialization between the Bakun and Lapui periods (Petrie 2011).

The red wares that characterize the deposits from Phases 30–20 at Tol-e Spid have close parallels with Lapui ceramics from the KRB but show clear signs of gradual change in production technology and style over time (Petrie et al. 2013). Judging by the Tol-e Spid sounding, Lapui fine red ware, particularly the red-slipped variety, increased in frequency and proportion through time and continued in use during the Banesh period (Petrie et al. 2013). Pilot compositional analysis of fourth millennium BC ceramics from several sites in Mamasani has shown that several local sources of raw materials were exploited during the Lapui period and that the coarse and fine wares were produced using compositionally distinct raw materials (Petrie et al. forthcoming). Kiln sites dating to the Lapui period have been discovered in various areas in the KRB, suggesting that ceramic production remained both specialized and centralized, as it had been in the Bakun period (Sumner 1988b: 33).

Alden identified a Terminal Lapui phase beneath the earliest Banesh layers at Tal-e Kureh and proposed that the ceramics used during this phase were akin to the Lapui fine ware forms found on the surface of the site (Alden 2003a: 187–8, 195–6; 1979: fig. 52). He also identified an Initial Banesh phase characterized by the appearance of bevel-rim bowls, but the absence of low-sided trays, incised shoulder decoration, and the reserved slip decoration so common in Susiana and Mesopotamia (Alden 1979: 152–6; 2003a: 196–8, table D1). Subsequent to the Lapui period phases at both Tol-e Spid and Tol-e Nurabad, there is evidence for what appears to be a transitional period during which the use of Lapui-type grit-tempered and red-slipped wares continued but in which distinctive vessels made from vegetal and vegetal and grit-tempered wares began appearing, including bevel-rim bowls (TN Phase A12a–A11, Weeks et al. 2009: 76; TS Phase 19; Petrie et al. 2009a: 129).

With the shift to the Early Banesh period proper, the bevel-rim bowl appeared more frequently in the highlands (Potts 2009), but this form is one of the few indicators of contact with the lowlands at this time (Alden 1979, 1982, 2003a). The Early Banesh phase was marked by the appearance of distinctive highland forms such as pinched rim bowls, goblets, and trays (Alden 1979: 50; 2012). Surveys have shown that chaff-tempered goblets and trays were produced at Tal-e Qarib, while grit-tempered vessels that were being redistributed from Tal-e Qarib were being produced at Tal-e Kureh (Alden 1979: 50, 2003a, 2013; Sumner 1986: 200). There was thus centralized production along product-specific lines (Alden 1979; Blackman 1981, 1989; see Petrie 2011) and organized redistribution taking place in the KRB (Alden 2013).

The ceramics produced and used during the Middle Banesh period in the KRB were largely a continuation of the Early Banesh material, with the addition of chaff-tempered goblets with necked bases and concave chaff-tempered goblet rims (Alden 2012). It appears that the production and redistribution center at Tal-e Qarib was abandoned at this point, and production presumably shifted to Tal-e Malyan (Blackman 1981: 16–17). The Middle Banesh ceramic assemblage at Tol-e Spid is largely similar to that seen at sites in the KRB, but there is also evidence of continuity in the tradition of manufacturing red-slipped ware vessels, which has not been observed in the KRB (Petrie et al. 2009a). It is notable that the Middle Banesh deposits at Tol-e Nurabad produced no examples of the Banesh low-sided trays or goblet bases and few examples of chaff-tempered goblet rims. The variation between the ceramic assemblages of the two Mamasani sites, and between them and those in the KRB, may indicate a degree of regional variability in Banesh period ceramic assemblages in Fars (Petrie et al. 2009b).

There is clear evidence of changes in the organization of ceramic production during the fourth millennium BC and a dramatic shift toward simplicity and efficiency in both the production process and the finished products (Petrie 2011). Many of the technological changes were related to the minimization of energy expenditure and the maximization of the rate of production of individual vessels. Although new techniques were introduced, the new material culture elements such as wheel- and mold-made vessel forms were nested within the existing local material culture assemblages, and preexisting production technologies were maintained for the production of certain vessel forms in some areas (Petrie 2011, 2015). Given the clear shift toward the use of more efficient production techniques through time, it seems likely that the role of ceramics themselves also underwent a change with the start of the fourth millennium BC.

Socioeconomy

Various interpretations of the changing socioeconomy for the fourth millennium BC in southwestern Iran have been put forward, typically involving nomadic pastoralism. Sumner (1988b: 39) argued that the decline in settlement numbers during the Lapui period that he observed reflected an initial shift away from field crops toward more intensive pastoralism and ultimately a mobile pastoralist way of life. In contrast, Alizadeh (2006: 49–50) has suggested that the Lapui period actually saw a population increase and argued that the shift toward a mobile pastoralist way of life occurred in the Late Bakun period. It is important to note, however, that there is considerable evidence for continued occupation of settlement mounds, particularly at Tol-e Spid and Tappeh Mir Ali, which suggests that a significant proportion of Lapui populations continued to be settled agriculturalists, who might have engaged in one or more approaches to pastoralism (Abdi 2003).

We know almost nothing about the internal settlement dynamics and the nature of socioeconomic organization in the Lapui period, as the excavations at Tappeh Mir Ali and Tol-e Spid have exposed only small areas of domestic dwellings (Sardari 2012; Petrie et al. 2013). Signs of ceramic production have been found at many but not all of the surveyed sites in the KRB, and no evidence for ceramic production has been recovered at Tappeh Mir Ali or Tol-e Spid, suggesting that a production system similar to that seen in the Bakun period may have been in place. The range of luxury or imported goods at Lapui sites is very limited and includes stone vessels that were probably made locally, at least in Fars (e.g., Petrie et al. 2009a). The excavations at Tappeh Mir Ali have, however, revealed evidence of the use of stamp seals that are akin to those found at Tal-e Bakun A, indicating that similar sealing and administrative practices may have been practiced there (Sardari 2012).

The absolute chronologies of the later fifth millennium BC ceramic assemblages from Kerman (see above) and Khuzestan (Petrie 2011) suggest that burnished red wares were in use in both of these regions before they was used in Fars, where they did not appear with any frequency until the very end of the fifth millennium BC, at which time they completely replaced painted buff wares. Although this suggests that the technology was introduced from Fars, Blackman (1989: 104–6) has argued that the observed changes are unlikely to have been the result of the introduction of new, previously unknown technology, through diffusion, innovation, or migration, but are more likely to have been the result of cultural responses to changing socioeconomic requirements.

The shift from the Lapui to Initial Banesh periods, as seen at Tol-e Spid, Tol-e Nurabad, and Tal-e Kureh, witnessed the introduction of new vessel forms from the lowlands, and although this indicates that communication took place between the lowland and highland regions of southwestern Iran, the significance of the appearance of bevel-rim bowls is not entirely clear (Petrie et al. 2009b; Petrie 2011; Potts 2009). Alden (1979: 157; 1982: 620–21) initially proposed that it marked the arrival of lowland traders eager to secure control over the importation of numerous highland resources. Similar vessels are also known from the Bard Sir, which is an area of precocious metalworking technology, and also in the Halil Rud region and even at Miri Qalat in Paksitani Baluchistan (see below), but their presence in all of these regions need not be a result of control being exerted from lowland Khuzestan or Mesopotamia. For example, Potts (2009) has shown that bevel-rim bowls are very widely distributed across Iran, and although they may be indicative of contact, they are unlikely to be a proxy for lowland control, and might in fact be indicative of culinary influence, perhaps in breadmaking (Goulder 2010). This suggests that the level of lowland influence in the mid- to late fourth millennium BC has been overstated.

Evidence of Banesh period architecture is very limited. As with the Lapui period, the excavations at Tol-e Spid exposed only very small areas of Banesh period domestic dwellings (Petrie et al. 2013), while the excavations at Tal-e Kureh and Banesh levels at Tol-e Nurabad revealed no architectural remains (Weeks et al. 2009). This means what little we know of the nature of socioeconomic structure in the Early Banesh period comes from the evidence for centralized ceramic production along product-specific lines at Tal-e Qarib and Tal-e Kureh and the organized redistribution taking place from Tal-e Qarib (Alden 1979, 2012; Blackman 1981, 1989; see Petrie 2011). This evidence implies a degree of economic and potentially also political integration that presaged the appearance of urbanism in the KRB (Alden 2012).

The Early Middle Banesh phase is distinguished by the foundation of Tal-e Malyan, which began as a town-sized settlement and then grew to c.45–50 ha in size to become a major regional urban center in the Late Middle Banesh phase (Sumner 1988a: 309; 2003: 113–17). The importance of Tal-e Malyan is emphasized by the evidence for specialized craft production, monumental architecture decorated with wall paintings, and proto-Elamite or Susa III protocuneiform tablets, seals, and sealings, attesting to the operation of a complex administrative system (Sumner 1988a: 309; 2003: 113–17; Voigt and Dyson 1992 1: 131ff.; Potts 1999: 81–3; Petrie 2015; see Chapter 13).

Alden has previously argued that the rise of Banesh period complexity was an indigenous highland development, accompanied by substantial immigration into the KRB from Khuzestan (Alden 1979: 166; 1982: 620; Lamberg-Karlovsky 1978: 116; see below). In contrast, Sumner (1986b: 200) argued that similar evolutionary processes were operating in both Susiana and the Zagros highlands, which "simultaneously produced the first stages of Proto-Elamite civilization," and suggested that these developments were internally motivated and connected to the transition to mobile pastoralism that involved the rise of tribal *khans*, resulting from a progressive agricultural crisis (Sumner 1986: 200, 207; 2003: 113). More recently, Alden (2012) has revisited Sumner's proposal and advocated the role of tribal *khans* and mobile pastoralism in this process. It is worth pointing out that the Middle Banesh phase shows no major transformation in the faunal assemblage to that of earlier phases (e.g., Mashkour 2009; Petrie et al. 2013). It is therefore entirely possible that scenarios for the rise of highland urbanism that do not involve mobile pastoralists should be explored.

Southeastern Iran

Our understanding of the archaeology of the fourth millennium BC in southeastern Iran is limited, though increasing. Although most of our evidence comes from Kerman, there is an increasing amount of survey data for occupation in Sistan, Baluchistan, and Hormuzgan (see below). In addition to evidence of connections to the southwest, there is also evidence for linkages with the eastern reaches of Pakistani Baluchistan through the excavations at Miri Qalat and Shahi-Tump (Mutin 2012, 2013).

In many ways, the fourth millennium BC in southeastern Iran was a period of profound transformation, marked by dramatic changes in settlement distribution and cultural connections with the surrounding regions. The significance and rationale for these connections are of considerable importance to our understanding of models of long-range interaction throughout south Iran.

Basis of knowledge

For the fourth millennium BC it is again the survey of the Shah Maran and Daulatabad Basin (Prickett 1986a, 1986b) and the excavations at Tepe Yahya (Beale 1986) and the surveys of the Bard Sir and the excavations at Tal-e Iblis (e.g., Caldwell 1967; Chase, Fehérvári. and Caldwell 1967; Chase, Caldwell, and Fehérvári 1967; Khosrowzadeh 2005) that provide the clearest evidence for the chronological sequences, settlement dynamics, cultural material, and socioeconomics of the core of southeastern Iran. This includes a building in Yahya Period IVC2 that is unlike any before or after it at the site and contains evidence for sealings, tablet blanks, and tablets inscribed in proto-Elamite (Potts 2001: 1, 10ff.).

Surveys of the Bampur, Shahdad, and Halil Rud regions, and the Sistan Basin (Stein 1937; Tosi 1968, 1970; Hakemi 1997; Sajjadi 2004, Sajjadi et al. 2008; Madjidzadeh 2008), have revealed evidence of settlements dating to the fourth millennium BC. There is now excavated evidence of fourth millennium BC occupation at Mahtoutabad in the Halil Rud (Vidale and Desset 2013), and there also appears to be a large fourth millennium BC mound in the Shahdad region (Potts 1980: 430; Salvatori and Vidale 1982; Tepe I, Vidale et al. 2012).

Chronology

There are several problems with the absolute chronology of the fourth millennium BC in southeastern Iran. In addition to problems with the size of the standard deviation and calibration of the available radiocarbon dates, there are also gaps in the excavated sequences and instances of settlement discontinuity in the available survey data that make it difficult to interpret the available evidence and to clearly outline its significance for socioeconomic and political dynamics.

The fourth millennium BC occupation at Tepe Yahya begins with Yahya Period VA, which correlates with the Late Bakun and Lapui periods and thus spans the late fifth to early fourth millennium BC (Voigt and Dyson 1992: 148–9; Petrie 2011: table 1). At the end of Yahya VA, the settlement was abandoned and there is evidence of a protracted hiatus in the form of erosion deposits visible in the south trench (Beale 1986: 11; Potts 2001: 1). Elsewhere there is evidence in the Soghun valley, and even at Yahya itself, that there was some occupation in this region during the hiatus (Prickett 1986b; Voigt and Dyson 1992 1: 149). After this hiatus, Tepe Yahya was resettled for a short time in Phase IVC2, and was then subsequently abandoned once again, although there is disagreement over the duration of this abandonment (Potts 2001: 199–202; Lamberg-Karlovsky 2001: 271–6; Petrie forthcoming a).

The precise duration of Yahya VA is unclear, as the three radiocarbon dates have large standard deviations and recalibration shows that they span a period of 2500 years (c.4950–2355 cal BC), which does not conform to any of the relative comparanda for the Yahya VA cultural material. The recalibrated age for the most coherent radiocarbon date from Yahya VA is 4225–3640 cal BC, which matches the suggestion that this period was contemporaneous with the Late Bakun and Lapui periods in Fars. Various dates have been proposed for the end of Yahya VA, ranging from 3900 BC (Prickett 1986a: table 3.2) to 3400 BC (Lamberg-Karlovsky 1970: 5) or 3300 BC (Beale 1986: 11). Of these, a date of 3400 BC, or even 3600 BC, conforms best with the recalibrated date. However, as Potts (2001: 195) has pointed out, each of these possibilities has a different set of ramifications for the duration of the subsequent hiatus, the end of which is controlled by the dating of the beginning of the Yahya IVC2 occupation, which has typically been dated to the final centuries of the fourth millennium BC, c.3400–3000 BC (Potts 2001: 195). As noted above, there are problems with radiocarbon dating the end of the fourth millennium BC because of a plateau in the calibration curve, and this, combined with the large standard deviations for most of the Tepe Yahya radiocarbon dates, means that the Yahya fourth millennium BC dates are not informative. Analysis of the relative and absolute chronology of Susa III and proto-Elamite tablets has indicated that the tablets from Tepe Yahya date to the very end of the sequence, so presumably c.3100–2900 BC (Dahl et al. 2013). If this is the case, then it would mean that the length of the hiatus between Yahya VA and IVC2 may have been up to 500 years. The date of the end of Yahya IVC2 is also unclear and may be as late as 2800 BC, as indicated largely by a range of relative parallels between material from Tepe Yahya and Jamdat Nasr and Early Dynastic I material from Susa and sites in Mesopotamia (Potts 2001: 196; Amiet 1976; Dittmann 1986).

At Tal-e Iblis, the fourth millennium BC is represented by Iblis III and IV. There is relatively limited evidence for the Iblis III or Dashkar period, primarily from poorly stratified contexts (Voigt and Dyson 1992 1: 145). Parallels between the various types of Iblis III and Dashkar pottery, Yahya VA and Lapui wares from Fars indicate an early fourth millennium BC date (Voigt and Dyson 1992; Petrie 2011). The material that characterized Iblis IV, Aliabad ware, is also poorly stratified at Tal-e Iblis and the site of Aliabad, and has also been recovered from sites in the Soghun valley, including Tepe Yahya (Prickett 1986b; Voigt and Dyson 1992 1: 145). The dating of the end of the Iblis IV/Aliabad period is unclear, but Voigt and Dyson (1992 1: 145–6) have suggested that it correlates with the Early Banesh period in Fars, though this relies on the presence of bevel-rim bowls and trays and assumes that there is no internal change in ceramic types during Iblis IV. On the basis of their excavations of deposits contemporaneous with Iblis IV/Aliabad at Mahtoutabad, Vidale and Desset (2013) have suggested that there was an Early Aliabad phase marked by the classic Aliabad painted ware, while the introduction of bevel-rim bowls and trays dates to a Late Aliabad phase. This interpretation supports the suggestion that Iblis IV/Aliabad corresponds with the Early Banesh and also possibly the Middle Banesh phase in Fars, though the precise end date of this phase is not clear. After the Iblis IV period, there was a decrease in settlement size and density in the Bard Sir region.

Settlement distribution

Most Yahya VI–VB sites continued to be occupied in Yahya VA (Yahya Phase), and those that were abandoned lay at the distal end of the fan and appear to have been replaced by sites further north (Prickett 1986a: 593ff., 1986b: 236). New sites also appeared on the silts of the basin center and on the distal fans that lie at the south and southeast edge of the basin (Prickett 1986b: 236). The Rud-e Gushk settlement system changed dramatically in the fourth millennium BC. After the intensification of settlement seen during the Yahya VI–VB and VA phases, there was a sharp decline in settlement density on the Shah Maran and Daulatabad plain: the number of settlements halved, entailing the abandonment of most of the northern part of the Rud-e Gushk fan and its terraced field system, as well as the distal fan area (Prickett 1986b: 236). Most of the settlement of the subsequent transitional Iblis IV/V period (Aliabad Phase) lay beyond the distal fan zone (Prickett 1986a: 599ff., 1986b: 236–7).

Surface remains of Aliabad phase occupation (Iblis IV/V Aliabad Phase) have been found in the Shah Maran and Daulatabad region and also at Tepe Yahya (Prickett 1986a: 774, 1986b: 236–7; Voigt and Dyson 1992 1: 149). Although the excavations at Tepe Yahya suggest that the site was abandoned at this time, there is evidence of occupation elsewhere in the Soghun valley (Prickett 1986a: 776) and small numbers of Aliabad sherds have been found in excavated contexts (Prickett 1986a: 450–51; Potts 2001: 198). Prickett (1986b: 237) noted that the slight increase in settlement area in the Rud-e Gushk in this period matched the absence of settlement at Tepe Yahya. Most of these settlements lay beyond the distal fan zone that had been occupied extensively during the fifth millennium BC (Prickett 1986a: 599ff., 1986b: 236–7; see below). Although there is clear evidence of settlement, the Iblis IV/V Aliabad Phase saw the fragmentation and ultimate collapse of the settlement pattern and farming system that had developed during the previous two millennia (Prickett 1986a: 774, 776). This same period, however, saw a dramatic fivefold increase in the number of settlements in the Bard Sir plain (from four to twenty) (Prickett 1986a: 777; after Chase, Fehérvári, and Caldwell 1967). The significance of this reorientation of settlement is difficult to assess but may have resulted from a wide range of cultural and environmental factors.

The Shah Maran and Daulatabad Basin appears to have been abandoned or at least depopulated after the Iblis IV/V period (i.e., during Yahya IVC), and only one site, 30 km to the south of the basin, and Tepe Yahya, 25 km to the east in the Soghun valley, were occupied (Prickett 1986a: 616ff., 782, 1986b: 237). After Iblis IV, there was a decrease in settlement size and density in the Bard Sir region, and the focus of settlement in the later third millennium BC appears to have shifted further to the east to areas like Shahdad and the areas around Shahr-e Sokhta and the Halil Rud valley (Prickett 1986a: 784; also Madjidzadeh 2008).

Settlement structure

Our understanding of settlement layout and organization during the fourth millennium BC is very limited and is primarily based on the IVC2 structures exposed at Tepe Yahya. There are no structural remains from this protracted period in the Bard Sir, and Tepe Yahya was abandoned for much of the fourth millennium BC (Voigt and Dyson 1992 1: 149; Potts 2001: 1). However, once Tepe Yahya was reoccupied, there was a dramatic change in the nature and function of the architecture that was constructed. The proto-Elamite building that was built on top of the eroded surface of the mound was constructed according to a specific unit of measure that closely conforms to one used in similar structures at Habuba Kabira in Syria (Beale and Carter 1983) and has interesting implications for the transmission of standard units of measurement and construction styles. The excavated portion of the IVC2 building consisted of five complete rooms and other elements and contained a range of inscribed proto-Elamite tablets, tablet blanks, cylinder seals, and sealings, as well as small finds, including chlorite vessels, stone balls, beads, and figurines (Potts 2001: 10–11). The layout and construction of this building is regarded as "western," and has parallels with buildings exposed in Susa Acropole 18 (Potts 2001: 10) (see below).

Ceramics

Yahya Period VA saw Chaff-tempered Ware replaced by a Plain Coarse Ware, and Black-on-Buff Ware was gradually replaced by Black-on-Red ware, which has clear affinities to material from areas east of Tepe Yahya, particularly at sites like Chah Husseini (Beale 1986: 67–82, fig. 4.1, 1992: 284; Beale and Lamberg-Karlovsky 1986: 257; Lamberg-Karlovsky and Beale 1986: 266; Voigt and Dyson 1992: 149; Mutin 2013). Parallels with Iblis Painted Ware suggest that Yahya VA correlates with Late Iblis II and Iblis III, as well as with the very Late Bakun and the Lapui phase in Fars (Beale 1986: 86; Voigt and Dyson 1992 1: 145, 149). The introduction of potters' marks on beakers during Period VA may be indicative of increasingly organized production and Beale and Lamberg-Karlovsky (1986: 255) have suggested that this might be related to the large-scale production of similar-looking vessels and/or the necessity for groups of pots to be identifiable in communal kilns.

Beale (1986: 67–82, 86–7, 257, fig. 4.1) suggested that the importation of black-on-buff ware vessels from Fars in the mid-fifth millennium BC may explain the adoption of related technologies for the local production of black-on-buff ware and also that it influenced production of the later black-on-red ware. While this may be the case, it is also important to point out that there were various local developments in production technology during the late fifth and early fourth millennia BC, including the development of Lapui wares in the southeast before they began being used in the southwest (see above). Mutin (2012) has emphasized that in Yahya VA there are very clear connections to the sites in the Bampur valley in the southeast.

In the Bard Sir, there appears to be a break between Iblis II and III (Caldwell 1967: 36), and in Iblis III, a range of wares labelled Dashkar wares appear, which is similar to material seen in Yahya VA (Voigt and Dyson 1992 1: 145). Similar fabrics and forms appear during the Lapui phase in Fars. The Iblis IV/Aliabad pottery is typically hand made and buff slipped and appears in plain, monochrome, and bichrome varieties (Chase, Fehérvári, and Caldwell 1967: 79; Chase, Caldwell, and Fehérvári 1967: 184; Voigt and Dyson 1992 1: 145). What have been described as large and carelessly drawn geometric designs in various colors are characteristic (Voigt and Dyson 1992 1: 145). In addition, there are several forms referred to as "Aliabad Ridged Ware" that have string-cut bases and these also appear in Iblis IV along with mold-made bevel-rim bowls and shoulder spouts (Chase, Fehérvári, and Caldwell et al. 1967: 82, 86–7; Chase, Caldwell, and Fehérvári 1967: 188–9, 200; Voigt and Dyson 1992 1: 145). The presence of these vessels suggests the use of the fast wheel and molds to mass-produce vessels (Caldwell 1968: 182). It is these latter vessel forms that Vidale and Desset (2013) have suggested might date to a later phase of Iblis IV.

There is a gap in the occupation sequence at Tepe Yahya between Period VA and IVC, which is believed to correlate with these various Aliabad wares from Iblis IV (Chase, Fehérvári, and Caldwell 1967: 75–9; Prickett 1986b; Voigt and Dyson 1992 1: 145, 149). The subsequent phase at Tepe Yahya, Period IVC, sees the appearance of a range of distinctive vessel forms and production techniques also found in the Middle Banesh phase in Fars, including bevel-rim bowls, trays, and conical cups (Voigt and Dyson 1992 1: 149; Potts 2001: 6–53, 195–9). In addition to this "western" material, Yahya IVC2 was also marked by the appearance of unpainted and potentially local vessels, and fine black-on-orange ware with parallel sets of zigzag lines, black-on-orange ware with hatched wavy bands, burnished gray ware and black-on-gray ware that show affiliations with other sites in southeastern Iran (Potts 2001: 198, table 8.1). Mutin (2013) has noted that, at the end of the fourth millennium BC, sites in this part of the Indo-Iranian borderlands often have "Late" Shahi-Tump ware, Burnished Ware, and "Eastern Pakistani Balochistan wares." Vandiver (1986: 99) has shown that in the later fourth millennium BC in Kerman, sequential slab construction continued to be used, in combination with the newly adopted technologies of wheel throwing, coiling and mold-making.

Socioeconomy

There is relatively little information on the fourth millennium BC socioeconomy of southeastern Iran, but that which exists is compelling. Yahya VA saw continued occupation of the single-family complexes with their own walls and courtyard seen in Yahya VB, which Beale and Lamberg-Karlovsky (1986: 254, 262) argued housed single nuclear or extended family units, but after this Tepe Yahya was abandonned. Another major transformation occurred with the abandonment of the Shah Maran and Daulatabad Basin after the Iblis IV/V transition. There is similar evidence for settlement disjuncture between Iblis II and III in the Bard Sir. It is in this transformative situation that we see what has been interpreted as evidence for overt communication and interaction with southwestern Iran and areas further west, in the form of bevel-rim bowls and other contemporaneous vessel forms like trays and spouted vessels. There has been considerable debate about the significance of the presence of these vessel forms in this relatively isolated part of eastern Iran, and much has been made of the proximity of the Bard Sir to copper sources and the evidence for early copper production at Tal-e Iblis (e.g., Algaze 2005: 71). Although models have been proposed that would regard Tal-e Iblis and the Bard Sir as being peripheries of a Mesopotamian core (e.g., Algaze 2005, 2009), it is essential to remember that the precocious copper-working technology seen in Iblis 0/I was indigenous and, similarly, the "western" vessel forms seen at Tal-e Iblis, Aliabad, and Mahtoutabad appeared as components of a ceramic assemblage that included a wide variety of local vessel forms and ware types. This prompts questions about the nature of the relationship between the population of Tal-e Iblis and their distant interlocutors.

In the knowledge that there was earlier fourth-millennium interaction with the west, the reoccupation of Tepe Yahya (IVC2) during the late fourth millennium BC becomes particularly interesting. The reestablishment of occupation at the site appears to have been a foreign initiative, possibly emanating from Susa (Lamberg-Karlovsky 1978; Potts 2001: 198) and involving the adoption of technologies used to produce bevel-rim bowls, trays, and conical cups as well as the use of proto-Elamite/Susa III tablets (Damerow and Englund 1989). Potts (2001: 198) also pointed to a range of southeast Iranian ceramic wares and vessel forms in the IVC2 assemblage (cf. Mutin 2013), which indicates that the inhabitants of Yahya IVC2 were unlikely to have been an isolated foreign enclave but were interacting with the local population of southeastern Iran.

Conclusions

The fifth and fourth millennia BC constitute a protracted period of transformation that saw varying degrees of interaction and isolation between the different regions that make up the enormous geographical area of southern Iran. Both southwestern and southeastern Iran saw progressive increases in settled populations over time, but there is considerable variation in the distribution of that population both between and within the two zones. There are clear signs of technological innovations developing and spreading from one region to another, but significantly the patterns of dispersal are multidirectional. Moreover, mobility was a key dynamic in south Iran throughout prehistory, and both people *and* goods were moving in southern Iran during the fifth and fourth millennia BC (Petrie 2011). In discussing the Tepe Yahya sequence, Beale and Lamberg-Karlovsky (1986) observed that there were intermittent phases of long-range cultural influence, which they compared to the concept of punctuated equilibrium, and Prickett (1986a: 780) described this as a process of "pulsations of influence." The author has proposed that there were phases during which populations were open to innovation and outside influence and periods where populations were more closed and overtly displayed what may well have been regional identities through material culture (Petrie 2011).

The later fourth millennium BC saw the adoption of a number of distinctive ceramic vessel forms (e.g., bevel-rim bowls and low trays), the rise of the first city-sized settlements, the implantation of what appear to be foreign colonies or outposts (Yahya IVC2), and the adoption of protoliteracy in the form of protocuneiform tablets, which are all clear signs of long-range interaction within highland Iran (e.g., Lamberg-Karlovsky 1978; Alden 1982; also Algaze 2005, 2009). While the presence of these elements is suggestive of connectivity and interaction, our understanding of the nature of those processes is largely speculative. They may represent only a material veneer that overlay local assemblages of material culture showing clear signs of regional distinctiveness. This is particularly marked when comparing southwestern and southeastern Iran, though even within the better-studied southwest, there are clear indications of variation in the use of material between the populations living in regions that are relatively close together (e.g., KRB and Mamasani). The new evidence from Mamasani and Mahtoutabad shows that there were at least two phases of contact with the lowland areas to the west, one that corresponds to the Late Uruk period and another which corresponds with the proto-Elamite period. The significance of this will be established only by further, problem-oriented research.

Further reading

There is a range of publications that provide insight into aspects of the archaeology of south Iran during the fifth and fourth millennia BC, but by and large these lack a comprehensive scope. Voigt and Dyson (1992) provide a good overview of the relevant archaeological evidence as it stood until 2000, with a particular focus on chronological issues. Several works address processes of cultural development over this period. Alizadeh (2006), and Potts et al. (2009) and Petrie et al. (2009) provide contrasting opinions of the archaeology of the southwest, while volumes by Beale (1986), Prickett (1986a), and Potts (2001) provide insight into the archaeology of the southeast. Petrie (2012) (*AIN*) seeks to contextualize the archaeology of fourth millennium BC Iran as a whole, while Petrie (2011) looks at processes of innovation and interaction across southern Iran for both the fifth and fourth millennia BC.

References

Abdi, K. 2003. The early development of pastoralism in the central Zagros Mountains. *JWP* 17/4: 395–448.

Abdi, K., S. Pollock, and R. Bernbeck. 2003. Fars Archaeology Project 2003: Excavations at Toll-e Bashi. *Iran* 41: 339–44.

Alden, J. R. 1979. Regional economic organization in Banesh Period Iran. Unpublished PhD diss., University of Michigan.

———. 1982. Trade and politics in Proto-Elamite Iran. *CA* 23: 613–40.

——. 2003a. Appendix D: Excavations at Tal-e Kureh. In *Early urban life in the land of Anshan: Excavations at Tal-e Malyan in the highlands of Iran*, ed. W. M. Sumner, 187–98. Philadelphia: UMM 117.

——. 2003b. Appendix E: Inventory of Banesh Sites. In *Early urban life in the land of Anshan: Excavations at Tal-e Malyan in the highlands of Iran*, ed. W. M. Sumner, 199–204. Philadelphia: UMM 117.

——. 2003c. Sherd size and the Banesh phase occupation in the ABC Operation at Malyan, Iran. *YBYN*: 109–20.

Alden, J. R. 2013. The Kur River Basin in the late 4th and 3rd millennia BC—Proto-Elamite ceramics, settlement, and socio-political organization. *AIN*.

Alden, J. R., K. Abdi, A. Azadi, G. Beckman, and H. Pittman. 2005. Fars Archaeological Project 2004: Excavation at Tal-e Malyan. *Iran* 43: 39–47.

Algaze, G. 2005. *The Uruk world system: The dynamics of expansion of early Mesopotamian civilization*, 2nd ed. Chicago: University of Chicago Press.

——. 2008. *Ancient Mesopotamia at the dawn of civilization: The evolution of an urban landscape*. Chicago: University of Chicago Press.

Alizadeh, A. 1988. Socio-economic complexity in southwestern Iran during the fifth and fourth millennia BC: The evidence from Tall-i-Bakun A. *Iran* 26: 17–34.

——. 1994–5. Archaeological surveys in northern Fars. *Oriental Institute 1994–1995 Annual Report*: 29–32.

——. 2003. Some observations based on the nomadic character of Fars prehistoric cultural development. *YBYN*: 83–97.

——. 2006. *The origins of state organizations in prehistoric highland Fars, southern Iran: Excavations at Tall-e Bakun*. Chicago: OIP 128.

——. 2008. *Chogha Mish II. The development of a prehistoric regional center in lowland Susiana, southwestern Iran: Final report on the last six seasons of excavations, 1972–1978*. Chicago: OIP 130.

——. 2010. The rise of the highland Elamite state in southwestern Iran: "Enclosed" or enclosing nomadism? *CA* 51/3: 353–83.

Amiet, P. 1976. Antiquités du désert du Lut, II. *RA* 70: 1–8.

Askari Chaverdi, A., C. A. Petrie, and H. Taylor. 2008. Early village settlements on the Persian Gulf littoral: Revisiting Tol-e Pir and the Galehdār Valley. *Iran* 46: 21–42.

Azizi Kharanaghi, M. H., H. Fazeli Nashli and Y. Nishiaki. 2014. The second season of excavations at Tepe Rahmat Abad, southern Iran: The absolute and relative chronology. *ANES* 51: 1–32.

Beale, T. W. 1986. *Excavations at Tepe Yahya, Iran, 1967–1976: The early periods*. Cambridge: ASPR Bulletin 38.

——. 1992. Ceramics v. The Chalcolithic period in southern Persia. *EnIr* 3: 282–4.

Beale, T. W., and S. M. Carter. 1983. On the track of the Yahya large Kuš: Evidence for architectural planning in the period IVC complex at Tepe Yahya. *Paléorient* 9: 81–8.

Beale, T. W., and C. C. Lamberg-Karlovsky. 1986. Summary of change and development in the early periods at Tepe Yahya, 4900–3300 B.C. In *Excavations at Tepe Yahya, Iran 1967–1976: The Early Periods*, ed. T. W. Beale, 215–46. Cambridge: ASPR Bulletin 38.

Bernbeck, R., H. Fazeli, and S. Pollock. 2005. Life in a fifth-millennium BCE village: Excavations at Rahmatabad, Iran. *NEA* 68/3: 94–105.

Bernbeck, R., S. Pollock, and K. Abdi. 2004. Reconsidering the Neolithic at Toll-e Bashi (Iran). *NEA* 66: 76–8.

Besenval, R. 2005. Chronology of protohistoric Kech-Makran. In *South Asian Archaeology, 2001*, vol. 1, ed. C. Jarrige and V. Lefèvre, 1–9. Paris: Éditions Recherche sur les Civilisations.

Besenval, R., V. Marcon, C. Buquet, and B. Mutin. 2005. Shahi-Tump: Results of the last field-seasons (2001–2003). In *South Asian archaeology 2003*, ed. U. Franke-Vogt and J. Weisshaar, 49–56. Berlin: Forschungen zur Archäologie Außereuropäischer Kulturen 1.

Blackman, M. J. 1981. The mineralogical and chemical analysis of Banesh period ceramics from Tal-i Malyan, Iran. In *Scientific studies of ancient ceramics*, ed. M. J. Hughes, 7–20. London: British Museum.

———. 1989. Ceramic technology and problems of social evolution in southwest Iran. In *Materials Issues in Art and Archaeology: Symposium held April 6–8, Reno, Nevada, U.S.A.*, ed. E. V. Sayre, P. Vandiver, J. Druzik, and C. Stevenson, 103–8. Pittsburgh: Materials Research Society.

Bobek, H. 1968. Vegetation. *CHI* 1: 280–93.

Caldwell, J. R. 1967. The setting and results of the Kerman Project. In *Investigations at Tal-i Iblis*, ed. J. R. Caldwell, 21–40. Springfield: Illinois State Museum Preliminary Reports 9.

———. 1968. Pottery and the cultural history of the Iranian plateau. *JNES* 27: 178–83.

Caldwell, J. R., and M. Sarraf. 1967. Exploration of Excavation Area B. In *Investigations at Tal-i Iblis*, ed. J. R. Caldwell, 272–308. Springfield: Illinois State Museum Preliminary Reports 9.

Carter, E. 1994. Bridging the gap between the Elamites and the Persians in southeastern Khuzistan. In *Continuity and change*, ed. H. Sancisi-Weedenburg, A. Kuhrt, and M.C. Root, 65–95. Leiden: AchHist 8.

Carter, R. A., K. Challis, S. M. N. Priestman, and H. Tofighian. 2006. The Bushehr hinterland: Results of the first season of the Iranian-British Archaeological Survey of Bushehr Province, November–December 2004. *Iran* 44: 63–103.

Chase, D. W., J. R. Caldwell, and I. Fehérvári. 1967. The Iblis Sequence and the exploration of excavation areas A, C and E. In *Investigations at Tal-i Iblis*, ed. J. R. Caldwell, 111–201. Springfield: Illinois State Museum Preliminary Reports 9.

Chase, D. W., G. Fehérvári, and J. R. Caldwell. 1967. Reconnaissances in the Bard Sir Valley. In *Investigations at Tal-i Iblis*, ed. J. R. Caldwell, 65–72. Springfield: Illinois State Museum Preliminary Reports 9.

Dahl, J. L., C. A. Petrie, and D. T. Potts. 2013. Chronological parameters of the earliest writing system in Iran. *AIN*: 353–78.

Damerow, P., and R. K. Englund. 1989. *The proto-Elamite texts from Tepe Yahya*. Cambridge: ASPR Bulletin 39.

Delougaz, P., and H. J. Kantor. 1996. *Chogha Mish, vol. 1, The first five seasons of excavations, 1961–1971*. Chicago: OIP 101.

Dittmann, R. 1986. Susa in the Proto-Elamite period and annotations on the painted pottery of Proto-Elamite Khuzestan. In *Ğamdat Naṣr: Period or regional Style?* ed. U. Finkbeiner and W. Röllig, 171–98. Wiesbaden: L. Reichert.

Dougherty, R. C., and J. R. Caldwell. 1967. Evidence of early pyrometallurgy in the Kerman Range in Iran. In *Investigations at Tal-i Iblis*, ed. J. R. Caldwell, 17–20. Springfield: Illinois State Museum Preliminary Reports 9.

Egami, N., and S. Masuda. 1962. *Marv-Dasht I: The excavation at Tal-i-Bakun, 1956*. Tokyo: Tokyo University Iraq-Iran Archaeological Expedition Reports 2

Egami, N., and T. Sono. 1962. *Marv-Dasht II: The excavation at Tall-i-Gap, 1959*. Tokyo: Tokyo University Iraq-Iran Archaeological Expedition Reports 3.

Evett, D. 1967. Artifacts and architecture of the Iblis I period: Areas D, F and G. In *Investigations at Tal-i Iblis*, ed. J. R. Caldwell, 202–255. Springfield: Illinois State Museum Preliminary Reports 9.

Frame, L. 2004. Investigations at Tal-i Iblis: Evidence for copper smelting during the Chalcolithic period. Unpublished BA thesis, Massachusetts Institute of Technology.

Fraser, J. A. 2008. An alternate view of complexity at Tall-e Bakun A. *Iran* 45: 1–19.

Ganji, M. H. 1968. Climate. *CHI* 1: 212–49.

Goff, C. 1963. Excavations at Tall-i Nokhodi. *Iran* 1: 43–70.

———. 1964. Excavations at Tall-i Nokhodi, 1962. *Iran* 2: 41–52.

Gotch, P. 1968. A survey of the Persepolis plain and Shiraz area. *Iran* 6: 168–70.

———. 1969. The Persepolis plain and Shiraz: Field survey 2. *Iran* 7: 190–92.

Goulder, J. 2010. Administrators' bread: an experiment-based re-assessment of the functional and cultural role of the Uruk bevel-rim bowl. *Antiquity* 84: 351–62.

Hakemi, A. 1997. *Shahdad: Archaeological excavations of a Bronze Age center in Iran*. Rome: IsMEO Reports and Memoirs 27.

Helwing, B., and M. Seyedin. 2010. Bakun period sites in the Darre-ye Bolághi, Fars. *BTU*: 277–92.

Heskel, D., and C. C. Lamberg-Karlovsky. 1986. Metallurgical technology. In. *Excavations at Tepe Yahya, Iran 1967–1976: The early periods*, ed. T. W. Beale, 207–14. Cambridge: ASPR Bulletin 38.

Johnson, G. A. 1973. *Local exchange and early state development in southwestern Iran*. Ann Arbor: Anthropological Papers of the Museum of Anthropology 51.

Kamilli, D., and C. C. Lamberg-Karlovsky. 1979. Petrographic and electron microprobe analysis of ceramics from Tepe Yahya, Iran. *Archaeometry* 21/1: 47–59.

Kerner, S. 1993. *Vakilabad-Keramik*. Berlin: BBVO 13.

Khosrowzadeh, A. 2005. The settlement pattern of Bard Sir Plain from prehistoric to Islamic period. Unpublished paper presented at the 20th Biennial Conference of the European Association of South Asian Archaeologists, British Museum, July 4–8, 2005.

Kole, J. E. 1980. Bakun Settlement Patterns. Unpublished paper presented in the session *Problems of large scale, multi-disciplinary regional archaeological research: The Malyan Project*, at the Annual Meeting of the Society for American Archaeology, 1980.

Lamberg-Karlovsky, C. C. 1970. *Excavations at Tepe Yahya, Iran, 1967–1969: Progress report 1*. Cambridge: ASPR Bulletin 27.

———. 1978. The Proto-Elamites on the Iranian plateau. *Antiquity* 52: 114–20.

———. 2001. Afterword. Excavations at Tepe Yahya: Reconstructing the past. In *Excavations at Tepe Yahya, Iran 1967–1975: The third millennium*, ed. D. T. Potts, 269–80. Cambridge: ASPR Bulletin 45.

Lamberg-Karlovsky, C. C., and T. W. Beale. 1986. Conclusion: Tepe Yahya in the context of a wider core-periphery interaction sphere in the fifth and fourth millennia B.C. In *Excavations at Tepe Yahya, Iran, 1967–1976: The early periods*, T. W. Beale, 265–8. Cambridge: ASPR Bulletin 38.

Langsdorff, A., and D. E. McCown. 1942. *Tall-i Bakun A: Season of 1932*. Chicago: OIP 59.

Madjidzadeh, Y. 2008. Excavations at Konar Sandal in the region of Jiroft in the Halil Basin: first preliminary report (2002–2008). *Iran* 46: 69–104.

Mashkour, M. 2009. Faunal remains from Tol-e Nurabad and Tol-e Spid. *MAPSO*: 135–46.

Mashkour, M., A. Mohaseb, and K. Debue. 2006. Towards a specialized subsistence economy in the Marvdasht Plain: Preliminary zooarchaeological analysis of Tall-i Mushki, Jari B, Jari A and Bakun A. In *The origins of state organizations in highland Fars, Iran*, ed. A. Alizadeh, 101–5. Chicago: OIP 128.

McCall, B. K. 2009. The Mamasani Archaeological Survey: Epipalaeolithic to Elamite settlement patterns in the Mamasani district of the Zagros Mountains, Fars Province, Iran. Unpublished PhD diss., University of Sydney.

McCown, D. E. 1942. *The comparative stratigraphy of early Iran*. Chicago: SAOC 23.

Miller, N. F., and M. Kimiaie. 2006. Some plant remains from the 2004 excavations at Tall-e Mushki, Tall-e Jari A and B, and Tall-e Bakun A and B. In *The origins of state organizations in prehistoric highland Fars, southern Iran: Excavations at Tall-e Bakun*, ed. A. Alizadeh, 107–118. Chicago: OIP 128.

Miller, N. F., and W. M. Sumner. 2004. The Banesh-Kaftari interface: The view from Operation H5, Malyan. *Iran* 42: 77–89.

Miroschedji, P. de. 1973. Prospections archéologiques dans les vallées de Fasa et de Darab (rapport préliminaire). *PASARI* 1: 1–7.

———. 2003. Susa and the highlands: Major trends in the history of Elamite civilization. *YBYN*: 17–38.

Mutin, B. 2012. Cultural dynamics in southern Middle-Asia in the fifth and fourth millennia B.C.: A reconstruction based on ceramic traditions. *Paléorient* 38: 159–84.

———. 2013. Ceramic traditions and interactions on the south-eastern Iranian plateau during the 4th millennium BC. *AIN*: 253–76.

Nicholas, I. M. 1990. *The Proto-Elamite settlement at TUV*. Philadelphia: UMM 69.

Nishiaki, Y. 2010. A radiocarbon chronology for the Neolithic settlement of Tall-i Mushki, Marv Dasht plain, Fars. *Iran* 48: 1–10.

Petrie, C. A. 2011. "Culture," innovation and interaction across southern Iran from the Neolithic to the Bronze Age (6500–3000 BC). In *Investigating archaeological cultures: Material culture, variability and transmission*, ed. B. Roberts and M. Vander Linden, 151–82. New York: Springer.

———. Forthcoming a. Radiocarbon. In *ARCANE, Western Iran*, ed. B. Helwing. Turnhout: Brepols.

———. 2015. Iran and Uruk Mesopotamia: Chronologies and connections in the 4th millennium BC. In *Preludes to urbanism in the Ancient Near East: The Late Chalcolithic of Mesopotamia*, ed. A. McMahon, and H. Crawford, 137–55. Cambridge: McDonald Institute Monographs.

Petrie, C. A., A. Asgari Chaverdi, and M. Seyedin. 2009a. Excavations at Tol-e Spid. *MAPSO*: 89–134.

Petrie, C. A., A. Sardari, R. Ballantyne, M. Berberian, C. Lancelotti, and M. Mashkour, B. McCall, D.T. Potts and L. Weeks 2013. The 4th millennium BC occupation in the Mamasani District. *AIN*: 171–94.

Petrie, C. A., A. Sardari Zarchi, and A. Javanmardzadeh. 2007. Developing societies and economies in 4th millennium BC Fars: Further Excavations at Tol-e Spid. *Iran* 45: 301–9.

Petrie, C. A., and H. Taylor. Forthcoming. Trench C, stratigraphy, phasing and dating. In *The Mamasani Archaeological Project Stage Two*, ed. A. Askari Chaverdi, A. Javanmardzadeh, A. Lashkari, C. A. Petrie, D. T. Potts, A. Sardari, and L. R. Weeks. Oxford: BAR Int Ser.

Petrie, C. A., and K. D. Thomas. 2012. The topographic and environmental context of the earliest village sites in western South Asia. *Antiquity* 86: 1055–67.

Petrie, C. A., L. R. Weeks, D. T. Potts, and K. Roustaei. 2009b. Perspectives on the cultural sequence of Mamasani. *MAPSO*: 169–96.

Pigott, V. C., and H. Lechtman. 2003. Chalcolithic copper-base metallurgy on the Iranian Plateau: A new look at old evidence. In *Culture through objects: Ancient Near Eastern studies in honour of P.R.S. Moorey*, ed. T. F. Potts, M. Roaf, and D. Stein Culture, 291–312. Oxford: Griffith Institute.

Pittman, H. 2013. Imagery in administrative context: Susiana and the West in the fourth millennium BC. *AIN*: 293–336.

Pollock, S., R. Bernbeck, and K. Abdi. 2010. *The 2003 excavations at Tol-e Baši, Iran: Social life in a Neolithic village*. Mainz: AIT 10.

Potts, D. T. 1980. Tradition and transformation: Tepe Yahya and the Iranian plateau during the third millennium BC. Unpublished PhD diss., Harvard University.

———. 1999. *The archaeology of Elam: Formation and transformation of an ancient Iranian state*. Cambridge: Cambridge University Press.

———. 2001. *Excavations at Tepe Yahya, Iran, 1967–1975: The third millennium*. Cambridge: ASPR Bulletin 45.

———. 2008. review of A. Alizadeh, *The origins of state organizations in prehistoric highland Fars, southern Iran: Excavations at Tall-e Bakun*. *BiOr* 65/1–2: 195–206.

———. 2009. Bevel-rim bowls and bakeries: Evidence and explanations from Iran and the Indo-Iranian borderlands. *JCS* 61/2: 1–23.

———. 2011. Nomadismus in Iran von der Frühzeit bis in die Moderne—Eine Untersuchung sowohl aus archäologischer als auch historischer Sicht. *Eurasia Antiqua* 16: 1–18.

Potts, D. T., K. Roustaei, L. R. Weeks, and C. A. Petrie. 2009. The Mamasani District and the archaeology of southwestern Iran. *MAPSO*: 1–16.

Prickett, M. 1986a. Man, land and water: Settlement distribution and the development of irrigation agriculture in the Upper Rud-i Gushk drainage, southeastern Iran. Unpublished PhD diss., Harvard University.

———. 1986b. Settlement during the early periods. In *Excavations at Tepe Yahya, Iran 1967–1976: The early periods*, ed. T. W. Beale, 215–46. Cambridge: ASPR Bulletin 38.

Roustaei, K., K. Alamdari, and C. A. Petrie. 2009. Landscape and environment in Mamasani. *MAPSO*: 17–30.

Sajjadi, S. M. S. 2004. Sistan and Baluchistan Project. *Iran* 42: 247–50.

Sajjadi, S. M. S., M. Cassanova, L. Constantini, and K. O. Lorentz. 2008. Sistan and Baluchistan Project: Short reports on the tenth campaign of excavations at Shahr-i Sokhta. *Iran* 46: 307–34.

Salvatori, S., and M. Vidale. 1982. A brief surface survey of the proto-historic site of Shahdad (Kerman), Iran: Preliminary report. *Rivista di Archeologia* 6: 5–10.

Sami, A. 1956. *Pasargadae: The oldest imperial capital of Iran*. Shiraz: Musavi Printing Office.

Sardari, A. 2013. Northern Fars during the 4th millennium BC: Cultural developments during the Lapui phase. *AIN*: 195–206.

Sardari, A., and A. Rezaei. 2007. Report of the rescue-archaeological investigations on the Tappeh Mehr Ali, Eghlid Fars. *Archaeological Reports* 7: 155–72 (in Persian).

Shaikhi, S. 2008. Archaeozoological study of the Chalcolithic site of Tepe Mehr Ali Fars, Iran. Unpublished MA thesis, Tehran University (in Persian).

Smith, C. S., T. A. Wertime, and R. Pleiner. 1967. Preliminary report of the metallurgical project. In *Investigations at Tal-i Iblis*, ed. J. R. Caldwell, 318–26. Springfield: Illinois State Museum Preliminary Reports 9.

Stein, M. A. 1935. An archaeological tour in the Ancient Persis. *GJ* 86/6: 489–97.

———. 1937. *Archaeological reconnaissances in north-western India and south-eastern Īrān*. London: Macmillan.

Sumner, W. M. 1972. Cultural development in the Kur River Basin, Iran: An archaeological analysis of settlement patterns. Unpublished PhD diss., University of Pennsylvania.

———. 1986. Proto-Elamite civilization in Fars. In *Ğamdat Naṣr: Period or regional style?* ed. U. Finkbeiner and W. Röllig, 199–211. Wiesbaden: TAVO Beiheft 62.

———. 1988a. Maljan, Tall-e (Anšan). *RlA* 7/3–4: 306–20.

———. 1988b. Prelude to Proto-Elamite Anshan: The Lapui phase. *IrAnt* 23: 23–44.

———. 1990. Full-coverage regional archaeological survey in the Near East: An example from Iran. In *The archaeology of regions: A case for full-coverage survey*, ed. S. K. Fish and S. A. Kowalewski, 87–115. Washington: Smithsonian Institution Press..

———. 1994. The evolution of tribal society in the southern Zagros Mountains, Iran. In *Chiefdoms and early states in Near East: The organizational dynamics of complexity*, ed. G. J. Stein and M. S. Rothman, 47–66. Madison: Monographs in World Archaeology 18.

———. 2003. *Early urban life in the land of Anshan: Excavations at Tal-e Malyan in the highlands of Iran*. Philadelphia: UMM 117.

Taylor, H. 2007. The Stein Collection: Periodisation of Bakun period survey material collected by Sir Marc Aurel Stein in highland Fars, Iran. Unpublished MA thesis, University College London.

———. Forthcoming. Bakun ceramics, Trench C, stratigraphy, phasing and dating. In *The Mamasani Archaeological Project Stage Two*, ed. A. Askari Chaverdi, A. Javanmardzadeh, A. Lashkari, C.A. Petrie, D. T. Potts, A. Sardari, and L. R. Weeks. Oxford: BAR Int Ser.

Thornton, C. P., and C. C. Lamberg-Karlovsky. 2004. A new look at the prehistoric metallurgy of southeastern Iran. *Iran* 42: 47–59.

Tosi, M. 1968. Excavations at Shahr-i Sokhta, a Chalcolithic settlement in the Iranian Sistan: Preliminary report on the first campaign, October–December 1967. *EW* 18: 9–66.

———. 1970. Shahr-i Sokhta. *Iran* 8: 188–9.

Vanden Berghe, L. 1952. Archaeologische opzoekingen in de Marv Dasht Vlakte. *JEOL* 12: 211–20.

———. 1954. Archaeologische navorsingen in de omstreken van Persepolis. *JEOL* 13: 394–408.

Vandiver, P. B. 1986. The production technology of earthenware ceramics, 4900–2800 B.C. In *Excavations at Tepe Yahya, Iran 1967–1975: The early periods*, T. W. Beale, 91–100. Cambridge: ASPR Bulletin 38.

———. 1987. Sequential slab construction; a conservative southwest Asiatic ceramic tradition, ca. 7000–3000 B.C. *Paléorient* 13/2: 9–35.

Vidale, M., O. Craig, F. Desset, G. Guida, P. Bianchetti, G. Sidoti, M. Mariottini, and E. Battistella. 2012. A chlorite container found on the surface of Shahdad (Kerman, Iran) and its cosmetic content. *Iran* 50: 27–44.

Vidale, M., and F. Desset. 2013. *Mahtoutabad I (Konal Sandal South, Jiroft): Preliminary evidence of occupation of a Halil Rud site in the early fourth millennium BCE. AIN*: 233–52.

Voigt, M. M., and R. H. Dyson, Jr. 1992. The chronology of Iran, ca. 8000–2000 B.C. In *Chronologies in Old World archaeology*, 3rd ed., ed. R. W. Ehrich, vol. 1, 122–78 vol. 2, 125–53. Chicago: University of Chicago Press.

Weeks, L. R. 2012. Metallurgy. In *A companion to the archaeology of the Ancient Near East*, vol. 1, ed. D. T. Potts, 295–316. Oxford/Malden: Wiley-Blackwell.

Weeks, L. R., K. Alizadeh, L. Niakan, K. Alamdari, A. Khosrowzadeh, and M. Zeidi. 2009. Excavations at Tol-e Nurabad. *MAPSO*: 31–88.

Weeks, L. R., K. Alizadeh, L. Niakan, K. Alamdari, M. Zeidi, A. Khosrowzadeh, and B. McCall. 2006. The Neolithic settlement of highland SW Iran: New evidence from the Mamasani District. *Iran* 44: 1–31.

Weeks, L., C. A. Petrie, and D. T. Potts. 2010. 'Ubaid-related-related? The "black-on-buff" ceramic traditions of highland southwest Iran. *BTU*: 247–78.

Weiss, H. 1986. *The origins of cities in dry-farming Syria and Mesopotamia in the third millennium B.C.* Guilford: Four Quarters.

Wright, H. T. 1985. Problems of absolute chronology in protohistoric Mesopotamia. *Paléorient* 6: 93–8.

Zeidi, M., B. McCall, and A. Khosrowzadeh. 2009. Survey of Dasht-e Rostam-e Yek and Dasht-e Rostam-e Do. *MAPSO*: 147–68.

PART III

THE BRONZE AGE

CHAPTER 9

THE EARLY BRONZE AGE IN NORTHWESTERN IRAN

GEOFFREY D. SUMMERS

Geographic and cultural parameters

Northwestern Iran approximately corresponds to the three modern provinces of East and West Azerbaijan and Ardabil, this last being part of East Azerbaijan until 1993. Principle modern cities are Tabriz, Urmia, formerly Rezayieh, and Ardabil. Of these Tabriz has retained its superior importance since medieval times as a result of its centrality. This large area covers some 100,000 sq km and has a population now in excess of 8,000,000. The region is both high and mountainous, its dominating feature being the internal basin of Lake Urmia into which all major drainage flows. Today the lake itself is almost dry, although only a few decades ago it was one of the saltiest bodies of water on earth. The lake water would have been highly saline from the time of the earliest permanent human settlement in the region, which occurred sometime in the Neolithic period. The eastern side of the Urmia basin is dominated by a large extinct volcano, Kuh-e Sahand, which attains an altitude of approximately 3700 masl. To the northeast, at an elevation of some 4800 m, lies the permanently snow capped Kuh-e Sabalan. Both mountains provide water that permits gravity-fed irrigation throughout the growing season. To the east our region is bordered by the hot, humid, fertile margins of the Caspian Sea whereas to the north and south modern administrative and political borders do not follow natural geographic boundaries. To the west lies the northern end of the Zagros Mountain range that divides the higher and colder region around Lake Van and the highland massif of eastern Turkey from the Urmia Basin. The climate of northwestern Iran is characterized by hot summers and cold winters. In the majority of years there is sufficient rainfall for rain-fed agriculture.

At first glance, then, this large region of northwestern Iran would appear to have a certain degree of homogeneity. In the Early Bronze Age, however, it turns out that our region was but one part of a huge zone dominated by a single, distinct, long-lived, and conservative archaeological culture that stretched from the Transcaucasus in the north to the Kangavar Plain in the south, and from the highlands bordering the Caspian Sea in the east to the Upper Euphrates catchment in the west (Fahimi 2005; Fazeli Nashli et al. 2005; Ökse 2005). Its most far-flung outposts were as distant as the southern Levant. Here I have followed the pioneering work of Charles Burney, the first scholar to really appreciate the extent and importance of this culture through his surveys in Eastern Turkey and subsequent excavations at Yanik Tepe and Haftavan Tepe in the Urmia basin. Burney originally coined the term Early Transcaucasian (ETC). Today the majority of archaeologists working with this material take ETC to stand for Early Transcaucasian Culture, but that was not Burney's usage. Some prefer the alternative term Kura-Araxes, first used by Boris Kuftin in the 1940s to emphasize the idea that the origins of this culture lay in the valleys of the Kura and Araxes Rivers (Kuftin 1941).

For a long time there was a general tendency to equate the ETC with the Early Bronze Age of Anatolia, and indeed to employ the same tripartite divisions. Early in the development of Iranian studies, however, Burney perspicaciously suggested that the end of the ETC in northwestern Iran and eastern Turkey should probably be placed well down into the second millennium BC, that is, in what is generally termed the Middle Bronze Age. In a series of radiocarbon dates from his excavations at Sos Höyük in the Erzurum plain of eastern Turkey, Antonio Sagona has demonstrated an even greater longevity. Thus neither the geographic area, northwestern Iran, nor the techno-chronological label, Early Bronze Age, are appropriate or useful. On the other hand, the creditable and up-to-date synthesis of the ETC by Giulio Palumbi (Palumbi 2008, 2011) brings together recent evidence from the Transcaucasus, eastern and southeastern Turkey and the Levant but, curiously, ignores the important evidence from Iran. The same lacuna is found in the very recent short summaries by Antonio Sagona (Sagona 2011). Thus this chapter is intended to fill a crucial gap for both the student and the general reader.

Brief history of investigation in northwestern Iran

In his pioneering use of aerial photography in the Ancient Near East in the late 1930s, Erich F. Schmidt brought to the attention of archaeologists the existence of substantial mounds in the Urmia Basin. Schmidt's original photograph of the western side of lake Urmia, then called Lake Riza'iyyah, "taken from an Altitude of 1300 M on July 25, 1937," can be viewed online (http://oi.uchicago.edu/museum/collections/pa/persepolis/surveys.html.). In 1948, Theodore Burton-Brown, director of the Manchester Museum in England, was granted permission to excavate one of the most prominent sites recognized in Schmidt's photographs, Geoy Tepe near the city of Urmia. Although Sir Aurel Stein had made soundings at several sites in the region, including Hasanlu (Stein 1940), it was Burton-Brown's work that provided the first stratigraphic sequences from the Chalcolithic period to the Middle Bronze Age (Burton-Brown 1951). Similar material was already known further north, in what were then the Soviet republics, although little information was available to Western scholars.

From 1960 to 1962, three seasons of excavation were conducted at Yanik Tepe, to the east of Lake Urmia, by Charles Burney. This site, selected following Burney's Eastern Anatolian survey (Burney 1958), has provided the best and fullest sequence of well-stratified material covering the entire ETC II–III in northwestern Iran and northeastern Turkey. Still known only through interim reports and brief descriptions, the ETC levels at Yanik formed the core of this writer's 1982 doctoral dissertation (Burney 1961a, 1961b, 1962, 1964, 1972a, 1977; Burney and Lang 1971; Summers 1982, 2004, and 2013). Results from Yanik Tepe were built on by Burney's excavations at Haftavan Tepe, close to the northwestern corner of the lake, in 1968, 1969, 1971, 1973, 1975, and 1978. Haftavan Tepe was primarily chosen to investigate the second millennium, and to thus fill the void between the third millennium and earlier levels at Yanik Tepe and the Late Bronze Age and Iron Age investigations of the Hasanlu project. Nevertheless ETC II levels (Hafatavan Level VIII; Summers 1982), were excavated in a limited exposure in the base of the trench dug though the mound by a mysterious Palestinian archaeologist called Butamin, while ETC III buildings of Haftavan Level VII were confined mainly to the high portion of this large mound. The ETC sequence and the material culture at Haftavan mirror those at Yanik.

A long, deep sequence that included 13 m of ETC occupation at Giljar Tepe north of Urmia was revealed in a small sounding excavated in 1978 by an Italian mission led by Paolo Pecorella. The results from this limited exposure complement the evidence from Yanik, Geoy, and Haftavan (Pecorella and Salvini 1984).

The only other major excavations of note were those of the Hasanlu Project, directed by Robert H. Dyson Jr., which investigated a number of sites in the Ushnu and Solduz regions of the Qadar River valley to the south of Lake Urmia (Dyson 1997). Investigation of Early Bronze Age levels was restricted to deep soundings at Hasanlu Tepe itself (Danti et al. 2004).

Published surveys include those by Stuart Swiny in 1971; Wolfram Kleiss and Stephan Kroll of the German Archaeological Institute at Tehran between 1967 and 1978; and Charles Burney in the Meskinshahr region in 1978. An Italian survey of the Urmia Basin by Paolo Pecorella and Mirjo Salvini between 1976 and 1978 included the excavation of a sondage at Tepe Giljar mentioned above. Hassan Tala'i worked in the eastern side of the basin in the 1980s (Ingraham and Summers 1979; Pecorella and Salvini 1984; Kroll 1984 with references; Swiny 1975; Tala'i 1984). In recent years Raffaele Biscione and Hamid Khatib-Shahidi have carried out surveys in East and West Azerbaijan (Biscione 2009 with references). At the small site of Ravaz, discovered by Wolfram Kleiss, the layout of the entire ETC settlement could be mapped (see below), thus complementing the excavated plans from Yanik Tepe.

Defining the Early Transcaucasian Culture

ETC culture is defined by a combination of characteristics. Foremost amongst these is the pottery, not because it is the most important but because it is unmistakable when found on archaeological surveys. As a result of the distinctiveness of this ceramic tradition, the broad extent of the ETC culture can easily be traced over a vast area that, in some portions of the ETC zone, including the northern Urmia Basin, persisted for perhaps a millennium and a half. Second, and more important, because of their connotations for the nature of ETC society and political structure, are the concepts that underlay individual house buildings and other structures in ETC villages. There were no towns, or at least no settlements yet recognized possessing public buildings of any kind that might be associated with even primordial levels of urban complexity, nor any excavated sites where the population might have attained urban proportions. Cult sites have been identified but no temples, and hence no priesthood, no palaces and no administrative buildings. No trace of writing, seals, or seal impressions occur. Architecture may be circular, as in ETC II at Yanik Tepe and Haftavan Tepe (Fig. 9.1), or rectangular, as in ETC III at these same sites (Fig. 9.3), where in both periods buildings were constructed of sun-dried mudbricks. In the Transcaucasus and in Eastern Turkey, most notably at Arslantepe and Norşuntepe, buildings were sometimes constructed of wattle and daub, their plans varying from curved to rectangular with rounded corners. In these Upper Euphrates Valley sites very distinctive portable hearths suggest, not surprisingly, that links were perhaps stronger with the Kura-Araxes region than with western Iran. In ETC II at Yanik Tepe and Haftavan Tepe many round buildings were provided with standardized, built-in kitchen ranges (Fig. 9.2). Huts containing these domestic installations may be considered houses. Whether these were the houses of nuclear families or whether group houses and other huts may have belonged to extended families or "clans" is unclear. The plan of Ravaz is very similar in character to that of the larger site of Yanik and raises the same difficulties of social interpretation. In ETC III, when the buildings were not only rectangular but agglutinative and sometimes two-storied, these kitchen ranges demonstrate that there had been no fundamental changes in either the system of kinship or the structure of society (Figs. 9.3–9.4). Similar installations are seen in ETC houses at Godin Tepe. It is therefore highly probable that this was the common pattern of buildings in village settlements in northwestern Iran at this time. Thus distinctive building forms, and what we would today call interior design, are characteristics of the culture. Taken together with the pottery, they demonstrate a considerable level of cultural cohesiveness and conservatism over a large and diverse geographic area. If these elaborate kitchen fittings are typical of northwestern Iran, an emphasis on hearths is found throughout the entire culture. In both the Caucasus and in Eastern Turkey elaborate, portable hearths and baked clay andirons, the latter often with anthropomorphic embellishments, are important cultural markers. It is presumably correct to associate these hearths with domestic cult and all that implies.

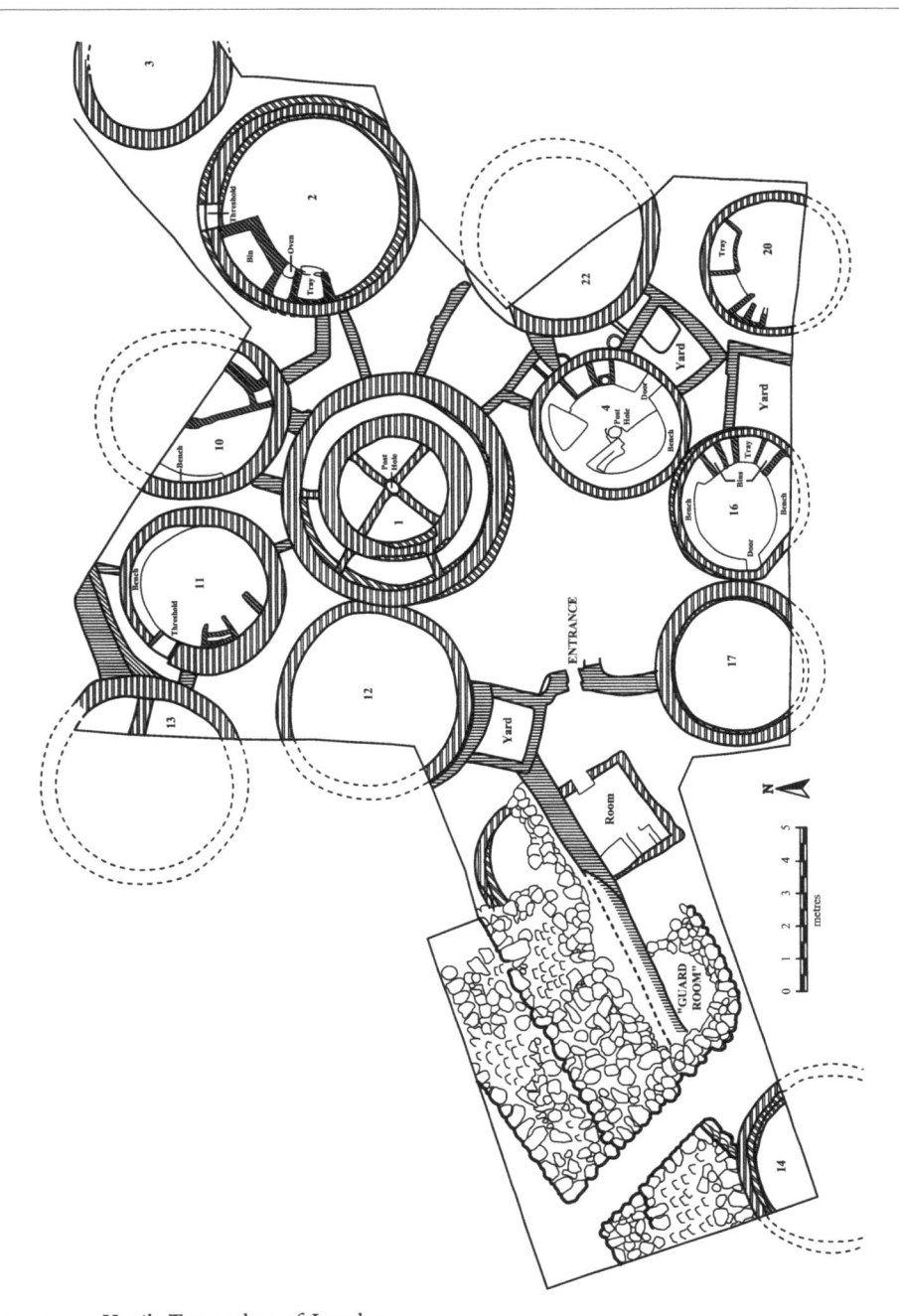

FIGURE 9.1 Yanik Tepe, plan of Level 15.

In contrast to, for instance, the famous Maikop culture on the other side of the Caucasian mountains, or the so-called Early Bronze Age II "royal cemetery" at Alaçahöyük in southern Pontus, the ETC has not produced a corpus of distinctive metalwork. This is often assumed to reflect archaeological visibility because no large ETC

FIGURE 9.2 Yanik Tepe, kitchen fittings in the early phase of Circle 45, early phase.

cemeteries have been excavated. But the seemingly unstoppable looting of archaeological sites in recent decades has not flooded the clandestine antiquities markets with the ETC metalwork that might have been anticipated half a century ago. Much of the archaeological literature has assumed that the ETC zone was an important source of metals and, concomitantly, that ETC communities would have had extensive metal workshops. This seems not, however, to have been the case in northwestern Iran.

Much, too, has been made of the idea that large elements of the ETC population were transhumant or nomadic, with an economy largely based on herding. In Iran at least there is no evidence to support such assumptions, and indeed there is little evidence in either Turkey or the Transcaucasus (Areshian 2005: 71–2; Kozbe 2004; Palumbi 2008: 314–15; Piro 2009). There are two caveats. First, permanently settled, mixed farming does not exclude small groups taking animals to pasture in the summer months, nor the existence of substantial but short-lived sites occupied on a seasonal basis. Temporary sites several kilometers from a village settlement could have been used on a daily basis at certain times while others, more distant but not necessarily at great altitudes, could have been occupied for longer periods. Such transhumance between permanent and seasonal settlements by a part of the population is still common in upland parts of the Near East. This is different from a truly nomadic way of existence in which herders and their animals are permanently on the move and rely on interaction with permanent settlements for agricultural produce as well as for tools and other manufactured items. Such a nomadic scenario in the ETC seems unlikely. Second, geographic and climatic diversity within the huge zone is so great that there would have to have been different, perhaps very different, agricultural and subsistence responses to regional environments. In northwestern Iran, the environment and thus conditions suitable for permanent settlement and mixed farming do not vary so greatly. This holds true even though some areas would have been more suitable for the raising of sheep and goats while others might have favored larger numbers of cattle. All permanent settlements, however, would have raised wheat, barley, and other crops and presumably possessed domestic oxen to draw plows.

Other Early Bronze Age ceramic assemblages

Painted Orange Ware

Painted Orange Ware is characteristic of the poorly known Hasanlu level VII. No architecture of this period has been revealed. The pottery has been found on a number of sites in the Urmia Basin, particularly in the southern portion. The floruit of this pottery would seem to have been in the third quarter of the third millennium according to the radiocarbon dates. The terminal date is unknown (Kroll 2005; Danti et al. 2004).

Hassan 'Ali Ware

Named after the site of Gerd-e Hassan 'Ali in the Solduz Plain excavated by Sir Aurel Stein in 1936. Occasional sherds have been picked up at a number of sites in and around the Urmia Basin and, according to Stephan Kroll, Hassan 'Ali Ware occurs in Hasanlu VIIC, below the Painted Orange Ware horizon (Kroll 2004, 2005). The single sherd from Yanik Tepe was found in an ETC II context.

Chronology

Periodization

In the general scheme adopted here the ETC is divided into three phases. The first, ETC I, beginning at least as early as the later fourth millennium BC, has not been found in Iran. Wherever the origins of this distinctive culture, there can be no doubt that it spread into the Urmia Basin from the north. It seems undeniable that this was brought about by the migration of farmers. Whatever the causes, and however rapid or slow the arrival of newcomers may have been, their presence in northwestern Iran can be taken to define the start of ETC II. In some studies ETC II as defined here is equated with Early Bronze Age I (EBA I), a term that might now be considered obsolete for northwestern Iran. At Yanik Tepe, the only extensively excavated site, the ETC II is characterized by circular buildings

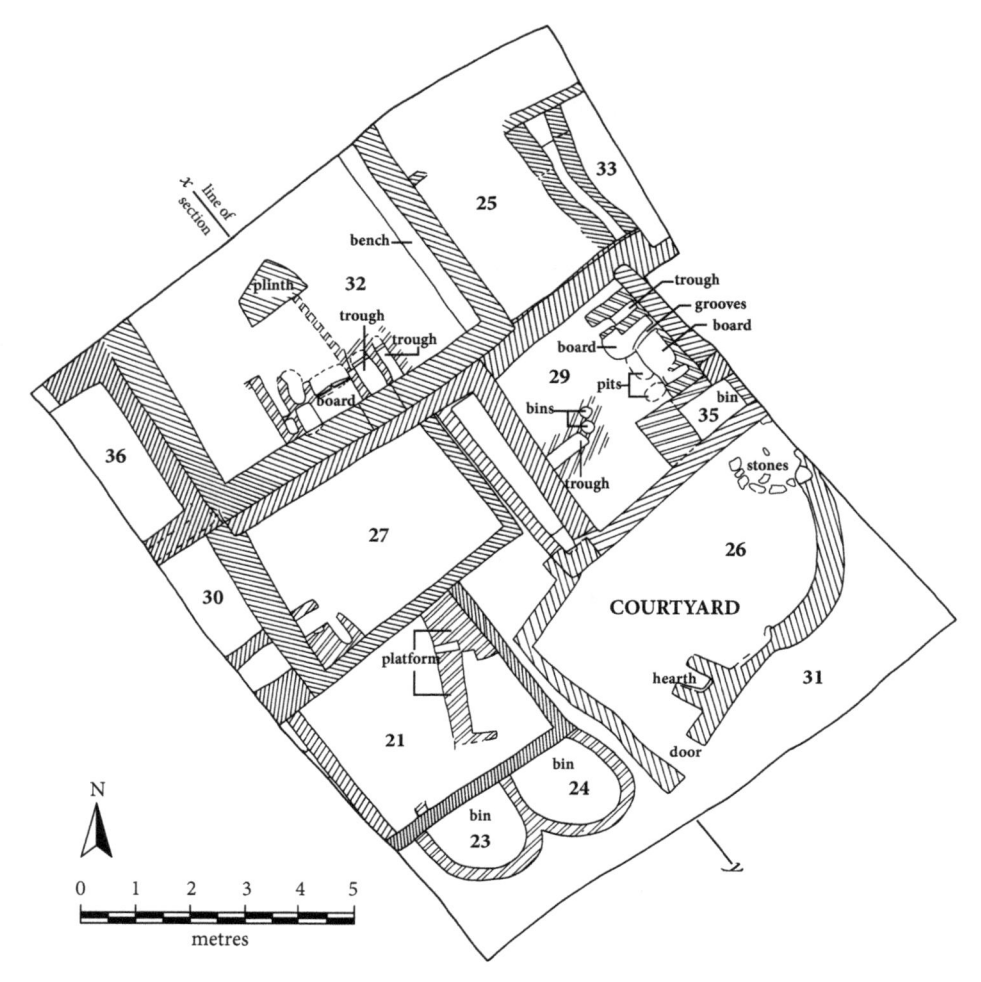

FIGURE 9.3 Yanik Tepe, plan of Level 10, Trench L 4/1.

(Fig. 9.1 and Summers 2004). This long period can be split into A and B on the basis of the ceramic repertoire; much of the pottery in ETC IIA was embellished with incised and excised decoration, very often filled with white paste, whereas the pottery of ETC IIB is almost entirely plain. In ETC III the buildings are agglutinative and entirely rectilinear, although domestic units continue to be discrete with, as in the previous period, each house possessing its own elaborate kitchen range (Figs. 9.3–9.4). It is almost certain that there was a hiatus of unknown duration between ETC II and III at Yanik Tepe.

Whether this Yanik-centric periodization can be usefully applied, or indeed recognized, in archaeological horizons elsewhere in northwestern Iran, let alone within the wider ETC cultural zone, is another matter which the current paucity of evidence does not permit us to address with confidence. Haftavan Tepe, where the complete ETC sequence has not been excavated, appears to mirror Yanik Tepe, while at Giljar (see below) there are but minor differences.

FIGURE 9.4 Yanik Tepe, Level 10, Trench L 4/1; detail of the kitchen range in Room 29.

Stratigraphy

Stratigraphically the ETC falls after the Late Chalcolithic period, but no excavated site has anything that looks like a transition or evidence for continuity between the two periods. Everywhere, it seems, there is discontinuity and very probably a hiatus. This certainly holds true for Yanik Tepe and is not contradicted by the scant evidence from other sites close to Lake Urmia, especially Giljar, Geoy Tepe, and Haftavan Tepe.

A hiatus before the arrival of the ETC culture is also attested further south at Godin Tepe, in central-western Iran, where there is some evidence for break in occupation between the ETC Period IV and the earlier Period VI (*OHR*: 160–67). Godin V, a term no longer used, comprised that area of Level VI:IB and IA when an oval enclosure was occupied by merchants from Mesopotamia as indicated by Late Uruk pottery, especially bevel–rim bowls and low-sided trays (Young 2004: 648).

At Hasanlu in the southern Urmia Basin the stratigraphy is less clear (Danti et al. 2004). Exposures of third-millennium levels are very restricted, the sequence being reconstructed on the basis of pottery from unclear contexts. Local Painted Orange Ware might be later than a very poorly known ETC horizon which may have been restricted to an unexplored area of this large mound.

At Yanik Tepe, Haftavan Tepe, Giljar, and other sites in the region where evidence is less robust, the end of the ETC was marked by abandonment. At Haftavan a phase of occupation restricted to a sparse settlement on the elevated, central portion of the site yielded sherds tentatively identified as Painted Orange Ware comparable to the better-known material of this type from Hasanlu. However, the radiocarbon dates from Hasanlu Period VII, which cluster in the mid-third millennium BC, create a chronological conundrum (see below).

No indications of final destruction have been recognized nor, as far as ceramics are concerned, any continuity into the widespread settlements characterized by polychrome painted Urmia Ware or, as it is called in Eastern Turkey, Yayla or Van-Urmia Ware (Edwards 1983, 1986; Rubinson 2004). A similar pattern of desertion is observed over much of the highland massif of Eastern Turkey, where the distribution of upland sites on which Yayla Ware has been found is strikingly different to the ETC pattern of village settlements (Özfirat 2001).

Absolute dating

There are no radiocarbon dates for the earliest ETC levels at any site in northwestern Iran. However, the generally accepted view that the Early Bronze Age in Anatolia began around or soon after 3100 BC is confirmed by the excellent sequence of radiocarbon dates from Arslantepe on the Upper Euphrates and Sos Höyük on the Erzurum Plain. More important than the absolute dates is the observation of some kind of convergence between the expansion of the ETC culture and the collapse of the Late Uruk culture and the northern manifestations of Mesopotamian-influenced urban complexity. As yet there is no evidence of direct Late Uruk influence in northwestern Iran, and it may be that none should be expected, although the presence of a Late Uruk enclave at Hasanlu has been postulated (Danti et al. 2004: 596–7). There is, however, evidence of a Late Uruk presence, indicated by bevelled-rim bowls, followed, after a gap of unknown duration, by ETC settlement, as far east as Qazvin (Fazeli Nashli and Abbasnezhad Sereshti 2005). Regardless of the geographical extent of Late Uruk presence and influence in the Urmia basin, it might not be wrong to link ETC expansion from the north with the Late Uruk collapse further south, and thus to consider it likely that the earliest appearance of the ETC in Iran should not be dated much before 3100 BC. In any event, when it did arrive the ETC culture was already fully developed.

A series of calibrated radiocarbon dates from Hasanlu VII cluster around the middle of the third millennium while a single date from Geoy Tepe seems to fall between 3000 and 2900 (Danti et al. 2004: 587, table 1). The radiocarbon dates from Godin Tepe, to the south of our area, are consistent with this general range, although the end of Godin IV falls much earlier than the end of the ETC in the Urmia Basin (*OHR*: 166, table 5.2). Mitchell Rothman would place the start of Godin IV in the early third millennium BC. However, if the succeeding Period III begins, as the radiocarbon dates and other evidence suggest, well before 2500 then Godin IV must have begun well before the start of ETC III, as defined by rectilinear architecture at Yanik Tepe (contra *OHR*: 163–5). A date early in the third millennium for the beginning of Godin IV is supported by the presence of incised and excised pottery which is very similar to what was found in ETC IIA at Yanik Tepe.

No less difficult to assess is the date of the end of the ETC in northwestern Iran. Charles Burney perspicaciously suggested that the rectilinear building phases that comprise ETC III at Yanik Tepe and Haftavan Tepe might extend well down into the second millennium, perhaps to 1600 BC or even later. This assessment has been supported by a comprehensive set of radiocarbon dates from Sos Höyük on the Erzurum Plain in northeastern Turkey (Sagona 2011 with references). However, in his study of Urmia Ware Michael Edwards used magnetic intensity dating to propose absolute dates for Haftavan VIC of about 2200–2000 BC, followed by Early VIB in the range of 1900–1550 BC and Late VIB from 1600/1550 to 1450 BC (Edwards 1983: 7–45, 354–5). At first glance all of the Haftavan dates appear to be some 400 years too early. There is clearly a chronological problem here because the radiocarbon dates for Painted Orange Ware at Hasanlu would suggest that the Haftavan IVC date is too late rather than too early. However, the identification of a few sherds of Painted Orange Ware at Haftavan has been questioned (Voigt and Dyson 1992: 177). A date of around 1900 BC for Haftavan IVB is surely too high. It is unfortunate that there are currently no other sets of radiocarbon dates, either for the ETC or the Urmia Ware horizon, from sites in northwestern Iran or Eastern Turkey.

In the Solduz Basin south of Lake Urmia the ETC is said to be contemporaneous with Hasanlu VIIC, although it was suggested above that ETC IIA levels at Hasanlu might lie unexcavated somewhere on the mound. Be that as it may, ETC IIB seems to have been contemporary with Hasanlu VIIA–B, dated to the second half of the third millennium BC. To what extent ETC cultural elements infiltrated the Hasanlu VII culture is unclear, as is the nature of the relationship between ETC and Hasanlu VII sites and their populations. Further south, in the Kangavar Plain, Godin Tepe IV and other, more substantial sites known only from archaeological surveys (Young 2004), seem to have been abandoned before 2500 BC, which might be well before the end of ETC II at Yanik Tepe. As noted above, parallels between decorated pottery from Godin Tepe IV and Yanik Tepe are not inconsistent with this date, although the construction of comparative chronologies of local and regional pottery styles is something of a fool's game in the absence of independent chronological pegs. There is some continuity in pottery traditions from Godin IV into Godin III, but this is to the south of our region and thus does not necessarily reflect developments in northwestern Iran.

One final chronological issue requires discussion, namely the date of the transition from ETC II to ETC III. Radiocarbon dates are of little help, except in demonstrating that at Yanik Tepe the change came well after 2600 BC, a date that sometimes appears in the literature. One way of trying to fix the date of this transition is to work backward from the end of the ETC at Yanik. But, as has just been shown, the date of the abandonment there is uncertain, as is the length of the hiatus between ETC II and III at the site.

Chronological summary

The beginning of the ETC in northwestern Iran is generally placed in the late fourth millennium BC. Whenever the exact date may have been, the ETC culture arrived from the north already fully formed. The speed of its expansion southwards, as far as the Hamadan Plain, is uncertain but the arrival of the new and distinctive culture, and therefore of people, at Godin Tepe followed the Late Uruk collapse. The few settlements found on the eastern edge of our region, in the highlands above the margins of the Caspian Sea, also seem to postdate the Late Uruk collapse, judging by the evidence from the Qazvin Plain. The principal settlements known are in the northern Urmia Basin. The most prominent of these have long sequences of occupation spanning as much as one and a half millennia. At Yanik Tepe there are two major phases: ETC II, distinguished by round buildings, and ETC III, with exclusively rectilinear ones. The earlier phase can be subdivided into IIA and IIB on the basis of a marked and fairly abrupt change from pottery with incised and excised decoration to plain pottery. It is uncertain if the Yanik Tepe sequence can be applied to all sites in northwestern Iran, or indeed in the northern Urmia Basin, but there is no evidence to the contrary.

To the south of Lake Urmia, at Hasanlu, the ETC appears to end late in the first half of the third millennium BC, to be replaced by a local tradition characterized by Painted Orange Ware. Apart from the ceramics themselves and their limited regional distribution, very little is known of this horizon. Further south, at Godin Tepe in central-western Iran, the ETC ends at around the same time as in the Solduz Plain, with some slight evidence of continuity into the following Godin III Period.

To the north, in the Transcaucasus, a great deal of new work is currently being undertaken in the republics of Azerbaijan, Georgia, and Armenia, as well as in the Autonomous Region of Nakhichevan. ETC I is found in the northeastern corner of Turkey, in the Araxes and Kura valleys, Nakhichevan and the area around Mount Ararat (Sagona 2010, 2011 with refs.). The chronology of the ETC in this diverse region remains vexed, and the transition from the third to the second millennium is poorly attested. While much of this large area lies outside Iran, the eventual resolution of many outstanding archaeological problems, including chronology, will impact on our understanding of the ETC in the Urmia Basin and lands to the east.

Key sites

Yanik Tepe

Yanik Tepe (37.980705° N, 46.003351° E) was selected for excavation by Charles Burney because of the exceptional incised, excised, and white-filled decoration applied to the ETC pottery found there. The mound sits on an alluvial plain near the northeastern edge of the Urmia Basin, close to the modern village of Tazekand and 5 km west of Khosrowshah. The region is fertile and well watered by the perpetually snow-covered peak of the volcanic Kuh-e Sahend to the south. In the 1960s only irrigated crops were grown, there being barely sufficient precipitation to permit rain-fed agriculture. Earlier periods represented include the Late Neolithic and Middle Chalcolithic, with a long hiatus between the latest Chalcolithic and the ETC. Following the ETC abandonment the site was unoccupied until the Iron Age.

The first ETC settlement was on the lower slopes of the earlier mound. The size of the ETC settlement is not easy to judge for at no time in the ETC period was the entire 8 ha site occupied. The mound rises some 6.5 m above the plain but, because the ETC village settlement was continually shifting, it proved possible to excavate substantial exposures of the ETC II without the need to remove deep ETC III levels which were themselves extensively uncovered on the summit of the mound.

The ETC II comprised round houses, circular huts, and circular buildings with internal partitions that were most probably silos (Fig. 9.1). Some of the huts had rectangular annexes that were generally unroofed. Walls were of mudbrick supporting lighter superstructures of wattle and reeds covered with mud. Rather than storage pits a plethora of built-in bins characterized these structures. Fires were not infrequent and had clearly engulfed considerable portions of the village. The frequent rebuilding of huts on the wall stubs of their predecessors demonstrates a continuity of place not explicable by space restrictions. Breaks in this continuity were often the result of fire. A total of fourteen stratigraphic levels were identified. Where there had been burning, the division between one level and another was distinct, but in other cases the levels reflected practicalities of excavation and recording rather than the complex phases through which each individual structure progressed between its construction and the end of its life. Huts reached diameters of 5 m, with central posts supporting the superstructure of the larger buildings. In many cases the walls of adjacent huts touched one another, demonstrating that there could not have been roofing beams or eaves that projected beyond the walls. Many of the huts were provided with standard kitchen ranges located immediately to the right of the doorway on entry. The most elaborate of these fixtures included large flat ovens with sunken fire pits filled with heat-retaining stones, presumably for cooking flat bread; gypsum-plastered trays for preparing food, with space beneath to accommodate knees; and storage bins of various sizes. Benches or platforms were commonly built around the side. Some houses were divided by low partition walls. The spatial distribution of houses, other circular huts, circular silos with discrete compartments, and external bins, suggest some complexity in the social organization of the village.

New analysis has suggested that the stone and mudbrick defences that appeared in the middle part of the ETC II sequence (Fig. 9.1) probably surrounded an elevated area at the center of the village rather than part of a defensive perimeter wall, as had been thought at the time of excavation (Summers 2013). Parallels with a small number of sites in the Transcaucasus, such as Mokhrablur (Areshian 2005, with references), suggest the possibility of an area set aside for cultic purposes. Whether or not such speculation is correct, the existence of this substantial wall is evidence of organized communal effort in bringing the stones from a considerable distance and in the large-scale production of mudbricks.

Long before the end of the ETC II Period of circular buildings a marked change in the ceramic repertoire is apparent, whereby the very common incised and excised decoration all but disappeared. Toward the end of the ETC II it may be possible to detect a more specialized mode of production in the form of finer cups with a very high black sheen that is sometimes called "graphite burnished," but the general household mode of production seems to have continued. It is noteworthy that, whatever the length of any hiatus in the settlement between ETC II and III, the ceramics show only gradual change throughout the entire ETC period, with no hint of centralized production. Pottery was handmade throughout the entire sequence.

ETC III architecture is in one way entirely different from that of ETC II, yet exactly the same in another. The dramatic change was from circular to rectilinear (Figs. 9.3–9.4). Hand in hand with this radical development went the transference of courtyards and open spaces from the ground to elevated flat roofs with instances of upper stories. However, this new, agglutinative style of building apparently involved nothing more than making round huts square. All of the internal features (kitchen fittings, benches, and central posts) were retained. Walls became more massive so as to bear the load of roof beams and mud, while mudbrick stair supports provided access via roofs, but even that was not so different from the elevated thresholds that were a common feature of the earlier round houses. There are obvious advantages in the rectilinear style: less frequent fires, dryer spaces on the flat roofs from which animals were perhaps excluded, and greater warmth through long and cold winters. Yanik ETC III had a total of four levels, but like the levels of ETC II, these divisions are little more than an archaeological convenience. More striking is the evidence of continuity and the continual rebuilding of individual areas. The absence of destructive fires in these less flammable structures reduced the amount of ceramics that was recovered. Nevertheless, pottery more than sufficient enough to demonstrate the continuity of local traditions as well as a general conformity to developments elsewhere in the northern Urmia Basin and the Van region of Eastern Turkey.

Haftavan Tepe

Located some 3 km from the district town of Salmas and close to the village of Haftavan (Burney 1970, 1972b, 1973, 1975, 1976), Haftavan Tepe (38.167319° N, 44.793612° E) is one of the largest settlement mounds in the Urmia Basin.

Levels belonging to both ETC II and ETC III were excavated. ETC II (Haftavan Level VIII) was investigated in a restricted area. Two successive circular houses, comparable to less elaborate examples at Yanik Tepe, were uncovered. Stratigraphically, this level in Test Trench 9 is floating. The pottery, some of which has dimples and grooves, is more reminiscent of Geoy Tepe and the Van region than of Yanik Tepe, while the restricted occurrence of incised decoration is suggestive of a date in the ETC IIB. Haftavan VII was investigated mainly on the mound summit where substantial buildings of mudbrick were relatively accessible. Haftavan VII replicated the evidence of the Yanik Tepe ETC III levels.

Geoy Tepe

Located in the Urmia Plain about 7 km south of the city of Urmia, Geoy Tepe (37.3104° N, 45.0842° E) was excavated in 1948 by Theodore Burton-Brown (Burton-Brown

1951). With circular buildings of ETC II in its lower levels, Period K spans much of the ETC period. The pottery recovered closely parallels that of Haftavan VIII, Tepe Giljar, and the Van region rather than the incised and excised fashion seen in Yanik. While this might suggest that, although there are several meters of stratified deposit, the Geoy Tepe ETC sequence is not necessarily complete, the evidence from Haftavan VIII and Giljar, summarized below, points to regional rather than chronological differentiation.

Tepe Giljar

Tepe Giljar (37.4242° N, 45.0434° E) is situated on the south bank of the Nazlı Çay, some 18 km north of Urmia. This substantial site rises 25 m above the plain. A sondage on the edge of the mound, where it had been cut away by the river, revealed a long sequence of ETC levels (Periods B and B/C) with 13 m of deposit. A long hiatus followed the late Neolithic Period C while Iron Age levels lay above the ETC. Phases VII and VIII at the base of Period B had circular houses and rectangular structures, whereas no walls were found in the preceding Phase IX in Period B/C. Above Phase VII were freestanding rectangular houses rather than agglutinative buildings, but the area exposed was very small. The ceramics closely parallel those at Geoy Tepe K and Haftavan Tepe VIII and VII. No Painted Orange Ware was reported.

Ravaz

Ravaz lies in the western portion of our region, a little to the northwest of Siah Ceshme in the area of Maku (Kleiss and Kroll 1979; Kroll 2005). The plan of features visible on the surface reveals groups of round huts with associated, smaller, rectilinear structures separated by streets. An irregular, open area occupies the center of the settlement, while terraces and isolated round huts to the west indicate gardens or fields. The plan closely resembles the largest excavated portion of Yanik Tepe ETC II. Ravaz does not, however, appear to have been occupied for long. Wolfram Kleiss and Stephan Kroll thought that a defensive wall with semicircular towers which cuts off the bluff on which the core of the site was located should also be dated to the ETC. If this wall really does date to the third millennium it would be of considerable interest.

Hasanlu Tepe

Hasanlu (37.004544° N, 45.458640° E) lies in northeastern Solduz which is itself situated in the eastern part of Quadar River valley to the south of Lake Urmia. The stratigraphic sequence revealed in small, deep soundings revealed a hiatus between Chalcolithic

Hasanlu VIII and ETC Hasanlu VII. Hasanlu VIII, which is known as the Pisdeli phase after a nearby site, is related to the Late Ubaid and Early Uruk periods in Mesopotamia while Hasanlu VII is considered contemporaneous with ETC II and III, that is, the Yanik Tepe, Haftavan Tepe, and related sequences (Danti et al. 2004).

Conclusions

The Early Bronze Age in northwestern Iran is dominated by a single, distinctive, cohesive and conservative complex, the Early Transcaucasian (ETC) culture. The geographical boundaries of the ETC extend across a vast area of which northwestern Iran is but a part, and over a chronological period which, due to the absence of ETC I assemblages, is not wholly represented within this region. In addition to its intrinsic interest, this distinctive cultural horizon is of great importance because it raises difficult and often controversial questions concerning relationships between archaeologically defined cultures, the migration of the bearers of those cultures, processes of acculturation, and, although currently out of favor perhaps, ethnicity and language. From a different perspective, questions about socioeconomic aspects of the ETC include how society was structured and what the roles of transhumance and nomadism may have been within a settlement pattern that, in the Urmia Basin, appears to have been dominated by permanently settled villages with an economy based on mixed farming. Beyond this, what is to be made of the absence of evidence of urbanism and of polity? What bound these settlements together? How was conflict resolved? There is no evidence of violence and weapons are precious few. These are all topics for ongoing and future research. Much new work in progress in nations to the north will, it is hoped, cast light on ETC origins and, more importantly, provide explanations for its extraordinary expansion. To the west, at Arslantepe on the Upper Euphrates, detailed evidence of the complexity that occurred in a contact zone between the ETC and the literate Syro-Mesopotamian world is being examined in exemplary fashion. In Iran, to the south of the area focused on here, Godin Tepe and other sites, some with large areas of ETC occupation according to surface survey, will surely reveal equally convoluted interactions with literate powers to the south and southwest. In the Urmia Basin, and perhaps as far west as the Erzurum Plain, on the other hand, cultural conservatism appears to have been dominant until well into the second millennium BC. One great challenge for archaeologists working in and on northwestern Iran is to document and explain the changes that happened between the disappearance of the ETC and the emergence of settlements like those at Dinkha Tepe and Hafvtavan VI, with architectural traditions and ceramic styles that were new and different. Here, too, it will be necessary to go beyond modern political borders in the search for answers to the archaeological questions posed by material found in northwestern Iran.

Acknowledgments

I am grateful to Antonio Sagona and Mitchell Rothman for supplying copies of papers before publication, to Toby Wilkinson for comments on an earlier draft, to Françoise Summers for help with illustrations, and to Daniel Potts for assiduous editing.

References

Areshian, G. E. 2005. Early Bronze Age settlements in the Ararat Plain and its vicinity. *AMIT* 37: 71–88.
Biscione, R. 2009. The distribution of pre- and protohistoric hillforts in Iran. *SMEA* 51: 123–43.
Burney, C. A. 1958. Eastern Anatolia in the Chalcolithic and Early Bronze Ages. *AnSt* 8: 157–209.
———. 1961a. Excavations at Yanik Tepe, north-west Iran. *Iraq* 23: 138–53.
———. 1961b. Circular buildings found at Yanik Tepe in north-west Iran. *Antiquity* 35: 237–40.
———. 1962. Excavations at Yanik Tepe, Azerbaijan, 1961: Second preliminary report. *Iraq* 24/2: 134–52.
———. 1964. Excavations at Yanik Tepe, Azerbaijan, 1962: Third preliminary report. *Iraq* 26/1: 54–61.
———. 1970. Excavations at Haftavân Tepe, 1968: First preliminary report. *Iran* 8: 157–71.
———. 1972a. Yanik Tepe. In *Excavations in Iran: The British contribution*, ed. P. R. S. Moorey, 13–14. Oxford: Organizing Committee of the Sixth International Congress of Iranian Art and Archaeology.
———. 1972b. Excavations at Haftavân Tepe, 1969: Second preliminary report. *Iran* 10: 127–42.
———. 1973. Excavations at Haftavân Tepe, 1971: Third preliminary report. *Iran* 11: 153–72.
———. 1975. Excavations at Haftavân Tepe, 1973: Fourth preliminary report. *Iran* 13: 149–64.
———. 1976. The fifth season of excavations at Haftavân Tappeh: brief summary of principal results. *PASARI* 4: 257–71.
———. 1977. *From village to empire: An introduction to Near Eastern archaeology*. Oxford: Phaidon.
Burney, C. A., and D. M. Lang. 1971. *The peoples of the hills, ancient Ararat and Caucasus*. London: Weidenfeld and Nicolson.
Burton-Brown, T. 1951. *Excavations in Azerbaijan, 1948*. London: John Murray.
Danti, M. D., M. M. Voigt, and R. H. Dyson, Jr. 2004. The search for the late Chalcolithic/Early Bronze Age transition in the Ushnu-Solduz Valley, Iran. *AVH*: 583–601.
Dyson, R. H., Jr. 1997. Hasanlu. *OEANE* 2: 478–81.
Edwards, M. 1983. *Haftavan, Period VI. Excavations in Azerbaijan (North-western Iran), I*. Oxford: BAR Int Ser 182.
———. 1986. "Urmia Ware" and its distribution in north-western Iran in the second millennium B.C.: A review of the results of excavations and surveys. *Iran* 24: 57–77.
Fahimi, H. 2005. Kura-Araxes type pottery from Gilan and the eastern extension of the Early Transcaucasian Culture. *AMIT* 37: 123–32.

Fazeli Nashli, H., and R. Abbasnezhad Sereshti. 2005. Social transformation and interregional interaction in the Qazvin plain during the 5th, 4th, and, 3rd millennia B. C. *AMIT* 37: 7–26.

Ingraham, M. L., and G. D. Summers. 1979. Settlements and stelae in the Meskinshah Plain, Iran. *AMI* 12: 67–102.

Kleiss, W., and S. Kroll. 1979. Ravaz und Yakhvali, zwei befestigte Plätze des 3. Jahrtausends. *AMI* 12: 27–47.

Kozbe, G. 2004. Activity areas and social organization within Early Trans-Caucasian Houses at Karagündüz Höyük, Van. *AVH*: 35–53.

Kroll, S. 1984. Archäologische Fundplätze in Iranisch-Ost-Azarbaidjan. *AMI* 17: 13–133

———. 2004. Aurel Stein in Hasan Ali. Bemalte frühbronzezitliche Keramik im Gebeit des Urmia-Sees: "Hasan Ali Ware." *AVH*: 677–92.

———. 2005. Early Bronze Age settlement patterns in the Orumiye Basin. *AMIT* 37: 115–22.

Kuftin, B. A. 1941. *Arkheologičeskie Raskopki v Trialeti*. Tiblisi: Akademii Nauk Gruzinskoj SSR.

Ökse, A. T. 2005. Early Bronze Age settlement pattern and cultural structure of the Sivas Region. *AMIT* 37: 35–51.

Özfırat, A. 2001. *Doğu Anadolu Yayla Kültüleri (M.Ö. II Binyil)*. Istanbul: Arkeoloji ve Sanat Yayınları.

Palumbi, G. 2008. *The red and black: Social and cultural interaction between the Upper Euphrates and the Southern Caucasus communities in the fourth and third millennium BC*. Rome: SPO 2.

———. 2011. The Chalcolithic of Eastern Anatolia. In *The Oxford Handbook of ancient Anatolia (10,000–323 BCE)*, ed. S. R. Steadman and G. McMahon, 205–26. New York: Oxford University Press.

Pecorella, P. E., and M. Salvini. 1984. *Tra lo Zagros e l'Urmia: Richerche storiche ed archaeologiche nell'Azerbaigiano Iranico*. Rome: Incunabula Graeca 78.

Piro, J. J. 2009. Pastoralism in the early Transcaucasian culture: The faunal remains from Sos Höyük. Unpublished PhD diss., New York University.

Rubinson, K. S. 2004. Dinkha Tepe, Iran, and so-called Urmia ware. *AVH*: 661–76.

Sagona, A. 2010. Past and present directions in the archaeology of the Transcaucasus. *TÜBA-AR* 13: 143–57

———. 2011. Anatolia and the Transcaucasus, themes and variations ca. 6400–1500. In *The Oxford Handbook of Ancient Anatolia (10,000–323 BCE)*, ed. S. R. Steadman and G. McMahon, 683–703. New York: Oxford University Press.

Stein, M. A. 1940. *Old routes of Western Īrān: Narrative of an archaeological journey*. London: Macmillan.

Summers, G. D. 1982. The architecture, pottery and other material from Yanik Tepe, Haftavan Tepe VIII and related sites. Unpublished PhD diss., University of Manchester.

———. 2004. Yanik Tepe and the early Trans-Caucasian culture: Problems and perspectives. *AVH*: 617–43.

———. 2013. *Yanik Tepe I: The Early Trans-Caucasian architecture*. Leuven: Peeters.

Swiny, S. 1975. Survey in northwest Iran, 1971. *EW* 25: 77–96.

Tala'i, H. 1984. Notes on new pottery evidence from the eastern Urmia basin: Gol Tepe. *Iran* 22: 151–6.

Voigt, M. M. and R. H. Dyson, Jr. 1992. The chronology of Iran, ca. 8000–2000 B.C. In *Chronologies in Old World archaeology*, 3rd ed., vol. 1, ed. R. W. Ehrich, 122–78. Chicago: University of Chicago Press.

Young, T. C., Jr. 2004. The Kangavar survey—Periods VI to IV. *AVH*: 645–60.

CHAPTER 10

THE BRONZE AGE IN NORTHEASTERN IRAN

CHRISTOPHER P. THORNTON

INTRODUCTION

Despite over 150 years of excavation, the northeast (Fig. 10.1) remains one of the least understood areas of prehistoric Iran. The reasons for this are varied, but the noticeable lack of a comprehensive excavation monograph from even one site in this region is the most likely culprit. Indeed, even the most important type-sites of this region such as Tepe Hissar (Hesar), which has been studied and discussed by some of the great prehistorians of the twentieth century (e.g., Childe 1942: 357–8; Piggott 1943; Mallowan 1965: 117–27), have seen less than 10 percent of the excavated finds published. This dearth of published data has caused considerable confusion among scholars attempting to use the incomplete publication record from such sites as a reference for their own research (e.g., Helwing 2006; Mousavi 2008; Mahfroozi and Piller 2009).

Since 2004, the author has been involved with a number of projects at the University of Pennsylvania Museum, working with Robert H. Dyson Jr., Holly Pittman, Ayse Gürsan-Salzmann, Michael Gregg, and others to publish its excavated Iranian collections. These include artifacts and/or archival records from a number of northeast Iranian sites, including Tepe Hissar, Tureng Tepe, Hotu and Belt (Pers. Ghar-e Kamarband) Caves, Shir-i Shian (Shir Ashian), and Sang-e Chakhmaq, as well as related sites in north-central Iran, such as Cheshmeh Ali (Rayy) and Murteza Gerd. In addition, the author has been fortunate enough to travel to northeastern Iran thanks to Dr. Hassan Fazeli and the ICAR. In Iran, the author benefited from numerous dialogues and site-visits with exceptional Iranian colleagues working in this region, including Ali Mahfroozi in Mazandaran; Kourosh Roustaei in Damghan-Shahrud; Qorban Ali Abassi and Hamid Omrani in the southern Gorgan Valley; Ali Vahdati around Jajarm; and

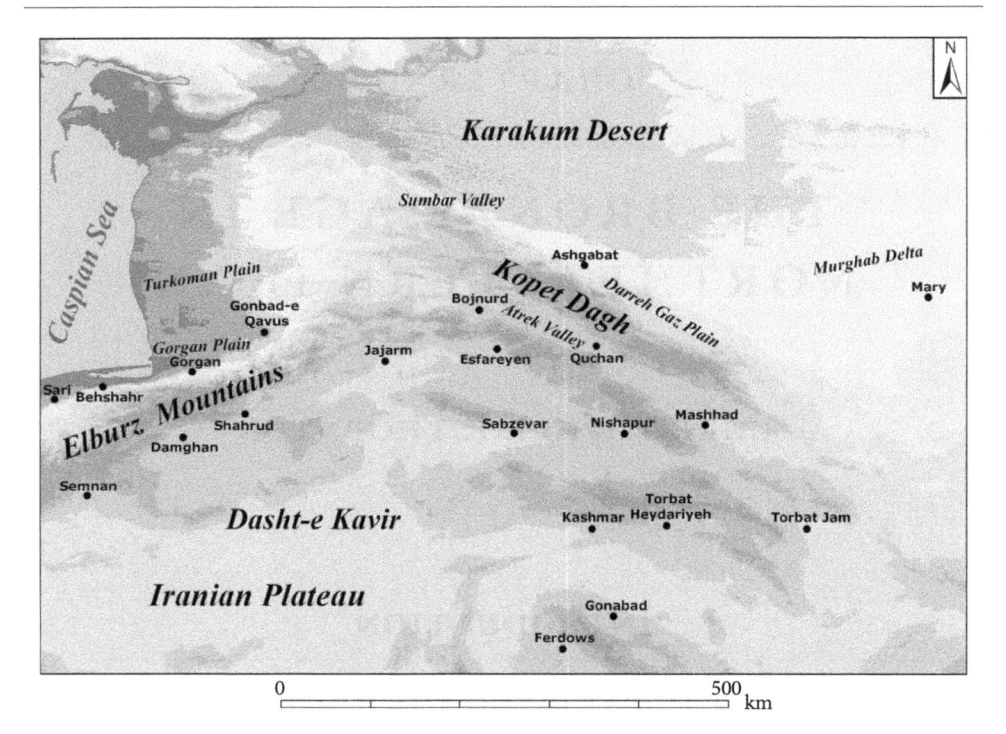

FIGURE 10.1 Topographic map of northeastern Iran (Sari to Mashad) (courtesy of David Massey, Ohio State University).

Emran Garajian in the northern Gorgan and Nishapur. Thus, much of the information synthesized in this chapter comes from personal observation of museum collections and personal communications from generous colleagues. Furthermore, this synthesis builds upon the pioneering work of J. Deshayes (1968, 1969a), R. H. Dyson Jr. (1977, 1991), V. I. Sarianidi (1971), S. Cleuziou (1986, 1991), M. Tosi (1973–4), P. L. Kohl (1984a), and others who attempted to bring the late prehistory of northeastern Iran to the attention of the wider archaeological world.

This chapter is divided into three main sections. First, the cultural geography of northeastern Iran will be summarized in order to outline the various environmental factors that have affected human behavior there over the past 10,000 years or so. Second, the history of archaeological investigation in this region will be summarized, with a focus on the major excavations and regional surveys that have provided data enabling a broader synthesis. Third, the culture history of the late prehistory of northeastern Iran, from Neolithic to Late Bronze Age (c.7000–1500 BC), will be summarized with a particular focus on those type-fossils (ceramics and small finds) that serve as chronological markers. While a chapter such as this cannot hope to be comprehensive, it should provide a useful reference for new excavations in the region as well as for projects aimed at publishing old excavations.

Cultural geography

The region of northeastern Iran can be divided, somewhat crudely, into three distinct cultural and ecological zones: the Caspian littoral, the Alborz highlands, and the relatively fertile plains of the Iranian plateau that gradually disappear into the salt deserts to the south. The southern Caspian littoral and the lush Gorgan plain provide some of the best agricultural land in all of Iran. Well watered by moisture coming off the Caspian Sea that collides with the high Alborz Mountains, the Caspian littoral has a semitropical climate and produces fantastic fruit, huge quantities of grain (including, today, rice), and fresh fish that is exported to the upland interior. Similarly, the Gorgan plain receives plentiful rainfall and provides superb land for irrigation, making this region a mini "breadbasket" for all of northern Iran. The northern part of the Gorgan plain gradually merges into steppe grassland (the Turkoman plain) more suitable for nomadic herdsmen than agriculturalists, while in the eastern part of the Gorgan plain low hills gradually transition into the Kopet Dagh Mountains along the Iran–Turkmenistan border.

The contrast between the semitropical lowlands along the Caspian Sea and the often snow-covered highlands of the nearby Alborz Mountains cannot be overemphasized. These mountains, many as high as 3500–4000 masl, are even today sparsely populated by only the hardiest of people. In recent centuries, loggers, miners, and transhumant pastoralists have comprised the majority of those living at such high altitudes. In reality, our knowledge of the prehistoric highland communities who inhabited northeastern Iran is minimal and studies of similar societies elsewhere in Iran, such as in the Bakhtiyari Mountains (Zagarell 1982), provide a poor substitute. However, we can infer that in prehistory, any peoples living in these areas would have had access to important resources such as timber, metal ore, gold, and semiprecious stones (notably turquoise), which they, in turn, could have purveyed to lowland populations to the northwest and to the societies of the Iranian plateau to the south and east.

Without a doubt, the Iranian plateau has been the heartland of Persian society for thousands of years, long before the modern nation-state of Iran was formed. Averaging 900 masl, the Iranian plateau was a rich but impenetrable landscape overlooking the agricultural populations of Mesopotamia and southern Central Asia for millennia. Until the twentieth century, the people of this region subsisted on both herding and irrigated agriculture using *qanat* technology to draw water from beneath the nearby mountains. These agro-pastoralists also engaged in resource procurement, craft production, and long-distance trade, making them almost entirely self-sufficient or, at least, symbiotically subsistent with their neighbors. The plateau does not, however, lend itself to large populations—water and irrigable land are scarce, so settlements were generally small until the Middle Ages brought new hydraulic technologies and extensive trade networks to feed large urban populations.

To my knowledge, there has never been a comprehensive geographical or anthropological study of northeastern Iran focusing specifically on land use and patterns of social movement (see, e.g., Adle 1971). The Turan Project of Brian Spooner and his students focused on important issues such as desertification and traditional village life on the plateau (Spooner 1965, 1974, 1985; Spooner and Horne 1980; Martin 1980; Horne 1994), but did not seek to understand interactive patterns of socially conscribed land use and population movement. Similarly, William Irons' (1972, 1975) study of the Yomut Turkmen along the Iran–Turkmenistan border has become a classic reference on tribal organization of steppe nomads, but it gives little insight into the totally different pastoral and agricultural communities in the rest of northeastern Iran.

The only study of northeast Iranian cultural geography that provides information on large-scale patterns of population movement and socioeconomic relationships across the varied landscape was carried out by Mohammad-Hossein Papoli-Yazdi (1991), who examined the movement of Kurdish groups along the Iran–Turkmenistan border. Most Kurds in northeastern Iran moved (or were moved) there in the sixteenth century to serve as a buffer against the raiding Uzbek nomads from the north. The Kurds were perfectly suited to this role, as their traditional east-to-west migration pattern (across the modern Iran–Iraq border within Kurdistan) helped them to monitor the long stretch of plateau south of the Kopet Dagh Mountains. While we cannot know whether such long-distance seasonal migration patterns existed in prehistory, the well-documented movement of goods such as lapis lazuli from east to west for thousands of years must have been orchestrated by groups familiar with such long-distance routes.

Papoli-Yazdi (1991: 213–50) also described the short-distance transhumance patterns of semisedentary pastoralists (seminomads) of Turkic, Persian, and Kurdish ethnicity in northern Khorasan. While the prevailing directions dominating such migratory patterns are "uphill" versus "downhill," many of the traditional routes taken by these pastoralists were north-to-south movements through the passes in the Kopet Dagh to the piedmont zone of southern Turkmenistan. One can imagine similar groups moving from the highlands of the Alborz Mountains or the Iranian plateau down to the Caspian littoral and the southern Gorgan plain. As such, Papoli-Yazdi provides us with a model for the cultural geography of northeastern Iran: intraregional, highland-lowland relationships complemented by interregional, east-to-west movement of people and trade goods.

History of excavation

In the mid-nineteenth century, the Russian diplomat Baron Clement Augustus de Bode published a short account of a hoard of gold and alabaster vessels, bronze weapons, and stone figurines found near the city of Astrabad (modern-day Gorgan) in northeastern Iran (Bode 1844). Although numerous Western explorers had previously traveled through this region and often noted archaeological sites and antiquities in their writing, the "Astrabad treasure" (Fig. 10.2) can be credited with sparking serious academic interest in the region (e.g., Rostovtzeff 1920). Indeed, it is probably no coincidence that many of the earliest surveys in northeastern Iran were carried out in the Gorgan Valley (Morgan 1896; Sykes 1911) and that some of the first archaeological excavations in this region were carried out at Tepe Khargush (Morgan 1896), Tureng Tepe (Wulsin 1932, 1938), and Shah Tepe (Arne 1935, 1945), just outside of historic Astrabad.

A second early source of information on the archaeology of this region was provided by A. Houtum Schindler (1877), who reported on some painted pottery from a mound near the city of Damghan called Tepe Hissar. Similar sherds were studied in the 1920s by the great Iranian expert Ernst Herzfeld (Dyson 2009), leading him to encourage the young German-American archaeologist Erich F. Schmidt to carry out the first systematic excavations at Tepe Hissar (Schmidt 1933, 1937) after the French monopoly over excavations in Iran ended in 1927. Schmidt's superb excavations and detailed (if incomplete) publications served as a model for archaeologists working across the Middle East, and made Tepe Hissar one of the best-known sites in Near Eastern archaeology.

With the onset of World War II, archaeological research in northeastern Iran slowed considerably and did not resume until the 1950s, when the lowlands of the Caspian littoral became a popular place to work. The anthropologist Carleton S. Coon excavated Belt and Hotu caves near Sari in Mazandaran (Coon 1951, 1952, 1957), inspiring Charles McBurney's excavations at nearby Ali Tappeh cave in the early 1960s (McBurney 1964, 1968). A French expedition headed by Jean Deshayes excavated Tureng Tepe from 1960 to 1977 and produced a number of important articles, yet no final monograph about the Bronze Age levels (Deshayes 1968, 1969b, 1977, and numerous preliminary reports in the journal *Iran*). In the early 1960s an Anglo-American team headed by David Stronach and Vaughn Crawford excavated further north in the Gorgan plain at the site of Yarim Tepe (Crawford 1963; Stronach 1972), but this site too remains incompletely published. Finally, a Japanese team headed by Matsuzaki Hisashi excavated a prehistoric site just southeast of Tureng Tepe called Tepe Hoseynabad in the early 1970s, but that has only recently been published outside of Japan (Ohtsu et al. 2010).

By the 1970s, archaeological interest in northeastern Iran had mostly moved back onto the plateau as Marxian ideas about craft production and trade networks drove scholars closer to such resources. A Japanese team headed by Seiichi Masuda excavated the Neolithic site of Sang-e Chakhmaq, near Shahrud, one of the most important (and least understood) Neolithic sites in the Middle East (Masuda 1974, 1977, 1984; cf. Thornton 2010, 2013). At the same time, an Italian–American team returned to Tepe Hissar under the direction of Maurizio Tosi and Robert H. Dyson Jr. to carry out limited excavations in order to retrieve stratified organic material for radiocarbon dating (Bulgarelli 1974; Dyson 1972, 1977; *THRRP*). In addition to these large projects, a number of important archaeological surveys were conducted in the 1970s, including a Japanese survey of the Gorgan (Ohtsu et al. 2010), a German survey of eastern Khorasan (Gropp 1995), an Italian survey of the Atrek Valley (Venco Ricciardi 1980), and an American survey of the Darreh Gaz (Kohl and Heskel 1980; Kohl et al. 1982).

The Islamic Revolution of 1978–9 and the ensuing Iran–Iraq War (1980–88) effectively ended prehistoric research in Iran until the 1990s, when Iranian scholars

184 THE BRONZE AGE

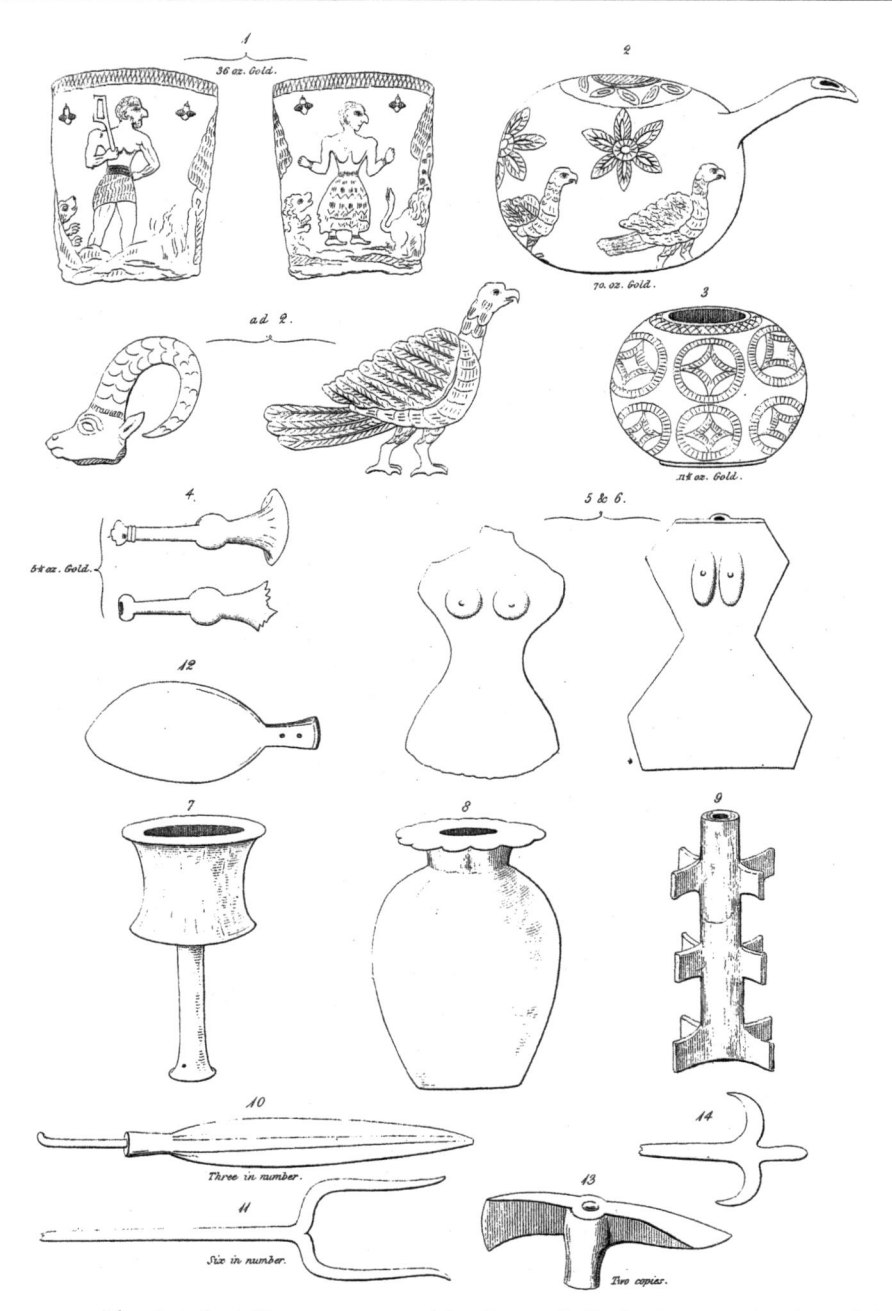

FIGURE 10.2 The Astrabad Treasure reported by Baron de Bode (1844: 250), adapted from Rostovtzeff (1920).

resumed survey and excavation. Much of this research is unknown to Western scholars as it is either unpublished or published only in Persian and often in journals and booklets that are difficult to access in the West. Notable work in this region by Iranian archaeologists after the revolution includes survey around Gorgan by the late M. Darvish Rouhani in 1984–5 (Abbasi 2007: 251); survey and test excavations across Semnan Province from 1988 to 1992 by Hassan Rezvani (1999); and salvage excavations at Tepe Hissar in 1995 by Ehsan Yaghmai (Mashkour and Yaghmayi 1996; Mashkour 1997).

Since the 1990s, a number of young, well-trained Iranian archaeologists have focused their attention on northeastern Iran. Much to their credit, these scholars often publish both in Persian and in Western languages (notably in English), which will no doubt have an enormous effect upon the wider world's appreciation of northeastern Iran. At the same time, a handful of Western scholars (and their students) have spent much of the 1990s and 2000s attempting to publish prerevolutionary excavations conducted in this region (e.g., Martinez 1990; Orsaria 1995; Hiebert and Dyson 2002; Leone 2004). Despite the tense political situation over the past decade, a lucky few have even carried out excavations in northeastern Iran with their Iranian colleagues (Mahfroozi and Piller 2009) or with their Iranian students (Fouache et al. 2010; Vahdati and Francfort 2011). Our understanding of the late prehistory of northeastern Iran is in its infancy, in spite of 150 years of interest in the region, but a new generation of both Iranian and Western archaeologists is seeking to change that.

Typological and chronological sequence

Northeastern Iran has long been recognized as an important frontier zone between the oasis settlements of Central Asia and the highland sites of the Iranian plateau in late prehistory (Sarianidi 1971; Tosi 1973–4; Kohl 1984a; Cleuziou 1986). Less well recognized is the important "social boundary" (Wright 1984, 1989, 2002) between the western and eastern halves of northeastern Iran (Biscione 1981; Kohl et al. 1982: 17–18), whereby the material culture of eastern Mazandaran, Semnan, Golestan, and western Khorasan is entirely different from the contemporary material culture of north-central and eastern Khorasan (southern Khorasan is archaeologically terra incognita). A useful model has been put forth by Emran Garajian (pers. comm. 2008), who suggested that the regions around Sari, Damghan, and Gorgan (up to the Sumbar Valley of western Turkmenistan) could be thought of as the eastern frontier of northern Iran, while Khorasan could be considered the northern frontier of eastern Iran. Recent surveys by Ali Vahdati (pers. comm. 2010) have placed this social boundary zone somewhere between Sankhast (east of Jajarm) and Touy (west of Esfareyen) in northwestern Khorasan (Vahdati 2011). Continued exploration and excavation by Iranian scholars in this region has done little to change this model of a divided frontier zone in late prehistory (Garajian 2006, 2008; Vahdati 2010a, 2010b, 2011; Vahdati and Francfort 2011).

Khorasan (east of the social boundary)

With the possible exception of the Kopet Dagh region along the northern border with Turkmenistan (Kohl and Heskel 1980; Venco Ricciardi 1980; Kohl et al. 1982; Rahbar 1997), our archaeological knowledge of Khorasan is quite limited (Korbel 1983; Gropp 1995). However, it is clear that this province shared the material culture of the relatively well-known Namazga-related sites of southern Turkmenistan in the fourth and third millennia BC (Masson and Sarianidi 1972; Lamberg-Karlovsky 1973; Kohl 1981, 1984b, 1992; Masson 1992; Sarianidi 1992, 2002). The association between Khorasan and southern Turkmenistan is attested at a number of excavated sites, including Tepe Borj (Garajian 2006) and Nishapur-P (Hiebert and Dyson 2002) near Nishapur; Tepe Damghani near Sabzevar (Vahdati and Francfort 2011); and Yam Tepe in the upper Atrek Valley (Biscione pers. comm., n.d.).

However, there are a few subtle differences between the sites of Khorasan and those in southern Turkmenistan. For one, Late Neolithic, Djeitun-style ceramics of the sixth and early fifth millennia BC are so far unknown in Khorasan—the earliest ceramics found are comparable to Anau IA black-on-red wares of the mid- to late fifth millennium BC (Vahdati 2010b: 28–30; see below). Second, in the Namazga II–III period (mid- to late fourth millennium BC), black-on-red wares with distinctive zoomorphic motifs such as those from Nishapur-P (Hiebert and Dyson 2002: 138) and the Kopet Dagh region (Kohl et al. 1982: 8) appear to be relatively common, while they remain quite rare (possibly imported?) at Namazga II–III sites of southern Turkmenistan. Third, burnished gray wares—the hallmark of the western region of northeastern Iran in the fourth through second millennia BC—appear with some regularity at third-millennium sites in Khorasan (Hiebert and Dyson 2002; Vahdati and Francfort 2011; Biscione and Vahdati in prep.; Garajian 2006), while they remain relatively rare at Namazga-sequence sites in southern Turkmenistan. Whether these three observations will continue to be correct after further excavation remains to be seen, but the highland-lowland dynamic between the intermontane valleys of northern Khorasan and the settlements along the northern piedmont of the Kopet Dagh in Turkmenistan is a topic worth pursuing.

Semnan, Mazandaran, Golestan, and western Khorasan (west of the social boundary)

The western side of northeastern Iran also exhibits an interesting highland-lowland dynamic—that is, between the plateau sites along the southern flanks of the Alborz Mountains (from Semnan to Jajarm) and the sea-level sites along the Caspian littoral (from Sari to Gonbad-e Qavus). Unlike in the east, where significant populations do not seem to appear until after Neolithic Djeitun-related villages had disappeared from the Turkmen piedmont (Harris 2010), settlements in the west arose on both the highland plateau and the lowland Caspian plain in tandem with developments in southern Turkmenistan. Despite extensive archaeological research in both the highlands and lowlands of the western region of northeastern Iran, the cultural and economic relationship between the two is a complete mystery. Was there seasonal migration between them? Did they share a symbiotic relationship based on production and trade? Did they rise and fall in tandem or did they alternate in significance over the millennia? The complete publication of excavated sites such as Tepe Hissar and Tureng Tepe, and perhaps new field investigations focused on these lacunae in our knowledge, are needed before these questions can be answered.

The earliest excavated sites in this region date from the eighth to seventh millennia BC and belong either to the Epipaleolithic/Mesolithic (on the Caspian coast) or the Aceramic Neolithic (on the plateau). Examples of the former include the cave sites near Sari, such as Belt and Hotu Caves (Coon 1951, 1952, 1957; Dupree 1952) and Ali Tappeh (McBurney 1964, 1968). Examples of Aceramic Neolithic sites are rarer still, with the incompletely published Japanese excavations at Sang-e Chakhmaq near Shahrud providing the best sequence (Masuda 1973, 1974, 1976, 1977, 1984). Although an updated synthesis of this site has been published elsewhere (Thornton 2010, 2013), a brief synopsis will be given here of the transition from the Aceramic Neolithic to the early Chalcolithic in northeastern Iran.

The sequence from the two mounds (West and East) at Sang-e Chakhmaq can be divided into four general periods (Table 10.1): Aceramic Neolithic (about the seventh millennium BC), Early Ceramic Neolithic (approximately late seventh to early sixth millennium BC), Late Ceramic Neolithic (about the sixth millennium BC), and Early Chalcolithic (approximately late sixth to early fifth millennium BC). The Aceramic Neolithic levels are exclusively on the West Mound and consist of large, well-built structures with prominent hearths containing evidence of *in situ* lithic production, groundstone tools for processing grains, and bone tools made from deer antlers and long bones. The Early Ceramic Neolithic levels above this period on the West Mound were mostly eroded, although a few sherds described as "burnt-umber colored with polished surfaces" (Kamuro 1977; Thornton 2013) suggest parallels with what Dyson (1991: 266) called "Caspian Neolithic Soft Ware" from Belt and Hotu Caves.

The Late Ceramic Neolithic levels at the base of the East Mound sequence are notable for their strong parallels with the Djeitun Culture of southern Turkmenistan (Harris 2010; Harris et al. 1996; Masson 1971, 1992). There are also notable connections with north-central Iran (specifically Sialk I) and with the Caspian cave sites, as well as a tradition of adapting these different influences in a local style of pottery, small finds, and architecture (Thornton 2010, 2013). The transition from the Early Ceramic Neolithic on the West Mound to the Late Ceramic Neolithic on the East Mound does not seem to have been abrupt, as many artifact types and burial styles remained unchanged.

The transition to the Early Chalcolithic levels at Sang-e Chakhmaq (called Early Transitional Chalcolithic period in Fazeli et al. 2009) tells a different story (see Masuda 1977). Burials changed from simple, flexed inhumations to those of extended corpses lying on their backs. The mudbricks used in house construction became shorter and

Table 10.1 Chronology of north-central and northeastern Iran.

DATE (BC)	n-c Iran	northeastern Iran			Turkmenistan
	Kashan	Damghan	Gorgan	Sumbar	
7000		?			
			?	?	?
		"Aceramic Neolithic"			
6500	?	West 4–5			
			Ali Tappeh B	Caspian	Mesolithic
		West 2–3	Belt/Hotu Caves	Mesolithic	
		"Ceramic Neolithic"			
6000	?	West 0–1			
					Early Djeitun
	I	"Djeitun Period"	(Aq Tappeh)		
		East 5–6	(Yarim 1)		
5500					
		East 3–4	IA		Middle Djeitun
	II	"Sialk II Period"			
5000		East 1–2			
					Late Djeitun
		?	(Hotu, Belt)		
			IB	?	
4500		(Shir-i Shian)			
	III.1–3				Anau IA
		IA			
					Anau IB1
4000		IB		SWT 7	
	III.4–5		(Shah III)		Namazga I
	(Qale Gusheh)	IC–IIA	IIA (early Yarim II)		Anau IB2
	III.6–7	"Early Hissar II"			
3500	(Arisman B)				Anau IIA
		IIB			Namazga II
	IV.1	"Mid Hissar II"	(Shah III-IIB)		
	(Arisman C)		IIB (late Yarim II)	SWT 6	
3000	IV.2	"Late Hissar II"			Anau IIB
	(Arisman A/D)		IIIA	SWT 5	Namazga III

Table 10.1 (Continued)

DATE (BC)	n-c Iran	northeastern Iran			Turkmenistan
	Kashan	Damghan	Gorgan	Sumbar	
	?	IIIA?			
			IIIB		
	"Kura-Araxes"		(Shah IIB)	SWT 4	Namazga IV
2500	(Qoli Darvish)		(early Yarim III)		
		IIIB			
	?	"Burned Building"			Namazga V
				SWT 3	
	Central	IIIC1	IIIC1		
2000	Gray Wares		(Shah IIA)		
		"BMAC burials"	(late Yarim III)	SWT 2	Namazga VI
	?	IIIC2?			
			IIIC2		Takhirbai

squarer, more standardized, and similar to Sialk II bricks in north-central Iran. Antler and deer bone essentially disappeared, to be replaced almost exclusively by cattle bone for the manufacture of tools (Masuda 1976: 64). While the multiple ceramic types of the Late Ceramic Neolithic levels still appeared in small quantities in this latest phase, the dominant ceramic type in these Early Chalcolithic levels is so-called Cheshmeh Ali Ware—a well-fired, black-on-red ceramic type of the early Sialk II period (c.5200–4700/4600 BC) found at every site in the western part of northeastern Iran around 5000 BC (Dyson and Thornton 2009: 4, n. 6).

The reasons and mechanism for the spread of the Cheshmeh Ali Ware technological style (including the use of grit temper, well-controlled kilns, elaborate painted designs, and possibly the fast wheel; see Fazeli et al. 2010) from north-central Iran to northeastern Iran remain unclear. It is important, however, to reiterate the key point made by Fazeli and Abbasnejad Sereshti (2005) that interregional ceramic styles such as Cheshmeh Ali Ware are notable only in relation to the relatively unknown *intra*regional ceramic styles of the Late Neolithic through Early Chalcolithic phases. This is particularly true in northeastern Iran, where discussions of long-distance connections with north-central Iran or southern Turkmenistan have superseded careful study of indigenous processes of social and cultural development in localized regions (Thornton 2013; Vahdati Nasab et al. 2013; Gregg and Thornton 2012).

The middle of the fifth millennium BC appears to have been a period of decline in both north-central and northeastern Iran, although very few sites of this phase have been found (Dyson and Thornton 2009). In this period (called "Late Transitional Chalcolithic" in Fazeli et al. 2009), the Cheshmeh Ali Ware style devolved into less finely made ceramics involving simple geometric and linear designs, abandoning the elaborate zoomorphic designs of the preceding period. These later ceramics are called Anau IA Ware after the famous site in southern Turkmenistan where they were first found and described (Schmidt 1908; Hiebert and Kurbansakatov 2003). While the western part of northeastern Iran may have retracted somewhat, it is important to note that in the Anau IA phase (c.4500 BC) sites first appeared in the Darreh Gaz, the Atrek Valley, and in the other intermontane valleys of the eastern part of northeastern Iran (discussed above).

For unknown reasons, the Anau IA phase ended somewhat abruptly with the rise of numerous localized cultural traditions toward the end of the fifth millennium BC. In north-central Iran, the late Sialk II phase gave way to the distinctive Sialk III_{1-3} phase (c.4300–4000 BC), distinguished by the return to robust mudbrick architecture and naturalistic motifs on painted pottery, as well as the rise of large, elaborately painted zoomorphic and anthropomorphic figurines (Thornton and Pittman forthcoming). In southern Turkmenistan, we see the development of the Namazga I–II culture out of the preceding Djeitun tradition. In northeastern Iran, the best known of these local styles is the Hissar I culture of the Damghan plain (Schmidt 1933, 1937), although so little of this material has been published from the Tepe Hissar excavations that it is difficult to reach any conclusions about it. Both Qaleh Khan (Garajian 2008) and Aq Tappeh (Shahmirzadi and Nokandeh 2001) in the upper Gorgan Valley appear to have post–Anau IA layers, but in the absence of comprehensive reports on these sites it is nearly impossible to define the local cultures.

By the mid to late fourth millennium BC, we have a much better understanding of the development of these localized cultures across northeastern Iran, thanks mainly to the pioneering work of the Italian-American team at Tepe Hissar (Fig. 10.3). In 1976 this team carried out one of the first restudy projects of an Iranian type-site utilizing modern methods of stratigraphic assessment, ceramic typological analysis, and radiocarbon dating (Dyson 1977; Dyson and Howard 1989). By cutting back old sections and placing small test-trenches in key locations, the team managed to contextualize the older excavations at Hissar (Schmidt 1933, 1937), Tureng Tepe (Wulsin 1932, 1938), and Shah Tepe (Arne 1935, 1945) and to situate these within an absolute chronology (Dyson 1991; Thornton et al. 2012). While the analysis of these data is still ongoing (Gürsan-Salzmann 2016), it is clear that the rise of the Hissar II culture (c.3600–2800 BC) was driven mainly by the creation of workshops dedicated to the large-scale processing of lapis lazuli and alabaster, and the equally large-scale production of copper-base alloys and lead/silver, presumably for export (Tosi 1984; Thornton 2009).

During this period of economic and cultural florescence in northeastern Iran, we also find the earliest evidence of complex societies in the fertile lowland plains along the Caspian littoral. While Djeitun-, Cheshmeh Ali-, and Hissar IC-style ceramics have all been found at sites in the Gorgan plain, they usually appear eroding out of later mudbricks as the strata to which these sherds originally belonged are unreachable below the water table—notable exceptions being Yarim Tepe (Crawford 1963) and Pookerdvall, near Gorgan, which has stratified, Djeitun-style ceramic layers above the water table (Abassi et al. in press). Thus, only in the Hissar II period can we begin to understand the complex dynamics of interaction between lowland sites like Tureng Tepe, Shah Tepe, and Narges Tepes (Abassi 2007) and their counterparts on the plateau, like Tepe

FIGURE 10.3 Mid- to Late Chalcolithic artifacts from Northeastern Iran.

Hissar. Interestingly, this was also the period in which reduction-fired, monochromatic gray wares first appeared at sites from north-central Iran to southern Turkmenistan. However, it was not until the end of the fourth or early third millennium BC that gray wares superseded other ceramic types, such as the distinctive burnished, incised, or black-painted red wares of the Gorgan and Mazandaran plains, which are found as far north as the Sumbar Valley in southwestern Turkmenistan (Khlopin 1997: pl. 13) and as far south as Tepe Hissar (Thornton et al. 2012). Other distinctive finds from this period across the western part of northeastern Iran include double-headed spiral pins, stone "handbags," and certain bead types.

The rapid expansion and collapse of the proto-Elamite phenomenon across the Iranian plateau at the beginning of the third millennium BC effectively ended complex society in north-central Iran for nearly a millennium, yet it had little overt effect upon the societies of northeastern Iran. Although Tepe Hissar seems to have declined in tandem with the proto-Elamite collapse (the nebulous Hissar IIIA period), due perhaps to some sort of economic interdependence with north-central Iran, the lowland sites flourished in the first half of the third millennium BC (Fig. 10.4). Whereas lapis lazuli production had peaked at Hissar in period IIB, c.3400–3000 BC, lapis production at Tureng Tepe peaked somewhat later, in period IIIA, c.3000–2500 BC (Deshayes 1968: 37; 1969a: 14). A similar situation can be observed further north at the contemporaneous Parkhai II cemetery of the Sumbar Valley, where richly adorned graves of Period IV (c.3000–2500 BC) contained elaborately decorated "altars" and ornaments of lapis, silver, and other valuable materials, suggesting a time of great prosperity (Khlopin 2002: 141). This shift to the north in the early third millennium BC parallels the rise of important centers of production and trade in the Namazga IV period of southern Turkmenistan, such as Ak-depe to the west (Kircho 1999; Gundogdyyew et al. 2010) and Altyn-depe to the east (Masson 1988; Kircho 2001; Masson and Berezkin 2005; Kircho et al. 2008).

Highland settlements in northeastern Iran such as Tepe Hissar returned to prominence in the mid- to late third millennium BC (Hissar IIIB period), due perhaps to their intermediary role between the rising centers of Margiana and the expanding trade routes of the plateau. The many burials from this period excavated by Schmidt (1937: 232–61), as well as the plethora of valuable items found in the Burned Building (Dyson 1972), all suggest that this was a phase of heightened socioeconomic status and increased wealth. This was also a time of great artistic achievement in the lowlands of northeastern Iran, as evidenced by the finely made, pattern-burnished gray ware ceramics and the decorative beads, pins, pendants, and vessels in various materials distributed from Gohar Tepe near Sari (Mahfroozi and Piller 2009: fig. 5) to the Period III graves of the Sumbar Valley (Khlopin 2002: 45–61). In addition, hoards of drinking vessels and fenestrated braziers from Hissar (incorrectly attributed to Hissar IIIC by Schmidt 1937: 158–9) and elaborately dressed figurines from Tureng Tepe (Olson 2012) bespeak a level of ritual activity not previously attested in northeastern Iran.

The end of the third millennium was a period of significant change in northeastern Iran, the sequence and drivers of which are still not understood. Dramatic changes in the architecture of settlements occurred at both highland and lowland sites. At Tepe Hissar, the well-planned architecture of Period IIIB was abandoned and replaced by the poorly organized structures of the early Hissar IIIC period (Deshayes' Period $IIIC_1$) that were laid out without regard to the plan of the earlier settlement (Schmidt 1937: 155; Gürsan-Salzmann 2016). At Tureng Tepe an enormous, mudbrick "haute

Third Millenium Artifacts from Northeastern Iran

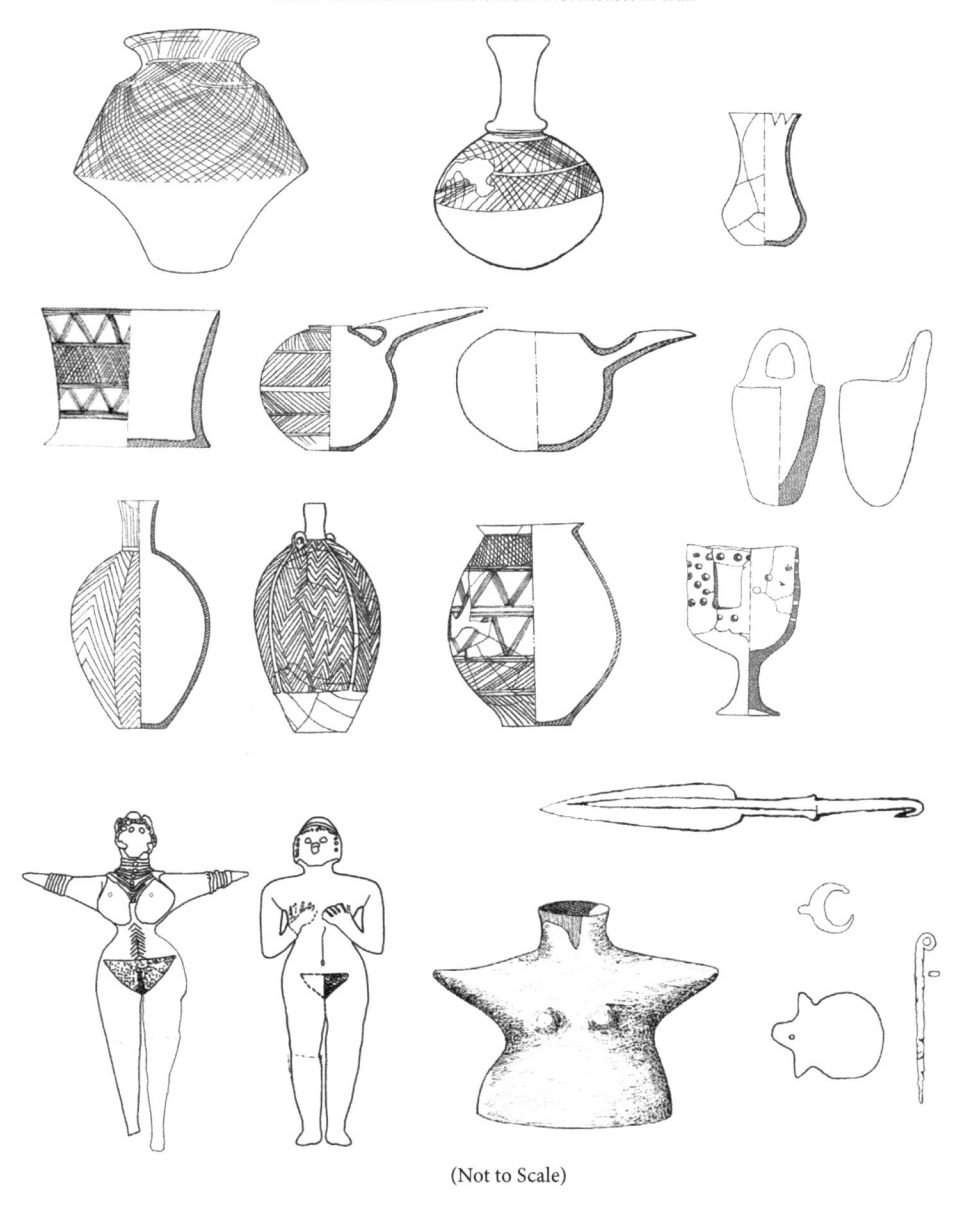

(Not to Scale)

FIGURE 10.4 Early Bronze Age artifacts from Tepe Hissar and Tureng Tepe, Periods IIIA–IIIC.

terrasse" (high terrace) was constructed in the center of the settlement, representing perhaps the earliest example of monumentality in this region (Deshayes 1977; Leone 2004). Paralleling this material evidence of social stratification and political centralization was the first appearance of truly elite burials, such as those of the "Warriors," the "Priest," and the "Little Girl" at Hissar (Schmidt 1933: 438–52).

194   THE BRONZE AGE

Stone columns

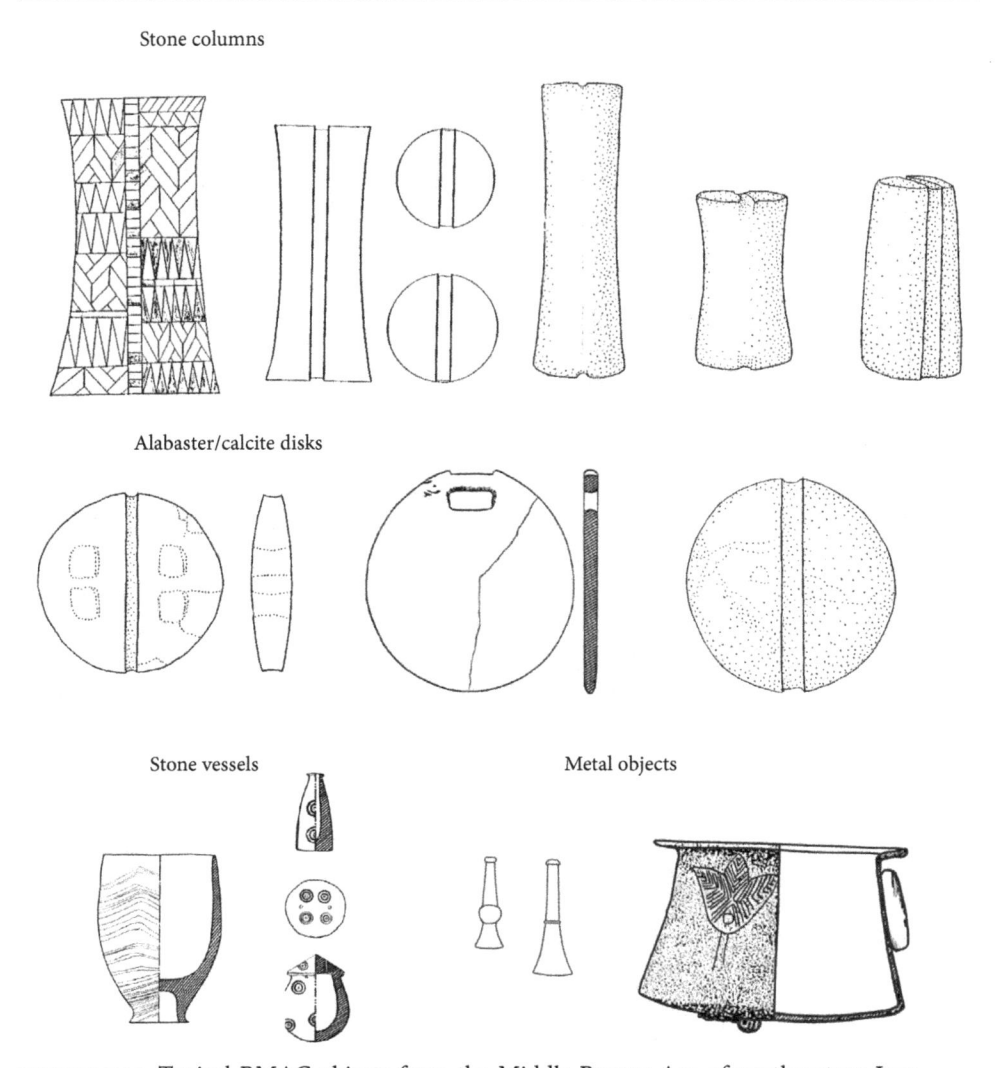

Alabaster/calcite disks

Stone vessels   Metal objects

FIGURE 10.5 Typical BMAC objects from the Middle Bronze Age of northeastern Iran.

At around the same time (whether before or after these architectural changes is unclear), material culture of the early Bactria–Margiana Archaeological Complex (early BMAC or Namazga V, c.2200–2000 BC) appeared at all of these sites (Fig. 10.5), sometimes intermixed with local gray ware ceramics (Hiebert and Lamberg-Karlovsky 1992). The most obvious examples of BMAC items are the grooved stone columns found atop the "haute terrasse" at Tureng Tepe (Deshayes 1975: fig. 1); in Period IIa levels at Shah Tepe (Arne 1945: 282); and in elite burials and hoards at Hissar (Schmidt 1937: pl. 61). The Astrabad treasure discussed above also contained a number of BMAC-related items, such as miniature "trumpets" (Rostovtzeff 1920: 6–7) with ready parallels at Hissar (Schmidt 1937: 209), but it also contained a number of Hissar IIIC-style (non-BMAC) artifacts, such as stylized female figurines made from stone plates (Schmidt 1933: pl. 132). Entirely missing from these purported BMAC assemblages in the western part of northeastern Iran is even a single sherd of Namazga V–VI pottery, with the sole exception of a BMAC necropolis found in the frontier zone between Jajarm and Isfareyan at Tepe Chalow near Sankhast (Biscione and Vahdati in prep.). Although the data are sparse, the archaeological and biological evidence (Hiebert 1998; Hemphill 1999) suggests that wealthy and influential immigrants from Margiana likely migrated into northeastern Iran around 2000 BC, where they seem to have integrated into local communities in ways that we do not yet understand.

The early second millennium levels at Tepe Hissar were mostly all eroded by the time Schmidt arrived at the site, although certain artifacts from near-surface contexts—such as jars with vertical handles (Schmidt 1937: pl. 41, H2871) and socketed spearheads (Schmidt 1937: pl. 50, H2779)—suggest that such layers may have existed. Far better evidence of early second millennium occupation comes from the lowlands of the western region of northeastern Iran, from Tepe Bazgir in the east (Nokandeh et al. 2006) to Tureng Tepe (period $IIIC_{1-2}$) in the west (Deshayes 1973). We know little about this "late BMAC" period in northeastern Iran (equivalent to Namazga VI), and even less about the Late Bronze Age, post-BMAC period ($c.1800–1500$ BC; equivalent to the Takhirbai period in Margiana). Many sites in the lowland areas contain Late Bronze Age assemblages that transition into the Early Iron Age, for example, at Gohar Tepe (Mahfroozi and Piller 2009: 183), in the Sumbar Valley (Chlopin 1986), and possibly at Tureng Tepe (Period $IIIC_2$; Deshayes 1973). However, most of this material is unpublished or from mortuary contexts, so our understanding of social development in this region remains limited.

Conclusion

Decades of anthropological and archaeological research have shown that so-called "frontier zones" were often areas of intense social and cultural innovation, where ideas and styles were hybridized and manipulated for local usage (Lightfoot and Martinez 1995; Parker and Rodseth 2005). While our understanding of the late prehistory of northeastern Iran is still quite limited, it is clear that we are dealing with a duel-frontier scenario. First, the entire region played an important role as a frontier zone between central Iran (and, by extension, the greater Near East) and southern Turkmenistan (and, by extension, Central Asia). This is what I would call an *interregional frontier zone*. Second, northeastern Iran was divided for millennia between the east (Khorasan) and the west (Semnan, Gorgan, Damghan, Mazandaran) for reasons that are still not entirely clear. This is what could be called an *intraregional frontier zone*, demarcated by a number of "social boundaries" over the millennia in the westernmost part of modern-day Khorasan province.

Northeastern Iran has long been a dynamic cultural landscape in which diverse groups of people interacted in various ways. Precious resources such as timber, semiprecious stones, salt from the *dasht*, and metal ores no doubt drew people to this region, while arable land and well-protected valleys encouraged them to stay. Just as Papoli-Yazdi's important study of the movement of pastoralists across this landscape in recent history raises a number of intriguing possibilities of relevance to traditional patterns of migration and trade, the archaeological record suggests even broader diachronic movements of ideas, trends, technologies, and people between central Iran and southern Turkmenistan through this critical frontier zone. Hopefully the forthcoming publication of a number of older excavations in this region, combined with new stratigraphic excavations by Iranian colleagues, will shed light on the intraregional interactions that caused northeastern Iran to play such an important role in the development of large-scale societies in the Middle East and Central Asia.

Acknowledgments

Thanks first and foremost to the editor for inviting me to contribute to this volume. Ali Vahdati and Raffaele Biscione provided important comments and new information that greatly improved this chapter, while Kyle Olson must be thanked for translating a number of articles from Persian to English for me. David Massey provided the topographic map, while Narges Bayani and Anne Bomalski provided the plates. Finally, this chapter would be impossible were it not for a number of fantastic colleagues, both in Iran and elsewhere, whose generosity and dedication to the late prehistory of northeastern Iran are truly inspiring.

Further reading

There has not been a compelling synthesis of the archaeology of northeastern Iran since the 1980s (see citations in text). A good reference for prehistoric Iranian material culture in general is Voigt and Dyson (1992), but that is somewhat out of date. The new research of Hassan Fazeli Nashli and his colleagues (e.g., Fazeli Nashli et al. 2009, 2010) and Barbara Helwing and her colleagues (e.g., Helwing 2004; papers in *EMM*) in north-central Iran provides the closest parallels to sites in the northeast and anchors the chronology of this region substantially.

References

Abassi, Q. A. 2007. Narges Tepe of the Gorgan Plain. In *The 9th Annual Symposium on Iranian Archaeology*, 247–6. Tehran: Archaeological Reports 7 (in Persian).

Abassi, Q. A., H. Omrani, and H. Zeyqami. In press. Tepe Pookerdvall: A Neolithic enclosure in the Gorgan Plain.

Adle, C. 1971. Contribution à la géographie historique du Damghan. In *Le Monde Iranien et l'Islam*, 69–104. Geneva: Hautes Études islamiques et Orientales d'Histoire comparée 4.

Arne, T. J. 1935. *The Swedish Archaeological Expedition to Iran, 1932–1933*. Copenhagen: Acta Archaeologica 6.

———. 1945. *Excavations at Shah Tepe*. Stockholm: Reports from the Scientific Expedition to the North-Western Provinces of China under the leadership of Dr. Sven Hedin Publication 27.

Biscione, R. 1981. Centre and periphery in late protohistoric Turan: The settlement pattern. In *South Asian Archaeology 1979*, ed. H. Härtel, 203–13. Berlin: Dietrich Reimer.

———. n.d. *The testing-pit at Tappeh Yam, Upper Atrek Valley, Xorasan*. Unpubl. report.

Biscione, R., and A. A. Vahdati. In prep. *Excavations at Tepe Chalow, northern Khorasan, Iran*.

Bode, C. A. de. 1844. On a recently opened tumulus in the neighbourhood of Asterabad, forming part of ancient Hyrcania, and the country of the Parthians. *Archaeologia* 30: 248–55.

Bulgarelli, G. M. 1974. Tepe Hissar: Preliminary report on a surface survey, August 1972. *EW* 24: 15–27.

Childe, V. G. 1942. Ceramic art in early Iran. *Antiquity* 16: 353–8.

Chlopin, I. N. 1986. *Jungbronzezeitliche Gräberfelder im Sumbar-Tal, Südwest-Turkmenistan*. Munich: Materialien zur Allgemeinen und Vergleichenden Archäologie 35.

Cleuziou, S. 1986. Tureng Tepe and burnished grey ware: A question of "frontier"? *Oriens Antiquus* 25: 221–56.

———. 1991. Ceramics ix. The Bronze Age in northeastern Persia. *EnIr* 5: 297–300.

Coon, C. S. 1951. *Cave explorations in Iran 1949*. Philadelphia: University of Pennsylvania Press.

———. 1952. Excavations in Hotu Cave, Iran, 1951, a preliminary report. *PAPS* 96/3: 231–49.

———. 1957. *The seven caves: Archaeological explorations in the Middle East*. New York: Alfred Knopf.

Crawford, V. E. 1963. Beside the Kara Su. *Metropolitan Museum of Art Bulletin* 22/8: 263–73.

Deshayes, J. 1968. Tureng Tepe and the plain of Gorgan in the Bronze Age. *Archaeologia Viva* 1/1: 35–8.

———. 1969a. New evidence for the Indo-Europeans from Tureng Tepe, Iran. *Archaeology* 22/1: 10–17.

———. 1969b. Tureng Tepe et la periode Hissar IIIC. *Ugaritica* 6: 139–63.

———. 1973. Rapport préliminaire sur les septième et huitième campagnes de fouilles à Tureng Tepe (1967 et 1969). *BAI* 3: 81–97.

———. 1975. Les fouilles récentes de Tureng Tepe: La terrasse haute de la fin du IIIe millénaire. *CRAIBL*: 522–30.

———. 1977. A propos des terrasses hautes de la fin du IIIe millénaire en Iran et en Asie centrale. In *Le Plateau iranien et l'Asie Centrale des origines à la Conquête islamique*, ed. J. Deshayes, 95–111. Paris: Éditions du CNRS.

Dupree, L. 1952. The Pleistocene artifacts of Hotu Cave, Iran. *PAPS* 96: 250–57.

Dyson, R. H., Jr. 1972. The Burned Building of Tepe Hissar IIIB: A restatement. *Bastan Chenassi va Honar-e Iran* 9–10: 57–83.

———. 1977. Tepe Hissar, Iran, revisited. *Archaeology* 30/6: 418–20.

———. 1991. Ceramics i: The Neolithic period through Bronze Age in northeastern and north-central Persia. *EnIr* 5/3: 266–75.

———. 2009. Tepe Hissar. *EnIr online edition*.

Dyson, R. H., Jr., and S. M. Howard. 1989. *Tappeh Hesār: Reports of the Restudy Project, 1976*. Florence: Monografi di Mesopotamia 2.

Dyson, R. H., Jr., and C. P. Thornton. 2009. Shir-i Shian and the fifth millennium sequence of northern Iran. *Iran* 47: 1–22.

Fazeli Nashali, H., M. Vidale, P. Bianchetti, G. Guida, and R. A. E. Coningham. 2010. The evolution of ceramic manufacturing technology during the Late Neolithic and Transitional Chalcolithic periods at Tepe Pardis, Iran. *AMIT* 42: 87–112.

Fazeli Nashli, H., and R. Abbasnezhad Sereshti. 2005. Social transformation and interregional interaction in the Qazvin Plain during the 5th, 4th, and 3rd millennia B.C. *AMIT* 37: 7–26.

Fazeli Nashli, H., A. Beshkani, A. Markosian, H. Ilkani, R. Abbasnejad Sereshti, and R. L. Young. 2009. The Neolithic to Chalcolithic transition in the Qazvin Plain, Iran: Chronology and subsistence strategies. *AMIT* 41: 1–21.

Fouache, E., H.-P. Francfort, J. Bendezu-Sarmiento, A. A. Vahdati, and J. Lhuillier. 2010. The Horst of Sabzevar and regional water resources from the Bronze Age to the present day (northeastern Iran). *Geodinamica Acta* 23/5–6: 287–94.

Garajian, O. 2006. Some traces of Turkmenistan prehistoric cultures in Khorasan Province in Iran. In *The Second Symposium of Iranian young archaeologists, Iran-Tehran*, ed. S. Zare, 69–98. Tehran: ICHTO.

———. 2008. Stratigraphic soundings and architectural documentation of Qaleh Khan: A preliminary report. In *The 9th Annual Symposium on Iranian Archaeology*, vol. 3. Tehran: ICAR (in Persian).

Gregg, M. W., and C. P. Thornton. 2012. A preliminary analysis of the prehistoric pottery from Coon's excavations of Hotu and Belt Caves in northern Iran: Implications for future research into the emergence of village life in western Central Asia. *IJAH* 19/3: 56–94.

Gropp, G. 1995. *Archäologische Forschungen in Khorasan, Iran*. Wiesbaden: TAVO Beiheft 84.

Gundogdyyew, O., T. Hojanyyazow, and A. Gurbanow. 2010. *Akdepe-The ancient archaeological site of Turkmenistan*. Ashgabat: Archaeological and Ethnographic Institute.

Gürsan-Salzmann, A. 2016. *The new chronology of the Bronze Age settlement of Tepe Hissar, Iran*. Philadelphia: UMM.

Harris, D. R. 2010. *Origins of agriculture in western Central Asia: An environmental-archaeological study*. Philadelphia: University of Pennsylvania Press.

Harris, D. R., C. Gosden, and M. P. Charles. 1996. Jeitun: Recent excavations at an Early Neolithic site in southern Turkmenistan. *PPS* 62: 423–42.

Helwing, B. 2004. Tracking the proto-Elamite on the central Iranian plateau. In *The potters of Sialk*, ed. S. M. Shahmirzadi, 45–58. Tehran: SRPR 3.

———. 2006. The rise and fall of Bronze Age centers around the Central Iranian Desert: A comparison of Tappe Hesar II and Arisman. *AMIT* 38: 35–48.

Hemphill, B. E. 1999. Foreign elites from the Oxus civilization? A craniometric study of anomalous burials from Bronze Age Tepe Hissar. *American Journal of Physical Anthropology* 110/4: 421–34.

Hiebert, F. T. 1998. Central Asians on the Iranian Plateau: A model for Indo-Iranian expansionism. In *The Bronze Age and Early Iron Age peoples of eastern Central Asia*, ed. V. H. Mair, 148–61. Philadelphia: Journal of Indo-European Studies Monograph.

Hiebert, F. T., and R. H. Dyson, Jr. 2002. Prehistoric Nishapur and the frontier between Central Asia and Iran. *IrAnt* 37: 113–50.

Hiebert, F. T., and K. Kurbansakatov. 2003. *A Central Asian village at the dawn of civilization: Excavations at Anau, Turkmenistan*. Philadelphia: UMM 116.

Hiebert, F. T., and C. C. Lamberg-Karlovsky. 1992. Central Asia and the Indo-Iranian borderlands. *Iran* 30: 1–15.

Horne, L. 1994. *Village spaces: Settlement and society in northeastern Iran.* Washington: Smithsonian Institution Press.

Houtum Schindler, A. 1877. Notes on some antiquities found in a mound near Damghan. *JRAS* 9: 425–7.

Irons, W. G. 1972. Variation in economic organization: a comparison of the pastoral Yomut and the Basseri. *Journal of Asian and African Studies* 7: 88–104.

———. 1975. *The Yomut Turkmen: A study of social organization among a Central Asian turkic-speaking population.* Ann Arbor: Anthropological Papers of the University of Michigan 58.

Kamuro, H. 1977. Ceramics. In *Tappeh Sang-i Chaxmaq*, ed. S. Masuda, 15–20. Tokyo/Hiroshima: University of Hiroshima.

Khlopin, I. N. 1997. *Eneolit Jugo-Zapadnogo Turkmenistana.* St. Petersburg: Evropeskij Dom.

———. 2002. *Bronze Age of south-west Turkmenistan.* Saint Petersburg: Russian Academy of Science (in Russian and English).

Kircho, L. 1999. *K izucheniju pozdnego eneolita juzhnogo Turkmenistana.* Saint Petersburg: Russian Academy of Sciences.

———. 2001. *Osobennocti Proizvodstva Pocelenija Altyn-depe v Epokhu Paleometalla.* Saint Petersburg: Materialy Juzhno-Turkmenistanskoj Arkheologicheskoj Kompleksnoj Ekspeditsii Vypusk 5.

Kircho, L., G. R. Korobkova, and V. M. Masson. 2008. *Tekhniko-Tekhnologicheskij Potentsial Eneoliticheskovo Naselenija Altyn-depe kak Osnova Stanovlenija Rannevorodskoj Tsivilizatsii.* Saint Petersburg: Proceedings of the Institute for the History of Material Culture Proceedings 28.

Kohl, P. L. 1981. *The Bronze Age civilization of Central Asia: Recent Soviet discoveries.* Armonk: M. E. Sharpe.

———. 1984a. Prehistoric "Turan" and southern Turkmenia: The problem of cultural diversity. In *Frontiers of the Indus civilization*, ed. B. B. Lal and S. P. Gupta, 321–31. New Delhi: Books & Books.

———. 1984b. *Central Asia: Paleolithic beginnings to the Iron Age.* Paris: Éditions Recherche sur les civilisations.

———. 1992. Central Asia. In *Chronologies in Old World archaeology*, 3rd ed., ed. R. W. Ehrich, 179–95. Chicago: University of Chicago Press.

Kohl, P. L., R. L. Biscione, and M. L. Ingraham. 1982. Implications of recent evidence for the prehistory of northeastern Iran and southwestern Turkmenistan. *IrAnt* 17: 1–20.

Kohl, P. L., and D. L. Heskel. 1980. Archaeological reconnaissance in the Darreh Gaz Plain: A short report. *Iran* 18: 160–72.

Korbel, G. 1983. Archäologische Ergebnisse einer Geländebegehung im Gebiet von Torbat-e Djâm und Tayyebat. *AMI* 16: 18–56.

Lamberg-Karlovsky, C. C. 1973. Prehistoric Central Asia. *Antiquity* 47: 43–6.

Leone, E. 2004. La piramide scalonata di Tureng Tepe e i suoi confronti con strutture cerimoniali nell'Iran orientale e nell'Asia Media. Unpublished MA thesis, University of Bologna.

Lightfoot, K. G., and A. Martinez. 1995. Frontiers and boundaries in archaeological perspective. *Annual Review of Anthropology* 24: 471–92.

Mahfroozi, A., and C. K. Piller. 2009. First preliminary report on the joint Iranian-German excavations at Gohar Tappe, Mazandaran, Iran. *AMIT* 41: 177–209.

Mallowan, M. E. L. 1965. *Early Mesopotamia and Iran.* London: Thames and Hudson.

Martin, M. 1980. Making a living in Turan: Animals, land and wages. *Expedition* 22/4: 29–35.

Martinez, L.-A. 1990. Les inhumations de l'Âge du bronze de Tureng Tepe, Iran. Unpublished MA thesis, University of Paris 1.

Mashkour, M. 1997. The subsistence economy of Hissar IIIB: The study of faunal remains. In *Archaeological Reports of Iran 1*, 125–32. Tehran: ICAR.

Mashkour, M., and E. Yaghmayi. 1996. Faunal remains from Tappeh Hessar (Iran), results of the 1995 excavation. In *Proceedings of XIII UISPP Congress*, ed. C. Arias, A. Bietti, L. Castelletti and C. Peretto, 543–51. Forli: Abaco Edizioni.

Masson, V. M. 1971. *Poselenie Djeitun*. Moscow: Materiali i issledovaniya po arkheologii SSSR 180.

———. 1988. *Altyn-depe*. Philadelphia: UMM 55.

———. 1992. The Bronze Age in Khorasan and Transoxiana. In *History of civilizations of Central Asia*, vol. 1, ed. A. H. Dani and V. M. Masson, 225–46. Delhi: Motilal Banarsidass.

Masson, V. M., and J. E. Berezkin. 2005. *Khronologija Epokhi Pozdnevo Eneolita—Srednej Bronzy Srednej Azii (pogrebenija Altyn-depe)*. Saint Petersburg: Proceedings of the Institute for the History of Material Culture 16.

Masson, V. M., and V. I. Sarianidi. 1972. *Central Asia: Turkmenia before the Achaemenids*. London: Thames and Hudson.

Masuda, S. 1973. Excavations at Tappe Sang-e Cagmaq. *PASARI* 1: 1–2.

———. 1974. Excavations at Tappeh Sang-e Caxmaq. *PASARI* 2: 23–33.

———. 1976. Report of the archaeological investigations at Sahrud, 1975. *PASARI* 4: 63–70.

———. 1977. *Tappeh Sang-i Chaxmaq*. Tokyo/Hiroshima: University of Hiroshima.

———. 1984. The excavation at Tappeh Sangh-e Caxmaq. *AfO* 31: 209–12.

McBurney, C. B. M. 1964. Preliminary report on Stone Age reconnaissance in north-eastern Iran. *PPS* 30: 382–99.

———. 1968. The cave of Ali Tappeh and the epi-Palaeolithic in N.E. Iran. *PPS* 34: 385–413.

Morgan, J. de. 1896. *Mission scientifique en Perse*, vol. 4. Paris: E. Leroux.

Mousavi, A. 2008. Late Bronze Age in north-eastern Iran: an Alternative approach to persisting problems. *Iran* 46: 105–20.

Nokandeh, J., H. Omrani, and G.-A. Abbasi. 2006. Preliminary report of discovery of the Bazgir Hoard in Gorgan Plain, 2001. In *Archaeological Reports 4*, ed. S. Etemadi, 113–29. Tehran: ICAR.

Ohtsu, T., K. Furuse, T. Adachi, M. Karami, H. Nojima, Y. Arimatsu, and K. Wakiyama. 2010. Preliminary report of the Iran Japan joint research study of the Gorgan material in the National Museum of Iran, Tehran. Unpublished report.

Olson, K. G. 2012. The figurines of Tureng Tepe: Ceramic bodies and social life at a Bronze Age site in northeastern Iran. Unpublished BA thesis, Ohio State University

Orsaria, F. 1995. Shah Tepe: A new approach to an old excavation. *Rivista degli studi Orientali* 69/3–4: 481–95.

Papoli-Yazdi, M.-H. 1991. *Le nomadisme dans le Nord du Khorassan, Iran*. Paris/Tehran: Institut français de Recherche en Iran.

Parker, B. J., and L. Rodseth. 2005. *Untaming the frontier in Anthropology, Archaeology, and History*. Tucson: University of Arizona Press.

Piggott, S. 1943. Dating the Hissar sequence—the Indian evidence. *Antiquity* 17: 169–82.

Rahbar, M. 1997. Excavations at Bandiyan, Darreh Gaz, Khorasan. In *Archaeological Reports of Iran* 1, 9–32. Tehran: ICAR.

Rezvani, H. 1999. Prehistoric settlement patterns and cultures in Semnan Province, Central Plateau, Iran. *IW*: 220–21.

Rostovtzeff, M. 1920. The Sumerian treasure of Astrabad. *Journal of Egyptian Archaeology* 6: 4–27.

Sarianidi, V. 1971. Southern Turkmenia and northern Iran: Ties and differences in very ancient times. *EW* 21/3–4: 291–310.

———. 1992. Food-producing and other Neolithic communities in Khorasan and Transoxania: Eastern Iran, Soviet Central Asia and Afghanistan. In *History of civilizations of Central Asia*, vol. 1, ed. A. H. Dani and V. M. Masson, 109–26. Delhi: Motilal Banarsidass.

———. 2002. *Margush: Ancient Oriental kingdom in the old delta of the Murghab River*. Ashgabat: Turkmendowlethabarlary.

Schmidt, E. F. 1933. Tepe Hissar Excavations 1931. *Museum Journal* 23/4: 322–485.

———. 1937. *Excavations at Tepe Hissar: Damghan*. Philadelphia: University of Pennsylvania Press.

Schmidt, H. 1908. Archaeological excavations in Anau and Old Merv. In *Explorations in Turkestan: Expedition of 1904*, ed. R. Pumpelly, 83–216. Washington, DC: Carnegie Institution of Washington Publication 73.

Shahmirzadi, S. M., and J. Nokandeh. 2001. *Agh Tepe, Miras-e farhangi, Ostan-e Golestan* Tehran: ICAR.

Spooner, B. 1965. Arghiyan: The area of Jajarm in western Khorasan. *Iran* 3: 97–107.

———. 1974. *City and river in Iran: Urbanization and irrigation of the Iranian Plateau*. New Haven: Society for Iranian Cultural and Social Studies.

———. 1985. Anthropology. *EnIr* 2: 107–16.

Spooner, B., and L. Horne. 1980. Cultural and ecological perspectives from the Turan program, Iran. *Expedition* 22/4: 4–10.

Stronach, D. 1972. Yarim Tepe. In *Excavations in Iran, the British contribution*, 21–23. Oxford: Organizing Committee of the Sixth International Congress of Iranian Art and Archaeology.

Sykes, P. M. 1911. A sixth journey in Persia. *GJ* 37/1: 1–19.

Thornton, C. P. 2009. The Chalcolithic and Early Bronze Age metallurgy of Tepe Hissar, northeast Iran: A challenge to the "Levantine paradigm." Unpublished PhD diss., University of Pennsylvania.

———. 2010. Sang-e Chakhmaq. *EnIr online edition*.

———. 2013. Sang-i Chakhmaq: A Neolithic site in northeastern Iran. In *The Neolithisation of Iran*, ed. R. J. Matthews and H. Fazeli Nashli, 241–55. Oxford: Oxbow Books.

Thornton, C. P., A. Gürsan-Salzmann, and R. H. Dyson Jr. 2013. Tepe Hissar and the fourth millennium of Northeastern Iran. *AIN*: 131–44.

Thornton, C. P., and H. Pittman. Forthcoming. The small finds. In *Cheshmeh Ali: A Neolithic and Chalcolithic site in north-central Iran*, ed. T. Matney, H. Fazeli Nashli, H. Pittman, and C. P. Thornton. Philadelphia: UMM.

Tosi, M. 1973–4. The northeastern frontier of the Ancient Near East. *Mesopotamia* 8–9: 21–76.

———. 1984. The notion of craft specialization and its representation in the archaeological record of early states in the Turanian Basin. In *Marxist perspectives in archaeology*, ed. M. Spriggs, 22–52. Cambridge: Cambridge University Press.

Vahdati, A. A. 2010a. *Archaeological investigations in Shahr-i Belqays (Medieval Isfarayen)*. Tehran: Iranian Cultural Heritage Publications.

———. 2010b. Tepe Pahlavan: A Neolithic-Chalcolithic site in the Jajarm Plain, north-eastern Iran. *IrAnt* 45: 7–30.

———. 2011. A preliminary report on a newly discovered petroglyphic complex near Jorbat, the Plain of Jajarm, north-eastern Iran. *Paléorient* 37/2: 177–87.
Vahdati, A. A., and H.-P. Francfort. 2011. Preliminary report on the soundings at Tappeh Damghani, Sabzevar. *IJAH* 24/2: 17–36 (in Persian).
Vahdati Nasab, H., C. P. Thornton, S. M. Mousavi Kouhpar, N. Sykes, and R. Naderi. 2013. Late Neolithic site of Rashak III rock shelter, Mazandaran, Iran. In *The Neolithisation of Iran*, ed. R. J. Matthews and H. Fazeli Nashli, 272–83. London: Oxbow Books.
Venco Ricciardi, R. 1980. Archaeological survey in the Upper Atrek Valley (Khorassan, Iran): Preliminary report. *Mesopotamia* 15: 51–72.
Voigt, M. M. and R. H. Dyson Jr. 1992. The chronology of Iran, ca. 8000–2000 B.C. In *Chronologies in Old World archaeology*, 3rd ed., vol. 1, ed. R. W. Ehrich. Chicago: University of Chicago Press.
Wright, R. P. 1984. Technology, style and craft specialization: Spheres of interaction and exchange in the Indo-Iranian borderlands, third millennium B.C. Unpublished PhD diss., Harvard University.
———. 1989. New tracks on ancient frontiers: Ceramic technology on the Indo-Iranian Borderlands. In *Archaeological thought in America*, ed. C. C. Lamberg-Karlovsky, 268–79. Cambridge: Cambridge University Press.
———. 2002. Revisiting interaction spheres: Social boundaries and technologies on inner and outermost frontiers. *IrAnt* 37: 403–17.
Wulsin, F. R. 1932. *Excavations at Tureng Tepe, near Asterabad*. New York: Supplement to the Bulletin of the American Institute for Persian Art and Archaeology 2/1 bis.
———. 1938. The early cultures of Astarabad (Turang Tepe). *SPA* 1: 163–7.
Zagarell, A. 1982. *The prehistory of the northeast Bakhtiyārī mountains, Iran: The rise of a highland way of life*. Wiesbaden: TAVO Beiheft 42.

CHAPTER 11

LURISTAN AND THE CENTRAL ZAGROS IN THE BRONZE AGE

D. T. POTTS

INTRODUCTION

Nowadays, Luristan is more or less synonymous with the Pish-e Kuh (lit. "before the mountain"), but prior to the Qajar period (1794–1924) it also included the Pusht-e Kuh (lit. "behind the mountain," i.e., the area east of the Kabir Kuh; Harrison 1946: 55; Amanolahi 2002: 194; Minorsky 2011). This unity dates to at least the Seljuq period when the Lur dynasty of Atabegs (Atabakan-e Luristan) was established (1184–1597), with its capital at Khorramabad. Together, the Pish-e Kuh and Pusht-e Kuh correspond to Lur-e Kuchek ("minor," "lesser," or "little Luristan"), whereas Lur-e Buzurg ("major" or "great" Lur) extended much further south, incorporating parts of Khuzestan (e.g., Dezful which, along with Kermanshah, was a traditional Lur market town; Harrison 1942: 127; 1946: 56) and the Bakhtiyari Mountains to the east (Rawlinson 1839: 49; Edmonds 1922: 335; Black-Michaud 1974: 210; Kunke 1991: 110; Mortensen 1993: 27). A third Lur area, between Shiraz and Kuh-Giluye—historic Shulistan—is yet further south and east of our area of concern, lying today in western Fars. Thus, the "land of the Lurs" has been neither a stable geographical entity nor one that was necessarily of great antiquity. The fact that the term "Luristan" is used by archaeologists, however, reflects the intensity of survey and excavation in the twentieth century in an area bounded, along its northern side, by the area of Kermanshah and Harsin (some, e.g., Minorsky 2011, consider Nehavand outside of it, but here it will be included); toward the east, by Malayer, Burujird, and the Dez River (Ab-e Dez); on the south by Khuzestan (to which Deh Luran and its sites are assigned); and on the west by the Iraqi frontier (Edmonds 1922: 335; Mortensen 1993: 26 and fig. 1.1). Although strictly speaking lying to the north of Luristan, the site of Godin Tepe in the Kangavar valley, so closely linked in the archaeological literature with Tepe Giyan and so important for chronological purposes, will be included here.

While the Pusht-e Kuh lies to the west of the Kabir Kuh and abuts the Iraqi frontier, most of the region is dominated by a series of seven, northwest–southeast trending mountain ranges ([1] Kabir Kuh and Tangavan; [2] Kuh-e Maleh, Kiyalan, and Taq-e Mani; [3] Kuh Astan, Dahlich, and Kuh Biab; [4] Kuh-e Ghazal and Kuh-e Gird; [5] Guraz, Dadabad, and Haftad Pahlu; [6]; Ispid Kuh and Mutba; and [7] Garru, Puneh, and Shahnishin; Edmonds 1922: 335) that form part of the great Zagros chain with peaks in excess of 3000 m. Some of these are snow capped for over five months of the year (Black-Michaud 1974: 210). As the geologist J. V. Harrison put it, "Luristan, north-west of the Kashgan, is pleasant country. It is walled in on the south-west by one long even range, Kabir Kuh, and is effectively blocked by high ranges between Khurramabad and Kermanshah. An inner barrier is formed by the escarpments above the Saimarreh at Varizard. Several large plains exist inside these barricades, divided up into separate ovals by lesser ranges. They are generally connected by easy passes. Many alternative ways are available through these inner parts, but the outer obstacles are hard to circumvent" (Harrison 1942: 127).

The region is bisected by three significant rivers: the Saimarreh, which descends from Kermanshah (where it is called the Qara Su), was traditionally fordable only at Hulailan (Harrison 1942: 127) and eventually becomes the Karkheh; the Kashgan, which rises south of Khorramabad and flows west and then south before joining the Karkheh; and the Dez, which arises in the mountains and flows southwest before joining the Karkheh at Dezful (Edmonds 1922: 335; Mortensen 1993: 33). Climate and rainfall in Luristan are highly variable, depending on elevation. Thus, whereas rainfall on the order of 400–500 mm per annum is not unusual in the higher reaches of the Zagros, the Pusht-e Kuh and the area close to Dezful are characterized by a much more arid regime, with summer temperatures easily reaching 40°C (Mortensen 1993: 37).

Brief history of Bronze Age research

Although Major Henry C. Rawlinson recorded Sasanian and early Islamic remains in the Pusht-e Kuh in 1836 (Rawlinson 1839: 53–60; Haerinck and Overlaet 2006b), modern archaeological exploration in Luristan began with the first Mission Scientifique en Perse undertaken by Jacques de Morgan who traversed 20,000 km in the course of twenty-seven months between 1889 and 1892 (see the review in Haerinck 2011: 56–7). Much of this time was spent in Luristan and neighboring portions of Kurdistan and, although he was mainly attracted by later sites, de Morgan also recorded a number of prehistoric ones (de Morgan 1896: 3–6; Jaunay 1997: 251ff.). Several decades passed, however, until further fieldwork was initiated. In what has been considered by some scholars the first "scientific" excavation of a tomb in the history of Iranian archaeology

(Calmeyer 1971: 375), Ernst Herzfeld excavated a Bronze Age tomb that had been discovered accidentally about 5 km from Gilviran in 1928 (Herzfeld 1929–30: 70–1). In the winter of 1929–30 bronzes, allegedly from the Harsin region, began appearing on the antiquities market in Kermanshah, Baghdad, and Europe. These so-called "Luristan bronzes" were quickly purchased by museums across Europe and the United States (Muscarella 1988), although neither their provenance nor their date were at all certain. In 1931, Freya Stark visited Luristan in the hope of ascertaining information on their origin and while this proved unsuccessful, she published notes on a number of cemeteries in the region (Stark 1932). In 1931–2 a French expedition under the direction of Georges Contenau and Roman Ghirshman conducted two seasons of salvage excavation at Tepe Giyan, near Nehavand, a site that was being looted by the local inhabitants and had been visited previously by Ernst Herzfeld, who had collected ceramics there (Contenau and Ghirshman 1935; Negahban 2001). The main goal of the excavations was the establishment of a ceramic chronology for the early periods on the Iranian plateau but the excavations, while recovering quantities of painted pottery, were anything but rigorous from a stratigraphic point of view. In 1933, investigations were also undertaken at Tepe Jamshidi, about 10 km southeast of Tepe Giyan. In 1934, E. F. Schmidt and G. C. Miles surveyed the Rumishgan area, some of which was later resurveyed in the 1960s by Clare Goff (Goff 1971), and in 1935 Schmidt undertook excavations at the Bronze Age sites of Kamtarlan, Chigha Sabz, and Mir Vali, returning in 1938 to work at Surkh Dum-e Luri, Chaman, and Qumish (Schmidt et al. 1989; Rickenbach 1992: 31–4). Sir Aurel Stein surveyed parts of Luristan in 1936, identifying Bronze Age material at Dum'avize in the Badawar valley and Telyab near Harsin (Stein 1938: 335; 1940: 292–8).

After World War II, the first major work in Luristan was undertaken by an expedition from the Danish National Museum (1962–4). Responding to an invitation from the civil engineering firm Kampsax, which was, at the time, building a road through Luristan, Jørgen Meldgaard and his team surveyed a number of valleys (Shabedagh, Hulailan, Bouluran, Tarhan, Kuh-e Dasht) and in Hulailan undertook soundings at several sites with Bronze Age occupation (e.g., Tang-e Hamamlan) and major excavations at Tepe Guran (Meldgaard et al. 1963; Mortensen 1975: 5; Thrane 2001). Once again, at least part of the impetus behind the project was the elucidation of the "chronology and cultural background of the Luristan bronzes" (Mortensen 1979: 3). From 1963 to 1967, a British expedition under the direction of Clare Goff worked in the Pish-e Kuh, with important results for Bronze Age studies (Goff 1971, 1976). In 1965 Louis Vanden Berghe and the Belgian Mission undertook the first of fifteen seasons of survey and excavation, lasting until 1979, originally with the purpose of better understanding the enigmatic Luristan bronzes but rapidly expanding the purview of the project to investigate Bronze Age cemeteries (e.g., Bani Surmah, Gululal-e Galbi, Kalleh Nisar, Sardant, Darvand, Takht-e Khan Abdanan, Tang-e sin Kazab; see, e.g., Vanden Berghe 1968, 1970a, 1970b, 1973a, 1973b, 1979b, 1979c; Vanden Berghe and Haerinck 1984; Vanden Berghe and Tourovets 1992; Haerinck 1987, 2008, 2011; Haerinck and Overlaet 2002, 2004, 2006a, 2006b, 2008). From 1973 until the Iranian Revolution, a Danish expedition under the direction of Peder Mortensen investigated Hulailan, concentrating principally on survey and prehistoric evidence but noting Bronze Age occupation at a number of sites as well (e.g., the caves of Mar Ruz and Mar Gurgalan Sarab, Tepe Faisala, Bagh Kahreh Sarab, Tepe Kazabad A, B, and C; Mortensen 1975: 36, 40, 43–4). Recently, Iranian archaeologists have excavated at the badly looted site of Tepe Nurabad (not to be confused with Tol-e Nurabad in Fars) where several graves date to the third and second millennia BC and at Tepe Giyan (Azarnoush and Helwing 2005: 231, n. 190). Important archaeo-metallurgical research has also been conducted at Deh Hosein (Nezafati et al. 2008: 84–6, fig. 4; 2009; Thornton 2009: 317). Helpful bibliographies of Iranian archaeology, arranged by region and site, are available to assist the student of Luristan's Bronze Age (Vanden Berghe 1979a; Vanden Berghe and Haerinck 1981, 1987; Haerinck and Stevens 1996, 2005)

In their publication of the material from the Holmes Expeditions, van Loon and Curvers (Curvers 1989: 131) adopted the following chronology: Early Bronze Age (EB: *c.*2900–2000 BC); Middle Bronze Age (MB: *c.*2000–1600 BC); and Late Bronze Age (LB: *c.*1600–1200 BC). Based on their work in the Pusht-e Kuh, where by far the bulk of the research conducted in Luristan has been carried out, the Belgians have proposed a refined periodization for the Early and Middle Bronze Age (Haerinck and Overlaet 2002; 2004: 122–8; 2008: 65–8; 2010a: 281–2) based on metal weaponry, ceramics, and tomb architecture: Phase I (cf. Jamdat Nasr and early ED I: late fourth to early third millennium BC); Phase II (ED I–II); Phase III (ED III and early Akkadian); and Phase IV (later Akkadian, "Gutian," Ur III and possibly early Isin-Larsa). These EB subphases will be referred to here as EB I/I, I/II, I/III, and I/IV. The Godin Tepe chronology (*OHR*) and standard Mesopotamian terms for contemporary periods (Jamdat Nasr, Early Dynastic [ED] I–III, Old Akkadian, Ur III) will be used when comparisons are made.

Early Bronze I

The Bronze Age of Luristan and the central Zagros did not emerge from a demographic vacuum. Although settlements are rare and graves far more abundant, it is nevertheless clear that, notwithstanding probable changes in social, economic, and political organization toward the end of the fourth millennium BC, the area was not depopulated at the end of the Chalcolithic period. The Late Chalcolithic/Uruk IV-related occupation at Godin Tepe (VI:1, formerly called V) was followed by the Godin IV settlement with ceramic ties (gray-black burnished ware) to the Early Transcaucasian Culture (ETC or Kura-Araxes culture) of the Caucasus and Yanik Tepe in Iranian Azerbaijan (Levine and Young 1987: 40; Ascalone 2006: 106–7; Rothman 2011). The time elapsed between Godin VI:1 and IV is uncertain but is likely to have been at least a century, with VI:1 ending *c.*3050 and IV:2 beginning *c.*2900 BC. About 1 m of deposit separated the latest Godin VI:1 deposits from the earliest Godin IV levels in the so-called Brick Kiln Cut (Rothman 2011: 162–3). The relationship between Godin IV and the succeeding Godin III:6 occupation, which began *c.*2600 BC (Henrickson 1987: 205), is also unclear (Haerinck 2011: 74) but it is now thought that Godin IV:1a1 ended *c*.2700 BC, which would imply a settlement hiatus of about one century (Rothman 2011: 163; cf. Levine and Young 1987: 42). Godin Tepe IV yielded two cylinder sealings (Young and Levine 1974: fig. 34.3) that have been dated on stylistic grounds to "late Proto-Literate or ED I" (Voigt and Dyson 1992: 162) but these are typically Piedmont Jamdat Nasr in style (Pittman 1994: 106, 326, cat. no. GD02:01; Marchetti 1996). Judging by the ceramic assemblage the situation is similar at Tepe Giyan. Despite the absence of stratigraphic control, it is clear that the Giyan VD tradition ended in the late fourth to early third millennium BC and the Giyan IV occupation commenced in the mid-third millennium, probably just prior to the beginning of the Akkadian period in Mesopotamia (Negahban 2001).

Evidence of continuity, however, is more abundant in burial contexts and in the ceramic repertoire than it is in the realm of settlement archaeology, for settlements from the turn of the fourth to the early third millennium BC remain elusive in much of the region. Some of the earliest examples have been excavated at Andjireh, in the Gulgul region south of Ilam (Haerinck 2011: 67) and at Mir Khair in the Badr area (Vanden Berghe 1979b). Among the sixty-four graves excavated at Mir Khair, most were predominantly small, subterranean cists lined with standing stone slabs, a floor of stone, and covered with either a gabled roof or large, flat, capstone slabs. Most (N = 35) were 0.9–1.4 m long, although several smaller ones (possibly for children) were found as well as six that ranged in length from 1.5 to 2.3 m. These larger tombs may have been collective, although one such tomb, containing the remains of two skeletons, seems to have been reused, while another contained neither human bones nor funerary artifacts of any kind (Vanden Berghe 1979b: 9–10). These graves contain Jamdat Nasr–related polychrome, bichrome, and monochrome ceramics (e.g., Vanden Berghe 1979b: fig. 17.1, pl. 10.B.B) comparable to material from contemporary graves at Ahmad al-Hattu in the Hamrin region (Eickhoff 1993; Haerinck 2011: 67, 73; contra Vanden Berghe 1979b: 31, who dated Mir Khair to the EB III [late ED III and Old Akkadian, *c*.2400–2200 BC]).

These graves are followed chronologically by a further nineteen in Area AI at Kalleh Nisar in the Aivan region (Haerinck and Overlaet 2008). Generally comparable to those at Mir Khair, the EB I graves at Kalleh Nisar included some as long as 4 m (internal length) and two with slightly vaulted roofs, prefiguring a form more common in EB II tombs (Haerinck and Overlaet 2008: 64). Polychrome/bichrome (black-brown and red) and monochrome ceramics attributed on stylistic grounds to the Jamdat Nasr and Early Dynastic (ED) I periods are paralleled at Ahmad al-Hattu, Gubba, and Tell Razuk in the Hamrin, and Tell Asmar and Tell Agrab in the Diyala (Haerinck and Overlaet 2008: 27–8; Haerinck 2011: 60, 72). In the town of Ilam itself, graves identified during construction contained carinated, painted pottery of Jamdat Nasr/ED I type, with parallels in the Hamrin and Diyala material as well as at Susa, Tepe Farukhabad, and Tepe Aliabad near Deh Luran (Soto Riesle 1983; Haerinck and Overlaet 2010a: 282; Haerinck 2011: 61). Graves at Tepe Jarali, excavated by the Danish expedition, north east of Mir Khair, have been dated to this horizon as well (Haerinck 2011: 68).

At Kunji Cave, near Khorramabad, up to eight burials (single primary inhumations, secondary deposits, and ossuaries) containing a minimum of thirty-three individuals were found in the slope below the entrance to the cave. These contained a minimum of sixty-two ceramic vessels, including biconical storage jars with nose-lugs and geometric decoration in bichrome or monochrome (Emberling et al. 2002: fig. 8b, 10d, 27a), showing parallels to Jamdat Nasr/ED I (3100–2800 BC) material from sites in southern Mesopotamia, as well as Tepe Farukhabad, Susa, and Tal-e Malyan. Other biconical storage jars, with or without nose-lugs, have raised rope-ridges (e.g., Emberling et al. 2002: figs. 10d, 20a–b, 21a, 25a–c, 30a) but the presence of "fruit stands" has led Emberling et al. (2002: 49, 54) to argue for an ED II date (2700–2600 BC). This has been rejected by Haerinck (2011: 69), who has argued that the Luristan fruit stands may not be Mesopotamian in inspiration or origin. Tomb G/B2 also contained a typical Susa III–type goblet base (Emberling et al. 2002: fig. 22c, "gobelet à base en moignon") also paralleled at Tepe Farukhabad and Tal-e Malyan in Jamdat Nasr/Middle Banesh levels as well as the rim of a bevel-rim bowl (Emberling et al. 2002: fig. 30e). The monochrome jars with simple, horizontal bands (e.g., Emberling et al. 2002: figs. 8c, 11a–f, 14b–d, 14f, 21c, 26a–f, and 30b) are also reminiscent of Banesh-era ceramics at Tal-e Malyan (Haerinck 2011: 73). A lead bowl (Emberling et al. 2002: fig. 23a) also points to an early date, as lead vessels are attested at Tal-e Malyan and Susa in Susa III/Banesh contexts; in ED I graves at Ur; and in the cemetery at Ahmad al-Hattu in the Hamrin region (see Haerinck 2011: 71 with full bibliography).

Metallurgically speaking, EB I/I is characterized by the relative rarity of metal weapons, tools, and ornaments. The limited répertoire available from Mir Khair and Kalleh Nisar includes tanged knives or daggers; blade axes; and coiled rings and bracelets of copper (Begemann et al. 2008: 4, fig. 2). Compositional analyses of five objects from Kalleh Nisar Area AI suggest the intentional alloying of copper and tin to produce bronze, as suggested by tin contents of 3.52 percent and 14.8 percent in two finger rings; 3.85 percent and 3.49 percent in two bracelets; and 3.74 percent in a pin (Fleming et al. 2005: table 1). For the moment, these are the earliest tin-bronzes known in Iran (Fleming et al. 2005: 37; Pigott 2008: 56–7). Their appearance is important in light of the discovery of a tin source at Deh Hosein in northeastern Luristan (Nezafati et al. 2009) which flatly refutes the view that "Luristan held no natural resources" that could not be obtained elsewhere (Hole 2007: 77). At Godin Tepe, on the other hand, tin-bronzes did not appear until Godin III:6, *c*.2600–2400 BC (Frame 2010: 1705).

Early Bronze II

The next phase in the Pusht-e Kuh, dating to the ED I and II periods in Mesopotamia, is represented at a number of cemeteries, including Bani Surmah, north of Ilam; Kalleh Nisar (AI tomb 2; C, tomb 4); Takht-e Khan (tomb 1); and other sites on the southern side of the Kabir Kuh including Bani Sol (Chavar area); Mehr War Kabud and Shatt-i Siah Safalaki (Arkavaz area); and Cheshmeh-e Takht-e Khan (Salihabad area) (Haerinck and Overlaet 2010b: 41ff.). The tombs of this phase have been described as "large communal corridor-shaped" structures (Begemann et al. 2008: 5). The largest tomb at Bani Surmah was 15.7 m long and 3.1 m wide, while most ranged between 9 and 14 m in length, and the smallest were still 5 m long (Haerinck and Overlaet 2004: 124; 2006a: 5). These tombs had massive capstones but no internal paving. In addition to cooking wares, the Bani Surmah tombs contained unpainted, carinated jars, some with raised shoulder ridges, easily paralleled in ED I–III contexts in the Diyala and Hamrin regions; round-bodied jars with punctate decoration in horizontal and diagonal lines, paralleled at Fara, Abu Salabikh, Khafajah, Tepe Aliabad, and Tepe Farukhabad; monochrome jars with geometric decoration of Susa D type; and polychrome jars with a combination of geometric and naturalistic motives, including caprids and birds, reminiscent of Scarlet Ware in the Diyala and Hamrin regions (Carter 1987: 79, fig. 3; Haerinck and Overlaet 2006a: figs. 12–13, pls. 20–22). Continuous use for over a millennium is suggested by the recovery of nine cylinder seals, four of which can be dated to the Jamdat Nasr or ED I period and five of which are of ED III and Old Akkadian type (Tourovets 1996; Haerinck and Overlaet 2004: 124), while pottery of Isin-Larsa and Old Babylonian date has also been recovered (Begemann et al. 2008: 5). It is important to note that these seals come from a site that is close to the Mesopotamian frontier and that similar seals have not been recovered in tombs in either the Pish-e Kuh or the Abdanan region, further south (Haerinck and Overlaet 2006a: 51). However, thirteen EB cylinder seals were recovered in Schmidt's excavations at Kamtarlan II and Surkh Dum-e Luri (Schmidt et al. 1989: pl. 132). These included two of Susa III/proto-Elamite type (Kamtarlan II, Level 2); one brocade style seal of ED I date (Surkh Dum-e Luri); one ED IIIB/Old Akkadian seal of "piedmont Early Dynastic" type (Kamtarlan II, Level 2); a clay seal of probable ED date (Kamtarlan II, Level 2); six seals of Old Akkadian date from Boehmer's stages Ib (c.2320–2295 BC) and Ic (2295–2279 BC); and two Old Akkadian seals with contest scenes datable to Boehmer's stage III (2254–2154 BC) (van Loon 1989d: 211–15).

The reuse of tombs in Area C at Kalleh Nisar from EB I through the early Old Akkadian period makes it difficult to distinguish trends in metallurgical development but genuine bronzes with 1.67 percent to 11.8 percent tin are found (Fleming et al. 2005: 37 and table 2)

Early Bronze II–III

In the Pusht-e Kuh this phase is represented by collective graves in three different zones, as defined by Haerinck (1987: 66–7). With respect to ceramics and metal weaponry, Zone I is "Mesopotamian-related" and includes assemblages at Bani Surmah, Kalleh Nisar C, and Mehr War Kabud; Zone II, near the southern end of the Pusht-e Kuh, is closely related to the Deh Luran sites (and includes tombs at at Qabr Nahi, Takht-e Khan, Tawarsa, and Pusht-e Qaleh-e Abdanan; and Zone III, to the north of the Kabir Kuh, is more closely related to the monochrome painted pottery tradition of Godin Tepe III:6 (Haerinck 1987: 66–7; 2011: 63–4, pls. 5–6; Begemann et al. 2008: 7; Ascalone 2006:

107–9; Haerinck and Overlaet 2010b: 14; Henrickson 2011b: 250ff.). Interestingly, construction of new tombs in EB III is presently unattested; rather, tombs of EB II continued to be used (Begemann et al. 2006: 5).

Material dating to this phase was also found by Schmidt at Mir Vali in the Rumishgan area (Haerinck 2011: 64; Ascalone 2006: 104–5). Generally this material is reminiscent of Scarlet Ware but with figurative decoration on the shoulder rather than the body. Quantities of monochrome with shapes reminiscent of Scarlet Ware in the Diyala and Hamrin regions but with decoration paralleled at Godin Tepe (period III:6; Henrickson 2011b: figs. 6.34a–b) were excavated at Dar Tanha and Ban Chaliah in the Badr region (Haerinck 2011: 68, 73), and Haerinck has suggested that some of the Dar Tanha ceramics may date to ED I/II and "represent a phase of its own, preceding the fully developed Godin III:6 style" (Haerinck 2011: 69). Based on parallels at al-Hiba in southern Iraq an ED III date, possibly beginning in ED II, has been suggested for Godin III:6 (Henrickson 1987: 207–8) but some scholars have suggested an ED IIIA or IIIB date (Haerinck 2011: 75). In any case, the painted, monochrome, buff ware ceramics of Godin III represent a significant departure from the gray-black burnished wares of Godin IV (Haerinck 2011: 76), though about 6 percent of the Godin III assemblage "consists of handmade burnished, gray-black ware, perhaps derived from a similar Godin IV ware … used for shallow carinated bowls, tankards, large concave-sided cylindrical vessels, and shallow dishes" (Henrickson 2011b: 251). To this phase belong also Giyan Tepe IVB–IVC and tomb 102.

The small settlements at Kamtarlan I and II excavated by Schmidt in 1935 yielded ceramics with Susa D parallels that have been generally dated to the late Early Dynastic and early Akkadian periods, c.2600–2300 BC (van Loon 1989a: 17; 1989b: 20; Curvers 1989: 131, 133–4). Kamtarlan I also yielded a Piedmont Early Dynastic–type cylinder seal (Schmidt, van Loon and Curvers 1989: pl. 132.10). The megalithic tomb investigated by Herzfeld at Gilviran (Herzfeld 1929–30; Calmeyer 1971) yielded two vessels with open spouts that have been dated stylistically to ED IIIB (Bellelli 2002: 16, 134 and Tav. 28.160–1).

At Godin Tepe, the period III settlement continued for over a millennium, terminating in the Late Bronze Age (LBA) c.1400 BC. Tepe Baba Jan IV, Level 5, was founded c.2300 BC and flourished until c.2100 BC. After a hiatus in settlement of about three centuries, the site was reoccupied in Baba Jan IV, Level 4, c.1800 and occupied until c.1500 BC (Henrickson 2011b).

Early Bronze IV

This poorly understood phase is attested only in Zone I (see above; Haerinck and Overlaet 2010b), for example, at Kalleh Nisar AII, Darvand A, Gululal-e Galbi, and Sardant. Small tombs (1.2–1.7 m long) of so-called "Gutian" type (Haerinck and Overlaet 2010b: 115ff.) may span the late Akkadian through early Isin-Larsa periods (late third to early second millennium BC) and include distinctive shafthole axes made of folded sheet bronze (Fleming et al. 2005: fig. 3); imported, monochrome Mesopotamian pottery showing distinctive Akkadian and Ur III shapes; and monochrome painted wares paralleled at Godin Tepe (Begemann et al. 2006: 7–8).

Tin bronze was less common in Kalleh Nisar Area AII than in previous periods, though some examples analyzed had tin contents up to 10.8 percent (Fleming et al. 2005: 38). A tomb at Dum'avize excavated by Schmidt dates to the end of the third millennium BC (van Loon 1989c: 61) and included a bronze vessel with outflaring rim, long neck, and sharply carinated shoulder (Bellelli 2002: Tav. 20.113).

Middle Bronze Age

In contrast to the earlier periods, Middle Bronze funerary remains in the Pusht-e Kuh are rare and usually occur in Early Bronze tombs that were reused (Haerinck and Overlaet 2004: 128). Excavations by Schmidt, however, identified graves at Chigha Sabz, Surkh Dum-e Luri, Chaman B and C, and Kamtarlan II containing MB ceramics with clear parallels at Godin Tepe and Tepe Giyan (Curvers 1989: 134–5, pls. 92–108; Ascalone 2006: 100–02). Nine Old Babylonian cylinder seals and one late Old Assyrian cylinder seal, heirlooms deposited in the Iron Age, were also discovered at Surkh Dum-e Luri (van Loon 1989d: 215–18). Bronze vessels of MB date (shallow bowls with carinated or rounded sides; tall beakers; concave beakers with rounded or ring bases; mugs with riveted handles) are relatively numerous and have been excavated in tombs at Godin Tepe (locus O, tomb I/B), Chigha Sabz (Area J7, tombs 2 and 4; Area H5, tomb 3; Area M7, tomb 3; Area N7, tomb 6), Tepe Jamshidi near Giyan (Level 4, tombs 10, 16 and 17), Sardant (tomb 2), Kamtarlan II (Area D, tombs 2, 4–6), Kalleh Nisar (Area A, tomb 2), Tepe Guran (grave 11), and Tepe Giyan (III, tombs 88, 97, 99, 107, 110) (Müller-Karpe 1995: figs. 7.13–16, 18; figs. 10.17; 40.6–8; Bellelli 2002: tables 14.51–2; 15.57–66; 17.75, 78–81, 84–5; 18.86–97; 19.99, 103, 104–8; 21.118, 27.157; cf. Ascalone 2006: 103–4).

Late Bronze Age

In the Pusht-e Kuh the last phase of the Bronze Age is represented by only a single grave at Sarab Bagh (Haerinck and Overlaet 2004: 128, fig. 5.13–16). In Rumishgan LB graves with parallels in Tepe Giyan II were identified by Schmidt at Zarde Savar. At Surkh Dum-e Luri, however, a multiroomed structure, interpreted as a sanctuary, was excavated. Lodged close to some of the stone walls of this structure were hoards of artifacts. Along with a sizable number of bronze objects, the excavations at Surkh Dum-e Luri yielded: a bead, on which the name is possibly to be restored as Burna-Buriaš II; an eye stone of Kurigalzu; a bead of Kurigalzu II; and a seal of an official serving one of the

Kassite kings named Kurigalzu (Brinkman 1976: 48 with references). Late Bronze Age glyptic recovered at Surkh Dum-e Luri included four Middle Elamite, one Kassite, three Mitannian, and three Middle Assyrian cylinder seals (van Loon 1989d: 218–220). These were most likely votive offerings, however, and need not reflect direct connections between the site or region and the powers of Late Bronze Age Babylonia and Assyria. Other bronze weapons with Kassite inscriptions said to be from Luristan (e.g., Dossin 1962) cannot be adduced as evidence of such links as all are from the art market and their origin in Luristan is unproven. Finally, the Neolithic mound of Tepe Guran was reused in the Late Bronze Age, both as a cemetery and as a settlement. A calibrated C14 date from one of the earliest graves falls in the period c.1500–1300 BC (Thrane 2001: 15). Vessels of "Khabur Ware" are attested (Area GI, Layer S) as are a number of tall, unpainted, wheelmade goblet fragments (Thrane 2001: fig. 60, pl. 30, from Area G II, Layer P) that are clearly reminiscent of Kassite and Middle Elamite types (Thrane 1999). Khabur ware is also attested in Godin III:2, Tepe Giyan II graves, Tepe Jamshidi, and Baba Jan (Henrickson 1987: 213). Godin Tepe also had a Late Bronze Age cemetery just off the main mound (Dellovin 2011).

Nomadism and sedentism

In 1972, Jacob Black wrote, "Until approximately forty-five years ago there was hardly a sedentary village in the whole of Luristan" and this situation only changed due to enforced sedentarization under Reza Shah in the 1920s and 1930s (Black 1972: 619; cf. Stein 1938: 327). Many scholars have speculated on what the situation may have been like in Bronze Age Luristan where settlements are generally rare in comparison with tombs. A general dearth of settlement led Vanden Berghe to suggest that nomadism prevailed across much of Luristan (cf. Hole 2007: 76) but as Begemann et al. have recently noted, far less attention has been paid to the search for settlements and "our concept of the settlement patterns in Luristan may be … distorted as villages are often located on the lower slopes of mountains, close to springs," and are "likely to be covered by sediments, making their detection difficult" (Begemann et al. 2008: 40–41; cf. De Meyer 2004 for a recent attempt to identify sites using satellite imagery). Certainly the Bronze Age tombs of Luristan, coupled with settlements like Godin Tepe, Tepe Giyan, and Surkh Dum-e Luri, give indications of a rich culture on which much research remains to be undertaken, building on the fundamental research of Schmidt, the Belgian Mission, the Danish work at Tepe Guran, and the Canadian excavations at Godin Tepe.

References

Amanolahi, S. 2002. Reza Shah and the Lurs: The impact of the modern state on Luristan. *Iran and the Caucasus* 6/1–2: 193–218.

Ascalone, E. 2006. *Archeologia dell'Iran Antico: Interazioni, integrazioni e discontinuità nell'Iran del III millennio a.C.* Messina: Nisaba 14.
Azarnoush, M., and B. Helwing. 2005. Recent archaeological research in Iran: Prehistory to Iron Age. *AMIT* 37: 189–246.
Begemann, F., E. Haerinck, B. Overlaet, S. Schmitt-Strecker, and F. Tallon. 2008. An archaeo-metallurgical study of the Early and Middle Bronze Age in Luristan, Iran. *IrAnt* 43: 1–66.
Bellelli, G.M. 2002. *Vasi iranici in metallo dell'Età del Bronzo.* Stuttgart: PBf II/17.
Black, J. 1972. Tyranny as a strategy for survival in an "egalitarian" society: Luri facts versus an anthropological mystique. *Man NS* 7/4: 614–34.
Black-Michaud, J. 1974. An ethnographic and ecological survey of Luristan, western Persia: Modernization in a nomadic pastoral society. *Middle Eastern Studies* 10/2: 210–28.
Brinkman, J. A. 1976. *Materials and studies for Kassite history*, vol. 1, *A catalogue of cuneiform sources pertaining to specific monarchs of the Kassite dynasty.* Chicago: Oriental Institute.
Calmeyer, P. 1971. Gīlvirān. *RlA* 3: 374–5.
Carter, E. 1987. The piedmont and the Pusht-i Kuh in the early third millennium B.C. *PM*: 73–89.
Contenau, G., and R. Ghirshman. 1935. *Fouilles de Tépé Giyan, près de Néhavend, 1931–32.* Paris: Geuthner.
Curvers, H. H. 1989. Bronze Age pottery and baked clay objects. *HEL*: 131–78.
Dellovin, A. 2011. A carpenter's tool kit from the Godin cemetery (central-western Iran). *IrAnt* 46: 107–32.
De Meyer, M. 2004. Archaeological research using satellite remote sensing techniques (Corona) in the valleys of Shirwan and Chardawal (Pusht-i Kuh, Luristan), Iran. *IrAnt* 39: 43–103.
Dossin, G. 1962. Bronzes inscrits du Luristan de la collection Foroughi. *IrAnt* 2: 149–64.
Edmonds, C. J. 1922. Luristan: Pish-i-Kuh and Bala Gariveh. *GJ* 59: 335–56, 437–53.
Eickhoff, T. 1993. *Grab und Beigabe: Bestattungssitten der Nekropole von Tall Aḥmad al-Ḥattū und anderer frühdynastischer Begräbnisstätten im südlichen Mesopotamien und in Luristān.* Munich: Profil Verlag.
Emberling, G., J. Robb, J. D. Speth, and H. T. Wright. 2002. Kunji Cave: Early Bronze Age burials in Luristan. *IrAnt* 37: 47–104.
Fleming, S. J., V. C. Pigott, C. P. Swann, and S. K. Nash. 2005. Bronze in Luristan: Preliminary analytical evidence from copper/bronze artifacts excavated by the Belgian Mission in Iran. *IrAnt* 40: 35–64.
Frame, L. 2010. Metallurgical investigations at Godin Tepe, Iran, Part I: The metal finds. *JAS* 37: 1700–15.
Goff, C. 1971. Luristan before the Iron Age. *Iran* 9: 131–52.
———. 1976. Excavations at Baba Jan: The Bronze Age occupation. *Iran* 14: 19–40.
Haerinck, E. 1987. The chronology of Luristan, Pusht-i Kuh in the late fourth and first half of the third millennium B.C. *PM*: 55–72.
———. 2008. Le Luristan à l'âge du bronze (vers 3100–1300 av. J.-C.). In *Bronzes du Luristan: Énigmes de l'Iran ancien, IIIe–Ier millénaire av. J.-C.*, ed. A.-J. Esparceil, 33–41. Paris: Paris musées.
———. 2011. Painted pottery of the first half of the Early Bronze Age (late 4th–first centuries of the 3rd millennium BC) in Luristan, W–Iran. *IrAnt* 46: 55–106.
Haerinck, E., and B. Overlaet. 2002. The Chalcolithic and Early Bronze Age in Pusht-i Kuh, Luristan (West-Iran): The chronology and Mesopotamian contacts. *Akkadica* 123: 163–81.

———. 2004. The chronology of the Pusht-i Kuh, Luristan: Results of the Belgian Archaeological Expedition in Iran. *FHK*: 119–35.

———. 2006a. *Bani Surmah: An Early Bronze Age graveyard in Pusht-i Kuh, Luristan.* Leuven: LED 6.

———. 2006b. Pošt-e Kuh. *EnIr* online edition.

———. 2008. *The Kalleh Nisar Bronze Age graveyard in Pusht-i Kuh, Luristan.* Leuven: LED 7.

———. 2010a. Bronze and Iron Age pottery from the Ilam graveyard (Pusht-i Kuh, Iran). *IrAnt* 45: 277–304.

———. 2010b. *The early Bronze Age graveyards to the west of the Kabir Kuh (Pusht-i Kuh, Luristan).* Leuven: LED 8.

Haerinck, E., and K. G. Stevens. 1996. *Bibliographie analytique de l'archéologie de l'Irān ancien. Supplément 3: 1986–1995.* Leuven: Peeters.

———. 2005. *Bibliographie analytique de l'archéologie de l'Irān ancien. Supplément 4: 1996–2003.* Leuven: Peeters.

Harrison, J. V. 1942. Some routes in southern Iran. *GJ* 99: 113–29.

———. 1946. South-West Persia: A survey of Pish-i-Kuh in Luristan. *GJ* 108: 55–70.

Henrickson, R. C. 1987. Godin III and the chronology of Central Western Iran circa 2600–1400 B.C. *AWI*: 205–27.

———. 2011a. Bābā Jān Tepe. *EnIr* online edition.

———. 2011b. The Godin Period III town. *OHR*: 209–82.

Herzfeld, E. 1929–30. Bericht über archäologische Beobachtungen im südlichen Kurdistan und in Luristan. *AMI* 1: 65–75.

Hole, F. 2007. Cycles of settlement in the Khorramabad Valley in Luristan, Iran. In *Settlement and Society: Essays dedicated to Robert McCormick Adams*, ed. E. C. Stone, 63–82. Los Angeles/Chicago: Cotsen Institute of Archaeology and the Oriental Institute.

Jaunay, A. 1997. *Mémoires de Jacques de Morgan, 1857–1924, Souvenirs d'un archéologue.* Paris: L'Harmattan.

Kunke, M. 1991. *Nomadenstämme in Persien im 18. und 19. Jahrhundert.* Berlin: Islamkundliche Untersuchungen 151.

Levine, L. D., and T. C. Young Jr. 1987. A summary of the ceramic assemblages of the Central Western Zagros from the Middle Neolithic to the late third millennium B.C. *PM*: 15–53.

Marchetti, N. 1996. The Ninevite 5 glyptic of the Khabur region and the chronology of the Piedmont style motives. *BaM* 27: 81–115.

Meldgaard, J., P. Mortensen, and H. Thrane. 1963. Excavations at Tepe Guran, Luristan: Preliminary report of the Danish Archaeological Expedition to Iran 1963. *Acta Archaeologica* 34: 97–133.

Minorsky, V. 2011. Luristan. *Encyclopaedia of Islam*, 2nd ed. Brill Online.

Morgan, J. de. 1896. *Mission scientifique en Perse*, vol. 4. Paris: E. Leroux.

Mortensen, I. D. 1993. *Nomads of Luristan: History, material culture, and pastoralism in western Iran.* London: Thames and Hudson.

Mortensen, P. 1975. A survey of prehistoric settlements in northern Luristan. *Acta Archaeologica* 45: 1–47.

———. 1979. The Hulailan Survey: A note on the relationship between aims and method. In *Akten des VII. Internationalen Kongresses für Iranische Kunst und Archäologie, München, 7.–10. September 1976*, ed. W. Kleiss, 3–8. Berlin: AMI Ergänzungsband 6.

Müller-Karpe, M. 1995. Zu den Erdgräbern 18, 20 und 21 von Assur: Ein Beitrag zur Kenntnis mesopotamischer Metallgefäße und —waffen von der Wende des 3. zum 2. Jahrtausend v. Chr. *Jahrbuch des Römisch-Germanischen Zentralmuseums Mainz* 42: 257–352.

Muscarella, O. W. 1988. The background to the Luristan bronzes. In *Bronzeworking centres of Western Asia c. 1000–539 B.C.*, ed. J. Curtis, 33–44. London/New York: Kegan Paul International.

Negahban, E. 2001. Giyan Tepe. *EnIr* online edition.

Nezafati, N., E. Pernicka, and M. Momenzadeh. 2008. Iranian ore deposits and their role in the development of the ancient cultures. In *Anatolian Metal IV*, ed. Ü. Yalç in, 77–90. Bochum: Der Anschnitt Beiheft 21.

———. 2009. Introduction of the Deh Hosein ancient tin-copper mine, western Iran: Evidence from geology, archaeology, geochemistry and lead isotope data. *TÜBA-AR* 12: 223–30.

Pigott, V. C. 2008. Le bronze et le fer au Luristan: Nouvelle confirmation d'une tradition technologique ancienne. In *Bronzes du Luristan: Énigmes de l'Iran ancien, IIIe–Ier millénaire av. J.-C.*, ed. A.-J. Esparceil, 55–65. Paris: Paris musées.

Pittman, H. 1994. *The glazed steatite glyptic style*. Berlin: BBVO 16.

Rawlinson, Major H. C. 1839. Notes on a March from Zoháb, at the foot of Zagros, along the mountains to Khúzistán (Susiana), and from thence through the province of Luristan to Kirmánsháh, in the year 1836. *JRGS* 9: 26–116.

Rickenbach, J. 1992. *Magier mit Feuer und Erz: Bronzekunst der frühen Bergvölker in Luristan, Iran*. Zurich: Museum Rietberg.

Rothman, M. S. 2011. Migration and resettlement: Godin Period IV. *OHR*: 139–206.

Schmidt, E. F., M. N. van Loon, and H. H. Curvers. 1989. *HEL*.

Soto Riesle, P. 1983. The population of the Konamazan Region of Luristan in the Late Bronze Age and in the Iron Period. *EW* 33: 177–216.

Stark, F. 1932. The bronzes of Luristan. *GJ* 80: 498–505.

Stein, M. A. 1938. An archaeological journey in western Iran. *GJ* 92: 313–42.

———. 1940. *Old routes of Western Īrān: Narrative of an archaeological journey*. London: Macmillan.

Thornton, C. P. 2009. The emergence of complex metallurgy on the Iranian plateau: Escaping the Levantine paradigm. *JWP* 22/3: 301–27.

Thrane, H. 1999. Pots and people—once again. The goblets from the Bronze Age settlement at Tepe Guran, Luristan. *IrAnt* 34: 21–40.

———. 2001. *Excavations at Tepe Guran in Luristan: The Bronze Age and Iron Age periods*. Aarhus: Jutland Archaeological Society Publications 38.

Tourovets, A. 1996. La glyptique de Bani Surmah, Pusht-i Kuh-Luristan. *IrAnt* 31: 19–45.

Vanden Berghe, L. 1968. La nécropole de Bani Surmah: Aurore d'une civilisation du Bronze. *Archeologia* 24: 52–63.

———. 1970a. La nécropole de Kalleh Nisar. *Archeologia* 32: 64–73.

———. 1970b. Prospections archéologiques dans la région de Badr. *Archeologia* 36: 10–21.

———. 1973a. Excavations in Luristan: Kalleh Nisar. *BAI* 3: 25–56.

———. 1973b. Le Luristan à l'âge du Bronze: Prospections archéologiques dans le Pusht-i Kuh central. *Archeologia* 63: 24–36.

———. 1979a. *Bibliographie analytique de l'archéologie de l'Irān ancien*. Leiden: Brill.

———. 1979b. La nécropole de Mīr Khair au Pusht-i Kūh, Luristān. *IrAnt* 14: 1–37.

———. 1979c. La construction des tombes au Pusht-i Kūh, Luristān au 3e millénaire avant J.-C. *IrAnt* 14: 39–50.

Vanden Berghe, L., and E. Haerinck. 1981. *Bibliographie analytique de l'archéologie de l'Irān ancien. Supplément 1: 1978–1980*. Leiden: Brill.

———. 1984. Prospections et fouilles au Pušt-i Kūh, Luristān. *AfO* 31: 200–9.

———. 1987. *Bibliographie analytique de l'archéologie de l'Irān ancien. Supplément 2: 1981–1985.* Leiden: Brill.

Vanden Berghe, L., and A. Tourovets. 1992. Prospections archéologiques dans le district de Shīrwān-Chardawal (Pusht-i Kūh, Luristān). *IrAnt* 27: 1–73.

van Loon, M. N. 1989a. Kamtarlan I. *HEL*: 15–18.

———. 1989b. Kamtarlan II. *HEL*: 19–22.

———. 1989c. Dum'avize. *HEL*: 61.

———. 1989d. Bronze Age cylinder seals. *HEL*: 211–27.

Voigt, M. M., and R. H. Dyson, Jr. 1992. The chronology of Iran, ca. 8000–2000 B.C. In *Chronologies in Old World archaeology*, 3rd ed., vol. 1, ed. R. W. Ehrich, 122–78. Chicago and London: University of Chicago Press.

Young, T. C., Jr., and L. D. Levine. 1974. *Excavations of the Godin Project: Second progress report.* Toronto: ROMAAOP 26.

CHAPTER 12

KHUZESTAN IN THE BRONZE AGE

JAVIER ÁLVAREZ-MON

Introduction

In many ways the province of Khuzestan can be considered a periphery as much as a center. From the Mesopotamian perspective it was a principal gateway to the highlands, the plateau beyond, and material resources such as quality timber, hard and precious stones, and tin. From the highland perspective it was the gateway to a web of riverine urban centers, luxury goods, and sociocultural complexity. At the same time, the geomorphology and fluvial characteristics of Khuzestan provided the potential for tremendous economic wealth based on agricultural surpluses and animal husbandry.

The urban settlements of lowland Khuzestan were concentrated on the plains of Deh Luran (*EASDLP*), Susiana (Kouchokos and Hole 2003), and Ram Hormuz (Carter 1971: 282). In addition, a range of small, central Zagros valleys, such as Izeh/Malamir (*AINX*), seem to have played determinant roles as cultic and regional centers. In this chapter, I shall be overstepping the boundaries assigned to the traditional beginning of the Bronze Age (*c.*3300 BC) and begin around 3700 BC toward the end of the "Village Period," which lasted from *c.*7000 to 4000 BC (Hole 1987; Kouchokos and Hole 2003: 55).

From village to state (c. 3700–2675 BC)

According to most accounts, the rise of the state in the province of Khuzestan was one of economic and political reorganization believed to have been closely related to events taking place in neighboring lower Mesopotamia. The more visible manifestations of these changes are the end of the distinctive "local" Susa I pottery, an increase in the number and size of settlements, and the emergence of numerical accounting systems and related sealing practices. The significance of these changes has been interpreted variously. It is believed that there was a cultural break associated with the arrival of migrant populations from the Mesopotamian plain. Differences of opinion exist, however, with respect to the degree of political influence exercised by the newcomers. The view that Susiana took part in a broader regional process of colonization emanating from Uruk is moderated by a more nuanced approach that sees progressive adaptation and integration into Mesopotamian economic networks combined with the reorganization of older exchange structures (Wright and Johnson 1975; Potts 1999: 52–71; Steve et al. 2002–3, 409–14).

During the Uruk period (Susa II or Susa B, c.3700–3100 BC) the settlement of Susa doubled in size by expanding eastwards into the areas called the Ville Royale ("royal town") and Donjon ("dungeon"), reaching no less than 25 ha. Archaeological levels corresponding to the Susa II period at Susa include Acropole I levels 22–17, and Acropole II levels 6–1 (cf. Johnson 1973: 60 for correspondences with Uruk, Nippur, and Tepe Farukhabad in the Deh Luran plain, and Tal-e Ghazir in the Ram Hormuz plain). Visible changes can be discerned in the orientation of buildings, brick sizes, and ceramics. The Acropole was dominated by residential houses and monumental architecture decorated with large numbers of conically shaped wall nails. The appearance of an accounting system that evolved from counters (*calculi*) to counters contained in clay balls (*bullae*) and finally to written texts (tablets) suggests participation in major regional socioeconomic transformations. The earliest cylinder seals in Acropole I levels 18–17 (Late Uruk period c.3200–3100 BC) and at neighboring Chogha Mish display mythological and animal scenes together with scenes of daily life, such as people engaged in weaving, possibly butter-churning, and grain storage in tall buildings topped by cupolas. The presence of a figure, often identified as a "big man" or "priest-king," shown engaged in hostile acts, is considered symptomatic of institutional elites, centralized authority, and regional conflict (Delougaz and Kantor 1996: 25, pls. 133, 148ff.; Amiet 1986: 64; Johnson 1987: 124). The final occupation of the Acropole high terrace at the end of Susa II (level 17) included large ash deposits suggesting destruction by fire. The residences in the northern part of the terrace next to the city wall, however, do not seem to have been affected by the conflagration.

The nature of settlement at Susa during the "proto-Elamite" period (Susa III or Susa C, c.3100–2675 BC) is fraught with preconceptions and ambiguity due, in large part, to the fact that the material excavated before 1957 (Le Breton 1957) was not recorded properly and because the later excavations of Susa III levels undertaken by Steve and Gasche (1971), Le Brun (1971), and Carter (1981; cf. Carter and Wright 2010: 11–14) were limited in scope and little material was recovered. Archaeological levels corresponding to the Susa III period include Acropole 1 (16–14 B); period IIIA on the Apadana (A. Le Brun) and Ville Royale I (18–13); and Period III B–C (?) (E. Carter). A significant development was the appearance (Acropole I, level 16 and Ville Royale I, levels 18 B–A) of the first so-called "proto-Elamite" or "Susa III" tablets, a writing system originally interpreted by V. Scheil as an archaic form of the later Elamite language (Scheil 1905: 59; cf.

Dahl 2002). This view has stimulated abundant discussion regarding possible links to the earlier (Susa II) numerical systems, the old Elamite language (*c.*2300 BC), and the later so-called "linear-Elamite" texts from the reign of Puzur-Inshushinak (*c.*2100 BC). The fact that Susa III/proto-Elamite tablets have been found at sites distributed across the Iranian plateau (Tal-e Ghazir, Tal-e Malyan, Tepe Yahya, Shahr-e Sokhta, Tepe Ozbaki, Tepe Sofalin) adds an intriguing aspect to the puzzle. Their spatial distribution has given rise to the notion that a supraregional economic enterprise (a "proto-Elamite civilization") sponsored by Susa or, conversely, by the large settlement of Anshan (Tal-e Malyan) may have existed (for earlier discussions see, e.g., Amiet 1979: 199; 1986: 210; Alden 1982; Sumner 1997: 406; Potts 1999: 71–83; Steve et al. 2002–3: 414–17; for radiocarbon dates see Wright and Rupley 2001: 96–7). Despite differences of interpretation, we appear to have a writing system and a technical apparatus of bookkeeping procedures that developed independently from Mesopotamia and were used across a network of Iranian towns. This technological revolution was paralleled by changes in glyptic and ceramic styles and by the continuing advancement of alloying and metalworking (Tallon 1987: 316–22).

SUSIANA AND THE EMERGENCE OF ELAM, AWAN, AND SHIMASHKI (C. 2675–1900 BC)

The Early Dynastic period at Susa (Susa IV or Susa D, *c.*2675–2100) is represented to the north of the High Terrace on the Acropole mound by architectural complexes containing large jars and grain storage facilities. Archaeological levels corresponding to the Susa IV period include Acropole Chantier (Steve and Gasche 1971; levels 4–3) and Ville Royale I (levels 12–9). As attested by the probable existence of a temple ornamented with votive limestone wall plaques exhibiting relief decoration (Pelzel 1977), the Acropole continued to be the religious heart of the city. The ceramics of this period included cream-colored vessels painted with red-orange-black motifs and distinctive imagery such as a chariot pulled by an ox, running horses, and fish. These wares are known as "second" or "Susa II" style and are distributed throughout a broad swath of the central Zagros (Potts 1999: 85–159; Steve et al. 2002–3: 418–39). The extent of the inhabited city at this time is difficult to estimate. The hundreds of tombs and related material uncovered in the Ville Royale (I) and Donjon by R. de Mecquenem, while poorly documented, suggest a large urban center supporting high levels of metallurgical production represented by metal vessels, pins, arrowheads, and other weaponry. Burials containing chariots with wooden wheels and nailed copper tires are also attested (Mecquenem 1943: 123, fig. 89; Amiet 1966: 143, fig. 103; for the chariot wheels see Tallon 1987: 297–307).

At around 2675 BC the first unequivocal reference to Elam appears in the so-called Sumerian King List. The text states that after "kingship was lowered from heaven [Col. i.1] the king of Kish (En)Mebaragesi carried away the spoil of the weapons of the land of Elam [Col.ii. 35–7] and (Sumerian) kingship went from Kish to Uruk, from Uruk to Ur, from Ur to Awan, and from Awan back to Kish [Col. ii. 45–iv. 19]" (Jacobsen 1939: 83–97). The inclusion of Elam and Awan in this list is intriguing. At this stage in history, the extent to which Sumerian scribes distinguished between Awan (the city) and Elam (the highland territory) is uncertain. The fact that they are generally mentioned separately, that two of the earliest kings of Awan bore Elamite names, and that later Elamite kings traced their political (and cultural) identity to Awanite rulers suggests that Awan and Elam may have possibly been coterminous or, more likely, that Awan was a part of the Elamite highland territory. At the same time, the fact that Awan is mentioned amongst the cities of the Sumerian heartland suggests that it must have been relatively close by, even if its precise location remains unknown. Based on parallels between burial goods from Susa IV, the Deh Luran plain, and the Pusht-e Kuh region (Luristan), D. T. Potts suggested that Awan may have been centered on the Kangavar valley (marked by the settlement of Godin Tepe, Potts 1999: 92). Regardless of where Awan was located, the Sumerian King List announces the beginning of a documented pattern of antagonism, trade exchanges, and alliances between Mesopotamia and the Zagros polities associated with Elam that lasted for millennia.

Except for the brief interval marked by the reign of the last king of Awan, Puzur-Inshushinak, it appears that Susiana was for all practical purposes an extension of the Mesopotamian socioeconomic and political network. From the Akkadian period (c.2334–2154) to the collapse of the Ur III dynasty in 2004 BC a sequence of Mesopotamian kings ruled over Susa, sending their armies on incursions into the highlands and pursuing alliances through interdynastic marriages. It can be speculated that a continuous pattern of asymmetric exchanges and aggression was responsible for fostering the emergence of highland alliances eventually culminating in the creation of an Elamite state in the form of a multicentered federation.

A key document from this period is a fragmentary Elamite text found at Susa that records a treaty between Naram-Sin of Akkad (2254–2218 BC) and an Elamite ruler whose name remains uncertain (Scheil 1911: 1–11; König 1965: 29–34; Hinz 1967). The content of this text is highly relevant for the history of the Elamite language and for the construction of an Elamite religious identity, as it begins with an invocation to more than thirty deities, twenty-six of whom are Elamite. The "treaty" part of the document states, "the enemy of Naram-Sin is my enemy; the friend of Naram-Sin is my friend." The physical manifestations of this period are attested on the Acropole (levels 1 and 2) in the form of a building interpreted as a granary and in a small area of domestic remains in Ville Royale I. For the most part, ceramics, metalwork, and glyptic styles follow Mesopotamian norms although there is evidence of continuing relations with the highlands, the Iranian plateau, and the Persian Gulf. Native traditions are most pronounced in the production of clay figurines.

The last ruler of Awan, Puzur-Inshushinak, engaged in territorial expansion. He incorporated Susa and Anshan into the Awanite kingdom, conquered more than seventy Iranian towns, raided northern Babylonian settlements seeking control of the great

Khorasan road, and defeated the king of Shimashki. His reign was marked by the creation of a unique script known as linear-Elamite (or proto-Elamite B) that survives in only nineteen inscriptions. Of the 103 signs recorded, over forty are attested only once. The restricted number of signs and inscriptions has thus far thwarted linear-Elamite's decipherment. The identity of Puzur-Inshushinak, the political character of Awan, and the characteristics of the "national" language of the kingdom remain matters of scholarly debate. At Susa, the evidence of a decorative votive nail with a text stating "Puzur-Inshushinak, ensi of Susa, šakkanaku of Elam, son of Šimbišhuk-Inšušinak, the temple of Šugu he has restored," together with a large statue of the enthroned goddess Narundi, flanked by two lionesses (and bearing a bilingual inscription), and the remains of an alabaster statuette possibly representing Puzur-Inshushinak himself (found in what has been identified as the temple of the goddess Ninhursag), suggest that Puzur-Inshushinak subscribed to a tradition that adopted (and coopted) many of the main cultural accoutrements of this ancient religious and urban center (Mecquenem 1911: 71; Amiet 1966: 227, fig. 166; Steve and Gasche 1971: 61, nn. 71 and 73, pl. 8.4–7; on Shimashki see Potts 2008: 188, n. 54).

After Puzur-Inshushinak, Susiana was once again integrated into the Mesopotamian political orbit under the Ur III dynasty. Textual information for this period is abundant, albeit heavily filtered through a Mesopotamian–Susian lens. The Sumerian kings left ample evidence of their religious zeal and administrative practices at Susa through monumental royal constructions and inscriptions (Malbran-Labat 1995). Foundation nails inscribed by Shulgi (2094–2047 BC) suggest he erected temples to Inshushinak and Ninhursag above the remains of earlier constructions on the Acropolis (Amiet 1966: 238). Sixteen foundation nails made of copper with a male upper body and inscribed with the name of Shulgi were found in the Acropole, eight in the temple of Inshushinak and eight in the temple of Ninhursag (Tallon 1987: 308–10). Another temple probably founded at this time was erected on the southwestern flank of the Ville Royale and included at least three pairs of large, painted terracotta lions guarding the main entrance (Amiet 1966: 292–3). Shulgi's political position was solidified through a series of diplomatic marriages between his daughters and the kings of Anshan, Marhashi, and Bashime.

The Sumerian appointees used the titles "governor of Susa" and "viceroy of the land of Elam." During the reign of Shulgi's son, Amar-Sin (2046–2038 BC), the city of Girsu (modern Telloh) became the chief urban entrepôt for trade with the eastern territories and the governor of Girsu assumed the title SUKKAL.MAH "Grand Vizier/Regent." The last Ur III rulers, Shu-Sin (2037–2029 BC) and Ibbi-Sin (2028–2004 BC), pursued a policy that combined dynastic marriages with military incursions into the highlands. Yet, in 2004 BC a coalition of Elamites and *Su*-people (LU.SU^{ki}) from the land of Shimashki captured Ur. In the *Lamentation over the destruction of Sumer and Ur* we read that the statues of Nanna and other Sumerian divinities were taken prisoner to Anshan, Ibbi-Sin was taken to the land of Elam in fetters, and Ur was reduced to "mounds of ruin and ashes" (Van Dijk 1978). The Elamite king responsible for the fall of Ur may have been the ruler of Shimashki, Kindattu. Like Awan, Shimashki's location remains unclear, as does the extent of its territory (Potts 2008: 189–94 proposes the Oxus Civilization or Bactria–Martiana Archaeological Complex [BMAC] was the original homeland of the founders of the Shimashkian dynasty).

With the unification of Susiana and the highlands by the dynasty of Shimashki the basic dual political and territorial structural unity of the Elamite kingdom was inaugurated (the sociopolitical composition of the kingdom, however, remains a subject of debate, see Potts 1999: 156–7). With Susiana secured, the pattern of military aggression appears to have shifted from the Elamite highlands to Mesopotamia proper. Politically, the beginning of the twentieth century BC witnessed periods of warfare alternating with diplomatic marriages and peace treaties. For instance, Ishbi-Erra of Isin (2017–1985 BC) named his 12th regnal year after a victory over Elam while giving his daughter Libur-nirum to Humban-shimti, the son of the Elamite *sukkal*; the following year was again named after the defeat of Elam and the Su-people; and his 23rd year was named after the expulsion of the Elamites from Ur. His descendant, Shu-ilishu of Isin (1984–1975 BC), commemorated the return of the cult statue of Nanna, possibly after a period of captivity in Anshan.

Around 1980 BC Bilalama, the ruler of Eshnunna (Tell Asmar), gave his daughter Me-Kubi in marriage to Tan-ruhurater, the governor of Susa. Me-Kubi was responsible for building a temple to Inanna in the religious quarter on the Acropole (Steve et al. 2002–3: 439). In his 1st regnal year Iddin-Dagan of Isin (1974–1954 BC) gave his daughter Matum-niattum in marriage to Imazu, king of Anshan, son of Kindattu. And king Gungunum of Larsa (1932–1906 BC) named his 3rd and 5th regnal years after wars against eastern Elamite territories, first Bashime and then Anshan.

The Old Elamite period: The Grand Viziers of Elam (c. 1900–1500 BC)

Shilhaha was the first Elamite ruler to be called *sukkalmah* and is thus considered the founder of a new dynasty. He claimed to be the "chosen son of Ebarat" (assumed to be Ebarti II of the Shimashki line) and used the title "king of Anshan and Susa." The relationship between the last rulers of Shimashki (c.1900 BC) and the first *sukkalmahs* is, however, uncertain. There is no indication of a sharp break between the two dynasties, suggesting temporal overlap and interdynastic links (Vallat 1996: 302, 310; Potts 1999: 160–87; Steve et al. 2002–3: 440–52).

From the Mesopotamian perspective, the early centuries of the second millennium BC were a period dominated by the cities of Isin and Larsa, followed by the empires of Shamshi-Adad of Assyria (1813–1781 BC) and Hammurabi of Babylon (1792–1750 BC). Recent revision of this Mesopotamo-centric view of international politics has brought Elam to the forefront of discussion. In Elam the early second millennium BC was marked by a political (and territorial?) reorganization under the *sukkalmahs*, followed by an expansionistic period in which Elamite political and economic interests went beyond their "natural" territorial boundaries, forming a kingdom whose prestige and influence were unprecedented. By the late nineteenth century BC the authority of the "great king of Elam" (*šarrum rabûm ša elamtim*) had reached the point where Elam was orchestrating political changes in Mesopotamia and the Levant. During the reign of Shamshi-Adad the *sukkalmah* Shiruk-tuh and a 12,000-strong force of Elamite soldiers campaigned on the upper course of the Lower Zab in eastern Mesopotamia. The death of Shamshi-Adad opened the northwestern territories to Elam's expansionist interests. Babylon and Mari joined in an alliance with the Grand Vizier to conquer Eshnunna, recognizing the leading authority of the Elamite king Siwepalarhuppak (Sheplarpak), "*sukkalmah, sukkal* of Elam and Shimashki." Letters from the Mari royal archives explicitly document threats made by the Elamite king against Hammurabi of Babylon, demanding that he leave Eshnunna or risk an invasion and counseling him to break off all correspondence with Zimri-Lim of Mari (1776–1761 BC). A similar tone was used with Zimri-Lim, Atamrum of Allahad, and Ishme-Dagan of Isin. Elamite influence extended all the way to the Mediterranean where the prince of Qatna in Syria proposed to submit to the Elamite king if the latter would take up the fight against the kingdom of Halab (Aleppo) on his behalf. A telling expression of the submissive status of the Amorite kings appears in the correspondence between the Syrian and Babylonian rulers, in which they address each other as "brother" but considered themselves "sons" of the Grand Vizier (Durand 1990; Charpin and Durand 1991: 62; Wu 1994: 169; Villard 1995: 881; dated to 1765–1763 BC according to the Middle Chronology, see Heimpel 2003).

The Mari archives provide an historical snapshot of the authority of the Elamite "emperor" in the western and northern regions. The particular treatment of the Elamite king can be explained by the historical status of Elam, the vast resources of the Iranian plateau and some degree of Elamite control over the lucrative interstate commerce in tin, which involved the securing of trade routes and commercial links with eastern Iran and possibly Afghanistan (the actual origin of the tin remains unknown, but see Joannès 1991; Potts 1994: 153–9; Potts 1999: 169). Elamite western expansion resulted in the creation of a Mari–Babylon–Aleppo alliance and perhaps in the emergence of a "national" Amorite conscience that shared a common interest against the *sukkalmah*. In three consecutive campaigns, from 1764/3 to 1762/1 BC, Hammurabi confronted the Elamites and attacked their western proxies: Eshnunna, Larsa, Subartu, and Gutium. To consolidate the victory Hammurabi put an end to the kingdom of his former Amorite associate, Zimri-lim of Mari. To date, we lack Elamite versions of these captivating accounts. On the other hand, the reference in Genesis 14 to a military expedition by an Elamite king named Chedor-Laomer against five Canaanite kings is perhaps a reflection of these events. Chedor-Laomer may be a corruption of the Elamite name Kutir-Lakamar (Hinz 1971a: 666) and the Babylonian name Kudar-Lagar[mar], alias Lagamaru (Scheil 1896: 600–601). Lakamar was an Elamite goddess attested from the Middle Elamite period onward (Hinz 1971b: 666, n. 4). According to some authors, the Biblical account might have been based on historical sources going back to the early Old Babylonian period (Albright 1961: 49; Sarna 1966: 110–15; for the so-called "Kedor–Laomer" texts see Potts 1999: 237).

The Elamite kingdom was characterized by distinctive systems of government, succession, and titulature. The organization of power followed a tripartite structure along the lines of a "triumvirate" composed of a *sukkalmah* or Grand Vizier, a *sukkal* of Elam or senior Vizier (often a brother of the *sukkalmah*), and a *sukkal* of Susa or junior Vizier (often a son or nephew of the *sukkalmah*). This system may have insulated Elam against debilitating dynastic struggles. Another much-discussed singularity of Elamite kingship consists of the use of the royal title "sister's son" (*ruhu šak*). A number of interpretations of this title have been suggested, some scholars seeing it as a sign of incestuous, close-kin marriages between brother and sister and others highlighting the possibility of determining royal succession through the maternal line (Potts 1999: 163–6; Frandsen 2009: 120–24). Whatever its interpretation, it seems *ruhu šak* also assumed a symbolic dimension, legitimating the royal line. This expression, taken together with terms of family affiliation and iconographic evidence, underscores the singular role played by women in Elamite history.

The general politically expansionistic outlook of the *sukkalmah* period is reflected in the material culture of the times by a wealth of archaeological and monumental remains. New sites emerged in the Susiana plain and Susa expanded toward the east with a succession of new constructions in the so-called Ville Royale (Chantier A levels XV to XII), reaching $c.85$ ha in extent and marked by a continuous sequence of about 250 years of building tradition. These neighborhoods provide important evidence of Elamite mudbrick vernacular architecture (Badawy 1958, 1966; Fathy 1986; Kubba 1987; Manzoor 1989). Houses were constructed following an agglutinative "plan" (i.e., buildings shared common walls along narrow streets to reduce the total surface area exposed to the sun). Town level XIV of the Ville Royale combined modest houses with large villas following an architectural convention which prioritized a central courtyard associated with a "reception" hall characterized by two pairs of pilasters. A courtyard with a central basin and four columns associated with a "reception" hall with pilasters is also seen in the Royal Palace of Qatna (Hall B) probably built at the time of king Ishhi-Addad, a contemporary of Shamshi-Adad (Mesnil du Buisson 1935: pl. 16; Morandi Bonacossi and Eidem 2006). This suggests that the political links between the prince of Qatna and the Elamite Grand Vizier referred to in the Mari archives may also be reflected in monumental architecture at both sites. Moreover, the main sanctuary of Qatna was dedicated to the goddess NIN.É.GAL who may have been introduced in Qatna during the Ur III period (Astour 2002: 122). She was also worshiped at Susa, beginning in the reign of Ebarat/Ebarti II ($c.1900$ BC), and was later honored at Chogha Zanbil (Gasche 2010: 452, n. 21).

The house of Temti-Wartash, the great chamberlain of the Elamite palace at Susa, was a monumental residence with no fewer than six courtyards and fifty ground-floor rooms divided into private and public reception areas. Ville Royale levels XIII and XII contained similar monumental domestic architecture; a substantial city wall to the north; a building interpreted as a school; and, in Ville Royale XII, a building that may have been a tavern or perhaps a brothel, with a network of large underground jars, presumed to have contained beer. Building also continued in the religious area of the

Acropole with a large ramp leading to the *Ekikuanna* (a temple of Inshushinak) and to the temple of Ishmekarab (the goddess who escorted the dead to the netherworld).

Additional aspects of Elamite religious beliefs are revealed in a number of Elamite texts dating to the late Old Elamite period (Ville Royale level XII, *c*.1500 BC), which have no parallel in Mesopotamian literature. These identify Inshushinak as the lord of the underworld and judge in charge of ordaining the destiny of the dead. As such, they illustrate the Elamite belief in the importance of the judgment of the deceased (Bottéro 1982: 394).

The Middle Elamite period: The golden age (c.1500–1100 BC)

The interval between the last Grand Vizier and the "king(s) of Susa and Anshan" is not well documented. There is no textual or archaeological indication of a sudden rupture, but later royal inscriptions employ a rhetoric of continuity suggesting dynastic links between the two periods. Whatever the true state of affairs, the geopolitical situation during the fifteenth century BC in Mesopotamia was severely affected by the gradual penetration and ascent to power of the Kassites (probably with links to a homeland in the central Zagros Mountains). The Middle Elamite period has been traditionally divided according to three ruling dynasties or houses: the Kidinuid House (*c*.1500–1400 BC), the Igihalkid House (*c*.1400–1200 BC), and the Shutrukid House (*c*.1200–1100 BC). This division is far from perfect as the Igihalkids may have been related to the Shutrukids.

Although neither genealogical nor political kinship can be demonstrated between Tepti-ahar and the houses of Kidinu or Igi-halki (Potts 1999: 188–258; Steve et al. 2002–3: 452–70), an important synchronism has been established between Tepti-ahar and the father of the Kassite king Kurigalzu I, Kadashman-Harbe I, who ruled in the late fifteenth century BC, following a new reading for Kadashman ᵈKUR.GAL (Cole and De Meyer 1999; Potts 1999: 192–3). Tepti-ahar used the title "king of Susa and Anshan, servant of Kirwashir and Inshushinak," which suggests a conscious reference to the house of Kidinu, who also used the title "king of Susa and Anshan," and to the legitimacy provided by a tradition going back to the king of Shimashkian king Ebarat (Ebarti II) who prioritized the eastern territories by using the inverted title "king of Anshan and Susa." Tepti-ahar is best known for his association with the ancient city of Kabnak, located in the most fertile part of the Khuzestan plain, about 10 km southeast of Susa.

Kabnak (Haft Tepe)

The town of Kabnak covers an area of *c*.1.5 km² and includes fourteen major mounds, the largest of which rises about 17 m above the plain. Only a small percentage of the site has been excavated, revealing massive architectural compounds combining two high terraces (complexes I and II) and a funerary complex. Most constructions are made of mudbrick, with baked brick used for important buildings and open areas. Gypsum was used to cover baked brick pavements and for plastering the walls and inner surfaces of roofs. Bitumen was used to line basins and water channels. Flat roofs were supported by large palm-tree beams covered with reed matting. The halls and ceilings were coated with gypsum plaster painted with polychrome motifs. Terrace complex I included a scribal school and workshops dedicated to specialized craft and artistic production. A small hall contained the skeletal remains of an elephant and exquisite, life-size, painted terracotta heads possibly representing members of the Elamite elite. Most of the small objects and craft debris recovered suggest relationships with both local and foreign lands from the Persian Gulf in the east to the kingdom of Mitanni in the west. On the other hand, most of the cylinder sealings collected display a thread of local conservatism (Álvarez-Mon 2005a, 2005b).

The funerary compound included a royal tomb tentatively ascribed to Tepti-ahar. The walls of the tomb stood 3.75 m high and the chamber itself was 3.25 × 10 m and covered with a massive barrel vault made of bricks in slanted position. This is the largest and oldest standing example of this type of vaulting system in the Near East. Parallel to and just to the west of the burial was another vaulted chamber of smaller dimensions containing a mass burial of twenty-three individuals. Fourteen skeletons had been carefully arranged side by side with their heads oriented to the west, with nine additional skeletons piled over them. Who these individuals were and how they died is unknown (Negahban 1991).

Al Untash-Napirisha (Chogha Zanbil)

The Kassite king Kurigalzu I may have been responsible for the destruction of Kabnak and for placing a new ruling family claiming descent from Igi-halki on the Elamite throne. This family may have originated at Deh-e Now (Khuzestan Survey site 120), a mound of c.9.5 ha situated about 20 km east of Haft Tepe and 7.5 km north of Chogha Zanbil. The males of the Igihalkid house engaged in a succession of interdynastic marriages over five generations with a number of Kassite princesses from Mesopotamia. Thus the eldest son of Igi-halki, Pahir-ishshan (c.1380–1370 BC), married the eldest daughter of Kurigalzu I; their grandson Humban-Numena married a Kassite princess; Humban-numena's son Untash-Napirisha (c.1340–1300 BC) married a daughter of the Kassite king Burna-Buriash II; Untash-Napirisha's son Kidin-Hutran (II) married another Kassite princess; and the founder of the Shutrukid house, Shutruk-Nahhunte (c.1190–1155 BC), married a daughter of the Kassite king Meli-Shipak. The enduring association by marriage between the Elamite and Kassite royal families resulted in the establishment of an Elamite claim to the Babylonian throne, which eventually led to the downfall of the Kassite dynasty and the sack of Babylon c.1150 BC. The influence and degree of political power held by this distinctive Elamo-Kassite elite "class" remains a matter of ongoing investigation (Pintore 1978: 24; Van Dijk 1986; Vallat 1994, 1999, 2006; Goldberg 2004).

Perhaps the most important Elamite king of the Igihalkid house was Untash-Napirisha (*c*.1340–1300 BC), himself of Kassite ancestry through his mother and, curiously enough, related by marriage to both the Egyptian Pharaoh Amenhotep IV/Akhenaten and the Hittite king Shuppiluliuma. His reign witnessed an artistic golden age and, as some authors have stressed, a religious "revolution" linked to the foundation of a vast religious complex called Al Untash-Napirisha (modern Chogha Zanbil). This complex was built on a high plateau overlooking, to the northeast, the plain drained by the Ab-e Dez River and the (presumed) ancestral city of Deh-e Now. The sacred city complex covering about 100 ha included three surrounding perimeter walls (the outermost of which was more than 4 km long) and was organized around a stepped temple platform or ziggurat *c*.53 m high that was dedicated to Napirisha and Inshushinak. The ziggurat consisted of four levels and, unlike Mesopotamian examples, was scaled internally (and indirectly) via two staircases, which were flanked at ground level by pairs of large, glazed bulls and bird-headed griffins. The façade of the high shrine (Elamite *kukunnum*) atop the ziggurat was made of brightly glazed, baked bricks decorated with geometric patterns and glazed knob plaques and nails of different colors. More than twenty-five temples were built at Chogha Zanbil for the worship of both highland and lowland Elamite deities with a smattering of originally Mesopotamian deities, including Nusku, the god of fire and light (Ghirshman 1968: 84–7).

The so-called Royal Quarter in the northeastern part of the site had large building complexes arranged around open courtyards and five monumental, vaulted, subterranean tombs. Tomb II included the remains of eight cremated bodies; Tomb IV had two cremated bodies and a mature female skeleton. It has been suggested that these remains may have belonged to Elamite royalty, including perhaps a queen of Kassite origin. A significant and still poorly understood aspect of the planning of Chogha Zanbil pertains to the function of a sophisticated network of drainpipes, wells, and a massive basin, all part of an intricate hydraulic installation situated at the edge of the city (Auberson 1966: 113–18; Margueron 1994; Corfù 2006; Nasrabadi 2007).

Susa

Associated with Untash-Napirisha is a corpus of metallurgical sculptural masterpieces, which continue a long tradition of superior metalwork but which, at this time (viz. the practice of the lost-wax method of casting, attested at the site by *c*.2100 BC; see the Elamite "God with the Golden Hand," Tallon 1987: 310), reached unprecedented levels of technological sophistication. One of the most significant examples is the 1.29 m tall, headless statue of queen Napir-Asu, found in the temple of the Ninhursag at Susa. The statue weighs 1750 kg and was cast in two parts, initially using a clay core that allowed the making of a single shell of copper by the lost-wax technique. Once the core was removed the shell was filled with solid bronze. The molded and engraved surface of Napir-Asu's garment was probably once covered with gold and silver leaf (Meyers 2000).

It is uncertain if the Igihalkid dynasty ended with the arrival of Shutruk-Nahhunte, c.1150 BC. The cultural accomplishments of the Shutrukid dynasty are often overshadowed by their infamous deeds in Mesopotamia. Shutruk-Nahhunte and his sons Kutir-Nahhunte (1155–1150 BC) and Shilhak-Inshushinak (1150–1120 BC) continued a foreign policy of vindication that asserted the claim of the Elamite kings to the Babylonian throne. This claim entailed numerous raids on Mesopotamian cities and eventually led to the collapse of the Kassite dynasty in 1155 BC, the death of the last Kassite king, and the "retirement" to Elam of the statues of Marduk and other deities from Babylon. Amongst the most celebrated artifacts dedicated to Inshushinak on the Acropole at Susa as votive offerings were large numbers of Kassite *kudurrus* (boundary stones), the victory stele of Naram-Sin, and the stele from Sippar on which Hammurabi's law code is inscribed.

The resources accumulated during this period of Elamite imperial expansion produced a golden age of exceptional building activity throughout Elamite territory. From Anshan to the shores of the Persian Gulf and the Susiana plain new temples were constructed and old ones restored (Potts 2010). Examples of monumental decorative architecture from Susa include the remains of glazed mudbrick panels depicting a royal couple from the façade of a building on the Acropole and the remains of a molded mudbrick façade showing bull-men grasping date palms and female deities holding their breasts, from a temple located in the Apadana area. This façade may have symbolized the "sacred grove" housing the "exterior chapel" of the temple of Inshushinak built by Shilhak-Inshushinak. The Shutrukid dynasty may also be responsible for incorporating two relief panels representing the royal family carved c.8.5 m high on the cliff-side of the highland grotto sanctuary of Shekaft-e Salman near Izeh/Malamir (De Waele 1976a: 321; 1981: 50–2; for the inscriptions and dating see Stolper 1988). One relief exhibits a fire altar, two adult males, a boy, and an adult female; another relief depicts a single adult male, a boy, and an adult female. All participants are represented in worshiping attitudes oriented toward the grotto.

Around 1120 BC the Babylonian king Nebuchadnezzar I (1125–1104 BC) entered Elamite territory. He defeated Hutelutush-Inshushinak by the banks of the Ulai (Karkheh) River, forcing the retreat of the Elamite king to the highlands and the eastern capital of Anshan. Traditionally, this event marks the end of the Shutrukid dynasty and, hence, the end of the Bronze Age in Khuzestan.

FURTHER READING

The essential sources for the study of the history and archaeological context of Bronze Age Khuzestan can be found in Johnson (1987), Potts (1999), and Steve et al. (2002–3). Since 2011 material from R. de Mecquenem's excavations at Susa (1912–39) has been available online (http://www.mom.fr/mecquenem/). Individual monographs related to trade and exchange in the third and second millennia BC include Amiet (1986) and Potts (1994). For metallurgy at Susa see Tallon (1987) and for bituminous materials see Connan and Deschesne (1996).

References

Albright, W. F. 1961. Abram the Hebrew: A new archaeological interpretation. *BASOR* 163: 36–54.
Alden, J. R. 1982. Trade and politics in Proto-Elamite Iran. *CA* 23: 613–40.
Álvarez-Mon, J. 2005a. Elamite Funerary Clay Heads, *NEA* 68/3: 114–22.
———. 2005b. Aspects of Elamite wall painting: New evidence from Kabnak (Haft Tepe). *IrAnt* 40: 149–64.
Amiet, P. 1966. *Elam*. Auvers-sur-Oise: Archée Éditeurs.
———. 1979. Archaeological discontinuity and ethnic duality in Elam. *Antiquity* 53: 195–204.
———. 1986. *L'âge des échanges inter-iraniens, 3500–1700 avant J.-C*. Paris: Réunion des Musées Nationaux.
Astour, M. C. 2002. A reconstruction of the history of Ebla (Part 2). In *Eblaitica: Essays on the Ebla archives and Eblaite language*, vol. 4, ed. C. H. Gordon and G. Rendsburg, 57–196. Winona Lake: Eisenbrauns.
Auberson, P. 1966. Étude des gouttières (Annexe 2). In *Tchoga Zanbil (Dur-Untash) I. La ziggurat*, R. Ghirshman, 113–18. Paris: MDP 39.
Badawy, A. 1958. Architectural provision against heat in the Orient. *JNES* 17/2: 122–8.
———. 1966. *Architecture in Ancient Egypt and the Near East*. Massachusetts: MIT Press.
Bottéro, J. 1982. Les inscriptions cunéiformes funéraires. In *La mort, les morts dans les sociétés anciennes*, ed. G. Gnoli and J.-P. Vernant, 373–404. Paris: Maison des Sciences de l'Homme.
Carter, E. 1971. Elam in the second millennium B.C.: The archaeological evidence. Unpublished PhD diss., University of Chicago.
———. 1981. Elamite ceramics. *ETDLP*: 196–223.
Carter, E., and H. T. Wright. 2010. Ceramic phase indicators in surface assemblages. *EASDLP*: 11–22.
Charpin, D., and J.-M. Durand. 1991. La suzeraineté de l'emperor (Sukkalmah) d'Élam sur la Mésopotamie et le «Nationalisme» Amorrite. *ME*: 59–66.
Cole, S. W., and L. De Meyer. 1999. Tepti-ahar, King of Susa, and Kadašman-^{d}KUR.GAL. *Akkadica* 112: 44–5.
Connan, J., and O. Deschesne. 1996. *Le bitume à Suse: Collection du Musée du Louvre*. Paris: Réunion des Musées Nationaux.
Corfù, N. A. 2006. Die Wasseraufbereitungsanlage von Čogā Zanbil, Iran. *AMI* 38: 137–40.
Dahl, J. L. 2002. Proto-Elamite sign frequencies. *CDLB* 2002/1: 1–3.
Delougaz, P., and H. J. Kantor. 1996. *Chogha Mish: The first five seasons of excavations, 1961–1971*, 2 vols. Chicago: OIP 101.
Durand, J.-M. 1990. Fourmis blanches et fourmis noires. *MJP*: 101–8.
Fathy, H. 1986. *Natural energy and vernacular architecture: Principles and examples with reference to hot arid climates*. Chicago: University of Chicago Press.

Frandsen, P. J. 2009. *Incestuous and close-kin marriage in Ancient Egypt and Persia: An examination of the evidence*. Copenhagen: CNIP 34.

Gasche, H. 2010. Les palais Perses Achéménides de Babylone. *PDS*: 446–63.

Ghirshman, R. 1968. *Tchoga Zanbil (Dur-Untash), vol 2. Temenos, temples, palais, tombes*. Paris: MDP 40.

Goldberg, J. 2004. The Berlin letter, Middle Elamite chronology and Šutruk-Nahhunte I's genealogy. *IrAnt* 39: 33–42.

Heimpel, W. 2003. *Letters to the King of Mari*. Winona Lake: Eisenbrauns.

Hinz, W. 1967. Elams Vertrag mit Narām-Sīn von Agade. *ZA* 58: 66–96.

———. 1971a. Persia, c. 2400–1800 BC. *CAH* 1/2: 644–80.

———. 1971b. Religion in Ancient Elam. *CHI* 1/2: 662–73.

Hole, F. 1987. Archaeology of the Village Period. *AWI*: 29–78.

———. 1987. 1992. The cemetery of Susa: An interpretation. *RCS*: 26–31.

Jacobsen, T. 1939. *The Sumerian King List*. Chicago: Assyriological Studies 11.

Joannès, F. 1991. L'étain, de l'Élam à Mari. *ME*: 67–76.

Johnson, G. A. 1973. *Local exchange and early state development in southwestern Iran*. Ann Arbor: Anthropological Papers of the Museum of Anthropology 51.

———. 1987. The changing organization of Uruk administration on the Susiana plain. *AWI*: 107–39.

König, F. W. 1965. *Die elamischen Königsinschriften*. Graz: *AfO* Beiheft 16.

Kouchoukos, N., and F. Hole. 2003. Changing estimates of Susiana's prehistoric settlement. *YBYN*: 53–59.

Kubba, S. A. A. 1987. *Mesopotamian architecture and town planning from the Mesolithic to the end of the proto-historic period c. 10,000–3,500 B.C.* Oxford: BAR Int Ser 367.

Le Breton, L. 1957. The early periods at Susa: Mesopotamian relations. *Iraq* 19: 79–124.

Le Brun, A. 1971. Recherches stratigraphiques à l'Acropole de Suse, 1969–71. *CDAFI* 1: 163–216.

Malbran-Labat, F. 1995. *Les inscriptions royales de Suse: Briques de l'époque paléo-élamite à l'Empire néo-élamite*. Paris: Réunion des Musées Nationaux.

Manzoor, S. 1989. *Tradition and development: An approach to vernacular architectural patterns in Iran*. Gothenburg: School of Architecture, Division for Housing Design, Chalmers tekniska högskola.

Margueron, J.-C. 1994. Fondations et refondations au Proche Orient au Bronze récent. In *Nuove fondationi nel Vicino Oriente Antico: Realtà e Ideologia*, ed. S. Mazzoni, 3–27. Pisa: Università degli studi di Pisa.

Mecquenem, R. de 1911. Constructions élamites du Tell de l'Acropole de Suse. In *Recherches archéologiques*, M.-C. Soutzo, G. Pézard, G. Bondoux, R. de Mecquenem, M. Pézard, J.-E. Gautier, and P. Toscanne, 65–78. Paris: MDP 12.

———. 1943. Fouilles de Suse, 1933–1939. In *Archéologie susienne*, R. de Mecquenem, G. Contenau, R. Pfister, and N. Belaiew, 3–161. Paris: MMAI 29.

Mesnil du Buisson, R. du. 1935. *Le site archéologique de Mishrifé-Qatna*. Paris: Collection de textes et documents d'Orient 1.

Meyers, P. 2000. The casting process of the statue of Queen Napir-Asu in the Louvre. *Journal of Roman Archaeology Supplementary Series* 39: 11–18.

Morandi Bonacossi, D., and J. Eidem. 2006. A royal seal of Ishhi-Addu, King of Qatna. *Akkadica* 127: 41–57.

Nasrabadi, B. M. 2007. *Archäologische Ausgrabungen und Untersuchungen in Čogā Zanbil*. Münster: Agenda.

Negahban, E. O. 1991. *Excavations at Haft Tepe, Iran*. Philadelphia: UMM 70.
Pelzel, S. M. 1977. Dating the Early Dynastic votive plaques from Susa. *JNES* 36/1: 1–15.
Pintore, F. 1978. *Il matrimonio interdinastico nel Vicino Oriente durante i secoli XV–XIII*. Rome: Orientis antiqui collectio 14.
Potts, D. T. 1999. *The archaeology of Elam: Formation and transformation of an ancient Iranian state*. Cambridge: Cambridge University Press.
———. 2008. Puzur-Inšušinak and the Oxus Civilization (BMAC): Reflections on Šimaški and the geopolitical landscape of Iran and Central Asia in the Ur III period. *ZA* 98/2: 165–94.
———. 2010. Elamite temple building. In *From the foundations to the crenellations: Essays on Temple building in the Ancient Near East and Hebrew Bible*, ed. M. J. Boda and J. Novotny, 49–70, 479–509. Münster: AOAT 366.
Potts, T. F. 1994. *Mesopotamia and the East: An archaeological and historical study of foreign relations, ca. 3400–2000 BC*. Oxford: Oxford University Committee for Archaeology Monograph 37.
Sarna, N. M. 1966. *Understanding Genesis, the heritage of Biblical Israel*. New York: Shocken.
Scheil, V. 1896. Chodorlahomor dans les inscriptions Chaldéennes. *Revue Biblique* 5: 600–1.
———. 1905. *Textes élamites-sémitiques, troisième série*. Paris: MDP 6.
———. 1911. *Textes élamites-anzanites, quatrième série*. Paris: MDP 11.
Steve M.-J., and H. Gasche. 1971. *L'Acropole de Suse*. Paris: MDP 46.
Steve, M.-J., F. Vallat, H. Gasche, and F. Jullien. 2002–3. Suse. *SDB* 73: 360–512 (bibliog. in *SDB* 74: 620–52).
Stolper, M. 1988. Mālamīr. B. Philologisch. *RlA* 7: 276–81.
Sumner, W. M. 1997. Malyan. *OEANE* 3: 406–9.
Tallon, F. 1987. *Métallurgie susienne I, de la fondation de Suse au XVIIIe siècle avant J.-C*, 2 vols. Paris: Musée du Louvre.
Vallat, F. 1994. Succession royale en Elam au IIéme millénaire. *CDR*: 1–14.
———. 1996. L'Élam à l'époque paléo-babylonienne et ses relations avec la Mésopotamie. In *Amurru 1, Mari, Ébla et les Hourrites, Dix ans de travaux*, ed. J.-M. Durand, 297–319. Paris: Éditions Recherche sur les Civilisations.
———. 1999. L'hommage de l'élamite Untash-Napirisha au Cassite Burnaburiash. *Akkadica* 114–15: 109–17.
———. 2006. La chronologie méso-élamite et la lettre de Berlin. *Akkadica* 127: 123–35.
Van Dijk, J. 1978. Išbi'erra, Kindattu, l'homme d'Elam, et la chute de la ville d'Ur. *JCS* 30/4: 189–208.
———. 1986. Die dynastichen Heiraten zwischen Kassiten und Elamern: Eine verhängnisvolle Politik. *Or* 55: 159–70.
Villard, P. 1995. Shamshi-Adad and sons: The rise and fall of an Upper Mesopotamian empire. In *Civilizations of the Ancient Near East*, vol. 2, ed. J. M. Sasson, 121–35. New York: Charles Scribner.
Waele, E. de. 1976. Les reliefs rupestres élamites de Shekāft-e Salmān et Kūl-e Farah près d'Izeh (Mālamir). Unpublished PhD diss., Catholic University of Louvain.
———. 1981. Travaux archéologiques à Šekaf-e Salman et Kul-e Farah près d'Izeh (Malamir). *IrAnt* 16: 45–61.
Wright, H. T., and G. A. Johnson. 1975. Population, exchange, and early state formation in southwestern Iran. *American Anthropologist* 77: 267–89.

Wright, H. T., and E. S. A. Rupley. 2001. Radiocarbon age determinations of Uruk-related assemblages. In *Uruk Mesopotamia and its neighbors: Cross cultural interactions in the era of state formation*, ed. M. S. Rothman, 85–122. Santa Fe: School of American Research.

Wu, Y. 1994. *A political history of Eshnunna, Mari and Assyria during the early Old Babylonian period*. Changchun: Institute of History of Ancient Civilizations.

CHAPTER 13

EARLY WRITING IN IRAN

JACOB L. DAHL

INTRODUCTION

Writing emerged at Uruk, in southern Mesopotamia, around the middle of the fourth millennium BC and it spread quickly to the north and east (Nissen 2001: 159–66). Many examples of protowriting are found at sites on the periphery, with fewer at Uruk itself. However, the resulting invention of a more advanced writing system and the sustained use of writing took place only in southern Mesopotamia and in the areas to its east, not in northern Mesopotamia or Syria where writing was reintroduced many hundred years after the initial spread of the bookkeeping techniques of the Uruk V period (Susa Acropole I levels 18–17). The exact locus where writing was first invented cannot be established, but most scholars agree that Uruk is the most likely candidate. The reasons for Uruk's preeminence in the history of writing, in the absence of samples of the very earliest stages of writing there, is the sheer number of (later) texts found at Uruk (from the Uruk IV and III periods), as well as the complexity of early writing at Uruk, the place of Uruk in the history of Mesopotamia, and the antiquity of other archaeological discoveries there. Susa, on the other hand, has produced examples of virtually all the stages leading up to the invention of writing; however, no Susa texts can compete in scope and complexity with the Uruk protocuneiform texts (Uruk IV and III periods).

The independent writing system invented in Iran, which followed the spread of the knowledge of writing and certain technological inventions associated with it, is traditionally called proto-Elamite, as it was early on believed to have preceded an indigenous Iranian, or Elamite, writing system used to write the language of Elam, originally termed Anshanite (Scheil 1900: vii). None of these names correspond to ancient Iranian terms for the land or languages spoken there, but proto-Elamite has been retained here for the sake of convenience. Elamite usually denotes the language of people in western Iran from around the middle of the third millennium to some time at the end of the first millennium BC or perhaps even later.

The proto-Elamite writing system was abandoned quickly after its invention, and thereafter, for perhaps 500 to 600 years, no writing is attested in Iran. When writing was reintroduced into Iran it was in the form of cuneiform, by then a full-fledged writing system well adapted to writing both Akkadian and Sumerian. At the end of the third millennium BC cuneiform was used for the first time to write also Elamite, a native language of unknown origin, and although writing was never widespread in Iran, cuneiform remained in use as late as the time of the Achaemenid kings.

At the time of Puzur-Inshushinak (André and Salvini 1989), an Iranian ruler of unknown pedigree associated with Awan (Potts 1999, 2008), yet another writing system was invented in Iran. This system, called linear-Elamite, had a very restricted scope and never became widely used. It is likely that linear-Elamite was invented by elite administrators for display purposes, rather than growing organically from a previous system (Dahl 2009).

Susa in Elam was known in Europe from the Hebrew Bible (e.g., Daniel 8.2: "And I saw in a vision; and it came to pass, when I saw, that I was at Shushan in the palace, which is in the province of Elam; and I saw in a vision, and I was by the river of Ulai"). Susa is widely recognized as the burial place of the prophet Daniel, a claim it shares with several other locations across Iraq and Iran. It is mentioned as such already by Benjamin of Tudela (1130–1173 AD) (Adler 1907: 52–3), and a popular Arab story relates how Abu Burda (legendary governor of Kufa, died c.722 AD) had a ring with a carved gem showing a man holding two lions that was found during the (re)burial of Daniel at Susa (the tradition is reported by Ibn Kathir on the authority of Ibn Abu al-Dunya [d. 894 AD] and appears in a variety of popular collections; reference courtesy of Professor Jeremy Johns).

The first Europeans to excavate at Susa were Loftus (1851–4) and Jane and Marcel Dieulafoy (1885–6). The Dieulafoys brought back substantial finds to the Louvre and are otherwise credited with preparing the only reliable plan of the outline of the Acropole prior to the arrival of Jacques de Morgan's excavation team (Dyson 1968; Steve et al. 2003: 375–403; cf. Dieulafoy 1888 for a quasi-literary account of their work). Excited perhaps by the initial finds of the Dieulafoys, Morgan had ambitious goals when he sat out to investigate Susa at the end of the nineteenth century. He wanted to lay bare the evolution of human civilization, and he believed that the topography of Susa, with its tall Acropole mound, would allow him to do this. After having secured the right from Naser al-Din Shah to both excavate and keep the finds, Morgan, originally trained as an engineer in Paris's École des Mines, first dug tunnels or galleries, as he called them, at 5 m intervals deep into the side of the mound (Morgan 1900: 81ff.). After having thus established the overall stratigraphy of the site, Morgan began his ambitious project to excavate the entire mound. He divided the mound along its central north-south axis and opened 5 m wide trenches on either side of it. Eventually, he would have the first trench dug 5 m down and expanded by 5 m on either side, before the central trench was excavated a further 5 m down. Working this way, Morgan in fact managed to dig away the top 10 m of almost the entire mound within the first ten to twelve years of work. These top 10 m represented the last c.5000 years of culture. Morgan had correctly proposed that a cultural change took place *c.*10 m below the surface of the mound where bevel-rim bowls were found in one of the tunnels (Gallerie F, see Morgan 1900: 86; dug between January 13 and March 1, 1898, over a length of 45 m).

During his tenure as chief of the mission to Persia from 1897 to 1912, Morgan made many extraordinary finds. About two-thirds of the known proto-Elamite tablets were excavated during these years, unfortunately without much attention to recording their exact find-spots. Information about find-spots in the published record poorly matches evidence from later excavations at Susa. This is perhaps best exemplified by the close archival relationship between some texts from the old excavations, often said to have been found in large lots, and the isolated, seemingly randomly located, tablets found in the recent excavations (see, e.g., Le Brun 1971: fig. 58.12 from Le Brun's excavations, a tablet with the same scribal design [see below] as Scheil 1905: nos. 263 and 387 from the old excavations; or Le Brun 1971: fig. 58.14 from the recent excavations, which can be compared to Scheil 1923: nos. 96+, etc.; cf. Dahl 2005a).

Later, Roland de Mecquenem continued the excavations of Morgan. His soundings at the southeastern perimeter of the mound produced a majority of the tablets published in MDP 26 (Scheil 1935). These tablets seem to form a separate group, although their poor state of publication should caution us against drawing any broad conclusions from them.

History of publication and decipherment

Early work on the decipherment of proto-Elamite aimed at either identifying signs based on purely graphical similarities to early (or standard) cuneiform signs (see, e.g., the list drawn by Morgan for MDP 6 [Scheil 1905: 83ff.] or Mecquenem's *tableau comparatif* in MDP 31 [Mecquenem 1949: 147–50]; the frequently made claims of sign borrowings between proto-Elamite and the Indus system can be largely ignored, cf. Potts 1981), or postulating a language of the texts (usually, and probably most credibly, Elamite). Both methods have failed. The team of Jacques de Morgan included the epigrapher Father Vincent Scheil among whose many merits we should count the extraordinary speed with which he published the epigraphic finds from Susa. The first two proto-Elamite tablets found at Susa were quickly recognized as examples of early writing perhaps comparable to the first examples of protocuneiform discovered in Iraq, and were published about a year after their discovery (probably discovered during the 1898–9 season, mentioned the following year [Morgan 1900: 138], and published by Scheil in the same year [Scheil 1900: 130–1]; republished in Scheil 1905: nos. 399 and 4996). Ironically, when describing the most archaic writing samples from Susa known in 1900, Scheil gave the prize to a cylinder seal with what looks like an Indus scene complete with Indus signs (Scheil 1900: 129). An assessment of its antiquity was based solely on the hieroglyphic character of the signs. Scheil even went so far as to compare this object with an ED I–II text from southern Mesopotamia (Gelb et al. 1991: 34, see entry in the Cuneiform Digital

Library Initiative [CDLI] at http://cdli.ucla.edu/P005987), which he claimed was clearly younger, again based solely on a supposed evolution from "hieroglyphic" to more abstract sign-forms. The writing of the two proto-Elamite texts was described as already cuneiform (something that is often overlooked in later publications), and well advanced with some good parallels in known (Mesopotamian) documents (Scheil had published a paleography of early cuneiform in 1898, as a supplement to Amiaud and Méchineau's 1887 "comparative table" of cuneiform, which included many correct observations on the development of cuneiform). Scheil correctly identified the numerical system in the proto-Elamite texts as "Babylonian."

PUBLICATIONS IN THE MDP SERIES AND THE WORK OF MORGAN, SCHEIL, AND MECQUENEM

MDP 6 (Scheil 1905) and 26 Supplement (Scheil 1935)

It can be difficult to trace the Susa objects from trench to paper, but from the finds reported in MDP 1 (Morgan 1900) we must assume that excavations in the central trench had reached what corresponds to Le Brun's Susa Acropole I level 14 already in the 1898–9 season, when workers went below Morgan's "level II" (as perhaps already indicated by the finds of bevel-rim bowls in Gallerie F). All of the tablets published in MDP 6 in 1905 (Scheil 1905), and most of the tablets published in the supplement to MDP 26 (MDP 26S, Scheil 1935) in 1935 (except perhaps for the two numerical tablets 4775 and 4781 which, due to the absence of nonnumerical signs, are ascribed to earlier stages of writing, as well as the numerical tablet 4778 and the numero-ideographic tablet 5224, both of which belong to the group of area calculation tablets identified by J. Friberg and which cannot be dated based on the absence of nonnumerical signs alone [Friberg 1997/8: 16–19]), can be ascribed to Le Brun's Susa Acropole I levels 14–15. MDP 26S (Scheil 1935) contains texts that were not published in MDP 6 (Scheil 1905) but that were sent to Paris together with the texts published there. This is confirmed both by the notes to MDP 26S as well as by the many close parallels between the two groups and several joins of fragments published in the two volumes (e.g., Scheil 1905: no. 366 which was joined with Scheil 1935: no. 5025 by the author in 2004 [for a complete list of joins in the proto-Elamite material made since their original publication see Dahl 2012a]).

The tablets mentioned in the catalog of MDP 6 (Scheil 1905) were given four-digit excavation numbers. The proto-Elamite tablets in the Louvre Museum have since been given museum numbers with the sigla Sb.

As early as 1905 Scheil understood that the content of all proto-Elamite tablets proper was administrative. He based this observation on the fact that all texts have numerical signs (see Scheil 1905: 60 and 115–18 for his attempt to analyze the numerical systems). Scheil and most scholars after him grouped what we today call linear-Elamite with proto-Elamite, suggesting that the difference between the two systems was dictated primarily by the medium on which the texts were inscribed, that is, inscriptions on stone would be more linear than those in clay.

The first 198 proto-Elamite texts were published by Scheil in 1905 in MDP 6 (Scheil 1905). The drawings were made from photographs. Photographs of ninety-three tablets were published on plates (using the heliogravure technique); a few of these were not copied, and remain de facto unpublished. Among these we find perhaps the most important of all proto-Elamite tablets, Sb 2801 (listed as number 5242 in the catalog and with a photo of the obverse and reverse on pls. 23–4), but also three further tablets (Sb 15222, 15229, and 15231). A further ten tablets were mentioned in the catalog but not published. Kathryn Kelley at the University of Oxford is preparing a new edition of Sb 2801; a preliminary copy and new images are available at the CDLI (http://cdli.ucla.edu/P272825). Unfortunately, not all surfaces of the tablets were published, in many cases not even the reverse. An administrative text often contains crucial information on the reverse (total), or the sides (summaries), and collations have shown that many tablets were in fact inscribed on the uncopied sides.

A substantial sign list, drawn by Morgan, complete with cuneiform parallels for many of the signs, was appended to the texts published in MDP 6 (Scheil 1905). However, there does not seem to have been any attempt at isolating graphical variants or grouping the signs according to semantic classification. Instead, signs seem to have been grouped together according to graphical shape and ordered more or less the same way as most cuneiform sign lists were ordered (starting with signs beginning with one horizontal wedge); unfortunately, this principle has been followed in all subsequent lists. The first sixty-three signs are from the linear-Elamite inscriptions, and the list included markings found on some tablets that are in fact not signs in the writing system but function much like seals (nos. 885–95; see below). The list has a total of 989 signs. It is followed by an excursus on the numerical system(s) (Scheil 1905: 115–18).

MDP 17

Following the expeditious appearance of the first several hundred texts found at Susa, publication slowed, perhaps in reaction to waning enthusiasm with regard to the prospects of a decipherment of proto-Elamite. In any case, the next publication of proto-Elamite texts did not appear until 1923, when almost 500 texts were published by Scheil in MDP 17 (Scheil 1923). About half of these texts came from strata that can be best compared to Le Brun's Acropole I level 16 and earlier; the other half originated, most likely, in contexts equivalent to Acropole I levels 14 and 15. It should be noted that these identifications are mainly based on indicators such as tablet format and sign-string complexity, and are therefore not absolute (for the relative date of the tablets see below). MDP 17 (Scheil 1923) contained a discussion of the individual texts (but no real catalog); a new sign list (with 1582 signs) replacing that of MDP 6 (Scheil 1905); and a list of scribal designs (Scheil 1905: 67–8; see below).

MDP 26, MDP 31, and minor publications

In 1935 Scheil published 485 tablets and fragments that had remained in Iran in the volume MDP 26 (Scheil 1935). The drawings were made by the daughter of R. de Mecquenem using a camera lucida. The unusually poor quality of the copies, and the lack of any photographic documentation, has meant that these tablets are of limited value for palaeographic analysis, while they offer some new insights into early administrative practices. The tablets seem to have come from the upper layers of the proto-Elamite occupation of Susa, but they most likely belong to a different "archival" context than the rest of the published material. According to Scheil (1935: i; cf. Steve et al. 2003: 395) these tablets were found in the so-called "sondage sud" at the southeastern end of the Acropole. MDP 26 does not contain a sign list or a catalog.

With the publication of MDP 26 and 26S most of the tablets from Susa had been published. In 1949 Mecquenem published the remaining fifty more or less complete tablets in the Louvre in MDP 31 (Mecquenem 1949). Unfortunately, his copies were not up to the standards of most publications of cuneiform tablets at the time. MDP 31 contains a sign list numbering 5529 signs. This sign list includes proto-Elamite and linear-Elamite signs as well as scribal designs (see below), and figures from seal impressions (e.g., no. 4567). Later, Mecquenem also published fifteen small tablets and fragments in the Louvre (Mecquenem 1956: 200–4). One of these (no. 1) came from the 1939 campaign, while the rest came from the earlier campaigns.

The proto-Elamite corpus is exceptional in being kept almost exclusively in two large collections, the Louvre in France and the National Museum in Iran. Otherwise, nine tablets and fragments are in the Couvent Saint-Étienne, Jerusalem; at least eight tablets and fragments are in the Ethnological Museum of the University of Sao Paolo in Sao Paolo, Brazil; one tablet was reported to have been found amongst the papers of the late E. Porada (Columbia University; said to be in Columbia Art Properties); one tablet is in the Hermitage Museum, St. Petersburg; one tablet is in Marseille (anonymous collection); one proto-Elamite tablet is in the Ashmolean Museum (Oxford; Ashm 2002-2); an unknown number of tablets from Susa are in Susa and Tehran; and many unpublished fragments are in the Louvre.

TEXTS FROM SITES OTHER THAN SUSA

The first proto-Elamite tablets found outside Susa appeared during R. Ghirshman's excavations of Tepe Sialk (Ghirshman 1934: 116; 1938: 85, pls. 92–3). Five of the twenty-three tablets and fragments from Sialk are proto-Elamite (Sialk 2, 1621, 1624, 1626, and 1630; but see Glassner 1998), while the rest are numero-ideographic or numerical tablets. Although few in number, these tablets were to be the first in a long list of proto-Elamite tablets found at sites spread throughout modern Iran. Proto-Elamite tablets have also

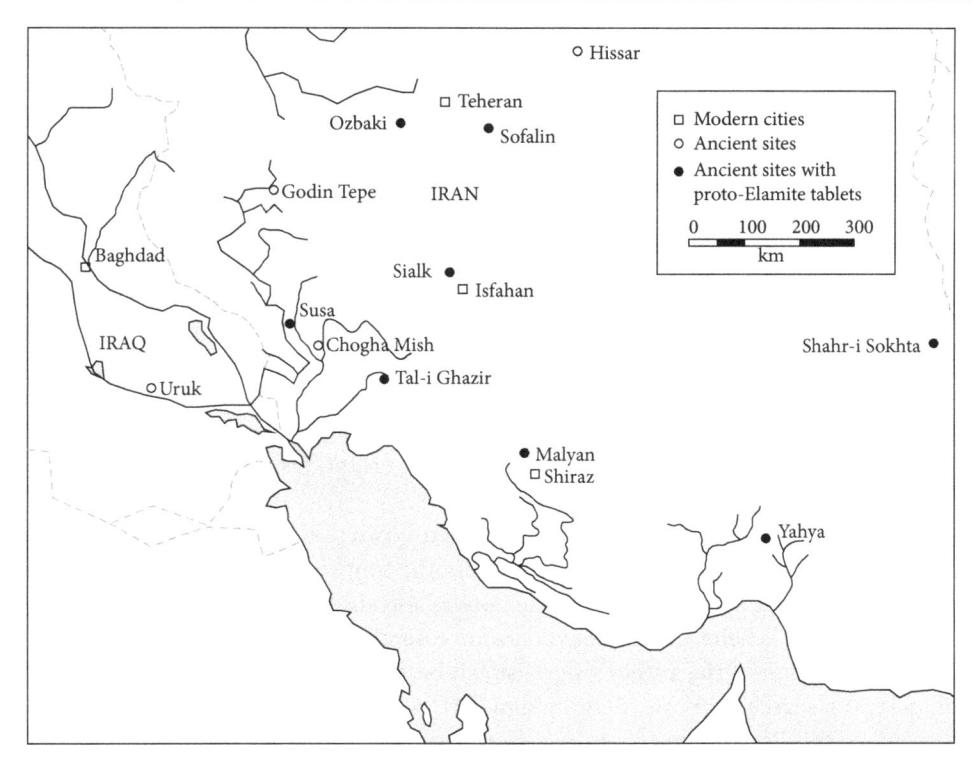

FIGURE 13.1 Map of sites discussed in the text.

been found at Tepe Yahya (twenty-seven texts; Damerow and Englund 1989); Tal-e Ghazir (one text, Whitcomb 1971: 37, pl. 11A.; cf. Alden 1982); Shahr-e-Sokhta (one text, for a photograph see Salvatori, Tosi, and Vidale 2001: 36); Tal-e Malyan (thirty-three texts, Stolper 1985; the complete corpus to be published by M. W. Stolper and the author); Tepe Ozbaki (one text, Vallat 2003); and Tepe Sofalin (many texts reported, see, e.g., http://cdli.ucla.edu/P393079). However, none of the texts from these sites rival in structure, complexity or scale the Susa documents. A few late texts from Tal-e Malyan are more complex, and even repeat certain strings, also attested at Susa, that are currently believed to be syllabic writings of personal names. Stamp seals were used on a few Tal-e Malyan tablets but never on the Susa tablets, which were sealed exclusively with cylinder seals.

History of decipherment

Following the publications of Scheil work on the proto-Elamite tablets slowed. Already in 1923 Scheil wrote in disappointment about the missing key to the texts and the stalled decipherment ("Il est malheureusement douteux qu'aucune fouille nous livre jamais la clef des problèmes que pose cette écriture proto-élamite" [Scheil 1923: iv]). Few advancements were made before the monumental studies of P. Meriggi (Meriggi 1969, 1971, 1974a, 1974b; but see for example Brice 1962–3 and 1963). Meriggi restudied all of the tablets in the Louvre and produced a commentated sign list which was a significant improvement on earlier lists and which forms the basis for current work on the proto-Elamite signary. However, a very different sort of advance in the study of proto-Elamite occurred when J. Friberg published his *The third millennium roots of Babylonian mathematics* (1978–9), a two-volume work outlining a new approach to decipherment. Friberg used the content-specific numerical systems to identify many text groups. In 1989 two of the members of the Berlin project to publish the protocuneiform texts from Uruk, P. Damerow and R. K. Englund, published the tablets from Tepe Yahya. Their seminal work on this small group of tablets included a complete discussion of the form and content of the most important Susa tablets (Damerow and Englund 1989).

Current work on the proto-Elamite texts is focused on the complete digital capture of the form and content of all proto-Elamite tablets, the continued edition of the remaining unpublished tablets and fragments in the Louvre and elsewhere, and the production of a new sign list. It is believed that these data are essential for an eventual decipherment. A working version of the author's sign list can be found on the CDLI website (http://cdli.ucla.edu; search for proto-Elamite sign list). All references below to proto-Elamite signs follow this list. In some cases related protocuneiform signs are given in parentheses after the proto-Elamite signs; their readings follow the Uruk sign list (Green and Nissen 1987).

Invention of writing

Although overall the invention of writing can be said to be a linear, evolutionary process—leading from the use of nonpermanent counting devices, through the encapsulation of these in clay envelopes, to the impression of marks representing counting devices in the surface of flat clay tablets (Nissen 2011)—early examples of protowriting exhibit a very low degree of standardization. It can be difficult to establish, for example, the numerical systems used even within one site (see most famously the Jebel Aruda text JA 75–104, Van Driel 1982), and it may be altogether impossible to establish rules for the values of counters or early numerical marks that are valid across the region (Englund 2006: 29–30). Once the idea of protowriting had been invented we must assume that practitioners in different locations experimented with this new technology and local counting preferences and vessel types of standardized size and form influenced the arithmetic rules underlying these texts.

Simple tokens are found across Mesopotamia and Iran, beginning shortly after the Neolithic revolution. Simple tokens resemble plain, geometric forms such as balls, disks, and cones. They are made of clay or, from the mid-fourth millennium BC onward, stone, and resemble similar objects found in later periods enclosed in clay envelopes. This observation, combined with many anthropological parallels, have led to the widespread notion that these tokens were used as counting devices to perform basic arithmetic operations (addition and subtraction). Unfortunately, nowhere in the archaeological record has a discrete group of tokens been recorded that could help us understand how, if at all, these devices functioned to aid administration. According to the standard understanding of the use of these counters (from at least the time they appear encased in clay envelopes), these would have stood in a one-to-one relationship to the object they represented, with probably very simple bundling rules applied as well (based perhaps on standardized vessel sizes). The complex tokens that D. Schmandt-Besserat suggested were the precursors of the nonnumerical signs of the Uruk IV and III period (Schmandt-Besserat 1992 1: 129ff., esp. 143–9) are never found in a context that supports this theory (cf. Englund 1994; Michalowski 1993; Shendge 1983). The invention of nonnumerical signs should rather be sought in a combination of stimuli from seals, storage locations and containers, texture and shape of perishable materials used in administrative and economic contexts, and pre-existing symbols, to mention only a few possible sources (Nissen et al. 1993: 11).

At some point in the Late Uruk period, probably before Uruk V (Susa Acropole level 18), clay tokens began to be encased in clay envelopes, so-called *bullae* (note that whereas Assyriologists call hollow clay balls containing tokens *bullae*, archaeologists usually call these "clay balls" and reserve the term *bullae* for solid lumps of clay, often bearing seal impressions). We can only speculate how tokens may have been stored before, but the new media enabled administrators to seal transactions and eventually to make impressions of the content on the outside of the *bulla*. The sample of *bullae* that have been opened under controlled circumstances remains deplorably low compared to the total number of complete, unopened *bullae* found. It is therefore impossible to conclude that the content of *bullae* and the impressions found on the outside of these always correspond (Englund 2006: 20). It is also impossible to establish whether the tokens inside *bullae* belonged to a fixed numerical system with precise bundling rules. *Bullae* with tokens have been found at Susa (in both the early excavations of Morgan and Mecquenem and the later excavations of Le Brun). During the excavations of Le Brun, *bullae* were found only in Acropole I levels 18/1–2, 3 and 4, barring the envelope fragment S.Acr 1903.1 found in room 830 in level 17B (Glassner 2003: 115; Englund 205: 115, and cf. the plan in Le Brun 1978: 60). *Bullae* have also been found at other sites in Iran including Chogha Mish, where several fragments and two complete *bullae* were recovered (Alizadeh 2008: fig. 76.AA and DD); Tepe Yahya, where one *bulla* was found (Schmandt-Besserat 1992 1: 111, fig. 58); and Tepe Sofalin, which also yielded one *bulla* (unpublished).

Whereas numerical tablets (i.e., flat clay tablets with impressions of tokens or impressions made by a stylus in the shape of tokens and often sealed) follow *bullae* on an evolutionary trajectory, there was most likely an overlap of these two technologies leading to a somewhat unclear picture in the archaeological record (Englund 2005: 115). Overall, the process of invention probably proceeded much faster than the archaeological record allows us to differentiate. Hence, *bullae*, numerical tablets, and numero-ideographic tablets are assigned to the archaeological level contemporary with Uruk V (Susa 18 and 17; only one bulla fragment is recorded from Susa 17, see Englund 2005: 115 and above). The singular find of a *bulla* at Middle Babylonian Nuzi only supports the interpretation that such techniques were quasi-universal, but does not argue for an independence of writing from arithmetical devices such as tokens and *bullae* (for the Nuzi *bulla*, see Oppenheim 1959; Lieberman 1980).

As mentioned above, it has proven impossible to identify the system of bundling of smaller into larger numerical units within groups of numerical tablets from one site as well as across the region. It can furthermore be difficult to judge whether a tablet is "numerical" when the term "numerical" is used as a typological designation for tablets from a certain period (probably Uruk V; Susa 18 and 17), as opposed to an archaic tablet with numbers only (see above and add, e.g., Englund 1994: pl. 11, W 6613,a, from Uruk, where the text, entirely numerical, is divided into cases, something usually believed to be a further development following the stage of numerical tablets). Numerical tablets have been found at Susa (e.g., Scheil 1923: nos. 11, 20, and 58), and at sites elsewhere in Iran, such as Chogha Mish (Alizadeh 2008: 78–9); Godin Tepe (Hallo 2011: 116–18); Tepe Sialk (Ghirshman 1938: pls. 92–3); and most recently, Tepe Sofalin.

It can be equally difficult to identify a numero-ideographic tablet without good stratigraphic information. The term "numero-ideographic" was coined by Englund (1998: 51–6) to cover those early tablets (from both Iran and Iraq) that predate protocuneiform proper, but nevertheless have the first nonnumerical signs. Some of the best examples come from Iran, with Godin Tepe in particularly yielding important finds (e.g., Gd 73–295, Englund 1998: 56, fig. 16, which has a sign representing perhaps a dairy vessel and a numerical notation; cf. Hallo 2011: 116–18; eight tablets were published in Weiss and Young 1975: 9–10). At Susa, numero-ideographic tablets were found only in level 17 (probably corresponding to Uruk V). The nonnumerical signs on the numero-ideographic tablets represent in all cases a simple product sign, making the associated numerical notation a qualifier. Information about owner and destination would have been indicated by other means. The numero-ideographic tablets were followed by protocuneiform tablets proper in Mesopotamia (Uruk IV–style tablets), and proto-Elamite tablets in Iran.

The split between Mesopotamian and Iranian writing

In more mature texts from Mesopotamia and Iran we can establish rules for the order of objects and qualifiers (mostly numerical signs). In protocuneiform the numerical signs always precede the object they qualify, whereas the opposite is true in proto-Elamite. It may also be possible to show the same distinction in the very earliest numero-ideographic tablets, where examples from Iran invariably have nonnumerical signs preceding the numerical. However, the sample of numero-ideographic tablets from Uruk itself is not representative enough to allow for the same sort of conclusive remarks (only two Uruk tablets with nonnumerical signs have been assigned to level V—Englund 1994: pl. 16, W 6782,a with a vessel sign, and pl. 17, W 6881,b with the sign "UDU," each preceded by a numerical notation).

In 2004 Englund suggested that the choice at Susa of writing the sign representing one-fifth of N1 with N39b indicated contact between the users of the two writing systems during the Uruk IV—Susa 17 period (Englund 2004: 125–7). Until then Uruk scribes seem to have freely alternated between N39a and its inverted version, N39b, but after that time Uruk scribes fixed the direction using only N39a. Another similar indicator for the discontinuation of contact after the Uruk IV period is the way in which the line rulings were made in the two corpora (Englund 2004: 126). Line dividers in Uruk IV texts were made by pressing the shank of the stylus into the clay, whereas one Uruk III tablet's lines were drawn with the pointed edge of a stylus. Line dividers in the proto-Elamite tablets were always made like those in the Uruk IV corpus, suggesting that contact between the two systems broke at the end of the Uruk IV period.

The structure of proto-Elamite texts

Whereas the global structure (Fig. 13.2) of protocuneiform and proto-Elamite tablets is similar with "headings," as well as "entries" and "subentries" consisting of objects and qualifiers, there is a major difference between the layout of the texts in the two writing systems (Englund 2004: 106, n. 12, and fig. 5.3b). This difference is not so much a product of the much greater complexity of many protocuneiform texts, but rather a reformulation of the principle of writing when in Iran. Whereas protocuneiform texts were arranged in visual hierarchies, thus poorly masking their weak link to spoken language (Damerow 2006), the same information was written continuously in lines in proto-Elamite texts, at least on a superficial level, much better resembling spoken language. In our publications of proto-Elamite tablets we turn these 90° counterclockwise to conform with standards in Assyriology. The description of tablet layout given below is in accordance with this.

Most proto-Elamite tablets begin with a single, sometimes complex (see below), sign that functions as a header for the entire text. This sign may indicate the household to which or person to whom the transactions belong. In protocuneiform texts this information would be found at the very end of the text, but would otherwise be similar in function and to some extent in sign category (Englund 2004: 106, n. 12). In some instances, in particular in early texts, there is no header and we must surmise that other factors such as storage location functioned as a replacement for a header. Following the header, a text can have any number of entries, from one to hundreds (Scheil 1923: no. 292; 1905: no. 316+ [cf. Dahl 2012a], and Sb 2801 are examples of very long texts). The entries can

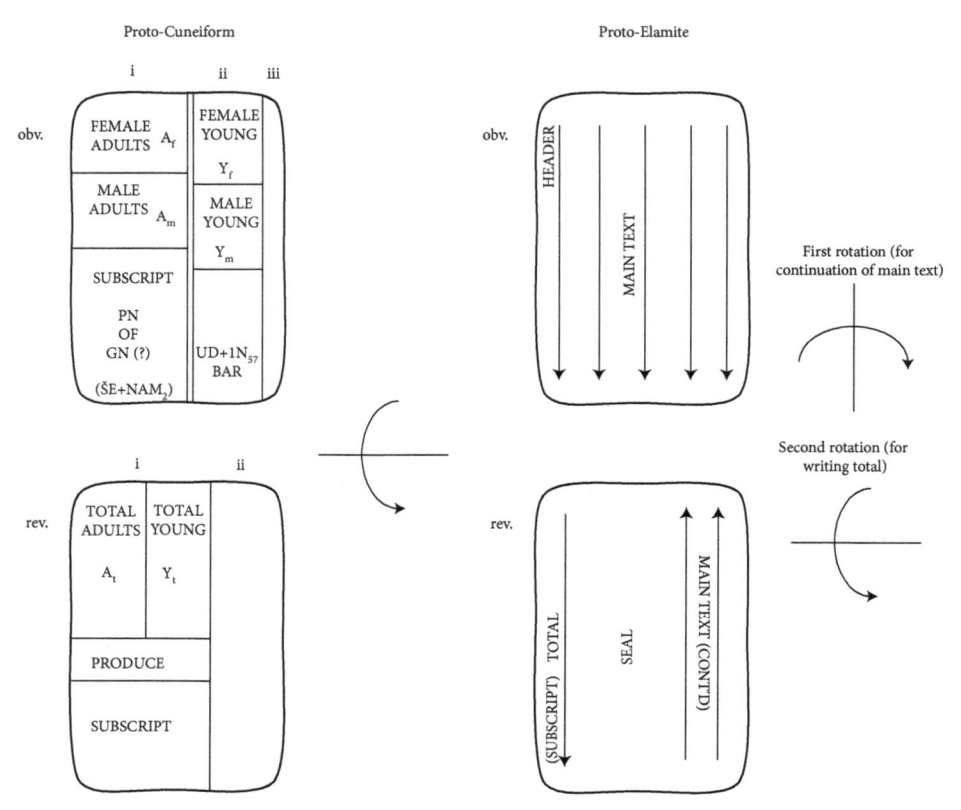

FIGURE 13.2 Structure of the content of protocuneiform and proto-Elamite texts.

be divided into subentries. A typical example of a text with a complex structure is Scheil (1923: no. 112; a new edition of that text is being prepared by Laura Hawkins of the University of Oxford). In that text workers of different categories are assigned to a number of persons (?). The first entry on the reverse, for example, begins with what may be the title of a person (M51a M388), followed by the same person's name or designation (M218 M229e M371), followed by a count of one worker (M317). The next two subentries list other workers assigned to the person with the title in the main entry (M54 and M46). In other words, these two entries can not stand alone, but belong together with the main entry. In schematic form that entry may look like this:

M51a M388   M218 M229e M371   M317   1N1
M54   1N1
M46   1N1

In a proto-Elamite text, however, this is all written continuously: M51a M388 M218 M229e M371 M317 1N1 M54 1N1 M46 1N1. For this reason we separate entries and not lines, made up of a series of ideographic signs followed by a numerical notation, in our transliterations of proto-Elamite texts. Within one entry the only distinction is between numerical and nonnumerical parts of an entry. Following conventions adopted for the protocuneiform corpus, the two parts are separated by a comma in our transliterations. The same entry with subentries above will therefore appear like this in our transliterations:

2a. M051a M388 M218 M229e M371 M317, 1(N01)
2b. M054, 1(N01)
2c. M046, 1(N01)

Among the worker categories in this short excerpt it is only M54 that we have any clear knowledge about, as it graphically seems to resemble a yoke and semantically seems to stand for either an able worker or a team of workers employed in agricultural work (cf. Damerow and Englund 1989: 57–8). M317 is placed at the start of this short list of workers, and is equally prominently attested in related texts; it can therefore be surmised that it stands for an important worker. M46 is a famous sign in proto-Elamite studies, as it is graphically identical to Mesopotamian DINGIR (the sign for star or a deity, or indeed the chief of the pantheon An). Semantically, the two are not related of course. The proto-Elamite sign M46 represents rather a low-ranking worker, as can be inferred from this and other texts (note that the sign NAB has no cognates in proto-Elamite: the sign that Meriggi copied as DINGIR over DINGIR [his no. 78] is in fact a graphical depiction of a vessel with a stroke down the middle).

Most proto-Elamite account entries are totaled. The totals can be complex, with multiple, different products individually totaled. The total is always written on the reverse of the tablet which is rotated around its vertical axis. Because text from the obverse can spill over onto the reverse, rotating the tablet around its horizontal axis, the text on the reverse of the tablets can run in two opposite directions, generally with a blank space between the two.

A number of proto-Elamite texts have an inscription on the top edge of unknown meaning. Unfortunately, early copies of proto-Elamite tablets included only the obverse, and only rarely the reverse. A detailed study of the top edge inscriptions is therefore still lacking, but these may relate to a simplistic time notation system otherwise not identified in proto-Elamite despite its existence in the Uruk-based protocuneiform system.

Late proto-Elamite tablets were ruled using the side of a rounded stylus (see above). Some proto-Elamite texts have other marks that may convey meaning. Most important among these is the corner mark found on a number of proto-Elamite tablets. A similar mark is found on all twenty Uruk IV texts using the so-called EN-system (a particular numerical system of unknown properties, see Damerow and Englund 1989 and Falkenstein 1936 for the archival mark which he thought was used to distinguish obverse from reverse). On the proto-Elamite tablets it is always found on the upper right corner (lower right according to the original direction of writing) and was usually made with the side of the stylus.

Seals and scribal designs

Seal impressions are common on proto-Elamite tablets, but contrary to Mesopotamia where the growing complexity of the writing system seemed to increasingly exclude seal impressions on tablets, so that by the Uruk III period virtually no Uruk text was sealed (although texts from other localities occasionally were; e.g. Englund 1998: 215), the opposite seems to be true in Iran (see also below).

The iconography of proto-Elamite seals is entirely devoid of human beings and those seals and sealings with human beings from Susa all predate the proto-Elamite period (humans are depicted, e.g., on seals found in levels 18 and 17, never on seals from levels 16–14, *pace* Pittman 1992: 75, who claims that fewer than five proto-Elamite seals have depictions of humans without reference to these). This accords well with other forms of proto-Elamite art which seem to prohibit depiction of the human body. It is important in this connection to note also that no proto-Elamite signs were based on the human body or any part thereof (including the head), except for two signs that were part of the package of early signs borrowed from Mesopotamia. These two signs, SAL and KUR_a in protocuneiform, M72 and M388 in proto-Elamite, had presumably lost their immediate graphical referent by the time they were adopted in Iran (Damerow and Englund 1989: 55–7). The fact that proto-Elamite is thus devoid of signs such as HAND, or HEAD, significantly impairs our understanding of the texts. Similar signs have proven to be cornerstones in the decipherment of other scripts (Gelb and Whiting 1975: 101).

The iconography of proto-Elamite seals was even more restricted than that of the Uruk period (for the Uruk material see Collon 1987: 14–15; Brandes 1979: 115–16; for the proto-Elamite material see Pittman 1997: 139–40). The scenes on the vast majority of proto-Elamite seals include animals, real or imagined: animals (in nature); mythical animals; processions of mythical and ordinary animals; and animals doing human tasks. Decorative elements appear on some seals, alone or with animals. A few seals have "texts" consisting of a single sign from the writing system (e.g., the famous "seal of the ruler of Susa" on Sb 2801, Pittman 1992: 75–6).

In a few instances there seems to be an overlap between the glyptic scene of the seal and the administrative activities of the tablet on which the seal is rolled, suggesting that seal iconography was related to administrative duties. A few sheep- and goat-herding tablets were sealed with a seal whose imagery relates to goats (Dahl 2005b: 119). Further, the seal of the ruler with bull-man holding lions and lion-man holding bulls is found on extremely high-level texts such as Sb 2801 (Pittman 1992: 75–6).

On some late proto-Elamite tablets (see below), we find a graphical design, often in the form of two intertwined geometric shapes, instead of a seal. These designs are attested on several tablets, with similar content. The presence of such a design precludes the rolling of a seal. The designs are placed in exactly the same areas on the tablets where we would expect to find a seal, namely on the obverse after the text, and on the middle of the reverse. Most of these designs were included in the sign lists accompanying the early publications. They have been dealt with separately only in the introduction to MDP 17 (Scheil 1923: 66–7) and more recently by the author (Dahl 2012b). An unpublished clay sealing from Tepe Sofalin has a rather similar design, but another clay sealing from the same site has a clumsily etched hairy triangle (see below). These finds challenge the way we understand the formation of early writing, by suggesting a fluid interaction between writing and symbols used in society.

THE SIGNARY

As already alluded to above, there are no signs that represent humans or human parts except for two signs of a common origin with Mesopotamian signs, namely SAL and KUR_a. These two classic signs depicting female and perhaps male genitalia are found on proto-Elamite texts of all periods and at all sites with more than a few tablets (i.e., excluding Tepe Ozbaki, Tepe Sialk, Shahr-e Sokhta, and Tal-e Ghazir). We can divide the proto-Elamite signs into four categories: loans from Mesopotamia or common origin signs (including numerical signs); signs depicting natural objects such as plants, plant parts, or animals; signs depicting cultural objects such as a yoke, a vessel, or a standard; and entirely abstract signs. Many of these signs have meanings that are not immediately tied to their graphical referent. For example, many of the animal signs never represent counted animals. Many of the signs that appear to depict cultural objects in fact stand for human beings.

A small number of signs and almost all the numerical signs and systems are either direct loans from protocuneiform or have a common origin, depending on how the history of writing ultimately is understood (Englund 2004: fig 5.14). If the invention of writing is understood as having taken place in Uruk alone and subsequently spread from there, in one or more waves, to other sites such as Susa, then we must accept that these signs are true loans. However, one could also suggest that writing was invented simultaneously over a larger area, Susa being one of the key locations, in which case these signs can be viewed as having a common origin.

Numerical systems (Fig. 13.3) in early writing systems in the Ancient Near East were context-specific, often allowing modern specialists to decipher the category of goods being counted (Englund 1998: 111–21 with literature). The primary differentiation in early numerical systems was between systems used to count discrete objects (at Uruk a sexagesimal system was used; in Iran a decimal system in addition to a sexagesimal system, see below) and systems used to count measures of barley or related grain products (the so-called ŠE-system). In addition, a special system used to count rations, the so-called bisexagesimal system, is attested in both writing systems, albeit with a restricted use in proto-Elamite.

Except for a few derived numerical signs and one numerical system, proto-Elamite essentially used a restricted version of the Mesopotamian system. Proto-Elamite used only seven systems compared to the thirteen or more in use at Uruk; and only

Numerical signs found in proto-Elamite.

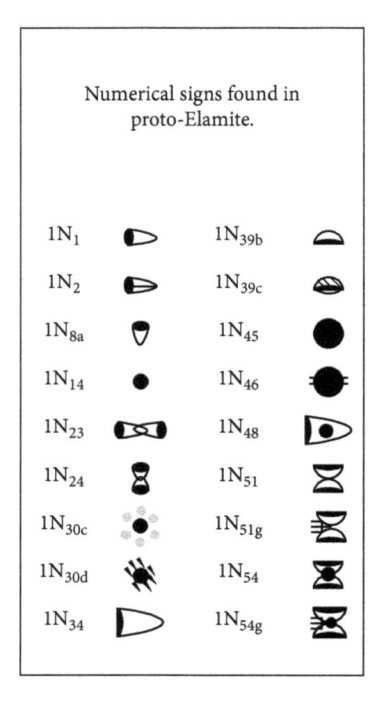

$1N_1$	▷	$1N_{39b}$	◠
$1N_2$	▶	$1N_{39c}$	◈
$1N_{8a}$	▽	$1N_{45}$	●
$1N_{14}$	•	$1N_{46}$	⦿
$1N_{23}$	⋈	$1N_{48}$	▷
$1N_{24}$	⧗	$1N_{51}$	⧗
$1N_{30c}$	⋰	$1N_{51g}$	⧗
$1N_{30d}$	✻	$1N_{54}$	⧗
$1N_{34}$	▷	$1N_{54g}$	⧗

Sexagesimal System S
System used to count discrete inanimate objects.

● ←6— ▶ ←10— ▷ ←6— • ←10— ▶ ←2— ▽
"3,600"   "600"   "60"   "10"   "1"   "1/2"

Decimal System D
System used to count discrete animate objects, in particular domesticated animals and human laborers.

⧗ ←10— ⧗ or ⧗ ←10— ⋈ ←10— • ←10— ▶
"10,000" "1,000"   "100"   "10"   "1"

Bisexagesimal System B
System used to count discrete grain products; objects noted with this system may, as in archaic Babylonia, belong to a rationing system.

⧗ ←10— ⧗ ←2— ▷ ←6— • ←10— ▶
"1,200"   "120"   "60"   "10"   "1"

Bisexagesimal System B#
System derived from the bisexagesimal system B, used to count rations (?) of an unclear nature.

⌈⧗⌉ ←10— ⌈⧗⌉ ←2— ⌈▷⌉ ←6— ⌈•⌉ ←10— ⌈▶⌉
"1,200"   "120"   "60"   "10"   "1"

Capacity System C
System used primarily to note capacity measures of grain, in particular barley; some of the small units also designate bisexagesimally counted cereal products.

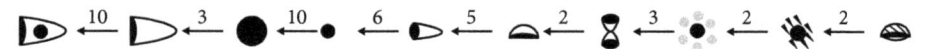

▶ ←10— ▷ ←3— ● ←10— • ←6— ▶ ←5— ◠ ←2— ⧗ ←3— ⋰ ←2— ✻ ←2— ◈

Capacity System C#
System derived from the capacity system C, possibly related to system B#

⌈▷⌉ ←3— ⌈●⌉ ←10— ⌈•⌉ ←6— ⌈▶⌉ ←5— ⌈◠⌉ ←2— ⌈⧗⌉ ←3— ⌈⋰⌉ ←2— ⌈✻⌉

Capacity System C"
System derived from the capacity system C, graphically related to the Babylonian system used to measure emmer.

⋰ ←6— ✻ ←5— ✻ ←2— ⧗ ←3— ✻ ←2— ✻

FIGURE 13.3 Numerical signs in the proto-Elamite writing system and a reconstruction of the numerical systems, explained as factor diagrams (adapted from Englund 2004).

about half of the more than sixty distinct numerical signs attested at Uruk are found in proto-Elamite texts (Damerow and Englund 1989: 18–28). Two proto-Elamite numerical signs were formed by adding the proto-Elamite version of the Uruk sign GAL (meaning "big" in later periods) to higher-order signs (named N51gal and N54gal), and two of the signs for subdivisions of the basic capacity sign (N39b, N30c and d) were executed as graphical representations of the Uruk signs N30a and N30c. N30d, representing a uniquely small capacity notation, is unmatched in protocuneiform (Damerow and Englund 1989: 26). The proto-Elamite numerical ŠE-system has a less elaborate system of subdivisions of N39a/b than its Uruk counterpart. Finally, as has been remarked upon above, the scribes of the proto-Elamite texts employed a decimally based system, which nevertheless used signs from the other systems. This system seems to have been reserved for counting low-status objects, such as herded animals and dependent workers (Damerow and Englund 1989: 24; Englund 2004: 112).

A large number of signs depict natural objects, such as a plant, an animal, or a part thereof. There is no evidence for the existence of signs depicting humans or human body parts, as discussed above, and no conclusive evidence for signs depicting inanimate natural objects such as stones, rivers, or the like.

Probably the largest group of signs are graphical representations of artifacts produced by humans. The proliferation of signs belonging to this group may have been due to the way in which new signs could be generated. Signs for vessels are a case in point. The signs M262 and related signs are probably graphic representations of vessels. M262 can be modified by adding strokes in different directions, by adding one or more dots at the base, or by adding to the body of the vessel a sign indicating the specific content of the vessel or the amount it held. M262 is probably a container for beer. Another prolific group of signs are those that stand for households, most famously the so-called hairy triangle sign (M136). This sign, which is found on tablets across Iran, only occurs framing other signs (the sole example when M136 is empty, Scheil 1923: no. 459, should be understood still as M136 + M36d, as the juxtaposition of a container sign and an indicator sign, a type of complex grapheme that is not uncommon; see Dahl 2005a).

M136 has been understood as a sign for the ruler of a certain political entity, thus M136g (M136 with an inscribed sign) has been identified as the sign of the ruler of Susa (Lamberg-Karlovsky 1986). We should probably understand this sign as a graphical representation of the ruler's standard with his mark drawn inside of it. The mark drawn inside M136g appears to be a spearhead. The sign appears on the sealing of Sb 2801, a high-level account mentioned above. Although Sb 2801 is by far the most important proto-Elamite text ever to have been recovered it remains unpublished (it appears in the photographic plates of MDP 6, i.e., Scheil 1905). More than two dozen variants of M136 are known today, but with every new settlement with an archive of proto-Elamite tablets we must expect to find new variants of the sign, as indeed has been the case with Tal-e Malyan, Tepe Yahya (M136 + M71a), and most recently Tepe Sofalin. However, some of the variants of M136 are not specific to geographical location, in particular M136 with an inscribed four-pointed star (M365), which is found at Susa, Tal-e Malyan, Tepe Sofalin, and Tepe Yahya, all sites with substantial finds of proto-Elamite tablets.

Another subgroup of signs depicting cultural objects are those that depict tools or instruments. As mentioned above, none of these stands for the object it actually depicts.

I shall discuss briefly the signs for yoke (M54) and plow (M56) below. Another sign that may be a graphical depiction of an object is M124. This sign has a slight resemblance to TI, the sign for a bow and arrow in Mesopotamia. The proto-Elamite variant is never used for a counted object but only as a sign for a human being, perhaps a soldier. For the plow and yoke signs, the obvious explanations are that the yoke stands for one or two workers or animals, the plow for a team of workers or an area of land (see below).

Yet another example of a sign depicting a cultural object without representing it is M329, most likely a graphical representation of a lyre or harp or a similar musical instrument. In most of the approximately forty instances of this sign it is likely to be interpreted as a sign with a pseudosyllabic value (see below).

A large number of signs remain impossible to classify according to the criteria used above, and we are forced to judge them as abstract (Damerow and Englund 1989: 22). For most we have probably failed to find the intended graphical referent, but there remain a number of signs whose use in fact suggests that they are entirely abstract. Strikingly, these include many of the signs assigned to the subclass that may make up a sort of syllabary (see below). We must of course be careful with such statements since, for instance, M1, a horizontal line (or vertical according to the original direction of writing), could just as well be a drawing of a (reed)-stalk or something similar, and the sign appears to have multiple semantic values, both syllabic and pictographic.

Many signs in proto-Elamite consist of a combination of one or more otherwise discrete signs inscribed one within the other to form complex graphemes. This way of increasing the repertoire of signs and adding meaning to signs is well known from most other early writing systems (see, e.g., Wagensonner 2010: 299–302 for protocuneiform). Proto-Elamite, which lacks any signs of standardization, creates complex graphemes more freely than any other system. Faced with a container sign that lacked the internal room to place a modifying sign inside it, this was simply placed next to it. Additionally, signs could frame other signs to create complex graphemes (Dahl 2005a).

Most signs are used in a one-to-one correspondence with the objects they signify. For example, the proto-Elamite equivalent of Mesopotamian SAL (M72), which depicts the female genitals, is used for a dependent female worker, and is always followed by a count in the decimal system (the system used to count discrete, low-status objects); similarly, simple signs depicting objects such as vessels are representations of actual vessels, followed by a numerical sequence representing the count of objects. Certain signs depicting containers of plants, or plant parts, are direct representations in a similar way but followed by counts in the capacity system; perhaps these numerical signs originally represented different capacity vessels. Yet other signs such as the so-called hairy triangle, described above, signify an owner or a household through a graphical representation of a symbol representing this. However, one group of signs stands out, since they do not seem to represent any actual object. These signs are used, it appears, primarily to describe owners by combining two to four signs. About 80–120 signs at present can be said to belong to this group, but more graphical variants may be identified, reducing the number to fewer than eighty. This group of signs may represent a never fully standardized syllabary (Fig. 13.4; Dahl 2009; cf. Meriggi 1971).

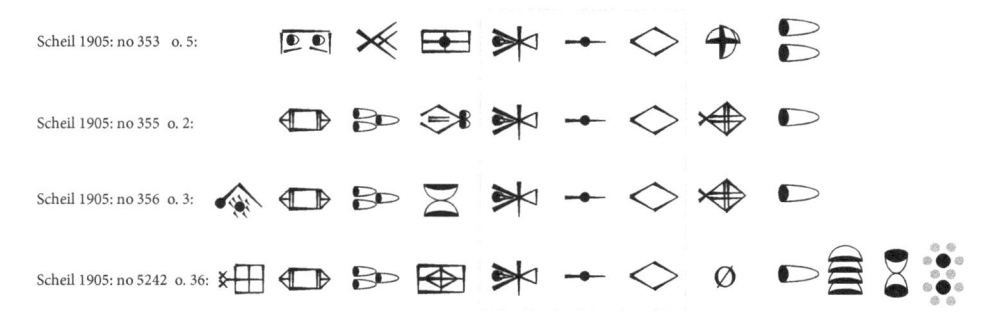

FIGURE 13.4 Graphotactical analysis of four entries from four different texts showing the possible existence of restricted syllabaries used for specific information, in this case probably to write syllabically the name of the owner/recipient of the counted objects (example 1. 2 sheep; ex. 2. 1 vessel; ex. 3. 1 vessel; ex. 4. an amount of cereals).

THE DATE OF THE TEXTS

It is notoriously difficult to date samples of early writing which lack references to historical events. Archaeological information is only rarely available, as most texts were excavated during the early years of exploration or during clandestine excavations. Even with good archaeological information we often come up short, as tablets are often found in a secondary context, such as in dumps or fill. Finally, the archaeological dating of texts rarely provides the sort of precision that philologists hope for. Nevertheless, a combination of traditional philological and archaeological data has produced a framework for an internal chronology of the documents. Three internal criteria—form, structure, and textual complexity—can be used to divide the proto-Elamite tablets into three main groups. When compared with the tablets found during stratigraphically controlled excavations, and with information mined from old publications, it can be shown that these groups correspond to a chronological sequence (Dahl et al. 2013).

The earliest tablets are thick and oblong. The signs often appear clumsily written, and the text is placed randomly on the surface of the tablet. The texts are rarely totaled and have often one entry on either side. The syntactic structure of the entries is much less sophisticated than in later texts. These tablets are known mainly from the early excavations at Susa (e.g., Scheil 1923: nos. 21, 37, 40, 51 and 111), though a single examples was found at Tal-e Ghazir.

Another group, consisting of very large, flat, and thick tablets (e.g., Scheil 1923: nos. 456, 466, and 476) was also found during the early excavations. Although these tablets presumably belong to an early group, based on the structure and complexity of the texts, this cannot be proven since no comparable examples were found in context during later excavations (S.ACR 1237.1 may belong to this group but it was found in the suspicious contact level 17a–16, and may very well belong to any of the levels above, i.e., 16c–14). This group is as yet poorly understood.

Later tablets tend to be thin and rectangular. The long side of the tablet is always parallel to the direction of the text. Most of the standard proto-Elamite tablets are ruled using the edge of a thin, rounded stylus. Unruled tablets may represent a chronologically earlier subgroup, followed by ruled tablets. The signs are more regularly executed and the text structure tends to be more rigid. The individual entries are increasingly complex, with sometimes very long strings of nonnumerical signs expressing information that was previously represented with one or a few signs. The first two proto-Elamite tablets found by Morgan (probably during the 1898–9 season, see above), and essentially all of the early finds published in MDP 6 (Scheil 1905) and MDP 26S (Scheil 1935), belong to this type. In addition, tablets of this type were found during Le Brun's excavations in levels Acropole I 16c–14b (16c: S.ACR 1018.1, 1067.1, 929.1, 964.1; 15b: S.ACR 736.1, 733.1; 15a: S.ACR 710.1, 838.1, 482.1; 14b: S.ACR 316.1, 316.2; 16–15b contact: S.ACR 845.1).

A subgroup of the standard tablets can also be identified. These are "cushion-" or pillow-shaped tablets with a highly developed internal structure. They are always ruled. One tablet belonging to this subgroup was found during stratified excavations (S.ACR 316.2, cf. Scheil 1923: nos. 23 or 43 found during Morgan's or Mecquenem's excavations).

The content of the proto-Elamite texts

As correctly observed by Scheil in 1905 the content of all proto-Elamite tablets is administrative. The only exceptions are two possible metro-mathematical texts (Scheil 1923: nos. 328 and 362, discussed by Scheil 1935: vii–viii, Damerow and Englund 1989: 18–19, nn. 51, 53, and J. Friberg, pers. comm.). The biggest difference between proto-Elamite and early writing in Mesopotamia is therefore the absence of school texts in Iran. Approximately 15 percent of the material from Uruk is made up of lexical texts. It is possible, but difficult to prove, that this lack of lexical material resulted in less standardization in the signary than can be observed in protocuneiform where the number of signs decreases by the Uruk III texts (Dahl 2003; Damerow 2006). As far as can be estimated, the subject matter of the proto-Elamite texts is rather restricted. The reasons for this may lie in the fact that proto-Elamite is not a complete system and that it never developed into a real writing system. Although it certainly progressed in that direction it suffered from serious systemic deficiencies, in particular the lack of a lexical tradition that could have fostered standardization.

Almost all proto-Elamite texts are related to agricultural products, labor, and animal herding. Although it may be predictable that these three categories should make up the majority of texts, it is nevertheless surprising that the texts give no hint of trade or manufacture of stone, metal, or wooden objects. We are accustomed to seeing Mesopotamia's eastern mountainous neighbor as a supplier of raw materials and objects not available in lowland Mesopotamia (Algaze 1989, but note criticism in Steinkeller 1993), and writing is often seen as facilitating this exploitation of natural resources (Algaze 2005, 2008). However, the absence of textual sources dealing with the manufacture and trade of these objects is not limited to the proto-Elamite corpus but is in fact a constant throughout the third millennium and beyond. The flow of objects from the highlands to the lowlands, which certainly took place, probably followed other, more complex channels (Englund 2006). A few signs in the proto-Elamite repertoire seem to represent wooden or metal objects or tools made of metal and wood. However, in no instance are we dealing with a count of the actual object. In the case of the sign representing a plow, for example, we can be rather sure that the texts do not count the physical objects but rather the work (through rations) of plowmen, or the area plowed (through rations or seed-ration) (Damerow and Englund 1989: 27, n. 88 and 57, n. 159, and see above). In the case of the sign probably representing a harp the situation is yet more complex, as that sign in fact never appears as a counted object but rather it is one of the signs for which a pseudo-syllabic value has been proposed.

A number of key texts appear to deal with the actual or projected yields of fields. One text (Scheil 1905: no. 221), for example, lists perhaps five plots, indicated by the sign M391, and the projected yield from each of these is indicated by an amount of cereal counted with M288. The yields are large and they total more than 10,000 liters (see Damerow and Englund 1989: 26 for an estimate of the absolute size of capacity notations in protocuneiform and proto-Elamite; Damerow and Englund argued that the numerical sign N30c is the proto-Elamite version of an Uruk numerical sign used to count the capacity of a vessel usually identified as the bevel-rim bowl, and therefore about equivalent to 0.5 to 0.9 liters). Many other texts list agricultural products, mainly in what appear to be ration texts.

Numerous texts detail the rations given to dependent workers and possibly higher-ranking members of society (Fig. 13.5). Starting with the former, one should mention the largest proto-Elamite text ever discovered (Scheil 1923: no. 292), and one of the largest examples of early writing from anywhere in the world. This fragmentary account, which originally would have had some 300–400 entries, deals presumably with the monthly rations for small groups of what we assume are dependent workers. These groups are not unlike those described above found in Scheil (1923: no. 112), but they include variants of a sign believed to be akin to TUR in Mesopotamian cuneiform (M370b), and which thus probably refers to children (Damerow and Englund 1989: 57 and n. 156; Englund 2004: 124 and fig. 5.14; Dahl 2005a: §4.4). Whereas Scheil (1923: no. 112) lists numbers of individuals of different categories, Scheil (1923: no. 292) adds amounts of M288, most likely a grain product, counted in the capacity system ŠE. Based on the relationship between amounts of M288 and numbers of workers classified by either of the signs M388 (KUR_a) or M124 (~ TI), it can be suggested that the text covers, roughly, one month (see Desset 2011: 261–2; but note that either the value of the basic capacity sign N30c was twice as big as the Mesopotamian counterpart or rations in Iran were half the size of the Mesopotamian ones; see Damerow and Englund 1989: 27). Several shorter texts (e.g., Scheil 1935: nos. 4773, 4783, and 4802) employ the same relationship between what appears to be workers and rations. These last three texts are part

Scheil 1935: no 4773   Scheil 1935: no 4783   Scheil 1935: no 4802

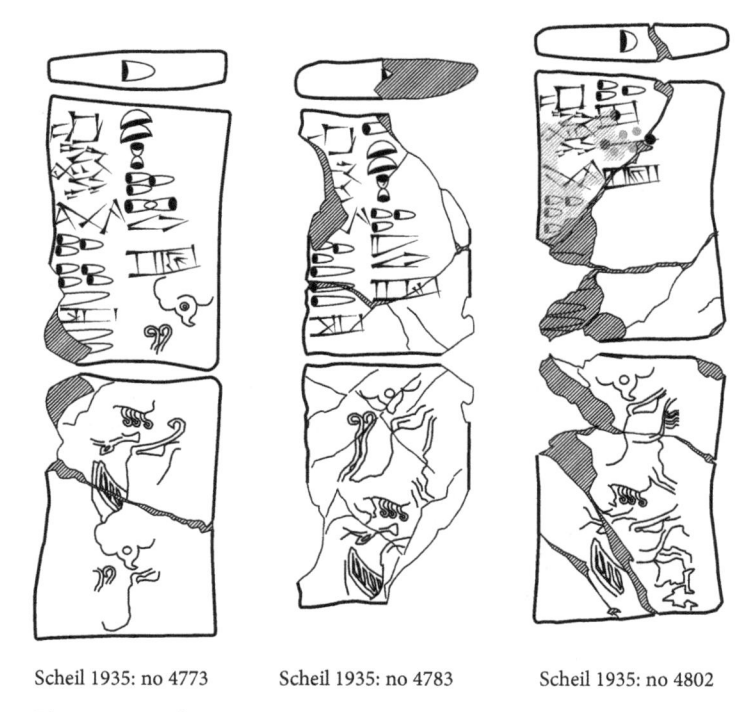

FIGURE 13.5 Three proto-Elamite texts concerning monthly rations for teams of field workers (drawing at 75 percent of original).

of a group of about eleven texts with similar content that are all sealed with the same seal (no. 329 in Legrain 1921, not included in Amiet 1972). Damerow and Englund (1989: 57, n. 159) speculated that they could be rations for small teams of field workers. All of these texts have an inscription on the top edge of a single numerical sign (N34), which may indicate the time period covered by the transaction recorded in the text (see above).

The key text Sb 2801, mentioned above, that most commentators have suggested represents a very high-level document, appears to total the equivalent of almost precisely 100 day-rations for dependent workers for one year (or more than 25,000 liters). This may somehow relate to the odd fact that a common, high-ranking administrator title is written with the numerical sign for 100 (units in the decimal system). Other texts, such as Scheil (1923: nos. 81, 347) suggest that ten such administrators formed one unit. Perhaps Sb 2801 lists the rations for 100 workers associated with such a unit of ten administrators

Many texts list what appear to be dependent workers without detailing their rations. These texts are understood as inventories of staff. Among the more interesting such texts is one which long resisted analysis due to the many errors in the published copy (Scheil 1923: no. 112, briefly discussed above, and see http://cdli.ucla.edu/P008310). However, renewed collations by the author and Laura Hawkins in 2011 and 2012 clarified most uncertainties. This text is introduced by a header, presumably indicating the household to which the transactions that follow belong. The header is followed by twelve main entries, each with one or several subentries. Each main entry consists of a long string of signs, perhaps describing the subunit of the household or an individual, followed by a sign for a dependent worker (M317) of unknown quality. Most of the main entries are followed by several subentries listing further workers belonging to the main entry. One of the many peculiarities in this text is the usage within the same text of the sign M386a as both a numerical and a nonnumerical sign. M386a is a graphical variant of the numerical sign N1, distinguished by a stroke down the middle. N1 represents one unit in both the sexagesimal and the decimal system. M386a is therefore identical to N2 in Mesopotamia, which it has been suggested was used for dead animals and was the precursor to the sign BAD with the later readings uš$_2$/ug$_7$, "dead or slaughtered," in Sumerian (Damerow and Englund forthcoming); note that a proto-Elamite version of the Mesopotamian system S' has not been identified.

The signs for sheep and goat and some of the products obtained from these (Fig. 13.6) have been identified in the sign repertoire (Damerow and Englund 1989: 53–5; Dahl 2005b). These animals were probably the most important, economically, to the population of Susa and the other cities using the proto-Elamite writing, as evidenced by zoo-archaeological data (for prehistoric highland Fars [Tal-e Bakun] see Alizadeh 2006: 23, 65, and 103–5; for Tal-e Malyan see Zeder 1991: 137 and table 26; but note that the textual record suggests that goat was favored over sheep; see Dahl 2005b: 101–2). However, judging from the archaeological evidence, they were not the only animals herded during this time. Both the archaeological and glyptic records suggest that cows were herded in no small numbers. However, neither texts nor terminology related to cow herding or products from this trade have been identified so far. It is perhaps less surprising that we have not been able to identify the signs for pigs and pig-herding since the pig was often herded in marginal circumstances escaping state accounting. Cow herding, on the other hand, was normally closely managed by the state in comparable societies. Sheep and goats were presumably herded for meat, dairy products, and secondary products such as hides, horns, and tendons. Two Susa texts (Scheil 1923: nos. 85 and 97) list eight different products obtained from sheep and goat herding, but only four of these have been identified. These are in all likelihood dried cheese and clarified butter from either sheep or goats milk. The products were differentiated with regard to the origin of the raw dairy product. Cheese and clarified butter from goats milk were written with signs with extra strokes. These identifications were made using both production rates and comparisons with Uruk signs and bookkeeping procedures (Dahl 2005b, 2009).

One very famous text (Scheil 1923: no. 105) lists a number of owners and their animals (the text is fragmentary, but should be compared to Scheil 1923: 96+, a similar text dealing with herds of sheep and goat). The signs for the animals are animal heads. The shape of these signs remains the only evidence for herding equids in the proto-Elamite texts. There is no evidence of equids used for traction, for example.

The only good candidate for record keeping concerning wild animals is a Susa text (Mecquenem 1949: no. 31) which lists exceedingly high numbers (probably 23,600) of an animal identified by a variant of the common sign used for billy goats (M367c). Such large numbers are otherwise unattested in the Susa records, and are therefore unlikely to represent the yearly cull of goat kids or similar, but could represent the harvest of wild

a) List of products in the texts Sb 22276 and 6353 (MDP 17, 85 and 97):

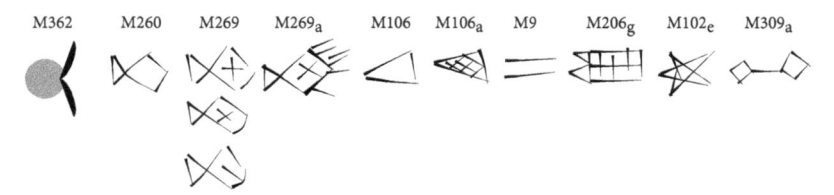

M362   M260   M269   M269$_a$ M106   M106$_a$ M9   M206$_g$ M102$_e$ M309$_a$

b) order of signs: products listed in order of importance
                            dairy products listed first

c) differentiation of signs: hatching indicate semantic variants
                            as in sheep and goats milk

d) comparison with the related   most basic shapes, and concepts (order and
    proto-cuneiform system: differentiation) identical in both systems

e) yield ratios: fixed production rates (corroborated using
                                comparative data):

                         1   :   1

                 M362, 1N$_1$ M111$_a$, 1N$_{30c}$

"one nanny (delivering) 2 liters of dry cheese (per year)"

f) proposed decipherment:

Product Base	Butter oil		Dry cheese	
	Susa	Uruk	Susa	Uruk
Sheep's milk	M260	KISIM$_a$	M106	GA'AR$_a$
Goat's milk	M269(a)	KISIM$_b$	M106$_a$	(only attested for dairy cattle)

FIGURE 13.6 Sheep and goat and the secondary products they provided in proto-Elamite.

gazelle, for example, using hunting techniques such as driving animal herds over a cliff or hunting with nets. Some other texts have signs that look like graphical representations of wild animals, but they are never counted objects (Dahl 2005b: 97 and fig. 11).

The disappearance of proto-Elamite

Proto-Elamite seems to have disappeared relatively shortly after its invention. Whereas many protocuneiform sign values are known through the later usages of these, the fact that proto-Elamite left no successor script has obviously obscured its decipherment. The collapse of the social system that created and sustained the use of the proto-Elamite script is seen as the most obvious reason for its disappearance, disregarding obvious signs of failure of the system itself. When the administrators at Susa adopted the new administrative technology we call protowriting from their neighbors in southern Mesopotamia they failed, however, to bring with them one, perhaps crucial, aspect of this new system, namely the scholarly tradition that at all times seems to have gone hand in hand with the often very practical applications of writing. Contrary to protocuneiform, which developed into cuneiform and thus lived on for more than three millennia, and did indeed become a communicative system, proto-Elamite was very short lived and left no trace in later writing system traditions in Iran. As the workings of the proto-Elamite writing system become clearer a high number of errors become visible. Many of the key texts used in this overview contain errors of the sort that would not occur in Mesopotamian texts of the same kind: an entry was forgotten in one case (Scheil 1923: no. 112) and squeezed in between two lines, and the scribe who wrote another (Scheil 1905: 316+) made crucial errors in the bundling of the totals. It may seem far fetched to try and connect the lack of standardization, the many errors, and the absence of any scholarly tradition to the rapid demise of this system, but it is hard to see how a system with so much inconsistency could have continued to function even without a general collapse of the social organizations sustaining it.

Linear-Elamite

A few dozen objects with inscriptions in a writing system obviously not related to cuneiform, but graphically remotely similar to proto-Elamite, were found during the early excavations at Susa (Glassner 2003: 57). The exact find locations are unknown but a majority may have been found in the same general part of the great trench where the Mesopotamian objects looted in the late second millennium by Shutruk-Nahhunte (e.g., the Code of Hammurapi and the Victory Stele of Naram-Sin) were found and where a number of "Elamite" statues were also found. Morgan seems to have excavated a monumental access route where sculptures would have been deposited over time. Unfortunately the excavation reports do not allow us to understand much of the topography of this vital part of ancient Susa. Eleven linear Elamite inscriptions were found on bricks from the steps of a monumental staircase and sculpture associated with it; nine more were found on a few minor objects and clay or gypsum tablets at different locations at Susa. Following the 1966 discovery of a silver beaker with a linear-Elamite inscription, apparently near Persepolis (see Hinz 1969 for a description of the circumstances of discovery; cf. Potts 2008 for this vessel and a similar one from Gonur Tepe in Turkmenistan; note that the Gonur vessel is without an inscription), several more silver vases with linear-Elamite inscriptions have appeared on the art market. The linear-Elamite texts are numbered A–Z (André and Salvini 1989; CDLI http://cdli.

ucla.edu subperiod "linear Elamite"). Sixteen texts were published in various MDP volumes (see the list in Mecquenem 1949: 5 and the catalog in Hinz 1969: 28) (A–P); the Persepolis silver vessel, labeled Q, was published by Hinz (1969), who also published a small tablet fragment from Susa in the Louvre and now labelled R (drawing by P. Amiet; Hinz 1969: 43). In 1971 Hinz published one further text (S, see below; Hinz 1971). B. André and M. Salvini published two further fragments in the Louvre (T and U) in 1989 (André and Salvini 1989: 58ff.). Text V (Winkelmann 1999; Laursen 2010) appears on what looks like a seal (with Indus affinities). A preliminary publication of X, Y, and Z appeared several years ago (Mahboubian 2004: 50–5), and the whereabouts of W are unknown (for an image, see http://cdli.ucla.edu/P332981).

The corpus can meaningfully be divided into three groups according to material and origin. The first group consists of objects (bricks, statuary) relating to the monumental structure discussed above. The text on all of these objects is virtually identical (noted already by Frank 1912: 32; 1923: 7; cf. Mecquenem 1949: 6–7; Dahl 2009: 27–8). The smaller objects found at Susa, but not necessarily associated with the staircase, can be grouped together based on their structural similarities, or dissimilarities depending on one's perspective. All of these objects have texts with very high numbers of singletons (signs occurring only once in the writing system). Finally the inscriptions on metal objects seem to form another discrete group showing little overlap with the other texts. The display texts can with some confidence be dated to the time of Puzur-Inshushinak (c.2100 BC), but it remains difficult to date any of the other inscriptions.

Despite the existence of a presumed bilingual (text A, first published in Scheil 1905)—a linear-Elamite text written adjacent to an Akkadian one—known for more than one hundred years, linear-Elamite remains undeciphered. Several attempts at decipherment have been made (e.g., Hinz 1962, 1969: 18–44; Meriggi 1969, 1971: 172–84; but see already Frank 1912: 32 and 1923: 7 for an approach closer to the one suggested by the author). However, no breakthrough has been achieved. The texts on all of the display objects from Susa are identical, but occasionally truncated, and with significant inconsistencies in the execution of identical signs. Furthermore, there appears to be no fixed direction of the writing. These features all suggest that linear-Elamite was not a system with a large corpus and an independent tradition of writing, but rather a limited system with few practitioners probably invented rather than organically developed, and most likely very short lived (Dahl 2009).

Although some of the signs in linear-Elamite show close affinity to signs in proto-Elamite it is very unlikely that the two writing systems are related. The main reason for this is the gap of time between the two writing systems during which not a single example of indigenous writing is known in Iran. Proto-Elamite can conservatively be dated to around 3200–3000 BC, perhaps as late as 2900 BC, whereas linear-Elamite is dated to around 2100 BC. Affinities in sign forms between the two systems can be explained without suggesting that one system was a successor of the other (Dahl 2012b).

It has been claimed that a few other objects from Iran have have linear-Elamite (or proto-Elamite) inscriptions on them. Most notable is a jar-rim from Shahdad (inscription S listed above). Although about half of the signs there have cognates in linear-Elamite, there is no reason to include it in the corpus of linear-Elamite inscriptions, as one can show the same overlap in sign forms with other systems such as potter's marks (Potts 1981; Dollfus and Encrevé 1982; Dahl 2009). More recently, objects with inscriptions said to be a new, but related, writing system have been discovered at Konar Sandal (Jiroft). These interesting objects await publication.

Further reading

For an overview of the world's writing systems, both ancient and modern, see Daniels and Bright (1996). A more detailed description of early writing systems and the question of script invention is Houston (2004). For a theoretical discussion of scripts and decipherments see Gelb (1952) and Sampson (1985). For a comprehensive introduction to early cuneiform see Nissen et al. (1993). The most detailed study of a group of proto-Elamite texts to date is Damerow and Englund (1989).

References

Adler, M. N. 1907. *The itinerary of Benjamin of Tudela: Critical text, translation and commentary*. London: Phillip Feldheim.

Alden, J. R. 1982. Trade and politics in proto-Elamite Iran. *CA* 23: 613–40.

Algaze, G. 1989. The Uruk expansion: Cross-cultural exchange in early Mesopotamian civilization. *CA* 30: 571–608.

———. 2005. The Sumerian takeoff: Structure and dynamics. *eJournal of Anthropological and Related Sciences* 1/1: article 1.

———. 2008. *Ancient Mesopotamia at the dawn of civilization: The evolution of an urban landscape*. Chicago/London: University of Chicago Press.

Alizadeh, A. 2006. *The origins of state organizations in prehistoric highland Fars, southern Iran: Excavations at Tall-e Bakun*. Chicago: OIP 128.

———. 2008. *Chogha Mish II: The development of a prehistoric regional center in lowland Susiana, southwestern Iran: Final report on the last six seasons of excavations, 1972–1978*. Chicago: OIP 130.

Amiaud, A., and L. Méchineau. 1887. *Tableau comparé des écritures babylonienne et assyrienne archaïques et modernes avec classement des signes d'après leur forme archaïque*. Paris: Ernest Leroux.

Amiet, P. 1972. *Glyptique Susienne: Des origines à l'époque des Perses achéménides. Cachets, sceaux-cylindres et empreintes antiques découverts à Suse de 1913 à 1967*, 2 vols. Paris: MDP 43.

André, B., and M. Salvini. 1989. Réflexions sur Puzur-Inšušinak. *IrAnt* 29: 3–78.

Brandes, M. 1979. *Siegelabrollungen aus den archaischen Bauschichten in Uruk-Warka*, 2 vols. Wiesbaden: FAOS 3.

Brice, W. C. 1962–3. The writing system of the Proto-Elamite account tablets of Susa. *Bulletin of the John Rylands Library* 45: 15–39.

———. 1963. A comparison of the account tablets of Susa in the Proto-Elamite script with those of Hagia Triada in Linear A. *Kadmos* 2: 27–38.
Collon, D. 1987. *First impressions: Cylinder seals in the Ancient Near East*. Chicago: University of Chicago Press.
Dahl, J. L. 2003. Proto-Elamite sign frequencies. *CDLB* 2002/1:1.
———. 2005a. Animal husbandry in Susa during the Proto-Elamite period. *SMEA* 47: 81–134.
———. 2005b. Complex graphemes in proto-Elamite. *CDLJ* 2005: 3.
———. 2009. Early writing in Iran, a reappraisal. *Iran* 47: 23–31.
———. 2012a. New and old joins in the Louvre proto-Elamite tablet collection. *CDLN* 2012: 6.
———. 2012b. The marks of early writing. *Iran* 50: 1–12.
Dahl, J. L., C. A. Petrie, and D. T. Potts. 2013. Chronological parameters of the earliest writing system in Iran. *AIN*: 353–78.
Damerow, P. 2006. The origins of writing as a problem of historical epistemology. *CDLJ* 2006: 1.
Damerow, P., and R. K. Englund. 1989. *The proto-Elamite texts from Tepe Yahya*. Cambridge: ASPR Bulletin 39.
———. Forthcoming. *The proto-cuneiform texts from the Erlenmeyer Collection*. Berlin: Materialien zu den frühen Schriftzeugnissen des Vorderen Orients 3.
Daniels, P. T., and W. Bright. 1996. *The world's writing systems*. New York: Oxford University Press.
Desset, F. 2011. Éléments d'archéologie du Plateau iranien, de la 2ème motié du 4ème au début du 2ème millénaire av. J.-C. (ca. 3500–1800 av. J.-C.). Unpublished PhD diss., University of Paris I.
Dieulafoy, J. 1888. *A Suse: Journal des fouilles, 1884–1886*. Paris: Hachette.
Dollfus, G., and P. Encrevé. 1982. Marques sur poteries dans la Susiane du Ve millénaire: Réflections et comparaisons. *Paléorient* 8/1: 107–115.
Dyson, R. H., Jr. 1968. Early work on the Acropolis at Susa: The beginning of prehistory in Iraq and Iran. *Expedition* 10/4: 21–34.
Englund, R. K. 1994. *Archaic administrative texts from Uruk: The early campaigns*. Berlin: Archaische Texte aus Uruk 5.
———. 1998. Texts from the Late Uruk Period. In *Späturuk-Zeit und frühdynastische Zeit*, ed. P. Attinger and M. Wäfler, 15–233. Göttingen: OBO 160/1.
———. 2004. The state of decipherment of Proto-Elamite. In *The first writing: Script invention as history and process*, ed. S. D. Houston, 100–149. Cambridge: Cambridge University Press.
———. 2005. review of J.-J. Glassner, *The invention of cuneiform: Writing in Sumer*. *JAOS* 125: 113–6.
———. 2006. An examination of the "textual" witnesses to Late Uruk world systems. In *A collection of papers on Ancient Civilizations of Western Asia, Asia Minor and North Africa*, ed Y. Gong and Y. Chen, 1–38. Beijing: Oriental Studies.
Falkenstein, A. 1936. *Archaische Texte aus Uruk*. Berlin/Leipzig: Harrassowitz.
Frank, C. 1912. *Zur Entzifferung der altelamischen Inschriften*. Berlin: Verlag der Königl. Akademie der Wissenschaften.
———. 1923. *Die altelamischen Steininschriften*. Berlin: Verlag Karl Curtius.
Friberg, J. 1978-9. *The third millennium roots of Babylonian mathematics, I–II*. Göteborg: University of Göteborg, Department of Mathematics.
———. 1997-8. Round and almost round numbers in proto-literate metro-mathematical field texts. *AfO* 44/45: 1–58.

Gelb, I. J. 1952. *A study of writing: The foundations of grammatology*. London: Routledge and Kegan Paul.

Gelb, I. J., P. Steinkeller, and R. W. Whiting. 1991. *Earliest land tenure systems in the Near East: Ancient kudurrus*. Chicago: OIP 104.

Gelb, I. J., and R. W. Whiting. 1975. Methods of decipherment. *JRAS*: 95–104.

Ghirshman, R. 1934. Une tablette proto-élamite du plateau iranien. *RA* 31: 115–19.

———. 1938–9. *Fouilles de Sialk, près de Kashan, 1933, 1934, 1937*, 2 vols. Paris: Geuthner.

Glassner, J.-J. 1998. Les tablettes dites "urukéennes" de Sialk IV1. *NABU* 1998/113.

———. 2003. *The invention of cuneiform: Writing in Sumer*. Baltimore/London: The Johns Hopkins University Press.

Green, M. W., and H. J. Nissen. 1987. *Zeichenliste der Archaischen Texte aus Uruk*. Berlin: Archaische Texte aus Uruk 2.

Hallo, W. W. 2011. The Godin Period VI tablets. *OHR*: 116–18.

Hinz, W. 1969. *Altiranische Funde und Forschungen*. Berlin: De Gruyter.

———. 1971. Eine alt-elamische Tonkrug-Aufschrift vom Rande der Lut. *AMI* 4: 21–4.

———. 1972. Zur Entzifferung der elamischen Strichschrift. *IrAnt* 2: 1–21.

Houston, S. D. 2004. *The first writing: Script invention as history and process*. Cambridge: Cambridge University Press.

Lamberg-Karlovsky, C. C. 1986. Third millennium structure and process: From the Euphrates to the Indus and the Oxus to the Indian Ocean. *Oriens Antiquus* 25: 189–219.

Laursen, S. T. 2010. The westward transmission of Indus Valley sealing technology: Origin and development of the "Gulf type" seal and other administrative technologies in Early Dilmun, c. 2100–2000 BC. *AAE* 21: 96–134.

Le Brun, A. 1971. Recherches stratigraphiques à l'Acropole de Suse, 1969–1971. *CDAFI* 1: 163–216.

———. 1978. Le niveau 17B de l'Acropole de Suse (campagne de 1972). *CDAFI* 9: 57–154.

Legrain, L. 1921. *Empreintes de cachets élamites*. Paris: MDP 16.

Lieberman, S. T. 1980. Of clay pebbles, hollow clay balls, and writings: A Sumerian view. *AJA* 84: 346–51.

Mahboubian, H. 2004. *Elam: Art and civilization of ancient Iran, 3000–2000 BC*. London: Mahboubian Gallery.

Mecquenem, R. de. 1949. *Epigraphie proto-élamite*. Paris: MMAI 31.

———. 1956. Notes protoélamites. *RA* 50: 200–4.

Meriggi, P. 1969. Altsumerische und proto-elamische Bilderschrift. *ZDMG* 119/1: 156–63.

———. 1971. *La scrittura proto-Elamica. Parte Ia: La scrittura e il contenuto dei testi*. Rome: Accademia Nazionale dei Lincei.

———. 1974a. *La scrittura proto-elamica. Parte IIa: Catalogo dei segni*. Rome: Accademia Nazionale dei Lincei.

———. 1974b. *La scrittura proto-elamica*. Parte IIIa: *Testi*. Rome: Accademia Nazionale dei Lincei.

Michalowski, P. 1993. Review: Tokenism. *American Anthropologist* 95: 996–9.

Morgan, J. de. 1900. *Recherches archéologiques*. Paris: MDP 1.

Nissen H. J., P. Damerow, and R. K. Englund. 1993. *Archaic bookkeeping: Early writing and techniques of economic administration in the ancient Near East*. Chicago/London: University of Chicago Press.

Nissen, H. J. 2001. Cultural and political networks in the Ancient Near East during the fourth and third millennia B.C. In *Uruk Mesopotamia & its neighbors: Cross-cultural Interactions in the era of state formation*, ed. M. S. Rothman, 149–79. Santa Fe: School of American Research.

———. 2011. Schule vor der Schrift. In *The empirical dimension of Ancient Near Eastern Studies/ Die empirische Dimension altorientalischer Forschungen*, ed. G. J. Selz and K. Wagensonner, 589–602. Vienna: Wiener Offene Orientalistik 6.

Oppenheim, A. L. 1959. On an operational device in Mesopotamian bureaucracy. *JNES* 18: 121–8.

Pittman, H. 1992. Proto-Elamite seals and sealings. *RCS*: 70–7.

———. 1997. The administrative function of glyptic art in Proto-Elamite Iran: A survey of the evidence. In *Sceaux d'Orient et leur emploi*, ed. R. Gyselen, 133–61. Bures-sur-Yvette: RO 10.

Potts, D. T. 1981. The potter's marks of Tepe Yahya. *Paléorient* 7/1: 107–22.

———. 1999. *The archaeology of Elam: Formation and transformation of an ancient Iranian state*. Cambridge: Cambridge University Press.

———. 2008. Puzur-Inšušinak and the Oxus Civilization (BMAC): Reflections on Šimaški and the geopolitical landscape of Iran and Central Asia in the Ur III period. *ZA* 98/2: 165–94.

Salvatori, S., M. Tosi, and M. Vidale. 2001. Crocevia dell'Asia. L'Iran orientale e l'evoluzione delle civiltà protostoriche ad oriente della Mesopotamia. In *Antica Persia, I Tresori del Museo Nazionale di Tehran e la Ricerca Italiana en Iran*, ed. A. Gramiccia, 32–7. Rome: Edizioni de Luca.

Sampson, G. 1985. *Writing systems: A linguistic introduction*. Palo Alto: Stanford University Press.

Scheil, V. 1898. *Recueil de signes archaïques de l'écriture cunéiforme*. Paris: H. Welter.

———. 1900. *Textes élamites-sémitiques, première série*. Paris: MDP 2.

———. 1905. *Documents archaïques en écriture proto-élamite*. Paris: MDP 6.

———. 1923. *Textes de comptabilité proto-élamites*. Paris: MDP 17.

———. 1935. *Texte de comptabilité*. Paris: MDP 26.

Schmandt-Besserat, D. 1992. *Before writing*, 2 vols. Austin: University of Texas Press.

Shendge, M. J. 1983. The use of seals and the invention of writing. *JESHO* 26: 113–36.

Steinkeller, P. 1993. Early political development in Mesopotamia and the origins of the Sargonic Empire. In *Akkad, the first world empire*, ed. M. Liverani, 107–29. Rome/Padua: Herder Editrice e Libreria.

Steve, M.-J., F. Vallat, and H. Gasche. 2003. La découverte de Suse: Les données archéologiques. *SDB* 73: 375–403.

Stolper, M. W. 1985. Proto-Elamite texts from Tall-I Malyan. *Kadmos* 24: 1–12.

Vallat, F. 2003. Un fragment de tablette proto-élamite découvert à Ozbaki, au nord-ouest de Téhéran. *Akkadica* 124: 229–31.

Van Driel, G. 1982. Tablets from Jebel Aruda. In *Zikir šumim: Assyriological studies presented to F.R. Kraus on the occasion of his seventieth birthday*, ed. G. Van Driel, T. J. H. Krispijn, M. Stol and K. R. Veenhof, 12–25. Leiden: Studia Francisci Scholten memoriae dicata 5.

Wagensonner, K. 2010. Early lexical lists revisited: Structures and classification as a mnemonic device. In *Language in the Ancient Near East: Proceedings of the 53e Rencontre Assyriologique Internationale*, vol. 1/1, ed. L. Kogan, N. Koslova, et al., 285–310. Winona Lake: Eisenbrauns [= Babel und Bibel 4A].

Weiss, H. and T. C. Young Jr. 1975. The merchants of Susa: Godin V and plateau-lowland relations in the late fourth millennium B.C. *Iran* 13: 1–17.

Whitcomb, D. S. 1971. The Proto-Elamite period at Tall-i Ghazir, Iran. Unpublished MA thesis, University of Georgia.

Winkelmann, S. 1999. Ein Stempelsiegel mit alt-Elamischer Strichschrift. *AMIT* 31: 23–32.

Zeder, M. 1991. *Feeding cities: Specialized animal economy in the Ancient Near East*. Washington: Smithsonian Institution Press.

CHAPTER 14

THE USE OF AKKADIAN IN IRAN

KATRIEN DE GRAEF

INTRODUCTION

The use of Akkadian in Iran has never been studied as a whole, either from the perspective of the textual corpus or from that of the language itself and the changes it might have undergone in its country of adoption. This overview aims to present what is known on both counts, taking the denomination Akkadian as a general term, covering all stages of the language in Mesopotamia. It is clear to anyone who has come into contact with the ancient civilizations of Iran that this was a multilingual society with an evolving use of and proportion between different languages: Elamite, Sumerian, Akkadian, Old Persian, and no doubt a number of other old Iranian languages that were never written down. This multilingualism is most apparent in the part of Iran that is closest to its equally ancient Mesopotamian neighbor, because this is a region where languages came in contact with each other and where writing appeared very early on. It was mainly in this region that Akkadian documents were found but I shall discuss a few other places as well.

As to the textual corpus, I shall distinguish two types of sources: royal inscriptions and economic–administrative–juridical texts. Clearly the choice of language in both groups of texts can be prompted by very different motives. Kings can conform to the at times dominant Mesopotamian culture and language or they may want to express their own cultural identity in contrast to it. The higher strata of society who had archives with economic, administrative, and juridical texts could follow the ready-made Mesopotamian models, adapt them to their own usage and needs, or replace them altogether with Elamite ones. Since history is never a straight, linear development, changing fortunes of dynasties and empires and changing relations with the outside world are reflected in changing choices of languages. This means that, although in a very general way one can observe a "semitization" (meaning a growing dominance of Akkadian over Elamite) during the first part of the second millennium BC and an "elamitization" during the second part of this and the first millennium, this picture is in need of specification and differentiation. Although this is an undertaking far beyond the scope of this overview, I shall try to give indications here and there along the way.

A note must be added concerning the writing systems used. Mesopotamian cuneiform is in part logographic, which means that it is not always possible, especially in very short inscriptions or seal legends, to determine whether it is to be read in Sumerian or Akkadian. Two different writing systems were used to render Elamite. A short-lived linear writing was replaced after some time by Mesopotamian cuneiform which then slowly started to differentiate itself in Iran from the Mesopotamian original.

On a practical level, I shall refer to inscriptions by citing their most recent publication; all absolute dates given in this article follow the short chronology (Gasche et al. 1998).

Old Akkadian domination (Old Elamite period IB, c.2200–2020 BC)

Gelb and Kienast (1990: 34) mention one inscription on a ceramic vessel (their VP 16; original publication Scheil 1905: 1). Its three lines are so damaged that only an NI and part of an IM are legible on the second line and part of an ÉNSI sign on the third line. Scheil had originally read UR-*i*-[*li*]-ʿ*im*ʾ, which would mean that this is an inscription in Akkadian—the oldest one to date—but Gelb and Kienast doubt the UR which puts the whole reading of the name in doubt.

The conquest of Susa and Elam by Sargon of Akkad and their integration into the Old Akkadian Empire not only brought a number of Akkadian speaking officials, administrators, and military personnel to the region (Potts 1999: 111) but also resulted in the use of the official language of the kingdom in economic and administrative documents (cf. Stolper 1992). The main reason for this was doubtless the fact that the administration and economy were now run according to the Old Akkadian model and Akkadian terminology had to be used (Foster 1982b). A group of about eighty-five Old Akkadian administrative, economic, and juridical texts from Susa (Scheil and Legrain 1913: 61–133) show that transactions were noted with Old Akkadian cuneiform in the Akkadian language. The presence of some private contracts and letters, also in Akkadian, shows that Akkadian models also penetrated further into (at least) the higher circles of Susian society. Further proof of this Akkadization is the fact that, according to Zadok (1991: 225), many personal names were Akkadian, clearly also among Elamites.

The only proof of building activity by the Old Akkadian kings are two brick fragments of Narām-Sîn found at Susa (Scheil 1900: 56, pl. 13, no. 1; Malbran-Labat 1995: no. 1). These are inscribed on their sides with a rather rare title of Narām-Sîn: he is called king of Ur, not Agade. Unfortunately, the name of the building from which these bricks came is not preserved.

Although it is certain that Akkadian was the language used by the kings, their representatives, and the scribes of the administration, this is not always immediately apparent in the inscriptions because of the frequent use of logograms. I shall cite the inscriptions in which at least some syllabically written Akkadian words appear, attesting to the use of this language in the written record.

Inscriptions of administrators, found at Susa, attest to the presence of an Akkadian, or at least Akkadian-led bureaucratic organization. The well-known high and influential official Suaš-takal (Westenholz 1987: 55), scribe and majordomo (šabra é), dedicated a statue to ᵈNIN.KIŠ.UNU (perhaps Erra, see Steinkeller 1987: 164, n. 18a) for the life of Narām-Sîn (Frayne 1993: E2.1.4.2002). The inscription is fifteen lines long and mostly in syllabic Akkadian.

Ešpum was governor of Elam under Maništušu, as we learn from an inscribed statue. The inscription has a typical formulary: "Maništušu king of Kiš: Ešpum, his servant (ìr-sú), has dedicated (this statue) to (a-na) Narundi" (for this interpretation of ìr.ZU see Frayne 1992: 622). His seal (Frayne 1993: E2.16.1 with previous literature), the legend of which calls him governor (ensí) of Elam, is also known. He is also mentioned in the legend on the seal of his majordomo: Egigi/šabra é/ir₁₁/Ešpum (Frayne 1993: E2.16.1.2001). As is usual for seal legends, their inscriptions are completely logographic (except of course for the names).

Inscriptions of two more governors are known: Epirmupi, a "military governor" (gìr. níta), is called "the mighty" (da-núm) in the seal legends of ME.DU and Libūr-bēli, his "servants" (ìr-sú) (Frayne 1993 E2.16.2.2001 and 2002). Ilišmani is called scribe and military governor of the land (ma-ti) of Elam on a bronze axe found at Susa (Frayne 1993 E2.16.3). M. Lambert proposed the sequence Ešpum, Epirmupi, and Ilišmani for these officials (Lambert 1979).

Under Šar-kali-šarri, Susa seems to have been a part of the province of Girsu-Umma, and some of the Old Akkadian texts found at Susa might stem from the "official records of the imperial administration there" (Foster 1982b: 7).

Several stone mace-heads inscribed in Akkadian with the name of Narām-Sîn (*IRSA* IIA4q and r) and dedications to gods are known from Luristan. Also found in Luristan but from the end of the Akkadian period is an inscription of Elul-dan on a copper dagger and on a bronze cup (*IRSA* IIA6a) and one of Šū-turul (*IRSA* IIA8a). Both are very brief, which causes uncertainty as to the logographically written "Elul-dan, king of Akkade," but the "Šū-turul, strong one, king of Akkade" leaves no doubt because of the syllabic writing *da-núm*.

2. Freedom from Mesopotamia: Puzur-Inšušinak (?–c.2015 BC)

Puzur-Inšušinak is the first Elamite king of whom a sizable number of royal inscriptions are known. In all, there are twelve inscriptions of his, all from Susa. All are in Akkadian but three also have a Linear Elamite text which was probably devised by Puzur-Inšušinak's scribes and disappeared with him (according to Meriggi 1971, the shape of these signs was derived from the proto-Elamite but cf. Chapter 13). Puzur-Inšušinak is called king of Awan in one of his inscriptions (our no. 7 below) and in the Susa king list in which he appears as the last in the Awanite dynasty (Gelb and Kienast 1990: 316). He also took the titles governor (énsi) of Susa, until then used by the representatives of the Akkadian kings, and military governor (gìr.níta) of Elam. In the Elamite texts of his inscriptions he is *sunkik halmeak*, "king of the land" (our no. 3 below) and *halmenik Šušīm*[ki], "sovereign of Susa" (our nos. 3, 9, and 11 below). Thus a correspondence between the Akkadian and Elamite titles can be assumed. At the height of his power he set out to conquer northern Babylonia but there his ambitions were stopped by Ur-Namma, founder of the Ur III kingdom. His origins and career are still a matter of debate: was he an original Susian, as his name seems to imply, or did he come from Awan or even Anšan? Was he originally in the service of the Akkadian kings before gaining his independence? (The arguments are conveniently summarized in Potts 1999: 122–4).

Steve et al. (2002-3: 427–8) reconstruct the following sequence of events. Puzur-Inšušinak started out as king of Awan, conquered Susa as mighty king of Awan, and then called himself ensí of the city. He then took Anšan and called himself gìr.níta of Elam. Finally he conquered a major part of Babylonia and the adjoining Diyala Region but was stopped by Ur-Namma; the final blow was landed by Gudea of Lagaš. Most recently, Steinkeller (2013) reconsidered this episode in early Elamite history, showing the huge scale of Puzur-Inšušinak's conquests—from Awan and the Zagros territories as far as the Hamadan plain in the east and part of Babylonia and the adjoining Diyala region in the northwest—that resulted in his hegemony over the entire western section of the Iranian plateau, including the incorporation of Susiana into Elam. As such, Puzur-Inšušinak's empire, though short-lived, gave impetus to the formation of the Šimaškian state some decades later. With Puzur-Inšušinak's fall, the Ur III kings took over and reimposed the Mesopotamian model, writing, and language.

The phase in which Elamite inscriptions were added to the Akkadian ones can be examined further in light of the twelve inscriptions of Puzur-Inšušinak. These are as follows:

1. Part of a sitting statue (Gelb and Kienast 1990: 321–4, Elam 2) with an inscription of 113 lines. The same text also seems to have been written on a stele (Gelb and Kienast 1990: 321, Text B), two fragments of which were found but later stolen. The inscription calls Puzur-Inšušinak governor (énsi) of Susa, military governor (gìr.níta) of Elam, and son of Šimpi-išhuk. It reports that he subdued a rebellion, took eighty-one cities in one day, and received the submission of the king of Šimaški.
2. Another inscription on a stele (Gelb and Kienast 1990: 325–8, Elam 3). It has eighty-five lines and describes Puzur-Inšušinak's embellishment of the Inšušinak temple, his votive offerings and dedication of precious objects, and his opening of a canal to Sidari. According to the inscription, he was governor (énsi) of Susa, military governor (gìr.níta) of Elam.
3. A stone block decorated with the head of a lion facing a god holding a foundation

peg followed by a Lama goddess bears a twenty-six-line inscription concerning the dedication of such a peg, with a curse on anyone who would remove the inscription. The top of the block shows part of a snake. The block also has an inscription in Linear Elamite, only five lines long, in which the name of the king is thought by some scholars to read Kutik-Inšušinak. Steve et al. (2002–3: 427) cast doubt on this, without further explanation, although Gelb and Kienast (1990: 329) had no problem with it. Steinkeller (2013) argues that the Elamite reading of Puzur-Inšušinak's name as Kutik-Inšušinak is unwarranted since the Linear Elamite remains undeciphered. Puzur-Inšušinak's titles here are "king of the land" (*sunkik halmeak*) and "sovereign of Susa" (*halmenik Šušim*). The Elamite version is no simple translation of the Akkadian one and does not contain a curse formula (Gelb and Kienast 1990: 328–9, Elam 4). According to the inscription, he was governor (énsi) of Susa, military governor (gìr.níta) of Elam.

4–5. Parts of two statuettes in alabaster have very similar inscriptions, with dedications to two different gods by Puzur-Inšušinak (Gelb and Kienast 1990: 329–31, Elam 5–6). According to the inscription, he was governor (énsi) of Susa, military governor (gìr.níta) of Elam.

6–7. Parts of stairs (as described in the inscription) on which Puzur-Inšušinak is called the strong one (*da-núm*) and king (lugal) of Awan. Dedication of the staircase to Inšušinak and curse formula. On one of the stair fragments the complete inscription in twenty-five lines is preserved; on the other only nineteen lines remain (Gelb and Kienast 1990: 332–4, Elam 7–8).

8. Clay pegs with a foundation inscription of the temple of the god ŠU.GU (Gelb and Kienast 1990: 334–5, Elam 9). According to the inscription, Puzur-Inšušinak was governor (énsi) of Susa, military governor (gìr.níta) of Elam.

9. A small statue of a headless goddess bears an Elamite inscription followed by an Akkadian one. The latter, nine lines long, is a dedication to Narunte by Puzur-Inšušinak, governor of Susa (the title gìr.níta is not added), with a plea to hear his request. The Elamite one has five lines: Kutik-Inšušinak calls himself inheritor of the territory (*halmenik*) of Susa and also addresses a plea to Narunte for help. Again, these are not literal translations of each other (Gelb and Kienast 1990: 336, Elam 10).

10. Door socket with a short inscription: Puzur-Inšušinak governor of Susa (the title gìr.níta is not added) (Gelb and Kienast 1990: 336–7, Elam 11).

11. Fragment of a small alabaster statue with a Linear Elamite inscription in which Kutik-Inšušinak calls himself inheritor (*halmenik*) of Susa, dedicates the statue, and calls himself victorious and son of Šimpi-hišhuk. The four Akkadian lines following this contain only the curse (Gelb and Kienast 1990: 337, Elam 12)

12. Bas-relief of a lion. The broken inscription does not preserve a name or titles, but on the basis of the formulas used it is ascribed to Puzur-Inšušinak. The seventeen lines contain only a curse and a plea to an (unnamed) god for help (Gelb and Kienast 1990: 337–8, Elam 13).

Potts (1999: 124) sees the bilingual inscriptions as an effort to integrate the highland and lowland regions to which Puzur-Inšušinak laid claim. This may well be so but, as stated above, the Elamite inscriptions are never a pure translation of the Akkadian ones. It is clear that an Elamite oral tradition of royal epithets existed, and when Puzur-Inšušinak wanted to put these in writing, the link between the cuneiform writing system and the Old Akkadian language was felt to be so strong that it could not be used to do this. It is interesting to note that advantage could have been taken of the logographic use of the cuneiform writing to render Elamite, just as it could express Akkadian or Sumerian, but this was not done. When Puzur-Inšušinak wanted to write Elamite he devised a new writing system, no doubt also as a graphic expression of Elamite identity. It is remarkable that his name had an Akkadian and an Elamite form: *puzur*/kutik (but recall the questions surrounding this reading, noted above). Either the Elamite was the original, which was Akkadianized when written in Akkadian inscriptions, or he translated his original Akkadian name in Elamite as an expression of his elamiteness.

As to the contents of the inscriptions, it is clear that there was no Elamite tradition of adding a curse on anyone who would remove the inscription since there was no earlier Elamite tradition of writing down royal inscriptions. This is obvious in no. 3 and especially in no. 11 where a curse in Akkadian was added to an otherwise completely Elamite text. Why Elamite texts were added on some of his inscriptions and not on others cannot be determined.

Ur III domination (Old Elamite period II, c.2015–1930 BC)

The conquest and subsequent integration of Susa and Susiana into the Ur III kingdom left only one royal inscription, about fifty economic documents from Susa, and an unknown number from Anšan.

Some of the royal inscriptions of the Ur III kings were written in Akkadian, no doubt a reflection of their Old Akkadian antecedents, and executed in the Old Akkadian style of writing. One of these is an inscribed brick of Šulgi's commemorating his victory over Kimaš and Ḫurtum and the digging of a ditch. Although bought on the antiquities market, its contents suggest it came from Susa (Frayne 1997: E3/2.1.2.33). The important point is that, if we accept the suggested provenance, this is a unique attestation of the continued, albeit reduced use of Old Akkadian language and writing for royal inscriptions in Iran.

A small number of administrative and economic documents dating to this period were found at Susa. A group of thirty-eight dating to the end of the Ur III period were excavated by Ghirshman in Chantier B of the Ville Royale and published in 2005 (De Graef 2005). Another eleven Ur III texts from Susa have been identified by the author in the previously published material (De Graef 2005: chapter 4; cf. Scheil 1908, 1930a, 1939; Dossin 1927).

Tal-e Malyan (ancient Anšan), the capital of the Šimaškian confederation, yielded numerous (precise number unknown) Ur III and Old Babylonian documents (Sumner 2003), most probably in Sumerian/Akkadian. Nothing more can be said about them since they are as yet unpublished.

Four rock reliefs, the oldest of this type, probably all of Anubanini, king of the Lullubi, were discovered at Sar-e Pol-e Zohab. The king is identified in the accompanying Akkadian inscriptions. He is to be dated to the very end of the Ur III or the beginning of the Old Babylonian period (Gelb and Kienast 1990: 373–7, Varia 6 and 7). The Akkadian used is later than Old Akkadian as exemplified by the use of signs with a /š/. Another Lullubum rock relief with an inscription in Akkadian is that of a certain ... irbirini, son of Ikkipšaḫmat, celebrating his annexation of the land of Awan (*IRSA* IIIG2a). The Lullubi, a people without a written tradition, took over Mesopotamian models to perpetuate the names and glorious deeds of the most successful of their kings and in order to do so they chose to write in Akkadian, the dominant language in Mesopotamia at that time.

During both the Old Akkadian and Ur III periods the Mesopotamian model of writing and choice of languages was followed. Just as in Mesopotamia itself, after the fall of the Ur III dynasty, Sumerian was replaced by Akkadian for documentary texts.

THE ŠIMAŠKIAN KINGDOM AND SUKKALMAH REGIME (OLD ELAMITE PERIOD III, C.1930–1450 BC)

Recent research has shown that after the Šimaškians expelled the Sumerians from Susiana, regained control of their territories and annexed Susa, a state structure with a king, sukkalmahs, and sukkals came into being. I therefore suggest deleting what we have called up to now the Šimaški dynasty as a period between the Ur III occupation and the Sukkalmah period at Susa. The Šimaški kings ruled both during and after the Ur III occupation: during the Ur III period they reigned over their territories under the authority of or in alliance with the Sumerian kings; after they expelled the Sumerians, they expanded their territory and instituted the Sukkalmah system (De Graef 2012, forthcoming a).

When the Ur III domination came to an end the Elamites even conquered parts of Mesopotamia, including the city of Ur itself. After they withdrew they continued to use Mesopotamian models in their administration and economy as well as for private contracts and letters. In this period the Akkadian language clearly dominated in all kinds of texts, as well as in the onomastics of Susa (Zadok 1991: 225).

Sources

Royal inscriptions

The first king of Šimaški of whom we have an inscription is Idattu I or Idattu-Inšušinak. The inscription is in Akkadian on a limestone basin. He declares that he rebuilt the wall of Susa and dedicated the basin to the god Inšušinak (*IRSA* IVO1a). Idattu I, king of Anšan and king of Šimaški and Elam, is also mentioned in a Sumerian inscription preserved in duplicate on two bronze vessels of unknown provenance. This inscription identifies him as the son of Kindattu and the grandson of Ebarat I. The bronze vessels were fashioned for him by his servant, Kiten-rakittapi, who was Sukkalmah of Elam and *teppir* (scribe, chancellor) (Steinkeller 2007: 221–2).

The fact that Idattu I used Akkadian for at least one of his inscriptions stands in contrast to his son Tan-ruhurater (who married Me-Kubi, daughter of Bilalama of Ešnunna) who used only Sumerian on his bricks commemorating his building of the temple of Inanna at Susa (Malbran-Labat 1995: nos. 24–7), as did his wife (Frayne 1990: E4.5.3.4). Our view may be distorted by the scarcity of the sources: both Idattu I and Tan-ruhurater may have had inscriptions in both Sumerian and Akkadian. But the situation is even more complicated. All of the known inscriptions of Tan-ruhurater's father-in-law, Bilalama, as well as the seal inscriptions of Bilalama's servants, excavated at Ešnunna (mod. Tell Asmar), are in Akkadian. In contrast, all of the inscriptions of his daughter and one of her servants, excavated at Susa, are in Sumerian. Clearly, she was Akkadian speaking and the use of Sumerian by the Šimaški rulers was a conscious choice. This is also apparent in their use (albeit scarce) of year formulae in Sumerian after the Mesopotamian model (De Graef 2008).

This seems to be less true of the contemporary or slightly later local ruler in Susa, Atta-hušu, who is attested in eight inscriptions from his own time (two seal legends in which he is mentioned are not relevant here because of their purely logographic nature; cf. De Graef 2009, 2012), most of which are in Akkadian (for the dating of Atta-hušu's reign at the beginning of the Sukkalmahat, contemporary with king Ebarat II and his Sukkalmah Šilhaha, see De Graef 2006: chapter 4; 2009; 2012). Two sets of bricks mention his construction of a bridge (Malbran-Labat 1995: nos. 10, 12). A clay "lentil" or "bun" records his building of a temple (*IRSA* IVO6d) as does a clay cylinder (*IRSA* IVO6e). A brick fragment also bears an Akkadian inscription (Malbran-Labat 1995: no. 13). A bronze gunagi vessel and an axe were dedicated to him by his *teppir* Ibni-Adad (*IRSA* IVO6g and h). Two Sumerian inscriptions on a clay cylinder and on small ceramic vessels mention his building of yet more temples (*IRSA* IVO6a and Malbran-Labat 1995 no. 11).

The fact that Akkadian predominates over Sumerian reflects what was happening in Mesopotamia but could also be a reference to the period before the Ur III domination. Somewhat later, the Šimaškian king Idattu II still maintained this Sumerian–Akkadian bilingualism since he documented his building of a new wall for the Ekikununa on bricks in Sumerian (of which we have 179) and Akkadian (of which we only have twelve). The texts on bricks mentioning the building of the rampart of the Acropolis of Susa (*IRSA* IVO3b) and on a seal given to the *teppir* Kuk-simut (*IRSA* IVO3c) are in Sumerian. This again shows that the kings of Šimaški maintained strong, Sumerian-Akkadian bilingualism (cf. Malbran–Labat 1996).

Only a few inscriptions mention Ebarat II and Šilhaha. For Ebarat II there are two seal legends (*IRSA* IVO4a and b) which, due to their logographic nature, can be read in either Sumerian or Akkadian. Šilhaha is mentioned on these same seals and on a clay lentil in Sumerian (*IRSA* IVO5c).

Kuk-kirwaš had an inscription written on bricks according to which he restored the Acropolis of Susa and built a wall. No fewer than 144 of these bricks have been found (*IRSA* IVO11a). The use of the verb *utiš* ("he restored") shows they are to be read in Akkadian. The later king Šilhak-Inšušinak cited one of his Akkadian inscriptions at the beginning of another in Elamite (Malbran-Labat 1995: no. 49; the copy is mostly logographic but Malbran-Labat cites [p. 112] a much shorter variant inscription that was written completely in Akkadian syllabic writing [Steve 1987: no. 17]; the former was probably a literal copy of the original, the latter rendered the way it was read).

At Liyan, on the coast of the Persian Gulf, an alabaster base was found with a short Akkadian inscription of Simut-wartaš (without a title) dedicated to the goddess Kiririša (*IRSA* IVO7).

Siruktuh was the supposed author of an inscription on an alabaster stele (Farber 1974). The text is only partially preserved and we have only the first sign of the royal name, but the editor of the text, W. Farber, makes a convincing case for this identification. This is a most important document because it constitutes a turning point in the languages used for official inscriptions. The choice was no longer between Sumerian and Akkadian but between Akkadian and Elamite. This is most important because it is the first inscription we have in Elamite since the Old Akkadian period, when the so-called treaty of Narām-Sîn was written (*EKI*: no. 2).

With the next sukkalmah, Şiwepalarhuppak, a contemporary of Hammurabi of Babylon, this linguistic choice is confirmed. The only inscription we have of his is also in Elamite and comes from Susa (*EKI*: no. 3, in two fragments). E. Reiner cast doubt on the authenticity of this inscription, noting that the writing and language are similar to Middle Elamite and as such could have been written much later (Reiner 1969: 58). Although it was the only Elamite royal inscription of its time when Reiner expressed this view, the publication of the Elamite inscription of Siruktuh removes any obstacle to accepting its early date (Farber 1974).

From the reign of Temti-Agun comes an Akkadian inscription on bricks commemorating his building of a temple for Išme-Karab (Malbran-Labat 1995: no. 14). The word used for temple in this text is El. *siyan*, replacing the older É, to which an Akkadian accusative ending was added, making *si-a-nam*. The same text also uses the Elamite expression *amma haštuk*, gracious mother. Another inscription of Temti-Agun's in Akkadian is cited in a later inscription of Šilhak-Inšušinak (Scheil 1939: 69). Two inscriptions in Elamite have also been attributed to Temti-Agun (*EKI*: nos. 67 and 70C lists them as *incerta* but Vallat 1990: 137 attributes to him).

Kuk-našur II commissioned inscribed bricks stating that he built the high temple of the Acropolis of Inšušinak. Malbran-Labat (1995: 40) notes a return to a more logographic writing. Indeed, only the use of *šà* reveals that they are to be read in Akkadian. As noted above, Šilhak-inšušinak cited an inscription of his in Akkadian in one of his Elamite inscriptions (Scheil 1905: 56–8).

The last but one of this line, Temti-halki, had brick inscriptions concerning the building of a temple written in Akkadian (Malbran-Labat 1995: nos. 15–16).

Economic and juridical texts

More than 1400 tablets from the first half of the second millennium have been unearthed at Susa. The majority of personal names in these are Sumerian/Akkadian and the economic organization is purely Mesopotamian as well (Steve et al. 2002–3: 426–7). There are even some lexical documents among them, attesting to the training of scribes at Susa according to purely Mesopotamian conventions. Some 930 texts were unearthed during the early excavations (1890s–1930s) by the French Délégation archéologique en Perse led by J. de Morgan and R. de Mecquenem and published by Scheil (1908, 1930a, 1930b, 1933, 1939) and Dossin (1927). Nearly 500 tablets were found during Ghirshman's excavations in Chantier A and B in the Ville Royale (1950s–1960s), only a fraction of which have been published (De Graef 2005, 2006). Apart from two texts in Old Elamite and one bilingual (Akkadian–Old Elamite) text, all of these tablets are written in Akkadian (with Sumerograms) and follow the Mesopotamian models of the time, albeit with various peculiarities as shall be shown further on.

According to Sumner (2003), numerous Ur III and Old Babylonian documents (most probably in Sumerian/Akkadian) were unearthed at Tal-e Malyan (ancient Anšan), the capital of the Šimaškian confederation. The exact number is unknown and nothing more can be said about them since they are as yet unpublished.

A special case is the site of Chogha Gavaneh (ancient name unknown) now Islamabad-e-Gharb, located some 60 km west of Kermanshah in the central Zagros Mountains, on the main road from the Mesopotamian alluvial plain to the Iranian highlands. In 1970, an Iranian team excavated eighty-four early Old Babylonian tablets (Abdi and Beckman 2007). The tablets are in Akkadian, with Sumerograms, as is usual in Mesopotamia. According to Beckman the syllabary is that of the Diyala region, the names are Akkadian or Amorite and the tablets should date to around the reign of Hammurabi (Abdi and Beckman 2007: 47–8). He assumes that a link with the kingdom of Ešnunna is possible. Since there does not seem to be any trace of Elamite influence, notwithstanding the location of the site, Chogha Gavaneh must be considered, at least provisionally, a Mesopotamian enclave.

Literary and religious texts

Fragments of the Etana legend were found at Susa by de Mecquenem (André-Salvini 1992: 274). These probably date to the later Old Babylonian period, as proposed by André-Salvini, and must be the product of an advanced apprentice-scribe, as were the fragments of the Sumerian King List also found at Susa.

A remarkable find, probably dating from the very end of the Sukkalmah period, is a group of seven texts, in Akkadian, labeled "funerary documents" by their editors (Steve and Gasche 1996). This text genre is unparalleled in Mesopotamia and shows how Akkadian could be used to render even purely Elamite concepts and proceedings.

Writing and orthography

At this point writing began to show a divergence in sign shapes: Elamite cuneiform was no longer a servile copy of Mesopotamian cuneiform and a specific Elamite syllabary was developing (Steve 1994: 5).

Salonen (1962: 10–11) noted a number of orthographic differences with Mesopotamian Old Babylonian writing, in part harking back to Old Akkadian usage (e.g., the use of the sign TI for /di/). He remarked that these differences tended to disappear in the course of this period which he divided into an "older linguistic period," a "transitional period" and a "younger" period. The use of ŠÀ for /ša/ alongside ŠA within words but (nearly) exclusively for the relative pronoun is characteristic of all periods. Remarkably, the so-called Malamîr texts, which are younger than the Old Babylonian Susa texts, show a few orthographic characteristics of the "older period" (Salonen 1962: 23). These sixteen tablets were bought by Scheil at the beginning of the twentieth century from a Persian dealer from the Malamîr region. Scheil described them as Elamite juridical texts written in Semitic from c.1000 BC (Scheil 1902). Stolper (1987–90: 280) showed that these tablets are much earlier, namely early Middle Elamite, and that they probably came from Haft Tepe rather than Malamîr (cf. Glassner 1991: 117).

This development in sign shapes and orthography was a local evolution of the Susian scribes, rather than the result of an influx of Mesopotamian ones. The large groups of exercise tablets found at Susa which date to different periods prove, if proof were needed, that scribal education was well established there and displayed some typical Susian features, both in mathematical (Bruins and Rutten 1961) and lexical texts (Tanret and De Graef 2010).

Akkadian and Elamite

Steve et al. (2002–3: 451) suggest that Elamite kingship underwent a process of "semitization," which is apparent in the language, religion, and titles of the kings. As to the language, they refer to the paucity of texts in Elamite: only three texts found at Susa and one from Tal-Malyan, to which they add an inscription concerning the conquests of Siruktuh of unknown provenance. As noted above, most juridical and economic texts from this period are in Akkadian. The large groups of exercise tablets of the scribal apprentices testify to Mesopotamian influence in this domain. From this Steve et al. conclude that the everyday language of this period, which lasted no less than four centuries, was Akkadian, pushing Elamite to the side. A word of caution may be added, however: all of the textual material reflects the situation in the higher strata of society, where there can indeed be no doubt that Akkadian was extensively used and written. The fact that here and there an Elamite word (*sí-a-nam*) or expression (*amma haštuk*) and various Elamite titles such as *teppir* seeped into the texts shows, however, that Elamite was certainly not nonexistent, even in these circles. As to the vast majority of the population who never had any reason to Akkadianize, they must have continued to speak Elamite. Best documented are the rulers and here too there seems to be an evolving situation. Up to the reign of the Šimaškian king Šilhaha there seems to have been a strong tendency to write royal inscriptions in Sumerian and Akkadian, maybe even a preference for the former. In this way the earlier rulers may have wanted to continue the Ur III tradition. At Susa, on the other hand, as shown by the inscriptions of Atta-hušu, this tendency seems to be the other way round, for official inscriptions were written more often in Akkadian than Sumerian. Of course Susa is closer to Mesopotamia and would have adapted more quickly to changes in the use of language there but there may have been a desire to distinguish between the Šimaškian king and the lower echelons of power. A new factor is the use of Elamite by Şiwepalarhuppak (if the inscription is authentic) and Temti-Agun, another proof that Elamite was still thriving during this period. In his dealings with those Mesopotamian kings whom he considered to be his vassals, Şiwepalarhuppak used Akkadian but in at least one of his own inscriptions (again, if authentic) he made a conscious choice to no longer express his identity in the language of his neighbors but in Elamite, in keeping with the domineering tone he assumed when ordering the Mesopotamian kings about (Durand and Charpin 1989: 63).

Spoils of war

The best-known object with an Akkadian inscription dating to this period is of course Hammurabi's Codex, which we know was taken to Susa by the later king Šutruk-Nahhunte, together with the Old Akkadian stele of Narām-Sîn.

Two further Mesopotamian objects with Akkadian inscriptions, dating to this period, were found at Susa and as such cannot be counted among the documents written there. One is a granite block (Scheil 1900: 84 = *IRSA* IVC6k) with an unfinished inscription of Hammurabi. Since Hammurabi never conquered this city, it must have been a spoil of (a later) war. The second is a statue with an Akkadian inscription of Ur-Ningiszida, king ("governor") of Ešnunna, who dedicated it to his god Tišpak and installed it in his temple. This was obviously a war trophy as well, probably from the conquest of Ešnunna in 1765 BC by the Elamite ruler Siwepalarhuppak who took up residence there. Ur-Ningiszida himself was the predecessor of Ipiq-Adad I, a contemporary of Sumu-abum of Babylon. His use of Akkadian is in line with his predecessors.

Another piece that must have reached Susa in the same way is a fragment of a *kudurru* from the Kassite period (Ghirshman 1968: 19–20).

Kidinuid, Igihalkid, and Šutrukid dynasties (Middle Elamite period c.1450–1050 BC)

Kidinuids (c.1450–1400 BC)

As stated by Steve et al. (2002–3: 452) this short-lived dynasty of only about fifty years constitutes a transition toward the Igihalkid and Šutrukid dynasties.

Royal inscriptions

All of the extant inscriptions or references to the Kidinuids are in Akkadian. The only known inscription mentioning Kidinu is a seal legend (Steve et al. 1980: 92) showing the first use of the logogram eššana for king so far attested.

At Susa a number of brick inscriptions testify to Inšušinak-šar-ilani's restoration of the temple (sí-i-a-ni) of Inšušinak (this is another king whose Elamite inscriptions reveal his name in that language, viz. Inšušinak-sunkir-nappipir; see Steve et al. 2002–3: 454). Inšušinak-šar-ilani states that the building (é.dù.a) of Temti-halki was falling in ruins and that he restored its brickwork. Malbran notes that the composition of the text is new and original (Malbran-Labat 1995: no. 19).

Tan-ruhurater II is known from one contemporaneous inscription only: the eight-line Akkadian legend of his seal (Porada 1971: 32). Among the so-called Malamîr texts are twelve with an Akkadian oath formula in which the name of Šalla, another Kidinuid ruler, appears.

The last Kidinuid, Tepti-ahar, left us a remarkable brick inscription. In nine lines this describes a ritual to be executed at night by four women, in front of statues (Malbran-Labat 1995: 20). Another inscription of his was found at Haft Tepe, a city where he did extensive building work. This is a stele in Middle Babylonian (Reiner 1973: 37–102). The text has fifty-six lines and its paleography allows us to date it to the late Middle Babylonian period (Steve et al. 1980: 80). The contents are also ritual in nature and concern the regulation of sacrifices and funerary offerings.

Economic and juridical documents

Thus far, more than 650 juridical and economic tablets, all dating to the early Middle Elamite period (Negahban 1991) and all written in Akkadian, have been excavated at the site of Haft Tepe (ancient Kabnak). About half of them were published by Herrero (1976), Beckman (1991), and Herrero and Glassner (1990, 1991, 1993, and 1996; only handcopies). Since documents mentioning Attar-kitah are included, this corpus also covers the beginning of the Igihalkid dynasty. As Herrero remarked (1976: 93–4), however, most of the personal names in these texts are Elamite, as is the sign use (ŠÀ for Mesopotamian ŠA, ŠÍ for Mesopotamian ŠI and the like).

In his Chantier A in Susa's Ville Royale (A XII and A XI), Ghirshman unearthed more than 120 tablets dating from the (end of the Old Elamite and) early Middle Elamite period (Steve et al. 1980: 122–8). None of these tablets has yet been published.

In this short period it is clear that Akkadian language and writing were still culturally dominant, both in royal inscriptions and in documentary texts, although, for the first time, Elamite personal names outnumbered Akkadian ones.

Igihalkids (1400–1210 BC)

Igi-halki's only inscription up to now is in Akkadian. All of the extant exemplars were found at Deh-e-Now (possibly his "birthplace and/or powerbase," see Potts 1999: 206), 20 km east of Haft Tepe. The inscription is a dedication to Manzat-Ištar, by Igi-halki, king of Susa and Anšan (Steve 1987: no. 2). His son Attar-kitah is also mentioned in Akkadian economic-juridical texts from Haft Tepe and on two mace heads (Steve 1967: vi).

An important change occurred, according to our available sources, with Igi-halki's grandson Humban-Numena. He was the first ruler for a very long time to use Elamite in his official inscriptions, although not exclusively. These include only a few extant bricks and a knob (Scheil 1901: no. 1), both from Susa and both in Elamite. In addition, an unprovenanced stone inscribed with a nine-line Akkadian dedication to Išnikarab and another (an agate) dedicated to Ištar (Steve 1987: nos. 3–4) are known.

Untaš-napiriša, Humbanumena's son, was the founder of a completely new city, Dūr-Untaš (mod. Chogha Zanbil), at which he built a ziggurat dedicated to Napiriša and Inšušinak, the gods of Anšan and Susa. Other religious buildings there are devoted in equal measure to the older gods of the Mesopotamian pantheon and to those "descended" from the highlands, according equal importance to the different geopolitical entities of Elam (Steve et al. 2002–3: 461). In other words, Untaš-Napiriša wanted to create a unique ideological center representing and uniting all parts of his realm (Malbran-Labat 1995: 53). After his death the site was probably abandoned.

This syncretic endeavor was to be expressed in one language, Elamite, which now almost completely replaced Akkadian in the royal inscriptions. Most inscriptions at Dūr-Untaš are in Elamite but some are in Akkadian, such as the inscription concerning the building of the High Temple with gold and silver, obsidian and alabaster for the Great God and Inšušinak of the *syian-kuk* (the term for the entire religious compound, see Steve et al. 2002–3: 461), with a curse against anyone who would rob the precious metals or stones (Malbran-Labat 1995: no. 32). Some brick inscriptions are in Akkadian but most are in Elamite (Rutten 1953: nos. I, II, and II-bis in Akkadian, but the next twenty-three inscriptions, nos. III to XXV, are all in Elamite). In fact, both languages sometimes appear in the same inscription: the first half in Elamite, the second half, containing the curse, in Akkadian (Steve 1962, 1963, 1967; and Rutten 1953: no. XXV/2). At Susa, bricks in Akkadian or bilingual Elamite–Akkadian ones seem to have been even more exceptional (Malbran-Labat 1995: 78).

An Akkadian curse formula was also added to a statue and two statue fragments taken as booty probably, from Tuplias (Scheil 1939: 32ff.).

A remarkable *novum* is a brick inscription from Haft Tepe (Scheil 1962: 72ff., cf. Reiner 1969: 116–18). This is a building inscription ending with a curse against anyone who would attack and/or destroy the temple compound (*siyan-kuk*). What is remarkable is that, for the first time, the curse is formulated not only in Akkadian, as was normal, but in Elamite, confirming the advance of this language.

Another interesting point is Steve's comparison of the Elamite and Akkadian inscriptions of this king (Steve 1992: 5). He concludes that they were made by the same bilingual Elamite scribes, using two divergent syllabaries.

With Untaš-Napiriša, Akkadian does not completely disappear from the official inscriptions but is superseded by Elamite. Even the curse formulas, typically Akkadian until then, are translated. Scribal bilingualism shows that this is a bi-(or multi)lingual society and not one composed of different language communities.

The Šutrukids (*c*.1210–1050 BC)

Steve et al. (2002–3: 464) adduce a number of arguments to closely link this dynasty with the preceding one and propose considering them as belonging to the same Igihalkid family. This dynasty returned to Susa where numerous religious buildings were (re) built.

Royal inscriptions

There still are a few short votive inscriptions in Akkadian of the type "*ša eššana* RN *ipušu*" ("[object] that the King RN made") of Šutruk-Nahhunte (Steve 1987: nos. 11–12), and his son and second successor Šilhak-Inšušinak (e.g., a votive axe, Ghirshman 1960: 210–12; Dossin 1962: 157–8). Of the eldest son and first successor, Kutir-Nahhunte, only five inscriptions have survived, all in Elamite. Scheil published a fragment of a brick statue base of Kutir-Nahhunte, on which is preserved "*Ṣa-al-mu ša* [Ku-ti]/ir-ᵈnah-hu-[un]/te," that is, "statue of Kutir-Nahhunte" (Scheil 1900: 117), which might seem Akkadian, but Scheil adds that the word *Ṣalmu* had, by this time, become a loanword in Elamite (with which *EKI*: 211 agrees).

Continuing and amplifying the tradition established by the Igihalkids (even more explicable if they were in fact of the same family), the overwhelming majority of the Šutrukid inscriptions are in Elamite. As mentioned above, Šilhak-Inšušinak had older building inscriptions, in Akkadian, copied above his own, in Elamite.

Walker (1980: 76) published a tablet fragment which he identified as part of an Elamite copy of a Babylonian lexical text listing temple personnel, probably dating to the Middle Elamite period. The text shows Elamite orthographies. As such, it is testimony to scribal training in Akkadian, in an "elamitized" Babylonian model.

Since Akkadian was the international diplomatic language of the time, it is not surprising that, when Šutruk-Nahhunte wrote to the Kassite king to claim his throne (Van

Dijk 1986), he used this language (we only have a Neo-Babylonian copy of this document, cf. the remarks in Steve and Vallat 1989). As a result of the refusal to comply Šutruk-Nahhunte invaded Babylonia and brought back, amongst other things, the stele of Narām-Sîn, as a trophy.

Economic and juridical documents

Ghirshman found about seventy tablets in Chantier A in Susa's Ville Royale (A IX) dating from the late Middle Elamite period (Steve et al. 1980: 119–22), none of which are published yet.

Over 300 late Middle Elamite tablets were found at Anšan. Only 114 of them have been published (Stolper 1984). The proportion of logograms used in them is high and they also include a number of Akkadian loanwords (Stolper 1984: 10–28). It is noteworthy that the units of measure, the dating formulae, and a large number of words designating objects are Mesopotamian (both logograms and loanwords) whereas the administrative formulae are written in Elamite. The addition of Elamite postpositions to Akkadian words is interesting in this regard as is the often pleonastic use of the Akkadian relative pronoun *ša*.

The linguistic situation is now the reverse and more like it was under the Šimaškians and Sukkalmahs: royal inscriptions as well as economic and juridical documents were written in Elamite. There are a few royal inscriptions in Akkadian, which can be seen as a reference to the tradition. In the economic and juridical documents Akkadian loanwords testify to an earlier situation as well as continued commercial contacts with Elam's western neighbor.

NEO-ELAMITE PERIOD (1050–539 BC)

From this period we have only a few short Akkadian brick inscriptions of Šutruk-Nahhunte II (717–699 BC) found at Susa (Malbran-Labat 1995: nos. 55–6). They are of the exact same type as those used by the first king of that name several centuries earlier and may well be a reference to him.

Spoils of war again

The Akkadian inscriptions from Susa of Nebuchadnezzar, on a barrel-shaped cylinder (Scheil 1900: 123–5) and on an inscribed brick with his name (Scheil 1902: Pl. 18.4; 1927: 47–8), as well as fragments of vases with the name of Amel-Marduk or Neriglissar (Scheil 1904: 96), could have been Achaemenid war trophies.

Apart from the few short inscriptions of Šutruk-Nahhunte II, Akkadian had disappeared from the royal inscriptions as well as in economic and juridical documents.

Achaemenid period (c.539–331 BC)

Royal inscriptions

In general the Achaemenid kings had trilingual inscriptions carved with texts in Old Persian, Akkadian, and Elamite. Lecoq (1997: 49–50) makes the interesting observation that the language of these inscriptions that we call Old Persian was in fact never spoken. Rather, it was an artificial construct based on Old Persian but with an admixture of Median and probably other old Iranian languages. The aim was to unite all of these peoples in one culture expressed in one language and in artistic representations, for example, mixing Medes and Persians. If the Persian kings wanted to unite the peoples of ancient Iran and provide them with a political and cultural identity, why then did they use the other two languages in their inscriptions, Elamite and Babylonian, as well? Elamite was the ancient culture of the west of their realm, the only autochthonous one with a writing system going back thousands of years and, at the same time, a language still in use in large parts of the empire. Since, as newcomers, they made every possible effort to integrate themselves in ancient traditions, the Persians must have seen themselves as the heirs of Elamite culture. Their Babylonian neighbor was of even greater antiquity and prestige and when they conquered Babylonia they took great care not to impose their own culture but to inscribe themselves in the local one, as is abundantly expressed by the fact that the cylinder inscription of Cyrus II was written in Akkadian only, not as a copy of an Old Persian original but with standard Babylonian phraseology.

As to the Babylonian version of the Achaemenid royal inscriptions in general, Lecoq (1997: 55) remarks that there is a clear difference vis-à-vis the Elamite version. Whereas the Elamite was a literal translation of the Old Persian text, the Babylonian one differs, using typical Babylonian phraseology and presenting the facts according to the general Babylonian tradition.

At Bisotun, right from the start there is a striking difference: The Old Persian version has (1) I am Darius, the great king, the king of kings, (2) The king in Persia, the king of peoples, (3) The son of Vištāspa, the grandson of Arsames, (4) The Achaemenid; and the Elamite version has only a slight variant in line 2: the king *with the Persians*. The Babylonian version is built on a completely different model: (1) I am Darius, the king, (2) the son of Vištāspa, the Achaemenid, (3) the king of kings, the Persian, (4) the king of Persia. This difference reflects the difference between the Persian and the Babylonian royal titles: in Babylonia the king's descent is mentioned first, in Old Persian it comes last.

Other differences can be seen in the month names used and the specification of the numbers of enemies. In line 25, when recounting a victory over a Median army and the Kampa(n)da, the Babylonian text, in good Mesopotamian tradition, adds: they killed 3827 and took 4329 (prisoner). The Old Persian and Elamite versions do not give any numbers.

Economic and administrative texts

A few economic and juridical documents written in Akkadian (Joannès 1990; Rutten 1954) were found at Susa. These are considered to be the remains of Babylonians who lived there and cannot be taken as an indication that Akkadian was still spoken by the local population. At Persepolis more than 15,000 administrative documents have been found dating to the early fifth century, the so-called Persepolis Fortification Tablets, written in Elamite, with a few in Aramaic, Phrygian, Old Persian, or Greek (Chapter 27). The last evidence of Akkadian usage in Iran, under the Achaemenid dynasty, thus shows that this was done for reasons of prestige, not because it was a language still spoken there.

FURTHER READING

No synoptic works exist on the use of Akkadian in ancient Iran. For the Akkadian used at Susa see De Meyer (1962), Salonen (1962), and Malbran-Labat (1995).

REFERENCES

Abdi, K., and G. M. Beckman. 2007. An early second-millennium cuneiform archive from Choga Gavaneh, western Iran. *JCS* 59: 39–91.
André-Salvini, B. 1992. Historical, economic and legal texts. *RCS*: 261–5.
Beckman, G. 1991. A stray tablet from Haft Tepe. *IrAnt* 26: 81–3.
Bruins, E., and M. Rutten. 1961. *Textes mathématiques de Suse*. Paris: MDP 34.
De Graef, K. 2005. *Les archives d'Igibuni: les documents Ur III du Chantier B à Suse*. Gent: MDP 54.
———. 2006. *De la dynastie Simashki au Sukkalmahat: les documents fin PE IIb—début PE III du Chantier B à Suse*. Gent: MDP 55.
———. 2008. Annus Simaškensis: L'usage des noms d'année pendant la période simaškéenne (ca. 1930–1880) av. notre ère. *IrAnt* 43: 67–87.
———. 2009. Count your sheep! Doings and dealings of Kûyâ: trader in small stock during the Early Sukkalmaḫat. *RA* 103: 5–18.
———. 2012. Dual power in Susa. Chronicle of a transitional period: From Ur III via Šimaški to the Sukkalmaḫs. *BSOAS* 75: 525–46.
———. Forthcoming a. *A socio-economic history of the Early Sukkalmaḫat*.
De Meyer, L. 1962. *L'accadien des contrats de Suse*. Leiden: Brill.
Dossin, G. 1927. *Autres Textes Sumériens et Accadiens*. Paris: MDP 18.
———. 1962. Bronzes inscrits du Luristan de la collection Foroughi. *IrAnt* 2: 149–64.
Durand, J.-M., and D. Charpin. 1989. La suzeraineté de l'empereur (sukkalmah) d'Elam sur la Mésopotamie et le "nationalisme" Amorrite. *ME*: 59–66.
Farber, W. 1974. Eine elamische Inschrift aus der 1. Hälfte des 2. Jahrtausends. *ZA* 64: 74–86.

Foster, B. 1982a. Archives and record-keeping in Sargonic Mesopotamia. *ZA* 72: 1–27.

———. 1982b. *Umma in the Sargonic period*. Hamden: Memoirs of the Connecticut Academy of Arts and Sciences 20.

Frayne, D. 1992. review of I. J. Gelb and B. Kienast, *Die altakkadischen Königsinschriften des dritten Jahrtausends v. Chr. JAOS* 112/4: 619–38.

———. 1993. *Sargonic and Gutian periods (2334–2113 BC)*. Toronto: RIME 2.

———. 1990. *Old Babylonian period (2003–1595)*. Toronto: RIME 4.

Gasche, H., J. A. Armstrong, S. W. Cole, and V. G. Gurzadyan. 1998. *Dating the fall of Babylon: A reappraisal of second-millennium chronology*. Ghent/Chicago: MHE Memoirs 4.

Gelb, I. J., and B. Kienast. 1990. *Die altakkadischen Königsinschriften des dritten Jahrtausends v. Chr*. Stuttgart: FAOS 7.

Ghirshman, R. 1960. Une hache votive du roi élamite Šilhak-Inšušinak (c. 1165–1151). *Iraq* 22: 210–12.

———. 1968. Suse au tournant du IIIe au IIe millénaire avant notre ère. *Arts Asiatiques* 17: 3–44.

Herrero, P. 1976. Tablettes administratives de Haft-Tépé. *CDAFI* 66: 93–116.

Herrero, P., and J.-J. Glassner. 1990. Haft-Tépé: choix de Textes I. *IrAnt* 25: 1–45.

———. 1991. Haft-Tépé: choix de Textes II. *IrAnt* 26: 39–80.

———. 1993. Haft-Tépé: choix de Textes III. *IrAnt* 28: 97–135.

———. 1996. Haft-Tépé: choix de Textes IV. *IrAnt* 31: 51–82.

Joannès, F. 1990. Textes babyloniens de Suse d'époque achéménide. *MJP*: 173–80.

Lambert, M. 1979. Le prince de Suse Ilishmani et l'Elam de Naramsin à Ibisîn. *JA* 217: 11–40.

Lecoq, P. 1997. *Les inscriptions de la Perse achéménide*. Paris: Gallimard.

Malbran-Labat, F. 1995. *Les inscriptions royales de Suse: Briques de l'époque paléo-élamite à l'Empire néo-élamite*. Paris: Éditions de la Réunion des Musées Nationaux.

———. 1996. Akkadien, bilingues et bilinguisme en Elam et à Ougarit. In *Mosaïque de langues, mosaïque culturelle: Le bilinguisme dans le Proche Orient ancien*, ed. F. Briquel-Chatonnet, 33–61. Paris: Antiquités sémitiques 1.

Meriggi, P. 1971. *La scrittura proto-Elamica, Parte Ia: La scrittura e il contenuto dei testi*. Rome: Accademia Nazionale dei Lincei.

Negahban, E. O. 1991. *Excavations at Haft Tepe, Iran*. Philadelphia: UMM 70.

Porada, E. 1971. Aspects of Elamite art and archaeology. *Expedition* 13: 28–34.

Potts, D. T. 1999. *The archaeology of Elam: Formation and transformation of an ancient Iranian state*. Cambridge: Cambridge University Press.

Reiner, E. 1969. The Elamite language. In *Altkleinasiatische Sprachen*, ed. B. Spuler, 54–118. Leiden: HdO 2/2.

———. 1973. Inscription from a royal Elamite tomb. *AfO* 24: 87–102.

Rutten, M. 1953. *Les documents épigraphiques de Tchoga Zembil*. Paris: MDP 32.

———. 1954. Tablette no 4. In *Village perse–achéménide*, ed. R. Ghirshman, 83–5. Paris: MDP 36.

Salonen, E. 1962. *Untersuchungen zur Schrift und Sprache des Altbabylonischen von Susa*. Helsinki: StOr 27.

Scheil, V. 1900. *Textes élamites-sémitiques, première série*. Paris: MDP 2.

———. 1901. *Textes élamites-anzanites, première série*. Paris: MDP 3.

———. 1902. *Textes élamites-sémitiques, deuxième série*. Paris: MDP 4.

———. 1904. *Textes élamites-anzanites, deuxième série*. Paris: MDP 5.

———. 1905. *Textes élamites-sémitiques, troisième série*. Paris: MDP 6.

———. 1908. *Textes élamites-sémitiques, quatrième série*. Paris: MDP 10.

———. 1930a. *Actes juridiques susiens*. Paris: MDP 22.
———. 1930b. *Actes juridiques susiens, suite n° 166 à n° 327*. Paris: MDP 23.
———. 1933. *Actes juridiques susiens, suite n° 328 à n° 395*. Paris: MDP 24.
———. 1939. *Mélanges épigraphiques*. Paris: MDP 28.
Scheil, V., and L. Legrain. 1913. *Textes élamites-anzanites, cinquième série*. Paris: MDP 14.
Steinkeller, P. 1987. The name of Nergal. *ZA* 77: 161–8.
———. 2007. New light on Šimaški and its rulers. *ZA* 97: 215–32.
———. 2013. Puzur-Inšušinak at Susa: A pivotal episode of early Elamite history reconsidered. *SE*: 293–318.
Steve, M.-J. 1962. Textes élamites de Tchoga Zanbil. *IrAnt* 2: 22–76.
———. 1963. Textes élamites de Tchoga Zanbil. *IrAnt* 3: 102–23.
———. 1967. *Tchoga Zanbil (Dur Untash) III. Textes élamites et accadiens de Tchoga Zanbil*. Paris: MDP 41.
———. 1987. *Nouveaux mélanges épigraphiques. Inscriptions royales de Suse et de la Susiane*. Nice: MDP 53.
———. 1992. *Syllabaire élamite: Histoire et paléographie*. Neuchâtel/Paris: Civilisations du Proche-Orient, Série 2, Philologie 1.
———. 1994. Suse: La couche XII du Chantier "A" de la "Ville Royale" et la fin de l'époque des sukkalmah. *CDR*: 23–30.
Steve, M.-J., and H. Gasche. 1996. L'accès à l'au-delà, à Suse. *CO*: 329–48.
Steve, M.-J., H. Gasche, and L. De Meyer. 1980. La Susiane au deuxième millénaire: Àpropos d'une interprétation des fouilles de Suse. *IrAnt* 15: 49–154.
Steve, M.-J., and F. Vallat. 1989. La dynastie des Igihalkides: nouvelles interprétations. *AIO*: 223–38.
Steve, M.-J., F. Vallat, H. Gasche, and F. Jullien. 2002-3. Suse. *SDB* 73: 360–512 (bibliog. in *SDB* 74: 620–52).
Stolper, M. W. 1982. On the dynasty of Šimaški and the early Sukkalmahs. *ZA* 72: 42–67.
———. 1984. *Texts from Tall-i Malyan 1. Elamite administrative texts (1972–1974)*. Philadelphia: Occasional Publications of the Samuel Noah Kramer Fund 6.
———. 1987-90. Malamir. *RlA* 7: 279–81.
———. 1992. Cuneiform texts from Susa. *RCS*: 253–60.
Sumner, W. M. 2003. *Early urban life in the land of Anshan: Excavations at Tal-e Malyan in the highlands of Iran*. Philadelphia: UMM 117.
Tanret, M., and K. De Graef. 2010. The exercise tablets from Chantier B in Susa revisited. *IrAnt* 45: 225–57.
Vallat, F. 1990. Reflexions sur l'époque des sukkalmah. *MJP*: 119–27.
Van Dijk, J. J. A. 1986. Die dynastischen Heiraten zwischen Kassiten und Elamern: eine verhängnisvolle Politik. *Or* 55: 159–70.
Walker, C. B. F. 1980. Elamite inscriptions in the British Museum. *Iran* 18: 75–81.
Westenholz, A. 1987. *Old Sumerian and Old Akkadian texts in Philadelphia, part two. The "Akkadian" texts, the Enlilemaba texts, and the Onion Archive*. Copenhagen: CNIP 3.
Zadok, R. 1991. Elamite onomastics. *SEL* 8: 225–37.

CHAPTER 15

BRONZE AGE FARS

BERNADETTE MCCALL

INTRODUCTION

Although the chronological term Bronze Age has little technological significance when applied to Iranian archaeology, due to the predominance of regional material sequences and cultural developments (Voigt and Dyson 1992 1: 122), it provides a useful label to differentiate the period from the end of the Chalcolithic, c.3500 BC, to the beginning of the Iron Age, c.1400–1300 BC (Voigt and Dyson 1989). Within Fars itself there is also some variation in material culture but in general terms the Bronze Age is marked by a series of archaeological sequences first identified in the Kur River Basin, which consist of the Banesh (c.3500–2600 BC), Kaftari (c.2200–1600 BC), and Qaleh to Shogha-Teimuran archaeological periods (later second millennium BC) (Sumner 2003: table 12; Potts et al. 2009: fig. 1.3).

Alternative chronological schemes used to describe this broad time period build on links established between archaeological and later historical sequences of highland Fars and the lowlands of Khuzestan to the northwest, which border Mesopotamia (Table 15.1; Carter 1984; Miroschedji 2003). Correlations have been drawn between Banesh-period Fars and the variously named Late Uruk/Susa II–III/proto-Elamite phases of southwestern Iran, and while this period preceded the development of an Elamite polity, the widely used term "proto-Elamite" (based on erroneous interpretations of contemporaneous texts), is essentially a misnomer (cf. Nicholas 1990; Potts 1999: 71–4). During the period of actual Elamite political sovereignty, the Kaftari, Qaleh, and Shogha/Teimuran sequences are broadly aligned with archaeological periods V–VIII at Susa and historically with the Old to Middle Elamite dynastic phases (Carter 1984; Miroschedji 2003: table 3.1; Potts 1999).

The precise chronological definition of Bronze Age Fars here has also been adjusted slightly to better address the main concerns of this period: changing population dynamics, the nature of settlement strategies and highland-lowland interaction. The Bronze

Table 15.1. Comparative chronology of Fars and Susa in the third and second millennia BC.

Date (BC)	Archaeological periods		Historical phases
	Fars	Khuzestan	
c.2900–2600	Late Banesh	Susa III C	
c.2600–2200	Banesh–Kaftari transition	Susa IVA–B	
c.2200–1900	Early Kaftari	Susa V	Old Elamite/Shimashki
c.1900–1800	Middle Kaftari	Susa V	Old Elamite/Sukkalmah
c.1800–1600/1500	Late Kaftari	Susa VI	Old Elamite/Sukkalmah
c.1600/1500–1300	Qaleh	Susa VII–	Middle Elamite I
c.1300–1000	Qaleh/Middle Elamite Shogha-Teimuran	Susa VIII–	Middle Elamite II–III

Age could be seen as commencing with the Terminal Lapui to Early Banesh phases, but the gradual adoption of Banesh material culture alongside Lapui wares in the Early to Middle Banesh phases and the lack of any distinct change in Lapui to Middle Banesh settlement patterns, provide the rationale for beginning with the Late Banesh phase, c.2900–2600 BC (Sumner 2003, 1989, 1986; Alden 1979; Petrie et al. 2009b: 176–8; McCall 2009: 222–3). By this time, the population of Fars declined markedly and no further examples of the widely distributed Susa III texts were recovered from the highlands (Alden 1979: 80; 1982a: 620; Sumner 1986: 206; Stolper 1984a: table 1; Potts 1999: 82–3). This coincided with the disappearance of these texts elsewhere, c.2800 BC, evidence that the economic system that had united much of southern Iran had collapsed (Alden 1982a: 613–14; Carter 1984: 132–3; Stolper 1984a; Potts 1999: 81–2; cf. Chapter 8 for further discussion), along with sedentary settlement systems elsewhere in Fars and southwestern Iran (Miroschedji 1973; Zeidi et al. 2009; McCall 2009; cf. Sumner 2003: 109–10).

These events mark a logical introduction to cycles of population growth and decline that characterize the third and second millennia and how they have been interpreted in respect of social, political, and economic organization (Sumner 1989: 155, table 4; 2003: 54–5; Miroschedji 2003; Petrie et al. 2009b: 180–1). Of specific interest are Late Banesh population decline and the ensuing "third millennium hiatus" marking the Banesh–Kaftari transitional phase (Sumner 2003: 54–5); rapid settlement growth during the early Kaftari period followed by a more gradual reduction in population by the later Kaftari and Qaleh phases; and the appearance of lowland Middle Elamite materials, and presumably people, during the second half of the second millennium (Sumner 1986, 1989, 2003; Carter 1996).

A continuing theme that underpins the history and archaeology of Fars during this period stems from the ongoing relationship with lowland areas to the northwest, principally centered on Susa, and the shifting nature of influence exercised by one area over the other (Potts 1999; Miroschedji 2003; Potts et al. 2009: 2–3). Apart from the distribution of Susa III economic texts, highland connections within the broader region are attested in Mesopotamian and Elamite sources dating from the late third millennium BC onward that refer to Anshan or Anshanites (e.g., Hansman 1972; Stolper 1984a: 10–43, Zadok 1994: 39; Potts 1999: 106, 137–8, 147–8; Petrie et al. 2005: 51) which, following the identification of Tal-e Malyan in the Kur River Basin as ancient Anshan (Reiner 1973, 1974), demonstrate that this region was known in lowland sources by the Kaftari period, if not earlier (cf. Potts 1999; Stolper 1984a; Zadok 1994). This discovery also confirmed the general geography of a land route connecting the dual kingdoms of Susa and Anshan attested in Elamite royal titles and the potential for archaeological finds in the areas between them (cf. Hansman 1972: 114–17; Stolper 1984a: 42, nn. 340–1 for full references; Potts et al. 2009: 2).

GEOGRAPHICAL AND ARCHAEOLOGICAL BACKGROUND

The geographic range of the present chapter takes in the modern Iranian province of Fars in southwestern Iran, dominated for much of its expanse by the Zagros Mountains, within which most archaeological research has been conducted. The most significant regions for this period are the large plains of the Kur River Basin, the Mamasani district in northwestern Fars, and the valleys of Fasa and Darab to the southeast (Map 0.1). The following brief summary focuses only on the archaeology from these three core areas that is significant for the Bronze Age.

Kur River Basin and surrounds

The Kur River Basin (henceforth KRB) is a large, internal drainage system to the north of Shiraz comprising several plains with a total area of $c.3400$ km^2 (Sumner 1989: fig. 3; 1990: 93–4). The average altitude of the valleys is $c.1600$ masl, surrounded by mountains which rise to $c.3400$ masl. The climate is highly seasonal with hot dry summers and winter rainfall, as for the smaller mountain valleys of Fars (Chapter 2). Average precipitation does not generally exceed 350 mm per year and dry farming is possible, but additional water sources for irrigation are available from rivers and springs (Alden 1982b: 89; Sumner 1989: 141–6). During different archaeological phases the regional economy was based on mixed agriculture (wheat and barley) and animal husbandry (goat, sheep and cattle) in varying proportions (Miller 1985; Zeder 1991).

Regional surveys have been largely responsible for identifying population growth and decline (Sumner 1972; Alden 1979), and the main excavated sites are Tal-e Malyan, containing Banesh, Kaftari, Qaleh, and Middle Elamite deposits, and Darvazeh Tepe dominated by later second millennium BC Shogha-Teimuran ceramic assemblages (Jacobs 1980; Carter 1992). Tal-e Malyan is approximately 45 km north-northwest of Shiraz in the western part of the basin (Fig.13.1). It consists of several low mounds covering a maximum of c.200 ha, but for much of its settlement history only parts of the site were occupied (Sumner 1986). Darvazeh Tepe is c.80 km from Tal-e Malyan, at the southeastern end of the basin (Jacobs 1980). One further site of note with an Early Kaftari assemblage is Tal-e Nokhodi, immediately northeast of the KRB, near Pasargadae (Goff 1963: 43; 1964). The remains of an open air rock relief at Naqsh-e Rustam in the eastern part of the basin provide further evidence of an Elamite presence dating to the Sukkalmah phase (Stolper 1984a: 31; Carter 1984: 154–5; Seidl 1986; Miroschedji 2003: 35; Potts et al. 2009: 12).

Mamasani valleys

The Mamasani (or Fahliyan) district is the next most extensively studied region in Fars (Potts et al. 2009). The area investigated to date consists of three small, intermontane valleys in the Zagros Mountains, c.90 km west-northwest of Tal-e Malyan (Anshan) and c.370 km southeast of Susa. The Mamasani valleys form an important link in modern and ancient routes connecting the Zagros highlands with lowland Khuzestan (Speck 2002), and are a nexus for other localized routes to the north and south. The plains are between 1000 and 780 masl, the climate has less extreme seasonal variation than the KRB, average annual rainfall is c.570–600 mm, and the region is well watered by perennial rivers and springs. Although considerably smaller than the KRB (248 km^2), the district makes up one of the larger areas of cultivable land between Khuzestan and Fars with an economy currently based on mixed agriculture (wheat, barley, and rice), horticulture, and animal husbandry (see Roustaei et al. 2009: 17–26; McCall 2009: 31–3).

Tol-e Spid and Tol-e Nurabad are the only sites outside of the KRB with stratified sequences containing Banesh, Kaftari, Qaleh, and Middle Elamite assemblages, but there are gaps in occupation at both sites between the Banesh and Kaftari phases (Potts et al. 2009: fig. 1.3; Petrie et al. 2009a; Weeks et al. 2009). Regional survey has also identified Banesh, Kaftari, Qaleh, and Middle Elamite period settlements in surface assemblages (McCall 2009; Zeidi et al. 2009). The presence of open-air rock carvings at Kurangun, of the same date as Naqsh-e Rustam, shows this region was also significant to Elam during the second millennium BC (Potts 2004; Potts et al. 2009: 3–4 for references).

Fasa and Darab

The valleys of Fasa and Darab are c.130 km and 185 km in a direct line southeast of Shiraz, respectively, and over 250 km southeast of Mamasani. At an altitude of c.1100 to 1400 masl the climate is warmer and less humid than the KRB and Mamasani (Chapter 2, Table 2.1), but there is evidence of irrigation during the prehistoric periods (Miroschedji 1973: 2, fig. 1). The valleys are larger than the individual Mamasani plains, but considerably smaller than the KRB.

Regional surveys have recorded evidence of prehistoric settlement from the Neolithic to Kaftari periods (Stein 1936; Miroschedji 1973), and re-analysis of soundings undertaken in the 1930s by Stein at Tal-e Vakilabad and Tal-e Zohak revealed a sequence of Bakun to Kaftari period ceramics (Kerner 1993). No Banesh wares, however, have been recorded in the area and there is some difficulty correlating ceramics with KRB sequences (Kerner 1993:187, 195–6; Miroschedji 1973: 3). Perhaps one of the more important sites is the burial mound of Tepe Jalyan, located in a narrow pass near the northeastern end of the Fasa valley (Miroschedji 1974: fig.1). A series of communal tombs contained a unique style of painted ceramics, with specific parallels to Susa IV and central Zagros painted pottery styles of the mid-third millennium BC (Miroschedji 1974; Carter 1984: 136). No related occupation sites have been recorded elsewhere in Fars and the site has been interpreted as evidence of a Zagros-wide nomadic population due to the similarity of tomb construction and ceramic styles with regions outside of Fars (Miroschedji 1974: 32–3; 2003: 24).

Bronze Age chronology and regional sequences

Chronology

The chronology of Bronze Age Fars was based initially on the relative dating of material from soundings and surface finds made in the KRB (Vanden Berghe 1952, 1954; Sumner 1972; Alden 1979), supplemented by stratigraphy and radiocarbon dates from Tal-e Malyan, Tal-e Kureh and Darvazeh Tepe (cf. Voigt and Dyson 1992 1: 140–42; Sumner 2003: 53–7, tables 12–13; Alden 2003: D3; Jacobs 1980: 22–3, 48–52, 117–19, 186, tables 2–3). This incomplete and occasionally problematic data (Petrie et al. 2005: 55–61; Potts et al. 2009: 11) is augmented by relative and absolute dates from deep soundings at Tol-e Nurabad and Tol-e Spid in Mamasani (Weeks et al. 2009: 67–70, table 3.2; Petrie et al. 2009a: 124–5, table 4.4; Potts et al. 2009: fig.1.3). Unfortunately, neither has a continuous sequence during the Bronze Age, but absolute dates from each site correlate with the KRB to confirm the general regional chronology (Table 15.1).

The Late Banesh phase is known from limited excavation exposures and surface collections in the KRB and Mamasani (Table 15.2; Sumner 1972, 1985; Alden 1979; Abdi 2001; Miller and Sumner 2004; Alden et al. 2005). It is generally dated from c.2900 to 2600 BC (Sumner 2003: 57, table 12; Voigt and Dyson 1992 1: 141–2), but a revision of parallels from Late Banesh strata at Tal-e Malyan (H5) now supports a final relative date of c.2500–2400 BC based on affinities with Susa IV and Godin III wares in the central Zagros (Miller and Sumner 2004: 87). A radiocarbon determination from Phase A6 at Tol-e Nurabad returned a broad calibrated range of c.2890–2580 BC, in general agreement with proposed dates from Tal-e Malyan (Weeks et al. 2009: 70, table 3.2).

The mid-third millennium Banesh to Kaftari transitional period is characterized by an almost complete disappearance of permanent settled occupation in Fars (Sumner 1986, 1989). At Tal-e Malyan most Kaftari deposits were separated from Banesh levels by extensive erosion layers of unknown duration, especially evident in reconstructed sections of the city wall (Sumner 1985: 153; 2003: 530). But rather than signifying a complete break between the two periods, it now seems from the H5 sounding that a smaller settlement remained. Nonstructural deposits up to 2.3 m thick continue into the early Kaftari phase and the few ceramic parallels to Susa IV and Godin III5 wares in transitional phases (Units B–C), support a relative mid-third millennium BC date (Miller and Sumner 2004: 85, figs. 1, 2; Voigt and Dyson 1992 2: fig. 2). Judging by ceramic parallels, Tepe Jalyan is the only other site of this period—*c.*2600 BC through to *c.*2000 BC—though most of the parallels suggest a date of *c.*2500–2400 BC (Miroschedji 1974: 31–2).

Although this transitional phase may have been shorter than previously thought, settlement decline is still thought to have lasted for at least 400 to 600 years in the KRB, and probably longer in Fasa, Darab, and Mamasani (Miller and Sumner 2004: 87; Sumner 2003: 54). Radiocarbon determinations from Tol-e Nurabad indicate an occupation gap of up to 800 years between Late Banesh and Middle Kaftari phases and up to 1300 years between Middle Banesh and Kaftari phases at Tol-e Spid (Petrie et al. 2009a: 125; 2009b: 177–9). Abandonment at Tol-e Spid may have followed a major earthquake, as signs of a vertical fault are visible in the stratigraphy, buried under an accumulation of sterile deposits separating Banesh from Kaftari levels (Petrie et al. 2009a: 95–6; pl. 12)

Leaving aside transitional wares, the start date proposed for the Kaftari period, *c.*2200 BC, refers to the first appearance of fully developed Kaftari ceramic styles (Sumner 2003: 55, table 12; Sumner 1992: 286–7: Nickerson 1983: 135–8; Petrie 2009). This period has been divided into three phases on the basis of radiocarbon dates from Tal-e Malyan: Early Kaftari, *c.*2200–1900 BC; Middle Kaftari, *c.*1900–1800 BC; and Late Kaftari, *c.*1800–1600 BC (Sumner 1989: table 4; 2003: 55; Voigt and Dyson 1992 2; Petrie et al. 2005: 55–6). Excavated assemblages from Tal-e Nokhodi are attributed to the early phase due to the high proportion of red to buff wares (Goff 1963, 1964; Sumner 1972: 44; 1974: 164–7). Mamasani Kaftari deposits cover the Middle to Late Kaftari phases and date accordingly from the second quarter of the second millennium BC, but some inconsistencies between stratigraphy and the respective age of the radiocarbon-dated samples mean they cannot offer any further precision to the existing date of *c.*1600 BC for the Late Kaftari to Qaleh transition (Weeks et al. 2009: 70; Petrie et al. 2009a: 125).

Qaleh wares first appeared in contexts with Late Kaftari ceramics and are assumed to have been the major ceramic class at Tal-e Malyan from *c.*1600/1500 to 1300 BC, but only a limited group of the later wares has been studied in detail (Carter 1992: 296; 1996; Sumner 1994: 99, 1988: 312; Alden et al. 2005: 41). These occurred in conjunction with Middle Elamite II–III (*c.*1300–1000 BC) lowland ceramic styles in later contexts and the chronological development of the early to late Qaleh period remains unknown (Carter 1984: 174; 1992: 296). The sequence of radiocarbon dates from Darvazeh Tepe suggests a longer time span than seems likely for the use of Shogha and Teimuran wares (Jacobs 1980: 115–19; cf. Sumner 1994: 100–101, for full references), but there is some overlap in the sample range from *c*.1600 BC to 800 BC which correlates better with Sumner's assessment that Shogha and Teimuran wares were contemporary with the Qaleh-Middle Elamite phase, particularly as no Kaftari ceramics were found there, whereas small quantities of Qaleh wares were (Jacobs 1980: tables 10, 60–3, 115–19; Sumner 1994: 99). No additional absolute dates are available from Mamasani for the remaining Qaleh or Middle Elamite phases.

Bronze Age regional assemblages

Late Banesh Phase

Ceramic assemblages form the major class of material culture used to determine the Bronze Age chronological framework of Fars. Banesh period wares were first identified in surface collections (Sumner 1972), their relative chronology refined through targeted resurvey of KRB Banesh sites (Alden 1979). The two main Banesh ceramic groups, grit- and vegetal- (straw-) tempered wares, continued into the Late Banesh phase, but the increased frequency of small, grit-tempered carinated jars and bowls with mainly painted decoration is diagnostic of the phase. Decoration consists of geometric or animal motifs in brown, black, or maroon, sometimes over a white slip or horizontal lines; incised decoration on the vessel rim is also typical (Sumner 1985: 156, figs. 3–4; 2003: 53; Miller and Sumner 2004: 84–5; Abdi 2001: fig. 22). Stylistic parallels with Susiana are found in Susa IIIC and IVA sequences (Sumner 2003: 53; Voigt and Dyson 1992 1: 133–4, 141–2).

Evidence of Late Banesh occupation at Tal-e Malyan is more limited than during the previous Banesh phases (Table 15.2; cf. Sumner 2003: 53, table 12; Nicholas 1990: 3; Sumner 1985: 154; Abdi 2001: 81–90; Miller and Sumner 2004: 84–5; Alden et al. 2005: 42–3). Architectural remains are restricted to traces of a stone and mudbrick perimeter wall with internal rooms, up to 5 m thick and 5 km long, which could have enclosed a space of *c*.200 ha (Sumner 1985: 117, 153–4, 159; 1986: 207; Abdi 2001). Excavation and surface collections show the area of settlement to have been much smaller, at *c*.40 ha, with little evidence of continuity in Middle Banesh buildings (Sumner 2003: 53; Miller and Sumner 2004).

In Mamasani, Late Banesh stratified deposits are found only at Tol-e Nurabad, Phase A6 (Weeks et al. 2009: 37). Some Middle to Late Banesh components were recorded in surface collections, but in numbers that indicate continued settlement decline from the Lapui period (McCall 2009: 159, 222). Finds from Mamasani survey sites display affinities with KRB Banesh assemblages, as well as limited parallels with Susa IIIC ceramics and with contemporary sites in Ram Hormuz and Deh Luran (McCall 2009: 154–5, 226). No Banesh ceramics have been found in Fasa or Darab, nor were any local wares of early third millennium date identified, raising the possibility that permanent settlements in eastern Fars had already been disbanded (Miroschedji 1973; Kerner 1993: 195–6).

Table 15.2. Comparative chronology of the Marv Dasht, Mamasani and Fasa–Darab regions in the third and second millennia BC.

Archaeological Phase	Date (approx.)	KRB region	Mamasani	Fasa-Darab
Late Banesh	2900–2600/2500	T. Malyan, TUV, L.1; By8, str. 8A–13; H5, Units D–E; TTW1, 13–10; YBR trench *Limited surface collections*	T. Nurabad, Ph. A6 *Limited surface collections*	
Banesh–Kaftari transition	2600/2500– 2300/2200	T. Malyan, H5, Units B–C		Tepe Jalyan (Tal-i Zohak?)
Early Kaftari	2200–1900	T. Malyan, H1s; H5, Unit A; GHI, L.4, str. 8–25; By8, str. 6B–7B; GGX98, str. 8–17c; FX106, str.4–23; T. Nokhodi, Levels I–II	*Surface collections only*	Tal-i Zohak Vakilabad, Ph. IIb–IIc *Surface collections (Kheyrabad/ Zohak wares)*
Middle Kaftari	1900–1800	T. Malyan, GHI, L.3; ABC, L.1c, str. 6–7; GGX98, str. 5–7; By8, upper strata	T. Nurabad, Ph. A5 T. Spid, Ph.17	
Late Kaftari	1800–1600	T. Malyan, GHI, L.2, str.3–6d ABC, L.1, str. 1–5 GGX98, str. 2–4 FX106, L.1, str.3	T. Nurabad, Ph. A4–A3 T. Spid, Ph. 16	
Late Kaftari/Qaleh	1600–1300	T. Malyan GHI, L.2; TT D Darvazeh Tepe, Ph. I	T. Nurabad, Ph. A2 T. Spid, Ph. 15	
Qaleh/Middle Elamite II–III	1300–1000	T. Malyan, GHI, L.1; BB33; EDD, L.3–4 Darvazeh Tepe, Ph. II	T. Nurabad, Ph. A1, B9 T. Spid, Ph. 14	

Sources: Sumner 1988; 2003: table 12; Potts et al. 2009: fig. 1.3; Petrie et al. 2005: table 1 and sources in text.

Banesh–Kaftari transitional phase

The H5 sounding at Tal-e Malyan yielded the only excavated, nonburial-context ceramics attributed to the mid-third millennium BC, including vessels that combine elements of both Late Banesh and Early Kaftari ceramics (Sumner 2003: 54–5; Miller and Sumner 2004: 85; Table 15.2). The changing proportion of ceramic types suggests a gradual transition from Late Banesh to Early Kaftari ceramics, evidence for either a small, permanent settlement during the mid-third millennium BC, or a settlement hiatus of much shorter duration than first assumed (Miller and Sumner 2004: 78, 87–8; Sumner 2003: 53–4).

It is premature to characterize the very small, transitional pottery assemblage from H5 (Units B–C), but in general these wares display decorative motifs, forms, or techniques that appear in both Banesh and Kaftari traditions, in atypical or unparalleled combinations (Miller and Sumner 2004). Forms include small jars or bowls in straw- and grit-tempered pastes, decorated with simple banded decoration, similar to Kaftari wares (Miller and Sumner 2004: 85–7, figs. 5–6). There are general parallels to Susa IV and Godin III 6–5 wares, but the combination of traits would imply a local development of Kaftari ceramics (Miller and Sumner 2004: 87). No similar ceramics or artifacts from this phase have been found in settlement sites in Mamasani or in Fasa and Darab (McCall 2009: 159; Miroschedji 1973).

The only other mid-third millennium BC assemblage in Fars comes from the tombs at Tepe Jalyan and is dominated by large, mainly monochrome, elaborately decorated jars with an array of geometric and naturalistic motifs (Miroschedji 1974). Less common forms include small carinated jars and bottles and spouted jars. Mineral- and vegetal-tempered fabrics were uniformly fired reddish brown or light brown and often covered with a thick self-slip. A single bichrome jar is decorated with dark brown and reddish brown painted motifs on a pale olive slip, depicting birds, fish, and a lion attacking two ibex (or caprids), separated by geometric patterns (see Miroschedji 1974: 23–32, figs. 5–14).

KAFTARI PERIOD

The Kaftari period is characterized by the appearance of two major ceramic wares: Kaftari Red wares and Kaftari Buff wares, which occur in plain and painted varieties (Sumner 1972: 45–6; Nickerson 1983: 135–8; Sumner 1992: 286–7; Petrie 2009). Less common are Kaftari coarse or burnished gray wares with incised and filled decoration (Sumner 1972: 45–6; Nickerson 1983: 135–8; Sumner 1992: 286–7). Red wares have a smoothed or polished red slipped surface over light brown to buff grit- and vegetal-tempered fabrics. The range of forms and decoration (black painted and relief) is limited compared with buff wares (Nickerson 1983: 135–6, figs. 39–41).

Buff wares are generally light brown with a self-slip and fine vegetal and grit inclusions (Nickerson 1983: 132–4; Sumner 1992: 287). The most common decoration consists of dark brown, painted horizontal bands near the rim and shoulder, with a variety of motifs between the bands: vertical or diagonal strokes, wavy lines, cross-hatching, filled geometric shapes, or naturalistic plant and animal motifs, including the distinctive left-facing bird motif, found in the KRB, but nowhere else in Fars (Nickerson 1983: figs. 39–40; Sumner 1999; Miller and Sumner 2004: 86; Petrie et al. 2005: 61). Occasional relief decoration consisted of incised lines or strokes and plain or impressed, applied ridges in a variety of shapes (Nickerson 1983: fig. 41).

Kaftari deposits at Tal-e Malyan cover roughly six centuries of use (Table 15.2; Nickerson 1983: 198; Sumner 2003: 55; Petrie et al. 2005: table 1) but much of this material relates to the Late Kaftari period (cf. Petrie et al. 2005: 55, table 2). While the early development of the style is still largely unknown, decreasing proportions of red to buff wares over time demonstrate that Kaftari Red wares are chronologically earlier than other wares (Sumner 1974: 164; Nickerson 1983: 194–5; Miller and Sumner 2004: 85; Alden et al. 2005: 42). Surface collections and excavated areas indicate that the maximum extent of Kaftari-period Tal-e Malyan was up to 130 ha, enclosed within a city wall rebuilt over the earlier Banesh structure (Sumner 1989: 137, tables 4–5). Kaftari population dynamics modeled on survey data from the KRB indicate a trajectory of rapid growth early in the period, peaking in the Middle Kaftari phase, followed by gradual decline throughout the Late Kaftari to Qaleh periods (Sumner 1989: 138–9, table 4). This pattern of early Kaftari resettlement was played out on a much smaller scale in Mamasani and in Fasa and Darab (McCall 2009: 231–2; Miroschedji 1974).

Early Kaftari settlements containing predominantly Kaftari red wares or parallels to Shimashki-phase ceramics at Susa were found only in surface collections in Mamasani (McCall 2009: 201), whereas buff and red wares from Middle to Late Kaftari phases were present in stratified contexts (Petrie et al. 2009a; Weeks et al. 2009). However, regional variation in Mamasani buff wares has led to the identification of "Kaftari-related" ceramics (Petrie et al. 2005). The term distinguishes typical KRB Kaftari wares from those in other regions that exhibit slight variations in decorative motifs, while retaining an overall similarity to Kaftari forms and decorative composition (Petrie et al. 2005: 51, 67). Mamasani may have been more closely affiliated with highland areas to its north as there are closer affinities with Kaftari-related ceramic motifs from a burial site c.125 km north of Nurabad, near the village of Lama, than with classic Kaftari traditions from the KRB (Potts 2013: 131–2).

There are two local ceramics similar to Kaftari wares in Fasa and Darab: red-slipped Kheyrabad wares and a variant of Kaftari Buff ware known as Zohak ware (Miroschedji 1973: 4–5). Apart from survey collections, these have been recovered in soundings at Tal-e Zohak and Vakilabad, in contexts contemporary with Early Kaftari strata at Tal-e Malyan (Kerner 1993: 212–13, fig. 90). Their presence in Fasa and Darab marks the southeastern extent of known Kaftari-related wares in Fars.

Qaleh or Middle Elamite wares

Ceramics of the Qaleh period are mostly well-fired, plain or painted buff wares with black or brown painted decoration (Sumner 1972: 48–9; Nickerson 1983: 138–9; Carter 1992: 296; Carter 1996: 25–6). They share forms and design elements with painted Kaftari wares, but differ in the finer execution and position of their decoration (Carter 1992: 296; 1996: 25–6). Common motifs are horizontal bands or strokes around the rim and parallel bands around the upper body, which sometimes enclose simple geometric or naturalistic motifs (Carter 1992: fig. 33; 1996: table 1B, figs. 26–7).

Later Qaleh wares from the EDD building at Tal-e Malyan, c.1300–1000 BC, are similar to Middle Elamite II–III ceramics (Carter 1992: 295–6; 1996). These lowland wares were found in the same levels, but the timing of their arrival is unclear. By the later second millennium BC there was also greater regional variation in ceramic styles, with the appearance of Shogha and Teimuran ceramics (Jacobs 1980: 60–3). Hand-made Shogha wares occurred in limited forms with painted decoration restricted to the upper body or neck (Jacobs 1980: 63–4; Carter 1992: 296, fig. 34; Sumner 1972: 49). Teimuran pottery was better fired and wheel turned; decoration is similar to Qaleh ware but not as well executed (Jacobs 1980: 83, app. I, figs. 25–7, 30.29–33; Carter 1992: fig. 35).

Site numbers in the KRB were almost halved during the Qaleh period. Tal-e Malyan shrank to c.40 ha but Qaleh-period occupation was located on older Kaftari sites, except for Darvazeh Tepe (Sumner 1989: 155, table 4; 1994: 104; Jacobs 1980: 60–3). In the KRB Middle Elamite ceramics were found only at Tal-e Malyan. Very little Qaleh ware was found at Darvazeh Tepe and a clear geographic division may be observed in the relative distribution of Middle Elamite, Qaleh, and Shogha-Teimuran wares (Sumner 1994: 97–9, 101; Carter 1996: 29–30; Jacobs 1980: 184). No data are available for Fasa and Darab from this period.

Clues regarding the role of Tal-e Malyan and the highlands come from administrative texts in Elamite recovered from level IVA of the EDD building. These document the receipt, storage, and distribution of raw materials (metals) and specialist goods at Anshan in the late second millennium BC (Stolper 1984b: 5–9, 99). Texts also refer to decorative objects for use in temples in or near Anshan (Stolper 1984b: 125, no. 86), suggesting that the Middle Elamite presence in the KRB was more substantial than survey results would suggest. Reuse of the building for temporary kilns producing Qaleh pottery toward the end of the millennium indicates a cessation of administrative activities in this area, if not at the site completely.

At present the Mamasani region is the only other area in Fars outside of Tal-e Malyan where Qaleh and Middle Elamite materials and sites have been recorded. Their distribution shows a higher degree of interaction between highland and lowland cultures than in the KRB and a continuing trend toward regionally specific ceramic traditions (McCall 2009: 235–6; Petrie et al. 2009b: 179). Unfortunately, stratified Qaleh and Middle Elamite sequences in Mamasani were either interrupted by later activity or composed of mixed contexts, making them difficult to interpret (Weeks et al. 2009: 72; Petrie et al. 2009a: 110–13). But a Middle Elamite brick recording the dedication of a temple was found in the early twentieth century at Tol-e Spid, providing evidence of building works (Petrie et al. 2009a: 89) and an established Middle Elamite presence, as does a newly recorded early Middle Elamite settlement, Tappeh Dozak (MS24) founded some time in the mid-second millennium BC. This site probably formed part of the regional network implied by the Malyan administrative texts (McCall 2009: 241).

Issues and Recurrent Themes: Population Dynamics, Settlement Strategies, and Regional Politics

The changes in regional archaeology and demographic shifts outlined above raise questions about how Bronze Age societies in Fars were organized, inviting speculation on the potential social and political changes they represent (cf. Sumner 1986). The expanded archaeological sequences from Mamasani and the KRB also invite reexamination of regional settlement patterns. Considering the previous dearth of settlement evidence covering the mid-third millennium BC hiatus, the more recent Tal-e Malyan data are especially significant. However, the Mamasani soundings confirm that contemporaneous site abandonments occurred in northwestern Fars. The overall trend begs the question, initially proposed by Sumner (1986: 207), of whether the lack of settlements is an archaeological reality or a case of archaeological invisibility. Should the data be interpreted as periods of actual population decline followed by a local recovery in the Kaftari period, or do they represent fundamental widespread shifts in how people lived and interacted within the highland environment?

One potential explanation of archaeological invisibility relates to methodology and local deposition processes. Geomorphological studies in the central Zagros documented active alluviation that buried archaeological evidence under meters of soil, rendering it invisible to surface surveys. Prehistoric settlement was often found on mounds where later activity or occupation had brought earlier material to the surface (Brookes 1989: 36–7; Brookes et al. 1982: 295–6). Similar deposition events are not as well recorded in Fars, but the Mamasani soundings show that some prehistoric deposits are buried beneath the modern ground surface, for example Banesh levels at Tol-e Spid, and most prehistoric sites in alluvial areas were occupied in later periods (Petrie et al. 2009a: fig. 4.10; McCall 2009: fig. 3.2, 198–9). Targeted excavation of the low mounds at Tal-e Malyan located Banesh–Kaftari deposits in limited areas, but only after intensive investigation (Miller and Sumner 2004). It is possible that Banesh–Kaftari transitional sites are buried under meters of alluvial buildup, or located in areas not yet subjected to intensive survey, or that they lie outside of assumed habitation areas in the unexplored regions of Fars.

POPULATION DECLINE AND THE ROLE OF PASTORALISM

Problems of sampling aside, do the changes in settlement patterns represent an unprecedented decline in regional population, or a radical change in how people occupied their environment? The drastic decline in Late Banesh settlements and the fundamental reorganization of any remaining highland population implies a crisis that could not be recovered from readily, but such situations are not unusual over the course of human history, nor are they limited to Fars for this period (cf. Shennan 2000: 817; Miroschedji 2003: 22; Sumner 2003: 109–110; Hole 1987: 23–4; Schmidt et al. 2011). Sumner interpreted the lack of settlement data in the KRB as a case of archaeological invisibility, but attributed this to a gradual change from a sedentary, agricultural society to full nomadic pastoralism, assuming that this large and previously populous region would not have remained unoccupied for several centuries (Sumner 1986). He argued that the start of this process was reflected by declining site numbers from the Bakun period, culminating in the eventual failure of irrigation agriculture by the Banesh period (Sumner 1989: 207). He cited two main forms of evidence to support a shift to fully nomadic pastoralism: the growing importance of animal husbandry by the later Banesh period and the location of several Banesh settlements away from the alluvial plains toward the valley fringes (Sumner 1986: 199, 207–9).

Sites located away from the alluvial plains might not represent a complete sample of Banesh activity (cf. Brookes et al. 1982) or reflect fully nomadic pastoralists, but faunal assemblages from the KRB do show that caprids, mainly goats, had become the dominant species, and proportions of cattle, equids, and wild animals decreased, a pattern associated with increasing reliance on mobile pastoralism (Zeder 1991: 53–63; 137–9, 160, tables 24–5). By the Late Banesh period, the proportion of sheep to goats had grown and though sheep are more often associated with settled animal husbandry, the overall high caprid component was cited as evidence that nomads, that is, fully mobile pastoralists, maintained control over meat supplies (Zeder 1991: 160–4). But pastoralism can take many forms and these data could equally represent village-based pastoralism or seasonal transhumance; they do not unequivocally represent completely nomadic pastoralism in the mid-third millennium BC (cf. Abdi 2003: 398).

An initial, defensive hypothesis for the Late Banesh wall at Tal-e Malyan was based on the assumption that local "dissident" pastoralists were in conflict with sedentary villages (Sumner 1986: 207–9; 2003: 117) but this interpretation is highly speculative on several grounds (cf. Potts 1999: 81). The practice of nomadic pastoralism in prehistoric Iran is not without some basis (cf. Abdi 2003; Potts 2008), but the discussion of nomadism in the highlands and the choices of analogy (e.g., Sumner 1986: 207; Alizadeh 2010) often have little relevance to the time periods under discussion and to fertile mountainous regions (Potts 2008: 196–7). Banesh Fars consisted of settled villages and a large urban center with no physical evidence of damage or conflict, and while the wall represents an impressive investment in time and labor, its purpose remains unclear (cf. Sumner

2003: 57, 117). The evidence of a small, ongoing settlement at Tal-e Malyan with poorly known ceramics hints at the existence of other permanent sites during the mid-third millennium BC that were significantly smaller and difficult to identify from surface finds alone. The mid-third millennium cemetery in Fasa, its similarity to others in the central Zagros, and the lack of contemporary local settlements provide the most compelling, albeit circumstantial, evidence that some of the population of Fars had shifted to a nomadic lifestyle (Miroschedji 1974: 36; Sumner 2003: 54).

But while initial estimates of a mid-third millennium hiatus lasting between 400 and 600 years have been revised for Tal-e Malyan (Miller and Sumner 2004), the abandonment of sites affected the rest of Fars and southwestern Iran implying that the triggers behind these changes were enduring and widespread (cf. Sumner 2003: 109–110). Earthquake damage at Tol-e Spid might have been enough reason to abandon this site, but there is no evidence that earthquake activity affected a wider area, and archaeological and historical studies have shown that people tend to rebuild rather than settle elsewhere (Ambraseys and Melville 1982: 24; Quigley et al. 2011). Environmental reconstructions based on pollen data from Maharlou Lake, southeast of Shiraz, indicate a period of moderate aridity from c.3200 to 2600 BC that could have led to decreasing agricultural returns and may have been a factor in regional settlement decline (Djamali et al. 2009: fig. 5; cf. Chapter 2). A long, dry period coinciding with the Late Banesh to Early Kaftari phases is attested by declining woodland and an increase in open, steppe vegetation with further evidence of landscape degradation, probably from intensification of land use, overgrazing, and tree removal (Djamali et al. 2009: 129–30). All of this points to an increasingly marginal (at least in local terms) landscape and more extensive use of available resources.

What becomes apparent is that people used the landscape differently, leaving few archaeological traces. The widespread phenomenon of near complete site abandonments cannot be explained unequivocally and could plausibly represent a move toward low-density or isolated small communities, the adoption of mobile lifestyles, or radical changes in building techniques. It is likely, yet unproven, that a combination of settled agriculture and pastoral occupancy became the norm with a reduced population base. A breakdown in local connections may be argued by the variations in material assemblages in Fars, including the distinctive Jalyan ceramic style, which is in contrast to the broader regional cultural affinities the latter share with burial sites in the central Zagros (Miroschedji 1974). Changes in highland settlement were probably affected by similar mechanisms (including climatic variation) behind the slightly earlier depopulation of Susiana, and other regions of Iran, and the subsequent collapse of the Susa III economic and administrative network (Miroschedji 2003: 24; Sumner 2003: 110).

Kaftari growth and regional interaction

Population growth during the Early Kaftari period could have been realized from a population reservoir of small but viable settlements remaining during the transitional phase (cf. Read and Leblanc 2003). Small populations can maintain and pass on cultural information and practices to their descendants, a mode of cultural transmission termed "descent with modification" (cf. Shennan 2000: 217), that may well fit the development of Banesh–Kaftari transitional ceramic traditions. This little-known assemblage could represent a formative phase in the development of mature Kaftari ceramic traditions and may help explain the widespread distribution of regional variations by the later third millennium BC (cf. Petrie et al. 2005; Miller and Sumner 2004).

Documentary sources from Mesopotamia refer to Anshanites by $c.$2300 BC and slightly later ($c.$2269–2255 BC) to the conquest of Anshan by Manishtushu of Akkad (Stolper 1984a: 13; Zadok 1994: 39; Potts 1999: 106), implying that a populous area or city (Anshan) with a distinct geographic identity was already of some consequence to Mesopotamia. Continuing conflict in southwestern Iran, lasting into the Ur III period (Potts 1999: 137), may have created additional regional instability that limited the growth of large settlements and discouraged expansion of the Kaftari network until late in the third millennium BC. These historical considerations may also have had some bearing on the rebuilding of the wall at Tal-e Malyan by or during the Early Kaftari period (see Sumner 1985: table 1; 2003: 55; Abdi 2001: 90).

The widest distribution of Kaftari-related wares between core regions of Fars and the Persian Gulf, including Tol-e Peytul (ancient Liyan), occurred early in the period (cf. Petrie et al. 2005; Pézard 1914). Limited finds from across the Gulf suggest a maritime connection (Potts 2003), but the nature of the network itself remains unclear (Petrie et al. 2005: 70–6). By the Middle Kaftari phase the distribution of Kaftari-related wares again centered on Fars. Settlement growth was experienced in the KRB and Mamasani (Sumner 1989; McCall 2009: 176, 201–2). A four-tiered settlement hierarchy with an economy based on irrigation agriculture and animal husbandry developed in the KRB (Sumner 1989: 140–3), implying internal political complexity and self-sufficiency.

Although the former links appear not to have been crucial to a highland Kaftari polity, the network they represented remained in place, presumably controlled to some degree by Sukkalmah-period Elamite expansion into the highland valleys (cf. Stolper 1984a: 31, n. 235; Bayani 1979; Wright and Carter 2003; Moghaddam and Miri 2003, 2007). The growth in settlement in Mamasani provides archaeological evidence for its incorporation into a land route connecting Susa and Anshan, and the region may also have been the conduit through which links with the Persian Gulf were maintained (Potts 1999: 180; Petrie et al. 2005: 75; McCall 2009: 191–5, 232). The importance of Fars to the Elamites is clearly demonstrated by the religiously significant rock reliefs at Kurangun and Naqsh-e Rustam (cf. Carter 1984: 154–5; Potts 1999: 182; 2004; Seidl 1986; Miroschedji 2003: 27–9). This presence signals another shift in highland–lowland relations in the first half of the second millennium BC. Elamite consolidation of power in the region is further adduced from titles such as "king of Anshan and Susa" or "king of Anshan," which appear in texts from Susa (Stolper 1984b: 28–9). Settlements of this period in Mamasani display greater evidence of Elamite and highland interaction than those nearer to the Kur River, a trend which continues into the Qaleh to Middle Elamite period (McCall 2009: 240–2).

Theories of nomadism and its juxtaposition with sedentary lifestyles have also been proposed for the Kaftari–Elamite period (Miroschedji 2003: 23; Alizadeh 2010: 374), but there is little archaeological evidence to support these views. Kaftari faunal remains consisted of cattle and roughly equal proportions of sheep and goats, showing a trend toward local animal management; and their differential spatial distribution at Tal-e Malyan indicated a high degree of economic organization and social hierarchy (Zeder 1991: 201–5), patterns consistent with repeated activity in the same locations. The charcoal record from Tal-e Malyan also shows signs of the negative environmental impact of an expanding sedentary population, as trees commonly used for fuel in the Banesh period were no longer present and various species secured from further afield or alternative fuels such as dung were used (cf. Miller 1985: 14–15). Cultivation of introduced tree species (*Juglans*, *Platanus*, *Olea*, *Vitis*) increased from c.2300 to 1800 BC, again consistent with a long period of sedentary occupation (Djamali et al. 2009: 130, fig. 4). The same pollen data also suggest more intensive cultivation of these species during the Late Kaftari–Qaleh period, between c.1700 and 1350 BC.

Mid-second millennium decline starting in the Qaleh period might not therefore be an accurate reflection of Late Bronze Age population dynamics (contra Sumner 1989: 139), as later survey data from Mamasani also suggest (McCall 2009: 202). Qaleh faunal assemblages show the same general pattern as the Kaftari period (Zeder 1991: 208–219), but with higher proportions of horse and camel bones, interpreted as evidence for greater interaction and exchange with nomads in the documented movement of goods and raw materials (e.g., metals, but also including animals) (Zeder 1991: 208, 236–7; Stolper 1984b). Pack animals would have been necessary to move goods locally and over longer distances, and perhaps provide food, but there is little evidence to explicitly favor a nomad-based explanation over more localized management of specialist herders and other traders.

The Bronze Age seemingly ends in much the same way as it started, with the abandonment of Tal-e Malyan, and the differing ceramic traditions and settlement locations may be seen as a corollary of apparent growing fragmentation in the highlands (Jacobs 1980: 169; Sumner 1994: 100–3; Carter 1996: 47). The picture emerging from Mamasani is somewhat different and suggests that a more enduring population remained in Fars, which retained links to other essentially Elamite groups throughout Khuzestan (Petrie et al. 2009b: 180–1; McCall 2009: 237–8).

Conclusions

Understanding the complexity of highland Fars over this long time period will be resolved only by continuing research-driven methodologies that target the archaeological gap in the third millennium (Miller and Sumner 2004; Alden et al. 2005) and by addressing the ongoing debate regarding nomadic and sedentary lifestyles using archaeological evidence rather than analogy. The theme of nomadism permeates the archaeology of Fars and is underpinned by assumptions that this formed a default way of life during periods when there is little archaeological or historical evidence for centralized political or economic control. Further, the assumption of nomadism is linked to expectations of limited environmental potential within the Zagros valleys (Miroschedji 2003: 23; Alizadeh 2010). Given the sometimes marked differences in environmental zones that make up the landscape of southwestern Iran (Chapter 2; Roustaei et al. 2009: 30; McCall 2009: 30–44) and varying microclimates within Fars that can accommodate year-round settlement, it is clear that a single approach to subsistence strategies and social organization does not fit all areas.

Mobile pastoralism may have been an important part of Banesh and third millennium BC Fars, but evidence from the Kaftari period suggests a high degree of sedentary settlement. The resolution of this ongoing discussion may yet be played out with recourse to semantics, with more consistent definitions of various forms of mobility related to pastoralism and agricultural practices and from reexamination of perceptions surrounding nomadic and sedentary interaction (Abdi 2003: 398; Weeks et al. 2010; Potts 2008; Alizadeh 2010: 353–5). The Bronze Age of Fars presents an intriguing and complex dilemma for understanding human settlement dynamics and political landscapes within the Iranian highland environment.

Acknowledgments

I would like to thank D. T. Potts for his invitation to author this chapter and my colleagues in the joint Iranian–Australian Mamasani Project team, particularly L. R. Weeks, C. A. Petrie, M. Jones, and J. Álvarez-Mon for their assistance. The chapter aims to build on the exemplary quality of the scholarship that has preceded it and owes a great debt to the foundation provided by ongoing archaeological investigations in Fars, primarily in the Marv Dasht region and surrounding KRB. This work and several key syntheses of the archaeology of southwestern Iran have guided much of this overview. Any omissions or oversights regarding this period, however, remain the responsibility of the author.

Further reading

For further background reading to help contextualize this chapter and, more generally, the Bronze Age of southwestern Iran, readers should consult Carter (1984), Potts (1999), and the overview of settlement dynamics and regional archaeology in Miroschedji (2003). The articles by W. M. Sumner and various colleagues on the archaeology of the Kur River Basin and Tal-e Malyan provide the framework for the archaeological sequence of Fars, which has been considerably expanded by the more recent publication of *MAPSO*.

References

Abdi, K. 2001. Malyan 1999. *Iran* 39: 73–98.

———. 2003. The early development of pastoralism in the central Zagros Mountains. *JWP* 17/4: 395–448.

Alden, J. R. 1979. Regional economic organization in Banesh Period Iran. Unpublished PhD diss., University of Michigan.

———. 1982a. Trade and politics in Proto-Elamite Iran. *CA* 23/6: 613–40.

———. 1982b. Marketplace exchange as indirect distribution: An Iranian example. In *Contexts for prehistoric exchange*, ed. J. E. Ericson and T. K. Earle, 83–101. New York: Academic Press.

———. 2003. Appendix D: Excavations at Tal-e Kureh. In *Early urban life in the land of Anshan: Excavations at Tal-e Malyan in the highlands of Iran*, ed. W. M. Sumner, 187–98. Philadelphia: UMM 117.

Alden, J. R., K. Abdi, A. Azadi, G. Beckman, and H. Pittman. 2005. Fars Archaeological Project 2004: Excavation at Tal-e Malyan. *Iran* 43: 39–47.

Alizadeh, A. 2010. The rise of the highland Elamite state in southwestern Iran: "Enclosed" or enclosing nomadism? *CA* 51/3: 353–83.

Ambraseys, N. N., and C. P. Melville. 1982. *A history of Persian earthquakes*. Cambridge: Cambridge University Press.

Bayani, M. I. 1979. The Elamite periods on the Izeh Plain. *AINX*: 99–105.

Brookes, I. A., L. D. Levine, and R. W. Dennell. 1982. Alluvial sequence in central west Iran and implications for archaeological survey. *JFA* 9: 285–99.

Brookes, I. A. 1989. *The physical geography, geomorphology, and Late Quaternary history of the Mahidasht project area, Qara Su Basin, Central West Iran*. Toronto: ROM Mahidasht Project 1.

Carter, E. 1984. Archaeology. In *Elam: Surveys of political history and archaeology*, E. Carter and M. W. Stolper, 103–277. Berkeley/Los Angeles/London: University of California Publications, Near Eastern Studies 25.

———. 1992. Ceramics viii. The Early Bronze Age in southwestern and southern Persia. *EnIr* 5/3: 294–7.

———. 1996. *Excavations at Anshan (Tal-e Malyan): The Middle Elamite period*. Philadelphia: UMM 82.

Djamali, M., J.-L. de Beaulieu, N. F. Miller, V. Andrieu-Ponel, P. Ponel, R. Lak, N. Sadeddin et al.. 2009. Vegetation history of the SE section of the Zagros Mountains during the last five millennia: A pollen record from the Maharlou Lake, Fars province, Iran. *VHA* 18: 123–36.

Goff, C. 1963. Excavations at Tall-i-Nokhodi. *Iran* 1: 43–70.

———. 1964. Excavations at Tall-i-Nokhodi, 1962. *Iran* 2: 41–52.

Hansman, J. 1972. Elamites, Achaemenians and Anshan. *Iran* 10: 101–25.

Hole, F. 1987. Themes and problems in Iranian archaeology. In *The archaeology of western Iran: Settlement and society from prehistory to the Islamic conquest*, ed. F. Hole, 19–27. Washington: Smithsonian Institution Press.

Jacobs, L. 1980. Darvazeh Tepe and the Iranian highlands in the second millennium B.C. Unpublished PhD diss., University of Oregon.

Kerner, S. 1993. *Vakilabad-Keramik*. Berlin: BBVO 13.

McCall, B. K. 2009. The Mamasani Archaeological Survey: Epipalaeolithic to Elamite settlement patterns in the Mamasani district of the Zagros Mountains, Fars Province, Iran. Unpublished PhD diss., University of Sydney.

Miller, N. F. 1985. Paleoethnobotanical evidence for deforestation in ancient Iran: A case study of urban Malyan. *Journal of Ethnobiology* 5/1: 1–19.

Miller, N. F., and W. M. Sumner. 2004. The Banesh-Kaftari interface: The view from Operation H5, Malyan. *Iran* 42: 77–89.

Miroschedji, P. de. 1973. Prospections archéologiques dans les vallées de Fasa et de Darab (rapport préliminaire). *PASARI* 1: 1–7.

———. 1974. Tépé Jalyan, une nécropole du IIIe millénaire av. J.-C. au Fars oriental. *Arts Asiatiques* 30: 19–64.

———. 2003. Susa and the highlands: Major trends in the history of Elamite civilization. *YBYN*: 17–38.

Moghaddam, A., and N. Miri. 2003. Archaeological research in the Mianab plain, lowland Susiana, south-western Iran. *Iran* 41: 99–137.

———. 2007. Archaeological surveys in the "Eastern Corridor," south-western Iran. *Iran* 44: 23–55.

Nicholas, I. M. 1990. *The proto-Elamite settlement at TUV*. Philadelphia: UMM 69.

Nickerson, J. L. 1983. Intrasite variability during the Kaftari Period at Tal-e Malyan (Anshan), Iran. Unublished PhD diss., Ohio State University.

Petrie, C. A. 2009. Kaftari ware. *EnIr* online edition.

Petrie, C. A., A. Asgari Chaverdi, and M. Seyedin. 2005. From Anshan to Dilmun and Magan: The spatial and temporal distribution of Kaftari and Kaftari-related ceramic vessels. *Iran* 43: 49–86.

———. 2009. Excavations at Tol-e Spid. *MAPSO*: 89–134.

Petrie, C. A., L. R. Weeks, D. T. Potts, and K. Roustaei. 2009b. Perspectives on the cultural sequence of Mamasani. *MAPSO*: 169–96.

Pézard, M. 1914. *Mission à Bender-Bouchir: Documents archéologiques et épigraphiques*. Paris: MDP 15.

Potts, D. T. 1999. *The archaeology of Elam: Formation and transformation of an ancient Iranian state*. Cambridge: Cambridge University Press.

———. 2003. Anshan, Liyan and Magan c. 2000 BC. *YBYN*: 156–9.

———. 2004. The numinous and the immanent: Some thoughts on Kurangun and the Rudkhaneh-e Fahliyan. *FHK*: 143–56.

———. 2008. review of A. Alizadeh, *The origins of state organizations in prehistoric highland Fars, southern Iran: Excavations at Tall-e Bakun. BiOr* 65/1–2: 195–206.

Potts, D. T., K. Roustaei, C. A. Petrie, and L. R. Weeks. 2009. The Mamasani district and the archaeology of southwestern Iran. *MAPSO*: 1–16.

———. 2013. In the shadow of Kurangun: Cultural developments in the highlands between Khuzestean and Anšan. *SE*: 129–37.

Quigley, M., M. Fattahi, R. Sohbati, and A. Schmidt. 2011. Palaeoseismicity and pottery: Investigating earthquake and archaeological chronologies on the Hajiarab alluvial fan, Iran. *Quaternary International* 242/1: 185–95.

Read, D. W., and S. A. Leblanc. 2003. Population growth, carrying capacity, and conflict. *CA* 44/1: 59–85.

Reiner, E. 1973. The location of Anšan. *RA* 67/1: 57–62.

———. 1974. Tall-i Malyan, epigraphic finds, 1971–72. *Iran* 12: 176.

Roustaei, K., K. Alamdari, and C. A. Petrie. 2009. Landscape and environment in Mamasani. *MAPSO*: 17–30.

Schmidt, A., M. Quigley, M. Fattahi, G, Azizi, M. Maghsoudi, and H. Fazeli. 2011. Holocene settlement shifts and palaeoenvironments on the Central Iranian Plateau: Investigating linked systems. *The Holocene* 21/4: 583–95.

Seidl, U. 1986. *Die elamischen Felsreliefs von Kurangun und Naqš-e Rustam*. Berlin: Iranische Denkmäler 12/2/H.

Shennan, S. 2000. Population, culture history, and the dynamics of culture change. *CA* 41/5: 811–35.

Speck, H. 2002. Alexander at the Persian Gates: A study in historiography and topography. *American Journal of Ancient History* 1/1: 7–234.

Stein, M. A. 1936. An archaeological tour in the ancient Persis. *Iraq* 3/2: 111–225.

Stolper, M. W. 1984a. Political history. In *Elam: Surveys of Political History and Archaeology*, ed. E. Carter and M. W. Stolper, 1–100. Berkeley/Los Angeles/London: University of California Publications, Near Eastern Studies 25.

———. 1984b. *Texts from Tall-i Malyan, 1. Elamite administrative texts*. Philadelphia: Occasional Publications of the Samuel Noah Kramer Fund 6.

Sumner, W. M. 1972. Cultural development in the Kur River Basin, Iran: An archaeological analysis of settlement patterns. Unpublished PhD diss., University of Pennsylvania.

———. 1974. Excavations at Tall-i Malyan, 1971–72. *Iran* 12: 155–80.

———. 1985. The Proto-Elamite city wall at Tal-i Malyan. *Iran* 23: 153–61.

———. 1986. Proto-Elamite civilization in Fars. In *Ğamdat Naṣr: Period or regional style?* ed. U. Finkbeiner and W. Röllig, 199–211. Wiesbaden: TAVO Beiheft B 62.

———. 1988. Maljan, Tall-e (Anšan). *RlA* 7/3–4: 306–20.

———. 1989. Anshan in the Kaftari phase: Patterns of settlement and land use. *AIO*: 135–61.

———. 1990. Full-coverage regional archaeological survey in the Near East: An example from Iran. In *The archaeology of regions: A case for full-coverage survey*, ed. S. K. Fish and S. A Kowalewski, 87–115. Washington: Smithsonian Institution Press.

———. 1992. Ceramics vi. Uruk, proto-Elamite, and Early Bronze Age in southern Persia. *EnIr* 5: 284–87.

———. 1994. Archaeological measures of cultural continuity and the arrival of the Persians in Fars. In *Continuity and change*, ed. H. Sancisi-Weerdenburg, A. Kuhrt, and M. Cool Root, 97–105. Leiden: AchHist 8.

———. 1999. The birds of Anshan. *IW*: 85–100.

———. 2003. *Early urban life in the land of Anshan: Excavations at Tal-e Malyan in the highlands of Iran*. Philadelphia: UMM 117.

Vanden Berghe, L. 1952. Archaeologische opzoekingen in de Marv Dasht Vlakte. *JEOL* 12: 211–20.

———. 1954. Archaeologische navorsingen in de Omstreken van Persepolis. *JEOL* 13: 394–408.

Voigt, M. M., and R. H. Dyson Jr. 1989. Bronze Age. *EnIr* online edition.

———. 1992. The chronology of Iran, ca. 8000–2000 B.C. In *Chronologies in Old World archaeology*, 3rd ed., ed. R. W. Ehrich, vol. 1, 122–78, vol. 2, 125–53. Chicago: University of Chicago Press.

Weeks, L. R., K. S. Alizadeh, L. Niakan, and K. Alamdari. 2009. Excavations at Tol-e Nurabad. *MAPSO*: 31–88.

Weeks, L. R., C. A. Petrie, and D. T. Potts. 2010. Ubaid-related-related? The 'black-on-buff' ceramic traditions of highland southwest Iran. In *The Ubaid and Beyond: Exploring the transmission of culture in the developed prehistoric societies of the Middle East*, ed. R. A. Carter and G. Philip, 245–76. Chicago: SAOC 63.

Wright, H. T., and E. Carter. 2003. Archaeological survey on the western Ram Hormuz plain. *YBYN*: 61–82.

Zadok, R. 1994. Elamites and other peoples from Iran and the Persian Gulf region in early Mesopotamian sources. *Iran* 32: 31–51.

Zeder, M. 1991. *Feeding cities: Specialized animal economy in the Ancient Near East*. Washington: Smithsonian Institute Press.

Zeidi, M., B. McCall, and A. Khowsrowzadeh. 2009. Survey of Dasht-e Rostam-e Yek and Dasht-e Rostam-e Do. *MAPSO*: 147–68.

CHAPTER 16

EASTERN IRAN IN THE EARLY BRONZE AGE

HOLLY PITTMAN

INTRODUCTION

Eastern Iran consists of three modern-day provinces—Kerman, Hormuzgan, and Sistan-Baluchistan. Taken together and combined with Afghanistan and Pakistan, the region is frequently referred to in the archaeological literature as the "Indo-Iranian borderlands," a term that captures its character as a deeply connected zone of cultural interaction during the Early Bronze Age (3200–1800 BC; hereafter EBA). Although it is still poorly known, this large area was prosperous, densely settled along rivers and closely connected in all directions through long-distance interaction during the third millennium BC. The topography of the region is highly varied with mountains, rich in minerals and metals and having permanent snow cover, rising over 4000 m and fertile, alluvial valleys associated with extensive oasis drainage systems (Fisher 1968). While rainfall is generally minimal and often comes in torrents, there are abundant underground springs. Although climate studies are lacking for the region, it is generally assumed that increasing aridity in the late Holocene intensified toward the end of the third millennium, contributing to the gradual depopulation of the area in the early second millennium BC.

At its western edge, the Zagros range divides the province of Kerman into several zones of unequal size. In the north a narrow strip of land wedged between the southern edge of the Lut and Kavir Deserts and the mountains is known through excavations and survey at the site of Shahdad. Occupied since the Neolithic, the mountain valleys to the south saw a radical abandonment in the mid-fourth millennium BC that was reversed at the beginning of the EBA when settlers from the west reoccupied Tepe Yahya. This highland zone was directly connected to the Persian Gulf through the Shur River and during the EBA was culturally oriented eastward toward the Halil River valley.

Recent surveys and excavations at Konar Sandal South (KSS) and Konar Sandal North (KSN) demonstrate that during the EBA the Halil River valley was densely settled with a hierarchy of sites ranging from small villages to large urban centers. After running for almost 400 km, the Halil River debouches into the Jaz Murian oasis, which marks the provincial boundary between Kerman and Sistan-Baluchistan. A second important water-course, the Bampur River, flows east to west from the Karvandar mountains of the Makran range for about 120 km before being absorbed into the Jaz Murian oasis on its eastern side. Although no large-scale excavations have been undertaken at sites along the Bampur River, survey and smaller-scale efforts at Bampur, Damin, and Khurab, among others, show that this river basin was also densely occupied during the EBA. The Bampur River is the natural route east toward the Persian and Pakistani Makran where such sites as Shahi-Tump, Miri Qalat, and Mehi are found. The route continues north into the enormous oasis lake of the Helmand River, which drains a huge area that is now in Afghanistan and Pakistan. During the EBA, this river valley was also the center of dense population that is known from excavations at Shahr-e Sokhta in Iran and Mundigak in Afghanistan. To the south of Kerman and Sistan-Baluchistan is the relatively new province of Hormuzgan. Its rugged mountainous terrain and torrid climate have discouraged exploration and no systematic archaeological work at EBA sites has been undertaken. It can be assumed, however, that the region around modern Bandar Abbas hosted settlements and provided portage to the seafaring merchants who plied the Persian Gulf during the third millennium BC.

Compared to western Iran, this vast and highly diverse region has received little sustained archaeological interest in spite of its obvious importance during the EBA. Most of the sites discussed here were identified and in some cases sounded by Sir Aurel Stein during his travels through the region in 1932–3 (Stein 1937). As his important narrative describes, the region is extremely rich in archaeological remains that are now located in hostile and remote settings. After his investigations, work in the region was undertaken by both Iranian and Western teams from the 1960s until the Islamic revolution in 1979. After a hiatus, Iranian archaeologists again began work in the region during the late 1990s. The issues that have engaged the scholarship on the EBA of eastern Iran have focused on intercultural interaction, regional chronology, technologies of craft production, and the evolution of urban settlement. EBA intercultural interaction, appropriately termed the "age of exchange" by P. Amiet (1986), has demonstrated that the Iranian plateau was the central participant in a system that extended from the western reaches of the Euphrates River to the Indus valley, including both Central Asia and the Persian Gulf. With no indigenous historical sequence to draw on, the construction of a cultural chronology for the region has had to depend on the blunt instruments of relative dating through typological comparisons and radiocarbon. However, with the accumulation of numerous newly calibrated dates and with the careful correlation of imports with refined ceramic sequences, the relative chronology of the region is now quite secure, at least in its broad outlines. The region was occupied throughout the third millennium, notwithstanding gaps at individual sites. The survey that follows is organized by region, beginning in the Halil River Basin; moving north to Shahdad before returning to the zone to the east of the Jaz Murian oasis along the Bampur River; and ending with the Helmand oasis. While the region is unified by a widespread tradition of black- and brown-on-buff pottery and the highly distinctive Emir Grey ware (Wright 1984, 1989a, 1989b, 2002), as well as artifacts such as compartmented stamp seals (Baghestani 1997), each zone has a distinct ceramic and artifactual profile. Previous summaries of the region with extensive bibliography include Carter and Stolper (1984) and Voigt and Dyson (1992).

THE HALIL RIVER BASIN: IBLIS V–VI, KSS, TEPE YAHYA IVC–B

The transition from Late Chalcolithic to EBA in the Halil River Basin is marked by the appearance of western-related bevel-rim bowls and other ceramic types together with administrative artifacts. The local, late Chalcolithic pottery tradition, defined at Tal-e Iblis IV–VI as Aliabad ware (Caldwell 1967, 1968; Sarraf 1981), was found at twenty-seven sites in the Soghun valley (Lamberg-Karlovsky 1977; Prickett 1986). This pottery appeared after the abandonment of Yahya VA and marks a phase that ended with the complete abandonment of the Soghun and surrounding valleys. The reasons for this apparent collapse are uncertain but may be related to local management of scare water resources. At the beginning of the third millennium Yahya was resettled in level IVC by outsiders arriving from the west (Lamberg-Karlovsky 1968, 1970, 1975, 1977, 2001; Lamberg-Karlovsky and Tosi 1973; Potts 2001). A different pattern of transition has been observed in the Halil River valley where the combination of bevel-rim bowls, seal impressions, and Aliabad ware have been recently documented in occupation levels of the initial EBA under the looted cemetery at Mahtoutabad (Vidale and Desseet 2013), as well as in the earliest levels at KSS (Madjidzadeh 2008). While needing to be confirmed through further excavation, this initial evidence suggests that at least in the river valley proper, if not in the surrounding valleys, the Aliabad ceramic assemblage not only predates but also overlaps with the arrival of the proto-Elamites. The fact that this phase is absent in the excavations at Yahya IVC2 may reflect a local phenomenon, specific either to the site or to the valley.

The proto-Elamite phase in the Halil River Basin is to date only clearly defined in Yahya IVC2. The general consensus situates this phase in the early centuries of the third millennium, ending sometime around 2800 BC (Carter and Stolper 1984; Voigt and Dyson 1992; Potts 2001; Tosi and Salvatori 2005). It is the first stage of the era of interaction that would ultimately engage the entire Iranian plateau for the remainder of the millennium. The remains of the proto-Elamite period at Yahya consist of a single level of occupation in which a well-planned building was revealed (Beale and Carter 1983; Potts 2001). In both the building and the surrounding area were found clay accounting tablets inscribed with the proto-Elamite script (Damerow and Englund 1989) and occasionally impressed with seals of distinctly proto-Elamite style and iconography together with seal-impressed clay jar sealings (Pittman 2001). Although first developed and introduced from the west, the administrative tools found in Yahya IVC2 are closely contemporary with their counterparts elsewhere. This is supported independently by such time-sensitive indicators as imported Jamdat Nasr pottery (Potts 2001: figs. 1.40–43, 3.13.A–B). Local wares include the continuation of Chalcolithic (see Chapter 8) black-on-orange fine wares, black-on-red, as well as black-on-gray wares that are found in Levels IVC2, IVC1, and IVB6. At Tepe Yahya, the transition from proto-Elamite IVC2 to the following phase of occupation is unclear. From the limited exposure it appears that the proto-Elamite building was abandoned and was followed by two levels (IVC1, IVB6) that lack architectural and stratigraphic clarity. At some later point a coherent complex was constructed in Yahya IVB5 (the Persian Gulf Room) that produced ceramics and glyptic art in a clearly defined architectural context.

The date of IVB5 has been the subject of an ongoing debate (Potts 2001; Lamberg-Karlovsky 2001; Kohl 2001) that we can now begin to clarify through excavations at KSS (Madjidzadeh 2003b, 2008), where continuous occupation is documented from the early to late third millennium. Survey of the river valley has shown that the northern part of the valley was densely occupied during the third millennium with sites of varying sizes dominated by the large sites of KSS, KSN, and Qaleh Kuchek, which may have been occupied sequentially (Fouache et al. 2005; Sajjadi and Tosi 1987; Sajjadi 1989; Madjidzadeh 2003b, 2008). First identified by Sir Aurel Stein (1937: 35–6), KSS is a large, low mound of about 100 ha that, toward the end of the third millennium, merged to the north with the settlement of KSN. A high citadel mound was built during the last phases of its occupation. Preliminary reports (Madjidzadeh 2003b, 2008) describe excavations in fourteen operations that exposed four sequential phases of occupation beginning no later than the Aliabad phase, identified both on the mound (Trench IX) and in the salvage project in Mahtoutabad cemetery (Vidale and Desset 2013). The earliest phase (Lower Town Phase 1) is dated by radiocarbon (Trench XI lowest level) to 2880–2540 cal BC (2-sigma). Black-on-red, black-on-buff, and fine orange ware with fugitive geometric and zoomorphic motifs in black are common in this phase and closely comparable to examples from Yahya IVC2 through IVB5. The most significant find for the relative dating of this early phase is an impression of a city seal of a type identical to those known from Ur SIS (seal-impression strata) on a door sealing (Pittman in Madjizadeh 2008, Pittman 2012; Legrain 1936). Found in trash in Trench XIV with three other impressions and a dense concentration of pigments, this seal impression establishes that relations with the west included not only the proto-Elamite presence at Yahya but also people from southern Mesopotamia. While the proto-Elamites certainly arrived over land, the early relations with the west must have followed the sea route, established in the Ubaid period and well attested in the Jamdet Nasr phase and later (Potts 1993, 1994; Ratnagar 2004).

Lower Town Phase 2 follows at KSS without a hiatus. It is the most extensively exposed phase of the current excavations including a large domestic complex (Trench IV), several craft production areas (Trenches XI, VIII, and IX), and an administrative quarter (Trench III). Black-on-orange pottery continues along with black-on-red and black-on-buff. Snake-cordoned wares begin at this time. Goblets are no longer present but a new form, the so-called scorpion bowl with upturned handle, appears for the first time and in large numbers. This highly diagnostic vessel type is found at Yahya IVC and IVB, Bampur II–IV, and Shahr-e Sokhta III. It is certainly most common at KSS, where it is represented by dozens of examples, including one in Emir Grey ware. Emir Grey ware is found at virtually all third millennium sites in eastern Iran. The earliest shapes of this gray ware are limited to deep bowls. By Lower Town Phase 2, the distinctive Emir Grey ware canister shape is documented at KSS. This context is certainly earlier than Bampur V–VI, Shahr-e Sokhta IV, or Tell Abraq on the other side of the Persian Gulf (Potts 2003, 2005) and may indicate that this shape was developed in the Halil River valley (R. P. Wright, pers. comm.). The construction of the Citadel revealed in Trench III began during this phase. It is not raised but rather consists of a thick, niched wall surrounding a complex of large rooms that served an administrative function, to judge from the large number of seal impressions found on the floors and in the fill. Two radiocarbon dates from the floor of this administrative area anchor it in absolute terms between 2450 and 2290 cal BC (2-sigma). Artifacts found in the administrative area include a unique collection of stamp and cylinder seal impressions that find their closest parallels in the SIS at Ur (Legrain 1936), Fara (Martin 1988), and Susa Ville Royale 18–17 (Carter 1980). They also find parallels among the stamp seals from Shahr-e Sokhta II. On the floor of the administrative area was found a large plaque of chlorite carved in the shape of a scorpion man. It was in this level that material of the distinctively carved, green softstone (also known as the *série ancienne* or Intercultural Style, see below) first appeared in considerable quantity.

Also belonging to this phase and perhaps continuing a bit later is the large platform and associated trash in Trench V, about 50 m to the north of the citadel. The platform produced thousands of fragments of debitage from the working of colorful stones, including agates, jaspers, and lapis lazuli, along with many used flint drill bits. To its side was an extended trash area in which pottery, bones, and hundreds of seal impressions were found, including multiple impressions of a stamp seal that was also found in the Trench III administrative area. Among the seal impressions in the trash were a dozen impressions that were made by seals engraved with combat scenes identical to those associated with Early Dynastic III in southern Mesopotamia (Pittman 2008, 2014). The importance of these impressions made by imported seals found together with completely local styles closely comparable to seals from Tepe Yahya IVB5 and in the graves at Shahdad cannot be overstated. They provide a secure, relative chronological cross date with a well-known and well-dated tradition in Mesopotamia (Reade 2001). Further, like the door sealing carrying an impression of a city seal from Ur, they stand as witness to the presence of Mesopotamians in the Halil River valley, who must have been participating in the market place for the luxury materials in such great demand in the west and so clearly manifest in the royal graves at Ur (Woolley 1934). Among the seal impressions is no evidence for seals of an Akkadian date (cf. Amiet 1976, Potts 1981a; Pittman 2014). This Lower Town Phase 2 can be equated with Tepe Yahya IVB5.

The following phase in the Halil River Basin must accommodate Tepe Yahya IVB4–1 as well as the two final phases of the Citadel at KSS. Tepe Yahya IVB 4–2 is not a well-defined sequence of architectural levels but rather a series of ephermal floors with disarticulated walls. These have been interpreted as open-air workshop spaces in which carved chlorite objects were produced, to judge from the hundreds of fragments of unfinished stone and debitage found there (Potts 2001). Only in Level IVB1 was architecture clearly articulated, including a *tholos* and rectangular structures. Brown-on-buff, snake-cordoned jars and combed-incised pottery continue in use. A new ceramic form appears in these levels, the truncated pot, which finds strong parallels in Central Asia in Namazga V levels (Potts 2001).

Although carved chlorite was found in all levels at Tepe Yahya, it was in the later levels of IVB that evidence for workshops in which the highly distinctive, carved chlorite objects that have been identified as the *série ancienne* by P. de Miroschedji (1973) and Intercultural Style by P. L. Kohl (1974, 1977, 1978, 1987, 2001) and C. C. Lamberg-Karlovsky (1988, 1993) were made. Although we still do not yet have good stratigraphic control for the long span of production of this distinctive artifact, several things are now clear. Excavations in ephermal levels of Tepe Yahya IVB4–2 established that these objects were produced on the Iranian plateau (Kohl et al. 1979). The large numbers of them (more than 700 were confiscated) that were looted from the graves in the Halil River valley in 2000–2001 make it clear that these highly symbolic objects were made solely for local consumption (Madjidzadeh 2003a). Further, the variety that exists in both the nature of the chlorite (color, consistency) and the style of carving indicates that they were produced in the region in multiple workshops over a considerable period of time. The fact that very few were found in the graves at Shahdad, and at sites along the Bampur River, allows us to conclude that this artifact was culturally salient only in the Halil River valley. About 100 examples of this carved softstone artifact have been found in temple and other contexts in Mesopotamia (Kohl 1974) and hundreds of small fragments were found on the small island of Tarut (Zarins 1978). Only closed vessels are documented among these exported examples—no goblets, inlay plaques, sculptures, or weights—which may suggest that they were exported for their contents. It is possible as well that they arrived at these western destinations in the company of their Iranian owners, traders, or craftsmen.

Lower Town Phase 3 at KSS saw the continuation of domestic occupation and craft production while the Citadel was consolidated through a campaign of building that included monumental structures. Two building levels of the Citadel (Shrine Phase and Upper phase) certainly extend into the later centuries of the third millennium. Two radiocarbon dates from the Shrine phase are 2490–2290 and 2470–2210 cal BC (2-sigma). On the floor of a monumental structure in the Shrine phase, a corner of a baked inscribed brick was found (Madjidzadeh 2008, 2011). In the same phase, attached to an external wall of monumental structure was a clay sculpture in high relief of a male figure, probably divine to judge from the mountain pattern on his skirt and bare chest. The ceramics of this phase saw a decrease in the fine orange wares and an increase of black-on-buff and black-on-red wares with simple, geometric decorations. Emir Grey wares including the distinctive canister-shaped vessels are present but in smaller numbers than before. Buff-ware jars with snake-cordon decoration are also found in this phase. Associated with this later phase of occupation are two varieties of small, mass-produced bowls in buff-ware that have no close parallels in the region. The last phase at KSS seems to be limited to rebuilding and fortifying an even smaller, highly fortified citadel. The deep accumulation of collapsed mudbrick in this part of the mound is consistent with seismic activity, which is a continual challenge in this part of the Iranian plateau.

Yahya IVA and KSN

The final centuries of the EBA are difficult to assess in the Halil River Basin. KSS was abandoned or more likely its population gradually shifted about 1 km north to what is now known as KSN (Madjidzadeh 2008). The mounded occupation of this period is covered by a later, huge, niched rectangular platform with a second stage that may date to the first millennium BC. Excavations penetrated the platform at points revealing architectural contexts in which large jars impressed with stamp seals were found, similar to ones from Shahdad and Shahr-e Sokhta. The pottery associated with this site is overwhelmingly plain, consisting of bottles and jars with sharply carinated profiles. At Tepe Yahya IVA the pottery is similarly plain but comparisons are limited by the lack of publication of material from both sites (Lamberg-Karlovsky 1970, 1975; Potts 1981b). It would appear however, that the relationship between the river valley and the surrounding highlands was more distant than previously. At this time the settlement at Yahya extended considerably beyond the conical mound, onto the surrounding plain. Survey of the area revealed that this was a period of high settlement density in the Soghun valley (Lamberg-Karlovsky 1977).

Khinaman and Shahdad

Another important concentration of EBA settlements has been investigated some seven days walk north of the Halil River Basin in the zone between the Beias and Laherzar Mountains and the edge of the Lut Desert. The first indications of EBA presence in the region came from the site of Khinaman near the modern town of Rafsanjan. Artifacts of arsenical copper (ceremonial weapons, pins, and vessels) collected from graves found their way to the British Museum (Curtis 1988; Maxwell-Hyslop 1988). These are identical to those revealed through systematic investigations of a burial ground at Shahdad, c. 100 km to the east. Excavated by Ali Hakemi, the enormous site of Shahdad sites in a region watered by mountain run-off and underground springs (Hakemi

1972, 1986, 1992, 1994, 1997a, 1997b, 2000; Hakemi and Sajjadi 1989; Salvatori and Tosi 1997; Amiet 1997; Salvatori and Vidale 1982). Hakemi excavated there for seven years and the site is still under excavation by Iranian archaeologists (Curtis and Simpson 1997, 1998; Kaboli 1989, 1997, 2001, 2002). Excavations focused on a large burial ground and an associated craft production area. Although the settlement was never located, isolated craft production structures have been identified and survey suggests that the site was large, with concentrated evidence for the processing of luxury stones, as well as vast quantities of pottery and copper slag indicating that ceramics and metal smelting and manufacture were undertaken at the site, certainly enough to meet the robust local demand for grave goods (Salvatori and Vidale 1982). While the majority of the graves belong to the later third millennium, the surface survey revealed that a large portion of the huge site dates to the fourth millennium, as shown by diagnostic pottery of the Iblis I–II period, Lalehzar coarse ware and contemporary fine ware.

The excavations in the graveyard revealed around 380 graves, in most cases badly preserved, at a variety of depths. The chronology of the graves has been difficult to assess but the cemetery appears to have been used over a period of centuries beginning in the mid-third millennium BC. Nothing in the content of the graves suggests a date earlier than Yahya IVB and the later phases of KSS. More than 90 percent of the pottery found in the graves is plain, either buff ware or much more frequently red ware. This lack of decorative treatment is characteristic of the later EBA in Kerman. Further, there is a small amount of ceramics that is closely comparable to the Oxus Civilization (BMAC). Especially typical are the flaring cups on narrow bases with a notched rim. Although no analysis has determined that such vessels are imports, the absence of earlier prototypes on the Iranian plateau, along with other artifacts in the graves, have led scholars to suggest that people from Central Asia were buried at Shahdad (Hiebert and Lamberg-Karlovsky 1992). These foreign elements, however, constitute but a small component of the overall assemblage and do not reflect a mass migration. More probably they are a material manifestation of the fact that the entire region was linked into a vast interaction network that connected the plateau with both the Indus Valley and Central Asia as well as with the Persian Gulf and Mesopotamia. It was not a case of unidirectional movement, but rather people moved freely in all directions across the entire region (Pittman 2014). Shahdad, like the sites in the Halil River valley, was a thriving, self-sustaining urban community that successfully practiced agriculture and animal husbandry and engaged in the exploitation and processing of abundant raw materials that were both consumed locally and were transmitted along the routes of interaction.

The material remains indicate that the Halil River Basin and Shahdad were closely related but there are differences that reflect both chronology and cultural identity. For example, there is virtually no Emir Grey ware at Shahdad and there are only four examples of carved softstone vessels, so abundant in the looted graves of the Halil River valley and the archaeological contexts of both KSS and Yahya IVB. However, there are a number of symbolic elements common to both regions that suggest shared ideological categories. These are manifest primarily in glyptic art, burial furniture, and the use of painted effigy figures sculpted in clay.

In addition to pottery, metal (copper, silver) artifacts, especially vessels and tools, are abundant. Large copper lids with repoussé figural imagery emerging from the center and a curved and flaring rim represent a distinctive type. One was found in the mouth of a large vessel. This lid type is also found in the graves of the Halil River and in graves of Hissar IIIC (Schmidt 1937) along with long alabaster rods and grooved columns. Ceremonial axes with long, curved butts and splayed blades from the Shahdad graves are also paralleled at Hissar (Schmidt 1937) and in the Oxus (Pottier 1984). Compartmented and openwork stamp seals in copper, sometimes with loop handles and sometimes functioning as the head of pin, are frequent in the Shahdad graves. Similar seals were stamped onto the sides of red-ware jars. These compartmented stamps have a very wide distribution at Shahr-e Sokhta II and III in Sistan and the Halil River valley. Although they are most common in the Oxus, they are certainly an Iranian type that was adapted in Central Asia along with other symbolic and administrative tools (Baghestani 1997; Winkelmann 1997, 2000a, 2000b).

Six cylinder seals—five of light or white, fine-grained calcite or magnetite and one of silver—and four stone stamps were found in the Shahdad graves. This corpus is very similar in overall character to the glyptic from Yahya and KSS. The primary difference is that the overwhelming majority of glyptic from KSS comes in the form of ancient impressions, while only seals were recovered at Yahya and Shahdad. The value of impressions found in controlled context is obvious for determining both the date and the primary function of seals as administrative tools. In light of the variety manifest in the glyptic from KSS, it is striking that the stone cylinder seals from Yahya and Shahdad have such a narrow iconographic range, limited to female deities. The silver seal from Shahdad stands out as an example of the Linear Style well attested at KSS where it was used for official or royal seals (Pittman 2008). While the community at Yahya must have been closely involved with the administrative practices in the valley, the presence of glyptic art at Shahdad does not necessarily suggest a close administrative connection to the centers south of the mountains. It is likely that, although the iconography of these seals was culturally familiar and meaningful, their presence in the graves might say nothing more than that they were special heirlooms valued as objects and not as administrative tools in the market place. Alternatively, the seals might flag a familial or kinship relation south of the mountains.

Unique among the artifacts from the graves is the "standard of Shahdad." This remarkable object depicts a ritual ceremony. The main actor is a male figure seated on a volute chair gesturing toward a squatting female wearing an enveloping garment. Surrounded by standing and kneeling figures, the scene is set in a garden of palms and deciduous trees. Above is a guilloche pattern, surely denoting water, while below is a scene of predation between felines and a humped bull. The imagery on this remarkable visual text is found on seals from KSS as well as on double-sided disks and carved chlorite objects from among the looted materials. While the precise meaning eludes us, reference to bedrock cultural institutions involving marriage, family, and rulership seems clear.

The Bampur River complex: Bampur, Damin, Khurab

Turning to the oasis culture southeast of the Jaz Murian, the EBA communities along the Bampur River participated in the general material trends of their neighbors to the west, while being even more closely part of the distinctive cultural traditions to the east (Franke 2008; Besenval 2011). The Bampur River is the route linking central Iran to southern Baluchistan, Pakistan, and ultimately Afghanistan (Tosi 1974). The dominant material artifact of these sites is ceramics, with a few stamp seals, stone bowl fragments and copper alloy objects.

The pottery of this zone is broadly of the familiar painted tradition consisting in the earlier periods of black-on-red and black-on-orange wares that were gradually replaced by black-on-buff and Emir Grey wares. Furthest west, the site of Bampur at the mouth of the river was first tested by Sir Aurel Stein and then revisited in 1966 by B. de Cardi, who excavated (Cardi 1967, 1970) two very small soundings (total area of 24 m^2) that produced abundant pottery. Cardi identified six architectural levels that she divided into two main periods on the basis of ceramics. During the earlier levels, Bampur I–IV, buff ware predominated, but with gray wares present. Recent surveys and tests undertaken at Bampur have not added substantially to previous results (Mortazavi 2006; Sajjadi 2003). Comparative analysis suggests general contemporaneity between Bampur I–IV and Shahr-e Sokhta II–III, while Bampur IV–VI has strong ties to Shahr-e Sokhta IV that are especially emphasized by the cooccurrence of incised gray ware in each assemblage (Tosi and Salvatori 2007; Potts 2003). This type of pottery was also found at KSS in very small amounts. Another chronologically relevant marker consists of Emir black-on-red or black-on-gray canisters that are familiar at Tepe Yahya IVB, Konar Sandal Lower Town phase 2, the late Umm an-Nar grave at Tell Abraq, and Shahr-e Sokhta IV (Potts 2005). While this type certainly had an extended life, it seems clear that it originated in southeastern Iran from whence it was disseminated to the east and to the other side of the Persian Gulf.

Damin and Khurab are both small sites that produced closely comparable ceramic sequences of painted pottery together with some interesting bronze objects. At Damin, two bronze stamp seals were found, one of which shows a whorl of raptor heads almost identical to an impression found in the administrative building of the first phase of the Citadel at KSS (Tosi 1970a). The other important find excavated by Stein at Khurab is a copper-alloy axe with the three-dimensional image of a recumbent Bactrian camel from Grave E (Lamberg-Karlovsky 1969; Lamberg-Karlovsky and Schmandt-Besserat 1977). Such a depiction suggests the importance of the Bactrian camel, which was certainly familiar in the region, where it was far from its natural habitat (Potts 2004). While the object itself is unique in southeastern Iran, the ceramics from the grave are closely comparable to Bampur V.

Shahr-e Sokhta

The 1400 km long Helmand River is the most extensive of the inland river systems that supported dense urban settlement concentrations during the EBA. Originating in the Hindu Kush, the Helmand is fed by four rivers that ultimately connected the region to its northern oasis neighbor, the Oxus Civilization. Unlike the tiered system of the Halil River valley, the EBA settlement pattern in Helmand consists of a few large cities surrounded by many very small, dependent sites. In the north is Mundigak (Casal 1961) in modern Afghanistan, while Shahr-e Sokhta is its counterpart to the south, located in a large, intermontane basin at the mouth of the river where it enters the Helmand oasis. Investigated over eleven seasons by Italian archaeologists led by M. Tosi and now explored by Iranian archaeologists, the EBA occupation at Shahr-e Sokhta is the most thoroughly analyzed and best understood among the sites in eastern Iran (Tosi 1968, 1969, 1983, Lamberg-Karlovsky and Tosi 1973; Sajjadii 2003; Sajjadi et al. 2003; Piperno and Salvatori 2007 for further refs.).

The mound rises 18 m above the plain and extends over 150 ha. At its southwest is the necropolis. About 20 km to the southeast is Rud-e Biyaban 2, a craft production site. First settled around 3000 BC, Shahr-e Sokhta was occupied continuously through eleven phases that are clustered into four main periods on the basis of ceramic and architectural features (Tosi and Salvatori 2007). The site reached its greatest extent during Period II (phases 8/7–5), which spans several centuries in the mid-third millennium BC, when it was deeply embedded in the long-distance interaction network that connected Central Asia, the Indus Valley, the Iranian plateau, and the Mesopotamian alluvial plain. In Period III (phases 4–2), the site experienced an economic and social reorganization that is reflected in the centralization of craft production, removing ceramic and other craft activities from the household. The result was a trend toward simplification and efficiency. This was followed by a sharp period of contraction in Period IV (phase 1), when occupation ended in a massive conflagration, the remains of which gives rationale to the meaning of its name in Persian, as the Burnt City.

In addition to the graveyard, three main areas of the site were investigated. The lowest levels of the housing complex were uncovered in the Eastern Residential Quarter (Tosi 1968, 1969, 1983). This is an elevated area of about 16 ha where the only evidence was found of Period I occupation, whose date around 3000 BC is confirmed by both radiocarbon and relative dating. Mirroring Tepe Yahya IVC2, the earliest phase of Period I (phase 10) occupation at Shahr-i Sokhta produced a proto-Elamite tablet (Chapter 13) and twenty seal impressions that sit squarely within the proto-Elamite tradition best known at Susa, Tal-e Malyan, and Tepe Yahya (Amiet 1979, 1983; Amiet and Tosi 1978). The Period I ceramic assemblage consists of buff pottery made on a slow wheel that was painted with stereometric patterns of triangles and squares. Ovoid jars and hemispherical bowls along with cylindrical beakers are common. Nal pottery imported from the

Makran shows strong connections to Quetta (Tosi and Salvatori 2007). Emir Grey ware bowls show strong connections to sites in Pakistani Makran, especially to Shahi-Tump and Miri Qalat IIIa–b (Besenval 2011), dated to between 3200 and 2800 BC, as well as to the sites in the Halil River Basin. An imported bowl from Turkmenistan of Namazga III type (Tosi and Salvatori 2007) suggests the same date range. Cylinder seals and their impressions occur only in phase 10, while in phases 9 and 8, stone and bone stamp seals bearing geometric and abstract designs are documented both as seals and through ancient impressions on clay (Ferioli et al 1979; Fiandra and Pepe 2000).

During Period II (phases 7–5), the Eastern Residential Area expanded to the west and consisted of a variety of large house compounds separated by streets. Black-on-buff ceramics continued as the most common ware, with beakers assuming for the first time a distinctive pear-shaped profile that continued into the following period (Vidale 1984). Stereometric patterns fell out of use. This was the period of greatest complexity in the decorative schemes of the pottery which now include horned animals, birds, and vegetation in addition to geometric patterns. Emir Grey ware bowls continue from the previous period. In addition, a new, highly distinctive type of pottery with polychrome decoration applied after firing appeared for the first time in phase 8, finding great popularity during Period II. The only close parallels for this ware are to the north, at Mundigak. While the other forms of ceramics underwent simplification during the course of Period III, this polychrome ware and a bichrome variant remained basically unchanged until the very end, when they too became more simplified. Its unusual appearance has been associated with females, perhaps a salient object in matters related to marriage and reproduction (Mugaverol and Vidale 2003).

Occupation expanded beyond the Eastern Residential Area during Period II to include the Central Quarter (Salvatori and Vidale 1997), a 20 ha expanse surrounded on three sides by large depressions. This was the period of the site's greatest extent, surpassing 100 ha. Several large building complexes were exposed in the Central Quarter that are organized differently than those in the Eastern Residential Area. Evidence for intense craft production was found in the North-western Area of the Central Quarter. Remains of copper and bronze processing as well as the working of lapis and other semi-precious stones were found over an extended area. Workshops for alabaster vessels were also identified. These were both used locally and exported across the plateau and beyond (Ciarla 1979, 1981; Casanova 1991). Phase 8/7, which the excavators estimate to have lasted fifty years, was brought to an end both in the Central Quarter and the Eastern Residential Area by a fire. Imported ceramics of Nal and Kot Dijian type and close ceramic connections between Mundigak III_6 and Shahr-e Sokhta phase 8 illustrate the continuing external relations of the site. Radiocarbon dates for phase 7 converge between 2750 and 2650 BC (Tosi and Salvatori 2007).

Period II saw a great increase in the use of glyptic for administrative purposes. Distributed throughout the domestic contexts were more than 180 examples of seal-impressed clay used both for immobile (door) and mobile storage (containers of various types) (Fiandra and Pepe 2000). Found in the same contexts were clay disks and balls with marks that have been interpreted as counters (Cattini 2000). After Period I, stamp seals were used exclusively at the site. Both copper alloy and stone stamp seals were found, primarily in Period II contexts. Many have geometric designs made with a drill, and among the metal stamps, zoomorphic and floral patterns are common. In addition to their use for marking clay locking devices, seals were also impressed occasionally on ceramic vessels before firing, a practice also documented at Shahdad, Tepe Yahya IVA, and KSN. Also found in great abundance in Period II were small, usually unbaked, figurines of animals, most often zebu (*Bos indicus*) (Santini 1990).

Period III (phases 4–2) is best known from excavations in the Central Quarter. In particular, the House of the Foundations, built over the remains of earlier Period II structures, was very large and is thought to have served other than a simple residential function. Two separate architectural complexes were surrounded by a threefold rectangular wall with internal partitions that enclosed an area of about 6000 m². The whole complex was apparently outfitted with ceramic piping that provided for the disposal of waste in a systematic and efficient fashion. Copper or bronze stamp seals find parallels in Central Asia. Survey identified many small villages in the vicinity. It was in this period that the satellite site of Rud-e Biyaban 2 was first occupied. Its surface is covered with pottery slag and wasters. Fifty large and small pottery kilns of one or two chambers were full of Period III–IV pottery (Tosi 1970, 1983). Clearly there was a radical reorganization of craft production that involved the migration of craft production to specialized quarters, the introduction of the fast wheel, drastic simplification of pottery decoration and much more extensive use of pottery marks. Emir Grey ware continued from Period I. Rud-e Biyaban 2 and several other sites were the pottery production sites for the entire region.

Period IV (phase 1) (Tosi 1983, Biscione 1979) saw a radical decrease in size of the site. Occupation was limited to the southeastern corner of the mound where the heavily Burnt Building was uncovered. The conflagration was judged to be the result of conflict on the basis of the body of a boy who died when apparently trying to escape. Incised gray-ware sherds were found for the first time in this level linking the site chronologically to Bampur VI. Snake-cordoned decoration also appeared for the first time in this level. Also present are canister jars in black-on-red ware which provide strong connections to Bampur V–VI and Mehi IIIc. Finally, there are clear links to late Namazga V and early VI in Margiana and Bactria. Administrative activity was reduced to a minimum and the very rare compartmented stamp seals found were made of highly fired clay (Tusa 1977). Radiocarbon dates from phase 1 have a maximum range of 2200–2000 BC.

The reason for the contraction of the site is unclear. The excavators concluded that increasing aridity was less important than a crisis in the structure of urban social organization and hierarchy. The new settlement structure, as revealed by survey, was no longer organized around a single concentration of population but was extended across the oasis, distributed within small villages that interacted with nomadic herders. The final stage of occupation at Shahr-e Sokhta was a squatter level (phase 0) on the remains of the Burnt Building which must reflect a new subsistence strategy in the region.

All of the deceased at Shahr-e Sokhta were found in the necropolis covering nearly 30 ha in the southwest of the site (Bonora et al. 2000; Piperno 1976, 1977, 1979, 1986;

Piperno and Salvatori 1982, 1983, 2007; Piperno and Tosi 1975). Sampling over a broad area led to an estimate of c.20,000 graves from all periods. Six seasons of excavation uncovered 230 graves with over 300 deceased. A number of different types of graves were used in all periods. Simple pits and pits divided with a mudbrick wall were the most common, followed by a niched or domed chamber approached through a rectangular shaft. This type was reused to receive new bodies. Much rarer were the few burials that were defined by low mudbrick walls, sometimes only one brick high. One collective grave was a circular, mudbrick structure that was repeatedly reopened, presumably for successive interments.

The earliest burials dated to Period I phase 9. Period II was the time of the greatest use of the graveyard. The grave goods varied in quantity but always included ceramics. Beads, stamp seals, stone vessels, bone, and metal objects were frequently present in the graves of males and females of all ages. In many, organic materials, wood, textiles, and hair were preserved. Some graves had more grave goods than others, but none stood out as extraordinarily rich in precious or luxury goods. Reused graves were interpreted as collective family burials. Excavators observed that graves tended to be grouped by profession and that there was a meaningful cooccurrence of sacrificed kids (i.e., young goats), lapis lazuli, and chalcedony beads, and Emir Grey ware. The meaning of these and other associations is uncertain but it has been suggested that they may reflect ethnic or other social groupings.

Conclusion

Over the course of more than one thousand years, the inhabitants of eastern Iran were linked together both by shared ceramic and lithic technologies and by a system of extraction and craft production of raw materials into objects for local consumption and long-distance commerce. This period of loose unity was initiated by the arrival—into the midst of local, Late Chalcolithic cultures—of individuals using and familiar with administrative and symbolic technologies that originated in the west (the proto-Elamites). While our knowledge still does not allow us to agree in all of the details of relative chronology, it is now possible to see that there were three distinct cultural zones (north of the mountains; the Jaz Murian oasis cultures of Halil and Bampur Rivers; and the Helmand River complex) that shared similar lifeways based on agricultural production and intensive craft production within a ranked society of low complexity. Certainly there were elites, but society here never had the hierarchical structure that characterized the Mesopotamian political and social system of the late third millennium dynastic regional states. While the political and social structure of the Harappan civilization to the east is poorly understood, the Iranian cultures did not share its profound cultural uniformity. It would be a mistake, however, to consider the Iranian plateau cultures of the third millennium simply as secondary states (Kohl 2007) whose existence depended on interaction with the flanking riverine civilizations. Perhaps they would have developed differently without contact, but so would have the better-known civilizations as well. The only way forward in our understanding of these fascinating worlds on the plateau is to pursue further excavation and survey in order to illuminate the dimly grasped material traditions that we currently study. The collapse of the Early Bronze Age cultures of eastern Iran must be considered both locally and globally. Each had a long trajectory of contraction, transformation, and ultimate decline. While increasing aridity must have certainly played a significant role, each culture responded through adaptation and resilience. These processes deserve our attention as well.

Further reading

For an introduction to the early exploration of eastern Iran and Central Asia by Sir Aurel Stein, see Mirsky (1977). T. F. Potts (1994) provides a fine summary of the trade relations that linked eastern Iran to Mesopotamia through overland and sea routes in the Early Bronze Age. Lamberg-Karlovsky and Tosi (1973) introduce the problem of long distance interaction and the place of eastern Iran and the Indo-Iranian borderlands. The evidence for environmental factors in the collapse of the Early Bronze Age urban communities of Western and Middle Asia is summarized in Dalfes et al. (1997).

References

Amiet, P. 1976. Antiquités du désert de Lut, II. *RA* 70: 1–8.
———. 1979. Les sceaux de Shahr-i Sokhta. In *South Asian Archaeology 1975*, ed. J. E. van Lohuizen-de Leeuw, 3–6. Leiden: Brill.
———. 1983. The archaic glyptic at Shahr-i Sokhta (Period I). In *Prehistoric Sistan 1*, ed. M. Tosi, 127–71. Rome: IsMEO Reports and Memoirs 19.
———. 1986. *L'âge des échanges inter-iraniens, 3500–1700 avant J. -C.* Paris: Réunion des Musé es Nationaux.
———. 1997. Introduction. In *Shahdad: Archaeological excavations of a Bronze Age center in Iran*, ed. Ali Hakemi, vii–xii. Rome: IsMEO Reports and Memoirs 27.
Amiet, P., and M. Tosi. 1978. Phase 10 at Shahr-i Sokhta: Excavations in square XDV and the late 4th millennium BC assemblage of Sistan. *EW* 28: 9–31.
Baghestani, S. 1997. *Metallene Compartimentsiegel aus Ost-Iran, Zentralasien und Nord-China*. Rahden: AIT 1.
Beale, T. W., and S. M. Carter. 1983. On the track of the Yahya large Kuš: Evidence for architectural planning in the Period IVC complex at Tepe Yahya. *Paléorient* 9: 81–8.
Besenval, R. 2011. Between east and west: Kech-Makran (Pakistan) during protohistory. In *Cultural relations between the Indus and the Iranian plateau during the third millennium BCE*, ed. T. Osada and M. Witzel, 41–164. Cambridge, MA: Harvard Oriental Series Opera Minora 7.
Biscione, R. 1979. The Burnt Building of Shahr-i Sokhta Period IV. an attempt of functional analysis from the distribution of pottery types. In *Iranica*, ed. G. Gnoli and A.V. Rossi, 291–306. Naples: Istituto Universitario Orientale, Seminario di Studi Asiatici, Series Minor 10.

Bonora, G. L., C. Domanin, S. Salvatori, and A. Soldini. 2000. The oldest graves of the Shahr-i Sokhta graveyard. In *South asian archaeology 1997*, ed. M. Taddei and G. de Marco, 495–520. Rome: SOR 90/1.

Caldwell, J. R. 1967. *Investigations at Tal-i Iblis*. Springfield: Illinois State Museum Preliminary Reports 9.

———. 1968. Tal-i Iblis and the beginning of copper metallurgy at the fifth millennium. *Archaeologia Viva* 1: 145–50.

Cardi, B. de. 1967. The Bampur sequence in the 3rd millennium B.C. *Antiquity* 41: 33–41.

———. 1970. *Excavations at Bampur: A third millennium settlement in Persian Baluchistan, 1966*. New York: Anthropological Papers of the American Museum of Natural History 51/3.

Carter, E. 1980. Excavations in Ville Royale I at Susa: the third millennium BC occupation. *CDAFI* 11: 11–134.

Carter, E., and M. W. Stolper. 1984. *Elam: Surveys of political history and archaeology*. Berkeley: University of California Publications, Near Eastern Studies 25.

Casal, J.-M. 1961. *Fouilles de Mundigak*. Paris: MDAFA 17.

Casanova, M. 1991. *La vaisselle d'albâtre de Mésopotamie, d'Iran et d'Asie centrale aux IIIe et IIe millénaires avant J. -C.* Paris: Éditions Recherche sur les Civilisations.

Cattini, G. 2000. Administrative indicators in the Shahr-i Sokhta Eastern Residential Area of Period II (2800–2600 BC). In *South Asian Archaeology, 1997*, ed. M. Taddei and G. de Marco, 485–94. Rome: SOR 90/1.

Ciarla, R. 1979. The manufacture of alabaster vessels at Shahr-i Sokhta and Mundigak in the 3rd millennium BC: A problem of cultural identity. In *Iranica*, ed. G. Gnoli and A.V. Rossi, 319–35. Naples: Istituto Universitario Orientale, Seminario di Studi Asiatici, Series Minor 10.

———. 1981. A preliminary analysis of the manufacture of alabaster vessels at Shahr-i Sokhta and Mundigak in the 3rd millennium BC. In *South Asian Archaeology 1979*, ed. H. Härtel, 45–63. Berlin: Dietrich Reimer.

Curtis, J. 1988. A reconsideration of the cemetery at Khinaman, south-east Iran. *IrAnt* 23: 97–124.

Curtis, V. S., and St.-J. Simpson. 1997. Shahdad. *Iran* 35: 140–2.

———. 1998. Shahdad. *Iran* 36: 193.

Dalfes, H. N., G. Kukla, and H. Weiss. 1997. *Third Millennium BC climate change and old world collapse*. New York: Springer.

Damerow, P., and R. K. Englund. 1989. *The proto-Elamite texts from Tepe Yahya*. Cambridge, MA: ASPR Bulletin 39.

Ferioli, P., E. Fiandra, and S. Tusa. 1979. Stamp seals and the functional analysis of their sealings at Shahr-i Sokhta II–III (2700–2200 B.C.). In *South Asian Archaeology 1975*, ed. J. E. van Lohuizen-de Leeuw, 7–26. Leiden: Brill.

Fiandra, E., and C. Pepe. 2000. Typology and distribution of the administrative indicators in Eastern Residential Area of Shahr-i Sokhta during Period II (2800–2600 BC): The sealings. In *South Asian Archaeology 1997*, ed. M. Taddei and G. de Marco, 467–84. Rome: SOR 90/1.

Fisher, W. B. 1968. Physical geography. *CHI* 1: 3–110.

Fouache, E., D. Garçon, D. Rousset, D. Sénéchel, and Y.Madjidzadeh. 2005. La vallée de l'Halil Roud (region de Jiroft, Iran): Étude géoarchéologique et résultats préliminaires. *Paléorient* 31/2: 107–22.

Franke, U. 2008. Baluchistan and the borderlands. In *Encyclopedia of Archaeology*, vol. 1, ed. D. M. Pearsall, 651–70. Elsevier: San Diego.

Hakemi, A. 1972. *Catalogue de l'exposition: LUT, Xabis (Shahdad)*. Tehran: Premier Symposium annuel de la Recherchéarchéologique en Iran.

———. 1986. Les maquettes de Shahdad: Modèles de bâtiments sacrés du troisième millénaire av. J. C. *FHE*: 45–9.

———. 1992. The copper smelting furnaces of the Bronze Age in Shahdad. In *South Asian Archaeology 1989*, ed. C. Jarrige, 119–32. Madison: Prehistory Press.

———. 1994. Some statues discovered in the excavations at Shahdad. In *South Asian Archaeology 1993*, ed. A. Parpola and P. Koskikallio, 217–24. Helsinki: Annales Academiae Scientiarum Fennicae B 271.

———. 1997a. *Shahdad: Archaeological excavations of a Bronze Age centre in Iran*. Rome: IsMEO Reports and Memoirs 27.

———. 1997b. Kerman: The original place of production of chlorite stone objects in the 3rd millennium BC. *EW* 47/1: 11–40.

———. 2000. Comparison between the plates of Shahdad and other plates that exist in a few museums. In *South Asian archaeology 1997*, ed. M. Taddei and G. de Marco, 943–59. Rome: SOR 90/1.

Hakemi, A., and S. M. S. Sajjadi. 1989. Shahdad excavations in the context of the oases civilization. In *Bactria, an ancient oasis civilisation from the sands of Afghanistan*, ed. G. Ligabue and S. Salvatori, 143–53. Venice: Erizzo Editrice.

Hiebert, F. T., and C. C. Lamberg-Karlovsky. 1992. Central Asia and the Indo-Iranian borderlands. *Iran* 30: 1–15.

Kaboli, M. A. 1989/1368. Shahdad. In *Cities of Iran*, ed. M. Y. Kiani, 66–106. Tehran (in Persian).

———. 1997/1376. Dasht-e Lut archaeological expedition: excavations at the ancient site of Shahdad, preliminary report on the tenth campaign. In *Archaeological Reports*, 89–124. Tehran: ICAR (in Persian).

———. 2001/1380. Dasht-e Lut archaeological expedition: Excavations at the ancient site of Shahdad, preliminary report on the eleventh campaign 1994/1373. *Azhouheshnameh* 2: 239–66 (in Persian).

———. 2002/1381. Dasht-e Lut archaeological expedition: excavations at the ancient site of Shahdad, preliminary report on the twelfth campaign 1995/1374. *Azhouheshnameh* 4: 141–81 (in Persian).

Kohl, P. L. 1974. Seeds of upheaval: The production of chlorite at Tepe Yahya and an analysis of commodity production and trade in southwest Asia in the mid-third millennium. Unpublished PhD diss., Harvard University.

———. 1977. A note on chlorite artefacts from Shahr-i Sokhta. *EW* 27: 111–31.

———. 1978. The balance of trade in southwestern Asia in the mid-third millennium BC. *CA* 19/3: 463–92.

———. 1987. The ancient economy, transferable technologies and the Bronze Age world-system: A view from the northeastern frontier of the Ancient Near East. In *Centre and periphery in the ancient world*, ed. M. J. Rowlands, M. T. Larsen, and K. Kristiansen, 13–24. Cambridge: Cambridge University Press.

———. 2001. Reflections on the production of chlorite at Tepe Yahya: 25 years later. In *Excavations at Tepe Yahya, Iran, 1967–1975: The third millennium*, ed. D. T. Potts, 209–30. Cambridge, MA: ASPR Bulletin 45.

———. 2007. *The making of Bronze Age Eurasia*. Cambridge: Cambridge University Press.

Kohl, P. L., G. Harbottle, and E. V. Sayre. 1979. Physical and chemical analyses of soft stone vessels from southwest Asia. *Archaeometry* 21/2: 131–59.

Lamberg-Karlovsky, C. C. 1968. Survey and excavations in the Kirman area. *Iran* 6: 167–8.
———. 1969. Further notes on the shaft-hole pick-axe from Khurab, Makran. *Iran* 7: 163–8.
———. 1970. *Excavations at Tepe Yahya, Iran, 1967–1969: Progress report 1*. Cambridge, MA: ASPR Bulletin 27.
———. 1975. Urban interaction on the Iranian plateau: Excavations at Tepe Yahya 1967–1973. *Proceedings of the British Academy* 59: 282–319.
———. 1977. Foreign relations in the third millennium at Tepe Yahya. In *Le plateau Iranien et L'Asie Centrale des origines à la conquête islamique*, ed. J. Deshayes, 33–43. Paris: CNRS.
———. 1988. The "Intercultural Style" carved vessels. *IrAnt* 23: 45–95.
———. 1993. The biography of an object: The Intercultural Style vessels of the third millennium BC. In *History from things: Essays on material culture*, ed. S. Lubar and W. D. Kingery, 270–92. Washington/London: Smithsonian Institution Press.
———. 2001. Afterword. In *Excavations at Tepe Yahya, Iran, 1967–1975: The third millennium*, ed. D. T. Potts, 267–80. Cambridge, MA: ASPR Bulletin 45.
Lamberg-Karlovsky, C. C., and D. Schmandt-Besserat. 1977. Evaluation of the Bampur, Khurab and Chah Husseini collections in the Peabody Museum and relations with Tepe Yahya. *ML*: 113–34.
Lamberg-Karlovsky, C. C., and M. Tosi. 1973. Shahr-i Sokhta and Tepe Yahya: Tracks on the earliest history of the Iranian plateau. *EW* 23: 21–53.
Legrain, L. 1936. *Archaic seal-impressions*. Philadelphia/London: Ur Excavations III.
Madjidzadeh, Y. 2003a. *Jiroft: The earliest Oriental civilization*. Tehran: Printing and Publishing Organization of the Ministry of Culture and Islamic Guidance.
———. 2003b. La première campagne de fouilles à Jiroft dans le basin du Halil Roud. *DA* 287: 64–75.
———. 2008. Excavations at Konar Sandal in the region of Jiroft in the Halil Basin: First preliminary report (2002–2008), with a Contribution on Glyptic Art by Holly Pittman. *Iran* 46: 69–104.
———. 2012. Jiroft tablets and the origin of linear Elamite writing system. In *Cultural relations between the Indus and the Iranian plateau during the third millennium BCE*, ed. T. Osada and M. Witzel, 219–44. Cambridge, MA: Harvard Oriental Series Opera Minora 7.
Martin, H. 1988. *Fara: A reconstruction of the ancient Mesopotamian city of Shuruppak*. Birmingham: C. Martin.
Maxwell-Hyslop. K. R. 1988. A comment on the finds from Khinaman. *IrAnt* 23: 129–38.
Miroschedji, P. de. 1973. Vases et objets en stéatite susiens du Musée du Louvre. *CDAFI* 3: 9–80.
Mirsky, J. 1977. *Sir Aurel Stein, archaeological explorer*. Chicago/London: University of Chicago Press.
Mortazavi, M. 2006. The Bampur valley: A new chronological development. *Ancient Asia* 1: 53–61.
Mugavero, L., and M. Vidale. 2003. The use of polychrome containers in the Hilmand civilization: A female function? *EW* 53: 67–94.
Piperno, M. 1976. Grave 77 at Shahr-i Sokhta: further evidence of technological specialization in the 3rd millennium BC. *EW* 26/1–2: 9–12.
———. 1977. La necropoli. In *La città bruciata nel deserto salto. Archeologi e naturalisti italiani alla riscoperta di una civiltà protourbana nel Sistan iraniano: dieci anni di ricerche archeologiche*, ed. G. Tucci, 251–62. Venice: Editions Erizzo.

———. 1979. Socio-economic implications from the graveyard of Shahr-i Sokhta. In *South Asian Archaeology 1977*, ed. M. Taddei, 123–39. Naples: Istituto Universitario Orientale, Seminario di Studi Asiatici Series Minor 6.

———. 1986. The aspects of ethnical multiplicity across the Shahr–i Sokhta graveyard. *Oriens Antiquus* 25: 257–70.

Piperno, M., and S. Salvatori. 1982. Evidence of western cultural connections from a phase 3 group of graves at Shahr-i Sokhta. In *Mesopotamien und seine Nachbarn: Politische und kulturelle wechselbeziehungen im alten Vorderasien vom 4. bis 1. jahrtausend v. Chr.*, vol. 1, ed. H. J. Nissen, and J. Renger, 79–85. Berlin: BBVO 1.

———. 1983. Recent results and new perspectives from the research at the graveyard of Shahr-i Sokhta, Sistan, Iran. *AION* 43/2: 173–91.

———. 2007. *The Shahr-i Sokhta graveyard (Sistan, Iran): Excavation campaigns 1972–1978*. Rome: IsIAO Reports and Memoirs 6.

Piperno, M., and M. Tosi. 1975. The graveyard of Shahr-i Sokhta, Iran. *Archaeology* 28: 186–97.

Pittman, H. 2001. Glyptic art of Period IV. In *Excavations at Tepe Yahya, Iran, 1967–1975: The third millennium*, ed. D. T. Potts, 231–67. Cambridge, MA: ASPR Bulletin 45.

———. 2012. Glyptic art of Konar Sandal South, observations on the relative and absolute chronology in the third millennium BCE. In *NĀMVARNĀMEH: Papers in honour of Massoud Azarnoush*, ed. H. Fahimi and K. Alizadeh, 79–94. Tehran: Ganjine-ye Naghsh-e Jahan.

———. 2014. Hybrid imagery and cultural identity in the Age of Exchange: Halil River basin and Sumer meet in Margiana. In *My life is like the summer rose. Maurizio Tosi e l'archeologia come modo di vita*, ed. B. Cerasetti and C. C. Lamberg-Karlovsky. Oxford: BAR Int Ser *MLSR*: 625–36.

Pottier, M.-H. 1984. *Matériel funéraire de la Bactriane méridionale de l'Âge du Bronze*. Paris: Éditions Recherche sur les Civilisations.

Potts, D. T. 1981a. Echoes of Mespotamian divinity on a cylinder seal from southeastern Iran. *RA* 75: 135–42.

———. 1981b. The potter's marks of Tepe Yahya. *Paléorient* 7/1: 107–22.

———. 2001. *Excavations at Tepe Yahya, Iran, 1967–1975: The third millennium*. Cambridge, MA: ASPR Bulletin 45.

———. 2003. Tepe Yahya, Tell Abraq and the chronology of the Bampur sequence. *IrAnt* 38: 1–24.

———. 2004. Camel hybridization and the role of *Camelus bactrianus* in the Ancient Near East. *JESHO* 47: 143–65.

———. 2005. In the beginning: Marhashi and the origins of Magan's ceramic industry in the third millennium BC. *AAE* 16: 67–78.

Potts, T. F. 1993. Patterns of trade in third-millennium BC Mesopotamia and Iran. *WA* 24/3: 379–402.

———. 1994. *Mesopotamia and the East: An archaeological and historical study of foreign relations ca. 3400–2000 BC*. Oxford: Oxford University Committee for Archaeology Monograph 37.

Prickett, M. E. 1986. Settlement during the early periods. In *Excavations at Tepe Yahya, Iran, 1967–1975: The early periods*, ed. T. W. Beale, 215–46. Cambridge, MA: ASPR Bulletin 38.

Ratnagar, S. 2004. *Trading encounters: From the Euphrates to the Indus in the Bronze Age*. New Delhi: Oxford University Press.

Reade, J. 2001. Assyrian king-lists, the Royal Tombs of Ur, and Indus origins. *JNES* 60/1: 1–29.

Sajjadi, S. M. S. 2003. Excavations at Shahr–i Sokhta: First preliminary report on the excavations of the graveyard 1997–2000. *Iran* 41: 21–98.

Sajjadi, S. M. S., F. Foruzanfar, R. Shirazi, and S. Baghestani. 2003. Excavations at Shahr-i Sokhta: First preliminary report on the excavations of the Graveyard, 1997-2000. *Iran* 41: 21-97.

Sajjadi, S. M. S., and M. Tosi. 1987. Prehistoric settlements in the Bardsir plain, south-eastern Iran. *EW* 37: 11-129.

———. 1989. A class of Sasanian ceramics from southeastern Iran. *Rivista di Archeologia* 13: 31-40.

Salvatori, S., and M. Tosi. 1997. Postscriptum: Some reflections on Shahdad and its place in the Bronze Age of Middle Asia. In *Shahdad: Archaeological investigations of a Bronze Age center in Iran*, A. Hakemi, 121-38. Rome: IsMEO Reports and Memoirs 27.

———. 2005. Shahr-i Sokhta revised sequence. In *South Asian archaeology 2001*, ed. C. Jarrige and V. Lefèvre, 281-92. Paris: Éditions Recherche sur les Civilisations. reference is now in the text

Salvatori, S., and M. Vidale. 1982. A brief surface survey of the protohistoric site of Shahdad (Kerman), Iran: Preliminary report. *Rivista di Archeologia* 6: 5-10.

———. 1997. *Shahr-Sokhta, 1975-1978: Central Quarters excavations, preliminary report*. Rome: IsIAO Reports and Memoirs, Series Minor 1.

Santini, G. 1990. A preliminary note on animal figurines from Shahr-i Sokhta. In *South Asian Archaeology 1987*, ed. M. Taddei, 427-51. Rome: SOR 66/1.

Sarraf, M. R. 1981. *Die keramik von Tell-i Iblis und ihre zeitliche und räumliche Beziehung zu den anderen iranischen und mesopotamischen Kulturen*. Berlin: AMI Ergänzungsband 7.

Schmidt, E. F. 1937. *Excavations at Tepe Hissar, Damghan*. Philadelphia: University of Pennsylvania Press.

Stein, Sir M. A. 1937. *Archaeological reconnaissances in north-western India and south-eastern Īrān*. London: Macmillan.

Tosi, M. 1968. Excavations at Shahr-i Sokhta, a Chalcolithic settlement in the Iranian Seistan: Preliminary report on the first campaign, October-December 1967. *EW* 18: 9-66.

———. 1969. Excavations at Shahr-i Sokhta: Preliminary report on the second campaign, September-December 1968. *EW* 19: 283-386.

———. 1970a. A tomb from Damin and the problem of the Bampur sequence in the third millennium B.C. *EW* 20: 9-50.

———. 1970b. Shahr-i Sokhta. *Iran* 8: 188-9.

———. 1974. Bampur: A problem of isolation. *EW* 24: 29-50.

———. 1983. Development, continuity and cultural change in the stratigraphical sequence of Shahr-i Sokhta. In *Prehistoric Sistan 1*, ed. M. Tosi, 127-71. Rome: IsMEO Reports and Memoirs 19.

Tusa, S. 1977. I sigilli e le impronte. *In La cittàbruciata nel deserto Salto. Archeologi e naturalisti italiani alla riscoperta di una civiltàprotourbana nel Sistan iraniano: Dieci anni de ricerche archeologische*, ed G. Tucci, 251-62. Venice: Editions Erizzo.

Vidale, M. 1984. The pear-shaped beaker of Shahr-i Sokhta: Evolution of a ceramic morphotype during the 3rd millennium BC. In *South Asian archaeology, 1981*, ed. B. Allchin, 81-97. Cambridge: Cambridge University Press.

Vidale, M., and F. Desset. 2013. *Mahtoutabad I (Konar Sandal South, Jiroft): Preliminary evidence of occupation of a Halil Rud site in the early fourth millennium BCE. AIN*: 233-52.

Voigt, M., and R. H. Dyson Jr. 1992. The chronology of Iran, ca. 8000-2000 B.C. In *Chronologies in Old World archaeology*, 3rd ed., vol. 1, ed. R. W. Ehrich, 122-78. Chicago: University of Chicago Press.

Winkelmann, S. 1997. Southeast Iranian and Indo-Iranian elements on Bactrian and Murghab style seals. In *South Asian archaeology 1995*, ed. R. and B. Allchin, 265–77. Enfield: Science Publishers.

———. 2000a. Intercultural relations between Iran, the Murghabo-Bactrian Archaeological Complex (BMAC), northwest India and Failaka in the field of seals. *EW* 50: 43–95.

———. 2000b. Some new ideas about the possible origin of the anthropomorphic and semi-human creature depictions on Harappan Seals. In *South Asian archaeology 1997*, ed. M. Taddei and G. de Marco, 341–62. Rome: IsIAO SOR 90/1.

Wright, R. P. 1984. Technology, style and craft specialization: Spheres of interaction and exchange in the Indo-Iranian borderlands, third millennium B.C. Unpublished PhD diss., Harvard University.

———. 1989a. New tracks on ancient frontiers: Ceramic technology on the Indo-Iranian Borderlands. In *Archaeological thought in America*, ed. C. C. Lamberg-Karlovsky, 268–79. Cambridge: Cambridge University Press.

———. 1989b. New perspectives on third millennium painted grey wares. In *South Asian Archaeology 1985*, ed. K. Frifelt and P. Sørensen, 137–49. London: Scandinavian Institute of Asian Studies Occasional Paper 4.

———. 2002. Revisiting interaction spheres: Social boundaries and technologies on inner and outermost frontiers. *IrAnt* 37: 403–17.

Woolley, C. L. 1934. *The Royal Cemetery*. Philadelphia: Ur Excavations II.

Zarins, J. 1978. Typological studies in Saudi Arabian archaeology: Steatite vessels in the Riyadh Museum. *Atlal* 2: 65–93.

PART IV

THE IRON AGE

CHAPTER 17

THE LATE BRONZE AND EARLY IRON AGE IN NORTHWESTERN IRAN

MICHAEL D. DANTI

Introduction

The Late Bronze Age (hereafter LBA; 1450–1250 BC) and Early Iron Age (1250–550 BC) of northwestern Iran comprise one of the most compelling and disputed eras in Iranian archaeology. Traditionally archaeologists have treated this time span as a single analytical unit dubbed the "Early Iron Age," at variance with prevailing Near Eastern terminology owing to a modicum of happenstance in the early development of the archaeology of Iran and a generally accepted degree of continuity in the archaeological record, particularly in ceramic horizons. This chapter presents a new chronological assessment of the LBA and early Iron Age and the immediately preceding transitional period: the Middle Bronze III (hereafter MBIII; 1600–1450 BC, Table 17.1; Danti 2013).

The location of mountain passes and other features of terrain truly make northwestern Iran a crossroads between Mesopotamia, the southern Caucasus, eastern Anatolia, and the Iranian Plateau. Accordingly, the region's material culture evinces far-flung interconnections, syncretisms, and synchronisms (Piller 2004b). What the northwestern Zagros lacks in indigenous written records in the concerned time periods, it surely compensates for in historical import. Scholars have long sifted through the archaeological and historical data sets in search of migrant proto-Iranian and other Indo-European groups who appear in neighboring Mesopotamia and Anatolia at this time and who are also mentioned there in textual sources in association with western Iran. The prevailing view on northwestern Iran holds that the LBA begins with a punctuated and sweeping change in material culture, best exemplified by, but not confined to, changes in the predominant ceramic wares and forms with so-called Western Grey Ware appearing in significant and rapidly increasing amounts. Scholars have long attributed this to migrations of newcomers, and accordingly issues of ethnicity, and archaeology's capacity to cope with such an anthropologically slippery concept, have occupied center stage in interpretative works. The written records of Mesopotamia and later, Urartu, paint a picture of ethnic and sociopolitical diversity with sedentary and transhumant Mannaean, Hurrian, Urartian, Semitic, Kassite, and Iranian populations interspersed throughout the verdant, well-watered mountain valleys. In the early Iron Age, this area was a target of Assyrian expansion and exacting tribute, and part of northwestern Iran formed a portion of the nascent and geographically unfixed Urartian state (Reade 1995; Piller 2010; Fuchs 2004, 2011; Lanfranchi 2003). Later, it was the stage for violent struggles between Assyria and Urartu, eventually leading to a military stalemate. With the coming of the Scythians and the political ascendancy of the Medes and Persians, the area played a more peripheral and poorly understood role in broader regional developments, and our archaeological view of the Iron III is increasingly variegated and complex.

The region

The distinction between the modern Iranian provinces of Eastern and Western Azerbaijan and Kurdistan is artificial, and this area traditionally shared tribal and ethnic groups in antiquity. In archaeological terms, the region of interest extends beyond the northern border of Iran into Nakhichevan, southern Armenia, and the Republic of Azerbaijan, and it is closely affiliated with eastern Anatolia, the southern and western Caspian littoral, and the region from Takab and Qazvin eastward along the southern flanks of the Alborz and southward skirting the eastern Zagros to Kashan. Over the last fifty years, many archaeological surveys have been conducted in the region, but the results have not always been published and methodologies have differed markedly (see the annual reports of Kleiss in *AMI*; Kroll 1994a, 2005 and sources cited therein; Pecorella and Salvini 1984; Swiny 1975).

The core of the region of interest is the Lake Urmia basin, today one of the most densely settled and agriculturally productive parts of Iran, the preeminent urban center being the illustrious city of Tabriz. Lake Urmia, a large salt lake, and its adjacent valleys are hemmed in by high mountains in most places; the valleys provide important lines of communication to nearby high mountain passes. A number of rivers flow into the lake and water the valleys, and hence they were settled fairly continuously from the sixth millennium BC (Voigt 1983). The largest are those of Urmia, Ushnu-Solduz, Mahabad, and Miyandoab on the western and southern sides of the lake. The eastern shore, dominated by the stratovolcano Mt. Sahand, was not as densely settled and is fringed by extensive salt flats. The area east of the lake was settled (Shahidi and Biscione 2007). The Salmas valley forms a smaller fertile enclave at the northwest corner of the basin. To the north of the lake lie the intermontane valleys of Maku, Khoy, and Marand (Kroll 2004). The valleys of the northern part of the region may be viewed as "terrestrial archipelagos" (Zimansky 1990: 12), exhibiting marked regional variations and close links to eastern Anatolia, in particular the Lake Van region, and the southern Caucasus. These influences were also strong in the northern Lake Urmia Basin in antiquity and diminish and were more intermittent to the south near the east-west Ushnu-Solduz valley, which was more closely aligned to northern Mesopotamia. The southern lake region was linked to Assyria via routes through passes at Kel-i Shin and Khaneh to the Rowanduz Gorge and the headwaters of the Upper Zab. The lake basin is connected to the mountains and rolling hills of Kurdistan by the river valleys of the Lower Zab, Simineh Rud (Tatau Çay), and Zarineh Rud (Jaghatu Çay). Other mountain passes in the vicinity of modern Sardasht and Lake Zeribar, near modern Marivan, offer prized east-west routes through the *chaîne magistrale* westward to Erbil and Mosul and to the Diyala River, Suleimaniyeh, and Baghdad. To the south and east roads led to the caravan city of Hamadan on the Great Khorasan Road via Nausud or Sanandaj. Accordingly, ties with Mesopotamia and the Iranian Plateau are manifest in the archaeological record of Kurdistan as well, particularly in the Iron III.

Early definitions of the Iron Age

The definition of the Iranian Iron Age has been almost inextricably linked to the development of theories on Iranian migrations into the Persian Plateau, and excavations in Iranian Azerbaijan and Kurdistan played a crucial role in both subject areas following the pioneering research conducted at Tepe Hissar (1931–3), Tepe Giyan (1931–2), Tepe Sialk (1933–4, 1937), and Susa (1946–67). Incomplete archaeological coverage, the poor quality of some early excavations, and a dearth of publication hamper our current view of protohistoric Iran, and this is especially true for the later second and early first millennia. Roman Ghirshman established the broad outlines of an archaeological sequence and an influential theoretical stance, positing multiple waves of migration driving culture change, in large part drawing on his excavations at Cemeteries A and B of Tepe Sialk, near modern Kashan, and Giyan Tepe in Luristan (Ghirshman 1939; Contenau and Ghirshman 1935). Ghirshman's work engendered a new paradigm within Iranian archaeology that connected the major archaeological horizons of northern and western Iran of the second and early first millennia with Indo-Iranian migrations (Ghirshman 1954: 70–1). While this theoretical movement generally met with acceptance in western scholarship and was greatly expanded (see esp. Young 1965, 1967), albeit with differences in opinion regarding the timing, relevant archaeological horizons, migratory routes, and the ethnos of the migrants (e.g., Deshayes 1969; Burney and Lang 1971; Dyson 1977), Soviet/Russian scholarship has been largely characterized by dissenting viewpoints (see esp. Kuz'mina 2007: 367–70).

In Sialk Cemetery A (Period V), Ghirshman excavated fifteen tombs containing a monochrome gray-to-black burnished ware, and in Tomb 4 he found two iron objects—a dagger and "punch" (Ghirshman 1939: 9, pl. 58)—that stand out from the ubiquitous items of bronze. The graves of Tepe Giyan I, particularly Grave 23, had already yielded ceramics similar to Sialk A in association with copper/bronze artifacts and an iron dagger (Contenau and Ghirshman 1935: 240, 245). Ghirshman reasoned the scarcity of iron indicated this ceramic "horizon," characterized by burnished gray-black ware, dated to the end of the Bronze Age. Sialk Cemetery B (Period VI), located some distance from Cemetery A and separated in time by a hiatus of unknown duration, provided evidence of a significantly different material culture, with painted ceramics, little burnished gray-black ware, and a higher incidence of iron artifacts. Ghirshman originally dated Sialk A to 1400–1200 BC and Sialk B to no earlier than 1200–1100 BC (Ghirshman 1935: 245). He later revised his dating of Sialk A to 1200–1000 BC, linking the phase to the graves of Giyan I^4 and I^3, which in turn were compared to graves at Babylon of the twelfth to eleventh centuries (Ghirshman 1939: 20; 1964: 277–8). He noted similarities between Sialk A gray-black burnished vessels with white-infilled incised designs with similar wares from the Caucasus, where such material was then erroneously dated to around 1000 BC (Ghirshman 1939: pl. 38 s. 431, s. 432; 1964: 277–8). He revised the start of Sialk B to 1000 BC (Ghirshman 1964: 280) based on the dating of the earlier Sialk A, a Neo-Assyrian cylinder seal in one Sialk B tomb, and his belief that this archaeological culture represented the Medes, who are first mentioned in the records of Assyria in 834 BC and therefore the start of Sialk B must predate this. As early as 1948, Schaeffer questioned the logic of Ghirshman's dating (Schaeffer 1948: 469–70, 477), preferring a range of 1400–1200 (LBA) for Sialk A and 1250–1100 for Sialk B (Iron I); this latter dating of Sialk B cannot be maintained (see Young 1963; Dyson 1965a: 200–1; Medvedskaya 1983). The earlier graves of Sialk A and Giyan I would now be more properly termed MBIII, LBA, and Iron I (cf. Tourovetz 1989; Helwing 2005: 40–1; Dittmann 1990; Piller 2004a). The association of gray-to-black monochrome burnished ware and early iron, as well as Ghirshman's grouping of the graves into a single period, would influence later scholars, as would his diffusionist theories of culture change driven by multiple waves of immigrants (Ghirshman 1954: 71, 74–5; 1964: 3, 277–8). Excavations by Erich Schmidt in northeastern Iran at Hissar had revealed generically similar gray-black burnished ceramics of the late third and early second millennia BC, ending with a destruction and abandonment (Schmidt 1937). Subsequently, the field would be dominated by theories attempting to "connect the dots" of Iranian migrations (Mousavi 2005)—the primary data often consisted of material salvaged from looted cemeteries, such as Hasanlu and Khurvin, that proved challenging to date (Hakemi and Rad 1950; Vanden Berghe 1964).

The Hasanlu Project in Ushnu-Solduz represents the next major chapter in the development of an archaeological sequence for the Iranian Iron Age. Work conducted at Hasanlu Tepe, Dinkha Tepe, and Agrab Tepe, as well as a short salvage project at Ziwiyeh in Kurdistan, greatly expanded understanding of the period (Dyson 1965a; Young 1965, 1985; Muscarella 1994). Excavations in the Solduz and Ushnu valleys served as the basis for the development of an archaeological sequence spanning the pottery Neolithic to the Achaemenid period. In a pioneering synthesis, T. Cuyler Young Jr. divided the archaeology of northern and western Iran's early Iron Age into "groups" or archaeological horizons chronologically structured by the results of the Hasanlu Project from 1956 to 1962 (Young 1965). In a related study, Robert H. Dyson Jr. rather tacitly introduced the terms Iron I–III, based on essentially the same data set (1965a: 211, table 2). Young defined an Early Western Grey Ware Group (EWGW), Late Western Grey Ware Group (LWGW), and Late Buff Ware Group (LBW) that generally corresponded to Dyson's Iron I, II, and III. Dyson's Iron I–III were often confused with cultures, but eventually their status as absolute time ranges was reemphasized (Levine 1987: 232–4, 243; Young 1985: 362, n. 1). The term Grey Ware, as applied to the pottery of LBA and early Iron Age Iran, does not aptly describe the ware's range of variation and has caused some confusion given the use of the term for other gray-colored wares of the second millennium BC (cf. Hamlin 1971), and so it is referred to here as Monochrome Burnished Ware (MBW). Over the years, the Hasanlu Project and other scholars maintained the link between MBW contexts and the designation "Iron Age." New radiocarbon dates from Dinkha and Hasanlu and the recalibration of the radiocarbon sequence steadily lowered the starting date of the Iron I to the fifteenth century BC. In terms of its development, the definition of the Iron Age was dissociated from absolute time ranges or the use of iron, which becomes ubiquitous in Iran only in the ninth century BC (Pigott 1981: 180; 2004), rather the terminology was imbued with cultural connotations supporting a theoretical movement. We read of "Iron Age cultures," and an "Iron Age expansion" (e.g., Dyson 1968: 31) represented by Grey Ware in western Iran. Over the years, various scholars have pointed out the problems with this singular application of chronological terminology (Muscarella 1974: 79; 1994: 140; Pigott 1977: 209; Haerinck 1988: 64; Kroll 1994b: 163, n. 23). A revised chronology based on a recent reassessment of Hasanlu and other sites in northwestern Iran is presented here (Table 17.1).

MBIII (1600–1450 BC)

This important transitional period is poorly known outside of northern Iranian Azerbaijan, and it is typified by affinities with the southern Caucasus. We can say little regarding the region's cultures beyond the prevalent styles and distribution of ceramics, especially painted pottery. This is most unfortunate since it is during this period that the MBW Horizon is first identifiable in the region.

In Kurdistan, the MBIII is known only from archaeological surveys; Giyan and Godin in Luristan provide grave groups and a fragmented occupational sequence for the area to the south in the environs of Nehavand (Contenau and Ghirshman 1935; Young 1965; Henrickson 1983–4; 2011: table 6.2). In the north, the period is characterized by painted wares, most notably polychrome painted Urmia Ware (Edwards 1981, 1983, 1986; Rubinson 2004) and Early MBW (Figs. 17.1–2A). Urmia Ware develops out of the MBII painted pottery traditions of the northern part of the region best attested at Haftavan Early VIb and Geoy Tepe early D (Edwards 1983; Burton-Brown 1951). In contrast, the MBII assemblage of the southern Lake Urmia Basin contains an important

Table 17.1 Periodization of northwestern Iran in the second and first millennia BC.

BC	Period	Horizon	Hasanlu	Dinkha	Geoy	Kordlar	Haftavan
550–300	Achaemenid Iron IV	Classic Triangle Ware	IIIa/II	–	–	–	–
800–550	Iron III	Late Buff Ware/ Ziwiyeh Ware	IIIb	–	–	–	–
	Iron III (Urartian)	Late Buff Ware/ Urartian	IIIc	–	–	–	III
1050–800	Iron II	Late MBW	IVb	II	Geoy A	IIb–I	IV
1250–1050	Iron I	Middle MBW/ Painted Ware (North)	IVc	Late III	Geoy B	IV/III–IIb	?
1450–1250	"Later Late Bronze"	Early MBW/ Painted Ware (North)	Late V	III	Geoy B	IV	?
	"Early Late Bronze"	Early MBW/ Painted Wares (North)	Early V	III	Tomb K	V?	V
1600–1450	Middle Bronze III	Early MBW/ Polychrome Painted Wares	VIa	Early III	Late D–C	V?	Late VIb
1700–1600	"Terminal MB II"	Painted Wares/ Early MBW?	VIb	IV Phase D	Geoy D	–	Early VIb
1900–1700	Middle Bronze II	Painted Wares	VIb	IV Phases A–C	Geoy D	–	Early VIb
2100–1900	Middle Bronze I	Simple Ware/ Painted Ware (North)	VIc	V	Geoy G	–	VIc

Khabur Ware component, indicative of strong ties with northern Mesopotamia (Hamlin [Kramer] 1971, 1974). Painted Khabur Ware rapidly falls out of the assemblage already in the Terminal MBII (seventeenth century). In Phase B (MBII) of the Dinkha Control Sounding, Painted Khabur Ware (Kramer's Ware Ie) is at a high at 24 percent of the assemblage, while in Phase D, the Terminal MBII, it comprises a mere 8 percent. There is a strong trend toward the production of unpainted wares in the Terminal MBII as well as annular band-painted ware. The MBII Khabur Ware assemblage is highly localized, having been found in significant amounts in excavations at Dinkha Tepe and Hasanlu and being known from surveys at sites stretching east to west along the Gadar Çay (Kroll 1994b: 165). The southeastern Lake Urmia Basin and the valley of the Zarineh Rud and Simineh Rud form a third second-millennium painted pottery tradition linked to Giyan Tepe III–II and Godin III (Swiny 1973; Tala'i 1984; Edwards 1986: 69; Henrickson 2011).

The MBIII is well known at Haftavan, near modern Salmas, where it is designated Period Late VIB (Burney 1970, 1972, 1973, 1975; Edwards 1981, 1983, 1986). Haftavan, like other sites in the region, provides evidence for disruptions during the mid-second millennium BC. The Early VIB settlement (MBII) was burned. In some parts of the

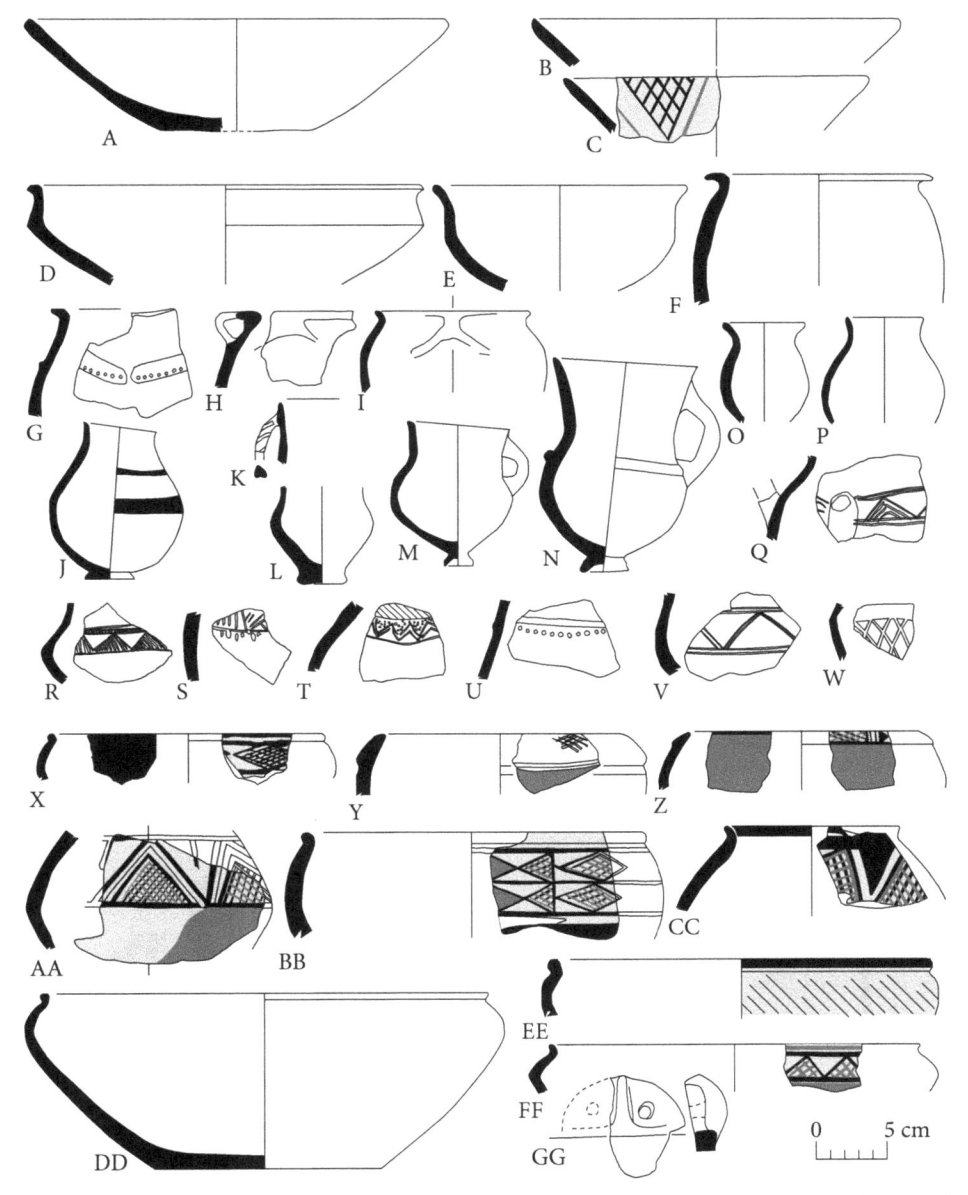

FIGURE 17.1 Middle Bronze III ceramics from Dinkha (A, D–H, K–L, Q–CC, GG), Hasanlu High Mound (EE), Hasanlu graves (J, M, N, DD), and Geoy Tepe (B, C, I, O, P, FF). MBW: A, B, D–F,H, I, K–P, DD, GG; pattern-burnished MBW: W; incised and impressed MBW: G, Q–V; Khabur ware: J; Urmia ware: X–CC, EE, FF.

site, this was followed by an ephemeral occupation attested by stake holes and pits. Elsewhere, a mudbrick and timber structure was terraced into the slope of the mound resting on the burned debris of the earlier settlement. MBIII Haftavan has multiple architectural phases, consisting of flimsy construction repeatedly rebuilt, including

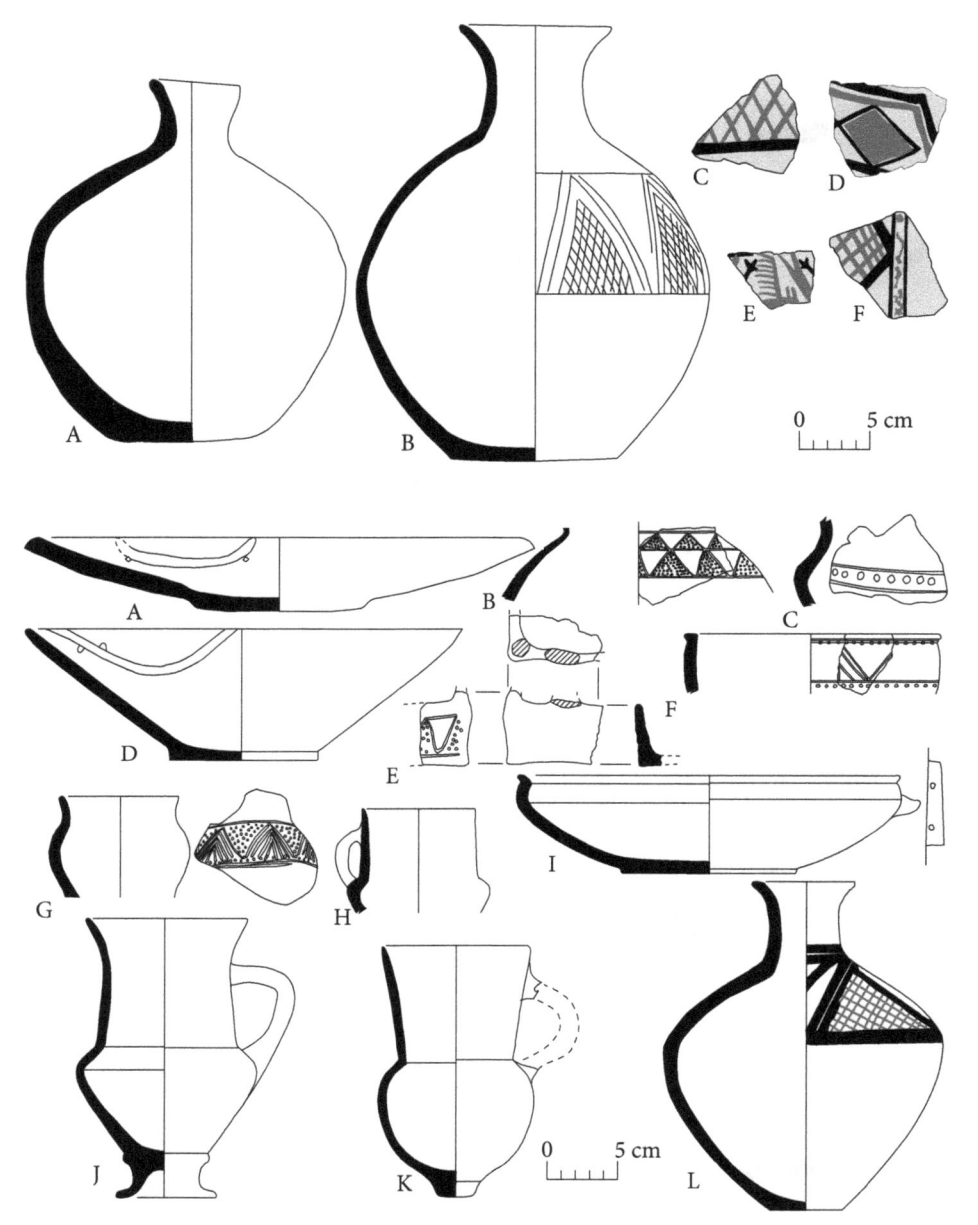

FIGURE 17.2 Upper (A–F): Middle Bronze III ceramics from Hasanlu Graves (A–B) and Geoy Tepe (C–F). MBW: A; Urmia Ware: B–F. (2a: B after Stein 1940). Lower (A–L): Early Late Bronze Age ceramics from Hasanlu and Dinkha. Hasanlu Graves: I–K; Dinkha: A–C, E–H; Dinkha Graves: D, L. MBW: A, D, H–K; White-filled Incised and Impressed MBW: B, C, F, G; Incised and Impressed MBW: E; Urmia Ware: L.

rectilinear mudbrick structures on stone footings and an area of large ovens suggesting intensive industrial or residential activities (Edwards 1983: 73). The MBIII settlement was also destroyed by fire.

In the Urmia valley to the south, Burton-Brown's excavations at contemporary Geoy Tepe provide one small exposure of MBIII architecture and graves, generally referred to as Geoy late D–C (Figs. 17.1: B, C, I, O, P, FF; 2A.C–F). The division of Geoy D into an earlier and later subperiod is based on analysis conducted by Dyson (Dyson 1968: 16–17; Edwards 1986: 58–60). The distinction is necessitated by the mixing of two separate periods through the digging of arbitrary levels defined by absolute elevations through sloping deposits in Pit [Operation] IV (cf. Burton-Brown 1951: figs. 16, 17b–c). In Pit III, a deposit containing Urmia Ware and early MBW sealed stone-built tombs initially dated to Geoy Tepe D (MBII, Burton-Brown 1951: 110). Dyson (1968: 18) dates Tombs A and J to Period late D–C (MBIII) based on their elevations, and Tombs B and H "could belong to the earlier state," that is, early Period D (MBII), while Edwards dates the tombs to the MBIII (Edwards 1986: 60–1). Polychrome painted Urmia Ware is not found in MBIII graves, which tend to contain undecorated ceramics. The overlying MBIII deposit was in turn cut by inhumation graves with MBW of likely early Iron Age date (Burton-Brown 1951: 123–6). Poorly preserved architectural remains were recovered in Pit IV, immediately above structures of Period D (Burton-Brown 1951: 72, figs. 17b–c, 18). The situation at Kordlar Tepe in the same valley is difficult to ascertain. Kordlar V, the earliest extensively known level, was revealed in limited soundings and provides a possible intermediate assemblage of ceramics (Heinsch 2004; Lippert 1979: figs. 6.6, 9.2, 10.1–2, 11.2), falling somewhere in the MBIII to early LBA, based on similarities to Dinkha (see below) and Kizylvank (Schaeffer 1948: fig. 270.1–5), as noted by Edwards (1986: 64), and radiocarbon dates from overlying Kordlar III–IV (Lippert 1979: 117–18, 137; Felber 1979).

Excavations at Dinkha Tepe in the Ushnu Valley to the south show the Terminal MBII settlement (Dinkha IV Phase D) was destroyed by fire. This marks the end of the Khabur Ware presence in Ushnu-Solduz with sharply diminishing amounts of annular band-painted buff ware and plain buff ware in later assemblages. The small excavated exposure of the late Terminal MBII provided no evidence for MBIII rebuilding, but the deposit immediately overlying the collapse of the MBII structures contained Urmia Ware (Fig. 17.1.X–CC; Rubinson 2004) and early MBW (Fig. 17.1.A, D–F, H, L, GG). In contrast to other MBIII sites, the early MBW of Dinkha also occurs in an Incised and Impressed variety (Fig. 17.1.G, Q–V). The MBIII level was overlain by "trash deposits" of the early LBA, and the MBIII and LBA strata were cut by graves of the LBA and Iron I (Muscarella 1974; see below). At nearby Hasanlu Tepe in the Solduz Valley, MBIII occupation is suggested by a few sherds from the Well Sounding, a deep sounding dug near the center of the main mound by a professional well-digger (Fig. 17.1.EE). Other stray sherds of Urmia Ware were found on the mound's surface. Graves probably dating to the period were found on the Low Mound (Figs. 17.1.J, M–N, DD and 17.2 (Upper).A–B). The MBIII is almost certainly present at Hasanlu, and sampling and site formation processes have contributed to a seeming hiatus (the Terminal MBII and MBIII) in the archaeological sequence between the MBII and early LBA.

The Late Bronze Age (1450–1250 BC)

The historical record sheds little light on this period in northwestern Iran; archaeological evidence offers a glimpse of a time of increasing prosperity and a gradual return to urbanism on the scale of the MBII, evincing new settlement types and the proliferation of Early MBW. The material record exhibits connections to the Kassite, Hurro-Mitanni, and Middle Assyrian kingdoms, as well as the southwestern Caspian littoral, southern Caucasus, and northeastern Iran. However, our view is based largely on ceramics with other artifact categories being comparatively rare until the latter LBA.

The LBA is best known at Hasanlu V, Dinkha III, and perhaps Haftavan V and Kordlar IV (see below). Graves, not always associated with settlements, have been excavated at Dinkha, Hasanlu, Geoy, Haftavan, Dalma Tepe, Hajji Firuz, and Yanik Tepe. Dinkha, Hasanlu, and Kordlar provide a range of radiocarbon dates. The LBA previously formed the early portion of Hasanlu V (Dyson 1977), the Early Western Grey Ware Group/Horizon (Young 1965), and the Iron I of northwestern Iran (Dyson 1965a; Muscarella 1994). The period is primarily identifiable by its Early Monochrome Burnished Ware component with an assemblage related to the MBIII but, overall, more limited in the number of ware types in the south. Painted wares continue in greater frequency north from the Urmia valley. At Hasanlu and Dinkha the period is divisible into early and late subperiods based on the prevalent vessel forms in occupation deposits and graves (Figs. 17.2B–17.6). Future research may justify the designation of an LBA I and II.

Built environment

Architecture of the LBA is known from Hasanlu and Kordlar. The exposures for early Hasanlu V, the early LBA, are quite limited and we can say little about the prevalent architectural styles and typical urban forms—a row of small, square rooms occupied the northwestern High Mound. In the later LBA, part of this structure was demolished and was replaced by a small columned-hall building (the RS22–23 LBA Building), likely an elite residence (Fig. 17.3A). The building was entered at the southeast, possibly through an antechamber, which opened onto a hall with two columns, a raised hearth, and a "throne seat." The sidewalls were lined with mudbrick benches, where there was evidence for possible side columns, and storage jars had been set into mudbrick benches in the northeast corner. The structure also contained a long, narrow storeroom(s) in the north and possibly a stairway to the north of the main entrance. The building's date largely rests on radiocarbon samples; finds from secure contexts were rare. The later Iron

I–II citadels contained several such structures on grander scales but with similar internal features and overall plan, and scholars have cited the appearance of the RS22–23 LBA Building as evidence for punctuated culture change attendant with the emergence of the MBW Horizon (Dyson 1977; Young 2003). However, the MBW ceramic horizon dates to at least the MBIII, well before this earliest attested columned hall of the later LBA, and the levels below the RS22–23 LBA Building provided evidence of a markedly different style of early LBA architecture associated with MBW. Another early columned-hall building of the later LBA–early Iron I is known from Kordlar IV. This fortified manor house had corner towers, a modest columned hall with a single central column and probable side columns, narrow benches, and a central sunken hearth (Lippert 1977: fig. 22). The building's construction can be dated to as early as the late LBA on the basis of radiocarbon samples from Kordlar IV and III (Lippert 1979). The building was destroyed by fire and contained human victims and a fairly large number of artifacts. Comparisons of the artifactual finds with Hasanlu indicate Kordlar IV was likely destroyed in the early Iron I, and therefore this material is treated herein under the Iron I below. At Kordlar we see a concern with fortifying a single structure, while at Hasanlu the later LBA buildings were likely located within a fortified citadel. No circumvallation is known for Hasanlu V, but other evidence suggests a fortified citadel occupied the High Mound. On the southern High Mound, a buttressed internal gateway with a tower, the YZ27–29 Building (Dyson 1977: 158, fig. 2), is similar to the Lower Court Gate of the Iron II citadel located in the same general area (Fig. 17.3B). The YZ27–29 Building dates at least to the later LBA and was repeatedly rebuilt and modified through the Iron I. Eventually Burned Building I East of the Iron II replaced it, and together with the Lower Court Gate formed the main fortified entrances to the Iron II Lower Court (Fig. 17.12). The YZ27–29 gateway suggests long-term continuity in the use of space on the High Mound and that the settlement centered on a fortified citadel from the late LBA to the Iron II. Burney and Lang (1971: 118) cite unfortified settlements as being typical of the "early Iron Age," but this is not the case with regard to Hasanlu. Other limited soundings beneath the Iron II monumental buildings of the Hasanlu citadel show similar continuities in the built environments of the later LBA, Iron I, and Iron II. On the Low Mound, several soundings reached deposits of the LBA, and occupation is attested on the northeastern Low Mound. Other areas served as cemeteries, especially in the north (the North Cemetery) and one early LBA grave was found on the northwest Low Mound in Operation LIII. The North Cemetery continued to be used in the Iron I–II and also contained graves of the MBII–III and Early Bronze Age.

Haftavan V (1450–1000 BC) provides two superimposed exposures of residential structures on the western low mound, but these are difficult to date precisely (Burney 1973: 162–4). They exhibit new construction techniques and their low density suggests a decline in the settlement's population. No architecture is known from LBA Dinkha Tepe, although the presence of "trash deposits" in the cemetery area suggests an occupation somewhere on the mound. Geoy Tepe B might have been occupied and fortified at this time (Burton-Brown 1951: 141), but little else is known and the period likely dates to the late LBA–Iron I, based on ceramic parallels with Hasanlu and Kordlar.

338 THE IRON AGE

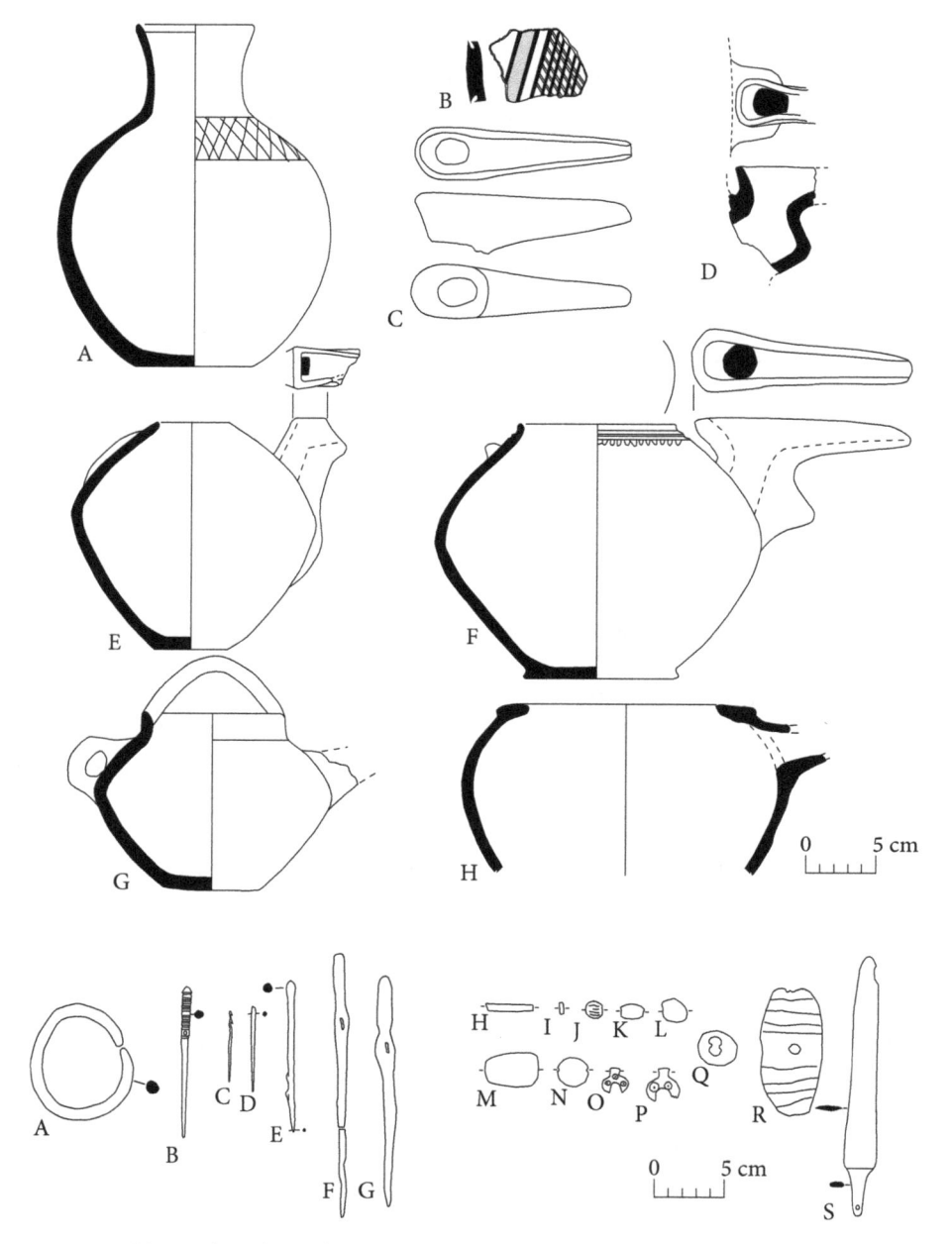

FIGURE 17.3 Upper (A–H): Early Late Bronze Age ceramics from Dinkha (D, H), Dinkha graves (E–G), Hasanlu High Mound (B–C) and Hasanlu graves (A). MBW: C–H; Pattern-burnish MBW: A; Urmia Ware: B.Lower (A–S): Early Late Bronze Age objects from Dinkha graves (A, D, S), Hasanlu graves (E–G) and Geoy Tepe Tomb K (B, C, H–R). Copper/bronze: A–G, Q, S; stone: I, L, M, P, R.

Mortuary patterns

Single interments in pits typify the burials of the LBA. At Hasanlu, the dead were buried almost exclusively in this manner, while single inhumations in pits and mudbrick tombs occur at Dinkha (Muscarella 1974: 37). In contrast, stone-built Tomb K at Geoy Tepe contained multiple interments in at least two separate episodes (Burton-Brown 1951: 142–5), and such tombs are well known in the southwestern Caspian littoral (de Morgan 1905; Negahban 1964, 1996; Egami et al. 1965; Piller 2008). Single inhumation pit graves also occur at Yanik (Burney 1962: 136, 146–7, pl. 42c.24–29), Haftavan (Burney 1970: 165, fig. 8.1, 7), Dalma (Young 1962: 707–8, fig. 8), and Hajji Firuz (Voigt 1976: 810–14, fig. 116, pls. 61–2). The development of extramural cemeteries in the LBA has often been linked to the appearance of the MBW Horizon (Dyson 1965a: 197; Burney and Lang 1971: 118; Muscarella 1994: 143), the attendant assertion being that intramural cemeteries typify the Middle Bronze Age (MBA). If true, such a shift in mortuary practices lends credence to the arguments of many scholars that the appearance of the MBW horizon represents punctuated, widespread, and wholesale culture change rather than merely a gradual shift in the predominant ceramic ware. Such cemeteries have also been linked to nomadic populations (Mousavi 2008: 117)—an interpretation not necessarily at odds with punctuated culture change models. There is certainly marked variation in mortuary patterns in the MBII, not only between sites, but also in the contemporary graves of the same cemetery. Two intramural tombs with multiple interments are known from the MBII Dinkha settlement (Muscarella 1968; Rubinson 1991; Dyson 1968), and as mentioned previously four such tombs were found at MBII/MBIII Geoy Tepe. Stein excavated four MBA graves at Dinkha, ranging from one simple pit inhumation, one stone-covered pit inhumation, one pithos burial, and a stone-built tomb with a single interment (Stein 1940: 142–3). These graves were not clearly associated with architectural remains. At Hasanlu, MBII graves in the extramural North Cemetery include one stone-built tomb with a single interment, a stone-covered pit grave, two multiple inhumations with at least one secondary burial each, a pithos burial, a single pit inhumation, and a single secondary pit burial. MBIII graves at Hasanlu exhibit less variation with three single pit inhumations and a single secondary pit burial. By contrast, the LBA graves of Hasanlu are nearly all single, primary inhumations in pits. The distinction between extramural versus intramural burial is not attested at Hasanlu, with the LBA graves located in the same cemetery as those of previous periods, and no evidence of MBA intramural burials, although the small sample of MBA contexts on the High Mound leaves this question open. Overall, we see the primary evidence for intramural burial in the MBA rests on the two stone-built tombs from Dinkha and perhaps the MBII/III tombs at Geoy Tepe. This does not constitute a pattern, and caution should be exercised when using Dinkha to characterize broader developments in northwestern Iran given its obvious connections to northern Mesopotamia. Rather than a clear cut intramural versus extramural cemetery dichotomy marking the transition from the MBA to the LBA, we see a reduction in variability in MBIII–LBA mortuary practices with the single pit inhumation predominating. Isolated cemeteries, that is, those unassociated with settlements, become increasingly common in northwestern Iran at this same time, and this too seems far more meaningful than the supposed intramural–extramural dichotomy.

At Hasanlu and Dinkha, the two largest excavated LBA cemeteries, a number of alignments and positions were used in the interment of the dead. The body was placed in a pit or, in the case of Dinkha, often a mudbrick tomb with walls on three sides. In some cases, traces of reed mats were found beneath the skeletons. In the earlier LBA, adult males were provided with an MBW tankard (Fig. 17.2B.J–K) and usually at least one larger ceramic container, be it a jar or, rarely at Dinkha, a bridgeless-spouted holemouth jar (Fig. 17.3A.A, E–F). Only one adult female from Hasanlu and Dinkha was found with a tankard (Fig. 17.2B.K). Drinking vessels were generally positioned near the deceased's head, often before the face. Sheep or goat bones were found in most of the graves piled near the deceased, usually at the lower body in a large bowl (Fig. 17.2B.D, I). The frequency of drinking vessel, container, and bowl with animal bones strongly suggests a final meal for the journey to the afterlife. In the earlier LBA, weapons and items of personal ornament are quite rare (Fig. 17.3B). Toggle pins represent a continuation of a common MBA type (Fig. 17.3B.B, F–G). The later LBA graves of Dinkha—few were found at Hasanlu—reveal increasing affluence and include two copper/bronze torques (Fig. 17.5.E, L), a copper/bronze socketed spear (Fig. 17.5.DD), glass beads, a Mitanni-style cylinder seal (Fig. 17.5.AA), and a copper/bronze omphalos bowl (Fig. 17.5.Y). Iron is unattested. The socketed spear, omphalos bowl, a convex boss (Fig. 17.5.J), and a bent-head pin (Fig. 17.5.A) foreshadow mortuary assemblages of the early Iron Age. Tall tankards quickly fell out of mortuary assemblages in the later LBA, a development paralleled by the contemporary occupation deposits at Hasanlu, and the typical mortuary ceramics were a large, double-drilled bowl (Fig. 17.4.E, G); mid-body carinated jar with low neck and everted simple rim (Fig. 17.4.J, N); and a bridgeless-spouted, mid-body carinated jar with low neck and simple everted rim (Fig. 17.4.Q–R).

Material culture

Ceramics

The LBA saw the decline of painted pottery traditions in southern Iranian Azerbaijan and the development of a ceramic horizon recognizable by a significant Early Monochrome Burnished Ware component. Painted wares continue in the north alongside MBW, while in the south a few Urmia Ware jars are the only notable exceptions. Incised and Impressed MBW continues at Dinkha Tepe, but Urmia Ware all but disappears, presenting a MBIII–LBA sequence similar to sites such as Shirakavan in the southern Caucasus (Smith, Badalyan, and Avetisyan 2009: 68).

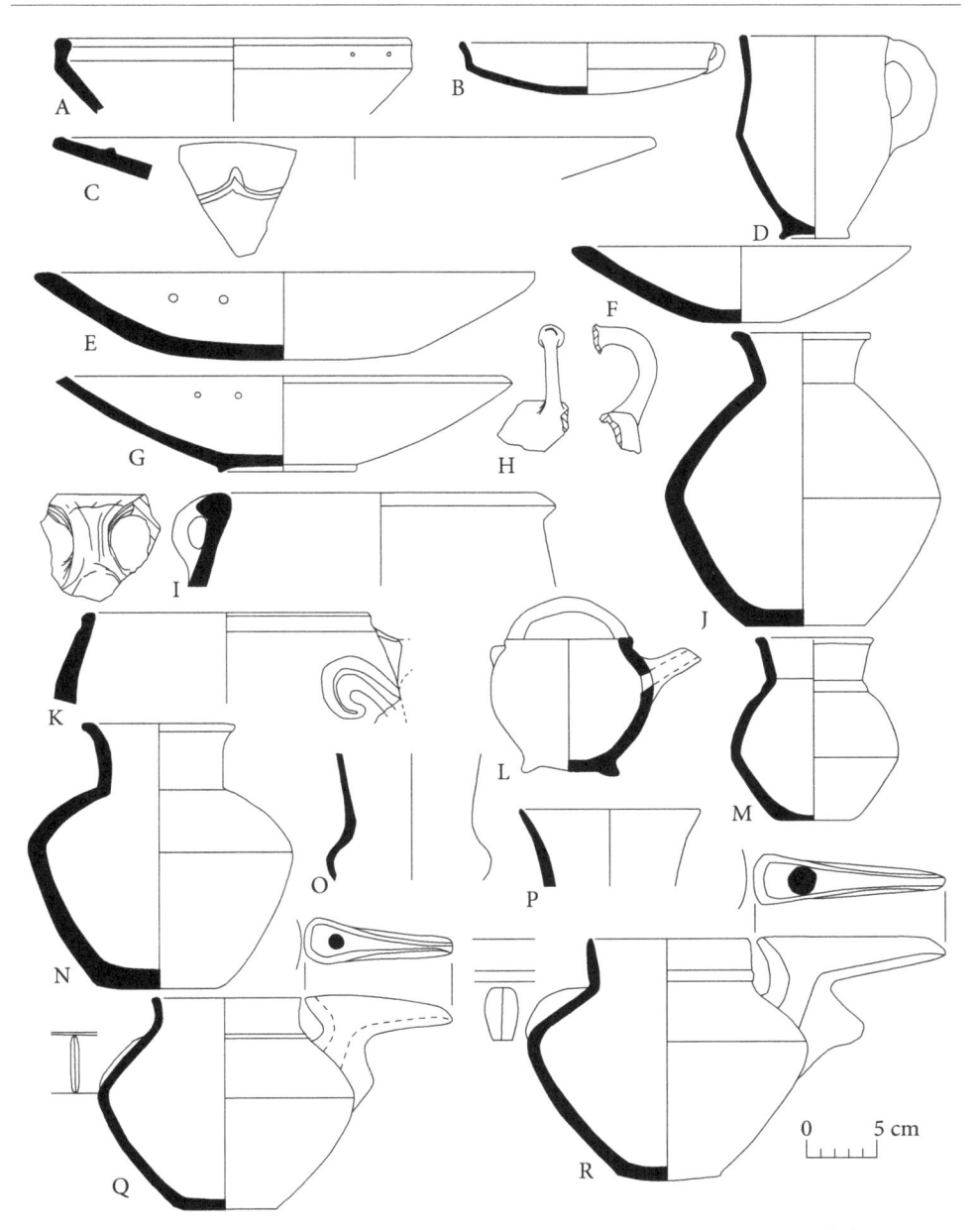

FIGURE 17.4 Later Late Bronze Age MBW Ceramics from Hasanlu High Mound (A–C, H, I, K, O, P), Dinkha graves (E–G, J, L–N, Q, R), and Hajji Firuz graves (D).

We are reliant on certain MBW vessel forms and formal and stylistic attributes to distinguish the major periods spanning the MBIII, LBA, and Iron I. The diagnostic forms of the early LBA in graves and occupation deposits are tall tankards, normally with pedestal bases (Fig. 17.2B.J–K), slightly incurving carinated bowls with simple everted rims and

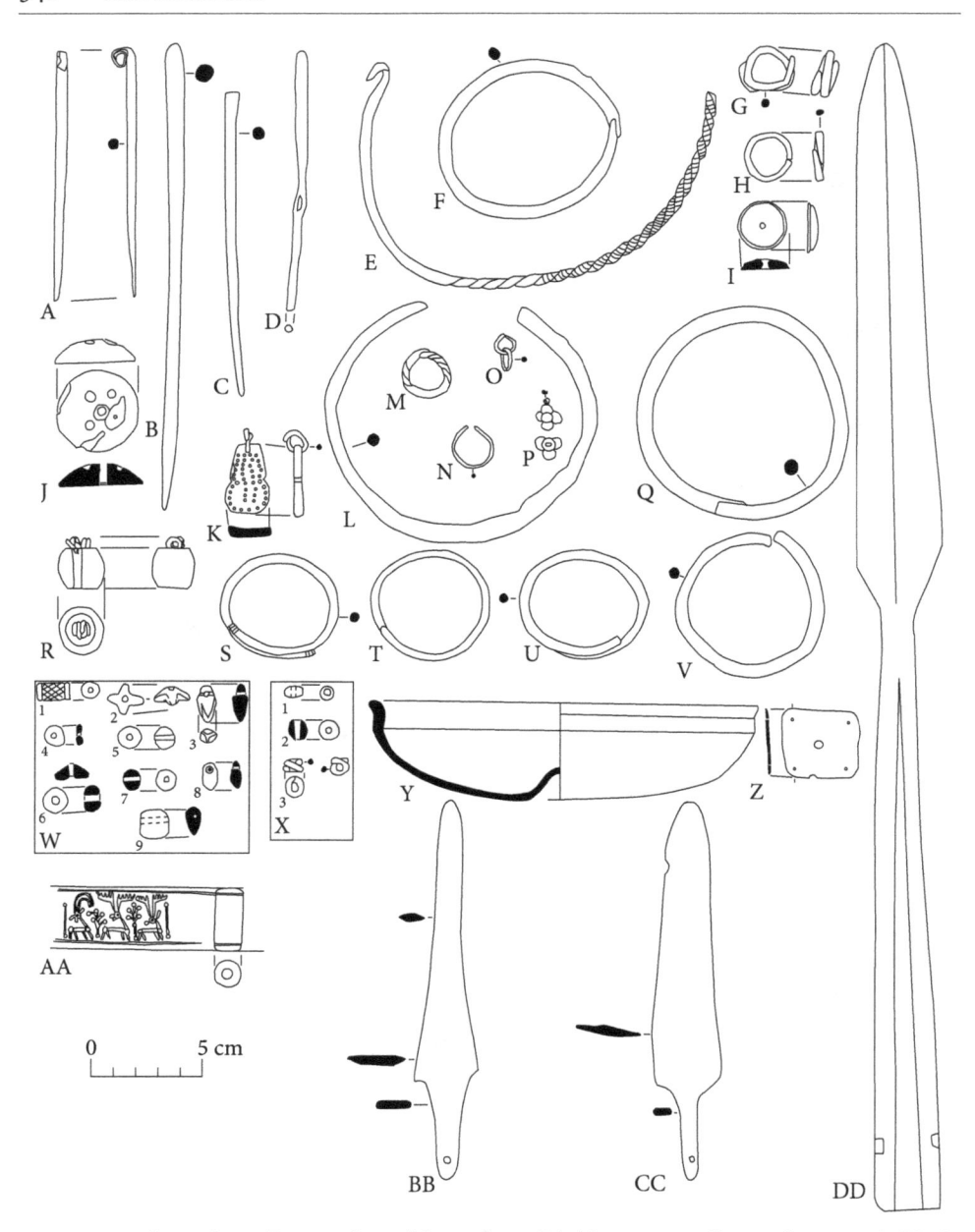

FIGURE 17.5 Later Late Bronze Age objects from Dinkha graves. Copper/bronze: A–H, L, Q–V, Y, Z, BB–DD; calcite: I; stone: J, W6; bone: K; gold: N–P; faience: W1–3, AA; paste: X1; glass: W4–5; carnelian: W7–9, X2.

occasionally vertically pierced lugs (Fig. 17.2B.I), and flaring-sided high bowls often with a crescent appliqué lug and two drilled holes—so-called "worm bowls" (Fig. 17.2B.D). A lower-sided variety is also attested (Fig. 17.2B.A). Holemouth jars are common in occupation deposits and occasionally occur in graves (Fig. 17.3A.E, F, H).

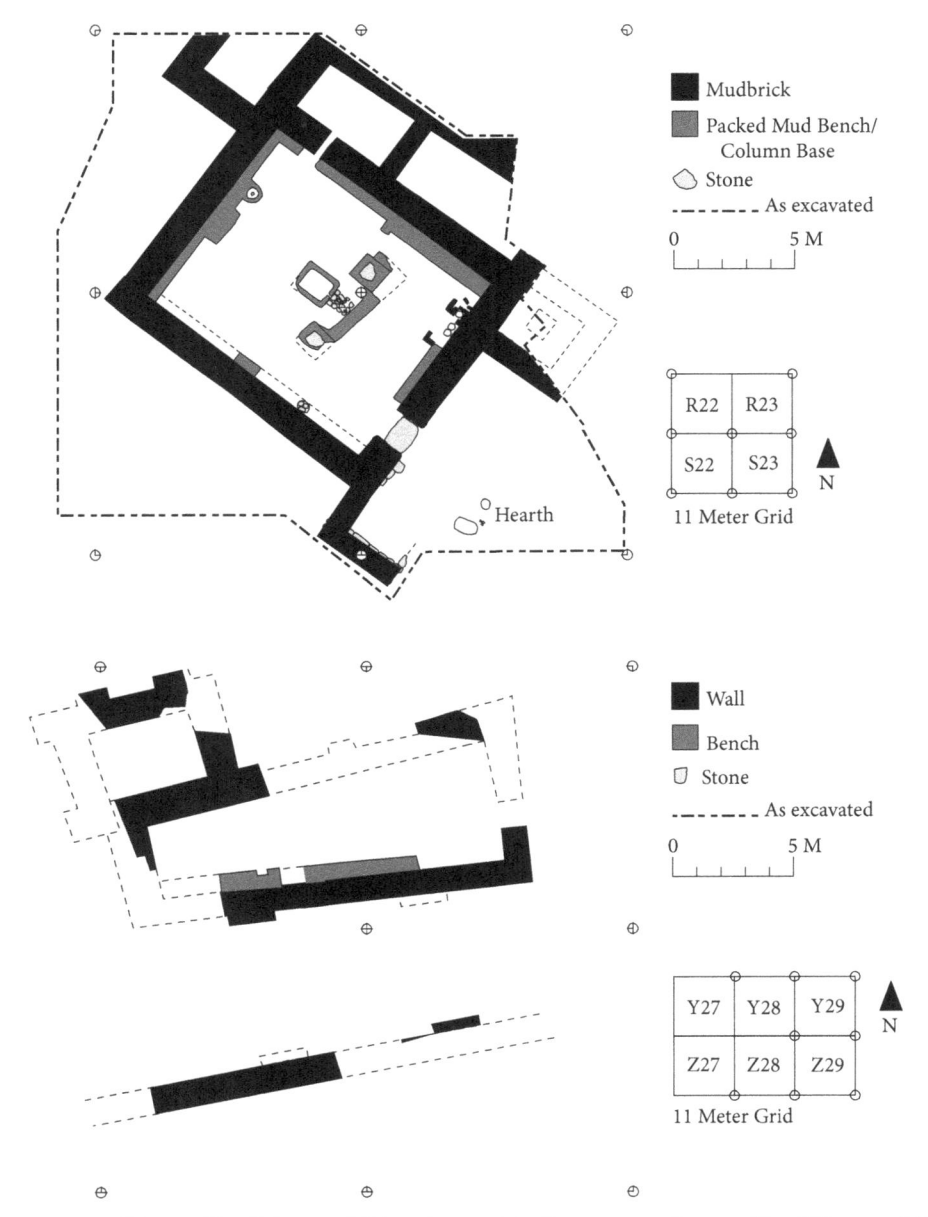

FIGURE 17.6 Upper: The RS22–23 LBA columned hall structure. Lower: The YZ27–29 LBA internal gate.

The tall tankards likely developed out of the shorter, button-base tankards and goblets of the MBIII (Fig. 17.1.J–P), and the flaring-sided bowls are attested in the MBIII in MBW at Dinkha, Hasanlu, and most notably at Geoy Tepe C (Fig. 17.1.A–C), where they occur in early MBW and with polychrome painting (Burton-Brown 1951: fig. 30.949–50, 961). In the later LBA, there is an increase in the occurrence of bridgeless-spouted jars in Dinkha graves; none come from the graves of Hasanlu and only one bridgeless spout was found in a secure LBA occupation context (Fig. 17.4A.C). Another comes from the early LBA trash deposit at Dinkha (Fig. 17.3A.D). Pedestal-base tankards are present in occupation deposits at Hasanlu (Fig. 17.4.O–P) as are worm bowls. The later LBA worm-bowl class tends to be more open and often lacks the crescent lug but usually retains the double drilling (Fig. 17.4.C, E–G). In general, jars have mid-body carinations and low-to-medium necks and everted simple rims (Fig. 17.4.J, M–N, Q, R). Holemouth jars still form a significant part of the assemblage (Fig. 17.4.I, K). Decoration on MBW is rare in the LBA and increases in the latter part of the period and includes pattern burnishing, incising, and appliqué. While undecorated MBW dominates the assemblages of Hasanlu, at Dinkha Incised and Impressed MBW, often with white granulation in the decoration, is also common (Fig. 17.2B.B–C, E–G). This represents a continuation of the pattern established in the MBIII and provides another important link to ceramic sequences in the Caucasus of the LBA Metsamor-Lchashen 1–2 complex (Smith, Badalyan, and Avetisyan 2009: 73–81) and may also provide links to Sialk A (see above). Attested forms include a prism-shaped "box basin," yet another connection to the southern Caucasus (Fig. 17.2B.E; Smith, Badalyan, and Avetisyan 2009: 73, 79, figs. 24.M, 27.R). The contrasts between Hasanlu and Dinkha in the early LBA are striking given the propinquity of the ceramic assemblages, suggesting a higher degree of regionalization in the early MBW horizon than scholars have previously acknowledged. These differences disappear in the later LBA in the southern Lake Urmia Basin but continue to the north. Other categories of material culture from secure contexts are rare in the occupation deposits of Hasanlu, and the graves of Hasanlu and Dinkha offer our best picture of developments (Figs. 17.3B, 17.5).

Our current evidence for the LBA of northwestern Iran does not support theories of punctuated, widespread culture change. The diagnostic attributes of Young's EWGW Horizon and Dyson's "Iron I" do not appear in the region simultaneously, and many ceramic diagnostics can be shown to develop out of the local MBIII. Influences from the southern Caucasus appear more pervasive than previous assessments of the LBA have indicated, and there is a fairly high degree of regionalization in material culture.

Iron I (1250–1050 BC)

This period previously formed the latter part of Dyson's Iron I and Young's EWGW Horizon. In the revised Hasanlu chronology, the Iron I is defined archaeologically using Hasanlu IVc (Table 17.1), and another important exposure is known from Kordlar IV–III/IIb. Geoy B likely also partly dates to this period. A short explanation is necessary to avoid confusion. As originally defined, and as is widely known, "Hasanlu V" comprised a pastiche of the MBII, MBIII, LBA, and Iron I (see esp. Young 1965: fig. 8; Dyson

1965b: fig. 3). Over time, the archaeological definition of the period changed to include what is now termed the LBA and Iron I (Dyson 1977), but there was no systematic reappraisal of previous results and little redaction of older publications. Dyson defined Hasanlu Period IVc as an earlier architectural phase of the Iron II monumental structures of the Hasanlu citadel (Dyson 1965a: 198, table 2). This phase, actually a subperiod, was later shown to date to approximately 1250–1050 BC, based on radiocarbon samples (Dyson and Muscarella 1989: fig. 15). Much material used to define "Period V" in earlier publications derives from Period IVc contexts in terms of absolute dating and stratigraphy. Given its absolute date ranges, material culture, and the conventional chronological terminology of surrounding regions, Hasanlu IVc should be the local variant of the Iron I. Iron is extremely rare with only two finger rings at Hasanlu securely attested, and like earlier periods the chronological distinction is based on changes in the prevalent MBW ceramic forms in the southern and western Lake Urmia Basin. In historical terms, Iron I begins during a period of widespread disruption in the Near East. While destruction levels are known from the major sites of the Lake Urmia Basin, particularly Kordlar IV–III and Terminal Hasanlu IVc, the pattern of growth and development established in the LBA continued unabated into the Iron II.

Built environment

There are no cities during the LBA and Iron I of northwestern Iran, rather the elite fortified centers established in the LBA continue to grow and develop—both small compounds and extensive citadels. These sites occupy strategic locations in the agriculturally fertile river valleys and were likely surrounded by villages, hamlets, and isolated cemeteries. The larger valleys have multiple, evenly spaced centers of roughly equal size suggesting a low order of sociopolitical centralization. Part of the population was almost certainly composed of pastoral groups practicing vertical transhumance and closely linked to agricultural areas given the need for conserved fodder and shelter in the cold season and the increasing threats posed by the region's neighbors. These settlement and land-use patterns are better attested in the Iron II (Kroll 2005; 2011a: 150–1), but there is strong evidence at Hasanlu and Kordlar that they extend back to at least the later LBA.

The largest and best-known excavated site, Hasanlu IVc, consisted of a fortified citadel covering roughly 2–3 ha (Fig. 17.7). The citadel provides extensive evidence for a destruction by fire in the eleventh century, and Dyson (1965a) used this event to mark the beginning of the Iron II (Hasanlu IVb). There is no evidence for a period of abandonment, and all the major buildings of Hasanlu IVc were rebuilt at the start of the Iron II with similar architectural plans, often incorporating the wall stubs of Iron I structures as foundations and footings. A similar architectural practice is attested at contemporary Kordlar. At least the eastern part of Hasanlu's Low Mound was also occupied and provides evidence of destruction by fire (Danti 2011).

A large columned-hall structure, Burned Building II (BBII), dominated Hasanlu's southern High Mound and likely served as a temple in the Iron I–II (Fig. 17.7; Dyson

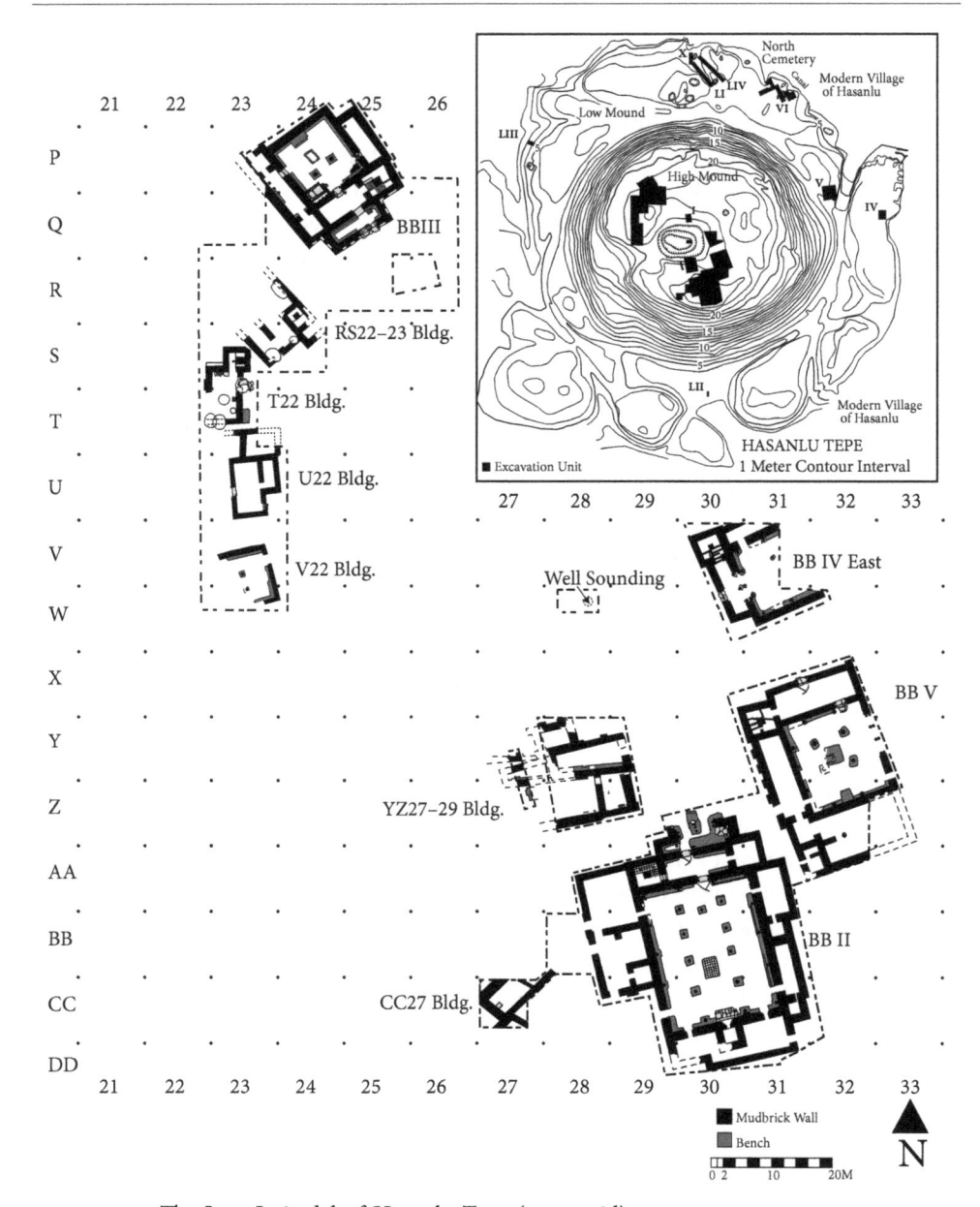

FIGURE 17.7 The Iron I citadel of Hasanlu Tepe (11 m grid).

and Voigt 2003). This building was newly constructed sometime during the Iron I. An internal gateway lay to the northwest of BBII, the YZ27–29 Iron I Building, and another monumental columned hall, BBV, occupied the area to the northeast. North of BBV lay columned hall BBIV East. The buildings of the southern citadel were organized around a courtyard based on analogy with the Iron II citadel plan. The northwest citadel evinces a different use of space in the Iron I. A group of smaller structures formed a north-south arc that likely bordered another open space to their east (Fig. 17.7). Again, this is similar to the arrangement of buildings in the Iron II. The northwest corner of this open space was filled by at least one, probably two columned halls, likely elite residences—the monumental columned-hall structure BBIII and the poorly preserved RS22–23 Iron I Building. The latter, the preserved front of a building, is likely a columned-hall structure since it represents a rebuilding of the LBA RS22–23 columned-hall building. The extant Iron I rooms lay immediately over those of the earlier structure and closely followed its wall alignments. The overall impression is of a well-planned citadel with separate building compounds dedicated to elite secular and religious activities. The larger columned halls BBII and BBIII were entered through porticos (contra Young 1966; 2002: 386–8; cf. Dyson and Voigt 2003: 232 regarding BBII) and BBIII had a niched-and-buttressed façade (Fig. 17.7). Few artifacts were found in the Period IVc structures. The buildings were destroyed by fire, probably simultaneously although this remains an open question, in the mid-eleventh century, based on radiocarbon dates (Dyson and Muscarella 1989: 9–12, fig. 15). There is also evidence for a destruction and rebuilding on the Low Mound at about this same time in BBXIII in Operation V (Danti 2011).

Following the destruction of Kordlar IV, the columned-hall structure was reconstructed using the stubs of the earlier walls as foundations, and the building was provided with a new enclosure wall with towers. Radiocarbon dates and the important ceramic assemblages show Kordlar IV–III date from the late LBA to the Iron I. The building sequence at Kordlar reveals repeated destructions by fire with some human victims. The rebuilt versions of the structure are progressively more fortified, probably in response to this threat. The interior features such as the columns and hearth are not attested in Period III, which was also destroyed by fire. Other sites such as Geoy Tepe and Haftavan were likely occupied in the Iron I, but little can be said of their built environments.

Mortuary patterns

Our knowledge of the graves of this period is largely confined to Dinkha and Hasanlu with some probable Iron I graves also from Geoy. The patterns in burial types previously discussed for the LBA continue. The graves of Dinkha and Hasanlu document access to preciousities and include copper-bronze weapons (Fig. 17.10B.GG–HH), headdresses (Fig. 17.10B.U), and a cylinder seal (Fig. 17.10B: LL). The graves of children indicate ascribed status with a wide range of ceramics, glass beads, and copper/bronze torques. In general, graves include a mid-body carinated jar with medium neck, everted simple rim, and at Dinkha an occasional bridgeless spout (Figs. 17.9.L and 17.10A.C); a large bowl, either hemispherical with tripod lug feet (Fig. 17.8.C, F) or carinated with an inverted or straight simple rim and often drilled holes (Fig. 17.8.E, J, N); and the graves of children have low pedestal-base carinated cups (Fig. 17.9.C, D, F).

Occupation deposits at Hasanlu IVc and Kordlar IV–III show such cups were common to the period (see below).

Material culture

Ceramics

The Middle Monochrome Burnished Ware of the Iron I is characterized by new forms of worm bowls, bridgeless spouted vessels, and short, carinated cups with handles and pedestal bases that develop from the tall LBA pedestal-base tankards (Fig. 17.9.A–F). Mid-body carinated jars continue to be an important form (Figs. 17.9.L and 17.10A.A, C). Although the "worm bowl" class continues (Fig. 17.8.A–D, F, H), the term is something of a misnomer since these large bowls usually lack the distinctive crescent lug and only have double drilling. A large open bowl approaching a charger is attested, in this case with a distinctive double crescent (Fig. 17.8.A), as well as a large hemispherical bowl, usually with a tripod lug base, pedestal base, or tripod legs (Fig. 17.8.C–D, F, H). In the later Iron I, the worm bowl class of large bowl is increasingly replaced by large carinated bowls—typically tall bowls with simple or rounded rims and often having inverted sides (Fig. 17.8.E, G, I–J, L–N). The worm bowl class disappears early in the Iron II, and carinated forms proliferate. Bilobed lugs, usually with horizontal double piercing, are the precursor to the animal-head lugs of the Iron II (Fig. 17.8.J, L). Segmented handles also appear and are more common in the Iron II (Fig. 17.8.K). Bridgeless-spouted jars are usually of the mid-body carinated type with a low neck and simple rim (Fig. 17.10A). These jars tend to be more elaborately decorated with incising, excising, and appliqué. This trend is also apparent in other vessel forms, and such decoration typifies the pottery of the Iron II. Many of the stylistic innovations are linked to the emulation of metal vessels (see below). Bridgeless spouts remain extremely rare at Hasanlu (Fig. 17.10A.B), but are comparatively well attested at Dinkha. Such spouts do not co-occur with bridge-spouted vessels, diagnostic of the Iron II, in graves or occupation deposits. Other important markers of the period are carinated and hemispherical mugs and beakers and channel-spouted bowls (Fig. 17.8.O–T, V, X). Decoration in excising and painting occurs in the assemblage of Kordlar, Geoy, and Gijlar A (Figs. 17.8.D, M, U, W and 17.9.I, J; Pecorella and Salvini 1984: fig. 51.1, pl. 41a–b), but decoration in the southern Lake Urmia Basin is largely confined to appliqué, pattern burnish, and simple incising (Fig. 17.9.G). Iron I closed forms, and more rarely bowls, have single horizontal ribs (Fig. 17.8.V, X), which is also common in the Iron II. Finally, high-swung handles, sometimes with thumbstops (Fig. 17.8.W), appear in the Iron I of Hasanlu and Kordlar and are ubiquitous in the Iron II–IV.

Iron I objects are fairly rare, with some material from the graves of Hasanlu and Dinkha supplemented by the occupation deposits of Kordlar IV–III (Lippert 1979) and a few finds from Hasanlu IVc (Fig. 17.10B). Iron makes its first limited appearance with two finger rings at Hasanlu—one from a grave and another from an occupation deposit

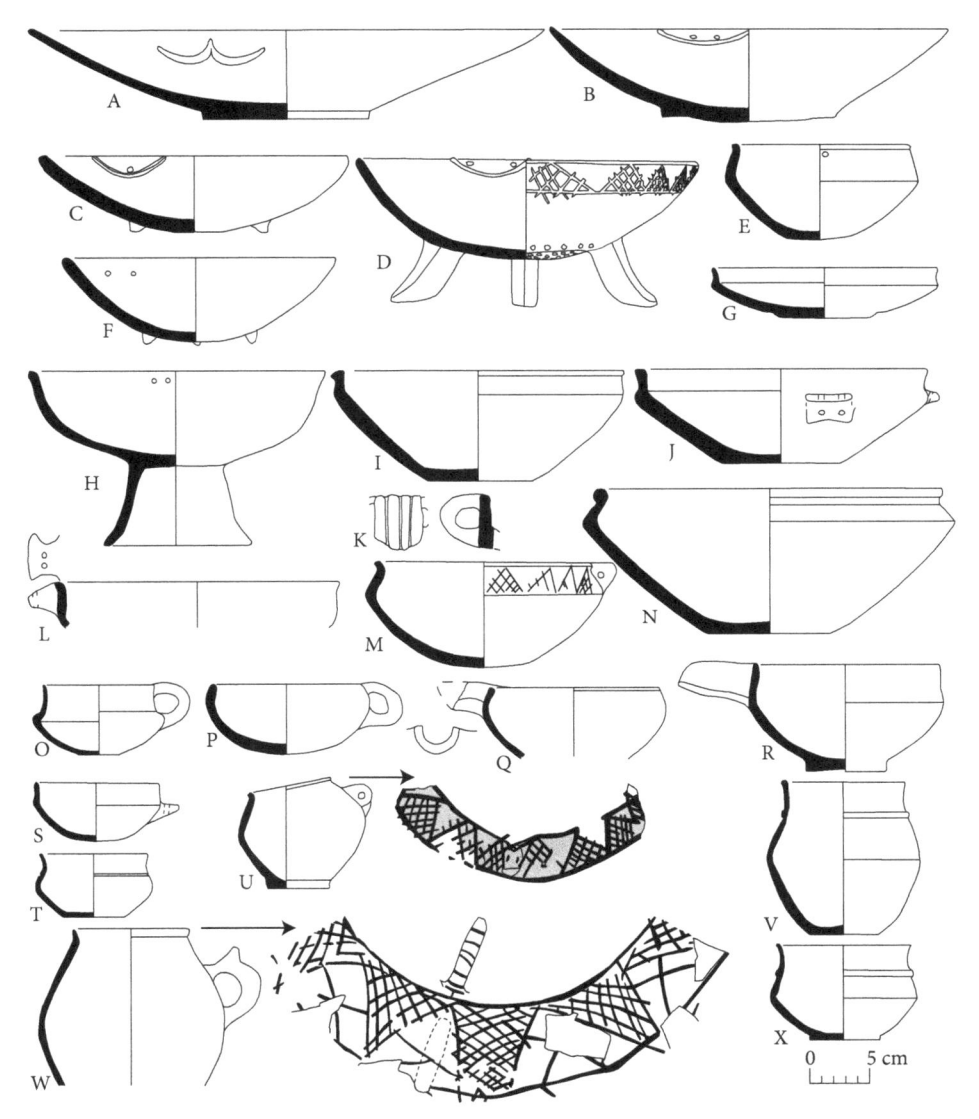

FIGURE 17.8 Iron I ceramics from Hasanlu High Mound (A, G, K, L, Q, T, V, X), Hasanlu graves (E, J, O), Dinkha graves (C, F, N) and Kordlar (B, D, H, I, M, P, R, S, U, W). MBW: A–T, V, X; Kordlar Painted Ware: U, W.

on the High Mound. Simple copper/bronze torques, anklets, bracelets, and rings, and earrings typify the personal ornament in graves (Fig. 17.10B.H–O, Q–T, W–Y). Pins tend to have incision or cast designs at the head (Fig. 17.10B.A–D). A wide range of beads is attested with glass and frit more common (Fig. 17.10B.U–V, EE–FF) with the appearance of a few large spheroid beads, typical of the Iron II, appearing (Fig. 17.10B.Z). Only a few weapons and items of horse gear are known (Fig. 17.10B.AA–DD, GG–KK). Overall, we see the beginnings of stylistic trends better documented in the Iron II.

FIGURE 17.9 Iron I ceramics from Hasanlu High Mound (G, H, K, M), Hasanlu graves (F), Dinkha graves (C, D, L), Geoy (I) and Kordlar (A, B, E, J). MBW: A–F, H, J–M; Pattern-Burnish MBW: G; Kordlar Painted Ware: I, J.

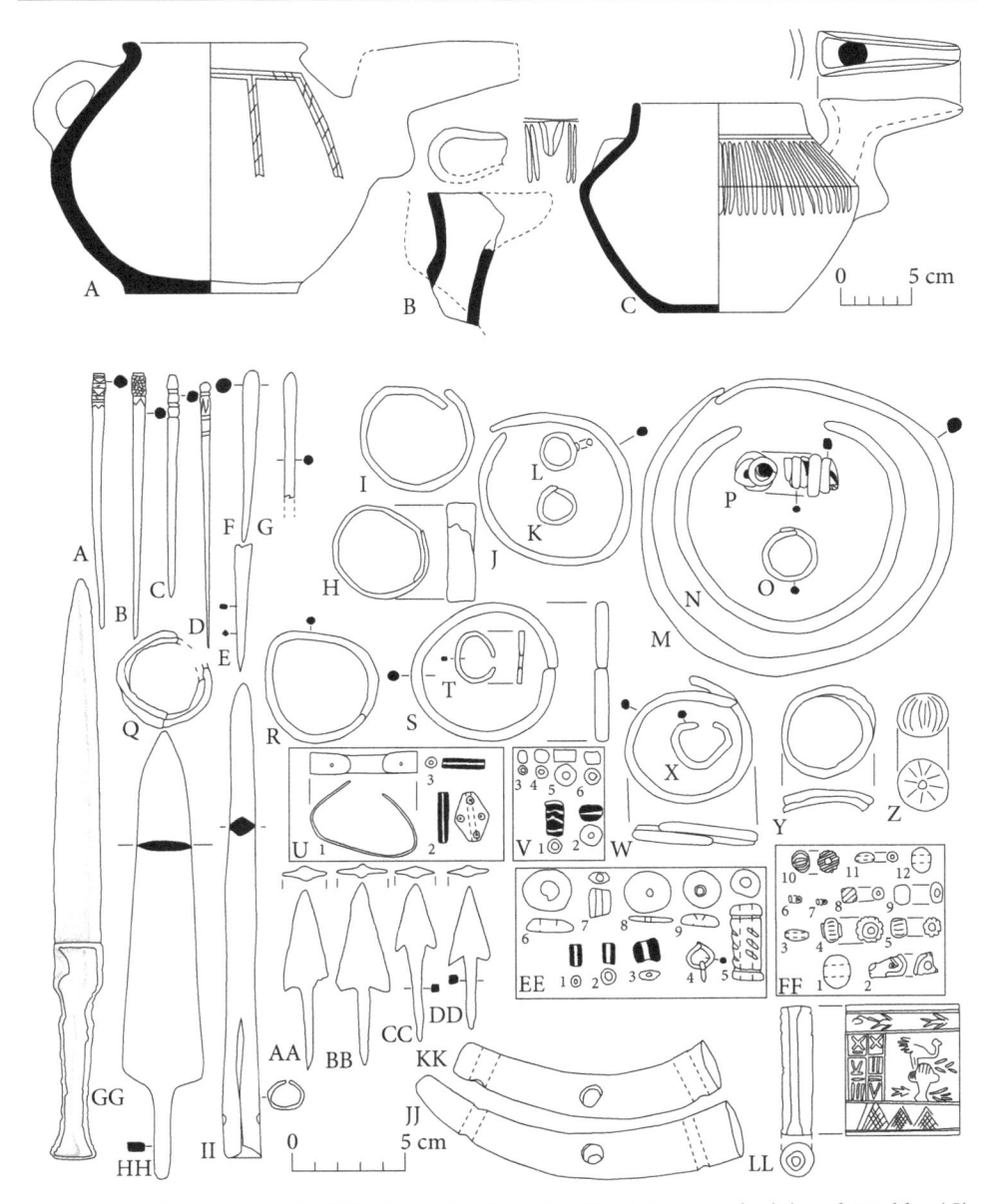

FIGURE 17.10 Upper: Iron I MBW Ceramics from Kordlar (A), Hasanlu (B) and Dinkha (C); Lower: Iron I objects from Hasanlu Graves (D, F, G, I, Q, S–V, Y, Z, EE, GG, LL), Dinkha graves (A–C, E, H, J–P, R, W, X, FF, HH) and Kordlar (AA–DD, II–KK). Copper/bronze: A–U1, W–Y, AA–DD, GG–II, EE4, FF1; glass V1–4, EE1–3, FF2; Frit V5, EE5, LL; glazed frit: V6; Egyptian blue: FF3–4; paste: Z, FF5–12; shell: EE6–7; stone EE8–9; antler: JJ, KK.

Iron II (1050–800 BC)

Assyria's and Urartu's steady rise to power had profound and lasting effects on neighboring regions in the Iron II, inspiring military coalitions, political centralization, and secondary state formation. The first stage in the development of these empires and the initial confrontation between them climaxed toward the end of the period in the reigns of the Assyrian kings Shalmaneser III (859–824 BC) and Shamshi-Adad V (824–811 BC) and the Urartian king Ar(r)ame, a contemporary and adversary of Shalmaneser III (Fuchs 2011). Urartu subsequently enjoyed territorial gains in northwestern Iran in the reigns of Ishpuini and Menua. The rich historical records of Assyria, Babylonia, and Urartu indicate northwestern Iran represented an economically and militarily prized region inhabited by an ethnically and linguistically diverse population. Part of the area may have formed an important part of the fledgling Urartian state, depending on where one locates the early Urartian capital of Arzaškun. Similarities in early Urartian and northwestern Iranian costume and military equipment suggest strong cultural affinities if not geographic overlap (Piller 2011). Urartu had certainly expanded into the western or southern Lake Urmia region by 859 BC, taking the settlement of Sugunia. The onomastics and prosopographics of Assyrian and Urartian texts reveal that a process of Iranianization had occurred in northwestern Iran at the end of the second and in the early first millennia (Diakonoff 1956; Diakonoff and Kashkai 1979; Grantovskiy 1971, 1998; Zadok 2002). Other attested ethno-linguistic groups include Kassites, Hurro-Urartians, and other autochthonous populations already well established in the second millennium (Zadok 2002: 140). Of special interest is the sociopolitical designation "Parsua" and its variants in Assyrian and Urartian texts, a coalition of rulers that some scholars link to early Iranians residing in the Lake Urmia Basin and/or the central Zagros. Parsua's location, character, association with an Iranian population, and the number of contemporary places bearing the name have long been debated (Diakonoff 1956: 69, 161, 224; 1967: 90–1; 1971: 130; Young 1967, 2003; Grantovskiy 1971: 312; Levine 1974; Zimansky 1990; Waters 1999: 99–101; Zadok 2002: 100–110). The coalition of Mannaean polities in Kurdistan and the southeastern Lake Urmia region is better known (Postgate 1989), and wielded formidable power in the Iron II–III, but locating the *topoi* of Assyrian and Urartian texts, mainly occurring in accounts of military campaigns, has proven difficult with few fixed points in the Zagros (Boehmer 1964; Eph'al 1999; Fales 2003; Lemaire 1998; Pecorella and Salvini 1984; Reade 1979; Sokoloff 1999; Levine 1973, 1974, 1977; Zimansky 1990; Zadok 2002). The archaeological record has played a lesser, supporting role in these debates. As previously discussed, there have been various attempts to match spatiotemporal patterns in the archaeological record with theories on the timing and routes of Iranian migration constructed from textual sources (Young 1965, 1967, 1985; Ghirshman 1977; Dandamaev and Lukonin 1989: 1–45), but the degrees of uncertainty in both have frustrated efforts. Assyrian influences are ubiquitous in the material culture of northwestern Iran, especially in southern

Azerbaijan in the Iron II and southern Kurdistan in the Iron III, and we suffer somewhat from a recent trend of loosely applying the designation "Mannaean" to all Iron II–III finds without explicit statements regarding the relevant archaeological correlates. In comparison with our knowledge of the growth of the Urartian Empire, much work remains to be done regarding the Assyrian presence.

The Iron II corresponds to Young's Late Western Grey Ware Horizon (1965), defined locally by Hasanlu IVb, which develops smoothly from the Iron I. Besides Hasanlu, which remains largely unpublished (Muscarella 2006), important excavations have been conducted at Dinkha Tepe II, Geoy Tepe A, Kordlar II–I, and Zendan-e Suleiman I. The last two sites provide our best view of the late part of the period—for lack of a better term, the Iron II–III transition. Geoy A likely also contains some Iron III material. The transition to the Iron III roughly corresponds to declining Assyrian fortunes under Adad-nerari III (811–783 BC) and his immediate successors and the expansion of Urartu under kings Ishpuini (828–810 BC) and his son Menua (810–786 BC) into the southern Lake Urmia basin. Hasanlu IVb ends with the site's destruction around 800 BC. This dating, based on short-lived radiocarbon samples (carbonized stored foodstuffs from a kitchen in BBIII) has not gone unchallenged (Magee 2008), but 800 BC remains the best estimate for the destruction, based on a review of the primary data currently available (Danti 2011). Other scholars have questioned the 800 BC destruction date with regard to the styles of certain objects in the Hasanlu destruction level (Medvedskaya 1988, 1991), but the excavators maintain such arguments are unsupported (Dyson and Muscarella 1989; Voigt 2011: xxxiii, nn. 1–2). More radiocarbon dates are needed from Hasanlu and other Iron II sites to clarify our archaeological chronology. Other sites, particularly in the southwestern Lake Urmia Basin such as Kordlar IIa, were also destroyed but we are still overly reliant on Hasanlu for our understanding of the Iron II. Following Hasanlu's destruction, an Urartian presence is well attested in the western and southern Lake Urmia region defined by the distribution of Urartian fortresses, settlements, and inscribed stele of Ishpuini/Menua and Menua distributed from Kel-i Shin and Qalatgah (Muscarella 1971; Van Loon 1975) near modern Urmia in the west to Tash Tepe near modern Miyandoab and Mahabad in the east (Kroll 2005: 75–6; Pecorella and Salvini 1984: 65–9). The end date of Hasanlu IVb does not seem the most precise means for defining the termination of the Iron II: occupation continues at other sites, such as at Zendan-e Suleiman and, following a hiatus, Kordlar I (Lippert 1979; Thomalsky 2006), revealing that trends in Iron II material culture continued into the early eighth century (Kroll 2005).

Built environment

Hasanlu IVb is the best-known urban center for the period, with an extensive Iron II citadel skirted by a lower settlement known from only a few excavations on the Low Mound that provided evidence of craft production and residential architecture (Stein 1940: 393–5; Danti 2011). In at least one area of the Lower Town, Period IVb ends with the burning of buildings, and human and animal victims were found in the destruction level along with a relatively high number of *in situ* artifacts (Danti 2011). Iron II cemeteries occupied large parts of the lower town. The exact extent of the lower settlement is unknown due to the encroachment of modern villages and agriculture, and it is unclear whether the area was fortified and how densely it was occupied.

The Iron II fortifications of the citadel are poorly known, but evidence for a probable circumvallation was found in three locations on the northern and northwestern citadel (Fig. 17.11; Danti 2013). A series of buildings on the southwest slopes of the mound formed the fortified entry to the Iron Age citadel (Dyson 1989: 110–11). The built environment of the citadel interior was designed to control access to its inner reaches (the Lower Court) and contained internal gateways and towers, supporting the conclusion that the entire citadel was strongly fortified in concentric fashion. The extant architectural exposures are divisible into three areas: the western slopes, the northwest citadel, and the Upper and Lower Courts. The western slope remains poorly understood and is not shown in Fig. 17.11. Architecture in this area has been interpreted as a triple road system (Dyson 1975) or, more recently and plausibly, stables (Kroll 1992, 2010: 25–6, forthcoming). This area certainly also provided the main access up to the citadel based on mound morphology and the location of Iron II internal gateways and access patterns (Fig. 17.11).

The Hasanlu citadel consisted of a large number of mudbrick and timber structures on stone footings (Fig. 17.11). Many of these buildings were sprawling compounds with multiple stories and internal open-air courts. Architecture was well preserved due to the violent sacking and burning of the citadel, and over 14,000 objects and 285 human victims and combatants were associated with the burned level. The northwest citadel was occupied by structures of likely military function such as gateways—the so-called Chariot Gate (BBVI south), Foot Gate (BBVI north), and Double Gate (BBVII East)—and possible arsenals (BBVII and BBVIII). In the northwest corner stood Burned Building III (BBIII), an elite residential compound centered on a monumental columned hall (Fig. 17.11). Access to the southern citadel was gained through the Lower Court Gate or through the Upper Court formed by BBI West and BBI East. The function of BBI West is difficult to determine since a later Urartian fortification wall cut away its western end. Objects found inside the building suggest that parts of its upper stories served as a treasury/arsenal. The ground floor was a formal meeting space. To the east was BBI East, one of the entries to the large stone-paved Lower Court. The main structure of this area was Burned Building II, a monumental columned-hall temple (Dyson and Voigt 2003). To the northeast stood columned-hall BBV—the columned hall served as a horse stable at the time of the settlement's destruction. The northern end of the Lower Court was defined by BBIV and BBIV East. Aniconic stone stelae stood at the entrance to BBIV East and BBII. The architecture and rich assortment of elite material culture indicate the buildings of the Lower Court served religious and elite residential functions.

Important but limited architectural exposures of Iron II date are also available at Dinkha II and Kordlar IIa, which was a small fortress. Late Iron II–Iron III Zendan-e

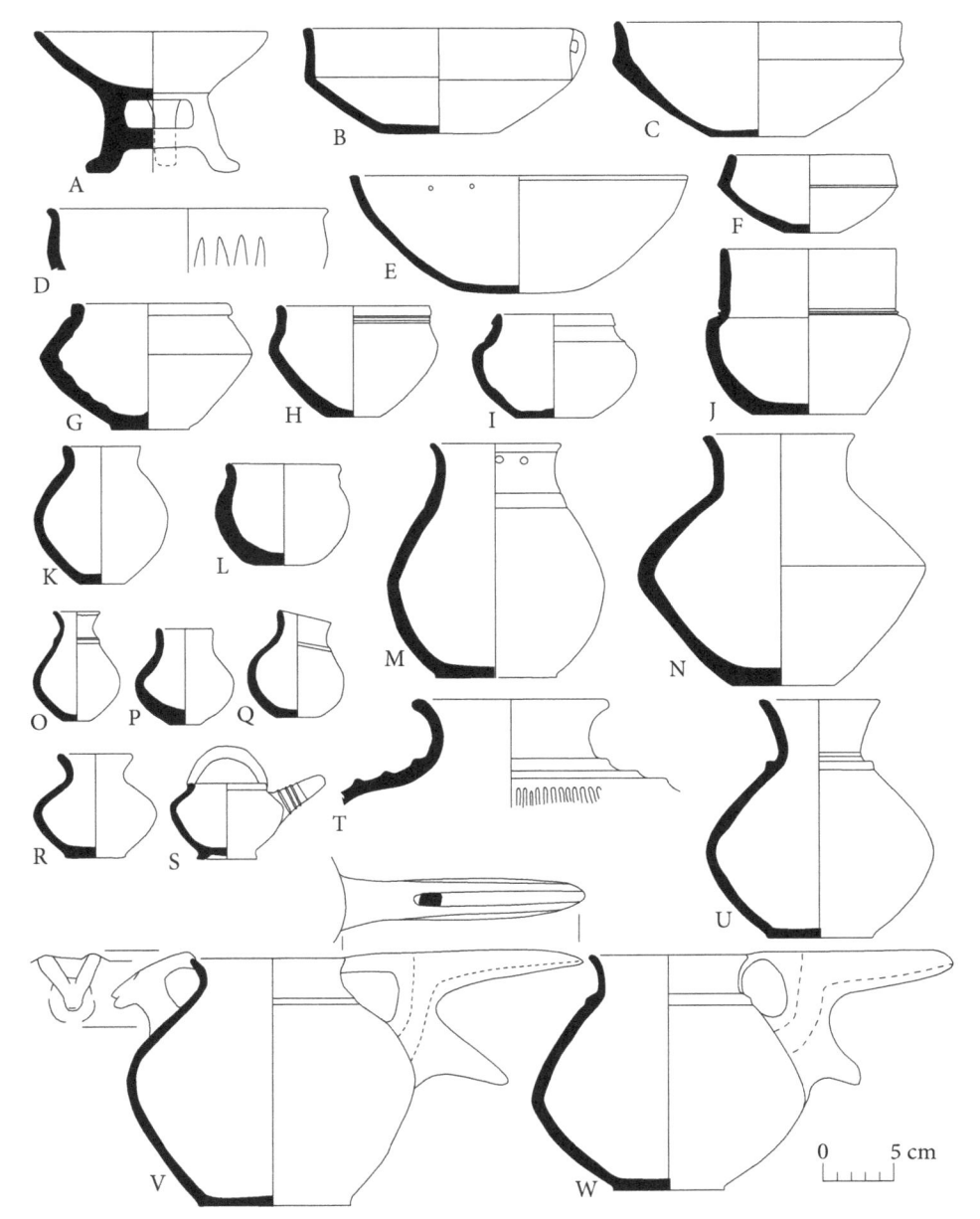

FIGURE 17.11 Late Iron I – Early Iron II MBW ceramics from Hasanlu Tepe High Mound (D, F–L, T), Hasanlu graves (B–C, E, M, O–R, U, W) and Dinkha graves (A, N, S, V).

Suleiman I provides a radically different built environment. In the eighth to seventh centuries, the site functioned as a mountain sanctuary consisting of a ring of square rooms and terraces surrounding a hollow conical peak containing a crater lake. Later, the ceremonial function lapsed and the site was fortified and apparently served as a Mannaean stronghold (Boehmer 1961, 1967, 1986; Kleiss 1971; Naumann 1977).

Small site archaeology is in its infancy in this region for the protohistoric and early historic periods beyond the initial surveys conducted by the German Archaeological Institute (see Kroll 2005 and sources cited therein). This is most unfortunate given the extensive settlement pattern that obtains in the period, as well as the habitation of marginal upland areas and emphasis on pastoralism.

Mortuary patterns

Approximately 100 graves of the Iron II were excavated at Hasanlu's Low Mound and another sixty-eight are known from Dinkha II (Muscarella 1974: 58ff.). At Haftavan, twenty-five graves date to the Iron I–II (Tala'i 2007; Tala'i and Aliyari 2009). In Tabriz, excavations at the important cemetery of Masjed-e Kabud have uncovered 108 graves of the Iron I–II (Hojabri Nobari 2004). Simple inhumations typify Haftavan and Hasanlu, and all graves were located in extramural low mound cemeteries at what were likely the shifting peripheries of the contemporary settlements. Mudbrick and stone tombs and simple inhumations are all attested at Dinkha, as well as nineteen infant urn burials (Muscarella 1974). The graves of Masjed-e Kabud were of three types: inhumations; stone-covered inhumations; and horseshoe-shaped mudbrick tombs similar to those of Dinkha (Hojabri Nobari 2004). There are also rectangular stone-built hypogea at Hasanlu with one stone-built tomb containing the secondary burials of two warriors in the North Cemetery (Danti and Cifarelli 2015) and a large rectangular hypogeum containing at least twelve bodies (Hakemi and Rad 1950: 30–1, Fig. 12). A similar hypogeum was documented by the Hasanlu Project at nearby Naqadeh.

Burial customs established in the LBA and Iron I continue with far more objects interred with the dead and a wider range of object types and materials. The presence of long (14–36 cm) copper/bronze and iron shroud pins indicates the wrapping of the deceased prior to burial (Fig. 17.18.F1–2, H4, I1–2, M–R; Marcus 1994: 4–5, figs. 4–6). The graves of Hasanlu and Dinkha typically contain bridge-spouted jars (Fig. 17.14.K; 15.A, F); *hydriae* (Fig. 17.14.L); carinated cups, mugs, and goblets (Fig. 17.13.K–L, N–Q); carinated incurving bowls (Fig. 17.13.A–C, E–G); and pyxides and small jars often occurring in groups (Fig. 17.13.U, 14.A, D–F). Tripod stands (Fig. 17.14.M) were found at Hasanlu. These vessel classes are also well attested in the contemporary settlement of Hasanlu (see below). Iron weapons and personal ornament occur with some frequency, but copper/bronze remains abundant. Weapons were relatively rare in graves at Hasanlu and Dinkha (Fig. 17.16.D, I, N, U; Muscarella 1974: 59). Copper or bronze drinking bowls gain in popularity (Fig. 17.15.E, I, K). Most noticeable, a diverse assortment of personal ornament was interred with the deceased, including headdresses, possible penannular hair rings (Fig. 17.19.S), pins (Fig. 17.18.M–BB), breast plaques with beads and dangles (Fig. 17.18.F3–4, G, H1–3, I3–7), bead necklaces, pendants (Fig. 17.19.II), segmented and plain penannular finger rings (Fig. 17.19.R, T), bronze and iron archer's rings (Fig. 17.19.GG, HH; Muscarella 1974: Fig. 36, no. 195), plain and incised band bracelets (Fig. 17.19.X, CC), plain round-section bracelets (Fig. 17.19.Y), bracelets

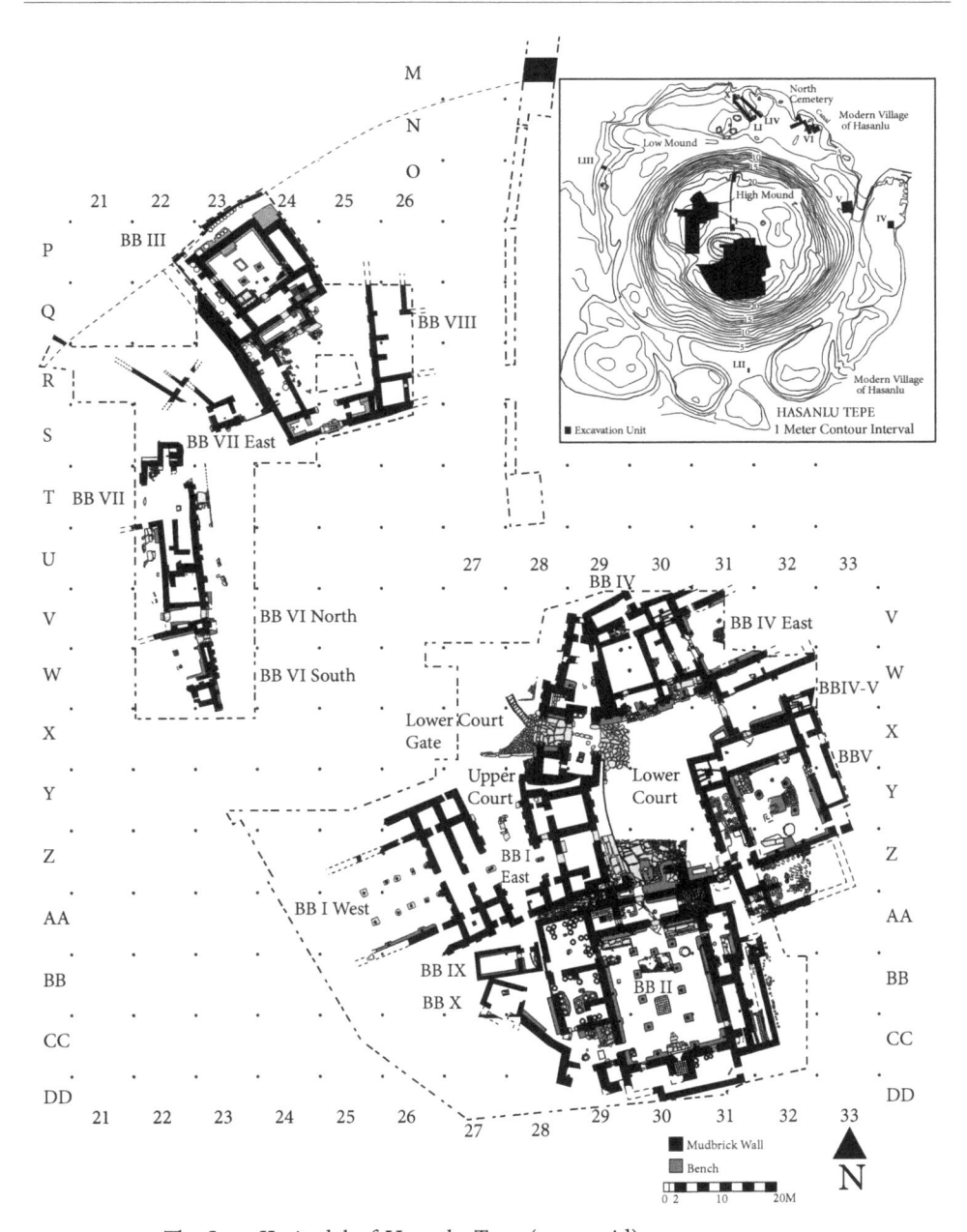

FIGURE 17.12 The Iron II citadel of Hasanlu Tepe (11 m grid).

with overlapping flattened ends (Fig. 17.19.Z–AA, DD), anklets (Fig. 17.19. OO), earrings (Fig. 17.19.U), armlets (Fig. 17.19.BB), and torques (Fig. 17.19.KK, LL; Muscarella 1974: figs. 27.1039, 28.187, 32.1040, and 39.115). Breast plaques were found only with adult females in burials, and at least one such plaque comes from the High Mound (Fig. 17.18.J). They were likely an important marker of identity, much like the lion pins found

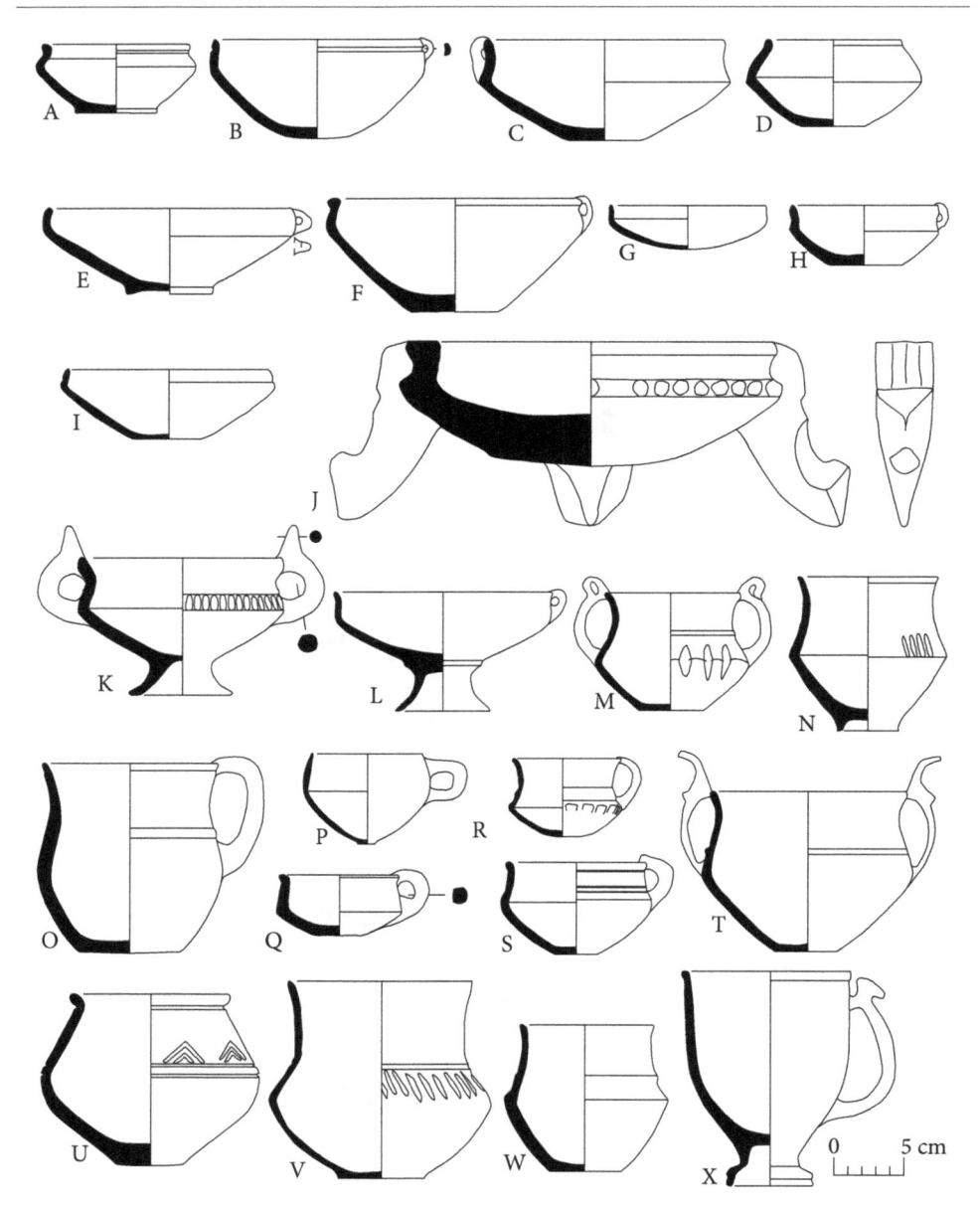

FIGURE 17.13 Iron II MBW ceramics from Hasanlu Tepe High Mound (D, H–J, M, R–T, V–X) and graves (A–C, E–G, K, L, N–Q, U).

mainly with female victims of the citadel destruction (Marcus 1993, 1994; Muscarella 2004). Incised bone cosmetic containers occur in graves and in occupation deposits (Fig. 17.19.NN; Muscarella 1974: 81, fig. 45.1047). A myriad of beads was found in the Iron II graves of Hasanlu and Dinkha—the most notable development is the popularity of large incised beads of paste, frit, glass, and bone. Glass, frit, Egyptian blue, and faience are far more abundant. Cylinder seals were included in a few of the graves at Hasanlu (Marcus 1996: 59–60). We gain the overall impression from the graves of the southern Lake Urmia Basin that the Iron II was a time of prosperity with far-flung trade connections.

Material culture

The destruction of Hasanlu IVb left a treasure trove of objects providing a vivid picture of elite material culture within a citadel of northwestern Iran. Less is currently known of other segments of society. In the citadel, only a small number of inscribed objects were found, and all came from neighboring regions and some substantially predate the level. Object styles attest to international influences with Assyrian objects and Assyrianizing local imitations being quite popular (Winter 1977), and more recently scholars have acknowledged strong ties with the southern Caucasus and Caspian littoral (Rubinson and Marcus 2005; Thornton and Pigott 2011). A compelling local style is also apparent and is best known from the carved ivories, cylinder seals, and clay sealings (Winter 1977; Muscarella 1980; Marcus 1996). Other major object and material categories include iron and bronze weapons, armor, and implements (Pigott 1989; Fleming et al. 2011; Thornton and Pigott 2011); horse gear (De Schauensee and Dyson 1983); a copper or bronze equestrian breastplate (Winter 1980); textiles (Love 2011); glazed ceramics and tile; glass and frit (Stapleton 2011); mosaic glass (Marcus 1991); Egyptian blue; amber; precious and semiprecious stone; and shell (Reese 1989). Undoubtedly the most famous objects from the destruction level are the repoussé gold beaker from Burned Building IW, found in association with three soldiers, and a silver beaker (Winter 1989; Porada 1959, 1959, 1967; Danti 2014). A large number of copper/bronze vessels were recovered (Fig. 17.17) and evince the formal and stylistic overlap with the contemporary MBW assemblage (Dyson 1965a: 198).

The citadel provides a detailed picture of personal ornament, including a multitude of plain round and segmented rings (Fig. 17.19.P–Q, EE–FF), breast plaques (Fig. 17.18.J), beads, band bracelets (Fig. 17.19.B, D, L, O), ball bracelets, and anklets (Fig. 17.19.G), segmented bracelets (Fig. 17.19.C, H, J–K), armlets with animal-head terminals (Fig. 17.19.V–W), and lion pins (Fig. 17.18.A–E). Iron II pins typically have decorated grooved heads or bent heads and occasionally attached chains (Fig. 17.18). Snake-headed terminals appear in the period and are another marker of the early Iron Age (Fig. 17.19.E, M–N; Moorey 1971: 220) and have been linked to the Caucasus (Rubinson and Marcus 2005). A wealth of armor and weapons was stored within the buildings of the citadel and was also found in association with some of the combatants and victims, providing an important line of evidence for determining the identity of the attackers (Thornton and Pigott 2011). Major categories are pear-shaped stone maceheads, copper/bronze spiked and star maces, shortswords, knives/daggers with upturned ends, iron socketed spears, and arrowheads (Fig. 17.16). Despite the richness of Hasanlu IVb, we currently do not know the settlement's ancient name, ethnic and linguistic composition, or the identities of those who destroyed it.

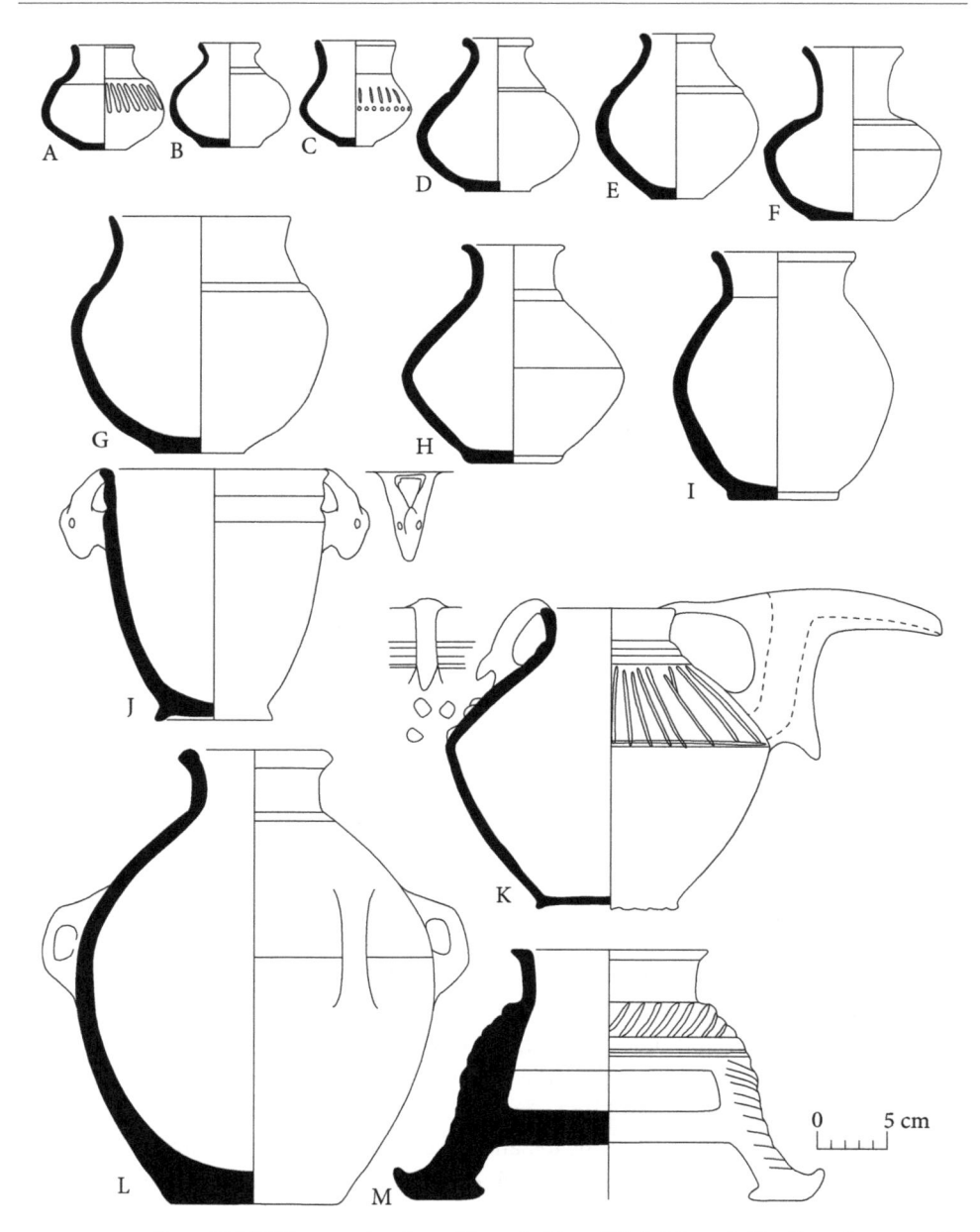

FIGURE 17.14 Iron II MBW ceramics from Hasanlu Tepe High Mound (B, C) and graves (A, D–M).

Ceramics

Iron II ceramics are best documented in the Lake Urmia Basin (Young 1965) and the Takab area (Thomalsky 2006). The period can be identified through the appearance of

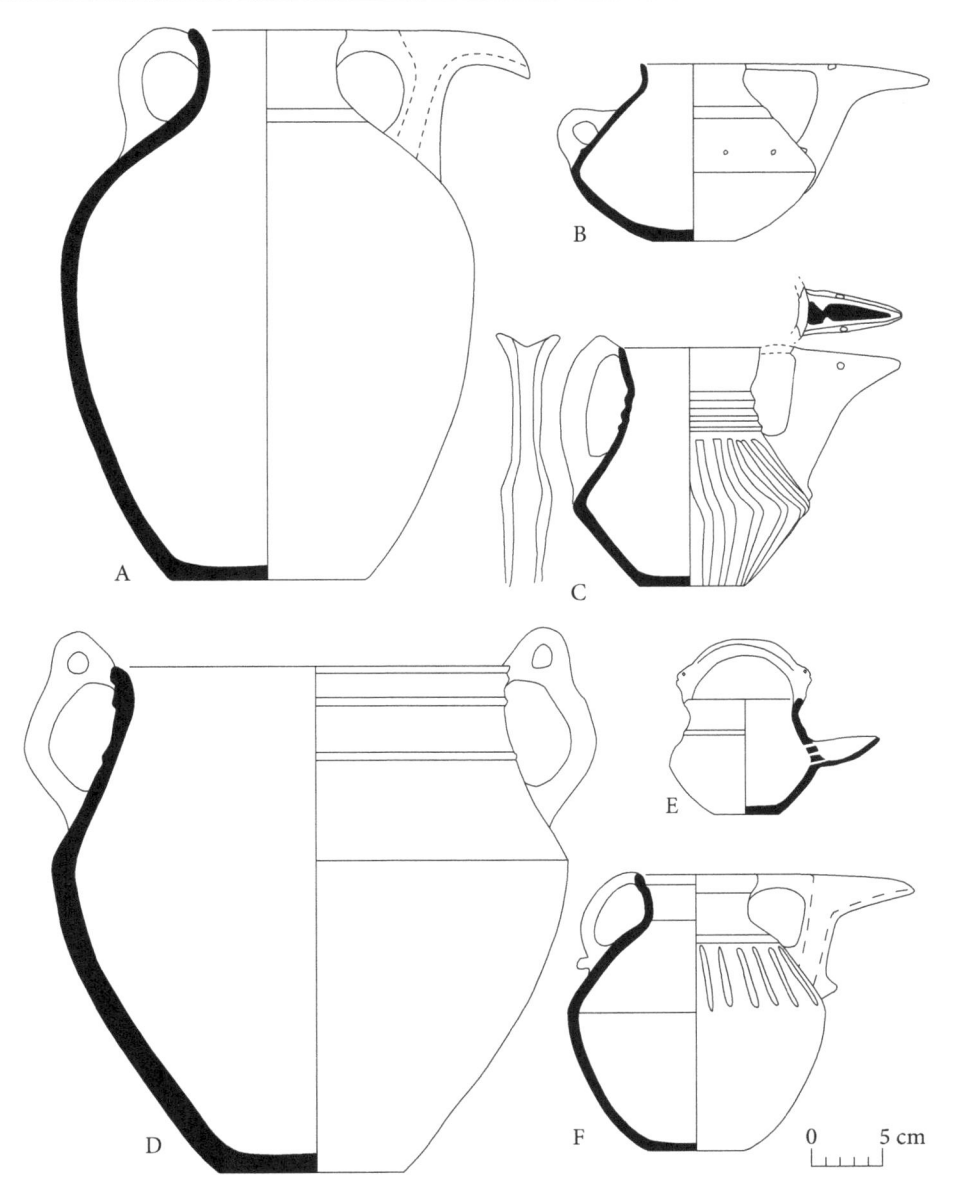

FIGURE 17.15 Iron II MBW ceramics from Hasanlu Tepe High Mound (B–E) and graves (A, F).

a number of new vessel forms and formal and stylistic attributes attested at Dinkha and Hasanlu, where both graves and occupation deposits are available. The latter part of the period is documented in occupation deposits at Zendan-e Suleiman I (Thomalsky 2006).

Overall, there is developmental continuity with the Iron I. Certain occupation deposits at Hasanlu and graves at Hasanlu and Dinkha can be dated to the late Iron I to early

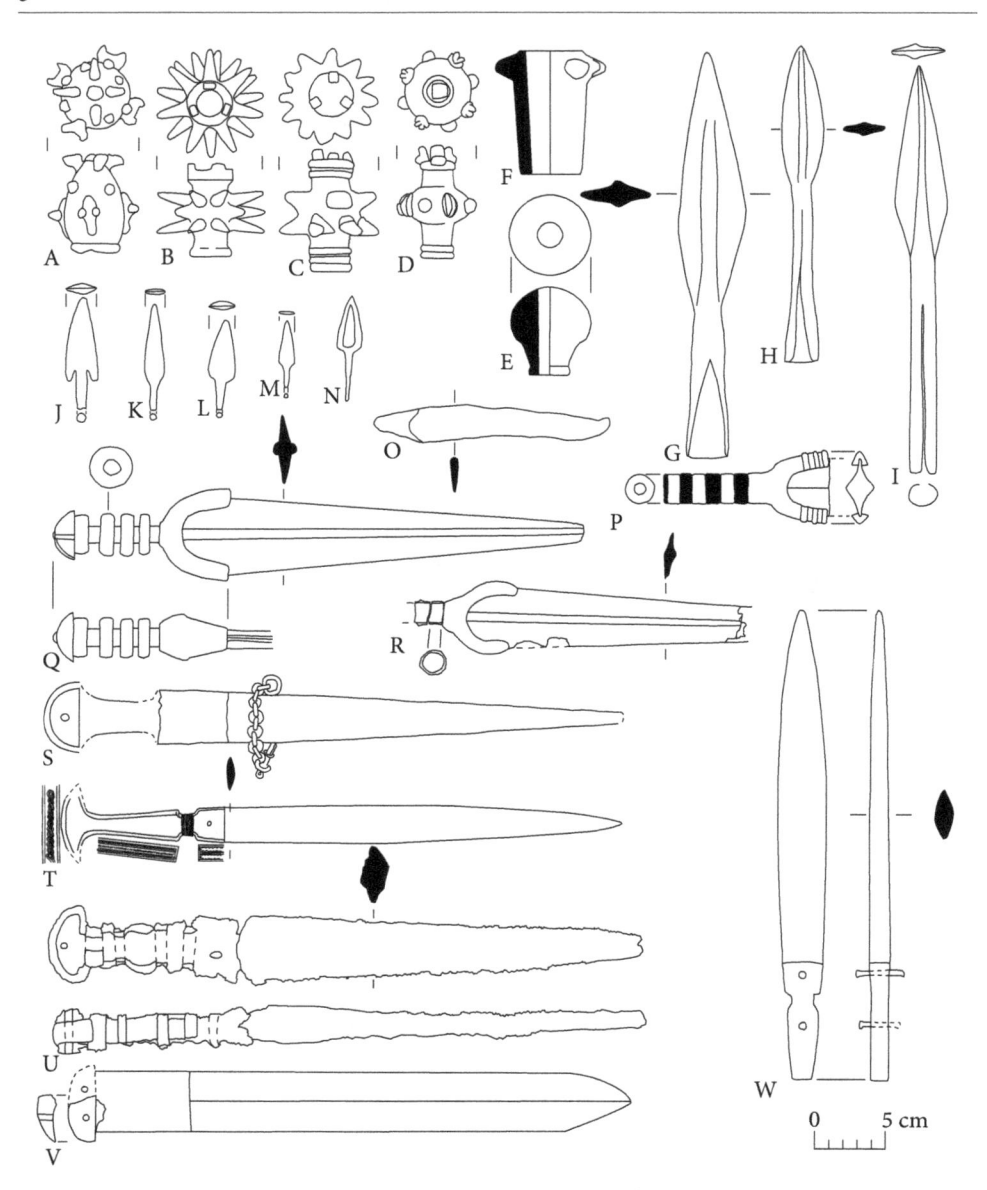

FIGURE 17.16 Iron II weaponry from Hasanlu Tepe High Mound (A–C, E–H, J–M, O–T, V, W) and graves (D, I, N, U). Iron: G, H, J–M, O, P (blade), Q, R (blade), S (blade), T (blade), U (blade), V (blade); copper/bronze: A–D, I, N, P (hilt), R (hilt), S (chain), U (grip); stone: E, F, P (grip); bone: S (handle inlay); gold: T (hilt trim); wood: C (grip), W (grip).

Iron II, providing a limited view of the transition. Bowls tend to be of the tall carinated or incurving carinated types (Fig. 17.11.B–C, F), with hemispherical bowls also present (Fig. 17.11.D). A few bowls of the worm-bowl class (Fig. 17.11.E)—one with a tripod stand (Fig. 17.11.A)—represent the latest attestations of this type. Pyxides and small jars are found in groups in graves (Fig. 17.11.G–L, O–R). A globular jar with double piercing retains attributes of earlier MBW assemblages (Fig. 17.11.M). Mid-body carinated jars continue with ribbing at the shoulder and fluting, features derived from metal vessels (Fig. 17.11.N, T, U). Most diagnostic of the transition from Iron I to Iron II is the appearance of the bridge-spouted jar (Fig. 17.11.V–W). The two attested early occurrences are mid-body carinated jars with prominent "beards" below the spout and in one case an animal-head protome handle, another marker of the Iron II.

Our understanding of the Iron II is greatly enhanced by the large number of whole vessels found in the Hasanlu destruction level, which duplicate and expand the assemblage known from the contemporary graves. At Hasanlu, so-called Palace Ware, a thin, well-manufactured variety of MBW, and glazed wares serve as markers of the Iron II in the citadel (Young 1965: 55). Small amounts of Urartian pottery appear (Kroll 2010: 27–8), and there are some formal and stylistic influences from Assyria.

Typical open forms are inverted, incurving, and high-sided carinated bowls (Fig. 17.13.D, H–I), distinctive pedestal-base cups and tankards (Fig. 17.13.X), and carinated beakers and mugs (Figs. 17.13.R–T, V–W and 14.C). Drinking vessels often have high swung handles with thumbstops (Fig. 17.13.T). Small pyxides and small and medium jars with restricted necks or wide shoulders with high necks often have a horizontal rib or incision at the shoulder (Fig. 17.14.B). The mid-body carinated jar remains a common form. Bridge-spouted jars in a wide range of shapes and sizes (Fig. 17.15.B–C) typify the period, as well as basket-handled lustration vessels with channel spouts (Fig. 17.15.E). Gadrooning, cannelures, appliqué, modeling, excising, and incision were used liberally during the Iron II.

At Kordlar I, MBW largely drops out of the assemblage, and Groovy Ware (*Rillenkeramik*) and Knob Ware (*Buckelkeramik*) represent some of the more important diagnostics (Lippert 1979; Kroll 2005: 65–6). Surveys have shown there are other sites with this horizon in the southern Lake Urmia Basin. Sites with this ceramic mix may represent "proof of the disruptions at the end of the Iron II period in the Urmia area" (Kroll 2005: 74).

Iron III (800–550 BC)

Throughout the Iron III, Azerbaijan and Kurdistan continued to be ethnically diverse and politically divided between many small kingdoms organized into coalitions aligned to the major neighboring powers. The period ends with the rise of the Achaemenid Empire. The early Iron III is characterized by disruption with shifting political borders and heightened tensions as Urartu and Assyria vied for control of Azerbaijan and Kurdistan. The Mannaeans and other smaller states of northwestern Iran were caught in the middle of this conflict. Urartu rapidly absorbed the northwestern part of the region not already under its control in the reigns of Ishpuini and Menua. As previously discussed, the Urartian presence is manifest in stelae and rock inscriptions, settlement patterns, urban form, architecture, and artifact assemblages.

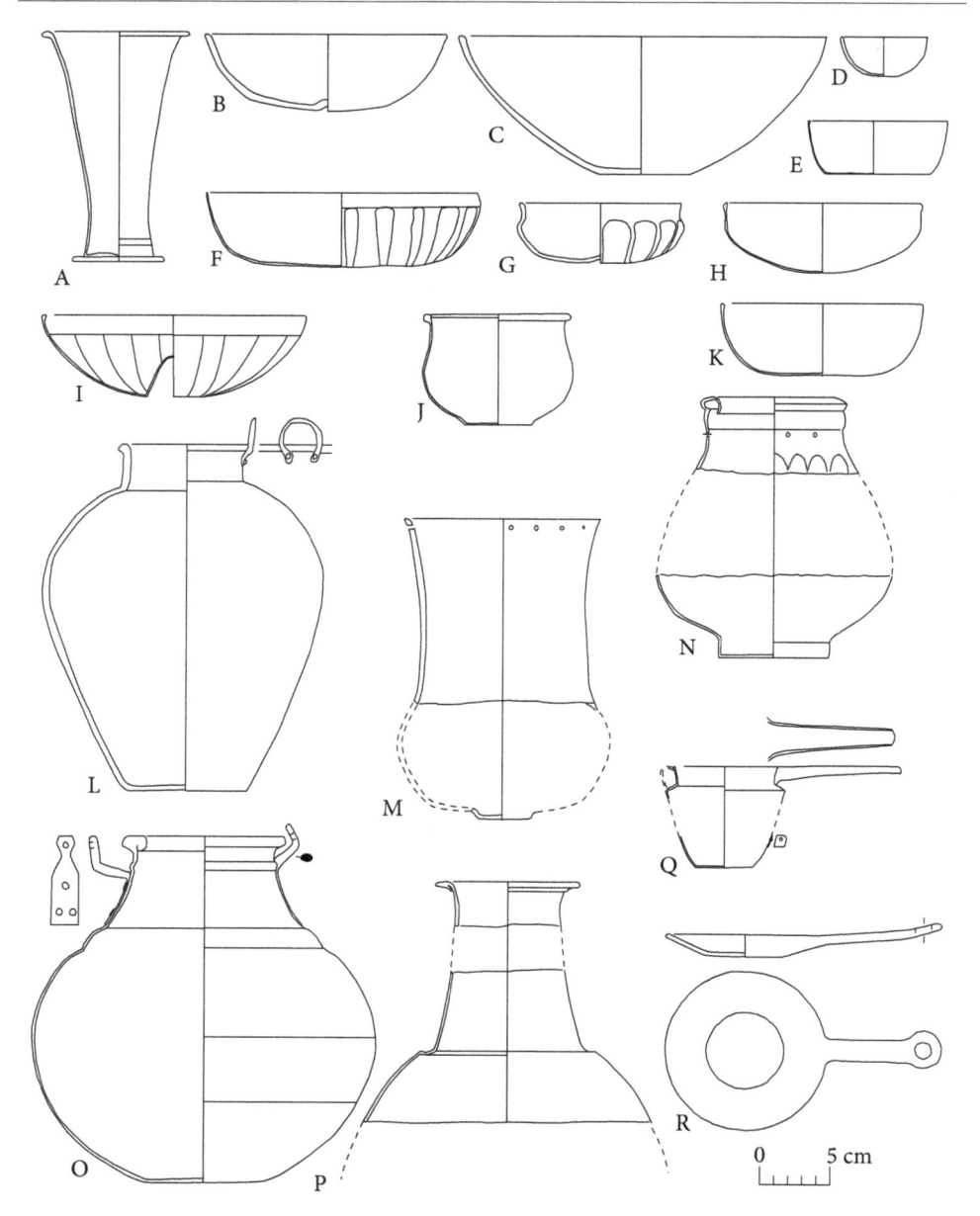

FIGURE 17.17 Iron II copper/bronze vessels from Hasanlu Tepe High Mound (A–D, F–H, J, L–R) and Hasanlu graves (E, I, K).

In Kurdistan, we see a landscape with sparse settlement typified by small, fortified citadels and manor houses, and fairly strong links with Assyria. The best-known Iron III sites lie further south in the central Zagros, key among them are Baba Jan (Goff 1977, 1978, 1985) and the Median sites of Nush-e Jan (Stronach and Roaf 2007) and Godin II (Young 1969; Young and Levine 1974; *OHR*). Here Iron II architectural trends continue

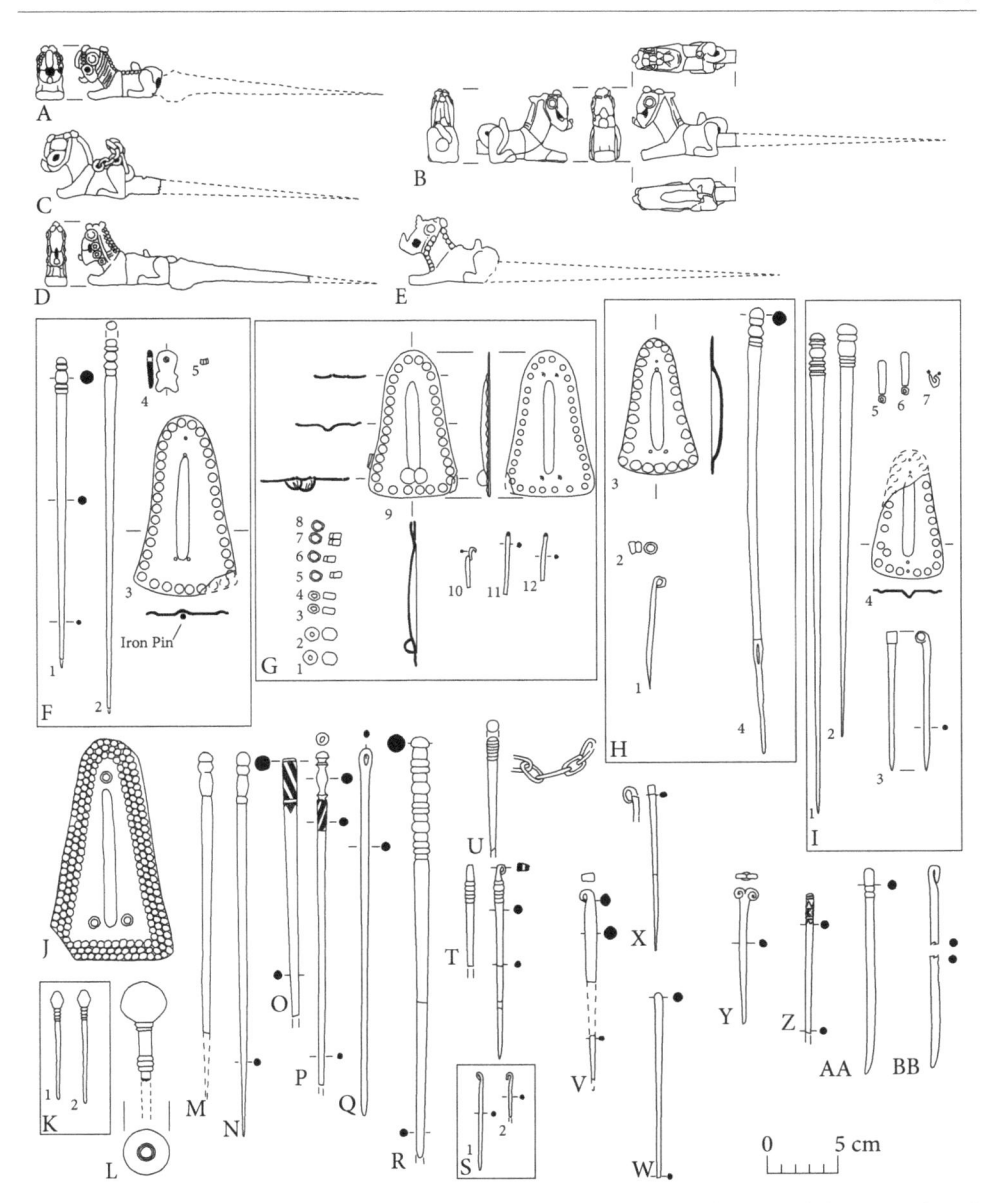

FIGURE 17.18 Iron II pins and pin groups from Hasanlu Tepe High Mound (A–E, J–L) and Hasanlu graves (F–I, M–BB). Copper/bronze head with iron pin: A–E; copper/bronze: F1–3, G5–12, H2–4, I–BB; iron: G3–4, H1; bone: F4; paste: F5; glass: G1–2.

with the use of columned halls key among them (Young 2002), and the rare traces of architecture in Kurdistan from Ziwiyeh (Motamedi 1997a, 1997b) and Qalaichi (Kargar 2004; Mollazadeh 2008) hint at this as well. Our view of historical events continues to be Assyrian and Urartian texts, and less reliable information is provided by Classical sources for the latter part of the period. Recent excavations at Iron III sites and ongoing

366 THE IRON AGE

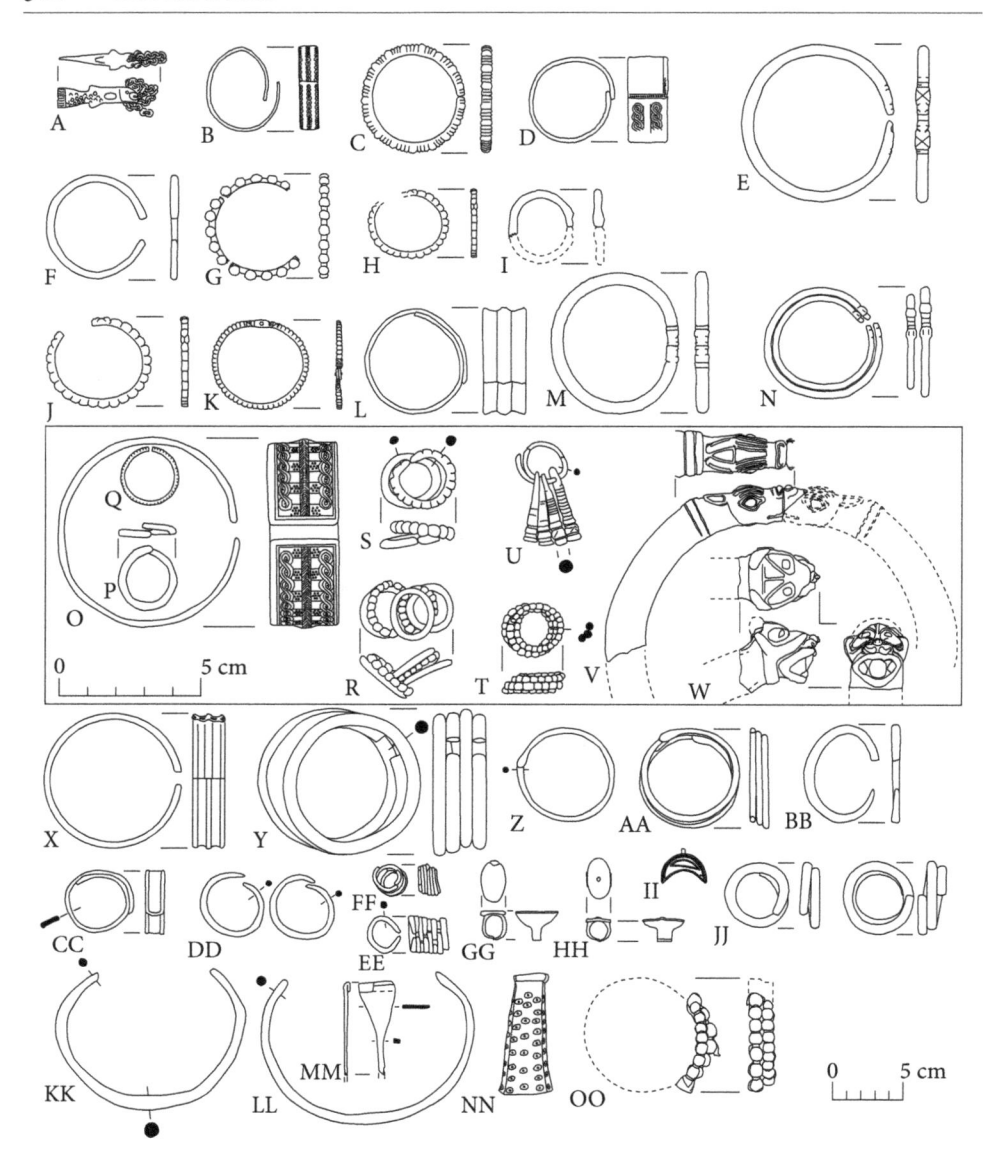

FIGURE 17.19 Iron II personal ornaments from Hasanlu Tepe High Mound (A–P, W, V) and Hasanlu graves (R–U, X–OO). Copper/bronze except copper/bronze head cast-on iron circlet (W); iron (DD2, OO); bone (NN); Egyptian blue (V); and gold (II).

revisions to Hasanlu III, critical in the development of definitions of this period and its subperiods (Young 1965; Dyson 1965a), promise to improve our chronological precision and our understanding of the later Mannaean kingdoms, Assyrian influence in Kurdistan, and the impacts of the ascendancy of the Medes and the formation of the Achaemenid Empire.

The beginning of the Iron III was originally pinned to the dating of the destruction of Hasanlu IVb around the end of the ninth century BC—a time of Assyrian weakness and Urartian expansion. Based on circumstantial evidence, the destruction of Hasanlu has often been ascribed to Urartu; however, this needs further investigation. Fuchs has shown that Urartu was already increasingly at odds with the Mannaeans, probably located to the southeast of Hasanlu, in the later ninth century, and likewise Assyria was campaigning around Lake Urmia at this time (Fuchs 2004 as cited in Kroll 2011a: 167–8; Kroll 2011b). Moreover, areas of northwestern Iran likely formed part of the early Urartian state (Fuchs 2011; Piller 2011).

In Young's threefold division, the LBW horizon corresponds with Dyson's Iron III (Young 1965). Besides a prevalence of buff burnished ceramics, Urartian architecture and artifacts appear in significant numbers in northwest Iran, and for a time Iron II LWGW trends continue. Surveys show over 100 Urartian sites in the northern, western, and southern Lake Urmia Basin (Biscione 2003, 2009; Muscarella 2011).

To be sure, the LBW horizon/period must be redefined since Young and Dyson mixed the Iron III and Iron IV. Dyson and Young drew heavily on the results of salvage excavations at the plundered site of Ziwiyeh (Godard 1950; Dyson 1963; Young 1965: 59–61, figs. 3–4) and the highly problematic Hasanlu III (cf. Muscarella 2006: 82–8 for an overview), which was until recent a veritable stratigraphic and chronological *Mischwesen*. In the traditional view, "Hasanlu III" follows a "squatter occupation" dubbed Hasanlu IVa (Dyson 1965a: 203), but recent reanalysis by Kroll shows this subperiod lacks substance (Kroll 2010: 22). Early in the Hasanlu Project, Period III was divided into subperiods Hasanlu IIIb and IIIa (Dyson 1963); however, even after this refinement Period III remained a mix of different periods. Period IIIb eventually came to signify Hasanlu's Urartian "fortress" and Period IIIa the ephemeral post-Urartian occupation. This "Hasanlu knot" has been recently disentangled by the meticulous work of Kroll (Kroll 2010, 2013; see below). The Iron III has also been brought into sharper focus with the publication of the ceramics from Zendan I–II (Thomalsky 2006), recent excavations in Kurdistan at Rabat Tepe (Heydari 2007; Kargar and Binandeh 2009), Qal'e Bardine (Hassanzadeh 2009), Qalaichi (Kargar 2004), the cemetery of Kul Tarike (Rezvani 2004; Rezvani and Roustaei 2007), and renewed work conducted at Hasanlu (Khatib Shahidi 2006) and Ziwiyeh (Motamedi 1997a, 1997b). The starting date of the Iron III has been archaeologically significant and identifiable in parts of northwestern Iran insofar as it corresponds to an intensified Urartian presence, but elsewhere in Iran it remains a rather arbitrary and tenebrous division.

Urartian conquests can be traced by spatiotemporal patterns in the distribution of inscribed stele and rock inscriptions. This pattern is paralleled by the destruction and abandonment of some settlements and the appearance of Urartian sites exhibiting new preferences in settlement location and the introduction of distinctive architectural forms and artifacts. Hasanlu was destroyed and Dinkha and Geoy Tepe were at the very least abandoned. Kordlar has multiple destruction levels, Haftavan III represents a small eighth-century Urartian site, and Qaleh Ismail Agha was the site of Urartian fortresses in the seventh century. Other Iron II settlements in the Lake Urmia Basin known from surveys were also destroyed in the late ninth or early eighth century. Over time, the Urartians established a network of fortresses in the northern, western, and southern Lake Urmia Basin and in the more isolated valleys to the north. Large fortresses occupied mountain spurs at strategic points, and smaller forts were built along important lines of communication (Kroll 1976: 173–214; Zimansky 1985: 36–40). The Urartian strategy was to draw on the wealth of this fertile region, deny the Assyrians access to an ideal staging ground for their campaigns in the Zagros, and block the strategic mountain passes leading into northwest Iran and southeastern Anatolia. It is important to emphasize that the Urartian connection to the physical evidence of devastation is often circumstantial, yet the overall pattern is compelling and, in adumbrated form, agrees with the historical record. Bastam, located north of Khoy, provides our best view of a major Urartian fortress in the area and a reliable starting point for defining Urartian material culture (Kroll 1970, 1979; *BAuA*). In Ushnu, we see the construction of the large hilltop fortress of Qalatgah overlooking a spring (Muscarella 1971) and controlling the head of the valley. An inscription of Ishpuini and Menua dates the site to around 800 BC, and it has been identified as either the Ulhu or the Uishi/Uajais of Assyrian texts (Muscarella 1986; Zimansky 1990: 17–18). In Solduz, the site of Agrab Tepe, commanding a rocky prominence, in keeping with Urartian practice, provides a compelling view of a smaller fortress (Muscarella 1973). The situation at Hasanlu is more complex. The construction of an Urartian fortification wall on the *tepe*, first identified by Kroll (Muscarella 2006: 83–5), ends a period of abandonment and represents an uncharacteristic location for an Urartian stronghold. Following the construction of the Urartian fortifications there is little sign of occupation, and there are hints that the fortifications were not finished (Kroll 2010: 25). Later, something like a "squatter occupation" occurred (Kroll 2010: 23) with a ring of structures built against the wall's interior, which, along with the fortification wall, were previously designated Hasanlu IIIb; however, there is little basis for identifying this later phase as Urartian and it postdates the Urartian wall. Much of the material originally used by Young and Dyson to define the LBW Horizon comes from this later occupation, and thus the dating of the construction of the Hasanlu IIIc Urartian fortification wall (formerly IIIb, Kroll 2010: 23) provides a critical *terminus post quem* for dating the IIIb occupation. Kroll has preliminarily suggested a date in the eighth to seventh centuries, based on similarities between the Hasanlu fortifications and those of Karmir Blur (Kroll 2010: 23–4). A major turning point was reached in 714 with Sargon II's momentous eighth campaign, which drove the Urartians out of the southern Lake Urmia Basin and largely pacified Mannaea. The Mannaeans continued to be major players in northwest Iran until the fall of Assyria in the closing decades of the seventh century. The Medes, a key member of the coalition that conquered Assyria, were on the political ascendant in the seventh century, exercising steadily increasing power and influence in northwest Iran from their strongholds in the central Zagros. The later Iron III is not well known in northwestern Iran, and the development of the Achaemenid Empire is difficult to discern.

Hasanlu IIIa represents the late Achaemenid period, and is identified by the presence of painted "Triangle Ware," which occurs at other sites in the region as well (Dyson 1999a, 1999b; Kroll 2000; Kroll forthcoming b).

CONCLUSION

When the Monochrome Burnished Ware Horizon emerges in the mid-second millennium BC, it is characterized by marked regional variation, contrary to previous assertions that view the horizon as arriving fully developed and *subsequently* regionally diversified. Closer inspection of the evidence suggests the MBW Horizon gradually developed in place out of the Terminal MBII (seventeenth century BC) and MBIII (1600–1450 BC), and previous arguments for a punctuated and wholesale cultural break between the MBW Horizon and the archaeological cultures of the so-called LBA (MBII) have been flawed by poor chronological resolution, over-reliance on data sets from chronologically floating cemeteries, and invalid comparisons between the highly localized Khabur Ware Horizon of the MBII in Ushnu-Solduz and the chronological pastiche of the former Iron I/EWGW (*sensu* Dyson and Young). Ushnu-Solduz received much interpretative weight since it provided archaeological sequences from occupational deposits. These sequences, based on small soundings at Hasanlu and Dinkha, largely missed the Terminal MBII and MBIII—the evidence certainly indicates these periods are attested in the region. The archaeological correlates identified with the horizon—columned-hall architecture, certain MBW vessel forms and attributes, extramural cemeteries, unfortified settlements—do not appear simultaneously in northwestern Iran, often can be shown to emerge from the MBA, or are not valid. To understand MBW origins in northwestern Iran, we should direct our attention to the Terminal MBII and MBIII and place more emphasis on the important connections with the southern Caucasus, eastern Anatolia, and northern Mesopotamia.

The MBW Horizon reaches its developmental zenith in the later ninth century BC. It was associated with a number of cultures and sociopolitical units. At this point, following at least 700 years of *in situ* development, the horizon exhibits its highest degree of homogeneity and maximum spatial extent. The southward expansion of the Urartian state appears to be closely linked to its decline, and the related LBW Horizon develops rapidly in the eighth century during widespread and fairly constant disruption. The late Iron II and Iron III witnessed the weakening of the more urban and agrarian-based societies of western and southern Iran, key among them the Mannaeans and Elamites, by Urartu and Assyria, which surely favored the political ascendancy of tribal confederacies largely made up of transhumant pastoralist groups such as the Medes and Persians who were already present in the region by at least the early first millennium BC.

FURTHER READING

Curtis (2005) provides the most balanced and current overview of the Early Iron Age within the framework of its relevance to the emergence of the Achaemenid Empire. The articles in Dyson and Voigt (1989) remain the best general introduction to the discoveries at Hasanlu Tepe. Burney and Lang (1971) provides a solid background and general synthesis of the archaeology of the larger region, but is somewhat dated. For a recent evaluation of the Hasanlu Project in terms of its methods, development, and findings see Muscarella (2006).

References

Biscione, R. 2003. Pre-Urartian and Urartian settlement patterns in the Caucasus two case studies, the Urmia Plain, Iran, and the Sevan Basin, Armenia. In *Archaeology in the borderlands*, ed. A. T. Smith and K. S. Rubinson, 167–84. Los Angeles: Cotsen Institute of Archaeology.

———. 2009. The distribution of pre- and protohistoric hillforts in Iran. *SMEA* 51: 123–43.

Boehmer, R. M. 1961. Die Keramikfunde vom Zindan-i Suleiman. In *Takht-i Suleiman. Vorläufiger Berichtüber die Ausgrabungen 1959*, ed. H. H. von der Osten and R. Naumann, 82–6. Berlin: Tehraner Forschungen 1.

———. 1964. Volkstum und Städte der Mannäer. *BaM* 3: 11–24.

———. 1967. Forschungen am Zendan-i Suleiman in Persisch-Aserbeidschan, 1958–64. In *Archologische Gesellschaft zu Berlin 1966, Sitzung am 8. Februar 1966*, 573–85. Berlin: AA Supplement.

———. 1986. Ritzverzierte Keramik aus dem mannäischen(?) Bereich. *AMI* 19: 95–115.

Burney, C. A. 1962. Excavations at Yanik Tepe, Azerbaijan, 1961: Second preliminary report. *Iraq* 24/2: 134–52.

———. 1970. Excavations at Haftavân Tepe, 1968: First preliminary report. *Iran* 8: 157–71.

———. 1972. Excavations at Haftavân Tepe, 1969: Second preliminary report. *Iran* 10: 127–42.

———. 1973. Excavations at Haftavân Tepe, 1971: Third preliminary report. *Iran* 11: 153–72.

———. 1975. Excavations at Haftavân Tepe, 1973: Fourth preliminary report. *Iran* 13: 149–64.

Burney, C. A., and D. M. Lang. 1971. *The peoples of the hills*. New York: Praeger.

Burton-Brown, T. 1951. *Excavations in Azerbaijan, 1948*. London: John Murray.

Contenau, G., and R. Ghirshman. 1935. *Fouilles du Tépé Giyan, près de Néhavend, 1931-32*. Paris: Geuthner.

Curtis, J. 2005. Iron Age Iran and the transition to the Achaemenid period. In *Birth of the Persian Empire*, vol. 1, ed. V.S. Curtis and S. Stewart, 112–31. London: I. B. Taurus.

Dandamaev, M. A., and V. G. Lukonin. 1989. *The culture and social institutions of ancient Iran*. Cambridge: Cambridge University Press.

Danti, M. D. 2011. The Artisan's House of Hasanlu Tepe, Iran. *Iran* 49: 11–54.

———. 2013. *Hasanlu V: The Late Bronze and Iron I periods*. Philadelphia: UMM.

———. 2014. The Hasanlu gold bowl in context: All that glitters ... *Antiquity* 88: 791–804 online supplement.

Danti, M. D., and M. Cifarelli. 2015. Iron II warrior burials at Hasanlu Tepe, Iran. *IrAnt* 50: 61–157.

De Schauensee, M., and R. H. Dyson Jr. 1983. Hasanlu horse trappings and Assyrian reliefs. In *Essays on Near Eastern art and archaeology in honor of Charles Kyrle Wilkinson*, ed. P. O. Harper and H. Pittman, 59–77. New York: Metropolitan Museum of Art.

Deshayes, J. 1969. New evidence for the Indo-Europeans at Tureng Tepe, Iran. *Archaeology* 22/1: 10–17.

Diakonoff, I. M. 1956. *Istoriya Midii ot drevneishikh vremen do kontsa IV veka do n.e.* Moscow and Leningrad: Izd-vo Akademii nauk SSSR.

———. 1967. *Iazyki drevnei Perednei Azii.* Moscow: Nauka.

———. 1971. Vostochnyj Iran do Kira. In *Istoriya Iranskogo gosudarstva i kul'tury,* ed. B. G. Gafurov, 122–54. Moscow: Glavnaya redaktsiya vostochnoi literatury.

Diakonoff, I. M. and S. M. Kashkai. 1979. *Geographical names according to Urartian texts.* Wiesbaden: RGTC 9.

Dittmann, R. 1990. Eisenzeit I und II in West- und Nordwest-Iran zeitgleich zur Karum-Zeit Anatoliens? *AMI* 23: 105–138.

Dyson, R. H., Jr. 1963. Archaeological scrap: Glimpses of history at Ziwiye. *Expedition* 5/3: 32–7.

———. 1965a. Problems of protohistoric Iran as seen from Hasanlu. *JNES* 24/3: 193–217.

———. 1965b. Notes on weapons and chronology in northern Iran around 1000 B.C. In *Dark ages and nomads c. 1000 B.C.,* ed. M. Mellink, 32–45. Istanbul: Historisch-Archaeologisch Instituut te Istanbul.

———. 1968. The archaeological evidence of the second millennium B.C. on the Persian plateau. *CAH* 2: 1–36 (appeared in book form in *CAH* 2/1: 686–715 in 1973).

———. 1975. Hasanlu, 1974: The ninth century B.C. gateway. *PASARI* 3: 179–88.

———. 1977. Architecture of the Iron I period at Hasanlu in western Iran and its implications for theories of migration on the Iranian Plateau. In *Le Plateau Iranien et l'Asie centrale des origines à la conquête Islamique,* ed. J. Deshayes, 155–69. Paris: Éditions du CNRS.

———. 1989. The Iron Age architecture at Hasanlu: An essay. *Expedition* 31/2–3: 107–127.

———. 1999a. The Achaemenid painted pottery of Hasanlu IIIA. *AnSt* 49: 101–110.

———. 1999b. Triangle-Festoon Ware reconsidered. *IrAnt* 34: 115–44.

Dyson, R. H., Jr., and O. W. Muscarella. 1989. Constructing the chronology and historical implications of Hasanlu IV. *Iran* 27: 1–27.

Dyson, R. H., Jr., and M. M. Voigt. 1989. East of Assyria: The highland settlement of Hasanlu. *Expedition* 31/2–3: 1–127.

———. 2003. A temple at Hasanlu. *YBYN*: 219–36.

Edwards, M. 1981. The pottery of Haftavan VIB (Urmia Ware). *Iran* 19: 101–40.

———. 1983. *Excavations in Azerbaijan (North-western Iran). Haftavan, Period VI.* Oxford: BAR Int Ser 182.

———. 1986. "Urmia Ware" and its distribution in north-western Iran in the second millennium B.C.: A review of the results of excavations and surveys. *Iran* 24: 57–77.

Egami, N., S. Fukai, and S. Masuda. 1965. *Dailaman I: Excavations at Ghalekuti and Lasulkan, 1960.* Tokyo: Tokyo University Iraq-Iran Archaeological Expedition Report 6.

Eph'al, I. 1999. The Bukan Aramaic inscription: Historical considerations. *IEJ* 49: 116–21.

Fales, F.M. 2003. Evidence for west-east contacts in the 8th century BC: The Bukān stele. *CE*: 131–48.

Felber, H. 1979. Vienna Radium Institute Radiocarbon Dates VIII. *Radiocarbon* 21/1: 113–19.

Fleming, S. J., S. K. Nash, and C. P. Swann. 2011. The archaeometallurgy of Period IVB bronzes at Hasanlu. *PCPIVB*: 103–34.

Fuchs, A. 2004. Bishinzum Berg Bikni. Zur Topographieund Geschichte des Zagrosraumes in altorientalischer Zeit. Unpublished Habilitation, Eberhard Karls University of Tübingen.

———. 2011. Urartu in der Zeit. *BU*: 153–85.

Ghirshman, R. 1935. Rapport préliminaire sur les fouilles de Tépé-Sialk. *Syria* 16/3: 229–46.

———. 1939. *Fouilles de Sialk, prs de Kashan, 1933, 1934, 1937,* vol. 2. Paris: Geuthner.

———. 1954. *Iran, from the earliest times to the Islamic conquest.* Baltimore: Penguin.

———. 1964. *The art of Ancient Iran*. New York: Golden Press.
———. 1977. *L'Iran et la migration des Indo-aryens et des Iraniens*. Leiden: Brill.
Godard, A. 1950. *Le Trésor de Ziwiyé*. Haarlem: H. Enschedel.
Goff, C. 1977. Excavations at Baba Jan: The architecture of the east mound, Levels II and III. *Iran* 15: 103–40.
———. 1978. Excavations at Baba Jan: The pottery and metal from Levels III and II. *Iran* 16: 29–65.
———. 1985. Excavations at Baba Jan: The architecture and pottery of Level I. *Iran* 23: 1–20.
Grantovskiy, E. A. 1971. *Rannyaya Istoriya Iranskikh Plemen Predney Azii*. Moscow: Nauka.
———. 1998. *Iran i Irancy do Akhemenidov*. Moscow.
Haerinck, E. 1988. The Iron Age in Guilan: proposal for a chronology. In *Bronze-working centres of Western Asia c. 1000–539 B.C.*, ed. J. Curtis, 63–78. New York: Kegan Paul International.
Hakemi, A., and M. Rad. 1950. Rapport et resultants de fouilles scientifques à Hasanlu, Solduz. *GB* 1: 87–103.
Hamlin, C. 1971. The Ḫabur Ware ceramic assemblage of northern Mesopotamia: An analysis of its distribution. Unpublished PhD diss., University of Pennsylvania.
———. 1974. The early second millennium ceramic assemblage of Dinkha Tepe. *Iran* 12: 125–53.
Hassanzadeh, Y. 2009. Qal'e Bardine, a Mannaean local chiefdom in the Bukan area, north-western Iran. *AMIT* 41: 269–82.
Heinsch, S. 2004. Korldar Tepe. Stratigraphie und Keramik. Unpublished MA thesis, University of Innsbruck.
Helwing, B. 2005. Tappeh Sialk South Mound: Operation 3. In *The fishermen of Sialk*, ed. S. M. Shahmirzadi, 27–66. Teheran: SRPR 4.
Henrickson, R. C. 1983–4. Giyan I and II reconsidered. *Mesopotamia* 18–19: 195–220.
———. 2011. The Godin Period III town. *OHR*: 209–81.
Heydari, R. 2007. The results of second season of archaeological projects at Rabat, Sardasht. In *Archaeological reports on the occasion of the 9th annual symposium on Iranian archaeology*, 7/1, 201–229. Tehran (in Persian).
Hojabri Nobari, A. 2004. Excavations of Masjed-e Kabud in Tabriz: Its place among contemporaneous Iranian Iron Age Sites. *PISIANR*: 265–76.
Kargar, B. 2004. Ghalaichi, Zirtu: Mannaean capital. *PISIANR*: 229–45.
Kargar, B., and A. Binandeh. 2009. A preliminary report of excavations at Rabat Tepe, northwestern Iran. *IrAnt* 44: 113–29.
Khatib Shahidi, H. 2006. Recent investigations at Hasanlu and reconsideration of its upper strata. *International Journal of Humanities of the Islamic Republic of Iran* 13/3: 17–29.
Khatib Shahidi, H., and R. Biscione. 2007. Iranian-Italian archaeological survey in Eastern Azerbaijan: Provisional report on the 2006–1385 season. *GB* 7: 25–34 (in Persian).
Kleiss, W. 1971. *Zendan-i Suleiman, Die Bauwerke*. Wiesbaden: Beiträge zur Archäologie und Geologie des Zendan-i Suleiman II.
Kroll, S. 1970. Die Keramik aus der Ausgrabung Bastam 1969. *AMI* 3: 67–92.
———. 1976. *Keramik urartischer Festungen in Iran: Ein Beitrag zur Expansion Urartus in Iranisch-Azarbaidjan*. Berlin: AMI Ergängzungsband 2.
———. 1979. Die urartäische Keramik aus Bastam. *BAuA*: 203–20.
———. 1992. Ein "Triple Road System" oder Stallbauten in Hasanlu IVb? *AMI* 25: 65–72.
———. 1994a. Festungen und Siedlungen in Iranisch-Azarbaidjan. Untersuchungen zur Siedlungs- und Territorialgeschichte des Urmia-Sees-Gebiets in vorislamischer Zeit. Unpublished Habilitation, Ludwig Maximilians University of Munich.

———. 1994b. Ḫabur-Ware im Osten oder: Der TAVO auf Irrwegen im Iranischen Hochland. In *Beiträge zur altorientalischen Archäologie und Altertumskunde*, ed. P. Calmeyer, K. Hecker, L. Jakob-Rost, and C. B. F. Walker, 159–66. Wiesbaden: Harrassowitz.

———. 2000. Nordwest Iran in achaimenidischer Zeit: Zur Verbreitung der Classic Triangle Ware. *AMIT* 32: 131–8.

———. 2004. Prehistoric settlement patterns in the Maku and Khoy regions of Iranian western Azerbaijan. *PISIANR*: 45–53.

———. 2005. The southern Lake Urmia basin in the Early Iron Age. *IrAnt* 40: 65–85.

———. 2010. Urartu and Hasanlu. In *Urartu and its neighbors*, ed. A. Kosyan, A. Petrosyan, and Y. Grekyan, 21–35. Yerevan: Aramazd V/2.

———. 2011a. Urartian cities in Iran. In *Urartu/Biainili: Transformation in the East*, ed. K. Köroğlu and E. Konyar, 150–69. Istanbul: YapıKredi Yayınları.

———. 2011b. Salmanassar III. und das frühe Urartu. *BU*: 187–94.

———. 2012. On the road(s) to nowhere: A re-analysis of the Hasanlu "Tripartite Road System" in light of the excavated evidence. In *Stories of long ago. Festschrift für Michael D. Roaf*, 277–84. Münster: AOAT 397.

———. Forthcoming b. Hasanlu III und die stratigraphische Evidenz der Triangle Ware. In *Der archäologische Befund und seine Historisierung. Dokumentation und ihre Interpretationsspielräume*. Innsbruck: Zentrum für Alte Kulturen, Universität Innsbruck.

Kuz'mina, E. E. 2007. *The origin of the Indo-Iranians*. Leiden: Indo-European Etymological Dictionary Series 3.

Lanfranchi, G. B. 2003. The Assyrian expansion in the Zagros and the local ruling elites. *CE*: 79–118.

Lemaire, A. 1998. Une inscription araméenne du VIIIe siecle av. J.-C. trouvée à Bukan. (Azerbaidjan iranien). *StIr* 27: 15–30.

Levine, L. D. 1973. Geographical studies in the Neo-Assyrian Zagros I. *Iran* 11: 1–27.

———. 1974. Geographical studies in the Neo-Assyrian Zagros II. *Iran* 12: 99–124.

———. 1977. Sargon's eighth campaign. *ML*: 135–51.

———. 1987. The Iron Age. *AWI*: 229–50.

Lippert, A. 1977. Kordlar-Tepe. *Iran* 15: 174–7.

———. 1979. Die österreichischen Ausgrabungen am Kordlar-Tepe in Persisch-Westaserbeidschan (1971–1978). *AMI* 12: 103–37.

Love, N. 2011. The analysis and conservation of the Hasanlu IVB textiles. *PCPIVB*: 43–56.

Magee, P. 2008. Deconstructing the destruction of Hasanlu: Archaeology, imperialism and the chronology of the Iranian Iron Age. *IrAnt* 43: 89–106.

Marcus, M. I. 1991. The mosaic glass vessels from Hasanlu, Iran: A study in large-scale stylistic trait distribution. *Art Bulletin* 73: 536–60.

———. 1993. Incorporating the body: Adornment, gender, and social identity in ancient Iran. *CAJ* 3: 157–78.

———. 1994. Dressed to kill: Women and pins in early Iran. *Oxford Art Journal* 17/2: 3–15.

———. 1996. *Emblems of identity and prestige: The seals and sealings from Hasanlu, Iran*. Philadelphia: UMM 84.

Medvedskaya, I. 1983. Horse harness from the Sialk B cemetery. *IrAnt* 18: 59–79.

———. 1988. Who destroyed Hasanlu IV? *Iran* 26: 1–15.

———. 1991. Once more on the destruction of Hasanlu IV: Problems of dating. *IrAnt* 26: 149–61.

Mollazadeh, K. 2008. The pottery from the Mannaean site of Qalaichi, Bukan (NW-Iran). *IrAnt* 43: 107–25.

Moorey, P. R. S. 1971. *Catalogue of the ancient Persian bronzes in the Ashmolean Museum.* Oxford: Clarendon Press.

Morgan, J. de. 1905. Recherches au Talyche persan. In *Recherches archéologiques, troisième série,* 251–341. Paris: MDP 8.

Motamedi, N. O. 1997a. Ziwiye: A Mannaean-Median fortress. In *Proceedings of Iranian architecture and city building congress,* ed. B. A. Shirazi, 320–57. Tehran: Iranian Cultural Heritage Organization (in Persian).

———. 1997b. Excavation at Ziwiyeh, 1995: Architecture and ceramics. *GB* 1: 143–70 (in Persian).

Mousavi, A. 2005. Comments on the Early Iron Age in Iran. *IrAnt* 40: 87–99.

———. 2008. Late Bronze Age in north-eastern Iran: An alternative approach to persisting problems. *Iran* 46: 105–20.

Muscarella, O. W. 1968. Excavations at Dinkha Tepe, 1966. *Bulletin of the Metropolitan Museum of Art* 27/3: 187–96.

———. 1971. Qalatgah: An Urartian site in northwestern Iran. *Expedition* 13/3–4: 44–9.

———. 1973. Excavations at Agrab Tepe, Iran. *MMJ* 8: 47–76.

———. 1974. The Iron Age at Dinkha Tepe, Iran. *MMJ* 9: 35–90.

———. 1980. *The catalogue of ivories from Hasanlu, Iran.* Philadelphia: UMM 40.

———. 1986. The location of Ulhu and Uiše in Sargon II's eighth campaign, 714 B.C. *JFA* 13/4: 465–75.

———. 1994. North-western Iran: Bronze Age to Iron Age. In *Anatolian Iron Ages* 3, ed. A. Çilingiroğlu and D. H. French, 139–54. Ankara: BIAAM 16.

———. 2004. The Hasanlu lion pins again. *AVH:* 693–710.

———. 2006. The excavations of Hasanlu: An archaeological evaluation. *BASOR* 342: 69–94.

———. 2011. Hasanlu and Urartu. *BU:* 311–26.

Naumann, R. 1977. *Die Ruinen von Takht-e Suleiman und Zendan-e Suleiman und Umgebung.* Berlin: Führer zu archäologischen Plätzen in Iran 2.

Negahban, E. O. 1964. *A preliminary report on Marlik excavation. Gohar Rud Expedition, Rudbar, 1961–1962.* Tehran: Offset Press.

———. 1996. *Marlik: The complete excavation report,* 2 vols. Philadelphia: UMM 87.

Pecorella, P. E., and M. Salvini. 1984. *Tra lo Zagros e L'Urmia. Ricerche storiche ed archeologiche nell'Azerbaigian Iraniano.* Rome: Incunabula Graeca 78.

Pigott, V. C. 1977. The question of the presence of iron in the Iron I period in western Iran. *ML:* 209–34.

———. 1981. The adoption of iron in western Iran in the early first millennium B.C.: An archaeometallurgical study. Unpublished PhD diss., University of Pennsylvania.

———. 1989. The emergence of iron use at Hasanlu. *Expedition* 31/2–3: 67–79.

———. 2004. Hasanlu und das Auftreten des Eisens in Westiran im frühen 1. Jahrtausends v. Chr. *PAP:* 350–7.

Piller, C. K. 2004a. Zur Mittelbronzezeit im nördlichen Zentraliran—Die zentraliranische Graue Ware (Central Grey Ware) als mögliche Verbindung zwischen Eastern und Western Grey Ware. *AMIT* 35–6: 143–73.

———. 2004b. The Iranian highlands in the 2nd and 3rd millennium BC: The period of early history. *PAP:* 310–27.

———. 2008. Untersuchungen zur relativen Chronologie der Nekropole von Marlik. Unpublished PhD diss., Ludwig Maximilians University of Munich.

———. 2010. Northern Iran in the Iron Age II and III: A neighbor of Urartu? In *Urartu and its Neighbors,* ed. A. Kosyan, A. Petrosyan, and Y. Grekyan, 53–75. Yerevan: Aramazd V/2.

———. 2011. Bewaffnung und Tracht urartäischer und nordwestiranischer Krieger des 9. Jahrhunderts v. Chr.: Ein Beitrag zur historischen Geographie des frühen Urartu. *BU:* 441–55.

Porada, E. 1959. The Hasanlu gold bowl. *Expedition* 1/3: 18–22.

———. 1967. Notes on the gold bowl and silver beaker from Hasanlu. *SPA*: 2971–8.

Postgate, J. N. 1989. Mannäer. *RlA* 7/5–6: 340–2.

Reade, J. E. 1979. Hasanlu, Gilzanu and related considerations. *AMI* 12: 175–81.

———. 1995. Iran in the Neo-Assyrian period. *N-AG*: 31–42.

Reese, D. S. 1989. Treasures from the sea: Shells and shell ornaments from Hasanlu. *Expedition* 31/2–3: 80–6.

Rezvani, H. 2004. Kul Tarikeh cemetery. *PISIANR*: 81–110.

Rezvani, H., and K. Roustaei. 2007. Preliminary report on two seasons of excavations at Kul Tarike cemetery, Kurdestan, Iran. *IrAnt* 42: 139–84.

Rubinson, K. S. 1991. A mid-second millennium tomb at Dinkha Tepe. *AJA* 95/3: 373–94.

———. 2004. Dinkha Tepe, Iran and so-called Urmia Ware. *AVH*: 661–76.

Rubinson, K. S., and M. I. Marcus. 2005. Hasanlu IVB and Caucasia: Explorations and implications of context. In *Anatolian Iron Ages 5*, ed. A. Çilingiroğlu and G. Darbyshire, 131–8. Ankara: BIAAM 31.

Schaeffer, C. F. A. 1948. *Stratigraphie comparée et chronologie de l'Asie occidentale*. London: Oxford University Press.

Schmidt, E. F. 1937. *Excavations at Tepe Hissar, Damghan*. Philadelphia: University of Pennsylvania Press.

Smith, A. T., R. S. Badalyan, and P. Avetisyan. 2009. *The foundations of research and regional survey in the Tsaghkahovit Plain, Armenia*. Chicago: OIP 134.

Sokoloff, M. 1999. The Old Aramaic inscription from Bukan: A revised interpretation. *IEJ* 49: 105–15.

Stapleton, C. P. 2011. Glass and glaze analysis and technology from Hasanlu, Period IVB. *PCPIVB*: 87–102.

Stein, M. A. 1940. *Old routes of Western Īrān Narrative of an archaeological journey*. London: Macmillan.

Stronach, D., and M. Roaf. 2007. *Nush-i Jan I: The major buildings of the Median settlement*. Leuven/Paris/Dudley: British Institute of Persian Studies and Peeters.

Swiny, S. 1973. Survey in northwestern Iran, 1971. *EW* 25: 77–96.

Tala'i, H. 2007. The Iron II (ca. 1200–800 B.C.) pottery assemblage at Haftavan IV: NW-Iran. *IrAnt* 42: 105–23.

Tala'i, H., and A. Aliyari. 2009. Haftavan IV (Iron II) settlement cemetery: NW-Iran, Azerbaijan. *IrAnt* 44: 89–112.

Thomalsky, J. 2006. Die eisenzeitliche Keramik von Zendān-e Soleimān in Iranisch-Āzarbāijān. *AMIT* 38: 219–89.

Thornton, C. P., and V. C. Pigott. 2011. Blade-type weaponry of Hasanlu Period IVB. *PCPIVB*: 135–82.

Tourovets, A. 1989. Observations concernant le matériel archéologique des nécropoles A et B de Sialk. *IrAnt* 24: 209–44.

Vanden Berghe, L. 1964. *La ncropole de Khurvin*. Istanbul: UNHAII 17.

Van Loon, M. 1975. The Inscriptions of Ishpuini and Meinua at Qalatgah, Iran. *JNES* 34/3: 201–7.

Voigt, M. M. 1976. Hajji Firuz Tepe: An economic reconstruction of a sixth millennium community in western Iran. Unpublished PhD diss., University of Pennsylvania.

———. 1983. *Hajji Firuz Tepe, Iran: The Neolithic settlement*. Philadelphia: UMM 50.

———. 2011. Foreword. *PCPIVB*: xxix–xxxiv.

Waters, M. W. 1999. The earliest Persians in southwestern Iran: The textual evidence. *IrSt* 32: 99–107.

Winter, I. J. 1977. Perspective on the "local style" of Hasanlu IVb: A study in receptivity. *ML*: 371–86.

———. 1980. *A decorated breastplate from Hasanlu, Iran*. Philadelphia: UMM 39.

———. 1989. The "Hasanlu gold bowl": Thirty years later. *Expedition* 31/2–3: 87–106.

Young, T. C., Jr. 1962. Taking the history of the Hasanlu area back another five thousand years: Sixth- and fifth-millennium settlements in the Solduz Valley, Persia. *ILN* 241/6431: 707–9.

———. 1963. Proto-historic western Iran, an archaeological and historical review: Problems and possible interpretations. Unpublished PhD diss., University of Pennsylvania.

———. 1965. A comparative ceramic chronology for western Iran, 1500–500 B.C. *Iran* 3: 53–85.

———. 1966. Thoughts on the architecture of Hasanlu IV. *IrAnt* 6: 48–71.

———. 1967. The Iranian migration into the Zagros. *Iran* 5: 11–34.

———. 1969. *Excavations at Godin Tepe: First progress report*. Toronto: ROMAAOP 17.

———. 1985. Early Iron Age Iran revisited: Preliminary suggestions for the re-analysis of old constructs. In *De L'Indus aux Balkans. Recueil la mémoire de Jean Deshayes*, ed. J.-L. Huot, M. Yon, and Y. Calvet, 361–78. Paris: Éditions Recherche sur les Civilisations.

———. 2002. Syria and Iran: Further thoughts on the architecture of Hasanlu. In *On pots and plans: Papers on the archaeology and history of Mesopotamia and Syria presented to David Oates in honour of his 75th birthday*, ed. L. el-Gailani Werr, J. Curtis, H. Martin, A. McMahon, J. Oates, and J. Reade, 386–98. London: NABU Publications.

———. 2003. Parsua, Parsa, and potsherds. *YBYN*: 242–8.

Young, T. C., Jr., and L. D. Levine. 1974. *Excavations of the Godin Project: Second progress report*. Toronto: ROMAAOP 26.

Zadok, R. 2002. The ethno-linguistic character of northwestern Iran and Kurdistan in the Neo-Assyrian period. *Iran* 40: 89–151.

Zimansky, P. 1985. *Ecology and empire: The structure of the Urartian state*. Chicago: SAOC 41.

———. 1990. Urartian geography and Sargon's eighth campaign. *JNES* 49/1: 1–21.

CHAPTER 18

LURISTAN DURING THE IRON AGE

BRUNO OVERLAET

Introduction

From about 1300/1250 to 650/600 BC a local culture thrived in the Luristan region, that is, the mountainous part of the Zagros between the Iraqi border, the Great Khorasan Road, and the roads connecting Kermanshah, Sahneh, Nehavand, Borudjird, Dorud, and the Ab-e Dez River to the Dezful plain (modern Luristan and Ilam provinces). Although iron seems to have been absent in the first centuries, the period is conventionally referred to as the Iron Age as an indication of the distinct change in the material culture of the region vis-à-vis the preceding Bronze Age (Overlaet 2003: 6–10). Iron Age Luristan is renowned for its unique bronzes: hammered and engraved sheet-metal objects (e.g., pins with large disk-heads, vessels, quiver plaques) and *cire perdue* (lost-wax) cast objects (e.g., axheads, horse-bits with decorated cheek-pieces, whetstone handles, clothing pins, idols). These display a specific style with a mixture of animals, humans and fantastic creatures. In the later phase of the Luristan Iron Age, similar decorated objects were produced in a combination of bronze and iron or even completely in iron.

Although some of these bronzes were already known in the nineteenth century, it was only in the late 1920s that they started to appear in large numbers on the art market and their true place of origin became known: graveyards and sanctuaries in the—at that time—very inaccessible tribal area of Luristan. Since the region was controlled by nomadic tribes and the central government could exert only limited authority, systematic field research there became possible only in the second half of the twentieth century.

Luristan is dominated by three northwest–southeast trending mountain chains, the Kabir Kuh, Kuh-e Sefid and Kuh-e Garin, reaching heights of around 3000 masl.

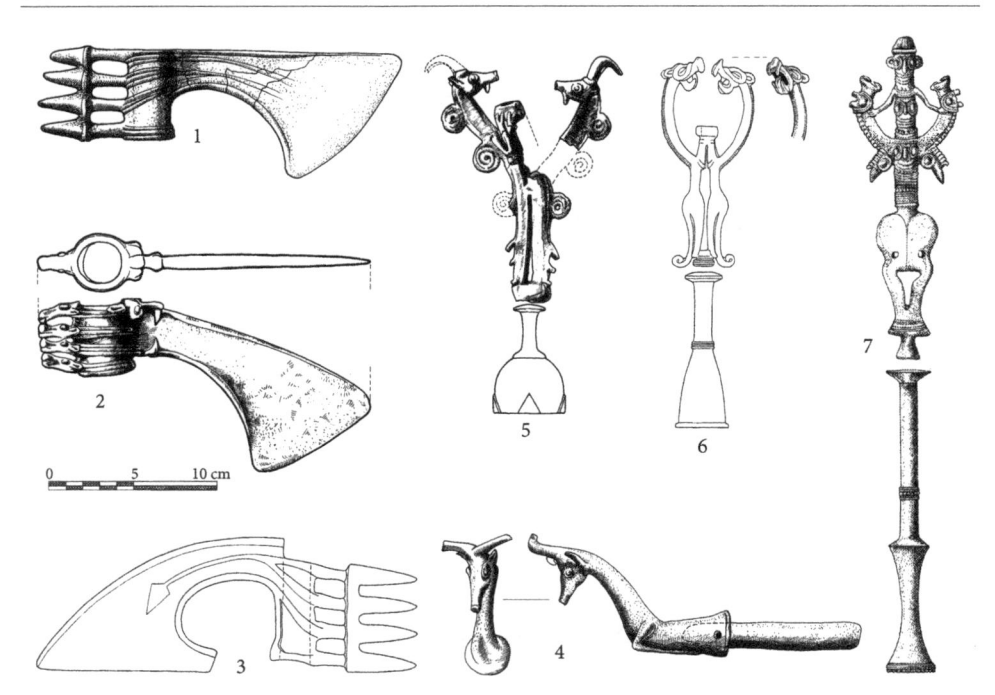

FIGURE 18.1 Selection of excavated Luristan bronzes: 1–3. axes; 4. whetstone with bronze grip; 5–7. idols (1, 4, 5: Bard-i Bal; 2: Kutal-i Gulgul; 3, 6: Khatunban B; 7: Tattulban) (© BAMI).

The Kabir Kuh divides Luristan into the Pusht-e Kuh and the Pish-e Kuh ("over" and "before" the mountain, as seen from the Iranian plateau). The region is known for its rainy winters and dry summers, but its mountainous character creates local microclimates (Potts 1999: 12–15). These regional differences explain the seasonal migration of seminomadic groups. The Kuh-e Sefid divides the Pish-e Kuh in two climate zones. The northeastern high valleys—the *sardsir* or summer quarters—provide a cooler climate in summer while the lower southwestern valleys—*garmsir* or winter quarters—enjoy a milder climate in winter. Because of the presence of a nomadic populace in Luristan at the time of the bronzes' discovery, the "Luristan bronzes" were ascribed exclusively to a nomadic people (Godard 1931: 21). Sedentary and nomadic lifestyles may always have coexisted in Luristan, however, just as they do today, with changing circumstances merely favoring one or the other. Nomadism became the dominant lifestyle only following the Mongol invasion and its destruction of irrigation systems (Mortensen 1993: 39–42).

For a long time, Luristan research focused on hearsay and unprovenanced objects, including forgeries and pastiches, that is, fantasy objects assembled from authentic fragments (Overlaet 2008: 29–31, figs. 4–5). "Luristan" had become a lucrative commercial label and bronze objects from different regions or of types that were also found outside Luristan were presented as Luristan bronzes (Fig. 18.1). As early as 1963, J. H. Potratz underscored the extent of this problem by listing objects in major museums that he considered to be forgeries (Potratz 1963: 131–45). O. W. Muscarella later introduced the term "canonical Luristan bronzes" for those items that were unambiguously in the local Iron Age style (Muscarella 1988b).

Meanwhile, fieldwork and documented chance finds have somewhat clarified the situation, making it possible to establish the general chronology and to define the main characteristics of the "Luristan bronzes." But even now, the number of excavated canonical bronzes is very limited and constitutes only a fraction of the objects held in museums and private collections. Our knowledge of the Iron Age Luristan cultures, particularly about the Pish-e Kuh, remains deficient. In the following pages, a short survey of the general chronology is provided, followed by a discussion of the main corpus of canonical bronzes.

Chronology and lifestyle

The chronology of the Luristan Iron Age is mainly based upon the investigation of cemeteries (Fig. 18.2) in the Pusht-e Kuh (Overlaet 2005), the chronological framework from which has been extended tentatively to the Pish-e Kuh. Important regional variations are known to have existed, however, and in particular it is clear that, because of its location, the Pusht-e Kuh was more prone to Mesopotamian influence.

The transition from Bronze to Iron Age is marked by the desertion of settlements in the Pish-e Kuh valleys. This phenomenon was observed at sites such as Tepe Baba Jan, Tepe Djamshidi, and Girairan and confirmed by surveys (Goff 1968: 127; 1971: 150–1; Schmidt et al. 1989: 486–7). Nevertheless, some sites remained settled, albeit

FIGURE 18.2 View of the Chavar plain with the excavations at War Kabud amidst the numerous pits of looted tombs (photo: BAMI 1966/© BAMI).

on a reduced scale. A small Iron Age settlement was found at Tepe Guran, but it is unclear whether it was occupied on a permanent or seasonal basis (Thrane 2001; Overlaet 2003: 25–8, figs. 14–16). There is no information about Late Bronze Age or Iron Age settlements in the Pusht-e Kuh. Some *tepes* are known to exist in the Aivan valley but they have not been studied. The desertion of Bronze Age settlements in Luristan is mirrored by events in the Kangavar valley, west of the Great Khorasan Road, where a more complete picture of events can be drawn. Whereas the main Bronze Age settlements located in the plain either shrank significantly in size or were deserted, the hill sites increased in number, suggesting a change to a subsistence economy based more on herding than agriculture (Young 2002: 424–6). The reason behind this parallel change in both the Kangavar valley and Luristan must be of a climatic or ecological nature since there are no reports of military destruction at any of the sites. Possibly the period of increased rainfall, known to have peaked between 1350 and 1250 BC, had a devastating effect on agricultural systems in these areas (Neumann and Parpola 1987: 164).

The beginning of the Iron Age in the Pusht-e Kuh is attested at several graveyards. The earliest phase, period IA (*c.*1300/1250 to 1150 BC), is known from graveyards with cist tombs of modest size that were, however, regularly reused. Pottery shapes, colorfully inlaid shell finger rings (Fig. 18.3.9) and small faience buckets (Fig. 18.3.5) represent imports from Kassite Mesopotamia that included the neighboring Hamrin region. Painted ceramics, which were characteristic of the Bronze Age, rapidly disappeared and were replaced by plain wares. Iron was absent and bronze was the material commonly used for weapons, utensils, and jewelry. The first objects in the canonical Luristan style were discovered in these tombs: spike-butted axheads and simple finials consisting of opposed animals mounted on a bottle-shaped support (Fig. 18.1.1–2, 5).

Kassite influence in the Pusht-e Kuh came to an end when the Elamite king Shutruk-Nahhunte destroyed the Hamrin sites around 1160 BC (Boehmer and Dämmer 1985: 80). This military event must be seen in the context of the widespread twelfth-century conflicts and migrations following a long, dry period with crop failures and resultant calamities. The disappearance of Kassite imports from the grave contents illustrates the isolation of the region and marks the beginning of a new phase in the Pusht-e Kuh (*c.*1150–900/950 BC). To facilitate the correlation with chronologies used in other areas of Iran, it is referred to as the Iron Age IB–IIA; it spans the later part of Iron Age I and the first part of Iron Age II. Although the construction of cist tombs did not fundamentally change, there was more variation in tomb size and shape (Fig. 18.4). Some tombs were reused over and over again and were packed with grave goods and skeletal remains. At Kutal-e Gulgul it was customary to push the grave goods and skeletons to the back of the tomb and sometimes to place skulls together along the side of the tomb chamber to make room for a new interment. In other cases, burial goods and skeletons were simply removed. As in most of the Near East, iron gradually became more available during this phase but it remained a rare and valuable material. Because it was associated with value and prestige, iron was initially reserved for jewelry (pins, finger rings, bracelets, anklets, etc.). It was only during the following phase, toward the

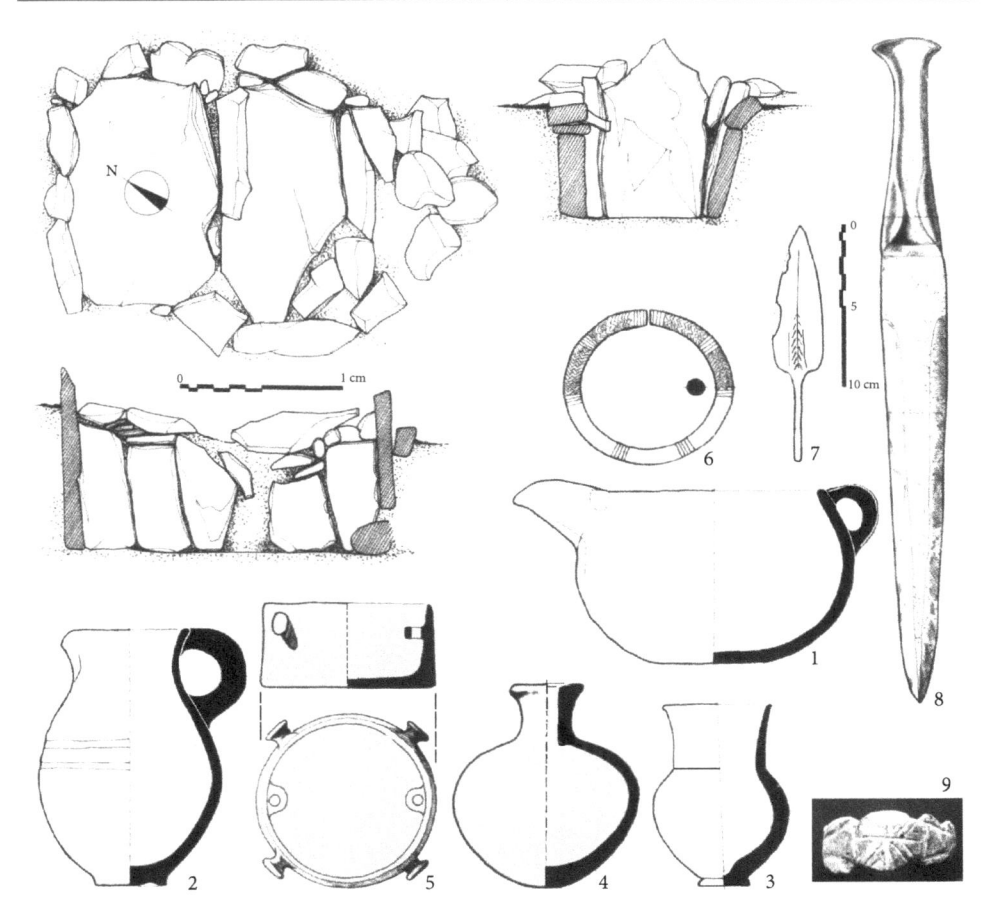

FIGURE 18.3 Characteristic Iron Age IA tomb and gravegoods from Kutal-i Gulgul: top view and sections of the tomb after removal of the cap stones; 1–3. pottery; 4–5. faience vessels; 6–8. bronze weapons and jewelry; and 9. a shell fingerring (© BAMI).

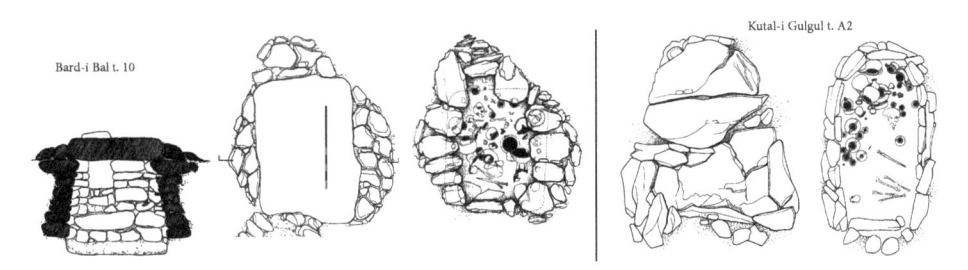

FIGURE 18.4 Iron Age IB–IIA cist tombs of Bard-i Bal and Kutal-i Gulgul (© BAMI).

end of the ninth century, that it became more common and was used for weaponry (Fig. 18.5). The canonical bronzes, which include axes, whetstone handles, and horse-bits with decorated cheek-pieces and finials, became more elaborate in Iron Age IB–IIA (Figs. 18.6–7).

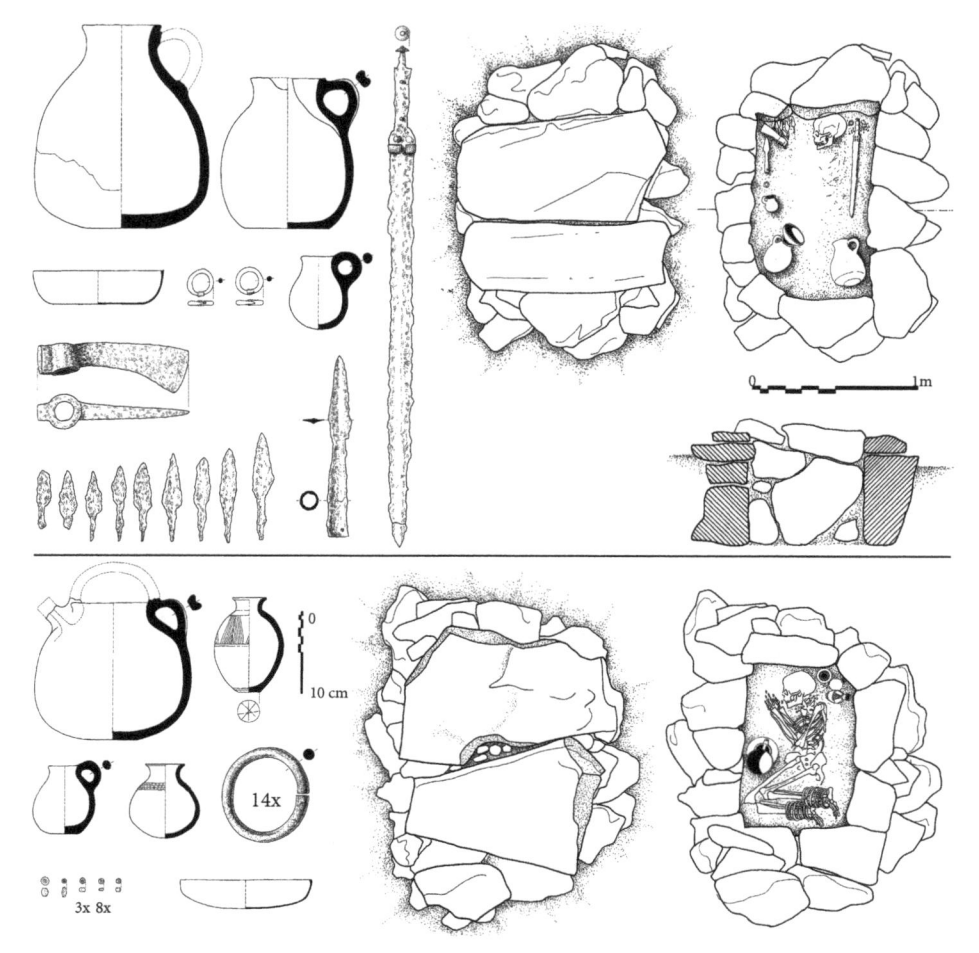

FIGURE 18.5 Iron Age III tombs and burial goods of a man (top) and woman (bottom) at War Kabud (© BAMI).

Around 950/900 BC another cool period with slightly more precipitation began (Neumann and Parpola 1987: 175). Some of the larger Bronze Age *tepes* in the Pish-e Kuh were resettled, and new, small habitation centers were founded (Goff 1968: 127–8), indicating that these changes had a positive effect on agriculture, enabling the sustenance of a larger (settled) population. Although we do not have information on settlements in the Pusht-e Kuh, other changes can be noticed in later Iron Age II or "Iron Age IIB" (*c.*900–800/750 BC). Small, individual tombs replaced the tradition of reusing existing tombs. Iron became more common amongst the grave goods. Although still used for jewelry, weaponry (daggers, knives) was also made of it. Bronze was still used for expendable weapons such as arrowheads, however, indicating that the value of iron remained high.

In the Pish-e Kuh a major settlement was excavated at Baba Jan, where a manor house was identified on one mound and a fort and temple with a ceiling decorated with painted tiles stood on another mound. The site's heyday was in the following Iron Age III, however (eighth century BC with only a limited occupation in the seventh century). This culture was characterized by a painted ware with pendant triangles and crosses, referred to as "Baba Jan III" or "genre Luristan" ware (Henrickson 1988; Overlaet 2003: 38–41, figs. 25–7). The settled population of Baba Jan cannot be linked to the mainstream users of Luristan bronzes and may have been newcomers to the area. No canonical bronzes were found in the Baba Jan III settlement or in tombs with Baba Jan III ceramics.

In addition to graveyards, important sanctuaries also existed. One was located at Surkh Dum-e Luri in the Kuh-e Dasht plain, while another probably existed at Sangtarashan, some 50 km from Khorramabad. Both sites were largely plundered before rescue excavations took place and the information available is incomplete, but both are characterized by stone architecture and *favissae* (Overlaet 2012). Probably dedicated to a female deity, the Surkh Dum-e Luri shrine (Schmidt et al. 1989; Overlaet 2003: 34–7; 2012: fig. 6, pls. 11–21) may have been founded in the ninth century but it certainly underwent several alterations in Iron Age III. It was built on the location of a Late Bronze Age building with stone foundations up to 1.5 m thick and a no-longer-preserved mudbrick superstructure. Although this must have been an important building, its function is unknown and a sterile layer separated it from the Iron Age shrine. Nevertheless, many votive objects in the Iron Age shrine were considerably older than its date of construction, raising the question whether an older shrine existed in the vicinity. In the walls and under the successive floors of the Iron Age sanctuary were deposits of objects, mostly seals and jewelry, many of which were ancient heirlooms dating to the Chalcolithic or Bronze Age. Pins, some very simple, others with lavish cast or hammered decorative pinheads, constituted an important group of objects. Although a number can be dated to the Early Iron Age, those with large sheet-bronze heads were found in the latest *favissae*, which suggests an Iron Age II or more probably Iron Age III date. The latest building phase of the Surkh Dum-e Luri sanctuary seems to belong to the early seventh century. During this phase, a room in a building opposite the sanctuary may have been used as some sort of chapel. It contained Neo-Elamite faience pottery, possibly reflecting increasing Elamite influence in the region at that time. The end of the temple as a religious center may be placed around 650 BC. The limited excavations conducted at the site were unable to establish the construction date and function of the architecture around the shrine (settlement or subsidiary buildings of the sanctuary?).

At Sangtarashan, the *favissae* contained objects of a very different nature than those found at Surkh Dum-e Luri. These included bronze vessels; bronze, iron, and bimetallic weaponry, including miniature spike-butted axheads; and canonical Luristan bronzes such as idols and whetstone sockets, most of which can be dated to Iron Age I and II. These *favissae* were spread over a large area but although traces of boulder architecture were found, a shrine or religious building has not yet been identified (Azarnoush and Helwing 2005: 222–3, figs. 49–51; Oudbashi et al. 2013).

Iron Age III (c.800/750–650 BC) was generally a very prosperous period in the Near East and this is also reflected in the finds from Luristan. Imports among the grave goods indicate regular contacts with both Mesopotamia and Susiana. The large number of graveyards in the Pusht-e Kuh (Vanden Berghe 1987; Haerinck and Overlaet 1998, 1999, 2004) also suggests an increase in population density. Burial goods were more diverse, reflecting increased wealth. Tombs were mostly individual and among the burial goods were bronze vessels, iron weaponry, and new shapes and types of ceramics (Fig. 18.5). A group of fine gray and fine buff ware, often decorated with incised geometric patterns, is related to contemporary painted Baba Jan III ware in the Pish-e Kuh. Iron was no longer preferred for jewelry but was the material of choice for weaponry, including arrowheads. Bronze continued to be used for decorative elements on arms, for jewelry, and occasionally also for more complex weapons such as maceheads and ax-adzes. The presence of Assyrian imports, such as polychrome glazed vases, indicates that the area was again in regular contact with Mesopotamia. Assyrian rock reliefs at Shikaft-e Gulgul (Reade 1977) and Heydarabad-e Mishkhas (Alibaigi et al. 2012) reflect the occasional military incursions of Neo-Assyrian armies into Luristan. The people of the Pusht-e Kuh can probably be identified with the Parnakians, a group mentioned by the Assyrians as fierce enemies (Zadok 1981–2: 135). A Neo-Assyrian outpost may have existed at Tepe Giyan in a region known to the Assyrians as Bit-Barua. This was part of the Ellipi confederacy that once included most of the Pish-e Kuh (Medvedskaya 1999: 63–4).

We have little or no information about the transitional phase from Iron Age III to the Persian Achaemenid Empire. An exceptional treasure with silver and gold vessels and human masks, accidentally discovered in a cave at Kalmakarra, is now widely dispersed (Motamadi 1992). It must have been hidden in the late seventh or early sixth century BC. Several vessels bear Elamite cuneiform inscriptions mentioning private individuals and rulers of a local "kingdom of Samati," probably situated somewhere in southern Luristan (Henkelman 2003: 214–27, pls. 9–15; Overlaet 2012: fig. 4, pls. 6–10).

The canonical Luristan style

Although thousands of bronzes in museums and private collections are claimed to come from Luristan, only a limited number are "canonical" Luristan objects, items that were exclusively produced in Luristan during the Iron Age (Figs. 18.1, 6–10). These display a distinctive decorative style with stylized humans, felines, birds, bovids, horses, and several species of goats as the main components, often combined into fantastic creatures. Vegetal elements are either combined into a "tree of life" or used as border or filler motif between the principal iconography. Particularly on the engraved sheet-metal work there is a strong tendency toward *horror vacui*. Although the number of canonical bronzes from controlled excavations is still limited, there are clear indications of a chronological evolution from simple, naturalistic to more complicated and fantastic creations.

Technically, a distinction can be made between cast bronzes (mainly in the *cire perdue* or lost-wax technique) and hammered sheet bronze. Decorated iron objects comprise a

FIGURE 18.6 Left: Luristan horsebit discovered at Khatunban B (Iran Bastan Museum, Tehran, after Haerinck, Overlaet and Jaffar–Mohammadi 2004: pl. 5); right: cheekpiece of a horsebit in the Royal Museums of Art and History, Brussels (inv. IR.790/© KMKG–MRAH).

separate category. Decorated bone pins and plaques from the Surkh Dum-e Luri shrine testify to the existence of the same style and type of object in perishable materials.

Several groups of cast Luristan bronzes exist. Horse gear includes horse-harness trappings and horse-bits with decorative cheek-pieces (Fig. 18.6). Arms and equipment include spiked axheads and adzes, halberds, daggers or swords, and whetstone handles (Figs. 18.1 and 18.8). Another important series are the so-called "idols," also known as "finials" or "standards," that were placed on tubular or bottle-shaped stands (Fig. 18.1.7). Jewelry, including bracelets, various types of pins with decorated heads, finger rings, and pendants, was also cast. Some of the "Luristan bronzes" are completely made of bronze, while others are bimetallic, consisting of iron with cast-on bronze decorations. Some exceptional objects made entirely of iron copy counterparts cast in bronze. Since these display the same style, they should be included under the rubric "Luristan bronzes" (Moorey 1991).

The horse-bits vary from naturalistic images of animals to complicated creations that can combine characteristics of various animal species and humans. Of all known Luristan horse-bits, only one with decorative cheek-pieces has a known provenience. This was a chance find made at Khatunban (Pish-e Kuh) that was seized by the local authorities (Haerinck et al. 2004: 105–9, pl. 5). It shows a winged gazelle treading on a defeated one (Fig. 18.6 left). Fig. 18.6 (right) illustrates a more complex animal: a fantastic creature that stands on two hares combines a bovid's body (horns, hoofs) with a human face, the long curled tail of a feline (Fig. 18.7 left) and a curved wing ending in an animal's head. Iron Age horse-bits with decorative cheek-pieces are also known outside Luristan. At Marlik Tepe (southwest of the Caspian Sea) a pair was discovered in an early Iron Age tomb (Negahban 1996: 305–6, pl. 135), and similar examples were depicted on Assyrian reliefs of the seventh century BC. These examples do not display the fantastic creatures that are typical of Luristan, however, but display more naturalistic depictions of horses. Some of the Luristan cheek-pieces can be extremely large and heavy, suggesting that they were not meant for daily use. Traces of wear are often visible, however, indicating they were used, either intensively or over a long period of time.

Finials or idols are amongst the most enigmatic items from Luristan (Moorey 1971: 140–68, pls. 30–9; Muscarella 1988a: 136–54, nos. 215–49; Overlaet 2003: 185–93, figs. 153–9). The earliest examples, discovered in Iron Age IA tombs in the Pusht-e Kuh and at Sangtarashan, consist of a pair of rampant predators or goats with more or less naturalistic proportions, placed on a hollow tubular or bottle-shaped support (Fig. 18.1.5). They are either arranged around a sheet-metal tube or hold rings between their paws or hoofs. It may be that a branch was once inserted in the middle to create the image of a tree of life flanked by animals, a widespread theme in the Ancient Near East. There seems to be a chronological evolution from more or less naturalistic animals to more stylized ones, with the predators or goats displaying long, curved necks (Fig. 18.7.1). Sometimes these predators hold a Janus-type head between their front paws. This is a transition to another group, often called the "master-of-animals standards" (Figs. 18.1.7, 18.7.2–3). These combine two predators with a human figure, occasionally with additional human heads, bird heads or complete birds added on. The fronts and backs of these idols are always identical, indicating that the image was designed to be seen from both sides. Whereas the two felines and the human torso are easily recognized on the earlier types, it becomes more difficult when parts become fused and human heads and birds are added to the image. The latest variant is a complex one: the lower part shows the opposing hips and hind legs of the predator, above which is a tube with two or three human heads and the arms of a human who grasps the long, curving necks of the predators. Small birds or bird heads were sometimes added to the felines' hips or at the base of the necks. Only one such master-of-animals finial has ever been discovered in controlled excavations, in an early Iron Age III tomb of a warrior at Tattulban in the Pusht-e Kuh (Overlaet 2003: 188–9, figs. 155–6) (Fig. 18.1.7). As this was the only finial ever discovered in an Iron Age III tomb and represents the very end of their stylistic evolution, it seems that the heyday of these complex finials should be dated to Iron Age II.

A third group of mostly small idols is related to the master-of-animal type because they often mix predator and human elements (Fig. 18.7.4–6). This affiliation suggests that they date from to Iron Age II, possibly extending into Iron Age III. These are small, mostly female figurines, often with a no longer identical front and back. The lower part may consist of the hind parts of the predators (Fig. 18.7.5) or predators may be flanking their legs (Fig. 18.7.4). The simplest of these idols is merely a bronze tube crowned with a human head.

The discovery of bottle-shaped supports without any idols in tombs at Khatunban (Schmidt et al. 1989: 63, pls. 64, 175) and Gul Khanan Murdah (Haerinck and Overlaet 1999: 169–70, pls. 107, 125–6) suggests that "idols" may also have been made of perishable materials such as ivory or bone. The discovery of decorative pinheads, boxes, and other utensils in such materials at Surkh Dum-e Luri underscores their use in Luristan. The significance of these finials, however, remains enigmatic. Those from tombs were associated with weaponry, suggesting they specifically belonged to male burials.

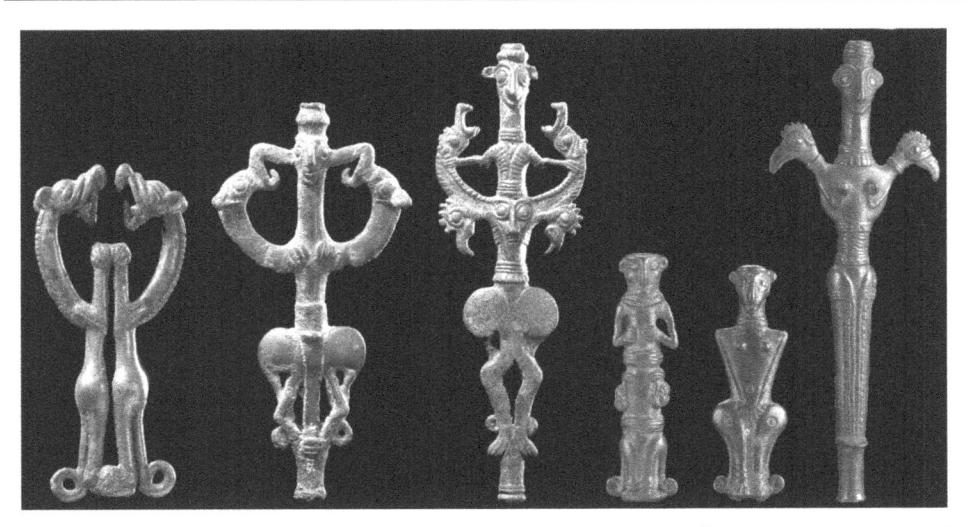

FIGURE 18.7 Luristan idols in the collection of the Royal Museums of Art and History, Brussels (left to right: 1. IR. 611; 2. IR.622; 3 IR.39; 4. IR.620; 5. IR.619; 6. IR.616/© KMKG–MRAH).

Weaponry, principally spike-butted axheads, halberds, whetstones handles, and swords and daggers, forms another group of canonical bronzes. Many axheads, adzes, and halberds have three or more spikes on the butt. The axes have a downward curving blade with an oblique cutting edge or, in extreme cases, a cutting edge at right angles to the ax handle (Fig. 18.1.1–3). A wide variety of shapes and decorations is known. The blade sometimes springs from a predator's jaws. Spikes may take the shape of animals, and small animals are added to the top edge of the blade or the spikes. Figurative and/or decorative designs are sometimes present on the blade. Specimens have been discovered in Iron Age I and II tombs and in the Sangtarashan *favissae*, where miniature examples were also found. There seems to be an evolution from axes with modest-sized spikes and slightly curved blades toward specimens with long spikes and extremely curved blades. On these, the blade is often not sharpened, which suggests the spikes and the pointed tip of the blade were more important than the actual "cutting edge" of the weapon. This type of axhead was absent in Iron Age III tombs when a simple type of iron ax became the standard weapon (Fig. 18.5 upper left).

Spikes can also be found on adzes and halberds, often with blades springing from lion's jaws. Most halberds, however, have a reclining lion on the butt (Fig. 18.8) instead of spikes. Some of these weapons are bimetallic with an iron blade, illustrating the gradual introduction of iron in Iron Age II, after which bronze was used only rarely for weaponry with cutting edges. Only a few ax-adzes, sparingly decorated with human faces, are known from Iron Age III tombs (Fig. 18.8). Bronze continued to be used for blunt, impact weapons in Iron Age III, such as mace heads, but these lack the characteristic figurative decoration.

The presence of bronze cutting edges on axes, knives, and daggers in Iron Age I and II necessitated regular sharpening, for which stick-shaped whetstones were used, often with a decorative cast bronze handle (Fig. 18.1.4). Here, too, one can follow a stylistic

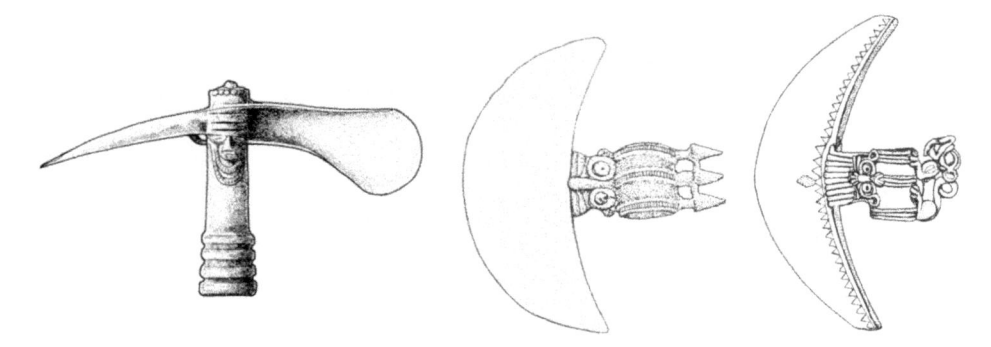

FIGURE 18.8 Bronze ax–adze from War Kabud (© BAMI) and unprovenanced bronze Luristan halbards (after Moorey 1991: 161).

and chronological evolution from simple naturalistic specimens to more complex ones (Moorey 1971: 98–100, pls. 11–12; Muscarella 1988: 182–3, nos. 298–301; Overlaet 2003: 180–5, figs. 146–52).

When iron was introduced in Luristan during Iron Age I, its rarity and novelty appeal gave it great value as a status symbol. Local craftsmen in Luristan had little knowledge of iron technology, however, and used it primarily for simple jewelry. Iron pins, anklets, and bracelets demonstrated personal wealth. Early, relatively low-carbon, wrought iron was hardly suitable for weaponry but in Iron Age II it began to be used for the blades of daggers, halberds, and adzes. The bronze decorated shaft in canonical Luristan style was simply cast on to the iron blade, a technique widely attested in western Iran (Pigott 1989).

A unique group of complete iron weapons comprises ninety or so short swords with decorated hilts that were assembled from a series of separately manufactured parts (Fig. 18.9). These may have been one of the first attempts to produce complex iron

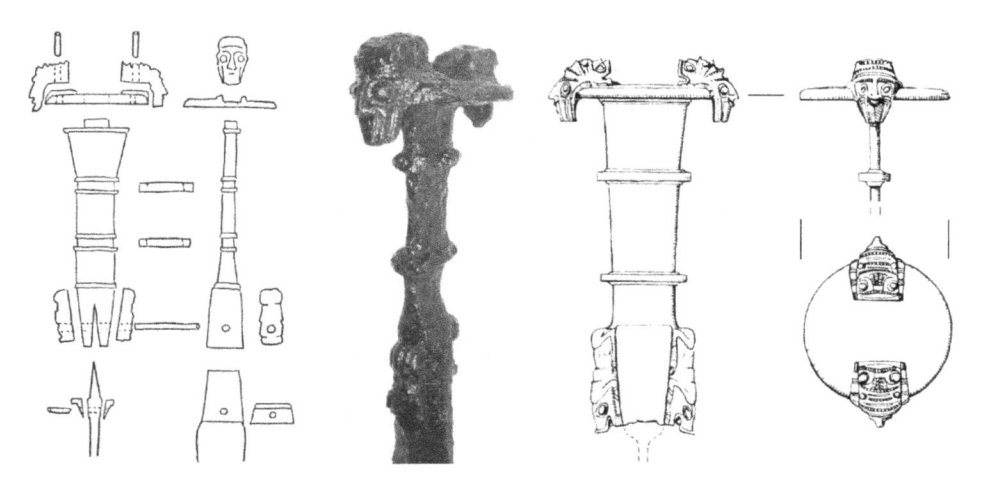

FIGURE 18.9 Iron swordgrip in the Royal Museums of Art and History, Brussels (inv. IR.546/ photo © KMKG–MRAH and drawing after Moorey 1991: 163).

FIGURE 18.10 Pins with large, decorated heads, allegedly from Surkh Dum-e Luri, in the Royal Museums of Art and History, Brussels. (inv. IR.672, IR.716, IR.647/© KMKG–MRAH).

objects. Two bearded human heads with the back of the head in the shape of a lion protome are placed on the rim of a flat pommel while two more lions lay outstretched on the hilt. None of these swords was found during controlled excavations, but the technology and style suggest they date from Iron Age II (tenth to ninth century BC) although much earlier (eleventh century BC: Moorey 1991; Rehder 1991) and later dates (c.750–650 BC: Muscarella 1989: 354–5) have also been suggested.

Cast bronze was also used for jewelry, mostly pins and bracelets but also pendants and small rattle bells that may have been worn as apotropaic items. Clothing pins (*fibulae*) often had decorative bronze heads cast on to an iron body. A large number of pins were found in the sanctuary at Surkh Dum-e Luri and although some were heirlooms, most date to the Iron Age. Among these are a number of pins with large, elaborately decorated heads, some cast, others made of hammered sheet bronze (Fig. 18.10). Some of these have geometric or floral motifs; others display scenes with humans, animals and fantastic creatures. A comparable iconography is present on other sheet-metal objects with repoussé and engraved decoration, such as vessels, shields, and quiver plaques, illustrating the importance of sheet-metal work in Luristan (Moorey 1999).

FURTHER READING

There is a vast literature on Luristan bronzes, but many of the older studies on examples held in museum collections are out of date. For a more recent catalog with current literature, see Engel (2008). For general orientation on their background, see Muscarella (1988). Overviews of fieldwork in Luristan and the chronology of the bronzes are provided in Overlaet (2006a, 2006b). Recent excavations of Iron Age assemblages of relevance include Haerinck et al. (2004) and Overlaet (2003).

References

Alibaigi, S., A.-M. Shanbehzadeh, and H. Alibaigi. 2012. The discovery of a Neo-Assyrian rock-relief at Mishkhas, Ilam Province (Iran). *IrAnt* 47: 29–40.

Azarnoush, M., and B. Helwing. 2005. Recent archaeological research in Iran: Prehistory to Iron Age. *AMIT* 37: 189–246.

Boehmer, R. M., and H.-W. Dämmer. 1985. *Tell Imlihiye, Tell Zubeidi, Tell Abbas*. Mainz: Baghdader Forschungen 7.

Engel, N. 2008. *Les bronzes du Luristan: Énigmes de l'Iran ancien (IIIe–Ier millénaire av. J.C.)*. Paris: Musée Cernuschi.

Godard, A. 1931. *Les bronzes du Luristan*. Paris: Ars Asiatica.

Goff, C. 1968. Luristan in the first half of the first millennium B.C.: A preliminary report on the first season's excavations at Baba Jan, and associated surveys in the eastern Pish-i Kuh. *Iran* 6: 105–34.

———. 1971. Luristan before the Iron Age. *Iran* 9: 131–52.

Haerinck, E., Z. Jaffar-Mohammadi, and B. Overlaet. 2004. Finds from Khatunban B—Badavar valley (Luristan) in the Iran National Museum, Teheran. *IrAnt* 39: 105–68.

Haerinck, E., and B. Overlaet. 1998. *Chamahzi Mumah, an Iron Age III Graveyard*. Leuven: LED 2.

———. 1999. *Djub-i Gauhar and Gul Khanan Murdah, Iron Age III sites in the Aivan plain*. Leuven: LED 3.

———. 2004. *The Iron Age III graveyard at War Kabud (Chavar district), Pusht-i Kuh, Luristan*. Leuven: LED 5.

Henkelman, W. F. M. 2003. Persians, Medes and Elamites: Acculturation in the Neo-Elamite period. *CE*: 181–231.

Henrickson, R. C. 1988. Baba Jan Tepe. *EnIr* 3: 292–3.

Medvedskaya, I. N. 1999. Media and its neighbours I: The localization of Ellipi. *IrAnt* 34: 53–70.

Moorey, P. R. S. 1971. *Catalogue of the ancient Persian bronzes in the Ashmolean Museum*. Oxford: Clarendon Press.

———. 1991. The decorated ironwork of the early Iron Age attributed to Luristan in Western Iran. *Iran* 29: 1–12.

———. 1999. The hammered bronzework of Iron Age Lurestan (Iran): Problems of chronology and iconography. *IW*: 146–57.

Mortensen, I. D. 1993. *Nomads of Luristan: History, material culture, and pastoralism in western Iran*. London: Thames and Hudson.

Motamadi, N. 1992. Report of the archaeological excavation of the Kalmakarra Cave. *Miras-e Farhangi* 10–11: 3–15 (in Persian).

Muscarella, O. W. 1988a. *Bronze and iron: Ancient Near Eastern artifacts in The Metropolitan Museum of Art*. New York: Metropolitan Museum of Art.

———. 1988b. The background to the Luristan Bronzes. In *Bronzeworking Centres of Western Asia c. 1000–539 B.C.*, ed. J. Curtis, 33–44. London: Kegan Paul International.

———. 1989. Multi-piece iron swords from Luristan. *AIO*: 349–66.

Negahban, E. 1996. *Marlik, the complete excavation report*, 2 vols. Philadelphia: UMM 87.

Neumann, J., and S. Parpola. 1987. Climatic change and the eleventh-tenth-century eclipse of Assyria and Babylonia. *JNES* 46/3: 161–82.

Oudbashi, O., S. M. Emami, M. Malekzadeh, A. Hassanpour, and P. Davami. 2013. Archeometallurgical studies on the bronze vessels from "Sangtarashan," Luristan, W-Iran. *IrAnt* 48: 147–74.

Overlaet, B. 2003. *The Early Iron Age in the Pusht-i Kuh, Luristan*. Leuven: LED 4.
———. 2005. The chronology of the Iron Age in the Pusht-i Kuh, Luristan. *IrAnt* 40: 1–33.
———. 2006a. Luristan bronzes i. The field research. *EnIr* online edition.
———. 2006b. Luristan bronzes ii. Chronology. *EnIr* online edition.
———. 2008. L'histoire des collections de «bronzes du Luristan», Les bronzes canoniques et l'Âge du fer. In *Les bronzes du Luristan, Énigmes de l'Iran ancien (IIIe–Ier millénaire av. J.C.)*, ed. N. Engel, 21–31, 43–53. Paris: Musée Cernuschi.
———. 2012. Čāle Ġār (Kāšā Area) and votives, favissae and cave deposits in pre-Islamic and Islamic traditions. *AMIT* 43: 113–40.
Pigott, V. C. 1989. The emergence of iron use at Hasanlu. *Expedition* 31/2–3: 67–79.
Potratz, J. A. H. 1963. Über ein Corpus Aerum Luristanensium. *IrAnt* 3/2: 124–47.
Potts, D. T. 1999. *The archaeology of Elam: Formation and transformation of an ancient Iranian state*. Cambridge: Cambridge University Press.
Reade, J. E. 1977. Shikaft-i Gulgul: Its date and symbolism. *IrAnt* 12: 33–44.
Rehder, J. E. 1991. The decorated iron swords from Luristan: Their material and manufacture. *Iran* 29: 13–19.
Schmidt, E. F., M. N. van Loon, and H. H. Curvers. 1989. *HEL*.
Thrane, H. 2001. *Excavations at Tepe Guran in Luristan: The Bronze Age and Iron Age periods*. Aarhus: Jutland Archaeological Society Publications 38.
Vanden Berghe, L. 1987. Les pratiques funéraires à l'Âge du Fer III au Pusht-i Kuh, Luristan: Les nécropoles "genre War Kabud." *IrAnt* 22: 201–66.
Young, T. C. 2002. The Kangavar Survey—The Iron Age. *IrAnt* 37: 419–36.
Zadok, R. 1981–2. Iranian and Babylonian notes. *AfO* 28: 135–9.

CHAPTER 19

THE CENTRAL ALBORZ REGION IN THE IRON AGE

ALI MOUSAVI

SITES TO THE SOUTH OF THE ALBORZ MOUNTAINS

The Alborz mountain chain stretches like an arc, 800 km long and some 200 km wide, from the Russian border near Astara toward the east as far as Jajarm in eastern Khorasan, where it diminishes substantially. It separates the Aralo-Caspian depression in the north (26 m below sea level) from the central Iranian uplands to the south (1100–1500 masl). With a width of 120 km, the central part of the Alborz constitutes the highest mass of the chain and is dominated by the volcanic peak of Damavand. To the south, Kuh-e Towchal at 3970 m dominates the city of Tehran, which is located at the foot of the southern flank of the chain (Bazin et al. 1985: 813).

The Iranian plateau encloses a dry, central area of irregular shape with inland basins, the westernmost of which is located along the Tehran–Qom–Kashan axis. To the east of this axis lies the Masileh Basin on the fringe of the Central Desert. This is the only route of communication between the foothills of the Alborz and the central part of the plateau. Human settlement in this area is concentrated around water streams coming from the Zagros such as the Qom-Rud or springs such as Cheshmeh Ali at Rayy and Fin near Kashan.

The first discoveries of Iron Age remains in the central region date to the beginning of the twentieth century and revealed pottery typical of the second millennium BC. In 1900, a group of gray ware vessels was accidentally found at Qeytariyeh near the summer compound of the British Embassy in Qolhak (Fig. 19.1), at the time a northern suburb of Tehran (Curtis 1987; Mousavi 2001: 159) and which, according to Sir Denis Wright, contained "forty-five acres of beautiful parkland, and well-watered qanats from the nearby mountains" (Wright 1977: 28).

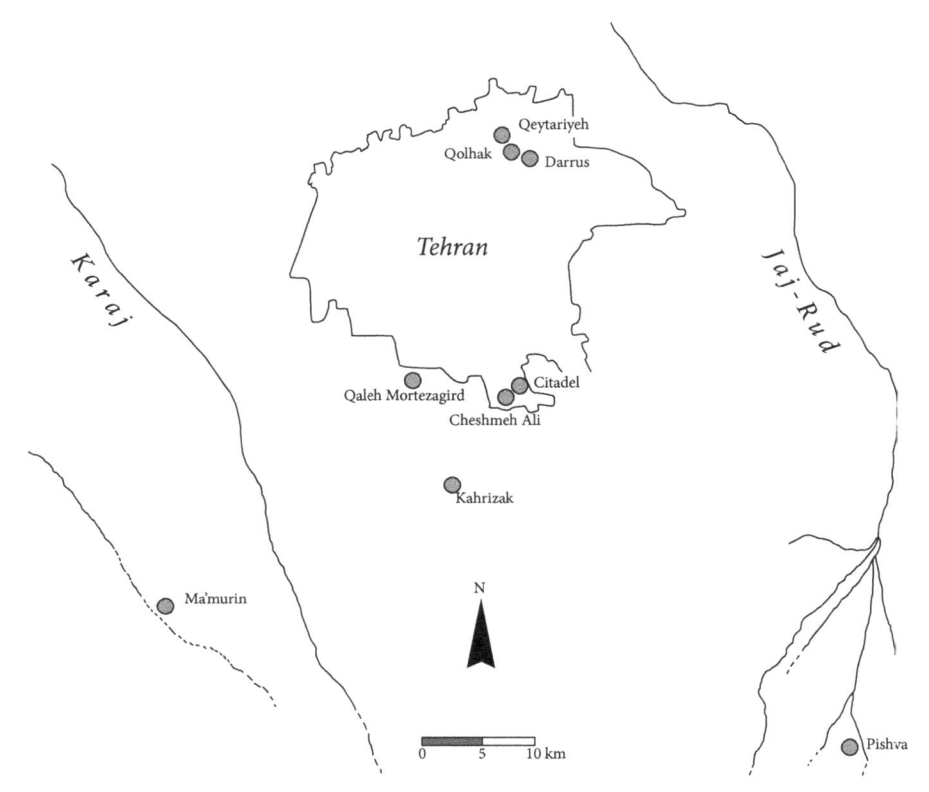

FIGURE 19.1 Map of Iron Age sites in the vicinity of Tehran.

In the early 1930s, Erich F. Schmidt excavated an area of 400 m² on the Citadel Hill at Rayy. The site consisted of the ruins of a poorly preserved mudbrick fort, a large part of which was still extant at the time of the excavations. Some 15 m below the surface of the mound Schmidt reached the base of the mudbrick fort. In the absence of stratigraphy, his short reports inform us that the excavations revealed five levels that were probably related to the following five major periods of occupation (Schmidt 1936: 133–6): (1) an upper stratum with remains of the late Islamic period; (2) a fifteenth-century level with a Timurid coin of Shah Rokh, minted in 1432/3; (3) an architectural level containing Saljuq ceramics (eleventh century); (4) a level showing an increase in "prehistoric gray ware no doubt pertaining to the Early Iron Age (roughly 1000 BC)"; and (5) a level containing a few painted sherds of Hissar IB type dating to c.3500–3200. Schmidt also carried out soundings in an old mudbrick fort called Qaleh Mortezagird (or Morteza-Kord) in the southeastern part of the plain (Fig. 19.1) where he identified an occupation associated with gray ware above a Hissar IB layer. In his view the gray ware stratum dated to the early Iron Age (Schmidt 1937: 323; Majidzadeh 1981: 142, 145–6).

The excavations at Tepe Sialk, near Kashan on the central plateau, conducted between 1933 and 1939, revealed two graveyards (Cemeteries A and B) containing "new material" that was thought to range from the mid-second to the early first millennium BC

(Ghirshman 1939: 3–72). This new material was, in fact, a new kind of pottery, which Ghirshman saw as the "first sign of change" associated with the intrusion of "tribes coming from the north and the northeast driven by some external pressure" (Ghirshman 1954: 70). Period V, attested only in Cemetery A, apparently has no affinity with the subsequent, flourishing Sialk VI (Iron II) settlement and cemetery. In Iran, Sialk VI pottery is almost unparalleled and cannot be said to represent more than a regional revival of painted pottery in the early first millennium BC. However, it has been observed that there are "foreign" elements in Sialk VI and Young has drawn parallels with painted pottery in Anatolia and the Caucasus (Young 1967: 26).

In 1949, Mahmoud Rad and Ali Hakemi excavated at Khorvin in the foothills of the Alborz mountains, 80 km to the west of Tehran. Five years later work there was resumed by L. Vanden Berghe, who discovered pottery and metals of second millennium BC date. The site consists of four mounds, the highest (35 m) and northernmost of which is called Ganj Tepe (Treasure Hill). Ganj Tepe is a natural hill and owes its name to fortuitous discoveries and clandestine digging which are said to have yielded a number of gold and silver objects.

Within the hilly area dominating the plain, the site of Chendar, on the northern bank of the Kordan Rud, was first reported by Vanden Berghe in 1955 (Vanden Berghe 1964: 38–9). He suggested that the pottery predated Khorvin and showed more affinities with the pottery of Cemetery A at Sialk. Many years later, Chendar was disturbed by construction activity.

A number of chance discoveries in the 1960s revealed significant Iron Age materials. A rescue excavation at Qeytariyeh (Fig. 19.1) was conducted by S. Kambakhsh Fard in 1969. The excavated area was vast (5000 m^2). In all, 158 trenches (5 × 5 m) were dug in three selected zones, almost all of which reached bedrock at about 1 m below the surface (Kambakhsh Fard 1991: 35). An examination of some of the rocky surfaces in one of the soundings suggested the existence of architectural remains made of light or perishable material such as wood. In one area the lower parts of a small, stone platform were discovered 80 cm below the surface. This may have supported several wooden structures (Kambakhsh Fard 1991: 36). Over 2000 objects were recovered in 350 graves (Fig. 19.2) including the most important quantity of Early Iron Age gray ware ever excavated in northern Iran (Kambakhsh Fard 1991; Mousavi 2001: 156–8).

In 1957 T. Burton-Brown excavated briefly at Qara Tepe (Burton-Brown 1979) and Barlekin Tepe (Burton-Brown 1981) in the Shahryar plain, west of Tehran. These excavations revealed very important material of the early second millennium BC which has often been neglected in the study of the Iron Age in northern Iran.

Kahrizak is located to the south of the city of Tehran (Fig. 19.1). The site consists of a series of low mounds located along the southern limit of Behesht-e Zahra cemetery (today the largest cemetery in the region of Tehran). The mounds are cut by small, seasonal water-courses flowing in the direction of the Central Desert, the largest of which is called Naqarreh-Khaneh. The ancient mounds stretch along the left bank of the stream. A short excavation in 1985 exposed three pottery kilns, some 0.50 m below the surface of the mound, with gray ware sherds typical of the early Iron Age (Kambakhsh Fard

FIGURE 19.2 Excavation of a grave at Qeytariyeh.

1991: 144). One of the kilns contained a very large, dark gray jar which had been misfired and consequently warped. Another yielded the gray ware sherds of a storage jar decorated with two registers of snakes in applied relief.

In the summer of 1970, Ezat O. Negahban began the first campaign of excavations in the Qazvin plain on behalf of the Archaeological Institute of the University of Tehran. Excavations at Sagzabad yielded second-millennium material including some architectural remains (Shahmirzadi 1977; Tala'i 1983a). Two Iron Age graves were excavated at another adjacent site, Tepe Qabrestan, without any trace of an associated settlement (Majidzadeh 1977: 69; Malekzadeh 1977).

In 1948, Ali Hakemi excavated the fifth millennium BC site of Tepe Mushalan, which yielded the celebrated black-on-red painted pottery known as Esmailabad Ware (Hakemi 1949; Varjavand 1971: 9–19; Tala'i 1983b). These excavations revealed the first reliable evidence of second millennium BC occupation in the Savajbulaq plain (Hakemi 1950; Vanden Berghe 1964). In the 1980s, the German Archaeological Institute conducted a series of surveys in the region where surface sherds indicated the presence of a number of Iron Age settlements (Kleiss 1997). Two short surveys of the Savajbulaq plain, between Tehran and Qazvin (2001–2), covering an area of about 400 km^2, identified and mapped twenty-one sites (Mousavi 2005). Located in the western part of the plain, the high mound (20 m) of Tepe Mohammadabad in the western part of the plain had gray wares of late second-millennium date along with examples of a polished gray/dark ware similar to that found in Hissar II (Schmidt 1937: pls. 97–100) in its lower strata. In addition, recent excavations have revealed a long sequence at Tepe Ozbaki, the largest mound in Savajbulaq, consisting of four major architectural periods. The latest period represents the remains of a late Iron Age or Median mudbrick building similar in plan to the Median forts at Nush-e Jan and Godin Tepe (Majidzadeh 2000) that was built on top of a second millennium BC settlement which in turn was above a fourth-millennium settlement.

During the past thirty years, Iron Age occupations have been excavated at Pishva, in the Varamin plain (Tehrani Moghaddam 1996); Ma'murin, south of Tehran (Mehrekiyan 1995, 1996); Qoli Darvish (Kleiss 1983: 74–6; Sarlak and Aghili Niaki 2004; Sarlak and Malekzadeh 2005); Sarm (Sarlak 2004); and Shamshirgah, south of Qom (Kleiss 1985: 69–74; Fahimi 2003). To sum up, the region of Tehran, including adjacent areas in the vicinity of Qom, Saveh, and Qazvin, has a more or less continuous sequence of occupation from the end of the Bronze Age to the late Iron Age, in the northwestern part of the plain (Majidzadeh 1999: 60, 80).

SITES AROUND THE CASPIAN SEA

The lowlands of the southern shore of the Caspian Sea are divided into three provinces: Gilan in the west, Mazandaran in the center, and Gorgan (now called Golestan) in the east. In fact, this tripartite division is reflected in a number of geographical differences. Each of these provinces is composed of two contrasting areas, one coastal and the other mountainous. The lowland region of Gilan consists principally of the delta of the Sefid Rud (White River), which stretches for about 100 km from Manjil to the sea. To the east of the Sefid Rud valley lie the mountains of Deylaman and Eshkevar, separating Gilan from Mazandaran to the east. To the west of the Sefid Rud are the Talesh Mountains, a natural continuation of the Alborz chain. The narrow coastal corridor linking the three Caspian provinces is c. 10 km wide.

Annual precipitation in the Caspian region is high (600–1000 mm), especially in coastal Gilan, which is located within an angle between the Talesh-Zagros and the eastward-trending systems. The climate there is also very humid. Accordingly, human occupation is mostly concentrated in the foothills, while the littoral may have been used principally for agriculture (Brown-Jones 1969: 597–8). The Caspian forests provide excellent wood for construction, a fact that was mentioned both by Istakhri in the tenth and Yāqut in the early thirteenth century (Barthold 1984: 230–1). Other areas lie mostly in the hinterland: the district of Amarlu in the western foothills of the Deylaman Mountains is particularly rich in archaeological remains and includes sites such as Marlik and Kaluraz on opposite sides of the Sefid Rud (Mousavi 1995: 535–8).

Three regions on the northern flank of the Alborz have yielded evidence of Iron Age occupation: the Rudbar valley on both sides of the Sefid Rud, the region of Amlash, and the mountainous region of Deylaman. Marlik or Cheraq-Ali Tepe (Fig. 19.3) is located on the western side of the valley, 1.5 km from the juncture of the Gowar Rud and the Sefid Rud. The site consists of a natural, rocky hillock with two peaks, a southeastern and a southwestern one, on the summit. In 1961–2 a mission from the Archaeological Institute of the University of Tehran under E. O. Negahban uncovered fifty-three

FIGURE 19.3 View of the mound of Marlik.

generally rectangular tombs during a fourteen-month campaign (Negahban 1996: 16). Located between the natural outcrops of the hill, the tombs were constructed of unworked stone with mud mortar (Negahban 1996: 13–14, fig. 1). In most cases the skeletal remains had disintegrated, but the few tombs that still contained skeletal material had evidence of elaborate interments in which the dead had been carefully laid out on stone slabs accompanied by precious objects (Negahban 1996), including vessels of gold and silver cups, bowls, beakers, vases, and, most typically, pots with long spouts.

Kaluraz is a village on the left bank of the Sefid Rud, 1 km to the west of the Qazvin-Rasht road, and about 85 km from the sea. The site sits at an altitude of 360 masl on a water-course joining the Sefid Rud and was excavated for two seasons (1965, 1967) by Ali Hakemi on behalf of the Iranian Department of Archaeology (Hakemi 1968, 1973). Further excavations by the Iranian Cultural Heritage Organization took place between 1996 and 2001 (Khalatbari 1997, 2007). Kaluraz consists of a series of tombs near the stone foundations of several wooden (?) buildings on both banks of the Kaluraz River. The tombs were particularly rich in gray-black vessels of various forms as well as gold and silver objects (Hakemi 1968: pls. 33–7; Tadahiko and Takuro 2006: figs. 1–49). The skeletal remains are no less interesting since some of the tombs revealed equid skeletons. The number of excavated tombs is unclear but, according to schematic plans published in one of the reports, ten tombs were uncovered. Recent excavations have yielded ceramics very similar to the early Iron Age gray ware known from Marlik (Khalatbari 1997), Lameh Zamin (Fukai and Matsutani 1982: 21–40, pls. 4–22, 34–55), and Tepe Jamshidabad (Fallahian 2004: 230–3). Although Hakemi dated most of the objects that he recovered to the eighth to the seventh centuries BC (Hakemi 1968: 63, 81; 1973: 2), some may date to the late second millennium (Haerinck 1988: 73).

In 2001, a Japanese mission from the Middle Eastern Culture Center in Japan undertook a survey in the Kaluraz area and excavated one of the nearby mounds named Tepe Jalaliyeh (Tadahiko et al. 2003: 39; 2005). The excavations revealed three layers (I–III) extending from the ninth century BC to the late Sasanian period. A number of architectural remains in mudbrick and stone were also uncovered, bearing witness to a late Iron Age settlement (Ohtsu et al. 2005: figs. 4–20; Ryuji 2006: 144). The Iron Age pottery at Tepe Jalalyieh belongs to the same horizon as that found in later tombs of Marlik and Ghalekuti (Takuro 2005: 72). A small female figurine from Layer III (Takuro 2005: fig. 33) closely resembles examples from Kaluraz and Jamshidabad (Fallahian 2004: 237, figs. 13–14; Fallahian et al. 2006: 150-1, fig. 201) which probably date to 800–700 BC.

The region of Deylaman is dotted with graveyards of the Iron Age. One of the best documented is Ghalekuti, 5 km to the east of the village of Deylaman. A wave of clandestine excavations in the 1960s revealed the presence of tombs and drew the attention of archaeologists to the area. The graveyard at Ghalekuti was the object of three seasons of excavations (1962–4) by the University of Tokyo in three different areas of the site (Ghalekuti I–III), the first of which yielded early Iron Age material. At Lasulkan, 2 km east of Deylaman, clandestine excavators discovered a graveyard. The Japanese mission later excavated two soundings there (Egami et al. 1965: 22–3, pls. 20–3, 84–90).

Architecture

It has been suggested that the people who made the distinctive Iron Age pottery of this region may not have established permanent settlements (Young 1985: 373) and this has often been taken as fact (Kambakhsh Fard 1991: 36; Dyson 1965: 196, n. 6). Most of our data for the early Iron Age come from cemeteries and no architectural remains have yet been found in association with the early Iron Age graveyards at Qeytariyeh, Khorvin or Sialk V. To the northwest, Hasanlu (Chapter 17) probably had a small early Iron Age settlement, the details of which are still unpublished (Dyson 1989: 108, fig. 2a–b). A similar building at Sagzabad on the Qazvin plain, built directly on top of a Late Bronze Age mudbrick feature (Talai 1983a: 54–5, fig. 3; 1995: 53–4), has been cited by H. Talai as evidence of early Iron Age architecture. Negahban's claim of having found the settlement of the inhabitants of Marlik at the nearby site of Pilla Qaleh has yet to be verified (Negahban 1964: 18; 1996: 11). Recent excavations at Ma'murin and Qoli Darvish have revealed mudbrick houses dating to the Iron Age II period (Mehrekiyan 1996; Sarlak 2004). At Tepe Ma'murin, 40 km south of Tehran, two excavation seasons revealed three occupation levels with rectangular mudbrick structures that had apparently been in use for a long period of time, judging by the fact that floors there had been replastered several times. According to brief reports by the excavator, most of the pottery found in these building levels is typical gray ware of early Iron Age date (Mehrekiyan 1996: 347).

At Qoli Darvish a mudbrick platform (30 × 3 × 10 m) was discovered that resembles the *Grande construction* (56 × 45 × 23 m) of Sialk VI (Malekzadeh and Sarlak 2005: 53–4). According to Ghirshman, the Sialk platform was built by the people whose dead were buried in Cemetery B (Ghirshman 1939: 23–5, 106, pl. 34).

Pottery

Pottery constitutes the most important body of data in the study of the second millennium BC cultures of northern Iran. The pottery of this period comes almost exclusively from tombs. Although published site reports do not provide as much data as might be desired, it is evident that this pottery accounts for 80 percent of the finds made at Qeytariyeh, and almost 50 percent of the finds at Marlik. The majority of the pottery is either gray/dark gray (75 percent) or red/orange. The Early Iron Age pottery is wheel made with a number of surface treatments including incisions and dots. There is no evidence of painted pottery in the Early Iron Age in Iran. The ware is usually fine and completely burnished. However, unlike the Late Bronze Age pottery of northeastern Iran, Iron Age pottery almost never displays pattern burnishing. It should be stressed that information on the technical aspects of Iron Age pottery is often incomplete. Laboratory studies are lacking, and neither thermoluminescence dating nor petrographic analyses are available.

The pottery of the late second millennium BC shows a remarkable diversity of forms and material, which varies from region to region in northern Iran. The examination of such a multiplicity of ceramic evidence cannot be undertaken without a practical classification and typology. The first comprehensive typological study of Iron Age ceramics in Iran was published by Ina Medvedskaya in 1982 (Medvedskaya 1982: 77–80; cf. her study in Dandamaev and Lukonin 1989: 26–8). A second classification was made by Kambakhsh-Fard, who distinguished twenty-three ceramic types and subtypes, mostly based on the Qeytariyeh material (Kambakhsh-Fard 1991: 51–102). Early Iron Age pottery is almost exclusively gray or dark and highly burnished. It seems that the production of gray ware in quantity became popular in regions where wood for firing was readily accessible, for example in the foothills of the Alborz Mountains.

Late Iron Age pottery is known from Sialk VI, Sagzabad, and Qoli Darvish, the most impressive of which is the corpus of decorated, beak-spouted pots from Cemetery B at Sialk. This pottery is buff with a cream slip and is decorated with geometric patterns and naturalistic figures of ibexes, horses, and goats. This contrasts with the earlier Iron Age I–II tradition of pottery making which prevailed from 1400 to 800 BC in most of the central and northern half of the Iranian plateau.

Whether or not these differences in the pottery traditions of the Iron Age reflect changes in the local population is unclear. Interpretation of the remarkable spread of gray-ware pottery production during the second millennium BC has always been a challenging problem in Iranian archaeology. The nature of the varied causes which led to such an expansion over the central and northeastern regions of the Iranian Plateau and its adjacent zones (southwestern Turkmenistan and western Iran) still represents a conundrum for archaeologists. One of the earliest and still prevalent solutions to the problem of change in material culture of the second millennium BC has been the migration thesis proposed and developed by Roman Ghirshman in his celebrated *Iran from the earliest times to the Islamic conquest* (1954). The Ghirshman "paradigm," written in the same spirit as V. Gordon Childe's *The Aryans* (1926), attempted to explain archaeological data in accordance with historical patterns involving the intrusion of new, Iranian-speaking populations (the Medes and the Persians) into the northern half of the Iranian plateau (Ghirshman 1954: 60–3). Ghirshman's thesis was largely accepted and followed by T. Cuyler Young Jr. in the 1960s and 1970s. The major disagreement between Ghirshman and Young concerned the route followed by these immigrants. Ghirshman favored migration from the north or northwest, most probably via the Caucasus (Ghirshman 1951: 59), whereas Young, with the support of excavation results from Hasanlu and his own surveys in the northwest, favored the coming of the Iranians from the east and suggested a link between the archaeological material in the northwest, for example at Hasanlu, and the northeast, for example at Tepe Hissar and Tureng Tepe (Young 1967: 24). In Dyson's words, "both interpretations, however, suffer from a lack of full data as to the cultural patterns of the sites being compared" (Dyson 1968: 30).

Metal objects

Apart from a few ceremonial weapons in gold or silver that have been found in Gilan, almost all of the weapons from the central Alborz are made of bronze. The northern and southern areas of the central Alborz present a strong contrast in the quantity and quality of bronze weapons. Fifty bronze objects, consisting of bronze tools such as knives, blades, and small daggers of varying shapes, are classified as weapons at Qeytariyeh. These, however, seem to have had a domestic rather than a military function. The number of actual published weapons is only thirty-six, which means only about one in ten tombs contained weaponry (Kambakhsh Fard 1991: 67–8, 103–5, figs. 117–18). Vanden Berghe's excavations at Khorvin yielded only two weapons: a tanged dagger and an arrowhead, each of bronze (Vanden Berghe 1964: 4, 6). The twenty-four weapons illustrated in Vanden Berghe's final report (Vanden Berghe 1964: pls. 34–6) in fact come from the Maleki Collection and their exact provenience is unknown. In contrast, the northern areas of the central Alborz have revealed a considerable quantity of bronze weapons. The tombs at Marlik contained a large number of weapons. Tomb 26 alone contained eleven mace heads, three swords, fourteen spearheads, twenty-five daggers, two axes, and about one hundred arrowheads (Negahban 1996: 251).

The quantity of precious metals vessels from the northern areas of the Alborz is quite remarkable. The discovery of such vessels dates from the 1930s, when the construction of a royal villa at Kelardasht revealed a hoard of gold objects, including a famous gold bowl (Samadi 1959: 179, figs. 11–13). Marlik and Kaluraz have provided far and away the greatest number of such vessels found in official excavations, and many metal vessels from illegal excavations are also attributed to one or the other of these sites (Amiet 1989). Some of the most celebrated vessels from Marlik and Kaluraz, such as the Marlik Gold Bowl from Tomb 26, can be dated to the late second millennium (Calmeyer 1982: 340–1; 1989: 427; Negahban 1996: 58–63, pl. 19.8, and color pl. 13). This spectacular object is decorated with winged bulls on either side of a "tree of life." The bodies of the winged bulls are represented in profile, while their heads are twisted in such a way as to appear in frontal view in high relief; the heads are hollow, made in one piece with the bowl itself, while the horns and ears were made separately and attached. According to Negahban, the body of the bowl itself and the figures of the winged bulls were hammered outward (*repoussé*) in high relief to a depth of almost 2 cm. However, a closer examination of the object suggests that several techniques were used in producing it. First, the flexible and soft sheet of gold was lightly hammered to produce small designs in repoussé. The sheet was supported on a bed of firm but soft material, such as pitch mixed with brick dust and linseed oil, and the design was hammered from behind with tracers, which are like blunt chisels with rounded corners. But the head of the bulls required another technique. They were probably cast by means of the lost-wax technique and then soldered onto the body of the vessel (Kambakhsh Fard 1995: 20). It seems that some of the other metal vessels of Marlik were produced and decorated by a combination of of repoussé, soldering, plating, and inlaying.

SEALS AND BRICKS WITH IMPRESSIONS

Fourteen cylinder seals and five stamp seals were found at Marlik, the majority of which consist of gypsum or frit seals in the Mitannian style, dating to *c*.1400–1100 BC. Other seals betray Assyrian influence and date to *c*.1200–800 BC. These include two inscribed seals, only one of which is legible, that may date to the reign of the Middle Assyrian kings Adad-nerari I or Tiglath-pileser I (Negahban 1996: 212–13). The Marlik seals may have been heirlooms or precious objects rather than functional, administrative devices. Only two cylinder seals were found in Cemetery A at Sialk, one of which is an imported Old Babylonian seal while the other, in Ghirshman's opinion, is of mediocre quality and probably local manufacture (Ghirshman 1939: 11, pls. 5.6, 46.S.661). In contrast, Cemetery B yielded twenty cylinder seals, three stamps seals, and two scarabs (Ghirshman 1939: 62–8, pls. 30–1). Most of the cylinder seals are comparable in both style and manufacture to Middle Assyrian seals.

Five decorated bricks or *briques de revêtement* were found in the excavation of the *Grande construction* at Sialk, where they may have decorated the outer faces of the platform (Ghirshman 1939: 42, pls. 98–9). Six others were discovered during the recent excavations at Sialk (Chegini 2002). A similar brick was found at Qoli Darvish and was probably part of the decoration of the mudbrick platform there (Malekzadeh and Sarlak 2005: 57, 66, fig. 1). A brick found at Shamshirgah, near Khowrabad, south of Qom, shows an armed man behind a chariot (Malekzadeh 2005: 83, fig. 1).

Burial types

The early Iron Age cemeteries of the Tehran region consist of simple pit-graves. Kambakhsh Fard suggested, however, that some of the tombs at Qeytariyeh had side walls in mudbrick covered with reeds (Kambakhsh Fard 1991: 48). Similar tombs were found at Khorvin and Pishva. The graveyards on the northern side of the Alborz show a greater variety of tomb types. At Lasulkan two types of tombs were found. The first is a "tumulus" type, also referred to as a "dolmen" or "megalithic tomb." These graves have an inner face constructed of stone blocks, and a circle of boulders on the surface. After inhumation, graves of this sort were covered with a mass of boulders and pebbles. Most of the boulder circles on the surface had disappeared by the time of excavation (Egami et al. 1965: 22–3, pls. 20–3, 84–90). This type of tomb is also found in the Talesh region, where Morgan noted tumuli marked with stone circles (Morgan 1896; 1905: 259–65). The second type here is the simple pit-grave. Two types of tombs were encountered at Ghalekuti I: simple or pit-graves and "stone chamber" tombs. Unlike the graveyard at Lameh Zamin where grave shape was related to the sex and age of the deceased, the size and the shape of the tombs at Ghalekuti apparently reflected the social status of the deceased. Most of the tombs measure 2 × 0.70–1 m. In Area A, the majority of the tombs were on the western slope of the hill, distributed in relation to the large tomb A–V. It seems that the location of the graveyard was initially occupied with a prepared pattern. In fact, the majority of the tombs at Ghalekuti I were placed in reference to the large Tomb A–V. Tombs that did not respect this orientation were mostly disturbed graves containing secondary inhumations (Cinquabre 1978: 336). At Kaluraz, Hakemi distinguished two types of tombs. The first type consisted of elliptical tombs dug out of the bedrock, to a depth of 1–1.80 m. The second type included square tombs which varied in depth from 2 to 4.50 m. The excavator observed that the dead were buried in a contracted position along a north–south axis (Hakemi 1968: 64–5).

At Marlik, Negahban identified three tomb types: (1) tombs with stone slabs laid in horizontal courses; (2) tombs built with a mixture of fragmentary shale and stone slabs which were again laid in horizontal courses; and (3) tombs built with heavy, roughly shaped blocks of stones. The tombs at Marlik were not built according to any rigorous pattern. Negahban classified them as large (6 × 8 m); medium-sized, rectangular tombs (4 × 4.5 m); and small, irregularly shaped tombs (2.5 × 3 m), to which must be added a small number of horse tombs (Negahban 1996: 16). Two types of graves were recognized at Lameh Zamin: inhumations placed directly below a circle of boulders and shaft graves, in which the body was placed in a side chamber at the base of the shaft (LZ 103, 105 and 107). According to the excavators, the tombs of adults were circular or oval (LZ 105) while those of children were roughly rectangular (Fukai and Matsutani 1982: 21–5).

Cemetery B at Sialk had seventy-one individual graves with gable roofs made of terracotta or stone slabs (Ghirshman 1939: pls. 7, 48–53). The novelty of such an inhumation type on the Iranian plateau has been interpreted as a sign of newcomers, namely, the Iranians (Ghirshman 1954: 83). Similar graves have been excavated at Sarm, 20 km south of Qom (Sarlak 2004: 160, figs. 4–6).

Conclusion

The archaeology of the Tehran region is marked by periods of disruption. At Rayy, Schmidt's excavations did not reveal any material immediately following the Hissar IB period (c.3500–3200 BC) and a gap separated this occupation from the "layer of gray ware" that Schmidt dated to the late second millennium BC (Schmidt 1936: 135). Other sites in the Tehran region such as Qeytariyeh and Pishvāwere founded only in the second half of the second millennium BC. On the Savajbulaq plain to the west of Tehran a period of abandonment followed the flourishing Neolithic culture of Cheshmeh Ali and Esmailabad (Mousavi 2005: 90). It seems, however, that human settlement shifted to the northwestern part of the plain, around Tepe Muhammadābād, where a continuous second millennium BC sequence has been recently documented.

The appearance and the density of archaeological data for the second and early first millennia BC in the central regions, especially in the piedmont zone of Tehran and the Qazvin plain, reflect archaeological developments to the northeast. The dynamics of change further south (near Sialk) also impacted on the region of Rayy and Tehran. None of the regions of the central Alborz range—from Tehran in the south to the Caspian in the north—has so far revealed traces of a major Late Bronze Age presence. There is a sharp contrast in the richness and variety of grave goods between the materials found on the northern and southern flanks of the Alborz. The often rich and varied finds in the north bear witness to flourishing settlements in contact with highly developed regions in western and northwestern Iran (Malekzadeh 1995). The Iron Age occupation of the southern flank needs to be further investigated, but the finds from Qeytariyeh, Khorvin, and Cemetery A at Sialk bespeak a society in isolation with a large population. This pattern changed with the introduction of a new culture reflected in the *Grande construction* and Cemetery B at Sialk and at Qoli Darvish and Sarm near Qom. The dynamics of change from the early to late phases of the Iron Age, as well as the settlement patterns of this transition period, which finally led to the rise of the Medes and Persians, have yet to be explored.

References

Amiet, P. 1989. Autour de Marlik. *AIO*: 311–22.
Barthold, W. 1984. *An historical geography of Iran*. Princeton: Princeton University Press.
Bazin, M., E. Ehlers, and B. Hourcade. 1985. Alborz: iii. Geography. *EnIr* 1: 813–21.
Burton-Brown, T. 1979. *Kara Tepe*. Woodstock: T. Burton-Brown.
———. 1981. *Barlekin*. Woodstock: T. Burton-Brown.
Calmeyer, P. 1982. Mesopotamien und Iran im II. und I. Jahrtausend. In *Mesopotamien und seine Nachbarn: Politische und kulturelle Wechselbeziehungen im alten Vorderasien vom 4.–1. Jahrtausend v. Chr.*, ed. H. J. Nissen and J. Renger, 339–48. Berlin: BBVO 1.
———. 1989. Marlik Tepe. *RlA* 7: 426–9.
Chegini, N. N. 2002. Ājorhāy-e bānaqsh-e mohr. In *The Ziggurat of Sialk*, ed. S. Malek Shahmirzadi, 171–5. Tehran: SRPR 1 (in Persian).
Childe, V. G. 1926. *The Aryans: A study of Indo-European origins*. London: Kegan Paul, Trench, Trubner.
Cinquabre, D. 1978. Les tombes de l'Âge du Fer en Iran du Nord-Ouest. *Paléorient* 4/4: 335–46.
Curtis, J. 1987. A grave-group from Qeytariyeh near Teheran (?). *AIO*: 323–33.
Dandamaev, M. A., and V. G. Lukonin. 1989. *The culture and social institutions of ancient Iran*. Cambridge: Cambridge University Press.
Dyson, R. H., Jr. 1965. Problems of protohistoric Iran as seen from Hasanlu. *JNES* 24/3: 193–217.
———. 1968. The archaeological evidence of the second millennium B.C. on the Persian plateau. *CAH* 2: 1–36 (appeared in book form in *CAH* 2/1: 686–715 in 1973).
———. 1989. The Iron Age architecture at Hasanlu: An essay. *Expedition* 31/2–3: 107–27.
Egami, N., S. Fukai, and S. Masuda. 1965. *Dailaman I: Excavations at Ghalekuti and Lasulkan, 1960*. Tokyo: Tokyo University Iraq-Iran Archaeological Expedition Report 6.
Fahimi, H. 2003. Sokunatgāh-e gurkhoftegān-e Sarm: gozāreshi darbārey-e mohavatey-e Shamshirgāh dar jonub-e Qom. *IJAH* 35: 61–9 (in Persian).
Fallahian, Y. 2004. Tajalliy-e farhang-e asr-e ahan 1 dar gurestan tarikhiy-e Jamshidabad, Gilan. *GB* 2: 217–37 (in Persian).
Fallahian, Y., O. Tadahiko, and A. Takuro. 2006. Figurines from Jamshid Abad. In *Report of the Iran-Japan Joint Expedition to Gilan, Fifth Season*, ed. O. Tadahiko, J. Nokandeh, Y. Kazuya, and A. Takuro, 150–1. Tehran/Tokyo: ICHO and Middle Eastern Culture Center in Japan.
Fukai, S., and T. Matsutani. 1982. *Halimehjan II. The Excavation at Lameh-Zamin, 1978*. Tokyo: Tokyo University Iraq-Iran Archaeological Expedition Report 18.
Ghirshman, R. 1939. *Fouilles de Sialk près de Kashan 1933, 1934, 1937*, vol. 2. Paris: Geuthner.
———. 1951. *L'Iran des origines à l'Islam*. Paris: Payot.
———. 1954. *Iran from the earliest times to the Islamic conquest*. Harmondsworth: Penguin.
Haerinck, E. 1988. The Iron age in Guilan: Proposal for a chronology. In *Bronze-working centres of Western Asia, c.1000–539 B.C.*, ed. J. Curtis, 63–78. London: Kegan Paul International.
Hakemi, A. 1949. Haffāri dar tappeh Mushalān, Esma'ilābād, Sāvajbulaq. *Sālnāmey-e Keshvar-e Iran* 14: 203–7 (in Persian).
———. 1950. Kāvoshhāy-e ejmāli dar tappehāy-e Khorvin va Ajin-Dojin. *GB* 1: 1–100 (in Persian).
———. 1968. Kaluraz et la civilisation des Mardes. *Archéologie Vivante* 1: 63–5.
———. 1973. Excavations in Kaluraz, Gilan. *BAI* 3: 1–3.
Kambakhsh Fard, S. 1969. Fouilles dans les tombes anciennes de Gheytariyeh. *Bastan Chenassi va Honar-e Iran* 2: 58–68 (in Persian with a résumé in French).

——. 1991. *The three thousand two hundred years of Tehran, on the basis of archaeological excavations.* Tehran: Faza Editions (in Persian).

——. 1995. An account of the archaeological investigations in the eastern foothills of Gīlān, northern Iran. *IJAH* 17: 16–23.

Khalatbari, M. R. 1997. Kavosh dar Kaluraz. In *Archaeological Symposium at Suse, February 1995*, ed. M. Mousavi, 65–98. Tehran: ICAR.

——. 2007. Tappey-e bāstāniy-e Kaluraz: neheshtehāy-e me'māriy-e asr-e āhan-e Gilān. *GB* 7: 233–53 (in Persian).

Kleiss, W. 1983. Khowrabad und Djamgaran, zwei vorgeschichtliche Siedlungen am Westrand des zentraliranischen Plateaus. *AMI* 16: 69–104.

——. 1997. Fundorte des 2. und 1. Jahrtausends v. Chr. mit grauer Ware in Iran. *AMI* 29: 3–64.

Majidzadeh, Y. 1977. Excavations in Tepe Ghabristan: The first two seasons, 1970 and 1971. *Marlik* 2: 53–71 (Persian), 45–61 (English).

——. 1981. Sialk III and the pottery sequence at Tepe Ghabristan: The coherence of the cultures of the Iranian plateau. *Iran* 19: 141–6.

——. 1999. Gozareh-e moqadamātiy-e nakhostin fasl-e hafriyāt-e bastanshenakhti dar mohavatey-e Ozbaki, sharestan-e Savajbulāq, pa'iz 1377. *IJAH* 25: 57–81.

——. 2000. Gozareh-e moqadamātiy-e dovvomin fasl-e hafriyāt-e bastanshenakhti dar mohavatey-e Ozbaki, sharestan-e Savajbulāq, pa'iz 1378: Dezh-e Madiy-e Ozbaki. *IJAH* 28: 38–49.

Malekzadeh, F. 1977. A preliminary report on the excavation of trench E, Qabrestan third season, 1972. *Marlik* 2: 73–80 (Persian), 63–6 (English).

Malekzadeh, M. 1995. Andiyeh, shāhakneshini dar sarzamin-e Mād va shāhkārhāy-e honariy-e Marlik. *IJAH* 16: 12–18 (in Persian).

——. 2005. Ājorhāy-e manqush-e asr-e ahan-e pāyāniy-e Mād-e sharqi: yek tiq-e Mādiy-e digar. *Bāstānshenāsi* 1: 82–4 (in Persian).

Malekzadeh, M. and S. Sarlak. 2005. Ājorhāy-e manqush-e asr-e ahan-e pāyāniy-e Mad-e sharqi. *Bāstānshenāsi* 1: 52–66 (in Persian).

Medvedskaya, I. 1982. *Iran Iron Age I.* Oxford: BAR Int Ser 126.

Mehrekiyan, J. 1995. Ofoqi novin dar pajuheshhāy-e sofāl-e khākestari. *Mirās-e Farhangi* 3: 74–5 (in Persian).

——. 1996. Pajuhesh dar memāriy-e noshenākhtey-e sofāl-e khākestari dar Tappeh Ma'murin. In *History of architecture and urbanism in Iran, symposium of Bam, March 1996*, 345–56. Tehran: National Cultural Heritage Organization.

Morgan. J. de. 1896. *Mission scientifique en Perse.* Paris: Recherches archéologiques 4.

——. 1905. Recherches au Talyche persan. In *Recherches archéologiques, troisième série*, 251–341. Paris: MDP 8.

Mousavi, A. 2001. La région de Téhéran à l'aube de l'âge du Fer: Reflexions et commentaires sur les nécropoles du IIe millénaire av. J.-C. *IrAnt* 36: 151–212.

——. 2005. Comments on the Early Iron Age Iran. *IrAnt* 40: 87–100.

Mousavi, M. 1995. Bāstānshenāsiy-e Gilān. In *Ketāb-e Guilān*, vol. 1, ed. E. E. Arabāni, 510–38. Tehran.

Negahban, E. O. 1964. A brief report on the excavations of Marlik Tepe and Pileh Qaleh. *Iran* 2: 13–19.

——. 1996. *Marlik: The complete excavation report*, 2 vols. Philadelphia: UMM 87.

Ohtsu, T., J. Nokandeh, and Y. Kazuya. 2003. Kaluraz, Jalalye A, B, C. In *Preliminary Report of the Iran Japan Joint Archaeological Expedition to Gilan, First Season, 2001*, ed. O. Tadahiko,

J. Nokandeh, and Y. Kazuya, 39–43. Tehran/Tokyo: ICHO and Middle Eastern Culture Center in Japan.

Ohtsu, T., J. Nokandeh, and A. Takuro. 2005. Exacavation at Tappe Jalaliye. In *Preliminary Report of the Iran Japan Joint Archaeological Expedition to Gilan, Fourth Season*, ed. O. Tadahiko, J. Nokandeh, and Y. Kazuya, 61–8. Tehran/Tokyo: ICHO and Middle Eastern Culture Center in Japan.

Ohtsu, T., and A. Takuro. 2006. Outline of the research during the 2005 fiscal year. In *Report of the Iran-Japan Joint Expedition to Gilan, Fifth Season*, ed. O. Tadahiko, J. Nokandeh, Y. Kazuya, and A. Takuro, 6–29. Tehran/Tokyo: ICHO and Middle Eastern Culture Center in Japan.

Ryuji, S. 2006. Excavation at Tappe Jalaliye. 1. Pottery analysis from Tappe Jalaliye. In *Report of the Iran-Japan Joint Expedition to Gilan, Fifth Season*, ed. T. Ohtsu, J. Nokandeh, Y. Kazuya, and A. Takuro, 144–8. Tehran/Tokyo: ICHO and Middle Eastern Culture Center in Japan.

Samadi, H. 1959. Les découvertes fortuites. *Arts asiatiques* 6: 175–94.

Sarlak, S. 2004. Avāmel-e mo'asser dar shekl giriy-e anvā'e me'māriy-e qobur-e Va shivehāy-e tadfin dar gurestān-e asr-e ahan-e Tappeh Sar-Kohak, Qom. *GB* 2: 129–64 (in Persian).

Sarlak, S., and S. Aghili Niaki. 2004. Gozāresh-e lāy-e negāriy-e mohavatey-e bāstāniy-e Qoli-Darvish, Jamkarān, Qom. *Archaeological Reports* 3: 60–96 (in Persian).

Sarlak, S., and M. Malekzadeh. 2005. Decorative bricks of the Late Iron Age in eastern Media [1]: Mud-brick platform of Qoli-Darvish-e Jamkarân and æLa grande construction" of Sialk. *Bāstānshenāsi* 1/1: 52–66 (in Persian).

Schmidt, E. F. 1936. Rayy research, 1935, part II. *University Museum Bulletin* 6: 133–6.

———. 1937. *Excavations at Tepe Hissar, Damghan*. Philadelphia: University of Pennsylvania Press.

Shahmirzadi, S. M. 1977. The excavation of Sagzabad mound, Qazvin plain, Iran, 1970–71. *Marlik* 2: 81–98 (Persian), 67–79 (English).

Takuro, A. 2005. The Iron Age pottery from Tappe Jalaliye. Layer II, III. In *Preliminary Report of the Iran-Japan Joint Expedition to Gilan, Fourth Season*, ed. T. Ohtsu, J. Nokandeh, Y. Kazuya, and A. Takuro, 69–95. Tehran/Tokyo: ICHO and Middle Eastern Culture Center in Japan.

Tala'i, H. 1983a. Late Bronze Age and Iron Age I architecture in Sagzabad-Qazvin Plain—the Central Plateau of Iran. *IrAnt* 16: 51–7.

———. 1983b. Stratigraphical sequence and architectural remains at Islamabad, the Central Plateau of Iran. *AMI* 16: 58–68.

Tehrani Moghaddam, A. 1996. Gurestān-e hezārey-e avval qabl az milād-e Pishvā. In *Papers of the First Archaeological Symposium after the Islamic Revolution, Susa 14–18 April, 1993*, vol. 1, 53–62. Tehran: ICAR.

Vanden Berghe, L. 1964. *La nécropole de Khūrvīn*. Istanbul: UNHAII 17.

Varjavand, P. 1971. *Sarzamin-e Qazvin*. Tehran: Silsila-i Intišārāt-i Anğuman-i Ātār-i Millī.

Wright, D. 1977. *The English amongst the Persians during the Qajar period, 1787–1921*. London: Heinemann.

Young, T. C., Jr. 1967. The Iranian migration into the Zagros. *Iran* 5: 11–34.

———. 1985. Early Iron age Iran revisited: preliminary suggestions for the re-analysis of old constructs. In *De l'Indus aux Balkans, Recueil à la mémoire de Jean Deshayes*, ed. M. Yon, Y. Calvet, and J.-L. Huot, 361–78. Paris: Éditions Recherche sur les Civilisations.

CHAPTER 20

LINGUISTIC GROUPS IN IRAN

RAN ZADOK

Introduction

The main pre-Iranian *ethnoi* in Iran are from south to north: Elamites in southern Iran, Kassites in Luristan and in the fluvial valleys of the Zagros, Lullubians in southeastern Kurdistan, Gutians somewhere in the Zagros, Manneans in northeastern Kurdistan, and Hurrians in the piedmont of the northern Zagros and near Lake Urmia. The Iranians are not autochthonous to the Iranian plateau: all the onomastic and lexical material from or about Iran before 881 BC is non-Iranian. From the third millennium BC onward this material was recorded in Sumerian, Akkadian, Elamite, Urartian, and Aramaic sources. Most of the statistics presented below are based on Zadok (2002).

Elamites

Elamite is so far an unaffiliated language: its hypothetical relationship to Proto-Dravidian (McAlpin 1981) has no practical consequences due to the considerable chronological gap. Elamite lexical material is documented (both in Elamite and non-Elamite sources) from the second half of the third through the second third of the first millennium BC, a period of nearly 2000 years. Moreover, the Elamite onomasticon is documented during a period of no less than 2500 years, viz. from the middle of the third millennium BC through the first half of the first century AD. Thus Elamite is one of the oldest and most continuously used languages of the Ancient Near East. Since there are no texts in Elamite before the last third of the second millennium BC, all the early Elamite names are recorded in Sumerian and Akkadian sources from Susiana, which culturally formed part of Mesopotamia. In practice, "Elamite" denotes the dialects written in cuneiform since the Elamite hieroglyphs (from the earliest period) are as yet undeciphered. There is no proof that the linear script is in Elamite (see Chapter 13), but Elamite is the most likely candidate. Elamite has four chronological phases ("dialects"), namely Old, Middle, Neo-, and Royal Achaemenid Elamite (OE, ME, NE, and RAE, respectively). Elamites inhabited a vast territory, namely Fars (ancient Anšan with Huhnuri and Adamshah), Khuzestan (Susiana), and adjacent regions (e.g., Pashime and Iabrat, see Carter and Stolper 1984; Carter et al. 1998). Hence their language must have had considerable regional diversification, but hardly any diatopic dialectal information is available. The documentation from each phase is very uneven. OE has only two more or less intelligible texts (a treaty and a royal inscription, Farber 1975). Other OE texts (all from Mesopotamia) are largely incomprehensible incantations and related texts; even their linguistic affiliation is obscure in several cases. In addition, there are some OE words (mostly referring to officials, craftsmen, realia, and peculiar Elamite numinous notions) in early Akkadian sources from Susa, where rare instances of Elamite formulae and epithets occur. Contrary to the OE scanty material, which is almost exclusively from Susa, the richer ME corpus has a wider geographical distribution. In addition to texts from Susa there are documents from several sites in Khuzestan (notably Kapnak, modern Haft Tepe) as well as from Liyan (Tol-e Peytul, near modern Bandar Bushehr). Noteworthy is a short text with an almost identical Akkadian version, that is, practically a bilingual inscription (*EKI*: 67ff., 13B) from Dur-Untash (Chogha Zambil). Several such ME texts contain repetitive formulae (*EKI*: 46ff., 84ff.). Some Elamite lexemes are contained in Babylonian lexical lists, which generally belong to the Standard Babylonian "dialect." The latter is post-Old Babylonian, that is, in this case coeval with ME and early NE (see below). Most of them do not appear in Elamite texts (Reiner 1969: 66; several words are not defined as Elamite and at least one defined as such is possibly Kassite). The relatively abundant NE material is diverse and has a wide geographical distribution: administrative documents from Anshan (Tal-e Malyan; early NE according to Steve 1992) and Susa (late NE); royal inscriptions from Susa and several mountainous sites in western Elam; as well as epistolary documents which were found in Sargonid Nineveh, but might have originated in Susiana. The very few religious texts are also from Susiana. There are some NE inscribed seals. A list of Susian deities and designations of Elamite classes of priests are recorded in a Neo-Assyrian royal inscription concerning Elam. RAE has not only the richest documentation (statistically outweighing all the earlier material) and the widest geographical distribution (cf. Jones and Stolper 1986: 248), but is also the most intelligible "dialect." This is largely due to the fact that many of the royal inscriptions have parallel versions in languages which are much better understood than Elamite (Akkadian and Old Persian; to a very limited extent Aramaic). In addition, the abundant administrative documentation from Persepolis contains numerous Iranian (notably Old Persian) loanwords and Aramaic notations, thereby enhancing its comprehensibility. On the other hand, the number of Sumerian and Akkadian loanwords in earlier dialects is very limited. The Elamite dictionary (Hinz and Koch 1987) is practically also a thesaurus and a concordance where, in addition to words (including *c*.240 verbal bases), most of the pertinent names (outweighing the words) are registered (for criteria, classification, and characterization, cf. Zadok 1984). Most of the toponyms are listed and discussed in Vallat (1993). It should be remembered that most of the lexemes resist any analysis (cf. Reiner 1969: 65ff.). Regarding degrees of plausibility, many items recorded in bilinguals as well as in Akkadian texts and lexical lists (Sumerian texts do not seem to contain any discernible Elamite vocables except for names) have a transparent meaning. At least the semantic category may be inferred if found in a relatively clear context. Elamite loanwords in nonperipheral Akkadian are very rare: *kidinnu* "divine protection, divinely enforced security," which is recorded in Old Babylonian Susiana, appears in Akkadian texts from Mesopotamia after the Old Babylonian period. Elamite names are recorded in sources from Mesopotamia, especially Ur III (where the Elamites were the most frequently mentioned non-Semitic foreign group) and Old Babylonian. The sources from Susiana where the population was mixed, viz. Elamite and Semitic, also contain many Semitic (Akkadian, Amorite) and hybrid (Semitic-Elamite) names. The latter reflect Elamite-Akkadian interaction there. The Semites seem to have been dominant in early Susiana as all the Susians mentioned in Sargonic texts bore Semitic names (Edzard et al. 1977: 154ff.) and most names from Old Babylonian Susa are Semitic. The percentage of the Semitic names there is much lower than that of the Elamite ones in the later (ME and NE) onomastic documentation, which contain some Kassite names as well. The onomasticon of NE and RAE reflects the intensive Iranian penetration into Elam. Gershevitch observed that most names recorded in RAE are Iranian (1969: 168). Since there were numerous foreigners at Persepolis, RAE has an especially wide spectrum of strange names. Apart from "nuclear" Elam in Fars and Khuzistan, ELAM (NIM) prefixed numerous entities in the central Zagros and its piedmont (excluding its northwestern section with Gutium and Lullubum), notably Shimashki, Sabum, Zapshali, Sigrish, Kimash, and Hu'urti. However, it is impossible to prove that the few individuals associated with this vast territory were ethnic Elamites, as most of their names are obscure and inexplicable in Elamite terms. One hardly expects ethnolinguistic unity in this huge territory of the central Zagros and east of it, with many almost inaccessible mountainous regions. The limited onomasticon of Marhashi, another region defined as ELAM, which is mostly unexplained, includes several Hurrian names. If this has any significance, it would weaken the case for locating it in the southeastern part of the Iranian Plateau (see Steinkeller 1982: 263, who regards Marhashi as an intermediary between Elam and Meluhha in the east), for Hurrians were found in northwestern Iran. However, a location in Margiana (advocated by Francfort and Tremblay 2010) would extend the geographical horizon of the early Mesopotamian sources to almost incredible dimensions. Much more archaeological investigation is needed to fill the geographical gap, which such a suggestion creates in order to enhance its credibility. Moreover, the year name of Hammurapi 30 has: "He (Hammurapi) overthrew the army of Elam, which had mobilized Subartu, Gutium, Eshnunna and Malgium *en masse* from the border of Mar-ha-ši^{ki}" (van Dijk 1970: 65; Horsnell 1999: 2, 139:132). Subartu and Gutium form the northwesternmost points, whereas Eshnuna and Malgium mark the southwesternmost ones, in which case Marhashi shared a border with Elam in the east. Therefore Marhashi is not to be sought far away beyond Elam.

Kassites

The Akkadian name *Kaššû* originates from Kassite *G/Kalž-. Middle Babylonian documents from Nuzi have the form *Ku-uš-š u (-hé)*, that is, with the Hurrian adjectival ending *-ḫḫe* (>*Kunšu-*), resembling the much later Greek name *Kossaioi*, "Kassites." The opinion that the Kassites originated in the central Zagros is based on the assumption that their geographical distribution before they took over the Babylonian alluvium, which they might have penetrated via the lower Diyala and the Sippar region during the late Old Babylonian period, was the same as their distribution after the demise of Kassite rule in Babylonia (Zadok 2005a). Since they do not appear among the peoples who inhabited the central and southern Zagros according to Sargonic and Ur III sources, the Kassites seem to have been relatively new to the region. Apart from several suspected Kassite names in Ur III economic documents, no Kassite anthroponyms or toponyms are recorded in these regions according to these early sources. However, it is not known whence the individuals bearing these names originally came. There may be several Kassite names at Old Babylonian Shusharra (mod. Tall Shemshara) in the Zagros. The fact that the river ordeal, which in the Old Babylonian period is mainly recorded in texts from Susa, became more common in Babylonia during the Kassite period than it had been in the preceding Old Babylonian period may point to an origin of the Kassites east of Babylonia, but this is not conclusive evidence. In view of some affinities between their pantheon and that of the Indo-Aryans, the Kassites might have once been neighbors of Indo-Europeans. Brinkman (1976–80) points out that the earliest evidence for Kassites is from northern Babylonia and to the west of it, that is, the Middle Euphrates and Alalakh VII. The earliest occurrence of an individual with a Kassite name in Babylonia is from 1770 BC. The Kassites first appeared as a political factor in Babylonia in 1742 (or 1741) BC. Thereafter, Kassite groups and individuals are recorded in northern Babylonia. A *terminus post quem* for the Kassites' penetration into the Middle Euphrates region and Upper Mesopotamia in general can be deduced from the absence of Kassite names in the rich documentation from early Old Babylonian Mari, Tuttul, Tall Lelan, and Chaghar Bazar. This absence, compared with the hypothetical appearance of Kassite names in the documents from Old Babylonian Susa, may strengthen the case for an eastern origin of the Kassites. Kassite names are recorded in Tikunani in the sixteenth century BC and in Terqa perhaps in the same period. Richardson (2005: 282–6) points out that the communication of the Kassites, who were integrated in the Babylonian social structure, with the authorities was facilitated by interpreters who also acted as informers. Since Kassites had chariots, they were not nomadic, but were fully settled in segregated rural encampments. The foreign inhabitants of the fortresses, who were mercenaries forming a garrison system, gradually gained control over the northern Babylonian countryside.

The emergence of the Kassite state in Babylonia took place in the sixteenth and fifteenth centuries BC. The Sealand was incorporated into Babylonia *c.*1465 BC. By the fourteenth century BC the Kassites controlled the whole of Babylonia, including the

Diyala region. Tilmun (mod. Bahrain) in the Persian Gulf was ruled by a Kassite governor. Amarna *Ša-an-har-ra*, *Ša-an-ha-ar* (from Mitanni and Alashia), Hittite *Ša-an-ha-ra(-az)*, Egyptian *Šngr*, Old Testament *Šnʿr* < **Šamġara* (Old Babylonian gentilic *Samharû*), presumably a Kassite tribe, gave its name to Babylonia while it was occupied by the Kassites, but the Kassite name of Babylonia was Kar(an)duniash. Elam's raids caused the demise of the Kassite dynasty in 1150 BC. The Kassite termini surviving in Akkadian are mainly from the realms of horse breeding and chariot building. With respect to the assimilation of Kassites in Babylonia, in most of the pertinent filiations the father has a Kassite and the son a Babylonian name. Several Kassite tribes and clans bore Akkadian and atypical names. Those of the Kassites who remained seminomads were organized in family and tribal units. It cannot be proven that the Kassites living in Babylonia had an essentially different social organization from that of the Babylonians. Kassites are recorded at Nuzi during the fifteenth century BC, as well as in Middle Assyrian documents. After the fall of the Kassite dynasty, Kassites still held important positions in the state sector, as late as the mid-tenth century BC. As late as the Achaemenid period some prebendaries in Babylonian temple cities bore Kassite ancestors' names. Kassites stayed in Babylonia, but their main concentration was in the central Zagros northeast of Babylonia, notably in Namri and Bīt-Hamban. Both regions remained linked with the Babylonian government during the eleventh and tenth centuries BC, but from 850 BC onward they passed to the Assyrian sphere of influence. Nevertheless, some Babylonian cultural influence presumably persisted there. The only named ruler of Bīt-Hamban bore the Kassite anthroponym (though originally a title) Ianzu. Namri was called *Babilū*, that is, "Babylon," in Urartian inscriptions. Kassites are recorded in Media during the first half of the first millennium BC. Sennacherib's eighth campaign was conducted against the Kassites and Yasubigalleans there. The rulers of Allabria, Hubushkia, and Ginguhtu, regions in the direction of present-day West Azerbaijan province, bore Kassite names (Ianzi-buriash, Ianzu, and Ursi, respectively). At least three toponyms in Mannea, another three in Gizilbunda, and one in eastern Media are explicable in Kassite terms. Five prominent individuals, several places in Inner Media and several members of the ruling family of Ellipi bore Kassite names. Kassite toponyms refer to three polities in western Media. The individuals bearing Kassite names comprise 7.72–5.31 percent of the general sample from Greater Media, that is, the second group after the Iranians, whose percentage was 45.37–32.36 percent. Traces of Kassites in Iranian nomenclature are negligible. There is not a single connected text in the Kassite language. The number of Kassite appellatives is restricted (slightly more than sixty vocables, mostly referring to colors, parts of the chariot, irrigation terms, plants, and titles). About 200 additional lexical elements can be gained by the analysis of the more numerous anthroponyms, toponyms, theonyms, and horse names used by the Kassites. As is clear from this material, the Kassites spoke a language without a genetic relationship to any other known tongue. The opinion of Eilers (1957–8), namely that Kassite is related to Elamite, is unlikely to be correct. Ancillotti's attempt to demonstrate that Kassite was originally an Indo-Aryan language (Ancillotti 1981) is unconvincing.

LULLUBIANS

Lullubians were people who probably originated in southern Kurdistan (Zadok 2005b). The heart of their country is thought to have been the valley of Shehrizor (Eidem 1992: 50–54), but it is impossible to indicate the boundaries of the land of the Lullubians. In the third millennium BC their abodes are still delimitable to some extent. The only description of Lullubum, albeit partial, is found in the "Sargon Geography," which goes back to an Old Babylonian—if not earlier—tradition. The land of *Lu-lu-mi-i* is identified in the first millennium BC with Zamua. The name of their country, *Lulubum*, ends with the Akkadian nominative ending; the same form was borrowed in Sumerian. Early Dynastic *Lu-lu-bu-na* and Old Akkadian *Lu-lu-ba-an* referring to a city in modern Halabjah (southwest of Lake Zeribor) may render the indigenous form. A shorter form is Old Babylonian *Lu-ul-li-im*, Middle Babylonian Nuzi *Lu-lu-ú-e > Nu-ul-lu-e* (with dissimilation), and the Assyrian variants *Lu-lu-i, Lu-(ul)-lu* (Middle and Neo-Assyrian, respectively).

Speiser and Klengel followed Hüsing in suggesting that the Lullubian language was related to Elamite. Their only argument is that *bi>* of the ethnonym (whose function—if any—eludes us) is identical to the animate plural marker (/p/) in Elamite. On a purely descriptive level, the segmentation of the ethnonym into *Lullu-* and *-bi* is defensible in view of the synchronic occurrences of forms with and without the second component. However, the second component is spelled not only with *b>*, but also with *m>* (/v/, /w/?): Middle Babylonian Nuzi *Nu-ul-lu-ma-i < *Lullumāyu*, Middle Assyrian *Lu-lu-mi/ mì-i, Lu-lu-me-e* and Neo-Assyrian *Lul-lu-mi-i, Lu-(ul-)lu-me-e*. There is no evidence that this alternating second component has the same function as /p/ in Elamite.

It cannot be proven that the pre-Iranian Lullubians, who inhabited part of southern Kurdistan, are the ancestors of the modern Iranian-speaking Lurs, who dwell further south in Luristan. The only known Lullubian word is *ki-ú-ru-um* = Akk. *ilu* "god" (recorded in a late Assyrian vocabulary). The inhabitants of the region of Sipirmena in Zamua "twitter like women," according to a Neo-Assyrian royal inscription. Due to the fact that we know next to nothing about the language of the Lullubians, it is not even clear whether they ever formed a distinct ethnolinguistic group. The ascription of any corpus to a distinctive "Lullubian" group is very doubtful. The thorough treatment of the "Lullubian" onomasticon by Speiser is necessarily tentative and overly optimistic. In fact, there are hardly any discernible name components in this restricted corpus (except perhaps *-ara* of *Ki-ir-te/ti-a-ra* and *Me-eg-di-a-ra, Ni-ig-di-a-ra)*. Moreover, there seems to be a late and secondary geographical extension of Lullubum (in the second millennium BC: "mountain dwellers, strangers") and there is no definite delimitation between Gutium and Lullubum. Gutium seems to overlap Lullubum to some extent: Mt. Nimušis located in Gutium according to a *lipšur* litany, but this is a relatively late literary source. On the whole, a clear-cut differentiation of the considerable, linguistically unaffiliated onomasticon cannot be attained, as a specific ascription to the languages of the autochthonous peoples is generally impossible (very little is known about the language of the historical Gutians). On the descriptive level, one can at best distinguish between names which have homonyms or parallels in other regions (notably toponymic interregional duplicates) and entirely isolated anthroponyms and toponyms. The number of Lullubian anthroponyms is negligible and all the Lullubian deities are anonymous. The comparable material comes partially from the earlier sites in the region or near it, such as Old Babylonian Shusharra and Middle Babylonian Nuzi. In addition, one has always to bear in mind the practices and conventions of the Akkadian scribes, and to reckon with folk etymologies and generations-old Mesopotamian designations of indigenous locales on the Iranian plateau (e.g., names beginning with Bīt—continuing the Middle Babylonian practice of naming regions after Kassite and other tribes). Naram-Sin of Akkad (2254–2218 BC) defeated Ía-tu-ni, the ruler of Lulubum. Lulubum and Akkad were still at war in the time of Naram-Sin's successor. Kanishba, king of Simurrum, incited his people, as well as the Lullubians, to rebel against Erridu-pizir, king of Gutium, according to the latter's inscription. Madga is located in the centre of Erridu-pizir's arena of operations in Simurrum and Lulubum. Lullubians are recorded at Girsu in the time of the Second Dynasty of Lagash. There may be an indication that the Lullubians were under the control of the Neo-Sumerian (Ur III) state. It is not certain whether Anubanini (end of Ur III or beginning of the Old Babylonian period) was a Lullubian or not. The numerous kings of *Lu-ul-li-im* are described in documents from Old Babylonian Shusharra. Old Babylonian sources show the extension of the term Lullu to an international "social" label. So far there is no evidence for an ethnolinguistic reality behind the opposition Lullean: Turukkean. "Lullean" become a designation for "highlander" ~ "barbarous" at Old Babylonian Shemshara. They inhabited the less accessible mountains, not the plain or the intermontane valleys (Eidem 1992: 50–54). They were basically engaged in herding and hunting, not in agriculture.

Urartian *Lulu(ine)* denotes "enemy of the mountains; foreigner, stranger" in the time of King Argishti (first half of the eighth century BC). Im-ma-aš-ku king of *Lulu* is recorded in an historical-mythological fragment from Böghazköy belonging to the Hurrian tradition. According to this tradition, there were several Lullubian kings at the same time, presumably a great king controlling several chieftains ("kings"). This find is in accordance with Neo-Assyrian sources, in which several kings of Zamua (< Lulubum) are recorded simultaneously. Zamua was a region characterized by a low level of political integration.

The emergence of Assyria as a world power in the fourteenth and thirteenth centuries BC brought the Assyrian army to the border of Lulubum. Assyrian involvement in Lulubum itself began in the second year of Tiglath-Pileser I's reign (1113 BC). Idu of Zamua was under Assyrian control then. At the beginning of the first millennium BC the Neo-Assyrian inscriptions treat the land of *Lu-lu-me/mi* separately from Zamua. Adad-nerari II (911–891 BC) reached the border of Lulubum while his son, Tukulti-Ninurta II (890–884 BC), conquered the region of *La-da-a-ni*, which was accessible through the passes of Habruri and bordered on the Lower Zab. It is described as inhabited by Lullubians. The late and secondary geographical extension of Lulubum does not necessarily apply to this region, which was very close—if not adjacent—to Lulubum.

Dagara (in the basin of the Tauq Chai) and Kiṣirtu in Western Zamua were ruled and inhabited—at least partially—by Arameans, who revolted against Assurnasirpal II. His campaign in 881 BC caused the Zamuan rulers to form an anti-Assyrian alliance and to build a wall in the Babite (now Bazian) pass, the gateway to Zamua. Assurnasirpal II had to conduct an anti-Zamuan campaign in the following year as well; Zamua became an Assyrian province. Shalmaneser III (858–824 BC) conducted more campaigns against Zamua. His first campaign was via Mt. Kullar to Inner Zamua (including Sumbi). This was followed by the conquest of the cities of Niqdira and Niqdime and the extermination of the remainder of the retreating Zamuan troops in the Sea of Inner Zamua (presumably Lake Zeribor). However, local rulers are recorded later as well, namely *Da-da-a* of Arzizu in Sargon II's time (722–705 BC) and *La-ar-ku-ut-la*, city lord of Zamua, at the end of Esarhaddon's reign (690–669 BC). *Ba-a-u-ri* was the ruler of the land of Idu (modern Sātu Qala; van Soldt 2008) sometime before 800 BC (see Salvini in Pecorella and Salvini 1984: 55; the reading *Qa-a-u-ri* is unlikely in view of his namesake *Ba-iu-ú-ri*, who sold a Lullubian-speaking female slave; see Postgate 1988: 52). The name of Idu's ruler, *Ab-bi-ze-ri* (kindly communicated to me by Cinzia Pappi), is hardly Semitic (the logographic spelling *Ab-bi-NUMUN* is due to reinterpretation).

Gutians

The Gutians originated in the central and northern Zagros mountain area as well as, perhaps, northwest of Mesopotamia. The geographical name Sum. Gu-ti-um^{ki}/Gu-tu-um^{ki}, Akk. K/Qutium, and the indication of people as Gutians, are attested in the Mesopotamian record from the mid-third to the late first millennium BC. Gutium is mentioned by Sargon of Akkad among his subject lands, together with Lullubum, Armanu, and other regions northeast of Mesopotamia. The Gutian kings came to power in Mesopotamia in the middle of the twenty-second century BC (short chronology) after the demise of the Akkad dynasty. T. Jacobsen and R. Kutscher tentatively suggest regarding Erridu-pizir as the successor of the Akkad dynasty (i.e., sometime after 2154 BC), thereby being the first recorded member of the Gutian dynasty that ruled over Mesopotamia as well (Kutscher 1989: 62ff., 67ff.). The last Gutian king was Tirigan, who was preceded by twenty-one kings. The Gutian dynasty ruled over certain parts of Mesopotamia for no more than forty years (Hallo 1957–71: 713ff.; 2005: 153) as many of these kings were coeval with local Mesopotamian rulers (Glassner 1986: 46–50). According to the Sumerian King List, Tirigan was defeated by Utu-hengal of Uruk, who expelled the Gutians from the country (*c.*2050 BC short chronology; Westenholz and Sallaberger 1999: 59, 94ff., 132, 134). The Gutian dynasty was succeeded by the Third Dynasty of Ur, whose founder, Ur-Nammu, devastated Gutium. Later their land was raided by Anubanini of Lullubum. Indaššu, the king of the Gutians somewhere in Luristan, is mentioned in texts from Old Babylonian Shemshara (Læssøe and Eidem 2001: 31–2). In the late second and first millennia BC "Gutians" designated as an anachronistic and pejorative term people in the Zagros who were hostile to Assyria. These people basically had no special relationship to the earlier Gutians. Cyrus (II) the Great attacked Babylonia in 539 BC, with the support of Ugbaru, governor of the land of Gutium (Oppenheim 1969: 306; cf. Briant 2002: 41–2). An interpreter for the Gutian language is recorded at Sargonic Adab (Hallo 2005: 149). Only three Gutian vocables (partially damaged) and one theonym are known (Hallo 1957–71: 719).

Based on their name (Kuti > Kuči) and the Gutian kings' names from the Sumerian King List, namely Inkishush, Zarlagab, Shulme (or Yarlagash), Silulumesh (or Silulu), Inimabakesh (Duga), Igeshaush, Yarlagab, Ibate, Yarla (or Yarlangab), Kurum, Laerabum, Irarum, Yarlaganda, Si-um (?), and Tirigan (leaving out the Semitic names Apilkin, Hablum, Ibranum, and Puzur-Suen), Henning (1978) inferred that the Gutian language was close to the Tocharian languages (a forerunner of which might have been the Old Babylonian toponym Tu-ug/k-ri-iš^{ki}; Groneberg 1980: 239) of the Indo-European family (not belonging to the Indo-Iranian subfamily), which was spoken later in Chinese Turkestan.

MANNEANS

The kingdom of Mannea was located in northern Kurdistan, south of Lake Urmia (Zadok 2006). The ending of Neo-Assyrian ^{kur}Ma/Man-na/nu-A + A (etc.) > Old Testament *Mny* is adjusted to the Neo-Assyrian and Aramaic gentilic suffix. The earlier forms, *Mu-un-na* and ^{kur}*Man-an-áš* (829 BC), lack this ending. One may distinguish between Mannea proper and Greater Mannea. Zig/k/qirtu and Andia were basically autonomous and Allab/pria belonged only temporarily to Mannea. The location of ^{uru}*I-zir/zi-ir-ti/tu*, the permanent capital of Mannea, is unknown. Its identity with Aramaic Z'tr, a seat of the god Haldi at the end of the eighth century BC, is not beyond doubt (see Eph'al 1999: 119ff.). ^{uru}*(I-)zi-bi-ia* is identified with modern Zīvya (Ziwiye). Mannea bordered the Assyrian province of Zamua in the southwest, the Median polities in the east and southeast, and Urartu in the northwest. It is attested mostly in Neo-Assyrian royal inscriptions (where a Mannean interpreter is also mentioned). Much less information is contained in Urartian sources and in the only indigenous document, an Aramaic inscription from Bukan. Mannean rulers are recorded between 829 BC and the second half of the seventh century BC. A Mannean named Zimaga is mentioned at Sippar in 527/6 BC. ^{lú}*Ba/Ma-na-i-ka-nu*, the name of a *hatru*-organization at Nippur (422/1–421/0 BC), may mean "Manneans." In the absence of any Mannean texts or vocables in foreign traditions, a determination of the ethnolinguistic character of the Manneans from the mid-ninth to the mid-seventh centuries must rely on an analysis of twenty-seven anthroponyms. Four out of twenty-seven anthroponyms (14.81 percent) are Old Iranian. Hurro-Urartians are the second-largest group (1–4 individuals = 14.8–3.7 percent compared with one individual with a Kassite name = 3.7 percent). Their presence there was probably due to the proximity of Mannea to Urartu. The ethnic characterization of Mannea naturally refers only to its ruling class, as very few commoners' names are mentioned in the sources. It is unlikely that there was any ethnolinguistic unity in Mannea. Like other peoples of the Iranian plateau, the Manneans were subjected to an ever-increasing Iranian (i.e., Indo-European) penetration. The Mannean toponymy (mostly unexplained) is more conservative. It preserved several pre-first millennium and Kassite names and was less affected by the Iranian penetration.

Hurrians

Hurrians and bearers of Hurrian names are not recorded before the end of the Akkadian dynasty. Is it a coincidence that they appear shortly before the Gutian incursions? Did the Hurrian infiltration into the northwestern Zagros impact the original abodes of the Gutians? The Turukkeans, who inhabited several riverine valleys in Kurdistan and possibly Azerbaijan in the Old Babylonian period (Læssøe and Eidem 2001: 20), bore Hurrian names. Such names were common later in Mannea and Kurdistan.

Indo-Iranians

There is no evidence for the presence of Iranians (see Chapter 21) on the Iranian plateau before 881 BC. There is no direct and continuous connection between the slight Indo-Aryan (or Dardic-Nuristani, according to Diakonoff 1996) presence on the Armenian plateau and the Fertile Crescent c.1600–1400 BC and the later Indo-Iranians who settled across the entire Iranian plateau. Indo-Aryans and Dardians belong to different branches of the Indo-Iranian linguistic family. The written sources are mainly Assyrian royal inscriptions and official letters (from or to the king), covering much of the relevant territory, as well as Urartian royal inscriptions referring only to the northwesternmost part of the territory under discussion. The only Aramaic inscription from Iran (Bukan in Mannea) does not contain any Iranian names. The direct evidence consists of territories, political entities, settlements, rulers, and to a much lesser extent officials in the northwestern section of the Iranian plateau. Commoners are totally absent. The numerous gentilicia recorded in the Neo-Assyrian sources refer to territories and settlements, not to tribes. The only tribes mentioned are the Medes and Scythians. There is no proof of a physical link between the territory of Parsua in the northwest and the Persians in Persis/Anshan. Most of the Median entities were located between the two big and crystallyzed polities of northwestern Iran, viz. Mannea in the northwest and Ellipi in the southeast. The Median presence on the fringe of the eastern desert ("the distant Medes" in the Assyrian inscriptions) has a special relevance to the issue of the direction of the Iranian penetration to northwestern Iran, although they are first mentioned in c.680 BC, long after the beginning of the Iranian wandering.

The earliest attestations of Iranian names date to 881 BC. They refer to rulers of Zamuan entities located in the northwest. However, the chronology in this case is less significant, taking into account that the references are a function of the direction and depth of the Assyrian penetration. The Assyrians first invaded Zamua and adjacent regions in the central Zagros, then the other sections of the Zagros, and only later did they come into contact with the eastern Medes. Moreover, the percentage of Iranian anthroponyms is highest in the east, high in the center, and negligible in the west. This indicates that the Iranians penetrated from the east rather than from the Caucasus, since the percentage of Iranian anthroponyms in the northwest, near Azerbaijan, is low. All together there are 128 entities, practically half Iranian and half non-Iranian. Eastern Media is entirely Iranian whereas the westernmost region, viz. Kurdistan, is overwhelmingly non-Iranian; central Media is mostly Iranian. A comprehensive analysis of the anthroponymy and toponymy (207 and 447 names, respectively) of Media and adjacent regions leaves no doubt that Greater Media underwent a process of Iranianization during the Neo-Assyrian period.

The Iranians were the largest group (max. 45.37, min. 32.36 percent) in Greater Media. All the other discernible ethnolinguistic groups (non-Iranians) are far behind. Next come the Kassites (7.72–5.31 percent) and the Hurro-Urartians (6.74–0.96 percent). The Iranians were the largest group in all Median regions. Only in Kurdistan (excluding Zamua) were the Hurro-Urartians (with various degrees of plausibility) the largest group (22.21–7.4 percent). Elsewhere the Kassites were the second-largest group ("Inner" and Western Media: 18.18–15.15 percent and 12.24–6.12 percent respectively; northwestern Media and Parsua: 6.66 percent and 6.88–3.44 percent, respectively). Only in Mannea and its environs, which were on the Urartian border, were the Hurro-Urartians the second-largest group (14.8–3.7 percent compared with 3.7 percent Kassites). In Kumme, a very old Hurrian cultic center, the Hurrian names are in the majority. The northwesternmost expansion of Old Iranian anthroponymy reached Muṣaṣir and Hubushkia.

There is a fairly high degree of accord between the toponymy and the anthroponymy of most regions. As expected, the pre-Iranian substratum is better represented in the toponymy than in the anthroponymy. The Iranian toponymy prevails in Eastern Media (54.54–27.27 percent), "Inner" Media (32.28–12 percent), Western Media (18.74–14.58 percent), and Parsua (10.41–4.16 percent). It has the same percentage as the Kassite toponymy in Gizilb/punda and environs (16–4 percent). The Hurro-Urartian toponymy prevails in Mannea and Northwestern Media (10.95–2.43 percent and 22.63–3.77 percent, respectively) which bordered on Urartu. In both regions the Iranian toponymy is the second-largest group (9.72–1.21 percent and 7.54–5.66 percent, respectively), whereas in the regions with predominantly Iranian toponymy Kassite is almost always the second-largest group (Parsua: 4.16–2.08 percent; "Inner" Media 12–4 percent; and Western Media 11.46–7.29 percent). The Zamuan toponymy has limited Kassite and Hurro-Urartian components (5.95–2.38 percent and 3.57 percent, respectively). Iranian is the second-largest group (4.76–2.38 percent). The low percentage of Akkadian anthroponyms and toponyms accords well with the Babylonian influence, which was already a thing of the past (but discernible in southwestern Media, notably Bīt-Hamban).

In addition to the textual evidence and considerable onomastic material, there is some archaeological evidence for the appearance of Iranians in western Iran. Young (1967) linked the gray-black monochrome ware with the appearance of the Iranians in northwestern Iran. Based on the rich find from a series of mounds in northwest Iran and cemeteries rich in ceramic and metallurgic material in Luristan, he pointed out that there is an absolute rupture between the material culture of the Late Bronze and that of the early Iron Age. A decade later, Pogrebova (1977) cast doubt on the linkage between the gray-black monochrome ware and the Iranians. Following her, and under the influence of Kramer (1977), Medvedskaya (1982) made a thorough analysis of ceramics, metallurgy, and burial practices arguing for continuity from the Late Bronze to early Iron Age, under steady Syro-Mesopotamian influence, whereas a connection between northwestern Iran and Trans-Caucasus is clear only in the first millennium BC. However, the proponents of the linkage between material culture and new ethnic elements (for the methodological problems, see Burmeister 2000) were still left with important arguments in their arsenal, namely the burial of horses (cf. Kuzmina 2007: 21, 23, 26) and the appearance of extramural cemeteries.

There are two possible routes of Iranian penetration (neither of which excludes the other): via south Central Asia, through northern Khorasan and Gorgan; and via the Caspian gates in the eastern Caucasus. The first possibility is supported by finds from a series of mounds in the submontane zone along the Turkmenistan border with Iran, especially Namazga Tepe. Masson and Sarianidi (1972: 137ff., 146, 155ff.) consider the possibility that the later Namazga assemblage (Later Bronze until *c.*1000 BC) is connected with the Iranian tribes. More meaningful seems to be the striking resemblance of the plan of the fortress at Ulug Depe near Namazga Depe to that of Nush-e Jan in early Iron Age Media, as well as Tepe Ozbaki near Teheran (Lecomte 2007: 213ff., 217). The second possibility is not supported by archaeological finds, but inspired by an analogy with the Cimmerian–Scythian invasion from the Caucasus to Iran and Anatolia in the eighth century BC and the survival of the name Sakasene, referring to a region between the Kura and the Aras rivers in Azerbaijan (Grantovskiy 1971). This argumentation is not decisive since the route is too narrow for a sizable migration capable of changing the ethnolinguistic character of a huge territory. After all, the Cimmero-Scythian invasion was ephemeral. Geopolitical considerations thus favor the eastern route. Massive migrations to western Iran are possible, mainly via Khorasan, which form a very wide front for penetration. This is supported by well-recorded, later analogical incursions, such as that of the Parnoi into Parthia and the Sakas into Drangiana (Sakastan > Sistan). Regarding chronology, the fact that Iranians are found in 881 BC as far west as the westernmost region of Iran indicates that their migration to eastern Media must have started several generations earlier, *c.*1000 BC. Earlier penetration remains speculative.

The eastern part of Elam, which is basically a plateau, gradually became Iranianized in the course of the second third of the first millennium BC. It then came under the domination of the Persians. This part, notably ancient Anshan, was renamed Pārsa (Persis). Rollinger (1999: 124) points out that the current theory of the Persian wandering into Anshan from the northwestern Zagros is unlikely due to the difficult topography. It seems to me that certain Iranian groups entered Anshan from Ellipi, which probably bordered on Elam, and were influenced by Elamite culture and that its population included people bearing Iranian names as early as the eighth century BC. Does the occurrence of the "yurt" on the Arjan bowl (Álvarez-Mon 2010: 126) indicate another wave of Iranians who penetrated Anshan from the east (via Sistan and Kerman)? This must remain highly hypothetical as long as this "yurt" is an isolated find. Even if the artist's acquaintance with the "yurt" is based on gift-exchange among the elites (as proposed by Stronach 2004: 12; cf. Álvarez-Mon 2010: 127), it is highly unlikely that the upper class of a small entity in eastern Elam had a special relationship with a Central Asian polity. The horizon of such gift-exchange was not very broad, presumably only within Greater Elam and adjacent regions. Later analogies may be helpful for the reconstruction of migration routes from northeastern Iran, as well as, perhaps, a quest for Persian–Eastern Iranian isoglosses (cf. Zadok 2011: 121–2). Based on early medieval models from central Europe, Rollinger (1999: 124–7) proposes that the process of Persian ethnogenesis took place in Anshan/Persis. It should be remembered that several hundred years later, most individuals who are recorded in the sizable prosopographical sample from Persepolis in the heart of Anshan/Persis bore Iranian names. The most likely assumption is that the gradual Iranianization of Anshan/Persis would have been impossible without the penetration of a significant number of Iranian-speaking people into this region during the Sargonid period, the more so since the very ancient and sophisticated Elamite sociocultural structures were more prestigious than those of the newcomers: a case in point is the use of Elamite script and language for administrative purposes, even after hundreds of years of Persian presence and domination (cf. Henkelman 2003, 2008), despite the fact that people with Iranian names had become the majority. Persians settled in Susiana as well (see Tavernier 2011: 240). Eastern Iranians (Arachosians, Drangianians, Bactrians, and Gandharians) and Indians are mentioned in the rich documentation from Persepolis, where western Iranians (Medes, Parthians, Parikanians, Carmanians, and Akaufachiyans) are also recorded (Henkelman and Stolper 2009). Except for the Persians, who left texts in Old Persian, none of the other numerous Iranian groups left any written remains. Nevertheless, there is no doubt that the most important Iranian group in northwest Iran was the Medes. Median is the most common dialect judging from lexical material in NE and Late Babylonian texts (Tavernier 2011: 243).

OTHERS

The Assyrians deported Israelites, Tabalians (Cappadocians), and probably other westerners to Media. Babylonian refugees settled in Elam. In the long run, these deportees probably assimilated with the indigenous population (some of the Babylonian exiles presumably returned to their country). The Achaemenid authorities brought workmen from all over the empire to Fars and Khuzestan: Babylonians (Henkelman and Kleber 2007), Transpotamians and upper Mesopotamians ("Assyrians"), Arabians, Egyptians,

Armenians, southeastern Anatolians ("Hattians"), Lycians, Lydians, Cappadocians, Carians, Thracians ("Skudrians"), and Greeks (including Cyprians) (Henkelman and Stolper 2009).

FURTHER READING

The relevant sources are listed below but for Elamite personal names and their linguistic affiliation, the reader is advised to consult Zadok (1984). For toponyms, tribal and personal names in western Iran as conveyed in Neo-Assyrian cuneiform sources, see especially Zadok (2002). Iranian personal names in the later Neo- and Late Babylonian sources are conveniently surveyed in Zadok (2009).

References

Álvarez-Mon, J. 2010. *The Arjān Tomb: At the crossroads of the Elamite and the Persian Empires*. Leuven: Acta Iranica 49.
Ancillotti, A. 1981. *La lingua dei Cassiti*. Milan: Unicopli Universitaria 103.
Briant, P. 2002. *From Cyrus to Alexander: A history of the Persian Empire*. Winona Lake: Eisenbrauns.
Brinkman, J. A. 1976–80. Kassiten (Kaššu). *RlA* 5: 464–73.
Burmeister, S. 2000. Archaeology and migration: Approaches to an archaeological proof of migration. *CA* 41: 539–67.
Carter, E., and M. W. Stolper. 1984. *Elam: Surveys of political history and archaeology*. Berkeley/Los Angeles/London: University of California Publications, Near Eastern Studies 25.
Carter, E., R. K. Englund, F. Grillot-Susini, S. Lackenbacher, M. Salvini, and F. Vallat. 1998. Elam. *EnIr* 8: 301–44.
Diakonoff, I. M. 1996. Pre-Median Indo-Iranian tribes in northern Iran? *BAI* 10: 11–13.
Edzard, D. O., G. Farber, and E. Sollberger. 1977. *Die Orts- und Gewässernamen der präsargonischen und sargonischen Zeit*. Wiesbaden: RGTC 1.
Eidem, J. 1992. *The Shemshāra archives 2: The administrative texts*. Copenhagen: The Royal Danish Academy of Sciences and Letters, Historisk-fil. Skrifter 15.
Eilers, W. 1957–8. review of K. Balkan, *Kassitenstudien*. *AfO* 18: 133–8.
Eph'al, I. 1999. The Bukān Aramaic inscription: historical considerations. *IEJ* 39: 116–21.
Farber, W. 1975. Eine elamische Inschrift aus der 1. Hälfte des 2. Jahrtausends. *ZA* 64: 74–86.
Francfort, H.-P., and X. Tremblay. 2010. Marhaši et la civilisation de l'Oxus. *IrAnt* 45: 51–224.
Gershevitch, I. 1969. Amber at Persepolis. In *Studia Classica et Orientalia Antonino Pagliaro Oblata*, vol. 2, 167–251. Rome: Istituto di Glottologia.
Glassner, J.-J. 1986. *La chute d'Akkadé: l'événement et sa mémoire*. Berlin: BBVO 5.
Grantovskiy, E. A. 1971. *Rannyaya Istoriya Iranskikh Plemen Predney Azii*. Moscow: Nauka.
Groneberg, B. 1980. *Die Orts- und Gewässernamen der altbabylonischen Zeit*. Wiesbaden: RGTC 3.
Hallo, W. W. 1957–71. Gutium. *RlA* 3: 708–20.

———. 2005. New light on the Gutians. In *Ethnicity in Ancient Mesopotamia*, ed. W. H. van Soldt, R. Kalvelagen, and D. Katz, 147–58. Leiden: PIHANS 102.

Henkelman, W. F. M. 2003. Persians, Medes and Elamites: Acculturation in the Neo-Elamite Period. *CE*: 181–231.

———. 2008. *The other gods who are: Studies in Elamite-Iranian acculturation based on the Perspolis Fortification Texts*. Leiden: AchHist 14.

Henkelman, W. F. M., and K. Kleber. 2007. Babylonian workers in the Persian heartland: Palace building at Matannan in the reign of Cambyses. *PR*: 163–76.

Henkelman, W. F. M., and M. W. Stolper. 2009. Ethnic identity and ethnic labelling at Persepolis: The case of the Skudrians. In *Organisation des pouvoirs et contacts culturels dans les pays de l'empire achéménide*, ed. P. Briant and C. Chauveau, 271–329. Paris: Persika 9.

Henning, W. B. 1978. The first Indo-Europeans in history. In *Society and history: essays in honor of Karl August Wittfogel*, ed. G. L. Ulmen, 215–30. Hague: Mouton.

Hinz, W., and H. Koch. 1987. *Elamisches Wörterbuch*, 2 vols. Berlin: *AMI* Ergänzungsband 17.

Horsnell, M. J. A. 1999. *The year names of the first dynasty of Babylon*, vols. 1–2. Hamilton: McMaster University Press.

Jones, C. E., and M. W. Stolper. 1986. Two late Elamite tablets at Yale. *FHE*: 243–54.

Kramer, C. 1977. Pots and peoples. *ML*: 91–112.

Kutscher, R. 1989. *The Brockmon tablets at the University of Haifa: Royal inscriptions*. Haifa: Shay Series of the Zinman Institute of Archaeology.

Kuz'mina, E. E. 2007. *The origin of the Indo-Iranians*. Leiden: Leiden Indo-European Etymological Dictionary Series 3.

Læssøe, J., and J. Eidem. 2001. *The Shemshāra Archives 1: The Letters*. Copenhagen: Royal Danish Academy of Sciences and Letters, Historisk-fil. Skrifter 23.

Lecomte, O. 2007. Entre Iran et Touran: Recherches archéologiques au Turkménistan méridional (2001–2006). *CRAIBL*: 195–226.

Masson, V. M., and V. I. Sarianidi. 1972. *Central Asia: Turkmenia before the Achaemenids*. New York/Washington: Thames and Hudson.

McAlpin, D. W. 1981. *Proto-Elamo-Dravidian: The evidence and its implications*. Philadelphia: Transactions of the American Philosophical Society 71.

Medvedskaya, I. N. 1982. *Iran: Iron Age*. Oxford: BAR Int Ser 126.

Oppenheim, A. L. 1969. Babylonian and Assyrian historical texts. In *Ancient Near Eastern texts relating to the Old Testament*, 3rd ed., ed. J. B. Pritchard, 265–317. Princeton: Princeton University Press.

Pecorella, P. E., and M. Salvini. 1984. *Tra lo Zagros e l'Urmia. Ricerche storiche ed archeologiche nell'Azerbaigian iraniano*. Rome: Incunabula Graeca 78.

Pogrebova, M. N. 1977. *Iran i Zakavkaz'e v Rannem Železnem Veke*. Moscow: Akademiia nauk SSSR, Institut vostokovedeniia.

Postgate, J. N. 1988. *The archive of Urad-Šerūa and his family: A Middle Assyrian household in government service*. Rome: Pubblicazioni del Progetto "Analisi elettronica dei Cuneiforme."

Reiner, E. 1969. The Elamite language. In *Altkleinasiatische Sprachen*, ed. B. Spuler, 54–118. Leiden: HdO I/2/2.

Richardson, S. 2005. Trouble in the countryside *ana tarṣi* Samsuditana: Militarism, Kassites, and the fall of Babylon I. In *Ethnicity in Ancient Mesopotamia*, ed. W. H. van Soldt, R. Kalvelagen, and D. Katz, 273–89. Leiden: PIHANS 102.

Rollinger, R. 1999. Zur Lokalisation von Parsu(m)a(š) in der Fārs und zu einigen Fragen der frühen persischen Geschichte. *ZA* 89: 115–39.

Soldt, W. H. van. 2008. The location of Idu. *NABU* 2008/55.
Steinkeller, P. 1982. The question of Marhaši: A contribution to the historical geography of Iran in the third millennium B.C. *ZA* 72: 237–65.
Steve, M.-J. 1992. *Syllabaire élamite: Histoire et paléographie.* Neuchâtel: Civilisations du Proche-Orient, Série 2, Philologie 1.
Stronach, D. 2004. On the antiquity of the Yurt: Evidence from Arjān and elsewhere. *Silk Road* 2/1: 9–18.
Tavernier, J. 2011. Iranians in Neo-Elamite texts. *EP*: 191–261.
Vallat, F. 1993. *Les noms géographiques des sources suso-élamites.* Wiesbaden: RGTC 11.
van Dijk, J. J. A. 1970. Remarques sur l'histoire d'Elam et d'Eshnuna. *AfO* 23: 63–71.
Westenholz, A., and W. Sallaberger. 1999. *Mesopotamien: Akkade-Zeit und Ur III-Zeit.* Fribourg/Göttingen: OBO 160/3.
Young, T. C., Jr. 1967. The Iranian migration into the Zagros. *Iran* 5: 11–34.
Zadok, R. 1984. *The Elamite onomasticon.* Naples: AION Supplement 40 to 44/3.
———. 2002. *The ethno-linguistic character of Northern Iran and Kurdistan in the Neo-Assyrian period.* Tel Aviv: Archaeological Center Publications.
———. 2005a. Kassites. *EnIr* online edition.
———. 2005b. Lulubi. *EnIr* online edition.
———. 2006. Mannea. *EnIr* online edition.
———. 2011. The Babylonia-Elam connections in the Chaldaean and Achaemenid periods. *Tel Aviv* 38: 120–43.

CHAPTER 21

IRANIAN MIGRATION

MICHAEL WITZEL

INTRODUCTION

During the Iron Age, peoples speaking Iranian (Ir.) languages were present from the borders of Romania in the west to Xinjiang (western China) and the Kamboja land in Afghanistan in the east; in the south they extended down to the Persian Gulf and the Indian Ocean. They included the Scythians of the Ukraine and their Saka relations in western and eastern Central Asia (former Soviet Central Asia, and Eastern Turkistan, now Xinjiang). While only small fragments of the Scythian language are known from Classical Greek sources, Saka texts have been preserved in manuscripts of the first millennium AD. Both groups survive as the Ossete of the Caucasus and the Sariqoli in southwest Xinjiang.

The Iranians of Greater Iran (modern Iran, Afghanistan, and Baluchistan) were linguistically divided into a western and an eastern group. The western Iranians included the Medes and the Persians proper, in the Tehran and Fars areas respectively. Eastern Iranian languages were spoken in most of Afghanistan (Avestan, Bactrian), the Pamirs (Muža land; see below on Muža/Mūja-, and Burusho), and in the Greater Ferghana area (Sogdian). They survive in modern Pashto, Yaghnobi (from Sogdian), and a number of Pamir languages. Baluchi is a more recent addition in the east of a western Iranian language, spoken by immigrants from westernmost Greater Iran (*c*.1000 AD), where western Iranian Kurdish is spoken now (eastern Turkey, northern Syria and Iraq, and northwestern Iran).

The Iranians constituted a cultural, not always sufficiently appreciated, link between the Mediterranean, East Asia, and South Asia from early on. After the horse was domesticated around 4000 BC, and especially so after horseback riding became prominent in the early Iron Age (*c*.1000 BC), the steppe belt, stretching from the plains of Hungary and Romania up to the borders of Korea, favored the quick movement of people (Sherratt 2006; on the beginning of the Iron Age in northwestern South Asia, at *c*.1000 BC, see

Possehl and Gullapalli 1999; consequently, the date *ante quem* of the Bronze Age Ṛgveda must predate 1000 BC).

Sources: Languages, Texts, Archaeology, Genetics

Language

The split of Iranian from Indo-Iranian (IIr)—and thus from its continuants Indo-Aryan (IA: Vedic, etc.) as well as Nuristani—is marked by a number of common innovations (mutations, to use the genetic term). Innovations include the very typical IIr. **gh*, **dh*, **bh* > Iran. *g, d, b*; IE **k'* > IIr. **ć* > Iran. *s* :: Ved. *ś*; IE **g'(h)* > IIr. **dz'(h)* > Iran. *z*; *p, t, k* + consonant > *f, ϑ, x* + consonant, and so on. Prominently, this included—around 1000 BC (Hintze 1998)—that of IIr. *s* > Iran. *h*, which functions as a shibboleth for all Iranian languages (IIr. **sapta* "seven" > Iran. **hafta* [Avest. *Hapta*]: Vedic *sapta*). This development is not found in Mitanni-Indo-Aryan, Vedic and Nuristani. Harmatta (1992) was wrong with his "eleven stages" of changes and the dates attributed to them (see below; for correct details, see Hoffmann 1988). Similarly, his discussion of the "movements of Proto-Indians and Proto-Iranians and their migration routes" (Harmatta 1992: 370–8) is flawed in its historical reconstruction and is full of unwarranted speculation.

Subsequently, the eastern and western Iranian languages are differentiated from each other by a number of innovations. Eastern Iranian (Avestan) has a large number of developments (Hoffmann 1988) that separate it both from Proto-Iranian and from Old Persian. In addition, we have some indications of early local dialect developments in Bactria, such as the name of the area itself: Iran. *bāxϑrī* > local Bactrian *bāxδī* (loaned into Indo-Aryan as Atharvavedic *bahli-ka/balhi-ka*, cf. Patañjali, *Mahābhāṣya Bāhlī*, see Witzel 1980).

Persian, too (we know little about the Old Median [Med.] language that nevertheless differed from Old Persian [OP], such as Med. [recorded in OP] *aniyāha [bagāha]*: OP *aniyai*, Ved. *anye*), differs by a number of independent developments, most notably, Iran. *s* > OP *ϑ* (from IE *k',* pronounced as interdental spirant, as in English *thin; t*his seems to have been felt as so typical that it is imitated in some Avesta passages, *Yašt* 19.61 *iϑe*, 19.63 *yaϑna* for regular Avestan *yasna*, and also occurs, occasionally, in some dialect forms of regular words, see Hoffmann 1988) and Iran. *z* > OP. *d* [δ] (from original < IE *g'*; pronounced as a voiced interdental spirant as in English *the*, thus Persian *dipi* [δ*ipi*] > Skt. *lipi* "script") or the disappearance of *h* in *hu*, in the royal inscriptions.

These differences are embodied in the earliest Iranian texts, that is, the Zoroastrian *Avesta* and the Old Persian inscriptions. The latter were incised on stone and other objects in a newly invented cuneiform script during the Achaemenid empire, from 519 BC down to Artaxerxes II (405–359) or III (358–338), and represent the southwestern language that later developed into modern Persian (cf. Chapter 32). We do not have old texts from the Median area (a northwestern Iranian language), but we have first millennium AD texts in later forms of both western languages, found in manuscripts recovered in Xinjiang.

The language of Zoroaster (Zaraϑuštra) and his followers, Avestan, is preserved in manuscripts stemming only from the thirteenth century AD. It is still in use in Zoroastrian rituals. However, the Zoroastrian texts were composed in the Late Bronze Age and faithfully transmitted orally up to their first writing down during the Sasanian Empire; they are very similar in language and content to the Vedic texts of neighboring northwest India. We distinguish Old Avestan, that is the hymns (gāϑā) of Zaraϑuštra and a contemporary ritual text, the Yasna Haptaŋhāiti dealing with fire worship, and the Later or Young Avestan texts. These are more voluminous; they deal with ritual (Yasna), the poetic praise and description of important deities next to Ahura Mazdā (Yašt), and with the rituals concerning pollution and death (Vīdēvdād). The texts indicate a geographic area mostly concentrated on Bactria and Arachosia: in general, the countries surrounding the Hindu Kush mountains are mentioned (Witzel 2000); western Iran is by and large excluded, as is any mention of the Medes, Persians, or their empires. The *Avesta* does mention, however, Hyrcania/Gorgān (Vəhrkāna), and west of Gorgān, the country Gilān (Xnənta), as well as Rayi, whose geographic position is debated (on Avestan data in general, see Skjærvø 1995; Witzel 2000).

There are no early Sogdian, Scythian, and Saka texts. However, we can piece together some information from Classical Greek sources, notably Herodotus, on the Scythians (*Histories*, on the royal and other Scythians; cf. Witzel 2009a on Central Asian myth materials), and there are more limited materials in old Chinese texts that mention the eastern Central Asian Saka from about 700 BC onward. In addition, we have secondary sources, such as the many transcriptions of western Iranian names and loanwords in Classical Greek (Schmitt 1995; Mayrhofer 1979).

Archaeology

Archaeology provides a further important facet of the picture of the early Iranians. It must be emphasized, however, that the simplistic linkage of archaeological cultures with languages is just as dangerous as that with genes and ethnicities. Note especially the unbridled, free-associative accounts of Parpola (e.g., 1988, 2002) that even link—in spite of his own general caveats (Parpola 2002: 66ff.)—(sub)sections of Vedic texts with a particular archaeological culture. This approach completely neglects the fact that the superficial linkage of archaeological remains with languages and ethnicities remains extremely tenuous, if not impossible to achieve, in the absence of texts from the period. Unfortunately such speculations have been taken as fact by nonspecialists, resulting in the vicious cycle described above. Likewise, the linguistic–historical account by Harmatta (1992) and the archaeological–historical one by Lamberg-Karlovsky (2002) of the origin and development of the Indo-Iranians are similarly flawed and often factually wrong (for a detailed discussion of the questions involved, see Witzel 2000, 2003; cf. Francfort 2005: 262ff.). Instead, we have to refrain from unrestrained speculations, which are consequently avoided in this chapter. The data from various fields of study need to be presented separately, and should only rather cautiously be linked (as is done below in the case of the Andronovo–Sintashta culture). We just have to recall a case like that of France: a Celtic population speaking a Latin language but having a Germanic ethnic name (the Franks). Without written sources we cannot be certain whether a particular archaeological culture was mono- or multilingual, or whether a certain language or its dialects were spoken in several adjacent archaeological cultures. In addition, scholars are generally unaware of the theoretical suppositions and working methods of the various fields of study involved (archaeology, linguistics, genetics, texts) other than their own, but they still take over the results and speculations of these other fields, and then build their own theories based on those results and speculations (unrelated to their own specialization). Obviously these procedures lead to increasingly shaky results. When we employ the results of other fields of study we must be aware of the nature of such data and the tentative nature of the conclusions drawn from them.

Genetics

Over the past two decades, human population genetics based on the study of DNA has held out the promise of shedding further light on early human history. However, most genetic data are derived from currently living humans; data from ancient DNA, when available, pose serious problems of contamination (past or present) and of reliability due to the frequently very fragmentary nature of the genetic material recovered. In addition, while the relative dates derived from the reconstruction of the genetic pedigree (in technical terms, a phylogenetic approach based on the cladistic arrangement of mtDNA or Y chromosome haplogroups that are transmitted via the female versus the male line only) are reliable (depending on the "molecular clock" of genetic mutations, based on the chimpanzee–human split at seven or five million years ago), they have huge error bars of several thousand years even for the Indo-Iranian (c.2000 BC) and the subsequent Old Iranian period. That makes them, in the present state of the art, virtually useless in determining dates of assumed genetic character of the populations speaking Old Iranian.

However, the male Y chromosome haplogroup R1 (subclade R1a1a [R–M17 or R–M198]) has frequently been linked to the Indo-Europeans and Indo-Iranians. It is widespread both in Eastern Europe and in South Asia, where it may have originated, albeit at a date *much* earlier than Indo-European language or Indo-Iranian migrations. These movements into Greater Iran and India cannot yet been traced genetically due to wide error bars and the lack of sufficient resolution of the subclade R1a1.

At any rate, our genes have little to do with the languages we speak: changes in language can occur within one or two generations and are not restricted to periods of immigration or foreign dominance but can result from cultural influences emanating from a prominent neighboring civilization. Nevertheless, in spite of these caveats, we can discern a large degree of genetic continuity (Di Cristofaro et al. 2013; cf. Wells 2002, who was, however, not correct about early Central Asian settlements as Central Asia was settled comparatively late, from the west and the east), even after the Turkic migrations (*c*.600 AD), both in Xinjiang and western Central Asia: in both areas the genetic setup of the pre-Turkic periods has been largely preserved, and the "East Asian" overlay (of various percentages) can be clearly discerned. It must be noted, however, that *some* influx from the east predates the Turkic expansion, as demonstrated by the Pazyryk mummies (note the East Asian features of a man [burial no. 2] among the mummies found at Pazyryk in the Altai mountains, about the sixth to third centuries BC).

Patterns of Iranian migrations

A definition of the prehistoric and Old Iranian peoples would include: first, speaking one of the Iranian languages mentioned earlier; second, a (reconstructed) culture based on the vocabulary of the Iranian languages, preferably based on their actual texts; and third, better yet, a culture evidenced in archaeology. Obviously, such facts are progressively more difficult to obtain for periods that predate the actual texts composed in Iranian languages. In addition, we have to reckon with quick shifts in the adherence to existing polities (see below).

Importantly the speakers of Old Iranian did not enter a void: the Greater Iran area was occupied by other languages and peoples, such as the Elamites, Guti, Lullubi, Urartu, and those speaking entirely unknown languages: the inhabitants of Shahr-e Sokhta, Mundigak, and other archaeological sites, including the Bactria-Margiana Archaeological Complex (BMAC) area. Some of these populations have left substrate influences in Iranian languages.

The Indo-Iranian parent, an "offspring" of Indo-Europeans in the steppe belt

The earliest indications of Iranian speaking populations—who called themselves *arya* (the name *Iran* is derived from *aryānām xšaϑra* "the realm of the Aryans," Middle Persian *ērān šahr*; cf. Kellens 2005)—can be found in the linguistic reconstruction of the Indo-European (IE; technically speaking, we should use Proto-IE, Proto-IIr., etc., for languages that are reconstructed and not yet attested, such as the Old Iranian language Avestan, Old Persian, etc.) language family (Beekes 1995; Szemerényi 1996; Fortson 2010). Iranian is a branch of the Indo-Iranian subfamily (IIr.) that is closely related both to Indo-Aryan (Vedic, Sanskrit, Pali and later forms, down to Hindi, Kashmiri, Kalasha, etc.) and to the Nuristani (Kafiri) language group in northeastern Afghanistan. Indo-Iranian is very well reconstructed (e.g., Bartholomae, 1895–1911;

cf. Hoffmann and Forssman 1996; Oranskij 1977; Sims-Williams 2002) based on the materials found in Avestan, Old Persian, and Vedic Sanskrit texts: the innovations that have occurred between Indo-European and Indo-Iranian are obvious and well circumscribed. In addition, a comparison of the religion, ritual, and society mentioned in these texts allows a fairly comprehensive reconstruction of Indo-Iranian culture (see the summary in Witzel 2000).

These data are reconfirmed by many early loanwords transmitted from Indo-Iranian to the Uralic (Finno-Ugric, etc.; see Carpelan et al. 2001; Rédei 1986, 1988), due to a cultural cline, and to the Yeneseian (Ket, Kott, etc.) languages (Witzel 2003, cf. 2009a). Loans include the central Indo-Iranian concept of *ṛta* "active truth," according to which even the gods must act: Yeneseian: Kott *artʽa* "true, veritable" < IIr. **ṛta*; also Kott *c̓ak* "force," Kott *c̓aga* "strong" < IIr. *c̓ak* "to be able; force;" perhaps Ket *kuʾš*, Yug *kuʾs*, Kott *husa*, Arin *kus*, Pumpokol *kut* "cow" < IIr. **gāus/gu*, Iran. *gauš* and Tocharian A *ko*, B *keu*. Amusingly, Finnish *orja* (from Indo-Iranian *Arya*) means "slave" (cf. Pre-Saami **orja* > *oarji* "southwest," *årjel* "southerner," and Mordvin *urʽe, urä*, Votyak *var*, Syry. *ver* "slave" (Rédei 1986: 54). Clearly the Aryans were situated south of the Uralic peoples and caught as slaves.

There also are a few loans from Uralic into Indo-Aryan, such as the word for bee: Uralic **mekše* > Ved. *makṣ, makṣikā* "fly, bee" (note the importance of bees and beeswax for producing copper objects using the lost wax or *cire perdue* technique, a prominent feature in the Andronovo culture). This linguistic evidence allows us to locate the Indo-Iranian language and its speakers in the steppe belt, south of the Russian Taiga forests that were inhabited by Uralic speakers (Sherratt 2006: 48ff. points to the "edge of the forest zone" since bees live in the Taiga forests but not in the open steppe due to the absence of suitable nesting sites). In addition, we can discern a general time frame. The reconstruction of the ancestral IIr. language points to the Bronze Age—there was no word for "iron" yet—and to the early use of the horse-drawn, spoke-wheeled chariot (**ratha*), early forms of which have indeed been discovered at the Sintashta excavations dated to c.2000/1800 BC. IIr. *ratha*, Ved. *ratha*, Ir. *raϑa*, (Mitanni *Tuš-ratta*, Kassite *Abi-rattaš*) and related words: **rathin* "chariot driver," **rathai-štha* "the one who stands on the chariot: chariot driver," parts of the chariot, different from the earlier (IE) oxen wagon with heavy tripartite wheels (Ved. *anas*). The chariot has a yoke modified for horses (Ved. *yoga*), reins, and so on (the heavy bridle is later: *khalīna* is loaned from Hellenistic Greek; for further details see Raulwing 2000). However, the Sintashta "chariot" still was a rather clumsy vehicle that could not turn easily and was probably intended mainly for ceremonial purposes. Importantly, the grave in which it was found also contained the remains of horses, sacrificed for the deceased person. Based on this cumulative evidence we can be fairly sure that Indo-Iranian language and culture existed in the steppe belt *somewhere* between the Ukraine and the Tien Shan mountains. The exact location is more difficult to determine.

Some additional help comes from the early links that existed with the northern Caucasus languages, the ancestors of modern Cherkes and Chechen, among others. There are clear loanwords borrowed in both directions, such as **ajʽa* "goat" (Witzel

2003: Circassian *aća* "goat," Kabardian *aza* "goat for breeding"; Proto-North Caucasian has *ˀējZˀwē* Proto-Burushaski *aćas*, both of which are closest to PIE *Hag̑* [Indo-Iranian *ajˀa-*, Avestan *aza-*, Latvian *âzis* etc.]; note however Greek as *áiks*) and *aća* "horse" in Caucasian [Northeast Caucasian Udi *ek-, ekw-* < IE *h_1ekwos*; from IIr *aćwa-*: Northwest Caucasian: Circass. *šˀə*, Abkhaz (*a-*)*ćə* "the horse"]; Kartvelian [Georgian] *ačuća* ["horse," in children's language], cf. Harmatta 1992: 369).

However, the area where these languages were spoken may have extended much farther north, which would limit the location of the Indo-Iranian parent language to a narrower, north-south strip between the Taiga and the Caucasus languages (cf. Nichols 1997, 1998; however, her location of the homeland of the Indo-European speaking peoples in the eastern part of western Central Asia [Sogdia/Greater Ferghana, Bactria etc.] is to be rejected, as this region was inhabited by people speaking the Central Asian [Macro-Caucasian] substrate language; see Witzel 2003). Importantly, the connection with the northern Caucasus languages additionally allows us to tentatively posit the Indo-Iranian homeland in the steppe belt east of the Ukraine in Russia and western Kazakhstan near the Urals and the Yenesei plains languages (spoken in a much wider area of western Siberia, see Vajda 1998; cf. Witzel 2003). Therefore, the Indo-Iranians have frequently been linked to the widespread archaeological Andronovo culture (*c*.2200 BC) and its various regional variations such as the prominent Sintashta-Petrovka-Arkhaim culture (2200–1600 BC).

However, whole populations or smaller sections (notably the IIr. [and IE] sodalities or *Männerbund*; see Bollée 1981; Falk 1986) could, and indeed have, moved very quickly across the steppes—in an extreme case (the Mongolian mail riders) all the way from Mongolia to southern Poland in just a few weeks (cf. Hiebert 1995, 1998, on steppe–BMAC relations: steppe objects are found in the late BMAC levels, including a recently discovered foal, as well as some axe handles in the alleged image of a horse [or rather onager?]). In addition, the Indo-European and Indo-Iranian polities were very fluid: "tribes" coalesced and split up easily, as we can still witness in the oldest Indian (Vedic) text, the Ṛgveda (Witzel 1997a, 1997b) and in later Iranian history with Scythians, Sarmatians, Massagetai, and so on, down to the five, originally non-Iranian Yueji/Kushana tribes that quickly took over the eastern Iranian Bactrian language after *c*.140 BC, and later the multiethnic Hun realm, followed by the Avars and Pechenegs. A hint of the easy movement of people, *realia*, and ideas is presented by the strong influence of Indo-Iranian religion and ritual, across Mongolia, to the Koguryo realm of Manchuria/Korea as well as to their close relatives in Kofun-era Japan (at *c*.400 AD; cf. Witzel 2009a on the close connections between western Central Asian [Indo-Iranian] and Japanese mythology).

If we assume, according to the (later Indo-Iranian) texts, a reconstructed, steppe-based, mainly pastoral culture (summary in Witzel 2000, introduction) with a preponderance of cows (*gau*) and horses (*aćwa*); with a number of polities (*vić, *jˀana*); without permanent settlements, tenuously overlorded by a great chieftain (*rājan*), then a *tentative* link can be made with the Sintashta/Arkhaim culture, where a number of circular "towns" have been found that point to a temporary occupation and metalworking. They may have served as cultural centers of a polity for part of the year, notably during great rituals and festivals. One of them, for instance Sintastha (*c.*1800 BC), may have been connected with the great chieftain represented in religion by Varuṇa (one of the "other" half of the IIr. deities, those not connected with nature [Heaven, dawn, fire, water, wind, etc.], but that are abstractions turned into IIr. [Vedic/Iranian] deities: Varuṇa [Mitanni *uruuana/aruna*], Mitra/Miϑra "agreement," Aryaman/ Airiiaman "Arya-hood" [note the artificial formation: the suffix *-man* is allowed only after verbal roots, not after nouns/adjectives], Bhaga/Baga "share in bounty"/"God," Aṃśa "lot, part," Dakṣa "dexterity"]). Yet, all of this must remain tentative—probable, informed speculation that cannot be proven due to the absence of texts around 2000 BC.

Early Indo-Iranian migrations

Whatever the exact location of the Indo-Iranian-speaking people may have been around 2000 BC, it is clear that some of them started a move southward, across the western Central Asian deserts, soon after that date. This may have followed the great streams, and also the mountain-range pastures of the Tien Shan, down to the high mountain pastures of the Pamirs where, according to the *Ṛgveda* and *Avesta*, the best Soma/Haoma was found at Mount Mūjavant (cf. the later Saka Haumavarga in Achaemenid times; Houben 2003). An Indo-Iranian-speaking people first appears with the Indo-Aryan words and personal names preserved in the texts of the Mitanni, a Caucasus people related to Urartu and the North Caucasus languages, such as Chechen, among others (Diakonoff 1971; Diakonoff and Starostin 1986) written on cuneiform tablets in northern Syria and northern Iraq around 1400 BC. Their language clearly is neither Proto-Indo-Iranian nor Old Iranian but has typical Indo-Aryan (Vedic) features such as *aika* "one" instead of Ir. *aiva* (Thieme 1960; note the horse-race terms in Kikkuli's training manual and the Indo-Aryan names of Mitanni nobility, as far south as Jericho; see Mayrhofer 1974, and the new edition of Kikkuli by Starke 1995). Notably, in a related Mitanni–Hittite agreement, the great Indo-Iranian (and thus Indo-Aryan) gods Varuṇa, Mitra, Indra, and the Nāsatyas (Aśvins) are mentioned and the importance of horses and horse racing is indicated by Kikkuli's training manual preserved in Hittite.

This Indo-Aryan move toward the Zagros Mountains and the Mitanni was a precursor of the waves of Indo-Iranian and Iranian migrations that were to follow (cf. the Indo-Aryan loanwords in the more or less contemporary Kassite realm of southern Mesopotamia, see Balkan 1954; there also are some very doubtful IA words attested at the time of the Guti/Lullubi). Some of this is visible in the many loanwords that have entered from local languages into both the Old Iranian and Old Indo-Aryan (Vedic) languages, albeit sometimes in slightly divergent forms.

Having moved across the pastures along the desert rivers and the pastures of the Tien Shan mountain ranges toward the area of the BMAC culture (*c.*2200–1700 BC) in southern Turkmenistan (Margiana) and northern Afghanistan (Bactria), the Indo-Iranian speaking populations must have interacted with the BMAC population(s). The extent of the BMAC language clearly excludes the southern belt of Iran, where Elamite was spoken, not just in Susiana (Khuzistan) and Anšan (Fars and surroundings), but also in southern and central Iran, in the areas of Tepe Yahya (Simaški?), and Shahdad (Tukriš?), but apparently not farther east than Marhaši/Parahšu in the Bampur/Jiroft area (on some of these place names see now Steinkeller 2014a); otherwise the southern boundary of the BMAC language is not clear.

Indo-Iranian interaction with the BMAC is clearly visible in the many terms reflecting agriculture, village life (Witzel 2003: §3.3ff.: plowshare, seed, semen, sheaf, mark, lump; well, source, pit, canal; yeast, bread; firm structure, permanent house, pillar, brick, wooden peg, sand, gravel; dish, bowl, spit, axe, pointed knife, club, cloak, hem, thread, coarse garment, cloth, needle), and religion that appear in Old Iranian and Vedic, including even highly prominent religious terms (black magic, *atharwan "priest," ṛṣi "seer," *učig "sacrificing priest," gift, offering, sacrifice) such as Indra (*Indra), Gandharva (*g[h]andharw/b[h]a "a demi-god or demon"), Śarva (*ćarwa "name of Rudra"), and Soma (to heal, *anću "Soma plant"). This sacred drink is not of Indo-European antiquity but was clearly added to the Indo-Iranian heritage in Central Asia, building on the Indo-European heritage of the sacred mead drink (ambrosia) including its Indo-European mythology. Another clear indication of strong cultural ties is the transformation that the Indo-European dragon myth has undergone in this area (Witzel 2000, 2009a). Even more than in the Vedic version, the Avestan form of the myth of killing the dragon shows BMAC features that we can discern in the art and sculptural remains of that culture.

Exactly when this interaction took place is open to further study, notably in archaeology as we do not have texts of this period, unless we project the data from the Ṛgveda and Avesta back into this period. Some indication is provided by the cultures that were transformed in contact with the BMAC. As James Mallory has put it, "[During the] Indo-Iranian migrations from the steppe lands south into the historical seats of the Iranians and Indo-Aryans … these steppe cultures were transformed as they passed through a membrane of Central Asian urbanism. The fact that typical steppe wares are found on BMAC sites and that intrusive BMAC material is subsequently found further to the south in Iran, Afghanistan, Nepal, India and Pakistan, may suggest then the subsequent movement of Indo-Iranian speakers after they had adopted the culture of the BMAC" (Mallory and Adams 1997: 73). A different view was expressed by Pinault (2011: 503), who wrote, "les Indo-Aryens, s'il sont passés par cette région, n'ont pas transporté plus au Sud des elements materiels de la culture du BMAC" (cf. religious and mythological elements).

How far the Indo-Iranian populations had adopted BMAC cultural features is open to question as the first Indo-Aryan and Iranian texts show comparatively little influence— apart from the Central Asian village-type loanwords noted above—of the urban civilization of the BMAC. Instead, the Indo-Aryans continued with their mostly pastorally oriented culture when they moved on into the Hindu Kush (including Proto-Nuristani speakers? see Degener 2002 with various scenarios for their immigration to northeastern Afghanistan; the curious case of western IE strata in the New IA Bangani language of the western Himalayas should be noted; I assume that they moved in from north of the Himalaya [like the Ossetes in the Caucasus], and that they once were distinct neighbors of the Tocharians, who share certain "western" [or rather, pre-Satem] IE features; see Zoller 1988, 1989) and northwestern India (Gandhāra and Panjab) during the posturban periods following the collapse of the BMAC (c.1700–1400 BC) and Harappan civilization (1900–1300 BC). Vedic language and texts were present in these areas well before the onset of the Iron Age, c.1000 BC (note the Akra excavation in Bannu, northwest Pakistan, see http://www.arch.cam.ac.uk/bannu-archaeological-project/bannu.pdf). The linguistic relationship between Mitanni-Indo-Aryan and Vedic indicates that Vedic is younger by a few hundred years than the Mitanni-IA of Mesopotamia (c.1400 BC). But this is as far as we can go; we cannot yet date the first entry into India archaeologically. Some late Bronze Age pastoral sites, excavated in southern Tajikistan, may however provide a hint (Litvinsky and P'yankova 1992, especially on Beshkent and Molali, with various types of steppe influences). As in the Indus area after the collapse of the Harappan civilization, many people in the Bactrian area had taken to pastoralism. Some of them may have been Indo-Aryan speaking. These sites, and possible continuants in the Hindu Kush and Gandhāra, need to be explored further.

Iranian migrations

We may speculate, but obviously cannot be sure, that the southward move of the early Indo-Aryans to the Mitanni and BMAC areas left a certain void in the northern steppe belt, which was then "filled" by their Proto-Iranian speaking relatives. It has long been asserted (Burrow 1973; Parpola 1999) that the "Iranians," that is, the populations speaking Proto-Iranian and Old Iranian languages, moved south only after the early Indo-Aryans had left, and thus occupied their areas in Greater Iran as well as all across the steppe belt. In doing so they must have "acculturated" any remaining Indo-Aryan speaking populations in these areas, such as possibly the Sindoi, reported by Greek authors in the Kuban area north of the Caucasus (Witzel 2003), and others in Bactria and Arachosia (note the non-Zoarastrian features of some eastern Iranian populations, see Witzel 2011: 509, n. 99). However, the arrival of horse-riding tribes must not automatically be connected with the arrival of speakers of Iranian, just as the arrival of horses in the Near East, more than a thousand years earlier, is not directly linked to that of IA speakers. Potts has stressed that horse burials in northern Iran in the later second millennium BC are preceded by a long tradition of horse breeding in the northern Zagros, for example, in Lullû, as reported in an Old Babylonian cuneiform text (Potts 2010: 6).

The Iranian group was characterized by several innovations: the linguistic ones have been characterized above; culturally and technically speaking, they made use of the newly developed metal, iron, and of the horse in a new fashion: horseback riding (OP *asbri*) replaced the "old-fashioned" chariot (Anthony 2007). Riding made their herdsmen and warriors much more mobile than before. It is, however, not correct that riding was invented only at the beginning of the Iron Age.

Their Indo-Aryan neighbors have preserved a few accounts of riding in their oldest, Bronze Age text, the Ṛgveda (Coomaraswamy 1941; Falk 1994). The handful of relevant passages, however, points to riding as a commoner's occupation: the gods ride chariots, while their "people," the Aśvins (the IA *Dioskuroi*), polluted by contact with human illnesses, ride horses. Riding may also have been looked down upon for another reason: the sweating of horses. An early Mesopotamian king is advised by his courtiers not to ride, for precisely this reason (Drews 1989). We do not know whether the general use of the horse for riding actually originated with the Iranians, however, it appears so in the texts (OP *asbāri,* Avestan *aspāyaoδa* "fighting on horseback?") while the usage is rare even in later Vedic (*aśvasāda*), and much of the terminology is loaned from Greek only in the post-Alexandrian period (*khalīna* "bit," *pariṣṭoma* "blanket," etc; the date of the stirrup is still disputed: one may be seen, at *c*.150 BC, in a sculpture from the Sanchi Stūpa in western India). Be that as it may, we can discern overlays of Iranian language on preexisting Indo-Aryan layers in greater Iran (Hintze 1998).

Preexisting populations

At this stage, it is opportune to review the linguistic and ethnic situation in Greater Iran (cf. Chapter 20). Apart from Indo-Aryan forays into northern Mesopotamia (Mitanni-IA), there is clear evidence of a number of preexisting local populations. To begin with, the linguistically isolated Elamites were located in what is now southwestern Iran: Susiana (OP Ūvja) and the mountainous areas east of it (Anšan, ancient Persis); however, it is not entirely clear how far their settlements extended to the east (Vallat 1980, see now Maekawa and Mori 2011; Steinkeller 1982, 1998, 2007, 2008, 2011a, 2014b). Similarly, the northwest had been occupied by various groups such as the Guti (*c*.2150 BC) and Lullubi; and some Caucasian populations (Mitanni, Urartu; on their languages see Diakonoff 1971; Diakonoff and Starostin 1986: 74ff.). The Gilan area on the southern shores of the Caspian Sea (Avest. *Xnənta*) was regarded as alien even at the time of the Younger Avesta and the only record of its language is its name.

The same is true of the languages of eastern Greater Iran, west of the Indus civilization. We do not have written records, though this has been claimed for Jiroft (Madjidzadeh 2011). This applies to the Bronze Age Mundigak culture just as well as to the BMAC in the north. One may call this area, along with the Indus (Farmer et al. 2004; note also that there was some back and forth between periods with written documents and those without them in northern Iraq in early prehistory), a "no-script zone." The languages of the BMAC area, and even the desert areas and riverine oases north of it, can be reconstructed to some extent by triangulation of known languages in the surrounding areas (Yeneseian, Caucasian, Tocharian, and Indo-Iranian, including its daughter languages Iranian and Vedic Sanskrit). It can be seen, then, that large parts of this area reflect remnants of the newly reconstructed Macro-Caucasian language family (Bengtson 1990, n.d.), situated between its North Caucasian and Burushaski (Pamir) members (Witzel 2003). All of the above stands in contrast to the general opinion that, in contrast to Vedic, Old

Iranian does not have a non-Indo-Iranian substrate, a point now disproven by the discovery of Central Asian substrate languages (Witzel 2003; Lubotsky 2001, Pinault 2003; in addition, scores of substrate words, in addition to Elamite ones, have been documented in a pilot project [2004, not yet published] for OP and Avestan).

It is into this general western Central Asian area that speakers of the Indo-Iranian languages intruded. As mentioned above the Indo-Aryans came first. When Iranian speakers followed them sometime during the late second millennium BC, they encountered both the local languages just mentioned as well as that of their relatives, the Indo-Aryans. It is clear that they substituted the Iranian version of certain river names (Sarasvatī, Proto-Iran. *Harahvaitī, OP Hara[h]uvatiš, local Young Avestan Harax^{v}aitīš, Greek Arachosia; Hintze 1998), while the move from IIr. *s* to Old Iranian *h* was still underway, as is seen in the Assyrian attestation in the northwest of Ahura Mazdā as *Ašara Mazaš* (^{d}aš-ša-ra ^{d}ma-za-aš) at about 1000 BC (Hintze 1998). Around this time we have to assume the activity of the religious reformer Zaraθuštra (and his colleagues), who probably stemmed from the Afghan–Iranian–Turkmen border area. His Gāθās (and the ritual text, Yasna Haptaŋhāiti) were composed in a dialect older than the bulk of the Avesta texts. However, even the Young Avestan text Vīdēvdād still mentions, several hundred years later, some areas with aberrant, non-Zoroastrian behaviors (such as burying the dead, noted above) that in part reflect older, Indo-Iranian or Vedic ideas, some of which were retained, until 1895, by the third IIr. group, the Nuristani, and their eastern neighbors, the IA Kalasha in Chitral, Pakistan, who still worship *Indr* and other IIr. deities (cf. Degener 2002: 114; and in detail, Witzel 2004). Other areas such as the high mountains—"At the sources of the Raŋhā" Vīdēvdād 1.19; probably the Burusho of Hunza, northern Pakistan (Avestan *Muža*, Vedic *Mūja-vant*, Tibetan *Bru-ža*, first-millennium colophons: *Prūṣava*, Sanskritized as *Puruṣa*)—are characterized as having "non-Aryan overlords." The lands north of the "Avestan area" had their own eastern Iranian languages such as Sogdian (modern Yaghnobi), and the Pamir languages, unknown until little more than a century ago.

In sum, we notice a gradual linguistic (later Vedic and early Indian grammatical sources [Yāska's *Nirukta*, Patañjali's *Mahābhāṣya*] know of the language of the Kamboja in eastern Afghanistan, who said *śavati* "he goes," which reflects Late Avestan *šauuati*, instead of Vedic *gacchati*) and cultural replacement of Indo-Aryan by Iranian (even Muža/Mūja, the originally much more extensive Burusho land in the Pamirs, is already called Zoroastrian in *Yašt* 13.125; apparently some part of the area was Indo-Aryan speaking: in the local name *Dāštāgni* we find *agni* "fire deity" instead of Avestan *ātar* [seen, e.g., in the names at *Yašt* 13.102], however, some Muža had become Zoroastrians) in the area of Greater Iran (no such problems in the northern steppe belt: fluid tribal unions: Arya, Saka, Massagetai, Saka *tigraxauda/haumavarga*, Sarmatians, etc., and later: the Huns, Hungarians, Khazars, Cumans, Pechenegs, etc.), finally leading up to the current situation with the western languages, Kurdish in the extreme west and Baluchi in the extreme east of Greater Iran, while another western language, Persian, has occupied all other areas from Persis and Media (Tehran) to Afghanistan and southern Tajikistan (in its Dari and Tajik forms).

First appearances of Iranians in history

Western Iranian

As mentioned above, some of the earliest mentions of Iranian languages and populations occur in Mesopotamian sources of the early first millennium BC, beginning in 879 BC. Several Assyrian kings then conducted campaigns against Paršuas (from 843 BC). In 836/7 BC Shalmaneser III campaigned in the east, venturing through Paršuas and receiving tribute from twenty-seven "kings." Median tribes (cf. Chapter 22) are first mentioned under the Assyrian king Tighlath-Pileser III (744–727 BC), and numerous times later along with other highland peoples. In 744 BC a new *Paršua* province was created. By the time of Sargon (*c*.715 BCE), Iranian names (e.g., *Ašpabarra*, "horse rider") appear and Iranians were depicted at the new palace of Dūr-Šarrukin (mod. Khorsabad) near Niniveh.

After the Cimmerian invasion of northwestern Iran around 715 BC, the Scythians, who followed them according to Herodotus, founded a kingdom in Azerbaijan (under Kaštaritu) and governed Media (*c*.652–625) until the emergence of a Mede kingdom under Cyaxares. The western Iranians thus appear on the eastern horizon of the Mesopotamians, in the Zagros mountains and the highlands east of it, just as the Guti, Lullubi, Kassite, and Mitanni IA did up to a millennium earlier.

Eastern Iranians

It is much more difficult to chronicle the arrival of Iranian speakers in the eastern parts of Greater Iran. The earliest Indian text, the *Ṛgveda*, helps to some extent as it mentions certain locations and names in the area, notably in book 8, the Kāṇva *maṇḍala*. Certain western Afghan place names occur, in their IA, however, not yet in their Avestan form: the Sarasvatī and the Herat River, Sarayu, still have *s*, while the Iranian forms have *h*: Haraxvaitī, and so on, and OP Haraiva and Avestan Harōiiu (for the Herat province, Areia). Furthermore, apart from the occurrence of camels that are rare even in later Vedic texts (attested in the late Vedic ritual text *Baudhāyana Śrauta Sūtra* [*c*.500 BC?] which is set in eastern Uttar Pradesh [Kosala]; for this connection see Witzel 2011 on the close relations of eastern North India with the Northwest [Gandhāra]), we have a number of personal names such as Kānīta (the Scythian *Kanítēs* of Greek sources, see Hoffmann 1939 [= 1975–6: 9]; further names include *Parśu, Kaśu*, etc.).

Other names are more difficult to assign and correlate. There is the enigmatic mentioning of *Tugra, tugrya* in the *Ṛgveda* (an enemy of Indra and Kutsa, 6.26.4; 6.20.8; 10.49.4, etc.; Tugrya = the legendary Bhujyu 8.32.20), usually explained from *tuj* "to impel." However, the word may sometimes refer to the central Iranian settlement of Tukriš, compare later Iranian *Tuyrān, Turyastān* (Mayrhofer 1986–2001 1: 65). Vedic

Paṇi may be the IA form of the Iranian tribal name Parna who were located in the area north of Herat. The linguistic development of *-rn-* would have led to Vedic **paṇa*. As the Paṇi usually appear as the enemies of the Vedic tribes, it may be that we are dealing here with semimythical memories of older foes in northern Afghanistan or the BMAC area and that this name simply has been transferred to contemporary Ṛgvedic enemies in the Panjab, whose fortifications *(pur)* and cattle the Arya wanted to conquer. Another name for enemies, *dasyu*, is more generic: Iranian has *dahyu* (OP) that indicates the provinces of the Persian Empire, except for the area of the Persians themselves *(Pārsa)*. Thus the *dahyu* areas are the "foreign," originally hostile areas (in Avestan the equivalent *daiŋ'hu* merely means "country, area"). Closely related is the term for "slave," Vedic *dāsa* (Greek *doûlos*, from Mycenean *dosero-* [**doselos*]). However, it turns up in Iranian, with a Saka form, as Dāha (Avestan *då:ha*), the name of a population in the western BMAC area (Greek *Dáiai*, *Dáoi*, Latin *Dahae* as the name of a Saka tribe east of the Caspian Sea; cf. Bartholomae 1904: 744). Apparently it was at first a denigrating nickname, just like Finnish *orja* < *arya* "slave."

As for later Indian and Iranian interactions, in the early post-Ṛgvedic text, the *Atharvaveda* (c.1000 BC), and also later on, the Bactrians (Avestan *Bāxδī*) appear as Balhika/Bāhlika (in Vādhūla Śrautasūtra's Mantra section; Patañjali's *Bāhlī* 4.2.99: 292.2; note especially Śatapatha Brāhmaṇa: Balhika, the designation of an eastern North Indian king, "the Bactrian," next to a *Cākra*, perhaps the Avestan land *Caxra* V. 1.16 [?]; for more on the Saka [Śaka/Śākya] influx into eastern North India just before the period of the Buddha, c.400 BC, see Witzel 2009b) and toward the end of the Vedic period, an Iranian speaking people in eastern Afghanistan appears as Kamboja (cf. OP Kambujiya [Cambyses], cf. Mayrhofer 1986–2001 1: 307; Witzel 1980; the identification of the Pashto/Pakhto with *Paktha*, a tribal name, "the fifth" in the *Ṛgveda*, is rejected by Mayrhofer 1986–2001 2: 61).

Movements of Eastern and Western Iranians, Again

As far as the exact route of migration of Iranian-speaking populations is concerned, we must distinguish between those speaking western and eastern Iranian. Theoretically one could assume an osmosis-type spread of Iranian. However, even this currently more "fashionable" model would require two different routes (see above). It has been assumed by some that the western Iranians (Medes and Persians) moved into Greater Iran using the narrow Daghestan plain east of the Caucasus because they first appear in Mesopotamian sources east of the Zagros Mountains. However, just like their predecessors, the Mitanni-Indo-Aryans (note Mitanni-IA *mani* "jewel, ornament," for Ved. *maṇi*, Mayrhofer 1986–2001 1: 293), they must have passed through the BMAC area as they have a number of BMAC loanwords (such as *mani* "jewel"). Like the Indo-Aryans first, and the eastern Iranians later, who settled in eastern Greater Iran (Avesta*n speakers, Kamboja*), they will rather have moved through the Bādgīš gap (Avestan *Vāiti. yaēsa*) along the Herat (Tedzhen) River. From there, they will have split up, moving west versus south and east.

Apart from these several migrations, we must also take into account later, secondary regionalism among the West and East Iranian languages (modern Persian has many Median [Parthian] elements; similar, secondary mutual influences of neighboring ethnicities are not uncommon, note, e.g., the language of the Anglo-Saxons and Jutes, later also the Vikings, in first millennium AD England), with mutual influences of the languages involved, resulting in the "eastern block" of Bactrian, Sogdian, and the pre-Pashto/Pamir languages, and the "western block" of Median and Old Persian, including the much later Kurdish and Baluchi. The development of the "northern Iranian block," from the Ukraine Scythians to the Xinjiang Saka (it must be noted, however, that Khotanese Saka has undergone strong influences from the Greater Pamir/Hindu Kush area that constituted a local *sprachbund;* this includes the retroflex consonants, unknown to Iranian, except for the *sprachbund* area's Pashto, and the latecomer at *c.*1000 AD, Eastern Baluchi), was facilitated by the relatively effortless exchanges in the steppe belt.

FURTHER READING

The two seminal papers on the migration of the Iranians are Burrow's (1973) and Thieme's (1960) articles on the Indo-Aryan, not Indo-Iranian, loanwords in Mitanni. A general, more or less up-to-date overview—though uneven in parts (e.g., Parpola)—is Sims-Williams (2002). The archaeological side of the argument is best represented by Anthony (2007), Hiebert (1995), and Mallory (1998, 2002). The ever-increasing genetic data are best approached through Underhill et al. (2010) and Underhill and Kivisild (2007), as well as the paper by Julie Di Cristofaro et al. 2013 that deals with the Greater Hindu Kush area.

REFERENCES

Anthony, D. 2007. *The horse, the wheel, and language: How Bronze-Age riders from the Eurasian steppes shaped the modern world*. Princeton: Princeton University Press.

Balkan, K. 1954. *Kassitenstudien*, vol. 1, *Die Sprache der Kassiten*. New Haven: AOS.

Bartholomae, C. 1895–1911. *Grundriss der iranischen Philologie. Ester Abschnitt. Sprachgeschichte*, vol. 1, *Vorgeschichte der iranischen Sprachen*. Strassburg: Trübner.

———. 1904 (repr. 1961). *Altiranisches Wörterbuch*. Berlin: De Gruyter.

Beekes, R. S. P. 1995. *Comparative Indo-European linguistics: An introduction*. Amsterdam/Philadelphia: John Benjamins.

Bengtson, J. D. 1990. An end to splendid isolation: The Macro-Caucasian phylum. *Mother Tongue* 10.

———. n.d. Genetic and cultural linguistic links between Burushaski and the Caucasian languages and Basque. Presentation at the 3rd Harvard Round Table on the Ethnogenesis of South and Central Asia, 2001.

Bollée, W. B. 1981. The Indo-European sodalities in Ancient India. *ZDMG* 131: 172–91.

Burrow, T. 1973. The Proto-Indo-Aryans. *JRAS*: 123–40.

Carpelan, C., A. Parpola, and P. Koskikallio. 2001. *Early contacts between Uralic and Indo-European: Linguistic and archaeological considerations.* Helsinki: Suomalais-Ugrilainen Seura.

Coomaraswamy, A. K. 1941. Horse-riding in the Ṛgveda and Atharvaveda. *JAOS* 62: 139–40.

Degener, A. 2002. The Nuristani languages. *IILP*: 103–17.

Diakonoff, I. M. 1971. *Hurrisch und Urartäisch.* Munich: Kitzinger.

Diakonoff, I. M., and S. A. Starostin. 1986. *Hurro-Urartian as an Eastern Caucasian language.* Munich: Kitzinger.

Di Cristofaro, J., E. Pennarun, S. Mazières, N.M. Myres, A.A. Lin, S.A. Temori, M. Metspalu, E. Metspalu, M. Witzel, R.J. King, P.A. Underhill, R. Villems, and J. Chiaroni. 2013. Afghan Hindu Kush: Where Eurasian sub-continent gene flows converge. *PloS One* 8/10: e76748. doi: 10.1371/journal.pone.0076748.

Drews, R. 1989. *The coming of the Greeks.* Princeton: Princeton University Press.

Falk, H. 1986. *Bruderschaft und Würfelspiel.* Freiburg: Hedwig Falk.

———. 1994. Das Reitpferd im Vedischen Indien. In *Die Indogermanen und das Pferd*, ed. B. Hänsel and S. Zimmer, 91–101. Budapest: Archaeolingua Series Minor 4.

Farmer, S., R. Sproat, and M. Witzel. 2004. The collapse of the Indus-Script thesis: The myth of a literate Harappan Civilization. *Electronic Journal of Vedic Studies* 11/2: 19–57.

Fortson, B. W., IV. 2010. *Indo-European language and culture: An introduction*, 2nd ed. Malden/Oxford: Wiley-Blackwell.

Francfort, H.-P. 2005. La civilization de l'Oxus et les Indo-Iraniens et Indo-Aryens en Asie Centrale. *AAIAC*: 253–328.

Harmatta, J. 1992. The emergence of the Indo-Iranians: The Indo-Iranian languages. *HCCA* 1: 357–78.

Hiebert, F. T. 1995. South Asia from a Central Asian perspective. In *The Indo-Aryans of ancient South Asia*, ed. G. Erdosy, 192–212. Berlin/New York: De Gruyter.

———. 1998. Central Asians on the Iranian Plateau: A model for Indo-Iranian expansionism. In *The Bronze Age and Early Iron Age peoples of eastern Central Asia*, ed. V. H. Mair, 148–61. Washington/Philadelphia: Journal of Indo-European Studies Monograph 26.

Hintze, A. 1998. The migrations of the Indo-Aryans and the Iranian sound-change $s > h$. In *Sprache und Kultur der Indogermanen*, ed. W. Meid, 139–53. Innsbruck: Innsbrucker Beiträge zur Sprachwissenschaft 93.

Hoffmann, K. 1975–6. *Aufsätze zur Indoiranistik*, vols. 1–2, ed. J. Narten. Wiesbaden: L. Reichert Verlag.

———. 1988. Avestan language. *EnIr* 3: 47–62.

Hoffmann, K., and B. Forssman. 1996. *Avestische Laut- und Flexionslehre.* Innsbruck: Innsbrucker Beiträge zur Sprachwissenschaft 84.

Houben, J. E. M. 2003. The Soma-Haoma problem [1. Introductory overview and observations on the discussion (J. E. M. Houben); 2. Report of the Workshop (J. E. M. Houben); 3. Report concerning the contents of a ceramic vessel found in the "white room" of the Gonur

Temenos, Merv Oasis, Turkmenistan (C. C. Bakels); 4. Margiana and Soma-Haoma (Victor I. Sarianidi); 5. Soma and Ecstasy in the Rgveda (G. Thompson). Proceedings of a Workshop on the Soma-Haoma problem organized by the Research school CNWS, Leiden University, July 3–4, 1999]. *Electronic Journal of Vedic Studies* 9. http://www.ejvs.laurasia.com/~india/ejvs/. Accessed October 29, 2011.

Kellens, J. 2005. Les Airiia- ne sont plus des Āryas: Ce sont déjà des Iraniens. *AAIAC*: 233–52.

Lamberg-Karlovsky, C. C. 2002. Language and archaeology: The Indo-Iranians. *CA* 43: 63–88.

Litvinsky, B. A., and L. T. P'yankova. 1992. Pastoral tribes of the Bronze Age in the Oxus Valley (Bactria). *HCCA* 1: 379–94.

Lubotsky, A. 2001. The Indo-Iranian substratum. In *Early contacts betwen Uralic and Indo-European: Linguistic and archaeological considerations*, ed. C. Carpelan, A. Parpola, and P. Koskikallio, 301–17. Helsinki: Suomalais-Ugrilainen Seura.

Madjidzadeh, Y. 2011. Jiroft tablets and the origin of linear Elamite writing. In *Cultural relations between the Indus and the Iranian plateau during the third millennium BCE*, ed. T. Osada and M. Witzel, 219–44. Cambridge, MA: Harvard Oriental Series, Opera Minora 7.

Maekawa, K., and W. Mori. 2011. Dilmun, Magan, and Meluhha in early Mesopotamian history. In *Cultural relations between the Indus and the Iranian plateau during the third millennium BCE*, ed. T. Osada and M. Witzel, 245–69. Cambridge: Harvard Oriental Series, Opera Minora 7.

Mallory, J. P. 1998. A European perspective on Indo-Europeans in Asia. In *The Bronze Age and Early Iron Age peoples of eastern Central Asia*, ed. V. Mair, 175–201. Washington/Philadelphia: Journal of Indo-European Studies Monograph 26.

———. 2002. Archaeological models and Asian Indo-Europeans. *IILP*: 19–42.

Mallory, J. P., and D. Q. Adams. 1997. *Encyclopedia of Indo-European culture*. London/Chicago: Fitzroy Dearborn.

Mayrhofer, M. 1974. *Die Arier im vorderen Orient—ein Mythos?* Vienna: Sitzungsberichte der Österreichischen Akademie der Wissenschaften, phil.-hist. Kl 294/3.

———. 1979. *Iranisches Personennamenbuch*, vol. 1. *Die Altiranischen Namen*. Vienna: Verlag der Österreichischen Akademie der Wissenschaften.

———. 1986–2001. *Etymologisches Wörterbuch des Altindoarischen*. Heidelberg: C. Winter.

Nichols, J. 1997. The epicentre of the Indo-European linguistic spread. In *Archaeology and language I: Theoretical and methodological orientations*, ed. R. Blench and M. Spriggs, 122–48. New York: Routledge.

———. 1998. The Eurasian spread zone and the Indo-European dispersal. In *Archaeology and language II: Correlating archaeological and linguistic hypotheses*, ed. R. Blench and M. Spriggs, 220–66. New York: Routledge.

Oranskij, I. M. 1977. *Les langues iraniennes*. Trans. J. Blau. Paris: Klincksieck.

Parpola, A. 1988. The coming of the Aryans to Iran and India and the cultural and ethnic identity of the Dāsas. *StOr* 64: 195–302.

———. 1999. The formation of the Aryan branch of Indo-European. In *Archaeology and Language, III: Artefacts, languages and texts*, ed. R. Blench and M. Spriggs, 180–207. London and New York: Routledge.

———. 2002. From the dialects of Old Indo-Aryan to Proto-Indo-Aryan and Proto-Iranian. *IILP*: 43–102.

Pinault, G.-J. 2003. Une nouvelle connexion entre le substrat indo-iranien et le tokharien commun. *Historische Sprachforschung* 116/2: 175–89.

———. 2011. review of G. Fussman, J. Kellens, H.-P. Francfort, and X. Tremblay, *Āryas, Aryens, et Iraniens en Asie Centrale*. *ZDMG* 161: 499–503.

Possehl, G. L., and P. Gullapalli. 1999. The Early Iron Age in South Asia. In *The archaeometallurgy of the Asian Old World*, ed. V. C. Pigott, 153–75. Philadelphia: University Museum.

Potts, D. T. 2010. Nomadismus in Iran von der Frühzeit bis in die Moderne: Eine Untersuchung sowohl aus archäologischer als auch historischer Sicht. *Eurasia Antiqua* 16: 1–19.

Raulwing, P. 2000. *Horses, chariots and Indo-Europeans: Foundations and methods of chariotry research from the viewpoint of comparative Indo-European linguistics.* Budapest: Archaeolingua Series Minor 13.

Rédei, K. 1986. *Zu den indogermanisch-uralischen Sprachkontakten*. Vienna: Sitzungsberichte der Österreichischen Akademie der Wissenschaften, phil.-hist. Kl. 468 Band.

———. 1988. Die ältesten indogermanischen Lehnwörter der uralischen Sprachen. In *The Uralic languages: Description, history and foreign influences*, ed. D. Sinor, 638–64. Leiden: Brill.

Schmitt, R. 1995. Iranische Namen. In *Namenforschung. Name Studies. Les nomes propres. Ein internationales Handbuch zur Onomastik. An International Handbook of Ononastics. Manuel international d'onomastique*, vol. 1, ed. E. Eichler, G. Hilty, H. Löffler, and H. Steger, 678–90. Berlin: De Gruyter.

Sherratt, A. 2006. The trans-Eurasian exchange: The prehistory of Chinese relations with the west. In *Contact and exchange in the Ancient World*, ed. V. Mair, 30–61. Honolulu: University of Hawai'i Press.

Sims-Williams, N. 2002. *Indo-Iranian languages and peoples*. Oxford: Oxford University Press.

Skjærvø, P. O. 1995. The Avesta as a source for the early history of the Iranians. In *The Indo-Aryans of ancient South Asia*, ed. G. Erdosy, 155–75. Berlin/New York: De Gruyter.

Starke, F. 1995. *Ausbildung und Training von Streitwagenpferden, eine hippologisch orientierte Interpretation des Kikkuli-Textes*. Wiesbaden: Studien zu den Boğazköy-Texten 41.

Steinkeller, P. 1982. The question of Marhaši: A contribution to the historical geography of Iran in the third millennium B.C. *ZA* 72: 237–65.

———. 1998. Marḫaši. *RlA* 7/5-6: 381–2.

———. 2007a. New light on Šimaški and its rulers. *ZA* 98: 215–32.

———. 2007b. Addenda to 'New Light on Šimaški and Its Rulers'. *Zeitschrift für Assyriologie* 98 (2007): 215–32. NABU 2008/15.

———. 2014a. Marhaši and beyond: The Jiroft Civilization in a historical perspective. *MLSR*: 691–708.

———. 2014b. On the dynasty of Šimaški: Twenty years (or so) after. *EAC*: 287–96.

Szemerényi, O. 1996. *Introduction to Indo-European linguistics*. Oxford: Clarendon Press.

Thieme, P. 1960. The "Aryan" gods of the Mitanni treaties. *JAOS* 80: 301–17.

Underhill, P. et al. 2010. Separating the post-glacial coancestry of European and Asian Y chromosomes within haplogroup R1a. *European Journal of Human Genetics* 18: 479–84.

Underhill, P., and T. Kivisild. 2007. Use of Y chromosome and mitochondrial DNA population structure in tracing human migrations. *Annual Review of Genetics* 41: 539–64.

Vaijda, E. J. 1998. The Kets and their language. *Mother Tongue* 4: 4–16.

Vallat, F. 1980. *Suse et Elam*. Paris: Boccard.

Wells, S. 2002. *The journey of man: A genetic odyssey*. Princeton: Princeton University Press.

Witzel, M. 1980. Early Eastern Iran and the Atharvaveda. *Persica* 9: 86–128.

———. 1997a. Early Sanskritization: Origins and development of the Kuru State. In *Recht, Staat und Verwaltung im klassischen Indien/The state, the law, and administration in Classical India*, ed. B. Kölver, 27–52. Munich: R. Oldenbourg.

———. 1997b. The development of the Vedic canon and its schools: The social and political milieu (Materials on Vedic Sakhas 8). In *Inside the texts, beyond the texts: New approaches to the study of the Vedas*, 257–345. Cambridge: Harvard Oriental Series, Opera Minora 2.

———. 2000. The home of the Aryans. In *Anusantatyai: Festschrift für Johanna Narten zum 70. Geburtstag*, ed. A. Hintze and E. Tichy, 283–338. Dettelbach: Münchener Studien zur Sprachwissenschaft Beihefte NF 19.

———. 2003. *Linguistic evidence for cultural exchange in prehistoric western Central Asia*. Philadelphia: Sino-Platonic Papers 129.

———. 2004. The Rgvedic religious system and its Central Asian and Hindukush antecedents. In *The Vedas: Texts, language and ritual*, ed. A. Griffiths and J. E. M. Houben, 581–636. Groningen: Forsten.

———. 2009a. Chuo Ajia Shinwa to Nihon Shinwa [Central Asian mythology and Japanese Mythology]. *Annual Report of the Institute for Japanese Culture and Classics, Kokugakuin University Heisei* 21 (September): 85–96 (in Japanese).

———. 2009b. Moving targets? Texts, language, archaeology, and history in the Late Vedic and early Buddhist periods. *Indo-Iranian Journal* 52: 287–310.

———. 2011. Gandhāra and the formation of the Vedic and Zoroastrian canons. In *Travaux de symposium international. Le Livre. La Roumanie. L'Europe.* 3rd ed., 20–24 Septembre 2010. vol. 3, *Etudes euro- et afro-asiatiques*, 490–532. Bucharest: Bibliothèque de Bucarest.

Zoller, C. P. 1988-9. Bericht über besondere Archaismen im Bangani, einer Western Pahari-Sprache. *Münchener Studien zur Sprachwissenschaft* 49: 173–200; 50: 159–218.

CHAPTER 22

ASSYRIA AND THE MEDES

KAREN RADNER

INTRODUCTION

Western Iran has a long history of contacts with Mesopotamia. Continual Assyrian involvement in the Zagros and beyond is attested only from the second half of the ninth century BC onward. This is a consequence of the kingdom of Urartu emerging as the overlord of eastern Anatolia, which had immediate political and economic consequences for Assyria. Being cut off from its traditional horse supplies endangered Assyria's military power directly but also threatened to limit its political weight in the wider region.

Assyria reacted to this threat by turning its attention toward Western Iran. First, the incursion into the Zagros were raids undertaken with no view of establishing permanent control and primarily intended to capture horses (Radner 2003: 38–43). From the mid-eighth century onward, however, this changed to territorial conquest after the political rivalry between Assyria and Urartu had shifted to the east and increasingly concerned access to, and territorial control of, the ancient overland trade route known as the Great Khorasan Road. It is that part of the Silk Route that leads from the plains of Mesopotamia along the Diyala headwaters into the Zagros mountain range and onto the Iranian plateau.

This chapter is a survey of the Assyrian presence in Iran, with a particular focus on the empire's interaction with the Medes. In addition to the relevant historical documents, we will discuss sites in Iran that offer evidence for Assyrian and/or Median occupation in the eighth and seventh centuries BC.

The First Assyrian Provinces in Iran: Bit-Hamban and Parsua

During their excursions into the east, the Assyrians often encountered evidence of previous cultural contacts with Mesopotamia: for example, the city of Silhazi was also known under the name "Fortress of the Babylonian" and there was a temple for Marduk at the city of Til-Aššurî, whose name means "ruin mound of the Assyrians" (Kroll and Radner 2006: 221). The usual route from central Assyria led through the province of Mazamua (established in 842 BC; Radner 2008: 51–2, no. 22), which corresponded to the Shahrizor plain in the Iraqi province of Sulaimaniyah. The city of Dur-Aššur (Bakr Awa near Halabja; Miglus et al. 2011), conquered and renamed (from Atlila) by Assurnasirpal II (r. 883–859 BC), constituted Assyria's most important gateway into the east and fulfilled the function of a gathering point for the army before they set off into the Zagros, until the reign of Assurbanipal (r. 668–c.627 BC; Borger 1996: 220: Prism B III 21–2 and parallels).

While there was always an awareness of the long shared history of the regions on both sides of the Zagros range (cf. Reade 1978; Abdi and Beckman 2007), the political and cultural contacts gained significantly in depth and focus when Tiglath-pileser III of Assyria (r. 744–726 BC) established as the result of his very first military campaign in 744 BC two provinces in Iran, Parsua and Bit-Hamban (Radner 2003: 44, 49–50, 57). For the first time in its history, Assyria directly controlled territory situated on the eastern slopes of the Zagros and along the Iranian part of the Silk Road.

The province of Parsua was situated in the northeastern headwaters of the Diyala (= Ab-e Sirwan), in the region of modern Sanandaj in Kurdistan province (Zadok 2001). Its capital was Nikkur (Radner 2003: 57) but the location of that city is unknown. Parsua adjoined Mazamua and the boundary between these two Assyrian provinces coincides roughly with the modern border between Iraq and Iran. Parsua shared its northern border with the kingdom of Mannea (south of Lake Urmia, with Qalaichi Tepe near Bukan as one of its centers: Hassanzadeh and Mollasalehi 2011) while Tiglath-pileser's second Iranian province Bit-Hamban, with the capital of the same name (Radner 2003: 57), was situated to the south of Parsua in the region of Kermanshah (Reade 1978: 138–9) along the main route of the Great Khorasan Road.

The governor of Mazamua, Aššur-da'nanni (year eponym in 733 BC), was tasked with supporting the newly established provincial administrations of Parsua and Bit-Hamban. He was specifically charged with monitoring and controlling the Medes, who were Assyria's new neighbors in the east. This is clear from one of his letters to the king (NL 100; Luukko 2012: no. 90) but especially from the fact that he led the campaign "against the mighty Medes of the rising sun" (Tadmor and Yamada 2011: nos. 41: 13'–15' and 47: 42) in 737 BC. This expedition brought the Assyrian forces into Median territories as far east as Mount Bikni: if this is indeed the Damavand range just north of Tehran (Reade 1995: 40), then only this mountain ridge separated the Assyrian troops from reaching the Caspian Sea. Unlike the war of conquest in 744, this second campaign had the character of a reconnaissance mission, undertaken in order to gather knowledge and make new contacts in the east.

According to the Assyrian sources from Tiglath-pileser III onward, both in royal inscriptions and archival documents, the Medes were politically organized in small principalities led by a hereditary ruler called "city lord" (*bēl āli*), highlighting the limited geographical influence they exercised (Lanfranchi 2003: 92–6); while all Median states encountered by the Assyrians are said to be controlled by a city lord, this political setup is not exclusive to the Medes but shared by other small states along the Great Khorasan Road such as in Namri, Bit-Sangibuti and Bit-Abdadani (Radner 2003: 49–50). The local rulers entered vassals treaties with the Assyrian king which gave them protection—against the empire's aggression but also against other powerful territorial states such as Mannea and Urartu—in return for their loyalty in war and peace and regular tribute payments, which were expected in the form of horses (unlike Assyria's vassals elsewhere, whose tribute was calculated in metal moneys).

The army's horse supplies were now secured, but maintaining control over the new provinces was more than anything a diplomatic challenge, as the region's political geography was as complex and difficult to navigate as the physical environment.

Median centers turned Assyrian strongholds: Kišessim and Harhar

In 719 BC, Sargon II became actively involved in the succession war that tore apart the vassal kingdom of Mannea and threatened to destabilize the entire Zagros region: in Mannea and in several Iranian principalities, rulers who were allied with the empire were forcefully replaced by men actively promoting an anti-Assyrian agenda (Radner 2003: 50). The ensuing military engagement led to a permanent Assyrian presence east of Parsua and Bit-Hamban and to the establishment of two further provinces in what is today the province of Hamadan. After the conquest of the city of Kišessim, it was renamed Kar-Nergal ("trading quay of the god Nergal") and made the center of a new Assyrian province that included the territories of six other rulers. One of these principalities was Bit-Sagbat which had already once before, a century earlier around 820 BC, found the attention of an Assyrian king when Šamši-Adad V (r. 823–811 BC) plundered "Sagbita, the royal city of Hanaširuka the Mede" (Grayson 1996: A.0.103.1 iii 35). This place has been identified with reasonable certainty with Ecbatana, modern Hamadan (Medvedskaya 2002), famous as the capital of what Herodotus described as a Median territorial state. To commemorate his conquests, Sargon had a stele set up at Kišessim which has survived on the site and therefore allows us to identify this Median city with the tell of Najafehabad, a village in the valley of Asadabad in Hamadan province (find circumstances: Levine 1972: 25; Gopnik 2011: 292–3; I follow Reade 1995: 39 in assuming that the stele cannot have been moved far due to its weight).

FIGURE 22.1 The Median fortress of Kišessim as depicted in Room 2 of Sargon II's palace at Dur-Šarrukin (mod. Khorsabad). Reproduced from P.-E. Botta and P. Flandin, *Monument de Ninive*, vol. 1, Paris, 1849, pl. 68bis.

The site of Najafehabad (34°46′59″ N, 48°04′55″ E) has never seen systematic excavations and it is therefore impossible to check the accuracy of the depiction that Sargon's stone masons created of the city (Fig. 22.1) as part of the wall decoration for his palace of Dur-Šarrukin (Albenda 1986: pls. 125–6). Identified by name, Kišessim is shown as a strongly fortified city with three rings of walls, all equipped with towers at regular intervals, protecting the upper town on the settlement mound, and a single wall with heavily fortified gates and towers surrounding the lower town in the plain. The topmost fortifications are decorated with pairs of deer antlers. Satellite imagery of Najafehabad as available on Google Earth (dated 5/7/2007) certainly suggests that the tell (180 × 120 m) houses the ruins of a very substantial upper town, with the contours of the mound suggesting the triple fortification lines indicated by the Assyrian depiction, and the oval lower town (600 × 300 m) is clearly discernable in the surroundings of the tell. Judging from the satellite image, only a few modern houses would seem to encroach onto the northern part of the lower town but as the villagers dig tunnels deep into the mound in order to stable their sheep and goats in winter (Gopnik 2011: 293) the site is likely to be less well preserved than the satellite image would suggest. Nevertheless, excavating at Najafehabad would most certainly reveal the remains of one of the most important Median centers of the eighth century BC and the subsequent Assyrian provincial capital city of Kar-Nergal.

Sargon's troops continued their march to the Median stronghold of Harhar, which had been for the past four years in open contempt of an earlier treaty with Assyria by withholding the tribute after dethroning the pro-Assyrian city lord Kibaba. The city was taken and renamed Kar-Šarrukin, "Sargon's trading quay." It was made the capital of a second new province that was made up of Harhar's territories and those of six other Median cities that had hitherto been under the ruler of their own city lords (Radner 2003: 50).

Harhar has been traditionally identified with a city *Kar(a)har of the Ur III and Old Babylonian sources, but this reading has now been abolished in favor of Karakina (Wilcke 2006) and there is now even less reason to seek Harhar's location near Kermanshah, as advocated, for example, by Levine (1975: 120; 1990: 258; also Radner 2008: 57, to be corrected). Geographical considerations instead favor a location further east in the area of Nehavand and Malayer. The best candidate is Tepe Giyan, where remains of a fortified palatial building with distinctive Assyrian architectural elements, such as the typical decorated door-socket capstones, were excavated in Level I on the settlement mound (Ghirshman 1951: 72, 78; Reade 1995: 39–40 and pl. II). This is most likely the seat of the Assyrian provincial administration, the construction of which is discussed in some letters from the correspondence of Sargon II (Fuchs and Parpola 2001: nos. 84, 94). Tepe Giyan is located in the Nehavand valley in Hamadan province, 12 km west of the modern town of Nehavand (34°10′53″ N, 48°14′38″ E). When the French excavations started in 1931, the substantial tell covered an area of 350 × 150 m and rose 19 m above the surrounding area but, during a visit in 2002, the present author found the high mound to be very badly disturbed. The results of the work undertaken in 2003 by a team led by Mehrdad Malekzadeh of Tarbiat Modares University (Tehran) have not yet been published. A lower town is attested in a letter to Sargon II mentioning building work on the "outer city wall" (*dūru ša kidāni*), parts of which needed to be accessed by boat for plastering (Fuchs and Parpola 2001: no. 94). This indicates that the city wall ran along the creek to the west of the high mound. Other than that, however, the intensive cultivation of the region and the modern settlement to the south of the tell make it difficult to trace the perimeter of this lower town.

Like Kišessim and some other Median fortresses, Harhar is depicted on the wall decoration for Sargon's palace at Dur-Šarrukin (Albenda 1986: pl. 112). Identified by name, a strongly fortified city is shown (Fig. 22.2) alongside a narrow river, which runs next to the outer wall (shown without towers)—this matches well the evidence of the Assyrian letter. A single inner wall, with two gates and towers at regular intervals, encircles the high settlement mound whose buildings are illustrated in considerable detail: in addition to a tree, there is a high-rising pillared structure and five tower-like buildings in different sizes. The biggest one is in part supported by a terrace built into the flank of the hill. A fire is burning on the roofs of this building and of the two others situated prominently at the top of the mound, possibly indicating the presence of fire temples comparable to that excavated at Nush-i Jan (see below).

The task of liaising with the new provinces in Iran fell again to the governor of Mazamua whose correspondence with Sargon concerns Bit-Hamban and Parsua and now also Kar-Nergal/Kišessim and Kar-Šarrukin/Harhar (Lanfranchi and Parpola 1990: nos. 199, 207, 226; Fuchs and Parpola 2001: no. 100). The distance from Mazamua (in or near modern Sulaymaniyah) to Harhar (Tepe Giyan) is 300 km as the crow flies,

FIGURE 22.2 The Median fortress of Harhar as depicted in Room 2 of Sargon II's palace in Dur-Šarrukin (mod. Khorsabad). Reproduced from P.-E. Botta and P. Flandin, Monument de Ninive, vol. 1, Paris, 1849, pl. 55 (detail).

which although still considerable, is of course significantly shorter than the distance of 525 km that separates Harhar from the region of modern Mosul where Dur-Šarrukin and Nineveh are situated.

Besides Najafehabad and Tepe Giyan, one other site in Iran has long been rumored to have yielded substantial Assyrian remains. This is Chogha Gavaneh, the settlement mound of Islamabad-e Gharb (formerly Shahabad) in Kermanshah province. However, the Akkadian cuneiform tablets unearthed in 1970 in a palatial building turned out to be from the early second millennium BC (Abdi and Beckman 2007) rather than Neo-Assyrian as previously reported (Kordevani 1971). While it is of course perfectly possible that this substantial but, due to its urban location, very badly damaged site was inhabited in the early first millennium there is at present no pressing reason to assume that there is an Assyrian occupation.

A FAMILY OF MEDES AT ASSUR

The situation in the two provinces Kar-Šarrukin and Kar-Nergal, which Sargon established in 716, was initially far from stable. This emerges very clearly from the king's correspondence with his governors and vassals in the area. For one, the Assyrian administration suffered from the effects of the unfamiliar and unforgiving weather conditions which slowed down building up the necessary infrastructure (Fuchs and Parpola 2001: nos. 85, 98, 100), and the twin horrors of snow and cold often cut off the new provinces from communication with central Assyria (e.g., Fuchs and Parpola 2001: no. 83). But local insurgence was the most pressing problem. Already in 715, the new provinces rose in rebellion on a scale that the local Assyrian officials were unable to contain. The imperial army had to return in order to regain control. The ensuing fighting was bloody and resulted, according to the inscriptions of Sargon II (Fuchs 1994: 108–9, 319: Khorsabad Annals 109–15; 210–11, 346–7: display inscription 64–5), in 4000 enemy warriors losing their heads and in the deportation of 4820 persons from the region. Some of them were brought to the city of Assur where people from Harhar and Hundir, the hinterland of Kišessim, are attested from the reign of Sargon II onward.

One extended family from Hundir lived in the residential quarter situated within the monumental gateway leading into the northwestern part of Assur. The remains of their two adjoining houses were excavated and found reasonably well preserved as they were buried under the debris of the adjoining city wall, which collapsed at some point after Assur was conquered in 614 BC (Miglus 1999: 301: Haus 65 and Haus 66). The houses and especially the family's archive found there give us insight into the household and its social and economic standing, especially in the later seventh century BC (Åkerman 1999–2001). This was a well-to-do family with members of three generations and their servants living together in two sizable, well-constructed houses of a surface of 240 and 320 m². Unlike the Egyptians who came to Assur in 671, after Esarhaddon's conquest of Memphis and Thebes, and whose distinct cultural heritage, including names, deities, and material culture, is apparent in the surviving sources of the late seventh century, the Iranian deportees—who of course had arrived at Assur already two generations earlier—seem to have adopted an Assyrian lifestyle by that time: nothing recognizably Iranian was found in the remains of their houses and by then, the whole family used Assyrian names.

The men of the family held positions at the Aššur temple (as did most of the city's notables) since the reign of Sargon II but as their profession was called "Hundurean," after their place of origin, it is not immediately obvious to us what their actual occupation was. They worked with a certain type of textile (*massuku*), which Soden (1972: 619) tentatively—but unaware of the geographical connection with Iran—identified as a rug. If this is correct then we may perhaps credit these deportees from Western Iran with introducing to central Assyria the art of hand-knotting carpets with a pile, the oldest surviving examples of which are known from the fifth century BC burials of Pazyryk (Rudenko 1970). The family was also involved in overland trade (Radner 2007); the destination for their caravans is not mentioned in any of the surviving documents but as caravan staff were given contracts for seven to twelve months, which were to cover both legs of the trip, it is clear that these were long-distance journeys. Given the family's origins, it is the most likely assumption that they were trading with their former homeland in Iran.

Although the surviving textual and material sources would initially seem to suggest that the Median deportees were thoroughly assimilated, maintaining their own distinct occupation (whatever its nature), whose designation invoked their native land, and also trading with the old country will have ensured that the Medes at Assur always preserved some part of their Iranian identity. Nothing in the sources informs us about their role in the Median assault on Assur or their fate after the conquest in 614. It is of course tempting to link the swift Median success with the fact that Medes lived right next to one of the city's principal gates and were therefore in a prime position to help the besiegers enter the city. After all, it is otherwise surprising that the Medes succeeded so swiftly when the Babylonian army had failed to take Assur during its surprise attack in the previous year, especially as the city's fortifications and food reserves had been increased in anticipation of a further attack (Miglus 2000: 88–9). It is in any case clear that the Medes attacked Assur from the north and that the main assault on the city wall was staged in the close vicinity of the Hundureans' houses (at the Tabira Gate: Miglus 2000: 86–7); after the taking of the city, the ensuing lootings were centered on the northern part of the city, with its temples and palaces. But whether we see them in 614 BC as loyal Assyrian citizens or collaborators of the Median invaders, the attack of Cyaxares and his Median army (see below) happens to mark with the centennial of this family's arrival in the city of Assur as deportees from Hamadan province, 480 km to the east as the crow flies.

The Assyrian administration of the Iranian provinces

Let us turn our attention back to Western Iran. In all Iranian provinces, the Assyrian strategy was to maintain and strengthen the local dynasts and thereby ensure their cooperation. Rather than replacing them with Assyrian officials, a dual system was operated that established an Assyrian administration alongside the traditional local power structures, which were actively supported provided that the leaders swore allegiance to the empire (Radner 2003: 53; Lanfranchi 2003: 111–12). Despite ruling over people and areas formally considered part of the Assyrian provincial system the city lords were treated like vassal rulers and in an extraordinary concession to their influence, rather than being expected to come to central Assyria in order to pay homage and deliver tribute to the Assyrian king, the governors (and their troops) instead went out to meet with them and collected the all-important horses (Fuchs and Parpola 2001: xxviii–xxix). The loyalty oaths of the Iranian allies required more than just words and good intentions. Tiglath-pileser and his successors kept Medes and other Iranians at the royal court (Radner 2003: 44), and while these individuals will have enjoyed a luxurious lifestyle they of course served as hostages who guaranteed their communities' collaboration with their lives. Although usurpers tried on several occasions to gain political capital among the native population by agitating against the Assyrian occupation, this system proved to be successful as the local elites stood to gain much from their cooperation with the empire. Their political and economic status was enhanced, rather than damaged, by their association with the Assyrian king (Lanfranchi 2003: 116–17):

However, when the new Assyrian administrations were established in Kišessim and Harhar in 716 it took some time before the peaceful coexistence with the occupiers became the norm. As we have already heard, Sargon's army had to return to Iran in 715 to regain control over the rebelling regions. Once subdued, some of the most important Median strongholds were turned into Assyrian fortresses, sharing the fate reserved earlier only for the administrative centers Kišessim and Harhar.

One of these cities was Kišešlu, which was renamed Kar-Nabû "Trading quay of the god Nabû" after its conquest. This took place at some point before October 715 BC, as we know from a clay tablet found in Assur that documents the sale of a garden in Kar-Nabû on the 22nd day of the seventh month of the Assyrian calendar (Faist 2007: no. 15). The vendor is the Third Man of the chariot team of Emuq-Aššur, the Assyrian commander (*šaknu*) of Kar-Nabû, who had previously made him a present (*tidittu*) of this garden. The buyer's name is lost but the list of witnesses provides us with information on those present when the sale was agreed. The first and therefore highest-ranking witness is Šamaš-belu-uṣur, identified as an "Assyrian magnate"; he was very probably the governor of Arzuhina at the time (and certainly in 710 BC when he serves as year eponym with that title), and he and his troops were therefore part of the imperial army dispatched to Iran. As Arzuhina adjoins the province of Mazamua in the southwest, this makes good sense from a logistical point of view. Kar-Nabu's commander Emuq-Aššur is the next witness, followed by the eunuch Tarditu-Aššur. The horse trader Ibû is listed after three witnesses without titles. Horse traders were part of the Assyrian army and oversaw the acquisition of horses for military purposes. The presence of all these witnesses makes it clear that although the document was found in Assur, the sale transaction was conducted in Western Iran, at the time the Assyrian military and administrative presence was established in Kišešlu. Replacing the treacherous local city lord as the highest-ranking official, Emuq-Aššur commanded the Assyrian garrison at Kišešlu. It is likely that the garden that he gifted to his Third Man had come into his possession when he took over from the disposed city lord. The volatile situation in Western Iran at that time may explain why the recipient of the gift would sell it on so quickly and with the explicit endorsement of Emuq-Aššur, who witnessed the sale. A professional soldier in active service will have had more use for silver in his pocket than a garden in need of regular care in order to yield fruit and profit, especially one in a war zone.

The Third Man's decision to sell his garden proved wise. The conflicts in the new provinces did not end with the war of 715 and the Assyrian army had to return in the following two years to assert the empire's control (Radner 2003: 53–5). But the strategy to leave the city lords locally in power, provided they accepted Assyrian sovereignty, eventually paid off and the dual system with the Assyrian provincial administration on the one hand and the local city lords on the other hand found an equilibrium that was profitable to both sides. After 713, the troubles subsided.

Kišešlu was one of six Median cities renamed by Sargon II as "Trading quay of (a god or king)," highlighting their importance in the overland trade. Sennacherib (r. 705–681) later followed his father's example and added another case to the list, giving it his own name. Kar-Nergal (Kišessim), Kar-Šarruken (Harhar), Kar-Nabû (Kišešlu), Kar-Sin (Qindau), Kar-Adad (Anzaria), Kar-Issar (Bit-Bagaia), and Kar-Sin-ahhe-eriba (Elenzaš) were all situated along the Great Khorasan Road and must have profited enormously from the rich trade between Mesopotamia and Central Iran and beyond. One can easily imagine how the heavily fortified strongholds, as we find them depicted in Sargon's palace, which control the narrow valleys that traverse the Zagros offered excellent opportunities to extract tolls from the passing caravans (Radner 2003: 51–2).

After observing the intensity with which Tiglath-pileser III and Sargon II devoted themselves to military actions in the Zagros Mountains, we see that Sennacherib, despite being active in the area, operated only on a very low-key level compared to his predecessors. The Iranian provinces were still under Assyrian control under the reign of Esarhaddon (r. 680–669 BC) as the extant sources and especially the so-called Oracle Queries, which sought divine guidance for imperial decision making (Starr 1990: nos. 41–73), demonstrate. But while these highlight that Medes but also Cimmerians, Scythians, and others in the region were perceived as a threat against the Assyrian administration the political situation, while as ever in constant flux, was stable enough for regular tribute-collecting campaigns to be undertaken as far east as Mount Bikni (see above) and the salt desert of Dasht-e Kavir (Radner 2003: 58–61): the Assyrian sources for Esarhaddon's reign clearly indicate that, as already in the mid-eighth century BC, the region around Tehran was considered Median.

The last mention of Medes in an official Assyrian inscription dates to c.656 and describes how three city lords rebelled against Assurbanipal (r. 668–c.627 BC), only to be punished by seeing their cities sacked before being brought to Nineveh before the king (Radner 2003: 61–2). Two Neo-Assyrian rock reliefs at Shikaft-e Gulgul (33°29′28″ N, 47°27′40″ E; discovered 1972) and nearby Heydarabad-e Mishkhas (33°31′46″ N, 46°34′24″ E; discovered 2009), both situated some 30 km southwest of the modern city of Ilam (Alibaigi et al. 2012: 37, pl. 4), may date to that time; the near identical depictions show the Assyrian king with five divine symbols but the inscription that accompanies the first relief is too poorly preserved to allow a secure identification with Assurbanipal. No further Assyrian sources are available that discuss the political situation in Western Iran and would allow us to bridge the forty-year gap before we see Cyaxares leading a unified Median army into what is today northern Iraq, allying with Nabopolassar of Babylon after the sack of Assur in 614 and succeeding in bringing down the Assyrian Empire with the fall of Nineveh in 612. Let us therefore turn to the archaeological exploration of Media itself.

THE ARCHAEOLOGY OF MEDIA

The two best-known Median sites in Iran are Godin Tepe and Tepe Nush-i Jan where large-scale excavations were undertaken in 1965–1973 and 1967–1977, respectively. They share common architectural features (Gopnik 2011: 319–20) and the pottery is similar (Gopnik 2003: 253, 264).

Godin Tepe is situated in the valley of Kangavar in Kermanshah province (34°31′06″ N, 48°04′06″ E). In its Level II.2 phase, the top of the ancient settlement mound was taken up by an impressive fortified citadel (120 × 50 m; Fig. 22.3), which was constructed

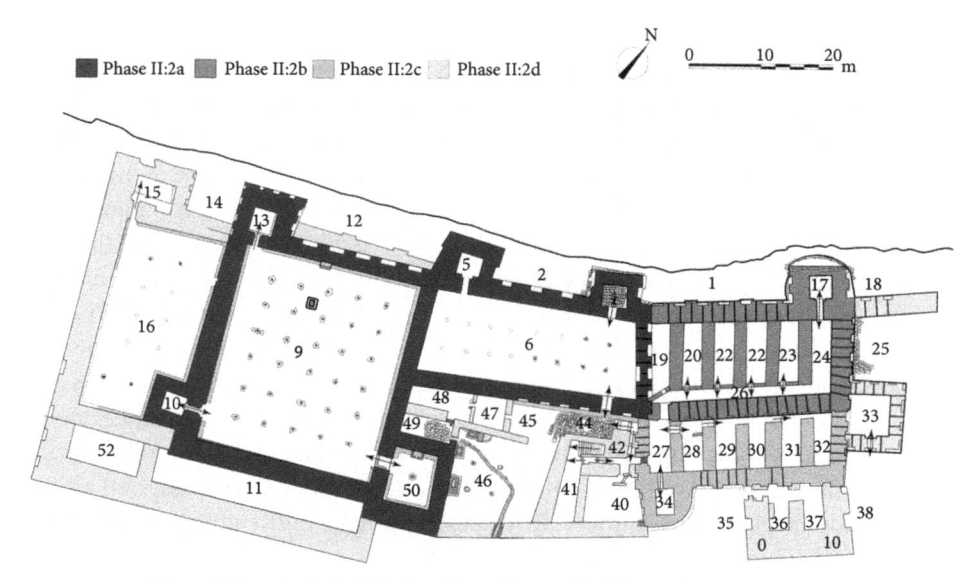

FIGURE 22.3 Plan of the citadel of Godin Tepe during building phase II: 2. Reproduced from Gopnik 2011: 304, fig. 7.7, with kind permission of Hilary Gopnik, Emory University.

in four consecutive building stages and consisted of three columned halls, an enormous kitchen with three huge hearths, and very substantial storage vaults (Gopnik 2011: 302–22). At some point in the mid-seventh century BC, as suggested by the radiocarbon analysis of charcoal excavated in the firebox of one of the kitchen hearths (Gopnik 2011: 343–5), the imposing fortress was peacefully abandoned by its inhabitants. Before that it certainly served as the seat of the Median city lord in control of the Kangavar valley but what was his territory's name?

Godin Tepe lies halfway between the Assyrian provincial capitals of Kar-Nergal/Kišessim (Najafehabad), situated further upstream of the Sarab Kangavar river, and Kar-Šarrukin/Harhar (Tepe Giyan), which is reached by following the river to its confluence with the Gamasiyab and then by tracking that river upstream. A possible candidate for identification with Godin Tepe is Araziaš (Aranzešu), which is located somewhere between Sagbita (Hamadan) and Harhar according to the Assyrian records (Grayson 1996: 68: l. 121 [Šalmaneser III, r. 858–824 BC]; 186–7: III 27–44 [Šamši-Adad V, r. 823–811 BC]; 212: l. 6 [Adad-nerari III, r. 810–783 BC]). Only from the reign of Sargon II is Araziaš explicitly designated as a Median principality controlling a region called the Upper Riverland (*nartu elitu*); it is one of the territories assigned to the new province of Harhar (Radner 2003: 50). Godin Tepe's identification with Araziaš is attractive also because the sources suggest that there was never any permanent Assyrian presence established at the site: its city lord is still attested under Esarhaddon (Starr 1990: no. 73).

Tepe Nush-e Jan lies further to the east in the valley of Malayer in Hamadan province (34°21′55″ N, 48°38′ E). Excavations there have yielded the extremely well-preserved ruins of a tower-like temple that was erected on the highest point of a prominent rock outcrop and held a freestanding altar with a fire bowl (Stronach and Roaf 2007: 212). Gradually, the so-called Central Temple was surrounded by additional buildings, including a second temple, a heavily fortified structure, and a columned hall, that were with the help of walls and arches combined into a coordinated building ensemble (Stronach and Roaf 2007: 203–9). Small finds, including a hoard of silver currency, make it certain that the citadel was in use in the seventh century BC (Curtis 2005) but beyond that, establishing the absolute chronology of the site remains difficult. At some point, the citadel and its buildings were systematically filled up with stones and bricks, creating a high terrace platform which, if it was indeed intended to serve as the base of a successor to the now-entombed Central Temple, does not seem to have ever been used for that purpose (Stronach and Roaf 2007: 171–6, 216–17). Why this enormous amount of labor was undertaken in the first place remains tantalizingly unclear.

Pottery parallels with Godin Tepe and Tepe Nush-e Jan in Level II of Tepe Baba Jan near Nurabad in Luristan province (34°01'14" N, 47°56'01" E; Levine 1987: 234–5, 238) suggest the possibility that the small fortified manor excavated there (Goff 1977) may have served as the residence of a minor Median city lord.

We have already highlighted that according to the Assyrian sources, the Medes controlled the region of Tehran and this was recently confirmed by the results of the excavations of Tepe Ozbaki at Nazarabad in Tehran province (35°58'47" N, 50°35'11" E; Madjidzadeh 2001) that began in 1998. On the top of the settlement mound the ruins of a fortress came to light whose architecture and pottery finds offer close parallels to those of Godin Tepe and Tepe Nush-e Jan (Stronach 2003: 237–40), both situated at a distance of some 250 km as the crow flies: the fortress of Tepe Ozbaki is certainly a Median site and, who knows? perhaps even one of the Median principalities mentioned in the accounts of Tiglath-pileser III and Esarhaddon (Radner 2003: 49, 58–9) about their campaigns deep into the eastern territories of the Medes.

INSTEAD OF CONCLUSIONS

What remains to be addressed is the elephant in the room—Herodotus' account of the early history of the Medes in the first book of the *Histories*. The Greek historian credits one Deioces with uniting the six Median tribes and thereby founding a Median empire, with Ecbatana (Hamadan, see above) as its capital; the Medes supposedly elected him to be their king, and Herodotus then traces Median history until the sixth century BC. According to Herodotus, the Median state reached as far west as the River Halys in Central Anatolia. Yet so far, contemporary evidence for a unified Median state in the eighth and seventh centuries has proven to be elusive. Excavations in sites such as Nush-e Jan, Baba Jan, and Godin Tepe support the idea of small independent states centered on fortresses controlling the region and passage through it, which emerges so clearly from the Assyrian sources. On the other hand, archaeological evidence for a unified Median state stretching from Iran to Inner Anatolia is conspicuously lacking while the Assyrian sources fail to back up any part of Herodotus' account on the genesis of such a state. Recent scholarship therefore prefers to see Herodotus' Medikos Logos as largely fictitious and cautions against its use as a historical source for the history of the Medes (cf. Waters 2005: 517–18).

Although the Assyrian sources and the archaeological evidence emphasize the political plurality of the Median (and non-Median) principalities in Iran, the testimony of the Babylonian Chronicles leaves of course no doubt that Cyaxares conquered Assyria at the head of a Median army that stayed united under his leadership for at least six years (Grayson 1975: 90–6: Chronicle 3). Whatever led to him being recognized as the "king of the Medes" by 615 BC remains tantalizingly unclear from the available sources (Liverani 2003: 6–7) although there is a possibility that the seemingly peaceful abandonment of Godin Tepe was the result of fundamental changes in the political organization of the Medes (Gopnik 2011: 345). Some answers at least could be reasonably expected to result from further exploration of Najafehabad and Tepe Giyan, where a clearer understanding of the end of the Assyrian occupation could offer a fresh perspective on the consolidation of Cyaxares' power. But the Medes' invasion of Assyria aside, it is important to remember that even less is known about the period from 610 to 550 BC, when Cyrus of Persia successfully replaced the Median king Astyages as the overlord of Iran (Liverani 2003: 7–9; Jursa 2003: 170–1 for the scarce Babylonian sources).

Our brief survey of the interaction between Assyrians and Medes in the early first millennium BC has left us with many uncertainties and open questions surrounding a crucial period of Iranian history. Reason enough, surely, to hope for an intensification of the archaeological fieldwork to be undertaken on the settlement mounds along the Iranian stretches of the Silk Route.

REFERENCES

Abdi, K., and G. M. Beckman. 2007. An early second-millennium cuneiform archive from Chogha Gavaneh, western Iran. *JCS* 59: 39–91.

Åkerman, K. 1999–2001. The "Aussenhaken Area" in the city of Assur during the second half of the 7th century BC. *SAAB* 13: 217–72.

Albenda, P. 1986. *The palace of Sargon King of Assyria*. Paris: Éditions Recherche sur les Civilisations.

Alibaigi, S., A.-M. Shanbehzadeh, and H. Alibaigi. 2012. The discovery of a Neo-Assyrian rock-relief at Mishkhas, Ilam Province (Iran). *IrAnt* 47: 29–40.

Borger, R. 1996. *Beiträge zum Inschriftenwerk Assurbanipals*. Wiesbaden: Harrassowitz.

Curtis, J. 2005. The material culture of Tepe Nush-i Jan and the end of the Iron Age III period in Western Iran. *IrAnt* 40: 233–48.

Faist, B. 2007. *Alltagstexte aus neuassyrischen Archiven und Bibliotheken der Stadt Assur*. Wiesbaden: Studien zu den Assur-Texten 3.

Fuchs, A. 1994. *Die Inschriften Sargons II. aus Khorsabad*. Göttingen: Cuvillier.

Fuchs, A., and S. Parpola. 2001. *The correspondence of Sargon II, Part III: Letters from Babylonia and the eastern provinces*. Helsinki: SAA 15.

Ghirshman, R. 1951. *L'Iran, des origines l'Islam.* Paris: Payot.
Goff, C. 1977. Excavations at Baba Jan: The architecture of the east mound, Levels II and III. *Iran* 15: 103–40.
Gopnik, H. 2003. The ceramics from Godin in the late 7th to the early 5th centuries BC. *CE*: 249–67.
———. 2011. The Median citadel of Godin Period II. *OHR*: 285–364.
Grayson, A. K. 1975. *Assyrian and Babylonian chronicles.* Locust Valley: TCS 5.
———. 1996. *Assyrian rulers of the early first millennium BC, II (858–745 BC).* Toronto: RIMA 3.
Hassanzadeh, Y., and H. Mollasalehi. 2011. New evidence for Mannean art: An assessment of three glazed tiles from Qalaichi (Izirtu). *EP*: 407–17.
Jursa, M. 2003. Observations on the problem of the Median "Empire" on the basis of the Babylonian sources. *CE*: 169–79.
Kordevani, M. 1971. Les fouilles de Tchoga Gavaneh. *Bastan Chenassi va Honar-e Iran* 7–8: 30–35 (French), 36–71 (Persian).
Kroll, S., and K. Radner. 2006. Ein Bronzedolch des Simbar-Šipak von Babylon (1025–1008 v. C.): Überlegungen zu Waffenweihungen im Vorderen Orient. *ZA* 96: 105–14.
Lanfranchi, G. B. 2003. The Assyrian expansion in the Zagros and the local ruling elites. *CE*: 79–118.
Lanfranchi, G. B., and S. Parpola. 1990. *The correspondence of Sargon II, Part II: Letters from the northern and northeastern provinces.* Helsinki: SAA 5.
Levine, L. D. 1972. *Two Neo-Assyrian stelae from Iran.* ROMAAOP 23.
———. 1975. Ḫarḫar. *RlA* 4: 120–1.
———. 1987. The Iron Age. *AWI*: 229–50.
———. 1990. Māhīdašt. *RlA* 7: 256–8.
Liverani, M. 2003. The rise and fall of Media. *CE*: 1–12.
Luukko, M. 2012. *The Nimrud letters: The correspondence of Tiglath-pileser III and Sargon II from Calah.* Helsinki: SAA 19.
Madjidzadeh Y. 2001. Les fouilles d'Ozbaki (Iran). Campagnes 1998–2000. *Paléorient* 27: 141–5.
Medvedskaya, I. N. 2002. Were the Assyrians at Ecbatana? *Journal of Kurdish Studies* 16: 45–57.
Miglus, P. A. 1999. *Städtische Wohnarchitektur in Babylonien und Assyrien.* Mainz: Baghdader Forschungen 22.
———. 2000. Die letzten Tage von Assur und die Zeit danach. *Isimu* 3: 85–100.
Miglus, P. A., U. Bürger, M. Heil, and F. M. Stepniowski. 2011. Ausgrabung in Bakr Awa 2010. *ZOA* 4: 136–74.
Radner, K. 2003. An Assyrian view on the Medes. *CE*: 37–64.
———. 2007. Hired labour in the Neo-Assyrian empire. *SAAB* 16: 185–226.
———. 2008. Provinz: Assyrien. *RlA* 11: 42–68.
Reade, J. E. 1978. Kassites and Assyrians in Iran. *Iran* 16: 137–43.
———. 1995. Iran in the Neo-Assyrian period. *N-AG*: 31–42.
Rudenko, S. I. 1970. *Frozen tombs of Siberia: The Pazyryk burials of Iron Age horsemen.* London: Dent.
Soden, W. von. 1972. *Akkadisches Handwörterbuch,* vol. 2. Wiesbaden: Harrassowitz.
Starr, I. 1990. *Queries to the Sungod: Divination and politics in Sargonid Assyria.* Helsinki: SAA 4.
Stronach, D. 2003. Independent Media: Archaeological notes from the homeland. *CE*: 233–48.
Stronach, D., and M. Roaf. 2007. *Nush-i Jan I: The major buildings of the Median settlement.* London/Leuven: British Institute of Persian Studies and Peeters.

Tadmor, H., and S. Yamada. 2011. *The royal inscriptions of Tiglath-pileser III (744–727 BC) and Shalmaneser V (726–722 BC), Kings of Assyria*. Winona Lake: RINAP 1.

Waters, M. 2005. Media and its discontents. *JAOS* 125: 517–33.

Wilcke, C. 2006. Kára-kín-naki. *NABU* 2006/20.

Zadok, R. 2001. On the location of NA Parsua. *NABU* 2001/28.

CHAPTER 23

ELAM IN THE IRON AGE

JAVIER ÁLVAREZ-MON

INTRODUCTION

The chronology of Elam during the first millennium BC is divided into two or three phases according to whether archaeological or textual evidence is followed. Here the archaeological division into Neo-Elamite I (hereafter NE), *c*.1000–725 BC, and Neo-Elamite II (*c*.725–520 BC) is adopted; this division nearly overlaps with the western Iranian Iron Age periods II and III (*c*.1100–800 BC and *c*.800–500 BC) (cf. Álvarez-Mon et al. 2011; 520 BC marks the suppression of the last of three Elamite revolts, which, according to the Bisotun inscription, challenged the authority of Darius I between 522 and 520 BC). The first part of the millennium is not well represented in either the archaeological or the textual records and corresponds with a presumed abandonment of the eastern Elamite capital of Anshan (Tal-e Malyan), often linked to the arrival of migrant populations of Iranian-speaking background. Equally entrenched in the scholarly literature is the emphasis given to the sack and devastation of the western Elamite capital of Susa in 647 BC. This date has been hailed as marking the political fragmentation of Elamite power and the disappearance of Elam from the historical record.

With the exception of the discovery of the Arjan tomb in 1982 and the Ram Hormuz burials in 2007, no major additions to the primary archaeological evidence available for the study of the Neo-Elamite period have been made since the Iranian Revolution in 1979. This hiatus, however, has provided an opportunity for the publication of data collected before 1979 and for a critical reexamination of earlier scholarship, leading to a significant revision of the traditional understanding of the Neo-Elamite period with important ramifications for the genesis of the Persian Empire (Álvarez-Mon and Garrison 2011). The following summary of archaeological, artistic, and textual evidence

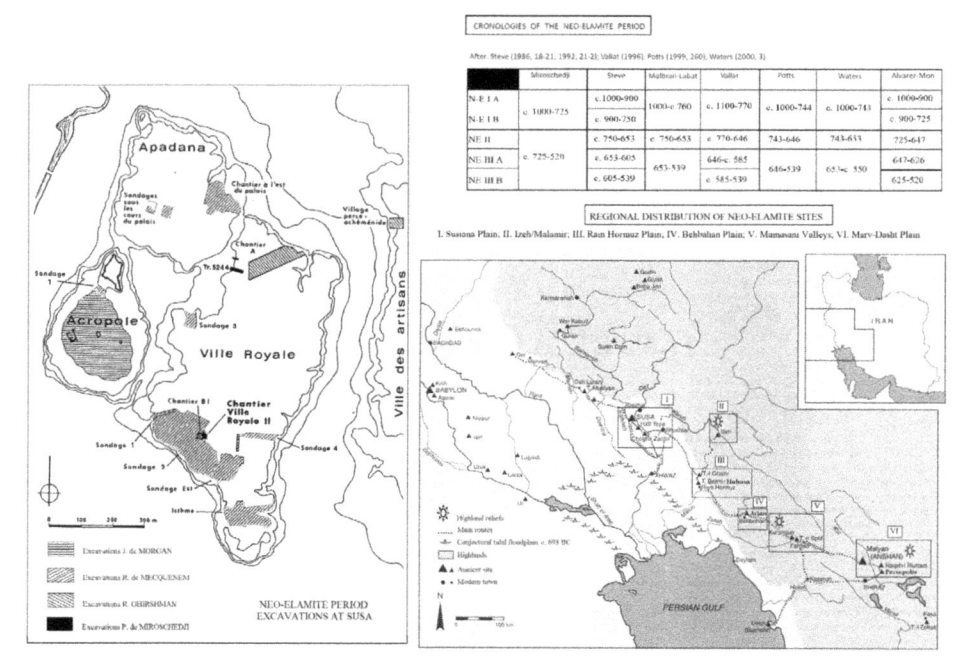

FIGURE 23.1 Maps and chronology of the Neo-Elamite period (c.1000–520 BC).

follows a broadly northwest to southeast trajectory (Fig. 23.1) encompassing the Susiana plain, the highland valley of Izeh/Malamir, the Ram Hormuz plain, the Behbahan plain, the Mamasani valleys, and the Marv-Dasht plain (for the Deh Luran plain, see Wright and Neely 2010).

Susiana: Susa

Surface surveys of the Susiana plain conducted between 1960 and 1977 charted the location of no fewer than 1200 ancient mounds. This undertaking was complemented by data analysis initiated in 1977 by P. de Miroschedji who identified twenty sites inhabited during the NE I and six during the NE II period (Miroschedji 1981c: 169, fig. 55). Of these, only Susa has been the object of any fieldwork of note.

The remains unearthed at Susa by Mecquenem (1912–46), Ghirshman (1946–67), and Miroschedji (1975–78) provide the foundation for an elaboration of NE stratigraphy and material culture. In particular, Miroschedji's careful excavations in the Ville Royale (VR) II (1974–7); Ville Royale–Apadana (VR–A), trench 5244 (1976); and Apadana–Ville Royale (A–VR) (1978) permitted the clarification of the NE ceramic sequence as well as providing important data on other categories of material.

NE I (c.1000–725 BC)

NE I remains were attested in Mecquenem's "élamite supérieur" or "Suse–Elam III"; Ghirshman's VR-A (Levels X–IX); and Miroschedji's VR II (Levels 9–8), A–VR (Trenches 2351 and 2384; P26–P28) and VR–A (Trench 5244, Level 7C). However, the stratigraphy in VR–A X–IX was highly disturbed and has been the source of much confusion. Both levels are dated to the end of the Middle Elamite period. The NE evidence is intrusive and comes mainly from pits and burials (Steve et al. 1980: 58, 60; fig. 1.6–10 shows wares dated to between the first and second quarter of the first millennium BC, while fig. 1.1–5 shows wares dated to the second half of the first millennium BC; cf. Steve et al. 2002–3: 395). Based on the absence of evidence of a clear transition, Miroschedji suggested a gap in habitation between VR X and IX (Miroschedji 1981a: 17; 1981b: 149).

Assemblage I: Pottery

Excavations in VR II and A–VR exposed isolated habitation remains and burials characterized by mudbrick walls and pits with skeletal remains accompanied by common and coarseware vessels (burials T. 2346, T. 2361 and materials from square P26; Miroschedji 1981a, 17–19, 23–4). Typical forms of this period include small and large bowls (Miroschedji 1981a: figs. 48.2–3, 8; 49.1–4) and small jars (Miroschedji 1981a: figs. 48.1, 49.8); cylindrical goblets (Miroschedji 1981a: figs. 49.6–7, 50.4–5); pots with molded walls (Miroschedji 1981a: fig. 48.9, "à paroi moulurée"); and the bowl with the pinched lip (Miroschedji 1981a: fig. 19.1–6, "jatte à bec pincé"). The presence of the tall, narrow "Elamite goblet" in VR-A 7C (Miroschedji 1981b: 146), A–VR, burial T. 2346—a male in a pit grave containing two 31 cm tall goblets and two other NE I vessels vessels (Miroschedji 1981a: fig. 48.6–7, pl. XVII.9–12)—and VR II Levels 9–8 (Miroschedji 1981a: fig. 21.6), combined with fragments of mold-made female figurines and a terracotta showing a couple having sex on a bed, may indicate some degree of continuity with the Middle Elamite period. The "Elamite goblets" here may not be intrusive in NE I but rather in their final phase of use before disappearing altogether in the NE II period.

Assemblage II: Vitreous industries

Relatively large numbers of frit figurines and containers and glazed ceramic vessels, containers and figurines, were also uncovered, as well as forty-five fragments of glazed pottery in VR II 9 (?) and 134 fragments in Level 8 (Miroschedji 1981a: 20, fig. 27). Bowls were covered with white, green, and possibly blue glaze. In addition, eighteen mainly green–clear glazed pyxides were found, one with a figurative tenon and three with decoration, the best preserved of which shows vegetal motifs (Miroschedji 1981a: fig. 27: 4). A turtle and a bird made of frit and ornamented with glaze find parallels at Chogha Zanbil (turtle: Miroschedji 1981a: fig. 27: 1; Ghirshman 1966: pl. 77.GTZ 440, Chapel III; bird: Miroschedji 1981a: fig. 27.2; Mecquenem 1953: 46, fig. 10.11; Ghirshman 1966: pls.

72.GTZ 700, 77.GTZ 441–442, 79.GTZ 529), raising the question of whether this important Middle Elamite site was still occupied in NE I. Based on the presence of a number of diagnostic artifacts, including the late form of the "Elamite goblet" in the Level III temple of Ishnikarab and in the *palais-hypogée* (Ghirshman 1966: pl. 88, GTZ 892, 893; 91), pots with molded walls (Mecquenem 1953: pl. 19.34), fragments of circular frit pyxides with white-green glaze (Mecquenem 1922: 128, fig. 9), and the above-mentioned frit turtle and bird, both Ghirshman (1966: 8) and Miroschedji (1978: 227, n. 30) suggested that Chogha Zanbil was occupied in the NE I period, "before the Assyrian conquest." Other scholars disagree (Pons 1994: 48; cf. Potts 1999: 262, 284).

NE II (c.730–520 BC)

Mecquenem called NE II "period e" and divided it into a "Babylonian period" (also called "Neo-Babylonian period") and "end of Elam" (also called "décadence élamite"). These are represented by material excavated by J. de Morgan and R. de Mecquenem on the Apadana, the Acropole, and the VR (cf. the Suse Archives of Mecquenem [1921–39], http://www.mom.fr/mecquenem/), Ghirshman's Village perse-achéménide (Level I), and Miroschedji's VR II Levels 7–6 and VR–A Trench 5244. According to Miroschedji (1981b: 149), the transition between NE I and NE II is not clear.

Assemblage I: Pottery

A large underground funerary chamber in VR II (burial 693) contained the skeletal remains of six individuals: two adult males (?), two females, and two infants. Given the context of deposition, they appear to have been brought into the chamber on three different occasions. The rich sample of funerary goods included no fewer than 150 vessels (a few containing the remains of dates) and objects such as an iron pin with golden head and an iron dagger. A white-glazed, faience cylinder seal with a scene showing a kneeling archer hunting a leaping, lion-headed griffin was found next to the chest of a female around fifty years old (Miroschedji 1981a: fig. 40). This seal was dated to the first half of the seventh century BC (Miroschedji 1982: 56, fig. 1). The most diagnostic group of wares from this period are amphora-like jars without handles, about 40–80 cm tall and made in two parts joined at the shoulder (the neck was turned on a wheel and the body was handmade using the coiling technique). Miroschedji divided these into three groups according to height (Miroschedji 1982: 53), the largest of which (60–80 cm tall) constitute a "fossile directeur de premier ordre" (Miroschedji 1981a: 32) for NE II (Fig. 23.3).

Assemblage II: Metalwork

Two types of bronze vessels exemplify the metallurgical corpus of this period: the peculiar inkwell-like vessel made of two pieces of hammered sheet metal joined at the shoulder (Miroschedji 1981a: 112, fig. 40.12); and the chalice-like vessel made of a single piece of hammered sheet metal (Miroschedji 1981a: 112, fig. 40.13; Álvarez-Mon 2010a: 165)

ELAM IN THE IRON AGE 461

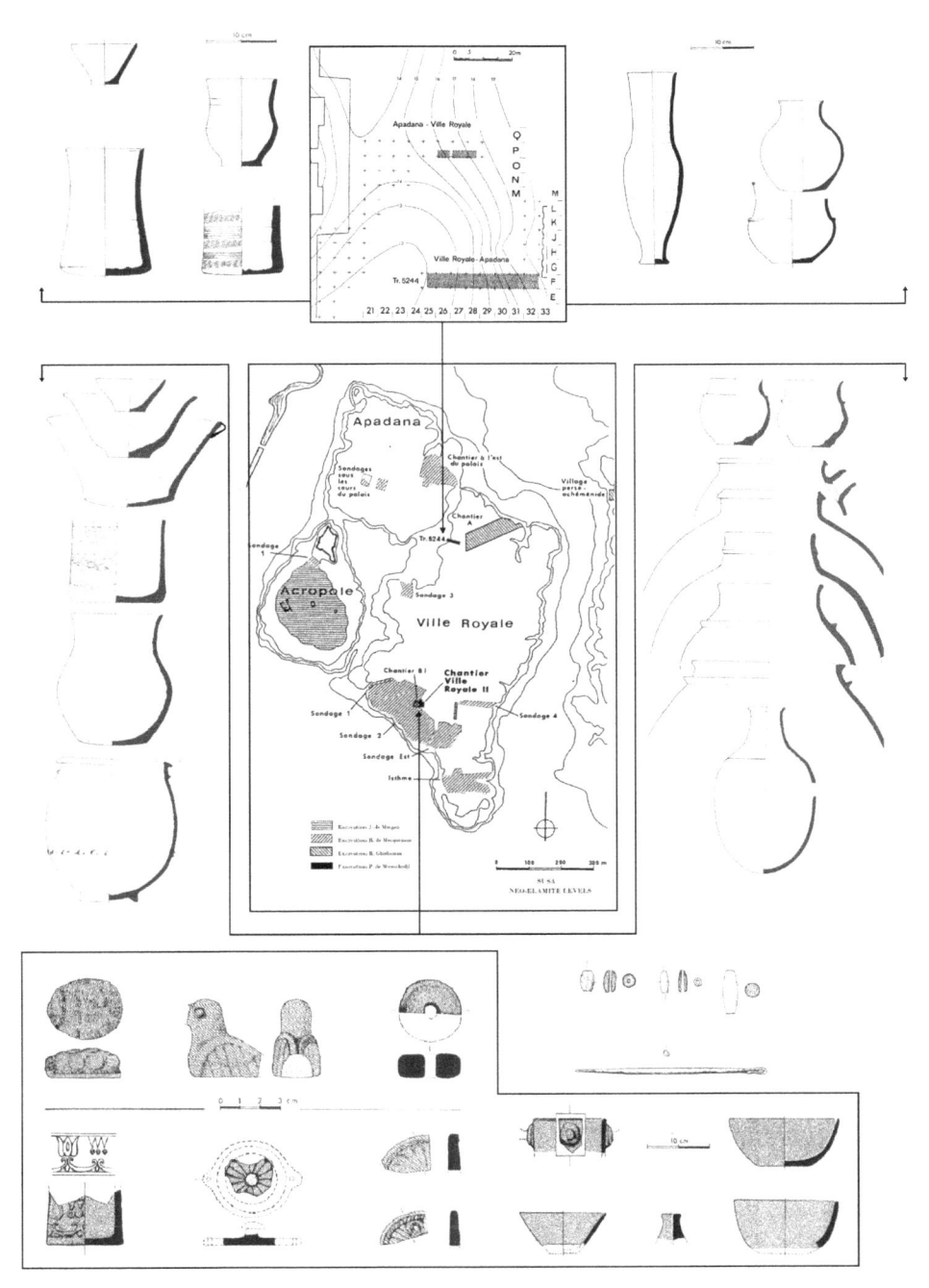

FIGURE 23.2 Neo-Elamite I ceramic vessels and vitreous wares from Susa.

(Fig. 23.3). Both vessels find counterparts at Susa, Luristan, Ram Hormuz, and Arjan. A bowl from burial T. 705 (VR II Level 7; Miroschedji 1981a: 114, fig. 41.1) has parallels in Luristan and at Ur. Additionally there is a distinctive corpus of at least sixteen hairpins combining an iron shaft with a head covered with gold leaf ornamented with filigree (Miroschedji 1981a: 113, fig. 40.4–5; 1990a). These are important indicators of the presence of female burials (with parallels at Susa, Luristan, and Ram Hormuz, where at least seven examples are known. Lastly, there is a small number of bronze lamps (Álvarez-Mon 2010a: 164–5) and some iron weaponry (Miroschedji 1981a: 113, fig. 40.14–15).

Assemblage III: Vitreous industries

Large numbers of fine glazed materials were unearthed at Susa, seven categories of which can be distinguished: (1) wall accessories I: plaques; (2) wall accessories II: pegs, knobs, protomes; (3) brick panels; (4) statuettes; (5) containers I: pyxides; (6) containers II: flasks; and (7) containers III: assorted vessels. A distinctive corpus is represented by a class of polychrome-glazed ceramic flasks and vessels decorated on the shoulder with a variety of geometric patterns including double triangles, double-dotted circles, and dotted diamonds (Fig. 23.3) (Álvarez-Mon 2010a: 235–81). This material represents an outburst of faïence production, which, along with an intrinsic mastery of technological skills, is distinguished by playfully vibrant colors and the adaptation of a vivid, numinous world populated by winged griffins, bearded sphinxes, winged horses, horned geniuses, protruding heads affixed to pyxides, bovine gods and goddesses, horses, lions, bulls, and human worshippers. Stylistically there is a peculiar treatment of the heads and necks of bulls and fantastic animals characterized by a lock-pompadour atop the forehead, a strip of hair (or side curl) dropping down from the ears, a collar-band marking the boundary of the neck and chest, slender curvature of the neck, and abstract divisions of the body. While the archaeological context of most artifacts is imprecise, the eastern necropolis and the palace courtyards on the Apadana produced some of the most important assemblages (http://www.mom.fr/mecquenem/, accessed November 14, 2012). Stylistic analysis would place this corpus of objects between the eighth and the sixth centuries BC (Álvarez-Mon 2010a: 235ff.).

Assemblage IV: Monumental sculpture

The remains of at least three terracotta lions at rest (1.26 m long × 0.65 m high), covered with blue or green glaze, were found in the vicinity of a temple–chapel dedicated to Inshushinak on the Acropole. One of the restored lions (Louvre Sb 2716) shows naturalistic rendering: the head is upright, covered with a heavy mane, the front paws are extended and claws are visible (Lampre 1905: 164–8; Amiet 1966: 525, fig. 402). The temple may have been founded in the late Middle Elamite period and later restored by Shutruk-Nahhunte II (716–699 BC) and his brother Hallutash-Inshushinak (c.698–693 BC) (for the temple and related "altar" of glazed brick see Álvarez-Mon 2010a: 236, 249).

Six fragments of a limestone stele of a king Atta-hamiti-Inshushinak (not mentioned in Mesopotamian sources; see Stolper 1992; Waters 2000: 85) were found in the Acropole

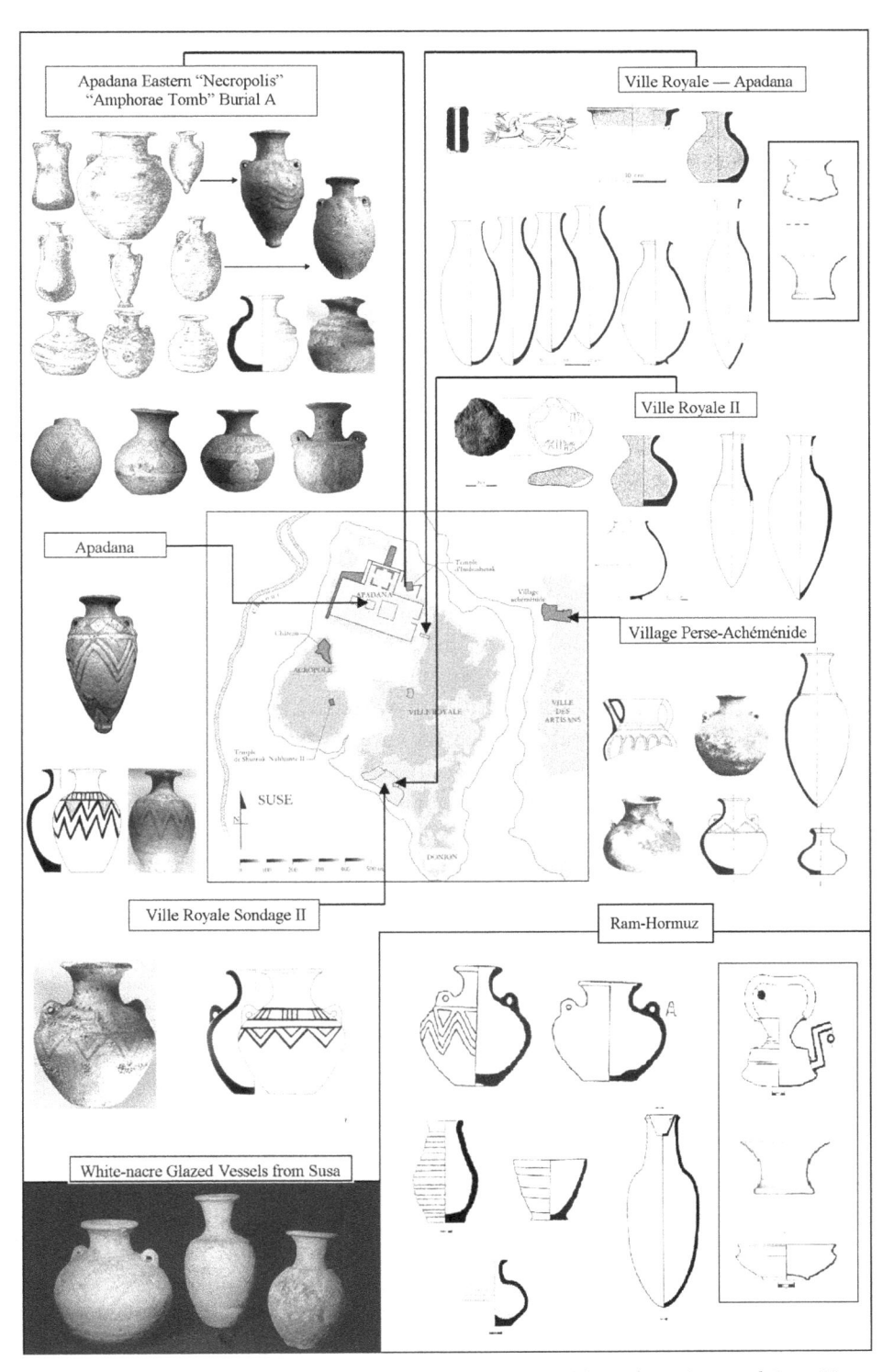

FIGURE 23.3 Neo-Elamite II ceramic and metal vessel assemblages from Susa and Ram Hormuz.

excavation by J. de Morgan, two of which (A–B) were published by V. Scheil (1911: 76–7). M. Pézard (1924: 1), following Scheil, recognized fragments C and E, and found a fifth one (D) amongst the Susa finds in the Louvre. These are carved in low relief with images of the royal Elamite couple. A short caption is located to the right of the king and a much larger inscription is situated below. The king wears a composite, hemispherical helmet decorated with rosettes. His beard is characterized by rows of small locks and long, straight locks of hair. A distinctive feature is the absence of hair over the tip of the chin. His garments are heavily ornamented. The Elamite queen, who wears a spherical, well-fitted bonnet and possibly a necklace linked at the back to a knob-shaped clasp and a long, hatched extension, faces the king. The headdress and necklace find close parallels on late Middle Elamite (twelfth century BC) representations of queens in the reliefs of Shekaft-e Salman (Izeh/Malamir) and in glazed architectural panels from the façade of a monumental building on the Susa Acropole (Amiet 2000: 4–5; Álvarez-Mon 2010c, 2013).

The inscription identifies Atta-hamiti-Inshushinak as son of Hutran-tepti "[king of Anshan and Susa, expander of the realm], master of Elam, sovereign of Elam," ("king of Anshan and Susa, expander of the realm" was restored by König 1965: 172, *EKI* 86.I) and author of a restoration project initiated by king Halkatash. King Halkatash has been tentatively identified with Humban-haltash III/Ummanaldaši (646–645 BC) (Potts 1999: 297; see Tavernier 2004 for further discussion). F. Vallat has suggested that Atta-hamiti-Inshushinak ruled between 646 and c.585 BC; and more precisely c.645–620 BC (Vallat 1996: 393; 2006; but see criticism by Henkelman 2008: 363, n. 848). On stylistic grounds both P. Amiet and O. Muscarella have dated the stele to c.650 BC (Amiet 1966: 566, fig. 431; Muscarella 1992: 198, fig. 140). More recently, M. Waters, J. Tavernier, and W. Henkelman have contemplated the possibility that Atta-hamiti (Inshushinak) could in fact be Athamaita (c.530–520 BC), the leader of the third Elamite revolt against Darius in 520 BC, mentioned (but not represented) in the great relief of Bisotun (Waters 2000: 85; Tavernier 2004: 24; Henkelman 2008: 14 and esp. 363, n. 848). The inscription reveals that Atta-hamiti-Inshushinak's political control may have centered on Huhnur (Tepe Bormi in the Ram Hormuz plain) and incorporated Susa to the west and Ayapir to the north (in or near Izeh/Malamir).

Assemblage V: Cylinder seals and sealings

Knowledge of late Neo-Elamite glyptic derives mainly from the corpus of seal impressions on the Acropole and Apadana tablets (Scheil 1907, 1911; Porada 1965: 50–51; Amiet 1966; 1972, 273–83, figs. 2121–201; 1973: 4); a single cylinder seal from Village perse-achéménide Level I (Ghirshman 1954: pl. 794); a faience seal from Ville-Royale II, Burial 693, dated to the first half of the seventh century BC; and a sealing from the Ville Royale-Apadana, dated to the first half of the sixth century BC (Miroschedji 1981a, 1981b, 1982). In addition, NE-related seals have been excavated in Luristan at Chigha Sabz (Van Loon 1988: pl. IIa) and Surkh Dum-e Luri (Schmidt et al. 1989: 429, pls. 236.81–2, 84, 93; 237.85–7; 238.923).

At the core of this corpus are sixteen seal impressions from the Acropole tablets and seven from the Apadana tablets (Garrison 2006). The question of their chronology is obviously intimately tied to the proposed dating of the tablets (see below). Some of the most salient, innovative artistic elements of this glyptic assemblage can be succinctly summarized as: (1) a minimalist arrangement of the composition; (2) a stylized, naturalistic attempt at treating the animal figure; and (3) the iconographic emergence of a distinctive equestrian art characterized by a rider on a leaping horse in the act of firing an arrow or throwing a spear at a rearing animal or human (Garrison 2010). Hunting scenes with a single horseman manifest an artistic iconography which emerged predominately in the seventh century BC and reflected a new sociocultural ideology (Amiet 1966: 569; Miroschedji 1982: 62–3; Van Loon 1988: 223–4; Garrison 2011).

Assemblage VI: Texts

The key foreign sources relating to Elam in this period originate in Assyria (annals, royal correspondence, epigraphs on wall reliefs) and Babylonia (chronicles) (Frame 1992; Brinkman 1984, in particular part VIII, "Notes on sources"; Gerardi 1987; Vallat 1996; Potts 1999; Waters 2000; Henkelman 2003a, 2003b; Álvarez-Mon, including Biblical sources, 2010a: 170; and Álvarez-Mon et al. 2011). For the most part, these concern political and military events spanning about 120 years (*c*.747–626 BC). In addition to these documents there exists a heterogeneous group of texts in Elamite: (1) economic and administrative tablets from Susa; (2) the Ururu bronze plaque from Persepolis; (3) the "Nineveh" letters; and (4) royal inscriptions. Scholars agree that these texts postdate the collapse of the Assyrian Empire with a noticeable trend in recent times to move the date of the Susa tablets and related texts to the sixth century BC or perhaps as late as the 520s BC (*c*.600–575 BC: Vallat 1998: 311; *c*.590/580–565/5 BC: Tavernier 2004: 32; *c*.550–520 BC: Garrison 2010: 401; Waters 2000, however, dates the Susa texts to the late seventh century BC).

The Elamite highlands: Kul-e Farah

To date no NE settlements have been identified in the Zagros valley of Izeh/Malamir, situated about 750 m above sea level. Layard (1846: 74–5) mentioned the "ruins of a very ancient city" on the eastern side of the valley but a test trench excavated by M. Sajjidi and H. T. Wright in the Izeh East Face mound encountered only Middle Elamite pottery and a related inscription (Sajjidi and Wright 1979: 107; cf. Stein 1940: 136: Bayani 1979: 99–105; Wright 1987). Artistic and textual evidence in the form of monumental carved reliefs and associated inscriptions, however, confirms the existence of political entities there in the late second and first millennium BC. Kul-e Farah (KF) is a ravine nestled on the eastern side of the valley, marked by a seasonal creek, where six NE reliefs were carved on the faces of cliffs (KF I, IV, and V) and boulders (KF II, III, and VI).

KF II, III, IV, V, and VI used to be considered a single group that was dated variously to the ninth to sixth centuries BC (De Waele 1976: 337; 1981: 52); the "époque Elamite récente" (Jéquier 1901: 142; Vanden Berghe 1963: 39); the period of "Elamite-Persian cohabitation" (Calmeyer 1973: 15); or the eighth to seventh centuries BC (Vanden Berghe 1983: 102–3; for KF III and VI, see Seidl 1997: 200–3; Álvarez-Mon 2010a: 39). In 1984, E. Carter proposed a pre–1000 BC date for KF IV (Carter 1984: 187). This was followed by P. Amiet who, while making exceptions for KF I and V, suggested that all of the other reliefs were the expression of a local monarchy that developed in eastern Elam after the invasion of the Babylonian king Nebuchadnezzar I (c.1104 BC), or perhaps slightly later, at the beginning of the first millennium BC (Amiet 1992: 81, 86; cf. Seidl 1997). More recently, a new study by the author has dated KF IV to the ninth to eighth centuries BC (Álvarez-Mon 2013). Of the six carvings, KF IV, III, and I are the most significant as they reveal key aspects of the religious and sociopolitical identity of Elam.

KF IV extends for almost 18 m along the vertical surface of the rock cliff (17.70 × 6 m). It depicts a communal banquet with no fewer than 141 participants. Social hierarchy is indicated by placement within (parallel) registers, activities, and dress. Seated on a high-backed throne framed by two tables holding food and vessels, a king presides over the ceremony. He is accompanied by attendants: a group of individuals wearing long garments, a weapon-bearer/chief archer (carrying a bow, quiver, and sword), archers, six harp players and conductor, and more than a hundred similarly represented individuals wearing short kilts. Of this last group, the best preserved wears his hair in a long, distinctive braid. One of his hands is positioned directly in front of his mouth holding a morsel of food, most likely a piece of meat (Seidl 1997: 200–3; Álvarez-Mon 2013).

The entire vertical surface of the boulder on which KF III was carved shows a procession of about 200 figures accompanied by flocks of domestic animals. At the head of the procession are four kneeling male individuals with head caps who support a large platform on which a large male figure (representing perhaps a king or a deity) stands. Behind him are two flocks consisting of eighteen rams and three zebus; groups of naked (?) individuals and others wearing long robes and short kilts; and three harp players facing another oversized figure followed by large numbers of worshippers arranged in parallel registers. A thorough study of this relief is lacking and its date remains to be determined (for recent discussion and references, see Álvarez-Mon 2010b, 2010c).

KF I was originally dated to between the eighth and the sixth centuries BC (Weissbach 1894; Scheil 1901: 102–13; Hinz 1962; König 1965: *EKI* 75, and captions *EKI* 75A–K; Stolper 1988). More recently, a date after the Assyrian campaigns has been preferred (between 585 and 539 BC: Vallat 1996: 387–9; 2006; last quarter of the seventh century BC: Tavernier 2004: 19, 21; 2006; "the very last part of the Neo-Elamite period": Henkelman 2008: 329; 650–c.550 BC: Álvarez-Mon 2010: 50, 201, 266). This is the latest relief in the group and assimilates artistic aspects of many of the reliefs at KF and Shekaft-e Salman. A large Elamite cuneiform inscription occupying the upper half of the relief identifies the large figure as Hanni, son of Tahhi, *kutur* ("prince" or "chief") of Ayapir and vassal of the Elamite king Šutur-Nahhunte, son of Indada. Hanni wears a bulbous cap, a waist-long braid, and heavily fringed garments with rosettes. Behind him stand the smaller figures of two court officials, a weapon bearer (labeled "Šutruru, the master of the palace," carrying a bow, quiver, and sword), and a long-garment bearer. A trio of musicians play a horizontal harp, a vertical harp, and a square drum as the butchering of a zebu is shown taking place next to the carcasses of rams and a fire altar or censer (for the headdress and garments, see Álvarez-Mon 2010c).

The presence of these reliefs at Kul-e Farah suggests the natural landscape of Izeh/Malamir was an essential component of the traditional Elamite cultic and religious ideology. The carving of two twelfth century BC reliefs on the eastern side of the valley (Shekaft-e Salman I and II), representing the Elamite royal family in attitudes of worship, underscores the significance of this locale. The same may be said of the open-air sanctuaries of Kurangun (II and III) and Naqsh-e Rustam (II). Apart from Hanni of Aiapir (KF I), we still do not know who these large groups of individuals were or where they originated. Nevertheless, the significance of these reliefs as artistic and ideological precursors of Persian sculptural and socioreligious traditions is becoming increasingly clear (Henkelman 2008, 2011; Álvarez-Mon 2010b, 2013).

Ram Hormuz plain

Recent archaeological survey in the eastern Zagros foothill corridor connecting Susiana with Ram Hormuz has revealed a new pattern of archaeological settlement and the identification of two NE sites (Moghaddam and Miri 2007). The Ram Hormuz plain itself is home to two large urban centers occupied in NE I and II, Tepe Bormi and Tal-e Ghazir (Carter 1994). Based on the chance discovery at Tepe Bormi of an inscription mentioning the dedication of a temple at Huhnur (Nasrabadi 2005), it is very probable that the site was the Elamite city of Huhnur/Hunar/Unar (cf. Miroschedji 1990b: 57; Carter 1994; Wright and Carter 2003). Excavations at Tal-e Ghazir (1946–8) by D. McCown uncovered funerary remains. Burial L consisted of a brick chamber coated with green–gray plaster and roofed with a slab-lid; burial M yielded iron bracelets, faience beads, and two glazed vessels comparable in form and decoration to examples from Susa (for more NE II material see Carter 1994).

In April–May 2007 an elite burial was found on the left bank of the Jarrahi River, in the Joobji district east of the city of Ram Hormuz. Two fragmentary bronze "bathtub" coffins contained the skeletal remains of two women, one about seventeen years old and the other thirty to thirty-five years old (Shishehgar 2008). The burial contained a sumptuous array of gold jewelry including bracelets of various styles (including some with animal terminals) (according to Shishegar, the younger woman was wearing a gold bracelet ornamented with agates and an inscription reading *Ani-Numa*); hair pins decorated with granulation (similar to ones found at Susa); pendants; rings; semiprecious stone beads with gold caps at both ends decorated with granulation; and about 155 assorted bracteates ornamented with filigree and incrusted with semiprecious stones. Bronze metalwork is represented by no fewer than seven chalice-style vessels; five inkwell-style vessels; and a unique candelabrum with a triangular frame composed of three duck-heads as feet supporting a trio of elongated bulls leaping toward the center and supporting the central shaft of the candelabrum with their knees. Equally original are a bronze figurine of a female balancing a vessel on her head (cf. two fragmentary figurines from Chigha Sabz in Luristan; Álvarez-Mon 2010a: pl. 111.h–i) and three bronze and one silver corner-terminals in the shape of sitting "mermaids" (females with a long fish tail and open palms turned upward), wearing ornate hairstyles, garments, and large number of bracelets (the British Museum has a "sitting mermaid" which was dated to the second millennium BC in light of popular terracotta female figurines with a similar hairstyle). In addition, the burials included glazed vessels and flasks, pyxides, and an amphora clearly paralleled in the NE II assemblage at Susa. The preliminary report of the finds indicates that four objects from the burial are inscribed. One gold disk is said to read: "Šutur-Nahhunte, son of Indada." If this is correct, then this inscription offers critical information for our understanding of NE chronology as it provides an important synchronism with both the unprovenanced seal of Huban-kitin, son of Šutur-Nahhunte, and the KF relief of Hanni, who is identified as a vassal of Šutur-Nahhunte, son of Indada. Following the chronology of this king proposed by F. Vallat in 2006, A. Shishegar dates the burial to c.585–539 BC (the seal of Huban-kitin represents a critical example of royal imagery closely related to the imagery represented in the Arjan ring discussed below; cf. Álvarez-Mon 2010a: 96–7; for differences of opinions on the date of Šutur-Nahhunte and Hanni, see Tavernier 2004; Henkelman 2008: 363, n. 848; Potts 2010b: 133, table I). The luxurious characteristics of the materials together with the royal inscription strongly suggest that the females buried at Ram Hormuz enjoyed royal status.

Behbahan plain: Arjan

The accidental discovery in 1982 of a burial chamber with stone walls next to the left bank of the Marun River near the ancient city of Arjan (also Arrajan), near modern Behbahan, has brought important additions to our knowledge of the end of the Elamite period (Álvarez-Mon 2010a). The Arjan funerary chamber represents a composite "foothill" (highland–lowland) style combining stone slabs for the construction of the roof with gypsum-plastered walls and floor. Inside the chamber a bronze bathtub coffin contained the skeletal remains of an adult male; an iron dagger ornamented with precious stones and gold filigree; and an intriguing gold object described as an open "ring" with flaring disk-shaped finials (both inner disks are decorated with matching designs: a palmette tree flanked by two rampant, winged, lion-headed griffins). In addition, there were twelve pieces of cotton textile (one with embroidered rosettes) and dozens of gold bracteates. To date, these are the earliest and best-preserved cotton garments found in the Near East. Outside the coffin was a silver vessel; a bronze lamp; bronze, chalice-style cups; a large bronze bowl engraved with a sequence of concentric narratives scenes; a bronze candelabrum (the upper part occupied by a spool-shaped platform held by six lions and a pedestal combining a triangular frame with three sets of three lions, bulls, and atlas figures); and a bronze beaker (the neck engraved with six identical running ostriches and a lower, bulbous, convex section worked in repoussé into the shape of four overlapping lion heads converging on a central rosette).

Four objects in the Arjan tomb—the large bronze bowl, the candelabrum, the silver vase, and the gold ring—were engraved with the late NE cuneiform label "Kidin-Hutran son of Kurluš" (Vallat 1984). On epigraphic grounds, the inscription has been dated to the end of the NE period, contemporary with the Acropole texts. The author has dated the assemblage to $c.600$ BC and the engraving of the inscriptions and the act of burial to about a generation later, $c.570$ BC (Álvarez-Mon 2010a).

Mamasani region

The region of Fahliyan and Nurabad-e Mamasani has been the focus of recent archaeological work by a joint Iranian–Australian team of archaeologists (Potts et al. 2007, 2009). The occupation at Tol-e Spid extends from the Chalcolithic to the Sasanian period while the occupation sequence of Tol-e Nurabad (a large site $c.25$ m high and covering $c.9$ ha) was occupied from the Neolithic ($c.6000$ BC) to the post-Achaemenid period. In addition, excavations at Jin-Jun (Qaleh Kali) have revealed a monumental portico recalling Persian palatial architecture. The building has been associated with Achaemenid (royal) way-stations mentioned in the Persepolis Fortification Tablets (Potts et al. 2007; 2009: 181).

Further architectural installations and related pottery have been observed atop an outcrop of the Kuh-e Pataweh Mountain adjacent to the open-air sanctuary of Kurangun (surface ceramics suggest Sasanian and Islamic occupation; see Zeidi et al. 2009: 165, MS40; this is confirmed by an unpublished sounding, D. T. Potts, pers. comm.). The Kurangun relief itself was carved on a rock-cliff about 80 m above the Fahliyan River (Potts 2004). The central panel (Kurangun I) is of Old Elamite date (seventeenth century BC). The original relief was expanded by incorporating parallel registers of worshipers on both sides of the central panel and along the staircases (Kurangun II). The peculiar group of individuals wearing a long braid are closely related to the ones on KF III and IV. Vanden Berghe believed these worshippers were eighth century BC additions (Vanden Berghe 1963: 32; 1986, worshipers 13–49) but U. Seidl, followed by E. Carter and P. Amiet, dated them to the end of the second millennium BC. Seidl (1986, 1997), Carter (1988: 146), and Amiet (1992: 81) based their opinion on the high dating of KF III and IV. In addition, the four individuals carved on the southeastern side (to the right of the central panel) are seen as further additions made at the end of the NE period

(Kurangun III) (Vanden Berghe 1986: worshipers 9–12). Seidl (1986: 12, n. 43) noted parallels between these four figures and those depicted at KF II, a relief she dates to the late NE period following Vanden Berghe (1963), Waele (1973), and Calmeyer (1973).

Finally, two tombs at Gur-i Dukhtar and Da-o Dukhtar somewhat outside the region—to the south and the northwest—have sometimes figured, erroneously, in discussions of this period (Stronach 1978: 300–304; Miroschedji 1985: 292, n. 113).

Marv-Dasht plain

The archaeological record of this region has been treated in general by Vanden Berghe (1966: 37–45), Sumner (1972, 1986), and Miroschedji (1990b: 52). The slightly earlier ceramic assemblage from Vanden Berghe's soundings at Tall-e Teimuran (B) (Vanden Berghe 1966: 44, pls. 60ff.; Miroschedji 1990b: 53) and the 1961 excavations at Tall-e Zohar by F. Tavalli (unpublished, see Miroschedji 1990: 52) are relevant but the bulk of the NE archaeological record of the Marv-Dasht plain comes from the large settlement of Tal-e Malyan (Anšan) which appears to have been abandoned at the beginning of the first millennium BC. The absence of late pre-Achaemenid occupation in Fārs after c.900 BC has been interpreted as reflecting a phenomenon of full pastoralization stimulated by the influence of migrant populations of Iranian-speaking background (Sumner 1986; Miroschedji 1985, 1990b; Steve et al. 2002–3: 471). There might be early NE I remains at Anshan (Carter 1994: 66, fig. 3; 1996: 47, fig. 46; Potts 1999: 285), including a metallurgical workshop attested in tablets which M. Stolper (1984: 9) dates to c.1300–1000 BC and M. J. Steve (1986: 9) dates to c.1000–900 BC. There are three main reasons to exert caution about this interpretation: only a very small portion of the large settlement of Tal-e Malyan has been excavated; the model of nomadic pastoralism should not be adopted uncriticlly; and the identification of early Achaemenid pottery remains problematic (for a critique of pastoral nomadism as a significant geopolitical force in ancient Iran, see Potts 2008, 2010; Weeks 2008: 309–313). According to W. Sumner, "early Achaemenid mounded sites exist and have not been discovered or such sites have been discovered but the Achaemenid ceramic components have not been recognized" (Sumner 1986: 4).

During the NE II period the open-air sanctuary additions were made to the main seventeenth century BC relief at Naqsh-e Rustam showing a male worshiper dressed in long ceremonial garment, wearing a distinctive, composite, pointed-visor headdress and carrying a small animal (he is generally believed to represent a king) and a female wearing a crown (generally believed to represent a queen). These added figures have been dated variously to the ninth century BC (Seidl 1986); the ninth to seventh centuries BC (Porada 1965: 66); the eighth to seventh centuries BC (Amiet 1966: 560–2; Vanden Berghe 1983: 103); and the seventh century BC (Miroschedji 1985: 280; 1990b: 74, n. 27). The presence at Naqsh-e Rustam of a crowned queen is a novelty within the Elamite artistic record. The existence of direct Assyrian prototypes (Álvarez-Mon 2009a) could suggest a period of close interaction between Assyrian and Anshanite-Elamite elites which, in the west, corresponds with an Elamo-Assyrian artistic period between c.674 and 626 BC. Nothing is known about who was behind these carvings, yet their addition to the Elamite sanctuary indicates continuity with Elamite religious traditions and political authority linked to an erstwhile Elamite cultic center.

Summary and conclusions

As we have seen, the NE I period (c.1100–725 BC) is scantily represented in the archaeological material record of Khuzestan and Fars. To date, the chief site of Susa has delivered meager data from poor funerary contexts characterized by common and coarse ceramic assemblages and polychrome vitreous material. The dearth of archaeological data at Susa stands in sharp contrast with the information provided by the two monumental rock reliefs at KF IV (ninth to eighth centuries BC) and III (eighth to sixth centuries BC) and the additions to Kurangun (II and III; eighth to sixth centuries BC?). These reliefs depict cultural traditions intimately attached to the notion of place (the Izeh/Malamir and Mamasani valleys), "ethnic" self-identification (a social group characterized by distinctive physical features, most particularly, braided long hair), and custom and ritual (animal sacrifice, a communal shared meal, and religious worship). Taken together, place, self-representation, communal ritual, and worship provide a nexus of identity markers defining a population characterized by a specific culture and sociopolitical ideology.

The international political background of the ninth and eighth centuries BC was dominated by the increasingly expansionistic aims of the Assyrian Empire. Their encroachment on areas of traditional Elamite influence, neighboring Babylon and the Zagros Mountains, during the reigns of Assurnasirpal II (883–859 BC) and Shalmaneser III (858–824 BC) (Potts 1999: 263) would have sent a powerful message to the Elamite elites. According to Mesopotamian sources (Brinkman 1968, 208–9), in 813 BC Elamite troops, alongside Kassite, Aramaean, and Chaldean units, came to the aid of the Babylonian king Marduk-balassu-iqbi, who was besieged at Dur-Papsukkal, a royal city near Der, by the Assyrian king Šamši-Adad V (823–811 BC). Yet, thirty years later, a letter from Nimrud dated to the end of the reign of Adad-nerari III (810–783 BC) mentions the presence on an Elamite ambassador at the Assyrian court and the manufacture and use of the Elamite bow (Dalley and Postgate 1984: 256, no. 145 iv.13 and iv.26).

The interlude between 720 and 674 BC was characterized by a pattern of Elamite confrontation against Assyria, directly challenging the authority of Sennacherib (705–681 BC). This drama peaked with the capture by the Elamites and probable execution in 694 BC of the Assyrian crown prince and king of Babylon Assur-nadin-shumi. The extent of Elamite influence was illustrated three years later when king Humban-Numena (692–688 BC) gathered a coalition of highlanders (from Parsuas, Ellipi, Pašeru, and Anshan) and lowlanders (Chaldeans, Arameans, and Babylonians) against Sennacherib. The subsequent period reveals moments of close, peaceful interaction which reached a climax in 674 BC when an *adê* peace treaty was concluded between Esarhaddon (681–669 BC) and the Elamite king Urtak (675–664 [?] BC). The treaty incorporated oaths sworn to Elamite and Assyrian gods and was sealed by an exchange of Elamite and Assyrian princes. In the end, neither the *adê* treaty nor the exile of the house of Urtak to Assyria (664–653 BC) prevented the looting and devastation of western Elam and Susa by Assurbanipal in 647 BC (Álvarez-Mon 2009a).

This latter event has dominated the traditional interpretative model for the end of Elamite civilization. However, the material, textual, and artistic assemblages at Susa, together with the reliefs from Izeh/Malamir (KF I, *c*.650–550 BC), Naqsh-e Rustam (*c*.674–626 BC), and the elite material from Arjan (*c*.600–570 BC) and Ram Hormuz (*c*.585–539 BC) provide evidence of the survival of Elamite political power, culture, and traditions after the Assyrian raids on western Elam. These assemblages manifest a period of close Elamite and Assyrian interaction that most likely began with the Elamo-Assyrian peace treaty of 674 BC and may have lasted until 626 BC, when the Babylonian king Nabopolassar returned "the gods of Susa" (implying the presence of a political authority and the restoration of the Susa shrines). This material also speaks in favor of a dynamic decentralization of Elamite territorial and political integrity that relied on multiple power centers such as Susa, Huhnur (Tol-e Bormi in the Ram Hormuz plain), and Hidalu (situated east of Huhnur). The political makeup of Elam during this time period, however, remains to be determined. Different views have been proposed to characterize the decentralized nature of NE political power along the lines of multiple royal courts and the degree to which these provincial centers were independent from the authority of a paramount Elamite king (e.g., Steve et al. 2002–3: 479, "l'empire désagrégé"; Henkelman 2003a: 255; Potts 2010).

The last century of an independent kingdom of Elam (*c*.626–520 BC) witnessed a revival of Elamite culture that integrated the recent Elamo-Assyrian past with western Elamite and highland artistic traditions. This period takes the form of a NE "renaissance" (Álvarez-Mon 2010a: 189, n. 48) emerging against a sociopolitical symbiosis conditioned by three fundamental events: the documented interaction of Elamite- and Iranian-speaking populations (distinctively labeled by P. de Miroschedji the genesis of the Persian *ethnos*; cf. Tavernier 2011); the vacuum left by the collapse of the Assyrian Empire after *c*.605 BC; and the increasing effects of new ideological (and possibly economic) orders dominated by an equestrian-based culture. In fact, the role played by the horse in both the collapse of the Assyrian Empire and the emergence of powerful polities in the Zagros and Fars has been generally underestimated by students of ancient history. In assessing the "Iranian" contribution to the culture of Achaemenid Persia, P. R. S. Moorey suggested that that equestrianism, "a repertory of distinctive personal equipment ... with no pedigree in the regions of the Near East west of the Zagros and no known antecedent in Iran before Iron II (1000–800 B.C.)," was one of the quintessential characteristics of Persian culture (Moorey 1985: 22).

Meanwhile, relatively sheltered from the upheavals of the west, the eastern highlands may have enjoyed the breathing space to channel these events in a proper "Anshanite" way. Much remains uncertain but it is highly possible that since 694 BC the old Elamite kingdom of Anshan enjoyed a substantial degree of political sovereignty that became cemented under the aegis of the House of Sheshpesh (Teispes). Various models have been articulated as to the characteristics of the kingdom of Anshan and the identity of Cyrus the Great (Vanden Berghe 1963: 39; Miroschedji 1985; Potts 2005, 2011; Henkelman 2008, 2011; Álvarez-Mon 2009b, 2010a; Álvarez-Mon and Garrison 2011; Quintana 2011; Vallat 2011; Waters 2011). What is becoming increasingly apparent, however, is that throughout this period Elamite civilization provided the crucible of legitimacy (Potts 2005: 70) and the traditional sociopolitical and religious nexus of continuity, which helped to forge the cultural foundations and imperial aspirations of Cyrus II "the Great" (c.559–530 BC).

Further reading

After the interlude caused by the Iranian Revolution in 1979 there was renewed interest in the Elamite Iron Age, beginning with a study of the history and broader archaeological context of Elam by Potts (1999). This work is complemented by the entry dedicated to Susa in the Supplement to the *Dictionnaire de la Bible* (Steve et al. 2002–3). The last few years have witnessed continuing interest in the later history of Elam and the Elamite heritage of Persia with studies stressing textual evidence (Waters 2000), religion (Henkelman 2008), and art (Álvarez-Mon 2010), as well as a comprehensive overview of the transition between Elam and Persia (Álvarez-Mon et al. 2011).

References

Álvarez-Mon, J. 2009a. Ashurbanipal's feast: A view from Elam. *IrAnt* 44: 131–80.
———. 2009b. Notes on the "Elamite" garment of Cyrus the Great. *AJ* 89: 211–33.
———. 2010a. *The Arjān tomb, at the crossroads of the Elamite and the Persian Empires*. Leuven: Acta Iranica 49.
———. 2010b. Platform bearers from Kul-e Farah III and VI. *Iran* 48: 27–41.
———. 2010c. Elamite garments and headdresses of the late Neo-Elamite Period (7th–6th century BC). *AMIT* 42: 207–35.
———. 2013. Braids of glory. Elamite sculptural reliefs from the highlands: Kūl-e Farah IV. *SE*: 207–48.
Álvarez-Mon, J., and M. B. Garrison. 2011. Postscript. *EP*: 489–93.
Álvarez-Mon, J., M. B. Garrison, and D. Stronach. 2011. Introduction. *EP*: 1–32.
Amiet, P. 1966. *Elam*. Auvers-sur-Oise: Archée Éditeurs.
———. 1972. *Glyptique susienne : Des origines à l'époque des Perses achéménides. Cachets, sceaux-cylindres et empreintes antiques découverts à Suse de 1913 à 1967*, 2 vols. Paris: MDAI 43.

———. 1973. La glyptique de la fin de l'Élam. *Arts Asiatiques* 28: 3–45.
———. 1992. Bronzes élamites de la collection George Ortiz. *AMI* 25: 81–9.
———. 2000. Glanes élamites. *VD*: 1–8.
Bayani, M. I. 1979. The Elamite periods on the Izeh Plain. *AINX*: 99–105.
Brinkman, J. A. 1968. *A political history of post-Kassite Babylonia, 1158–722 BC*. Rome: Analecta Orientalia 43.
———. 1984. *Prelude to empire: Babylonian society and politics, 747–626 BC*. Philadelphia: OPBF 7.
Calmeyer, P. 1973. Zur Genese altiranischer Motive. *AMI* 6: 135–52.
Carter, E. 1984. Archaeology. In *Elam: Surveys of political history and archaeology*, E. Carter and M. W. Stolper, 103–277. Berkeley/Los Angeles/London: University of California Publications, Near Eastern Studies 25.
———. 1988. review of U. Seidl, *Die elamischen Felsreliefs von Kūrāngun und Naqš-e Rustam*. *ZA* 78: 145–8.
———. 1994. Bridging the gap between the Elamites and the Persians in southeastern Khūzestān. In *Continuity and change*, ed. H. Sancisi-Weedenburg, A. Kuhrt, and M. C. Root, 65–95. Leiden: AchHist 8.
———. 1996. *Excavations at Anshan (Tal-e Malyan): The Middle Elamite period*. Philadelphia: UMM 82.
Dalley, S. and J. N. Postgate, 1984. *The tablets from Fort Shalmaneser*. London: CTN 3.
Frame, G. 1992. *Babylonia 689–627 BC: A political history*. Leiden: UNHAII.
Garrison, M. B. 2006. The "Late Neo-Elamite" glyptic style: A perspective from Fars. *BAI* 16: 65–102.
———. 2010. The heroic encounter in the visual arts of ancient Iraq and Iran c. 1000–500 BC. In *The Master of Animals in Old World iconography*, ed. D. B. Counts and B. Arnold, 151–74. Budapest: Archaeolingua.
———. 2011. The seal of "Kuraš the Anzanite, Son of Šešpeš" (Teispes), PFS 93*: Susa–Anšan–Persepolis. *EP*: 375–405.
Gerardi, P. 1987. Ashurbanipal's Elamite campaigns: A literary and political study. Unpublished PhD diss., University of Pennsylvania.
Ghirshman, R. 1954. *Village perse-achéménide*. Paris: MDP 34.
———. 1966. *Tchogha Zanbil (Dur-Untash): La ziggurat*. Paris: MDP 39.
Henkelman, W. F. M. 2003a. Defining Neo-Elamite history. *BiOr* 60/3–4: 251–63.
———. 2003b. Persians, Medes and Elamites: Acculturation in the Neo-Elamite period. *CE*: 181–231.
———. 2008. *The other gods who are: Studies in Elamite-Iranian acculturation based on the Persepolis Fortification Texts*. Leiden: AchHist 14.
———. 2011. Parnakka's feast: *šip* in Pārsa and Elam. *EP*: 89–166.
Hinz, W. 1962. Die elamischen Inschriften des Hanne. In *A locust's leg. Studies in honour of S. H. Taqizadeh*, ed. W. B. Hennig and E. Yarshater, 105–16. London: Lund, Humphries & Co.
Jéquier, G. 1901. Description du site de Malamir (Appendice). In *Textes élamites-anzanites, première série*, ed. V. Scheil, 133–44. Paris: MDP 3.
König, F. W. 1965. *Die elamischen Königsinschriften*. Graz: AfO Beiheft 16.
Lampre, G. 1905. La representation du lion à Suse. In *Textes élamites-anzanites, deuxième série*, ed. V. Scheil, 159–76. Paris: MDP 8.
Layard, A. H. 1846. A description of the province of Khúzistán. *JRGS* 16: 1–105.
Mecquenem, R. de. 1922. Fouilles de Suse: Campagnes des années 1914–1921–1922. *RA* 19: 109–40.

———. 1953. *Recherches à Tchogha Zembil*. Paris: MMAI 33.
Miroschedji, P. de. 1978. Stratigraphie de la période néo-élamite à Suse (c. 1100–c. 540). *Paléorient* 4: 213–28.
———. 1981a. Fouilles du chantier Ville Royale II à Suse (1975–1977). I. Les niveaux élamites. *CDAFI* 12: 9–136.
———. 1981b. Observations dans les couches néo-élamites au nord-ouest du tell de la Ville Royale à Suse. *CDAFI* 12: 143–67.
———. 1981c. Prospections archéologiques au Khūzestān en 1977. *CDAFI* 12: 169–92.
———. 1982. Notes sur la glyptique de la fin de l'Elam. *RA* 76: 51–63.
———. 1985. La fin du royaume d'Anšan et de Suse et la naissance de l'Empire Perse. *ZA* 75: 265–306.
———. 1990a. Note d'orfèvérie Neo-Elamite. *MJP*: 181–94.
———. 1990b. La fin de l'Elam: Essai d'analyse et d'interpretation. *IrAnt* 25: 47–95.
Moghaddam, A., and N. Miri. 2007. Archaeological surveys in the "Eastern Corridor," south-western Iran. *Iran* 44: 23–55.
Moorey, P. R. S. 1985. The Iranian contribution to Achaemenid material culture. *Iran* 23: 21–38.
Muscarella, O. W. 1992. Stele of Adda-hamiti-Inshushinak. *RCS*: 198–9.
Nasrabadi, B. M. 2005. Eine Steininschrift des Amar-Suena aus Tappe Bormi (Iran). *ZA* 95: 161–71.
Pézard, M. 1924. Reconstitution d'une stèle de Adda-hamti-In-Šušnak. *Babyloniaca* 8: 1–26.
Pons, N. 1994. Tchoga Zanbil après Untas-Napirisa. *CDR*: 43–51.
Porada, E. 1965. *The art of Ancient Iran: Pre-Islamic cultures*. New York: Praeger.
Potts, D. T. 1999. *The archaeology of Elam: Formation and transformation of an ancient Iranian state*. Cambridge: Cambridge World Archaeology.
———. 2004. The numinous and the immanent: Some thoughts on Kurangun and the Rudkhaneh-e Fahliyan. *FHK*: 143–56.
———. 2005. Cyrus the Great and the Kingdom of Anshan. In *Birth of the Persian Empire*, ed. V. S. Curtis and S. Stewart, 7–28. London: I. B. Tauris.
———.2008. review of A. Alizadeh, *The origins of state organizations in prehistoric highland Fars, southern Iran: Excavations at Tall-e Bakun*. *BiOr* 65/1–2: 195–206.
———. 2010a. Nomadismus in Iran von der Frühzeit bis in die Moderne: Eine Untersuchung sowohl aus archäologischer als auch historischer Sicht. *Eurasia Antiqua* 16: 1–19.
———. 2010b. Monarchy, factionalism and warlordism: Reflections on Neo-Elamite courts. In *Der Achämenidenhof/The Achaemenid Court*, ed. B. Jacobs and R. Rollinger, 107–37. Wiesbaden: CLeO 2.
———. 2011. A note on the limits of Anšan. *EP*: 35–43.
Potts, D. T., A. Asgari Chaverdi, C. A. Petrie, A. Dusting, F. Farhadi, I. K. McRae, S. Shikhi et al. 2007. The Mamasani Archaeological Project, Stage Two: Excavations at Qaleh Kali (Tappeh Servan/Jinjun [MS 46]). *Iran* 45: 287–300.
Quintana, E. C. 2011. Elamitas frente a Persas: El reino independiente de Anšan. *EP*: 167–90.
Sajjidi, M., and H. T. Wright. 1979. Test excavations in the Elamite layers at the Izeh East Face. *AINX*: 106–13.
Scheil, V. 1901. *Textes élamites-anzanites, première série*. Paris: MDP 3.
———. 1907. *Textes élamites-anzanites, troisième série*. Paris: MDP 9.
———. 1911. *Textes élamites-anzanites, quatrième série*. Paris: MDP 11.
Schmidt, E., M. N. Van Loon, and H. H. Curvers. 1989. *HEL*.

Seidl, U. 1986. *Die elamischen Felsreliefs von Kurangun und Naqš-e Rustam*. Berlin: Iranische Denkmäler 12/2/H.
———. 1997. Izeh. *OEANE*: 199–203.
Shishehgar, A. 2008. *Discovery of a tomb attributed to members of King Shutur-Nahhunte dynasty, son of Indid (or Indattu), Neo-Elamite III period (c. 585–539 BC)*. Tehran: ICAR (in Persian).
Stein, M. A. 1940. *Old routes of Western Īrān: Narrative of an archaeological journey*. London: Macmillan.
Steve, M.-J. 1986. La fin de L'Elam: A propos d'une empreinte de sceau-cyindre. *StIr* 15: 7–21.
Steve, M.-J., H. Gasche, and L. De Meyer. 1980. La Susiane au deuxième millénaire: À propos d'une interprétation des fouilles de Suse. *IrAnt* 15: 49–154.
Steve, M.-J., F. Vallat, H. Gasche, and F. Jullien. 2002–3. Suse. *SDB* 73: 360–512 (bibliog. in *SDB* 74: 620–52).
Stolper, M. W. 1984. Political history of Elam. In *Elam: Surveys of political history and archaeology*, E. Carter and M. W. Stolper, 1–100. Berkeley/Los Angeles/London: University of California Publications, Near Eastern Studies 25.
———. 1988. Mālamīr B. Philologisch. *RlA* 7: 276–81.
———. 1992. Stele of Adda-hamiti-Inshushinak (the inscriptions). *RCS*: 198–9.
Stronach, D. 1978. *Pasargadae: A report on the excavations conducted by the British Institute of Persian Studies from 1961 to 1963*. Oxford: Clarendon Press.
Sumner, W. M. 1972. Excavations at Tall-i Malyan, 1971–72. *Iran* 12: 155–80.
———. 1986. Achaemenid settlement in the Persepolis Plain. *AJA* 90: 3–31.
Tavernier, J. 2004. Some thoughts on Neo-Elamite chronology. *ARTA* 2004.003: 1–44.
———. 2011. Iranians in Neo-Elamite texts. *EP*: 191–262.
Vallat, F. 1984. Kidin-Hutran à l'époque néo-élamite. *Akkadica* 37: 1–17.
———. 1996. Nouvelle analyse des inscriptions néo-élamites. *CO*: 385–95.
———. 1998. Elam i. The history of Elam. *EnIr* online edition.
———. 2006. Atta-hamiti-Inshushinak, Shutur-Nahhunte et la chronologie néo-élamite. *Akkadica* 127: 59–62.
———. 2011. Darius, l'héritier légitime, et les premiers Achéménides. *EP*: 263–84.
Vanden Berghe, L. 1963. Les reliefs élamites de Malamir. *IrAnt* 3: 22–39.
———. 1966. *Archéologie de l'Iran ancien*. Leiden: Brill.
———. 1983. *Reliefs rupestres de l'Iran ancien*. Brussels: KMKG-MRAH.
———. 1986. Données nouvelles concernant le relief rupestre élamite de Kūrangūn. *FHE*: 157–67.
Van Loon, M. N. 1988. Two Neo-Elamite cylinder seals with mounted huntsmen. *IrAnt* 23: 212–26.
Waele, E. de. 1973. Une page d'Art iranien: Les reliefs rupestres d'Izeh Malamir. *Archeologia* 60: 31–46.
———. 1976. Les processions avec statues divines sur les reliefs rupestres élamites Kul-e Farah III et Kul-e Farah VI (Izeh). In *Akten des VII. Internationalen Kongress für Iranische Kunst und Archäologie*, ed. W. Kleiss, 93–101. Berlin: Dietrich Reimer.
———. 1981. Travaux archéologiques à Šekaf-e Salman et Kul-e Farah près d'Izeh (Malamir). *IrAnt* 16: 45–61.
Waters, M. W. 2000. *A survey of Neo-Elamite history*. Helsinki: SAAS 12.
———. 2011. Parsumaš, Anšan, and Cyrus. *EP*: 285–96.
Weeks, L. R. 2008. review of A. Alizadeh, *Chogha Mish*, vol. 2. *AMIT* 42: 309–13.

Weissbach. F. H. 1894. *Neue Beiträge zur Kunde der susischen Inschriften*. Leipzig: Abhandlungen der Königlichen Sächsischen Gesellschaft der Wissenschaften, phil.-hist. Klasse 14/7.

Wright, H. T. 1987. The Susiana hinterlands during the era of primary state formation. *AWI*: 141–55.

Wright, H. T., and E. Carter. 2003. Archaeological survey on the western Ram Hormuz plain. *YBYN*: 61–82.

Wright, H. T., and J. A. Neely 2010. *EASDLP*.

Zeidi, M., B. McCall, and A. Khosrowzadeh. 2009. Survey of Dasht-e Rostam-e Yek and Dasht-e Rostam-e Do. *MAPSO*: 147–68.

CHAPTER 24

ELAM, ASSYRIA, AND BABYLONIA IN THE EARLY FIRST MILLENNIUM BC

MATTHEW WATERS

Introduction

Elam, less explored and less well understood than its neighbors to the west in Mesopotamia, is often relegated to secondary status in modern treatments, if it is not simply an afterthought. When the Neo-Elamite period (c.1000–550 BC) is discussed, it is lowland (i.e., western) Elam, roughly equivalent to modern Khuzestan (Susiana) and its mountainous periphery that comes to the fore. This emphasis reflects the source preponderance and the attendant analytic problems, recurring issues throughout this chapter.

The archaeological evidence from Khuzestan as a whole is limited. The archaeological sequence from the main city, Susa, is inexact. Many cities beyond Susa that are mentioned in the extant sources are not excavated and, in some cases, not even confidently identified on the ground. The situation becomes more opaque as one proceeds beyond Khuzestan. Placing geographical demarcations upon "Elam" as a political entity thus becomes an elusive goal. Indeed, the term "Elam" itself is a Mesopotamian construct—written logographically ^{KUR}NIM.MA^{KI}, Akkadian *Elamtu*—a term that over time came to indicate the lowland component of what the Elamites themselves termed *Ha(l)tamti* (for overviews see Potts 1999: 1–9; Vallat 1993: cviii–cx; Miroschedji 2003).

Migrations of various Iranian groups into Iran during the late second and early first millennia add layers of complexity to historical analysis. Examining (if not fully apprehending) the processes of Elamite–Iranian acculturation is of particular import when one considers that the Achaemenid Persian Empire's core was the territory of modern Fars, an area that had been for centuries a distinctly Elamite territory, that is, Anšan: the name of both a capital city and its surrounding region. Around 1000 BC the city of

Anšan was abandoned, and the scant evidence suggests that semisedentary pastoralism became the dominant way of life over the succeeding centuries. It must be emphasized that the excavation of first millennium sites, including Anšan, is minimal, so the paucity of the archaeological record is not a reliable gauge (see *inter alia* Miroschedji 1990: 62–5; Boucharlat 2005; Henkelman 2008: 43–9; Potts 2011).

Neo-Elamite (NE) periodization

With regard to archaeological periodization there is an accepted break: some distinctive finds dated to the eighth century have been used to demarcate the NE I period, *c*.1000–725/700, and the NE II period, *c*.725/700–520 (Miroschedji 1981a, 1981b; Potts 1999: 260–2; Carter 1999). Historical periodization is more convoluted; paleographical, linguistic, or historical considerations all are applied, and all are fluid (see Steve 1992: 21–3; Vallat 1996; Waters 2000: 3–4; Tavernier 2004; and Henkelman 2008: 4–8 for overviews). Generally a tripartite structure is applied to Neo-Elamite history: NE I, *c*.1000–750, a "dark age" for which little evidence exists and even less guess is hazarded; NE II, *c*.750–646, characterized by a (relatively) massive amount of textual material from Mesopotamia, though significantly less from Elam itself, and demarcated at its end by the Assyrian sack of Susa; and NE III, *c*.646–550, with a fluctuating end date dependent upon when one chooses to give primacy to the Persians rather than the Elamites, especially in Susa. A tripartite system is also followed herein: a choice that allows some thematic categorization based upon the available evidence (for NE I, treated only in summary fashion, see Potts 1999: 262–3; Waters 2000: 10–11; and Steve et al. 2002–3: 470–1).

The NE II period

There is some paradox in that the mid-eighth to mid-seventh centuries are the most richly documented period for the study of Neo-Elamite history, since that rich documentation is mainly of Assyrian origin. We are thus reliant upon the perspective of Elam's enemy for assessment of Elam's history. This is rather like its parallel for the study of Achaemenid Persian history in the sixth through fourth centuries, for which period Greek sources provide such an integral (and quantitatively large) part of the narrative. However, Elam was a major rival of Assyria at the height of the latter's power. Yet beneath the conflict was a rich network of economic and cultural ties, far less obvious but nonetheless significant for both regions, the historical ramifications of which have yet to be studied in detail (see Zadok 2011 for a sampling of such during the Neo-Babylonian period).

Throughout the NE II period, a theme of Elamite–Babylonian cooperation against Assyria may be tracked. Babylonia often appears caught—figuratively, though the literal sense may also serve—between Elam and Assyria. Battle for control of the eastern

Babylonian hinterland, as well as the Zagros foothills with the lucrative trade routes leading across northern Iran, remained pressing concerns for all parties (see the overview in Henkelman 2008: 35–9). At times control of Babylonia itself, especially its shared border with Elam and its southern reaches (i.e., the Sealand), was at issue. Assyrian correspondence reveals that the Elamites had great influence, if not direct control, over many of the various Aramaean and Chaldean groups living in that region.

The Assyrians generally referred to a single "king of Elam," though there are some notable exceptions. The extant evidence is sufficient to attest that we are woefully uninformed about the political structure of the Neo-Elamite kingdom, or for that matter "kingdoms" at those times for which the plural applies. Our information is based almost entirely upon Assyrian annals and correspondence (among the kings and their officials or subjects) and later Babylonian chronicles; in other words, relatively few insights into political or dynastic history may be gleaned from the sporadic Neo-Elamite sources. Further difficulties arise from the fact that Neo-Elamite texts have no consistently identifiable chronological markers, an issue that will be treated below.

A list of NE II kings named in Mesopotamian sources, with regnal dates, is given in Table 24.1. The rulers listed bear the title "king of Elam" or its presumed functional equivalent in Assyrian and Babylonian texts. Even providing a dynastic chart is not uncomplicated. A seemingly straightforward list of rulers is not so straightforward: it necessitates explanations of the exceptions and interpretive difficulties involved in assessments of individual reigns. Vallat (1996: 389–90) assigns two additional kings—Huban-tahra and Huban-mena II (also spelled Huban-immena)—to the early eighth century. These kings are not attested or labeled as such in Mesopotamian sources but are identified as fathers of Huban-nikaš (I) and Šutruk-Nahhunte (II), respectively (cf. Waters 2000: 12–13, 17–18; Tavernier 2003: 203–4).

Table 24.1 Rulers labelled "king of Elam" in Mesopotamian sources, with regnal dates (italicized names indicate potential equivalents attested in NE sources).

Ruler	Date (BC)
Huban-nikaš I	743–717
Šutruk-Nahhunte II	717–699
Hallušu	699–693 (*Hallutaš-Inšušinak?*)
Kutir-Nahhunte	693–692
Huban-menanu	692–689
Huban-haltaš I	689–681
Huban-haltaš II	681–675
Urtak	675–664
Te'umman	664–653 (*Tepti-Huban-Inšušinak?*)
Huban-nikaš II	653–652
Tammaritu	652–649? and 647
Indabibi	649?–648?
Huban-haltaš III	648?–645?
Huban-habua	647?
Pa'e	646?

These issues will be discussed or referenced in what follows: a brief, diachronic overview of Neo-Elamite history, from which select themes and illustrative episodes will be discussed along with associated problems of historical interpretation. The first five kings in Table 24.1 (Huban-nikaš I through Huban-menanu) were related. There were at least two Šutruk- or Šutur-Nahhuntes in the Neo-Elamite period who were kings; there is disagreement whether the names Šutruk-Nahhunte and Šutur-Nahhunte are variant spellings of the same name, the position followed herein, or are distinct names (cf. Lambert 1967: 48; Vallat 1995, 1996; Waters 2000: app. B; Tavernier 2004: 7–15). The Šutruk-Nahhunte who ruled contemporaneously with Sargon II and Sennacherib of Assyria is considered by many scholars to be the same king from whom several dedicatory inscriptions at Susa are extant. A certain king Hallutaš-Inšušinak, who left a dedicatory inscription at the temple of Inšušinak in Susa, is only with immense difficulty equated with the Hallušu in the chart above. Akkadian *Hallušu* is considered a hypocoristicon of Elamite *Hallutaš-Inšušinak*, but some commentators—on paleographic and historical grounds—disassociate the two rulers (see below). Most NE inscriptions are short, and with few exceptions they seldom contain information regarding the kings political or military deeds, certainly not on par with the quality and quantity of information derived from Assyrian annals. A root cause of the usual neglect of NE inscriptional material involves the manifold uncertainties in their translation, chronology, and interpretation.

The four kings from Huban-haltaš I to Te'umman were brothers (Waters 2006 with references). Little is known of Huban-haltaš, either I or II, though some of their offspring may be tracked during the Assyrian–Elamite wars of the mid-seventh century. Much of the decade after the Til Tuba campaign in 653 BC was marked by more forceful and direct Assyrian involvement in Elamite affairs. The rapid succession of kings, as relayed in Table 24.1, is a manifestation of the resultant instability. Other Elamite rulers and challengers, not on the chart, also appear in the sources during this tumultuous period; among these other rulers were Ištarnandi and Tammaritu (a distinct Tammaritu from the one listed in Table 24.1), kings of Hidalu. Assyrian sources for Elam fade after the celebrated sack of Susa in 646 BC: a glorified assault that ranks with those of Sargon's sack of Musasir in 714 BC and Sennacherib's sack of Babylon in 689 BC. Beyond the haze of Assurbanipal's hyperbole, we know that that was far from the end of the story for Susa.

ELAM AND ASSYRIA: THE MIDDLE ZAGROS AND THE BABYLONIAN FRONTIER DURING THE NE II PERIOD

The site of Der, near modern Tell Aqar at Badra in eastern Iraq, was a gateway to one of the major trade routes into the Zagros Mountains. Near the end of the ninth century, the Assyrian Šamši-Adad V fought a battle at Dur-Papsukkal, near Der, against the

Babylonian king Marduk-balassu-iqbi supported by Elamite troops. Tiglath-pileser III (744–727 BC) campaigned against Aramaean groups in southern Babylonia along the Elamite border, campaigns that included acquisition of territory. We have no record of any Elamite response to this activity, but subsequent events reveal that this region remained volatile. Table 24.2, although not comprehensive, provides a schematic overview of Elamite–Assyrian conflict by kings' reigns, dates, and locations. Engagements noted are major campaigns as relayed in Assyrian and Babylonian sources; not recorded are ongoing skirmishes or related military maneuvers, echoes of which appear via opaque references in the annals, palace relief epigraphs, or correspondence. The Assyrian kings are listed in the first column to emphasize the Mesopotamian sources for this information. Most of the engagements listed involve Babylonia, whether the engagements were fought in or near Babylonian territory or included active involvement of Babylonian forces (for overviews and additional context see Stolper 1984: 44–53; Potts 1999: 259ff.; Waters 2000; and Steve et al. 2002–3: 471–8, all with references to previous literature).

Certain patterns recur in the annals (see Liverani 2011: 41 for a general overview of the phenomenon). With little exception, the Assyrians are victorious. Where more than one source for an engagement exists, comparisons are instructive. For example, differing reports on the outcome from battles at Der in 720 or at Halule in 691 BC make Assyrian claims to victory suspect; the Babylonian chronicle contradicts the Assyrian annals in both cases. Overall, however, Assyria was more effective at projecting its power: the most consistent fighting occurred along the Elamite–Babylonian frontier. Yet the necessity of frequent military activity there reveals that Assyria, even at its height, never effectively quieted the region. A persistent motif in the annals finds the Elamite king in flight from

Table 24.2 Main Assyrian engagements with Elamite forces during the NE II period.

Assyrian king	Elamite king	Year(s) BC	Region(s)
Šamši-Adad V	?	814	Der
Tiglath-pileser III	Huban-nikaš I	uncertain	Elamite–Babylonian frontier
Sargon II	Huban-nikaš I	720	Der
	Šutruk-Nahhunte II	710	Elamite–Babylonian frontier
	Šutruk-Nahhunte II	708	Ellipi (central Zagros)
Sennacherib	Šutruk-Nahhunte II	703	Kish (Babylonia)
	Šutruk-Nahhunte II	702	Ellipi (central Zagros)
	Šutruk-Nahhunte II	700	Babylonia
	Hallušu	694–693	Babylonia
	Kutir-Nahhunte	692	Elam
	Huban- menanu	691	Halule (Tigris River)
Esarhaddon	Huban-haltaš II	680–675	Sealand (southern Babylonia)
Ashurbanipal	Urtak	664	Elamite–Babylonian frontier?
	Te'umman	653	Til Tuba (Elam, Ulai River)
	Huban-nikaš II	652	Mangisi (Diyala region?)
	Tammaritu	650 or 649	Babylonia
	Huban-haltaš III	648–645	Elam

Assyrian forces. The Elamite king's refuge is often the "distant mountains" (e.g., around Hidalu). This phenomenon, in part, underlies Miroschedji's hypothesis (1986: 216–20; cf. Henkleman 2008: 12–13) of three royal capitals in the NE period: Susa, Madaktu, and Hidalu—a system parallel to that of the *sukkalmah* period in the early second millennium BC. The locations of Madaktu and Hidalu are still a matter of some debate, as are their relationships as regional power centers in the Neo-Elamite political structure (for their locations see inter alia Miroschedji 1986; Vallat 1993: 96, 162; Potts 2001; Waters 2000: 33; Stolper 2003; Henkelman 2008: 499–501 on Hidalu).

That the highland peripheries, particularly along the southern route toward Fars, served as important centers is demonstrable from both contemporary and later evidence. Thus, it is presumed that the Assyrian accounts depict a reality, even if they are understood to include elements of hyperbole.

Another Assyrian theme emphasizes the Babylonian purchase of Elamite military support. Two prominent Chaldeans, Merodach-baladan (during the reigns of Sargon and Sennacherib) and Nabû-bēl-šumāti (during the reign of Assurbanipal), frequently appealed for Elamite support by means of gifts or payments. And they were not unique in doing so. The frequency of cooperation and exchange, often termed by the Assyrians—again, it must be remembered, a hostile source—as a "bribe" (*ṭātu*), is telling. Babylonia and Elam (at least, Susiana) were joined geographically as parts of the Babylonian alluvium, and the Sealand was important to both; numerous Aramaean groups interlaced the border region. Periodic Assyrian activity in order to fortify this area, such as Sargon's establishment of a fortress (with garrison implied) at the city of Sagbat, speaks to Assyrian strategic concerns. That the problems there remained intractable also speaks to Elamite and Babylonian persistence and their capability to thwart Assyrian designs.

Through the early seventh century similar strategic concerns applied in the central Zagros. At the death of the Ellipian king Daltâ in 708 BC, his nephews Ašpa-bara and Nibê fought as proxies for, respectively, Sargon II and Šutruk-Nahhunte II. Assyrian success in Ellipi, in conjunction with the activity along the Elamite–Babylonian border, saw Elam pressured from buffer zones in the north and west. Subsequent campaigns by Sennacherib against Ellipi (702 BC) and against Babylonia (700 BC) reveal that Assyrian efforts to secure these contested peripheries with Elam required frequent maintenance. After the Battle of Halule (691 BC), however, Elamite reach in the central Zagros seems reduced, at least as one may discern from the extant sources.

If Elamite–Assyrian conflict may be demarcated into stages, the Battle of Halule marks the end of one. To judge from the decrease in clay dedicated to Assyrian actions against Elam, the former's southeastern front may have been quiet for a time, during the reign of Huban-menanu's successor, Huban-haltaš I (689–681 BC). Note that this is an observation from silence. We know little about Huban-haltaš I's reign—even whether or not he shared a familial relation with any of his predecessors (Waters 2006)—beyond the Babylonian Chronicle's notice of the odd medical emergency that brought his death. This may be compared with notations about Huban-menanu's protracted illness and Huban-haltaš II's sudden death "without becoming ill." If more were evident about the Chronicle's composition—by whom, for whom, and when—it would be easier to speculate about any conjunction of these episodes and the rationale for mentioning the mysterious maladies that afflicted some of the Neo-Elamite kings. This phenomenon is certainly to be paralleled with Mesopotamian omen literature, and the attendant religious and cultural significance, but it is in need of further study. No doubt these strange maladies were to be attributed to the gods' antipathy; compare Assurbanipal's descriptions of Te'umman's affliction (Borger 1996: 98–9) before the Til Tuba campaign and note a potential parallel in Liverani (2011: 36, 44ff. on the chronicles as a genre; see also Brinkman 1990).

Tension in southern Babylonia flared again during Huban-haltaš II's reign (681–675 BC), marked by the Elamite–Assyrian struggle for control of the Sealand. This sequence is somewhat unusual in that the Assyrian annals do not serve as our main sources for the conflict, but the particulars must be gleaned from Assyrian correspondence. While the exact sequence is uncertain, a conceptual outline is possible and, at the same time, illustrative for how the history of this period is reconstructed (Waters 1999). It is clear from the Sealanders' letters to Nineveh that the future king Te'umman was directing the Elamite enterprise, one that threatened to destabilize the region. It is not a coincidence that Esarhaddon (Assyrian king since 680 BC) chose to sponsor a sheikh among the Gambulu, Bēl-iqīša, and to fortify his stronghold Ša-pī-bēl, "like a locked door in the face of Elam" (Leichty 2011: 18–19). The Babylonian Chronicle is silent on this entire affair but does offer a laconic reference that Huban-haltaš II assaulted Sippar in 675 (Grayson 1975: 83), a raid that—in reading only the Chronicle's terse accounting—seems odd and out of place. But the Sippar raid is more easily contextualized when considered with the Elamite fomentation in the Sealand. Further, since Esarhaddon's annals have little to say on the subject, one wonders whether there was not much for the Assyrians to celebrate—that, though, is speculation from silence.

Urtak's reign (675–664 BC) is remarkable for a sea-change in recorded Elamite–Assyrian relations: within two years of Urtak's accession, a formalized peace with Assyria had been concluded, one that included sworn oaths, the return of captured gods, and even an exchange of royal children to the respective courts. One may only wonder at the preliminaries that led to this apparently unprecedented agreement, a situation completely at odds with what had pertained in the previous reigns. Peaceful relations continued into Assurbanipal's reign. Assurbanipal even offered assistance during a time of famine in Elam: grain delivered to Urtak and refuge offered to Elamites fleeing drought conditions. This tranquil state of affairs did not last, though, as the end of Urtak's reign witnessed a return to Assyrian–Elamite friction.

The aftermath of Urtak's death and Te'umman's accession occasioned scores of the extended Elamite royal family fleeing to Assurbanipal, an exodus that would have enormous consequences for subsequent Elamite history. Assyrian annals offer no information on Te'umman's reign (664–653 BC) until its end. Elamite sources do not assist, unless the Tepti-Huban-Inšušinak who commissioned several dedicatory inscriptions at Susa is considered to be this Te'umman—an equation maintained by many scholars through the twentieth century but which has undergone significant revision (see below). Elamite political history and relations with Assyrian and Babylonia during the late 660s and early 650s BC are thus largely unknown, before the epic battle at Til Tuba. The word "epic" is used here purposely to evoke Assurbanipal's account of the battle in the annals, epigraphs, and famous palace relief sequence at Nineveh. The battle itself and the palace relief sequence have been treated voluminously (see inter alia, Potts 1999: 278–9; Córdoba 1997; Russell 1999: 154–98; Waters 2000: 51–5; Nadali 2007).

This Assyrian–Elamite confrontation in 653 BC marked a turning point, specifically with regard to increased Assyrian involvement in the internal affairs of Elam. Despite the concomitant increase in source material it is seldom easy to date, even sequentially, letters about particular Assyrian operations against Elamite or Chaldean forces. Further, because Assyrian annals were redacted frequently, the chronology and sequence of the episodes described therein is not always straightforward. For example, during the aftermath of the Til Tuba campaign the Assyrians also were victorious against the Gambulian sheikh Bēl-iqīša and another Elamite king, Ištarnandi, the king of Hidalu. How are we to assess Ištarnandi? Did he rule concurrently with Te'umman, or did he fill a vacuum after the battle of Til Tuba (and Te'umman's death) but rule only part of Elam (i.e., with a base in Hidalu)? What does Ištarnandi's role as king of Hidalu imply about Neo-Elamite political structure? These are questions for which scholars have developed no compelling answer (note Stolper 2003 and Henkelman 2008: 12–17, the latter with emphasis on this episode as reflective of an integrated Elamite state).

Assurbanipal had an answer, as he implemented what he no doubt hoped would be a solution to Assyria's long-running Elamite problem. He arranged the installation of two brothers (both sons of Urtak and both refugees at the Assyrian court) as concurrent kings: Huban-nikaš (II) as king of Elam and Tammaritu as king of Hidalu. While the particulars are not fully understood, Assurbanipal's action implies that Ištarnandi's position as king of Hidalu was a regular one. There is the additional implication that the latter (king of Hidalu) was subordinate to the former (king of Elam). It is an ongoing question to what extent Assurbanipal's arrangement echoed previous Neo-Elamite dynastic structure, but in any event it appears that at this time Elam may have been made a formal province of Assyria (Waters 2000: 57–60).

The arrangement did not last, as Huban-nikaš soon turned against his benefactor. Assurbanipal's annals associate this treachery with a bribe from Šamaš-šum-ukīn (Assurbanipal's brother and King of Babylon)—again as per the theme of Babylonian purchase of Elamite military aid—thus an opening salvo of Šamaš-šum-ukīn's rebellion in 652 BC. Rejoined Babylonian–Elamite cooperation against Assyria, enjoined by the Chaldean Nabû-bēl-šumāti of the Sealand, saw Assyria's entire southeastern front aflame with war for several years. This is only a superficial and telescoped summary of a complex geopolitical situation, for which there is voluminous (and often confusing) evidence from royal correspondence and administrative documents, in addition to the annals. There is no Elamite evidence (for an overview see Frame 1992: 131ff.; Potts 1999: 281–8 and Waters 2000: chaps. 5–6). The resulting dynamic looks similar to the one that pertained two generations before, though subsequent Assyrian activity remained focalized on the Babylonian–Elamite frontier, and even within Elam itself, in particular under the direction of Assurbanipal's commander (Akkadian *turtānu*) in the south, Bēl-ibni (De Vaan 1995).

Between 652 and the mid-640s BC, Assyrian annals name several kings of Elam: Huban-nikaš (II), Tammaritu, Indabibi, and Huban-haltaš (III), and various challengers (e.g., Huban-habua and Pa'e). The interpretative problems involved with multiple Tammaritus and other homonymous Elamites are too convoluted to go into here (see Waters 2000: 62–4; Waters 2001; Henkelman 2008: 12–13). Relentless pressure from Assyria on Elamites and Babylonians resulted, so Assurbanipal claimed, in total Assyrian victory: manifest in the annals and palace reliefs by portrayals of the sacks of Babylon and Susa, the humiliation of Elamite kings, and also the capture (and suicide) of Nabû-bēl-šumāti. Coincidentally or not, after this catastrophic sequence Assyrian sources no longer provide any substantive information about Elamite affairs.

THE NE III PERIOD

The century after the sack of Susa is one of the most opaque in Elamite history, yet one of enormous historical importance as it immediately precedes (and thus informs) the rise of the Achaemenid Persian Empire. The textual and archaeological sources for this period are sporadic and their interpretation varied. Nevertheless, from them we discern not only a continuation of a vibrant Elamite civilization but also an ethnogenesis, or acculturation as it is sometimes termed (see Henkelman 2008: 47–57 with previous lit.), of Elamites and Persians in Fars—a phenomenon not necessarily exclusive to that area. The finds at the tomb of Arjan (see Chapters 23 and 26) provide a compelling case study: evidence of a veritable hybrid culture, squarely set in an ongoing Persian–Elamite acculturation process (for overviews, see Stronach 2005; Álvarez-Mon 2010; Álvarez-Mon et al. 2011: 19–21. Álvarez-Mon 2010 provides a full treatment of the tomb and its contents). The NE III period is often characterized as one in which the Persians became dominant over separate, ethnically Elamite groups; that is, if the Elamites are even acknowledged in the sequence, one that in modern scholarship generally starts with the Persian victory over the Medes.

It has become the norm to envision contemporaneous, Neo-Elamite kings ruling independent principalities throughout southwestern Iran—not only in Susiana—in the roughly 100 years between the sack of Susa and Cyrus the Great's conquest of the Medes (see Vallat 1996; Potts 1999: 288–306; 2005; Waters 2000: 81ff.; Steve et al. 2002–3: 477–85; Tavernier 2004; Henkelman 2008: 1–63; Quintana 2011). The network of political relationships, if any, among these Elamite rulers is unclear. Regardless, it is no longer sufficient to assume a strict dichotomy between Persians and Elamites in tension with one another. A variety of evidence testifies to the persistence of Elamite cultural traditions and administrative practices, many of which heavily influenced the Persians and are manifest during the Achaemenid period.

One firmly datable reference stems from the Babylonian Chronicle series. In 626/5 BC the Babylonian king Nabopolassar returned the gods of Susa to that city (Grayson 1975: 88). From this gesture it is generally assumed that: (1) there must have been some organized polity with which Nabopolassar arranged this return; and (2) his act continues the pattern of Babylonians seeking Elamite aid against Assyria. There is no other context for this episode, and if Elamites were ultimately involved in the Babylonian and Median operations that brought about the fall of Assyria—and one may easily imagine Elamite enthusiasm in this enterprise—it is not obvious (Reade 1976: 105; Nylander 1999; Henkelman 2003: 198–9 for interesting speculation about Elamite involvement in the sack of Nineveh). The oblique reference in the chronicle provides confirmation that Susa was not annihilated, as a literal reading of Assurbanipal's hyperbolic account of the sack of Susa would have the reader suppose. For this period information on Elam's internal, political history is minimal. Conversely, there is a great deal of data for economic and social exchange with Babylonia (e.g., Zadok 2011 for an overview; cf. Henkelman 2008: 20–7 for a convenient survey of Neo-Elamite officials and their titles in both Mesopotamian and Elamite sources). Reliance on Elamite documentation offers a number of enticing possibilities for reconstructing Neo-Elamite history, but the long-frustrating counter involves fundamental problems of methodology and interpretation. Table 24.3 provides a list of NE kings and rulers as attested in NE inscriptions (cf. Vallat 1996: 393; Tavernier 2004: 5–6, 39; Henkelman 2008: 5–7). This is not intended to be comprehensive, as some kings mentioned in Neo-Elamite documentation, such as Appalaya, king of the Zarians (Scheil 1907: no. 71), are probably not Elamite (cf. Tavernier 2011: 240). Caution applies also to the enigmatic "kings of Samati" named upon some of the objects of the infamous Kalmakarra hoard (Henkelman 2003: 214–27; 2008: 28–31).

Only one king from this list, Šutruk-Nahhunte (II), has been confidently correlated with a counterpart mentioned in Mesopotamian texts, as discussed above. The kings Hallutaš-Inšušinak, son of Huban-tahra, and Tepti-Huban-Inšušinak, son of Šilhak-Inšušinak (II), have been traditionally identified with the kings Hallušu and Te'umman of Mesopotamian sources (e.g., Cameron 1936: 185ff.; Hinz 1972: 138ff.;

Table 24.3 Neo-Elamite kings and rulers in Neo-Elamite inscriptions. Note the difficulties in correlating the various rulers of this name, with spelling variants (see above). Šutruk-Nahhunte II is considered distinct from the two Šutur-Nahhuntes listed below, even if the latter two may be one and the same individual.

Neo-Elamite king	References in Neo-Elamite inscriptions
Šutruk-Nahhunte (II)	EKI nos. 71–73; Malbran-Labat 1995: no. 57
Hallutaš-Inšušinak	EKI no. 77; Malbran-Labat 1995: no. 58
Šilhak-Inšušinak (II)	EKI no. 78
Tepti-Huban-Inšušinak	EKI nos. 79–85, Malbran-Labat 1995: nos. 59–62
Šutur-Nahhunte (son of Indada)	EKI no. 75 l. 10
Šutur-Nahhunte	Amiet 1973: 29, no. 34 (father of Huban-kitin)
Hanni, *kutur* of Ayapir	EKI nos. 75–76
Ummanunu	Scheil 1907: no. 165
Atta-hamiti-Inšušinak	EKI nos. 86–87
Huban-Šuturuk	Schmidt 1957: pls. 27–28

Stolper 1984: 47–51). Since the seminal treatment of F. Vallat (1996), some scholars have severed the links between those kings who left dedicatory inscriptions in Elamite and their seventh-century counterparts of the same name prominent in Sennacherib's and Assurbanipal's annals. Despite problems with the traditional identifications of the aforementioned kings, the challenges and uncertainties in assessing NE inscriptions make elements of Vallat's chronological scheme problematic (cf. Tavernier 2004; Waters 2006: 65–8; Henkelman 2008: 4–8).

A brief overview must suffice in this context. Among various paleographic considerations applied in dating these Neo-Elamite inscriptions—none of which, it must be emphasized, has any internal chronological markers—are broken writings of the type consonant + vowel$_1$ – vowel$_2$ + consonant, such as *ba-iš* (this example is taken from Tavernier's important discussion 2004: 32–6; cf. Stolper's cautionary remarks, 1988: 279). Other orthographic assessments have been applied and been found wanting (cf. Vallat 1995, 1996; Waters 2000: 114; Tavernier 2004: 12–14). Broken writings occur with much more frequency in Achaemenid and late NE, so NE inscriptions that contain them, especially in large quantity, are dated accordingly to NE III. Further precision within that range is often difficult, if not impossible. The texts most central to a late seventh or sixth century dating for many of the kings listed in Table 21.3—i.e. those of Hallutaš-Inšušinak, Šilhak-Inšušinak, and Tepti-Huban-Inšušinak—manifest one instance of broken consonant writing each (see the chart in Tavernier 2004: 34–5). A single example of broken consonant writing offers no compelling argument to securely date any of these inscriptions. The significance of such sporadic paleographic and orthographic variations is, in my view, overestimated, especially when they occur in singular or few instances in a given inscription. This phenomenon recalls Greek epigraphy's "three-bar sigma" controversy of the latter half of the twentieth century AD. That litmus test applied to the reconstruction and dating of Athenian inscriptions has proven untenable; as a consequence, a widespread revisiting of several fundamentally accepted "truths" about fifth-century Athenian imperialism has resulted (Chambers 1996; Rhodes 2008). A similar lesson, in outline if not in specific application, is worth bearing in mind for analysis of NE history based on epigraphical features of royal and monumental inscriptions.

The important study of Vallat (1998b) further established a number of synchronisms between disparate NE textual evidence: a small corpus of Elamite letters from Nineveh, tablets from the Susa Acropolis and Apadana, among others (cf. Steve et al. 2002–3: 479–85; Waters 2000: 81ff.; Henkelman 2008: 13–14). The mention of a king Ummanunu in one of the roughly 300 from the Susa Acropolis archive (Scheil 1907: no. 165) serves as a linchpin for Vallat's (1996) and Tavernier's (2004) NE III chronological schemata: the Susa Acropolis texts, and thus Ummanunu, are dated by them to the early sixth century BC. In his royal inscriptions Šilhak-Inšušinak names his father Ummanunu (König 1965: no. 78), whom Vallat sees as the king Ummanunu mentioned in Scheil (1907: no. 165). Šilhak-Inšušinak, in turn, is identified as the father of Tepti-Huban-Inšušinak in the latter's inscriptions. Neither Šilhak-Inšušinak nor Tepti-Huban-Inšušinak are attested outside their own inscriptions.

A synchronism between the Acropolis tablets and the so-called Nineveh Letters would appear to place these texts chronologically before the fall of Nineveh. One of the Nineveh letters (Weissbach 1902: no. 13) refers to the king of Assyria; by implication, this refers to a time before the fall of the Assyrian Empire. Despite the uncertainties surrounding the status of Nineveh after 612, there is no evidence for a king of Assyria after its fall. This difficulty has yet to be reconciled with any scheme dating the Nineveh Letters, and any texts synchronized with them, after 612 BC (this is minimized by Vallat in his important treatment of this corpus, 1998a: 100; cf. Reade 2000; Tavernier 2004: 36–8; Waters 2011: 289, n. 24; on Nineveh after 612, see inter alia Dalley 1993; Kuhrt 1995; Reade 2001: 428–9; Curtis 2003; Jursa 2003; Rollinger 2008: 57). Because of the manifold uncertainties, the dating of many of these texts should remain open in the NE III period.

On historical grounds, if one is able to countenance multiple, concurrent kings c.650–550 BC, there seems little disincentive to allow the possibility during the earlier periods as well, as per the Huban-nikaš (II)–Tammaritu example. It must be emphasized again that the structural dynamic of Neo-Elamite government, as indicated by the preceding, escapes us. Arguments based on inscriptional paleography that set some of these kings in the late seventh and early sixth centuries BC are no more compelling than keeping these kings linked to their like-named counterparts prominent in Mesopotamian sources.

For example, admitting an early seventh-century Hallutaš-Inšušinak as primary king of Elam, who dedicated a temple to an important deity at Susa, does not preclude his reigning as king elsewhere in Elam for years before, perhaps even as subordinate to another king, in this case Šutruk-Nahhunte II (Stolper 1986: 238–9). Miroschedji's *sukkalmah* model (1986) which, based on the extant evidence, seems impossible to apply literally to the NE period, does provide a model with historical antecedents (cf. Waters 2000: 32–3; Miroschedji 2003: 34–5; Henkelman 2008: 12–13). Because of the paucity of evidence, a bewildering number of scenarios for assessment of this episode (and others), each as plausible and problematic as the next, may be applied. Vallat's groundbreaking chronological scheme has much to recommend it, but it poses as many questions as answers, and any conclusions therefrom are tenuous until new evidence is brought to bear.

Further Reading

Accessible studies in English on the Neo-Elamite period as a whole are few. Good places to start for overviews and bibliography are Tavernier (2004), Miroschedji (2003), Waters (2000), Potts (1999), Vallat (1998a), Stolper (1984), Hinz (1972), and Cameron (1936). Some of the latter are dated but still contain much of value. Álvarez-Mon et al. (2011) and Henkelman (2008) offer updated assessments (with references) of the states-of-the-question, especially for the century immediately preceding the rise of the Persian Empire.

References

Álvarez-Mon, J. 2010. *The Arjān Tomb: At the crossroads of the Empire and the Persian Empires.* Leuven: Acta Iranica 49.
Álvarez-Mon, J., M. Garrison, and D. Stronach . 2011. Introduction. *EP*: 1–32.
Amiet, P. 1973. La glyptique de la fin de l'Élam. *Arts Asiatiques* 28: 3–45.
Borger, R. 1996. *Beiträge zum Inschriftenwerk Assurbanipals.* Wiesbaden: Harrassowitz.
Boucharlat, R. 2005. Iran. *AEA*: 221–92.
Briant, P. 2002. *From Cyrus to Alexander: A history of the Persian Empire.* Winona Lake: Eisenbrauns.
Brinkman, J. A. 1986. The Elamite-Babylonian frontier in the Neo-Elamite period, 750–625 B.C. *FHE*: 199–207.
———. 1990. The Babylonian Chronicle revisited. In *Lingering over words: Studies in Ancient Near Eastern literature in honor of William L. Moran*, ed. T. Abusch, J. Huehnergard, and P. Steinkeller, 73–104. Atlanta: Scholar's Press.
Cameron, G. G. 1936. *History of early Iran.* Chicago: University of Chicago Press.
Carter, E. 1999. Neuelamische Kunstperiod. *RlA* 9/3–4: 283–90.
Chambers, M. 1996. Foreword. In *The Athenian Empire restored: Epigraphic and historical studies*, ed. H. B. Mattingly, vii–xi. Ann Arbor: University of Michigan Press.
Córdoba, J.M. 1997. Die Schlacht am Ulāya-Fluß: Ein Beispiel assyrischer Kriegführung während der letzten Jahre des Reiches. In *Assyrien im Wandel der Zeiten*, ed. H. Waetzoldt and H. Hauptman, 7–18. Heidelberg: HSAO 6.
Curtis, J. 2003. The Assyrian heartland in the period 612–539 B.C. *CE*: 157–67.
Dalley, S. 1993. Nineveh after 612 BC. *AoF* 20: 138–47.
De Vaan, J. M. C. T. 1995. *Ich bin eine Schwertklinge des Königs: Die Sprache des Bēl-ibni.* Neukirchen-Vluyn: AOAT 242.
Frame, G. 1992. *Babylonia 689–627 BC: A political history.* Leiden: UNHAII.
Grayson, A. K. 1975. *Assyrian and Babylonian chronicles.* Locust Valley: TCS 5.
Henkelman, W. F. M. 2003. Persians, Medes, and Elamites: Acculturation in the Neo-Elamite period. *CE*: 181–232.
———. 2008. *The other gods who are: Studies in Elamite-Iranian acculturation based on the Persepolis Fortification Texts.* Leiden: AchHist 14.
Hinz, W. 1972. *The lost world of Elam: Re-creation of a vanished civilization.* Trans. J. Barnes. London: Sidgwick and Jackson.
Jursa, M. 2003. Observations on the problem of the Median "Empire" on the basis of the Babylonian sources. *CE*: 169–79.
König, F. W. 1965. *Die elamischen Königsinschriften.* Graz: *AfO* Beiheft 16.
Kuhrt, A. 1995. The Assyrian heartland in the Achaemenid period. In *Dans les pas des Dix-Mille*, ed. P. Briant, 239–54. Toulouse: Groupe de Recherches sur l'Antiquitéclassique et orientale.
Lambert, M. 1967. Shutruk-Nahunte et Shutur-Nahunte. *Syria* 44: 47–51.
Leichty, E. 2011. *The royal inscriptions of Esarhaddon, king of Assyria (680–669 BC).* Winona Lake: RINAP 4.
Liverani, M. 2011. Later Mesopotamia. In *The Oxford history of historical writing*, ed. A. Feldherr and G. Hardy, 29–52. Oxford: Oxford University Press.
Malbran-Labat, F. 1995. *Les Inscriptions royales de Suse: Briques de l'époque paléo-élamite à l'Empire néo-élamite.* Paris: Éditions de la Réunion des Musées Nationaux.

Miroschedji, P. de 1981a. Fouilles du chantier Ville Royale II àSuse (1975-1977). I. Les niveaux élamites. *CDAFI* 12: 9-136.

———. 1981b. Observations dans les couches néo-élamites au nord-ouest du tell de la Ville Royale à Suse. *CDAFI* 12: 143-67.

———. 1985. La fin du royaume d'Anšan et de Suse et la naissance de l'Empire perse. *ZA* 75: 265-306.

———. 1986. La localisation de Madaktu et l'organisation politique de l'Élam à l'époque néo-élamite. *FHE*: 209-26.

———. 1990. La fin de l'Élam: Essai d'anaylyse et d'interpretation. *IrAnt* 25: 47-95.

———. 2003. Susa and the highlands: Major trends in the history of Elamite civilization. *YBYN*: 17-38.

Nadali, D. 2007. Ashurbanipal against Elam: figurative patterns and architectural location of the Elamite wars. *Historiae* 4: 57-91.

Nylander, C. 1999. Breaking the cup of kingship: an Elamite coup in Nineveh? *IrAnt* 34: 71-84.

Potts, D. T. 1999. *The archaeology of Elam: Formation and transformation of an ancient Iranian State*. Cambridge: Cambridge University Press.

———. 2001. Madaktu and Badake. *Isimu* 2: 13-28.

———. 2005. Cyrus the Great and the Kingdom of Anshan. In *Birth of the Persian Empire*, ed. V. S. Curtis and S. Stewart, 1: 7-28. London: I. B. Tauris.

———. 2011. A note on the limits of Anšan. *EP*: 35-43.

Quintana, E. 2011. Elamitas frente a Persas: El reino independiente de Anšan. *EP*: 167-90.

Reade, J. 1976. Elam and Elamites in Assyrian sculpture. *AMI* 9: 97-106.

———. 2000. Elam after the Assyrian sack of Susa in 647 BC. *NABU* 2000/4.

———. 2001. Ninive (Nineveh). *RlA* 9: 388-433.

Rhodes, P. J. 2008. After the three-bar sigma controversy: The history of Athenian imperialism reassessed. *Classical Quarterly* 58: 501-6.

Rollinger, R. 2008. The Median "Empire," the end of Urartu, and Cyrus the Great's campaign in 547 BC (Nabonidus Chronicle II 16). *AWE* 7: 51-65.

Russell, J. M. 1999. *The writing on the wall: Studies in the architectural context of Late Assyrian palace inscriptions*. Indiana: Winona Lake: Eisenbrauns.

Scheil, V. 1907. *Textes élamites-anzanites, troisième série*. Paris: MDP 9.

Schmidt, E. 1957. *Persepolis II: The contents of the Treasury and other discoveries*. Chicago: OIP 69.

Steve, M.-J. 1992. *Syllabaire élamite: Histoire et paléographie*. Neuchâtel/Paris: Civilisations du Proche-Orient Série 2 Philologie 1.

Steve, M.-J., F. Vallat, H. Gasche, and F. Jullien. 2002-3. Suse. *SDB* 73: 360-512 (bibliog. in *SDB* 74: 620-52).

Stolper, M. W. 1984. Political history of Elam. In *Elam: Surveys of political history and archaeology*, E. Carter and M. W. Stolper, 1-100. Berkeley/Los Angeles/London: University of California Publications, Near Eastern Studies 25.

———.1986. A Neo-Babylonian text from the reign of Halluŝu. *FHE*: 235-41.

———. 1988. Mālamīr. B. Philologisch. *RlA* 7: 276-81.

———. 2003. Hidali. *EnIr* online edition.

Stronach, D. 2005. The Arjan tomb: Innovation and acculturation in the last days of Elam. *IrAnt* 40: 179-96.

Tavernier, J. 2003. review of Waters, A survey of Neo-Elamite history. *JNES* 62: 202-4.

———. 2004. Some thoughts on Neo-Elamite chronology. *ARTA* 2004.003.

———. 2011. Iranians in Neo-Elamite texts. *EP*: 191–262.
Vallat, F. 1993. *Les noms géographiques des sources suso-élamites*. Weisbaden: RGTC 11.
———. 1995. Šutruk-Nahhunte, Šutur-Nahhunte et l'imbroglio néo-élamite. *NABU* 1995/2.
———. 1996. Nouvelle analyse des inscriptions néo-élamites. *CO*: 385–95.
———. 1998a. Elam i. The history of Elam. *EnIr* online edition.
———. 1998b. Le royaume élamite de Zamin et les "lettres de Nineve." *IrAnt* 33: 95–106.
Waters, M. W. 1999. Te'umman in the Neo-Assyrian Correspondence. *JAOS* 119: 473–7.
———. 2000. *A survey of Neo-Elamite history*. Helsinki: SAAS 12.
———. 2001. Mesopotamian sources and Neo-Elamite history. In *Historiography in the cuneiform world*, vol. 1, ed. T. Abusch et al., 473–82. Bethesda: CDL Press.
———. 2006. A Neo-Elamite royal family. *IrAnt* 41: 59–69.
———. 2011. Parsumaš, Anšan, and Cyrus. *EP*: 285–96.
Weissbach, F. H. 1902. Susische Thontäfelchen. *Beiträge zur Assyriologie und semitischen Sprachwissenschaft* 4: 168–202.
Zadok, R. 2011. The Babylonia-Elam connections in the Chaldean and Achaemenid periods (part one). *Tel Aviv* 38: 120–43.

CHAPTER 25

IRON AGE SOUTHEASTERN IRAN

PETER MAGEE

Introduction

For the purposes of this chapter, southeastern Iran is defined as the three modern political provinces of Sistan/Baluchistan, Kerman, and Hormuzgan. These vary in extent: Sistan/Baluchistan and Kerman are quite similar in size, at 181,785 km² and 180,836 km², respectively, while Hormuzgan is a much smaller 70,669 km². Together they account for over 25 percent of the current landmass of Iran.

This region has certainly not held the attention of scholars proportional to its size. What research has occurred has tended to focus on the Neolithic, Chalcolithic, and Bronze Ages, for example at Tal-e Iblis, Tepe Yahya, Shahdad, Bampur, and Shahr-e Sokhta (see Chapters 8 and 16). An important component of this research has been tracing the emergence of Bronze Age trade systems which incorporated south Asia, Iran, the Gulf, and Mesopotamia. At many of these important Bronze Age sites, Iron Age remains (identifiable for the purposes of this chapter as dating to the period from 1300 to 600 BC), are scant or nonexistent. The exception is Tepe Yahya, which forms the basis for much of the discussion below. Together with finds from other sites, the data from this site permit us to sketch an outline history of this region during the Iron Age. Such a sketch is by necessity patchy and incomplete and it is to be hoped that future research will fill in many of the gaps apparent below.

The Bronze to Iron Age transition

Unlike the record from the west and northwest, there is no identifiable Bronze Age to Iron Age transition in southeastern Iran. At Tepe Yahya, the only site to have revealed

Iron Age remains in a long stratigraphic sequence, the final Bronze Age occupation (period IVA) came to an end around 1400 BC (Beale 1986: 11). The material from this period remains largely unpublished and it is entirely possible that this date may eventually be lowered by a century or two. Nevertheless, survey and excavations in other parts of southeastern Iran and adjoining regions would appear to confirm that archaeologically visible settlement is less apparent for these centuries than those prior and later. Caldwell's excavations at Tal-e Iblis revealed no remains dated to the very end of the second and early first millennia BC (1967). The excavators attributed the abandonment of the site to a shift in the course of the Ab-e Lalehzar River, which, up until that point, had run next to the settlement. Similarly, Bronze Age settlements in Sistan, such as Shahr-e Sokhta, were not occupied past the middle of the second millennium BC. Given the lack of firm chronological leitfossils for this period, it is perhaps unsurprising that Sajjadi's (1987, 1990) detailed survey in the Qobeira area and Bard Sir plain in southeastern Iran revealed very few—if any—settlements that could be securely dated to between *c*.1400 and 800 BC.

However, caution is certainly necessary in interpreting the results of such survey data, as the absence of stratigraphically definable "leitfossils" for these centuries at Tepe Yahya has obviously hindered the identification of relevant sherds. However, those areas adjacent to southeastern Iran—especially Pakistan and southeastern Arabia—display similar settlement lacunae during this period. In southeastern Arabia, the Iron Age I period (Magee and Carter 1991) witnessed a restriction of settlement while Franke-Vogt (2001) has recently reaffirmed the existence of an occupational gap between 1700 and 600 BC in the southern Indus.

In Iranian Sistan, Mortazavi (2007) has suggested that a combination of modern development and research interests in this area has obfuscated our understanding of the period between the demise of Shahr-e Sokhta and the foundation of Achaemenid Dahan-e Ghulaman. It is, however, difficult to understand how these factors would have selected against the recovery of Iron Age remains. Mortazavi (2007) also made the important point that the ecology of long-term agricultural settlement in Sistan is susceptible to small changes in climate.

Indeed, an underlying climatic cause is the most likely explanation for this widespread decline in archaeologically visible settlement. Today, southeastern Iran is located between two major weather systems, each of which has the ability to influence precipitation patterns in discrete areas as well as more generally across the whole region. Currently, westerlies bring winter rainfall to a large area of southeastern Iran around Kerman. In contrast, coastal areas to the south and east, specifically around Baluchistan, receive limited winter rainfall but some summer rainfall from the effects of the Indian Ocean monsoon. The discrepancy between these two systems is no more clearly indicated than by a comparison of the precipitation patterns between Bahrain, which receives virtually no summer rainfall, and Karachi in Pakistan, which receives 82 percent of its rainfall in summer (Regard et al. 2006: 38).

There is compelling evidence that both of these weather systems lessened in intensity around the end of the second and the beginning of the first millennium BC. Winter rainfall throughout southeastern Iran would have been affected by the decline of weather systems in the Mediterranean around the thirteenth century BC (Matthews 2002 with references). The effects of these climate changes in southeastern Iran are suggested by the Lake Awafi sequence in Ras al-Khaimah (UAE) which experienced aeolian sand deposition at this time (Parker et al. 2006). On the other hand, compelling evidence from palaeoclimatic proxies in the Indian Ocean (Lückge et al. 2001) suggest a decline in the intensity of both the summer and winter monsoon around 1000 BC. This would have had the effect of reducing summer rainfall and run-off throughout the arid margins and coastal zones of southeastern Iran. It is possible that this decline in rainfall would have affected settlement in southeastern Iran in a time or geographically transgressive fashion. A decline in winter rainfall would have first affected those areas of Kerman and Hormuzgan that regularly received some winter rainfall. It maybe possible to see the effects of this in the drying up of the Ab-e Lalehzar near Tal-e Iblis. Such a decrease in rainfall would have had a disastrous effect in Sistan, which today receives on average only 75 mm of rainfall per year, mostly in the winter (Whitney 2006). In combination with the "120-day winds" that blow from May to September, long-term, sedentary agriculture would have been difficult to sustain in these areas. It is interesting to note, however, that this decline in rainfall would not have affected the flow of the Helmand River, which derives from snow melt. This may help explain why the Helmand-Sistan Project of the 1970s discovered sites dating from 1300 BC in the Sar-o-Tar plain (Whitney 2006: 30) and sites located closer to the source of the Helmand River, like Nad-e Ali, likely continued to be occupied.

The decline in summer rainfall brought about by the Indian Ocean monsoon would have had a similarly negative effect along the coastal margins of Baluchistan. Although palaeoclimatic proxies are difficult to compare to each other within a century-level scale, so far as we can judge this decline in settlement postdated the decline in winter rainfall and may help explain why sites such as Pirak in the Kachi plain of (Pakistani) Baluchistan exhibit evidence of continued occupation from the late second to some time in the early first millennium BC (Magee and Petrie 2010). Such settlements were then abandoned, perhaps as a result of the decline of summer rainfall that fed local rivers in that area (Magee and Petrie 2010).

In summary, although one should not assume that correlation equals causality in reference to climate and human settlement, it seems very likely that the decline of rainfall throughout southeastern Iran would have had serious effects on the ability of humans to practice those methods of subsistence that had sustained them for millennia.

REEMERGENCE OF IRON AGE SETTLEMENT

The clearest archaeological evidence we have for the reemergence of human settlement in southeastern Iran can be found at Tepe Yahya in Kerman. In 1968, Iron Age remains were recovered in excavations on the central part of the mound, marking the first time such remains had been found in a stratified context in southeastern Iran. Over the next five years, Iron Age remains were found throughout the excavations. A preliminary assessment was published in 1970 (Lamberg-Karlovsky 1970) but, subsequently, important material was excavated in 1971 and 1973. A complete reanalysis of the finds and documentation of this material, along with new radiocarbon dates, was published in 2004 (Magee 2004). This provides detailed evidence of the reappearance of identifiable Iron Age occupation in southeastern Iran.

The earliest Iron Age remains at Tepe Yahya belong to Period III. These consist of two buildings in the main part of the mound, both roughly square and constructed of mudbrick and stone. Given their size, it is unlikely they were residential in nature and it is possible that they represented some sort of communal building, akin to a *majlis* in traditional Islamic architecture. A single stone channel ran between the buildings (Magee 2004).

Two radiocarbon dates from below, and connected with this architecture, provide a date for the construction of these two buildings. In combination with the dates from upper levels, these suggest that Period III at Tepe Yahya began no earlier than 800 BC and ended before 650 BC (Magee 2004: 75–6). A restricted artifactual assemblage was associated with these levels. Locally produced, simple jars and bowls dominated. While there are generic parallels to material from adjacent regions, none could be insisted upon as evidence of interaction. One particular storage jar form with a flattened collar rim finds parallels at a site in the Bard Sir plain documented by Sajjadi (Magee 2004: 32; Sajjadi 1987: 107), perhaps suggesting an Iron Age date for this otherwise undated settlement. One class of ceramics stands in contrast to the overwhelmingly local character of the assemblage. This comprises a highly burnished serving ware which has been labeled "Burnished Maroon Slipped Ware" (BMSW) (Magee 2005). This distinctive ware is attested in a series of very fine trays and bowls that were widely distributed from southeastern Arabia to Pakistan. Geochemical analysis of examples from Tepe Yahya and southeastern Arabia suggest that the former site was located near a production center.

Nonceramic finds from Period III confirm contact with southeastern Arabia at this time as well. Of particular importance is a complete soft-stone vessel. Soft-stone (probably chlorite) working had a long history at Tepe Yahya. While it is unknown whether the Period III example was locally made or imported, it was decorated and formed in a fashion identical to that seen on thousands of vessels discovered at Iron Age II sites in the United Arab Emirates and Sultanate of Oman (Magee 2004: fig. 41.2). Of some importance also from the Period III deposits is an iron scabbard confirming that iron working was practiced in southeastern Iran by the eighth century BC.

If shifts in climate were responsible for the decline in archaeologically visible settlement in southeastern Iran at the end of the second millennium BC, it is very likely that adaptation to these new, arid conditions provided the basis for the reemergence of settlement in the eighth century BC. The likely stimulus for the reappearance of visible settlement in southeastern Iran was the use of the *qanat* irrigation system. This unique and important water system involves tapping aquifers and transporting water to lower-lying areas. In our current understanding, *qanat* technology is present in southeastern Arabia from *c*.1000 BC onward, where it is associated with the emergence of a series of polities along the western edge of the al-Hajjar mountain range (Magee 2007). The possibility that the reemergence of settlement in southeastern Iran was due to transfer of *qanat* technology from Arabia to Iran receives some support from the presence of artifacts such as the southeast Arabian-style stone vessel at Tepe Yahya in Period III.

The expansion of Iron Age settlement

Two mudbrick platforms surmount the Period III village at Tepe Yahya. The date of these is fixed by radiocarbon dates to between 650 and 500 BC, thus placing them in the immediate pre-Achaemenid period (Magee 2004). Both were constructed sequentially, with square mudbricks. Although both platforms were oriented in the same general direction, the earlier one was considerably smaller than the later example, which was so large that its entire dimensions were not encompassed within the excavated trench. There was very little other architecture associated with this phase of settlement; only two walls extending from one of the baulks could be attributed to this building phase and little could be said about their function. The function of these platforms remains enigmatic. Comparisons have been drawn to examples from Nad-e Ali and Kandahar in Afghanistan and it has been suggested that they may have served as symbols of independence and authority within the landscape (Lamberg-Karlovsky and Magee 1999). The absence of broader contextual information means such an interpretation remains conjectural.

Those deposits associated with the use of these platforms provide an important insight into the material culture of pre-Achaemenid southeastern Iran. Wide-ranging parallels for the ceramics from these deposits can be drawn with finds from numerous sites extending from South Asia to southeastern Arabia (Magee 2004: 40–3). Of particular interest is a distinctive storage jar form that is characterized by a concave base with a smooth, often shaved, exterior and a sandy coarse exterior below the carination. This form has a wide distribution from Central Asia to the Gulf. According to Scerrato (1966: 28) the concave base facilitated the placement of the vessel in the ground. Recent survey and a reanalysis of the material collected by Andrew Williamson in the 1970s has revealed similar vessels at numerous sites in Hormuzgan around the Minab plain (S. Preistman, pers. comm). More generally, survey around Tepe Yahya indicated a reemergence of settlement that may date to this period—even if the criteria used for such a conclusion were based upon a generic Period III/II identification (Vidali et al. 1976). Lastly, it is worth noting that some of the thousands of stone cairns documented by Stein (1937) in the Dashtiari and adjoining plains in Baluchistan and by Lamberg-Karlovksy and Humphries in the Soghun Valley (1967) might date to this period, although it should be cautioned that these were likely used and reused over centuries.

The platforms and the ceramic parallels suggest that in the pre-Achaemenid period there existed some form of interaction in a zone that ran from Central Asia through eastern Iran to the Gulf. Neither the nature of this interaction nor the broader cultural dynamics it represents are known. It is interesting to consider, however, that connections between Central Asia, eastern Iran and the Indo-Iranian borderlands characterized earlier periods in prehistory, such as the early third millennium BC. The extent to which long-standing connections between these areas might help explain some of the revolts that beset the Achaemenid Empire after the death of Cyrus has been signaled (Lamberg-Karlovksy and Magee 1999). Indeed, recent survey and excavation in Baluchistan have revealed ceramic assemblages (e.g., the Durrah-i Bust assemblage) that appear in the Tepe Yahya sequence at roughly the same time as the emergence of the Achaemenid Empire. Such discoveries have the potential to tie together a number of archaeological assemblages which Stein and Fairservis ("Complex B") encountered on survey across southeastern Iran and Baluchistan (Franke-Vogt 2001). For now, however, the archaeological record from Iron Age southeastern Iran is perhaps the most incomplete of all those from ancient Iran. Renewed excavations in these regions will hopefully remedy this situation and throw light on a region that was a nexus between Arabia, Iran, Central Asia, and South Asia.

Further reading

There is no synoptic study of the Iron Age in southeastern Iran. For the principal evidence from Tepe Yahya see Lamberg-Karlovsky and Magee (1999) and Magee (2004).

References

Beale, T. W. 1986. *Excavations at Tepe Yahya, Iran, 1967–1975: The early periods.* Cambridge: ASPR Bulletin 38.
Caldwell, J. R. 1967. *Investigations at Tal-i Iblis.* Springfield: Illinois State Museum Preliminary Reports 9.
Franke-Vogt, U. 2001. The southern Indus valley during the late 2nd and 1st millennia BC. In *Migration und Kulturtransfer: Der Wandel vorder- und zentralasiatischer Kulturen im Umbruch vom 2. zum 1. vorchristlichen Jahrtausend*, ed. R. Eichmann and H. Parzinger, 247–90. Bonn: Kolloquien zur Vor- und Frühgeschichte 6.
Lamberg-Karlovsky, C. C. 1970. *Excavations at Tepe Yahya, Iran. 1967–1969: Progress report 1.* Cambridge: ASPR Bulletin 27.
Lamberg-Karlovksy, C. C., and P. Magee. 1999. The Iron Age platforms at Tepe Yahya. *IrAnt* 34: 41–52.
Lückge, H., H. Doose-Rolinski, A. Ali Khan, H. Schulz, and U. von Rad. 2001. Monsoonal variability in the northeastern Arabian Sea during the past 5000 years: Geochemical evidence from laminated sediments. *PPP* 167: 273–86.

Magee, P. 2004. *Excavations at Tepe Yahya, Iran, 1967–1975. The Iron Age settlement.* Cambridge: ASPR Bulletin 46.

———. 2005. Investigating cross-Gulf trade in the Iron Age III period: Chronological and compositional data on Burnished Maroon Slipped Ware (BMSW) in southeastern Arabia and Iran. *AAE* 16: 82–92.

———. 2007. Beyond the desert and the sown: Settlement intensification in late prehistoric southeastern Arabia. *BASOR* 347: 83–105.

Magee, P., and R. Carter. 1991. Agglomeration and regionalism: Southeastern Arabia between 1400 and 1100 BC. *AAE* 9: 236–54.

Magee, P., and C. A. Petrie. 2010. West of the Indus—East of the empire: The archaeology of the pre-Achaemenid and Achaemenid periods in Baluchistan and the North-West Frontier Province, Pakistan. *WAP*: 503–22.

Matthews, R. 2002. Zebu: Harbingers of doom in Bronze Age western Asia. *Antiquity* 76: 438–47.

Mortazavi, M. 2007. Mind the gap: Continuity and change in Iranian Sistan archaeology. *NEA* 70: 109–10.

Parker, A. G., A. S. Goudie, S. Stokes, K. White, M. J. Hodson, M. Manning, and D. Kennet. 2006. A record of Holocene climate change from lake geochemical analyses in southeastern Arabia. *QR* 66: 465–76.

Regard, V., O. Bellier, R. Braucher, F. Gasse, D.L. Bourlès, J. L. Mercier, J.-C. Thomas et al . 2006. 10Be dating of alluvial deposits from Southeastern Iran (the Hormoz Strait area). *PPP* 242: 36–53.

Sajjadi, S. M. 1987. Prehistoric settlements in the Bardsir Plain, southeastern Iran. *EW* 37: 11–129.

Sajjadi, S. M., and H. T. Wright. 1990. Archaeological survey in the Qobeira area, Province of Kerman, Iran. *AION* 50: 1–40.

Scerrato, U. 1966. Excavations at Dahan-i Ghulaman (Seistan-Iran): First preliminary report (1962–1963). *EW* 16: 9–30.

Stein, Sir M. A. 1937. *Archaeological reconnaissances in north-western India and south-eastern Irān.* London: Macmillan.

Vidali, M. L., E. Vidali, and C. C. Lamberg-Karlovsky. 1976. Settlement patterns around Tepe Yahya: A quantitative analysis. *JNES* 35: 237–50.

Whitney, J. W. 2006. *Geology, water and wind in the lower Helmand basin, southern Afghanistan.* Washington: US Geological Survey Scientific Investigations Report 2006–5182.

PART V
THE ACHAEMENID PERIOD

CHAPTER 26

SOUTHWESTERN IRAN IN THE ACHAEMENID PERIOD

RÉMY BOUCHARLAT

INTRODUCTION

Southwestern Iran is the region of origin of the Achaemenid dynasty. Two royal residences, Pasargadae and Persepolis, are located in the province of Fars. But neither in the pre-Achaemenid period nor at the time of Cyrus and his successors can we separate Fars from the neighboring province of Khuzestan, consisting of the foothills of the Zagros and a plain which is an extension of Mesopotamia. This link between the two regions is evinced in several decades of historical research, as well as in art historical and archaeological finds.

The archaeology of the Achaemenid period is mainly limited to data from the two royal residences in Fars and from Susa in the Elamite lowlands, sites that have been known to travelers since the seventeenth century. Archaeologists became interested in them in the late nineteenth century (Chevalier 2010) but it was only in the late twentieth century that the hinterlands of these centers began to be explored. The archaeology of ordinary settlements is still in its infancy.

According to Herodotus, the family of the Persian kings belonged to the Achaemenid clan, which was a part of the Pasargadae tribe and was the "most noble" (1.125). It is now accepted that the Persians as we know them resulted from the acculturation of Iranian-speaking people who arrived in Fars, probably at the end of the second millennium BC, and local, mostly Elamite groups. The texts and the iconography of glyptic and luxury objects recently discovered clearly show this mixing, at least among the elites (Briant 1984; Miroschedji 1985; Potts 2005; Henkelman 2008a: 41–57; Álvarez-Mon 2010, 2011; Garrison 2011). Judging by the material found so far, the Persian ruling classes were interwoven with local cultures (Elamites in the Bakhtiyari

Mountains and the Khuzestan plain) and in contact with neighboring ones (Babylonia and Assyria).

The emergence of Cyrus' empire was not a process involving a small, local prince from the distant east, but one that grew out of the milieu of Persian (Iranian–Elamite) chiefdoms. The Cyrus Cylinder found in Babylon indicates that Cyrus and his ancestors were kings of Anshan the kingdom or Anshan the city (Potts 2011) which had been the center of a flourishing state until the end of second millennium (see Chapter 15). Anshan (Tal-e Malyan) is located on the Marv Dasht plain about 50 km northwest of Persepolis.

Herodotus' account has long led scholars to believe that the Persian Empire of Cyrus was a continuation of the "Median empire." The Medes were thought to have been the ruling class in Western Iran during the eighth to seventh centuries BC. This Median legacy is unsupported by either written sources or archaeological data and has now been seriously challenged (e.g., Henkelman 2003a). The beginnings of the Persian kingdom before Cyrus remain a major issue in the history of Iran. Since the late twentieth century, however, the critical reexamination of texts and archaeological discoveries on the western fringes of Fars have begun to shed light on this phase.

The Neo-Elamite state did not disappear with the sack of Susa by Assurbanipal in 647 BC (Waters 2000: 81–107; Potts 1999: 288–308). Life continued there and at other cities in the lowlands and in the Bakhtiyari Mountains, as illustrated by inscriptions and rock reliefs. In Fars, and especially in the Marv Dasht plain, we are hampered by the lack of actual or apparent witnesses of settlement in the centuries preceding the Persian Empire. Evidence from the period corresponding elsewhere to Iron Age III (from the eighth century until the reign of Darius I, 522–486 BC) has not been found (Sumner 1986; Young 2003; contra Alizadeh 2003 with very little data). At Anshan (Tal-e Malyan), which had ruled the region for generations before Cyrus, evidence of post-Middle Elamite or pre-Achaemenid occupation is very rare (Carter 1994: 66, fig. 3; 1996: 47, fig. 46), as is evidence of Achaemenid settlement (Sumner 1986: 11). Despite the archaeologically barren record of first millennium occupation in the region, a seal bearing the legend "Kuraš the Anzanite [or: 'of Anzan'], son of Šešpeš," was still used by Darius at Persepolis (PFS 93, Garrison 2011). This shows that the owner had some power in that part of Fars before Cyrus II. This Kurash, who can be identified with Cyrus' grandfather, Cyrus I, belonged to a dynasty, the existence of which is confirmed by the Cyrus Cylinder from Babylon (l. 21): Teipses – [Cyrus I] – Cambyses – Cyrus II.

For the period from the late seventh to the third quarter of the sixth century BC, the archaeological and epigraphic data concerning elites comes from outside Fars but not from "the land of the Medes" around Hamadan (ancient Ecbatana), whose territory may have extended far to the east and northeast, but not southwards into Fars. South of Ecbatana, a kingdom (?) of "Samati" is attested in inscriptions on metal vessels allegedly found in Kalmakarra cave in the Rumishgan district of southern Luristan. Amongst the dozens of silver and bronze vases found there, about twenty bear a Neo-Elamite cuneiform inscription mentioning several names forming a short dynasty, though they are not called princes. Based on the personal names and language used in these inscriptions, they have been variously dated from the late seventh to the first half of the sixth century BC.

The shape of the vases and, for those that are decorated, the motifs and iconography are consistent with this dating, and they reflect a phenomenon of Elamo–Iranian acculturation (Henkelman 2003a).

In the lowlands of Susiana, Elamite tablets found at Susa in the early twentieth century, unfortunately from insecure archaeological contexts, are significant. Nearly 300 tablets from the Acropolis mound and elsewhere are to be dated from the very end of the seventh or the first half of the sixth century BC. Over 10 percent of the personal names are etymologically Iranian, attesting to economic relations between Iranians and Susians. This mixture of cultures is best illustrated by the glyptic of "the end of Elam" (Amiet 1973), especially the seals and seal impressions on tablets, which are in the tradition of local Elamite glyptic, but with some Assyrian elements. This group illustrates the emergence of themes that would become more common in later Achaemenid Persian glyptic, as illustrated by hundreds of seal impressions on tablets at Persepolis. These iconographic links and the small number of "antique" seals used on some Persepolis tablets (PFS 93 and three others, Garrison 2011) rightly invite us to reconsider this glyptic assemblage, previously called (Late) Elamite when Elam was thought to have been centered on Susa where the seals were found. On the contrary, this glyptic style might better be called "Anzanite" (indicating Fars as its place of origin) or perhaps, in the case of its latest manifestations, "Early Persian" (Garrison 2011: 401).

At the southeastern edge of the Khuzestan plain, near the foot of the Zagros Mountains toward the frontier of Fars, the discovery of rich tombs demonstrates the existence of other chieftains of territories, the extent of which is unknown. These political entities illustrate the fragmentation of Elam and the acculturation of Elamites and Iranians.

At Arjan, 9 km northeast of Behbahan near the border of Fars, a stone-built, subterranean tomb proved to be a revelation when it was discovered in 1982 (Alizadeh 1985; Chapter 23). Accidentally uncovered by a bulldozer, it contained a U-shaped bronze coffin of Mesopotamian type (reminiscent of Neo-Babylonian "bath-tub" coffins), with one straight and one rounded end. The rich furniture inside and outside the coffin included fragments of textiles carefully folded and placed in the sarcophagus; metal vases, one of which was compared to Phoenician bowls of the eighth to seventh centuries BC; and a "power ring," an unusually shaped gold bracelet, found on the chest of the deceased. The two ends of the ring (11 cm in diameter) are expanded into a flat disk, a shape in the Elamite tradition, one of which is decorated with a palmette flanked by two rampant, winged griffins. Such representations were known in Elam and Assyria and continued to appear in the glyptic of Persepolis. These objects, as well as a tall candelabrum with an elaborate tripod base and a silver vase, bear the short Neo-Elamite legend "Kidin-Hutran son of Kurluš." There is a consensus that these inscriptions date to the first half of sixth century (Vallat 1984), although the objects themselves may be a bit older (Álvarez-Mon 2010, 2011).

Another grave was found in 2006 near Ram Hormuz, about 100 km northwest of Behbahan, in an area with extensive Elamite settlement (Chapter 23). As in the case of Arjan, this underground tomb stone was badly damaged by a bulldozer. A rescue excavation (Shishehgar 2008) revealed two U-shaped coffins placed obliquely in a stone cist, parallel to each other. Nearly 500 objects were found both inside and outside the coffins: ceramic and stone vessels; a spouted bronze jug as well as other bronze vessels and candelabra; several "power rings"; decorated bracelets; over one hundred gold buttons and dozens of semiprecious stone beads. The date proposed by the excavator is Neo-Elamite IIIB (585–539 BC), according to the chronology of Miroschedji (1978; cf. Steve et al. 2002–3: 479–83), contemporary with the Arjan tomb, but some items, such as a sculpture of a female deity, are a millennium older and were probably heirlooms.

To summarize, Elamite texts and Assyrian annals mention a dozen kings but their exact dates are usually known. Some Elamite anthroponyms also are attested in inscriptions on metal vessels and jewelry found at Arjan (the cuneiform inscriptions from Ram Hormuz are unpublished) and Kalmakarra cave dated from the late seventh and/ or early sixth century BC based on style and iconography. Administrative texts from late Neo-Elamite Susa reveal the presence of Iranians or Persians in the lowlands at this time. Glyptic continues in the Elamite tradition, but obviously contains Assyrian elements and heralds the beginnings of early Persian art. All together these finds constitute the corpus available for the pre-Achaemenid period. The political unity of ancient Elam (lowlands and mountains of Fars) had been broken, weakened by external attacks and struggles between chieftains and pretenders. Despite the fragmentation of the ancient Elamite kingdom into chiefdoms fighting one another, recently likened to "warlordism" (Potts 2010), we observe cultural homogeneity in Elam (Henkelman 2003c: 255), exemplified by tombs, rock inscriptions, and bas-reliefs in the mountains.

The dynasty of Cyrus was probably no more important than the other petty kingdoms, but Elamite cultural unity may have facilitated the domination of the Teispes family over other kingdoms in Fars. Cambyses, Cyrus' father, was considered by the Mede Astyages a good match for his daughter. The domination of Anshan or its ability to unite the forces of other realms might have allowed Cyrus to raise a powerful army in its confrontation with the Medes about 550 BC, probably where Pasargadae (OP Batrakataš), was later founded, 40 km as the crow flies northeast of Persepolis (Waters 2004: 92).

The beginnings of the empire: Cyrus and Pasargadae

After this victory, Cyrus continued northwards into Asia Minor, where he conquered the Lydian kingdom of Croesus in 545 BC and the Greek cities. Babylon was taken over in 539 BC, as documented in the Cyrus Cylinder inscription (Kuhrt 2007: 70–4). No sources mention the taking of Susa, which was probably already within the orbit of the kingdom of Anshan. In conquering Transeuphrates, from the Euphrates River to the Phoenician cities, Cyrus very likely saw pharaonic royal images which later inspired him at Pasargadae.

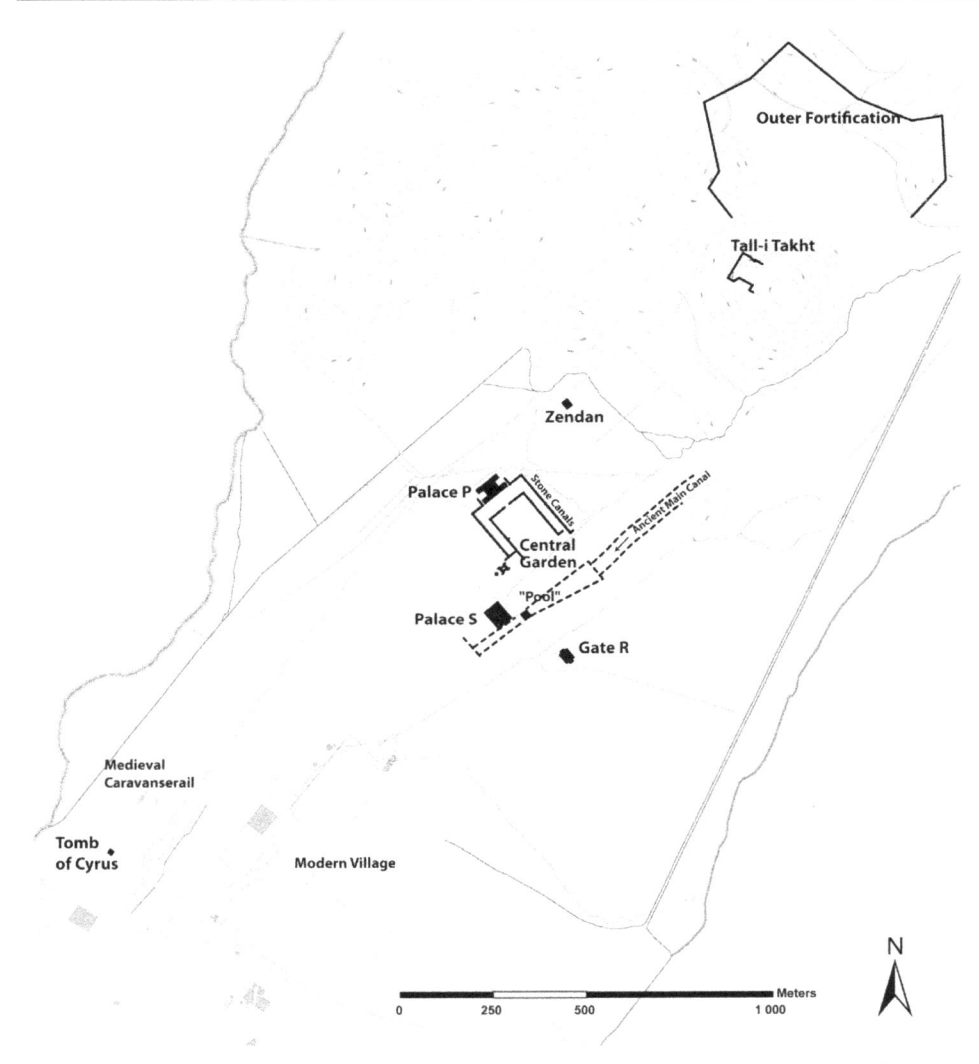

FIGURE 26.1 Plan of Pasargadae showing the main monuments and the results of the geomagnetic survey on the water stream widened into a pool along the central garden (© Iran France Archaeological Expedition in Pasargadae–Persepolis).

As evinced by the obvious influence of both Lydian and Ionian art and techniques, Cyrus' residence at Pasargadae was certainly built after the conquest of Asia Minor (Fig. 26.1). The work carried out between 545 and 530 BC resulted in a complex of stone buildings scattered over c.250 ha (Stronach 1978). Other buildings and structures remain buried amongst them and within a 30 ha enclosure to the north of the platform, where many large buildings have been identified by geophysical survey (Boucharlat and Benech 2002). Beginning in the north, a 30 m high hill, today called Tall-i Takht ("Throne Hill"), is crowned by a huge platform made of ashlar masonry, the longest side of which measures almost 100 m. The platform supported brick buildings from the

FIGURE 26.2 The central garden defined by the stone watercourses, photographed from a kite (© B. N. Chagny, Iran France Archaeological Expedition in Pasargadae–Persepolis 2002).

time of Darius. Some 350 m to the south, an isolated tower standing 14 m tall, although poorly preserved, is the twin of one at Naqsh-e Rustam, near Persepolis. Adjacent to the tower, an unsuspected, large stone building, more than 45 m on each side, was identified by geophysical prospection (Boucharlat and Benech 2002: fig. 12).

The next group of buildings further south is seen as the core of the royal site (Fig. 26.2). The buildings here are arranged on two sides of a central garden, marked by stone-lined channels punctuated by deeper basins which form two rectangles inside a larger rectangle (Boucharlat 2009). Altogether the watercourses define a garden measuring 250 × 165 m that is considered the ancestor of the classical, fourfold Persian garden, the *chahar bagh* (Stronach 1990). The two main buildings, Palaces S and P, are rectangular with one central hall flanked by rows of stone columns. The central room of Palace S is surrounded by four porticoes. Palace P has two long porticoes extending beyond the limits of the hall, the southern one opening onto the garden. In both buildings, the columns show contrast of color, gray-black stepped plinths supporting white drums (Palace S) and one step made of black stone under a white one and smaller white for the plinths of Palace P. Fragments of stone capitals shaped like animal protomes have only been found in Palace S. The plans do not suggest that these were residential buildings but rather audience halls or buildings with some other official function. The complex is connected with the other side of the river by a bridge. A monumental gateway on the left bank of the river was a quite new Persian concept. The gate is neither protected nor connected to a rampart. It is a rectangular hall with two rows of four columns.

The famous tomb of Cyrus is 1 km away from the central area, southwest of Palace S (Fig. 26.3). Departing from the Neo-Elamite vaulted, subterranean chamber or the pre-Achaemenid cist grave, Cyrus created an entirely new type of tomb in the shape

FIGURE 26.3 The tomb of Cyrus (c.530 BC), a free standing monument almost unique in the Achaemenid Empire (© Iran France Archaeological Expedition in Pasargadae–Persepolis).

of a house erected upon a large base with six steps. The monument, which is almost intact, was seen by Alexander in the midst of meadows and groves, with a house of priests (no longer preserved), a landscape that Alexander's companions called a "paradise" (Greek *paradeisos*) (Arrian, *Anab.* 6.29.4–9).

Thanks to geophysical prospections carried out from 1999 to 2008, following the excavations of D. Stronach (1978), the distribution of the buildings on the site is gradually forming a more coherent plan. The common people and/or military quarters were away from the central area. Probably the entire area from the tomb of Cyrus to the central garden should be considered the "paradise" of Pasargadae, a park of over 100 ha. This "landscaped" area was not restricted to the west of the stream, but extended on the east side as well. Moreover, according to the geophysical survey, this canal became a large trapezoidal pool with stone sides (c.250 × 100 m) alongside the central garden. The smallest side is nearest the bridge (Boucharlat 2011). Cyrus' residence heralded a new type of royal residence in the Near East. It was a vast area in which rectilinear rows of trees and plants, along with the architecture, created a visible, well-organized plan. Creating a colorful landscape and a distinctive pattern of water circulation was as important as the built architecture itself.

Before the Achaemenids, southwestern Iran had no tradition of stone architecture. At Pasargadae the most recognizable external influences are from Lydian and Ionian Greek cities (Nylander 1970; Stronach 1978; Boardman 2000). The involvement of architects, quarrymen, and masons brought by Cyrus from Asia Minor is obvious in both the stone masonry techniques and architectural features employed. The plain torus (Palace S) was known in Ionia and Syria, but the horizontally fluted torus (Palace P) was copied from models in Greece and Ephesus in Ionia.

The retaining walls of Tall-i Takht are made of perfectly horizontal courses of large blocks. Their joining sides are worked out by anathyrosis without mortar and the blocks are held together by iron clamps. Their visible faces exhibit a finely drafted margin and a carefully pecked, flat surface. These techniques, as well as the numerous masons' marks, may be compared with the architecture of Lydian Sardis and other Greek cities (Boardman 1998: 5–7). The cornice of the tomb of Cyrus and the horizontal denticulation of the Zendan-e Solaiman tower also testify to Ionian Greek influence. However, Pasargadae is also heir to Near Eastern artistic traditions: the capitals in the shape of animal protomes of Palace S represent an adaptation of the monsters that guarded Assyrian gates, as are certain themes of the reliefs in the palaces. In one of the four doorways of Gate R a relief depicts Cyrus himself or a genius (?) wearing Elamite dress with a double pair of wings in the Assyrian tradition, and an Egyptian crown. This is the best illustration of the king's desire to represent the cultural diversity of the empire: Above the relief an inscription, now lost, proclaimed, "I, Cyrus, the king, an Achaemenian." This is repeated several times in Palaces S and P, while a slightly different inscription on the reliefs of Palace P, says "Cyrus the great king, an Achaemenian." The question is hotly debated whether these inscriptions are from the time of Cyrus, who would then be the inventor of the written Old Persian language (Vallat 2010), or Darius, in which case the new king would have had them carved after the great relief and inscription at Bisotun (Stronach 1990; Huyse 1999).

Beyond the confines of the site, the area up to 30 km north of Pasargadae was developed by building several long earth dams on the Pulvar river. These may have been meant to store water, after first regulating the flow of water from melting snow during the spring thaw. Two of these dams display a sophisticated system, made of stone, consisting of a major conduit (1×1 m) divided into six small canals equipped with sluices. All of this is built of ashlar masonry, comparable in quality to that seen at Pasargadae with carefully polished blocks, anathyrosis for joining the 2 m long blocks, and iron clamps in dovetail-shaped holes filled with lead.

In the opposite direction, to the south of the tomb of Cyrus, canals run on each side of the narrow Pulvar valley for over 10 km. There are both rock-cut sections in the narrower parts of the valley, and longer, built sections in the wider parts, following the topographic contour lines. At the time of Cyrus, or shortly after, a twin-porticoed pavilion was built near one of these channels, downstream from which several farms and a village have been identified (Boucharlat and Fazeli Nashli 2009).

Pasargadae reflected a new conception of the royal residence which, together with the sophisticated monuments of water control in its hinterland, also displays the high technical level reached in the early days of Cyrus. Besides showing borrowings from conquered regions (e.g. Ionia), the architecture of the period reveals important Persian innovations that were later applied at Persepolis and Susa, 600 km to the west of it. This maturity in art and architecture is paralleled by the precise organization of administration throughout the empire, which included the creation of a system of satrapies (Xen. *Cyr.* 8. 6.1–15; Briant 2002: 63–5). After Cyrus and Cambyses, Pasargadae became a medium-sized city, equipped with a treasury, as demonstrated by references to it in the Persepolis tablets. It was mentioned by Arrian (*Anab*. 3.18.10) and retained its status as the city of the founder and an important place for the Achaemenid dynasty (Plutarch, *Artaxerxes* 3).

Cyrus was probably the builder of a palace near modern Borazjan (ancient Gr. Taoke/ OP Tahmaka), about 70 km from the Persian Gulf coast, north of Bushehr. A rectangular, pillared hall excavated there has two rows of square stone column bases, consisting of one black square between two white ones, topped by a black torus, which can be compared to those seen in the palaces at Pasargadae (Sarfaraz 1971). Two other buildings several kilometers further north (unpublished) are probably later. One of these was probably built or completed by Cambyses according to references in Babylonian tablets (Henkelman 2008b; Tolini 2008). These palaces reflect the interests of the early Achaemenid kings in the sea-lanes that allowed navigation to the mouth of the Tigris and Euphrates and thence to Babylon.

Cambyses

The short reign of Cambyses (530–522 BC) did not allow him the opportunity to engage in any great building activity, especially since he left to conquer Egypt in 525. Nothing is known of his activity at Pasargadae. The notion that the site for the construction of Persepolis was chosen by Cambyses, before Darius, is based on references to a locality named Humadešu in Babylonian texts dating to Cambyses' reign. This name was believed to be the equivalent of Matezziš, a town near Persepolis. However, it is now thought Humadešu must have been located closer to Babylon, in the lowlands. In addition, the remains of stone architecture near the Persepolis terrace have been considered transitional between that of Pasargadae and Persepolis, thus dating to the reign of Cambyses. However, they might instead represent the first style of Darius when he started to build the terrace. Nearby the stepped plinth of Takht-e Rustam, 3 km north of Persepolis and similar to the tomb of Cyrus, has long been a candidate for Cambyses' tomb. His tomb is probably to be sought elsewhere, according to some Persepolis tablets mentioning the šumar of Cambyses at Nerazzaš, modern Niriz, over 100 km southeast of Persepolis (Henkelman 2003b; Bessac and Boucharlat 2010).

Darius

After his victory over the magus Gaumata (the "Smerdis" of Herodotus), and after suppressing revolts in many parts of the empire, including Fars, as narrated in the large relief and trilingual inscription carved on the cliff of Bisotun, near Kermanshah, Darius consolidated and extended the conquests of Cyrus and Cambyses. Moreover, he went on to complete the administrative organization of the empire.

Like Cyrus, Darius did not establish a permanent capital. The movements of the king and the court did not signify a nomadic lifestyle in the alleged style of the earlier Persians. Rather, the king visited peoples and countries (*dahyu*) and the royal administration followed. In this way, he displayed his power and guaranteed the protection of the population. This mode of government, "an itinerant State" (Briant 2002: 187), had two important consequences. First, the empire had no single capital. Conversely, the king must have multiple residences, some of which were in very significant locations such as the ancient capitals of conquered nations, like Babylon, Susa, and Ecbatana. According to textual evidence Darius was active at Babylon and Ecbatana, but no archaeological remains have yet been found of his building activities at either site. Persepolis was a place of great importance in Persia itself. Other residences built elsewhere to host the king and his entourage were perhaps also permanently inhabited by the local governor or satrap.

The construction of Persepolis, which replaced Pasargadae as the royal residence in the Persian heartland, was begun shortly after 520, simultaneously with the construction of a palace at Susa, the ancient Elamite capital and a center located midway between Fars and the agriculturally rich province of Babylonia.

Persepolis

Persepolis (OP Barsa/Parsa) was not mentioned by the Greek authors until the time of Alexander, while Susa was regarded by them as the Persian capital at the time of Xerxes (cf. Aeschylus, *The Persians*) and later. This ignorance is all the more surprising since numerous Greek Ionian craftsmen worked on the construction and decoration of the two residences; later delegations of Greek city-states came to the royal court, though it was always traveling. Ctesias, a Greek physician who remained fifteen years at the royal court in the late fifth century, does not mention Persepolis. This is further evidence showing that neither Persepolis nor Susa was the capital.

The extent of Persepolis is much greater than that of Pasargadae, reaching 20 km². The Persepolis Settled Area encompasses the terrace and its surroundings in the south, the royal necropolis of Naqsh-e Rustam 6 km to the north and a large area to the west of this line. Within this vast area, the distribution of architectural and archaeological remains and empty areas shows a loose layout that was to include the residential area of the king and the court, which could not be accommodated on the terrace, as well as houses of the elite. Of the latter, some stone architectural remains were found, including column bases, doorways, and floor slabs *c*.3–4 km west of the terrace (Tilia 1978). This recalls Diodorus Siculus' description of the rich houses of the Persians (17.70.3–5). The Royal City should also have included administrative and military quarters as well as housing for artisans working on the site, traders, and so on (Sumner 1986). As we have seen at Pasargadae, gardens or parks may have been located in some of the seemingly "empty zones" within this area. Beyond the Settled Area, the Marv Dasht plain (80 × 30 km) also witnessed important agricultural development, as evinced by archeological remains of dikes, dams, and irrigation canals and small-scale settlements. All of this evidence echoes data contained in the Persepolis Fortification Tablets (Sumner 1986), which mention many places in the area at which textiles, food, and livestock were produced, exchanged, and delivered to the palace and elsewhere. Classical writers praised the agricultural wealth of the region (Quintus Curtius 5.4.6–7, 20).

To reconstruct the landscape of the Persepolis region, the thousands of clay tablets found in two rooms of the Fortification north of the terrace are an invaluable source. Whether they represent living or dead/discarded archives, remains uncertain (Razmjou 2008). The vast majority are written in Achaemenid Elamite cuneiform and date from the years 509 and 494, during the reign of Darius I. Over 2000 of these texts have been published (Hallock 1969), while thousands more are available to specialists. These documents, strictly administrative in nature (there are no Achaemenid annals), are copies of originals on clay tablet or parchment. They were issued at Persepolis by the supervisor of the transaction recorded, whose name is usually mentioned, and bear one or more seal impressions corresponding to the person or the office who controlled the transaction or the goods. The tablets mention the receipt, taxation, storage, transport, and disbursement of goods and livestock to members of the royal family or other nobles living in Fars or traveling in the region or beyond it. Deliveries also concern temple personnel in Fars (Henkelman 2008a) and very often workers (*kurtaš*), both small and large teams of people, including women; craftsmen employed in the building of Persepolis or other places under construction, like Susa (Briant 2010); and peasants working on estates in Fars. For the Persepolis plain, these estates are not described according to their size. Sometimes they are called El. *partetaš*, a term very likely equivalent of the Greek *paradeisos*, derived from OP *paridaida*. From the tablets it is clear that *partetaš*/paradise cannot be rendered "garden" or "pleasant retreat." It covers a wide array of forms, sizes, and functions: orchards, estates, parks, hunting preserves, and so on. Until now, the only place identified that might illustrate this kind of estate/paradise in Fars is located in the Pulvar valley south of Pasargadae (see above).

At Persepolis the royal precinct extended beyond the famous terrace occupying 12 ha, and measuring 450 × 300 m. To the south of the terrace the *Barzan-i jonubi* ("South Quarter") is an area almost equal in size to the terrace itself that consists of several stone buildings with hypostyle halls, sometimes with porticoes, and a series of smaller rooms and courtyards. Some seven buildings have been excavated and more are probably still buried (Tadjvidi 1976; Mousavi 2012: 26–41, pls. 4–9). A column base inscribed with the name of Xerxes gives a chronological clue to the date of the complex. To the east, overlooking the platform, the steep slope of the mountain was largely terraced, showing signs of canals and perhaps buildings, extending up the ridge along which a mudbrick fortification ran, complete with an inner gallery and towers (Tadjvidi 1976; Mousavi 1992).

The construction of the terrace probably began around 520 but the first Fortification texts date only to 509 (Roaf 2004). The mountain slope was leveled and used as the

FIGURE 26.4 The Persepolis terrace seen from the north, photographed from a balloon (© B. N. Chagny, Iran France Archaeological Expedition in Pasargadae–Persepolis 2004).

foundation of a retaining wall that reached 14 m in height and was built of huge blocks of limestone quarried from the mountain itself or from quarries nearby (Fig. 26.4). The masonry is cyclopean, not as it was on the elegant Pasargadae platform but certainly more impressive. Darius began the construction of the Apadana at the edge of the terrace, and changed it during construction from a rectangular (cf. Pasargadae) to a square plan. He began the monumental "Gate of All Nations" in the north, a square hall with four columns. The two main doorways are flanked by sculptures of human-headed, winged bulls (*lamassu*) in Assyrian style. To the south, the "palace of Darius" or *tačara* is a columned hall with a southern portico, flanked by rooms on the sides. This is the best-preserved building at Persepolis and the prototype of later "palaces." The southeastern quarter of the terrace was occupied by the Treasury, a set of hypostyle rooms of varying size, separated by narrow corridors (Cameron 1948).

The column shafts and capitals of the Apadana (Fig. 26.5) and the Gate of All Nations are made of stone, and reach a height of 21 m. Later, only the Hall of 100 Columns (or Throne Hall) of Xerxes had stone columns and capitals, but of much smaller dimensions. In all of the other hypostyle buildings, only the column bases were made of stone. The columns themselves were made of stuccoed and painted wood. The Apadana consists of a square room, 53 m on each side, with six rows of six columns, and porticoes (two rows of six columns) on the northern, eastern, and western sides; the southern side consists of rooms and corridors giving access to other buildings. When the porticoes are added onto the Apadana itself, the overall plan measures 109 m on each side. The

FIGURE 26.5 The main columned hall (Apadana) on the Persepolis terrace, photographed from a balloon (© B. N. Chagny, Iran France Archaeological Expedition in Pasargadae–Persepolis 2004).

mudbrick walls are exceptionally thick, 5 m, whereas they are 1.50–2.50 m thick in other buildings on the terrace. In contrast, the doors, window frames and niche frames of the various buildings are made of stone extracted from nearby quarries, the closest of which is adjacent to the terrace itself. The higher quality of limestone, for example the sort used for the reliefs, was quarried about 30 km away from the terrace.

The buildings begun by Darius hardly occupy one-third of the surface of the terrace (Roaf 1983: figs. 153, 156). The king may have chosen to preserve large uncovered areas, courtyards, or gardens. Though much less loose than the layout of Pasargadae, Darius' plan broke with the tradition of earlier Near Eastern palatial architecture, which normally consisted of compact blocks built around courtyards that provided light and allowed the circulation of movement. The only buildings on the terrace of Persepolis had official and/or ceremonial functions but were not suitable as residential buildings.

The sculptural program on the staircases of the Apadana was probably begun by Darius and completed by his son Xerxes. The reliefs are not narrative but, like the architecture, they were intended to exalt the power of the king. More specifically they display the wealth and diversity of the empire as well as the peace conferred upon it by the king (Root 1979; Roaf 1983). Unlike the Assyrian reliefs, there were scenes of neither war nor hunting. On one side of the stairs north and east of the Apadana, the Medes and Persian guards are shown armed, but in a peaceful march. Symmetrically arranged on the staircases, the delegations of the peoples and lands of the empire are represented in several registers, each group dressed in the costume and hairstyle of his country and carrying objects that illustrate the region's products—precious vessels, textiles, animals, and so on. After Darius' lifetime the same program was repeated on the staircases of other buildings, without innovation. Religious scenes seem to be absent (contra Razmjou 2010); they are at least not immediately identifiable. On some doorjambs the king is shown seated on a huge symbolic throne carried by the peoples of the empire. In other places (e.g., the Hall of 100 Columns) the king is shown fighting a monster.

Naqsh-e Rustam

The royal necropolis at Persepolis is on the edge of the Settled Area, just as Cyrus' tomb is at Pasargadae. However, Darius completely changed the design for his tomb. He chose a cliff 60 m high in which he had a rock chamber cut, perhaps inspired by Anatolian models (Fig. 26.6). He had a large space carved into the rock containing three rooms with three, in-built sarcophagi (Schmidt 1970). Outside, below the door, where an inscription glorifying the king was carved, a large, smooth surface made the room inaccessible. Two panels were carved above the door (Fig. 26.7). The upper one shows the king standing on a gigantic throne carried by a representative of each "people" or "land" of the empire, identified by his costume and a short inscription such as, "This is a Lydian," "This is an

FIGURE 26.6 The Royal necropolis of Naqsh-e Rustam with the rock-cut tombs of Darius I and three of his successors, one is not visible on the right. On the left, the free standing tower of unknown function, photographed from a balloon (© B. N. Chagny, Iran France Archaeological Expedition in Pasargadae–Persepolis 2004).

Armenian." The king, one arm raised, faces an altar bearing a fire. Between the king and the altar, but higher than both, is a bust emerging from wings in a circle. This represents, probably not the god Ahuramazda, but *Farr(ah)/x^{v}arənah* "royal fortune/luminous glory" (Gnoli 1999), the symbol of royalty given by Ahuramazda. The lower, wider panel shows the façade of a palace, a portico with a row of columns, including the base, drum, and capital supporting a denticulate entablature. This representation was instrumental in the first reconstructions of the elevation of the "palaces" of Persepolis (Krefter 1971). The first three successors of Darius followed exactly this tomb model on the same cliff. Later, Artaxerxes II and III had their similar tombs cut overlooking the Persepolis terrace (Schmidt 1970; Calmeyer 2009).

Susa

Cyrus and Cambyses apparently built nothing at Susa. Darius, however, erected a residence that required a colossal amount of labor. Workers and skilled craftsmen were brought in from all over the empire. Their contributions are symbolically listed on "foundation tablets" in Elamite (DSz) and Akkadian (Dsaa) (Steve et al. 2002–3; Vallat, 2010) and in a number of texts from Persepolis and Babylon that record the sending of workers, materials, and goods to Susa over a period of fifteen years (Joannès 1990; Briant 2010).

The overall plan (*PDS*) of Darius' residence at Susa differs from Persepolis while sharing several features (Boucharlat 2010: 33–4; Boucharlat and Gasche 2010) including

FIGURE 26.7 The bas-relief carved above the tomb of Darius I at Naqsh-e Rustam (© Iran France Archaeological Expedition in Pasargadae–Persepolis).

a high platform, a large, pillared hall (Apadana), and an isolated, monumental gate (Fig. 26.8). On a plain devoid of stone, the 12 ha platform at Susa was created by leveling the summit of an archaeological mound (Ladiray 2010: 161–70). Some of this material is embedded within a huge mudbrick retaining wall faced with baked brick, standing 14 m, the same height as the terrace at Persepolis. The huge pillared hall or Apadana was the creation of Darius as evinced by a foundation tablet (DSf). The building is called Apadana in an inscription of Artaxerxes II (A²Sa) recording its reconstruction in the early fourth century BC. The Susa Apadana is similar to that of Persepolis in plan, dimensions (109 × 109 m), and column height (21 m). To secure such walls and columns in the ground, foundation trenches over 10 m deep were dug and then filled with gravel and pebbles.

The same technique was applied to the main walls of the Residence, a building identified as such on the basis of its plan, which is derived from the Mesopotamian and probably Susian tradition (Elamite prototypes of the immediately preceding centuries, if they existed, have not been found). The Residence is rectangular (246 × 155 m) with an entrance on the east that provides access to three aligned courtyards of different sizes. As one moved from the exterior toward the interior, access was increasingly controlled by a complex plattern of circulation. Some of the walls of the first courtyard, the most official, were decorated with glazed brick panels representing lines of archers, and lions and griffins *en passant* (Muscarella 1992; Caubet 1992; Caubet and Daucé 2010). The original location and arrangement of these wall decorations, now reconstructed in the Louvre museum, are poorly understood because of the very imprecise nature of the Susa excavations in the late nineteenth century. The third courtyard to the west provided access to the royal apartment. Beyond an oblong antechamber and a square room lay the square king's chamber. On both sides of the royal apartment, a series of five blocks of two rooms were either apartments for the king's family (*PDS*) or, more likely, offices and rooms for scribes or archives. They may have supported a second story, which was for the residential apartments (Amiet 2010). On both sides of the door to the royal apartment inscribed stone slabs were buried in the foundation. These are inscribed on all six faces, one in Elamite the others in Akkadian. The text describes the work accomplished by order of the king: the countries of the empire that supplied the materials—stone, wood, gold, and so on—transported from their place of origin to Susa and worked on site. These tablets, invisible to all mortal eyes, were copied on stone, baked brick, and glazed brick in order to publicize the works of the king (Potts 1999: table 9.4).

The Apadana and Residence occupy only 5 ha of the 12 ha terrace at Susa. Some 50 m to the east of the Residence, an isolated monumental gate stands on the edge of the terrace. According to an inscription on the column bases (XSd) there, Darius began this 40 × 28 m building and Xerxes completed it. The square room (21.10 m on each side) with four columns is generally similar to the Gate of All Nations at Persepolis, except that rooms have been added on the long sides and staircases at the corners. On one side of the passage to the palace was found a statue of Darius. Although the upper part of the statue is missing, when complete it probably stood about 3.50 m tall. Made in Egypt, it was brought to Susa by Xerxes. Although the king wears a Persian garment, he stands

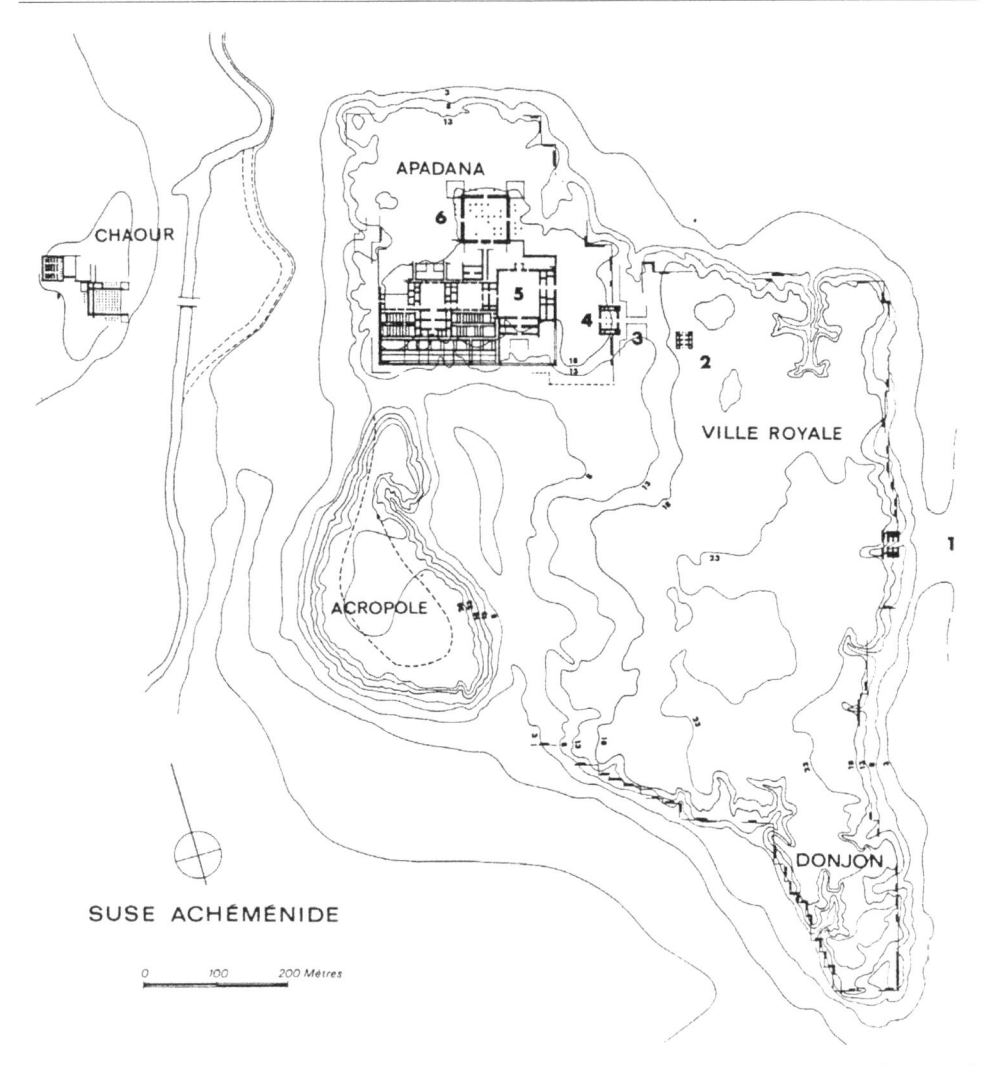

FIGURE 26.8 Map of the Royal City (Ville Royale) of Susa modeled by Darius (late sixth century BC) (after Perrot 2010: fig. 108).

in an Egyptian pose, backed by a pillar. The garment bears a quadrilingual inscription, the three cuneiform languages (Akkadian, Elamite, and Old Persian) of the empire to which a hieroglyphic text was added with the legend, "Here is the stone statue of the king Darius who ordered it to be made in Egypt." The square base is decorated front and back with the symbols of Upper and Lower Egypt. On the sides of the base are engraved twenty-four cartouches in the shape of fortresses, each with the name of the people in hieroglyphs and a representation of a kneeling *dahyu* (Stronach 1974; Roaf 1974; Yoyotte 2010).

From the Gate, a mudbrick bridge crossed the deep ditch between the Terrace and another mound which was leveled to the same height. Called the "Royal City" (Ville

Royale) by the early excavators, this second mound was home to a square building, 24 m on each side. According to a trilingual inscription (XSa) on the column bases, it was built by Xerxes and consisted of two parallel, oblong rooms opening on each side onto a portico with two columns. The building had foundations several meters deep, similar to those beneath the palace of Darius (Ladiray 2010: 180–3).

Covering *c.*100 ha., the only partially explored Royal City had a monumental city gate to the east which was built on an impressive 18 m high *glacis* without rampart that demarcated it. Apart from Darius' palace and associated buildings, no other constructions of similar prestige, nor indeed any ordinary living quarters, were found in the Royal City. Is this an artifact of excavation, even though these were extensive, or a real reflection of the situation in this part of the site? Apparently there was in fact no "city" inside the royal perimeter wall, judging by the paucity of material recovered after decades of excavations (Amiet and Frank 2010). Even more so than Persepolis, Susa raises the question of the environment around the royal residence, though both sites functioned as the capital of a satrapy (Boucharlat 1997).

The Achaemenid inscriptions at Susa are mainly the work of Darius (Potts 1999: table 9.4). Some are attributable to Xerxes, who completed the constructions of his father, while others are those of Darius II (423–405 BC) and, especially, Artaxerxes II (405–359 BC) (Vallat 2010). Many of these inscriptions refer to constructions using terms which are poorly understood (e.g., *hadiš*, *tačara*, *bītu*, etc.) and which remain unidentified archaeologically. They may have either disappeared or refer to parts of existing buildings (Boucharlat 2000). Apart from stone inscriptions, sometimes copied on bricks, Susa has not yielded official archives like those found at Persepolis.

Xerxes and his successors

It is a commonplace inherited from the Greek writers to see the empire after Darius as a period of decline or decay, governed by weak and incompetent kings. Actually, the textual sources and archaeological data are far fewer from the time of Xerxes and his successors. However, their activities at both Susa and Persepolis were important. Of all the successors, Artaxerxes II was one of the most active at Susa. He rebuilt or repaired the Apadana of Darius and recorded this in an inscription (A^2Sa) engraved on four column bases in the Apadana, which was in fact the first Achaemenid inscription found at Susa when excavations began there in 1854 (Kent 1953; Lecoq 1997: 272–3).

Artaxerxes II also built outside the walls of Susa, on the other side of the Shaur River. The plan of his new palace, covering 4 ha, was original. Unlike Darius' palace, the Shaur palace consisted of several buildings positioned around a garden. The main building, in the east, was a columned hall (six rows of six columns), flanked on each side by a portico. On one side of the garden was a small construction built on a terrace 2 m high. This consisted of a foundation of intersecting walls forming rectangular cavities filled with gravel and pebbles. Above this stood a pillared hall, flanked by two side rooms and a portico opening onto the garden. The entire complex evokes a Persian paradise, situated in the plain, near water, in contrast to the palace of Darius erected on the top of the nearby mound (Boucharlat 2010).

Neither of the two Susa palaces was destroyed by Alexander but instead died a "natural" death, whereas Persepolis was burned down in 330 BC (Boucharlat 1990). To its end, Susa was active, as evinced by the small number of nonroyal inscriptions found there.

Elite residences and roads in Fars

Despite the lack of later Achaemenid texts and testimony in the works of Classical authors, it is likely that the "itinerant state" continued after Darius. Recent excavations and surveys have revealed some new sites that are relevant in this regard. The results remain modest, but they are an improvement on our knowledge of some decades ago (Boucharlat 2005). To start with, in south-central Fars, a group of buildings, close to one another, is reported at Farmeshgan near Kavar. Few remains are visible apart from stone platforms showing stone-cutting techniques of Achaemenid type (Razmjou 2005a)

In western Fars, a "pavilion" at Jinjun (Qaleh Kali), first detected by Herzfeld in 1924 and known from brief Japanese excavations in 1959, has recently been investigated (Potts and Roustaei 2006; Potts et al. 2007, 2009). The site is situated near Nurabad, in an intermontane valley in western Fars, within sight of the Elamite rock relief of Kurangun and the multiperiod settlement of Tol-e Spid. Excavations have shown that this was much more than a small pavilion, rather the portico of a larger building. A row of columns rested on bell-shaped bases, decorated with ribbed leaves and palm leaves, comparable in size to the larger bases in the Hall of 100 Columns at Persepolis. The portico was delimited by a parapet with stepped merlons. Three short steps indicate that the building was raised on a small terrace. The main part of the building, very poorly preserved, is not yet defined. Remains of another building were identified nearby but this is not yet securely dated to the Achaemenid period. Importantly, column bases have been reported a few kilometers to the south at Tol-e Gachgaran (Potts et al. 2009: 212) and further north (Yaghma'i 2006), clearly showing that Achaemenid occupation in the area is not limited to a single building.

Further west, near Ram Hormuz in eastern Khuzestan, the construction of a road in 2009 led to the discovery of eighteen column bases, only five of which appear to be *in situ* (unpublished). Nurabad/Jinjun and Ram Hormuz are located on what is considered to be the extension of the Royal Road from Sardis to Susa, along the Susa–Persepolis route unknown to the Classical authors. However, there is no reason to link these elite or temporary royal residences to roads and "stations" (Potts 2008: 279). The latter were used by officials, messengers, soldiers, and groups of workers to whom food was delivered. Attempts to match the place names attested in the Persepolis texts with modern place names are largely hypothetical and have led to very different results (Hallock 1959, 1969; Kleiss 1981; Koch 1986, 1990; Arfa'i 1999; Yaghma'i 2006) that invite caution (Potts 2008). Nevertheless, during the Achaemenid period the Fars and more westerly road segments (Behbahhan–Ram Hormuz) in Khuzestan must have been crossed frequently by kings, officials, and many ordinary people, and later by Alexander on his way to Persepolis. This is the natural route between the lowlands of Elam and the mountainous region of Anshan.

Places of worship and burial practices

During the Achaemenid period, many religions were tolerated, even in the heart of the empire. On the religion of the kings we have very little information: at most, the royal inscriptions indicate that Auramazdā/Ahuramazda is "the great god (*baga*)" (DNb) or "the greatest of the gods" (DPd) (Lecoq 1997: 154–9), from whom the Achaemenid kings derived their power. In this respect we can therefore say that the Achaemenid kings were Mazdeans (avoiding the term Zoroastrian; see the discussion in Chapter 28). Under Artaxerxes II, other gods (*baga*) are mentioned, such as Anahita and Mithra. Moreover, fire, as an object or instrument of worship, was important, as shown in the bas-reliefs carved above the royal tombs.

In keeping with Herodotus' statement "The Persians have no temples" (*Hist.* 1.121), no places of worship have been identified. The only candidate for an open-air shrine is at Pasargadae where two cuboid, monolithic bases, about 2 m on each side, are located, one of which is equipped with a staircase. Although these have been compared to depictions on the bas-reliefs of the tombs, any connection remains hypothetical. The existence of built or unbuilt open-air places of worship is attested by Darius, since he says in his Bisotun inscription that he restored the *ayadana* previously destroyed by the usurper Gaumata (DB 1.14). Permanent places of worship are referred to in many of Persepolis tablets that mention the provision of food for religious personnel and plant products and animals for sacrifice (Henkelman 2008a). The deities worshiped at these sanctuaries were most often non-Iranian, either Elamite or of unidentified affiliation (Henkelman 2008a). There was no state religion in Fars, or in the other satrapies, where people continued to worship their own gods.

The known tombs of the Achaemenid period are all royal, apart from one of an elite person at Susa (Amiet and Frank 2010). These tombs indicate that burial practices did not follow the requirements of the *Avesta*. The sacred book recommends the exposure of the body to beasts of prey and then the gathering of bones in a secondary burial. As confirmed by Classical writers, cremation was abhorred (Ctesias, *Persika* §57; Strabo 15. 3.18). Herodotus (1.140) indicated that the practice of body exposure was reserved only for magi, but said that in-ground burial was the norm (7.10), an opinion confirmed by Plutarch (*Artaxerxes* 18.7). At Pasargadae, Cyrus is said to have been laid on a bed with rich grave furniture (Arrian, *Anab.* 6. 29.5–6). The rock-cut sarcophagi in the burial chambers of Naqsh-e Rustam and Persepolis are human sized with a heavy lid, also clearly suggesting burial of the complete corpse.

Ceremonies were performed at Cyrus' tomb by a group of professional priests. According to the Persepolis texts, they received food rations for themselves and similar products for the sacrifices, like the clergy of the shrines. According to Arrian, one horse per month was delivered for sacrifice (*Anab.* 6.29, 7). This is confirmed by the Persepolis texts, which also mention products for the *šumar* of Cambyses at Narezzaš and that of Hystaspes at Persepolis (Henkelman 2003b). These practices presuppose buildings that have left no trace near the tomb of Cyrus, an area deeply disturbed by medieval occupation and modern activities.

Daily life

The archaeology of Fars mainly reflects royal achievements. Hundreds of articles have been published about Achaemenid art, while very limited research has been carried out on what went on in the vicinity of the palaces at Persepolis and Susa. The investigation of human settlement and urbanization around these royal residences remains a major archaeological concern. One should probably consider the absence of densely built settlement on the outskirts of these residences as an expression of the king's desire to isolate the royal quarter from the town. The survey and sounding program launched west of the platform of Persepolis will, one hopes, provide new information on the organization of this area.

Although data on cities and villages elsewhere in Fars and neighboring regions has long been almost nonexistent, this situation is slowly changing. In the Nurabad region, research has not been limited to the exploration of the Achaemenid building at Jinjin, but includes regional surveys and the demonstration of significant levels dating to the Achaemenid period at Tol-e Spid (Potts et al. 2007). Rescue excavations in the Tang-e Bolaghi valley also revealed Achaemenid-period occupation, probably corresponding to one or more estates (*partetaš*) under royal or elite authority. These investigations are changing our vision of the Achaemenid period in Fars by revealing evidence of nonroyal activities in the heart of the empire.

Further reading

For general history see Briant (2002). On the pre-Achaemenid period, see Potts (1999) and the papers in *EP*. For the art and archaeology of the Achaemenid Empire, mainly Iran, see the papers in *WAP*. On the excavations of the Cyrus' residence, see Stronach (1978). For Persepolis see the volumes by Schmidt (1953–70), Henkelman (2008), Mousavi (2012), and Boucharlat et al. (2012). On Susa see Harper et al. (1992) and *PDS*.

References

Alizadeh, A. 1985. A tomb of the Neo-Elamite period at Arjān, near Behbahan, *AMI* 18: 49–73.

———. 2003. Some observations based on the nomadic character of Fars prehistoric cultural development. *YBYN*: 83–97.

Álvarez-Mon, J. 2010. *The Arjān tomb: At the crossroads of the Elamite and the Persian Empires*. Leuven: Acta Iranica 49.

———. 2011. The golden griffin from Arjan. *EP*: 299–373.

Amiet, P. 1973. La glyptique de la fin de l'Elam. *Arts Asiatiques* 28: 3–32.

———. 2010. Le palais de Darius à Suse: Problèmes et hypothèses. *Arta* 2010.001.

Amiet, P., and C. Frank. 2010. L'art mobilier à Suse à l'époque perse. *PDS*: 350–73.

Arfa'i, A. 1999. La grande route de Persépolis-Suse. Une lecture des tablettes provenant des Fortifications de Persépolis. *Topoi* 9/1: 33–45.

Bessac, J.-C., and R. Boucharlat 2010. Le monument de Takht-e Rustam, près de Persépolis dit "tombeau inachevé de Cambyse": note technique et reconsidérations. *Arta* 2010.003.

Boardman, J. 1998. Seals and signs: Anatolian stamp seals of the Persian Period revisited. *Iran* 36: 1–13.

———. 2000. *Persia and the West: An archaeological investigation of the genesis of Achaemenid art*. London: Thames and Hudson.

Boucharlat, R. 1990. La fin des palais achéménides de Suse: une mort naturelle. *MJP*: 225–33.

———. 1997. Susa under Achaemenid rule. In *Mesopotamia and Iran in the Persian Period: Conquest and imperialism 539–331 BC*, ed. J. Curtis, 54–67. London: Trustees of the British Museum.

———. 2000. Les autres palais achéménides de Suse. *VD*: 141–52.

———. 2005. Iran. *AEA*: 221–92.

———. 2009. The "Paradise" of Cyrus at Pasargadae, the core of the royal ostentation. In *Bau- und Gartenkultur zwischen 'Orient' und 'Okzident'. Fragen zu Herkunft, Identität und Legitimation*, ed. J. Ganzert and J. Wolsche-Bulmahn, 47–64. Hannover: Beiträge zur Architektur- und Kulturgeschichte 3.

———. 2010. Autres travaux de Darius et successeurs. *PDS*: 374–419.

———. 2011. Gardens and parks at Pasargadae: Two Paradises? In *Herodot und das Persische Weltreich/Herodotus and the Persian Empire*, ed. R. Rollinger, B. Truschnegg, and R. Bichler, 457–74. Wiesbaden: CLeO 3.

Boucharlat, R., and C. Benech 2002. Organisation et aménagement de l'espace à Pasargades: Reconnaissances archéologiques de surface, 1999–2002. *Arta* 2002.001: 1–41.

Boucharlat, R., and H. Fazeli Nashli. 2009. Tang-i Bulaghi Reports. *Arta* 2009.001–006.

Boucharlat, R., and H. Gasche 2010. Suse dans l'architecture iranienne et orientale. *PDS*: 420–65.

Boucharlat, R., T. De Schacht, and S. Gondet. 2012. *Dariosh Studies II. Persepolis and its settlements: Territorial system and ideology in the Achaemenid state*, ed. G.P. Basello and A.V. Rossi, 123–66. Naples: Università degli Studi di Napoli "L'Orientale".

Briant, P. 1984. La Perse avant l'empire (un état des questions). *IrAnt* 19: 71–118.

———. 2002. *From Cyrus to Alexander: A history of the Persian Empire*. Winona Lake: Eisenbrauns.

———. 2010. Suse et l'Élam dans l'empire achéménide. *PDS*: 22–48.

Calmeyer, P. 2009. *Die Reliefs der Gräber V und VI in Persepolis*. Mainz: AIT 8.

Cameron, G. G. 1948. *Persepolis Treasury Tablets*. Chicago: OIP 65.

Carter, E. 1994. Bridging the gap between the Elamites and the Persians in southwestern Khuzistan. In *Continuity and Change*, ed. H. Sancisi-Weerdenburg, A. Kuhrt, and M. C. Root, 65–95. Leiden: AchHist 8.

———. 1996. *Excavations at Anshan (Tal-e Malyan): The Middle Elamite period*. Philadelphia: UMM 82.

Caubet, A. 1992. Achaemenid brick decoration. *RCS*: 223–5.

Caubet, A., and N. Daucé 2010. Les arts du feu. *PDS*: 322–47.

Chevalier, N. 2010. Les découvreurs du palais de Darius. *PDS*: 74–115.

Garrison, M. 2011. The Seal of «Kuraš the Anzanite, son of Šešpeš» (Teispes), PFS 93*: Susa—Anshan—Persepolis. *EP*: 375–405.

Gnoli, G. 1999. Farr(ah). *EnIr* online edition.

Hallock, R. T. 1959. The Elamite texts from Persepolis. In *Akten des vierundzwanzigsten internationalen Orientalisten-Kongresses München, 28. August bis 4. September 1957*, ed. H. Franke, 177–9. Wiesbaden: Deutsche Morgenländische Gesellschaft.

———. 1969. *Persepolis Fortification Tablets*. Chicago: OIP 92.

Henkelman, W. 2003a. Persians, Medes and Elamites: Acculturation in the Neo-Elamite period. *CE*: 181–231.

———. 2003b. An Elamite memorial: The *šumar* of Cambyses and Hystapes. *APP*: 101–72.

———. 2003c. Defining "Neo-Elamite history." *BiOr* 60/3–4: 251–63.

———. 2008a. *The other gods who are: Studies in Elamite-Iranian acculturation based on the Persepolis Fortification texts*. Leiden: AchHist 14.

———. 2008b. From Gabae to Taoce: The geography of the central administrative province. *AFP*: 303–15.

Huyse, P. 1999. Some further thoughts on the Bisitun monument and the genesis of the Old Persian cuneiform script. *BAI* 13: 45–66.

Joannès, F. 1990. Textes babyloniens de Suse d'époque achéménide. *MJP*: 173–80.

Kent, R. 1953. *Old Persian: Grammar, texts, lexicon*, 2nd ed. New Haven: AOS 33.

Kleiss. 1981. Ein Abschnitt der achaemenidischen Königsstraße von Pasargadae und Persepolis nach Susa, bei Naqsh-i Rustam. *AMI* 14: 45–53.

Koch, H. 1986. Die achämenidische Poststraße von Persepolis nach Susa. *AMI* 19: 133–47.

———. 1990. *Verwaltung und Wirtschaft im persischen Kernland zur Zeit der Achämeniden*. Wiesbaden: TAVO Beiheft B 89.

Krefter, F. 1971. *Persepolis Rekonstruktionen*. Berlin: Teheraner Forschungen 3.

Kuhrt, A. 2007. *The Persian Empire: A corpus of sources from the Achaemenid period*. London/New York: Routledge.

Ladiray, D. 2010. Les données archéologiques. *PDS*: 160–221.

Lecoq, P. 1997. *Les inscriptions de la Perse achéménide*. Paris: Gallimard.

Miroschedji, P. de. 1978. Stratigraphie de la période néo-élamite à Suse (c. 1100–c. 540). *Paléorient* 4: 213–28.

———. 1985. La fin du royaume d'Anshan et de Suse et la naissance de l'empire perse. *ZA* 75: 265–306.

Mousavi, A. 1992. Parsa, a stronghold for Darius: A preliminary study of the defense system of Persepolis. *EW* 42/2–4: 203–26.

———. 2012. *Persepolis: Discovery and afterlife of a world wonder*. Berlin: De Gruyter.

Muscarella, O. 1992. Achaemenid art and architecture at Susa. *RCS*: 216–19.

Nylander, C. 1970. *Ionians in Pasargadae: Studies in Old Persian architecture*. Uppsala: Boreas, Acta Universitatis Upsaliensis 1.

Potts, D. T. 1999. *The archaeology of Elam: Formation and transformation of an ancient Iranian state*. Cambridge: Cambridge University Press.

———. 2005. Cyrus the Great and the Kingdom of Anshan. In *Birth of the Persian Empire*, ed. V. S. Curtis and S. Stewart, 7–28. London: I. B. Tauris.

———. 2008. The Persepolis Fortification Texts (PFTs) and the Royal Road: Another look at the Fahliyan area. *AFP*: 275–300.

———. 2010. Monarchy, factionalism and warlordism: Reflections on Neo-Elamite courts. In *Der Achämenidenhof/The Achaemenid court*, ed. B. Jacobs and R. Rollinger, 107–37. Wiesbaden: CLeO 2.

———. 2011. A note on the limits of Anshan. *EP*: 35–43.

Potts, D. T., A. Asgari Chaverdi, C. A. Petrie, A. Dusting, F. Farhadi, I. K. McRae, S. Shikhi et al. 2007. The Mamasani Archaeological Project, Stage Two: Excavations at Qaleh Kali (Tappeh Servan/Jinjun [MS 46]). *Iran* 45: 287–300.

Potts, D. T., A. Askari Chaverdi, I. K. McRae, K. Alamdari, A. Dusting, J. Jaffari, T. M. Ellicott et al. 2009. Further Excavations at Qaleh Kali (MS 46) by the Joint ICAR–University of Sydney Mamasani Expedition: Results of the 2008 Season. *IrAnt* 44: 208–82.

Potts, D. T., and K. Roustaei. 2006. *The Mamasani Archaeological Project Stage One: A report on the first two seasons of the ICAR–University of Sydney expedition to the Mamasani District, Fars Province, Iran*. Tehran: ICAR.

Razmjou, S. 2005a. Notes on a forgotten Achaemenid site at Farmeshgan, Iran. *AEA*: 293–312.

———. 2005b. Religion and burial customs. In *Forgotten empire: The world of Ancient Persia*, ed. J. Curtis and N. Tallis, 150–6. London: British Museum Press.

———. 2008. Find spots and find circumstances of documents excavated at Persepolis. *AFP*: 51–8.

———. 2010. Persepolis: A reinterpretation of palaces and their function. *WAP*: 231–45.

Roaf, M. 1974. The subject peoples on the base of the statue of Darius. *CDAFI* 4: 73–160.

———. 1983. Sculptures and sculptors at Persepolis. *Iran* 21: 1–164.

———. 2004. Persepolis. *RlA* 10: 393–412.

Root, M. C. 1979. *The king and kingship in Achaemenid art: Essays on the creation of an iconography of empire*. Leuven: Acta Iranica 19.

Sarfaraz, A. A. 1971. Un pavillon de l'époque de Cyrus le Grand à Borazjan. *Bāstān-Šenāsī va Honar-e Īrān* 7–8: 22–5.

Schmidt, E. F. 1953. *Persepolis I. Sculptures, reliefs, inscriptions*. Chicago: OIP 68.

———. 1957. *Persepolis II. Contents of the Treasury and other discoveries*. Chicago: OIP 69.

———. 1970. *Persepolis III. The royal tombs and other monuments*. Chicago: OIP 70.

Shishehgar, A. 2008. *Discovery of a tomb attributed to members of King Shutur-Nahhunte dynasty, son of Indid (or Indattu), Neo-Elamite III period (c. 585–539 BC)*. Tehran: ICAR (in Persian).

Steve, M.-J., F. Vallat, H. Gasche, and F. Jullien. 2002–3. Suse. *SDB* 73: 360–512 (bibliog. in *SDB* 74: 620–52).

Stronach, D. 1974. Une statue de Darius découverte à Suse. *CDAFI* 4: 61–72.

———. 1978. *Pasargadae: A report on the excavations conducted by the British Institute of Persian Studies from 1961 to 1963*. Oxford: Clarendon Press.

———. 1989. The royal garden at Pasargadae: Evolution and legacy. *AIO*: 475–502.

———. 1990. On the genesis of the Old Persian cuneiform script. *MJP*: 195–203.

———. 2003. The Tomb at Arjan and the history of southwestern Iran in the early sixth century B.C. *YBYN*: 249–59.

Sumner, W. M. 1986. Achaemenid settlement in the Persepolis Plain. *AJA* 90: 3–31.

Tadjvidi, A.A. 1976. *Dānestanīhā-ye novīn darbāreh-ye honar va bāstānšenāsi-ye aṣr-e hakhāmaneši bar bonyād-e kāvoshā-ye pang̈ sāleh-ye Takht-e Ğamšīd*. [New knowledge about Achaemenid art and archaeology based on five years of excavations at Persepolis]. Tehran.

Tilia, A.B. 1978. *Studies and restorations at Persepolis and other sites of Fārs*, vol. 2. Rome: IsMEO Reports and Memoirs 18.

Tolini, G. 2008. Les travailleurs babyloniens et le palais de Taokè. *Arta* 2008.002.

Vallat, F. 1984. Kidin-Hutran à l'époque néo-élamite. *Akkadica* 37: 1–17.

———. 2010. Les principales inscriptions achéménides à Suse. *PDS*: 300–17.

Waters, M. 2000. *A survey of Neo-Elamite history*. Helsinki: SAAS 12.

———. 2004. Cyrus and the Achaemenids. *Iran* 42: 91–102.

Yaghmaee, E. 2006/[1385]. Čand manzelgāh-e rāh-e šāhī-ye hakhāmanešī: az Nūrābād-e Mamasanī tā Arğān-e Behbahān. *Bāstānpazhuhi* 2: 32–49.

Young, T. C., Jr. 2003. Parsa, Parsua, and potsherds. *YBYN*: 242–48.

Yoyotte, J. 2010. La statue égyptienne de Darius. *PDS*: 256–99.

CHAPTER 27

ADMINISTRATIVE REALITIES: THE PERSEPOLIS ARCHIVES AND THE ARCHAEOLOGY OF THE ACHAEMENID HEARTLAND

WOUTER F. M. HENKELMAN

Introduction

Together with the foothill areas of eastern Khūzestān, a larger part of modern Fārs formed an administrative unit of the Achaemenid Empire (c.550–330 BC). Its ancient name, Pārsa, was also used for Persepolis (Pārsa-the-city, not "city of the Persians") itself. This area, the Achaemenid heartland, comprises a series of northwest-southeast-oriented valley systems and some larger intermontane plains. A series of dams in the area north of Pasargadae; rock-cut canals between Pasargadae and Persepolis; and sluices and extensive canals in the Persepolis plain all attest to a massive investment of energy and organizational power to bring the Achaemenid heartland under cultivation. As a testimony to this endeavor PFa 33 may be mentioned. This Elamite administrative text lists tree seedlings to be planted in five "paradises." In so far as the terminology can be understood, the list may include apple, mulberry, pear, quince, olive, date, and pomegranate trees (Hallock 1978: 116, 135–6, Tavernier 2007: 458–60; Henkelman 2010: 742–3). The total of 6166 seedlings in a single text gives an impression of the scale of Achaemenid tree cultivation and fruit production, but also, by implication, of the irrigation effort required to sustain the plantations. Classical descriptions, mostly from the end of the Achaemenid period, convey a similarly impressive image of a well-watered, fertile heartland interspersed with lush paradises (landscape: see, e.g., Quintus Curt. *Hist.* 5.4.5–9, 4.20, Diodorus Siculus 17.67.3, Strabo, *Geog.* 15.3.1, 3.6, Arrian, *Indika* 40.3–4; paradises with fruit trees: Diod. Sic. 19.21.2–3; on Persian paradises see Tuplin 1996; Briant 2002: 442–4, 942–3; and Henkelman 2008a: 427–52, all with refs.). Even outlying regions were brought under cultivation by the Achaemenids and were still blooming in the later fourth century. Such was the case in the area of Mesambria (the Būšehr peninsula) on the Persian Gulf coast, described by Arrian as having many gardens where all sorts of fruit trees grew (*Ind.* 39.2).

Two important royal roads intersected in the heartland area: one that descended from Ecbatana (modern Hamadan) and eventually reached the Persian Gulf, and another that ran from Babylon via Susa to Persepolis (Potts 2008) and thence eastwards to northwestern India. Way stations were built at regular intervals and were provided with sufficient stock for issuing rations to travelers on official missions. Furthermore, the area was dotted with representative structures of different sizes (and, probably, functions) which consciously cited the architecture of the royal residences. Such structures could serve the king, the royal women, and probably the highest administrators, on their regular itineraries through Achaemenid Pārsa. The famous "Table of the King," a social and economic institution that fed thousands of individuals associated with the itinerant court, was held at many different places in the heartland. But the sites, confusingly known as "pavilions," were probably also nodal points in the administrative grid, just as the many storage centers and other facilities mentioned in the textual sources must have been (see below).

The Achaemenid landscape was thus highly developed and highly integrated, even if the density of the (settled) population does not seem to have reached that of earlier periods (Miroschedji 2003: 19–21; Boucharlat 2005: 226–7, both referring to W. M. Sumner's work in the Kūr River Basin and Miroschedji's work in Khūzestān). It was also a highly institutional landscape in the sense that much of the cultivation and livestock breeding, construction of irrigation canals and bridges, upkeep of the way stations, and management of the large labor force was organized centrally and involved an extensive and complex bureaucracy. Although it would certainly be wrong to assume that the institution known as the "Persepolis economy" comprised the entirety of manpower, livestock, arable land, and productive activities in the Achaemenid heartland, it must have been a major if not the predominant entity. It is this iconic emblem of Achaemenid administrative performance that is documented by the Fortification and Treasury archives from Persepolis.

This chapter is paired with another one, by the same author (in Jacobs and Rollinger forthcoming). To avoid excessive duplication, that survey concentrates more on the contents of the Persepolis archives, whereas the present one privileges find circumstances, formal characteristics, and connections with the archaeology of the Achaemenid heartland. The bibliography lists all key studies on the contents of the archives (for other surveys see, e.g., Hallock 1969: 1–69, 1985; Briant 2002: 422–71, 938–47, Henkelman 2008a: 65–179, 2013; Azzoni et al. forthcoming; see also the rich, commented sample in Kuhrt 2007: 763–825).

The Persepolis Fortification archive

The Persepolis Fortification archive (PFA) is so named after its discovery, in March 1933, in the northeastern section of the defense system of the Persepolis terrace. Ernst E. Herzfeld, then field director of the Persepolis excavations on behalf of the Oriental Institute at the University of Chicago, had ordered a brief investigation before leveling part of the wall in order to create an exit for the debris cleared from the terrace. Since Herzfeld resigned in 1934 and never published a full report, the circumstances of the discovery remain unclear.

The northeastern Fortification represented a two-storied casemate system. Thousands of clay tablets and fragments were found at two different locations within this structure, apparently in two small spaces (near an interior staircase) that were sealed off in antiquity. It is possible that (some of) the larger tablets had been stored in the upper story. Available descriptions of the find contexts suggest a secondary deposit; still, it may have been part of a larger administrative sector on the northeastern (and eastern) terrace. At any rate the tablets appear to have been deposited, not dumped. Perhaps they retained a certain legal function (accountability), even though they had lost their immediate bureaucratic relevance. When laid out by their field numbers, the tablets indeed show residual traces of organization according to content (discovery and archival deposit: Recent discoveries at Persepolis 1934: 231–2; Root 1996: 6–9; Garrison and Root 2001: 23–9; Razmjou 2008: 51–5; Henkelman 2008a: 69–71, 162–71).

Following their discovery, the tablets were covered with paraffin, wrapped in cotton, packed, and sent on long-term loan to the Oriental Institute, where they became available for study in 1937. In 1948, 153 Elamite tablets, 23 anepigraphic tablets, and a loom weight were returned to the National Museum of Iran, followed by over 35,000 small fragments in 1951, and 300 Elamite tablets in 2004. The larger part of the archive remains in Chicago, but its immediate future is uncertain and overshadowed by a legal dispute. The current Persepolis Fortification Archive Project is working toward the complete documentation and publication of the entire Fortification corpus so as to preserve, at least electronically, its greatest value: its integrity as an ancient archive (return of tablets: Stein 2004; Razmjou 2004b; legal crisis: Stein 2007; Heath and Schwarz 2009; PFA project: Stolper 2011; cf. http://persepolistablets.blogspot.com/).

PFA is a single ancient artifact integrating Elamite and Aramaic texts in a bureaucratic and archival system in which tablet formats and, especially, sealings and seal protocols played key roles. It belongs to the branch of regional administration that organized and controlled the intake, storage, and notably the redistribution of locally produced food commodities within the Persepolis economy. The most frequently attested transaction is the disbursal of food commodities as fodder, rations, wages, and offerings. The most common format is a sealed, roughly tongue-shaped tablet formed around a knotted string, the ends of which protruded from the left and right corners of the flattened left edge.

Elamite is by far the most common language used (95 percent or more of all discrete texts) and it was also the preferred language in seal inscriptions. Though an inherited administrative language used in Elam (southwestern Iran) since at least the later third millennium BC, the language of the tablets is new in the sense that it represents a morphosyntactically restructured variety with reduced complexity. The majority of the scribes evidently were speakers of an Old Iranian vernacular (related to inscriptional Old Persian, an archaizing acrolect of the language). They imposed features of their mother tongue on their version of Elamite, the language Persians used for writing. Thanks to the pioneering efforts of George G. Cameron, Richard T. Hallock, and others, Achaemenid Elamite is nowadays reasonably well understood (seal inscriptions: Garrison 2006: 70–1; Henkelman 2008a: 99–100; Achaemenid Elamite: Henkelman 2011a: 586–95, 614–22; lexicon and grammar: Hallock 1969: 663–776; Stolper 2004 with references; dictionary: Hinz and Koch 1987).

Dated Elamite tablets cover the period from April 509 to April/March 493 BC (Darius I, years 13–28). The size of the original Elamite corpus for this period may have amounted to as many as 100,000 texts; the Fortification find, impressive as it was, yielded much less than that. Current estimates indicate that preserved tablets and fragments with Elamite cuneiform stem from 15,000 or more original documents. The expectation is that the published corpus will eventually include no more than 6000–7000 legible tablets and analytically meaningful fragments (Henkelman 2008a: 79–82, 177–9; cf. Jones and Stolper 2008). To date, 2403 texts have been published, mostly by R. T. Hallock: 2187 in 1969 (siglum PF) and 33 in 1978 (PFa); almost all texts sent back to Tehran in 1948, and some additional texts (total: 167), were recently published by A. Arfaee (2008a, siglum Fort., Teh.). At his death, Hallock left a manuscript with 2551 additional editions (PF-NN); these and sixty-seven texts, previously read by C. E. Jones, have been prepared for publication by the author. A total of sixteen out of these 2618 texts have already been published (Henkelman 2003, 2008a, 2010, 2011a–d, Henkelman and Stolper 2009). M. W. Stolper is preparing editions of the remaining 1000–2000 (legible) Elamite tablets in Chicago (Fort.). Twelve Fortification-like texts in various collections were probably pocketed and sold by Herzfeld (Henkelman 2008: 77; cf. Henkelman et al. 2006).

The use of Elamite for administrative purposes was not confined to Persepolis: a few Elamite, Fortification-like tablets were found at Susa and even at distant Kandahār. Though limited in number, they necessarily imply institutional economies with a regional scope, like the one documented by the Fortification archive. Similar systems, with Elamite documentation, can plausibly be assumed for Ecbatana and perhaps other places on the Iranian plateau (e.g., the Kermān, Esfahān, and Borāzğān regions). The willful proliferation of administrative Elamite in the Iranian parts of the empire went *pari passu* with the much wider spread of imperial Aramaic over the entire Achaemenid realm, which, in turn, continued the increasing use of Aramaic seen in the Neo-Assyrian and Neo-Babylonian Empires. As is becoming clear from comparable syntax, technical Iranian loanwords and calque translations, and formal redaction (in case of letters and reports) in administrative Aramaic sources from Achaemenid Egypt, Bactria, Idumea (Palestine), and elsewhere, the Persians must have set up scribal schools that furthered uniformity in terminology and bureaucratic practice. Moreover, the organizational structures evidenced by the Elamite, Aramaic and other sources betray the same imperial blueprint. What we are seeing, then, is not so much the spread of administrative languages or bureaucratic techniques per se, but the replication of entire systems for the development and control of regional economies (spread of Elamite: Henkelman 2008a: 78–9, 110–15; 2008b; 2010: 696–7, 714 n.174; Aramaic: Naveh and Shaked 2012: 37–60 (Bactria); Briant 2002: 447–71; 2009: especially 148–55; Iranian loans: Tavernier 2007).

From the above contexts it becomes understandable that at Persepolis, too, Aramaic played an important role. Apart from some seal inscriptions, Aramaic is used in two kinds of texts in PFA: monolingual documents, incised or written in ink on clay tablets, and epigraphs added in ink to Elamite cuneiform texts. Both kinds are also attested in Neo-Assyrian and Neo-Babylonian contexts. A reconstructed fourth group is referred to in the Elamite texts: Aramaic documentation on leather, drafted, copied, or received in the office of the director of the Persepolis economy. It must have included original letter orders, travel vouchers, and top-level administrative correspondence. The recently found Aramaic documents from Bactria represent such a director's archive and as such felicitously complement the surviving part of the Fortification archive.

PFA includes some 800 monolingual Aramaic texts on clay tablets. They are triangular or tongue-shaped, pertain to the same types of transactions, use technical expressions directly paralleling Elamite terminology, and appear to belong to the same date range, but their contents are often more terse than those of the Elamite texts. In many cases they lack dates, quantities, and/or other core data. They may therefore not represent unique and independent records in the diplomatic sense, but rather additional sources of information used in tandem with other documents. As such they are comparable to the c.250 short Aramaic epigraphs on tablets with Elamite writing. Such epigraphs generally add information not given (explicitly) in the Elamite text. They imply, minimally, passive knowledge of Elamite by some Aramaic scribes. Other contexts provide evidence for active command of both administrative languages by individual scribes. As in the Elamite texts, Iranian influences (loanwords, calque translations) occur in Persepolis Aramaic alongside some influence of Elamite orthography. There is, then, ample indication that Elamite and Aramaic documents were part of the same system, but the ways in which they interacted remain incompletely understood. Part of the Aramaic tablets (PFAT) and epigraphs were studied by R. A. Bowman; the corpus is currently being edited by A. Azzoni. E. R. M. Dusinberre is preparing the publication of the seals on the Aramaic tablets (Azzoni 2008; Dusinberre 2008; Azzoni and Dusinberre 2014; Azzoni and Stolper 2015; Neo-Babylonian and Neo-Assyrian contexts: Oelsner 2006; Fales 2007: 99–105; Lemaire 2008 with references; multilingualism and Elamite-Aramaic interaction: Tavernier 2008; Henkelman 2008a: 89–93, 147–53; Azzoni and Dusinberre 2014).

All Aramaic monolingual tablets and most Elamite tablets are sealed. In addition, there are up to 5000 anepigraphic or uninscribed tablets that bear the impressions of one or more seals. The Elamite, Aramaic, and anepigraphic tablets were found intermingled and undoubtedly belong to a single archival system. This is also borne out by the fact that the anepigraphic tablets too are triangular or tongue-shaped. What appears to apply to the terse Aramaic texts is a fortiori true for the anepigraphic tablets: they do not constitute *records* in the technical sense. They do not identify a unique collocation of place, date, and transaction, but a repeatable grouping of jurisdictions. It is likely that the anepigraphic tablets functioned with other documents, perhaps Elamite or Aramaic tablets. The loop of string that was a standard feature of the triangular or tongue-shaped tablets may have played a role here. Also relevant is the growing number of seals identified on two or three types of media (Elamite, Aramaic, anepigraphic tablets). Such glyptic connections may eventually elucidate the complex relations between the various types of documentation (anepigraphic tablets: Garrison 2008, 2014; for various theories on the use of the strings see Vallat 1997; Henkelman 2008a: 154–62; E. Dusinberre [pers. comm.] estimates that at least 10 percent of the seals found on the Aramaic tablets also occur on Elamite or anepigraphic tablets; in statistical terms, since many seals occur only a few times and only a small part of the archive survives, this is a significant number; cf. Henkelman, Jones and Stolper 2004 on similar objects in other collections and compare Kaptan 2010 on the oval tags from Seyitömer Höyük).

With now over 3000 discrete seals identified, the Fortification archive is by far the richest corpus of Achaemenid glyptic and indeed of Achaemenid iconographic material at large. In addition to their art historical value, seal impressions are also crucial for understanding the archive as a complex system. They were, as Margaret Root puts it, "legible image[s]" and served as prime identifiers of document and transaction categories. As such, they constituted another mode of communication, a "language" spoken and understood by everyone. All individual actors (excluding the myriad nameless laborers) in the organization, from travelers on the royal roads to the director of the Persepolis economy, and from Persian queens to team leaders directing work in the fields, had their own cylinder or stamp seal. Seals expressed jurisdiction and administrative rank, but also inherited or acquired status, the latter most conspicuously bestowed by royal name seals (for the Fortification seals see Garrison and Root 2001 and forthcoming volumes; on Persepolitan glyptic see, e.g. Garrison 1991, 1996, 2000, 2002, 2010, 2011, forthcoming a, 2014 [royal name seals]; Root 1991, 1996, 1997, 2008 [importance of seals]; cf. Chapter 29).

The Fortification find also included single texts in Greek (*IEO* no. 230), Old Persian (Stolper and Tavernier 2007), Akkadian (Stolper 1984), and, presumably, Phrygian (Brixhe 2004: 118–26), as well as seals with Egyptian hieroglyphs (Garrison and Ritner 2010). With the exception of the apparently intrusive Akkadian text, these *unica* appear to have functioned in a manner similar to regular (Elamite) records in the archive. This is particularly clear in the case of the Greek tablet, where the format (tongue-shaped tablet), the two seals used (counter sealing), and the amount indicated by two simple vertical strokes (besides the Greek δύω) probably sufficed to convey its message. Put differently, these exceptional texts underline the strength of the administrative and archival machinery of the Persepolis economy.

The Persepolis Treasury archive (PTA)

In 1936–8, the much smaller Treasury archive was found by Herzfeld's successor, Erich F. Schmidt, in several rooms of the Treasury building on the southeastern section of the Persepolis terrace. From a find of 746 tablets and fragments, 138 sealed, tongue-shaped Elamite tablets and one rectangular Akkadian tablet are published; 199 sealed clay bullae and tongue-shaped anepigraphic tablets are provisionally published in the excavation report. The finds were divided between Tehran and Chicago.

Aramaic occurs only in seal impressions, not in epigraphs or monolingual tablets in PTA; there are, however, again some references (colophons) to Aramaic documentation in a lost director's archive. The Elamite texts date between July/August 492 and January 457 (Darius I/30 to Artaxerxes I/7), the Akkadian text to 502 BC. Contrary to PFA, PTA deals with (partial) payments in silver in lieu of, or in addition to, payments in kind, often to specialized craftsmen (the Akkadian text deals with taxation). As such, it represents a different branch of administration and a different archive, *not* a subsequent, new way of remunerating laborers. Moreover, PFA and PTA do not represent all branches of administration. A feature of foremost interest in the Treasury texts is the fluctuation in the silver/barley rate (Elamite tablets [PT]: Cameron 1948, 1958, 1965; Arfa'i 2008b; Jones and Yie 2011; cf. Hallock 1960; find context, seal impressions, anepigraphic tablets: Schmidt 1957: 4–41, pls. 2–14; cf. Garrison 1998; Garrison and Root 2001: 33–4; Akkadian text: Briant 2002: 441; Zournatzi 2000: 257, 259; surveys: Cahill 1985; Briant 2002: 422–71, 938–47; other administrative branches—textiles, craft products, labor organization, etc.: Hallock 1973; Henkelman 2011c: 3).

The Mountain Fortification

A group of about sixty sealed bullae and clay tags (and three cylinder seals) were found in a tower, the so-called Mountain Fortification, directly east of the Persepolis Terrace. Some of these are triangular or tongue-shaped and have two string holes; they are therefore similar to the anepigraphic tablets from the Fortification archive, some of the anepigraphic tablets from the Treasury archive, and to several other smaller corpora. Others are flat, roughly square, oval or trapezoid in outline, and with vertical string impressions on the reverse. They are similar to some bullae in the Treasury archive, some bullae in the Aršāma correspondence (Egypt), from Daskyleion (Hellespontine Phrygia), Seyitömer Höyük (Phrygia), and Achaemenid Bactria. Objects in the second category must have been attached to Aramaic letters on folded leather or papyrus (Tadjvidi 1970, 1973, 1976; Rahimifar 2005; bullae with string impressions: Garrison 2014 [Aršāma]; Kaptan 2002 1: 14–16 [Daskyleion]; Naveh and Shaked 2012 [Bactria]; cf. Amiet 1972 1: 284–7; 1972 2: pls. 189–90; Garrison and Root 2001: 35–9; Henkelman et al. 2004). Given the empire-wide parallels for both anepigraphic tablets and bullae, they are another witness to standardization in bureaucratic protocol and document format.

Territory, procedure, and contents

There is, or has been, a controversy about the extent of the territory under purview of the administration centered at Persepolis. Whereas some have held that it stretched all the way to Susa, there is convincing evidence that this major residence had its own administrative structures and bureaucracy. The border zone of the two administrative regions probably lay in the Zagros foothills between Khūzestān and Fārs. Beyond this general statement, little can be said with certainty since only a few of the hundreds of toponyms in the Fortification and Treasury tablets have been identified on the map. With that caveat in mind, it may be suggested, however, that the administrative region comprised a roughly oval-shaped territory defined by Nīrīz (possibly Narezzaš/*Nareča) in the southeast and Rām Hormuz and Īzeh in the northwest. It seems that the coastal region of Borāzğān (Tamukkan/*Tauka-/Ταόκη) and the region of Esfahān (Kab[b]aš/*Gaba-/Γάβαι) in the north were not integrated, yet in close contact with, the Persepolis administration.

The territory thus described has roughly the size of present-day Switzerland; as such, it matches the only other Achaemenid regional administration of which we can estimate the extent, that is, the one documented by the newly found documents from Achaemenid Bactria. The PFA territory was divided in three administrative subregions: the Fahliyān (northwest), Kāmfīrūz (central), and Persepolis (southeast) regions. This particular division probably relates to the two major routes that crossed the administrative territory and met in the small Kāmfīrūz region. The one that descended from Ecbatana ran via Kab(b)aš and eventually reached the Borāzğān area at the Persian Gulf coast. The other route connected Babylon to Susa, reached Persepolis, and thence continued to India (extent: Arfaee 1999; Henkelman 2008a: 110–17, 2008b, with references; contra Koch 1986, 1990: 302, 307–10; cf. Naveh and Shaked 2012 on Bactria, and Briant 2010 on Susa; subregions: Arfa'i 2008c; Henkelman 2008a: 118–20; cf. Metzler 1977 on connections with Ptolemy, and Vallat 1993 for an index of toponyms).

The basic layout of the administrative system is reasonably clear, but many particulars remain elusive. The three main organizational principles were commodity, time, and location. Monthly rations of wine and barley to, for example, a group of workers active near Tirazziš (ancient Šīrāz) would always be documented on separate tablets since different jurisdictions (and accountabilities) were involved. This means that, for a period of twelve months, a total of twenty-four tablets would be written. Other commodities that were documented separately included beer, fruit, poultry, and both small and large livestock.

Elamite tablets documenting single transactions of the kind just described mostly are sealed and tongue-shaped; they are known as memoranda. There is a near consensus that memoranda were made locally, in the hundreds of way stations, fortresses, hamlets, villages, and towns within the territory under purview of the Persepolis administration. At certain intervals, but at least once a year, the memoranda would be collected from local storekeepers and regional officials and brought to Persepolis, perhaps after a first audit on the spot. There is some evidence for groups of tablets from the same location, i.e. a single file, being transported and kept in a sealed textile or leather bag. It seems plausible that letter-orders sent from Persepolis and other centres to local officials remained there after effectuation of the order and then were included in the file sent to Persepolis.

Once at Persepolis, the contents of the memoranda from a single file would be subjected to control and summarized on rectangular tablets known as journals (registers). These, in turn, alongside other data, would be processed into accounts stating total amounts carried over from the previous year, yield of the current year and amounts withdrawn, as well as additional figures, including taxation or exchanges. Accounts come in several clearly distinct formats, depending on the commodity and type of account.

Throughout the administrative process, commodity, time, and location remained guiding principles: journals almost exclusively pertain to a single location (with satellites), a single commodity, and a single year; accounts sometimes pertain to several years, but those would be presented in separate paragraphs. A small number of accounts of a particular type pertain to more than one type of commodity.

Elamite, Aramaic, and anepigraphic tablets were sealed according to a range of fixed sealing protocols; this is particularly true and clear for the Elamite memoranda. The most common pattern found here is that of countersealing. It involved, for example, a storekeeper and traveler receiving travel rations at a way house, or a storekeeper and a team leader responsible for dependent workers. Another protocol involves the seal of only one individual or office; it characterizes noble and royal Persians (including royal women) and administrators or offices with overarching authority. Other patterns entail up to six different seals. In each of these protocols, seals expressed the various jurisdictions involved in the transaction. The implications are often obscure to us, but were so clear for ancient administrators that the names of the relevant officers could often be omitted from the texts.

Accountability and control formed the main *raisons d'être* of the Persepolis archives. The overall system was set up in such a way that mutual checks existed between a sub-organization dealing with "storage and supply" and another one that could be dubbed "logistics and rationing." Officers belonging to the latter kept rosters for the labor force and cooperated with the storekeepers to ensure the distribution of rations. The countersealing protocol often reflects the intertwined and mutually controlling parts of administration (administrative system, tablet format, sealing protocols: Hallock 1977; Hinz 1971; Aperghis 1998, 1999; Garrison and Root 2001: 11–13; Brosius 2003; Henkelman 2008a: 95–109, 126–62; "matrix management," administrative hierarchy: Hallock 1985; Aperghis 1999; taxation: Tuplin 2008 with references).

Although PFA concerns the intake (and storage) as well the redistribution of locally produced food commodities, the thrust of the documentation is on the second category. This also explains the generally more prominent rank of "logistics and rationing" officers and the importance of their seals. Although one witnesses withdrawals on behalf of the royal domain, transports of commodities, livestock inventorying, and exchange with third parties, many such procedures may actually relate indirectly to feeding animals and people. Even in the case of sacrifices, the prime interest seems to have been the officiant and/or other consumers of commodities offered to the gods. In other words, PFA is not concerned primarily with producing or storing food commodities, or with the organization of labor or cultic activity per se, but represents the bookkeeping of a truly redistributive economy. In being centered on the palace, having direct control over extensive production and apportioning systems, and feeding large numbers of dependent laborers, it differed from the economic institutions centered on temples in contemporary Mesopotamia. In layout, and partially in administrative vocabulary, it is comparable to the institutional economy attested in Elam about 150 years earlier (Stolper 1978; Henkelman 2008a: 18–19; cf. Basello 2011 on administrative terminology). The difference is its markedly imperial character, which, among other elements, is shown by its responsibility for part of the network of royal roads and in the expansion of existing status terminology to new social categories (cf. notably the developed use of *kurtaš*; see below).

Gods and royal court formed the top end of the social pyramid. Various types of sacrifices are known for a host of deities. Officiants with Elamite and Old Iranian names and titles performed the sacrifices; some of them are also known in administrative roles. Since there is no evidence for different religious spheres, PFA bespeaks large-scale acculturation between Elamites and early Persians. As for the royal court, the archive yields abundant evidence on the status and economic activities of Persian royal women (notably Irdabama, possibly Darius' mother), royal itineraries (also within Pārsa), the size and organization of the Royal Table, court titles, individuals such as Xerxes and Hystaspes, and funerary sacrifices for Cambyses and others (cults: Henkelman 2003, 2005, 2008a, 2011d, 2011e, forthcoming a–b [responding to Koch 1977, 1987, 1991; Handley-Schachler 1998; Kreyenbroek 2010]; Razmjou 2001, 2004; Tuplin 2008: 322–4; cf. Garrison forthcoming on cultic iconography; royal (and queenly) tables, royal domain, royal court, royal women: Lewis 1987; Koch 1994; Brosius 1996; Tuplin 1998; Briant 2002: 463–71; Henkelman 2008a: 217–24; 2010).

The institution's middle levels comprised, among many others, administrators of varying rank, craftsmen, treasurers, cedar-carpenters and builders, fortress guards, fruit producers, caretakers of the royal mules, road inspectors, express messengers, and a conspicuous number of female team leaders with relatively high rations. Especially in travel contexts one finds *šalup*, "free men" (*vel sim.*); their status may have partly overlapped with that of the *taššup*. These seem to have been the able-bodied men known in OP as *kāra-*. Depending on the context, *taššup* may be "(military) troops" or "people" in the sense of nondependent Persians of a certain class.

The free smallholders (αὐτουργοί) mentioned in Greek sources (Xenophon, *Cyropaedia* 7.5.67, Aelian *Varia Historia* I.31–3) are hard to identify in Fortification terms. They may have included *taššup*, but also *kurtaš*. These dependent worker(s) (*grda-*, lit. domestic staff, workman) are found in the thousands at the bottom of the pyramid. They remain nameless, with the exception of women receiving maternity bonuses. Minimal ration levels were much lower than in contemporary Mesopotamia. Unless one is willing to accept sustained and institutionalized malnutrion, these levels strongly suggest that the *kurtaš* generally were expected to have additional sources of income.

Whereas the status of dependent worker seems to have been at home in Neo-Elamite and presumably in early Persian contexts, it gained a new meaning with the rise of empire. At Persepolis, *kurtaš* with twenty-seven ethnic labels are attested; some of these groups, such as the Lydians and "Skudrians," consisted of hundreds of individuals and may reflect the well-attested Achaemenid policy of deporting populations. Other groups may have been sent to the Persian heartland on short-term corvée duty, that is, within the framework of tax obligations. Though their lives may have been hard, the *kurtaš* were not slaves in the strict sense. The relative term *libar*, lit. "servant, subordinate," could in some contexts denote slavery; *libap* (pl.) did not constitute a significant part of the labor force (administrators, officials, middle levels: Hinz 1971; Koch 1983; Kawase 1984; Brosius 1996: 146–63; Henkelman 2002; Tavernier 2007: 414–37; status of *kurtaš* and *libap*: Zaccagnini 1983; Uchitel 1989; Dandamaev in Dandamaev and Lukonin 1989: 158–77, Aperghis 2000, Briant 2002: 429–39, 455–60, 940–2; Brosius 2003: 163–80; Henkelman 2003: 129–37; 2011f; contemporary Mesopotamia: Jursa 2008; foreign groups in the Achaemenid heartland: Uchitel 1991; Tavernier 2002; Henkelman and Kleber 2007; Tolini 2008; Henkelman and Stolper 2009; Henkelman and Rollinger 2009; Henkelman forthcoming b; Tavernier 2015).

Goats and sheep were consigned to semiexternal herdsmen in a share-breeding system; the same was true for ducks, but not for geese. The outsourcing of herding reveals a human landscape beyond the seemingly enclosed world of the Persepolis archives. The royal domain, too, appears but partially in the Fortification archive, as do the "Houses" of royal women and the estates of noble Persians, entities that were coopted by the institutional economy, but not fully integrated with it. Members of the elite—some, such as Gobryas and Mardonios, known from Greco-Roman sources—make occasional appearances as travelers, commanders or otherwise, but rarely remain within view of the Persepolis archives. At still greater distance we find various Persian tribes, as well as evidence for exchanges with (agro-)pastoralist groups beyond the institution's direct control (share-breeding: Kawase 1980, 1986; Henkelman 2005: 157–9; 2010: 736–7; Henkelman et al. 2006; cf. Gabrielli 2006 and Tuplin 2010 on horses; estates: Uchitel 1997; Briant 2002: 442–6, 460–63; tribes, exchange with external parties: Aperghis 1997; Henkelman 2005, 2011c; Henkelman and Stolper 2009: 284–7; noble Persians: Hallock 1985; Lewis 1984, 1985; Henkelman 2003, 2010).

Archives and Archaeology

Until recently, the connections between the Fortification archives and the physical world of the Achaemenid heartland were largely limited to Persepolis and Pasargadae. The last ten years have witnessed the steady reemergence of the institutional landscape through new excavations and surveys, particularly in the Mamasanī region and in the Tang-e Bolāḡi.

The impressive harvests documented in the Fortification archive, as well as the many plantations known as *partetaš* (OPers. *pardēda-; cf. Gk. παράδεισος) necessarily imply vast irrigation and water-management efforts. This assumption is indeed corroborated by the dams and sluices north of Pasargadae, extensive canals and sluices in the Marv Dašt plain, and rock-cut and earthen canals in the Tang-e Bolāḡi between Pasargadae and Persepolis.

The road system was one of the decisive elements of the Persepolis economy. It constituted not only a communication network that effectively enhanced the integration of the empire, but it also opened up the hinterlands of the Persepolis economy and connected the institution to an interregional network of such entities. The exact courses of two main roads will probably remain disputed as long as the entire relevant area has not systematically been surveyed and more way stations have not been identified. Perhaps more interesting is the functioning of the system, which certainly can be elucidated on the basis of available Fortification texts, other textual evidence, and material remains. Several shorter stretches of the roads, some stone paved, are identified in the heartland, among others near Naqš-e Rustam, where also two way stations were found (at a distance of 26 km from each other). Other such structures are tentatively identified in the Tang-e Bolāḡi and elsewhere (Nicol 1970; Sumner 1986; Kleiss 1992; Atai and Boucharlat 2009; survey in Henkelman 2012).

Based on the Fortification archive, the institutional landscape presumably included numerous granaries, storage facilities, local administrative centers, "treasuries" (craft centers) plantations of various types and sizes, bird farms, livestock stations, fortified structures, and elite and royal residences and domains. Some archaeological evidence matches these expectations. Most notable is the so-called Circular Structure at Čoḡā Miš, which was certainly used and perhaps also constructed in the Achaemenid period and presumably functioned as a central granary. Tantalizing snippets of administrative evidence were found nearby: an Achaemenid-Elamite tablet, a cylinder seal, and a sealing on what appears to be a Persepolis-type anepigraphic tablet (Delougaz and Kantor 1996: 10–12, 17–18, comparing Achaemenid granaries in Palestine; cf. the possible farmstead in the Tang-e Bolāḡi: Helwing and Seyedin 2009).

Structures referred to as *halmarraš*, lit. "fortified place, fortress," seem to have included a function as storage center. An example could be the fortified structure excavated in the Tang-e Bolāḡi. Other recognizable structures are, obviously, the so-called pavilions, characterized by stone column bases and sometimes stone staircases, merlons, and relief slabs, that is, structural elements referring to the architecture of the residences. About a dozen "pavilions" can be identified in the Achaemenid heartland. Best known are a small structure in the Tang-e Bolāḡi, a more extensive complex at Qalēh-ye Kalī, and various sites at and near Borāzḡān. In all three cases, the stone architecture was part of a larger complex that served production, storage, and perhaps administrative purposes (fortified structure: Askari Chaverdi and Callieri 2009: 27–32; cf. Boucharlat 2005: 245–6 on Khūzestān;

pavilions: Atai and Boucharlat 2009 [Tang-e Bolāḡi]; Potts et al. 2007, 2009 [Qalēh-ye Kalī/Ḡīnḡīn]; see generally Boucharlat 2005: 272–4; Henkelman 2012 with references).

Though sites known through surveys and excavations in the Mamasanī region, in the Tang-e Bolāḡi, and elsewhere have not yet yielded new identifications with toponyms from the Persepolis archives with Achaemenid sites, the increasing number of such sites, their distribution patterns, and presumable clustering along the royal roads, are obviously highly relevant. In the end, they will enable us to read the Fortification tablets less as the paperwork of an abstract entity and more as the documentation and institutional landscape that was as real as it was impressive (Mamasanī: *MAPSO*; McCall 2009; Asgari Chaverdi et al. 2010; Tang-e Bolāḡi: Fazeli Nashli 2009; Atai and Boucharlat 2009; Askari Chaverdi and Callieri 2006, 2009: 3–27; cf. references cited above; other surveys: references in Henkelman 2012; Sumner's [1986] attempt to relate a site hierarchy based on the Fortification texts to his survey in the Marv Dašt is problematic due to many uncertainties that lie at the basis of the analysis).

Further reading

The history and culture of the Achaemenid Empire are the subject of P. Briant's 1996 synthesis (English translation: Briant 2002), which is the current standard reference. The source book by A. Kuhrt (2007) should be seen as a complement to this monograph and is very useful for teaching and easy access to the relevant sources (in translation, with notes). For the Fortification archive, see Henkelman (2008a) as well as the *AFP* conference volume that appeared in 2008. For seals in the Fortification archive see Garrison and Root (2001).

References

Amiet, P. 1972. *Glyptique susienne: Des origines à l'époque des Perses achéménides. Cachets, sceaux-cylindres et empreintes antiques découverts à Suse de 1913 à 1967*, 2 vols. Paris: MDP 43.

Aperghis, G. G. 1997. Surplus, exchange and price in the Persepolis Fortification Tablets. In *Économie antique. Prix et formation des prix dans les économies antiques*, ed. J. Andreau, P. Briant, and R. Descat, 277–90. Saint-Bertrand-de-Comminges: EAH 3.

———. 1998. The Persepolis Fortification Tablets: Another look. *SPH*: 35–62.

———. 1999. Storehouses and systems at Persepolis: Evidence from the Persepolis Fortification Tablets. *JESHO* 42: 152–93.

———. 2000. War captives and economic exploitation: Evidence from the Persepolis Fortification Tablets. In *La guerre dans les économies antiques*, ed. J. Andreau, P. Briant, and R. Descat, 127–44. Saint-Bertrand-de-Comminges: EAH 5.

Arfaee [Arfa'i], A. 1999. La grande route Persépolis–Suse. Une lecture des tablettes provenant des Fortifications de Persépolis. *Topoi* 9/1: 33–45.

———. 2008a. *Persepolis Fortification Tablets, Fort. and Teh. Texts*. Tehran: Ancient Iranian Studies 5.

———. 2008b. PT 10a, collated and completed. *ARTA* 2008.001.

———. 2008c. The geographical background of the Persepolis Tablets. Unpublished PhD diss., University of Chicago.
Asgari [Askari] Chaverdi, A., A. Khosrowzadeh, B. McCall, C. A. Petrie, D. T. Potts, K. Roustaei, M. Seyedin et al. 2010. Achaeological evidence for Achaemenid settlement within the Mamasani Valleys, western Fars, Iran. *WAP*: 287–97.
Askari Chaverdi, A., and P. Callieri. 2006. A rural settlement of the Achaemenid period in Fars. *JIAAA* 1: 65–70.
———. 2009. Achaemenid and post Achaemenid remains at TB 76 and TB 77. *ARTA* 2009.004.
Atai, M. T., and R. Boucharlat. 2009. An Achaemenid pavilion and other remains in Tang-i Bulaghi. *ARTA* 2009.005.
Azzoni, A. 2008. The Bowman MS and the Aramaic tablets. *AFP*: 253–74.
Azzoni, A., and E. R. M. Dusinberre. 2014. Persepolis Fortification Aramaic Tablet Seal 0002 and the keeping of Horses. *EAC*: 1–16.
Azzoni, A., E. R. M. Dusinberre, M. B. Garrison, W. F. M. Henkelman, C. E. Jones, and M. W. Stolper. Forthcoming. Persepolis administrative archives. *EnIr*.
Azzoni, A., and M. W. Stolper. 2015. The Aramaic epigraph *ns(y)ḥ* on Persepolis Fortification Elamite tablets. *ARTA* 2015.004.
Basello, G. P. 2011. Elamite as administrative language: From Susa to Persepolis. *EP*: 61–88.
Boucharlat, R. 2005. Iran. *AEA*: 221–92.
Briant, P. 2002. *From Cyrus to Alexander: A history of the Persian Empire*. Winona Lake: Eisenbrauns.
———. 2009. The empire of Darius III in perspective. In *Alexander the Great: A new history*, ed. W. Heckel and L. Trittle, 141–70. Chichester/Malden: Wiley-Blackwell.
Briant, P. 2010. Suse et l'Élam dans l'empire achéménide. *PDS*: 22–48.
Brixhe, C. 2004. Corpus des Inscriptions Paléo-Phrygiennes, Suppl. II. *Kadmos* 43: 1–130.
Brosius, M. 1996. *Women in Ancient Persia 559–331 BC*. Oxford: Clarendon Press.
———. 2003. Reconstructing an archive: Account and journal texts from Persepolis. In *Ancient archives and archival traditions: Concepts of record-keeping in the Ancient World*, ed. M. Brosius, 264–83. Oxford: Oxford University Press.
Cahill, N. 1985. The treasury at Persepolis: Gift-giving at the City of the Persians. *AJA* 89: 373–89.
Cameron, G. G. 1948. *Persepolis Treasury Tablets*. Chicago: OIP 65.
———. 1958, Persepolis Treasury Tablets old and new. *JNES* 17: 161–76.
Cameron, G. G., and I. Gershevitch. 1965. New tablets from the Persepolis Treasury. *JNES* 24: 167–92.
Dandamaev, M. A., and V. G. Lukonin. 1989. *The culture and social institutions of ancient Iran*. Cambridge: Cambridge University Press.
Delougaz, P., and H. J. Kantor, eds. 1996. *Chogha Mish*, vol. 1. *The first five seasons of excavations, 1961–1971*. Chicago: OIP 101.
Dusinberre, E. R. M. 2008. Seal impressions on the Persepolis Fortification Aramaic tablets: Preliminary observations. *AFP*: 239–52.
Fales, F. M. 2007. Multilingualism on multiple media in the Neo-Assyrian period: A review of the evidence. *SAAB* 16: 95–122.
Fazeli Nashli, H. 2009. The Achaemenid/post-Achaemenid remains in Tang-i Bulaghi near Pasargadae: A report on the salvage excavations conducted by five joint teams in 2004–2007. *ARTA* 2009.001.
Gabrielli, M. 2006. *Le cheval dans l'empire achéménide—Horse in the Achaemenid Empire*. Istanbul: Studia ad Orientem Antiquum Pertinentia 1.

Garrison, M. B. 1991. Seals and the elite at Persepolis: Some observations on Early Achaemenid Persian art. *Ars Orientalis* 21: 1–29.

———. 1996. A Persepolis Fortification seal on the Tablet MDP 11 308 (Louvre Sb 13078). *JNES* 55: 15–35.

———. 1998. The seals of Ašbazana (Aspathines). *SPH*: 115–31.

———. 2000. Achaemenid iconography as evidenced by glyptic art: Subject matter, social function, audience and diffusion. In *Images as media: Sources for the cultural history of the Near East and the Eastern Mediterranean (1st millennium BCE)*, ed. C. Uehlinger, 115–63. Fribourg: OBO 175.

———. 2006. The "Late Neo-Elamite" glyptic style: A perspective from Fars. *BAI* 16: 65–102.

———. 2008. The uninscribed tablets from the Fortification Archive: A preliminary analysis. *AFP*: 149–238.

———. 2010. Archers at Persepolis: The emergence of royal ideology at the heart of the empire. *WAP*: 337–68.

———. 2011. The seal of "Kuraš the Anzanite, Son of Šešpeš" (Teispes), PFS 93*: Susa–Anšan–Persepolis. *EP*: 375–405.

———. 2014. The royal-name seals of Darius I. *EAC*: 67–104.

———. Forthcoming. Visual representation of the divine and the numinous in early Achaemenid Iran: Old problems, new directions. In *Iconography of Ancient Near Eastern religions*, vol. 1, *Pre-Hellenistic periods: Introductory essays*, ed. C. Uehlinger and F. Graf. Leiden: [www.religionswissenschaft.unizh.ch/idd/prepublication_4.php].

Garrison, M. B., and R. K. Ritner. 2010. From the Persepolis Fortification Archive Project, 2: Seals with Egyptian hieroglyphic inscriptions at Persepolis. *ARTA* 2010.002.

Garrison, M. B., and M. C. Root. 2001. *Seals on the Persepolis Fortification Tablets*, vol. 1, *Images of heroic encounter*. Chicago: OIP 117.

Giovinazzo, G. 1994. Les documents de voyage dans les textes de Persépolis. *AION* 54: 18–31.

Hallock, R. T. 1960. A new look at the Persepolis Treasury Tablets. *JNES* 19: 90–100.

———. 1969. *Persepolis Fortification Tablets*. Chicago: OIP 92.

———. 1973. The Persepolis Fortification Archive. *Or* 42: 320–3.

———. 1977. The use of seals on the Persepolis Fortification Tablets. In *Seals and sealings in the Ancient Near East*, ed. M. Gibson and R. D. Biggs, 127–33. Malibu: Bibliotheca Mesopotamica 6.

———. 1978. Selected Fortification Texts. *CDAFI* 8: 109–36.

———. 1985. The evidence of the Persepolis Tablets. *CHI* 2: 588–609.

Handley-Schachler, M. 1998. The *lan* ritual in the Persepolis Fortification Texts. *SPH*: 195–204.

Heath, S., and G. M. Schwarz. 2009. Legal threats to cultural exchange of archaeological materials. *AJA* 113: 459–62.

Helwing, B., and M. Seyedin. 2009. The Achaemenid period occupation at Tang-i Bulaghi site 73. *ARTA* 2009.006.

Henkelman, W. F. M. 2002. Exit der Posaunenbläser: On lance-guards and lance-bearers in the Persepolis Fortification archive. *ARTA* 2002.007.

———. 2003. An Elamite memorial: The *šumar* of Cambyses and Hystaspes. *APP*: 101–72.

———. 2005. Animal sacrifice and "external" exchange in the Persepolis Fortification tablets. In *Approaching the Babylonian economy*, ed. H. D. Baker and M. Jursa, 137–65. Münster: AOAT 330.

———. 2008a. *The other gods who are: Studies in Elamite-Iranian acculturation based on the Persepolis Fortification texts*. Leiden: AchHist 14.

———. 2008b. From Gabae to Taoce: The geography of the central administrative province. *AFP*: 303–16.

———. 2010. "Consumed before the King." The table of Darius, that of Irdabama and Irtaštuna, and that of his satrap, Karkiš. In *Der Achämenidenhof/The Achaemenid court,* ed. B. Jacobs and R. Rollinger, 667–75. Wiesbaden: CLeO 2.

———. 2011a. Cyrus the Persian and Darius the Elamite: A case of mistaken identity. In *Herodot und das Persische Weltreich/Herodotus and the Persian Empire,* ed. R. Rollinger, B. Truschnegg, and R. Bichler, 577–634. Wiesbaden: CLeO 3.

———. 2011b. Xerxes, Atossa, and the Persepolis Fortification Archive. *Netherlands Institute for the Near East Annual Report* 2010: 26–33.

———. 2011c. Of Tapyroi and tablets, states and tribes: The historical geography of pastoralism in the Achaemenid heartland in Greek and Elamite sources. *BICS* 54/2: 1–16.

———. 2011d. Parnakka's feast: *šip* in Pārsa and Elam. *EP*: 89–166.

———. 2011e. Šimut. *RlA* 12: 511–12.

———. 2011f. Elam. In *Handwörterbuch der antiken Sklaverei* 3, ed. H. Heinen. Stuttgart: Akademie der Wissenschaften und der Literatur Mainz (CD-ROM-Lieferung 3).

———. 2012. The Achaemenid heartland: An archaeological-historical perspective. In *A companion to the archaeology of the Ancient Near East,* ed. D. T. Potts, 931–62. Oxford/Malden: Wiley-Blackwell.

———. 2013. Persepolis Tablets. In *The encyclopaedia of ancient history,* ed. R. S. Bagnall, K. Brodersen, C. B. Champion, A. Erskine, and S. R. Heubner, 5179–81. Oxford/Malden: Wiley-Blackwell.

———. 2014. Turmira. *RlA* 14/3–4: 199–200.

———. Forthcoming a. Festivals. In *A companion to the Achaemenid Persian Empire,* ed. B. Jacobs, and R. Rollinger. Oxford/Malden: Wiley-Blackwell.

———. Forthcoming b. Pantheon and practice of worship. In *A companion to the Achaemenid Persian Empire,* ed. B. Jacobs and R. Rollinger. Oxford/Malden: Wiley-Blackwell.

———. Forthcoming c. On the road: The travel files in the Persepolis Fortification Archive. In *The world of Arshama,* vol 2, *Thematic essays,* ed. J. Ma and C. Tuplin.

Henkelman, W. F. M., C. E. Jones, and M. W. Stolper. 2004. Clay tags with Achaemenid seal impressions in the Dutch Institute of the Near East (NINO) and elsewhere. *ARTA* 2004.001.

———. 2006. Achaemenid Elamite administrative tablets, 2: The Qaṣr-i Abu Naṣr tablet. *ARTA* 2006.003.

Henkelman, W. F. M., and K. Kleber. 2007. Babylonian workers in the Persian heartland: Palace building at Matannan during the reign of Cambyses. *PR*: 163–76.

Henkelman, W. F. M., and R. Rollinger. 2009. New observations on "Greeks" in the Achaemenid Empire according to cuneiform texts from Babylonia and Persepolis. In *Organisation des pouvoirs et contacts culturels dans les pays de l'empire achéménide,* ed. P. Briant and M. Chauveau, 331–51. Paris: Persika 14.

Henkelman, W. F. M., and M. W. Stolper. 2009. Ethnic identity and ethnic labelling at Persepolis: The case of the Skudrians. In *Organisation des pouvoirs et contacts culturels dans les pays de l'empire achéménide,* ed. P. Briant and M. Chauveau, 271–329. Paris: Persika 14.

Hinz, W. 1970. Die elamischen Buchungstäfelchen der Darius-Zeit. *Or* 39: 421–40.

———. 1971. Achämenidische Hofverwaltung. *ZA* 61: 260–311.

Hinz, W., and H. Koch. 1987. *Elamisches Wörterbuch,* 2 vols. Berlin: *AMI* Ergänzungsband 17.

Jacobs, B., and R. Rollinger. Forthcoming. *A companion to the Achaemenid Persian Empire.* Oxford/Malden: Wiley-Blackwell.

Jones, C. E., and M. W. Stolper. 2008. How many Persepolis Fortification Tablets are there? *AFP*: 27–50.

Jones, C. E., and S. Yie. 2011. From the Persepolis Fortification Archive Project, 3: The first administrative document discovered at Persepolis: PT 1971-1. *ARTA* 2011.003.

Jursa, M. 2008. The remuneration of institutional labourers in an urban context in Babylonia in the first millennium BC. *AFP*: 387–427.

Kaptan, D. 2002. *The Daskyleion bullae: Seal images from the western Achaemenid Empire*, 2 vols. Leiden: AchHist 12.

———. 2010. Clay tags from Seyitömer Höyük in Phrygia. *WAP*: 361–8.

Kawase, T. 1980. Sheep and goats in the Persepolis royal economy, *ASJ* 2: 37–51.

———. 1984. Female workers "pašap" in the Persepolis royal economy. *ASJ* 6: 19–31.

———. 1986. *kapnuški* in the Persepolis Fortification Texts. *FHE*: 263–75.

Kleiss, W. 1992. Dammbauten aus achaemenidischer und aus sasanidischer Zeit in der Provinz Fars. *AMI* 25: 131–45.

Koch, H. 1977. *Die religiösen Verhältnisse der Dareioszeit: Untersuchungen an Hand der elamischen Persepolistäfelchen*. Wiesbaden: Göttinger Orientforschungen 3.4.

———. 1983. Zu den Lohnverhältnissen der Dareioszeit in Persien. In *Kunst, Kultur und Geschichte der Achämenidenzeit und ihr Fortleben*, ed. H. Koch and D. N. Mackenzie, 19–50. Berlin: *AMI* Ergänzungsband 10.

———. 1986. Die achämenidische Poststraße von Persepolis nach Susa. *AMI* 19: 133–47.

———. 1987. Götter und ihre Verehrung im achämenidischen Persien. *ZA* 77: 239–78.

———. 1990. *Verwaltung und Wirtschaft im persischen Kernland zur Zeit der Achämeniden*. Wiesbaden: TAVO Beiheft B 89.

———. 1991. Zur Religion und Kulten im achämenidischen Kernland. In *La religion iranienne à l'époque achéménide*, ed. J. Kellens, 87–119. Gent: *IrAnt* Supplement 5.

———. 1994. Zu den Frauen im Achämenidenreich. In *Iranian and Indo-European Studies: Memorial Volume of Otokar Klíma*, ed. P. Vavroušek, 125–41. Prague: Enigma Corp.

Kreyenbroek, P. G. 2010. Zoroastrianism under the Achaemenians: A non-essentialist approach. *WAP*: 103–9.

Kuhrt, A. 2007. *The Persian Empire: A corpus of sources from the Achaemenid period*. London: Routledge.

Lemaire, A. 2008. Remarks on the Aramaic of Upper Mesopotamia in the seventh century B.C. In *Aramaic in its historical and linguistic setting*, ed. H. Gzella and M. Folmer, 77–92. Wiesbaden: Veröffentlichungen der Orientalischen Kommission 50.

Lewis, D. M. 1984. Postscript. In *Persia & the Greeks: The defence of the West, c. 546–478 B.C.*, 2nd rev. ed., A. R. Burn, 587–609. London: Stanford University Press.

———. 1985. Persians in Herodotus. In *The Greek historians: Literature and history, Papers presented to A.E. Raubitschek*, Department of Classics, Stanford University, 101–17. Saratoga: ANMA Libri.

———. 1987. The king's dinner (Polyaenus IV 3,32). In *The Greek sources*, ed. H. Sancisi-Weerdenburg and A. Kuhrt, 79–87. Leiden: AchHist 2.

———. 1990, The Persepolis Fortification texts. In *Centre and Periphery*, ed. H. Sancisi-Weerdenburg and A. Kuhrt, 1–6. Leiden: AchHist 4.

———. 1994. The Persepolis tablets: Speech, seal and script. In *Literacy & power in the Ancient World*, ed. A. K. Bowman and G. Woolf, 17–32. Cambridge: Cambridge University Press.

McCall, B. K. 2009. The Mamasani Archaeological Survey: Epipalaeolithic to Elamite settlement patterns in the Mamasani district of the Zagros Mountains, Fars Province, Iran. Unpublished PhD diss., University of Sydney.

Metzler, D. 1977. Ptolemaios' Geographie und die Topographie der Persepolis Fortification Tablets. In *XIX. Deutscher Orientalistentag vom 28. September bis 4. Oktober 1975 in Freiburg in Breisgau: Vorträge*, ed. W. Voigt, 1057–60. Wiesbaden: ZDMG Supplement 3.2.

Miroschedji, P. de. 2003. Susa and the highlands: Major trends in the history of Elamite civilization. *YBYN*: 17–38.

Naveh, J., and S. Shaked. 2012. *Ancient Aramaic documents from Bactria (fourth century B.C.E.)*. London: CII 1/5/2.

Nicol, M. B. 1970, Rescue excavations near Dorūdzan. *EW* 20: 245–84.

Oelsner, J. 2006, Aramäische Beischriften auf neu- und spätbabylonischen Tontafeln. *Die Welt des Orients* 36: 27–71.

Potts, D. T. 2008, The Persepolis Fortification texts and the Royal Road: Another look at the Fahliyan area. *AFP*: 275–301.

Potts, D. T., A. Asgari Chaverdi, I. K. McRae, K. Alamdari, A. Dusting, J. Jaffari, T. M. Ellicott et al. 2009. Further excavations at Qaleh Kali (MS 46) by the Joint ICAR—University of Sydney Mamasani Expedition: Results of the 2008 Season. *IrAnt* 44: 207–82.

Potts, D. T., A. Asgari Chaverdi, C. A. Petrie, A. Dusting, F. Farhadi, I. K. McRae, S. Shikhi et al. 2007. The Mamasani Archaeological Project, Stage Two: Excavations at Qaleh Kali (Tappeh Servan/Jinjun [MS 46]). *Iran* 45: 287–300.

Rahimifar, M. 2005. Mo'arafi-ye barkhī az barčasbhā-ye geli-ye Takht-e Ğamšīd. *Bāstān Šenāsī* 1: 72–6, 10 (with English summary).

Razmjou, S. 2001. Des traces de la déesse Spenta-Ārmaiti à Persépolis et proposition pour une nouvelle lecture d'un logogramme élamite. *StIr* 30: 7–15.

———. 2004a. The Lan ceremony and other ritual ceremonies in the Achaemenid period: The Persepolis Fortification Tablets. *Iran* 42: 103–17.

———. 2004b. Project report of the Persepolis Fortification Tablets in the National Museum of Iran. *ARTA* 2004.004.

———. 2008. Find spots and find circumstances of documents excavated at Persepolis. *AFP*: 51–8.

Recent discoveries at Persepolis. 1934. *JRAS* 1934: 226–32.

Root, M. C. 1991. From the heart: Powerful Persianisms in the art of the Western Empire. In *Asia Minor and Egypt: Old cultures in a new empire*, ed. H. Sancisi-Weerdenburg and A. Kuhrt, 1–29. Leiden: AchHist 6.

———. 1996. The Persepolis Fortification Tablets: Archival issues and the problem of stamps versus cylinder seals. In *Archives et sceaux du monde hellénistique*, ed. M.-F. Boussac and A. Invernizzi, 3–27. Paris: BCH Supplement 29.

———. 1997. Cultural pluralisms on the Persepolis Fortification Tablets. In *Recherches récentes sur l'Empire achéménide*, ed. M.-F. Boussac, 229–52. Lyon: *Topoi* Supplement 1.

———. 2008, The legible image: How did seals and sealing matter in Persepolis? *AFP*: 87–148.

Schmidt, E. F. 1957. *Persepolis II. Contents of the Treasury and other discoveries*. Chicago: OIP 69.

Stein, G. J. 2004. Persepolis Fortification Tablets. *Oriental Institute 2003–2004 Annual Report*: 121–4.

———. 2007. A heritage threatened: The Persepolis Tablets lawsuit and the Oriental Institute. *Oriental Institute News and Notes* 192: 3–5.

Stolper, M. W. 1978. Šarnuppu. *ZA* 68: 261–9.

———. 1984. The Neo-Babylonian text from the Persepolis Fortification. *JNES* 43: 299–310.

———. 2004. Elamite. In *The Cambridge encyclopedia of the world's ancient languages*, ed. R. D. Woodard, 60–94. Cambridge: Cambridge University Press.

———. 2011. Persepolis Fortification Archive Project. *Oriental Institute 2010-2011 Annual Report*: 102-11.
Stolper, M. W., and J. Tavernier. 2007. From the Persepolis Fortification Archive Project, 1: An Old Persian administrative tablet from the Persepolis Fortification. *ARTA* 2007.001.
Sumner, W. M. 1986. Achaemenid settlement in the Persepolis Plain. *AJA* 90: 3-31.
Tadjvidi, A. A. 1970. Persepolis. *Iran* 8: 186-7.
———. 1973. Persepolis. *Iran* 11: 200-1.
———. 1976. *Dānestanīhā-ye novīn darbāreh-ye honar va bāstānšenāsi-ye aṣr-e hakhāmaneši bar bonyād-e kāvoshā-ye pang sāleh-ye Takht-e Gamšīd*. [New knowledge about Achaemenid art and archaeology based on five years of excavations at Persepolis]. Tehran.
Tavernier, J. 2002. Non-Elamite individuals in Achaemenid Persepolis. *Akkadica* 123: 145-52.
———. 2007. *Iranica in the Achaemenid period (ca. 550-330 B.C.): Lexicon of Old Iranian proper names and loanwords, attested in non-Iranian texts*. Leuven/Paris/Dudley: OLA 158.
———. 2008. Multilingualism in the Fortification and Treasury archives. *AFP*: 59-86.
———. 2015. Des Lyciens à Persépolis en Mésopotamie durant la période achéménide (c. 521-331 av. J.-C.). In *De Lycia Antiqua*, ed. R. Lebrun, 147-74. Leuven: Hethitica 18.
Tolini, G. 2008. Les travailleurs babyloniens et le palais de Taokè. *ARTA* 2008.002.
Tuplin, C. 1996. The parks and gardens of the Achaemenid Empire. In *Achaemenid Studies*, ed. C. Tuplin, 80-131, 178-82. Stuttgart: Historia-Einzelschriften 99.
———. 1998. The seasonal migration of Achaemenid kings. *SPH*: 63-114.
———. 2008. Taxation and death: Certainties in the Persepolis Fortification Archive? *AFP*: 317-86.
———. 2010. All the King's horse: In search of Achaemenid Persian cavalry. In *New perspectives on ancient warfare*, ed. M. Trundle and G. Fagan, 101-82. Leiden/Boston: Brill.
Uchitel, A. 1989. Organization of manpower in Achaemenid Persia according to the Fortification archive. *ASJ* 11: 225-38.
———. 1991. Foreign workers in the Fortification Archive. *ME*: 127-35.
———. 1997. Persian paradise: Agricultural texts in the Fortification archive. *IrAnt* 32: 137-44.
Vallat, F. 1993. *Les noms géographiques des sources suso-élamites*. Wiesbaden: RGTC 11.
———. 1997. L'utilisation des sceaux-cylindres dans l'archivage des lettres de Persépolis. In *Sceaux d'Orient et leur emploi*, ed. R. Gyselen, 171-4. Bures-sur-Yvette: RO 10.
Zaccagnini, C. 1983. Patterns of mobility among Ancient Near Eastern craftsmen. *JNES* 42: 245-64.
Zournatzi, A. 2000. The processing of gold and silver tax in the Achaemenid Empire: Herodotus 3.96.2 and the archaeological realities. *StIr* 29: 241-71.

CHAPTER 28

AVESTA AND ZOROASTRIANISM UNDER THE ACHAEMENIDS AND EARLY SASANIANS

PRODS OKTOR SKJÆRVØ

ZOROASTRIANISM

Zoroastrianism as we know it from the *Avesta* was a religious tradition that took shape among the Iranians in Central Asia in the second millennium BC, after they separated from their Indo-Aryan relatives, but, probably, before some of the tribes, among them the Medes and Persians, migrated onto the Iranian plateau around 1000 BC and later founded the Median polity and the Achaemenid Empire. This was the religious tradition of the Achaemenid kings and, later, of the Parthian and Sasanian kings until the Arab conquest, *c*.650 AD. After some 300 years under Arab rule, a group of Iranian Zoroastrians migrated to India, where they settled on the west coast and became known as the Parsis (Parsees). Today there are members of the Zoroastrian diaspora all around the world.

This tradition is referred to as Zoroastrianism, from Zoroaster, the Greek name for Zarathustra (Zarathushtra, etc.), or Mazdaism (Mazdayasnianism), from the Avestan term *mazda-yasna* "someone who sacrifices to Ahura Mazdā," the supreme deity. The Sasanian Zoroastrian priests referred to themselves by the latter term, Middle Persian (Pahlavi) *mazdēsn*, and to their sacred tradition as "the *dēn* of the Mazdayasnians."

In Western scholarship, Zoroastrianism has long been studied based on the untenable premise, formulated in the nineteenth century, of Zarathustra's reform, according to which Zarathustra was a prophet who rejected beliefs inherited from the Indo-Iranians and preached a reformed religion as reflected in his five *Gāthā*s, "songs" (e.g., Boyce

1975, 1982). Studies have therefore tended to focus on the precise nature of Zarathustra's reform and to what extent later religious beliefs remained true to Zarathustra's teachings (e.g., Duchesne-Guillemin 1962: 165–8), which in turn has generated somewhat divergent descriptions of Zoroastrianism.

IRANIANS, PERSIANS, AND ACHAEMENIDS

Because the Iranians (and the Indo-Aryans) left no written records in their original homelands, it is impossible to correlate them with any of the numerous archeological remains in the areas in question, and we have no certain evidence of them before they are mentioned in the Assyrian royal annals (Skjærvø 2006 with references). The Iranian migration onto the Iranian plateau probably proceeded in several waves and along different routes, and Iranian tribes may have been established throughout the northern and central plateau by the beginning of the first millennium BC (Skjærvø 1995). The earliest direct evidence for Persian and Median presence on the plateau is found in descriptions of campaigns by Assyrian kings, where peoples they came into contact with or subdued are commonly mentioned. Here, Parsuwash and Matai are first mentioned in the ninth century BC in the area of Lake Urmia in the records of Shalmaneser III (858–824 BC) who, in 835 BC, is said to have received tribute from twenty-seven kings of Parsuwash. Subsequent kings, including Shamshi-Adad V (823–811 BC) and Adad-nerari III (810–783 BC), also campaigned against them; in the annals of Shamsi-Adad, for the year 821 BC, a civil war is mentioned in a land stretching from Bīt-Bunaki to Parsumash. Tiglath-Pileser III (744–727 BC) campaigned against the Medes as far as Mount Bikni (= Mount Alvand). From Sargon II's reign (721–705 BC) we have the mention of a nephew of King Dalta of the Ellipi by the name Aspabara, which can hardly be other than Iranian (Median?) *aspabāra* "rider, knight." In 691 BC, Sennacherib (705–681 BC) faced an army of troops from Elam, Parsumash, Anzan (Anshan), and elsewhere (Waters 1999; Zadok 2001). The route of the Persian tribes from northwestern Iran down to Pārsa (modern Fārs) in southwestern Iran, where they replaced the Elamites as the ruling elite, is therefore fairly clear, although the exact origins of the Achaemenids remain unclear.

Numerous Iranian tribes remained in Central Asia and spread west, north, and east, where we find them under Darius, who lists Choresmians, Sogdians, and Sakas (= Scythians; western: "those beyond the Sea"; northern: "those wearing pointed-hats"; and eastern: "those beyond the Sogdians"). Of these, the Sogdians and eastern Sakas, the Khotanese, were Zoroastrians in the Achaemenid period and later (although the Khotanese were Buddhist by the time of their earliest written remains; Skjærvø 1991). Several tribes settled in the area of modern Afghanistan, in Bactria, Drangiana (Zranka), and Arachosia (Harakhwatī). In some of the later traditions, Bactria became the kingdom of Zoroaster.

THE TEXTUAL SOURCES

The *Avesta* is a collection of texts composed orally, presumably in the second and first millennia BC, and then transmitted orally until they were written down, perhaps a little after 600 AD (thus Kellens 1998), but the oldest manuscripts date only from the thirteenth and fourteenth centuries. The orality of the *Avesta* has not been emphasized until recently, and the texts have commonly been studied like written literature. It was therefore usual in both the nineteenth and twentieth centuries to speak of "the books" or "writings of Zoroaster." Yet, even with increased understanding in the twentieth century of oral literature and history, the oral nature of the *Avesta* has been little focused upon by either Iranists or non-Iranists (Skjærvø 1994; 2005–6).

The extant texts are in two linguistic forms, one older and one younger, hence referred to as Old and Young(er) Avestan, respectively. The two parts of the *Avesta* thus distinguished are accordingly referred to as the *Old* and *Young(er) Avesta* (see Skjærvø 2003–4; Panaino 2007, on issues of chronology). The *Old Avesta* is the more famous, as it contains the five *Gāthās*, whose literary authorship, since the late nineteenth century, has traditionally been ascribed in the West to Zarathustra. The *Yasna Haptanghāiti*, "Sacrifice in Seven Sections," is an Old Avestan hymn in praise of Ahura Mazdā and his creation (Humbach 1959; Insler 1975; Hintze 2007; see also the translations in Skjærvø 2011a).

Among the Young Avestan texts, the most extensive are the *Yasna*, the text accompanying the morning ritual (the *yasna* "sacrifice"); the *Yashts*, which are hymns to individual deities; and the *Videvdad*, "the rules for keeping the *daēwa*s [bad old gods] away" [not "anti-demonic" or similar], which contains rules for how to deal with pollution and purification (Skjærvø 2007).

The Old Persian cuneiform inscriptions of the Achaemenid kings at Persepolis, Susa, and elsewhere, mainly of Darius I (521–486 BC), Xerxes I (485–465 BC) and Artaxerxes II (405–359 BC), are the earliest written texts in an Iranian language and were also redacted in Akkadian and Elamite, with some also in Aramaic. The Old Persian inscriptions ascribed to their predecessors, Cyrus (558–530 BC), Ariaramnes, and Arsames, all postdate Darius; the Old Persian version of Cyrus' inscriptions at Pasargadae may have been added under the later Achaemenids, and those of Ariaramnes and Arsames are late fabrications (recent translations in Schmitt 2009; Skjærvø 2011a). The Cyrus cylinder, in which Cyrus describes his religious policy in Babylon, is written in Akkadian (Finkel 2013). This text does not tell us much about Cyrus' own religious views or his religious policy at home, and the question of Cyrus' religion has therefore been debated, though there are no conclusive arguments for any of the current opinions. Since the Old Persian inscriptions start only with Darius I, information about the history and beliefs of the Iranians before this period has to be sought in nonindigenous sources, the earliest of which include the Greek historians Herodotus (c.484–425 BC), Ctesias of Cnidus (fl. 400 BC), Xenophon (c.431–354 BC), and a few preserved only fragmentarily in quotations by later authors, such as Xanthus of Cnidus (fifth century BC).

The main corpus of texts complementing the Achaemenid inscriptions is the large number of clay tablets inscribed mostly in Elamite (Chapter 27) found during the excavations by the Oriental Institute, Chicago, led by Ernst Herzfeld at Persepolis in 1933–4 and published as the Fortification tablets, dating from 509–494 BC (Hallock 1969), and the Treasury tablets, dating from 492–458 BC, thus including the reign of Artaxerxes I (465–424 BC) (Cameron 1948). These texts, now in the Oriental Institute, and several more in Iran provide a wide range of information about the religion, not all of which is yet clearly understood. Only a part of the whole collection has so far been published.

During excavations at Persepolis in 1936–8, ritual implements used in the *haoma* ritual and inscribed in Aramaic were also found (Bowman 1970). This material contains numerous personal names, as do the Aramaic letters found on the island of Elephantine in the Nile (recent edition Porten 1996).

Written records from the Seleucid and Parthian periods are quite rare, as are those from the *fratarakas* (Chapter 36), a local Persian dynasty under the Parthians surviving in Pārs (Fārs) in southwestern Iran (Skjærvø 2000). The third century AD Sasanian kings all left inscriptions in which they expressed their religious stance, two of them substantial: Šābuhr I's (240–272) trilingual (Middle Persian, Parthian, Greek) inscription on the Ka'be-ye Zardosht at Naqsh-e Rustam (Huyse 1999) and his youngest son Narseh's (293–302/3) bilingual (Middle Persian, Parthian) inscription at Paikuli (Humbach and Skjærvø 1980–83). The most important sources for Zoroastrianism from this century, however, are the inscriptions of the high priest Kerdīr (Kartīr), who began his career under Šābuhr I and was still in office in 293 (MacKenzie 1989; Skjærvø 2011a, 2011b). Photographs of most of the inscriptions and reliefs are in Schmidt 1970.

We have no written Zoroastrian texts from the Sasanian period, but there must have existed a large corpus of oral traditions (referred to later as the *dēn*). These were committed to writing only from the ninth century onward, partly, perhaps, because the oral traditions were threatened with weakening and disappearance under Arab rule. This written corpus is what we refer to as the Pahlavi Books, that is, the Zoroastrian texts written in Pahlavi.

Iranian dualism

The basic tenet of Zoroastrianism is its so-called dualist approach to the problem of evil, which consists in positing two powers in the universe existing from eternity, one for good (Av. Ahura Mazdā, OP Ahuramazdā, Pahl. Ōhrmazd) and one for evil (Av. Angra Manyu, Pahl. Ahrimen). The present mixed world resulted when the evil one attacked the good creation. In the *Gāthās*, the origin of good and evil is represented as two "spirits" (Av. *manyu*), sleeping fetuses that are in every respect each other's opposites: the "life-giving spirit" (*spenta manyu*) and the "evil spirit" (*ahra, originally perhaps "dark"). While the *Avesta* contains no clear statement about whether the life-giving spirit was identical to Ahura Mazdā (they were probably separate), in the later literature they tended to be equated and a line of thought developed that Ōhrmazd and Ahrimen were twin brothers, a concept that was anathema to both Zoroastrians and Manicheans. This led to speculations about to whom the original womb belonged, and it was early on ascribed to the god of Time (Av. Zurwan), invoked at the end of the *yasna* and other rituals, together with the firmament (Thwāsha) and the empty space (Vāyu) as three eternal cosmic entities (*Yasna* 72.10).

Evil was frequently associated with evil smell (*gand-*); thus, Darius (DNb) prays that Ahuramazdā may protect him, his house, and his land from what smells evil (*gasta*), as does Artaxerxes II (A²Sa, d). In Pahlavi, Ahrimen is commonly called the Foul (*gannāg*, from *gand-*) Spirit.

The earliest version of this origin myth is found in Plutarch's (first to second century AD) *On Isis and Osiris*, where we are told that "some believe there are two gods, rival craftsmen [*antitekhnoi*], as it were, the one the creator [*dēmiourgos*] of good things, the other of evil things. Others call the better divinity 'god' [*theos*] and the other 'demon' [*daimōn*], as does Zoroaster the Magian, who they say lived five thousand years before the Trojan war. Zoroaster called the former Horomasdes and the latter Areimanios ... the one begotten of the purest light, the other of darkness, are at war with each other." The *Avesta* and especially the Pahlavi books contain several elaborate descriptions of the origins of this world and how it will end when evil has been overcome and removed from Ahura Mazdā's, Pahlavi Ōhrmazd's, creation (e.g., Skjærvø 2011a: nos. 23–5, 69–71).

Divine and demonic entities

In the world view of the *Old* and *Young Avesta*, the universe is divided into two parts, the other world (Av. the world of thought, Pahl. *mēnōy*), that of gods and demons, and this world (Av. the world that has bones, the world of living beings, Pahl. *gētīy*). The other world cannot be perceived by ordinary human perception, but can be reached by their souls (Av. *urwan*, Pahl. *ruwān*) and men's "visionary" capability, their *daēnā* (Pahl. *dēn*).

The head deity is Ahura Mazdā, originally epithets that signified approximately "the (ruling) lord who places all in his mind," that is, "the omniscient lord." He is "the greatest of the 'gods'" (*Yasht* 17.16) and beside him are numerous divine entities who help him establish, reestablish, and maintain the cosmic order (Av. *asha*, Old Pers. *erta*), many (or all) of them of stellar origin: Mithra (Pahl. Mihr) the morning star, who chases darkness and prepares a path for the sun; Ardwī Surā Anāhitā (Pahl. Ardwīsūr or Anāhīd), "the lofty unattached (or 'unsullied') one endowed with life-giving strength," the heavenly river, who purifies the semen and wombs of humans to prepare them for procreation; Tishtriya, Sirius, the dog star, who fights the demon of drought and other evil stellar beings to bring down the seasonal rains; Sraosha (Pahl. Srōsh), the principal enemy of darkness embodied in the demon Wrath "with the bloody club," who at nightfall bathes the creation in blood and who needs to be overcome in order for the "cover of good thought," i.e., the day sky, to be stretched out (*Yasna* 48.7); Rashnu (Pahl. Rashn), god of "straightness," who weighs the souls' good and evil deeds on a balance, determining which will go to paradise and which will fall into hell; Apām Napāt, "Scion of the Waters," deity associated with the fire in the heavenly waters; and others. The term *yazata* (Pahl. *yazd*), applied to male deities, originally meant "deserving of sacrifices" but later came to mean "god" in general.

The Life-giving Immortals (Av. *amesha spenta*s, Pahl. *amahrspand*s) are six divine entities sired by Ahura Mazdā: Good Thought, Best Order, Well-deserved (royal) Command, Life-giving Ārmaiti (the earth, Av. *Spentā Ārmaiti*, Ahura Mazdā's daughter and spouse), and Wholeness and Immortality (representing water and plants), Pahlavi Wahuman, Ardwahisht, (Kh)shahrewar, Spandārmad, Hordad, and Amurdad. The *frawashi*s (Pahl. *frawash* or *frawahr*) or *ashāunām frawashi*s, "*frawashi*s of the sustainers of order," depicted as mounted female warriors with raised banners, are Ahura Mazdā's assistants at the birth and rebirth of the cosmos, as well as of children in the wombs; together with the Fire, they also kept the Evil one contained when he attacked Ahura Mazdā's creation (*Yasht* 13.76–8).

The principal demonic entities are the Evil Spirit (Av. Angra Manyu, Pahl. Ahrimen) and the Lie (Av. female *druj*, Old Pers. masculine *drauga*), that is, the cosmic deception, which distorts the truth about the cosmic order for gods and men. Their commander-in-chief is Wrath.

In this universe, whoever upholds the cosmic order is a "sustainer of order, at one with order (once dead)" (Av. *ashawan*, OP *ertāwan*, Pahl. *ahlaw*); those who do not, because deceived by the Lie, are "possessed by the Lie" (Av. *dru(g)want*, OP. *draujana*).

The entity called in Avestan *khwarnah*, in Old Persian probably *farnah* (Pahl. *xwarrah, farr*), in the *Avesta* denotes a luminous object that, when the sun rises or the moon becomes visible, is bestowed on the world by the deities to further living beings and order (*Yasht* 6.1, 7.3); it is deposited in the earth (Pahl. *zamyād*) and provides the substance of the mountains (according to a Pahlavi text), with which it is closely related in the *Avesta* (*Yasht* 19, Hintze 1994: Skjærvø 1994: 218 n. 29a). It was in particular associated with the *kawi*s (later *kay*s), ancient poet-sacrificers (the kavian *khwarnah*, originally also a celestial entity); in the Pahlavi and modern Persian tradition, the *kay*s, together with the other mythical figures of the Iranian past, became kings, but there is no specific evidence that the kavian *khwarnah* was originally associated with kingship in particular; rather, it was a divine force needed to uphold the cosmic order and so also required to be possessed by rulers (Skjærvø 2013).

In the Achaemenid inscriptions, Ahuramazdā, who made the ordered cosmos, is "the great god (*baga*)" and the king's god, to whom Darius and Xerxes offer sacrifices in return for divine approval and assistance. As "the greatest of the gods," he is not alone, but Darius simply subsumes all others in the formula "and the other gods who exist" (DB IV 61) and "together with the other gods" (DPd). Only in the later inscriptions are some of these other gods mentioned by name: Ahuramazdā, Anāhitā, and Mithra are invoked by Artaxerxes II to protect him from all evil (A²Sa, d), and Ahuramazdā and the *baga* Mithra by Artaxerxes III (359–338 BC).

Numerous gods are mentioned in the Elamite texts (Koch 1977), many of them Elamite (e.g., Humban, the chief Elamite god, and Napir irshara "the Great God") and Babylonian (e.g., Adad, the weather god, and KI, the Earth), others clearly Zoroastrian: Ahuramazdā, Ispandāramaiti (Av. Spentā Ārmaiti), and Naryasanga (Av. Nairya Sangha, the divine messenger); as well as the Ertāna Fraverti (Av. *ashāunām frawashi*s). Deities with Old Persian names include Visai Bagā "all the gods," with which compare Middle Persian as *pad wispān yazdān nām* "in the name of all the gods" in the Paikuli inscription of Narseh; *Druvā, either the god of Time (Av. Zruwā) or a god or goddess of Health (cf. OP *duruva* "healthy, unharmed," Av. Druwāspā "she who keeps the horses healthy"); Mizhdushi, perhaps a female deity, "the reward-granting one" (Av. *mizhda* "reward"). Divinities of rivers, mountains, places, and cities are also revered.

The Aramaic letters from the Achaemenid military colony at Elephantine in the Nile, most of them from the fifth century BC, contain Iranian personal names that clearly reflect the Avestan beliefs, such as Artaxwant "*possessing Order;" Ātr-farna "enjoying the *farnah* of the fire;" Ārma(n)ti-dāta "given by (Spentā) Ārmaiti;" Baga-farna "enjoying the *farnah* of the gods;" Baga-zushta "in whom (in whose sacrifice) the gods take pleasure, approved by the gods;" Hōm-dāta "(child) given by Haoma;" Mazda-yazna "who sacrifices to/worships (Ahura) Mazdā;" Mithra-dāta "(child) given by Mithra;" Mithra-yazna "who sacrifices to/worships Mithra;" Spenta-dāta "(child) given by Spentā (Ārmaiti?);" Tīri-pāta "protected by Tīri" (another name for Tishtriya); and Zhāmāspa, an Iranian epic name.

Calendars and festivals

The Avestan months are named after deities and first attested in historical times in a local form in Cappadocia (Panaino 2010). 1. The *frawashi*s (Capp. Artana, corresponding to the Elamite Ertana Fraverti), 2. Best Order, 3. Wholeness, 4. Tishtriya (Tīri), 5. Undyingness, 6. Well-deserved Command, 7. Mithra, 8. (Scion of) the Waters, 9. Fire, 10. the Creator, 11. the Sky, 12. Life-giving Humility, the Earth.

In the Achaemenid inscriptions, a "farmer's calendar" is used, in which the month names refer to meteorological, agricultural, and ritual events (some are known only in their Elamite transcription), but correspond closely to the Avestan month names, such as, 1. Ādu-kanaisha probably refers to sowing, celebration of the Frawardīgān–New Year festival; 2. Thūra-vāhara "(the month) of life-giving spring"; 4. Garma-pada "station of heat," perhaps the month of the Tīragān festival; 7. Bāga-yādi "(the month) for sacrificing to the god (Mithra?)," perhaps the month of the Mihragān festival; 9. Āçi-yādiya "(the month) for sacrficing to/at the fire"; 10. the much-discussed Ānāmaka "(month) dedicated to (sacrificing to the creator) by name"(?); and 12. Viyaxana assumed to refer to the cleaning out of the irrigation canals in the ground.

According to the traditions recorded in the Pahlavi and later literature, the new year beginning at the spring equinox was said among Iranians to have been instituted by

Jamshēd (Av. Yima), first king according to the *Avesta* (*Videvdad* 2, Skjærvø 2008). On the first day of the new year, Jamshēd would receive presents from ambassadors from all the provinces of his empire. The great relief at the *apadāna* at Persepolis illustrates such an event and is likely to have been where the Achaemenid kings celebrated the new year. The event is also illustrated by reliefs showing a lion killing a bull (otherwise not referred to in the Zoroastrian literature). The implication of the king in the role of Jamshēd is underscored in the Pahlavi texts where we are told that, when the *khwarrah* of good kingship as in Jamshēd is combined with the *khwarrah* of the good Zoroastrian tradition (*dēn*), the Evil Spirit will be destroyed and the universe will become permanently *frasha* (Skjærvø 2011a: 233).

Kingship in the Achaemenid inscriptions

In the Achaemenid inscriptions, the kings are portrayed as sacrificing to the great god Ahuramazdā, who produced and maintains the ordered cosmos and who bestowed the royal command upon them, so that they might (re)establish and maintain order on earth. The purpose of the established order is to provide *happiness* (*shiyāti*) for man and to guide his life so that he may be among Ahuramazdā's chosen after death.

Darius states his appurtenance to Ahuramazdā in DSk: "King Darius announces: Ahuramazdā is mine, I am Ahuramazdā's. I sacrificed to Ahuramazdā. May Ahuramazdā bring me support!" Thus, the relationship between Ahuramazdā and the kings is portrayed as one of possession and mutual indebtedness between god and his worshiper, in which Ahuramazdā in return for worship and sacrifice assists the king in maintaining his land.

Most of Darius' statements are introduced by the formula "King Darius announces," where the verb is Old Persian *thātiy*, from *thah-*, the equivalent of Old Avestan *sangh*: "to announce." The kings' statements announce their knowledge and purpose, praise of Ahuramazdā and his work, denunciation of those possessed by (on the side of) the Lie, and thus serve to uphold the order of the land. Similarly, the *Old Avesta* is the poet-sacrificer's oral announcement of his knowledge, praise of Ahura Mazdā and his work, and denunciation of those possessed by the Lie. Besides the simple word "speak," the term *sangh* is used about both the sacrificer and Ahura Mazdā's utterances, which are by themselves capable of combating the Lie and its evil and protecting all living beings (*Yasna* 44.14), as are, indirectly, those of the Achaemenid kings.

Like the Old Avestan poet, who identifies himself as Zarathustra and who states his side in the cosmic battle and how he fights evil (by praise and conferring fame on Ahura Mazdā; *Yasna* 43.7–8), the king, by his announcements, states his name and his ancestry; his appurtenance to Ahura Mazdā, who bestowed the royal command upon him; and his activities: supporting the work of Ahuramazdā and combating the forces of the Lie. When Darius saw chaos reign in the land, he would put it back in order (DNa, cf. XPh 30–35), matching Ahuramazdā's efforts in the other world: "When Ahuramazdā saw this earth was in turmoil, he gave it to me. He made me king. I am the king. By the greatness of Ahuramazdā, I set it down in its place." It is up to the king to maintain the peace and happiness established for mankind by Ahuramazdā, as it is the job of the Gathic sacrificer to maintain "peace and pasture" for the settlements (*Yasna* 29.10, etc.). Similarly, after the Gaumāta debacle, Darius "restored to the people the pastures, cattle and household (slaves)" (Skjærvø 2011a: 230).

Throughout his inscriptions, Darius assures us that he is an active participant in the battle against the Lie (cf. DB I 34–5, DB IV 33–40), and he regards his opponents as having been bewildered and deceived by the Lie or the Evil one and so having become their minions: "When Kambūjiya had gone to Egypt, then the people sided with the Evil one (became *ahrīka*); the Lie became rampant in the lands" (DB I 30–35). The opponents all present themselves falsely, as in DB I 77–8: "And a certain Babylonian, Nidintu-Bēl, son of Ainaira, rose up in Babylon. He lied to the people: 'I am Nebuchadrezzar, the son of Nabonidus.'" Similarly, in the *Old Avesta*, the old gods (*daēwa*s) were bewildered by deception and chose the wrong side (*Yasna* 30.6).

Although it is not stated in the inscriptions that the Achaemenid kings' achievements in this world parallel and match those of Ahura Mazdā in the other world, it is implicitly clear in the reliefs and other representations in which the kings are shown battling monsters, as well as in the relief accompanying the Bisotun inscription and elsewhere, where the king's opponents are led to him bound and he seizes the first in line by the hand. Although also known from Mesopotamia, this illustrates repeated statements to this effect (DB IV 33–6, cf. DB I 82–3, II 73) and matches several passages in the *Gāthā*s (*Yasna* 30.8, 44.14).

Being on the side of the Lie therefore manifests itself in the worship of the wrong gods, the *daiva*s. Both Darius and Xerxes used the proscription of the worship of wrong gods as a means of subduing and punishing local rebellions (DB V 14–18, XPh 35–41); Darius explicitly prescribes punishment for the evil-doers (e.g., DB I 20–24), and Xerxes tells us how he destroyed the places where *daiva*s were worshiped (*daiva-dāna*) and proscribed worship of the *daiva*s, replacing it with the worship of Ahuramazdā (XPh §5 35–41). They fulfill their duties to Ahuramazdā by upholding the law and pursuing and punishing those who do not, those who are liers and rebels or foreigners who worship the wrong gods, and Darius' advice to other kings is to behave in that same manner (DB IV 61–65). These functions of the kings are summarized in Darius' "prayer" (DPd): "May Ahuramazdā bear me aid together with all the gods! And may Ahuramazdā protect this land from the enemy army, from bad seasons, and from the Lie! May there not come upon this land an enemy army, bad seasons, or the Lie!"

The ultimate purpose of the Gathic poet–sacrificer is to give Ahura Mazdā a gift valuable enough for the god to enable him to constantly remake the ordered world as his countergift, making it *frasha*, leading to the final "*frasha*-making" (Av. *frashōkerti*, Pahl. *frashkerd*) at the end of time. Darius, however, uses the term to refer to his work on earth (DSf 55–7): "in Susa much (*paruv*) *frasha* had been ordered, much *frasha* has been made." In Akkadian, the word is rendered as *būnu* "good," which is also how it was understood by Xerxes, who uses *naiba* "good" instead of *frasha* (XPg 3–5): "By the greatness of Ahura

Mazdā (there was) much (*paruv*) good that Darius the king, my father did and ordered."
The original meaning of this term, probably "full of the juices of fecundity and fertility,"
was perhaps lost already in the *Young Avesta*, where we find similar phrases (*Yasht* 19.10):
"Ahura Mazdā made his creations many (*pouru*) and good, many and beautiful, many
and marvelous, many (*pouru*) and *frasha*." In this light we must also, no doubt, see the
constructions of "paradises," that is, royal gardens imitating and anticipating the heavenly existence awaiting the followers of Order after death (see, e.g., Briant 1996: 244–50;
Henkelman 2008: 434ff.). Note especially the name Vispa-shiyātish, "All Happiness," of a
paradise (El. *partetash*) known from the Persepolis tablets (Cameron 1948: 207; see also
Skjærvø 2005 for further details).

The Parthians (Arsacids)

One of the most interesting kings from the Parthian period is Antiochus of Commagene
(r. second century BC), a vassal of the Parthians (*c*.247 BC–224 AD), who called himself
"just, manifest god, friend of Rome and Greece." On his grave, located at Nemrud Dağ,
is a row of seated deities, who are identified in the inscription accompanying the statues
as Zeus Oromasdes, Apollo, Mithra Helios, Hermes, Artagnes Heracles, and Ares. The
same identification is seen in a Parthian-Greek inscription from the mid-second century
AD, by Arsakes Vologeses, son of Mitridates, written on the thighs of a statue, which the
Greek identifies as Hercules and the Parthian as Warthragn. According to these inscriptions, the statue was part of the booty acquired by a Parthian king and brought back
from Mesene to be put in the temple (*bagin*) of the god Tīri.

The Parthian inscriptions from Nisa in modern Turkmenistan provide evidence of
Zoroastrianism in the calendar and in onomastics. We also find there the term *āyazan*,
place of sacrifice (or similar), which matches Old Persian *āyadana*, the places of worship
that Gaumāta destroyed and Darius restored (DB I 63–4). It was also in the Parthian
period or earlier that the three major sacred fires are thought to have been founded:
Ādur Burzēnmihr, Ādur Farrōbag (or Farnbag), and Ādur Gushnasp, located at Takht-e
Solaymān (see the entries in *EnIr* online edition).

The third-century Sasanians

The Sasanian kings were the heirs of a local dynasty under the Parthians, the *fratarakas*
(Chapter 36) in Pārs (Fārs). The *frataraka* kings struck coins showing a fire temple on the
reverse, and their names, such as Dārāyān (or Dārēw) and Artakhshahr (Ardakhshahr),
were inherited from the Achaemenids.

The last in the line of the *frataraka* kings and the founder of the Sasanian dynasty
(224–651 AD), Ardakhshahr (Ardašīr) I, son of King Pābag, minted a new coinage, on

which the king presents himself as *mazdēsn*, a Mazdayasnian, and states that his *chihr* is from the "gods" (*bay* from OP *baga* "distributor [of good things], god"). The meaning of the term *chihr* has been much discussed, and no consensus exists (Panaino 2009). It is not unlikely, however, that its meaning is close to Pahl. *chihr*, which is found in contexts suggesting some inner quality, such as "(inherited) nature," but which is also characterized as something luminous, no doubt because of its origin in the other world. The same formula is found in the inscriptions of the early Sasanians, and in their reliefs the kings are represented as receiving the royal diadem directly from Ōhrmazd or another deity, from which it is clear that, like their remote ancestors, they regarded themselves as the carriers and protectors of the Mazdayasnian tradition and as god's principal ally in the divine scheme of overcoming and abolishing evil and establishing god's order on earth.

We now also find the idea that the kings' achievements in this world parallel and match those of Ahura Mazdā in the other world expressed in the royal reliefs, where the victory of the king's enemy is equal to Ahura Mazdā's victory over the Evil Spirit. In Ardašīr's investiture relief at Naqsh-e Rustam, the bust of the vanquished Parthian lies under the forelegs of the king's horse, while that of the vanquished Evil Spirit himself lies under the forelegs of the god Ōhrmazd's horse.

The core of Šābuhr's trilingual inscription is his victory over the three Roman emperors Gordian, Philip the Arab, and Valerian (Alram et al. 2007). This is preceded by a description of his empire and followed by a description of the court under Pābag, Ardašir, and himself; by a list of the fires he founded; and, finally, by an apostrophe addressed to his successors to revere the gods the way he himself had revered them. The narrative of his engagements with the Romans contains several references to the themes discussed above of the king's role in upholding the cosmic and political order. He uses the terms "lied" and "did wrong, sinned" (*wināh*) of the emperor's attack upon Armenia, and he captures Valerian with his own hand, as also illustrated in the victory relief at Naqsh-e Rustam. Remarkably, Šābuhr does not mention Ōhrmazd by name in the inscription on the Ka'be, where, in his apostrophe to his successors, he refers only to the gods (*yazd*).

Narseh's inscription was composed in order to legitimize his becoming king of Iran instead of his grandnephew, Warahrān III, who was under the influence of an evil councillor, Wahunām, inspired by Ahrimen and the demons (*dēws*). Narseh, viceroy of Armenia, upon being approached by the dignitaries of the realm, sets out in the names of Ōhrmazd, Anāhīd the Lady, and all the (other) gods, and, having overcome Warahrān and the evil Wahunām and concluded negotiations with the dignitaries of the realm, mounts the throne in the name of the gods, his father, and his ancestors. In what has long been regarded as his investiture relief at Naqsh-e Rustam, he appears to receive the ribboned ring of kingship from Anāhīd, although this interpretation has now been contested (Weber 2012).

Still later, in the two reliefs at Tāq-e Bustān, the investiture of Šābuhr II (309/10–379) by Ōhrmazd takes place in the presence of Mihr (Mithra), represented with a "spiked" solar nimbus and a sword wielded against the powers of evil, with the vanquished emperor Julian (d. 363) lying below the king and Ōhrmazd, and the investiture of Xosrow II takes place in the presence of Anāhīd pouring water from a ewer.

Kerdīr's inscriptions

Kerdīr's two identical long inscriptions at Naqsh-e Rustam on Šābuhr's victory relief and at Sar-e Mashhad are divided into four sections: description of Kerdīr's career under Šābuhr (240–272), his son Ōhrmazd (272–273), his other son Warahrān I (273–276), and his grandson Warahrān II (276–293); a continued account of his achievements under Warahrān II and reflections on his life achievements; the narrative of a vision of a heavenly journey; and the results of the heavenly journey and conclusion (Skjærvø 2011a: nos. 84 and 130; 2011b).

While the vision narrative is interesting for the study of the fate of the souls after death, the first two sections provide first-hand information about the activities of the clergy in general and of Kerdīr in particular. In the first section, we are told how Šābuhr I bestowed upon him, while still an *ēhrbed* (religious teacher), various high clerical honors and gave him the highest authority in the priestly community. He also assigned a "basic resource" to him, with which (?) he would perform the various rituals for the gods, founding Warahrān fires and caring for the priests; sealing charters for fires and Magi; and making priests "happy and prosperous," all of which brought profit to Ōhrmazd and the other gods, but harmed Ahrimen and the demons. Ōhrmazd I in addition bestowed upon him the hat and belt (or necklace?), insignia of high rank. Under Warahrān II, the rituals for the gods were increased, and great "satisfaction" came to the good creations, the gods, water, fire, and kine, while Ahrimen and the demons received "blows" and were "opposed, hated" so that "(false) beliefs" in them were no longer adhered to in the land and were "made untrustworthy." At this time, non-Mazdayasnians were "struck down" in the land, including Jews, shamans (Buddhists), Bramans (Hindus), Christians, Nāṣrā (Nazarenes or Nazoreans), Makdags (baptists?), and Zandīgs (Manicheans). Idols were destroyed, the "dens" of the demons (cf. Xerxes's *daiva-dāna*s) were obliterated and turned into thrones and seats for the gods.

In the second section, we are told about Kerdīr's activities in Anatolia while in Šābuhr I's retinue, when the enemy was struck down and captured and the land burned and devastated, while Kerdīr, ordered by the king, looked after existing priests and fires, protecting them from harm, and sent home those who had been taken captive. He held good priests in the land in high honor, but reprimanded the nonconformists in the Magian community who did not abide by the Mazdayasnian tradition and thus "improved" them. At home, he founded fires and established next-of-kin marriages, turned unbelievers into believers, making those who held the "(false) beliefs" in demons give them up and embrace that of the gods. He also details the number of *yasna*s celebrated in one year, almost seven thousand.

Of special interest are his references to a variety of documents carrying his seal, something that was common practice in view of the many seals of Magi that have been recovered (Gyselen 2001). The sealing of documents, including religious ones, is also attested in the Pahlavi literature. For instance, Mānushchihr, high priest of Kermān and Pārs in the late ninth century, in the colophon to his *Judgments from the Tradition* (*dādestān ī dēnīg*), says he ordered it (i.e., the manuscript) to be written and then sealed it, and the author of the *Dēnkard* (3.374) lists three seals (*muhr*) as being reliable for sealing important documents. Mānushchihr, in his *Letters* (2.1.8), also tells us that when there were differences of opinion regarding practices and interpretations of the "tradition," the Magi assembled (sometimes, even, at the court in Pārs?), and put their seals on the agreed-upon versions.

Rituals

The principal Young Avestan ritual activity is the *yasna*, "sacrifice" (OP **yashna*, cf. Pers. *jashn*, any ritual celebration) from the verb *yaza-* (Old Indic *yajña* and *yaja-*, OP *yada-*), implying offering up to the deities sacrificial gifts accompanied by hymns and other ritual utterances. The ritual is performed in the presence of a fire, which is the earthly representative of the heavenly fire, the Sun, who is also Ahura Mazdā's son. During the ritual, a sacred drink is prepared from the *haoma* plant (Old Indic *soma*) by crushing its twigs with a mortar and pestle (*hāwanā*). It is mixed with milk and consumed by the priest. The basic purpose of the ritual is to place Ahura Mazdā back in command, banish evil, and reestablish the cosmic order by bringing down the heavenly waters and making the sun reappear.

The purpose of the Old Avestan ritual was, similarly, to regenerate the ordered cosmos and provide peace and pasture for those living according to Ahura Mazdā's cosmic order and his commands. The *Sacrifice in Seven Sections* contains hymns in praise of Ahura Mazdā's creations, including a rapturous invocation of the waters (*Yasna* 38.3–5).

The Aramaic inscriptions on mortars (*hāwan*, Av. *hāwana*) and pestles (*abishāwan*) found at Persepolis prove that the Avestan *haoma* ritual, the *yasna*, was performed there. The Elamite tablets contain references to several kinds of religious services and describe the amount of produce bought for religious services (Koch 1977; Razmjou 2001, 2004; the most comprehensive study is Henkelman 2008). Among the Avestan and/or Old Persian ritual terms are the priests *magush* (OP *magush*), chiefly involved with the *lan* service, exceptionally services for Visai Bagā, Druvā, a river, and a mountain; *ātrwakhsha* (Av. *ātrewakhsha* "fire-tending priest"); *yashtā* (= Av.), generic "sacrificer." The terms *daussa* or *daussiya* are Old Persian **dauça*, liquid and nonliquid offerings (Av. *zaothra*, Pahl. *zōhr*).

Remarkably, Ahuramazdā does not appear to have a prominent position in the tablets, being rarely mentioned. The principal service was the *lan* service (Elamite *d.lan*), the only service that seems to have been celebrated on a grand scale, often listed together with names of deities, for example, PF 1956: *Druva, *Huwarīra, the Earth, and *Visai Bagā. The fact that it involves Iranian priests *magush* and *ātrwaxsha*, beside the Elamite *shātin* (Koch 1977: 154–70), and the offering of *dauças also suggests an Avestan-type ceremony, and, as Ahura Mazdā himself is only rarely mentioned in the tablets, it has sometimes been assumed that the *lan* service was for the supreme deity, who therefore was not mentioned by name himself (Koch 1977: 138). According to Razmjou (2004: 103–4), the meaning of Elamite *la*, "send forth," corresponds perfectly to Avestan *yaza-*, which refers to the sending off of offerings directed at the gods ("offering up in sacrifice"). Henkelman (2008: 181–304), however, has shown that the ceremony was not linked to any particular god or ethnicity, which means that the question of the rituals practiced at Achaemenid Persepolis in former Elamite territory does not yet have a complete answer.

The Old Persian inscriptions contain no details other than the kings' repeated statements that they "sacrificed" (*yada-*) to Ahuramazdā, who then assisted them, but, according to Herodotus (1.132), the Persian priest sacrificed in the presence of a Magus. After the victim had been cut in pieces and the flesh had been boiled it was laid out upon soft grass. A Magus chanted a hymn, which was said to recount the origin of the gods. The reliefs on the tombs at Naqsh-e Rustam, however, depict the kings, apparently sacrificing, in front of a fire altar. Above is seen a male figure in a winged disk (an ancient symbol representing the sun) holding up a ribboned ring. In the opinion of the present author, the scene should be interpreted in accordance with a statement in Xerxes' inscriptions: "I sacrificed to Ahuramazdā 'in the height' and 'in accordance with *erta* (the cosmic order),'" where "in the height" and "in accordance with *erta*" are likely to be quoted from the Achaemenid *Avesta*. This much-discussed symbol should then be interpreted as Ahuramazdā standing in the winged disk symbolizing the cosmic order, which, according to the Avesta, "contains the sun" (*Yasna* 32.2), while presenting the king with the ring of royal investiture (Skjærvø 2005, 2011c). There is no evidence that the male figure represents a (female) *frawashi* (Alram et al. 2007: 28–9), nor that the disks might refer to the *khwarnah* (Skjærvø 2013).

In order to acknowledge his relationship with the gods and their support for his victories and conquests, Šābuhr I lists in detail the various fires he founded and named for his own soul and renown and for those of his family: a fire named Xosrow-Šābuhr, "Šābuhr of good renown," for himself, one named Xosrow-Ādur-Anāhīd for his daughter, the queen of queens Ādur-Anāhīd, and so on for his sons Ōhrmazd-Ardaxshahr king of the Armenians, Šābuhr king of Mēshān (Mesene), and Narseh king of Hind, Sagestān (Sistan), and Tūrestān. He further lists donations made to these and other fires that were recorded individually in writing to be offered in sacrifice for his own soul (daily one sheep and specific amounts of bread and wine) and for those of his ancestor Sāsān, his grandfather Pābag and uncle Šābuhr, his father Ardashahr, and so on.

Some of these fires, at least, may have been kept in the domed square buildings with arches on the four walls referred to as *chahār-tāq*, "four arches," in modern times (Pahl. *chahār-tāg*), found scattered throughout Iran, notably those reportedly built by Ardašīr and Šābuhr.

Death and pollution

In the Zoroastrian dualist scheme of things, humans, water, and fire were constantly in danger of being polluted by agents of death, especially by corpses, but also impurities such as those resulting from menstruation. Already Herodotus (1.139) mentions that the Persians revered the rivers and never polluted them with dirt from their own bodies, including by washing themselves in a river. Pollution of one's surroundings was a constant threat, and determining the extent and reach of pollution became an important issue for the priests, especially as it affected one's home or a fire temple.

Buildings with domes and *tāg*s are mentioned in the Pahlavi texts in connection with pollution when there is a question of the polluting effect of dead things on top of the dome and the potential for the pollution spreading to the *tāg*s and the rest of the building. For instance, if there are *tāg*s in the house (*xānag*) and there is a dead thing in one of the *tāg*s, then only that *tāg* is polluted. Other parts of buildings, too, are mentioned in similar contexts (roofs, ceilings, walls, stairs/ladders, floors, doors, doorways, entrance halls, rooms, porches, etc.); for example, if something dies on a plastered floor, the plaster is polluted, but if it is removed and new plaster poured, then the area is clean. These architectural features have not yet been studied, however. Pollution also works differently on various utensils, so that for instance if something dies on the outside of a jar containing wine, then the wine is clean, but if it contains oil, both the jar and the oil are unclean, because the oil seeps through an earthenware jar.

According to Mānushchihr, a container for bones (*astōdān*) that have been picked clean of bodily tissues by birds should be elevated above the ground and be covered by a roof so that the bones cannot be rained upon but can be exposed to the light. The container itself (*ast-kadag* "room for the bones") should be made from one "stone," and plaster and stone should be packed around it. The rock-cut tombs of the Achaemenid kings clearly conform to similar rules. We may also note Herodotus' remark that the bodies of dead males were buried only after they had been torn by dogs or birds of prey, and the Magi covered the bodies with wax before burying them (1.140).

Ethics

The main Zoroastrian ethical principles, based on Ahura Mazdā's "established Law" (*dāta*) and the eternal agreements between gods and men (Av. *urwata*) and among men (Av. *mithra*), are straightness, honesty, generosity, moderation, and so on, while crookedness, deviousness, deceit, and miserliness or greed, lust, hate, envy, slander, among others, are to be avoided. The most important values include care of the poor and fairness: treating all the same, whether high or low (Skjærvø 2011a: chapter 7).

According to their inscriptions (cf. Skjærvø 2011a: no. 91), the Achaemenid king represents himself as treating everybody equally and justly (DB I 20–22, DNb 16–24), and he rewards those who behave according to the Law he has laid down (*dāta*), but punishes those who do not (DB I 23). One should speak only what is true or real (*hashiya*), behaving with rectitude, and doing what is straight (*rāsta*), not abandoning the straight path (DNa 58–60). One should not lie (*durujiya-*), do wrong (*vināthaya-*), behave crookedly (*zūra kar-*) or deviously (*mitha*). Herodotus (1.140), indeed, points out that the Persians considered it the greatest disgrace in the world to tell lies, the next to owe a debt.

Also according to the Achaemenid inscriptions, the man who behaves according to the laws will be rewarded in both life and afterlife, becoming happy (*shiyāta*) while alive and at one with order (*ertāvan*) when dead (DB V 18–20, XPh). Similarly, according to Kerdīr (at Naqsh-e Rajab), he who sustains order, "fame and prosperity will come upon this his body with bones, and oneness with Order will come upon that his soul with bones" (Skjærvø 2011a: no. 84).

Were the Achaemenids Zoroastrian or not?

Throughout the twentieth century, historians of Iranian religion debated whether the Achaemenids were Zoroastrians or not, the answer to which was commonly sought in terms of similarities and differences between Zoroastrianism and the Achaemenid religion as expressed in their inscriptions. The differences were often defined in terms of "omissions and discrepancies" in the inscriptions as compared with Zoroastrianism as understood at the time, and it was argued that so many key terms and notions of Zoroastrianism were absent from the Old Persian inscriptions that the Achaemenid religion was at least not "pure" Zoroastrianism (e.g., Duchesne-Guillemin 1972; see also the articles in Kellens 1991). There were several problems with this approach. It was not taken sufficiently into account that the *Avesta* and the Old Persian inscriptions are different kinds of texts (royal proclamations versus ritual texts) and in different languages and that there was no particular reason to expect mention of Zarathustra, for instance, whose name is absent from both the Achaemenid and Sasanian inscriptions (also those of Kerdīr). Furthermore, the identification of differences and similarities was predicated upon the widespread assumption that Zarathustra was a historical reformer who had reformed the ancient religion of the Iranians and whose teachings were enshrined in the notoriously difficult *Gāthā*s. His teachings were deduced from these texts, but mostly according to how they were understood in the late nineteenth century. By the 1960s it was becoming increasingly clear that this interpretation was fundamentally flawed, and numerous new translations have appeared, though there is still no consensus about the overall meaning and function of the texts, other than that they were probably ritual rather than didactic texts.

To answer the question one must, obviously, define both "Achaemenid religion" and "Zoroastrianism." If one defines the former as the religion expressed in the various primary and secondary sources at our disposal and the latter as the religion expressed in the (entire) *Avesta*, it can be shown that the similarities between Achaemenid religion and Zoroastrianism are so numerous and fundamental that one must conclude that the Achaemenid kings, at least from Darius onward, were Zoroastrian. It is easy to verify that the Achaemenid king performs his Zoroastrian duties faithfully: he praises Ahuramazdā and his ordered cosmos; he worships Ahuramazdā and the other gods, those, that is, who are "worthy of worship"; he discards the wrong gods, the *daiva*s; he repeats time and again that Ahuramazdā is the greatest of the gods; and he represents himself as having all the good qualities of a sustainer of Ahuramazdā and his order.

Like Zarathustra, he is Ahuramazdā's chosen, and, in his function as mediator between the gods and men, as supreme sacrificer, he, like the Old Avestan sacrificer, becomes "like Zarathustra," in the same way that, in the *Young Avesta*, the sacrificer sacrifices like Zarathustra, the prototype of human sacrificers (*Yasna* 8.7, *Yasht* 13.41). Darius thus reunites in one and the same person the functions of supreme king and supreme sacrificer (see above and Skjærvø 2005: 75–80).

Serious questions remain, however. The origin of the Achaemenids is unknown, so it is also unknown whether their Zoroastrianism was inherited or adopted (Skjærvø 2005: 80–81).

Further reading

For a concise survey of Persian history in the period considered here, see Wiesehöfer (1996). Boyce (1979) and Rose (2011) contain broad overviews of Zoroastrianism; Malandra (1983) and Skjærvø (2011a) English translations of many of the relevant texts; and *LPII* a survey of the Old and Middle Persian literature. On the history of the *Avesta* and the Avestan language, see Skjærvø (1995, 2003–4, 2006, and 2012) and Panaino (2007). On religion in Achaemenid Iran, see also, for example, Boyce (1982), Schwartz (1985), Kellens (2002), and De Jong (2010). On Zoroastrian monotheism and dualism, see Skjærvø (2011d, 2011e). In addition, there are a number of useful digital resources, including http://www.achemenet.com/; http://www.humanities.uci.edu/sasanika/; http://www.iranicaonline.org/; and http://www.parthia.com/.

References

Alram, M., M. Blet-Lemarquand, and P. O. Skjærvø. 2007. Shapur, King of Kings of Iranians and Non-Iranians. In *Des Indo-Grecs aux Sassanides: Données pour l'histoire et la géographie historique*, ed. R. Gyselen, 11–40. Bures-sur-Yvette: RO 17.

Bowman, R. A. 1970. *Aramaic ritual texts from Persepolis*. Chicago: OIP 91.

Boyce, M. 1975. *A history of Zoroastrianism*, vol. 1, *The early period*. Leiden: HdO 1/8/1/2/2A.

———. 1979. *Zoroastrians: Their religious beliefs and practices.* London: Routledge and Kegan Paul.
———. 1982. *Zoroastrianism*, vol. 2, *Under the Achaemenians.* Leiden: HdO 1/8/1/2/2A.
Briant, P. 1996. *Histoire de l'Empire perse de Cyrus à Alexandre.* Paris: Fayard.
Cameron, G. G. 1948. *Persepolis Treasury Tablets.* Chicago: OIP 65.
De Jong, A. 2010. Religion at the Achaemenid court. In *Der Achämenidenhof/The Achaemenid Court*, ed. B. Jacobs und R. Rollinger, 533–58. Wiesbaden: CLeO 2.
Duchesne-Guillemin, J. 1962. *La religion de l'Iran ancien.* Paris: Presses universitaires de France.
———. 1972. La religion des Achéménides. In *Beiträge zur Achämenidengeschichte*, ed. G. Walser, 59–82. Wiesbaden: Historia-Einzelschriften 18.
Finkel, I. L. 2013. *The Cyrus Cylinder: The Great Persian edict from Babylon.* London: I. B. Tauris.
Gyselen, R. 2001. Les sceaux des mages de l'Iran sassanide. In *Au carrefour des religions: Mélanges offerts à Philippe Gignoux*, ed. R. Gyselen, 121–50. Bures-sur-Yvette: RO 7.
Hallock, R. T. 1969. *Persepolis Fortification Tablets.* Chicago: OIP 92.
Henkelman, W. F. M. 2008. *The other gods who are: Studies in Elamite-Iranian acculturation based on the Persepolis Fortification Texts.* Leiden: AchHist 14.
Hintze, A. 1994. *Zamyād-Yašt. Edition, Übersetzung, Kommentar.* Wiesbaden: L. Reichert.
———. 2007. *A Zoroastrian liturgy: The worship in seven chapters (Yasna 35–41).* Wiesbaden: Harrassowitz.
Humbach, H. 1959. *Die Gathas des Zarathustra.* Heidelberg: C. Winter.
Humbach, H., and P. O. Skjærvø. 1978–83. *The Sassanian inscription of Paikuli.* Wiesbaden: L. Reichert.
Huyse, P. 1999. *Die dreisprachige Inschrift Šābuhrs I. an der Kaʿba-i Zardušt (ŠKZ).* 2 vols. London: CII 3/1/1.
Insler, S. 1975. *The Gāthās of Zarathustra.* Tehran/Liège: Acta Iranica 8.
Kellens, J. 1991. *La religion iranienne à l'époque achéménide.* Gent: IrAnt Supplement 5.
———. 1998. Considérations sur l'histoire de l'Avesta. *JA* 286/2: 451–519.
———. 2002. L'idéologie religieuse des inscriptions achéménides. *JA* 290: 417–64.
Koch, H. 1977. *Die religiösen Verhältnisse der Dareioszeit. Untersuchungen an Hand der elamischen Persepolistäfelchen.* Wiesbaden: Göttinger Orientforschungen 3.4.
MacKenzie, D. N. 1989. Kerdir's inscription. In *The Sasanian rock reliefs at Naqsh-i Rustam 6*, ed. G. Hermann, 35–72. Berlin: Iranische Denkmäler 13/2/1.
Malandra, W. W. 1983. *An introduction to ancient Iranian religion: Readings from the Avesta and the Achaemenid inscriptions.* Minneapolis: University of Minnesota Press.
Panaino, A. 2007. Chronologia Avestica. In *Disputationes Iranologicae Vindobonenses*, vol. 1, ed. A. Panaino and V. Sadovski, 7–33. Vienna: Veröffentlichungen zur Iranistik 41.
———. 2010. Nuove considerazioni sul calendario cappadoce. Persistenze e adattamenti dell'eredità achemenide nella storia di un piccolo regno tra mondo macedone, seleucide, attalide, partico e romano. *Electrum* 18: 158–73.
———. 2009. The king and the gods in the Sasanian royal ideology. In *Sources pour l'histoire et la géographie du monde iranien (224–710)*, ed. R. Gyselen, 209–56. Bures-sur-Yvette: RO 18.
Porten, B. 1996. *The Elephantine papyri in English: Three millennia of cross-cultural continuity and change.* Leiden: Brill.
Razmjou, S. 2001. Des traces de la déesse Spenta-Ārmaiti à Persépolis et proposition pour une nouvelle lecture d'un logogramme élamite. *StIr* 30: 7–15.

———. 2004. The Lan ceremony and other ritual ceremonies in the Achaemenid period: The Persepolis Fortification Tablets. *Iran* 42: 103–17.
Rose, J. 2011. *Zoroastrianism: An introduction*. London: I. B. Tauris.
Schmidt, E. F. 1970. *Persepolis III: The royal tombs and other monuments*. Chicago: OIP 70.
Schmitt, R. 2009. *Die altpersischen Inschriften der Achaimeniden: Editio minor mit deutscher Übersetzung*. Wiesbaden: L. Reichert Verlag.
Schwartz, M. 1985. The religion of Achaemenian Iran. *CHI* 2: 664–97.
Skjærvø, P.O. 1991. Chinese Turkestan. ii. In pre-Islamic times: Iranian religious terms in pre-Islamic Central Asia and Inner Asia. *EnIr* 5: 469–71.
———. 1994. Hymnic composition in the Avesta. *Die Sprache* 36: 199–243.
———. 1995. The Avesta as source for the early history of the Iranians. In *The Indo-Aryans of Ancient South Asia*, ed. G. Erdosy, 155–75. Berlin: De Gruyter.
———. 2000. The joy of the cup: A pre-Sasanian Middle Persian inscription on a silver bowl. *BAI* 11: 93–104.
———. 2003–4. The antiquity of Old Avestan. *Nāme-ye Irān-e Bāstān* 3: 15–41.
———. 2005. The Achaemenids and the Avesta. In *Birth of the Persian Empire*, ed. V. S. Curtis and S. Stewart, 52–84. London: I. B. Tauris.
———. 2005–6. The importance of orality for the study of Old Iranian literature and myth. *Nāme-ye Irān-e Bāstān* 5: 1–23.
———. 2006. Iran iv. Iranian languages and scripts. *EnIr* 13: 344–77.
———. 2007. The *Videvdad*: Its ritual-mythical significance. In *The Age of the Parthians*, ed. V. S. Curtis and S. Stewart, 105–41. London: I. B. Tauris.
———. 2008. Jamšīd i. Myth of Jamšid. *EnIr* 14: 501–22.
———. 2011a. *The spirit of Zoroastrianism*. New Haven: Yale University Press.
———. 2011b. Kartir. *EnIr* 15/6: 608–28.
———. 2011c. review of Schmitt 2009. *OLZ* 106: 325b–28b.
———. 2011d. Zoroastrian dualism. In *Light against darkness: Dualism in ancient Mediterranean religion and the contemporary world*, ed. E. M. Meyers et al., 55–91. Göttingen: *Journal of Ancient Judaism* Supplement 2.
———. 2011e. Zarathustra: A revolutionary monotheist? In *Reconsidering the concept of revolutionary monotheism*, ed. B. Pongratz-Leisten, 325–58. Winona Lake: Eisenbrauns.
———. 2012. The *Avesta* and the Avestan languages. In *The Oxford Handbook of Iranian History*, ed. T. Daryaee, 57–119. Oxford: Oxford University Press.
———. 2013. Kayāniān. *EnIr*.
Waters, M. W. 1999. The earliest Persians in southwestern Iran: The textual evidence. *IrSt* 32: 99–107.
Weber, U. 2012. Narseh, König der Könige von Ērān und Anērān. *IrAnt* 47: 153–302.
Wiesehöfer, J. 1996. *Ancient Persia from 550 BC to 650 AD*. London: I. B. Tauris.
Zadok, R. 2001. On the location of NA Parsua. *NABU* 2001/28. http://www.achemenet.com; http://sepoa.fr/?page_id=208.

CHAPTER 29

ROYAL ACHAEMENID ICONOGRAPHY

MARK B. GARRISON

INTRODUCTION

Sometime in the early spring or summer of 522 BC, the Persian king Cambyses (r. 529–522 BC), son and legitimate successor to Cyrus the Great (558–530 BC), died. The death of Cambyses, of which we have conflicting ancient testimonia as to both cause and place, resulted in almost two years of civil war. The eventual successor was Darius I (521–486 BC). The exact events surrounding the death of Cambyses, the rival claimants to the throne, including possible impersonators of Cambyses' brother Bardiya (the first of whom is known by several names in the sources, Smerdis, Gaumata, etc.), and Darius' ultimate seizure of power have vexed historians for generations (the events and scholarship are most recently tracked in Briant 2002: 62–138, 898–9; cf. Kuhrt 2007: 135–77 with sources and commentary).

Darius claims in his victory monument at Bisotun (DB I 1–11) to be an Achaemenid, tracing his family back to the eponymous ancestor Achaemenes and giving his lineage as follows: Darius—Vištaspa (Gk. Hystapes)—Aršames—Ariaramna (Gk. Ariaramnes)—Čišpiš (Gk. Teispes)—Hakhaimaniš (Gk. Achaemenes). In this genealogy, the son of Achaemenes is one Teispes, whom most equate with the great-grandfather of Cyrus the Great. Thus, according to the Cyrus Cylinder (ll. 20–21) Cyrus' lineage is as follows: Cyrus – Cambyses – Cyrus I – Teispes. Darius' linkage to the Teispid royal house is suspect on several grounds, not least of which is the fact that in his inscriptions Cyrus always traces his ancestry back to a Teispes, not an Achaemenes, and styles himself and his ancestors as kings of Anšan. (On Cyrus' royal titulary, see Garrison 2011: 378–9, n. 5; Quintana 2011: 175–81; Waters 2011: 285–7, 289–93; for a translation with commentary of the Cyrus Cylinder, the most important text from Cyrus' reign, see Kuhrt 2007: 70–4, E.a.21; on the inscriptions at Pasargadae naming Cyrus as an Achaemenid, see below; for Darius' genealogy at Bisotun, see the refs. above and Vallat 2011. Henkelman 2011a is an important contribution that seeks to redress the traditional depiction of the antithesis between Cyrus and Darius; from an art historical perspective, as argued below, I see a distinct break in the visual presentations of kingship between Cyrus and Darius.)

The debates surrounding the nature of Darius' claim to kingship and his linkage to the Teispid line of kings at Anšan are significant in determining when and where one first identifies "royal Achaemenid iconography." This is not simply a trivial matter of nomenclature. For many years the architectural reliefs at Pasargadae, Cyrus' new imperial capital in the Persian heartland, have been treated as the first expression of "Achaemenid" art. In a narrative that now has considerable modern scholarly tradition behind it, Cyrus and the Achaemenids are linked to an emerging Indo-Iranian cultural consciousness (first attested in the literary tradition in Herodotus' *mēdikos logos*), one that marks a radical break with the millennia-old Sumero-Akkadian culture of the Mesopotamian flood plains and the Elamite culture of the lowlands and highlands of southwestern Iran.

This traditional narrative is now untenable. There is an emerging consensus on the nature of the ethnogenesis of the Persians in southwestern Iran. The Persian peoples in seventh to sixth century BC Fars were not ethnically pure Indo-Iranians, but were a culturally hybrid, multilingual group of Iranian clans whose experience (and bloodlines) were shaped by centuries of acculturation with Elamites in the highlands of eastern Elam (the scholarship on Elamite-Iranian acculturation is now considerable; the seminal study is Miroschedji 1985, but more recent summaries of the discussion may be found in Henkelman 2003a, 2008: 1–63, 2012; Garrison 2010; Álvarez-Mon, Garrison and Stronach 2011: 7–9). As Liverani (2003: 10) has so eloquently stated, "Persia is the heir of Elam, not of Media."

In many ways this recontextualizing of the formative period of the Persian empire was first initiated by the publication of two sets of administrative tablets written in cuneiform Elamite from Persepolis, known today as the Persepolis Fortification archive and the Persepolis Treasury archive, named after their find-spots in chambers of the fortification wall and the Treasury respectively (Hallock 1969; Cameron 1948; a comprehensive accounting of the texts and publications associated with the Fortification archive may be found in Henkelman 2008: 65–179; cf. *AFP*; Azzoni et al. forthcoming). The publication of 2087 Fortification texts by R. T. Hallock in 1969, followed slowly by the realization that there were thousands more Elamite documents from this archive, was especially critical in the growing awareness of the important role that Elam and Elamite culture had played in the formation of Persian culture.

Of the historicity of Darius' genealogy at Bisotun, there is still no consensus. A substantial number of scholars interpret Darius' claims of direct line of succession as, at best, a very generous understanding of the concept of the Old Persian *taumā*—("extended family, clan"), at worst an outright fabrication. There is no denying, however, that Darius was a leading member of one of the elite Persian clans, the Achaemenids, and that he successfully forged alliances with the leading members of other elite clans so as to become king. Briant (2002: 110–14) and Kuhrt (2007: 135–9) provide forceful presentations of the difficulties of accepting at face value Darius' account at Bisotun. As Henkelman notes, the issue is not that Darius came to power based upon a lie, but that, in the chaotic circumstances surrounding the death of Cambyses, he, amongst a number of claimants, emerged as the victor (Henkelman 2011a).

In his inscription at Bisotun, Darius seems at pains to downplay the house of Teispes. It is Darius' "Achaemenid-ness" that marks him as the legitimate heir. In a similar manner, Darius promotes his Aryan (OP *arya-*) lineage at Bisotun and in other royal texts. Henkelman (2012) eloquently states that, rhetorically, "the *use* of 'Aryan' strikes me as a conspicuous parallel to the use of 'Anšan' in Cyrus' titulature. 'Anšan' and 'Aryan' are both deployed to construct a royal self-image on top of an existing and widely-accepted ethnic and cultural identity" (on the term Aryan, cf. Briant 2002: 180–1). Darius' rhetoric of kingship and the visual expression of that rhetoric are very different from that of Cyrus and seem intended to mark a distinction with the Teispid rulers of Anšan. This distinction does not mark a cultural or ethnic rupture—both Cyrus and Darius are Persians from the highlands of Fars—but a political one (on continuities between Cyrus and Darius, see Henkelman 2011a). These observations carry far-reaching implications for our conceptualization of royal Achaemenid art. In a strict definition, one that will be followed in this chapter, royal Achaemenid art begins with the first Achaemenid king, Darius I (cf. Briant 2002: 110–11 on Darius' conceptualization of "Achaemenid" as a political phenomenon, "direct line" of succession within a particular family, rather than a clan designation).

The seminal work on Achaemenid imperial art by Margaret Cool Root (1979) was an important watershed in the discipline. Root articulated the overarching program of imperial Achaemenid art and dispelled the long-held notion that Achaemenid art was essentially debased Greek art (based upon the superficial resemblance of some formal aspects of Achaemenid art with Greek art of the late Archaic period). Her work not only firmly grounded the formative phases of imperial Achaemenid iconography in the visual traditions of Assyria, Babylonia, and Egypt, but also carefully articulated the complexity of the Achaemenid imperial message in art.

Root also provided a working definition of "Achaemenid art" that may provide a basis for the discussion of royal Achaemenid iconography. In her definition, Achaemenid art is the official art of the Achaemenid dynasty, an art that "speaks for that empire ... in the service of kingship" (Root 1979: 1). While the king figures prominently in this official art, the king per se is not a *sine qua non* for imagery to qualify as royal.

PREDECESSORS AND PRECEDENTS FOR ROYAL ACHAEMENID ICONOGRAPHY

After his initial seizure of power in 521 BC, Darius had to face down a series of revolts that lasted until July of 521 BC. Thereafter, the authority of Darius as the king of Persia was relatively secure and he could turn his attention to the expansion of the imperial domains and the creation of a program in art and texts to legitimize and solidify his rule. That territory eventually included a vast and ethnically diverse region that stretched from Thrace and Egypt in the west to India and Sogdiana in the east. The ideological program that he devised in images and texts may be one of the most sophisticated to have survived from ancient western Asia.

Darius did not emerge from a sociopolitical vacuum. Indeed, it was just the opposite. The Teispid line of kings at Anšan controlled an immense expanse of territory stretching from eastern Iran to Egypt. Darius himself was a member of an elite Persian family and had traveled to Egypt as a high-ranking official in Cambyses' imperial retinue. As Root (1979: 28–42) and Briant (2002: 17–18) have shown, Darius and his ancestors were not naïve, tent-dwelling nomads but sophisticated players accustomed to high-stakes politics on an international stage. The Persian clans were well versed in the cultural politics of their day and must have had a keen conception of not only the expanse and workings of the Teispid empire, but also its political predecessors in Babylonia and Assyria. As such, Darius had at his call various models for consideration in devising and articulating an imperial program in texts and images (see Root 1979 for potential prototypes of Achaemenid monumental art). These models existed not only as cultural memories, but also in the lived landscape in the form of capital cities and rock-reliefs.

In Fars itself were the two Teispid capital cites, long-lived Anšan (modern Tal-e Malyan), which had been a traditional Elamite highland capital for at least 1400 years, and Pasargadae, recently founded by Cyrus the Great. For us today, the status and very existence of Anšan in the first millennium BC are subjects of some debate (see the summary of the site in Hansman 1987; Garrison 2011 discusses connections between Persepolis and Anšan at the time of Darius; Potts 2005 and 2011 explores the issues surrounding Anšan from Cyrus II to Darius I; recently, two possible Achaemenid-period column bases were found near the site; see Boucharlat 2005: 230–1). The site is named in the Fortification archive, but whether this Anšan in any sense represents the remnants of the capital city (rather than simply a small settlement on or nearby the ancient remains of the site) is not known (see, for example, the discussion in Potts 2011; both Potts 2011: 41 and Waters 2011: 287 note what is often overlooked, the important passage at DB III 21–28, where "the Persian army which [was] in the palace, [and which had been called up] from Anšan previously" went over to the rebel Vahyazdāta; the passage is not, however, without some difficulties, see Schmitt 1991: 64, commentary on l. 26, whence the translation). That it figures so prominently in Cyrus' rhetoric and that it occurs in the inscription on the remarkable heirloom seal PFS 93* from the Fortification archive suggest that the site was a functioning capital city at the time of the early Teispids and, thus, visible in some form to Darius and his planners (Garrison 2011 discusses the historical context of PFS 93*, which carries an inscription naming one Kuraš, the Anzanite [or from Anšan], the son of Šešpeš; cf. the comments of Potts 2011: 41 concerning Darius and Anšan).

Pasargadae, Cyrus' capital city, must have been in good condition in the early years of Darius' reign, the existing monumental reliefs fully visible; many of the planners and workers from that site would also still have been alive and so available to Darius when he became king in 522 BC. There is a long-running debate concerning the possibility that Darius added inscriptions and even some reliefs to the architectural sculpture on the site. Certainly, the overall sculptural program at Pasargadae seems uneven, although the architectural sculpture from the site is in a poor state of preservation. So, too, stylistically there is a variety of carving styles in the surviving monumental sculpture (the monumental sculpture and architecture at the site were published by Stronach 1978; updated bibliography in Boucharlat 2005: 228-9 and Stronach and Gopnik 2009). A treasury may have been located there (Henkelman 2008: 431) and Classical sources indicate that in the later Achaemenid period royal investiture took place there (Henkelman 2011b: 109, 111) as well as ongoing sacrifices at the tomb of Cyrus (Henkelman 2003b: 152-6).

The relief of the four-winged figure from Gate R is exemplary of the problems one encounters in understanding the sculpture from Pasargadae. Although many of the reliefs from Pasargadae had been known, drawn, and studied much earlier, Stronach (1978: 44-55, pls. 40-9) stands as the official publication of the relief (cf. Root 1979: 46-9, 295, 300-3 for valuable commentary and Stronach 1997b: 42-4). Herzfeld had suggested that the doorways on the short sides of the building were lined with colossal winged bulls (on the southeastern door) and winged human-headed bulls (on the northwestern door) facing outwards, although this reconstruction has never been definitely confirmed (Stronach 1978: 44 reviews the evidence). Of the small fragments of these creatures that remain, Stronach (1978: 51) noted that they are carved in an Assyrian style.

The relief is preserved on the only standing doorjamb in Gate R, the eastern of the northeastern door. It is assumed that similar figures stood in the other three doorjambs. Above the four-winged figure, but no longer extant, was the trilingual inscription CMa: "I am Cyrus the King, an Achaemenid" (trans. Waters 1996, 14). The same inscription is found on corner wall blocks in Palace S and Palace P. The vexing problem of the date of all of the inscriptions that mention Cyrus at Pasargadae remains open, although the bulk of scholarly opinion now favors attributing all of these inscriptions to the reign of Darius I (Stronach 1978: 102-3, 1990, 1997a, 1997b: 48-9; Waters 1996; and Briant 2002: 63, 889 provide overviews of the arguments with previous literature).

The winged figure is clearly Assyrian in inspiration. Stronach (1978: 51, 1997a: 42-3), following Herzfeld, highlighted the late eighth-century winged genius from Sargon II's palace at Khorsabad as the conceptual source for the Pasargadae figure. Root (1979: 302) places the stylistic rendering of the internal parts of the wings of the figure in the time of Aššurnasirpal II. Boardman (2000: 102) identifies the inspiration for the Pasargadae figure in "Egyptianizing figures of the Levant coast, probably Phoenicia," and suggests that it "was Cyrus' bid to invoke divine support from the deities of the subject peoples." The iconography is, however, a mix, including an Egyptianizing headdress, Assyrianizing wings, an Elamite(?) garment, and so on, and there are some peculiarities of style. There is much speculation as to the identity of the winged figure and its function (Stronach 1978: 53-5, 1997a: 42-3; Root 1979: 301-3; and Garrison forthcoming a survey the various interpretations). Perhaps the one positive thing that one may conclude about the sculpture in Gate R is that the program and style are deeply rooted in the Assyrian tradition. The winged figure, its garment, and its headdress do not occur again in surviving Achaemenid monumental sculpture or coinage. Winged humanoid figures do occur in Persepolitan glyptic, but they never wear the type of garment and headdress seen on the winged figure in Gate R.

Doorjamb reliefs, in a very fragmentary state of preservation, are also found in Palace S at Pasargadae. Presumably all four doorways to the main hall carried sculpture, although nothing is preserved in the northeastern doorway above the level of the dado course (Stronach 1978: pl. 61b). The surviving reliefs are processional in character, consisting of human figures and composite creatures (Stronach 1978: figs. 34–6). The compositions and iconography of the sculpture on the northwestern and southeastern doorways are again deeply indebted to Assyrian prototypes (Stronach 1997b: 44); the particular figures found in these processional compositions do not occur in Achaemenid monumental art or coinage. The figure in a fish-skin cloak occurs on one known seal from Persepolis (PFUTS 3, Garrison 2008: figs. 14–17). Taloned, composite creatures, and rampant bulls (and bull creatures) are very common in Persepolitan glyptic. The processional scene on the southwestern doorjamb showing three human figures and a bovine recalls both Assyrian scenes and several tribute delegations on the Apadana at Persepolis (Stronach 1978: 69–70; Calmeyer 1994: 135–6).

The fragmentarily preserved architectural sculpture in Palace P at Pasargadae has a very different quality than that in Palace S and Gate R (Root 1979: 49–58; Calmeyer 1981). The jambs on the northwestern and southeastern doorways carried identical scenes: the Persian king wearing the court robe and strapless boots processes out of the hall followed by an attendant dressed in the Persian court robe and strapped boots (only the lower legs of the figures are preserved; holes for metal attachments are indicated). The king is at a larger scale than the attendant and holds a staff vertically in front of his body. A diagonal fold on each side of the central pleat of the royal figures carries the inscription CMc (in Babylonian and Elamite): "Cyrus, the Great King, an Achaemenid." A part of the Old Persian version of the inscription was found on a sleeve fragment from Stronach's excavations, but Stronach (1978: 93) judged that that fragment was not from the doorway reliefs of Palace P. Another trilingual inscription, CMb, decorated the upper part of the doorjambs (no longer *in situ*).

There has long been debate on the date of the execution of the reliefs in Palace P: Cyrus or Darius (Calmeyer 1987a: 571 surveys the arguments, with references)? The issue is not a purely chronological one. The reliefs in Palace P exhibit several of the hallmarks of what we could call "classical royal Achaemenid art," as seen at Naqsh-e Rustam and Persepolis:

1. the king in procession followed by attendant(s);
2. the king holding a long staff;
3. the Persian court robe rendered in a distinctive manner in which the lower part of the garment has a thick central vertical fold from which depend diagonal folds;
4. two different renderings of boots/shoes, one with straps, the other without (and worn only by the king);
5. trilingual inscriptions that name the king.

Thus, if the reliefs indeed date to the time of Cyrus, it would imply that classical royal Achaemenid art had its origins under this ruler. The evidence for this question is varied and its interpretation open to several lines of reasoning. The general consensus today is that the reliefs from Palace P and all the inscriptions from Pasargadae date to the reign of Darius (Stronach and Gopnik 2009; Boucharlat 2005: 228). Indeed, the reliefs in Palace P are so different in conception from those in Gate R and Palace S that, were they dated to the reign of Cyrus, they would imply a radical change in Cyrus' visual program *in medias res*. Here I am thinking not only with regard to compositional formula, for example, the inclusion of the royal figure, but also the greatly reduced Assyrianizing imagery. So, too, given how Darius seems at pains to articulate a new rhetoric of a distinctively Achaemenid (as opposed to Anšanite) kingship, it seems inconceivable that Darius would adopt such specific compositional, iconographical, and stylistic formulae so closely associated with Cyrus. Lastly, based upon the glyptic evidence from the Fortification and Treasury archives, the last decade of the sixth century BC appears to have been a time when classical royal Achaemenid art (in glyptic, at least) was canonized (see the discussion below). Of course, our evidence from those archives may have internal biases of which we are as yet not fully aware, but it seems striking that rather suddenly in 503/502 BC there appear in the Fortification archive two magnificent royal-name seals, PFS 7* and PFS 11*, that epitomize the classic Achaemenid court style in glyptic (see, e.g., the comments in Garrison 2014). It seems also noteworthy that of the now over 3000 distinct seals identified in the Fortification archive, relatively few are executed in the classic glyptic Court Style. The rarity of the Court Style in the glyptic from the Fortification archive may indicate that the formulation of the style was a recent phenomenon and that there were few examples of it in circulation.

Moving out of Fars, the two closest imperial capitals are the Median one at Ecbatana (modern Hamadan) and the lowland Elamite one at Susa. Both are, unfortunately, as opaque as the Teispid capital at Anšan. Suffice to say that there does not exist for the moment an archaeology of Median Ecbatana (see, e.g., Brown 1997, with extensive bibliography; Sarraf 2003; Boucharlat 2005: 253–4). The "Median question" is much debated (numerous contributions in *CE* question the existence of a united Median kingdom, cf. Rollinger 2008 and 2010 on the extent of Median political control), as is the lack of any securely identifiable Median art (Muscarella 1987; cf. Stronach 2003; Razmjou 2005; and Roaf 2010 for recent surveys of the evidence with more optimistic perspectives on the identification of Median material culture). Herodotus' *mēdikos logos* is also a topic of considerable debate with a lengthy bibliography (e.g., Briant 2002: 25–7, 879–80; Briant 1997: 45–6; 2001: 79; Rollinger 2010). Even the Achaemenid levels at Ecbatana are patchy (see Kuhrt 2007, 497–501, nos. 14–15, Fig. 11.13 for an inscribed column base said to have come from Ecbatana).

Neo-Elamite Susa is only marginally better represented in the archaeological record. For some 3500 years Susa had been one of the premier sites of the Elamite lowlands (Steve et al. 2002–3; Boucharlat 2005: 240–6). The condition of the site in the Neo-Elamite period and the century leading up to the reign of Darius is not well known, largely because Achaemenid building on the site, which was extensive, was highly destructive to earlier first millennium BC levels (Steve et al. 2002–3: 470). The Achaemenid building program at Susa has been discussed by a number of scholars (e.g., *RCS*: 216–18, 223–41; Steve et al. 2002–3: 486–95; essays in *PDS*; Henkelman 2012).

A few rock-cut reliefs of local kings of the first millennium BC do survive in the Elamite highlands; those at Kul-e Farah and Kurangun (located closer to Anšan than Susa) in particular resonate with some aspects of the visual program at Persepolis (Henkelman 2011b: 128–33 on Kul-e Farah; 2008: 44 on Kurangun, both with extensive bibliographies).

Farther to the northwest lay hoary Babylon, the premier religious site in Mesopotamia. Cyrus had placed particular importance in claiming kingship in Babylon (Kuhrt 2007: 70–84 for relevant texts). Despite the fact that Neo-Babylonian levels and monumental architecture are well preserved at the site, the evidence for visual strategies articulating late Neo-Babylonian imperial ideologies is, unfortunately, uneven. The scholarship on Neo-Babylonian imperial policy is considerable (Kuhrt 1995: 573–622; Joannès 2004: 112–202; on the Neo-Babylonian court, see Riva 2010; Jursa 2011) but few images of Neo-Babylonian kings actually survive in the archaeological record (Ehrenberg 2008). Thus, it is difficult to know precisely what imperial visual programs may have existed. This may be why, in general, Babylonian influences on Achaemenid royal imagery seem rare.

The Assyrian imperial capitals in northern Iraq, Nimrud, Nineveh, and Khorsabad, appear to have been quite influential in some aspects of the formation of the early Achaemenid imperial visual program (Root 1979: 202–18; Feldman 2007 attempts to link the relief at Bisotun with Akkadian visual prototypes). Assyrian glyptic seems also to have played a considerable role in the development of Achaemenid glyptic (Garrison 2000). The exact condition of these Assyrian capital cities at the time of Cyrus, Cambyses, and Darius I is not known. Were large sections of the wall reliefs in some or all of the palaces still visible? While the general scholarly consensus is that these sites were for the most part destroyed in 612 BC, the influence of Assyrian monumental sculpture in the surviving reliefs from the Achaemenid homeland is so pronounced that one suspects that large sections of the palaces were still standing and visible in the sixth century BC (on the condition of Assyrian palaces post–612 BC, see, e.g., Dalley 1993; Dandamaev 1997; Oates and Oates 2001: 257–9; Curtis 2003, 2005). Whether actually visible or not, by some mechanism much of the basic structure of Assyrian royal imagery, as well as stylistic idioms, were available to Darius and his planners. It is conceivable that this information had been preserved, and handled down, via imperial workshops and/or artisans at Babylon and Ecbatana and in local court settings in both the lowlands and highlands of Elam (see Álvarez-Mon 2011 for Assyrianizing imagery in local court contexts in the highlands of Elam; Parpola 2010: 39–42 identifies imperial courts, court scholars [scribes], libraries, and temples and mystery cults as "channels of transmission" for the perpetuation of the constituent elements of Neo-Assyrian kingship into later periods). The continued circulation of Assyrian seals would also have been a mode of transmission, but the thematic repertoire in Assyrian glyptic is in many ways very different from that in Assyrian monumental relief; it is difficult to envision Assyrian glyptic having served as a significant model for Achaemenid monumental sculpture in Fars.

Lastly, Darius spent time in Egypt in the retinue of Cambyses. He thus would have had some exposure to the millennia-old reliefs in royal mortuary complexes and temples (particularly those in the north) and perhaps even reliefs and painting in some tombs (Root 1979: 39, 138–47, 218–22, 240–50, 270–2).

Early royal Achaemenid art: Bisotun

In what follows, I concentrate on monuments and glyptic from the imperial heartland of southwestern Iran, consisting of the highlands of Fars and the Elamite lowlands centered on Susa, and western Iran. Many commentators (e.g., Calmeyer 1987a; Farkas 1974) distinguish multiple phases in the development of Achaemenid art; this is not necessary for the purposes of the present analysis. I distinguish between early royal Achaemenid art (Bisotun) and classical royal Achaemenid art (architectural sculpture at Persepolis and Susa, the royal tombs at Naqsh-e Rustam, coinage of types I and II, and glyptic from the Fortification and Treasury archives). I also expand the boundaries of the inquiry to include not only iconography, but also compositional formulae and carving styles.

Achaemenid royal iconography is easily recognizable, consisting of a distinctive assemblage of:

1. garments (the so-called Persian court robe and the Iranian tunic and trousers);
2. headdresses (generally a banded dentate crown for the king, fluted or domed headdresses or fillets for Persian nobility);
3. hairstyles and beards (long, curly, squared beard for the king, short-cropped, curly beards for Persian nobility);
4. weapons (bow, quiver, bowcase, spear, or dagger);
5. animals and creatures (lion, bull, often winged and human-headed);
6. figure in the winged ring/disk or the winged ring/disk;
7. plants (rosette, date palm, conifer, palmettes);
8. celestial symbols (star and crescent);
9. paneled inscriptions (Old Persian, Elamite, and/or Babylonian).

While the iconography of royal Achaemenid art is uniform, the compositional syntax is highly complex. Different media, monumental relief, glyptic, and coinage tend to have distinct compositional formats. Although admitting much variation, balanced compositions, often expressed as antithetical groupings, figure prominently. Other expressions of this interest in balanced composition are the many mirrored doorjambs that are such a distinctive feature of Persepolitan architecture. Conceptual themes that overlap the various media include control and order, spiritual and cosmic authority/legitimacy, and ascension (ascension: winged figures, raised platforms, pedestal creatures, atlantids, etc.; for an overview of the ideological aspects of Achaemenid monumental arts, see, e.g., Root 1979: 310–11; Ahn 1992; Briant 2002: 204–25; Jacobs 2002, 2010; Brosius 2005; Kuhrt 2010; Garrison 2011c).

Darius' first monument remains today his best known: the rock-cut relief and inscriptions at Bisotun (Gr. *Bagístanon*; OP **Bagastana*, "place/stand of the god(s)"; in modern times various other forms of the placename have been used; see Schmitt 1990a: 289–90). Carved on the sheer cliff face of the mountain, some 66 m above the springs on the plain, the relief looks out over the Great Khorasan Road that links the Tigris and Euphrates alluvial plains with Central Asia. Owing to the role that the inscriptions played in the initial study of the cuneiform script in the nineteenth century, the texts have tended to overshadow the relief (Schmitt 1990b: 299, "This inscription is the most important document of the entire ancient Near East"; cf. Dandamaev 1976: 1–22 for historiographic discussion of Bisotun; Luschey 1968 remains essential; see Borger 1982 and Schmitt 1990b on the stages of execution of the monument; Root 1979: 182–226 is a wide-ranging and important discussion; for bibliography see Kent 1953: 1–5; Root 1979: 59–61, 182–226; Schmitt 1990a, 1990b; Luschey 1990). There are four cuneiform inscriptions, one in Old Persian, one in Babylonian, and two in Elamite. The monument that we see today was modified at several stages in a relatively short period of time. It was completed before 519 BC, as attested by the added text (DB V) and relief (the rebel Skunkha the Scythian), the latter necessitating the partial destruction of the original Elamite text and the creation of a second Elamite text (Root 1979: 60–1). Some of the changes would seem to represent rather major modifications of the conception of the monument (Schmitt 1990b: 301).

There are many aspects of the composition, iconography, and style of the relief that are not repeated in classical royal Achaemenid art. For this reason, the relief at Bisotun is something of an outlier within the Achaemenid repertoire. The early date of the relief indicates that planning for it must have begun almost immediately after July 521 BC in a period of rapidly moving events (see above). The changes to the relief within a relatively short span of time may also suggest that planning was in a fluid state, the conception experimental.

The theme of defeated enemies being presented to the Achaemenid king is found only in a handful of Achaemenid seals of later date. So, too, the relief at Bisotun remains the only Achaemenid monument that unambiguously seeks to commemorate known and specific historical events. Root (1979: 182–226) has traced the complex origins of the imagery at Bisotun. The most critical models were the rock-cut relief of Anubanini at Sar-e Pol-e Zohāb (late Ur III or early Old Babylonian in date?) and Assyrian palace reliefs (ninth to seventh centuries BC).

While the overall theme is unique in Achaemenid monumental art, there are select aspects of the presentation that anticipate classical royal Achaemenid art. These include:

1. highlighting of the king through hieratic scale;
2. the presence of attendants who stand behind the king holding weapons;

3. the presence of a figure in a winged ring hovering above the scene;
4. the pose of the king standing, the one hand raised, palm cupped and facing forward, the other hand holding a bow.

Iconographic details that also anticipate classical royal Achaemenid art include:

1. the king wears a headdress that consists of a decorated headband topped by dentate extensions; the attendants wear headbands decorated with rosettes;
2. the king and his attendants wear a distinctive court garment (the Persian court robe) that is belted at the waist and has large, billowy sleeves; diagonal folds fall from a central vertical pleat on the lower part of the garment (see in general Sekunda 2010; Stronach 2011);
3. the king wears strapless boots, his attendants strapped ones;
4. the royal bow(s) and quiver; the bows have duck-head terminals;
5. the king has a long, curly, thick beard; his attendants have close-cropped curly beards;
6. the king and his attendants have curly locks of hair bunched in a mass at the back of the neck;
7. the king and attendants wear bracelets;
8. the figure in the winged ring holds a ring in one hand (Kuhrt 2010: 92 n. 41 distinguishes this ring from the traditional ring and staff or rod held by deities in Mesopotamia);
9. the figure in the winged ring is essentially a duplicate of the king as regards facial features, hair and beard, garment, and pose (with the exception of one hand holding a ring);
10. trilingual inscriptions are included.

Many of these iconographic details at Bisotun are, however, rendered in a unique or highly decorative manner. For example, the king's crown is very elaborate, the headband decorated with a frieze of alternating stars and interlocking lotuses, the dentals crenellated. The king's beard is very broad and squared; its shape and the arrangement of the curls are exceptionally Assyrianizing (Root 1979: 215, where the specific parallels noted are Sargon and Aššurbanipal). Later renderings of the royal beard have it narrowing at its tip and the curls are treated differently. At several places in the relief there are separate pieces of carved stone that have been inserted into the relief: Darius' beard; most of the bow held by Darius (with the exception of the terminals); a section of the top of the bow (below the upper terminal) held by the attendant immediately behind Darius; the top of the crown worn by the figure in the winged ring; the right hand of the figure in the winged ring. It is not known whether these insertions, especially those to the figure in the winged ring, simply represent corrections to rock unsuitable for carving or mark substantial programmatic changes. Stronach (1997b: 46) describes the circular device atop the crown worn by the figure in the winged ring as a "conscious addition to the original design."

The treatment of the diagonal folds on the lower part of the Persian court robe is softer and the hemline contours are more active than seen in the later period (cf. Root 1979: 215–17 on the Assyrianizing features of the hemlines on the Persian court robes). The figure in the winged ring wears an exceptional headdress consisting of a *polos* that carries four superimposed rings at its base (in classical royal Achaemenid art the figure in the winged ring or disk wears a headdress identical to that of the king). The front of the headdress is very damaged; in most reconstructions, no longer extant horns have been restored above these rings at the front of the headdress Luschey (1968: 80–1, fig. 4) restored along the top of the *polos* a scalloped edge (feathers?), which is difficult to see in published photographs of the rock surface itself (first-hand examination is needed in order to confirm its existence). Above the *polos* a polygonal-shaped piece of stone has been inserted into the rock, a metal clamp holding it in place. On this piece of stone is carved an eight-pointed star symbol within a disk: following Stronach (1997b: 48), "eight arms of the disk that caps the crown of Ahuramazda." The eight points can clearly be seen in a recent publication (Alram 2003: fig. 4; cf. Root 1979: 186: "a seven-pointed star symbol"). Of an iron peg jutting out more than three inches from the god's crown, Cameron (1950: 843–4) claimed that it "was surmounted by a silver or gold ball which glittered in the sun to indicate the deity." Finally, a ribbon or plait emerges from the back of the hair to hang down along the figure's back.

Lastly, it bears noting that while the chronicle-like nature of the texts at Bisotun is not repeated, the first-person narration is.

In conclusion, Bisotun is a monument that, while anticipating many of the conventions of classical royal Achaemenid art, is highly experimental and assertively Assyrianizing in composition and in select aspects of iconography and style.

CLASSICAL ROYAL ACHAEMENID ART: NAQSH-E RUSTAM, PERSEPOLIS, AND SUSA

The last decade of the sixth century BC appears to mark a turning point in Darius' reign. The period may have been something of an interlude for the king. The first ten years of his reign had been given over to quelling revolts followed by territorial expansion to the west (e.g., Samos, Egypt, Scythia, and Thrace) and the east (India) (Briant 2002: 139–46, 904–5). The next phase of expansion, the wars in the west, would not begin until *c*.500 BC. Thus, the last decade of the sixth century BC may have provided a respite, a space in which Darius could turn to articulating a more comprehensive statement of Achaemenid royal ideology. The evidence that we have is plentiful, consisting of the rock-cut tomb relief of Darius at Naqsh-e Rustam, architectural reliefs on the Apadana and the Palace of Darius at Persepolis, glazed relief bricks from the palace at Susa, royal coinage, and glyptic preserved in substantial numbers via impressions in the Persepolis

Fortification archive and the Persepolis Treasury archive (in the discussion that follows, relief on buildings postdating Darius at Persepolis is also noted: the Central Building [late Darius or Xerxes]; the "Harem" of Xerxes; the Palace of Xerxes; the Throne Hall [Xerxes–Artaxerxes I]; and Palace H [Xerxes–Artaxerxes I, with added reliefs of Artaxerxes III]).

This new program was a major conceptual break from Bisotun but, as we have seen, many aspects of iconography are carried over. Thematically, classical royal Achaemenid art stressed an ahistorical perspective on kingship, one that articulated a cosmic harmony based upon a divinely sponsored (and thus legitimate) kingship. Broadly speaking, six compositional formats account for the majority of scene types in classical royal Achaemenid art:

1. the seated or standing king, sometimes in reception, with trusted attendants who stand, sometimes holding the royal weapons (bow, quiver, battle-axe, and/or spear);
2. the king standing before an altar and/or tower-like structure;
3. the king controlling or in combat with animals or fantastical creatures;
4. the king shooting a bow and arrow;
5. antithetical compositions involving humans, animals, or fantastical creatures;
6. a lion and bull group.

The king always wears the Persian court robe. The issue of crowns (see, e.g., Calmeyer 1993; Henkelman 1995-6; Dusinberre 2002; Tuplin 2007, with extensive bibliography) is complicated at Persepolis owing to the use of metal attachments and paint (no longer preserved). At Naqsh-e Rustam the king and the figure in the winged disk wear dentate or crenellated crowns (Garrison 2011c). In coinage and glyptic, the king invariably wears a dentate crown. Attendants can wear either the Persian court robe or a garment consisting of a tunic and trousers, what is sometimes called the Iranian riding habit, and carry or wear weapons (Achaemenid garment types, and their origins, are much discussed; see, e.g., Sekunda 2010 and Stronach 2011, with very different readings of the evidence; the issue is clouded by the evidence of Greek sources, which do not accord with the Iranian visual evidence; the use of the term "Median garment" for the tunic and trousers is modern and erroneous; cf. Stronach 2011). Many of these compositional formats may include the figure in the winged ring or disk, a winged ring or disk, star, and/or crescent (Garrison forthcoming a, forthcoming b).

Seated or standing king with attendants

The Apadana is the *locus classicus* for the seated king with attendants (for the Apadana, see Schmidt 1953: 70–106; Walser 1966; Krefter 1971: 45–54; Tilia 1972: 127–36; 1978: 11–27; Root 1979: 86–95, 227–84; Roaf 1983: 47–64, 114–20; Calmeyer 1982, 1983,

1987b; Stronach 1987; Sancisi-Weerdenburg 1991; Root 1985, 2003, 2007, 2008, 2011; Jacobs 1997; Kleiss 2000; Huff 2010). The reliefs are disposed across two stairway façades of the building, the northern and eastern ones, in a complex and extended scene of gift or tribute reception (sometimes called an audience scene [Schmidt 1953: pls. 16–17, 19–22, 27–54, 57–61]). The royal retinue in the original central panels of the stairways is extensive (Schmidt 1953: pls. 121–3; Krefter 1971: Beilagen 4 [with replacement panels] and 16 [reconstructed original central panels]). Behind the king stands the crown prince, a figure holding a towel or scarf, and a weapon-bearer. In front of the king are two incense-burners and a figure who bows holding a hand before his mouth. All of these individuals stand beneath a canopy. At each edge of the composition, and outside of the canopy, are two figures: before the king, one holds a spear and the other a pail; behind the king, one holds a spear and the other a pole supporting a square standard. All figures wear the Persian court robe, with the exception of the figure who bows and the weapon-bearer, both of whom are dressed in the tunic and trousers. The king holds a flower and a long staff, the crown prince a flower. Both the standing crown prince and the seated king are on an elevated platform.

An abbreviated version of the central scene on the original Apadana panels, king and crown prince under a canopy, is repeated on one set of doorjambs of the Central Building, but here the king and crown prince are raised aloft by personifications of the subject peoples of the empire; a figure in a winged ring holding a ring hovers above the scene (Schmidt 1953: pls. 77–80; Root 1979: 95–100). The structure is also known as the Tripylon and the Council Hall. The building may date to late in the reign of Darius. Since there is no inscriptional evidence associated with the Central Building (unlike the Apadana and the Palace of Darius), a dating in the reign of Darius relies on stylistic analysis of the sculpture, comparison of iconographic details of that sculpture (e.g., the forms of the crowns) to other reliefs, the likelihood that the scene of the king and crown prince date to the reign of Darius, and the perceived topographical relationship of the building to the Apadana. Root (1979: 98–100), with some caveats, suggests late Darius; Roaf (1983: 142–4), late Xerxes for the main hall, Artaxerxes I for the north stairs. The so-called Throne Hall at Persepolis also shows abbreviated versions of the scene of the seated king with attendant(s) supported by personifications of the subject lands of the empire (two sets of doorjambs; Schmidt 1953: pls. 102–13) or antithetically posed guards (two sets of doorjambs; Schmidt 1953: pls. 91, 96–101).

Only a handful of seals show the seated king with attendants, the best known of which is the royal-name seal from Daskyleion (in Old Persian, naming Artaxerxes), showing an interesting adaptation of the central scene on the Apadana (Kaptan 2002: no. DS 4). Schmitt suggests that the seal may in fact exist in duplicate (Kaptan 2002: 194–5). Kaptan (2002: 31–40) discusses audience scenes of the Achaemenid period and beyond in some detail (cf. Root 1979: 227–84 on the Near Eastern prototypes and extensive analyses of the scene on the Apadana; Allen 2005: 39–62 on the royal audience scene in Achaemenid art and its reception in Greek and later periods).

The other iteration of this static scene shows the king standing followed by attendants holding a parasol, flywhisk, and/or towel and bowl. Variations of the scene are found on various structures on the *takht* including two sets of doorjambs in the Palace of Darius and two sets of doorjambs in the Central Building; those in the Central Building have a figure in a winged ring holding a ring hovering over the scene (Schmidt 1953: pls. 75–6 [Central Building], 138–41 [Palace of Darius]; the scene is also found on two sets of doorjambs in the "Harem" of Xerxes, see Schmidt 1953: pls. 193–4, and at least four sets of doorjambs in the Palace of Xerxes, see Schmidt 1953: pls. 178–82).

Perhaps conceptually connected to these static scenes of the seated or standing king with attendants are the many files of domestic attendants and palace guards that occur on numerous structures at Persepolis. Domestic attendants appear on seven sets of doorjambs and two stairways in the Palace of Darius (Schmidt 1953: pls. 132–5, 148–50); one stairway in the Central Building (Schmidt 1953: pls. 82, 85–6, 87B–C); four sets of doorjambs, two stairways, and eight windows in the Palace of Xerxes (Schmidt 1953: pls. 161, 163–5, 168–72, 181B, 183–8); and fragments of glazed brick reliefs from Susa (*RCS*: 224–5, fig. 51). Guards appear on two sets of doorjambs and one stairway in the Palace of Darius (Schmidt 1953: pls. 126, 136–7, 151); two stairways in the Central Building (Schmidt 1953: pls. 62–5, 71, 82–4, 87a); two sets of doorjambs in the "Harem" of Xerxes (Schmidt 1953: pl. 191A); two stairways and two sets of doorjambs in the Palace of Xerxes (Schmidt 1953: pls. 159–60, 166–9A, 173, 176–7); two sets of doorways in the Throne Hall (Schmidt 1953: pls. 94–5); and one façade in Palace H (Schmidt 1953: pl. 200).

Rarely mentioned are two relief fragments (unfinished) showing spearmen wearing the Iranian tunic and trousers from the area of where the "Harem" backs up onto the Palace of Xerxes; the one is cut into bedrock (Schmidt 1953: 160–1, figs. 111C; Calmeyer 1980: 59, pl. IIIa), the other a stone-relief block reused in the platform of the Palace of Xerxes (near the rock-cut northern wall of room 4 of the "Harem" [Schmidt 1953: figs. 111D, 112D]). Both reliefs would have been hidden by the construction of the "Harem." Calmeyer (1987a: 574) suggested that they may be the oldest reliefs on the site.

From Susa the famous glazed-brick guards, who hold a spear, have a bow and quiver slung over their shoulder, and wear elaborately decorated Persian court robes, may have also come from similar compositional contexts (*RCS*: 224, 226–7 on the disturbed find-spots of the bricks).

King standing before an altar or tower-like structure

The rock-cut tomb relief of Darius at Naqsh-e Rustam is the best-known example of the compositional format where the king stands before an altar or tower-like structure (Schmidt 1970: 80–90, pls. 18–39; Calmeyer 1975; Root 1979: 162–81; Garrison 2011c). The monument is cut into a recess of the Hosayn Kuh, approximately 6 km to the north of Persepolis. Here, the king and the stepped altar, on which there is a blazing fire, stand on a three-stepped podium which itself rests on a platform held aloft by personifications of the subject peoples of the empire. Above the scene hovers a figure in a winged ring, facing toward the king, and a crescent inscribed in a disk. The king wears the Persian court robe and a crenellated crown and holds a bow. The figure in the winged ring is garbed in a similar manner and holds a ring. Attendants are disposed to left and right of the main tableau. To left are three weapon-bearers stacked one above the other in registers, the top and bottom figures wearing the Persian court robe, the middle figure wearing the Iranian tunic and trousers; uniquely in the corpus of royal Achaemenid art, two of them (in the top and middle register) are named: "*Kambarma*, a Patischorian, spear-bearer of Darius the king" (DNc) and "*Ašbazana, lipte*-bearer, holds Darius the king's bow-and-arrow case" (DNd) (El. *Kambarma* is rendered more commonly by Gr. *Gobryas*, OP *Gaubaruva*; El. *Ašbazana*, Gr. Aspathines, OP *Aspacanā* has generally been equated with a person by the same name mentioned in the Fortification archive and with the Aspathines mentioned by Herodotus [*Hist.* 3.70.1; see Garrison 1998; Henkelman 2003: 117–29]; the translation of DNd is notoriously contested; I follow here the translation of the Elamite version of the text as given in Henkelman 2003: 117; both Schmitt and Henkelman translate *vaçabara* as "clothes-bearer"). Balancing these three weapon-bearers are three attendants, dressed in the Persian court robe with low, fillet-like caps on their heads and holding their left hands up to their mouths, to the right of the main scene. More attendants are found at left and right on wings of rock that project out perpendicular to the façade of the tomb. At left are four spear-bearers, wearing the Persian court robe with low fillet-like caps on their heads, disposed in three registers. At right are three attendants, dressed in the Persian court robe with low, fillet-like caps on their heads and holding their left hands up to their mouths, disposed in three registers. Below this figural scene is an architectural façade (the actual entrance to the tomb). Two long trilingual inscriptions, DNa and DNb, are also cut into the tomb façade, as well as captions identifying the subject peoples (DN I–IV, XVI–XVII and XXIX).

The scene itself of king before an altar or tower structure seems to be an innovation of the Achaemenid period. The carved tomb reliefs of succeeding kings at Naqsh-e Rustam and Persepolis followed the model set by Darius with only minor variations but, with one exception, without inscriptions (the exception is Tomb V at Persepolis; see Schmitt in Calmeyer 2009: 25–41; on the Achaemenid royal tombs, see Krefter 1968; Schmidt 1970: 90–107, pls. 40–79; Root 1979: 72–6; Calmeyer 1990 and 2009; Seidl 1999; Briant 2003: 39–52 on the unfinished tomb at Persepolis). These tombs are the only other known examples of the scene type in Achaemenid monumental art. There are a handful of scenes in Persepolitan glyptic that show the king before a stepped altar or a tower structure. The most elaborate is PFS 11*, a seal that carries a trilingual royal-name inscription of Darius. Here the royal figure is doubled around a tower structure with a distinctive crenellated top (cf. the comments below). It is noteworthy that there are a goodly number of seals in Persepolitan glyptic showing a figure who has no headdress and wears an Assyrian garment standing before a fire blazing on a stepped altar and/or a tower structure. These glyptic scenes may suggest that the compositional format of king standing before an altar or tower structure had its origins in a distinctly local tradition.

King controlling or in combat with animals and fantastical creatures

By far and away the two most common compositional formats in Achaemenid art, both monumental and glyptic, are the hero who controls two animals or creatures and the hero who fights in combat with one animal or creature (see Garrison and Root 2001 for some 312 examples of the scene type in seals from the Fortification archive and for discussion of the compositional distinctions). In monumental art this scene type always shows a figure wearing the Persian court robe. The identity of this figure is somewhat clouded by the fact that in Persepolitan architectural relief the hero wears only a banded headdress, not a dentate or crenellated crown, and strapped boots, not strapless. Despite these iconographic oddities, the figure is commonly labeled the royal hero (Root 1979: 303–8). The theme, in variations, is found on five sets of doorjambs in the Palace of Darius (Schmidt 1953: pls. 144–7); two sets of doorjambs in the "Harem" of Xerxes (Schmidt 1953: pls. 195–6); and four sets of doorjambs in the Throne Hall (Schmidt 1953: pl. 114–17). In Persepolitan glyptic, where we have hundreds of examples of heroic encounters, the hero more commonly has no headdress and wears an Assyrian garment. Nonetheless, a number of Persepolitan seals show the royal hero; in these examples he almost always wears a dentate crown. In monumental art by far and away the preferred compositional format is the combat encounter, while in glyptic it is the control encounter. The menagerie is varied, but lions and bulls, often winged or having avian features, are the most common antagonists. The best-known examples of the royal hero in glyptic are those seals that carry royal-name inscriptions: three from the Fortification archive, PFS 7*, PFS 113* (= PTS 4*), and PFUTS 18*, all trilinguals naming Darius; an additional seven from the Treasury archive, PTS 1*, PTS 2*, and PTS 3*, all trilinguals naming Darius, and PTS 5*, PTS 6*, PTS 7*, and PTS 8*, all monolingual Old Persian inscriptions naming Xerxes, with the exception of PTS 7* which is trilingual; one seal from Daskyleion, DS 3, a monolingual Old Persian inscription naming Xerxes (for the royal-name seals of Darius, see Garrison 2014; for those of Xerxes, see Schmidt 1957: 20–2, pls. 4–5; Kaptan 2002: DS 3 s.v.). While it has often been inferred that this glyptic evidence suggests a specific royal seal type, this is not the case since there are several examples of royal-name seals that carry different imagery and those seals that do show the royal hero are in fact quite varied in details (Garrison 2014).

In contrast to the previously discussed scene types of classical royal Achaemenid art, the heroic encounter shows a rather active and energetic king, although, as Root (1979: 310–11) has remarked, the scene in monumental relief communicates the same notion of timelessness. In this regard it is noteworthy that the glyptic examples involving the royal hero only once, PTS 1*, show the hero in a running pose, which is commonly seen in other Persepolitan examples of the hero (many examples of the hero in the running pose may be found in Garrison and Root 2001; e.g., PFS 795 [Cat. no. 214], PFS 815* [Cat. no. 215], PFS 98* [Cat. no. 217], etc.).

King shooting a bow and arrow

This compositional format shows a figure dressed in the Persian court robe, generally crowned, shooting a bow and arrow; perhaps on analogy with the heroic encounters, we may call this figure the "royal archer." I distinguish here compositionally the active archer imagery, the figure in the Persian court robe shooting a bow and arrow, from the static references to the bow and arrow; for example, the king or attendants carrying or holding bows, arrows, quivers, and/or bow cases, that figure so prominently in monumental art and coin types I, III, and IV. Semantically, the two types, active and static, have the same referent, the manly (and royal) qualities denoted by skill in archery. It is noteworthy that in monumental art, this semantic is universally expressed as a static attribute of kingship rather than as the action itself of shooting the bow and arrow (cf. the discussion in Garrison 2010).

The most famous expression of the royal archer is found on the type II imperial coin series. There a kneeling royal archer, depicted alone, shoots to the right (Garrison 2010 for detailed discussion with earlier bibliography). While Persepolitan glyptic preserves a relatively large number of archer scenes (including impressions of a type II coin), only a few show the archer in the Persian court robe and only one, PFS 390*, unambiguously has a crowned archer. This may be due to the fact that heads of human figures are very often not preserved, owing to the restricted space on the tablet surfaces (for archer scenes in Persepolitan glyptic, see Garrison 2010). In the glyptic examples, the archer almost always shoots toward an animal or fantastic creature. The only exceptions documented to date are PFUTS 251, a fragmentarily preserved scene in which a figure apparently wearing the Persian court robe sits on horseback and shoots a bow and arrow toward a standing archer (apparently wearing an Assyrian garment); PFS 2084*, a composite leonine creature shoots toward a winged human figure; and PFS 2454 and PFUTS 273, both of which show an archer shooting toward a figure carrying a spear.

On PFS 390* the royal archer stands, one leg raised onto the back of a winged goat couchant, shooting toward a rampant lion. In those scenes in which the archer wears the Persian court robe, the antagonists are most frequently lions. PFS 71* is an exceptionally sophisticated rendering of the archer shooting at a lion. Here the archer wears an elaborate Persian court robe, but no crown; a dagger is stuck in the belt. He shoots toward a rampant lion that has already been hit by two arrows; a second lion, also hit by two arrows, lies dead in the field. Interestingly, three seals show an archer in the Persian court robe shooting toward a boar (PFS 395 [although the identification of the archer's garment is not certain], PFS 545s, and PFS 2323; see Garrison 2011b). The archer on PFS 1568* wears a detailed Persian court robe and shoots toward a pair of fleeing wild goats; the larger of the pair has been hit by two arrows. The composition is very sophisticated and shows the stacking of figures as seen on the heirloom seals PFS 51 and PFS 93* (Garrison 2011). The archer on PFS 117, who wears the Persian court robe, shoots toward an antithetical group consisting of a rampant goat (?) and a winged, human-headed, lion (?). An interesting variation on the archer theme is PFS 261*; an archer wearing a triple-belted Persian court robe emerges from the back of a fantastical composite creature and shoots toward a rampant lion (the imagery is discussed in more detail in Garrison 2010: 346–51; forthcoming a, forthcoming b). His headdress appears to be some type of *polos* arrangement; he also has an elaborate quiver and, perhaps, an extra bow slung on his back.

The almost total absence of the royal archer and the rarity of court-centric iconography, such as Persian court robe, winged symbol, date palm, and so on, in archer scenes from the Fortification archive are striking given the critical role that archer imagery plays in imperial coinage issues. Two phenomena may account for this situation. Firstly, court-centric iconography in glyptic from the Fortification archive as a whole is rare, perhaps owing to the fact that its development is recent and, thus, there are few seals in circulation. It is probably no coincidence that almost all the seals mentioned in the previous paragraph are inscribed. That is, they are exceptional glyptic artifacts, perhaps attesting to the initial appearance of Achaemenid court-centric iconography in glyptic. PFS 71* in fact provides one of the earliest dated examples of the occurrence of the Persian court robe in glyptic; it seals two Fortification tablets dated to the fourteenth year of Darius, 508/507 BC. Secondly, we commonly see in early Achaemenid art that distinct themes or iconography (in this case, the royal archer) are deployed in distinct media (in this case, coinage).

Antithetical compositions involving humans, animals, and/or fantastical creatures

This scene type generally does not include the king (see, however, the comments below concerning PFS 11*), but it is clearly an important aspect of the Achaemenid visual program, occurring regularly in architectural sculpture at Persepolis and Susa and in Persepolitan glyptic.

At Persepolis the façade of the southern stairway of the Palace of Darius consists of a series of antithetical displays (Schmidt 1953: pls. 126, 130, 132–3). In the center is a long inscription (XPcb OP). Disposed to either side, and facing the inscription, are nine spearmen wearing the Persian court robe and a fluted headdress. Each spearman has a tasseled quiver and bow slung on his back and holds a spear vertically before his body. This grouping is then framed by the Elamite and Babylonian versions of XPcb. Finally, lion and bull groups and friezes of segmented stalks crowned by palmettes bracket the entire façade. Above this register, only fragmentarily preserved, is a second register carrying another antithetical group. Here a winged disk forms the central focal element to either side of which is a winged, human-headed lion sejant. Only the creature to the right is preserved; it raises one foreleg to place it on a segmented stalk crowned by a palmette. The creature is elaborately detailed and exquisitely rendered. The human head has a long, curly, squared beard and a bull's ear. It wears a pendant earring and a horned *polos* headdress topped with a row of feathers.

A similar antithetical arrangement is attested in the replacement central panels on the Apadana (Schmidt 1953: pls. 22, 53): an inscription panel (in this case blank) to either side of which are four spearmen dressed alternately in the Persian court robe and the Iranian tunic and trousers. The spearmen in the Persian court robe wear fluted headdresses and carry shields; those in the tunic and trousers wear domed headdresses. As in the Palace of Darius, this scene is then framed by lion and bull groups and friezes of segmented stalks crowned by palmettes. Above is a second register also arranged antithetically: a central winged disk to either side of which is a winged, human-headed lion sejant. Iconographical details of the human-headed lion are identical to the one surviving on the southern stairway of the Palace of Darius.

The stairway façade of the Central Building reworks this formula somewhat (Schmidt 1953: pls. 62–4, 66, 69). The central scene is a blank inscription panel to either side of which are four spearmen dressed in the Persian court robe, followed by a lion and bull group and a frieze of segmented stalks crowned by palmettes. Above in a second register a winged, human-headed lion sejant with paw raised is disposed to either side of the inscription; these creatures are framed by a frieze of segmented stalks crowned by palmettes and a line of nobles dressed in the Persian court robe. This central grouping occurs on a façade that is set back so that the stairs project in front of it (opposite the arrangement in the Apadana). The projecting stairway façades are decorated in such a manner to present a large, antithetical group, the recessed façade of the central stairway essentially acting as the central element of the group. To each side are a frieze of segmented stalks crowned by palmettes, a lion and bull group, and three spearmen, two dressed in the Persian court robe, one in the Iranian tunic and trousers. The arrangement thus is something of an inversion of that seen on the replacement panels of the Apadana.

The glazed bricks from Susa showing spearmen may have originated from similar antithetical groupings (see above). A beautiful glazed brick panel from the site has antithetical winged, human-headed lions sejant (*RCS*: no. 157). Like their counterparts from Persepolis, they each have a bull's ear, horned *polos* headdress with feather top (additionally there is a floral petal above), thick, squared beard, and earring. Above them is a winged disk. The winged, human-headed lions on the replacement panels of the Apadana (Schmidt 1953: pl. 22) appear to have a similar flower above the headdress, although Schmidt does not mention them in his description.

Antithetical animals or creatures occur regularly in Persepolitan glyptic. It is difficult to know for certain which of these designs may have direct royal connotations. Based upon the evidence of architectural sculpture from Persepolis and Susa, winged, human-headed or human-faced creatures may have carried particular references to Achaemenid kingship, especially those that wear elaborate headdresses and/or have long, squared beards. In Persepolitan glyptic, these creatures appear more often to be taurine, rather than feline. PFS 108*, which has winged, human-faced bulls (?) disposed around a central floral disk (or stylized tree), appears to have come from a court workshop; the carving is very similar to that found on the royal-name seal PFS 113* (Cat. no. 19 in Garrison and Root 2001). The creatures have elaborate horns and thick, squared beards with horizontal striations. On PFS 320* a similar creature is disposed to either side of an inscription panel in a manner very evocative of display patterns in monumental architecture at Persepolis. Winged, human-headed or human-faced bulls are in fact rare in Persepolitan glyptic. Their rarity, combined with the fact that the iconographic details and/or compositions are closely related to architectural sculpture at Persepolis, suggest that at the time of Darius at least, these creatures have intimate associations with Achaemenid kingship.

In addition to designs involving animals/creatures, there are several other composition formats in Persepolitan glyptic that exhibit strong antithetical dynamics. PFS 11*, mentioned above, is a rare example that involves the king. PFUTS 19* is very similar, crowned figures and a tower structure, but without the trilingual royal-name inscription and date palms (Garrison 2008: figs. 41–3; fig. 41 is a preliminary drawing). PFS 82* shows a very interesting variation, in some ways analogous to architectural sculpture from Persepolis (Garrison forthcoming a). The central focal elements are a winged, human-headed creature above which is a figure in a winged device. To either side is disposed a spearman who stands on the back of winged lions. This seal may reflect early experimental phases in Darius' visual program in glyptic. The spearmen wear Assyrian garments (rather than the Persian court robe) and domed headdresses, while the figure in the winged symbol is set into a yoke-like device (rather than a ring or disk). The carving style is a distinctive version of the Persepolitan Modeled Style (rather than the Court Style). The scene on PFS 1567* is very similar to that seen on PFS 82* (Garrison 1998: 117–22, figs. 1–3). A large figure in a winged ring is the central focal element, to either side of which is a figure dressed in an Assyrian garment standing on the back of a horned creature. Again, this seal may be very early in the Achaemenid visual program. The figures wear Assyrian garments and the carving style is Persepolitan Modeled Style. Each figure holds a flower in one hand and raises the other hand before his face, reminiscent of figures of the king and crowned prince in monumental architectural sculpture. Another interesting variation on this format is seen in PFS 389*; here the focal elements are a winged disk that hovers over an inscription panel (Elamite; Garrison 2000: 144–5, fig. 22, pl. 24.22; forthcoming a). To either side of this central group is disposed a winged fish-man; the one to the left wears a serrated crown. A human figure wearing a serrated crown stands on the tails of the fish-men, thus somewhat breaking the antithetical arrangement. The arrangement of an inscription over which a winged symbol hovers is, of course, directly analogous to the façades of stairways on the Palace of Darius, the Apadana (replacement panels), and the Palace of Xerxes (see above).

The prominence given the winged symbols in PFS 11*, PFS 82*, PFS 389*, and PFS 1567* recalls a goodly number of worship scenes in Persepolitan glyptic employing antithetical compositions. In these scenes the central focal elements are a stylized tree over which there is a figure in a winged ring or disk; disposed to either side are generally bull-men who act as atlantids to support the winged disk (e.g., PFS 122, PFS 310, etc., see Garrison forthcoming a). The exact referent for the winged symbol in all of its variations remains unresolved. A variety of opinions have been put forward, the most commonly accepted being the god Auramazdā (opinions are tracked in Garrison forthcoming a, forthcoming b). These scenes involving bull-men atlantids, the stylized tree, and a winged symbol are obviously highly Assyrianizing. Although the scenes have no overt references to Achaemenid kingship via court-centric iconography, they are intimately linked to one of the central thematic concerns of the Achaemenid visual program, ascension (Garrison 2010: 350–1, 355–6; 2011c).

PFUTS 1* is an interesting variation on this particular compositional format, wherein the central focal elements are the figure in the winged symbol and a stylized tree (Garrison 2008: figs. 35–8). Rather than bull-men atlantids, the attending figures are humans who wear Assyrian garments (PFS 82* and PFS 1567*) and serrated crowns (PFS 389*), hold flowers (PFS 389* and PFS 1567*), and stand on the backs of fish-men (PFS 389* and PFS 1567* as well as PFS 82*, which also employs pedestal creatures). As in PFS 1567* and PFS 389*, an inscription panel (Elamite) in PFUTS 1* is artfully arranged so as to be either a framing device (if rolled in an extended manner) or the central element itself (again, requiring an extended rolling).

Lastly, it bears noting that the control heroic encounter, which is the single most popular compositional format in the important royal-name seals, has a very strong antithetical quality. The hero serves as the central focal element to either side of which is disposed a rampant or upturned animal. While we are not normally accustomed to viewing the dynamics of the heroic encounter in this manner, one cannot avoid the obvious compositional, and, by extension, conceptual similarities with the worship scenes just discussed.

Lion and bull group

One of the most striking and often-discussed images in Persepolitan architectural sculpture is the lion and bull group that decorates numerous stairway façades, most famously those of the Apadana (Schmidt 1953: pls. 16B, 17, 19–20, 22, 53–4 [Apadana], 62–3, 66, 69 [Central Building], 126, 132 B, 133 B, 152–3, 155 B [Palace of Darius], 159, 161, 165C, 166, 168A, 169A [Palace of Xerxes], 203 D [Palace H]). The scene consists of a rampant bull moving in one direction, but turning its head back in the opposite direction toward a lion that wraps both paws around and bites down upon the haunches of the bull. The head of the lion is rendered frontally, a remarkable archaizing quotation of late Early Dynastic and Akkadian art (cf. Boehmer 1965: nos. 3–4, 6–8 [late ED], 12, 29, 37, 41, 51, etc. [Akkadian]).

Because of its prominence in Persepolitan architecture, it is assumed that the lion and bull group is a critical element in royal Achaemenid iconography. Nonetheless, there is no consensus on its exact significance (Root 1979: 236; 2002: 197–8, 201–3; Calmeyer 1980: 59). The lion and bull group is the only example of a major compositional theme that consists only of animals interacting with each other in Achaemenid monumental art. Otherwise, animals, outside of human or heroic contexts, occur in the animal protome capitals and the ubiquitous lion friezes in Persepolitan relief (Root 2002: 199–201).

Lions are the most common animal in Persepolitan glyptic, and lion friezes are conspicuous in Persepolitan architectural sculpture. The range of scene types in which lions occur in Persepolitan glyptic is extremely large, suggesting that the animal itself, outside of specific contexts involving the royal hero, did not have a consistently specific royal referent (on lions in Persepolitan architectural sculpture see Root 2002: 199–201, who links the lion friezes with the rosette as emblems of Ištar/fertility). Bulls are another matter. They are relatively rare in Persepolitan glyptic and often found in scenes with extensive court-centric iconography (e.g., the royal-name seals PFS 7* [Cat. no. 4, winged], PFS 113* [Cat. no. 19, winged and human-headed], PTS 5* [Schmidt 1957: pl. 4, winged and human-headed], PTS 7* [Schmidt 1957: pl. 4, winged]). As noted above the winged, human-headed or human-faced bull appears to be intimately linked with notions of Achaemenid kingship.

Scenes showing one animal or creature attacking another, what we could call animal combats (*Tierkampfszenen*), occur by the hundreds in Persepolitan glyptic in a range of compositional formats and various carving styles. These animal combats appear to convey the notion of a predator and prey. It seems noteworthy that these animal combats almost never carry any overt marker of court-centric iconography, such as a winged symbol, paneled inscription, and so on. The very large quantity of animal combats in Persepolitan glyptic, their wide-ranging compositional formats, and their lack of any distinct iconography associated with kingship would seem to indicate that the animal combat per se did not have a specific royal referent.

Despite the superficial resemblance of the lion and bull group in Persepolitan architecture sculpture with animal combats in Persepolitan glyptic, it is not at all clear that they are meant to understood in the same manner as the animal combats, that is, a predator and prey. Root (2002: 201–3) has suggested that the lion and bull imagery is not about predator and prey, but about a symbolic expression of the combined powers of nature harnessed by the empire. It seems significant that Persepolitan glyptic contains only a handful of seals that show a lion "attacking" a bull. This state of affairs may suggest that the repertoire of the animal combat as a scene type in Persepolitan glyptic did not normally admit the combination of a lion attacking a bull; thus, another instance in Achaemenid art of specific imagery occurring only in specific media. This observation brings us, however, no closer to understanding the significance of the lion and bull group in Persepolitan architectural sculpture.

OTHER DESIGN ELEMENTS

In addition to individual design elements already highlighted as recurring in royal Achaemenid iconography, for example, the king, the crown prince, attendants, the winged symbol, and so on, the following design elements occur repeatedly in court-centric contexts:

1. rosettes, date palms, and palmettes;
2. inscriptions.

Rosettes, date palms, and palmettes

The rosette occurs ubiquitously in Persepolitan architectural sculpture. Root (2002: 199–200) has suggested that it is a conscious revitalization of the age-old image of the goddess Ištar as a symbol of the link between kingship and fertility. It seems noteworthy that the rosette is virtually absent in Persepolitan glyptic. Its analog in glyptic may be the date palm. Indeed, every Achaemenid royal-name seal from Persepolis includes a date palm in its design (see Garrison 2014 on the royal-name seals of Darius; Root 1979: 120–2 for a list of all royal-name seals then known). Like the rosette, the date palm was an ancient symbol wherein one sees an intricate interlocking of the referents Ištar, fertility, and kingship (Garrison forthcoming a, 2011c). The clear separation of the contexts in which the rosette and date palm occur at Persepolis surely cannot be fortuitous, but must represent yet another example of media-specific programs in Achaemenid art; in this case analogous symbols (rosette/date palm) are deployed in different media (architecture/glyptic) (Garrison 2010).

Another common design element in Persepolitan architectural sculpture is the palmette, occurring generally as the crowning element on segmented stalks (e.g., the stairway facades of the Central Building and the Palace of Darius, Schmidt 1953: pls. 62–3, 69, 126–7, and glazed brick from the Apadana, Schmidt 1953: Fig. 35). Palmettes occur only rarely in Persepolitan glyptic. In Persepolitan architectural sculpture, palmettes would seem to function in a manner analogous to rosettes, as a symbol of the linkage between kingship and fertility.

Inscriptions

A striking feature of royal Achaemenid iconography is the inscribed word, often existing in triplicate: Old Persian, Elamite, and Babylonian. Textual displays are embedded into figural scenes generally in the form of paneled inscriptions, or set off in distinct zones within the imagery. Large inscriptions are a prominent feature in the premier imperial monuments of the Achaemenids, such as Bisotun, Naqsh-e Rustam, the Palace of Darius, among others; and of course, the royal-name seals contain, by definition, an inscription naming the king. These trilingual inscriptions are always set off in display panels. The original stairways of the Apadana are thus anomalous in this regard, having no inscriptions.

Outside of a few scribes, most individuals who encountered these inscriptions could not have read them. Their primary purpose would seem to have been iconographical rather than textual. That is, the primary semantic function of these inscriptions would be as a signifier of power via the control or application of specialized, indeed almost mystical, knowledge (Garrison 2011c explores the iconographic function of inscriptions in Achaemenid imperial monuments and Persepolitan glyptic in more detail).

Summation

The reign of Darius marks the most critical and formative phase in the development of royal Achaemenid iconography. It is perhaps no exaggeration to say that his reign was transformational, similar to those of other foundational kings such as Sargon of Akkad and Assurnasirpal II, wherein a distinct visual and textual language of empire was formulated and codified.

Further reading

The modern study of royal Achaemenid art was spearheaded by two scholars, Margaret Cool Root, whose 1979 book remains the seminal comprehensive study of the art of Achaemenid kingship, and Peter Calmeyer, who, in a series of individual studies (e.g., Calmeyer 1975, 1982, 1983, 1987b, 1994, etc.), explored a range of topics related to Achaemenid art, both royal and nonroyal. Root and Calmeyer were part of the revolution in Achaemenid studies resulting from the Achaemenid History Workshops initiated by Pierre Briant, Helen Sancisi-Weerdenberg, and Amélie Kuhrt. More recently, Bruno Jacobs (e.g., 2002, 2010) has revisited many of the issues surrounding the art of the Achaemenid kings. The ongoing publication of the seals preserved as impressions in the Persepolis Fortification archive (Garrison and Root 2001, Garrison 1998, 2000, 2010, etc.) has radically expanded the data available for the study of Achaemenid art on multiple levels during its most formative period, the middle and late years of Darius I.

References

Ahn, G. 1992. *Religiöse Herrscherlegitimation im achämenidischen Iran: Die Voraussetzungen und die Struktur ihrer Argumentation*. Leiden: Acta Iranica 31.

Allen, L. 2005. Le roi imaginaire: An audience with the Achaemenid king. In *Imaginary kings: Royal images in the Ancient Near East, Greece and Rome*, ed. O. Hekster and R. Fowler, 39–62. Munich: Oriens et Occidens 11.

Alram, M. 2003. *7000 Años de Arte Persa. Obras Maestras del Museo Nacional de Irán*. Barcelona: Fundacíon La Caixa.

Álvarez-Mon, J. 2011. The golden griffin from Arjan. *EP*: 299–373.

Álvarez-Mon, J., M. B. Garrison, and D. Stronach. 2011. Introduction. *EP*: 1–32.

Azzoni, A., E. R. M. Dusinberre, M. B. Garrison, W. F. M. Henkelman, C. E. Jones, and M. W. Stolper. Forthcoming. Persepolis administrative archives. *EnIr*.

Boardman, J. 2000. *Persia and the West: An archaeological investigation of the genesis of Achaemenid art*. London: Thames and Hudson.

Boehmer, R. M. 1965. *Die Entwicklung der Glyptik während der Akkad-Zeit*. Berlin: ZA Ergänzungsbänd 4.

Borger, R. 1982. Die Chronologie des Darius-Denkmals am Behistun-Felsen. *Nachrichten der Akademie der Wissenschaften in Göttingen, phil.-hist. Kl.* 3: 103–31.

Boucharlat, R. 2005. Iran. *AEA*: 221–92.

Briant, P. 1997. Bulletin d'histoire achéménide (I). In *Recherches récentes sur l'Empire achéménide*, ed. M.-F. Boussac, 5–127. Lyon: *Topoi* Supplement 1.

———. 2001. *Bulletin d'histoire achéménide II*. Paris: Persika 1.

———. 2002. *From Cyrus to Alexander: A history of the Persian Empire*. Winona Lake: Eisenbrauns.

———. 2003. *Darius dans l'ombre d'Alexandre*. Paris: Fayard.

Brosius, M. 2005. Pax Persica: Königliche Ideologie und Kriegführung im Achämenidenreich. In *Krieg-Gesellschaft-Institutionen: Beiträge zu einer vergleichenden Kriegsgeschichte*, ed. B. Meissner, O. Schmitt and M. Sommer, 135–61. Berlin: Akademie Verlag.

Brown, S. 1997. Ecbatana. *EnIr* 8: 80–4.

Calmeyer, P. 1975. The subject of the Achaemenid tomb reliefs. *PASARI* 3: 233–42.

———. 1980. Textual sources for the interpretation of Achaemenian palace decorations. *Iran* 18: 55–63.

———. 1981. Figürliche Fragmente aus Pasargadae nach Zeichnungen E. Herzfelds. *AMI* 14: 27–44.

———. 1982. Zur Genese altiranischer Motive, VIII. Die "Statistische Landcharte des Perserreiches": I. *AMI* 15: 105–87.

———. 1983. Zur Genese altiranischer Motive, VIII. Die "Statistische Landcharte des Perserreiches": II. *AMI* 15: 141–222.

———. 1987a. Art in Iran iii. Achaemenian art and architecture. *EnIr* 2: 569–80.

———. 1987b. Zur Genese altiranischer Motive, VIII. Die "Statistische Landcharte des Perserreiches"—Nachträge und Korrekturen. *AMI* 20: 129–46.

———. 1990. Das Persepolis der Spätzeit. In *Centre and periphery*, ed. H. Sancisi-Weerdenburg and A. Kuhrt, 7–36. Leiden: AchHist 4.

———. 1993. Crown i. In the Median and Achaemenid periods. *EnIr* 6: 407–8.

———. 1994. Babylonische und assyrische Elemente in der achaimenidische Kunst. In *Continuity and change*, ed. H. W. A. M. Sancisi-Weerdenburg, A. Kuhrt, and M. C. Root, 131–47. Leiden: AchHist 8.

———. 2009. *Die Reliefs der Gräber V und VI in Persepolis*. Mainz: AIT 8.

Cameron, G. G. 1948. *Persepolis Treasury Tablets*. Chicago: OIP 65.

———. 1950. Darius carved history on ageless rock. *National Geographic Magazine* 98: 825–44.

Curtis, J. 2003. The Assyrian heartland in the period 612–539 B.C. *CE*: 157–67.

———. 2005. The Achaemenid period in northern Iraq. *AEA*: 175–95.

Dalley, S. 1993. Nineveh after 612 BC. *AoF* 20: 138–47.

Dandamaev, M. A. 1976. *Persien unter den ersten Achämeniden*. Wiesbaden: L. Reichert.

———. 1997. Assyrian traditions during Achaemenid times. In *Assyria 1995*, ed. S. Parpola and R. M. Whiting, 41–8. Helsinki: Neo-Assyrian Text Corpus Project.

Dusinberre, E. R. M. 2002. King or god? Imperial iconography and the "tiarate head" coins of Achamenid Anatolia. In *Across the Anatolian plateau: Readings in the archaeology of Ancient Turkey*, ed. D. Hopkins, 157–71. Boston: Annual of the American Schools of Oriental Research 57.

Ehrenberg, E. 2008. Dieu et mon droit: Kingship in late Babylonian and early Persian times. In *Religion and power: Divine kingship in the ancient world and beyond*, ed. N. Brisch, 103–31. Chicago: Oriental Institute Seminars 4.

Farkas, A. 1974. *Achaemenid sculpture*. Leiden: UNHAII 33.

Feldman, M. H. 2007. Darius I and the heroes of Akkad: Affect and agency in the Bisitun relief. In *Ancient Near Eastern art in context: Studies in honor of Irene J. Winter by her students*, ed. J. Cheng and M. H. Feldman, 265–93. Leiden/Boston: Culture and History of the Ancient Near East 26.

Garrison, M. B. 1998. The seals of Ašbazana (Aspathines). *SPH*: 115–31.

——. 2000. Achaemenid iconography as evidenced by glyptic art: Subject matter, social function, audience and diffusion. In *Images as media: Sources for the cultural history of the Near East and the Eastern Mediterranean (Ist millennium BCE)*, ed. C. Uehlinger, 115–64. Fribourg/Göttingen: OBO 175.

——. 2008. The uninscribed tablets from the Fortification Archive: A preliminary analysis. *AFP*: 149–238.

——. 2010. Archers at Persepolis: The emergence of royal ideology at the heart of the empire. *WAP*: 337–68.

——. 2011a. The seal of "Kuraš the Anzanite, son of Šešpeš" (Teispes), PFS 93*: Susa—Anšan—Persepolis. *EP*: 375–405.

——. 2011b. Notes on a boar hunt (PFS 2323). *BICS* 54/2: 17–20.

——. 2014. The royal-name seals of Darius I. *EAC*: 67–104.

——. Forthcoming a. Visual representation of the divine and the numinous in early Achaemenid Iran: Old problems, new directions. In *Iconography of Ancient Near Eastern religions, Volume 1. Pre-Hellenistic periods, introductory essays*, ed. C. Uehlinger and F. Graf. Leiden: Brill.

——. Forthcoming b. The figure in the winged disk in Persepolitan glyptic: Select new evidence. In *Ō Šābuhr kē čihr az yazdān dāšt: Essays in Memory of A. Shapur Shahbazi*, ed. K. Abdi. Tehran/Persepolis.

——. 2011c. By the favor of Auramazdā: Kingship and the divine in the early Achaemenid period. In *More than men, less than gods: Studies in royal cult and imperial worship*, ed. P. P. Iossif, A. D Chankowski, and C. C. Lorber, 15–104. Leuven/Paris/Walpole: Studia Hellenistica 51.

Garrison, M. B. and M. C. Root. 2001. *Seals on the Persepolis Fortification Tablets*, Vol. 1. *Images of heroic encounter*. Chicago: OIP 117.

Hallock, R. T. 1969. *Persepolis Fortification Tablets*. Chicago: OIP 92.

Hansman, J. 1987. Anshan. *EnIr* 2: 103–7.

Henkelman, W. F. M. 1995–6. The royal Achaemenid crown. *AMI* 28: 275–93.

——. 2003a. Persians, Medes and Elamites: Acculturation in the Neo-Elamite period. *CE*: 181–231.

——. 2003b. An Elamite memorial: The *šumar* of Cambyses and Hystaspes. *APP*: 101–72.

——. 2008. *The other gods who are: Studies in Elamite-Iranian acculturation based on the Persepolis Fortification Texts*. Leiden: AchHist 14.

——. 2011a. Cyrus the Persian and Darius the Elamite: A case of mistaken identity. In *Herodot und das Persische Weltreich/Herodotus and the Persian Empire*, ed. R. Rollinger, B. Truschnegg, and R. Bichler, 577–634. Wiesbaden: CLeO 3.

——. 2011b. Parnakka's feast: *šip* in Pārsa and Elam. *EP*: 89–166.

———. 2012. The Achaemenid heartland: An archaeological-historical perspective. In *A companion to the archaeology of the Ancient Near East*, ed. D. T. Potts, 931–62. Oxford/Malden: Wiley-Blackwell.

Huff, D. 2010. Überlegungen zu Funktion, Genese und Nachfolge des Apadana. In *Der Achämenidenhof / The Achaemenid court*, ed. B. Jacobs and R. Rollinger, 311–74. Wiesbaden: CLeO 2.

Jacobs, B. 1997. Eine Planänderung an den Apadāna-Treppen und ihre Konsequenzen für die Datierung der Planungs- und Bebauungsphasen von Persepolis. *AMI* 29: 281–302.

———. 2002. Achämenidische Kunst—Kunst im Achämenidenreich. Zur Rolle der achämenidsichen Großplastik als Mittel der herrscherlichen Selbstdarstellung und der Verbreitung politischer Botschaften im Reich. *AMI* 34: 345–95.

———. 2010. Herrschaftsideologie und Herrschaftsdarstellung dei den Achämeniden. *CKA*: 107–13.

Joannès, F. 2004. *The age of empires: Mesopotamia in the first millennium BC*. Edinburgh: Edinburgh University Press.

Jursa, M. 2011. Der neubabylonische Hof. In *Der Achämenidenhof / The Achaemenid court*, ed. B. Jacobs and R. Rollinger, 67–108. Wiesbaden: CLeO 2.

Kaptan, D. 2002. *The Daskyleion bullae: Seal images from the western Achaemenid Empire*. 2 vols. Leiden: AchHist 12.

Kent, R. G. 1953. *Old Persian: Grammar, texts, lexicon*, 2nd ed. New Haven: AOS 33.

Kleiss, W. 2000. Zur Planung von Persepolis. *VD*: 355–68.

Krefter, F. 1968. Achaemenidische Palast- und Grabtüren. *AMI* 1: 99–113.

———. 1971. *Persepolis Rekonstruktionen*. Berlin: Teheraner Forschungen 3.

Kuhrt, A. 1995. *The Ancient Near East c. 3000–330 BC*. London/New York: Routledge.

———. 2007. *The Persian Empire: A corpus of sources from the Achaemenid period*. London/New York: Routledge.

———. 2010. Achaemenid images of royalty and empire. *CKA*: 87–105.

Liverani, M. 2003. The rise and fall of Media. *CE*: 1–12.

Luschey, H. 1968. Studien zu dem Darius-Relief von Bisutun. *AMI* 1: 63–94.

———. 1990. Art. Bīsotūn ii. Archaeology. *EnIr* 4: 291–99.

Miroschedji, P. de 1985. La fin du royaume d'Anšan et de Suse et la naissance de l'empire perse. *ZA* 75: 265–306.

Muscarella, O. W. 1987. Median art and Medizing scholarship. *JNES* 46: 109–27.

Oates, D., and J. Oates. 2001. *Nimrud: An Assyrian imperial city revealed*. London: British School of Archaeology in Iraq.

Parpola, S. 2010. Neo-Assyrian concepts of kingship and their Heritage in Mediterranean Antiquity. *CKA*: 35–44.

Potts, D. T. 2005. Cyrus the Great and the Kingdom of Anshan. In *Birth of the Persian Empire*, ed. V. S. Curtis and S. Stewart, 7–28. London: I. B. Tauris.

———. 2011. A note on the limits of Anšan. *EP*: 35–43.

Quintana, E. C. 2011. Elamitas frente a Persas: El reino independiente de Anšan. *EP*: 167–90.

Razmjou, S. 2005. In search of lost Median art. *IrAnt* 40: 271–314.

Riva, R. da. 2010. Dynastic gods and favorite gods in the Neo-Babylonian period. *CKA*: 45–62.

Roaf, M. 1983. *Sculptures and sculptors at Persepolis*. London: British Institute of Persian Studies [= *Iran* 21].

———. 2010. The role of the Medes in the architecture of the Achaemenids. *WAP*: 247–53.

Rollinger, R. 2008. The Median "Empire," the end of Urartu, and Cyrus the Great's campaign in 547 BC (Nabonidus Chronicle II 16). *AWE* 7: 51–65.

———. 2010. Das medische Königtum und die medische Suprematie im sechsten Jahrhundert v. Chr. *CKA*: 63–85.

Root, M. C. 1979. *The king and kingship in Achaemenid Art: Essays on the creation of an iconography of Empire*. Leiden: Acta Iranica 19.

———. 1985. The Parthenon frieze and the Apadana reliefs at Persepolis: Reassessing a programmatic relationship. *AJA* 89: 103–20.

———. 2002. Animals in the art of ancient Iran. In *A history of the animal world in the Ancient Near East*, ed. B. J. Collins, 167–209. Leiden/Boston/Cologne: HdO 1/64.

———. 2003. The lioness of Elam: Politics and dynastic fecundity at Persepolis. *APP*: 9–32.

———. 2007. Reading Persepolis in Greek: Gifts of the Yauna. *PR*: 177–224.

———. 2008. Reading Persepolis in Greek—Part two: Marriage metaphors and unmanly virtues. In *Ancient Greece and Ancient Iran: Cross-cultural encounters*, ed. S. M. R. Darbandi and A. Zournatzi, 195–221. Athens: National Hellenic Research Foundation.

———. 2011. Elam in the imperial imagination: From Nineveh to Persepolis. *EP*: 419–74.

Sancisi-Weerdenburg, H. 1991. Nowruz in Persepolis. In *Through travellers' eyes: European travellers on the Iranian monuments*, ed. H. Sancisi-Weerdenburg and J.-W. Drijvers, 173–201. Leiden: AchHist 7.

Sarraf, M. R. 2003. Archaeological excavations in Tepe Ekbatana (Hamadan) by the Iranian Archaeological Mission between 1983 and 1999. *CE*: 269–79.

Schmidt, E. 1953. *Persepolis I. Structures, reliefs, inscriptions*. Chicago: OIP 68.

———. 1957. *Persepolis II. The contents of the Treasury and other discoveries*. Chicago: OIP 69.

———. 1970. *Persepolis III. The royal tombs and other monuments*. Chicago: OIP 70.

Schmitt, R. 1990a. Bīsotūn i. Introduction. *EnIr* 4: 289–90.

———. 1990b. Bīsotūn iii. Darius' inscriptions. *EnIr* 4: 299–305.

———. 1991. *The Bisitun inscriptions of Darius the Great: Old Persian text*. London: CII 1/1/1.

Seidl, U. 1999. Naqš-i Rustam. *RlA* 9: 165–8.

Sekunda, N. V. 2010. Changes in Achaemenid royal dress. *WAP*: 256–72.

Steve, M.-J., F. Vallat, H. Gasche, and F. Jullien. 2002–3. Suse. *SDB* 73: 360–512 (bibliog. in *SDB* 74: 620–52).

Stronach, D. 1978. *Pasargadae: A report on the excavations conducted by the British Institute of Persian Studies from 1961 to 1963*. Oxford: Clarendon Press.

———. 1987. Apadāna ii. Building. *EnIr* 2: 146–8.

———. 1990. On the genesis of the Old Persian cuneiform script. *MJP*: 195–203.

———. 1997a. On the interpretation of the Pasargadae inscriptions. In *Ultra terminum vagari: Scritti in onore de Carl Nylander*, ed. B. Magnusson, 323–9. Rome: Quasar.

———. 1997b. Anshan and Parsa: Early Achaemenid history, art and architecture on the Iranian Plateau. In *Mesopotamia and Iran in the Persian Period: Conquest and imperialism 539–331 B.C.*, ed. J. Curtis, 35–53. London: British Museum Press.

———. 2003. The tomb at Arjan and the history of southwestern Iran in the early sixth century BCE. *YBYN*: 249–59.

———. 2011. Court dress and riding dress at Persepolis: New approaches to old questions. *EP*: 475–87.

Stronach, D., and H. Gopnik. 2009. Pasargadae. *EnIr* online edition.

Tilia, A. B. 1972. *Studies and restorations at Persepolis and other sites of Fārs*, vol. 1. Rome: IsMEO Reports and Memoirs 16.

———. 1978. *Studies and restorations at Persepolis and other sites of Fārs*, vol. 2. Rome: IsMEO Reports and Memoirs 18.

Tuplin, C. 2007. Treacherous hearts and upright tiaras: The Achaemenid king's head-dress. *PR*: 67–97.

Vallat, F. 2011. Darius, l'héritier légitime, et les premiers Achéménides. *EP*: 263–84.

Walser, G. 1966. *Die Völkerschaften auf den Reliefs von Persepolis: Historische Studienüber den sogenannten Tributzug an der Apadanatreppe*. Berlin: Gebr. Mann.

Waters, M. W. 1996. Darius and the Achaemenid line. *Ancient History Bulletin* 10: 11–18.

———. 2011. Parsumaš, Anšan, and Cyrus. *EP*: 285–96.

CHAPTER 30

COLOR AND GILDING IN ACHAEMENID ARCHITECTURE AND SCULPTURE

ALEXANDER NAGEL

Introduction

The importance of an overarching and systematic integration of the study of color in all of its many aspects (e.g., transmissions of knowledge of pigment production and ground layer preparation from earlier generations; architectural paint research as part of building analysis, preservation, and conservation; Achaemenid Persian aesthetics) is only just emerging from the scholarly shadows. The earliest prehistoric traces of recognizable, distinctive, ancient Iranian polychromatic cultures from the sixth millennium BC already bear the signs of a culture that would become deeply invested in the use of pigments and surface applications. Highly advanced technologies of metal and glass production attested at scientifically excavated sites from the early first millennium BC in Iran and the application of paints on the sculptures and monuments of Elam suggest that the production of pigments developed alongside other technologies. As stressed in material culture studies in recent years, *color* is an important yet little explored tool in studying early societies around the world (Young 2006). This is especially true in the case of architecture and sculpture, yet in every premodern society, decorative finishing played a crucial part in the sensory experiences of those who lived with or visited buildings and monuments. While evidence of these embellishments is in many cases scarce, there are important traces of color in Achaemenid Persian palace architecture, as will be shown in this chapter.

Analytical Methods

Today, there are excellent research facilities and laboratories in the Islamic Republic of Iran. Furthermore, museum collections around the world house fragments of Achaemenid Persian sculpture and pigments and allow access to experts for pigment analysis and identification. Techniques of pigment analysis include scanning electron microscopy with energy dispersive X-ray analysis (SEM/EDX) and Fourier transform infrared (FTIR) spectroscopy. Often, fairly small samples suffice to produce reliable results. In many cases one can identify pigments by matching them with existing samples in other scientific collections or databases, such as the Forbes pigment collection (Carriveau and Omecinsky 1983; http://cameo.mfa.org/pigments/index.asp). There are also nondestructive methods for identifying specific pigments such as Egyptian blue, and it is hoped that these can be applied more widely in the future (see, e.g., Verri 2009).

By their very nature, mineral-based pigments fade, change color, and disappear completely over time. For this reason the rendering of color reconstructions that satisfy the public's curiosity to see the way a monument "really looked" can be challenging. There are also challenges in verbally describing colors and hues in the archaeological record in ways that do not embed assumptions that cannot be sustained by the actual evidence. For many years the Munsell Color System has been used as a standard reference for describing hue in archaeological materials (e.g., ceramics, glass). The objectivity of this standard of reference has, however, been questioned (Gerharz et al. 1986). Thus, at the present time, much ambiguity exists in descriptions and discussions of what scholars see on ancient monuments as they now appear. Standardization of description, however, should be a goal, and efforts have been made to resolve this problem by employing colorimeters (Strudwick 1991). This underscores the importance of sample studies. By identifying chemical elements in samples that "produced" these hues, communication problems and the complexities of an objective measuring system can be partly resolved (Braenne 2009; Bregnhoi and Christensen 2009; Vandenabeele et al. 2009).

On the Concept of Polychromy and Some Theoretical Remarks

The modern term *polychromy* applied in studies of color and paint is derived from the ancient Greek word *polychrómatos*, which simply means many-colored or multicolored. It is important to note, however, that an equivalent term has yet to be identified in Ancient Near Eastern (including Iranian) and Egyptian texts, although we have plenty of color terms in, for example, ancient Iranian languages (Rossi 1996, 2006). Since the term polychromy in its basic lexical sense of many-colored is so broad, it can legitimately embrace, for the Achaemenid Persian court environment, myriad media. Besides painted wooden beams (for recently analyzed painted wooden beams discovered in Achaemenid Anatolia, see Summerer and Kienlin 2010) and wall paintings, these media included multicolored dyed and woven textiles as well as glazed brick reliefs and tiles, stucco, architectural and sculptural details made of other materials (e.g., stone), glass, and inlays, in short almost everything that belonged in an Achaemenid Persian palace and expressed the "rhetoric of abundance" considered characteristic of palaces in the Ancient Near East more generally (Winter 2003). As is evident on the extant sculpted façades of the palaces of Pasargadae, Persepolis, and Susa, aside from paints and gilding, craftsmen made use of other materials like gold, silver, and lapis lazuli to emphasize specific parts of a sculpture, such as hair, beards, or ornamented jewellery. How do the concept and process of polychromy (as generally applied to the coloring of preformed, modeled compositions) then relate to the concept and process of applying paints to walls in the form of murals?

From the craftsman's perspective, the raw materials of painted color (minerals, pigments, and binders) and the process of applying them to relief sculpture, statuary in the round, and wall painting are nearly identical. There is no reason to believe that the tools used to apply paints to walls and stone reliefs were different, and it has been observed that the "techniques of polychromy on sculpture often parallel those of two-dimensional painting in the same culture" (Marincola 2004: 1319). Particularly in the case of Neo-Assyrian palace art, one of the main predecessors of Achaemenid Persian palace art, Moorey (1994: 35) argued for the "close relationship of painter and sculptor," noting that the Neo-Assyrian palace reliefs were in fact "two-dimensional drawings rendered in relief," and that "it is likely that their execution was influenced from the outset by the techniques of wall painting ... The design would be sketched in, in ink, then the background cut away" (Moorey 1994: 35; cf. Moortgat 1959: 130–31). Moorey further remarked that the palette of colors used on relief sculpture and murals in Neo-Assyrian palaces was identical (1994: 326). The same applied in Achaemenid Persia, as recent studies of pigments and materials in wall paintings and on stone sculpture prove (see below). It is well known that wall paintings appeared directly above painted reliefs in the very same Neo-Assyrian palace interiors (Albenda 2005; Guralnick 2010). Wall paintings and painted reliefs must be considered part of one production process, the result of which was an integrated, polychromatic program.

A close connection between polychromatic murals and architectural reliefs is well attested at both Persepolis and Susa. Excavations at Susa in the 1970s revealed the remains of full-scale mural paintings (Labrousse and Boucharlat 1974; Boucharlat 2010: 402–3, figs. 466–9), rendering the motif of gift-bearers from the subject lands which echoed at approximately the same scale the famous carved stone reliefs on the Apadana at Persepolis. Crossovers between reliefs in stone (originally painted) at Persepolis and Susa are attested abundantly at both sites in colorful glazed brick relief and equally colorful, flat glazed tiles. The motif of servant carrying vessels and containers up staircases at Susa is a prominent example of this in all three media, and it would seem that there was no distinction between what motifs and scales of production were appropriate for polychrome renderings in mural work, glazed brick, and glazed brick relief. With respect to technical production (as opposed to decorative concept), Caubet compared the mode of application of polychromy on glazed bricks at Susa to the cloisonné technique of jewelry manufacture (Muscarella et al. 1992: 223).

The so-called Alexander Sarcophagus, excavated at Sidon (Lebanon) in 1887 and dated to the late fourth century BC, combines deeply carved, relief sculpture, with remnants of lavish polychromy and motifs painted on the interiors of the shields of the sculpted Persian warriors in the manner of miniature murals (Graeve 1970: 102–9; Brinkmann 2007: 154, figs. 284–7) directly inspired by Achaemenid monumental sculpture at Persepolis. We also know that at Persepolis paint was used to create patterns and motifs on certain architectural reliefs which, in other instances, were rendered in carved form. The walking lions, for instance, carved in low relief on the royal baldachins of the original central panels of the Apadana and the doorjambs of the Hall of 100 Columns, can be compared with the walking lions in paint that once decorated the throne-covers and royal robes preserved as incised painters' guidelines on figures from the Hall of 100 Columns, the main Hall of the Harem building and the Tripylon (Tilia 1978: figs. 3, 39–40; Schmidt 1953, pl. 105; Nagel 2010). All of these observations reinforce the impression of craft interconnectivity in the sphere of polychromatic vision, design, and implementation at the Achaemenid Persian court.

Questions of terminology in Elamite and Old Persian

The terminology used for relevant craft techniques at the Achaemenid Persian court was ambiguous, fluid, and hardly restrictive. Comparative anthropological studies of other premodern societies suggest that knowledge of pigment production and gilding techniques was part of the oral tradition of experts and craftsmen, often in closed circles. How would the ancient inhabitants of Achaemenid Iran have referred to the images created by applying paint on sculptures? The Old Persian term *patikarā* was translated by Kent as "picture, (sculptured) likeness" (Kent 1953: 194; cf. Cameron 1958: 166; Roaf 1980) and by Gershevitch as "counterfeit, re-production" (Roaf 1980: 73, n. 5). The word is rooted in the idea of likeness, not in the technique of sculpture per se. Kent's parenthetical suggestion of *sculptured* likeness was inferred from the fact that, in extant Achaemenid texts, the word refers to sculptural monuments. *Patikarā* is used in the inscriptions of Darius I at Bisotun (DB IV 66, ll. 72–7; Kent 1953: 132; Schmitt 1991: 72) and Naqsh-e Rustam (DNa 4, ll. 30–47, Kent 1953: 138), where it refers to the representational imagery on the two monuments (which in both cases happen to be rock reliefs). However, in discussing the terminology for sculptors and sculptures at the Achaemenid court, Roaf (1980: 65) argued correctly that the term *patikarā* must be interpreted like Akkadian *salmu*, which "had a similarly wide range of meanings: statue, relief, drawing."

Evidence from other Achaemenid texts does not provide a great deal more information that would allow us to see distinctions between *techniques* of wall painting versus painted relief sculpture versus polychrome-decorated glazed bricks in the rendering of "likeness" (for a variety of texts, see Nagel 2010).

Elamite administrative documents from Persepolis cast light on the subject in a context that was not governed by ideologically driven rhetoric. PT 27 (reign of Artaxerxes I, 462/1 BC) refers to "makers of inlay, makers of reliefs (?)" (Kuhrt 2007: 788, no. 19) and is interesting in that it unites two crafts in a reference to what appears to be a single work project. Several texts in the Persepolis Fortification archive refer to craftsmen, sometimes making explicit distinctions between types of crafts engaged in the decoration of Persepolis. Hallock translated El. *karsup* as "painter" (PF 1110, 1111, 1169 = Hallock 1969: 711). Cameron El. *hatena hutira* (PT 78) as "ornament maker," whereas Hallock suggested a "mirror maker" (Kuhrt 2007: 789, no. 21). El. *beasiskurraspe* (PT 30, PT 62) was understood as "ornament maker" by Hallock (1969: 677; 1959: 99–100). A "plasterer" (?) is perhaps attested as El. *du-uk-kaš* (PT 49a = Cameron and Gershevitch 1965: 175; PT 76:5 = Hallock 1969: 682; PT 10a = Arfa'i 2008). Gold- and silversmiths are also mentioned (PF 872 = Kuhrt 2007: 794, no. 29; PF 874 = Kuhrt 2007: 795–6, no. 33). The evidence reinforces the general impression that the Achaemenid court considered the production of various forms of ornamentation as part of a larger whole. Distinct specialties that contributed to the polychromy of the whole surely existed (such as inlay work vs. relief carving), but at the level of payments and disbursements, a craftsman employed in applying paints or surface décor was a craftsman to a large degree.

Ancient Texts

Colorful columns and reliefs adorning the walls of the palaces in Babylon are mentioned in the Bible and Classical texts. According to Ezekiel 23: 14–15 (perhaps recording scenarios of the sixth century BC) in the palaces of Babylon "there were men portrayed on the walls, the images of the Chaldaens portrayed with vermilion, girded with girdles upon their loins, exceeding in dyed attire upon their heads, all of them princes to look to, after the manner of the Babylonians at Chaldaea." According to Strabo, the Babylonians "wind ropes of twisted reed around the columns and then they plaster them and paint them with colors" (Strabo, *Geog.* 16.5.1).

Although the palaces and royal buildings in the Achaemenid heartland in Fars and Khuzestan were colorful throughout, there is surprisingly little Classical testimony that talks about color in relation to Achaemenid imperial built environments. Non-Oriental sources took note of colors in the Orient, but were often unspecific: the multicolored rings of fortifications at Ecbatana, the old capital of the Median Empire, were described by Herodotus (*Hist.* 1.98) in some detail and from a late source we are informed about the rich ornamentation of the palaces at Ecbatana. Polybius (10.27) stated that the woodwork in the palace "was all of cedar and cypress, but no part of it was left exposed, and the rafters, the compartments of the ceiling, and the columns in the porticoes and colonnades were plated with either silver or gold, and all the tiles were silver." Herodotus claims to have seen a mural painting, commissioned by Darius' engineers, depicting the bridge built by Darius I across the Bosporus showing "the whole bridge, with King Darius sitting in a seat of honor, and his army engaged in passage" (*Hist.* 4.88). Referring to the fourth century BC author Chares of Mytilene, Athenaeus (*Sophists at Dinner* 12.575) commented on "replicas of paintings of a famous myth of a Median princess and an Iranian ruler that can be found in temples and palaces, even in private dwellings" of the non-Greeks inhabiting the empire. Beyond these comments, though, the essential omission of references to color on Achaemenid monuments in the literary sources is an indication of a general silence on (lack of interest in?) colors in architectural and sculptural display that we get from most Classical authors. When Classical or Biblical texts refer to color it is usually to textiles. According to Esther 1: 16, for instance, the Persian king at Susa held a feast in the court of the garden of the royal palace, which was filled with "white, green, and blue hangings, fastened with cords of fine linen and purple to silver rings and pillars of marble; the beds (couches) were of gold and silver upon a pavement of red and blue, and of white and black marble." Plutarch wrote that Alexander found at Susa some 5000 talents of *porphyra hermionike*, "purple from Hermione," which had been stored for 190 years and "was still fresh in color" (*Alexander* 36.36).

Early Modern observations on polychromy

Surface applications and décor were early on observed and documented on the visible stone monuments of Achaemenid Persia (Nagel 2010, 2011). These early observations are critical pieces of information for us, for several reasons. On the one hand, they supply precious data on the original appearance of monuments before many fragile vestiges of pigments and overlays disappeared. On the other hand, they offer valuable instruction on several issues of which we must be aware. That a specific early traveler did not comment on surface coatings does not necessarily mean that these were not there when he visited. It may just not have seemed important or interesting to him. In other cases, a specific traveler may not indicate on which structures he saw the traces of paint that he refers to in his writing or "documents" in a visual presentation. In some cases, evidence expressed in written form may have been meant to serve a different purpose than the same early observer's characterization in the form of a graphic or other visual display. Finally, we cannot be sure if what may have appeared to an early observer as colorant may not have been remains of dust, vestiges of natural deterioration processes, or the like.

In one of the earliest preserved modern descriptions, Thomas Herbert (1606–1682), who visited Persepolis in 1630, described what appeared to him as gold inlays (1634: 59), although his comments were later considered fantastic (Weld-Blundell 1893: 557). Yet Herbert was not the only one to remark on what appeared to be gilding on stone reliefs;

only two generations later, in December 1685, Engelbert Kaempfer (1651–1716) visited the ruins at Naqsh-e Rustam and Persepolis and remarked specifically on the embellishment of inscriptions in cuneiform letters, apparently filled with metal (Kaempfer 1712: 338). According to Wiesehöfer (1991: 85), Kaempfer was specifically referring to the inscriptions of Darius on the south side of the Terrace (DPg). Gold in cuneiform letters carved on architectural surfaces on the Persepolis Takht is also mentioned by the French travelers André Daulier-Deslandes (1654–1719) and Jean Chardin (1643–1713).

More detailed comments on preserved polychromy were made by travelers who visited Persepolis in the nineteenth century: the Englishman James Buckingham (1786–1855) asserted (1829 1: 493), without further elaboration, that "the sculpture at Persepolis was also painted, *mostly in blue*, a favourite color of Egypt, but *sometimes in black and in yellow*." Charles Texier (1802–1871), who visited the Takht of Persepolis and Naqsh-e Rustam in January, 1840, can be considered the father of modern polychromy studies in Achaemenid archaeology. Not only was he the first to place the Achaemenid Persian monuments and reliefs in the broader context of Ancient Near Eastern building traditions, he was also the first to pay systematic attention to the surface embellishments of the monuments at Persepolis, providing a full set of observations on polychromy. It took another twelve years before these observations were published (1852). For example, after examining a particular relief depicting a king and two servants he noted,

> When I had to draw the figure of the king, followed by his two servants, I had to admit the certain, irrefutable presence of the paint of the bas-reliefs. Indeed I saw under the surface coating, which is nowadays as polished as a mirror, rosettes lightly drawn with a stylus, and that could only be the outline of a painted ornament on the coating; I saw the same ornament on the servants' hats. The king's tiara, as we know it today, is only a massive cylinder-shaped item; but we notice two holes on it that were used to seal a more decorated headgear made of bronze or a more precious metal. This one element would prove by itself that the sculpture was polychrome. Had the coating been designed to bear only one color, the ornaments that cover it would have been raised patterns, like the rosettes around the bas-reliefs; drawing simple ornaments on the sculptures with a chisel was never one of the ancient craftsmen's habits. (Texier 1852: 188–9)

Texier was also the first person to use a chemical technique to get "behind" the materials employed on the surface. He experimented with acid in order to identify the components of the surface finishing. Thus, he wrote,

> In another bas-relief, I identified the coating I previously mentioned, which had a blackish appearance; I scraped the stone smoothly, and dissolved the dust in hydrochloric acid, as I had kept a little box of reagents. I obtained a gray residue, and threw it in a pipe that contained ammonia, and twenty-four hours later I obtained a beautiful blue-colored solution. It was, without any doubt, an application of blue ash, the base of which is copper, and which was used as an ointment on the sculptures. (Texier 1852: 189)

Although he did not leave a published record of which part of which relief he subjected to analysis, Texier made a color reconstruction of a Persepolis relief depicting a king with two attendants (Texier 1852: pl. 111). Furthermore, in what became one of the most vivid and iconic modern reconstructions of the polychromy of Achaemenid Persepolis, Texier created a stunning, original portrayal of this relief in a chromolithograph. The rendering is quite faithful in composition and iconography to a motif well known from palace doorjambs on the Takht. The figures are set against a blue background. All details, including skin and hair, are deliberately covered with paint; there is no part of the relief where the stone itself shows through. The garments and headdresses are elaborately embellished. In the accompanying text, Texier stated that his reconstruction was based on observations of a number of reliefs, all depicting the same subject, though he admitted that his reconstructions did not necessarily approximate the original colors (Texier 1852: 188–90, 222). Texier's attention to polychromy as a key element on the remaining monuments of Persepolis was prescient in many respects. This episode is also an interesting attestation of the notion of "scientific" analysis at this early date, even though Texier's methods and results cannot today be used to verify the originally intended color.

By contrast, Eugène Flandin (1809–1871), a painter, and his architect-companion Pascal Coste (1787–1879) visited Persepolis only a year after Texier (December 1840 to early 1841), and their extensive documentation does not include *any* comments on traces of pigments on the standing remains there (Flandin and Coste 1851: 134–5). This is all the more remarkable in view of their profession.

Despite the practice of displaying painted plaster casts of Ancient Near Eastern monuments in both public and private collections during the nineteenth century, there is only one documented case of an attempt to restore the polychromy of Achaemenid Persian stone sculpture, and even in this instance, we lack important contextual information. At least one painted plaster cast from Persepolis must have been on display in the Louvre: Lottin de Laval's nineteenth-century tinted plaster cast of a Persian noble from wing A of the north façade of the Apadana, made between 1845 and 1850 after he had taken molds from a large number of relief façades at the site, has been dismissed as a fantasy based on little evidence (Nagel 2010: 76–7). Similarly, there is no information available on why the Achaemenid bull capitals recreated as part of the Assyrian palace in the upper floor of the Nineveh Court at the Crystal Palace in London were rendered in blue (Piggott 2004: 96).

In 1885 the botanist Frédéric Houssay (1860–1920) visited many sites in Khuzestan and Fars. He observed abundant traces of paint on the garments of the rulers on the Elamite rock reliefs at Kul-e Farah (Chapter 23), 150 km northeast of Susa (Dieulafoy 1885: 226). He also noted that the letters of the inscriptions on the façade of the tomb of Darius I at Naqsh-e Rustam stood out in blue against the natural gray of stone (Dieulafoy 1885: 227).

Although some travelers noted the presence of pigments on the visible structures above ground on the Persepolis Takht, Achaemenid Persia remained white in the minds of most European artists throughout much of the nineteenth century. This changed when a second major Achaemenid capital suddenly appeared on the radar of the European mindset, as French excavations at Susa began to offer a body of striking evidence for the original polychromy of the Achaemenid Persian architectural environment (Nagel 2010: 80–7).

Ernst Herzfeld (1879–1948), who began excavating in Iran in the early 1920s, is our closest witness, since he observed and documented significant traces of polychromy both at Pasargadae and Persepolis (Nagel 2011). At Pasargadae Herzfeld commented on traces of red paint in the wings and the dress of the "winged genius" on the doorjamb of Gate R, which served as the main entrance to the palace area on the plain. Excavating there in the spring of 1928, he noted traces of paint representing vestiges of mural paintings in Palace P. Samples of painted plaster, taken from Palace P at Pasargadae by Herzfeld, are today in the Freer Study Collection of the Freer Gallery of Art and Arthur M. Sackler Gallery of Art, Smithsonian Institution, Washington, DC, and are currently in the process of being analyzed.

Only five years earlier, during a visit to Persepolis in 1923, Herzfeld remarked that on the reliefs,

> in the Hall of 100 Columns, the throne legs laid bare were of a bright blue color. Also, remains of red paint were found higher above on the throne, and the feather wings of Ahuramazda have still their turquoise green color.... The lions of the eastern Hall of the Apadana had a more distinct layer of a red color.... I also investigated the Darius of the Tachara [Palace of Darius] with the lapis-beard in search of color: it is strange that the hair of the servants show traces of paint, the Darius heads not. The curls of the king have a deep yellow tone, which is not the original color of the stone (gray black). Was he perhaps blonde? (Herzfeld 1923; trans. A. Nagel)

Numerous fragments of lapis and other blue inlays for beards were subsequently discovered in the Treasury, the so-called Harem, a room beneath Palace D, one of the garrison quarters (Schmidt 1957: 73) west of the Apadana (Tilia 1978: pl. 100), and in other areas around Persepolis. Herzfeld repeatedly claimed that lapis was used in the beard and hair in the palace of Darius (e.g., Herzfeld 1931: 67; cf. Razmjou 2002a for paint on the statue of Darius found at Susa). According to his handwritten notes, the colorization of the doorjambs in the Hall of 100 Columns continued below the figure of Ahuramazda. In December 1923, Herzfeld noted what appeared to be pigment when examining the standing doorjambs—"Of those who support the dais, the negro still bears traces of black on the face" (Herzfeld 1923)—but he did not specify which of the four doorjambs in the Hall of 100 Columns with a depiction of a figure in the winged disk above the king supported by personifications of the subject lands he was referring to. Recent microscopic investigations of the supporting figures on these doorjamb reliefs have not revealed any traces of paint. However, the throne legs here still retain abundant traces of blue paint, substantiating Herzfeld's observations. On an ink drawing, on the same page on which Herzfeld had written about traces of paint on the "negro," he indicated the colors he mentioned seeing traces of greens, blues, and reds on another (?) sculpted winged symbol on one of the door jambs of the Hall of 100 Columns. It should also be recalled that there is abundant evidence of various skin tones on the glazed brick reliefs from Susa.

When doing exploratory work at Persepolis in 1928, Herzfeld harvested fragments that became part of his private collection and are important for the documentation of polychromy. Among these is a fragment of a glazed brick relief, today in the Freer Study Collection (Freer Gallery of Art, Washington, DC). In a sketchbook drawing, preserved in the same archive, Herzfeld noted the colors on this fragment. His letters and notes, written soon after the official excavations commenced on the Takht in early 1931, make frequent mention of color. From the so-called Harem, one of the building complexes on the southern side of the terrace, Herzfeld reported a typical Achaemenid ceramic "tulip" bowl with a blue mass inside (Nagel 2010: fig. 4.10). From unspecified parts of the same structure, Herzfeld listed ears of limestone bulls covered with red paint, a large number of wall pegs of Egyptian blue, and many fragments of glass paste in various colors. In a letter to the Oriental Institute in Chicago, dated November 5, 1932, Herzfeld noted a spectacular discovery in the Central Building (Tripylon):

> I nearly forgot to mention that yesterday, during the uncovering of a door in the Tripylon the lower part of a relief was found, which portrays a king with sunshade and servants, in its original bright colors. I did not allow it to be uncovered entirely, in order to make preparations for a color drawing when the uncovering was complete. The most striking color is a luminous bright red for the ground of the king's garment and for the shoes. It is not cinnabar, rather a little orange in tone: I assume there was such a bright purple in antiquity: it is closest to the red of the robes of cardinals. With the color remains found everywhere on the sculptures which had been buried under the soil, I first thought, that the reliefs essentially were the colors of the polished stone, i.e. black and only few parts, like ornaments, feather wings, lips, eyes, overlaid with red and bright blue, green, and yellow. *Now, it seems rather that all reliefs were entirely painted in brilliant, alternating colors, perhaps on the polished, black ground. What a strange impression this must have been!*

Herzfeld was obviously rather taken aback by the traces of paint detected by his workmen. Two weeks later he sent a set of photographs to Chicago. In the accompanying notes he offered another interesting observation: "Herewith I attach some more photographs.... (2) Gate building [i.e., the Central Building, Tripylon], back (northern) door. Lower part of the figures of the king and servants with vivid colors (we made watercolor sketches). (3) The same, hem of the robe of the king: besides the colors there was a layer of nearly 0.5mm gold." A watercolor of the same relief, by Herzfeld's assistant, Friedrich Krefter, was published only a few months later in April 1933; but no gold is indicated on it (Herzfeld 1933: 488, republished in Krefter 1989: pl. 1). In contrast to Herzfeld, Ann Britt and Giuseppe Tilia, who worked on the restoration of Persepolis from 1964 to 1979, described the traces of paint on the royal shoe on this doorjamb as red, not blue (Tilia 1978: 56–7). In 1986 P. Calmeyer (1930–1995) reexamined the door jambs of the Central Building and claimed to have identified red *and* blue paint on the king's shoes (Calmeyer 1989: 133; 1991). Subsequently, Krefter corrected Calmeyer, claiming that he saw *blue*, not red (and thus certainly also not blue *and* red) on the shoes when excavating the lower parts of this particular relief in 1932 with Herzfeld (Krefter 1991: 57–9). In support of his claim that both red and blue had been used on the royal shoes at Persepolis, Calmeyer (1989: 133) referred to Flandin's observations on the shoes of Sargon II on a relief at Khorsabad, which were striped in red and blue (Botta and Flandin 1846 1: pl. 14). While this comparison lends credence to Calmeyer's observation, the fact remains that we are left with divergent testimony, since no scientific analysis was conducted, nor were any color photographs or scientific documentation ever published. As already mentioned, Herzfeld's important observations regarding the applications of color and gilding to stone surfaces were only partially included in the final excavation reports, in which pigments on stone remains were only briefly mentioned (e.g., Schmidt 1953: 82, n. 90, 116, 134, n. 53, 257). In 1941, however, he remarked that "the excavations of the covered parts of the sculptures of the Tripylon also revealed their original colors unchanged: purple red and turquoise blue, with application of metal, possibly gold" (Schmidt 1941: 255).

Between 1969 and 1975 Judith Lerner worked as an independent researcher at Persepolis (thus overlapping with the era of the Tilias' restorations and investigations at the site). Lerner had previously worked on the polychromy of a fragment from the Hall of 100 Columns in the Harvard Museum collections. She was the first to observe and document the pigment remains on the Persepolis "figure in the winged disk" in the Harvard collection, on the basis of which she proposed a color reconstruction (Lerner 1971: 23, figs. 9–10; 1973: 120–1), later contested in part by Ann Britt Tilia. The traces of paint preserved on the matching segments of the same relief *in situ* at Persepolis were described by Tilia as follows: "on the first row of feathers from the bottom there were plenty of green pigments, and … the circular areas on the tips of the feathers showed traces of scarlet red color. The second row of feathers, on the other hand, showed numerous traces of red color, whereas the circles on the tips of the feathers had been painted blue" (Tilia 1978: 33, fig. 1a.). None of the alternating red and blue rows of small feathers at the top of the wings documented by Lerner on the Harvard relief were found on the fragments at Persepolis. The paint motif of the feathers inside the ring from which the figure emerges continues the lines of the carved elements of the relief (Tilia 1978: 36). An important feature of all the winged figures' feathers on the jambs are the incised circles on the tips. These had been observed by Herzfeld and later by Lerner and Tilia. The latter commented on a whitish substance along the edges, also visible on the small feathers on the top of the wings (Tilia 1978: pl. 26, figs. 22–4). Tilia observed that the outsides of these framings show a high degree of corrosion and argued that "a special color had been used for a special foundation, which had had a corroding effect on the stone, and possibly one that was meant to imitate a metal, perhaps gold" (Tilia 1978: 36). No chemical analysis has yet been conducted on these whitish substances. Photographs of the reliefs on both jambs of the western doorway taken in the early 1970s, still showed a whitish substance at the edge of the feathers that has since mostly disappeared. Recently, a microsample was taken from the whitish spots on the small feathers on the top of the wings of the jamb fragment at Harvard (Eremin and Kandhekar 2008). Analysis suggests that a hydrated iron oxide was used, perhaps indicating a yellow ocher. This may have been a ground layer for gilding, but without any further investigation and analysis of the reliefs *in situ*, Tilia's 1978 proposed gold reconstruction remains hypothetical.

Microscopic research has shown that the dress of the "figure in the winged disk" on the Harvard fragment was originally incised with patterns for ornamentation in color. By analogy with those depicted on garments of some of the guards on the glazed brick reliefs at Susa as well as on later images of Achaemenid rulers (e.g., the details on the border of the garment of Darius III in the so-called Alexander Mosaic, *c*.100 BC, from Pompeii: Hase 2009: 66, 71, figs. 4–5; Cohen 1997), golden appliqués adorning the dress may have been rendered in paint. Finds from unplundered tombs in Khuzestan (Arjan, Ram Hormuz; see Chapter 23) and elsewhere in the empire, as well as ancient texts, demonstrate that Elamite and Achaemenid royal dress was rich in gold ornamentation (Gleba 2008: 61; Shishehgar 2008; Álvarez-Mon 2010). The holes on the pleats of the garment and on the shoes of Cyrus on the reliefs adorning the door jambs of Palace P, the "residential palace" at Pasargadae, were intended to keep metal attachments in place (Tilia 1968: fig. 15; Root 1979: 51–2, pl. 2–3).

Recently, there has been much interest in textiles in the archaeological record and their depiction (Paetz 2009; Álvarez-Mon 2009; cf. Oppenheim 1949; Bovon 1963; Linders 1984). It is clear that only persons of high status wore garments with woven gold designs, bracteates, and embroidery (Kantor 1957). The recently excavated fourth century BC dress ornaments from burials at Vani in western Georgia (Kacharava and Kvirkelia 2009: 288–92, fig. 47, grave no. 24) and southern Siberia (Polosmak 2001), add to the already abundant evidence demonstrating the widespread use of such lavish garments among elites on the periphery of the Achaemenid Empire, a practice that may have been mirrored in the polychromy of the sculptures adorning Achaemenid palaces.

CASE STUDY I. THE FAÇADE OF THE TOMB OF DARIUS I AT NAQSH-E RUSTAM

Already in the nineteenth century, the rock-carved façade of the tomb of Darius I was the subject of important observations on polychromy by Houssay (see above). Schmidt, who published the findings of the Chicago expedition to Naqsh-e Rustam in 1970, does not seem to have been aware of this earlier testimony. Nevertheless, he did provide crucial new information about the original polychromy of this monument, although it is embedded in such a large documentary publication that it has perhaps not achieved the attention it deserves. Traces of blue pigment discovered by Boris Dubensky, the expedition photographer, in some cuneiform signs of the DNa inscription behind the king's figure are sufficient proof that all characters of at least the Old Persian and Elamite versions of the inscription were painted blue, and we see no reason to doubt that all inscriptions on the tomb were treated in the same manner (Schmidt 1970: 84). During restoration work conducted between 2001 and 2005 it was possible to make further observations on the polychromy of the façade. Abundant evidence of polychromy is now attested both in the inscriptions and elsewhere on the façade (Nagel and Rahsaz 2010). Blue pigment has been identified on the curls of the beard and hair of Darius. Traces of red paint have been identified on the visible eyelid, eyeball, and lips. Black lines accentuate the inner eyelid. Traces of blue and white pigment have been identified on Darius' headdress, the royal crown with three-stepped crenellations resembling the one Darius wears on his relief at Bisotun (Luschey 1968: 72, pl. 33), although no traces of paint have so far been documented on either the rock relief or the inscriptions at Bisotun (Luschey 1968: 83, "Von einer ursprünglichen farbigen Fassung.... konnten wir keine Spuren mehr feststellen").

On the tomb façade at Naqsh-e Rustam, Darius I is dressed in the Persian court robe. Detailed painted motifs detected on similar representations in Persepolis were meticulously reconstructed by Tilia (1978: 54, fig. 6; Kuhrt 2007: 532, fig. 11.25) and may provide a clue to the original appearance of the king as he appeared at Naqsh-e Rustam as well, even though no paint has been observed there on his robe. A dark red pigment has, however, been recorded on Darius' shoes on the tomb façade, perhaps a priming layer for an additional coat. No traces of paint have been identified so far on either the pedestal or the fire altar shown in front of Darius. Similarly, no traces have been identified on the figure in the winged disk.

Behind the image of Darius I are inscriptions in Old Persian, Babylonian, and Elamite. Recently, traces of blue paint from these inscriptions were recovered from paper squeezes made by Herzfeld in 1923 (in the Herzfeld Archives in the Freer Gallery of Art and Arthur M. Sackler Gallery, Washington, DC). These were examined in the Conservation Laboratory in October 2009 and identified as Egyptian blue. In 2003, traces of "red (?) color pigments" were mentioned to Adriano Rossi by Hassan Rahsaz, then director of the Parsa-Pasargad Research Foundation, as having recently been discovered in an inscription on the southern tomb above the Takht (Rossi 2006: 475, n. 105). One hopes that this material will be analyzed to determine its chemical composition. Even if it turns out that a red pigment was used, however, we must bear in mind that this could imply the use of red either for display or as a ground layer for an additional top layer (e.g., gilding?).

On the tomb relief of Darius I at Naqsh-e Rustam, courtiers and soldiers, representing the two columns of the Achaemenid Empire, are depicted on the side. The two uppermost figures to the left of Darius, Gobryas, and Aspathines are identified by inscriptions highlighted in blue. The inscriptions in Old Persian, Elamite, and Babylonian identifying the various peoples personifying the lands of the empire are also highlighted in blue. These labels were framed with finely chiseled lines, also infilled with blue. Blue was also found in the leaf-like ornaments which constitute the uppermost part of the throne platform. Furthermore, the leonine creature that is part of the furniture preserves remnants of blue on the body and mane and red in the mouth.

Traces of paint were also identified all over the entablature, presumably representing the wooden roof of a palace, that separates the middle and upper parts of the tomb façade. Red traces were observed on the dentils in the lower part of the entablature, while the background was painted in blue. Red, blue, and green pigments were identified on the fillet of the register. On the latest Achaemenid royal tombs (carved above the Persepolis Takht), these parts were adorned with a frieze of eighteen lions arranged antithetically with a lotus flower in the center (Schmidt 1970: pl. 75; Calmeyer 2009: pls. 17.3, 32.1). The painted pattern on the façade of Darius I's tomb is reminiscent of this animal frieze found in sculpted form on the later Achaemenid tomb façades at Persepolis.

The middle register of Darius I's tomb façade evokes an architectural façade featuring four plain columns on rectangular, two-stepped bases with a torus and bull capitals carrying a beam below the architrave. Schmidt identified traces of blue paint on the bull capitals here, mirroring the blue identified on the body of the animal protome capitals of the palaces at Persepolis. The horns of the bull protomes carrying the roof on the top register were made separately. No details have been observed that would suggest the type and original appearance of these horns.

Traces of paint were also identified on the Egyptianizing cavetto cornice in the central doorway of the middle register. The leaves of this cornice were decorated in an alternating blue and red color scheme, with a fin in the center of each of the individual leaves, known as "painted leaf" on contemporary Egyptian and Greek monuments (e.g., Brinkmann 2008: figs. 107–8, 119, 179). On the door leading to the tomb chamber of Darius I, the blue leaves were decorated with a red fin, while blue fins correspondingly filled the other scales.

Although all of the Achaemenid tomb façades at Naqsh-e Rustam and Persepolis appear superficially similar in form and detail, this does not necessarily mean that they originally looked the same. Clearly, they share much iconographically but color would have differentiated them. One example will perhaps suffice. Although Schmidt did not observe any traces of pigment on the tombs of Darius' successors (Schmidt 1970: 92), observations made by the author in 2008 revealed that the Egyptianizing cornice of the doorway in the middle register of Tomb V (= tomb of Artaxerxes II?) at Persepolis has green and blue leaves rather than the red and blue found on Darius' tomb façade at Naqsh-e Rustam (Nagel 2010: figs. 4.34–4.36). No painted fins could, however, be identified on the leaf scheme. It has been argued that the traces of paint on these later tomb façades are vestiges of the original polychromy, applied to the surface of the façade in the months immediately following their carving (Nagel and Rahsaz 2010). Naturally, the paints could also date to later episodes of repainting. Future investigations and technical analyses may well provide additional information about the existence of possible paint preparation layers or repainting. The interiors of the tombs may have been painted, too, but no evidence of this has yet been found.

Case Study II. The Pigment Bowls from the Apadana

From the time its construction began in the late sixth century BC, the Apadana was the landmark building on the terrace platform at Persepolis. Measuring c.110 m on each side, with thirty-six stone columns supporting the central hall and a group of storerooms between the two southern towers, this building was a colossal enterprise in many respects. Seen from afar the Apadana dominated the entire Marv Dasht Plain. Stairways in the corners of the building led to upper mezzanines and floors. The stairways leading up to the first floor on the north and east side are adorned with the famous reliefs of gift-bearers from the subject lands paying homage to the Great King. In the 1970s, unexpected evidence was discovered during soundings below the level of the façades. When removing the lower parts of the inner western flight of the northern stairway in order to repair them in the spring of 1978, Tilia discovered lumps of green, red, and blue colors spread over an area measuring c.2.50 × 0.60 m, some 26 cm below the bottom of the rosette border. Potsherds encrusted with pigments of the same color were also found (Tilia 1978: 69). In 2004, additional sherds encrusted with red and blue pigment were excavated in front of the east façade of the Apadana (Nagel 2010), again c.26 cm below the base of the visible façade. The distribution of these finds extended along the files of gift-bearing delegations toward the central panels of the two façades which originally depicted the king about to receive the offerings shown. Although we do not know at what point in the building's history the pigments were deposited, it may be hypothesized that this was done by the artisans themselves, as intentional offerings to the Apadana (and the King).

Evidence of painting activity was also found in the interior of the building. In Room 6 of the southern tower of the Apadana, Schmidt excavated a bowl lined with green pigment, which he suggested was used to touch up the walls and floors, but the substance has never been properly analyzed (Schmidt 1953: 74, fig. 32 "Room 6"). During the final excavation season in 1939 a sherd encrusted with Egyptian blue was found in Room 21 of the Apadana (Schmidt 1957: 133 [PT 7 381, Plot HE 41]). Pieces of gold foil were found in the same room (Schmidt 1953: 75), but their present whereabouts are unknown. All of this suggests ongoing activity by painters and we may infer that touch up work was a constant part of the maintenance of the polychrome reliefs and other architectural elements on the site.

Elsewhere on the Takht, paint bowls were also found. As noted above, Herzfeld found a bowl containing pigment in the so-called Harem area. In the Treasury, Schmidt excavated a "grinding bowl" of gray basalt, smoothed by use on the interior; a limestone polisher or grinder retaining traces of red pigment (Schmidt 1953: 191, room 81, PT 6 452; 1957: 102: pl. 80.10); and a small stone object covered with "pink matter" (Schmidt 1953: 185, Room 51; 1957: 102–3, pl. 80. 12, PT 6 213, lost at sea). In 2008, a large number of blue pellets (c.2 cm in dia.) were rediscovered in the storerooms of the Persepolis

Museum (Nagel 2010: 138–9, fig. 4.21), though their find circumstances are unknown today and they have not yet been analyzed. Many paint bowls were excavated by the Italian-Iranian team below the southwestern corner of the platform during work that continued until 1973 in the area of the so-called Palace H. This zone bears remnants of at least three successive buildings, two Achaemenid date and one post-Achaemenid (Tilia 1978: 239).

In December 1971, after excavations were conducted southwest of Palace H, samples from a bowl containing pigment were given to J. Lerner for analysis and in the summer of 1975 she photographed a large number of fragments bearing traces of pigment, from which four dozen pigment samples were taken for further chemical analysis (Stodulski et al. 1984). These included pure pigments from cleaning conducted below the eastern doorway of the Central Building in spring 1975.

While no paint containers per se have been documented from Susa, clumps of earth encrusted with paint were noticed by Ghirshman in the 1930s in the area of the Apadana, and by D. Ladiray at the Gate of Darius in the 1970s (*PDS*: 254, n. 17).

ON FIND CONTEXTS AND SYMBOLIC MEANINGS

Although little information is available on paint preparation or application in Achaemenid palaces, evidence from elsewhere in the ancient world provides glimpses into the work processes involving color and polychromy. Large lumps of pigment were excavated by Place in the corners of a room in the Neo-Assyrian palace at Khorsabad. A red lump "en quantité considérable" weighed about 20 kg (!), and a blue lump about 1 kg (Place 1867–70 2: 251). In the same chamber, Place noted three unfinished sculpted stone slabs with chips of the same stone and pigment lumps scattered on the floor (Place 1867–70 1: 92–3 and vol. 3: pl. 48). This evidence suggests that this was a workshop in which both painters and sculptors worked closely together. In Room SW 6 of Fort Shalmaneser at Nimrud, the excavators discovered "large lumps of bright Egyptian Blue… certainly stored" (Mallowan 1966: 408). Excavations of a Hellenistic/Roman temple at Petra in Jordan identified a subterranean painter's workshop inside the temple (Hammond 1996: 49–50; Shaer 2003: 125–8). This workshop was part of the original building plan at Petra, and it is assumed that it "was meant to be for activities related to the maintenance of the building" (Shaer 2003: 126). The same may have been the case on the Athenian Acropolis. "Closed jars containing actual pigments" were said to have been discovered near the southeast angle of the Parthenon during excavations in 1836 (Donaldson 1851: 44; Semper 1851: 43). Materials, tools, and contexts suggestive of a painter's workshop were excavated at Olympia as well (Heilmeyer 1981). In New Kingdom Egypt, a factory and paint shops, complete with paint boxes, was found at Tell Amarna (Spurrell 1895: 230–5). Several important studies of the technical process involved in the creation of painted Egyptian tombs have been published (e.g., Bryan 2001; Owen and Kemp 1994; Miller 2008).

Pigment and empire: Supplying the courts with material

The stone used in the palaces at Persepolis was supplied by local quarries (Tilia 1968; Krefter 1967, 1971; Zare 2004). With the exception of the statue of Darius, most of the stone monuments at Susa were made of local Susiana limestone (Trichet and Vallat 1990: 205; Razmjou 2002b: 102). It is interesting that Darius specifically boasted in his so-called Foundation Charter (DSf), that the stone for the soaring columns of the Susa palaces came from a certain village in Elam (Kent 1953: 142–4). Analysis has also shown that the raw materials for the bricks at Susa came from local sources (Ruben 1979; Trichet and Ruben 1980). Even without the benefit of similar provenience studies for Persepolis, Schmidt suggested that the glazed bricks there must have been made "in the neighborhood of the site" (Schmidt 1957: 93), but he went on to say "we are quite certain that the makers of these bricks were foreigners, presumably Babylonians, here as at Susa."

Were the pigments and gold used to embellish the monuments of Persepolis locally derived or did they come from further afield? Only recently have scholars attempted to reconstruct the process of supplying paint pigments and related materials for ancient capitals (e.g., Gliozzo 2007 [pigments] and Wilson 2007 [metal] for Rome; cf. Hejl 2005). In the case of Egyptian blue, F. R. Matson and Schmidt (Schmidt 1957: 133, n. 4) suggested two possible scenarios: the ingredients were imported and the artisans who made the objects were foreign experts, either from Egypt or Mesopotamia; or lumps or powder of Egyptian blue were imported for use as pigment, to be mixed locally with a carrying agent—water, egg white, and so on. These scenarios are not necessarily mutually exclusive. In dry form, pigment cakes and cubes could have been transported over long distances and then crushed, ground, and pulverized with mortars, mixed with binders, and converted into coloring agents, at the work site itself. In discussing the few traces of paint preserved on architecture and sculpture at Susa, Mecquenem suggested that some raw materials, such as red ocher, could have come from islands in the Persian Gulf (Mecquenem 1947: 95). Today, such an attribution is questionable, and only recently have the raw materials excavated at Susa been properly analyzed, though the results are difficult to interpret (Razmjou et al. 2004; Caubet and Daucé 2010).

The manufacture and distribution of raw materials, including pigments and gilding, must have played an important role in the economies of the Achaemenid and pre-Achaemenid era. Egyptian blues, as well as all other materials applied to the surfaces of Achaemenid monuments, required an understanding of techniques of manufacture, application, fixing, and color preservation. Among our earliest preserved records on how to produce red colors from yellow earth is an Old Assyrian cuneiform text from c.1700 BC (Campbell Thompson 1926: 31–2; Leicester 1971: 8).

Although archaeo-metallurgical studies focusing on pre-Islamic Iran have made much progress, our information about various raw material sources in Fars is still limited. Minerals were mined close to Persepolis in the Achaemenid period: for example, one copper and two iron mines have been investigated since 2003 (Emami 2005). A mine in the Bavanat deposit, with several tunnels up to 40 m deep, yielded copper sulfide and copper oxide. Two iron mines in the same region, Faryadan and Kan Ghobar, have deposits of magnetite and siderite. Both have two large gates some 14–17 m below ground, with several tunnels. Pottery found in them suggests use in the Achaemenid period (Emami 2005). Recent research has confirmed that the Iranian plateau was an important source of metals for societies in neighboring regions (e.g., Pigott 1999a, 1999b, 2004). More than 400 copper deposits are attested in Iran, and though widely distributed across time and space almost eighty of these show indications of ancient mining (Bazin and Hübner 1969; Momenzadeh 2004). Today, the Sar Cheshmeh copper porphyry mine in Kerman and the Sungun and Meiduk deposits in the same region make Iran one of the major copper producers of Asia (Momenzadeh 2004; Aliani et al. 2009). It is possible that the malachite used for green pigment ($Cu_2[(OH)_2|CO_3]$), a copper oxide identified on the monuments on the Takht and easily smelted in a crucible, originated near Persepolis, but further investigation is needed to confirm this.

Some materials needed for the embellishment and finishing of architectural sculpture on the Achaemenid monuments would, however, have come from distant parts. Gold, for example, was available in various places in the empire. More than 100 gold and gold-bearing deposits and occurrences have been identified in Iran. Thirteen were clearly exploited in the pre-Islamic period, some of which are located in southeastern Iran (Momenzadeh 2002, 2004). Gold was obtained from both hard rock and alluvia by panning (Momenzadeh 2002, 2004). In addition, the river Hyctanis in the province of Carmania (OP *Karmanâ*, El. *Kurman*, cf. PF 1348 in Hallock 1969: 381) is mentioned by Pliny as a source of gold (*Nat. Hist.* 4.98). There were also silver, copper, and ocher mines in Armenia. Strabo refers to a gold mine and other mines, particularly one in northern Armenia, that produced *sandyx*, "which they call Armenian color" (Strabo, *Geog.* 11.14.9; Kuhrt 2007: 706).

While the collation of actual data on the sources of the raw materials for Achaemenid polychromy in Fars and Khuzestan is important, perhaps even more important is the rhetorical dimension of the supply system. The very *concept* of raw materials (and labor) for palatial constructions coming from all over the empire to the centers of power was a significant rhetorical motif in the formative years of Darius I. Raw materials as prestige commodities of empire under the King's control were a key element in the royal expression of power. The Susa Foundation Charters (DSf, DSz, DSaa; e.g., Kent 1953: 142–4; Kuhrt 2007: 492–5, no. 13; Root 2010) make this clear even though they do not explicitly refer to pigments.

On color, materiality, and surface at Persepolis

Our discussion of blue paints and precious, colorful materials at Persepolis invites us to investigate some further aspects of color, materiality, and surface at Achaemenid

Persian sites. The first issue to discuss is the materiality of the limestones used for stone architectural/sculptural elements. For Pasargadae, for instance, Boardman (1959: 217) and Francovich (1966: 233–4) once argued that the mix of light and dark limestone in Palaces R and S was systematic and reflected Ionian influence. Similarly, Nylander (1970: 142–3) concluded that: (1) such systematic variation in color is attested only in selected contexts; and (2) such accentuation by color contrasts might have been used for purely aesthetic considerations that may or may not have reflected input from a specific craft tradition. He cited Palace P at Pasargadae, where the various stones were used in an "entirely unstructural way.... What we find in Pasargadae is thus not a bichromatism evincing structural analysis and an accentutation of the constituing parts but a predominantly optical, atectonic play of contrasts, based, no doubt, on purely aesthetic considerations" (Nylander 1970: 143). Tilia argued for a distinction between a purely decorative and a structural use, in which the dark stones were used as "decorative elements," while the light-colored stones were used for all "constructive elements" (Tilia 1968: 68). We must ask therefore, whether the bichromatism, where it does exist at Pasargadae, was originally meant to be seen, or whether a final coat of paint would have obscured these dark/light variations in the building material, bearing in mind that both Herzfeld and Lerner found clear evidence of paint on stone reliefs at Pasargadae.

Turning to Persepolis, Nylander observed that the systematic, if selective bichromatism in stone that does appear at Pasargadae is completely absent at Persepolis (Nylander 1970: 143) where, in contrast, we have abundant evidence of paint. Elsewhere it has been argued that it is important to systematically record the locations of the various limestones used at Persepolis (Nagel 2010) with the goal of revealing any possible pattern of systematic bichromatism. While such a finding would represent an exciting new discovery about polychromy at the site, I do not anticipate a reversal of our current understanding that the variegated colors do not reflect a consistently applied aesthetic principle intended to highlight the natural surface appearance of the stone. Rather, I would argue that such systematic documentation might help us to understand other important issues involved in the material aspects of the stone. Some quarries may have yielded better blocks for large-scale elements, such as bull capitals. Some limestones might have had different surface properties, enabling them to better receive and hold pigments. This in turn would potentially provide useful information about the processes of stoneworking and subsequent painting.

If we consider the different color schemes employed on the doors of the façades of the tomb of Darius at Naqsh-e Rustam and the tomb of one of his predecessors above the Persepolis platform, alternative readings can be suggested, in which color signified a remarkable degree of diversity. On the façade of the tomb of Darius I at Naqsh-e Rustam, the blue that filled in and framed the inscriptions certainly helped to make the forms visible to viewers looking at them high above their heads. On a microscopic level, the surface coatings on exterior façades like the Apadana reliefs or the stone bulls in the portico of the Hall of 100 Columns may have helped protect the stone from weathering (Nagel 2010).

The polychromy of Achaemenid Persepolis has two main characteristics:

1. the colors employed formed clear contrasts with their environment; and
2. within the Achaemenid palaces there was a system of cross-referencing between precious stones and paint applications. Blue-painted bull column capitals referred to precious lapis and painted plaster applied to wooden columns may have been intended to imitate expensive stone columns. The very colors of the stone, though, were hidden and remained largely invisible. Research indicates that the elaborate polychromy employed was intended to imitate precious stones.

Concluding remarks: Toward an archaeology of paint at Persepolis?

Achaemenid Persian architectural sculpture is rich in vestigial traces of original polychromy. The stone reliefs at Persepolis, as well as the carved tomb façades of the Achaemenid rulers above the Persepolis platform and at Naqsh-e Rustam, preserve traces of original polychromy to a remarkable degree. While we lack proper documentation for many decades of past research and even for the more recent treatment of the stone surface, the size of the terrace alone suggests that pigments and color schemes can still be identified, recorded, and analyzed. Once a sensitivity toward and awareness of polychromy has been established, necessary steps may be undertaken to document the remaining paints. Proper documentation and conservation will ideally go hand in hand, however difficult the integration of archaeological science and archaeological interpretation may be (Pollard and Bray 2007; Agnew and Bridgland 2006).

Perhaps the greatest potential in the study of Achaemenid Persian polychromy lies in the monumental tomb façades. Nearly inaccessible due to their position high above the ground, the carved and sculpted façades of the Achaemenid royal tombs are ideal candidates for detailed examination. Working toward an archaeology of paint in Persepolis is exciting. Paint archaeology is a relatively new field that presents its own complexities, but documenting and discussing the evidence available for the polychromies of Persepolis and Susa is an important component in any appraisal of material culture in the Achaemenid court environment. So *why* does the world need studies of the pigments of Persepolis? Because the pigments are a physical testament to ancient knowledge in art, chemistry, optics, and perception, and taken together they provide unique insights into the world of this empire. Looking back from the vantage point of the early third millennium AD, we can understand the excitement of Charles Texier, or Ernst Herzfeld, and everyone else of the late nineteenth and early twentieth centuries who spotted traces of paint and polychromy in the Achaemenid remains while visiting or excavating these sites. Mistakes were made, documents were lost, material was *whitewashed* (Nagel 2010). When we begin to analyze and investigate the surface of the monuments at Persepolis, uncovering paint layers and making cross-sections, it may at first be difficult to understand the historical consequences of such work. In order to fully understand Achaemenid painting and polychromy, however, it is crucial to study how the paints and surface treatments were made and applied, and how they deteriorated over time. This knowledge should become a fully integrated part of research in the archaeology of ancient Iran.

Further reading

An accessible introduction to aspects of color and gilding in Achaemenid architecture and sculpture at Persepolis remains Tilia's chapter "Color in Persepolis" (Tilia 1978: 29–70), even if detailed technological studies are missing entirely. Lee and Quirke (2000) provide a masterful introduction to "painting materials" in the Egyptian sphere. The observations made there are highly relevant for aspects of paint and gilding in Achaemenid Persia, too. The recently published papers from a session on color at the 7th International Congress on the Archaeology of the Ancient Near East, held in 2010 (Matthews and Curtis 2012), provide a good account of current work on color in the Ancient Near East.

References

Agnew, N., and J. Bridgland. 2006. *Of the past, for the future: Integrating archaeology and conservation.* Los Angeles: Getty Conservation Institute.

Albenda, P. 2005. *Ornamental wall painting in the art of the Assyrian empire.* Leiden/Boston: Brill.

Aliani, F., A. Alirezaei, A. Moradian, and Z. Abbaslo. 2009. Geochemistry and petrography of the Meiduk porphyry copper deposit, Kerman, Iran. *Australian Journal of Basic and Applied Sciences* 3/4: 3786–800.

Álvarez-Mon, J. 2010. *The Arjān tomb, at the crossroads of the Elamite and the Persian Empires.* Leuven: Acta Iranica 49.

Arfa'i, A. M. 2008. PT 10a, collated and completed. *ARTA* 2008.001.

Bazin, D., and H. Hübner. 1969. *Copper deposits in Iran.* Tehran: Geological Survey of Iran Report 13.

Boardman, J. 1959. Chian and early Ionic architecture. *AJ* 39: 170–218.

Botta, P. E., and E. Flandin. 1846–50. *Monument de Ninive*, 5 vols. Paris: Gide and Baudry.

Boucharlat, R. 2010. Autres travaux de Darius et successeurs. *PDS*: 374–419.

Bovon, A. 1963. La représentation des guerriers perses et la notion de barbare dans le la première moitié du Ve siècle. *BCH* 87: 579–602.

Braenne, J. 2009. Layers of misunderstanding: The challenge of understanding, interpreting and organizing the results from architectural paint research. In *Architectural finishes in the built environment*, ed. M. Jablonski and C. Matsen, 113–22. New York: Archetype.

Bregnhoi, L., and M. Christensen. 2009. Paint research, interpretation and communication. In *Architectural finishes in the built environment*, ed. M. Jablonski and C. Matsen, 87–96. New York: Archetype.

Brinkmann, V. 2007. The blue eyes of the Persians: The colored sculpture of the time of Alexander and the Hellenistic period. In *Color of gods: Painted sculpture of classical antiquity*, ed. V. Brinkmann and R.Wünsche, 150–67. Munich: Glyptothek.

———. 2008. *Bunte Götter: Die Farbigkeit antiker Skulptur*. Frankfurt: Liebighaus.

Bryan, B. 2001. Painting techniques and artisan organization in the tomb of Suemniwet, Theban Tomb 92. In *Colour and painting in ancient Egypt*, ed. W. V. Davies, 63–72. London: British Museum Press.

Buckingham, J. 1829. *Travels in Assyria, Media and Persia, including a journey from Bagdad by Mount Zagros*, vol. 1. London: Colburn and Bentley.

Calmeyer, P. 1989. Zur Genese altiranischer Motive: Die elamisch-persische Tracht. *AMI* 21: 27–53.

———. 1991. Die blauen Schuhe. *AMI* 24: 133.

———. 2009. *Die Reliefs der Gräber V und VI in Persepolis*. Mainz: AIT 8.

Cameron, G. G. 1958. Persepolis Treasury Tablets old and new. *JNES* 17: 161–76.

Cameron, G. G., and I. Gershevitch 1965. New tablets from the Persepolis treasury. *JNES* 24: 167–92.

Campbell Thompson, R. 1926. *A dictionary of Assyrian chemistry and geology*. Oxford: Clarendon Press.

Carriveau, G., and D. Omecinsky 1983. Identification of the Forbes Collection pigments: 1. Whites. *Journal of the American Institute for Conservation* 22/2: 68–81.

Caubet, A., and N. Daucé. 2010. Les arts du feu. *PDS*: 322–47.

Cohen, A. 1997. *The Alexander Mosaic: Stories of victory and defeat*. Cambridge: Cambridge University Press.

Dieulafoy, M. 1885. Mission de Susiane. Note relative à la découverte sur le tombeau de Darius de sept inscriptions nouvelles. *Revue Archéologique sér.* 3/6: 224–7.

Donaldson, T. L. 1851. Polychromatic embellishments in Greek architecture. *Civil Engineer and Architects Journal* 14: 42–50.

Emami, S. M. 2005. *Recent investigations into the archaeometallurgy and ancient mining of the Achaemenid period in Takht-i-Djamshid*. Shiraz: Parsa-Pasargadae Foundation (in Persian).

Eremin, K., and N. Kandhekar. 2008. Identification of pigments on the Persepolis relief: 1943.1062. Unpublished report, Harvard Strauss Center for Conservation and Technical Studies.

Flandin, E., and P. Coste 1851. *Voyage en Perse de mm. Eugène Flandin, peintre, et Pascal Coste, architecte ... entrepris par ordre de m. le ministre des affaires étrangères, d'après les instructions dressées par l'Institut*. Paris: Gide et J. Baudry.

Francovich, G. de. 1966. Problems of Achaemenid architecture. *EW* 16/3–4: 201–60.

Gerharz, R., R. Lantermann, and D. Spennemann. 1986. Munsell Farbtafeln: Eine Notwendigkeit für die Archäologen? *Acta praehistorica et archaeologica* 18: 177–87.

Gleba, M. 2008. You are what you wear: Scythian costume as identity. In *Dressing the past*, ed. M. Gleba, C. Munkholt, and M. L. Nosch, 13–28. Oxford: Oxbow Books.

Gliozzo, E. 2007. Supplying Italy with black and white pigments. In *Supplying Rome and the Empire: The Proceedings of an international seminar held at Siena-Certosa di Pontignano on May 2–4, 2004, on Rome, the provinces, production and distribution*, ed. E. Papi, 72–84. Portsmouth: *Journal of Roman Archaeology* Supplementary Series 69.

Graeve, V. von. 1970. *Der Alexandersarkophag und seine Werkstatt*. Berlin: Mann.
Guralnick, E. 2010. Color at Khorsabad: Palace of Sargon II. In *Proceedings of the 6th International Congress of the Archaeology of the Ancient Near East. 5th–10th May 2008, Rome*, vol. 1, ed. P. Matthiae, F. Pinnock, L. Nigro, and N. Marchetti, 781–92. Wiesbaden: Harassowitz.
Hallock, R. T. 1959. The Elamite texts from Persepolis. In *Akten des vierundzwanzigsten internationalen Orientalisten-Kongresses München, 28. August bis 4. September 1957*, ed. H. Franke, 177–9. Wiesbaden: Deutsche Morgenländische Gesellschaft.
———. 1969. *Persepolis Fortification Tablets*. Chicago: OIP 92.
Hammond, P. C. 1996. *The temple of the winged lions. Petra, Jordan, 1973–1990*. Arizona: Petra Publishing.
Hase, F.-W. 2009. Das Alexandermosaik—ein Mosaikgemälde und seine Interpretationsprobleme. In *Alexander der Große und die Öffnung der Welt: Asiens Kulturen im Wandel*, ed. S. Hansen, A. Wieczorek, and M.Tellenbach, 66–75. Mannheim: Publikationen der Reiss-Engelhorn-Museen 36.
Heilmeyer, W.-D. 1981. Antike Werkstattfunde in Griechenland. *AA*: 440–5.
Hejl, E. 2005. Prehistoric pigment mining on Santorini's neighbouring island Anafi. *Austrian Journal of Earth Sciences* 98: 22–33.
Herbert, T. 1634. *Description of the Persian monarchy now being the Oriental Indyes, Iles and other parts of the Greater Asia and Africk*. London: Stansby and Bloome.
Herzfeld, E. 1923. Ernst Herzfeld Papers, N-24 (8 December 1923). Unpublished papers held in the Freer Gallery of Art and Arthur M. Sackler Gallery Archives, Smithsonian Institution.
———. 1931. Die Magna Charta von Susa. *AMI* 3: 29–81.
———. 1933. Xerxes in ancient Persian art. The colour of treasures from the great Persepolis discovery. *ILN* April 8: 488–9.
———. 1941. *Iran in the Ancient East*. London/Oxford: Oxford University Press.
Kacharava, D., and G. Kvirkelia. 2009. Archaeological excavations at Vani in 2002: A preliminary report. In *Archaeology in Southern Caucasus: Perspectives from Georgia*, ed. A. Sagona and M. Abramischwili, 407–40. Leuven: Peeters.
Kaempfer, E. 1712. *Amoenitatum exoticarum politico-physico-medicarum fasciculi V, quibus continentur variæ relationes, observationes et descriptiones rerum Persicarum et Ulterioris Asiae, multâ attentione, in peregrinationibus per universum Orientem, collectæ*. Lemgo: Meyer.
Kantor, H. J. 1957. Achaemenid gold jewellry in the Oriental Institute. *JNES* 16: 1–23.
Kent, R. 1953. *Old Persian: Grammar, texts, lexicon*. 2nd ed. New Haven: AOS 33.
Krefter, F. 1967. Zur Steinmetztechnik von Persepolis. In *Festschrift für Wilhelm Eilers*, ed. G. Wiessner, 429–41.Wiesbaden: Harrassowitz.
———. 1971. *Persepolis Rekonstruktionen*. Berlin: Teheraner Forschungen 3.
———. 1989. Persepolis in Farbe. *AMI* 22: 131–2.
———. 1991. Die roten Schuhe. *AMI* 24: 57–9.
Kuhrt, A. 2007. *The Persian Empire: A corpus of sources from the Achaemenid period*. London/ New York: Routledge.
Labrousse, A., and R. Boucharlat. 1974. La fouille du palais du Chaour à Suse en 1970 et 1971. *CDAFI* 2: 61–167.
Lee, L., and S. Quirke. 2000. Painting materials. In *Ancient Egyptian materials and technology*, ed. P. Nicholson and I. Shaw, 104–20. Cambridge: Cambridge University Press.
Leicester, H. 1971. *Historical background of chemistry*. New York: Dover.
Lerner, J. 1971. The Achaemenid relief of Ahura Mazda in the Fogg Art Museum, Cambridge, Massachusetts. *BAI* 2: 19–35.

———. 1973. A painted relief from Persepolis. *Archaeology* 26: 116–22.
Linders, T. 1984. The kandys in Greece and Persia. *Opuscula Atheniensa* 15: 107–14.
Luschey, H. 1968. Studien zu dem Darius-Relief von Bisutun. *AMI* 1: 63–94.
Mallowan, M. 1966. *Nimrud and its remains*, 2 vols. New York: Dodd, Meade and Co.
Marincola, M. 2004. Polychromy. In *The Encyclopedia of sculpture*, ed. A. Bostroem, 1318–22. New York/London: Fitzroy Dearbon.
Matthews, R., and J. Curtis. 2012. *Proceedings of the 7th International Congress of the Archaeology of the Ancient Near East*, vol. 2, *Ancient and modern issues in cultural heritage, colour & light in architecture, art & material culture*. Wiesbaden: Harrassowitz.
Mecquenem, R. de. 1947. Contribution à l'étude du palais achéménide de Suse. In *Archéologie susienne*, ed. R. de Mecquenem, L. Le Breton, and M. Rutten, 1–119. Paris: MDP 30.
Miller, E. 2008. Painterly technique. In *The Nebamun wall paintings: Conservation, scientific analysis and display at the British Museum*, ed. A. Middleton and K. Uprichard, 61–70. London: Archetype Publications and British Museum.
Momenzadeh, M. 2002. Mining archaeology in Iran. An ancient gold mining site of Zartorosht (SW-Jiroft, SE-Iran). *Metalla* 9/1: 47–53.
———. 2004. Metallic mineral resources of Iran, mined in ancient times. *PAP*: 8–21.
Moorey, P. R. S. 1994. *Ancient Mesopotamian materials and industries: The archaeological evidence*. Oxford: Clarendon Press.
Moortgat, A. 1959. *Alt-Vorderasiatische Malerei*. Berlin: Safari.
Muscarella, O., A. Caubet, and F. Tallon. 1992. Susa in the Achaemenid Period, circa 559–330 BC. *RCS*: 215–52.
Nagel, A. 2010. Colours, gilding and painted motifs in Persepolis: Approaching the polychromy of Achaemenid Persian architectural sculpture, c. 520 to 330 BCE. Unpublished PhD diss., University of Michigan.
———. 2011. Farbe in Persepolis. In *Teheran 50: Ein halbes Jahrhundert deutsche Archäologen in Iran*, ed. B. Helwing and P. Rahemipour, 171–3. Mainz: AIT 11.
Nagel, A., and H. Rahsaz. 2010. Colouring the dead: New investigations on the history and the polychrome appearance of the tomb of Darius I at Naqsh-e-Rostam, Fars. In *Death and burial in Arabia and beyond: Multidisciplinary perspectives*, ed. L. R. Weeks, 289–98. Oxford: BAR Int Ser 2107.
Nylander, C. 1970. *Ionians at Pasargadae: Studies in Old Persian architecture*. Uppsala: Boreas, Acta Universitatis Upsaliensis 1.
Oppenheim, A. L. 1949. The golden garments of the gods. *JNES* 8: 172–93.
Owen, G., and B. Kemp. 1994. Craftsmen's work patterns in unfinished tombs at Amarna. *CAJ* 4/1: 121–9.
Paetzgen Schieck, A. 2009. Alexander der Große und das Ornat des persischen Großkönigs. In *Alexander der Große und die Öffnung der Welt: Asiens Kulturen im Wandel*, ed. S. Hansen, A. Wieczorek, and M. Tellenbach, 104–9. Mannheim: Publikationen der Reiss-Engelhorn-Museen 36.
Piggott, J. 2004. *Palace of the people: The Crystal Palace at Sydenham, 1854–1936*. London: Hurst.
Pigott, V. 1999a. The development of metal production on the Iranian plateau: an archaeometallurgical perspective. In *The archaeometallurgy of the Asian Old World*, ed. V. Pigott, 73–106. Philadelphia: MASCA Research Papers in Science and Archaeology 16.
———. 1999b. A heartland of metallurgy: Neolithic/Chalcolithic metallurgical origins on the Iranian Plateau. In *The Beginnings of Metallurgy*, ed. A. Hauptmann, E. Pernicka, T. Rehren, and Ü. Yalçin, 107–20. Bochum: *Der Anschnitt* Beiheft 9.

———. 2004. On the importance of Iran in the study of prehistoric copper-base metallurgy. *PAP*: 28–43.

Place, V. 1867–70. *Ninive et l'Assyrie. Avec des essais de restauration par Félix Thomas*. Paris: Imprimerie impériale.

Pollard, M., and P. Bray. 2007. A bicycle made for two? The integration of scientific techniques into archaeological interpretation. *Annual Revue of Anthropology* 36: 245–59.

Polosmak, N. 2001. Zur Kleidung der Pazyryk Bevölkerung aus Ukok, Suedaltaj. In *Migration und Kulturtransfer: Der Wandel vorder- und zentralasiatischer Kulturen im Umbruch vom 2. zum 1. vorchristlichen Jahrtausend*, ed. R. Eichmann and H. Parzinger, 101–26. Bonn: Habelt.

Razmjou, S. 2002a. Traces of paint on the statue of Darius. *Arta* 2002.3: 1–2.

———. 2002b. Assesssing the damage: Notes on the life and demise of the statue of Darius from Susa. *Ars Orientalis* 32: 81–104.

———. 2004. Glasierte Ziegel der Achaemenidischen Periode. *PAP*: 382–93.

Roaf, M. 1980. Texts about the sculptures and sculptors at Persepolis. *Iran* 18: 65–74.

Root, M. C. 1979. *The king and kingship in Achaemenid art: Essays on the creation of an iconography of empire*. Leiden: Acta Iranica 19.

———. 2010. Palace to temple—king to cosmos: Achaemenid foundation texts in Iran. In *From the foundations to the crenellations: Essays on temple building in the Ancient Near East and Hebrew Bible*, ed. M. Boda and J. Novotny, 165–210. Münster: AOAT 366.

Rossi, A. 1996. Perception et symbologie des couleurs dans le monde iranien et d'Asie centrale. In *Convegno internazionale sul tema: La Persia e l'Asie centrale da Alessandro al X secolo*. 87–97. Rome: Accademia Nazionale dei Lincei.

———. 2006. Colours and lexical taxonomies: Linguistic and cultural categories in Iranian. In *Proceedings of the 5th Conference of the Societas Iranologica Europaea, held in Ravenna, 6–11 October 2003*, vol. 1, *Ancient and Middle Iranian studies*, ed. A. Panaino and A. Piras, 459–80. Milan: Mimesis.

Ruben, P. 1979. Contribution à l'étude des matériaux naturels des environs de Suse (Khuzistan, Iran), et de leur utilisation pour la confection d'objects archéologiques. Unpublished PhD diss., University of Orléans.

Schmidt, E. F. 1953. *Persepolis I. Structures, reliefs, inscriptions*. Chicago: OIP 68.

———. 1957. *Persepolis II. Contents of the Treasury and other discoveries*. Chicago: OIP 69.

———. 1970. *Persepolis III. The royal tombs and other monuments*. Chicago: OIP 70.

Schmitt, R. 1991. *The Bisitun inscriptions of Darius the Great. Old Persian text*. London: CII 1/1/1.

Semper, G. 1851. On the study of polychromy. *Museum of Classical Antiquities* 1: 228–46.

Shaer, M. 2003. The decorative architectural surface of Petra. Unpublished PhD diss., Technical University of Munich.

Shishehgar, A. 2008. *Discovery of a tomb attributed to members of King Shutur-Nahhunte dynasty, son of Indid (or Indattu), Neo-Elamite III period (c. 585–539 BC)*. Tehran: ICAR (in Persian).

Spurrell, F. 1895. Notes on Egyptian colours. *Archaeological Journal* 52: 222–39.

Stodulski, L., E. Farrell, and R. Newman. 1984. Identification of ancient Persian pigments from Persepolis and Pasargadae. *Studies in Conservation* 29: 143–54.

Strudwick, N. 1991. The objective-colour measuring system for the recording of Egyptian tomb paintings. *Journal of Egyptian Archaeology* 77: 43–56.

Summerer, L., and A. von Kienlin, eds. 2010. *Tatarlı: renklerin dönüşü/The return of colours/ Rückkehr der Farben*. Istanbul: T. C. Kültür ve Turizm Bakanlığı; Yapı Kredi Yayınları.

Texier, C. 1852. *Description de l'Arménie, la Perse et la Mésopotamie*, vol. 2. Paris: Didot.
Tilia, A. B.. 1968. New restoration work at Persepolis. *EW* 18: 67–108.
———. 1978. *Studies and restorations at Persepolis and other sites of Fārs*, vol. 2. Rome: IsMEO Reports and Memoirs 18.
Trichet, J., and P. Ruben. 1980. Méthodes d'étude de l'origine des matériaux ayant servi à la confection de briques et de céramiques dans les sites de Suse et de Djaffarabad (Khuzistan, Iran). *Paléorient* 6: 129–58.
Trichet, J., and F. Vallat. 1990. L'origine égyptienne de la statue de Darius. *MJP*: 205–8.
Vandenabeele, P., R. Garcia-Moreno, F. Mathis, K. Leterme, E. van Elslande, F. P. Hocquet, S. Rakkaa et al. 2009. Multi-disciplinary investigation of the tomb of Menna (TT69), Theban Necropolis, Egypt. *Spectrochimica Acta A* 73: 546–52.
Verri, G. 2009. The spatial characterisation of Egyptian blue: A study by visible-induced luminescence digital imaging. *Analytical and Bioanalytical Chemistry* 394/4: 1011–21.
Weld-Blundell, H. 1893. Persepolis. In *Transactions of the Ninth International Congress of Orientalists*, vol. 2, ed. E. Delmar Morgan, 537–59. London: Ballantyne, Hanson & Co.
Wiesehöfer, J. 1991. Engelbert Kaempfer in Naqš-i Rustam und Persepolis. In *Through travellers's eyes: European travellers on the Iranian monuments*, ed. H. Sancisi-Weerdenburg and J. Drijvers, 71–87. Leiden: AchHist 7.
Wilson, A. 2007. The metal supply of the Roman Empire. In *Supplying Rome and the Empire: The Proceedings of an international seminar held at Siena-Certosa di Pontignano on May 2–4, 2004, on Rome, the provinces, production and distribution*, ed. E. Papi, 109–25. Portsmouth: Journal of Roman Archaeology Supplementary Series 69.
Winter, I. J. 2003. Ornament and the rhetoric of abundance in Assyria. *Eretz Israel* 27: 252–64.
Young, D. 2006. The colours of things. In *Handbook of material culture*, ed. C. Tilley, W. Keane, S. Kuechler, M. Rowlands, and P. Spyer, 173–85. London: Sage Publications.
Zare, A. 2004. *The identification of stone quarries in the Marvdasht Plain and comparing them with the stones used in the architecture of Persepolis complex on the base of archeological studies and petrographical results*. Shiraz: Parsa–Pasargad Research Foundation (in Persian).

CHAPTER 31

EASTERN IRAN IN THE ACHAEMENID PERIOD

BRUNO GENITO

Introduction

It is well known that archaeological evidence of the Achaemenid period in eastern Iran is limited. This is as true of excavated material remains as it is of direct and indirect written sources, which tend to be both rare and contradictory (cf. Boucharlat 2005 on the Iranian plateau; Francfort 2005 on Central Asia; cf. Vogelsang 1992 with regard to the importance of the eastern provinces and the scarcity of archaeological documentation compared to historical data). We must also remember that the territorial extent of the Achaemenid Empire is ambiguous and in this regard the cultural background of the different provinces, as well as relationships between center and periphery, were crucial factors affecting the visibility of the Achaemenid Empire in its easternost regions (Briant and Herrenschmidt 1989).

Similarly, the geographic definition of "eastern Iran" requires clarification as well because, as a geomorphological unit, the term "Iranian plateau" is not restricted to the borders of the Islamic Republic of Iran, but extends far beyond them toward the west and the east. In reality, the plateau can be considered as extending roughly from an imaginary line joining the Gulf of Alexandretta and Trebizond, to the Pamirs, that is, for about 3500 km. In the east the border is marked by the separation between the mountains of Afghanistan and the Indus depression; in the south, by the Indian Ocean coasts and the eastern shores of Persian Gulf; in the west by the outer chains of the Zagros Mountains extending from the Persian Gulf into the heart of Armenia; and to the north by the Caucasus and the Alborz Mountains, pressing up toward the coast of the Caspian depression, and eastward toward western Turkestan and the Pamirs. The area included within these limits comprises roughly 3,000,000 km^2, about 1,600,000 km^2 of which belong to the Islamic Republic of Iran and 635,000 km^2 to Afghanistan, with small portions lying in Iraq, Armenia, and the Cis-Caucasian region, Turkey, and the Republic of Azerbaijan.

The geographical issue, in fact, is fundamental to an understanding of the complex political nature and territorial integration of the Empire across its enormous extent (cf. Jacobs 2011 for the most up-to-date analysis of the historical questions of the provinces/satrapies). Moreover, based on lists of "lands" in the Achaemenid inscriptions and Herodotus, eastern Achaemenid Iran can be considered as including Parthava, Drangiana, and Maka, Gedrosia and Carmania having been recognized as territorially autonomous regions only in post-Achaemenid times. More broadly, "eastern Iran" may be understood as including areas located in Central Asia and adjacent territories, such as Margiana (Merv oasis in south Turkmenistan, never listed as an autonomous province), Areia, Arachosia, and Bactriana. Even more easterly regions included Gandhara, Sogdiana, Choresmia, and Hinduš. The identification of each of the areas mentioned in the Achaemenid and Greek sources with precise, present-day geographical units, is notoriously difficult. Their variable positions in the lists of provinces and regions, and the sequence of individual groups of people on the Achaemenid reliefs, defy easy interpretation and ethnogeographical attribution. In addition, many of the so-called Achaemenid remains in eastern Iran are beset by dubious chronology and cultural affiliation rendering their interpretation difficult (cf. Genito 1988d: 157, fig. 1, where the author scrutinizes issues related to the ethnic, chronological, and political/dynastic interpretation of the material evidence). Thus at least four different aspects of interpretation should be considered when considering the evidence of the Achaemenid Empire in the east (Abdullaev and Genito 2011: 11):

1. the dynastic—identifiable by inscriptions, coins, and seals;
2. the ethnic—possibly detectable on both physical anthropological and cultural grounds;
3. the political/imperial—recognizable both in macroscopic architectural and art historical remains and in the material traces of settlement patterns and economic investments, e.g. to secure the water supply;
4. the chronological—interpretable in the differing horizons connected to the period of Achaemenid politico-dynastic dominion in the area.

Most of eastern Iran has always been a frontier zone, both in relation to the steppe regions to the north and the desert and mountainous areas to the east. The recognition of an Achaemenid horizon in this area is more often based on chronological contemporaneity with the Achaemenid Empire and location within the assumed confines of one of the Achaemenid satrapies, than on the presence of unequivocally Achaemenid material culture.

IRAN

Parthava

Primarily located in present-day Turkmenistan, along the lower slopes of the Kopet Dagh mountain range, Parthava was originally a relatively small area, less than 200 km long and perhaps 40 km wide. According to the sources (cf. Isidore of Charax: Weißbach 1916: 2064–8; Miller 1855: 244–56; Schoff 1914) Parthava comprised two different subregions; the first, more arid one, in Turkmenistan, and the second in Iran (Gorgāni 1971). Although arid, the northern slopes of the Kopet Dagh and adjacent plains have supported communities practicing irrigation agriculture for thousands of years (Ehlers 1970, 1971). The southern slopes of the Kopet Dagh have more vegetation and the plains at their base are the proper Parthian homeland, extending southward and including much of the upper, fertile Atrek River valley, and the Kuhistan Hills, beyond the Kopet Dagh (Arne 1935). These areas today correspond to the Golestan and northern Khorasan provinces in Iran.

Parthava appears as Varkāna in the inscription of Darius I at Bisotun. In the Achaemenid lists of lands it appears variously as the 3rd (DSe 21–30; DNa 22–30), 5th (Darius Statue), 6th (XPh 19–28), 13th (DB I 14–17; DSaa 18–31), or 14th province (DPe 10–18). In Herodotus' army list (*Hist.* 7.61–96) the Paricanians appear after the Gandharians and before the Caspians, while in the "tribute list" (*Hist.* 3.90–4) the Paricanians belong to the 17th district and the Parthians to the 16th district. Paricania may be associated with Hyrcania, between the Hyrcanian Ocean (Caspian Sea) to the north and the Alborz Mountains to the south and west. Zadracarta, the capital of the satrapy, has been identified by some scholars with Sari city, in Mazandaran, or Qala Khandan, the ancient part of Gorgan city (Ehlers 2002).

In northern Parthia (southern Turkmenistan) sites such as El'ken (Kačuris 1967) and Ulug Depe (Boucharlat et al. 2005) have Iron Age occupation and may be considered regional centers (Košelenko 1985: 184–5), while smaller sites thrived as well (Pilipko 1986). Tureng Tepe (Deshayes 1967, 1968, 1969, 1973), an important site located 18 km from the modern city of Gorgan, at the edge of fertile foothills of the Alborz and the Turkmen steppe, consists of a main *tepe*, 30 m high, and a series of lower mounds. According to the chronology proposed in the long sequence of occupation at the site, extending from the fifth millennium BC to the Mongol period, the Achaemenid remains comprise level VA, and may be assigned to Iron Age IV (Boucharlat and Lecomte 1987: 11). The ceramics, mainly red wares, display forms (Deshayes 1976: fig. 10; Cleuziou 1985: figs. 18, 24) similar to those documented at Pasargadae while the Achaemenid-period architecture evinces a marked change from the preceding period, as square mudbricks (35 × 35 cm) replaced rectangular ones (Deshayes 1976: 306; 1979: 33; Cleuziou 1985: 182). Located between the Iranian plateau and southern Central Asia, Tureng Tepe is clearly related to the Iron Age II–IV cultures on the Iranian plateau. At the same time it clearly had ties to Iron Age II in archaic Dehistan (southwestern Turkmenistan), which itself represents a local development from the Bronze Age in that region.

Located 10 km south of Gonbad-e Qavus, Yarim Tepe contains Iron Age and later remains (Crawford 1963) ranging from at least 1100/1000 BC to 200 AD. Architecturally, the most remarkable feature is a massive mudbrick wall crowning the site. Some 16 km northeast of Gonbad-e Qavus is a cluster of sixteen tombs dating to the first millennium BC that were excavated in 2000. Among the ceramics recorded were Iron Age types and some "potsherds of the Achaemenid period" (Shahmirzadi and Nokandeh 2001: 3, figs. 20–1, pls. 15–16).

Archaeological research in northeastern Khorasan has been very limited. Explorations were conducted by the University of Turin in the Atrek valley between 1976 and 1978 (Venco Ricciardi 1980, 1981a, 1981b). Three sites have Iron Age material similar to that found in the Yaz Depe horizon in southern Central Asia (Hlopina and Hlopin 1976: 200–203), not to Iranian assemblages. In the Achaemenid period (Yaz III), a total of seventeen sites, some with earlier occupation, were recorded. These are modest in size and rarely cluster (Venco Ricciardi 1980: 60–62; 1981a: 98–9). Pottery consists mostly of carinated, cylindrical-conical vessels, a widespread type in Central Asia, Afghanistan, and eastern Iran dating back to Yaz II. Technically, the material differs from that of the earlier Iron Age (Yaz I–II): the pottery is wheel turned, smoothed, and unpainted (Venco Ricciardi 1980: fig. E; Cornelio 1981).

A survey conducted in 1978 (Kohl and Heskel 1980) in the Dargaz (Darreh Gaz) valley recorded thirty-six sites, the most important of which was Yarim Tepe, covering 8 ha. Following occupation in the Bronze Age, "substantial occupation was suggested for the Achaemenid period" in this region (Kohl 1996).

Drangiana

The modern Iranian province of Sistan and Baluchistan borders Khorasan province and Afghanistan to the north; Afghanistan and Pakistan to the east; the Gulf of Oman to the south; Kerman province to the west; and Hormuzgan province to the southwest. The first historical reference both to the territory around the Hamun Lake and to the Helmand River is found at Bisotun (DB I 16; Kent 1950: 116–35; Schmitt 1991; Lecoq 1997: 83–96, 187–217). In the Achaemenid inscriptions it appears variously as the 5th (XPh, 19–28), 8th (DSe, 21–30; DNa, 22–30), 9th (Darius Statue), 14th (DB I 14–17; DSaa 18–31), or 15th province (DPe 10–18). According to Herodotus' tribute list (*Hist.* 3.90–94) Drangiana was inhabited by Sarangians and other peoples, forming part of the 14th district, while in his army list (*Hist.* 7.61–96) the peoples inhabiting the area are said to have been the Sarangians, together with the Utians and Sagartians. These are listed after the Mycii (Maka) and before the Bactrians.

Nevertheless, despite its frequent attestation in the sources, the geographical limits of Drangiana in the Achaemenid period remain obscure. Of particular importance are references to Zarin, the capital of Achaemenid Drangiana, in Ctesias' *Persica*; Isidore of Charax's *Parthian Stations*; and the *Tabula Peutingeriana* (Daffinà 1967; Gnoli 1967: 45, n. 1; 1993: 584; König 1972; Gilmore 1888). Yet it is doubtful whether the administrative center of the region, though retaining the same name, remained in the same location over time and indeed it seems more likely that, because of changes in the ecosystem of the region—frequently attested in later periods, for example, in reference to the city of Zaranj, capital of the province during the Islamic period (Gnoli 1967: 104, n. 1)—it moved more than once.

The results of the excavations of the Italian Archaeological Mission at Dahan-e Ghulaman, for example, suggested that the site should be identified not with the

Zarin of Isidore of Charax, but rather, in view of the date of the site, with the Zarin of Ctesias (Scerrato 1962, 1966a, 1966b: 11; 1970, 1972, 1974, 1979; Gnoli 1967: 103–7). Dahan-e Ghulaman is still one of the most important settlements of the Achaemenid era in Iran. The plan of a building interpreted as a religious structure suggests it may have been a Zoroastrian or even pre-Zoroastraian fire temple (Genito 1986, 1987, 1990, 2010a, 2010b, 2012, 2013, forthcoming). An Iranian team has conducted further investations at the site, confirming its importance (Sajjadi and Saber-Moghaddam 2004; Sajjadi 2007).

Although the foundation of the upper terrace of Nad-e Ali in Afghan Sistan has been dated to the Bronze Age (Besenval and Francfort 1994), it is not impossible that it still retained a cultic function in the Iron Age, as shown by the dates of materials found in its upper part (Ghirshman 1939–42; Dales 1977).

Karmania

Karmania denoted a region east of Persis, corresponding roughly to modern Kerman province (Hinz and Koch 1987: 525ff.). It appears in the foundation tablet of Darius' palace at Susa (DSf 9) as the source of *Dalbergia sissoo* wood (the *jag* tree, also brought from Gandhara). In the Persepolis Fortification Tablets Karmania is frequently mentioned in connection with travelers to Susa. The OP ethnic name is possibly reflected in the Elamite version, which occurs in unpublished tablets (Hinz and Koch 1987: 526ff.), and in Greek Karmánioi (Lat. Carmāniī) (cf. Francfort 1988; Genito 1996).

Maka

As Gnoli showed (1987: 512–18), Gedrosia denoted a geographical area within which were populations who deemed themselves *Arya*, without any political or administrative implications. Several scholars have argued that the Persian satrapy Maka (DB I 17; cf. DSaa 18–31, DPe 10–18, DS3 21–30, DNa 22–30, Darius Statue, XPh 19–28; Herodotus, *Hist.* 3.90–4, 7.61–96) was identical to Gedrosia, emphasizing the similarity of the name Maka and modern Makran (Holdich 1896; Pozdena 1975), the southeasternmost coastal region of Iran and southwestern Pakistan. However, it is more likely that Maka is to be sought in modern Oman, the northern part of which was called Maketa in antiquity (Potts 1985). In southeastern Iran and Baluchistan there is a general lack of water, and this situation, judging from the Alexander's difficult crossing of Gedrosia, cannot have been much different in ancient times. It is therefore not surprising that Gedrosia is never mentioned in the Achaemenid sources and that its capital, Pura, cannot be located with certainty, though it is clear from the Alexander biographies that it lay west of the main Gedrosian deserts (Stein 1931, 1943). It should therefore be placed in Persian Baluchistan, possibly in the Bampūr oasis (Potts 1989; Vogelsang 2000).

Central Asia

As used here, the term Central Asia denotes the modern states of Afghanistan, Turkmenistan, Uzbekistan, Tajikistan, and part of Kazakhstan. As far as the Achaemenid period is concerned, one fundamental point must be emphasized: it is very difficult to recognize an Achaemenid horizon in the Central Asian Iron Age which comprises a 1500-year-long unit of archaeological time extending from the Late Bronze Age to the Hellenistic period, and sometimes even beyond (Košelenko 1985), to the end of the Kušan period in the third and fourth centuries AD (Francfort 2005).

The political-economic domination of the Achaemenid empire represented the first period of imperial political unity in Central Asia and one might have expected a large quantity of material remains belonging to military, administrative, and economic centers and large towns. Instead, these are almost completely absent. Moreover, Achaemenid epigraphic remains in Central Asia are very scarce, consisting of a fragment of an Achaemenid Elamite tablet from Kandahar (Helms 1997); an alabastron of Artaxerxes in Bactria inscribed in cuneiform and hieroglyphs (Schmitt 2001); newly discovered Aramaic letters from Bactria (Shaked 2004; Naveh and Shaked 2012); and an Aramaic ostracon found in the main temple of Aï Khanoum in a context dated to the late third century BC (Rapin 1992: 95–114).

Margiana

Drained by the river Murghab which originated in the mountains of Afghanistan and reached Merv oasis in modern-day Turkmenistan (Gubaev, Košelenko and Novikov 1990), Marguš was included in one of the other eastern satrapies of the empire (Genito 1998d). Margiana must have been conquered by Cyrus the Great because he fought against the Massagetae, a nomadic tribe living beyond Margiana. According to Darius' inscription at Bisotun, in March 522 BC, following the Magian revolt by Gaumata further to the east, the oasis of Margiana revolted as well. The leader of the Margian insurrection was one Frâda. The satrap of Bactria, Dâdarši, advanced against the rebels, whom he defeated on December 28, 521 BC, after a march of 300 km through the Karakum desert. In the Bisotun inscription, which was engraved immediately after these events, Dâdarši's victory is presented as if it was just as important as the victories over the rebels in Babylonia or Media. The Aramaic version of the text, although severely damaged, even mentions 55,423 Margians killed and 6972 taken captive, almost certainly an exaggeration (Struve 1949a. 1949b).

Apart from the excavations carried out at the beginning of the twentieth century by Raphael Pumpelly, the first archaeological research in the region of the lower Murghab dates to 1946 when the so-called JuTAKE (Južno-Turkmenistanskoj arheologičeskoj kompleksnoj ekspedicii—Archaeological Complex Expedition in South Turkmenistan) was established and undertook its first excavations in the Murghab delta under the direction of M. E. Masson. The most important sites, grouped by oasis, are: for the Iron Age, Takhirbaj, Uč-Depe, Ajrak, Aravali Depe, and Taip and for the Achaemenid period, Erk Kala. For Iron Age chronology Uč-Depe, partially investigated in the 1950s, provided, together with Yaz Depe further south, the first sequence of Iron Age through Achaemenid ceramic types in Margiana, and the following periodization: Yaz I (900–700 BC), Yaz II (700–500 BC), Yaz III (500–350 BC). Numerous sites have been identified in the Takhirbaj oasis, including Takhirbaj 1, a settlement mound, perhaps a fortress, with extensive living areas. Citadels of the Achaemenian period include Erk Kala (Usmanova 1969a, 1969b; Filanovič 1973, 1974; Košelenko 1985: 228–9) and Gyaur-Kala (Filanovič 1974; Usmanova et al. 1985: 226–42), and other Yaz III sites like Starij Kishman (Genito 2010c). Alignments of sites dated ceramically to the Achaemenid period have been discovered by surveys in the desertified delta (Genito 1998a, 1998b: fig. 1; 1998c, 2003), while some sections of the so-called Wall of Antiochus (Bader et al. 1998) are dated to the Achaemenid period. The function of this as a perimeter wall of the oasis is certainly more convincing than that of a primarily defensive structure, as the sources state.

The circular plan of Merv has definitely a defensive origin, perhaps arising from the fact that this made it more easily defensible than a rectangular town, and also perhaps because this would allow the interior space to be enclosed in multiple, concentric walls, less extensive than that required to encompass the equivalent rectangular area. Some trial-trenches have provided partial clarification of the walls. Occupation in the center on the highest part of the site dates, on ceramic grounds, to the Yaz I–III (900–350 BC) horizon.

Areia

Areia corresponded to the Hari Rud valley in northwestern Afghanistan. In the Achaemenid inscriptions it appears as the 4th (DSe, 21–30; Darius Statue), 7th (XPh, 19–28), 15th (DB I 14–17; DSaa, 18–31), or 16th (DPe 10–18) province. In Herodotus' taxation list (*Hist.* 3.89ff.), the Areians are listed together with the Parthians, Choresmians, and Sogdians, and according to him, the Areians were dressed in the Bactrian fashion. In his army list (7.61–96), the Aryans are mentioned after the Parthians and before the Choresmians.

The present town of Herat (Afghanistan), presumably the capital of the region, dates back to ancient times but its exact age remains unknown. In Achaemenid times, the surrounding district was known as OP *Haraiva* and in Classical sources the region was called Areia. In the *Avesta* (*Yašt* 10.14; *Vidēvdāt* 1.9), the district is mentioned as *Harōiva*. The name of the district and its main town are most probably derived from that of the Hari Rud (Old Iranian *Harayu*), the main river in the region, which traverses the district and passes just south of modern Herat (Vogelsang 2003). Herat dominates the productive part of ancient Areia, which was, and basically still is, a rather narrow stretch of land extending for *c.*150 km along both banks of the river. The city and district of

Areia/Herat occupied an important strategic place along the age-old caravan routes that crossed the Iranian plateau. In the texts Areia is grouped with Zranka (modern Sistān) to the south, Parthava (Parthia) to the northwest, and Bāxtriš (Bactria) to the northeast.

Representatives from Areia are depicted in reliefs at the royal Achaemenid tombs of Naqsh-e Rustam and Persepolis. They wear Scythian-style dress and a twisted turban around the head. This costume is also worn by the representatives from nearby Sistān (to the south) and Arachosia (to the southeast) and is reminiscent of the dress worn by the representatives from almost all of the northern lands strongly influenced by the Eurasian steppe cultures. On the Darius statue at Susa (Kervran et al. 1972), the representative from Areia is also shown wearing a long coat around the shoulders with empty sleeves, a type of coat known from Classical sources (Gk. *kandys*) and sometimes also worn by the Persians and the Medes, whose origin should be sought among the nomadic Scythians of Central Asia (Gervers-Molnár 1973). Herodotus (*Hist.* 7.61ff.) says that Areians served in Xerxes' army against Greece, around 480 BC.

Arachosia

Arachosia is the Latinized form of the Greek name of an Achaemenid (and later Seleucid) satrapy in the eastern part of the empire, corresponding to the middle Helmand valley in southwestern Afghanistan. It appears in the *Avesta* (*Vidēvdāt* 1.12) in the indigenous form Harax^{v}aitī. In Old Persian inscriptions the region is referred to as *Harahuvatiš*. Arachosia was named after the name of a river that runs through it, in Greek Arachōtós, today known as Arghandabad. In the Achaemenid inscriptions Arachosia appears as the 3rd (XPh, 19–28), 8th (Darius Statue), 9th (DSe, 21–30; DNa, 22–30), 21st (DPe 10–18), or 22nd (DB I 14–17; DSaa, 18–31) province. The inhabitants of Arachosia were called *Pactians*, a name which survives today in the form of Pakhtuns/Pashtun (Vogelsang 2002).

Isidore of Charax and Ptolemy (Ptolemy 6.20.4–5) provide a list of cities in Arachosia, among them an Alexandria on the Arachothos river, a tributary of the Helmand (see Allchin and Hammond 1978; Ball 1982), identified with modern Kandahar, the name of which would derive from Alexandria, reflecting Alexander the Great's refoundation of the city on his eastern campaign. Isidore, Strabo (*Geog.* 11.8.9), and Pliny (*Nat. Hist.* 6.61) also refer to the city as "metropolis of Arachosia." In his list, Ptolemy also refers to a city named Arachotus or Arachoti, which was the earlier capital of the land. Pliny the Elder and Stephen of Byzantium mention that its original name was Cophen (Κωφήν). The famous Buddhist pilgrim Hsuan Tsang refers to the name as *Kaofu*. This city has been identified with Zhob, which lies just east of Kandahar (Vogelsang 1987).

Although centered on Zhob and Kandahar, the extent of Arachosia remains unclear. According to Ptolemy (Ptolemy 6.20.1; cf Strabo, *Geog.* 15.2.9), Arachosia was bordered by Drangiana in the west, Bactria in the north, the Indus River in the east, and Gedrosia in the south. Strabo (*Geog.* 11.10.1), too, suggests that Arachosia extended eastwards as far as the Indus River. Pliny (*Nat. Hist.* 6.92) speaks of Dexendrusi in the south. Ptolemy (Ptolemy 6.20.3) mentions several tribes of Arachosia by name, including the Pargyetae and, to the south, the Sidri, Rhoplutae, and Eoritae. Despite attempts to connect Eoritae with "Arattas" of the *Mahabharata* or with the modern Aroras, who populated this region and migrated to India after partition, the identity of these tribes is unknown, and even Ptolemy's orthography is disputed ("Pargyetae" is given in some manuscripts as "Parsyetae" or "Aparytae").

Arachosia is first referred to in the Persepolis Fortification Tablets. It appears again in the Old Persian, Akkadian, and elamite inscriptions of Darius I and Xerxes I, among the lists of the subject peoples and countries noted above. It is also identified as the source of the ivory used in Darius' palace at Susa. In his Bisotun inscription (DB III 54–76), Darius says that a Persian was three times defeated by the Achaemenid governor of Arachosia, Vivana, who thereby ensured that the province remained under Darius' control. Chronologically speaking, the next reference to Arachosia appears in Quintus Curtius who recorded that, under Darius III, the Arachosians and Drangians were under the command of a governor who, together with the army of the Bactrian governor, contrived a plot against Alexander (Curtius Rufus 8.13.3).

Arachosia represents a transitional region on the Indo-Iranian and Central Asia border. The Achaemenid ceramic forms found at Kandahar are more like, if still distinct from, those at sites in Iran than those of the northern Yaz tradition (McNicoll 1978; Vogelsang 1985; McNicoll and Ball 1996; Helms 1997). This might suggest that areas south of the Hindu Kush, because of their proximity to the Achaemenid heartland, were better integrated into the empire than areas to the north of the Hindu Kush. The distribution area of Yaz II and III ceramics was approximately the same as that of the painted ceramics of Yaz I, repeating the distribution of the material culture of the Bronze Age Oxus Civilization, which occupied the same territory thousand of years earlier.

Bactriana

Bactriana corresponds to northeastern Afghanistan and southern Uzbekistan. In the Achaemenid inscriptions it appears as the 5th (DSe 21–30; DNa 22–30), 6th (Darius Statue), 8th (XPh 19–28), and 17th (DB I 14–17; DSaa 18–31; DPe 10–18) province. In Herodotus' tribute list (3.90–4) the Bactrians are mentioned in the 12th district. In Herodotus' army list (7.61–96) they are mentioned after the Sarangians and before the Sacae Amyrgians. The region was subjugated by Cyrus the Great, and from then on formed one of the satrapies of the empire.

The main center is Balkh, in the province and river of the same name, not far from Mazar-e Sharif, in a fertile agricultural region. It was a holy city of Zoroastrianism, and under the name Bactria it became the capital of Bactriana. In northern Bactria, sites with occupation dating from the sixth to the fourth centuries BC are distributed in the valleys of Surkhan Darya, Mirshade, Bandykhan Saj, Sherabad Darya and Ulanbulak Saj, whose fortifications were built in the eighth to seventh or sixth century (Košelenko

1985: 188). Apart from Balkh, large or significant Achaemenid sites have also been found as Kutlug-Tepe, At-Chapa, and Altyn-Dilyar (Kruglikova and Sarianidi 1976: 16, fig. 13; cf. Sarianidi 1985). In northern Bactria Achaemenid remains have been identified by Rtveladze (Rtveladze 1975, 1987) who documented and mapped and described five groups of oasis and other sites along the Surkhan Darya, including the major fortified sites of Kyzyl Tepe, Tepe Bandykhan, Talashkan Tepe I (Rtveladze and Pidaev 1993), and Kyzylča 6 (Sagdullaev 1987b).

Altyn 10 in Afghan Bactriana presents two buildings whose plans may be compared with those of Persian palaces (Sarianidi 1977: 121–8; 1985), in the first case with columns, and in the second with an anteroom and a corridor surrounding the central court. On the eastern Bactria plains of Dasht-i Qala, Taloqan and Bangui are remains of buildings with columns related to monumental Achaemenid architecture.

The Oxus treasure in the British Museum includes antiquities that have been identified as Achaemenid (Dalton 1964; Barnett 1968; Artamonov 1973; Kuz'mina 1977, 1979, 2002; Zejmal 1979; Boardman 2003; Muscarella 1987; Litvinskij and Pičikjan 2000: 13–36; *Treasures of ancient Bactria* 2002: 200–29; Litvinskij 2002). Mir Zakah 2 is an important Bactrian treasure that has sometimes been called "Oxus treasure 2" (Pičikjan 1992, 1997, 1998a, 1998b). Consisting of votive objects dated to between the sixth and the second centuries BC (*Treasures of ancient Bactria* 2002), it includes statuettes of officiants holding a barsom bundle, numerous plates of gold engraved with representations of male and female priests, often dressed in Persian or Scythian fashion, and a galloping Persian horseman, wielding a spear. Achaemenid-style gold vessels are numerous and include phiales, bowls, a lion's head from a situla, a deer protome from a rhyton a lion protome, and torques and bracelets. Obvious similarities to the Oxus treasure, Takht-e Sangin and Aï Khanoum have been noted (Bernard and Francfort 1978).

Takht-e Sangin, a sanctuary located on the Oxus and dedicated to the deity of the river, has traces of Achaemenid contact, though the architecture is later. Here one recalls a plate bearing the image of a man leading a camel (Pičikjan 1992: 32–5, fig. 143.17) and the famous ivory *akinakes* scabbard adorned with a lion preparing to devour a deer (Pičikjan 1992: 42–8, fig. 146). A rhyton with a lion protome does not look purely Afchaemenid, despite a high dating in the fifth or fourth century (Pičikjan 1992: 48–9; Litvinskij and Pičikjan 1994).

Although a Hellenistic foundation, Aï Khanoum has yielded Achaemenid pottery in the heroôn of Kineas, in a context of reuse (Bernard 1973) and finds elsewhere in the city suggest some Achaemenid activity there (Bernard 1985, 1990). These include bronze plaques with rosettes and palmettes (Francfort 1984: 58–9, n. 29, pl. 22.21); several Greco-Persian intaglios (Francfort 1984: 78–9, pls. 12 and 35.26; Guillaume and Rougeulle 1987: 55, no. 1002, and pl. 18.17, XIV.11); a stone rhyton adorned with a bull or a ram (Francfort 1984: 26–7, pl. 14.15); fragments of a painting of lions *en passant* similar to Persepolis and Pazyryk examples (Francfort 1984: 32–4, no. 19.20, pl. 15.16); and a fragment of a typically Achaemenid cylinder seal (Guillaume and Rougeulle 1987: 72, no. 1247).

Other eastern provinces

The remaining eastern provinces, such as Sogdiana, Choresmia, Gandhara, and Hindush are excluded here due to their distance from the Iranian core of the empire.

FURTHER READING

The eastern Iranian provinces of the Achaemenid Empire are treated in Vogelsang (1992) and in the survey of Briant (2002). For detailed issues regarding all of the eastern provinces the relevant entries in *EnIr* are invaluable.

REFERENCES

Abdullaev, K., and B. Genito. 2011. Trial trenches at Koj tepa, Samarkand area (Sogdiana) (Third interim report 2011). *Newsletter di Archeologia CISA* 2: 7–72.

Allchin, F. R., and N. Hammond. 1978. *The archaeology of Afghanistan: From earliest times to the Timurid period*. London: Academic Press.

Arne, T. J. 1935. La steppe turkomane et ses antiquités. *Geografiska Annaler* 17: 28–43.

Artamonov, M. I. 1973. *Sokrovišča Sakov. Amu-Darinskij klad, Altajskie kurgany, Minusinskie bronzy, Sibirskoe zoloto*. Moscow: Iskusstvo.

Bader, A., P. Callieri, and T. Hodžanijazov. 1998. Survey of the "Antiochus Wall": Preliminary report on the 1993–1994 campaigns. *AMMD*: 159–86.

Barnett, R. D. 1968. The art of Bactria and the treasure of the Oxus. *IrAnt* 8: 34–54.

Ball, W. 1982. *Archaeological gazetteer of Afghanistan/Catalogue des sites archéologiques d'Afghanistan*. Paris: Éditions Recherche sur les Civilisations.

Bernard, P. 1973. *Fouilles d'Aï Khanoum I*. Paris: MDAFA 21.

———. 1985. *Fouilles d'Aï Khanoum IV: Les monnaies hors trésor. Questions d'histoire gréco-bactrienne*. Paris: MDAFA 18.

———. 1990. L'architecture religieuse de l'Asie Centrale à l'époque hellénistique. In *Akten des XIII. Internationalen Kongress für klassische Archäologie*, 51–9. Mainz: von Zabern.

Bernard, P., and H.-P. Francfort. 1978. *Etudes de géographie historique sur la plaine d'Aï Khanoum*. Paris: Publications de l'URA 10 du CNRS.

———. 1994. The Nad-i Ali "Surkh Dagh": A Bronze Age monumental platform in Central Asia. In *From Sumer to Meluhha: Contributions to the archaeology of south and west Asia in memory of George F. Dales Jr.*, ed. J. M. Kenoyer, 3–14. Madison: Wisconsin Archaeological Reports 3.

Boardman, J. 2003. The Oxus Treasure scabbard in London: A closer look. In *Central'naja Azija istočniki, istorija, kul'tura. Tezisy dokladov konferencii, posvjaščennoj 80-letiju Eleny A. Davidovič i B.A. Litvinskikogo*, ed. T. K. Mkrtyčev, T. G. Alpatkina, S. B. Bolelov, and O. N. Inevatkina, 33. Moscow: RAN Institut Vostokovedenija, Gos Muzej Vostoka.

Boucharlat, R. 2005. Iran. *AEA*: 221–92.

Boucharlat, R., H.-P. Francfort, and O. Lecomte. 2005. The citadel of Ulug Depe and the Iron Age archaeological sequence in southern Central Asia. *IrAnt* 40: 480–514.

Boucharlat, R., and O. Lecomte. 1987. *Fouilles de Tureng Tepe 1. Les périods sassanides et islamiques*. Paris: Éditions Recherche sur les Civilisations.

Briant, P. 2002. *From Cyrus to Alexander: A history of the Persian Empire*. Winona Lake: Eisenbrauns.

Briant, P., and C. Herrenschmidt. 1989. *Le tribut dans l'Empire perse*. Paris/Louvain: Peeters.

Cleuziou S. 1985. L'Age du fer à Tureng Tepe (Iran) et ses relations avec l'Asie centrale. In *L'archéologie de la Bactriane ancienne*, 175–93. Paris: Éditions du CNRS.

Cornelio V. 1981. Ricognizioni e ricerche nell'Iran orientale dell'età preistorica ad oggi. Periodo achemenide. *Memorie della Accademia delle Scienze di Torino* Ser. 5 5/2: 117–25.

Crawford, V. E. 1963. Beside the Kara Su. *Metropolitan Museum of Art Bulletin* 21: 263–73.

Daffinà, P. 1967. *L'immigrazione dei Saka nella Drangiana*. Rome: IsMEO Reports and Memoirs 9.

Dales, G. F. 1977. *New excavations at Nad-i Ali (Sorkh Dagh), in Afghanistan*. Berkeley: Center for South and Southeast Asia Studies, University of California, Berkeley, Research Monograph 16.

Dalton, O. M. 1964. *The Treasure of the Oxus*. London: British Museum.

Deshayes, J. 1967. Aux confins des steppes d'Asie Centrale, un foyer de civilisation indo-européene: Tureng Tepe. *Archaeologia* 18: 33–7.

———. 1968. Tureng Tepe and the plain of Gorgan in the Bronze Age. *Archaeologia Viva* 1/1: 35–8.

———. 1969. New evidence for the Indo-Europeans from Tureng Tepe, Iran. *Archaeology* 22/1: 10–17.

———. 1973. Rapport préliminaire sur la neuvième campagne de fouilles à Tureng Tepe (1971). *Iran* 11: 141–52.

———. 1976. Rapport préliminaire sur la onzième campagne de fouilles à Torang Tappeh. *PASARI* 4: 298–321.

———. 1979. Les niveaux de l'Âge du Fer à Tureng Tépé. In *Akten des VII. internationalen Kongresses für iranische Kunst und Archäologie, München, 7.-10. September 1976*, 29–34. Berlin: *AMI* Supplement 6.

Edrisi, Abu ʿAbd-Allāh Moḥammad b. Moḥammad. 1970. *Ketāb nozhat al-moštāq fi eḵterāq al-āfāq*, Naples/Rome: Istituto Universitario Orientale di Napoli.

Ehlers, E. 1970. Die Turkmenesteppe in Nordpersien und ihre Umrandung: Eine landeskundliche Skizze. *Geographische Zeitschrift* 26: 1–51.

———. 1971. Klimageschichte und Siedlungsgang in vor- und frühgeschichtlicher Zeit in der Turkmenensteppe Nordpersiens. *AMI* 4: 7–19.

———. 2002. Gorgān ii. Dašt-e Gorgān. *EnIr* online edition.

Filanovič, M. I. 1973. K stratigrafii Gjaur-Kaly starogo Merva. *Izvestija Akademii Nauk Turkmenskoj SSR Serija obščestva nauka* 1: 60–4.

———. 1974. *Gjaur-kaly*. Ashgabat: Trudy Južno-Turkmenistanskoj arheologičeskoj kompleksnoj ekspedicii 16.

Francfort, H.-P. 1984. *Fouilles d'Aï Khanoum III. Le sanctuaire du temple à niches indentées 2. Les trouvailles*. Paris: MDAFA 27.

———. 1988. Central Asia and Eastern Iran. *CAH* 4: 165–93.

———. 2005. Asie Centrale. *AEA*: 313–52.

Genito, B. 1986. Dahan-i Ghulaman: Una città achemenide tra centro e periferia dell'impero. *Oriens Antiquus* 25: 287–317.

———. 1987. Altari a gradini nell'Iran antico. In *Orientalia Iosephi Tucci Memoriae Dicata*, ed. G. Gnoli and L. Lanciotti, 475–86. Rome: IsMEO.

———. 1990. The most frequent pottery types at Dahān-e Gholāmān (Sistan) and their spatial variability. In *South Asian Archaeology 1987*, vol. 2, ed. M. Taddei and P. Callieri, 587–604. Rome: SOR 66/2.

———. 1996. The Iranian empires and Central Asia: An archaeological perspective. In *La Persia e l'Asia Centrale da Alessandro al X secolo*, 401–21. Rome: Atti dei Convegni Lincei 127.

———. 1998a. The pottery chronological seriation of the Murghab Delta from the end of the Bronze Age to the Achaemenid period: A preliminary note. *AMMD*: 75–88.

———. 1998b. The Iron Age in Merv Oasis. *AMMD*: 89–96.

———. 1998c. Trial-Trench at Site no. 215. *AMMD*: 125–34.

———. 1998d. The Achaemenids in the history of Central Asia. *AMMD*: 149–58.

———. 2003. Al di là dei confini degli imperi iranici e oltre.... In *Scritti in onore di Umberto Scerrato per il suo settantacinquesimo compleanno*, ed. M. V. Fontana and B. Genito, 403–30. Napoli.

———. 2010a. From the Achaemenids to the Sasanians: Dāhān-e Gholāmān, Qal'a-ye Sam, Qal'a-ye Tapa: Archaeology, settlement and territory in Sistān, (Iran). In *South Asian Archaeology 2007*, vol. 2, ed. P. Callieri and L. Colliva, 101–10. Oxford: BAR Int Ser 2133.

———. 2010b. The Achaemenid Empire as seen as from its eastern periphery: The case of Dahan-i Ghulaman in Sistan. Forty years later, a revision of data. In *Proceedings of the 6th International Congress of the Archaeology of the Ancient Near East. 5th–10th May 2008, Rome*, vol. 1, ed. P. Matthiae, F. Pinnock, L. Nigro, and N. Marchetti, 77–92. Wiesbaden: Harrassowitz.

———. 2010c. The Building no. 546 at Uly Kishman Complex in the Merv Oasis. In *Problemy Istorii, Filologii, Kul'tury* [Journal of Historical, Philological, and Cultural Studies] 1/27: 200–16.

———. 2012. An Achaemenid capital of the imperial periphery: Zranka/Drangiana/Sistan. In *Territorial system and ideology in the Achaemenid state: Persepolis and its settlements*, ed. A. V. Rossi and G. P. Basello, 365–86. Viterbo: Dipartimento di Scienze Umane.

———. 2013. Landscape, sources and architecture at the archaeological remains of Achaemenid Sistan (East Iran): Dahan- i Ghulaman. In *Excavating an empire: Achaemenid Persia in longue durée*, ed. T. Daryaee, A. Mousavi and K. Rezakhani, 163–78. Los Angeles: Dr. Samuel M. Jordan Center for Persian Studies & Culture.

———. Forthcoming. Sistan ii. History in pre-Islamic period, *EnIr* online edition.

Gervers-Molnár, V. 1973. *The Hungarian Szűr: An archaic mantle of Eurasian origin*. Toronto: Royal Ontario Museum.

Ghirshman, R. 1939–42. Fouilles de Nad-i-Ali dans le Seistan Afghan (Rapport préliminaire). *Revue des Arts Asiatiques* 13/1: 10–22.

Gilmore, J. 1888. *The fragments of the Persika of Ktesias*. London: Macmillan.

Gnoli, G. 1967. *Ricerche Storiche sul Sīstān antico*. Rome: IsMEO Reports and Memoirs 10.

———. 1987. Βασιλεύς Βασιλέων Ἀριανῶν. In *Orientalia Iosephi Tucci Memoriae Dicata*, ed. G. Gnoli and L. Lanciotti, 509–32. Rome: SOR 56.

———. 1993. Dahan-e Ġolāmān. *EnIr* 6: 582–5.

Gorgāni, M. 1971 [1350]. *Eqteṣād-e Gorgān o Gonbad o Dašt*. Tehran: Bongah-e Matbuʿati-ye Safi–Alishah.

Gubaev, A. G., G. A. Košelenko, and S. V. Novikov. 1990. Arheologičeskie Issledovanija v Mervskom Oazise. *VDI* 3: 117–27.

Guillaume, O., and A. Rougeulle. 1987. *Fouille d'Aï Khanoum VII. Les petits objets*. Paris: MDAFA 31.

Helms, S. W. 1997. *Excavations at Old Kandahar in Afghanistan 1976–1978. Stratigraphy, pottery and other finds*. Oxford: BAR Int Ser 686.

Hinz, W., and H. Koch. 1987. *Elamisches Wörterbuch*, 2 vols. Berlin: *AMI* Ergänzungsband 17.

Hlopina, L. I., and I. N. Hlopin. 1976. K proishoždeniju kompleksa Yaz-tepe I Južnogo Turkmenistana. *SA* 4: 200–3.

Holdich, H. 1896. Notes on ancient and medieval Makran. *GJ* 7: 387–405.

Jacobs, B. 2011. Achaemenid satrapies. *EnIr* online edition.

Kačuris, K. 1967. Raskopki na El'ken-depe v Južnoj Turkmenii. *Arheologičeskie Otkritija* 1966: 336.

Kent, R. G. 1953. *Old Persian: Grammar, texts, lexicon*. New Haven: AOS 33.

Kervran, M., D. Stronach, F. Vallat, and J. Yoyotte. 1972. Une statue de Darius découverte à Suse. *JA* 260: 235–66.

Kohl, P. L. 1996. Darragaz, Dargaz, ii. Archaeological sites. *EnIr* 7: 60–1.

Kohl, P. L., and D. L. Heskel. 1980. Archaeological reconnaissance in the Darreh Gaz Plain: A short report. *Iran* 18: 160–72.

König, F. W. 1972. *Die Persika des Ktesias von Knidos*. Graz: *AfO* Beiheft 18.

Košelenko, G. A. 1985. *Drevnejšie Gosudarstva Kavkaza i Srednej Azii*. Moscow: Izdatel'stvo "Nauka."

Kruglikova, I. T., and V. I. Sarianidi. 1976. Pjat' let raboty sovetsko-afganskoj arheologičeskoj ekspedicii. In *Drevnjaja Baktrija. Materialy Sovetsko-Afganskoj ekspedicii 1969–1973 gg.*, ed. I. T. Kruglikova, 3–20. Moscow: Akademija Nauka.

Kuz'mina, E. E. 1977. Les relations entre la Bactriane et l'Iran du VIIIe au IVe siècle BC. In *Le plateau iranien et l'Asie centrale des origines à la conquête islamique*, ed. J. Deshayes, 201–14. Paris: Éditions du CNRS.

——. 1979. O dvuh pertnah amudarinskogo klada s izobraženiem carič. *SA* 1: 35–45.

——. 2002. *Mifologija i iskusstvo Skifov i Baktrijcev*. Moscow: Rossijskij Institut Kulturologii.

Lecoq, P. 1997. *Les inscriptions de la Perse achéménide*. Paris: Gallimard.

Litvinskij, B. A. 2002. Baktrijcy na ohote. *Zapiski Vostočnogo otdelenija Russkogo arheologičeskogo obščestva* 1/26: 181–213.

Litvinskij, B. A., and Pičikjan, I.R. 1994. A rhyton from Takht-i Sangin. *ACSS* 1/3: 355–64.

——. 2000. *Ėllinističeskij chram Oksa v Baktrii: južnyj Tadžikistan Raskopi, architektura, religioznaja žizn'*. Moscow: Izdat. Firma "Vostočnaja Literatura" RAN.

McNicoll, A. 1978. Excavations at Kandahar 1975: Second interim report. *Afghan Studies* 1: 41–66.

McNicoll, A., and W. Ball. 1996. *Excavations at Kandahar 1974 and 1975*. Oxford: BAR Int Ser 641.

Miller, C. 1855. *Geographi graeci minores*, vol. 1. Paris: Firmin Didot.

Muscarella, O. W. 1987. Median art and Medizing scholarship. *JNES* 46: 109–27.

Naveh, J., and S. Shaked. 2012. *Ancient Aramaic documents from Bactria (fourth century B.C.E.)*. London: CII 1/5/2.

Pichikyan [Pičikjan], I. R. 1992. *Oxos-Schatz und Oxos-Tempel: Achämenidische Kunst in Mittelasien*. Berlin: Antike in der Moderne 1.

——. 1997. Rebirth of the Oxus treasure: Second part of the Oxus treasure from the Miho Museum collection. *ACSS* 4/4: 307–83.

——. 1998a. Vozroždenie bol'šogo klada Oksa. Vtoraja čast' klada Oksa iz kollekcii Miho muzeja. I. *VDI* 1: 92–107.

——. 1998b. Vozroždenie bol'šogo klada Oksa. Vtoraja čast' klada Oksa iz kollekcii Miho muzeja. II. *VDI* 2: 161–86.

Pilipko, V. N. 1986. Rannij železnij vek Eteka (Južnij Turkmenistan). *Information Bulletin* 11: 9–19.
Potts, D. T. 1985. The location of Iz-ki-e. *RA* 79: 75–6.
———. 1989. Seleucid Karmania. *AIO*: 581–603.
Pozdena, H. 1975. Makran: Das rückstandigste Gebiet Irans. *Erdkunde* 29: 52–9.
Rapin, C. 1992. *La trésorerie du palais hellénistique d'Aï Khanoum. L'apogée et la chute du royaume grec de Bactriane*. Paris: MDAFA 8.
Rtveladze, E. V. 1975. K karakteristike pamjatnikov Surhandar'inskoj oblasti ahemenidskogo vremeni. *SA* 2: 263–66.
———. 1987. Novye baktrijskie pamjatniki na juge Uzbekistana. *Istorija Material'noj Kul'tury Uzbekistana, Taškent. Izdatel'stvo «Fan Uzbekskoj SSR»* 21: 56–66.
Rtveladze, E. V., and Š. R. Pidaev. 1993. Drevnebaktrijskaja krepost' Talaškan-tepe I. *Rossijskaja Arheologija*: 133–47.
Sagdullaev, A. S. 1987b. *Usadby drevnej Baktrii*. Tashkent: Izdatel'stvo «Fan Uzbekskoj SSR».
Sajjadi, S. M. S., and F. Saber-Moghaddam. 2004. Peintures et gravures murales découvertes à Dahan-e Gholāmān, Sistān. *StIr* 33/2: 285–96.
Sajjadi, S. M. S. 2007. Wall painting from Dahaneh-ye Gholaman (Sistan). *ACSS* 13: 129–54.
Sarianidi, V. 1977. *Drevnie zemledel'cy Afganistana*. Moscow: Akademija Nauk SSSR, Ordena Trydnogo Krasnogo Znameni Institut Arheologii, Isdatel'stvo "Nauka."
———. 1985. Monumental architecture of Bactria. In *De l'Indus aux Balkans: Recueil à la mémoire de Jean Deshayes*, ed. J.-L. Huot, M. Yon, and Y. Calvet, 417–32. Paris: Éditions Recherche sur les Civilisations.
Scerrato, U. 1962. A probable Achaemenid zone in Persian Sistan. *EW* 13: 186–97.
———. 1966a. L'edificio sacro di Dahan-i Ghulaman (Sistan). In *La Persia e il Mondo Greco-romano*, 475–7. Rome: Accademia Nazionale dei Lincei, Quaderno 76.
———. 1966b. Excavations at Dahan-i Ghulaman (Seistan-Iran): First preliminary report (1962–1963). *EW* 16: 9–30.
———. 1970. La Missione Archeologica Italiana nel Sistan Persiano. *Il Veltro* 14/1–2: 123–40.
———. 1972. Missions Archéologiques Italiennes au Sistan. In *The Memorial Volume of the Vth International Congress of Iranian Art and Archaeology. Tehran—Isfahan—Shiraz, 11th–18th April 1968*, vol. 1, 200–203. Tehran: Ministry of Culture and Arts.
———. 1974. A proposito dello "Airyana Vaējah." Notizie sulle possibilità di allevamento del bovino nella Drangiana come attività autonoma. In *Gururājamanjarikā. Studi in Onore di Giuseppe Tucci*, vol. 1, 101–12. Naples: Istituto Universitario Orientale Seminario di Studi Asiatici Series Minor 1.
———. 1979. Evidence of religious life at Dahan-e Ghulaman, Sistan. In *South Asian Archaeology 1977*, vol. 2, ed. M. Taddei, 709–35. Naples: Istituto Universitario Orientale Seminario di Studi Asiatici Series Minor 6/2.
Schmitt, R. 1991. *The Bisitun inscriptions of Darius the Great. Old Persian text*. London: CII 1/1/1.
———. 2001. Eine weitere Alabaster-Vase mit Artaxerxes-Inschrift. *AMT* 33: 191–201.
Schoff, W. H. 1914. *Parthian Stations by Isidore of Charax*. Philadelphia: Commercial Museum.
Shahmirzadi, S. M., and J. Nokandeh. 2001. *Agh Tepe, Miras-e farhangi, Ostan-e Golestan* Tehran: ICAR.
Shaked, S. 2004. *Le satrape de Bactriane et son gouverneur: Documents araméens du IVe s. avant notre ère provenant de Bactriane*. Paris: Persika 4.
Stein, M. A. 1931. *An archaeological tour in Gedrosia*. Calcutta: Government of India, Central Publication Branch.

———. 1943. On Alexander's route into Gedrosia: An archaeological tour in Las Bela. *GJ* 102: 193–227.
Struve, V. V. 1949a. Vosstanie v Margiane pri Darii I. *VDI* 2: 10–29.
———. (1949b). Vosstanie v Margiane pri Darii I. In *Materialy Južno-Turkmenistanskoj arheologičeskoj kompleksnoj ekspedicii*, vol. 1, 9–34. Ashgabat: Akademija Nauk Tyrkmenskoj SSR.
Treasures of ancient Bactria. 2002. Shiga: Miho Museum.
Usmanova, Z. I. 1969a. Erk-Qala-gorodisče Starogo Merva pory antičnosti i rannego srednevekov'ja (K istorii razvitija drevnih gorodov Srednej Azii). Unpublished diss., Tashkent.
———. 1969b. *Novye dannye k arheologičeskoj stratigrafii Erk-kala*. Ashgabat: Trudy Južno-Turkmenistanskoj arheologičeskoj kompleksnoj ekspedicii 14.
Usmanova, Z. I., M. I. Filanovič, and G. A. Košelenko. 1985. Margiana (v antičnuju epochu). In *Drevnejše gosudarstva Kavkaza i Srednej Azii*, ed. G. A. Košelenko, 226–42. Moscow: Arheologiya SSSR.
Venco Ricciardi, R. 1980. Archaeological survey in the Upper Atrek Valley (Khorassan, Iran): Preliminary report. *Mesopotamia* 15: 51–72.
———. 1981a. Prospezione archeologica nell'alta valle dell'Atrek (Khorâsân). *Memorie della Accademia delle Scienze di Torino*, ser. 5 5/2: 93–105.
———. 1981b. Ricognizioni e ricerche nell'Iran orientale dall'età preistorica ad oggi. Periodo partico e sasanide. *Memorie della Accademia delle Scienze di Torino*, ser. 5 5/2: 127–36.
Vogelsang, W. 1981. Kandahar and Arachosia in the early Achaemenid period. Unpublished diss., University of Leiden.
———. 1985. Early historical Arachosia in south-east Afghanistan. *IrAnt* 20: 55–99.
———. 1987. Southeast Afghanistan and the borderlands in the early historical period: Some further observations and suggestions. *Newsletter of Baluchistan Studies* 4: 47–59.
———. 1992. *The rise and organisation of the Achaemenid Empire: The Eastern Iranian evidence*. Leiden: Brill.
———. 2000. Gedrosia. *EnIr* online edition.
———. 2002. *The Afghans*. Oxford: Wiley-Blackwell.
———. 2003. Herat ii. History, pre-Islamic period. *EnIr* online edition.
Weißbach, F. H. 1916. Isidoros 20. *RE* 9: 2064–68.
Zejmal, E. V. 1979. *Amudarinskij klad*. Leningrad: Iskusstvo.

CHAPTER 32

OLD PERSIAN

JAN TAVERNIER

Introduction

It is generally known that the Achaemenid Empire was established by an Iranian-speaking people. More precisely they were speakers of Old Persian, which is one of the two Old Iranian languages (next to the language conventionally called Median), attested in the Achaemenid royal inscriptions.

Old Persian is an Indo-European language and as such is related to Old Indian, Hittite, Latin, Greek, and the modern Indo-European languages. It belongs to the Indo-Iranian branch of the Indo-European languages and, naturally, to the Iranian family within this branch. More precisely, Old Persian is a southwestern Old Iranian language (Schmitt 1989: 56), other Old Iranian languages being Median (Northwest), Avestan (East), and Scythic (North).

In all likelihood, the Persians settled in what is now the Fars area (Gr. Persis) in southwestern Iran during the first half of the first millennium BC. At that time this area, its main town being Anšan, was culturally under Elamite control, whereas its political situation is unclear.

The Old-Iranian-speaking people are attested in history for the first time through Neo-Assyrian royal inscriptions, which contain Median names as well as some information on the history of the Persian-speaking people. According to an inscription of Shalmaneser III (858–824 BC) twenty-seven kings of Parsuwa (written ᵏᵘʳPár-su-a; RIMA A.0.102.14:120) paid tribute to this Assyrian king in 835 BC. Shortly after 646, Kuraš, king of Parsuwa (ᵏᵘʳPar-su-ma-áš; *BIWA* 191 ii 7'), being impressed by Assurbanipal's victories, decided to pay tribute to the Assyrian king. It is now accepted that this Parsuwa was situated in the Lake Urmia area (probably to the southwest of it; Schmitt 1989: 56) and that the name Parsuwa is a forerunner of Pārsa-, the Old Persian indication for Fars (Eilers 1956: 188; Harmatta 1971: 221–2; Skalmowski 1995: 305–6). Nevertheless, the former idea that this Parsumaš was identical to modern Fars has been abandoned (Briant 1996: 28). Around 635 BC, Teispes set up a small kingdom in the region around Anšan. He was followed by Cyrus I (*c*.610–*c*.585 BC), Cambyses I (*c*.585–558 BC), and Cyrus II (558–530 BC), who founded the Achaemenid Empire.

Old Persian is a limited text corpus language, implying that there are not that many texts written in this language. Other examples of such languages are Elamite, Urartian, and Hurrian, among others. The textual corpus of Old Persian consists of three kinds of texts:

(1) The royal inscriptions of the Achaemenid kings: Achaemenid royal ideology was spread throughout the Empire by means of royal inscriptions mostly recorded in three languages: Old Persian, Babylonian, and Elamite. The oldest one and also the longest one is the well-known inscription of Bīsotūn (not far from actual Kermanshah), an inscription of Darius I (521–486 BC) describing the events which led to his kingship as well as the events of the first two years of his reign. It is recorded in Old Persian, Babylonian, and Elamite, but it should be stressed here that the first version was the Elamite one. Darius I and his son and successor Xerxes (485–465 BC) were responsible for the major part of the inscriptions, which are also the most narrative ones. After Xerxes, the number, size, and significance of the inscriptions decrease. This decrease and the use of stereotyped formulas could be the result of a decreasing knowledge of the language (Schmitt 2004: 718). The Old Persian inscriptional language, which was rather artificial (i.e., it did not reflect the spoken language very well) in the elder inscriptions, now reveals some grammatical mistakes. These can be explained only by a growing discrepancy between inscriptional Old Persian and spoken Old Persian, which was developing toward Middle Persian. It should, therefore, not be surprising that most of these mistakes are attested in inscriptions from Artaxerxes III (358–338 BC), one of the latest kings of the Achaemenid Empire who also produced the youngest written documents in Old Persian.

The inscriptions are usually referred to by sigla, naming the king who ordered the inscription and the place where the inscription was carved: for example, DB = Darius I Bīsotūn; DNa = Darius I Naqš-e Rustam a; XSc = Xerxes Susa c; A³Pa = Artaxerxes III Persepolis a; and so on.

The only publication of all inscriptions, together with their non-Persian versions, is Weissbach (1911). An edition of all Achaemenid Old Persian royal inscriptions was published by Schmitt (2009). Other editions contain specific inscriptions: Bīsotūn (Schmitt 1991), Naqš-e Rustam and Persepolis (Schmitt 2000), some texts from Susa (Steve 1987), and various inscriptions (Schmitt 1999).

(2) Short inscriptions on seals: Various Old Persian inscriptions on seals are attested: seven from Darius I as well as from Xerxes; one from Darius II; two from Artaxerxes III; and two from private persons (Schmitt 1981). Nevertheless, these short inscriptions add very little information to the language as known in the Achaemenid royal inscriptions.

(3) One administrative tablet (see below).

Sadly, it must finally be mentioned that Old Persian is all too often attested in fake inscriptions. There are two kinds: fakes from antiquity and modern fakes. The first category (Schmitt 2007: 25–34) includes inscriptions, whose Achaemenid date is certain but which cannot belong to the king from whom they are supposed to derive.

Examples include inscriptions ascribed to Ariaramnes, Arsames, and Cyrus II. The second category (Schmitt 2007: 35–116) consists of various modern fake Achaemenid inscriptions, such as the golden tablets of London and Hamadan, the clay tablets of Karahöyük, the stone tablet from Essen, and a wooden sarcophagus from Baluchistan, which allegedly contained the body of Rhodogoune, the daughter of Xerxes, the discovery of which has received considerable attention in the world's press since October 2000.

This chapter will discuss some aspects of the Old Persian language. It will, however, not treat the core grammar itself, for which interested readers are referred to the available grammars of Old Persian (Kent 1953; Brandenstein and Mayrhofer 1964; Schmitt 1989, 2004). An Old Persian reader by P. O. Skjærvø is freely available online at www.fas.harvard.edu/~iranian/OldPersian/index.htm.

History of decipherment

Proto-research: Classical Antiquity

The history of decipherment has been dealt with by a number of authors (cf. Weissbach 1896–1904: 64–72; Rogers 1900: 1–83; Booth 1902; Kent 1953: 10–11; Borger 1975–8; Schmitt 1989: 63–4). In Classical Antiquity the political interactions between the Greek city-states and the Persian Empire stimulated some Greeks to travel around the Persian Empire or, in some cases, to move there. Many Greeks are attested at the royal Persian court, such as Ctesias of Cnidus, a Greek physician who stayed at the court of Artaxerxes II from 404 to 398/7 BC and who wrote a history of the Persians.

Travelers and Greek authors must have seen the various Achaemenid royal inscriptions in Persepolis, Van, Susa, and other places, and indeed some reports are preserved in Greek literature. Although the translations or summaries given in this literature are manifestly wrong, they attest to a Greek interest in these Old Persian texts. One of the inscriptions mentioned by Greek authors is a tomb inscription of Cyrus II (Schmitt 1988: 18–25). According to the Alexander historian Aristoboulos (cited by Arrian, *Anab.* 6.29.4, 8; Strabo, *Geog.* 15.3.7) the tomb of Cyrus II was situated in a park at Pasargadae. On it was engraved an inscription "in Persian signs" (Περσικοι = ς γραμμασι). Aristoboulos even gave a translation of this inscription (και\ εθήλου Περσιστι\ τάδε):

> O human being, I am Cyrus, the son of Cambyses who has established power for the Persians and who has ruled as king over Asia. As a consequence, do not envy me because of this tomb.

In the same passage Strabo cited another Alexander historian, Onesicritus, according to whom the inscription was recorded in Greek, but written in Persian characters. Its translation was:

"Here I lie, Cyrus, King of Kings."

Plutarch (*Alexander* 69.4) stated that Alexander, after having read the Persian inscription, ordered the engraving of a Greek translation on this spot. Its text was:

> O human being, whoever you are and from wherever you will come, for I know that you will come, I am Cyrus, who has acquired power for the Persians. As a consequence do not envy me for this bit of earth, covering my body.

Finally, Strabo (*Geog.* 15.3.8) mentioned Aristos of Salamis (second century BC), who argued that there was a Greek as well as a Persian inscription having the same meaning. Apart from the discussion of the possibility of a Greek inscription at Pasargadae, it has been regularly argued (Weissbach 1894: 661; Jackson 1906: 290; Dandamayev 1976: 29; Schmitt 1988: 22) that some phrases are remarkably similar to Old Persian constructions, such as "I am Cyrus, King of Kings" (*adam Kuruš xšāyaθiya Haxāmanišiya*). Yet the perfectly hexametric character of Onesicritus' inscription and its similarity to Greek epigrams weaken this idea. To summarize, it must be accepted that these Greek tomb inscriptions are not authentic (Stronach 1978: 26; Schmitt 1988: 22–5).

Greek authors also mention the inscription on Darius' tomb. Again they present translations ("I was a friend to the friends," "I am a good horseman," "I am a good archer" in Strabo, and a more amusing one "I could drink large quantities of wine and I could bear it well" in Athenaeus [*c*.200 AD]). The two first examples are mere topoi which the Greeks ascribed to the Persians. It is thus improbable that the Greeks copied their texts from real exemplars of the Old Persian cuneiform inscriptions (Schmitt 1988: 26–30).

Other Old Persian inscriptions (e.g., the Tearos and Bosporus stelae), mentioned by *inter alia* Herodotus, are also problematic (Schmitt 1988: 30–36). Finally, the Bīsotūn complex was also noticed by authors, albeit only the relief, not the inscriptions, was discussed. It was mentioned by Ctesias, Diodorus (first century BC), and Tacitus (100 AD). Around 900 AD Ibn Hawqal, an Arab geographer, considered the relief to be a representation of a teacher who punished his students.

Pre-research (1320–1765)

The first European to travel to Persepolis was a wandering friar named Odoricus. Described as a "man of little refinement" (Yule 1866: 52 n.), he passed Persepolis about 1320 on his way to Cathay and described the ruin as follows:

> I came unto a certain city called Coprum, which was a huge and mighty city in old time, containing well nigh fifty miles in circuit, and had done in times past great damage unto the Romans. In it there are stately palaces altogether destitute of inhabitants, notwithstanding it abounded with great store of victuals (trans. by Hakluyt 1599: 54; the original Latin text reads, "Ab hac, transiens per civitates et terras, veni ad quamdam civitatem nomine Coprum, quae antiquitatus civitas magna fuit: haec maximum damnum quondam intulit Romae; eius autem muri bene

quadraginta miliarum sunt capaces. Et in ea sunt palacia adhuc integra, et multis victualibus haec abundant").

More than 150 years later, in 1472, the Venetian envoy Josaphat Barbaro also visited Persepolis and described in more details the various reliefs he saw. Nevertheless he did not mention any inscriptions.

By opening his land to European ambassadors and merchants, Shah Abbas (1586–1629) contributed greatly to the expansion of European knowledge about Persian antiquities. Gradually, Western Europeans started to rediscover the East. In 1602 Antonio de Gouvea, an ambassador of Philip III, king of Spain and Portugal, visited Persepolis and, upon seeing the cuneiform inscriptions there, described them as utterly strange:

> The inscriptions—which relate to the foundation of the edifice and no doubt also declare the author of it—although they remain in many parts very distinct, yet there is none that can read them, for they are not in Persian nor Arabic nor Armenian nor Hebrew, which are the languages current in those parts; and thus all helps to blot out the memory of that which the ambitious king hoped to make eternal.

Sixteen years later another envoy of Philip III, Don Garcia de Silva y Figueroa, who had met Antonio de Gouvea at the Spanish court, also visited the site, identified it correctly as Persepolis, and reported that

> The letters themselves are neither Chaldaean, nor Hebrew, nor Greek, nor Arabic, nor of any other Nation which was ever found of old, or at this day to be extant. They are all three cornered, but somewhat long, of the form of a Pyramid, or such a little Obelisk as I have set in the margin (Δ).

After a meeting at Isfahan between Don Garcia and the Italian traveler Pietro della Valle, the latter stayed two days in the Persepolis in 1621 and wrote that, "One cannot tell in what language or letters these inscriptions are written, because the characters are unknown." Nevertheless he made two substantial contributions to the decipherment of cuneiform writing: (1) he correctly deduced the direction of writing to be from left to right; and (2) in copying in 1621 five very common signs and publishing them in 1658, he was the first person to publish a cuneiform sign.

From then on things proceeded quickly. In 1674 Jean Chardin also copied some signs and argued that the inscriptions always appeared in sets of three parallel forms. Although he furnished a copy of three lines of cuneiform, Thomas Herbert (1677) contributed nothing of scientific importance to the study of cuneiform writing. Samuel Flower, an agent of the East India Company, copied several inscriptions, from which twenty-three signs were published in 1693. The first case of deception in the field was committed by an Italian traveler, Giovanni-Francesco Gemelli-Carreri, who slightly modified some of Herbert's copies and described them as his own in 1699–1700. The drawings of Persepolis by the Dutch artist Cornelius de Bruijn (1652–1727) were well known in the West.

The first inscription to be published completely was a text from Darius at Persepolis (siglum: DPc), published by Chardin in 1711. Nevertheless, progress in decipherment was not yet made.

The decipherment of the Old Persian script (1765–1851)

In 1765, a substantial advance in the research on these inscriptions was made by the German–Danish scholar Carsten Niebuhr (1733–1815) during his stay in Persepolis. His accurate drawings, published in 1778 in his *Reisebeschreibung nach Arabien und anderen umliegenden Ländern*, finally provided European scientists with reliable images of the texts. Although sharing the general belief that the texts were written in an alphabetic script, Niebuhr correctly argued that they were written in three different scripts and emphasized the simpler nature of Old Persian cuneiform writing (his class I) in comparison to the Babylonian and Elamite scripts (his classes II and III).

In 1798, Olav Gerhard Tychsen, professor at Rostock, discovered that the three scripts represented three different languages, but he assigned the inscriptions to the Parthian period (second century BC to third century AD), a mistake corrected by Friedrich Münter of Göttingen. In 1798, both authors independently discovered the word-divider, which was thus the first sign to be deciphered. Münter also correctly argued that recurring groups of characters must designate a word for "king."

All this was taken up in 1802 by the German scholar Georg Friedrich Grotefend (1775–1853), who was assisted by recent knowledge of Avestan grammar which provided him with a structure for the Old Persian tongue and by Silvestre de Sacy's decipherment of the royal titles in Pahlavi. By putting inscriptions next to each other and looking for royal names and titles Grotefend succeeded in deciphering several Old Persian signs. Grotefend continued to publish on Old Persian and remains a very important name in the decipherment history. While knowledge of Avestan and Old Indian grew, other scholars, such as Rasmus Rask (1787–1832), Eugène Burnouf (1801–1852), Christian Lassen (1800–1876; who discovered the mixed alphabetic–syllabic character of the Old Persian script and who may be credited as the final decipherer of the Old Persian script) and many others continued Grotefend's work.

The man who would earn imperishable prestige with his work on the Old Persian inscription of Bīsotūn is Henry C. Rawlinson (1810–1895). Located in the Orient and consequently deprived of European publications, he worked independently of other scholars and thus confirmed and extended the knowledge of European scholarship on the Old Persian language. On January 1, 1838, he sent his translation of the first two paragraphs of the Bīsotūn inscription to the Royal Asiatic Society and in 1839 he sent some additions, but unfortunately his work would be delayed due to his involvement in the First Anglo-Afghan War (1839–42). In 1846, his article on the Old Persian version of the Bīsotūn inscription was finally published (Rawlinson 1846–7).

This independent analysis of Old Persian was surprisingly followed by a third one: in January 1847, the *Dublin University Magazine* contained an anonymous article, "Some passages of the life of King Darius," which clearly bears the hand of Edward Hincks. This Irish clergyman, who spent the major part of his life as pastor at Killyleagh, a village twenty miles south of Belfast, had already published a Hebrew grammar and a series of articles on Egyptian before he turned to cuneiform. This he did only because he hoped it would shed light on the Egyptian hieroglyphics. On June 9, 1846, he presented his first paper on Old Persian and Elamite cuneiform to the Royal Irish Academy. It was published two years later. Independently, Jules Oppert (1825–1905) also made some discoveries on the nature of Old Persian cuneiform.

In 1851, the last syllabic sign, occurring only four times and indicating the non-Persian sound /l/, was deciphered by J. Oppert. From then on, the script was declared "deciphered." Nevertheless, various later studies have slightly modified our precise understanding of the script and the system behind it. In 1890, B. T. Evetts deciphered the last logogram (for Ahuramazda). Finally, it must be stressed that the decipherment of the Old Persian script provided the clue to the decipherment of the other cuneiform writing systems (Mesopotamian, Urartian, etc.).

The Old Persian writing system

Old Persian was written by means of a cuneiform script, counting thirty-six basic signs, a small number of signs compared to languages such as Sumerian and Akkadian. To these were added two word-dividers (one used exclusively in the Bīsotūn inscription, the other used in other inscriptions), nineteen number signs and eight logographic signs (Table 32.1).

The script is a mixture of alphabetic and syllabic principles (Jensen 1969: 98; Mayrhofer 1979: 293; Justeson and Stephens 1991–3: 30–1; Testen 1996: 134; some scholars, e.g., Mallowan 1972: 2–3; Lecoq 1974b: 32; Hincha 1974: 72, described it as an alphabetic script): whereas the vowel signs A, I, and U are alphabetic, the consonant signs all have an inherent vowel, for example, the sign B may represent /b/ as well as /ba/. Remarkably, the syllabary is not complete: the series of consonant signs with inherent /a/ is complete, but the series with /i/ and /u/ are not. As a result, it is often hard to determine what form is meant. To illustrate this: as there is no sign TI, both sequences -/tiy/ (act. pres. 3 sg. ending) and -/taiy/ (med. pres. 3 sg. ending) must be expressed by the same graphic sequence –ta–i–y, which leads to confusion (e.g., there is no graphic distinction between *vainatiy* "he sees" and *vainataiy* "he seems"), even for the ancient Persians themselves.

There has been much debate about the origin of the Old Persian cuneiform script, as well as on the date of its creation. Earlier scholars believed that the script was derived from the Neo-Babylonian cuneiform writing system (e.g., Oppert 1874: 239–45; Sayce 1884; Halévy 1885). According to Deecke (1878: 289), the script was directly derived from the Old Babylonian writing system. It is now apparent that the Old Persian writing system has no clear, systematic connection with the other major existing cuneiform

Table 32.1

A-series		I-series		U-series	
Sign	Value	Sign	Value	Sign	Value
	A		I		U
	B				
	C				
	Ç				
	D		DI		DU
	F				
	G				GU
	H				
	J		JI		
	K				KU
	L				
	M		MI		MU
	N				NU
	P				
	R				RU
	S				
	Š				
	T				TU
	Θ				
	V		VI		
	X				
	Y				
	Z				

writing systems of the Ancient Near East, such as Mesopotamian, Hittite, Hurrian, or Elamite (Kuryłowicz 1964: 563; Windfuhr 1970: 121; Kuryłowicz 1973: 274; Hoffmann 1976: 620; Mayrhofer 1979: 292), although the use of logograms must be related to the widespread Elamo-Mesopotamian cuneiform practice (Lecoq 1974b: 39). Equally clear is the fact that the script was specifically devised for Old Persian, as there is a sign for the typically Old Persian sound /ç/.

A peculiarity is the sign denoting /l/, which is a secondary sign since /l/ is not an indigenous Persian sound. Either it developed from Elamo-Sumero-Akkadian LA (; Oppert 1874: 241, 243; Halévy 1885: 494; Paper 1956: 24–5; Windfuhr 1970: 121, n. 4; Hinz 1973: 23; Lecoq 1974b: 39; Hoffmann 1976: 620; Mayrhofer 1979: 292, n. 15; Schmitt 1980: 18;

Table 32.2
Logograms

Sign	Name	Value	Sign	Name	Value
𒀭𒊕	AM₁	Auramazdā	𒀭𒊕	BU	būmiš
𒀭𒊕	AM₂	Auramazdā	𒀭𒊕	DH₁	dahyāuš
𒀭𒊕	AMha	Auramazdahā	𒀭𒊕	DH₂	dahyāuš
𒀭𒊕	BG	baga	𒀭𒊕	XŠ	xšāyaθiya

d'Erme 1983: 432, 440; Mayrhofer 1989: 174; Testen 1996: 134) or it was inspired by the shape of R, the sign expressing the sound closest to /l/ (Horn 1898–1901: 56; Oranskij 1963: 46, n. 19; 1988: 106; Justeson and Stephens 1991–3: 31).

Despite the apparent lack of contacts between the various major cuneiform writing systems and Old Persian, the Old Persian script shows some similarities to another cuneiform writing system, which itself was derived from the Neo-Assyrian cuneiform writing system, but still had some specific characteristics: the Urartian script. Features common to both writing systems include:

(1) the occurrence of a word-divider. According to D'jakonov (1970: 102; cf. Hoffmann 1976: 121, n. 4) the Old Persian word-divider is probably a descendant of the Urartian one.

Table 32.3
Numerals

Sign	Number	Sign	Number	Sign	Number
		𒌋	10	𒎙	20
𒁹	1				
𒈫	2	𒌋𒁹	12	𒎙𒁹	22
		𒌋𒈫	13	𒎙𒈫	23
		𒌋𒐗	14		
𒐙	5	𒌋𒐙	15	𒎙𒐙	25
				𒎙𒐚	26
𒐛	7			𒎙𒐛	27
𒐜	8	𒌋𒐜	18		
𒐝	9	𒌋𒐝	19	𒁹𒐏	120

Word divider: ⸱

(2) the fact that both in the Urartian and in the Old Persian cuneiform scripts horizontal and vertical wedges never really cross, contrary to the Neo-Assyrian cuneiform script (Jensen 1969: 92; Hoffmann 1976: 621, n. 4; Schmitt 1989: 61).

D'jakonov (1970: 121–2; cf. Hoffmann 1976: 622–3) also saw various similarities between the Urartian and Old Persian inscriptional traditions, where some formulas seem to be similar:

(1) The royal titles: the Old Persian royal titles PN *xšāyaθiya vazrka, xšāyaθiya xšāyaθiyānām, xšāyaθiya dahyūnām vispazanānām* "PN, great king, king of kings, king of all kinds of lands" (e.g., in DNa 8–11) is nicely paralleled by Urartian PN MAN dan-nu, MAN GAL-*ni* MAN KUR.KUR, MAN MAN^meš "PN, powerful king, great king, king of lands, king of kings" (Salvini 2008: A 9–7:8; cf. A 9–15:9–12).
(2) The Old Persian formula *vašnā Auramazdāha* "By the favour of Ahuramazda" also has Urartian relatives: *Ḫaldini alšuišini* "By the greatness of Ḫaldi" (e.g., Salvini 2008: A 5–8 Ro 10, A 11–4:1), *Ḫaldini baušini* "With the help of Ḫaldi" (e.g., Salvini 2008: A 5–11A:5, A 8–1 Ro 17) and, most frequently, *Ḫaldini ušmašini* "By the power of Ḫaldi" (e.g., Salvini 2008: A 2–6A:1, A 3–5 Vo 8, A 5–75:1–2, A 9–3 vi 1, A 11–8:2). Once *Ḫaldini baušini* appears in the Assyrian version of an Urartian-Assyrian bilingual text as *ina tukulti Ḫaldia* "With the help of Ḫaldi." The three formulae appear in free variation.
(3) The assertion of the greatness of Ahuramazda, often encountered in the Old Persian inscriptions, reminds one of the following formula, preceding the report of every campaign in the Urartian inscriptions: *Ḫaldini kuruni Ḫaldinini šuri kuruni* "Mighty is Ḫaldi, mighty are the Ḫaldian arms!" (Salvini 2008: A 9–3:2–3; D'jakonov 1970: 121). Admittedly the similarity between both traditions is not that great here, particularly as the translation is not certain. Salvini (2008: 422) translates *kurini* as "victorious."
(4) The phrase "This is what I did, by the favor of Ahuramazda, in one and the same year" (frequent in Achaemenid royal inscriptions of Darius I) could be compared with "With Ḫaldi these deeds I did there in one year" (e.g., Salvini 2008: A 8–2 Ro 12'–13,' 35'–36'; D'jakonov 1970: 121, n. 60).

These similarities should, however, be examined critically. Concerning the first similarity, one has to remember that "king of lands" as well as "king of kings," are also attested, albeit not that frequently, in Mesopotamian texts (CAD Š 2: 79–80). As to the second similarity, it should be noted that the expression *ina tukulti DN* is often attested in Akkadian texts too, certainly in the Neo-Assyrian royal inscriptions (CAD T: 463). The third and fourth similarities are rather generalities. In sum, the significance of these so-called similarities should not be exaggerated, although it is possible that Urartians and Persians had some contacts.

It should be noted, however, that the differences between both systems are still great: the Urartian script is basically the same as the Neo-Assyrian script and it does not permit the splitting of a word at the end of a line (Lecoq 1974b: 40). In addition, one should always be aware that the line between influence and autonomous invention is sometimes hard to draw. The Mycenaean and Cypriote scripts, as well as some archaic Greek scripts also have word-dividers (Lecoq 1974b: 43–4), but that does not mean that Old Persian is derived from these writing systems. Mittelberger (1965: 93–8; Lecoq 1974b: 42–8) also recognized various similarities between Eastern Mediterranean scripts (Luwian hieroglyphs, Linear B, Cypriote, archaic Greek) and Old Persian, but correctly concluded that both systems are fundamentally different. Furthermore, the Semitic alphabet also influenced the genesis of the Old Persian script: the absence of a graphic distinction between ĭ and ī and ŭ and ū as well as the fact that a sign C could render both /C/ and /Ca/ must be ascribed to Semitic influence (Kuryłowicz 1964; 1973: 274–5; Hincha 1974: 83).

By now, it has been generally accepted that the Old Persian cuneiform script was not the result of a longer evolution, but that it was created ad hoc for the rendering of Old Persian (Weissbach 1911: lix; Jensen 1969: 103; Hoffmann 1976: 621; Mayrhofer 1979: 292; 1989: 174, 180). The signs were also created in a deliberate order, for example, it seems logical that the sign PA (three horizontals over two verticals) was designed after the signs DA (one horizontal over two verticals) and ÇA (two horizontals over two verticals) (cf. Hoffmann 1976: 621; contra Windfuhr 1969: 991–2; 1970: 121–5). In all likelihood Babylonian, Elamite, and Aramaean experts participated in the creation of the Old Persian writing system (Kuryłowicz 1964: 563–4; Hoffmann 1976: 632).

The origin of the Old Persian script, as well as the date of its invention, are much debated. There are various factors which have to be taken into account:

(1) DB IV 88–92, where Darius says he has made a "new form of writing" (if correct) which is said to be "in Aryan."
(2) Some Old Persian inscriptions that are claimed to date from the reign of Cyrus II (558–530 BC). These can be divided in two categories: three inscriptions naming Cyrus from Cyrus' capital Pasargadae, and a tomb inscription of Cyrus, referred to by Greek authors. If these texts are authentic, then the script did exist during Cyrus' reign.
(3) The structural analysis of the Old Persian script itself.
(4) The 21st Letter of Themistocles (cf. below).
(5) A number of archaeological and iconographical issues concerning the oldest Old Persian inscription and monument, that of Bīsotūn.

The oldest opinions presented on the invention of the Old Persian script actually date from Antiquity itself. In the 21st Letter of Themistocles, two types of script are mentioned: The "Assyrian letters" (Ἀσσύρια γράμματα, probably indicating the Aramaic script; cf. Nylander 1968: 123–4) and "Those which Darius, the father of Xerxes, recently wrote for the Persians" (ἃ Δαρεῖος ὁ πατὴρ Ξέρξου Πέρσαις ἔναγχος ἔγραψε) (indicating the Old Persian script). The text is generally dated to the Roman period (Schmitt 1992: 28; Huyse 1999: 52), which means that the Greeks and Romans ascribed the invention of the Old Persian script to Darius I (D'jakonov 1970: 100). Unfortunately, the sources of this opinion, for it is sure that the author of this text used an older source who knew Iranian culture quite well (Nylander 1968: 134; Dandamayev 1976: 43), are unknown. Nylander believed the source to be a fifth-century author, probably Charon of Lampsacus, rather than Hellanicus.

Since then, many scholars have expressed their views on this issue, and these ideas fall into five groups:

(1) The Persians adopted their writing system from the Median writing system, which was influenced by or based upon another writing system, such as the Urartian one, the Aramaic one, or the Elamite one. The missing link between the older tradition and the Old Persian tradition was the Median annals (Hüsing 1900; Jensen 1901: 239; Hüsing 1908: 365; Struve 1951: 188–91; D'jakonov 1956: 367; Struve 1968: 49–50; D'jakonov 1970: 122; Dandamayev 1976: 39; Gershevitch 1979: 114). Sancisi-Weerdenburg (1988: 198–9) and Mayrhofer (1989: 178–9) rejected the idea of Median writings. The former, however, followed D'jakonov (1970: 114, n. 45) in accepting the existence of an oral tradition, which preceded the writing down of royal inscriptions.

(2) The script was invented during the reign of Cyrus II (Oppert 1874: 240; Herzfeld 1908: 65–8; 1910: 63; Schaeder 1930: 293; Weissbach 1936: *41*; Kent 1946: 210–12; 1953: 12; Kuryłowicz 1964: 569; Ghirshman 1965: 248; Hallock 1970; Mallowan 1972: 3; Kuryłowicz 1973: 274–80).

(3) The first Achaemenids wrote Old Persian by means of Aramaic characters (Lewy 1954: 178–88). Afterward Darius invented a proper writing system.

(4) It was Darius I who commanded a script to be designed in order to produce an Old Persian version of the Bīsotūn inscription (Sayce 1884: 24; Foy 1898: 597; Hommel 1904: 201–2; Weissbach 1911: lxix; Hinz 1938: 164–70, 1942: 349; 1952; Borger and Hinz 1959: 127; Brandenstein and Mayrhofer 1964: 17; Jensen 1969: 104–6; Duchesne-Guillemin 1972: 79; Hinz 1973: 15–21; Hoffmann 1976: 622; Huyse 1999: 51–5).

(5) More recently, a theory has been suggested claiming that the development of a script designed for the denotation of Old Persian probably began in the reign of Cyrus II, but that its use was really extended by Darius I (Hallock 1970: 54–5; Lecoq 1974b: 102–3; Mayrhofer 1979; 1989: 181; Schmitt 1989: 61; 2004: 721–2). A variant of this idea was defended by Werba (1983: 206), who believed that the script was first used under Bardiya/Smerdis, the successor of Cambyses, and that its use was later extended by Darius I.

In all probability the inscriptions ascribed to Cyrus II are not authentic: the inscriptions mentioned by the Greek authors rather reflect Greek topoi (Schmitt 1988: 18–25), whereas the Old Persian Pasargadae inscriptions (CMa–c) were probably added by Darius I. An important clue supporting this view is the fact that, if the texts were authentic, Cyrus would have called himself an Achaemenid, something which only happened from Darius' reign onward (Huyse 1999: 52). The nonauthenticity of these inscriptions can be used against theories 1 and 2, in other words, no Old Persian or Median texts predating Darius I exist.

A crucial argument for the last theory is the fact that the two simplest signs, KU (the only sign consisting of only two wedges) and RU, are the only signs in the *i*- and *u*-series with fewer than four wedges, even though the phonemic sequences expressed by them are not that frequent, and that both are used in writing the name of Cyrus (Kuruš). This does not mean that CMa, an inscription wrongly ascribed to Cyrus, was the basic text for the development of the Old Persian writing system, as Hallock believed.

Yet, this argument is not waterproof. Lecoq (1983: 38; cf. Huyse 1999: 51) wondered why, if KU and RU were the first signs to be designed, RU too was not composed of two wedges, as was KU. In addition, if the signs belonging to the *i*- and *u*-series were only designed to make proper names comprehensible to the public, why is there not a sign BU, needed to write the name Kambūjiya (Cambyses), or *NI (for Nisaya-), or *ΘU (for Aθurā), and so on? Huyse (1999: 51) also questioned why the frequently used sign A was composed of four wedges whereas rare signs such as F and J had only three wedges. In addition, the fact that no Old Persian texts from Cyrus' reign exist at this moment also argues against this theory.

No generally accepted solution has yet been presented regarding the date of invention of the Old Persian cuneiform writing system. Nevertheless, it seems that most objective arguments point to a genesis of the Old Persian cuneiform script early in the reign of Darius I, to be used for the first time in DBa-k and DB (Huyse 1999: 54).

When and by whom was Old Persian used?

Although the general view of Old Persian as a court language is still widespread, this theory needs some modification, and it seems appropriate to adopt a moderate stance, namely, that there were two fields in which the language could be used: court and administration. It should, however, be stressed, that Old Persian, as we know it from the inscriptions, was not the vernacular spoken by the Achaemenids and their Persian subjects. The inscriptional language is more an artificial language, peppered with non-Persian (e.g., Median) words (cf. Lecoq 1974a). The expression "Old Persian," as used here, may indicate two sociolects: inscriptional Old Persian and vernacular Old Persian.

Old Persian as a Court Language

As Old Persian was always found in royal inscriptions, it was quickly assumed that the language, as we know it, was a court language, used exclusively for the transmission of the royal ideology and propaganda, a language "confined to royal prestige purposes" (Gershevitch 1979: 122; Schmitt 1989: 57; 1992: 26; 2004: 717). Equally, its script was a

Prunkschrift. Indications for this are: (1) the fact that the inscriptions were mostly placed in spaces where they could not be read, so they were not intended for reading; and (2) the inscriptions are nearly never attested outside of Persia, Elam, and Media. It should, however, be noted that Darius explicitly stated that copies of the Bīsotūn Inscription were sent all over the empire (DB IV 91–92). It is still possible that Old Persian versions were spread to the Persian-speaking satraps in their satrapies.

Nevertheless, there is one text written in Old Persian of a purely administrative character. It belongs to the so-called Persepolis Fortification Archive, a collection of several thousand texts, written predominantly in Elamite and Aramaic (see Chapter 27). Nevertheless, this archive, a part of the Persepolitan administration dealing with various issues (e.g., rations to workers), contains some curiosities, such as one Greek text, one Phrygian text, and the recently discovered, unique Old Persian administrative text (Stolper and Tavernier 2007).

The text is not intrusive. It nicely fits the administrative pattern of the Fortification Archive, as can be seen from the transliteration. As half the text is broken, it is difficult to present a translation. What can we deduce from it? It refers to 6000 or more liters of some dry commodity, from a named person, at five named villages, for two years or more.

As it remains the sole nonroyal text in Old Persian, this text has not caused a revolution among the scholarly community. The ideological function of Old Persian is still overwhelming. In all likelihood the Old Persian text is proof of a general literacy among the scribes at Persepolis. Most of the Fortification Texts (Elamite, Aramaic, etc.) were probably written by scribes who spoke Iranian languages, but not necessarily Old Persian. Also Aramaic, at least basic Aramaic, must have been known by the scribes, since they had to be able to read the various Aramaic dockets on the Elamite tablets (Stolper and Tavernier 2007: 19–20). As the Old Persian script was relatively easy to learn and as the language used in the tablet was not that difficult, most scribes working around Persepolis could easily have written the Old Persian text.

Still, the question remains, why did someone write it? Probably the text was created as a kind of diversion or even sport. Nevertheless, with only one partial Old Persian document, this question is difficult to tackle. Almost certainly this tablet, just like the Greek and the Phrygian examples, was the result of extraordinary behavior rather than of a widespread practice.

Old Persian as a nonwritten administrative language

The idea of Old Persian as an exclusive court language has in part been challenged by the discovery of the Old Persian administrative tablet discussed above. Even before the discovery of the Old Persian administrative text, however, the notion that Old Persian was a court language had already been criticized by D'jakonov (1970: 123), who observed that, even if it was not used for administration in Fars itself, Old Persian might have been used elsewhere in that capacity. Now, of course, we know that Old Persian was used as an administrative language and in spite of the lack of written documents, two main phenomena justify the belief that Old Persian was used in an administrative way, apart from the logical assumption that the leaders of the Achaemenid Empire spoke Old Persian, were probably monolingual and thus uttered their commands in this Old Iranian tongue before they were later translated into Aramaic and from Aramaic into Egyptian, Elamite, and other local vernaculars. First of all, there are the many loanwords in non-Iranian texts (cf. Tavernier 2007: 78–90, 403–71). These loanwords are generally quite technical expressions, for which the target languages (Aramaic, Babylonian, Elamite, etc.) had no immediate or convenient equivalent. They belong most certainly to the official administrative language as used by high-ranking officials. Second, various expressions seem to have been translated literally from Old Iranian into Aramaic and Elamite. The latter, however, represents a special case. Because Iranian-speaking people settled in what is now the Fars province of Iran, Achaemenid Elamite was heavily influenced by Old Iranian. Intense contact between Iranians and Elamites in the seventh and sixth centuries BC gave rise to the specifically Irano-Elamite character of Achaemenid culture. Miroschedji called this phenomenon the "ethnogénèse des Perses" (1985: 295, 304).

The Aramaic language was selected by the Achaemenids as their linguistic gateway to the world. As they realized that there were many languages spoken in their immense empire, they also knew that they would need one administrative language that could be used by everyone. The choice of Aramaic was, in this sense, the most logical one, since this was already the lingua franca of the western parts of the empire (Mesopotamia, Palestine, Syria). This meant that all administrative documents, emanating from the satrapal administrations, were translated from Old Persian into Aramaic. If necessary, the document could also be translated into a third, indigenous language, such as Egyptian (Tavernier 2008: 64–74; forthcoming a, forthcoming b). As was to be expected, various Old Iranian expressions appeared in these Aramaic texts (Benveniste 1954: 305; Kutscher 1961: 127; 1969: 142; Kaufman 1974: 70, with older references; Whitehead 1978: 133–4; Stolper 1985: 21; Makujina 1997). A good example is Aramaic *br byt'* "prince," which is a calque (a word-for-word translation of a concept or phrase in one language into another) on Old Persian **vīsapuθra-* "son of the (royal) house, prince," as is Babylonian *mar bīti* "prince" (Kaufman 1974: 70, with older references; Whitehead 1978: 133–4; Stolper 1985: 21). Another example is *šym ṭ'm* "to issue an order" (in various forms). Kutscher (1969: 142) considered it to be a *passivum majestatis*, but the expression is also attested in the active form and therefore Makujina (1997) considered the formula to be Old Persian in origin, with the caveat, however, that it was not a servile rendering of OP **framānā(maiy) ništāta-* "A command was issued (by me)."

Scholars (e.g., Benveniste) have "discovered" other calques, but these are less convincing than the ones discussed here. In any case, these examples demonstrate that the administrative Aramaic language was influenced, logically, by administrative Old Iranian. It is therefore more than a pity that the only Old Persian administrative text is incompletely preserved, as it could have provided an interesting link between both languages.

Epilogue

Old Persian is nowadays especially referred to and used by Iranologists and scholars studying the Achaemenid Empire. Yet the language is not the exclusive property of these scholars. One may recall the spectacular celebrations to mark the 2500th birthday of Iran in 1971. A more humorous example dates from 1997–8 when the popular rock band the Rolling Stones held their "Bridges to Babylon" tour and had a poster designed with the famous "Babylonian Tongue." In reality, however, the language written on the tongue was neither Babylonian nor Akkadian but rather Old Persian, more precisely a fragmentary royal title of a king Darius (Schmitt 2007: 125–6).

Further reading

Various grammatical studies on the Old Persian language have been published. The most detailed remains Kent (1953). A more Indo-European approach can be found in Brandenstein and Mayrhofer (1964). More recent descriptions of Old Persian include Schmitt (1989 and 2004). For those more interested in the history of the Achaemenid Empire, see the monumental volume of P. Briant (1996).

References

Benveniste, E. 1954. Éléments perses en Araméen d'Égypte. *JA* 242: 297–310.
Booth, A. J. 1902. *The discovery and decipherment of the trilingual cuneiform inscriptions.* London: Longmans Green.
Borger, R. 1975–8. Die Entzifferungsgeschichte der altpersischen Keilschrift nach Grotefends ersten Erfolgen. *Persica* 7: 7–19.
Borger, R., and W. Hinz. 1959. Eine Dareios-Inschrift aus Pasargadae. *ZDMG* 109: 117–27.
Brandenstein, W., and M. Mayrhofer. 1964. *Handbuch des Altpersischen.* Wiesbaden: Harrassowitz.
Briant, P. 1996. *Histoire de l'Empire perse de Cyrus à Alexandre.* Paris: Fayard.
Dandamayev, M. A. 1976. *Persien unter den ersten Achämeniden (6. Jahrhundert v.Chr.).* Wiesbaden: Beiträge zur Iranistik 8.
Deecke, W. 1878. Ueber den Ursprung der altpersischen Keilschrift. *ZDMG* 32: 271–89.
d'Erme, G. M. 1983. Aspetti grafici e fonetici della scrittura antico-persiana. *AION* 43: 429–77.
D'jakonov, I. M. 1956. *История Мидии от древнейших времен до конца IV века до Н.Э.* Moscow: Akademia Nauk SSSR.
——. 1970. The origin of the "Old Persian" writing system and the ancient Oriental epigraphic and annalistic traditions. In *W. B. Henning memorial volume*, ed. M. Boyce and I. Gershevitch, 98–124. London: Lund Humphries.
Duchesne-Guillemin, J. 1972. La religion des Achéménides. In *Beiträge zur Achämenidengeschichte*, ed. G. Walser, 59–82. Wiesbaden: Historia-Einzelschriften 18.

Eilers, W. 1956. Der Name Demawend. *Archiv Orientalní* 24: 183–224.
Foy, W. 1898. Beiträge zur Erklärung der susischen Achaemenideninschriften. *ZDMG* 52: 564–605.
Gershevitch, I. 1979. The alloglottography of Old Persian. *Transactions of the Philological Society*: 114–90.
Ghirshman, R. 1965. A propos de l'écriture cunéiforme vieux-perse. *JNES* 24: 244–50.
Hakluyt, R. 1599. *The second volume of the Principal Navigations, Voyages, Traffiques, and Discoveries of the English Nation*. London: G. Bishop, R. Newberie, and R. Baker.
Halévy, M. J. 1885. Note sur l'origine de l'écriture perse. *JA* 8/6: 480–501.
Hallock, R. T. 1970. On the Old Persian signs. *JNES* 29: 52–5.
Harmatta, J. 1971. The literary patterns of the Babylonian edict of Cyrus. *AAASH* 19: 217–31.
Herbert, T. 1677. *Some years travel into divers parts of Africa, and Asia the great: Describing more particularly the empires of Persia and Industan*... London: R. Everingham.
Herzfeld, E. 1908. Pasargadae: Untersuchungen zur persischen Archäologie. *Klio* 8: 1–65.
——. 1910. Das Alter der altpersischen Keilschrift. *ZDMG* 64: 63–4.
Hincha, G. 1974. Zur Ursprung der altpersischen Keilschrift. in *Neue Methodologie in der Iranistik*, ed. R. N. Frye, 70–84. Wiesbaden: Harrassowitz.
Hinz, W. 1938. Das erste Jahr des Großkönig Dareios. *ZDMG* 92: 136–73.
——. 1942. Zur Behistun-Inschrift des Dareios. *ZDMG* 96: 326–49.
——. 1952. Die Einführung der altpersischen Schrift. *ZDMG* 102: 28–38.
——. 1973. *Neue Wege im Altpersischen*. Wiesbaden: Göttinger Orientforschungen III/1.
Hoffmann, K. 1976. Zur altpersischen Schrift. In *Aufsätze zur Indoiranistik*, vol. 2, 620–45. Wiesbaden: Reichert.
Hommel, F. 1904. *Grundriss der Geographie und Geschichte des Alten Orients, II*. Munich: Beck.
Horn, P. 1898–1901. Neupersische Schriftsprache. In *Grundriss der iranischen Philologie* I 2, ed. W. Geiger and E. Kuhn, 1–200. Strassburg: Trübner.
Hüsing, G. 1900. Die iranische Keilschrift. *OLZ* 3: 401–3.
——. 1908. Zur Schriftsprache Altirans. *OLZ* 11: 363–8.
Huyse, P. 1999. Some further thoughts on the Bisitun monument and the genesis of the Old Persian cuneiform script. *BAI* 13: 45–66.
Jackson, A. V. W. 1906. *Persia, past and present: A book of travel and research*. New York: Macmillan.
Jensen, H. 1969. *Die Schrift in Vergangenheit und Gegenwart*, 3rd ed. Berlin: VEB Deutscher Verlag der Wissenschaften.
Jensen, P. 1901. Alt- und neuelamitisches. *ZDMG* 55: 223–40.
Justeson, J. S., and Stephens, L.D. 1991–3. Evolution of syllabaries from alphabets: Transmission, language contrast, and script typology. *Die Sprache* 35: 2–46.
Kaufman, S. A. 1974. *The Akkadian influences on Aramaic*. Chicago: AS 19.
Kent, R. G. 1946. The oldest Old Persian inscriptions. *JAOS* 66: 206–12.
——. 1953. *Old Persian: Grammar, texts, lexicon*, 2nd ed. New Haven: AOS 33.
Kuryłowicz, J. 1964. Zur altpersischen Keilschrift. Zeitschrift für Phonetik. *Sprachwissenschaft und Kommunikationsforschung* 17: 563–9.
——. 1973. Zur altpersischen Keilschrift. In *Esquisses Linguistiques*, vol. 2, J. Kuryłowicz, 274–80. Munich: W. Fink.
Kutscher, E. Y. 1961. The language of the Aramaic letters of Bar-Koseva and his contemporaries. *Lešonenu* 25: 117–33.

———. 1969. Two "passive" constructions in Aramaic in the light of Persian. In *Proceedings of the International Conference on Semitic Studies held in Jerusalem, 19–23 July 1965*, 132–51. Jerusalem: Israel Academy of Sciences and Humanities.

Lecoq, P. 1974a. La langue des inscriptions achéménides. In *Commémoration Cyrus: Actes du Congrès de Shiraz 1971 et d'autres études rédigées à l'occasion du 2500ᵉ anniversaire de la foundation de l'Empire perse*, vol. 2, 55–62. Tehran: Acta Iranica 2.

———. 1974b. Le problème de l'écriture cunéiforme vieux-perse. In *Commémoration Cyrus: Actes du Congrès de Shiraz 1971 et d'autres études rédigées à l'occasion du 2500ᵉ anniversaire de la foundation de l'Empire perse*, vol. 3, 25–107. Tehran: Acta Iranica 3.

———. 1983. Observations sur l'écriture vieux-perse. In *Orientalia Romana. Essays and lectures 5: Iranian Studies*, ed G. Gnoli, 31–9. Rome: SOR 52.

Lewy, J. 1954. The problems inherent in section 70 of the Bisutun Inscription. *Hebrew Union College Annual* 25: 169–208.

Makujina, J. 1997. On the Possible Old Persian Origin of the Aramaic מעט טים, "to issue a decree." *Hebrew Union College Annual* 68: 1–9.

Mallowan, M. 1972. Cyrus the Great (558–529 B.C.). *Iran* 10: 1–17.

Mayrhofer, M. 1979. Überlegungen zur Entstehung der altpersischen Keilschrift. *BSOAS* 42: 290–6.

———. 1989. Über die Verschriftung des Altpersischen. *Historische Sprachforschung* 102: 174–86.

Miroschedji, P. de. 1985. La fin du royaume d'Anšan et de Suse et la naissance de l'Empire perse. *ZA* 75: 265–306.

Mittelberger, H. 1965. Zum Altpersischen. *Die Sprache* 11: 93–121.

Nylander, C. 1968. ΑΣΣΥΡΙΑ ΓΡΑΜΜΑΤΑ: Remarks on the 21st "Letter of Themistocles." *Opuscula Atheniensia* 8: 119–36.

Oppert, J. 1874. La formation de l'alphabet perse. *JA* 7/3: 238–45.

Oranskij, I. M. 1963. Иранские языки (Iazyki Zarubeznogo Vostoka i Afriki). Moscow: Izdatel'stvo Vostočnoj Literatury.

———. 1988. *Введение в иранскую филологию*. Moscow: Nauka.

Paper, H. H. 1956. The Old Persian /L/ phoneme. *JAOS* 76: 24–6.

Rawlinson, H. C. 1846–7. The Persian Cuneiform Inscription at Behistun, deciphered and translated; with a memoir on Persian cuneiform inscriptions in general, and on that of Behistun in particular. *JRAS* 10: 1–349.

Rogers, R. W. 1900. *A history of Babylonia and Assyria*. New York: Eaton and Mains.

Salvini, M. 2008. *Corpus dei Testi Urartei*, vol. 1. Rome: Documenta Asiana 8/1.

Sancisi-Weerdenburg, H. 1988. Was there really a Median empire? In *Method and Theory*, ed. A. Kuhrt and H. Sancisi-Weerdenburg, 197–228. Leiden: AchHist 3.

Sayce, A. H. 1884. The origin of the Persian cuneiform alphabet. *Zeitschrift für Keilschriftforschung* 1: 19–27.

Schaeder, H. H. 1930. *Iranische Beiträge I*. Halle: Schriften der Königsberger Gelehrten Gesellschaft, geisteswissenschaftliche Klasse 6/5.

Schmitt, R. 1980. Altpersisch-Forschung in den Siebziger-Jahren: *Kratylos* 25: 1–66.

———. 1981. *Altpersische Siegel-Inschriften*. Vienna: Sitzungsberichte der Österreichischen Akad. der Wiss., phil.-hist. Kl. 381.

———. 1988. Achaimenideninschriften in griechischer literarischer Überlieferung. In *A green leaf: Papers in honour of Prof. Jes P. Asmussen*, ed. J. Duchesne-Guillemin, W. Sundermann, and F. Vahman, 17–38. Leiden: Acta Iranica 28.

———. 1989. Altpersisch. In *Compendium Linguarum Iranicarum*, ed. R. Schmitt, 56–85. Wiesbaden: L. Reichert.

———. 1991. *The Bisitun inscriptions of Darius the Great: Old Persian text*. London: CII 1/1/1.

———. 1992. Assyria Grammata und ähnliche: Was wußten die Griechen von Keilschrift und Keilinschriften? In *Zum Umgang mit fremden Sprachen in der griechisch-römischen Antike*, ed. C. W. Müller, K. Sier, and J. Werner, 21–35. Stuttgart: Palingenesia 36.

———. 1999. *Beiträge zu altpersischen Inschriften*. Wiesbaden: L. Reichert.

———. 2000. *The Old Persian inscriptions of Naqsh-i Rustam and Persepolis*. London: CII 1/1/2.

———. 2004. Old Persian. In *The Cambridge Encyclopedia of the world's ancient languages*, ed. R. D. Woodard, 717–41. Cambridge: Cambridge University Press.

———. 2007. *Pseudo-altpersische Inschriften*. Vienna: Sitzungsberichte der Österreichischen Akad. der Wiss., phil.-hist. Kl. 762.

———. 2009. *Die altpersischen Inschriften der Achaimeniden: Editio minor mit deutscher Übersetzung*. Wiesbaden: L. Reichert Verlag.

Skalmowski, W. 1995. Old Persian Parθava. In *Immigration and emigration within the Ancient Near East: Festschrift E. Lipiński*, ed. K. Van Lerberghe and A. Schoors, 305–12. Leuven: OLA 65.

Steve, M.-J. 1987. *Nouveaux mélanges épigraphiques: Inscriptions royales de Suse et de la Susiane*. Nice: MDP 53.

Stolper, M. W. 1985. *Entrepreneurs and empire: The Murašû archive, the Murašû firm, and Persian rule in Babylonia*. Istanbul: UNHAII 54.

Stolper, M. W., and J. Tavernier. 2007. From the Persepolis Fortification Archive Project, 1: An Old Persian administrative tablet from the Persepolis Fortification. *ARTA* 2007.001.

Stronach, D. 1978. *Pasargadae: A report on the excavations conducted by the British Institute of Persian Studies from 1961 to 1963*. Oxford: Clarendon Press.

Struve, V. V. 1951. Реформа письменнности при Дарии I. *VDI* 3: 186–91.

———. 1968. Этюды по истории Северного Причерноморья, Кавказа и Средней Азии. Leningrad: Nauka.

Tavernier, J. 2007. *Iranica in the Achaemenid period (ca. 550–330 B.C.): Lexicon of Old Iranian proper names and loanwords, attested in non-Iranian texts*. Leuven: OLA 158.

———. 2008. Multilingualism in the Fortification and Treasury archives. *AFP*: 59–86.

———. Forthcoming a. "Numerous people who differed in speech": Multilingualism in the Elamite kingdoms and the Achaemenid Empire. In *Crossing boundaries: Multilingualism, Lingua Franca and Lingua Sacra*, ed. M. J. Geller. Berlin: Sources of the Max Planck Research Library for the History and Development of Knowledge.

———. Forthcoming b. Persian in official documents and the processes of multilingual administration. In *The Aršama Archive: Conclusions and prospects*, ed J. Ma and C. Tuplin. Oxford.

Testen, D. 1996. Old Persian cuneiform. In *The world's writing systems*, ed. P. T. Daniels and W. Bright, 134–7. Oxford: Oxford University Press.

Weissbach, F. H. 1894. Das Grab des Cyrus und die Inschriften von Murghāb. *ZDMG* 48: 653–65.

———. 1896–1904. Die altpersischen Inschriften. In *Grundriss der iranischen Philologie, Bd. 2. Litteratur, Geschichte und Kultur*, ed. W. Geiger and E. Kuhn, 54–74. Strassburg: Trübner.

———. 1911. *Die Keilschriften der Achämeniden*. Leipzig: Vorderasiatische Bibliothek 3.

———. 1936. Über die ältesten arischen Inschriften. *ZDMG* 90: *41*–*42*.

Werba, C. 1983. review of M. Mayrhofer, *Sanskrit-Grammatik mit sprachvergleichenden Erläuterungen*. *Wiener Zeitschrift für die Kunde Südasiens* 27: 203–7.

Whitehead, J. D. 1978. Some distinctive features of the language of the Aramaic Arsames correspondence. *JNES* 37: 119–40.

Windfuhr, G. 1969. Das System der altpersischen Schrift. In *XVII. deutscher Orientalistentag vom 21. bis 27. Juli 1968 in Würzburg: Vorträge*, ed. W. Voigt, 991–2. Wiesbaden: ZDMG Supplement 1.

———. 1970. Notes on the Old Persian Signs. *Indo-Iranian Journal* 12: 121–5.

Yule, H. 1866. *Cathay and the Way Thither, being a collection of medieval notices of China*. London: Hakluyt Society.

CHAPTER 33

GREEK SOURCES ON ACHAEMENID IRAN

MARIA BROSIUS

Achaemenid Iran began to feature in Greek poetic and tragic texts as a consequence of the Persian Wars of 490 BC and 480/79 BC. These—in the Greek view—monumental events also inspired the first Greek historical work, Herodotus' *Histories*. Among the literary documents that contain references to the Greek victories over the Persians feature the elegies of Simonides (*c*.557/6–468/7 BC) and the poetry of Pindar (*c*.522–446 BC). The tragedy *The fall of Miletus,* written by Phrynichus, whose subject was the sack of Miletus at the hands of the Persians in 494 BC, was banned after its first performance and its author fined 1000 drachmas (Herodotus, *Hist*. 6.21.2), as the Athenian audience was moved to tears by the tragic staging of the suffering of the Ionian Greeks. Phrynichus was more successful with his play *Phoinissai* (*The Phoenician women*), performed in 476 BC, which dealt with Xerxes' defeat at Salamis. Aeschylus' (525/4–456 BC) tragedy *Persai* (*The Persians*), performed in 472 BC, had the same subject matter. Though these literary documents contain ample references to the Persian king and his court, their historical value is difficult to extrapolate, as they need to be read and understood within their literary context as well as the occasion for which they were written. As Persia remained an important political entity in Greek politics, either as a diplomatic ally or as a political opponent, Persian history continued to be recorded to a limited extent by Herodotus' successors. The *Histories* was followed by the works of other Greek historians or compilers of world history who recorded Persian events in so far as they impinged on Greek history. In addition, there were Greek writers of specific *Persica*, or even writers who chose a Persian king as the subject of a biography in the widest sense, as in the case of Xenophon's *Cyropaedia* or Plutarch's *Life of Artaxerxes (II).*

Greek historical sources on Achaemenid Persia allow us to write a general outline of the history of events that considers political affairs as well as matters of the royal court, government, administration, culture, and religion. However, no single Greek source provides a full and comprehensive insight into the history of the empire. Other literary sources, especially those of the fourth century BC, such as philosophical texts, orations, tragedies, and comedies, likewise emphasize specific aspects of Persian monarchy with an aim to focus on, if not exaggerate, a particular Greek view on Persia. In these sources especially the image projected of Persia is determined by the contrast between two different forms of government, Persian monarchy on the one hand and Greek democracy, specifically that of the Athenian city-state, on the other.

Generally, the interest of Greek writers in Persia is limited to aspects of the political and military contact the empire had with the Greeks. As a result, an imbalance exists between the relatively full information we have on diplomatic contacts and military conflicts between the Greek city-states and Persia, including Persian interaction with Western Asia Minor, and the barely discernible data these sources provide on events relating to the eastern parts of the Persian Empire, and indeed on the center of Persian power itself. It is the military conflicts between Greece and Persia in particular, beginning with the Ionian Revolt (499–492 BC), the campaign of Datis and Artaphernes which resulted in the Battle of Marathon (490 BC), the Median or Persian War (480–479 BC), as well as Alexander's conquest of the Persian Empire (334/3–331/30 BC), that inform Greek writing on Persia.

As the Persian Wars were recorded by the Greeks, and the earliest surviving historical account was written about fifty years after the event, Greek writers on Persia were free to project a specific image of the empire, viewed through the lens of the victor. In addition, as already in antiquity, the Persian Wars became events of world historical importance, their account laid the foundations of a West–East divide that can be detected in many of the Greek historical and literary sources (Papenfuß and Strocka 2001; Wiesehöfer 1992). This view affected not only the way Greek historians described the Persian wars themselves, but also subsequent historiography of the fourth century and later periods. Persia was the first world empire in the ancient Mediterranean and Near Eastern world. Its extent was noted by Greek writers, beginning with Herodotus, and at least in part experienced by Greek diplomats traveling to the royal court and Greeks living in the Persian Empire. Its sheer geographic dimensions and its unlimited political and military might must have been unimaginable to most mainland Greeks. The unexpected Persian defeat at the hands of the Athenians at Marathon, and the Greek victories at Salamis and Plataea, therefore, had a major impact on Greece. Politically and militarily these victories catapulted Athens to the top of the Greek *poleis*. Her preeminent position saw her as leader of the Delian League and the most powerful opponent of Sparta and her Peloponnesian allies until Athens' political collapse at the end of the Peloponnesian War. Ideologically, too, the impact of the Greek victories over Persia from Marathon to Plataea and Mycale caused a seismic shift within Greece, giving rise to the recognition of a Greek identity, of the collective identification of the Greeks as *Hellenes*, as opposed to the *Barbaroi*, the barbarians, a term almost exclusively used to describe the Persians after 479 BC (Harrison 2002; Hutzfeld 1999; Hall 1991). Furthermore, the religious dimension given to these victories allowed the events to transcend history, becoming myth in Greek imagination (Cherf 2001; Hölteskamp 2001). Any Greek literary document commenting on Achaemenid Persia after 479 BC has to be viewed in this light.

Both categories, the Greek historical sources and the other literary documents, are subsequently defined by the predominantly negative attitude toward Persia. The "themes" of a Greek defense of freedom versus the despotism of the Persian monarch, the defense of democracy versus a single ruler, of the West versus the East, of Europe versus Asia, became political slogans used in oratory, pamphlets, tragedy, philosophical disputes, and historical writing. To emphasize the negative attributes ascribed to Persia, certain aspects of Persian politics, culture, and court life were highlighted. Episodes describing the luxury of court life, the influence of royal women on political affairs, and the willfulness of the king served to demonstrate the weakness of the Persian monarch per se, the corruption and intrigue at his court, and the decadence of the empire as a whole. Its seeming decline either from the reign of Xerxes onward, as Herodotus implied, or, in the case of Xenophon, following the reign of the founder of the empire, Cyrus II, gave the history of Achaemenid Persia little chance of a fair voice in the Greek sources.

The generally negative Greek attitude toward Persia continued in accounts of the second key military conflict impinging on Greek–Persian relations, the conquest of the empire by Alexander III of Macedon. While first Philip II, and then Alexander III, justified their planned campaign against Persia with the slogan of Greek revenge for Xerxes' destruction of Athens and Athenian temples in 479 BC, finding support in Greek pamphletic and philosophical fourth-century writing that emphasized the decadence of the Persian Empire, its condemnation also had to be kept in limits, as a victory over a weak king (Darius III) and a weak empire would have diminished the greatness of Alexander's achievement. This ambiguous attitude is discernible in the historical texts of the so-called Alexander historians who, writing considerably *post eventum*, were guided in their writing by the then already legendary status held by the deceased Alexander and, once again, by the perspective of the victor that allowed them to control the image they wished to portray of the Persian Empire.

The main source for the early history of the Persian Empire is Herodotus. He was born around 484 BC at Halicarnassus in Caria, and his family were subjects of the Persian king. His travels took him to Egypt, parts of the Near East, and possibly to Scythia, but he never visited Persia proper or the eastern satrapies. Herodotus compiled his *Histories* about 430 BC, while residing in Athens. With the "Enquiries" he wanted to describe the conflict between the Greeks and Persians, namely the Persian War of 480/79 BC. The stark contrast between these two civilizations, however, is set immediately in Book 1.1 by failing to identify the Persians and instead refer to them as "Barbarians." Herodotus also constructed a lengthy build-up to the war, and the actual conflict is described only in the last three of the nine books of the *Histories*. There are several reasons why Herodotus did this. He wanted to provide a historical context for the Persian Empire, and in order to convey his view of the inevitable rise and fall of empires he recalled the history of the Lydian kingdom and that of the Median Empire before turning his attention to Persia. A remarkable symmetry characterizes the description of all three kingdoms or empires, as their rise and fall occurs within the reigns of five kings, and is determined, as in the case of Media and Persia especially, by humble beginnings of the empire's founder, to increasing luxury, which signals the inevitable decline of the royal line in its fifth generation. It is thought that it is for this reason that Herodotus ended his account with Xerxes I, although he had knowledge of Xerxes' successor Artaxerxes I (465–424 BC). But ending his *Histories* with a story of intrigue at the king's court after Xerxes' return from Greece allowed Herodotus to construct a historiographical framework within which he placed his *Histories*. The so-called *Ringkomposition* (ring composition) begins with the story of the wife of the Lydian king Candaules who, betrayed by her husband, orders his murder and elevates the courtier Gyges to the throne as the founder of the last Lydian dynasty, while the story of Xerxes' betrayal of his wife Amestris, and her subsequent revenge leading to a revolt within the empire, brings Herodotus' stories of the rise and fall of empires full circle (Beck 1971).

A further aspect that determines Herodotus' view on Persia is the ethnographic discourses interspersing his histories of the empires. He includes extensive discussions on a number of ethnic groups, devoting entire books specifically to Egypt (Book 2) and Scythia (Book 4). These inclusions serve to introduce and explain "the Other" to his audience, peoples who are set apart from the Greeks through their different customs, religion, social and sexual behavior. Far from being merely diversions away from his main narrative, they too are part of Herodotus' build-up to his narrative of the Persian War. The ethnic descriptions of different peoples provide a context for the Persians themselves, and at the same time emphasize the Persians' place within the world of the Other (Bichler 2001). They are also a harbinger of events to come. As François Hartog has argued, the excursus on the Scythians mirrors the impending conflict between Athens and Xerxes, already telling the audience of a futile war and the Persian defeat (Hartog 2010). To that end, historical reality becomes distorted, since at least some parts of Scythia were conquered, as Persian inscriptions and reliefs attest. Furthermore, Herodotus' account of a single-front attack along the west coast of the Black Sea has recently been challenged by B. Jacobs who, on the basis of archaeological evidence, argues that Darius' Scythian campaign was a two-pronged attack from both the west and east coasts of the Black Sea (Jacobs 2006). Taking these issues into account, any modern engagement with Herodotus' *Histories* has to consider not only the historical account of Persia itself, but also aspects of historiographical constructs and the use of literary motifs.

Herodotus' relatively limited knowledge of Persian culture and customs is probably due to the fact that he did not travel to Persia proper and thus was dependent on oral information from the empire's periphery or even from external sources. He does, however, relate information about Persia's earliest history, offering an extensive account of the story of the birth and upbringing of the founder of the empire, Cyrus II (*Hist.* 2.1). While the story of Cyrus' familial link with the Median king Astyages through his daughter Mandane belongs to the category of the "official" version of conquest by legitimizing royal rule over a conquered people through a marriage alliance, the story of the exposure of the infant Cyrus, his upbringing by a couple of humble background, and his subsequent ascent to the throne follow an equally "official" royal tradition that traces its origins back to the story of Sargon of Akkad (2334–2279 BC) (Drews 1974).

However Herodotus learned of this version, it must have passed through Near Eastern channels. The story was accepted, with variants, by several other Greek writers, including Xenophon, as well as by the Latin authors Nicolaus of Damascus (c.64 BC–after 4 BC) and Justin (second century AD). Only Ctesias, eager to distance himself from Herodotus, disputes this version. As for Cyrus' campaigns, Herodotus is able to provide relatively comprehensive accounts of the conquests of Media, Lydia, and Babylonia, even though details may be queried (Rollinger 1993; papers in *CE*), but he has barely any knowledge of the conquests of the eastern parts of the empire.

His travels to Egypt account for his detailed knowledge of Egyptian customs, but they are especially important with regard to his view of Cambyses II, who conquered Egypt in 525 BC (*Hist.* 2.1). The exclusively negative characterization of Cambyses II in the *Histories* seems to stem entirely from oral Egyptian sources. Herodotus' portrayal of Cambyses II as a willful king who committed sacrileges and acts of *hybris*, also fits with his desire to alternate between "good" king and "bad" king in his description of the Persian kings Cyrus II—Cambyses II—[Bardiya]—Darius I—Xerxes I. Recent scholarship has reacted to this literary construct by arguing for a more critical view of Herodotus' depiction of Cambyses II, not only by deconstructing Herodotus' view, but also by considering Egyptian epigraphical evidence (Young 1988: 47–52). Similarly, his equally negative portrayal of Xerxes II as a weak king committing acts of sacrilege and *hybris* is regarded with skepticism (Kuhrt and Sherwin-White 1987).

Literary constructs apart, Herodotus appears in other respects to have had first-hand information about Persia, which he could have acquired only from (translated) Persian sources. This information relates to the events surrounding the accession of Darius I and to the satrapies of the empire. In regard to the revolt of Bardiya/Gaumata or, as he is named in Herodotus, Smerdis, and the conspiracy of the seven Persian nobles, including Darius I, Herodotus recalls the events in a similar vein to the manner in which they are described in Darius' inscription at Bisotun (DB I 11–15). Like the inscription, Herodotus refers to a false brother of Cambyses II, a *magus*, who took the throne of Persia after the "real" Bardiya had been killed and who reigned for several months before being uncovered by the Persian nobles and killed. Although there are differences in the details of the accounts of Bisotun and Herodotus, the main storyline matches that presented in Darius' inscription (Balcer 1987). Herodotus also has precise knowledge of the names of six of the seven Persian nobles. The one exception, Aspathines, may possibly be explained as being that of the successor of the original member, Ardumanish (DB IV 68). Overall, Herodotus could have known this information only if he had had access to a translated version of the Bisotun inscription, or to someone who had intimate knowledge of it almost 100 years after it had been carved on the rock face of Mount Bisotun and copies had been distributed in different languages across the empire.

Slightly more problematic is Herodotus' list of the tribute-paying satrapies (*Hist.* 3.89–96), one of the most intensely debated issues in Greek–Persian studies (Ruffing 2009; Wiesehöfer 1997; Jacobs 1994). The reason for this debate is the fact that both the number of satrapies given by Herodotus (twenty) and their composition cannot be matched with the list of lands (OP *dahyāva*) given in several Persian royal inscriptions, where their number varies from twenty-three to twenty-nine, and neither the order nor the ethnic and tribal groups identified for each land or satrapy corresponds with the list given in Herodotus. While the order given in Herodotus may be due to a local version of a satrapy list, beginning with Ionia, rather than the heartlands of the empire (Media, Elam, Babylonia), the very list itself may reflect fiscal units rather than the political and administrative division of the Persian satrapies.

Following Herodotus' account of the early history of Achaemenid Iran, up to the time of the Persian Wars, we rely on a variety of sources from which a general outline of events can be constructed, but which often lack a detailed record of a specific event. Their accuracy is hampered further by problems of chronology, affecting, for example, Kimon's campaigns to Cyprus, the battle at the Eurymedon, and crucially, the peace agreement between Athens and Persia, known as the Peace of Kallias, of 449 BC. Information about internal Persian politics was even more limited and tends to be inaccurate, as political issues were replaced with stories of court intrigue. Thus, the so-called Satraps' Revolt, identified by Diodorus as a single event dating to 362/1 BC (Diod. Sic. 15.90–1), in fact comprised four separate rebellions that took place over several years (Weisskopf 1989), and information about the kings, such as the death of Artaxerxes III, was sensationalized, with Greek sources describing his death as murder at the hands of a courtier (Diod. Sic. 17.5.1), whereas Near Eastern sources (BM 71537) record a natural death (Walker 1997: 22). Finally, the depiction of Darius III in the histories of the Alexander-historians is too dependent on the intention to depict the last Achaemenid king and the empire as weak and lacking in leadership and military skills to be regarded as historical (Briant 2003).

Herodotus' immediate successor, Thucydides (*c*.455 BC–404 BC), gave an account of the Persian War only in a summary fashion in his *Pentekontaetia* in order to convey the political situation that arose in Greece after the war, which saw Athens develop into an empire and brought her into a war against Sparta. Throughout his history of the Peloponnesian War, Thucydides' interest in Persia was limited to the extent to which Persian history infringed on Greek affairs. Most importantly, his account mentions Egypt's rebellion against Persia in 464–454 BC—as Athens supported the rebel Inaros and suffered her first major naval loss there with 250 ships—as well as the return of Persia onto the Greek political stage with the Spartan–Persian alliance of 411 BC, having detailed knowledge of three different versions of the terms of the alliance before its final agreement concluded in the spring of 411 BC. Crucially, he made no mention of the Peace of Kallias concluded between Athens and Persia in 449 BC. Reported only by Diodorus (Diod. Sic.12.4.4–6), who provided us with a seemingly accurate wording of the decree, its historicity has been the subject of an ongoing dispute in scholarship, even though scholars have to concede that Athenian–Persian aggression ceased after that date and an agreement of some kind is not implausible.

Xenophon (*c*.431–354 BC), whose *Hellenica* continues Thucydides' account, recording Greek history from 411 to 362 BC, referred to Persia only to a limited extent. Together with Diodorus Siculus' world history, the *Bibliotheca*, compiled in the first century BC and which, although flawed, includes references to Persian history down to Alexander's conquest of the empire based on fourth-century historians, these are the two main Greek sources from which fourth-century events relating to Persian history can be reconstructed. Apart from being used by Diodorus, the fragmentarily preserved works of the fourth-century writers Ephorus (FGrH 70), Deinon (FGrH 690), and Heracleides (FGrH 689; Lenfant 2009) are also reflected in the works of Plutarch and Arrian. The fragments of the *Hellenica Oxyrhynchia* are concerned mainly with Greek history, but include brief references to Persia in the accounts of the late fifth (409–407 BC) and early fourth century (396–394 BC). Scattered references to Achaemenid Iran can also be found in the *Geographia* of Strabo (64/3 BC–after AD 21).

In addition to the *Hellenica*, Xenophon was the author of two further works relating to Persian affairs. One is his *Anabasis*, a work which records the march of the Ten Thousand, the Greek mercenaries who found themselves in enemy territory having supported Cyrus the Younger in his rebellion against Artaxerxes II and, under the leadership of Xenophon, returned to Greece in a long march through the Persian Empire. The work does not effectively discuss Persian politics or historical events and contains only snippets of information. A work particularly difficult to assess as an historical text is Xenophon's *Cyropaedia*. Part biography, part romantic novel, the work, written in eight books, focuses on the birth and childhood of Cyrus the Great and his ascent to the Persian throne. Xenophon followed Herodotus' version of the exposure of the child by Cyrus' grandfather, the Median king Astyages; his humble upbringing by a poor herdsman and his wife; and the nobility of his character revealed despite the impoverished conditions in which he grew up, to find redemption with Astyages and succeed to the kingship. Versions of the humble upbringing of Cyrus II appear in the fragments of Nicolaus of Damascus (FGrH 90 F66.2–5) as well as in Justin's work (Justin 1.4.7–10), reflecting the great impact this depiction must have had in antiquity. Regardless of where Herodotus heard the story, its historicity is questionable, and the fact that its origin can be traced back to a Near Eastern source dated to the end of the third millennium BC, that is, the legend of Sargon of Akkad, places it in the realm of literary motifs used to highlight the goodness and nobility of a king. The *Cyropaedia* reveals barely any information on Cyrus' conquest or the organization of the empire. Instead, it retains a "romantic" tone throughout, placing the work between a biography and a novel. Though much of what Xenophon says about the Persian court appears to have some basis in historical reality, it is more likely that he projected contemporary knowledge about the Persian court back onto Cyrus II's reign (Tuplin 2010). Almost as an afterthought, the final book (Book 8) is a diatribe on the failure of the Persian Empire, in which the author attacks the successors of Cyrus II as weak and decadent kings and portrays the empire as being in permanent decline from the reign of Cyrus II onward. It has been suggested that Xenophon may not have been the author of this section, but that it was added on at a later date. In any case, it has been an effective tool to support the view of a weak and decadent empire.

The *Persica* of Ctesias of Knidos (FGrH 688; Lenfant 2004), a physician who claims to have practiced at the court of Artaxerxes II and to have been present at the battlefield of Cunaxa in 401 BC, was preserved in a compilation by the ninth-century Byzantine patriarch Photius of Constantinople. Ctesias' account of Persian history is rather summary and tends to favor court stories, especially those involving intrigues staged by royal women and eunuchs. Though claiming to have had information from royal records, his reliability and trustworthiness have been called into question, not only due to skepticism surrounding his ability to read non-Greek languages, but also due to doubts as to whether he actually ever stayed at the Persian court (Wiesehöfer et al. 2011).

In the fourth century BC Persia received mention in Athenian pamphletic writing and orations regarding contemporary politics. Isocrates' (436–338 BC) *Panegyricus*, dated to about 380 BC, and his *Address to Philip* of 346 BC, and, among the speeches of Demosthenes (384–322 BC), the *Philippics*, should be mentioned. While Isocrates was a fervent defender of Athens and indeed of Hellas in fending off any link with Persia at all costs, to the point of opposing the King's Peace, or the Peace of Antalcidas of 386 BC (Xen. *Hell.* 5.1.30–31), and blindly supporting the Macedonian king Philip II, Demosthenes took a more differentiated view, which recognized Philip's intentions in Greece and advocated an Athenian alliance with Persia as a protection against the Macedonian king. Both orators drew on past and contemporary history to remind the Athenians of the advantages or drawbacks of an alliance with Persia. In so far as Persia was mentioned in these orations at all, both authors pursued specific aims in the way they "used" Persia in their speeches.

The references to Persia in the philosophical works of Plato, especially the *Nomoi* (*Laws*), tend to serve Plato's argument about the ideal state. Persia served as an example of the decline of a monarchy after its initial success, due to a lack of discipline, the increasing influence of women, and the acceptance of a luxurious lifestyle. These images buy into a stereotypical view of Persia, prevalent in the fourth century, that wanted to see the empire as a weak opponent, an empire in decline and a monarchy that could not compete with the advantages of a democratic government, or, in the case of Plato, that could serve as a negative example of the failure of a monarchy not headed by a philosopher-king. Similarly, references in Aristotle, especially in the Ps.-Aristotelian *De Mundo*, only emphasize the negative view of Persia. As with the speeches, it is difficult to use these texts as historical sources, since they were not written as historical accounts of Persia, but as philosophical texts that used specific aspects and views of Persia to support a particular argument.

One of the latest Greek texts on Persia, the *Life of Artaxerxes* by Plutarch (c.AD 45– after 120), relied heavily on the fourth-century historians (Binder 2008). The work is much less a biography of Artaxerxes II's long reign (405–359 BC) than an anecdotal narrative that focuses on a Persian court beset with intrigues. The influence of women and eunuchs, the quarrel between the king and the heir to the throne, Darius, over a concubine, and the king's incestuous marriage to his own daughters, take preference over the political events of his reign, such as the revolt in Egypt or the rebellions in the satrapies of Western Asia Minor.

In his *Anabasis*, Arrian (second century AD) recorded the achievements of Alexander the Great, focusing on the military campaigns rather than on an historical account of the situation in Greece, Macedon, and Persia in the fourth century BC following the reign of Philip II. Yet details are recorded about the last Persian king, Darius III, as well as his family and court, which accompanied Darius on his campaign. We also can derive information from the *Anabasis* about the Persian nobles and the hierarchy of the court, as well as court procedure and court practice.

The few extant Greek inscriptions that contain references to the Persian Wars, to Persian interaction with Greek city-states, or to decrees recovered from Greek sources, are noteworthy exceptions in the neutral tone used when describing Greek–Persian relations. With the exception of Darius' letter to his Magnesian satrap Gadatas, whose historicity has been hotly disputed by scholars (Meiggs and Lewis 1989: no. 12; Tuplin 2009), the Greek epigraphic texts represent a body of ancient primary sources on Persia which demand recognition equal to that accorded the primary documentary evidence from the Persian Empire itself. Greek epigraphic records range from a few Athenian inscriptions commemorating their dead of the Persian Wars and an inscription from Delphi recording the Greeks who fought against the Persians in 479 BC (Meiggs and Lewis 1989: no. 27), to fourth-century inscriptions from Ionia referring to Persian involvement in Greek politics. The latter include references to Persia, affording a glimpse into the relationship between the cities of Asia Minor and the Persian authorities, as, for example, in the case of Persian intervention in a dispute between Miletus and Myus between 391 and 388 BC (Rhodes and Osborne 2003: no. 16); Athens' attitude toward Persia in regard to Clazomenae in 387/6 BC (Rhodes and Osborne 2003: no. 18); and a reaction to the Satraps' Revolt (Rhodes and Osborne 2003: no. 42). The Greek epigraphic evidence is perhaps most illuminating for the assessment of local rule within the Persian Empire, as in the case of inscriptions relating to the Carian king and satrap Mausolus from c.367/6–355/4 BC (Rhodes and Osborne 2003: nos. 54–6); the bilingual inscription of the Lycian dynast Arbinas from c.390–380 BC (Rhodes and Osborne 2003: no. 13); and the trilingual inscription of Pixodaros from Xanthus (337 BC) (Rhodes and Osborne 2003: no. 78).

Several decrees from Mylasa referring to Mausolus of Caria (377/6–353/2 BC attest to Mylasa's recognition of the political superiority of the Carian dynast (Rhodes and Osborne 2003: no. 54). Although written in Greek, they are dated to the reigning year of the Persian kings Artaxerxes II and Artaxerxes III, respectively, while using the Persian title "satrap" in referring to Mausolus himself. A later source, Polyainos' *Strategika* (*Stratagems*), dated to the second century AD, indicates that Mausolus was both a king and a satrap (*Strat.* 7.23.1).

The inscription of Arbinas (Erbbina), son of Gergis (Kheriga), was carved on the statue base of the Leto sanctuary at Xanthos and dates to c.390–370 BC. The text tells of Arbinas' efforts to gain control of the Lycians, including the cities of "Xanthos, Pinara, and Tel[messus]." While the statue was erected after seeking advice from the oracle at Delphi, the inscription also seems to indicate an adherence to Persian values in its reference to the ruler's outstanding achievements "in bowmanship, in courage, in horsemanship," which could be regarded as a direct reference to DNb §9.

The trilingual inscription of Xanthos, written in Greek, Aramaic, and Lycian, refers to Pixodaros, son of Hekatomnos, a member of the Hekatomnid dynasty, who ruled as Persian satrap, probably between 341/40 and 336/5BC. In the inscription Pixodarus appointed Hieron and Apollodotus as *archontes* of Lycia. It further relates the instigation of a local cult for Basileus Kaunios and Arkesimas and the installation of Simias as its priest.

The most contested Greek inscription, Darius' letter to Gadatas, is preserved only in a copy of the second century AD, but it purports to be the Greek translation of an authentic letter from Darius I to his Magnesian satrap. The text seemingly follows Persian royal scribal conventions in the way the king addresses his subject and deals with Gadatas' violation of the sacred ground of the Apollo sanctuary, for which Gadatas was to be punished.

FURTHER READING

The sources discussed above are conveniently assembled in two editions, Brosius (2000) and Kuhrt (2007). For Ctesias, see in particular Lenfant (2004).

REFERENCES

Balcer, J. M. 1987. *Herodotus and Bisitun: Problems in ancient Persian historiography*. Stuttgart: Historia—Einzelschriften 49.

Beck, I. 1971. *Die Ringkomposition bei Herodot und ihre Bedeutung für die Beweistechnik*. Hildesheim: Olms Verlag.

Bichler, R. 2001. *Herodots Welt. Der Aufbau der Historie am Bild der fremden Länder und Völker, ihrer Zivilisation und ihrer Geschichte*, 2nd ed. Berlin: Akademie Verlag.

Binder, C. 2008. *Plutarchs Vita des Artaxerxes*. Berlin: De Gruyter.

Briant, P. 2003. *Darius dans l'ombre d'Alexandre*. Paris: Fayard.

Brosius, M. 2000. *The Persian Empire from Cyrus II to Artaxerxes I*. London: London Association of Classical Teachers Original Records 16.

Cherf, W. J. 2001. Thermopylai: Myth and reality in 480 BC. In *Gab es das griechische Wunder? Griechenland zwischen dem Ende des 6. und der Mitte des 5. Jahrhunderts v. Chr.*, ed. D. Papenfuß and V. M. Strocka, 355–61. Mainz: von Zabern.

Drews R. 1974. Sargon, Cyrus, and Mesopotamian folk history. *JNES* 33: 387–93.

Hall, E. 1991. *Inventing the Barbarian: Greek self-definition through tragedy*. Oxford: Clarendon Press.

Harrison, T. 2002. *Greeks and barbarians*. Edinburgh: Edinburgh University Press.

Hartog, F. 2010. *The mirror of Herodotus: The representation of the Other in the writing of history*. Berkeley/Los Angeles: University of California Press.

Hölteskamp, K.-J. 2001. Marathon—vom Monument zum Mythos. In *Gab es das griechische Wunder? Griechenland zwischen dem Ende des 6. und der Mitte des 5. Jahrhunderts v. Chr.*, ed. D. Papenfuß and V. M. Strocka, 329–53. Mainz: von Zabern.

Hutzfeld, B. 1999. *Das Bild der Perser in der griechischen Dichtung des 5. vorchristlichen Jahrhunderts*. Wiesbaden: Serta Graeca 8.

Jacobs, B. 1994. *Die Satrapienverwaltung des Perserreiches zur Zeit Darius' III*. Wiesbaden: TAVO Beiheft 87 B.

———. 2000. Achaimenidenherrschaft in der Kaukasus-Region und in Cis-Kaukasien. *AMIT* 32: 93–102.

———. 2006. Caucasus, iii. Achaemenid rule in. *EnIr* online edition.

Kuhrt, A. 2007. *The Persian Empire: A corpus of sources from the Achaemenid period.* 2 vols. London: Routledge.

Kuhrt, A., and S. Sherwin-White. 1987. Xerxes' destruction of Babylonian temples. In *The Greek sources*, ed. H. Sancisi-Weerdenburg and A. Kuhrt, 69–78. Leiden: AchHist 2.

Lenfant, D. 2004. *Ctésias de Cnide: La Perse. L'Inde. Autres fragments.* Paris: Les Belles Lettres.

———. 2009. *Les histoires perses de Dinon et d'Héraclide.* Paris: Persika 13.

Meiggs, R., and D. Lewis. 1989. *A selection of Greek historical inscriptions to the end of the fifth century BC*, rev. ed. Oxford: Clarendon Press.

Papenfuß, D., and V. M. Strocka, eds. 2001. *Gab es das griechische Wunder? Griechenland zwischen dem Ende des 6. und der Mitte des 5. Jahrhunderts v. Chr.* Mainz: von Zabern.

Rhodes, P. J., and R. Osborne. 2003. *Greek historical inscriptions, 404–323 BC.* Oxford: Oxford University Press.

Rollinger, R. 1993. *Herodots babylonischer Logos: Eine kritische Untersuchung der Glaubwürdigkeitsdiskussion an Hand ausgewählter Beispiele.* Innsbruck: Innsbrucker Beiträge zur Kulturwissenschaft Sonderheft 84.

Ruffing, K. 2009. Die "Satrapenliste" des Dareios: Herodoteisches Konstrukt oder Realität? *AMIT* 41: 323–40.

Tuplin, C. 2009. The Gadatas letter. In *Greek history and epigraphy*, ed. L. Mitchell and L. Rubinstein, 155–84. Swansea: Classical Press of Wales.

———. 2010. Xenophon and Achaemenid courts. In *Der Achämenidenhof/The Achaemenid Court*, ed. B. Jacobs and R. Rollinger, 189–230. Wiesbaden: CLeO 2.

Walker, C. B. F. 1997. Achaemenid chronology and the Babylonian sources. In *Mesopotamia and Iran in the Persian period: Conquest and imperialism 539–331 BC*, ed. J. Curtis, 15–25. London: British Museum Publications.

Weisskopf, M. 1989. *The so-called "Great Satraps' Revolt," 366–360 BC: Concerning local instability in the Achaemenid far west.* Stuttgart: Historia-Einzelschriften 63.

Wiesehöfer, J. 1992. "Denn es sind welthistorische Siege" ... Nineteenth and twentieth century German views of the Persian Wars. In *The construction of the Ancient Near East*, ed. A. C. Gunter, 61–83. Copenhagen: Culture & History 11.

———. 1997. *Ancient Persia.* London: I. B. Tauris.

Wiesehöfer, J., R. Rollinger, and G. B. Lanfranchi. 2011. *Ktesias' Welt/Cteasias' World.* Wiesbaden: CLeO 1.

Young, T. C., Jr. 1988. The early history of the Medes and the Persians and the Achaemenid Empire to the death of Cambyses. *CAH* 4: 1–52.

PART VI

SELEUCID, POST-ACHAEMENID, AND ARSACID ARCHAEOLOGY AND HISTORY

CHAPTER 34

ALEXANDER THE GREAT AND THE SELEUCIDS IN IRAN

PAUL J. KOSMIN

Introduction

Interactions between the Iranian and Greek worlds in the late Archaic and Classical periods (the two centuries from Cyrus to Alexander, 540s–330s BC) were intense and complex, ranging from destructive invasion to artistic patronage, Common Peaces to ethnographic writings (see, e.g., Raaflaub 2009; Miller 1997; Lewis 1977; and Root 1985). The rise of Macedonia under Philip II, his son Alexander's conquest of the Persian kingdom, the disintegration of central authority after his death, and the emergence in its place of the Seleucid dynasty marked an entirely new phase of Iranian history and its relations with Hellenic politics and culture. For almost two centuries the Iranian lands were the colonized provinces of imperial formations whose centers lay far to the west. This chapter will examine the Greco-Macedonian presence and the progressive marginalization of Iran it brought about. Its texture will change from a finely grained war narrative to a more synchronic, structural analysis of Seleucid imperialism.

The Macedonian Conquest

In spring 334 BC Alexander III of Macedonia guided his flagship across the narrow strait of the Hellespont and from its prow hurled a spear onto the beach of Troy (Diod. Sic. 17.17.2; Just. *Epit.* 11.5.10); with this act of symbolic violence, explicitly recalling the Trojan War (Alexander claimed descent from Achilles) and avenging Xerxes' 480 BC invasion of Greece, began the remarkable decade-long invasion and takeover of the Achaemenid Empire. The details of the Macedonian campaign are complex and frequently unclear, not least because our extant Classical sources are late, biased, and literary. Although Alexander's campaign was extensively reported by his courtiers and peers (including Ptolemy I of Egypt), we possess no narrative earlier than book 17 of Diodorus Siculus' *Bibliotheke*, belonging to the reign of Augustus. Arrian's seven-volume *Anabasis*, Plutarch's biography, Quintus Curtius Rufus' ten-volume history (the first two volumes are lost), and Justin's *Epitome of the Philippic History of Pompeius Trogus*, books 11–12 are all of later Roman imperial date. Various other extant sources, such as Alexander's Letters, his Royal Diary, and the Alexander Romance, while of great cultural and political importance, are of limited use for historical reconstruction (for discussion of the lost contemporary accounts, see Pearson 1960; for the extant narratives, see Bosworth 1988). In brief, the conquest falls into three main arcs of movement. First, Alexander swept along the entire east Mediterranean coastline of the Achaemenid Empire, from Hellespontine Phrygia to Egypt; the Macedonian army was victorious in two battles, against Darius III's Asia Minor satraps at the Granicus River in May 334 and against the Great King himself at Issus, in the Gulf of Iskenderun, in November 333. Second, leaving Egypt in spring 331, Alexander began a five-year long eastward march, taking him from Phoenicia through Mesopotamia, Iran, Central Asia, and northwest India, right up to the limit of his conquests at the Hyphasis (modern Beas) River; this stretch of the campaign saw Alexander's victory over Darius III's immense army at Gaugamela, east of the Tigris, in October 331, and the pursuit of Darius III and then his assassin and usurper, the Bactrian satrap Bessus (who took the throne name Artaxerxes V). Finally, in 326, Alexander turned back to the west, following the shore of the Persian Gulf into Iran, and returned to Babylon, where he died in June 323. Accordingly, the itinerant Macedonian court twice wove its way through Iran—in 330, heading northward and eastward in pursuit of Darius III, and in 325, returning westward in a consolidation and reorganization of empire. As we shall see, the two journeys were strikingly different in action and ideology.

The invasion and integration of the Persian lands posed problems for the European conquistadors quite unlike any other Achaemenid province. For the Greek and Phoenician city-states of the Anatolian and Levantine coastlines, for the former territorial kingdoms of Lydia, Egypt, and Babylonia, Alexander was able to respond to indigenous expectations of hegemonic or monarchic behavior, acting as liberator from Persian oppression, restorer of local privileges, sponsor of temple cults, and patron of social elites. For instance, the Classical sources record that, having arrived at Babylon in Autumn 331, Alexander authorized and paid for the reconstruction of the Esagila, the temple of Babylon's patron deity Marduk, and performed sacrifices according to the instructions of Chaldaean ritual experts (Arr., *Anab.* 3.16.5; cf. Sherwin-White 1987); a contemporary though—alas!—fragmentary Babylonian astronomical cuneiform text records (in Akkadian) Alexander's assurance to the city's population that, "Into your houses I shall not enter" (Sachs and Hunger 1988: 179, –330 Rev. 7). By contrast, Iran, the political and ideological heartland of the Achaemenid Empire and its governing "ethno-elite," offered fewer opportunities for the liberator's pose and none for the invocation of pre-Achaemenid glories. As a result, local resistance was more determined and Macedonian retaliation more brutal (for Alexander in Iran, see, e.g., Briant 2002: 850–55; Wiesehöfer 1994: 23–49; Bosworth 1980).

In the half-year following Gaugamela, Alexander took control of the five major Achaemenid capitals. Four—Babylon, Susa, Pasargadae, and Ecbatana—were handed over peacefully by Darius' satraps or governors; these Persian noblemen retained their positions, albeit under the watchful gaze of Greco-Macedonian garrisons, citadel commanders, and treasurers. By contrast, Persepolis, the Achaemenid Empire's ceremonial and religious capital, was plundered and its population massacred (Diod. Sic. 17.70; Curt. 5.6.4–8). Worse was to come: at the end of a four-month sojourn at Persepolis, Alexander intentionally burned down the palaces and treasuries on the Royal Terrace (Arr., *Anab.* 3.18.11–12; Diod. Sic. 17.72; Plut., *Alex.* 38; Curt. 5.7.1–9; for discussion of archaeological evidence for the Persepolis conflagration see Sancisi-Weerdenburg 1993), whether as a sign to faltering Greeks that Xerxes' invasion had been avenged (Badian 1967: 185–90), to Asia that the Achaemenid yoke had been lifted (Borza 1972), or to local inhabitants that their hegemony was over (Briant 2002: 850–1). With Darius III still alive and maintaining a loyal escort, the destruction and depopulation of Persepolis once and for all denied the Achaemenid his ideologically potent capital, but, as general Parmenion forewarned and Alexander later lamented, the arson also deprived the Macedonian of the opportunity to adopt and deploy the Great Kings' rites of rule in their ancestral heartland. Furthermore, our sources indicate an unflagging hostility to Alexander on the part of at least some of the Persian population, an enmity that Alexander more than reciprocated. In the difficult passage from Susa to Persepolis Alexander faced down the brigandage of the mountain-dwelling Uxians and the much more serious opposition of Ariobarzanes' satrapal army (Arr., *Anab.* 3.17.1–18.9; Diod. Sic. 17.67.2–68; Plut., *Alex.* 37; Curt. 5.3–4). In a month of campaigning across the Iranian plateau the Macedonians devastated the inhabitants' fields and reduced their settlements (Diod. Sic. 17.73.1; Curt. 5.6.12–16). In an assessment unique to this region Diodorus informs us that Alexander "did not trust the inhabitants and felt bitter enmity toward them" (Diod. Sic. 17.71.3). When Alexander moved on in pursuit of Darius III he left behind a terrorized population, a razed capital, and a ruptured administration. It is revealing of both the violence of the Macedonian conquest and the limits of its transformational ambitions that the destruction layer at Persepolis constitutes the only archaeological footprint of Alexander's presence in Persia.

Given our sources' almost exclusive focus on the itinerant Macedonian court we have only a vague understanding of events in Iran in the period between Alexander's two visits. It seems that the destruction of the *ancien régime* and the immediate evacuation of the new one generated a deep rupture in administrative authority. During Alexander's campaigns in Central Asia and India a Median named Baryaxes had proclaimed himself king of the Medes and Persians, even wearing the royal upright tiara; Cyrus the Great's mausoleum at Pasargadae and the Achaemenid royal tombs at Naqsh-e Rustam had been looted; the temples of Susiana and Persepolis were despoiled; Orxines, who traced his descent from Cyrus, of his own accord had assumed control of Persis; and various abuses of power, from summary execution to rape, had gone unchecked (Arr., *Anab.*

6.27.5, 6.29.2–11, 6.30.1–2; Diod. Sic. 17.106.2–3, 17.108.4, 17.108.6; Curt. 10.1.1–5, 10.1.23, 10.1.30–5).

The Macedonian army, decimated from its passage through the waterless wastes of Gedrosia, returned to Iran in winter 325/4. Alexander's second, briefer visit opened with a bloody purge of Persian nobles and governors convicted, whether correctly or not, of disloyalty (Arr., *Anab.* 6.27.3–6, 6.29.2–3; Plut., *Alex.* 68.3–4; Curt. 10.1.22–42); according to Plutarch, Alexander ran through the son of Abulites, satrap of Susiana, with his own spear (*Alex.* 68.4). Greeks and Macedonians with no connection to the land or its population were appointed in place of the Iranian satraps, among them Peucestas over Persis (see below). At the same time, Alexander actively inscribed himself in the role of the defunct Achaemenid monarch. On entering Persia he distributed gold coinage to the female population (Plut., *Alex.* 69.1), reverently repaired the tomb of Cyrus at Pasargadae (Arr., *Anab.* 6.29.4–11; Curt. 10.1.32), publicly expressed regret for his burning of Persepolis (Arr., *Anab.* 6.30.1; Curt. 5.7.11), and conducted in the Persian manner a mass wedding of Macedonian officers to noble Iranian women at Susa, joining himself to Darius' daughter Stateira and perhaps also to Artaxerxes III Ochus' daughter Parysatis (Arr., *Anab.* 7.4.4–8; Plut., *Alex.* 70.2; Diod. Sic. 17.107.6).

Throughout his *anabasis* Alexander's treatment of Iranians, Persia, and Achaemenid kingship was driven by an awkward ideological incompatibility, nicely expressed by a passage in Plutarch: the Macedonian conqueror asked a statue of Xerxes, toppled at the sack of Persepolis, "Shall I pass on and leave you lying there, because of your expedition against the Greeks? Or shall I set you up again, on account of your magnanimity and excellence?" (After pondering in silence for a long time, he walked away) (*Alex.* 37.3). On the one hand, the expedition had been conceived at the outset as a Hellenic crusade against ancient and recent Persian aggression (Arr., *Anab.* 2.14.4–6; Diod. Sic. 16.89.1; Isoc., *Philip.* 146; Flower 2000), which specific acts of the campaign continued to highlight—the sending of 300 Persian panoplies to Athens after victory at the Granicus; the restoration from Persia of Greek statues; the massacre of the Branchidae of Sogdiana, descendants of Apollo's priests who, it was alleged, had supported Xerxes in his Persian invasion; and, perhaps, the celebration of Greek games in the Persian capitals (Arr., *Anab.* 1.16.7, 3.16.7–8; Strabo, *Geog.* 17.1.43; Plut., *Mor.* 557c; Diod. Sic. *list of contents* 17.20; Curt. 7.5.28–35; Parke 1985). Yet as early as 333 it appears that Alexander attempted to represent himself as legitimate "King of Asia" and rightful inheritor of the Achaemenid Empire (Plut., *Alex.* 34.1; Curt. 6.6.6; Muccioli 2004: 109–11; Fredricksmeyer 2000); Briant has demonstrated that Alexander's knowledge of Persian monarchic ideology was detailed if not comprehensive (1982b). So, full honors were given to Darius III's family, captured at Damascus after the battle of Issus (Arr., *Anab.* 3.22.1, 4.20.1–3; Curt. 3.12.13–26, 4.12.1; Diod. Sic. 17.37–8, 17.54; Plut., *Alex.* 21); Bessus, the satrap of Bactria who had conspired against and usurped Darius, was disfigured and executed in a traditional Persian way (Arr., *Anab.* 3.25.8, 3.30.3–5, 4.7.3; Diod. Sic. 17.82.9; Curt. 7.5.40, 7.10.10.); Alexander gave Darius a royal burial with full honors in the Achaemenid necropolis (Arr., *Anab.* 3.22.1; Justin, *Epit.* 11.15.15); at Susa Alexander married Darius' daughter (Arr., *Anab.* 7.4.4; Diod. Sic. 17.107.6; Plut., *Alex.* 70.2–4); and so on. Furthermore, Alexander cultivated the memory of Cyrus II—an apt prototype for a great conqueror and dynastic founder—by honoring the Ariaspians of Areia, who had helped Cyrus during his conquest of Central Asia (Arr., *Anab.* 3.27.4; Diod. Sic. 17.81.1–2; Curt. 7.2.3), and, as we have seen, by restoring his tomb at Pasargadae; it is no accident that Strabo calls Alexander *philokyros*, "Cyrus-lover" (*Geog.* 11.11.4).

The incongruity of Alexander's double-identity was pressed further by the Macedonian court's progressive incorporation of Achaemenid ceremony and governing structures. In 330, perhaps in response to the usurper Bessus' claim to Darius III's throne, Alexander added to his traditional Macedonian costume some parts of Persian royal dress and distributed Persian cloaks to his Companions (Plut., *Alex.* 45.1; Diod. Sic. 17.77; Curt. 6.6.1; for the context see Bosworth 1980: 5–7). During the Central Asian and Indian campaigns Achaemenid rituals were introduced to Alexander's reception ceremonies, select Persian nobles were entered into the highest court circles, and Iranian troops, especially cavalry, became fully integrated participants in the military (for references and bibliography, see Bosworth 1980). Of all Achaemenid court ceremonies, the introduction of *proskynesis*, or ritual obeisance, was the most fraught, not least for being misunderstood as an act of worship (Bickerman 1963). After the army's return to Iran and Babylonia, it seems that Alexander consciously attempted to bind the Persian aristocracy into his governing elite: at Susa in early 324, as we have seen, Alexander obliged eighty of his generals to marry noble Persian women (Arr., *Anab.* 7.4.4–8; Plut., *Alex.* 70.2; Diod. Sic. 17.107.6; Just., *Epit.* 12.10.9–10); a little later, at a great banquet at Opis on the Tigris, Alexander publicly prayed for partnership and harmony between Macedonians and Persians in the governance of his empire (Arr., *Anab.* 7.11.8–9). Against this king-led dynamic, the earlier Hellenic agenda was relocated to certain "traditionalists" within his court and to much of the Macedonian infantry: increasing resistance to the Persianizing agenda is a recurring motif of Alexander's court and a major complaint of the Hyphasis and Opis mutineers (for court conspiracies against Alexander, see Badian 2000). Nonetheless, we should not doubt that the extension of Macedonian rule over the former Achaemenid provinces necessitated the adoption, without change, of much of the governing structure and institutional arrangements that had worked so successfully during the preceding centuries. In this sense, Alexander acted not unlike his hero, Cyrus the Great, who seems to have incorporated the nobility and institutions of the conquered Medes into his new Persian Empire.

When Alexander died at Babylon in summer 323 much had changed, and little. For most of his decade in Asia, Alexander had been a conqueror on the move, with limited opportunity for a meaningful reconfiguration of Iranian landscapes, society, language, or material culture. No colonies were founded, no villages synoecized in Persia. We cannot know in what ways the monetization of thousands of talents of imperial bullion affected the local economy, but the repercussions may have been intense. Seen in the long view, the historical function of Alexander's campaign for Iran was double. First, to the extent that fragments of Achaemenid structures, ceremonies, and ideology survived into the dynastic formations established by the conqueror's Greco-Macedonian generals, Alexander's code-switching and courtly experimentation are responsible. Second, the geographical and ideological importance of the conquerors' southern Balkan homeland pulled the imperial center of gravity westward, to Babylon during Alexander's closing years, and even closer to the Mediterranean under his successors; Persia became increasingly marginalized and, while retaining a regional significance, would not reemerge as core region of empire until the rise of the Sasanian kingdom in the third century AD.

THE WARS OF SUCCESSION

Alexander's failure to beget an adult heir abandoned his empire to a violent, generation-long scramble for power, as the more ambitious of his generals competed either for the supreme command or for a more circumscribed regional dominance. The events of the so-called Diadoch Wars, known almost only from abbreviations of the lost history of Hieronymus of Cardia, are both bewilderingly complicated and immensely significant (sources for the Diadoch Wars are books 18–21 of Diodorus Siculus' *Bibliotheke*, Photius' summary of Arrian's *Ta meta Alexandron*, Plutarch's biographies of Demetrius Poliorcetes and Eumenes, and Justin's *Epitome of the Philippic History of Pompeius Trogus*; a limited number of inscriptions and Babylonian cuneiform texts give contemporary record; the best discussion of Hieronymus of Cardia is Hornblower 1981). In brief, after a couple of decades of fighting, Alexander's empire had fragmented into a number of successor kingdoms, returning the Near East to the kind of multistate international order that Cyrus' conquests had ended two and a half centuries earlier; the surviving generals, having taken the royal diadem and title, transformed the nature of legitimate kingship and engaged in the post-conquest state-building enterprises for which Alexander had neither opportunity nor inclination.

After Alexander's death, the general weakening of central authority and the removal to Macedonia of Alexander's ineffectual successors (his mentally handicapped half-brother, Philip Arrhidaeus, and his young child by Rhoxane, Alexander IV) impacted Iran at two levels. Intra-satrapal rivalries broke out between the different governors, who had been given space to construct strong and autonomous provincial power bases; in particular, Peithon, satrap of Media, attempted to extend his dominance over the rest of the Upper Satrapies, but was opposed by a coalition of Iranian and Central Asian governors, initially headed by Peucestas, satrap of Persis. This regional clash was, in its turn, implicated in a broader, pan-imperial conflict, the Second Diadoch War, between Antigonus Monophthalmus and Eumenes of Cardia. In two battles in Paraetacene and Gabiene (317/6), near modern Isfahan, Peithon brought to Antigonus' aid the forces of northern Iran, while the anti-Peithon satrapal coalition contributed their forces to Eumenes' core of Silver Shields, the Macedonian veterans of Alexander's campaign. Antigonus, after a shabby victory over Eumenes, became undisputed master of all the Asian provinces and seems to have received royal honors from the inhabitants of Persis (Diod. Sic. 19.48.1; the most detailed account of the sources and campaign is Bosworth 2002: 98–168).

The confrontations between Antigonus and Eumenes were the largest pitched battles ever fought on Iranian soil throughout the Hellenistic period. Although we lack any direct evidence for the impact of these non-stop conflicts on the local population, the effect must have been similar to that of Antigonus' attack on Seleucus in Babylonia half a decade later, which, according to cuneiform sources, brought about "weeping and mourning in the land" and sky-high food prices (BCHP 3 col. 4 l.37; for food-prices see van der Spek 2000). Even so, despite such bitter strife and rivalry among the conquerors, we have no record of an indigenous anti-Macedonian insurrection in Iran or, for that matter, anywhere else; after Alexander's death, only the Greek colonists in Central Asia and some city-states of the Greek mainland attempted to throw off the Macedonian yoke. This absence may be explained, at least in part, by the provincial governors' successful cultivation of local support. Such a policy of integration, followed by Seleucus in Babylonia (Sherwin-White 1987: 14-18 and Capdetrey 2007: 25-31) and Alcetas in Pisidia (Diod. Sic. 18.46-7) amongst others, is most clearly demonstrated for the Iranian territories by Peucestas, the satrap of Persis. After his appointment by Alexander, Peucestas adopted Persian clothing, learnt the Persian language, and in consequence earned the allegiance of the local elite (Arr., *Anab.* 6.30.2, 7.6.3, 7.23.3; Diod. Sic. 19.14.5), who resisted, albeit unsuccessfully, Antigonus' attempt following the battle of Gabiene to unseat him. Diodorus Siculus (19.48.5) reports that a Persian noble, Thespius, said that the Persians would not obey anyone else; Antigonus executed him. Peucestas seems to have entered the court service of Antigonus and his son Demetrius Poliorcetes (Phylarchus *FGrH* 81 F12 = Ath. 14.614e-615a). Such a strategy was dramatized at the large banquet for the troops of Eumenes and the anti-Peithon coalition hosted by satrap Peucestas in 317. Below the burnt-out terrace of Persepolis, Peucestas orchestrated his guests into four concentric circles with the innermost ring occupied by the senior Greco-Macedonian officers and the Persian nobility concurrently (Diod. Sic. 19.22); Henkelman has demonstrated that this kind of banquet was rooted in Achaemenid royal tradition (2011). The feast was opened with sacrifices to the gods (unspecified in Diodorus' account), to Alexander the Great, and to Philip II. Perhaps to be associated with these festivities are five small stone altar plaques, from within or near the so-called Frātadāra temple at Persepolis. These are carefully inscribed with the names in the genitive case of the gods Zeus Megistos, Apollo, Helios, Artemis, and Athena Basileia (*IEO* nos. 241-5; Wiesehöfer 1994: 72-3, 89). The inscriptions name exclusively Hellenic gods and thereby signify the introduction of formal Greek cult at Persepolis; however, we should acknowledge the possibility of their assimilation to traditional Persian deities, presumably Ahuramazda, Mithra, and Anahita, in the eyes of the local population (Herzfeld 1935: 44-7 and Iossif and Lorber 2009: 22 are in favor of syncretism, but note the caution of Boyce and Grenet 1991: 107 and Callieri 2007: 67). The style of lettering—an approximate indication at best—suggests that the plaques date toward the end of the fourth century BC (*IEO* nos. 241-5; Robert 1967: 282).

Following his victory at Gabiene, Antigonus murdered or drove out the long-established and independently minded satraps of western Iran, appointing in their place native administrators or officers of more limited prestige and ambition (Diod. Sic. 19.46, 55).

They quickly crushed a minor revolt of Peithon's loyal supporters, Greco-Macedonian and Median, indicating that, like Peucestas, the former satrap of Media had also won a following from at least part of the indigenous population (Diod. Sic. 19.47). Having reconfigured and subordinated Elam, the central Zagros Mountains, and the Iranian plateau, Antigonus returned to the Mediterranean coast, taking with him our eye-witness historian, Hieronymus of Cardia; as a result, our sources' spotlight shifts westward and Iran drops back into narrative obscurity.

The Antigonid glacis in western and central Iran did not last long. The final decade of the fourth century was marked by the meteoric rise to dominance of Seleucus Nicator, satrap of Babylonia, in Mesopotamia, Iran, and Central Asia. Seleucus, having fled Antigonus' march from Iran in 315, returned four years later to claim back his satrapy. With the strong support of the indigenous population he faced down an eastern invasion from the Antigonus-aligned governors of western Iran and seized Susiana, Media, and what Diodorus terms "the adjacent lands" (doubtless Persis) (Diod. 19.92). Between 310 and 308, using the resources and landscape of this newly acquired west Iranian region, Seleucus successfully resisted renewed assaults on Babylonia by Antigonus and his son Demetrius, and then embarked on a long campaign (308–c.305/4) to subordinate the east Iranian and Central Asian provinces. Our sources are all but silent on the nature of Seleucus' operations, mentioning only a battle against Bactrians (Just., *Epit.* 15.4.11–12), but it is possible that he may have been welcomed as a bulwark against the threats of nomadic razzia from the north (Tarn 1940: 91; Wolski: 1960; Gardiner-Garden 1987: 46–7) or Mauryan expansion from the south (Capdetrey 2007: 44). The exploitable ideological capital of his Iranian wife, Apame, daughter of Sogdian Spitamenes, should not be underestimated. Seleucus had consolidated his control of the Upper Satrapies sufficiently to descend into India in 305 or 304, where he secured peace with Chandragupta Maurya, the new potentate of northern India, exchanging the most easterly satrapies of the Macedonian empire for a force of five hundred war elephants (Just., *Epit.* 15.4.12, 20–21; Strabo, *Geog.* 15.2.9; App., *Syr.* 55). This "Treaty of the Indus" continued to be honored by Seleucus' and Chandragupta's successors right down to the late third century (according to Polyb. 11.34.11–12, Antiochus III formally "renewed the friendship" with Sophagasenus, king of the Indians). The Indian elephants defeated Antigonus at the Battle of Ipsus in 301, as a result of which Seleucus extended his territories to northern Syria (Diod. Sic. 21.12; Plut., *Demetr.* 19.3). Twenty years later, Seleucus defeated Lysimachus and absorbed his territories in Asia Minor and Thrace. By the time of Seleucus' murder in 281 his empire extended from the Central Asian steppe to European Thrace, or in modern terms, from Tajikistan to Bulgaria.

THE SELEUCID EMPIRE IN IRAN

The three violent decades from Alexander's invasion of Iran to Seleucus' conquest constitute the birth pangs of a new period of settled rule under the Seleucid dynasty, lasting over one and a half centuries. Seleucid imperialism represents a qualitatively different form of Greco-Macedonian presence in Iran. In the final section of this chapter we shall move away from the narrative of battles and actions, tedious for us and horrific for the ancient population, to a synchronic discussion of the institutions and military structures of Seleucid Iran.

For Seleucus I the Iranian lands were largely unfamiliar. At the beginning of his reign he sponsored a range of "scientific" practices and research ventures to generate, order, and deploy a governmentally useful geographic knowledge. Patrocles, a trusted courtier, was commissioned to explore the Caspian Sea and investigate opportunities for trade with its coastal populations; his published account determined the Classical understanding of the Caspian's geography for centuries (*FGrH* 712; see Neumann 1884). Demodamas, a Seleucid general from Miletus, seems to have published an ethnographic account of the kingdom's northeastern frontier (*FGrH* 428). Two milestones, found in Persis, give distances between locations in *stades* (the standard Greek distance unit); one has a fragmentary Aramaic précis (*IEO* nos. 247–8). Such inscriptions, new to the Near East, indicate an interest in maintaining and measuring roadways. The short distances inscribed on our two extant examples imply that others would have been erected at frequent intervals.

More significant was the organization of the new lands into a coherent provincial administration and hierarchy. Only the barest outlines can be detected from our sources: unlike the Achaemenid and Ptolemaic kings, the Seleucids never listed their territorial possessions in royal inscriptions or encomiastic poetry, and historiographical sources privilege the untypical crisis moments of war or revolt. Even so, it is clear that the Seleucid kingdom arranged its political landscape according to an imperial geography largely inherited from Alexander and the Achaemenids. Satrapies (large territorial blocks with some degree of ethnic or cultural identity organized around a capital city), governed by satraps or generals (*stratēgoi*), formed the basic administrative reference points. In the third century, the core satrapies east of the Tigris were Susiana, Media, Persis, Parthia-Hyrcania, Carmania, Gedrosia, and Bactria (Bengtson 1944: 18). Recall that the easternmost satrapies of Alexander's empire—Gandhāra, Paropamisadae, Areia, and parts of Arachosia—had been handed over to Chandragupta Maurya in the Treaty of the Indus (Mookerji 1995: 12 and Foucher 1942: 208 *contra* Tarn 1951: 100 and Schmitt 1964: 66, n. 4). We now have evidence that the coastline and islands of the Persian Gulf were grouped into an administrative archipelago called either the satrapy of the Erythraean Sea or of Tylos (Bahrain) and the Islands (Kosmin 2013). Moreover, at various moments Armenia, Media Atropatene, and Parthia were reduced to a state of vassalage. In the second century, following the independence of Greco-Bactria and the rise of Arsacid Parthia, the Seleucids lost control of all territories east of Media.

Official inscriptions, representing royal instructions in the form of letters cascading down administrative levels (for discussion of this form of authorized instruction, see Ma 1999), show both a clear bureaucratic hierarchy and the nonuniform and locally adapted satrapal subdivisions, ranging from colonies and forts to hyparchies and merides (hyparchies are attested at Parthian Avroman, see Capdetrey 2007: 260; merides in

Judea and the Hindu Kush, see Capdetrey 2007: 61). All satrapies east of the Euphrates or Tigris were united under the general commander of the Upper Satrapies. This post, created in 294 by Seleucus I on Achaemenid and Antigonid precedent, was occupied by crown princes or senior courtiers (Bengtson 1944: 78–90). It is likely that the position was filled continuously until the Parthian conquest of Media in the 140s, although only five general commanders are attested: Antiochus I until the death of his father Seleucus I in 281; Antiochus III during the short reign of his elder brother Seleucus III; the courtier Molon from Antiochus III's accession; the courtier Timarchus during the reign of Antiochus IV; and Cleomenes, in 148, according to a dedication in his honor at Bisotun in Media. The nonroyal general commanders also functioned as satraps of Media, based at Ecbatana. The post's royal associations and Media's resources and strategic importance seem to have allowed the general commanders' territorial authority to be transformed at moments of weakened central control into independent personal power: following in Peithon's footsteps (see above), Molon (222) and Timarchus (162) each revolted against the Seleucid house and declared themselves kings, the Roman Senate even acknowledging the latter as *rex Medorum* (for discussion of Molon's revolt see, amongst many, Schmitt 1964: 116–49; for revolt of Timarchus, see Ehling 2008: 124–9).

Within their circumscribed regions provincial governors functioned as local representatives of imperial authority and substitutes for the distant body of the Seleucid monarch. However, as the revolts of Molon, Timarchus, and several other satraps show, such administrative independence encouraged a centrifugal dynamic in the kingdom's Iranian and Central Asian territories. Accordingly, provincial tours by the reigning king were an important, if not the major, mechanism for imperial integration: the Seleucid Empire was a kind of territorial configuration that could only be operated by continuous royal movement through its satrapies. So, several third and second century kings led imperial armies into Iran in order to reduce rebellious satraps or insurgent populations, face down Parthian expansion, revivify the administration, and consolidate relationships of allegiance or vassalage. The most famous such journey (called *anabasis* in Greek) was Antiochus III's march through Media and northern Iran up to the Hindu Kush and return through southern Iran and the Persian Gulf (see, amongst many, Kuhrt and Sherwin-White 1993: 197–202 and Will 1979–82: 54–69), but similar, if shorter, campaigns are attested for Seleucus II (Lerner 1999: 33–44), Antiochus IV (Mittag 2006: 296–326 and Mørkholm 1966: 166–80), Demetrius II (Ehling 2008: 183–6), and Antiochus VII (Fischer 1970). Seleucus II and Demetrius II ended up as Parthian captives in northern Iran, while Antiochus III and Antiochus IV died in separate attempts to resubordinate the Elymaeans and their temples (Dabrowa 2004).

The satraps were responsible for the collection of imperial taxes, in coin or kind, about which we know next to nothing from Iran (for the kingdom's satrapal revenues, see Aperghis 2004: 137–79). In addition, it seems that they were required to recruit military forces for the imperial army from the local population. According to our Classical sources, the Seleucid kings at the battles of Raphia (217) and Magnesia (189) deployed thousands of Elymaean archers, Persian bowmen and slingers, Median cavalry, and Dahaean mounted archers (from the eastern coast of the Caspian). Antiochus IV displayed a troop of 1000 Median horsemen at his Daphne parade (166) (for a full discussion of the Seleucid battle-ranks and recruitment see Bar-Kochva 1976). These Iranian forces were almost always commanded by Greco-Macedonian officers, so it is important that at the battle of Raphia Aspianus, a native Mede, led a force of 5000 (Atropatenian?) Medes, Cissians, Cadusians, and Carmanians. These mountain-dwelling or peripheral peoples may have participated as auxiliaries or allies on the basis of some kind of exchange relationship with the Seleucid kings, much as they had served the Achaemenids (for the Achaemenid practice, see Briant 1982a: 93–5). The indigenous Iranian troops were always ballistic and cavalry support for the Seleucid military core, formed of phalanx infantry recruited from the kingdom's military settlements, to which we now turn.

The transformation of territorial conquests into a cohesive landscape of legitimate authority was achieved to a great extent by the creation of new centers of imperial power. A network of colonial settlements formed the key nodes of Seleucid administrative and military control. Whereas Alexander and Antigonus merely deposited campaign veterans in the former Achaemenid capitals and regional centers, the early Seleucid kings formally settled several new colonies of Greeks and Macedonians (Cohen 1978). In Elmyais Susa was refounded as Seleucia-on-the-Eulaeus and another Seleucia was built on the Hedyphon river. Laodicea, Apamea, and Heraclea were established in Media, where the ancient capital, Ecbatana, was later refounded as Epiphanea by Antiochus IV. Antioch-in-Persis and Seleucia-on-the-Erythraean-Sea were established on the Gulf coast. In northern and northeastern Iran, Rhagae was renamed Europos, after Seleucus I's Macedonian home-city; Sirynx and Hecatompylus in Hyrcania seem to have held Greco-Macedonian residents; Soteira, Calliope, and Charis were founded in Parthia and many more colonies further into Central Asia. The majority of these new settlements seem to have been established in the final decade of the fourth century by Seleucus I or in the first two decades of the third century by his son Antiochus I, in his capacity as viceroy of the Upper Satrapies.

It is sufficiently clear that the Seleucid colonies were established primarily as military communities to garrison the newly won provincial landscape. Settlement was encouraged and sustained by grants to individual colonists of *klēroi*, agricultural plots in the royal estate, whose size and quality appear to have depended on military rank (Cohen 1978: 55–7). *Klēros* ownership in Iran is attested for the garrison of Seleucia-on-the-Eulaeus (Susa), for settlers in Persis, and for a community in the western foothills of Media (Seleucia-on-the-Eulaeus: *IEO* no. 214; Persis: Polyainos, *Strat.* 7.40; Avroman: Minns 1915). The colonies' locations indicate a concern for controlling the key arteries of interregional movement: the important route from Seleucia-on-the-Tigris to Ecbatana, the Khorasan highway from Media to Central Asia, and the maritime routes of the Persian Gulf. Furthermore, the Seleucid colonies formed a settlement hierarchy, ranging in size and internal complexity from small, fortified outposts (*phylakai*), such as one commanded by a certain Thoas, near modern Kermanshah (*IEO* no. 272), to the large, dynastically named satrapal capital of, say, Seleucia-on-the-Eulaeus. The colonies no doubt interconnected with preexisting indigenous villages and cities, such as Ecbatana and Persepolis. The great majority of individuals' names known from these new settlements—evidence inevitably weighted toward office-holders and social elites—are well paralleled Greek, Macedonian, and southern Balkan appellations, with only a couple of Babylonian or Iranian examples from Seleucia-on-the-Eulaeus (Le Rider 1965: 285-7). As we would expect, the names indicate the colonial elite's Hellenic self-ascription and, presumably, family origins. The mix of names from different regions of the Aegean world makes a single, exclusive origin for any colony unlikely.

The majority of the Seleucid colonies in Iran are little more than names scattered in the works of Classical geographers and lexicographers. But epigraphic evidence from two of the larger settlements, Antioch-in-Persis, near Bushehr on the Persian Gulf, and Seleucia-on-the-Eulaeus, the former Susa in Elymais, indicates that their internal political organization corresponded to the traditional decision-making organs of the Greek city-state. So, an important late third-century decree from Antioch-in-Persis, inscribed on the wall of the Sacred Agora at Magnesia, records the colony's recognition of a panhellenic festival for the goddess Artemis Leucophryene ("of the white brow") promulgated by Magnesia-on-the-Maeander, an ancient Greek city in western Asia Minor. It is worth quoting in full the decree's opening sentences:

> (Decree) of the Antiochians-in-[Persis]. When Heraclitus son of Zoes was priest of Seleucus (I) Nicator and Antiochus (I) Soter and Antiochus (II) Theos and Seleucus (II) Callinicus and King Seleucus (III) and King Antiochus (III) and his son King Antiochus, in the first half-year, resolutions of a sovereign meeting of the assembly which were handed in by Asclepiades son of Hecataeus and grandson of Demetrius, the secretary of the council (*boulē*) and the assembly (*ekklesia*), on the third of the waning month of Pantheus. Resolved by the assembly on the motion of the *prytaneis* (*IEO* no. 252 ll. 1–10).

Antioch-in-Persis possessed a bicameral system of city council (*boulē*) and assembly (*ekklesia*), together with an executive body (*prytaneis*) to introduce motions for vote by the citizen-body (*dēmos*). Such a political system would not be out of place among the sovereign democracies of the Greek mainland and Asia Minor: only Asclepiades' service as secretary of both *boulē* and *ekklesia*—two separate jobs in most Greek *poleis*—offers any hint of the infrequency of civic decree and law making or the limited size of the colony's citizenry. Furthermore, the structure and style of the decree follow the standardized forms of the Hellenic world's civic epigraphy. It is possible that the colony possessed the specialized built architecture, such as a council building (*bouleuterion*), to accommodate such political process. We should place alongside this inscription evidence from Parthian-period Seleucia-on-the-Eulaeus (Susa) for the existence of elected annual magistracies with legally prescribed limitations on repeat office-holding, rules that surely date to the period of Seleucid colonization (*IEO* no. 218). Furthermore, an early second century letter from Menedemus, governor of Media, "to the magistrates (*archontes*) and *polis* of the Laodiceans" indicates that this colony (Laodicea-in-Media; modern Nehavend) possessed a civilian political organization (*IEO* no. 277). Similar political structures are attested for the Seleucid kingdom's major cities, such as Seleucia-on-the-Tigris in Babylonia and Antioch-near-Daphne and Seleucia-in-Pieria in northern Syria (Cohen 1978).

The rich inscriptional evidence from Seleucia-on-the-Eulaeus indicates that the colony possessed, alongside these formal political organs, the basic social institutions and cultural reflexes of Greek city-life—on the one hand a gymnasium and stadium, for education and exercise; and on the other, a developed epigraphic habit, *euergetism* (wealthy citizens' patronage), erection of statues, displays of honors, manumission of slaves, poetic composition, and a legal system of witnessed decisions and publicly imposed sanctions (*IEO* nos. 186–220, with Le Rider 1965: 277–87).

Unlike sovereign Greek *poleis*, however, these settlements had been founded by the Seleucid monarchs and continued to support the kingdom's interests and institutions. Important officials in the kingdom's bureaucracy resided at Seleucia-on-the-Eulaeus, including a financial executive, a person in charge of the royal palace, an overseer or city governor (*epistatēs*), and a town archivist (*chreophylax*) (in order: *IEO* nos. 184, 183, 192). Several of these posts are known from other Seleucid colonies. The city also contained a significant garrison of military settlers, both infantry and cavalry, who occupied the citadel (*akra*) and owned irrigated agricultural estates (*klēroi*) in the plain. It is likely that, as elsewhere in the kingdom, such a garrison constituted the original core of Seleucus I's settlement and thereby formed the colony's land-owning social elite; but it remains unclear how smoothly and by what formal and informal channels the civilian and military populations interwove. Certainly, a number of honorific and dedicatory inscriptions show that the garrison possessed a strong corporate identity and functioned as its own decision-making body. For example, a Seleucid-period Greek inscription reads, "Leon and the officers under him and the soldiers [honor] Arete, daughter of Timon, the prefect of the king's palace, and of Atheno" (*IEO* no. 183), indicating a hierarchical military community interacting with the elite civilian administration.

Many of our colonial inscriptions raise questions of religious behavior and change in Seleucid Iran. The decree from Antioch-in-Persis, quoted above, is dated by the priesthood of the Seleucid dynastic cult, honoring all recognized monarchs from the founder down to the then reigning Antiochus III and his eldest son. The cult is attested in various forms elsewhere in Iran. Inscriptions found in Media report Antiochus III's instructions, forwarded to both the large colony of Laodicea and Thoas' small *phylakē*, for the introduction of religious cult and appointment of a high priestess for his wife Laodice. The priestess, king Antiochus' and queen Laodice's own daughter Laodice, was to wear a gold crown bearing her mother's portrait and have her name mentioned in the prologue to all contracts (*IEO* nos. 271–2, 277–8; for a recent survey of the evidence for Seleucid dynastic cult see van Nuffelen 2004). Although not formally dynastic cult, manumitted slaves from Seleucia-on-the-Eulaeus and Hyrcania were dedicated on behalf of the royal family. Throughout the kingdom dynastic cult provided a regularized religious language for the articulation of political loyalty and dependence. Inevitably, our epigraphic evidence for the dynastic cult is Greek and colonial, but it is likely that the monarchs were also revered in major indigenous settlements or temples, as at Babylon or Jerusalem: fragments of a bronze statue from the Elymaean sanctuary of Shami may belong to that of a Seleucid monarch revered there (Callieri 2007: 70). Although deceased kings had received cult in Achaemenid and Diadoch times (recall Peucestas' sacrifices to Philip and Alexander) the mandated worship of reigning monarchs was new to the Iranian religious landscape.

The colonists brought with them their ancestral gods: we have already seen that Greek deities were formally introduced at Persepolis, probably during the satrapal rule of Peucestas. Inscriptions and coins reveal the range of deities worshiped in Seleucid Iran, including the dynastic patrons Apollo and Artemis, as well as Athena, Heracles, the Dioscuri, and Zeus Ammon (Le Rider 1965: 287–97). A peristyle temple with round altar was constructed at Laodicea-in-Media; six of its columns still stood in the early twentieth century (Callieri 2007: 79–80). In their decree recognizing the festival of Artemis Leucophryene, the Antiochians-in-Persis insisted that they worshiped the same Hellenic gods as the Magnesians-on-the-Maeander (*IEO* no. 252 ll. 40–1). In this light it may be significant that a marble statue of the Marsyas, the Phrygian satyr revered in the Maeander valley, has been found in the region of Antioch-in-Persis (Callieri 2007: 105–8). If authorized imperial or colonial media appear to have honored exclusively Hellenic deities, several manumission inscriptions from Seleucia-on-the-Eulaeus show that in their private dedications the colonists also revered the originally Babylonian deity Nanaya (*IEO* nos. 193, 197, and probably 192) and the Cappadocian goddess Ma (*IEO* no. 180); a manumitted slave from Hyrcania, by the Caspian Sea, was dedicated to the Greek-Egyptian god Sarapis (*IEO* no. 280).

The most successful religious innovation in Seleucid Iran seems to have been the introduction of Heracles worship, reaching particular prominence in Media and Elymais. The hero's bellicosity and soteriological qualities certainly allowed an identification with the Avestan war god Verethragna, an assimilation attested at Commagene, Seleucia-on-the-Tigris, and Armenia, but such syncretism was by no means systematic or necessary (on Heracles in Hellenistic Mesopotamia and Iran see Bonnet 1992; Ghirshman 1975: 229–37; Kaizer 2000). In Media his cult is attested by figurines and plaques from Laodicea-Nehavand, Masjed-e Solayman, and Tang-e Shimbar (Callieri 2007: 110–11), an apotropaic inscription from the Karafto cave complex (Bernard 1980 has shown that Heracles is invoked in an apotropaic inscription protecting a secular residence, probably a garrison barracks), a deep rupestral relief at Bisotun dated to 148 BC (*IEO* no. 274; Luschey 1974: 122–5), and perhaps the colonial foundation of Heraclea (Strabo, *Geog.* 11.514; Amm. Marc. 23.6.39; Ptol. 6.2.16; nothing is known about the colony). It is worth discussing in some detail the Bisotun sculpture as it constitutes our only extant instance of monumental Seleucid art in Iran and brings together various imperial phenomena. Round the corner and far below Darius' famous inscription, a stocky, nude Heracles reclines in sympotic pose on a lion skin; in his left hand, he raises a large wine cup; his club rests off to one side; at his back, his bow leans against an olive tree. Behind his shoulder a low-relief pedimental stele records the dedication in Greek: "Year 164, month Panemos. Hyacinthus, son of Pantauchus, [dedicates] Heracles Callinicus for the safety of Cleomenes, commander of the Upper Satrapies." There follows an almost illegible Aramaic inscription, beginning *šnt* … "In the year … ". If the sanctuary, rupestral relief, and lack of naturalism all betray the Zagros context and local workmanship, it should be emphasized that the iconography is entirely Greek; the inscription uses the imperial calendar (the Seleucid Era, the Macedonian month), the kingdom's administrative titulature, and the god's Greek name and epithet; Hyacinthus is otherwise unknown, but Pantauchus is a markedly Macedonian name; the inscribed stele recalls the form in which the Seleucid kings erected their letters and instructions in the region. The ensemble represents a colonial–imperial religious intervention at the Bisotun sanctuary, deploying the authorized iconographic and textual markers of the Seleucid kingdom.

Without doubt, Iranian pre-Hellenistic cults continued into the Seleucid period. With the important exception of Antiochus IV's persecution of the Jews, the Seleucid monarchs sought neither to uproot indigenous religious traditions nor impose the Greek pantheon in their place. Quite the contrary: much like their Achaemenid predecessors, the kings respected the sanctity of the Anatolian, Syrian, Babylonian, and Judean sanctuaries to the point of funding their monumentalization, bestowing tax exemptions on their estates, and incorporating priestly elites into their courtly circle. So it is jarring to realize that our only narratives of Seleucid-temple interactions in Iran report mutual hostility and imperial aggression—in 209 Antiochus III stripped the temple of Aine/Anahita at Ecbatana of almost 4000 talents' worth of precious metal (Polyb. 10.27); in 187 the same king died in an attempt to loot the sanctuary of Bel in Elymais (Diod. Sic. 28.3, 29.15; Strabo, *Geog.* 16.1.17; Just., *Epit.* 32.2.1; *1 Macc.* 6.1–16); and in 164 his son Antiochus IV attacked the Elymaean temple of Nanaya (Polyb. 31.9.1; *2 Macc.* 1.13–17; App., *Syr.* 66; Porphyry *FGrH* 260 F53, 56; Joseph, *Ant.* 12.9.1). It is likely that the latter two incidents formed part of broader Seleucid campaigns against an Elymaean insurrectionary movement (Dabrowa 2004), but it is not without significance that our Classical (and Jewish) sources focus on temple invasions and clerical resistance. Once again we are cursed by a complete lack of evidence for the first century of Seleucid domination and for the regular rhythms of provincial administration outside the specific moments of royal campaigning; but it is likely that the picture would more closely resemble the situation in the empire's other provinces.

The Seleucid presence in Iran, while peaceful and prosperous in comparison to Alexander's campaign and the Diadoch chaos, nevertheless repeatedly faced bitter challenge and resistance, in two modes. First, powerful Greco-Macedonian satraps revolted against the royal house during moments of dynastic strife or contested succession. In the troubled reign of Seleucus II (246–225), the far-off Diodotus, satrap of Bactria, and Andragoras, satrap of Parthia, gradually, peacefully, and successfully seceded from Seleucid sovereignty. As we have seen, Molon and Timarchus, governors of Media and general commanders of the Upper Satrapies during the reigns of Antiochus III and Demetrius I respectively, ruptured their ties and embarked on short-lived military expansion into Babylonia. Second, in the second century the empire was rocked by numerous indigenous uprisings led by powerful local elites, perhaps encouraged by Rome's defeat of Antiochus III at the battle of Magnesia (189), further dynastic squabbling, and the increasing appointment of local aristocrats to positions of regional authority. In the empire's western hemisphere the Hasmonaeans in Judea, the Orontids in Commagene, the Artaxiads in Armenia, and Hyspaosines and his successors in Mesene emancipated themselves. In Iran, the Fratarakā in Persis and the Kamnaskirids in Elymais broke from the Seleucids; Pliny the Elder reports an amphibious victory of Antiochus IV's general Numenius over Persians at the Straits of Hormuz (Pliny, *Nat. Hist.* 6.32.152). Most importantly, the Arsacids of Parthia, having already established a certain regional autonomy in the third century, rapidly expanded under Mithridates I to occupy Ecbatana in 147, Susa in about 140, and Seleucia-on-the-Tigris in 141 (the fullest recent examination of the late Seleucids is Ehling 2008).

The kingdom responded to these Iranian rebellions, insurrections, and invasions with episodic campaigns of reconquest from northern Syria led by reigning kings (Seleucus II in 230–227; Antiochus III in 222–220 and 212–205; Antiochus IV in 165–164; Demetrius I in 160; Demetrius II in 140–139; and Antiochus VII in 131–129). For obvious reasons the kings proved more successful against the closer Greco-Macedonian satraps, such as Molon and Timarchus, than against indigenous movements. Our accounts of these campaigns, brief and lacunose as they are, indicate a remarkable capacity for imperial rejuvenation based, to a large extent, on the continuing loyalty of the Greco-Macedonian colonies to the Seleucid house. For instance, Josephus reports that the colonists of the Iranian plateau dispatched envoy after envoy to Demetrius II promising to join him if he appeared among them (Josephus, *Jew. Antiq.* 13.185). However, with the exception of Antiochus III's great *anabasis*, the kings' brilliant early successes in lowland Mesopotamia or the rises to Media were followed hard by their defeat, imprisonment, and death on the Iranian plateau.

Ultimately, the kingdom was unable to adequately and consistently resist indigenous insurrection or Parthian expansion. The causes are numerous but three fault-lines stand out. The systematic concentration of imperial ideology and practice on the person of the monarch meant that neither subordinates nor regional administrators were effective substitutes for the king's body, while the ever-increasing centrality of northern Syria and the undeniable pull of the Mediterranean, marginalizing the Iranian territories, made the kings' absence the more typical provincial experience. Moreover, it seems that the kings had failed to cultivate a support base much beyond the nodes of colonial settlement, never sufficiently persuading indigenous elites to identify imperial interests with their own. Finally, dynastic strife (pretenders, usurpers, cadet branches), by no means uncommon in the third century but out of control from the 160s (and egged on by Rome, the Attalids, and the Ptolemies), shattered the kings' monopoly on sovereignty and the loyalties attendant on it, absorbed the empire's energies and resources, and offered opportunity for rebellion, emancipation, and expansion. After Antiochus VII's suicide in Media in 129, the rump of the once-great Seleucid Empire imploded in a paroxysm of decline. After one hundred and fifty years of Seleucid domination in Iran, Parthian hegemony was secured for the next three and a half centuries.

It is hard to resist the impression that the Seleucid footprint was light, that the imperial gaze lay far to the west, and that the provincialization of Iran, begun by Alexander, continued apace under his Seleucid successors. All that is certainly true. Yet the dynasty demonstrated a continual concern for western Iran (Media and Susiana) and repeatedly if infrequently attempted to reinforce or restore their control over this and more easterly regions. The foundation of Greco-Macedonian colonies profoundly altered the land's demography, culture, and religious life, and continued to do so long into the Parthian period. The modalities of rebellion and the forms of independent monarchy that followed underline the successful penetration of the Seleucid royal image and imperial discourse in this region.

FURTHER READING

The bibliography on Alexander the Great is immense. Briant (2010) offers a concise and useful introduction to the major issues. For Hellenistic epigraphy, see *IEO*; for Seleucid numismatics, see the recent catalogs Houghton and Lorber (2002) and Houghton et al. (2008). For Seleucid imperial structures, see Capdetrey (2007), and for the narrative of Seleucid decline, Ehling (2008).

REFERENCES

Aperghis, M. 2004. *The Seleukid royal economy*. Cambridge: Cambridge University Press.
Badian, E. 1967. Agis III. *Hermes* 95: 170–92.
——. 2000. Conspiracies. In *Alexander the Great in fact and fiction* ed. A. B. Bosworth and E. Baynham, 50–95. Oxford: Oxford University Press.
Bar-Kochva, B. 1976. *The Seleucid army*. Cambridge: Cambridge University Press.
Bengtson, H. 1944. *Die Strategie in der hellenistischen Zeit*. Munich: Beck.
Bernard, P. 1980. Héraclès, les grottes de Karafto et le sanctuaire du mont Sambulos en Iran. *StIr* 9/2: 301–24.
Bickerman, E. 1963. À propos d'un passage de Charès de Mytliène. *Parola del Passato* 91: 241–55.
Bonnet, C. 1992. Héraclès en Orient: interprétations et syncrétismes. In *Héraclès: d'une rive à l'autre de la Méditerrané*, ed. C. Bonnet and C. Jourdain-Annequin, 165–98. Brussels: Academia Belgica and Rome: École française de Rome.
Borza, E. 1972. Fire from Heaven: Alexander at Persepolis. *CP* 67: 233–45.
Bosworth, A.B. 1980. Alexander and the Persians. *JHS* 100: 1–21.
——. 1988. *From Arrian to Alexander*. Oxford: Clarendon Press.
——. 2002. *The legacy of Alexander: Politics, warfare and propaganda under the Successors*. Oxford: Oxford University Press.
Boyce, M. and F. Grenet 1991. *A history of Zoroastrianism*, vol. 3, *Zoroastrianism under Macedonian and Roman Rule*. Leiden: HdO 8/1/2/2/3.
Briant, P. 1982a. *État et pasteurs au Moyen-Orient ancient*. Cambridge: Cambridge University Press.
——. 1982b. Conquête territoriale et conquête idéologique: Alexandre le Grand et l'idéologie monarchique achéménide. In *Rois, tributs et paysans: Études sur les formations tributaires du Moyen-Orient ancien*, ed. P. Briant, 357–403. Paris: Centre de Recherches d'Histoire Ancienne 43 / Annales littéraires de l'Université de Besançon 269.
——. 2002. *From Cyrus to Alexander: A history of the Persian Empire*. Winona Lake: Eisenbrauns.

———. 2010. *Alexander the Great and his empire: A short introduction.* Princeton: Princeton University Press.

Callieri, P. 2007. *L'archéologie du Fārs à l'époque hellénistique.* Paris: Persika 11.

Capdetrey, L. 2007. *Le pouvoir séleucide: territoire, administration, finances d'un royaume hellénistique, 312–129 av. J.-C.* Rennes: Presses Universitaires de Rennes.

Cohen, G. 1978. *The Seleucid colonies.* Wiesbaden: Historia-Einzelschriften 30.

Dabrowa, E. 2004. Les Séleucides et l'Élymaïde. *Parthica* 6: 107–15.

Ehling, K. 2008. *Untersuchungen zur Geschichte der späten Seleukiden (164–63 v. Chr.).* Stuttgart: Historia-Einzelschriften 196.

Fischer, T. 1970. *Untersuchungen zum Partherkrieg Antiochos' VII.* Dissertation. Tübingen.

Flower, M. 2000. Alexander the Great and Panhellenism. In *Alexander the Great in fact and fiction,* eds. A. B. Bosworth and E. Baynham, 96–135. Oxford: Oxford University Press.

Foucher, A. 1942. *La vieille route de l'Inde de Bactres à Taxila.* Paris: Mémoires de la Délégation archéologique française en Afghanistan 1.

Fredricksmeyer, E. 2000. Alexander the Great and the kingship of Asia. In *Alexander the Great in fact and fiction,* eds. A. Bosworth and E. Baynham, 136–66. Oxford: Oxford University Press.

Gardiner-Garden, J. 1987. *Greek conceptions of Inner Asian geography and ethnography from Ephoros to Eratosthenes.* Bloomington: University of Indiana Research Institute for Inner Asian Studies.

Ghirshman, R. 1975. Un bas-relief parthe de la Collection Foroughi. *Artibus Asiae* 37: 229–39.

Henkelman, W. 2011. Parnakka's Feast: *šip* in Pārsa and Elam. *EP:* 89–166.

Herzfeld, E. 1935. *Archaeological history of Iran.* London: Oxford University Press.

Hornblower, J. 1981. *Hieronymus of Cardia.* Oxford: Oxford University Press.

Houghton, A., and C. Lorber. 2002. *Seleucid coins: A comprehensive catalogue. Part 1: Seleucus I through Antiochus III.* New York: American Numismatic Society.

Houghton, A., C. Lorber, and O. Hoover. 2008. *Seleucid coins: A comprehensive catalogue. Part 2: Seleucus IV through Antiochus XIII.* New York: American Numismatic Society.

Iossif, P. and C. Lorber. 2009. The cult of Helios in the Seleucid East. *Topoi* 16: 19–42.

Kaizer, T. 2000. The "Heracles figure" at Hatra and Palmyra: Problems of interpretation. *Iraq* 62: 219–32.

Kosmin, P. 2013. Rethinking the Hellenistic Gulf: The new Greek inscription from Bahrain. *JHS* 133: 67–79.

Kuhrt, A. and S. Sherwin-White. 1993. *From Samarkhand to Sardis.* Berkeley: University of California Press.

Le Rider, G. 1965. *Suse sous les Séleucides et les Parthes. Les trouvailles monétaires et l'histoire de la ville.* Paris: MMAI 38.

Lerner, J. 1999. *The impact of Seleucid decline on the eastern Iranian plateau.* Stuttgart: Franz Steiner Verlag.

Lewis, D. 1977. *Sparta and Persia.* Leiden: Brill.

Luschey, H. 1974. Bisutun: Geschichte und Forschungsgeschichte. *AA* 89: 114–49.

Ma, J. 1999. *Antiochus III and the cities of western Asia Minor.* Oxford: Oxford University Press.

Miller, M. 1997. *Athens and Persia in the fifth century BC: A study in cultural receptivity.* Cambridge: Cambridge University Press.

Minns, E. 1915. Parchments of the Parthian period from Avroman in Kurdistan. *JHS* 35: 22–65.

Mittag, P. F. 2006. *Antiochus IV. Epiphanes: Eine politische Biographie.* Berlin: Klio-Beiheft N.F. 11.

Mørkholm, O. 1966. *Antiochus IV of Syria*. Copenhagen: Gyldendal.
Mookerji, R. 1995. *Asoka*. London: Macmillan.
Muccioli, F. 2004. "Il regno dell'Asia": Ideologia e propaganda da Alessandro Magno a Mitridate VI. *Simbolos* 4: 105–58.
Neumann, K. 1884. Die Fahrt des Patrokles auf dem Kaspischen Meere und der alte Lauf des Oxus. *Hermes* 19: 165–85.
Parke, H. 1985. The massacre of the Branchidae. *JHS* 105: 59–68.
Pearson, L. 1960. *The Lost Histories of Alexander the Great*. New York: American Philological Association.
Raaflaub, K. 2009. Learning from the enemy: Athenian and Persian "instruments of empire." In *Interpreting the Athenian Empire*, ed. J. Ma, N. Papazarkadas, and R. Parker, 89–124. London: Duckworth.
Robert, L. 1967. Encore une inscription grecque de l'Iran. *CRAIBL*: 281–96.
Root, M. 1985. The Parthenon frieze and the Apadana reliefs at Persepolis: Reassessing a programmatic relationship. *AJA* 89: 103–20.
Sachs, A. J., and H. Hunger. 1988. *Astronomical diaries and related texts from Babylonia I. Diaries from 652 B.C. to 262 B.C*. Vienna: Denkschriften der Österreichischen Akademie der Wissenschaften, phil.-hist. Kl 195.
Sancisi-Weerdenburg, H. 1993. Alexander and Persepolis. In *Alexander the Great: Reality and myth*, ed. J. Carlsen, 177–88. Rome: Danish Institute.
Schmitt, H. 1964. *Geschichte Antiochos' des Grossen*. Wiesbaden: Franz Steiner Verlag.
Sherwin-White, S. 1987. Seleucid Babylonia: A case study for the installation and development of Greek rule. In *Hellenism in the East*, ed. A. Kuhrt and S. Sherwin-White, 1–31. Berkeley: University of California Press.
Tarn, W. 1940. Two Notes on Seleucid History: 1. Seleucus' 500 Elephants, 2. Tamita. *JHS* 60: 84–94.
———. 1951. *The Greeks in Bactria and India*. Cambridge: Cambridge University Press.
van der Spek, R. 2000. The effect of war on the prices of barley and agricultural land in Hellenistic Babylonia. In *Economie antique. La guerre dans les économies antiques*, ed. J. Andreau, P. Briant, and R. Descat, 293–313. Saint-Bertrand-de-Comminges: Entretiens d'archéologie et d'histoire 5.
van Nuffelen, P. 2004. Le culte royale de l'empire des Séleucides: Une réinterpretation. *Historia* 53: 278–301.
Wiesehöfer, J. 1994. *Die "dunklen Jahrhunderte" der Persis*. Munich: Zetemata 90.
Will, É. 1979–82. *Histoire politique du monde hellénistique*. 2nd ed. Nancy: Presses Universitaires de Nancy.
Wolski, J. 1960. Les Iraniens et le royaume gréco-bactrien. *Klio* 38: 110–21.

CHAPTER 35

MEDIA, KHUZESTAN, AND FARS BETWEEN THE END OF THE ACHAEMENIDS AND THE RISE OF THE SASANIANS

PIERFRANCESCO CALLIERI AND
ALIREZA ASKARI CHAVERDI

INTRODUCTION

Despite the existence of a series of sources (Wiesehöfer 1994), the period between the end of the Achaemenid empire and the rise of the Sasanian dynasty can be considered one of the "dark ages" in the history of Iran. Archaeological research on this period has been neglected for decades and only in recent years have comprehensive projects dedicated to it been conducted. On a historic level, the end of the Achaemenid empire and its conquest by Alexander the Great represent a crucial phase in the history of Iran because the complex process of encounter and fusion between Hellenism and Iranism (cf. Sherwin-White and Kuhrt 1993) that belongs to what is generally described as the "Hellenization" of Asia reached the core of the largest empire of the ancient Near East (Callieri 2001a). At the same time, the Seleucid kings did not reign everywhere for the same length of time before the Arsacid conquest of most of the Iranian plateau and adjoining areas in the mid-second century BC. In Media Seleucid power lasted until about 145 BC, when the region was conquered by the Arsacids. Elymais and Susiana were under Seleucid domination until the Arsacid conquest of the plateau, but the beginning of local coinage around 147 BC suggests that the local Kamnaskirid dynasty took advantage of these conflicts, retaining power in Elymais until the mid-first century AD, while Susa, on the other hand, had a more troubled history. A new, local dynasty bearing Arsacid names took power until the very end of the Arsacid period, when Susa at least was ruled by the Arsacid Artabanus V, who lost his city and his kingdom to Ardašīr I in 224. As for Fars, the end of Seleucid rule is linked to the beginning of the coinage issued by the local dynasts of Fars bearing the title *frataraka* (Chapter 36). While the traditional dating of 300–250 BC would assign Fars a very short-lived Seleucid rule, a new chronology for the coin issues (Alram 1986) and a reexamination of the historical sources (Wiesehöfer 1994) have shifted the beginnings of the *frataraka* coinage to 200–180 BC (contra Curtis 2010). In fact, Fars was never under direct Arsacid rule, and the use of the term "Arsacid" for Fars is only convention. Political history thus followed different paths in each of the three regions considered here.

In the more than five centuries of this period we can single out two main cultural phases. The first, lasting until the first century BC, including the Macedonian, Seleucid, and Early Arsacid periods, can be defined as Post-Achaemenid or Hellenistic according to the prevailing cultural orientation. On the Iranian plateau the Achaemenid heritage was strong, surviving the end of Achaemenid rule, particularly in Fars, the cradle of the dynasty, but at the same time the Seleucids continued the policy of interest in Asia that had characterized Alexander's kingdom, with the foundation of colonies and establishments that contributed to the diffusion of Hellenistic culture, lasting into the three first centuries of the Arsacid empire. If, on the whole, the Greco-Macedonian presence on the plateau differed from region to region, all three areas investigated in the present essay offer evidence of this presence. Media, corresponding to the present provinces of Hamadan, Kermanshahan, Kurdistan and Luristan in western-central Iran, represented the strategic point of contact between Mesopotamia and the Iranian plateau. Susiana, in modern-day Khuzestan, along with the Zagros piedmont of Elymais, was a particularly fertile agricultural region. Even Persis—modern Fars, Bushehr, and part of Hormozgan provinces—although generally considered of marginal importance in the Seleucid kingdom, seems to have had a Hellenistic presence.

For the second phase, starting in the first century AD, even though it is often termed "Parthian" in the literature, we use the term "Arsacid," because of the distinct cultural re-orientation of this dynasty, which also shaped the cultural milieu from which the Sasanian dynasty arose. Despite some important contributions to the study of pottery (Haerinck 1983), the difficulty in dating archaeological evidence from these centuries makes it impossible to attribute every piece of archaeological evidence to one or the other of these two phases. Therefore, the exposition of the archaeological evidence here will follow the chronological scheme used within each region and site, under a common heading for the two phases.

Media

Traversed by the major route linking the eastern capital of the Seleucid kingdom, Seleucia-on-the-Tigris, with the "Upper Satrapies" (i.e., the Iranian plateau and Central Asia), Media received great attention from the Seleucids and indeed, despite a shortage of archaeological research, the epigraphic and topographic evidence taken as a whole shows this to have been one of the major areas in Iran with a Hellenistic presence.

Ecbatana, the former summer capital of the Achaemenid empire (modern Hamadan), continued to be an important town during the Seleucid and Arsacid periods. Excavations there between 1983 and 1999 at Tepe-ye Hegmataneh, where the old houses of this quarter of the city center were demolished in order to allow archaeological investigation, brought to light parts of a great mudbrick architectural complex with a plan of remarkable regularity. The first report did not give any information on associated finds and refrained from suggesting a date (Sarraf 1997). The regularity of the residential complex was tentatively interpreted as possible evidence of use in the Seleucid period (Boucharlat 1998), when the older Achaemenid structures are said by Strabo to have been used by the Seleucid kings (*Geog.* 11.13.5). Further soundings produced reliable stratigraphic and ceramic evidence that dates the complex to the late Arsacid period (Azarnoush 2007). From Hamadan we also have a gray limestone male head which may be of Mithridates II (Kawami 1987: 51–3).

As for the famous Sang-e Shir ("lion of Hamadan"), an over life-size sculpture of a lion in the round revealing, despite its poor state of preservation, a naturalistic conception typical of Hellenistic sculpture, it has been suggested that this belonged to the cenotaph commissioned by Alexander to commemorate his companion Hephaestion on the site of his death (Luschey 1968). Excavations in a nearby cemetery revealed simple inhumations in flexed position, attributed to the late Achaemenid period; terracotta sarcophagi and jar burials of Seleucid date; and boat-shaped, terracotta sarcophagi dated to the early Arsacid period on the basis of associated coins from the late second century BC (Azarnoush 1975, 1976, 1979). The evidence of settlement in the Hamadan region has been expanded by the recent discovery of Arsacid-period sites on the northern slopes of Mount Alvand (Motarjem and Balmaki 2009).

The existence of Greco-Macedonian colonies in Media, structured exactly like other Hellenistic *poleis*, is attested by the important Greek inscription from Nehavand, ancient Laodicea (Robert 1949; Rougemont 2012). The inscription is carved on a stele crowned by a tympanum on small columns, now in the National Museum of Tehran. Dated to 193 BC, the text preserves an edict issued by Antiochus III upon the institution of the cult in honor of his queen Laodice. A second, fragmentary version of the same text was found near Kermanshah, while a third copy was discovered in Phrygia (Anatolia). In all three cases the text of the edict itself is preceded by a letter from the sovereign to the local authorities (Robert 1967).

These inscriptions are of considerable importance, both because they provide a picture of the administrative structure of the Seleucid satrapies in Iran and because they serve as evidence of a Seleucid royal cult practiced in the temples mentioned in the inscriptions. One of these was very probably the site in Nehavand that, as recently as the early twentieth century, still displayed six columns. Identified by Ghirshman as a Hellenistic building (Robert 1949: 21), it has never been investigated. Also found at this site were a small, circular stone altar adorned with a garland in relief and five bronze statuettes of Hellenistic divinities, all of Hellenistic craftsmanship, now in the National

Museum in Tehran. Regardless of the complexity of their dating (Invernizzi 2000: 247–9)—these objects have been variously considered late Hellenistic works of the first century BC or Roman products (Fleischer 2000: 223)—they reflect the historical importance of Laodicea, a point emphasized by yet another Greek inscription from 183/182 BC honoring the governor of the "Upper Satrapies" (Robert 1950). It is not, perhaps, by chance that the so-called "Karen treasure," which includes Hellenistic metalware, is supposed to have originated in Nehavand (Herzfeld 1928; Khachatrian 1989: 299).

On the main road between Ecbatana and Seleucia, at Bisotun—site of the rock relief of Darius I and of an open-air shrine (Kleiss and Calmeyer 1996)—is a relief depicting Heracles Kallinikos recumbent on a lion skin, accompanied by a Greek inscription dated to 148 BC (Hakemi 1958; Robert 1963: 76; Bonanno Aravantinos 1991: 170; Luschey 1996b). The addition of a quiver and arrows to the traditional iconography of Heracles depicts the god as a hunter and allows the identification of Bisotun Mountain with the Mount Sambulos mentioned by Tacitus (*Ann.* 12.13) in connection with the cult of a local Heracles (Boyce and Grenet 1991: 91–4). While the *leontis* in low relief could be an earlier—possibly Elamite—creation, the image of the naked Greek hero, holding a goblet in his hand, in high relief is nearly sculpture in the round. However, Heracles' physiognomy, particularly his body, betrays the sculptor's local origins in an area where, by the time the sculpture was made, naturalism had virtually disappeared. The dedicatory inscription is of particular interest since it expresses a sort of ex-voto wish for for Kleomenes, the Seleucid governor of the "Upper Satrapies," to achieve victory over the Parthians. The wish was expressed by one Hyakinthos, whose father bore the Macedonian name Pantauchos, thus attesting to the presence of Macedonian settlers in the region. Traces of an Aramaic translation of the text have been interpreted as a local, "nationalistic" proclamation (Huyse 1996: 66).

Moreover, two rock reliefs dated between the second and first centuries BC are also located at Bisotun, one of which depicts a king (?) (Mithridates II?) before four dignitaries, while the other shows a horseman named Gotarzes, identified, on no solid grounds, with the Arsacid sovereign of the same name. The continued use of Greek in the region is indicated by the inscriptions accompanying these reliefs.

The stone block in the *Partherhang* of Bisotun, preserving the frontal representations of a king standing before an altar, flanked by two assistants (Gall 1996), is evidence of the diffusion onto the Iranian plateau of so-called "Parthian art" of Syro-Mesopotamian origin in the later Arsacid period. The Parthian inscription on the altar mentions Vologases, king of kings (Gropp 1970: 200–1), probably a reference to Vologases II, who reigned in the early second century AD. Finds dated to the Seleucid and Arsacid periods have also been identified in the settlement and graves on the eastern slope of Bisotun Mountain (Kleiss 1970, 1996).

An imposing architectural complex at Kangavar, between Bisotun and Hamadan, was long attributed to the Seleucid period and later to the Arsacid era. Much of the enormous basement of this structure remains intact. An exterior wall of ashlar masonry has, on its south side, two flights of stairs meeting in the center. This building has been identified by various scholars as the temple of Anahita at Concobar mentioned by Isidore of

Charax in his *Parthian Stations* (§6) (Kambaksh Fard 2007), but M. Azarnoush demonstrated that it dates to the late Sasanian period and was probably a palace (of Xosrow II?) (Azarnoush 1981, 1999). On the other hand, graves attributed to the Arsacid period, both terracotta coffins covered with stone slabs and jar burials, have been excavated at the site (Azarnoush 1981: 69–71; Kambaksh Fard 2007 2: 9–50). Finally, a survey of the Kangavar Valley located ninety-five settlements dated to the Arsacid period (Young 1975).

Moving on to the region of Kermanshah, an Arsacid-period settlement with an adjacent graveyard has been identified at Kuh-e Paru, not far from the Sasanian reliefs at Taq-e Bustan (Matheson 1976: 131). From Denavar come three fragments of a large basin made of local, porous limestone rendered waterproof with yellow plaster (now in the National Museum, Tehran). Decorated with the heads of Silenus and a Maenad issuing forth from what has been interpreted as Dionysus' *nebris*, they are rendered in a naturalistic style and on stylistic grounds have been dated to the third or early second century BC (Parlasca 1991: 457; Luschey 1996a). Associated speculatively by Ghirshman (1972: 189) with a temple of Dionysus that he suggested was built by Greeks who saw the Kermanshah Plain as Dionysus' birthplace, these fragments should more cautiously be considered evidence of a sculptural school of Hellenistic inspiration, dating to the Seleucid period, but very probably consisting of local craftsmen, as suggested by both the stone used and the fairly massive dimensions of the pieces. Two further stone Silenus heads from the same area might have belonged to the same basin (Luschey 1996a: 266), as indeed might four other fragments now in private collections (Parlasca 1991: 457). In the early twentieth century a fragmentary Greek epitaph which probably preceded an epigram was found near Kermanshah (Robert 1967: 295).

Several monumental rock-cut tombs in Media (Qyzqapan, Dukkan-e Da'ud, Fakhriqa), although attributed by Herzfeld to the Medes, in fact date to the post-Achaemenid period. Their iconographic program seems to echo fairly closely the tombs of Darius I and his successors, with a palace façade and a ritual scene with fire altar. However, the presence of Ionic capitals and the distance between the two pairs of half-columns shown suggest a date in the fourth or third century BC (Gall 1966, 1974; Huff 1971).

Further north, a Greek dedication to Heracles incised on the entrance to a complex of rooms excavated in the rock at Karafto, in northern Kurdistan, and dated between the fourth and third centuries BC (Robert 1946–47: 364), has given rise to contrasting interpretations of the complex itself. Rather than a sanctuary dedicated to the cult of Heracles, as suggested by Sir Aurel Stein (Stein 1940: 340–2), it is now considered more likely to have been the residence of an officer in charge of the border between Media, then a part of the Seleucid kingdom, and Media Atropatene, where an Iranian dynasty ruled (Bernard 1980; cf. Hamzalu and Mir Eskandari 2002–3).

A new interpretation has also been proposed for the architectural complex at Khorheh, southeast of Qom in north-central Iran. On the basis of of two slender columns of Ionic type, Herzfeld had identified Khorheh as a peripteral temple of Seleucid date (Herzfeld 1941: 283–4). Excavations by A. Hakemi in 1955 (Hakemi 1990) yielded no material predating the Arsacid period, and showed that the columns belong to a colonnaded portico in front of three rooms—the central one larger than the two side rooms—and a square hall surrounded by corridors. Subsequent surface investigations led W. Kleiss to interpret the building as a palace of the Arsacid period (Kleiss 1981b, 1985). In the last few years the Organization for the Conservation of the Cultural Heritage of Iran has returned to the site, correcting some of Hakemi's reconstructions. The portico evidently had a single row of columns, while the central room had a pilaster base in the middle (Rahbar 1999a).

Khuzestan

Another region where the post-Achaemenid period is characterized by a profound and lasting Hellenistic cultural presence—at least to judge by the abundance of epigraphic finds in Greek—is Susiana, the core of ancient Elam, a particularly fertile agricultural region, corresponding to the lower part of present-day Khuzestan. Sources mention the towns of Seleucia-on-the-Eulaeus (ancient Susa) and Seleucia-on-the-Hedyphon, a site yet to be located with any certainty (Le Rider 1965: 261).

While a Hellenistic-type administration, a cult of the dynasts, a gymnasium and a Seleucid garrison are attested epigraphically at Seleucia-on-the-Eulaeus (Le Rider 1965), the presence of a substantial colony of Greco-Macedonians and the survival of Greek institutions, even after the Arsacid conquest, are evidenced by a considerable number of inscriptions in Greek dating right up to the turn of the Christian era (Chapter 41; Huyse 1996: 69–70). Over and above the city's importance as a commercial center, it seems likely that favorable conditions for agriculture and the availability of water, as highlighted by one of the few studies on the settlement patterns of the historic periods in Iran (Wenke 1975–6: 104–15), excited the interest of the Seleucid sovereigns, as they did in neighboring Mesopotamia, to which Susiana was a natural adjunct.

Unfortunately, the poor methodology of the French excavations at Susa in the late nineteenth and early twentieth centuries complicate our understanding of the Seleucid, Arsacid, and Sasanian levels exposed (Martinez-Sève 2002b: 45–9). Nevertheless, based on the large stratigraphic excavation carried out by Ghirshman between 1946 and 1966, unfortunately unpublished, and subsequent excavations in the 1970s, it has been possible for L. Martinez-Sève to reconstruct the life of the city from the fourth to the first century BC (Martinez-Sève 2002b), when the city extended beyond the main four mounds investigated by the French mission (Boucharlat and Shahidi 1987; Recherches archéologiques françaises 2001). In the early Hellenistic period very few areas on the old settlement mounds of Susa bear traces of new structures, probably because the explored areas were then still the Royal City ("Ville Royale," see Chapter 26). The first extensive, new occupation which extended to parts of the palace of Darius I began around the mid-third century BC. The main architectural evidence from this period is a large house with a peristyle court and a wooden roof complete with terracotta tiles and antefixes, the mudbrick walls of which were painted with large, monochrome panels. The area of Darius' monumental gate and causeway was not part of the city until the first century BC, as shown by the fact that an urn containing a cremation burial was found, pointing to a funerary custom unattested in Greek cities. We know also that Seleucid-era inhabitants used part of the Shaur palace of Artaxerxes II (Labrousse and Boucharlat 1972: 55–96) and the Acropole, which was also used in the Arsacid period. The so-called "Ville des artisans," on the other hand, contained craft workshops and a necropolis with jar burials, sarcophagi, and vaulted, underground tombs during the Arsacid period (Boucharlat et al. 1987).

The archaeological finds from these centuries include, first and foremost, a great many terracottas, some of decidedly Hellenistic inspiration, including figurines (Martinez-Sève 2002a) as well as architectural elements such as tiles and antefixes (Labrousse and Boucharlat 1972: 95–6; Martinez-Sève 2002b: 41, 51). A marble head of Tyche, with crenellated crown, that bears the incised signature of the sculptor with the Greek name Antiochos son of Dryas, was identified in the past as queen Musa (Cumont 1939, contra Colledge 1990). Although thoroughly Hellenistic from a stylistic point of view, the stepped merlons on the crown and the plastic rendering of the iris suggest production in an Asian workshop (Colledge 1979: 225–6) sometime between 100 BC and 45 AD (Colledge 1990). The gradual weakening of Hellenistic craft traditions at Susa can be considered complete with the appearance of Parthian art of Syro-Mesopotamian origin. This is well attested by a stele commemorating the investiture of the satrap of Susa, Khwasak, by the Arsacid king Artabanus V, found in 1947 in the Ville Royale, on which the two figures are represented frontally and the accompanying inscription is in Aramaic rather than Greek (Ghirshman 1950).

In the early twentieth century, several sarcophagi dated to the Arsacid period were discovered at Bulaylah in the hinterland of Susa (Unvala 1929). In the graveyard of Gelalak, near Shushtar, five tombs dated to the first century AD were excavated in 1968 and 1986. The best preserved of these (no. 1) consists of a rectangular, subterranean chamber accessible via a small stairway covered with a barrel vault, the bricks of which stand on edge. Three terracotta coffins decorated with garlands and covered with lids were placed along the sides of the tomb chamber while two more graves were placed under the arches, below the level of the coffins. Tomb nos. 2 and 3 also have rectangular chambers, while tomb nos. 4 and 5 have square chambers (Rahbar 1997). East of Shushtar, a survey of the Mianab plain carried out by A. Moghaddam located sixty-one sites dated to the Seleucid and Arsacid periods (Khosrowzadeh and Aali 2005). Of these, thirty-one are concentrated in the northern part of the plain, where the large site of Dastova is located. In 1969 A. A. Sarfaraz discovered graves of the Arsacid period there (Sarfaraz 1970: 12–13). From an unspecified site in Khuzestan comes a plain, stone statue base in Hellenistic style with an Aramaic inscription dated according to the Seleucid era. Two depressions in the shape of feet with mortises for dowels show that it originally supported a bronze statue, presumably of Hellenistic type (Bashshâsh Kanzaq 1996).

In the mountainous region coming between Susiana, Media, and Persis, the Greek name of which, Elymais, suggests a direct connection with the ancient Elamite population, archaeological evidence of the Seleucid period is represented mainly by the small sanctuary of Shami and the two extensive complexes of Masjed-e Solayman and Bard-e Neshanda. These represent a particular type of cult place known in the archaeological literature as a "sacred terrace," that is, a natural hilltop bounded by walls upon which podia, altars, statue bases, and temples were built in successive stages. Although their excavator, R. Ghirshman, dated the foundation of these two cult sites to the Achaemenid period and dated the construction of the temples of Masjed-e Solayman to the post-Achaemenid period (Ghirshman 1976), a reexamination of the available evidence suggests that only the first phase of the Bard-e Neshanda and Masjed-e Solayman complexes dates to the post-Achaemenid period. A reanalysis of Ghirshman's excavation data from the upper terrace at Bard-e Neshanda sanctuary by E. Haerinck suggested it was founded sometime between the end of the Achaemenid period and 150 BC. This date is supported by the presence of eight Hellenistic and two Elymaean coins of Kamnaskires I (to whom a fragmentary inscription is also ascribed) in deposits belonging to the second phase of occupation at the site (Haerinck 1983: 13). With a square vestibule giving access to an oblong cella and two side rooms, the Bard-e Neshanda temple was probably only built in the late Arsacid period (Hannestad and Potts 1990: 115). The sculptural reliefs at the site, all of which are in the frontal, Syro-Mesopotamian "Parthian" style, date to the same period.

Ghirshman (1976) attributed the earliest phase of the two temples at Masjed-e Solayman to the Seleucid period. On the evidence of two bronze images of Athena and a great many terracotta figurines depicting Macedonian horsemen, the principal temple ("Grand Temple"), known in this phase only through some limited sondages, was dedicated to Athena Hyppia, according to the French scholar. On the other hand, the images of Heracles found near the second temple in its Arsacid phase suggest that the temple was already sacred to this hero in its Seleucid phase. Closer examination of the evidence reveals that these attributions and dating are in fact unfounded. While the open-air terraces may indeed date to the Seleucid period, between the third century and 150 BC (Haerinck 1983: 13–14; Martinez-Sève 2004: 199–200; but see Boyce and Grenet 1991: 44), we lack any clear evidence that would allow us to date the temples erected upon them earlier than the Arsacid period (Hannestad and Potts 1990: 115), the period to which the stone sculptures found there must be referred as well.

The small sanctuary of Shami was subjected to a brief excavation and survey in the 1930s, and while not stratigraphic, the work was thorough enough to convey an indication of the organization of the site (Stein 1940). Within an enclosure wall built of mudbrick on stone foundations were a parallelepiped altar and two paved areas, all of baked brick, with seven stones bases—not found *in situ*—for eleven or twelve bronze statues of various sizes, the remains of which were found in the area, deliberately reduced to fragments. The great quantity of charcoal and ash suggests there may have originally been a wooden roof, possibly only partial, above the statues. Apart from the famous bronze statue of the "Parthian prince" in the National Museum (Tehran), certainly dating to the Arsacid period (Godard 1937), some fragments appear to be from bronze images of Greek divinities. Others belonged to a naturalistic head of a ruler (Seleucid or local in

Hellenistic guise), which suggests the existence of the sanctuary in the Seleucid period (Cumont 1936; Sherwin-White 1984; Callieri 2001b). A small head in white marble which Stein interpreted as a Hellenistic Aphrodite but which could just as well be an expression of a local version of Artemis (Stein 1940: 134; cf. Kawami 1987: 218, n. 56; Parlasca 1991: 460, with dating to the late fifth century BC) was also found at Shami, along with a small altar and various other artifacts of a cultic nature.

We also owe to the mountainous Bakhtiyari region a naturalistic marble torso from a small, composite statue now in the National Museum of Iran, representing a female deity. The piece shows iconographic traits common to both Artemis and Aphrodite but with some original features, and might represent Nanaya, the main goddess of Susa (see Chapter 41). It attests to the widespread nature of Hellenistic sculptural production and was probably crafted in an Oriental workshop between the third and the first centuries BC (Fleischer 2000: 229; Callieri 2003a).

Rock reliefs constitute the most typical genre of art production in Elymais during the later Arsacid period (see Chapter 38). These have been found at various sites including Tang-e Sarvak, Khong-e Azhdar, Khong-e Yar-e Alivand, Khong-e Kamalvand, Bidzard, Tang-e Butan, Shimbar, Kuh-e Taraz, Bard-e But, and Kuh-e Tina. Some of these are accompanied by Aramaic inscriptions. Expressions of local religiosity, these reliefs attest to the diffusion in the region, during the second and third centuries AD, of the main features of "Parthian art" (Vanden Berghe and Schippmann 1985; Mathiesen 1992). The main exception to this is the relief of Khong-e Azhdar (also known as Khong-e Nowruzi), where the image of a mounted, diademed figure in profile contrasts with a series of other figures shown in full frontal view. The hypothesis that the two scenes date to two different phases (Mathiesen 1992) has recently been confirmed by an Irano-Italian expedition (Messina and Mehr Kian 2010, 2011), whose work for the first time explains the presence of a second or first century BC profile bust alongside frontal figures of "Parthian" type. In the past, the mounted figure in profile has been identified with one of the kings named Mithridates, but it could also be one of the early Elymaean kings of the Kamnaskirid dynasty (Messina and Mehr Kian 2010, 2011). The Irano-Italian mission has also excavated some sondages at the foot of the boulder on which the reliefs were carved, revealing the presence of stone structures that were modified around the mid-first century BC.

FARS

In the post-Achaemenid period, Fars (Gr. Persis) does not seem to have enjoyed the same pre-eminence under the Seleucids that it had under the Achaemenids. Possible reasons for this may have been its limited agricultural potential, compared to Susiana, and the marginal position it occupied with respect to the major land route for traffic between the Mediterranean and Central Asia (the Great Khorasan Road) that crossed the plateau further north, between Media and Parthia, despite its importance as a conduit for traffic between eastern Iran and southern Mesopotamia (Wiesehöfer 1996b: 37). However, even though no important settlements of the Seleucid period have yet been identified—the locations of the main Greek foundations recorded in the sources, Antioch-in-Persis, Laodicea-in-Persis and Seleucia-on-the Persian Gulf, are uncertain Callieri 2007a: 24–8)—evidence of a Greek presence is not lacking.

Use of the Greek language is attested by inscriptions belonging to two distinct classes: the two milestones from Pasargadae (Lewis 1978: 161; Bivar 1978) and Persepolis (Kabiri 1993–4; Callieri 1995), which reflect the existence of a well-organized road system and thus of the involvement of Greco-Macedonians in territorial control, and inscriptions from the so-called "temple of the *fratarakas*," a monumental complex brought to light by E. Herzfeld *c.*200 m to the north-northwest of the main terrace of Persepolis. The latter, long unpublished apart from brief references by Herzfeld and the epigraphist L. Robert (Herzfeld 1935: 44; 1941: 275; Robert 1967: 282; Rougemont 1999: 6; see now *IGIAC*), consists of the names of five Olympian divinities in the genitive case typical of inscriptions on altars—*Dios Megistou, Heliou, Athenas Basileias, Artemidos, Apollonos*—incised on five thick limestone slabs (*c.*30 × 10 × 10 cm) that are in fact reused Achaemenid architectural elements. Unfortunately, the exact location(s) in which these were found is unknown (Callieri 2007a: 56).

A review of the archaeological evidence from Fars begins in the center of the province where archaeological work has been the most intensive. After the early surveys of L. Vanden Berghe (1952, 1953, 1954) and P. Gotch (1968, 1969), the main survey undertaken was that of the Marv Dasht Plain or Kur River Basin by W. M. Sumner. This work is particularly important because it was carried out before major leveling and earthmoving during the 1970s, conducted in connection with agricultural expansion, drastically altered the surface of the plain (Sumner 1986). Unfortunately, the set of type-fossils used by Sumner for the identification of Achaemenid sites on survey were taken from an excavation dump near the *frataraka* temple excavated by Herzfeld (Sumner 1986: 3, fig. 1), a monument very likely to date to the post-Achaemenid period. Moreover, even Sumner stressed the similarity of his type-fossils to material from Persepolis, dated by Schmidt to the late Achaemenid period, and Pasargadae, attributed by Stronach to the fourth and third centuries BC (Stronach 1978: 183–4; cf. Sumner 1986: 3–4). Indeed, Sumner based the Achaemenid attribution of his sites on comparanda which could just as easily be post-Achaemenid. Therefore, we can rely on Sumner's dating only when other diagnostics, such as architectural elements and techniques, are attested as well (Sumner 1986: 7).

The influence of Sumner's conclusions is evident in later works, such as the survey of the upper Kur River Basin by A. Alizadeh, who attributed only one site to the Arsacid period in contrast to thirty-nine sites of alleged Achaemenid date (Alizadeh 1997: 72). In fact, new material brought to light by the Irano-Italian excavations at Tang-e Bolaghi, Pasargadae, and Persepolis confirm the remarkable continuity of pottery production during the Achaemenid and post-Achaemenid periods already documented on the Tall-e Takht at Pasargadae by Stronach. Bearing this in mind, published chronological attributions of survey sites by Sumner and Alizadeh should be regarded with great caution and the hypothesized, predominantly nomadic occupation of Fars in the post-Achaemenid period put forward by R. Boucharlat (Boucharlat 2003: 265), which was influenced by Alizadeh's attributions, must be reconsidered.

Due to the difficulty of distinguishing Achaemenid from post-Achaemenid pottery, the date of the material from Qasr-e Abu Nasr, on the outskirts of Shiraz (Whitcomb 1985: 150; Sumner 1986: 19), and sites near Lake Maharlu (Kleiss 1973: 69) is still debated. Particularly in the case of Qasr-e Abu Nasr, dated by Sumner to the Achaemenid period, D. Whitcomb suggested a date range from "Seleucid or Parthian" (Whitcomb 1985: 150) to "probably late Parthian" (104), while R. Boucharlat wrote more generally of a post-Achaemenid date (Boucharlat 2005: 231). It is important to recall that, in the 1930s, hundreds of stone cairn tombs stood on the ridges behind Qasr-e Abu Nasr, similar to those found by Sir Aurel Stein at Baghan near Kavar (Stein 1936: 114). Twelve of these cairns were excavated by the Metropolitan Museum of Art and the few Arsacid coins recovered in them all date from the first century BC to the first century AD (Whitcomb 1985: 210–16; Boucharlat 1989: 687). The foot of a small Hellenistic-Roman statue was also discovered at Qasr-e Abu Nasr in a Sasanian context (Whitcomb 1985: 190, fig. 73j).

Further to north, on the western part of the Marv Dasht Plain, the "sparse Partho-Persis material" discovered at Tal-e Malyan includes evidence of the typically Greek custom of placing an obol for Charon in the mouth of the deceased (Balcer 1978: 86–7). Nearby at Qal'a-ye Now, surface survey suggested the existence of a "substantial Parthian site" (Balcer 1978: 90) where a large male head of limestone, belonging to a bust probably associated with architectural elements, was discovered that is remarkably similar to a head discovered at Tomb-e Bot in southern Fars (see below). The poor state of preservation of the head does not hide the naturalistic rendering of volume, while the presence of a mustache, beard, and tall headdress on bulging hair suggest a date in the late Arsacid period, immediately before the rise of the Sasanians (Kawami 1987: 138–9, 222; Curtis 1998: 65). This attribution brings us to the question of the location of the seat of the rulers of Fars who, according to Ṭabarī, lived at al-Bayḍa', identified with the present village of Bayza', near Tal-e Malyan, in the period immediately before the rise of Ardašīr ī Pābagān (Bosworth 1990: 6, n. 17). A careful survey of this site in the late 1980s by D. Huff identified pottery of the Seleucid-Arsacid period as well as several stone architectural elements of Achaemenid type and workmanship, which Huff believed were brought there from Persepolis in the Seleucid or Arsacid period. Huff put forward the hypothesis that they belonged originally to a monumental building at the seat of the rulers of Fars (Huff 1991: 63, 67).

At Persepolis, the southwestern corner of the Terrace has, in particular, yielded evidence of the post-Achaemenid period. Schmidt found the remains of a post-Achaemenid building on the site of the so-called Palace H, in which materials from destroyed Achaemenid palaces were recycled (Schmidt 1953: 43, 279–80). Subsequent study and restoration by G. and A. B. Tilia (Tilia 1972: 255–8, 315–16; 1977: 74–6; 1978: 258, 315; cf. Wiesehöfer 1994a: 68–79; Boucharlat 2006: 451–5) confirmed that the building included a podium, today visible in the unexcavated hillock, to which access was gained via a stairway that had been brought from the destroyed palace of Artaxerxes III (so-called Palace G). The podium was supported by a revetment wall built with reused blocks and filled with earth and fragments of sculptural and architectural elements. On it stood partition walls, the lowest courses of which are preserved, as well as columns, only the rough-hewn stone foundations of which remain. A mudbrick wall enclosed a courtyard to the north of the building, perhaps as far as the so-called *tačara* of Darius I, where Schmidt also found traces of reuse (Schmidt 1953: 279). Schmidt thought the courtyard probably belonging to the same phase as the pavillion to the south of Palace H, on an intermediate step at the southern edge of the terrace (Schmidt 1953: 43).

The attempted reoccupation of the Palace G area, indicated by the closing of a drain in the western part of the area using blocks from the horned parapet of the southwestern corner of the terrace, probably dates to a different phase (Tilia 1972: 316). The traces of this new occupation are all the more relevant when we remember that the excavators of the 1930s were not particularly concerned with the stratigraphy of the deposits overlying the imposing remains of Achaemenid date, and destroyed a precious series of occupation surfaces and collapsed mudbrick walls which no doubt would have allowed us to establish a secure sequence for these now isolated architectural episodes, leaving very little documentation of their work. If Schmidt gave only a very general chronological attribution to these deposits ("certainly prior to the Islamic era," Schmidt 1953: 279), A. B. Tilia attributed the post-Achaemenid architectural phases to the independent rulers of Fars whom she dated, according to the theory prevailing at the time, to about thirty years after the fire that destroyed Persepolis (see Chapters 34, 36; Tilia 1972: 315). A. S. Shahbazi also attributed the post-Achaemenid occupation of Persepolis to the *fratarakas* (Shahbazi 1977: 200).

There is also archaeological evidence at Persepolis which may be linked iconographically with the local rulers of post-Achaemenid Fars, thanks to comparisons with coinage. We refer to the finely engraved graffiti on some architectural stone blocks in Darius I's *tačara* and in the so-called "harem" of Xerxes. Whereas, initially, only isolated images of noble figures were discovered here (Allotte de la Fuÿe 1928; Herzfeld 1935, 1941; Schmidt 1953), more careful investigations have subsequently revealed at least two examples of more complex scenes, surprisingly reminiscent of Sasanian reliefs (Calmeyer 1976: 65–67), that were probably painted (Callieri 2006: 140). The figures show features that reflect their royal status: the diadem and tall tiara correspond to those on the coins of the *frataraka* between the early first century BC and the first quarter of the third century AD. More precise identification of most of the figures depicted is impossible (Callieri 2006: 135) and we cannot accept as certain the identifications proposed with specific rulers on the basis of coin portraits (Herzfeld 1941: 308; Huff 2008: 32–4). One of the personages is represented in profile, facing right, as are obverse portraits on Sasanian coinage. He wears a headdress consisting of a plain, hemispherical cap, surmounted by a seven-pointed, fan-like element extremely similar in shape to the five-pointed, fan-like element on the head of the figure represented on the reverses of some *frataraka* coins (Alram 1986: 185, nos. 653–5), such as those of Šābuhr, the penultimate king of Persis and predecessor of Ardašīr, who became first king of the Sasanians, interpreted subjectively by some scholars as the image of Ardašīr's father Pabag (contra Callieri 2006: 136). But in general we are unsure of the identity of the figures on the reverses of many of the *frataraka* coin types who may represent the biological father, forefather, or even the son or heir of the king (Alram 1986: 164; contra Lukonin 1969: 29, who, on the basis of the legend BRH bgy X MLK,' interprets the images on the reverse as those of the father of the king). At any rate, the iconographic similarities between the graffiti and the coin portraits suggest that the person depicted is the last of the series and closest in time to the Sasanian period.

The presence of these graffiti at Persepolis is easily explained if we remember that the site recalled the power and magnificence of the Achaemenid "ancestors," fictive or not, for the local rulers of Fars (cf. Frye 1975: 238). There is an evident continuity from the *fratarakas* to the first Sasanians in their privileged relationship with this site, at least until the fourth century AD, when the *sakashah* Šābuhr had his inscriptions engraved here (Frye 1966; cf. Wiesehöfer 1994: 139, n. 4). Engraving and painting on the walls of the old palaces probably constituted an homage to the "ancestors" and an expression of continuity with heroes of the past, be they the mythical Kayanids of the epic tradition or more probably the Achaemenids in mythical guise (Callieri 2011). The graffiti are even better explained when we remember, as shown above, that life at Persepolis had resumed after the site's destruction by fire, and new buildings had been erected: a sign of new ownership was indeed necessary.

The attribution of the Persepolis graffiti to the rulers of Fars does not, however, exclude the possibility that some of the post-Achaemenid evidence there might be even older, perhaps dating to the Seleucid period. As P. Bernard has proposed, Persepolis was probably the seat of the Seleucid satraps of Persis, the last of whom is mentioned in connection with the rebellion of Molon (222–220 BC), and later of the *frataraka* dynasts (Bernard 1995a: 84). However, a passage in Strabo's *Geography*, written between the first century BC and the first century AD, suggests that the terrace was no longer fully occupied in the Arsacid period: "These [i.e., Susa, Persepolis, Pasargadae] were the palaces in the times of the empire of the Persians, but the kings of later times used others, naturally less sumptuous, since Persis had been weakened not only by the Macedonians, but still more so by the Parthians. For although the Persians are still under the rule of a king, having a king of their own, yet they are most deficient in power and are subject to the king of the Parthians" (*Geog.* 15.3.3).

The so-called "temple of the *fratarakas*" at Persepolis, excavated by Herzfeld in 1932, where the above-mentioned Greek inscriptions were found, is a monument of great complexity, both in terms of its function and its chronology, which brings us again to the Hellenistic period. As far as function is concerned, the identification of it as a fire temple, advanced by Herzfeld (1935: 46–7; 1941: 275, 286) was based on the contemporaneity of a stone window jamb showing, in low-relief profile, one person with a long, priestly dress who was identified as a "priest" because of the barsom (the bundle of twigs characteristic of Zoroastrian cult) held in his right hand (Herzfeld 1941: pl. 86) and of a square hall (*c*.5 × 5 m) with four three-stepped column bases, displaying a layout similar to the so-called

Ayādana at Susa and other buildings considered at the time to be among the earliest fire temples. However, it has been pointed out that the complex to which the square hall (supposedly the temple, called the "Pedestal Temple" by Stronach 1985) belongs is separated from the room with the window jamb (Stronach's "Window Temple") by a road or a broad aisle, raising questions over Herzfeld's suggestion that the two belonged to the same complex (Schmidt 1953: 56; Boucharlat 1984: 130–2). Indeed, the rectangular, two-stepped molded base situated in the center of the rear wall in the square hall (Kleiss 1981a) bears traces of a socket for the tenon of a stone statue (Callieri 2003b) and is therefore not the base of a fire altar, as suggested by Herzfeld and others (Litvinskij and Pičikjan 2000: 230–1). Even if the plan of the square hall with the four column bases resembles that of the Hellenistic houses of Aï Khanoum (Bernard 1969: 337, n. 1; Boucharlat 1984: 130–2), it is also true that the position of the statue base suggests a cultic function, as does the lack of rear access to the square hall. However, rather than a fire temple, or one of the temples built by Artaxerxes II for a statue of Anahita (Stronach 1985: 616), the building was probably one of those temples for cult images that proliferated in Iran during the Hellenistic period. And indeed the three-stepped column bases in the square room, of a post-Achaemenid type, the dimensions of the baked bricks, differing from those used in the terrace, and the Hellenistic date of the comparanda for the molded base (Callieri 2007a: 61–3) all suggest that the presence of Achaemenid bases in the same building does not provide a valid basis for its attribution to the Achaemenid period as once thought (Francovich 1966: 207; Kleiss 1981a; Stronach 1985), but rather represents a case of reuse. Only a new survey of the monument and the documentation on Herzfeld's excavation, if extant, could eventually shed more light on the matter.

The general stylistic character of the priestly figure with the barsom bundle on the "temple" doorjamb, as well as that of the similar, though poorly preserved, female figure (?) on the opposite jamb, is far from the style of both Achaemenid sculpture and the Hellenistic tradition, particularly in the lowness of the relief. Rather, these look like products of a local tradition by second-rate craftsmen and recall a small ($c.50$ cm), badly preserved image of a praying female (?) shown in profile, facing right, carved on the wall of a stone quarry between Naqsh-e Rustam and Hajiabad, which D. Huff dated to the post-Achaemenid period (Huff 1984: 240–1, fig. 18). A similarity to the relief of Kel-e Dawud, a short distance from the "Median" tomb of Dokkan-e Dawud in Media (Huff 1984: 241), is even greater. From an iconographic viewpoint, the similarity with the images of officiants on *frataraka* coinage is also striking.

Further north, along the piedmont of the Kuh-e Rahmat, is the so-called "Persepolis Spring cemetery," a necropolis with terracotta sarcophagi containing few grave goods which, however, parallel material from the terrace of Persepolis. Dated to the late and post-Achaemenid period (Schmidt 1953: 56; 1957: 123; Boucharlat 2006: 454–5), the site must also be considered in any evaluation of occupation in the Persepolis area after 330 BC. Stone cairn tombs attributed to the late Arsacid period have also been found behind the Persepolis terrace on the Kuh-e Rahmat (Gotch 1971: 162–3).

Seveal scholars have dated the origins of Istakhr, the major settlement in the region from the Sasanian through the early Islamic period located 13 km north of Persepolis, to the Seleucid period. The idea that references to "Persepolis" in the Hellenistic sources relating to events after the Persepolis fire in fact refer to Istakhr, thereby confirming the city's foundation in the Seleucid period, dates to the late nineteenth century and is widely accepted (Tomaschek 1883: 32–3; Brunner 1983: 751). However, excavations by Herzfeld and Schmidt did not bring to light any post-Achaemenid phase remains below the Sasanian levels at the site, apart from several reused Achaemenid architectural elements, a few *frataraka* coins, and a fragmentary stone vessel. The limestone capitals and bases were taken by Herzfeld to show a local variant of Hellenistic orders (Herzfeld 1941: 276–9; cf. Bier 1983: 307). However, P. Bernard has suggested that these attest to the persistence of Hellenistic models in the Sasanian period (Bernard 1974: 284–8). Perhaps the foundation of Istakhr dates to the time of the *frataraka* dynasty. According to Middle Persian texts, Ardawān (Artabanus), the enemy of Ardašīr I, lived at Staxr (*Kārnāmag ī Ardaxšēr ī Pābagān*, Grenet 2003a: I. 4), a town which he himself had founded (*Šahrestānīhā ī Ērānšahr*, Daryaee 2002: 41). Even though neither text is strictly speaking historical, the basis of this information is likely to have been a Persian tradition concerning the pre-Sasanian foundation of Istakhr, which associated it with last Arsacid king (Callieri 2007b). Some scholars have also suggested that Istakhr was the seat of the *frataraka* dynasty (Chaumont 1959; Bivar 1998: 643) and the location of its mint (Schmidt 1939: 105). The late dating of this coinage brings the *frataraka* dynasty closer in time to the appearance of the Arsacid dynasty in Iran, and we cannot exclude the possibility that the new town was founded in this period, thus diminishing the occupation of Persepolis.

Coins are not the only archaeological evidence of the rulers of post-Achaemenid and Arsacid Fars, however. A silver bowl with a Middle Persian inscription mentioning the sequence of rulers Dārāyān II–Ardaxšahr II–Wahīxšahr, of unknown provenance and in a private collection, has been also published (Skjærvø 2000, 2003: 382; Lerner 2008: 186). The bowl has a central medallion containing the image of a humped bull (zebu), facing right, and conforms in its overall composition to eastern metalwork of the Seleucid and Arsacid periods (Lerner 2008: 186). The figural medallion in the center and multiple registers decorated with different motifs find comparanda on several bowls attributed to the Hellenized Near East (Pfrommer 1993: 22). The style of the bull is also naturalistic, pointing to the same cultural area and confirms the appreciation of Hellenistic craftsmanship we can see on coinage.

At Naqsh-e Rustam, the Aramaic inscription on the façade of Darius I's tomb was dated to the third century BC by W. B. Henning, who read the name Seleucus and interpreted it as a reference to a Seleucid king (Henning 1958: 24; Schmidt 1970: 12). Such an attribution suggests that the king in question would have shared in the great honor accorded to the Achaemenid kings (contra Frye 1982, who denies any Seleucid presence in the area and dates the inscription to the late Achaemenid period). The period between the Achaemenid and the Sasanian periods, which Schmidt called "Hellenistic," is represented at Naqsh-e Rustam by sparse remains (Schmidt 1970: 12). The possibility of a phase below the Sasanian mudbrick fortification walls was considered but then ruled out by Schmidt (1970:57).

The group of rock-cut tombs at Akhur-e Rustam, 8 km to the south of Persepolis, includes an isolated tomb at the northern edge of the site with a square cornice recalling Achaemenid architecture. Boucharlat dated this to between the late fourth and the third century BC (Boucharlat 2006: 454). Huff considered the site a "small dynastic cemetery" in use from late or post-Achaemenid times to the late Arsacid or early Sasanian period (Huff 2004: 597–8; cf. 2004: 187).

Between Persepolis and Pasargadae lies the Tang-e Bolaghi, a valley in which the British team working at Pasargadae in the 1960s documented stone cairn tombs dated to the Arsacid period (Stronach 1978: 167). In the framework of an international program of rescue excavations, a joint Irano-Italian team investigated a small, rural settlement (TB 76) where occupation began in the Achaemenid period and continued through the post-Achaemenid period with no evident interruption in the sequence. In particular, the last phase (Phase 2) of occupation in a house in the main trench (TB76-3) built of mud and stone above stone-block foundations is certainly post-Achaemenid. Despite the presence of several artifacts typical of the Achaemenid period, finds of post-Achaemenid date in earlier Phase 3 contexts suggest that this phase belongs to the same period (Askari Chaverdi and Callieri 2006, 2009, forthcoming).

An episode in the life of the site which C14 analyses have dated to the late or more probably post-Achaemenid period is represented by an isolated grave in Trench TB76-1 (Askari Chaverdi and Callieri 2007b, 2009). Here the deceased was deposited in an oval grave pit in a foetal position, along an east-west axis, with the head to the west, facing south. The sole grave furnishing was a handmade beaker of gray-buff ware with concave sides (Askari Chaverdi and Callieri 2007b: fig. 21) which can be compared in shape to a beaker decorated with black-painted bands found by Sir Aurel Stein in an "Early Historic" context during his sounding at Tol-e Zohak near Fasa, in eastern Fars (Stein 1936: 149, pl. 19.20).

If we move to Pasargadae, on the Tall-e Takht, the imposing Achaemenid platform on a hilltop which Darius I transformed into a proper citadel, the extensive British excavations of the 1960s demonstrated substantial continuity in occupation between the fifth century BC and a vast episode of diffuse destruction across the site apparently unrelated to the Macedonian conquest. Stronach linked the "large conflagration" to the uprising of the local rulers of Fars against the Seleucids, which he dated to the beginning of the third century BC in conformity with the then common opinion (Stronach 1978: 146). Recent excavation of a trial trench on the north side of the Tall-e Takht, carried out in 2006 and 2007 by a joint Irano-Italian Archaeological Mission, has revealed a much more complex sequence with nine stratigraphic phases (Askari Chaverdi and Callieri 2007a, 2010), confirming the need to review the sequence proposed by the British excavators, particularly the pottery (cf. Levine 1980; Boucharlat 2006: 460). Unfortunately, relatively little pottery was recovered. Nevertheless, some C14 analyses have provided interesting evidence. The second earliest phase (Phase 8), which ended with the plundering of the walls and a large-scale fire indicated by a considerable amount of ash, most likely dated to c.410–380 BC. It is indeed tempting to identify this fire with the "conflagration" of which Stronach found evidence throughout the excavation. However, whereas Stronach attributed the fire to events occurring at the end of Seleucid rule, which he dated to c.280 BC (Stronach 1978: 146), the date of the episode we recorded, instead, falls squarely within the Achaemenid period. As for the later deposits, Phase 7 dates to c.380–250 BC, while Phase 6 dates to c.250–200 BC. No C14 dates are available from the later deposits.

The presence of post-Achaemenid sherds on the surface of the area north of the Tall-e Takht, where geomagnetic surveys have shown the possible existence of a residential area (Boucharlat and Benech 2002: 29; Boucharlat 2002: 282), suggests that the settlement there could have been occupied after the end of the Achaemenid period, like that on Tall-e Takht. Nor should we forget that amongst the surface pottery picked up to the southwest of Palace S Boucharlat found sherds that he dated to the Seleucid or Arsacid periods (Boucharlat and Benech 2002: 14; Boucharlat 2006: 460, n. 6).

As for the northernmost areas of Fars, Stein found sherds of red ware with polished slip on the surface of the Qasr-e Bahram mound near Dehbid which he attributed to a pre-Sasanian period (Stein 1936: 215–6). In western Fars, the recent Irano-Australian investigations in the Mamasani district have revealed several stratigraphic sequences in which the Achaemenid phase is followed by a post-Achaemenid phase which is not always easy to define given problems of pottery chronology similar to those encountered in central Fars (Potts and Roustaei 2006: 12). Phases B5 and B4 at Tol-e Nurabad have been dated to the Achaemenid and post-Achaemenid period, while Phases B2–B1 are considered post-Achaemenid, based on the presence of a turquoise-glazed vessel base which can be compared to Parthian ceramics from Khuzestan (Potts and Roustaei 2006: 77). At Tol-e Spid the post-Achaemenid Phase 3 is C14 dated to between 370 and 50 BC (Potts and Roustaei 2006: 77; Askari Chaverdi et al. 2010: 290). Surface surveys in the area have shown that twelve sites of Achaemenid date continued to be occupied during the post-Achaemenid period (Askari Chaverdi et al. 2010: 292). In the same area, excavations of an Achaemenid building at Qaleh Kali (Jinjun) have revealed occupation dated by C14 to the Achaemenid and post-Achaemenid periods (Potts et al. 2007, 2009). The multiple architectural phases at the site date to between the sixth/fifth and fourth to mid-second centuries BC (I. K. McRae, A. Dusting, and D. T. Potts, pers. comm.)

Another important monument that can probably be assigned to the aristocracy of Fars during the Seleucid or early Arsacid period is the rock-cut tomb of Da o Dokhtar, also in the Mamasani district. Typologically this tomb belongs to the widespread group of so-called "Median rock-cut tombs" and therefore differs from the Achaemenid tombs. The monumental façade, cut into the rock of a cliff above a large smooth area, reproduces the façade of a building with central, rectangular door, flanked by two pairs of half-columns that support the entablature, thus perpetuating the scheme of the Achaemenid tombs of Naqsh-e Rustam in reduced dimensions though with obvious differences in architectural detail. The bases of the half-columns consist of a low torus on a two-stepped plinth. The half-columns themselves have smooth shafts and support simplified, pseudoarchaic Ionic capitals with volutes which project exaggeratedly from the shaft. The tomb proper consists of a funerary chamber cut into the rock, accessible through a door with raised threshold and projecting jambs on the sides, and has been assigned to the early post-Achaemenid period based on the fact that the intercolumniations occur in pairs (Gall 1993). Iconographic reference to the Achaemenid tombs is, however, explicit, and the grafting of Hellenistic architectural elements onto a Persian typology accords well with the date proposed by H. von Gall. Most probably, this was the work of "provincial" craftsmen. As for the tower monument of Dum-e Mil, near Nurabad-e Mamasani, which Ghirshman (1944–5) interpreted as a temple of the Seleucid period, this has been better interpreted by D. Huff as a building belonging to the proto-Sasanian period, having an either funerary (ossuary) or commemorative function (Huff 1975: 209).

Moving to the south of Shiraz, archaeological evidence of pre-Sasanian occupation in the Firuzabad area consists of a molded, square statuette base (15 × 15 × 4 cm) found at Qal'a-ye Dokhtar, carved in marble from Greece or Asia Minor and still bearing the right foot of the statuette which it originally supported (Huff and Gignoux 1978: 120, fig. 2). Considered a Roman object, it could have arrived at the time of the construction of the building in the early Sasanian period or in the preceding Arsacid period. In the surface layers of a trench dug at Tal-e Gawd-e Rahim, in the Sarvestan area between Shiraz and Fasa, Stein discovered sherds decorated with parallel bands typical of Achaemenid and post-Achaemenid pottery (Stein 1936: 182).

In eastern Fars the major evidence of post-Achaemenid period occupation is represented by Tal-e Zahak, near Fasa, where in 1934 Stein discovered the marble head (*c.* 11 cm tall) of a female Greek goddess (Aphrodite?). This has been dated stylistically to between the mid-third and mid-second century BC and attributed to a workshop in Asia Minor (Stein 1936: 140–1; Colledge 1979: 225; Schlumberger 1983: 1037, pl. 57). Although the site may have played an important role in the Elamite period, it is topped by a large settlement of the twelfth to thirteenth centuries AD. Although never excavated, surface survey has revealed ceramics of the Achaemenid period (Stein 1936: 140; Miroschedji 1973; Hansman 1999) as well as fragments of rounded-rim bowls of a less refined ware which Hansman took as an indication of probable "Hellenistic occupation" (Hansman 1975: 299, fig. 3.1–2; 1999: 391).

From Tal-e Zahak we also have a series of bell-shaped, stone column bases of Achaemenid type, datable to the Achaemenid and/or post-Achaemenid periods, as well as another group of bases with a thick torus, in some cases standing above a square plinth and in some cases with decoration (Pohanka 1983; Boucharlat 2005: 234; Callieri 2007a: 88–90, 94–6). The origin of this type of barrel-shaped torus seems to be the thick torus that was widespread throughout the Hellenized East, as far as Bactria (Bernard 1968: 132, 138, fig. 8; Boardman 2000: 206), itself derived from the elegant torus of Achaemenid architecture. These are similar to the toruses of bases discovered in Media, dated to the late or post-Achaemenid period and much more similar to Greek models (Huff 1989: 295).

Several stone cairn tombs have been recorded between Fasa and Darabgerd (Stein 1936: 158). As for Darabgerd itself, although the circular city was long considered an Arsacid foundation, it is now known to have been founded in the Islamic era (Huff 1993: 56). Nevertheless, three stone column bases, the shapes of which are derived from the bell-shaped bases of Achaemenid type but with a decorated or undecorated *cyma reversa* profile, could date to the Seleucid or the Sasanian period (Morgan 2003: 334).

Moving to southern Fars, on an isolated rock boulder near Qir-Karzin is a relief representing a life-sized bowman in profile, facing right, in the act of shooting an arrow (Huff 1984; Vanden Berghe 1986). Although badly eroded, it is possible to recognize several iconographic elements of Achaemenid type in the clothing and weaponry, but with peculiarities which led Vanden Berghe to date the relief to the post-Achaemenid period. Despite its flatness, the rendering of the figure is much more statuesque than other reliefs of the same period and the figure is shown in profile, with none of the frontality typical of the later Parthian period. Consequently a Hellenistic date, some time in the second century BC or earlier, has been proposed by D. Huff (Huff 1984: 246–7).

Further to the south, in the Lamerd district, the architectural complex of Tomb-e Bot, discovered by A. Askari Chaverdi, is characterized by architectural elements and other objects carved in a gray-white limestone of local origin (Askari Chaverdi 1999/2000, 2002). At least three capitals of Achaemenid type were found as well, the lower portions of which have volutes and the upper parts of which are decorated with well-preserved projecting, addorsed bull protomes. The rather poor sculptural quality and schematization of several iconographic elements suggest a post-Achaemenid date. More problematic, however, is the bust of a male figure in the round found at the same site. The figure is shown in frontal view, with physiognomic features rendered in a rather naturalistic way, particularly the eyes, which have well-carved eye-lids. This bust finds no comparanda in post-Achaemenid art, but is very similar to the yellow limestone bust from Qal'a-ye Now, between Malyan and Bayza,' that T. S. Kawami dated to the period immediately preceding the Sasanian ascent to power, when the artistic tradition of Arsacid Fars gave birth to Sasanian art (Kawami 1987: 138–9, 222). Since the same naturalistic qualities characterize the Tomb-e Bot bust, it is logical to attribute it to the same period and thus it seems reasonable to assign the same date to the other architectural elements found at the site (Callieri 2007a: 139). Moreover, capitals with bovine protomes, dating to the third and fourth centuries AD, are known at Bishapur and Hajiabad.

During his survey of the Lamerd valley, Askari Chaverdi discovered twelve sites attributed to the post-Achaemenid period, eight of which were new foundations (Askari Chaverdi and Azarnoush 2004). In the same area, Sir Aurel Stein located a site with pottery described as "early historical" at Tump-e Podu, less than 1 km east of Galehdar (Stein 1937: 220).

We arrive finally on the coast of the Persian Gulf, which was an integral part of Fars and fully connected to the plateau (Salles 1990: 125). The main site of historic date on the Bushehr peninsula (originally an island) is Reshahr, a site that has been identified with Rev-Ardašīr, founded, according to Tabari, by Ardašīr I (Schwarz 1896: 120–1; Marquart 1901: 27; Bernard 1995b: 402, n. 112). In the middle of a vast sherd scatter are the remains of an imposing, square, mudbrick fortress measuring $c.500 \times 500$ m (Stein 1937: 241; Mostafavi 1978: 279–80). Some 70 m from the southwest corner of the fortress are the foundations of a long platform projecting toward the sea, possibly a pier (Whitehouse and Williamson 1973: 35–42). Recently, an Iranian team has identified a white limestone, molded base, reused in one of the two walls supporting the platform. This limestone base is considered Hellenistic and has been attributed to the *frataraka* dynasts of Fars (Ata'i 2005). The surface pottery, dated by the Iranian team from the Achaemenid period onward (Ata'i 2005: 87), was dated by Whitehouse and Williamson to between the first and the fifth centuries AD (Whitehouse and Williamson 1973: 38–9) and by Whitcomb to the "Parthian and Sasanian" periods (Whitcomb 1987: 317–19). It is therefore possible that the site has a pre-Sasanian phase. However, the stone base is not Hellenistic, but rather an unfinished base of Roman type with comparanda of second to fifth century date (Callieri 2007: 96; cf. Pensabene 1998: 10, fig. 16). It is not, therefore, possible to link this alleged pier to the notice preserved by Pliny (*Nat. Hist.* 6.152), according to which a Persian fleet fought against a Seleucid fleet from Mesene, since the pier cannot predate the Roman Imperial period and most likely dates to the Sasanian period. Perhaps linked to the pre-Sasanian occupation of the area are the cairn burials directly behind the ruins of Reshahr (Stein 1937: 240–1; Whitehouse and Williamson 1973: 37) where sherds of glazed and unglazed pottery have been found.

A very interesting piece of evidence that has been attributed to the Hellenistic period is a fragment of a white marble statue representing Marsyas, found in 1988 at Tol-e Khandaq, near Borazjan, in an architectural complex of baked brick identified as a religious building, perhaps a fire temple. The lower part of a naked male figure with tail, sitting on a rock covered with a goat skin, against which a flute, a *pedum* and a syrinx lean, is supported on a rectangular, molded base (52 × 29.5 cm). Even in the absence of precise comparanda, the figure can be identified with Marsyas based on the associated objects (Rahbar 1999b). However, the use of a drill and the emphasis on light and shadow argue against the first century BC date proposed for the sculpture, which should rather be dated to the Roman Imperial age, the Flavian period or better yet the third century AD (Callieri 2007a: 108).

Further reading

An important contribution to the knowledge of the Hellenistic-Arsacid period in Iran is made by the ancient sources, particularly by the Greek and Roman historians. These sources describe the Iranian plateau according to the various regions of its historic geography, not from the unitarian perspective present in the Iranian tradition, at least from the third century AD onward, when the concept of Ērān was finally shaped. One of the most interesting Greek texts of descriptive geography is the *Geography* by Strabo of Amasia (end of first century BC to early first century AD), while the only ancient Iranian geographical text available dates to the late Sasanian period (Daryaee 2002).

References

Alizadeh, A. 1997. Preliminary report on archaeological surveys in Upper Kur River Basin and northeastern Marvdasht, Fars Province. *GB* 1: 67–88 (in Persian).

Allotte de la Fuÿe, F. M. 1928. Graffitis relevés en 1928 dans les ruines de Persépolis. *RA* 25: 159–68.

Alram, M. 1986. *Nomina propria iranica in nummis. Materialgrundlagen zu den iranischen Personennamen auf antiken Münzen*. Vienna: Iranisches Personennamenbuch 4.

Askari Chaverdi, A. 1999–2000. Fars after Darius III: New evidences from Lamerd District. *IJAH* 13/2–14/1: 66–71 (Persian), 6 (English).

———. 2002. Recent post-Achaemenid finds from southern Fars, Iran. *Iran* 40: 277–8.

Askari Chaverdi, A., et al. 2007. Archaeological excavations at Tol-e Espid: Radio-carbon dates from some Achaemenid and post-Achaemenid finds, Fars (550–50 BC). *Bastanshenasi* 5/3: 57–96 (Persian).

———. 2010. Archaeological evidence for Achaemenid settlement within the Mamasani Valleys, Western Fars, Iran. *WAP*: 287–98.

Askari Chaverdi, A., and M. Azarnoush. 2004. Barrasi-ye bāstānšenāxti-ye mohavvate-hā-ye bāstāni-ye paskarāne-hā-ye Xalij-e Fārs: Lāmerd va Mohr, Fārs. *IJAH* 18/2: 3–18 (Persian), 2 (English).

Askari Chaverdi, A., and P. Callieri. 2006. A rural settlement of the Achaemenid period in Fars. *JIAAA* 1: 65–70.

———. 2007a. Preliminary report on the stratigraphic study of the Toll-e Takht, Pasargadae: Investigations on the material culture of the Achaemenid and post-Achaemenid periods. In *Archaeological Reports 7. On the occasion of the 9th Annual Symposium on Iranian Archaeology*, vol. 1, ed. H. Fazeli Nashli, 5–23. Tehran: ICAR.

———. 2007b. Tang-e Bolaghi Site TB 76: 3rd excavation season (Ordibehesht-Khordad 1385). Preliminary Report. In *Archaeological Reports 7. On the occasion of the 9th Annual Symposium on Iranian Archaeology*, vol. 2, ed. H. Fazeli Nashli, 97–124. Tehran: ICAR.

———. 2009. Achaemenid and post Achaemenid remains at TB76 and TB77. *ARTA* 2009.004.

———. 2010. Preliminary report on the Irano-Italian stratigraphic study of the Toll-e Takht, Pasargad: Investigations on the material culture of the Achaemenid and post-Achaemenid periods in Fars. In *Ancient and Middle Iranian Studies: Proceedings of the 6th European Conference of Iranian Studies, held in Vienna, September 18–22, 2007*, ed. M. Macuch, D. Weber, and D. Durkin-Meisterernst, 11–28. Wiesbaden: Harrassowitz.

———. Forthcoming. *Tang-e Bolaghi (Fars), Sites TB76 and TB77: Rural Settlements of the Achaemenid and post-Achaemenid Periods. Report of the archaeological rescue excavations carried out in 2005 and 2006 by the joint Irano-Italian mission of the Iranian Center for Archaeological Research and the University of Bologna, with the collaboration of IsIAO, Italy*. Oxford: Archaeopress.

Ata'i, M. T. 2005. Report of archaeological survey at Rishehr (Liyan) Shores, Boushehr. *Bastanshenasi* 1/1: 85–93 (Persian), 12 (English).

Azarnoush, M. 1975. Kāvoša-ye gurestān-e mohavvate-ye Sang-e Šir. *PASARI* 3: 51–72.

———. 1976. Dovvomin fasl-e kāvoš dar mohavvate-ye bāstāni-ye Sang-e Šir dar Hamedān, 1356. *PASARI* 4: 40–59 (in Persian).

———. 1979. Deux saisons de fouilles à la necropole de "Sang-e Shir" (Hamedan). In *Akten des VII. Internationalen Kongresses für iranische Kunst und Archäologie, München, 7–10. September 1976*, ed. W. Kleiss, 281–6. Berlin: *AMI* Ergänzungsband 6.

———. 1981. Excavations at Kangavar. *AMI* 14: 69–94.

———. 1999. Kangavar. Un temple séleucide d'Anahita devient un monument sassanide. *DA* 243 (May): 52–3.

———. 2007. Gozāreš-e maqadamāti-ye kāvosha-ye lāyešenākhti-ye Tepe-ye Hegmatāneh Hamedān. In *Archaeological Reports, 7. On the occasion of the 9th Annual Symposium on Iranian Archaeology*, vol. 1, ed. H. Fazeli Nashli, 19–60. Tehran: ICAR.

Balcer, J. M. 1978. Excavations at Tal-i Malyan. Part 2. Parthian and Sasanian coins and burials (1976). *Iran* 16: 86–92.

Bashshâsh Kanzaq, R. 1996. Pāye-ye mojassame-ye sangi-ye katibedār-e dowre-ye Seluki. *Mirās-e Farhangi* 14: 46–9.

Bernard, P. 1968. Chapiteaux corinthiens hellénistiques d'Asie Centrale découverts à Aï Khanoum. *Syria* 45: 111–51.

———. 1969. Quatrième campagne de fouilles à Aï Khanoum (Bactriane). *CRAIBL*: 313–55.

———. 1974. Trois notes d'archéologie iranienne. *JA* 262: 279–97.

———. 1980. Héraclès, les grottes de Karafto et le sanctuaire du mont Sambulos en Iran. *StIr* 9/2: 301–24.

———. 1995a. Remarques additionnelles [to Callieri 1995]. *CRAIBL*: 73–95.

———. 1995b. Paysage et toponymie dans le Proche Orient hellénisé. *TOPOI* 5/2: 382–408.

Bier, L. 1983. A sculpted building block from Estakhr. *AMI* 16: 307–16.

Bivar, A. D. H. 1978. The Aramaic summary. In *Pasargadae. A Report on the Excavations Conducted by the British Institute of Persian Studies from 1961 to 1963*, ed. D. Stronach, 161–2. Oxford: Clarendon Press.

———. 1998. Eṣṭaḵr. i. History and archaeology. *EnIr* 8: 643–46.

Boardman, J. 2000. *Persia and the West: An archaeological investigation of the genesis of Achaemenid art*. London: Thames and Hudson.

Bonanno Aravantinos, M. 1991. Osservazioni sul tipo dell'Eracle sdraiato. In *Giornate di studio in onore di Achille Adriani, Roma, 26–27 novembre 1984*, ed. S. Stucchi and M. Bonanno Aravantinos, 155–79. Rome: Studi miscellanei 28.

Bosworth, C. E. 1990. Bayzā. *EncIr* 4: 14–15.

Boucharlat, R. 1984. Monuments religieux de la Perse achéménide. État de questions. In *Temples et sanctuaires*, ed. G. Roux, 119–35. Lyon: TMO 7.

———. 1989. Cairns et pseudo-cairns du Fars: L'utilisation des tombes de surface au 1er millénnaire de note ère. *AIO*: 675–712.

———. 1998. À la recherche d'Ecbatane sur le Tepe Hegmataneh. *IrAnt* 33: 173–86.

———. 2002. Pasargadae. *Iran* 40: 279–82.

———. 2003. The Persepolis area in the Achaemenid period: Some reconsiderations. *YBYN*: 261–5.

———. 2005. Iran. *AEA*: 221–92.

———. 2006. Le destin des résidences et sites perses d'Iran dans la seconde moitié du IVe siècle avant J.-C. In *La transition entre l'empire achéménide et les royaumes hellénistiques (vers 350–300 av. J.-C.)*, ed. P. Briant and F. Joannès, 443–70. Paris: Persika 9.

Boucharlat, R., and C. Benech. 2002. Organisation et aménagement de l'espace à Pasargades: Reconnaissances archéologiques de surface, 1999–2002. *ARTA* 2002.001.

Boucharlat, R., J. Perrot, and D. Ladiray. 1987. Les niveaux post-achéménides à Suse, secteur nord. Fouilles de l'Apadana-Est et de la Ville Royale-Ouest. *CDAFI* 15: 145–312.

Boucharlat, R., and H. Shahidi. 1987. Fragments architecturaux de type achéménide: Découvertes fortuites dans la ville de Shoush, 1972–1979. *CDAFI* 15: 312–27.

Boyce, M. and F. Grenet 1991. *A history of Zoroastrianism*, vol. 3, *Zoroastrianism under Macedonian and Roman Rule*. Leiden: HdO 8/1/2/2/3.

Brunner, C. 1983. Geographical and administrative divisions: Settlements and economy. *CHI* 3/2: 747–77.

Callieri, P. 1995. Une borne routière grecque de la région de Persépolis. *CRAIBL* 139: 65–95 (Persian trans. in *Asar* 28 [1376]: 96–103).

———. 2001a. L'Iran nel periodo macedone and seleucide. In *Antica Persia. I tesori del Museo Akbarzadeh Nazionale di Tehran e la ricerca italiana in Iran*, 101–8. Roma: De Luca.

———. 2001b. Frammento di testa bronzea raffigurante un personaggio maschile diademato (sovrano ellenistico?). In *Antica Persia. I tesori del Museo Nazionale di Tehran e la ricerca italiana in Iran*, 109–11. Roma: De Luca.

———. 2003a. Su una piccola statua in marmo dall'Elimaide (Iran). In *Transmarinae imagines. Studi sulla trasmissioni di iconografie tra Mediterraneo ed Asia in età classica ed ellenistica*, ed. E. Acquaro and P. Callieri, 149–63. Sarzana: Agorà.

———. 2003b. Some notes on the so-called temple of the Fratarakas at Persepolis. In *Studi in onore di Umberto Scerrato per il suo settantacinquesimo compleanno*, vol. 1, ed. M. V. Fontana and B. Genito, 153–65. Naples: Istituto Universitario Orientale Series Minor 65.

———. 2006. At the roots of the Sasanian royal imagery: The Persepolis graffiti. In *Ērān ud Anērān. Studies presented to Boris Il'ič Maršak on the occasion of his 70th birthday*, ed. M. Compareti, P. Raffetta, and G. Scarcia, 129–48. Venezia: Cafoscarina.

———. 2007a. *L'archéologie du Fārs à l'époque hellénistique*. Paris: Persika 11.

———. 2007b. Persepolis in the post-Achaemenid period: Some reflections on the origins of Estakhr. *Bastanpazhuhi-Persian Journal of Iranian Studies (Archaeology)* 2/4: 8–14.

———. 2011. Les Sassanides étaient-ils les héritiers des Achéménides ? L'évidence archéologique. In *Un impaziente desiderio di scorrere il mondo. Studi in onore di Antonio Invernizzi per il suo settantesimo compleanno*, ed. C. Lippolis and S. De Martino, 187–200. Firenze: Monografie di Mesopotamia 14.

Calmeyer, P. 1976. Zur Genese altiranischer Motive V. Synarchie. *AMI* 9: 63–95.

Chaumont, M.-L. 1959. Pāpak, Roi de Staxr, et sa cour. *JA* 247: 175–91.

Colledge, M. A. R. 1979. Sculptor's stone-carving techniques in Seleucid and Parthian Iran, and their place in the "Parthian" cultural milieu: Some preliminary observations. *EW* 29: 221–40.

———. 1990. Musa from Susa, or Tyche Revealed. *Études et Travaux* 15: 99–108.

Cumont, F. 1936. Bronzes hellénistiques en Perse de Shami. *Syria* 17: 394–5.

———. 1939. Portrait d'une reine parthe trouvé à Suse. *CRAIBL*: 330–41.

Curtis, V. S. 1998. The Parthian costume and headdress. *PSZ*: 61–73.

———. 2010. The Frataraka coins of Persis: Bridging the gap between Achaemenid and Sasanian Persia. *WAP*: 379–94.

Daryaee, T. 2002. *Šahrestānīhā ī Ērānšahr: A Middle Persian text on Late Antique geography, epic, and history*. Costa Mesa: Mazda.

Fleischer, R. 2000. Griechische Kunst in Iran vor der Partherzeit. In *7000 Jahre persische Kunst. Meisterwerke aus dem Iranischen Nationalmuseum in Teheran*, ed. W. Seipel, 221–9. Milan: Kunsthistorisches Museum Wien.

Francovich, G. de. 1966. Problems of Achaemenid architecture. *EW* 16/3–4: 201–60.

Frye, R. N. 1975. The rise of the Sasanians and the Uppsala School. In *Monumentum H. S. Nyberg I*, 237–45. Leiden/Tehran/Liège: Acta Iranica 4.

———. 1982. The "Aramaic" inscription on the tomb of Darius. *IrAnt* 17: 85–90.

Gall, H. von. 1966. Zu den "medischen" Felsgräbern in Norwestiran und Iraqi Kurdistan. *AA*: 19–43.

———. 1974. Neue Beobachtungen zu den sogenannten medischen Felsgräbern. *PASARI* 2: 139–54.

———. 1993. Dā o Doktar. *EnIr* 6: 529-30.

———. 1996. Der grosse Reliefblock am sog. Partherhang. In *Bisutun. Ausgrabungen und Forschungen in den Jahren 1963-1967*, ed. W. Kleiss and P. Calmeyer, 85-8. Berlin: Teheraner Forschungen 7.

Ghirshman, R. 1944-5. La tour de Nourabad. Étude sur les temples iraniens anciens. *Syria* 24: 175-93.

———. 1950. Un bas relief d'Artaban V avec inscription en pehlevi-arsacide. *Monuments Piot* 44: 97-107.

———. 1972. *La civiltà persiana antica*. Turin: Einaudi.

———. 1976. *Terrasses sacrées de Bard-è Néchandeh et Masjid-i Solaiman. L'Iran du Sud-Ouest du VIIIe s. av. n. ère au Ve s. de n. ère.* Paris: MDAI 45.

Godard, A. 1937. Les statues parthes de Shami. *Athār-é Īrān* 2: 285-305.

Gotch, P. 1968. A survey of the Persepolis plain and Shiraz area. *Iran* 6: 168-70.

———. 1969. The Persepolis plain and Shiraz: Field survey 2. *Iran* 7: 190-2.

———. 1971. The Imamzadeh high altar and subsidiary monuments. *Iran* 9: 162-3.

Grenet, F. 2003a. *Kārnāmag ī Ardaxšēr ī Pābagān, La geste d'Ardashir fils de Pābag*. Die: Éditions A Die.

Gropp, G., and S. Nadjmabadi. 1970. Bericht über eine Reise in West- und Südiran. *AMI* 3: 173-230.

Haerinck, E. 1983. *La céramique en Iran pendant la période parthe (ca. 250 av. J.C. à ca. 225 après J.C.): Typologie, chronologie et distribution*. Gent: IrAnt Supplement 2.

Hakemi, A. 1958. Mojasseme-ye Herkol dar Biztun. *Majalle-ye Bāstānšenāsi* 3-4: 3-12.

———. 1990. The excavation of Khurha. *EW* 40: 11-41.

Hamzalu, M., and M. Mir Eskandari. 2002-3. Qal'eh va ghār-e Karaftu. *Asar* 33-34: 278-304.

Hannestad, L., and D. T. Potts. 1990. Temple architecture in the Seleucid Kingdom. In *Religion and religious practice in the Seleucid Kingdom*, ed. P. Bilde, T. Engberg-Pedersen, L. Hannestad, and J. Zahle, 91-124. Aarhus: Studies in Hellenistic Civilizations 1.

Hansman, J. 1975. An Achaemenian stronghold. In *monumentum H. S. Nyberg*, vol. 3, 289-309. Leiden/Tehran/Liège: Acta Iranica 6.

———. 1999. Fāsā. ii. Tall-e Ẓaḥḥāk. *EnIr* 9: 389-91.

Henning, W. B. 1958. Mitteliranisch. In *Iranistik 1: Linguistik*, ed. B. Spuler, 20-130. Leiden/Cologne: HdO 1/4/1.

Herzfeld, E. 1928. The hoard of the Karen Pahlavs. *Burlington Magazine* 52: 21-7.

———. 1935. *Archaeological history of Iran*. London: Oxford University Press.

———. 1941. *Iran in the Ancient East*. London/New York: Oxford University Press.

Huff, D. 1971. Das Felsgrab von Fakhrikah. *Istanbuler Mitteilungen* 21: 161-72.

———. 1975. Nurabad, Dum-i Mil. *AMI* 8: 167-209.

———. 1984. Das Felsrelief von Qir. *AMI* 17: 221-47.

———. 1989. Säulenbasen aus Deh Bozan und Taq-i Bustan. *IrAnt* 24: 285-95.

———. 1991. Bayzā. *Šahrhā-ye Irān* 4: 46-69.

———. 1993. Architecture sassanide. In *Splendeur des Sassanides. L'empire perse entre Rome et la Chine 224-642*, 45-61. Brussels: KMKG-MRAH.

———. 2004. Archaeological evidence of Zoroastrian funerary practices. In *Zoroastrian rituals in context*, ed. M. Stausberg, 594-690. Leiden: Brill.

———. 2008. Formation and ideology of the Sasanian state in the context of archaeological evidence. In *The Sasanian era*, ed. V. Sarkhosh Curtis and S. Stewart, 31-59. London: I. B. Tauris.

Huff, D., and P. Gignoux. 1978. Ausgrabungen auf Qal'a-ye Dukhtar bei Firuzabad 1976: A. Vorläufiger Grabungsbericht. B. Pithos-Inschriften von Qal'a-ye Dukhtar. *AMI* 11: 117–50.

Huyse, P. 1996. Die Rolle des Griechischen im "hellenistischen" Iran. In *Hellenismus: Beiträge zur Erforschung von Akkulturation und politischer Ordnung in den Staaten des hellenistischen Zeitalters*, ed. B. Funck, 57–76. Tübingen: Mohr Siebeck.

Invernizzi, A. 2000. Die Kunst der Partherzeit. In *7000 Jahre persische Kunst. Meisterwerke aus dem Iranischen Nationalmuseum in Teheran*, ed. W. Seipel, 230–43. Milan: Kunsthistorisches Museum Wien.

Kabiri, A. 1993–4. Kašf-e masāfatnemā "sang-e kilumetr" dar Marvdašt. *Asar* 22–23: 196–200.

Kambakhsh Fard, S. 2007. *Archaeological excavations and research at Anahita Temple and Taq-e Gara (Kermanshah)*, 2 vols. Tehran: ICAR (in Persian).

Kawami, T. S. 1987. *Monumental art of the Parthian period in Iran*. Leiden: Acta Iranica 26.

Khachatrian, J. D. 1989. Silver bowls and basins of Armenia in the late Hellenistic period. *IrAnt* 24: 297–308.

Khosrowzadeh, A., and A. Aali. 2005. Towsif, tabaqebandi va gunehšenāsi-ye sofālhā-ye dowrān-e seluki, aškāni va sāsāni. In *Archaeological surveys in Mianab plain, Shushtar*, ed. A. Moghaddam, 166–247. Tehran: ICAR.

Kleiss, W. 1970. Zur Topographie des "Partherhanges" in Bisutun. *AMI* 3: 133–68.

———. 1973. Bericht über Erkundungsfahrten in Iran im Jahre 1972. *AMI* 6: 7–80.

———. 1981a. Bemerkungen zu achaemenidischen Feueraltären. *AMI* 14: 61–4.

———. 1981b. Bemerkungen zum Säulenbau von Khurha. *AMI* 14: 65–7.

———. 1985. Der Säulenbau von Khurha. *AMI* 18: 173–80.

———. 1996. Der sogenannte Partherhang. In *Bisutun. Ausgrabungen und Forschungen in den Jahren 1963–1967*, ed. W. Kleiss and P. Calmeyer, 73–84. Berlin: Teheraner Forschungen 7.

Kleiss, W., and P. Calmeyer, eds. 1996. *Bisutun. Ausgrabungen und Forschungen in den Jahren 1963–1967*. Berlin: Teheraner Forschungen 7.

Labrousse, A., and R. Boucharlat. 1972. La fouille du palais du Chaour à Suse en 1970 et 1971. *CDAFI* 2: 61–167.

Le Rider, G. 1965. *Suse sous les Séleucides et les Parthes. Les trouvailles monétaires et l'histoire de la ville*. Paris: MMAI 38.

Lerner, J. 2008. review of P. Callieri, *L'archéologie du Fārs à l'époque hellénistique*. *BAI* 18: 182–9.

Levine, L. D. 1980. review of D. Stronach, *Pasargadae*. *JAOS* 100: 68–9.

Lewis, D. M. 1978. The Seleucid inscription. In *Pasargadae*, ed. D. Stronach, 160–61. Oxford: Clarendon Press.

Litvinskij, V. A., and I. R. Pičikjan. 2000. *Ellinističeskij xram Oksa v Baktrii (Južnyj Tadžikistan). I. Raskopki Arxitektura. Religioznaja žizn*. Moscow: Akademija Nauk Respubliki Tadžikistan.

Lukonin, V. G. 1969. *Kul'tura sasanidskogo Irana*. Moscow: Nauka, Vostochnaia Literatura.

Luschey, H. 1968. Der Löwe von Ekbatana. *AMI* 1: 115–22.

———. 1996a. Dinavar. In *Bisutun. Ausgrabungen und Forschungen in den Jahren 1963–1967*, ed. W. Kleiss and P. Calmeyer, 265–6. Berlin: Teheraner Forschungen 7.

———. 1996b. Die seleukidische Heraklesfigur. In *Bisutun. Ausgrabungen und Forschungen in den Jahren 1963–1967*, ed. W. Kleiss and P. Calmeyer, 59–60. Berlin: Teheraner Forschungen 7.

Marquart, J. 1901. *Ērānšahr nach der Geographie des Ps. Moses Xorenac'i, mit historisch-kritischem Kommentar und historischen und topographischen Excursen*. Berlin: Abhandlungen der Königlichen Gesellschaft der Wissenschaften zu Göttingen, phil.-hist. Kl. NF 3/2.

Martinez-Sève, L. 2002a. *Les figurines de Suse: De l'époque néo-élamite à l'époque sassanide.* Paris: Réunion des Musées Nationaux.

———. 2002b. La ville de Suse à l'époque hellénistique. *Revue archéologique* 1/2002: 31–54.

———. 2004. Les figurines de Masjid-i Soleiman et les relations entre Suse et l'Elymaïde. *Parthica* 6: 179–201.

Matheson, S. A. 1976. *Persia: An archaeological guide,* 2nd ed. London: Faber.

Mathiesen, H. E. 1992. *Sculpture in the Parthian Empire: A study in chronology,* 2 vols. Aarhus: Aarhus University Press.

Messina, V., and J. Mehr Kian. 2010. The Iranian-Italian joint expedition in Khuzistan. Hung-e Azhdar: 1st Campaign (2008). *Parthica* 12: 31–45.

———. 2011. Ricognizione dei rilievi partici d'Elimaide. La piana di Izeh-Malamir. *Vicino & Medio Oriente* 15: 215–31.

Miroschedji, P. de. 1973. Prospections archéologiques dans les vallées de Fasa et de Darab (rapport préliminaire). *PASARI* 1: 1–7.

Morgan, P. H. 2003. Some remarks on a preliminary survey in eastern Fars. *Iran* 41: 323–38.

Mostafavi, S. M. T. 1978. *The land of Pars (The historical monuments and the archaeological sites of the Province of Fárs),* trans. R. N. Sharp. Chippenham: Picton.

Motarjem, A. and B. Balmaki. 2009. Barrasi va tahlil-e esteqrārhā-ye aškāni-ye dāmanehā-ye shomāli-ye Alvand (Hamedan). *Journal of Archaeological Research* [University of Tehran] 1/1: 135–53.

Parlasca, K. 1991. Zur hellenistischen Plastik im Vorderen Orient. In *O ellinismos stin Anatoli. Protos diethnous archaiologikou synedriou Delphi 6–9 Noembriou 1986,* 453–65. Athens: European Cultural Centre of Delphi.

Pensabene, P. 1998. Depositi e magazzini di marmi a Porto e Ostia in epoca tardoantica. *Bollettino di Archeologia* 49–50: 1–56.

Pfrommer, M. 1993. *Metalwork from the Hellenized East: Catalogue of the collection.* Malibu: J. Paul Getty Museum.

Pohanka, R. 1983. Zu einigen Architekturstücken von Tell-e Zohak bei Fasa, Südiran (Veröffentlichungen der Iranischen Kommission, nr. 14). *Anzeiger der Österreichischen Akademie der Wissenschaften, phil.-hist. Kl.* 120/7: 255–65.

Potts, D. T., A. Asgari Chaverdi, I. K. McRae, K. Alamdari, A. Dusting, J. Jaffari, T. M. Ellicott et al. 2009. Further excavations at Qaleh Kali (MS 46) by the Joint ICAR–University of Sydney Mamasani expedition: Results of the 2008 season. *IrAnt* 44: 207–82.

Potts, D. T., A. Asgari Chaverdi, C. A. Petrie, A. Dusting, F. Farhadi, I. K. McRae, S. Shikhi et al. 2007. The Mamasani Archaeological Project, stage two: Excavations at Qaleh Kali (Tappeh Servan/Jinjun [MS 46]). *Iran* 45: 287–300.

Potts, D. T., and K. Roustaei. 2006. *The Mamasani Archaeological Project. Stage One: A report on the first two seasons of the ICAR–University of Sydney expedition to the Mamasani District, Fars Province, Iran.* Tehran: ICAR.

Rahbar, M. 1997. Kāvosh-e ārāmgāhhā-ye elimā'i-ye "Gelalak" Shushtar. In *Yādnāmeh-ye gardhamā'i-ye bāstānšenāsi—Šuš,* 175–208. Tehran: ICAR.

———. 1999a. Khorheh. Une résidence parthe sur le Plateau iranien. *DA* 243: 44–6.

———. 1999b. Pojuheši dar bāre-ye yek mojassame-ye marmari-ye yunāni. *IW*: 192–210.

Les recherches archéologiques françaises en Iran. 2001. Tehran: National Museum.

Robert, J., and L. Robert. 1946–7. review of M. A. Stein, Old Routes of Western Īrān. *Bulletin Épigraphique* 2: 364–5, no. 227.

Robert, L. 1949. Inscriptions séleucides de Phrygie et d'Iran. *Hellenica* 7: 5–29.

———. 1950. Addenda au Tome VII. Inscription honorifique à Laodicée d'Iran (Nehavend). *Hellenica* 8: 73–5.

———. 1963. review of P. M. Fraser, *Samothrace. II/1. The inscriptions on stone*. *Gnomon* 35: 50–79.

———. 1967. Encore une inscription grecque de l'Iran. *CRAIBL*: 281–96.

Rougemont, G. 1999. Les inscriptions grecques d'Iran. *DA* 243: 6–7.

———. 2012. Les inscriptions grecques d'Iran et d'Asie centrale. Bilinguismes, interférences culturelles, colonisation. *Journal des Savants* 2012/1: 3–27.

Salles, J.-F. 1990. Les Achéménides dans le Golfe Arabo-Persique. In *Centre and periphery*, ed. H. Sancisi-Weerdenburg and A. Kuhrt, 111–30. Leiden: AchHist 4.

Sarfaraz, A. A. 1970. Šahr-e qadim-e Dastuva. *Bastan Chenassi va Honar-e Iran* 4: 12–13.

Sarraf, M. R. 1997. Neue architektonische und städtebauliche Funde von Ekbatana-Tepe (Hamadan). *AMI* 29: 321–39.

Schippmann, K. 1986. Archaeology iii. Seleucid and Parthian. *EnIr* 2: 297–301.

Schlumberger, D. 1983. Parthian Art. *CHI* 3/2: 1027–54.

Schmidt, E. F. 1939. *The Treasury of Persepolis and other discoveries in the homeland of the Achaemenians*. Chicago: OIC 21.

———. 1953. *Persepolis, I. Structures, reliefs, inscriptions*. Chicago: OIP 68.

———. 1957. *Persepolis, II. Contents of the Treasury and other discoveries*. Chicago: OIP 69.

———. 1970. *Persepolis. III. The royal tombs and other monuments*. Chicago: OIP 70.

Schwarz, P. 1896. *Iran im Mittelalter nach den arabischen Geographen*, vol. 1. Leipzig: Harrassowitz.

Shahbazi, A. S. 1977. From Parsa to Takht-e Jamšid. *AMI* 10: 197–207.

Sherwin-White, S. M. 1984. Shami, the Seleucids and dynastic cult: A note. *Iran* 22: 160–1.

Sherwin-White, S. M, and A. Kuhrt. 1993. *From Samarkhand to Sardis. A new approach to the Seleucid Empire*. London: Duckworth.

Skjærvø, P. O. 2000. The joy of the cup: A pre-Sasanian Middle Persian inscription on a silver bowl. *BAI* 11: 93–104.

———. 2003. Coupe portant une inscription en Moyen Perse. In *De l'Indus à l'Oxus. Archéologie de l'Asie Centrale*, ed. O. Bopearachchi, C. Landes, and C. Sachs, 378. Lattes: Association IMAGO Musée de Lattes.

Stein, M. A. 1934. Archaeological reconnaissances in southern Persia. *GJ* 83/2: 119–34.

———. 1936. An archaeological tour in the Ancient Persis. *GJ* 86/6: 489–97.

———. 1937. *Archaeological reconnaissances in north-western India and south-eastern Īrān*. London: Macmillan.

———. 1940. *Old routes of western Īrān: Narrative of an archaeological journey*. London: Macmillan.

Stronach, D. 1978. *Pasargadae. A report on the excavations conducted by the British Institute of Persian Studies from 1961 to 1963*. Oxford: Clarendon Press.

———. 1985. On the evolution of the early Iranian fire temple. In *Papers in honour of Professor Mary Boyce*, vol. 2, ed. J. Duchesne-Guillemin and J. R. Hinnells, 605–27. Leiden: Acta Iranica 25.

Sumner, W. M. 1986. Achaemenid settlement in the Persepolis Plain. *AJA* 90: 3–31.

Tilia, A. B. 1972. *Studies and restorations at Persepolis and other sites of Fārs*, vol. 1. Rome: IsMEO Reports and Memoirs 16.

———. 1977. Recent discoveries at Persepolis. *AJA* 81: 67–77.

———. 1978. *Studies and restorations at Persepolis and other sites of Fārs*, vol. 2. Rome: IsMEO Reports and Memoirs 18.

Tomaschek, W. 1883. *Zur historischen Topographie von Persien.* Vienna: Sitzungsberichte der Kaiserlichen Akademie der Wissenschaften zu Wien, phil.-hist. Kl. 102.

Unvala, J. 1929. Sarcophage de Suse. *RA* 26: 132.

Vanden Berghe, L. 1952. Archaeologische opzoekingen in de Marv Dasht-vlakte. *JEOL* 12: 211–20.

———. 1953. Monuments récemment découverts en Iran méridional. *BiOr* 10: 5–8.

———. 1954. Archaeologische navorsingen in de Omstreken van Persepolis. *JEOL* 13: 394–408.

———. 1986. Le relief rupestre de Gardanah Galumushk (Qir). *IrAnt* 21: 141–55.

Vanden Berghe, L., and K. Schippmann. 1985. *Les reliefs rupestres d'Elymaïde (Irān) de l'époque parthe.* Gent: *IrAnt* Supplement 3.

Wenke, R. J. 1975–6. Imperial investments and agricultural developments in Parthian and Sasanian Khuzestan: 150 B.C. to A.D. 640. *Mesopotamia* 10–11: 31–221.

Whitcomb, D. 1985. *Before the roses and nightingales: Excavations at Qasr-e Abu Nasr, Old Shiraz.* New York: Metropolitan Museum of Art.

———. 1987. Bushire and the Angali Canal. *Mesopotamia* 22: 221–72.

Whitehouse, D., and A. Williamson. 1973. Sasanian maritime trade. *Iran* 11: 29–49.

Wiesehöfer, J. 1994. *Die "dunklen Jahrhunderte" der Persis. Untersuchungen zu Geschichte und Kultur von Fārs in frühhellenistischer Zeit (330–140 v. Chr.).* Munich: Zetemata 90.

———. 1996. Discordia et Defectio—Dynamis kai Pithanourgia. Die frühen Seleukiden und Iran. In *Hellenismus. Beiträge zur Erforschung von Akkulturation und politischer Ordnung in den Staaten des hellenistischen Zeitalters*, ed. B. Funck, 29–56. Tübingen: J. C. Mohr Siebeck.

Young, T. C., Jr. 1975. Kangavar valley survey. *Iran* 13: 191–3.

CHAPTER 36

FRATARAKĀ AND SELEUCIDS

JOSEF WIESEHÖFER

Introduction

About ten years after Alexander's death, the Achaemenid heartland of Persis (Fars) became part of the Seleucid Empire, and in the second half of the second century BC it fell under Arsacid rule. In between, however, Fars experienced a short period of political independence. Scholars agree on the two phases of foreign suzerainty, but disagree fundamentally on the date and the duration of Persid independence. The main reason for that is an argument between numismatists over how to date and interpret the so-called *fratarakā* coins (Table 36.1) in whose inscriptions the names and titles of the sub-Seleucid dynasts and the independent rulers of Fars are mentioned. Historians and archaeologists contribute to that dispute by trying to harmonize the additional brief literary and epigraphic information and the archaeological findings with the numismatic material (Chapter 39; see the excellent recent overview and commentary in Callieri 2007: 115–46; cf. 1998, 2003; Wiesehöfer 2001, 2007, 2011b; Shayegan 2011: 168–87).

Fratarakā rule

Achaemenid rule ended, at least in western Iran, with Alexander's arson on the Persepolis terrace and the murder of Darius III. The Macedonian followed the Persian example in Fars, just as he had done earlier in the western part of the Persian Empire toward non-Greek subjects of the Great King, and he behaved like an Achaemenid in order to be recognized as a legitimate rival and, later, as a legitimate heir to Darius III. The destruction of Xerxes' palaces and treasuries on the terrace of Persepolis can probably be explained by Alexander's unsuccessful attempt to enlist support from the

Table 36.1 Dynasts of Persis (second century BC).

	Date	(Greek/Latin) Name	Indigenous (MP) Name	Comment
1	Late third/early second century BC	Artaxares I	Ardašīr	Sub-Seleucid dynast (MP title: *fratarakā*)
2	First half of second century BC	Oborzus	Wahbarz	Sub-Seleucid dynast—Rebel against Seleucids (MP title: *kāren*?)
3	First half of second century BC	Bagadates (Bades)	Baydād	Sub-Seleucid dynast (MP title: *fratarakā*)
4	Mid-second century BC	Autophradates I	Wādfradād	Independent dynast of Persis
5	Shortly after 140 BC	Autophradates II	Wādfradād	Parthian "vassal king" (*MLK'/šāh*)

inhabitants of Persis at the beginning of his rule and by his attempt to put an apparent end to the Greek war of revenge. However, it did not result in his giving up on these projects, nor did the later execution of the self-proclaimed satrap Orxines, who was probably seen by Alexander as a potential rival and adversary. Orxines' successor, the Persophile Peucestas, proved himself, on the one hand, to be a loyal follower of Alexander, and on the other hand, he turned out to be the man who gave the inhabitants of Persis (or rather their nobility) a feeling of continuity. He and the new king himself did not touch either the Achaemenid system of local dependencies and local administration or the basic ideas of the Persian ideology of kingship. We do not know anything about unrest in Persis after Peucestas' appointment, and the new satrap was even able to levy troops there without difficulty and guarantee the Persid nobles' collaboration (the Achaemenid traits of Alexander's ideology and actions were clearly brought out by Briant 2002: 817–71; 2003, 2005; cf. Wiesehöfer 1994a: 23–49). In my view, this support from the nobles for their new Persophile Macedonian masters continued until the second century BC, as will be shown below. There must have been opposition against Macedonian rule in Fars—the negative image of Alexander in the Zoroastrian part of Iranian tradition is proof of the hostile attitude of at least parts of the population (Wiesehöfer 1995, 2011a); however, for a long time, this hostility did not lead to unrest and revolts in Fars.

As far as religious policy is concerned, we can also find signs of Alexander's and Peucestas' efforts to receive recognition in Persis. First, Peucestas' Persepolitan feast in honor of the diadoch Eumenes (316 BC) (Diod. Sic. 19.22.2ff.), which was also meant to underline the satrap's own powerful position, was arranged in accordance with Achaemenid custom, as far as the sacrificial ceremony and the seating order were concerned (Wiesehöfer 1994a: 53–4 and especially Henkelman 2011: 115–18). Second, construction work at Persepolis, and especially the five Greek inscriptions with the names of Zeus Megistos, Athena Basileia, Apollon, Artemis, and Helios that were found in the so-called *fratarakā*-temple area below the terrace, probably date from the time of Peucestas and may have been used in a syncretistic Greco-Iranian manner (Wiesehöfer 1994a: 72–3; photographs of three of the inscriptions can be found in Rougemont 1999: 6; Callieri 2007: 57).

After Peucestas had been removed from office against the will of the local Persid nobility, Antigonus Monophthalmus became lord of Persis, but only a few years later, after 312 BC, Seleucus, by using the resources of his realm's heartland, Babylonia, conquered Fars. There is a scholarly dispute about when Seleucid supremacy over Persis ended and when those successors of Alexander in the East lost their province. This question is closely connected to the problem of the rule of the so-called *frataraka*, that is, the dynasts who gained a (short) period of independence from the Seleucids for their Persid subjects (it should be noted that other readings of this Iranian title in Aramaic writing can sometimes be found in the literature—*fratadāra*, *fratakara*, among others—but these are not as plausible as *frataraka*, see Wiesehöfer 1994a: 105–8; cf. Skjærvø 2000; for the debate on the interpretation of the coin legend *frataraka ī bayān*, see Callieri 2007: 128–30).

Since the middle of the nineteenth century, scholars have devoted their attention to the coins of these dynasts as the most important testimonies of their reign; on the one hand, they have regarded them as symbols of the *frataraka*'s political legitimacy, on the other, they have used their iconography and style and their respective archaeological contexts to find criteria for their dating. Only one dynast, Oborzus-Wahbarz, is mentioned in Greek literature (Polyaenus 7.40). Up to now the numismatic tradition has been unable to agree on an unequivocal date for the *frataraka*. Critical analysis of the written sources and new archaeological surveys in Fars, which started in the 1970s and showed that Persis remained a fertile and densely populated region even after the reign of Alexander (Wiesehöfer 1994a: 63), as well as archaeological research in the Gulf region, have not changed the minds of many numismatists: they still try to date the beginning of the *frataraka* coinage to the period around 300 or 280 BC (Klose and Müseler 2008: 15, "noch zu Lebzeiten oder unmittelbar nach dem Tod Seleukos' I. Nikator") and they associate the archaeologically detectable, partial destruction of the citadel of Pasargadae, the Tall-e Takht, with a rebellion of the Persians under the *frataraka* Baydad (for the older literature, see Wiesehöfer 1994a: 115–17; for newer studies cf. Müseler 2005–6; Mittag 2006: 310–16; Klose and Müseler 2008; Hoover 2008; Curtis 2010; for the Tall-i Takht, see Callieri 2004; Chapter 35). In the view of other numismatists, however, this thesis seems highly questionable, as numismatic-typological observations might indicate a close connection between the coins of the *frataraka* and those of the second-century sub-Parthian "kings" of Persis (Alram 1986: 162–86). Klose and Müseler (2008: 33), however, see a clear typological break between the first series of *frataraka* coins of Baydad, Ardakhshir, Wahbarz, and Wadfradad I, which they date to the mid to late third century BC, and the second series, including Wadfradad II, "Unknown King," Darayan I, Wadfradad III, and Wadfradad IV (= Wadfradad III, second series, according to Alram) which is said to have started only a short while before the Parthians came to power in Fars. Thus, they assume an interruption of minting at Persepolis of about one century. In my view, apart from the obvious numismatic debate on the significance of typological criteria, both authors underestimate the importance of the literary tradition and the general political situation. Furthermore, the literary, epigraphic, and archaeological evidence also speaks for a rather late date of the *frataraka* reign. For example, there is no indication whatsoever of a third-century loss or reconquest of Persis by the Seleucids. Some unrest is mentioned by Polyaenus (7.39), which can probably be dated to the rule of Seleucus I. According to Polyaenus, a Macedonian commander by the name of Seiles had instigated a massacre by his subordinate *katoikoi* of 3000 insurgent Persians under the pretense that these Iranians should have been his allies in his alleged fight against Seleucus. However, this indigenous rebellion seems to have been a unique episode and, by the way, turned into a disaster.

If a successful Persid revolt had occurred in the first half of the third century BC, Persis ought to have lost its independence again before the rebellion of Molon, in which a Seleucid satrap of Fars named Alexander is mentioned in the sources (Polyaenus 5.40ff.). Information about the founding of towns in southwestern Iran by Antiochus I (OGIS 233; Steph. Byz. *s.v.* Stasis), about the rebellion of Molon, about Persid *katoikoi* at Raphia in 217 BC (Polyaenus 5.79.3–8), and an inscription concerning Antiochus III's remarkable stay at Antioch-in-Persis (for the location, see Callieri 2007: 26–7) in the year 205 BC (OGIS 231) all seem to indicate that Fars had been loyal to the Seleucids in the third century BC. In addition, the archaeological evidence in the Persian Gulf region (Salles 1987: 91–9, 1994a, 1994b, 1996: 260–62; Potts 1990: 92–7, 178ff.) leaves no doubt about a clear, continuous, and assured military and trading presence of the Seleucids in this region until the end of the reign of Antiochus III (Sachs and Hunger 1989: 358ff., no. −183 A "rev. 12–13"). The loss of Persis would have certainly threatened the kings' presence and goals. Apart from that, the central and important neighboring provinces of Persis in the west, Babylonia and Elymais/Susiana, remained in the safe possession of the Seleucids up to the end of Antiochus' reign (for Elymais, see Shayegan 2011: 174–6, defection in summer 184 BC). Coin hoards from the Persepolis area, which contained coins of Seleucus I and the *fratarakā*, and which were used to prove an upheaval of Persis in the third century, do not necessarily point to an immediate succession from the first Seleucid king to the first *fratarakā* (Wiesehöfer 1994a: 93–6, 115ff.).

Apart from the close stylistic and iconographic link between the *fratarakā* coins and those of their sub-Parthian "successors," the literary evidence suggests a rebellious or even independent Persis in the second century BC. Thus, Livy does not mention any Persid units in Antiochus III's army at Magnesia (Livy 37.40ff.), and in Pliny the Elder's *Natural History* (6.152) the Seleucid *eparch* Numenius is described as having been attacked by Persians, presumably after 175 BC (Shayegan 2011: 176 dates this episode to the time before winter 164 BC), on land and on water at the Straits of Hormuz. Also, Trogus–Justin report that Demetrius II had had to turn to southwest Iranian troops for support when fighting the Parthian king Mithridates I in 140 BC (36.1.4). This seems to indicate that Persis was independent for a short period of time. Besides, other Iranian regions of the Seleucid realm attempted to break away from the center at the same time. According to the excavations on Bahrain and Failaka, the Seleucid presence in the Persian Gulf region grew weaker and became more endangered after 150 BC. The final loss of Babylonia, Susiana, and Characene was not until the reign of Antiochus VII, when Seleucid rule in that area came to an irrevocable end.

Of the *frataraka* who minted tetradrachms, most probably only two (Wahbarz and Wadfradad I) were rebellious and/or independent dynasts (in Wiesehöfer 1994a: 115–29, I postulated, like all other scholars, the following sequence of the first dynasts: Baydad, Ardakhshir, Wahbarz, Wadfradad I; with the help of overstrikes, however, Hoover [2008] was able to prove that the correct sequence should be Ardakhshir, Wahbarz, Baydad, Wadfradad I). According to the Augustan author Strabo, the contemporary Persians were ruled by kings who were subordinates of other kings. In earlier times these were the kings of Macedonia and, in Strabo's own day, the Parthian rulers (*Geog.* 15.3.24). Iconographic details of the coins and, furthermore, the historical comments of Polyaenus and Strabo, suggest that the first dynasts who minted coins, Ardakhshir and Wahbarz, did not rule without the approval of the Seleucids, irrespective of the question of their dating. The similarity of the images and certain symbols on the early *frataraka* coins to Achaemenid iconography has long been stressed, and it has often been concluded that Baydad, who until recently had been considered the first *frataraka* (as noted above), must already have rebelled against the Seleucids. The images of "ruler on the throne" or "ruler in devotional pose in front of a fire altar" on his coins and those of his predecessors were actually modeled on the so-called Treasury reliefs at Persepolis and the funerary reliefs of Naqsh-e Rustam. Although scenes and symbols of royalty such as the standard, the throne with arms, the scepter, and the pole may indicate that the *frataraka* saw themselves as custodians of Achaemenid heritage (Canepa 2010: 568–70), they are not necessarily signs of independent rule. These symbols of rulership and the dynastic *ductus* are similar but not identical to those of the Achaemenids; Ardakhshir and Baydad hold the Seleucid, not the Achaemenid scepter. Their coins use the same weight standard as Seleucid coins and both rulers adopted the title *frataraka*, which is known to have been the title of the Achaemenid sub-satraps in Egypt (Wiesehöfer 1994a: 106–8). And even Wadfradad I, an actual independent *frataraka*, was not totally devoted to the Achaemenids' symbolism and claim to power. His coins show some new details on the reverse. For the first time, the *khvarnah*-symbol in Achaemenid style, a well-known symbol of charisma and power, which is still interpreted as Auramazda by many scholars (Alram 1986: 168ff., pls. 17ff., nos. 533–43; for the man in the winged disk, see Wiesehöfer 2003), appears (Wiesehöfer 1994a: 110–12). In addition, another coin type of Wadfradad I shows the wreathing of the ruler by Nike. This gesture clearly imitates Seleucid coins, but also suggests the ruler's independence— not just a simple military victory—and his desire to commemorate this achievement.

Apparently, the second dynast Wahbarz, Polyaenus' Oborzus, had already given the starting signal for the shaking off of Seleucid rule. This second century AD author reports (7.40) that Oborzus, as commander of 3000 *katoikoi*, had planned the assassination of those military settlers. That he was still a Seleucid representative at the time of uprising is suggested by the fact that non-Iranian troops would hardly have been under arms in an already independent Persis. Accordingly, Oborzus' deed was probably an attempt to gain total autonomy for Fars through the elimination of those potential troublemakers (Shayegan 2011: 172–4 advances good reasons to date Wahbarz's rebellion after Antiochus III's unsuccessful Greek campaign; in his view, Wahbarz might even have been able to appoint a Persid *marzbān* [Sagdodonacus] in Characene, and he interprets the title *kāren/karanos* as a reflection of Wahbarz's exalted position). Since Strabo did not know of a period of independent dynasts (see above), we can conclude that any period of political independence in Persis can only have been quite short (but see Shayegan 2011: 176–7). Wahbarz's rebellion, which might have come to an end during Antiochus III's Elymaean campaign in 187 BC (Shayegan 2011: 174–6), cannot have been successful, since his successor, Baydad—as is proven by his coins and the historical circumstances—was again a loyal governor of the Seleucids (assuming they are not fakes, the two previously unknown coins that show Wahbarz–Oborzus killing a kneeling Macedonian soldier [Alram 1987: pl. 20.7; Bivar 1998: fig. 26b] would be proof of the rebellion and a visual expression of Polyaenus 7.40; cf. Shayegan 2011: 170–1, who believes in the coins' authenticity and suggests a new reading of the legend, giving Wahbarz the title of *kāren*, "commander"). However, some numismatists doubt this authenticity (M. Alram, pers. comm.), and the new sequence of Persid rulers which has Wahbarz's successor Baydad as a sub-Seleucid dynast again does not lend itself to diminish those doubts. For Baydad, Shayegan suggests a reign between 164 and 146 BC (2011: 178), with him and Wadfradad I ruling as rival dynasts, supported by different Seleucid factions, between 150 and 146 BC (for this last assumption, cf. Shayegan 2011: 178, n. 27). If Wahbarz had attempted a revolt, which might perhaps be connected with the destruction level at the end of Pasargadae's third settlement period (Wiesehöfer 1994a: 129), then Wadfradad I was the dynast who proclaimed Persid independence by means of his coins. He, who may have been a rival king to Baydad for a certain amount of time (this assumption is based on the presence of an Aramaic graffito with the name of Baydad on a coin of Wadfradad; see Hoover 2008: 215, and Hoover *apud* Curtis 2010: 388), was probably the man whom the Seleucid king Demetrius II asked for assistance against the Parthian ruler Mithridate I in 140 BC (if Shayegan's dating of the Numenius episode to 164 BC is correct, this battle on land and on water might illustrate either a second Persid attempt to break away from the Seleucids or the beginnings of Wadfradad I's independent rule; a third but less convincing solution would be to connect it with the end of Wahbarz's reign, cf. Shayegan 2011: 177 for possible explanations of such a long reign of Wahbarz; this would, however, imply an independent Persis in the late years of Antiochus III and under Seleucus IV and Antiochus IV; for Wadfradad I, Shayegan 2011: 178 suggests a reign as sole ruler between 146 and 138 BC). The immediate successor and namesake of Wadfradad, who was the last dynast to mint tetradrachms, presumably already ruled his subjects on behalf of the Arsacids.

That Mithradates I left the dynasts in office with their right to mint coins indicates a sub-Seleucid phase of *fratarakā* rule. The Parthians probably returned to the conditions in existence before Wadfradad I rather than granting partial autonomy and the coinage prerogative to the Persid dynasts as something completely new. This is all the more likely as the Arsacids came under heavy pressure from Antiochus VII and the Sakas (Scythians) between 140 and 129 BC.

The seat of the *fratarakā* in the second century BC was presumably Persepolis and not yet Istakhr (Chapter 35). In any case, there was intense building activity on and below the terrace during their time. Artaxerxes III's staircase façade was moved from Palace G to Palace H. To the west, a wall was erected, and the crenellated architectural elements, which appear on the *fratarakā* coins, were rebuilt. Below the terrace, there was building activity, too, as is indicated by the find of reliefs of a *fratarakā* and his spouse (Wiesehöfer 1994a: 68–78; cf. Callieri 2007).

Let us now turn our attention to the religious history of the *fratarakā* era. About 150 years of undisputed Seleucid rule in Fars can be explained only by far-sighted Macedonian politics and religious policy. First, there is no proof of the Seleucid ruler cult in Iranian holy shrines. Second, Wahbarz and Wadfradad I were not exponents of a religious opposition to Hellenism in Fars, nor priestly dynasts or magi themselves, nor, as Samuel K. Eddy suggested (Eddy 1961), initiators of an Iranian apocalyptic tradition, hostile to Alexander (Wiesehöfer 1994a: 129–36). Rather, the *fratarakā* Ardakhshir, Wahbarz, and Baydad were lords of Persis by order of the Seleucids, and only Wadfradad I became independent. From the second series of Baydad's coins onward, and not only after the beginning of their period of independence, the *fratarakā* are depicted in a devotional pose in front of a fire altar. The Achaemenid winged man, who should be interpreted as the embodiment of the *khvarnah* of a famous royal precursor, appears for the first time on Wadfradad's coins. The winged man wears the Achaemenid crenellated crown—the ruler himself wears a tiara—and as such the iconography of the coins reminds us of the triad king/fire altar/winged man on Darius I's tomb façade at Naqsh-e Rustam. This is probably an expression of Wadfradad's claim to being the legitimate heir of the Achaemenid kings in Persis (cf. Panaino 2003; Callieri 2007: 128–30).

However, the coin imagery is predominantly of a political style. The *fratarakā* wear the so-called "royal" tiara (on Baydad's first series; Alram 1986: 165, pl. 17, nos. 511–14) or the *tiara apagês* ("satrap's tiara"; Alram 1986: 165ff., pl. 17ff., nos. 515ff.), not the *tiara orthê* (the "upright tiara") of the Achaemenid Great King or the tiara of the magi. According to Strabo (*Geog.* 15.3.19), the latter is related to the satrap's tiara. The *fratarakā* are depicted in an Achaemenid fashion with royal insignia, but these are only partially genuinely Achaemenid: the bow is different (doubly convex instead of arched once), the scepter is Seleucid. Thus, their royal symbols, their diadem, and their title all indicate that the *fratarakā* saw themselves as stakeholders of an Achaemenid tradition, but did not lay claim to the ideas of universal kingship of the Great Kings. In fact, the diadem tied at the back of the head, which is worn by Baydad and his successors, was not reserved for the king alone in Achaemenid times, but was also worn by his *syngeneis* ("relatives"; Wiesehöfer 2012). It may be that the *fratarakā* claimed this Achaemenid honorary title for themselves.

As for religious life in Persis during the early Hellenistic period, the contemporary burial practices prove that early post-Achaemenid Persis was not completely Zoroastrian. The burials of the Persepolis Spring Cemetery, the cairn burials and the fact that most (Zoroastrian) *astodans* and ossuaries are to be dated to the Sasanian period, point to a religiously mixed southwestern Iran under the *fratarakā*, just as it was under the Achaemenids (Wiesehöfer 1994a: 83ff.).

Conclusion

To conclude, although the *fratarakā*—who were not magi themselves—stressed their close ties to the Achaemenids and recognized the close connection between Persid rule and divine choice and support, they did not consider themselves to be Achaemenids and "Great Kings." They did not adopt this title, did not wear the headgear of the Great King, or use other symbols of Persian royalty. With their choice of the satrap's tiara they expressed their claim to regional rule, first as subordinates of the Seleucids, later as independent rulers, but they did not take over the Achaemenid claim to power outside the borders of Persis. Thus, it is not surprising that their rule did not come to an end in Arsacid times. With their limited goals, the *fratarakā* were no serious danger and no obstacle to the legitimacy of the Parthians who called themselves Great Kings and acted as rulers of an empire that went beyond the borders of Iran. Presumably the Seleucids, for their part, had also not been afraid of their rule being threatened by these dynasts after long periods of Persid loyalty.

Both the Persid and contemporary Babylonian evidence testify to the fact that at least the early Seleucid kings up to Antiochus III—in accord with their Achaemenid predecessors—acted flexibly, wisely, and successfully toward their indigenous subjects, and respected and supported local traditions and institutions (Wiesehöfer 1996). Therefore, the Greek literary ignorance of Persian affairs in Hellenistic times should not be confused with the failure of that policy. On the contrary, the silence of the sources might even reflect its success. It is not surprising that the previously loyal, autochthonous Persian elite did not feel encouraged to break away from Seleucid rule until Antiochus III's defeat by the Romans (Wahbarz) and until the general weakness of that rule became apparent after the death of Antiochus IV (Wadfradad I).

Further reading

For a general overview of the history of this period see Wiesehöfer (2004). For the archaeological evidence from post-Achaemenid Fars see Callieri (2007). The coinage of the *fratarakā* dynasts is summarized in Curtis (2010). Shayegan (2011) is a wide-ranging study of political ideology in the period following Alexander's conquest of the Achaemenid Empire.

References

Alram, M. 1986. *Nomina propria iranica in nummis. Materialgrundlagen zu den iranischen Personennamen auf antiken Münzen*. Vienna: Iranisches Personennamenbuch 4.

———. 1987. Eine neue Drachme des Vahbarz (Oborzos) aus der Persis? *LNV* 3: 147–55.
Bivar, A. D. H. 1998. *The personalities of Mithra in archaeology and literature*. New York: Biennial Yarshater Lecture Series 1.
Briant, P. 2002. *From Cyrus to Alexander: A history of the Persian Empire*. Winona Lake: Eisenbrauns.
———. 2003. *Darius dans l'ombre d'Alexandre*. Paris: Fayard.
———. 2005. *Alexandre le Grand*, 6th ed. Paris: Presses Universitaires de France.
Callieri, P. 1998. A proposito di un'iconografia monetale dei dinasti del Fārs post-achemenide. *Ocnus* 6: 25–38.
———. 2003. Some notes on the so-called temple of the Fratarakas at Persepolis. In *Studi in onore di Umberto Scerrato per il suo settantacinquesimo compleanno*, vol. 1, ed. M. V. Fontana and B. Genito, 153–65. Naples: Università di Napoli "L'Orientale" Series Minor 65.
———. 2004. Again on the chronology of the Tall-e Takht at Pasargadae. *Parthica* 6: 95–100.
———. 2007. *L'archéologie du Fars à l'époque hellénistique*. Paris: Persika 11.
Canepa, M. P. 2010. Technologies of memory in early Sasanian Iran: Achaemenid sites and Sasanian identity. *AJA* 114/4: 563–96.
Curtis, V. S. 2010. The Frataraka coins of Persis: Bridging the gap between Achaemenid and Sasanian Persia. *WAP*: 379–94.
Eddy, S. K. 1961. *The king is dead: Studies in Near Eastern resistance to Hellenism (334–31 B.C.)*. Lincoln: University of Nebraska Press.
Henkelman, W. F. M. 2011. Parnakka's feast: šip in Pārsa and Elam. *EP*: 89–166.
Hoover, O. D. 2008. Overstruck Seleucid coins. In *Seleucid coins: A comprehensive catalogue*, vol. 2, pt. 1, ed. A. Houghton and C. Lorber, 209–30. New York: American Numismatic Society.
Klose, D. O. A., and W. Müseler. 2008. *Statthalter, Rebellen, Könige: Die Münzen aus Persepolis von Alexander dem Großen zu den Sasaniden*. Munich: Staatliche Münzsammlung.
Mittag, P. F. 2006,. *Antiochos IV. Epiphanes. Eine politische Biographie*. Berlin: Klio-Beiheft N.F. 11.
Müseler, W. 2005–6. Die sogenannten dunklen Jahrhunderte der Persis. Anmerkungen zu einem lange vernachlässigten Thema. *Jahrbuch für Numismatik und Geldgeschichte* 55–6: 75–103.
Panaino, A. 2003. The bayān of the Fratarakas: Gods or "divine" kings? In *Religious themes and texts of pre-Islamic Iran and Central Asia: Studies in honour of Prof. Gherardo Gnoli on the occasion of his 65th birthday on 6th December 2002*, ed. C. G. Cereti, M. Maggi, and E. Provasi, 265–88. Wiesbaden: Beiträge zur Iranistik 24.
Potts, D. T. 1990. *The Arabian Gulf in Antiquity*, vol. 2, Oxford: Clarendon Press.
Rougemont, G. 1999. Les inscriptions grecques d'Iran. *DA* 243: 6–7.
Sachs, A. J., and H. Hunger. 1989. *Astronomical diaries and related texts from Babylonia, vol. 2. Diaries from 261 B.C. to 165 B.C.* Vienna: Denkschriften der Österreichischen Akademie der Wissenschaften, phil.-hist. Kl. 210.
Salles, J.-F. 1987. The Arab-Persian Gulf under the Seleucids. In *Hellenism in the East*, ed. A. Kuhrt and S. Sherwin-White, 75–109. London: Duckworth.
———. 1994a. Le Golfe arabo-persique entre Séleucides et Maurya. *Topoi* 4/2: 597–610.
———. 1994b. Fines Indiae, Ardh el-Hind: Recherches sur le devenir de la mer Érythrée. In *The Roman and Byzantine army in the East*, ed. E. Dabrowa, 165–87. Krakow: Drukarnia Uniwerstyety Jagiellońskiego.
———. 1996. Achaemenid and Hellenistic trade in the Indian Ocean. In *The Indian Ocean in Antiquity*, ed. J. Reade, 251–67. London: Kegan Paul International.

Shayegan, M. R. 2011. *Arsacids and Sasanians: Political ideology in post-Hellenistic and Late Antique Persia*. Cambridge: Cambridge University Press.

Skjærvø, P. O. 2000. The joy of the cup: A Pre-Sasanian Middle Persian inscription on a silver bowl. *BAI* 11: 93–104.

Wiesehöfer, J. 1994a. *Die "dunklen Jahrhunderte" der Persis*. Munich: Zetemata 90.

———. 1994b. Zum Nachleben von Achaimeniden und Alexander in Iran. In *Continuity and Change*, ed. H. Sancisi-Weerdenburg, A. Kuhrt, and M.C. Root, 389–97. Leiden: AchHist 8.

———. 1996. Discordia et Defectio—Dynamis kai Pithanourgia. Die frühen Seleukiden und Iran. In *Hellenismus. Beiträge zur Erforschung von Akkulturation und politischer Ordnung in den Staaten des hellenistischen Zeitalters*, ed. B. Funck, 29–56. Tübingen: J. C. Mohr Siebeck.

———. 2001. Frataraka. *EnIr* 10: 195.

———. 2003. Tarkumuwa und das Farnah. In *A Persian perspective: Essays in memory of Heleen Sancisi-Weerdenburg*, ed. W. F. M. Henkelman and A. Kuhrt, 173–87. Leiden: AchHist 13.

———. 2004. *Ancient Persia*, 3rd ed. London/New York: I. B. Tauris.

———. 2007. Fars under Seleucid and Parthian rule. In *The age of the Parthians*, ed. V. S. Curtis and S. Stewart, 37–49. London: I. B. Tauris.

———. 2011a. The "Accursed" and the "Adventurer": Alexander the Great in Iranian tradition. In *A Companion to Alexander literature in the Middle Ages*, ed. Z. D. Zuwiyya, 113–32. Leiden: Brill.

———. 2011b. Frataraka rule in Seleucid Persis: A new appraisal. In *Creating a Hellenistic World*, ed. A. Erskine and L. Llewellyn-Jones, 107–21. Swansea: Classical Press of Wales.

———. 2012. Das Diadem bei den Achaimeniden: Die schriftliche Überlieferung. In *Das Diadem der hellenistischen Herrscher: Übernahme, Transformation oder Neuschöpfung eines Herrschaftszeichens?*, ed. A. Lichtenberger, K. Martin, H.-H. Nieswandt, and D. Salzmann, 55–62. Bonn: EUROS 1.

CHAPTER 37

THE ARSACIDS (PARTHIANS)

STEFAN R. HAUSER

INTRODUCTION

The Arsacid (or Parthian) Empire was one of the most extensive and long-lasting political entities not only in Iranian, but in Near and Middle Eastern history. Together with its indirect predecessor, the Achaemenid Empire, and its successor and continuator, the Sasanian Empire, it counts as one of the three ancient Iranian empires. Nevertheless, its general reputation is much lower than the other two and research on it remains comparatively limited.

Arsacid history should be divided into three phases. The early phase covers the period from the beginnings of Arsacid power in the mid-third century BC by the eponymous Arsaces I in Parthia and Hyrcania, east and south of the Caspian Sea, to its incorporation of what is today northern Iran and Turkmenistan. The middle phase begins with the transition to empire in the 140s BC, when the entirety of modern Iran and many neighboring regions, especially the southern part of modern Iraq, were conquered. Later northern Iraq and Armenia up to the upper Euphrates were added to the realm and with Mithridates II the Arsacid rulers assumed the title "King of Kings" (c.108 BC). The later Arsacid period began with the consolidation of Arsacid family rule in middle of the first century AD, after a period of internal strife. It lasted through several wars with Rome during the second century and ended with the defeat of the last Arsacid King of Kings by the Sasanian Ardašīr I (see Chapters 35, 39; Hauser 2012: 1003–5).

The Arsacid Empire thus existed for 475 years. From the early first century BC to the 220s AD, the Arsacid family ruled over a vast area from the Syrian Euphrates in the west to the Indus in the east, from the steppes of Central Asia in the north to the shores of the Red Sea (Mare Erythraeum) and the Indian Ocean. Despite this, the period is among the least known in Oriental history and archaeology.

This chapter first addresses some of the reasons for the comparative neglect of the Arsacid Empire. It then reviews the principal modern conceptions of Arsacid rule (the nomadic heritage, internal fragmentation and regionalization, and the idea of a Hellenized East). Finally, some explanations for the long duration and obvious success of the empire are proposed.

Sources and modern conceptions of the Arsacid Empire in Iran

Although the Arsacid period belongs to the "historical periods," the number of available written sources, especially from Iranian territory, is very limited. A number of ancient historiographies by indigenous (esp. Apollodorus) and Roman authors (e.g., Strabo), alluded to by various ancient authors, have not survived. No texts detail administrative or social matters. Some 2500 ostraca found at Nisa, mainly concerning the distribution of wine between 150 and 12 BC; a few Greek and Aramaic inscriptions from Susa and Elymean rock reliefs (see Chapters 35, 38, 40, 41; Vanden Berghe and Schippmann 1985); as well as two Greek and one Parthian parchment from Avroman concerning landed property (Chapter 40), provide incidental information on Arsacid rulers and genealogy (Thommen 2010: 467–91; Weber 2010: 492–561). Outside of Iran the Babylonian astronomical diaries as well as a few cuneiform archives and Greek inscriptions, all from Babylon, offer glimpses of historical events, while 500 short Aramaic inscriptions from Hatra and Assur shed light on local history (Böck 2010; Beyer 1998).

Due to the scarcity of written evidence from within the empire even the basic outline of Arsacid history depends on foreign and later sources. Islamic historians mainly preserve the Sasanian version of Arsacid history, but the Sasanians attempted to distance themselves from their predecessors in order to legitimate their rule. In contrast to the strong rule of the Sasanians, the preceding Arsacid period is denounced as a time of up to ninety (Tabarī 710; Schubert 2010: 458ff.) "party kings" (Pahlavi *kadag-xwadāy*, Ar. *molūk al-ṭawā'ef*) who paid homage to the Arsacid King of Kings. In Islamic times even the duration of Arsacid rule was no longer known. It is often reduced to 266 years, or even to "some 200 years" as in Ferdowsī's *Shah-nama* (VII 116), although the nearly correct number of 523 years between Alexander and the Sasanian Ardashir, based on Syriac chronicles, is likewise related by Tabarī (711) (Shahbazi 1986).

Since little concrete information is provided by Arabic and Persian texts, Arsacid history has been largely reconstructed from Roman sources (Debevoise 1938; Schippmann 1980, 1986), which call the empire "Parthian" after the region of origin. This term has been commonly used in modern Western literature, but should be abandoned as it conveys an incorrect idea of an ethnic ruling class within the multiethnic, multilingual population (Wolski 1993; Hauser 2005).

Only minor portions of the once extensive Roman literature on the Arsacids have survived. Nevertheless, Justin's *Epitome* of Pompeius Trogus' lost *Philippic History*; Tacitus' *Annals*; and Cassius Dio's *Roman History* provide the backbone for the narrative history of events from the rise of Arsaces I to the final doom brought by the Sasanian Ardashir I. These reports are supplemented by Appian; fragments of Arrian's lost *Parthica*; Plutarch's biographies; Flavius Josephus; and others (Thommen 2010). Excellent information on topography is provided by Strabo's *Geography*, Pliny the Elder's *Natural History*, Isidore of Charax's *Parthian Stations*, and Claudius Ptolemy's *Geography*. To these sources we may add some contemporary reports by Chinese embassies (Golze and Storm 2010), as well as later Armenian and Syriac chronicles of varying reliability (Traina 2010; Zehnder 2010).

The unavoidable reliance on Roman sources creates an awkward situation. As the extant Roman historians were not interested in the Arsacid Empire as such, the sources are skewed toward military actions and internal differences that prompted Roman (diplomatic) reactions. The administrative or social organization of the Arsacid Empire, particularly in Iran, remains a matter of debate. In the past, in the search for any scrap of information, even the most partisan Oriental and Western sources were often taken at face value. This resulted in constant negative comparisons with either Rome (presented as culturally superior enemies) or the Sasanians (in the role of mighty successors). This in turn had the effect of severely limiting historical and archaeological research on the Arsacid period.

Arsacid-period rock reliefs in Elymais belong to the earliest documented archaeological remains in Persia (Flandin and Coste 1851–4). But in accord with George Rawlinson's (1873: 388) judgment that the Parthians scarcely had an idea of art, the buildings and burials excavated in Susa before the 1960s largely remained unpublished (cf. now Boucharlat and Haerinck 2011). After the French monopoly on excavation in Iran ended many scholars preferred prehistoric or Achaemenid and Sasanian sites. Exceptions include Herzfeld's work at Kuh-e Khwaja (Chapter 46; Kawami 2005); E. F. Schmidt's investigations at Rayy; and Sir Aurel Stein's studies at Shami. Only in the 1960s and 1970s was fieldwork directed at Arsacid burials (Egami et al. 1966; Sono and Fukai 1968; Kambakhsh Fard 1998), settlements and religious architecture (e.g., Shahr-e Qumis: Hansman and Stronach 1974; Elymaean temples at Masjed-e Solayman and Bard-e Neshanda: Ghirshman 1976; Qal'eh Yazdegerd: Keall 2002; sites on the Gorgan plain: Kiani 1982). At many sites, in particular Susa, Arsacid levels were carefully studied (Haerinck 1983; Boucharlat 1987; de Miroschedji 1987) and surveys concentrating on evidence from the later periods were commenced (Wenke 1975/76; Venco Ricciardi 1980), although the Achaemenid and Sasanian periods were often preferred. With the Islamic revolution, interest in the Arsacids declined (cf. Boucharlat 2008). Only in recent years has a steadily growing interest appeared, especially in Arsacid burial patterns (e.g., Mohammadifar and Sarraf 2006; Khosrowzadeh 2007; Nemati et al. 2011; Roustaei and Azadi 2011) and specialized surveys (Niknami et al. 2007; Kaim 2008).

This renewed interest and additional material evidence allow us to revisit the question of whether the common images of and treasured prejudices about the Arsacid period can still be upheld. In this chapter three main ideas about the Arsacids are explored: (1) the nomadic character of the "Parthian" rulers and their empire; (2) the notion of political fragmentation; and (3) the Arsacid Empire as a Hellenized interlude between the Achaemenids and Sasanians.

The Arsacid Empire and "nomadic heritage"

Arsaces I gained independence from Seleucid authority in the former Achaemenid province of Parthyene, east of the Caspian Sea, around 247 BC. According to one among several conflicting Roman sources, this happened with the help of the Parni tribe, who were probably nomadic. Modern historians have accordingly interpreted this coup d'état as a nomadic takeover. Some believe that the nomadic descent of the Arsacids provides the key to an understanding of the empire's social, military and cultural constitution (Wolski 1993; Koshelenko and Pilipko 1994; Olbrycht 1998). The idea finds support in Roman notices on family relations between Artabanus II and Scythians in Central Asia; the peripatetic nature of the Arsacid court; and the importance of horses in Arsacid life and warfare. Archaeology adds evidence for shared dress and weaponry in the Arsacid Empire and on the steppes settled by nomads. But is this enough to prove that the Arsacids maintained a nomadic lifestyle even after coming to power?

Nomads and the early Arsacid state

The revolt of Arsaces I was part of the secession of several Central Asian provinces from the Seleucid Empire in the mid-third century BC (Wolski 1993: 37–65; Lerner 1999: 13–31). Unfortunately, conflicting versions of the events by Arrian, Strabo and Justin cannot be reconciled and they should be understood as literary works which employed *topoi* of foundation myths, like humble beginnings, and explained to a Roman audience the strength of their enemies, that is, the fierceness of Scythians (Hauser 2005: 175–8).

According to Justin (41.5.1–2), Arsaces I himself (whether a nomad or, following Strabo and Arrian, a former Bactrian or Parthian noble courtier) immediately secured his new possessions against Seleucids and nomads alike by strengthening existing and newly founded cities and building fortresses. His successors ruled over these areas from their capital at Nisa (in Turkmenistan) for nearly 100 years. Nisa is split into two, heavily fortified parts: a large settlement area (New Nisa) and a citadel and possible ceremonial center for Arsacid royalty (Old Nisa, renamed Mithradatkert in the first century BC; Invernizzi 2001; Pilipko 2008). Excavated since the 1930s, Old Nisa is of outstanding importance for our knowledge of early Arsacid culture. Of particular interest is an architectural complex consisting of several large buildings grouped around a courtyard. The center of this complex is the "Round Hall," a circular room with the diameter of 17 m set in a square building measuring 30 m on a side. The incurving walls led the excavators to reconstruct a hyperbolic dome. The vaulted and domed architecture of Old Nisa is of decidedly local, Central Asian style (cf. Baimatowa 2008). Hellenistic influence can be seen in architectural decoration and painted, larger-than-life clay sculptures. The monumentality of the Round Hall and the findings inside, including a portrait of Mithridates I, indicate its sacral nature as a royal memorial (Invernizzi 2007). The sculpture resembles the Yüechi (Kushan) palatial structure at Khalchyan in Uzbekistan from the late second century BC, which in turn shows local adaptation and transformation of Hellenistic influence in the depiction of humans (Pugačenkova 1971; Nehru 1999/2000).

More important in respect to the nomadic question are changes in land use and livelihood (on nomads in archaeology see Cribb 1991; Hauser 2006a; Barnard and Wendrich 2008; Hauser forthcoming). Archaeological surveys in the wider area governed by the Arsacids in the later third and early second centuries BC, especially the Serakhs oasis, the Atrek river and Damghan, show that at this time large irrigation systems, some dating from Achaemenid times but since collapsed, were newly created or revived (Kaim 2008; Venco Ricciardi 1980; Trinkaus 1983). Even north of the borders additional settlements sprang up which points to a stabile regime based on sedentary agriculture. Thus, already the earliest archaeological evidence for the Arsacids points to a sedentary, urbanized society with wide ranging contacts to centers of Hellenistic culture, not to a nomadic heritage.

Nomads and Empire

If a kernel of Arsacid nomadism still persisted, it will have been lost to the Arsacids with the expansion of their power and the transformation of their state into an empire in the mid-second century BC. After a number of former satraps in Media (central and western Iran), Elymais (southwestern Iran) and Mesene (southern Iraq) had seceded from the Seleucid Empire, the Arsacid Mithridates I (171–138 BC) took the opportunity and conquered Media (148 BC), Babylonia (141 BC), and Elymais (139/8–132 BC) in succession. Phraates II (138–127 BC) extended his territory eastwards into Margiana and established a common border with the Yüechi, a western Chinese tribal confederation that had ousted the Macedonian dynasty of Bactria (the so-called Greco-Bactrian rulers). By and large this border remained stable until the Sasanian conquests. Finally, early in his reign Mithridates II (123–88 BC) extended the Arsacid realm by conquering all the land up to the Syrian Euphrates.

Following this expansion the empire's economic center shifted to the densely settled, economically strong areas of Media, Elymais and, especially, Babylonia. Arsacid expansion was marked by the building of huge, fortified cities. First Hecatompylus (Shahr-e Qumis), a regional center south of the Alborz Mountains, became a capital. Only a palace-like building and a strongly fortified place with several towers have been explored at this enormous site (Hansman and Stronach 1974). At Rayy (Rhagae), which was renamed Arsakia (Chaumont 1973: 201–5), hundreds of coins confirm a resettlement of the site after a long gap in the second half of the second century BC. Excavations in 1932 at Cheshmeh Ali exposed a huge, central court building, identified as a temple (Schmidt 1940: 32–4). Recent work has demonstrated that the fortified city (*šahrestān*) and citadel were also enclosed by strong ramparts (Rante 2008, 2010). An impressive Arsacid foundation is the perfectly regular city plan with large building units exposed at Ecbatana (Sarraf 2003; Azarnoush 2007).

For some time the Arsacid court was peripatetic, seasonally migrating between Ecbatana and the winter residence at Ctesiphon, across the Tigris from the populous former Seleucid capital, Seleucia-on-the-Tigris. Later, Ctesiphon was chosen as sole capital and remained such throughout the Arsacid and Sasanian periods. Ecbatana housed the local king of Media. With the move to Babylonia the last vestiges of nomadic social practices or organization will certainly have disappeared in the new, urbanized imperial setting.

Dress and weaponry

Nevertheless, connections with the people of the steppe are indicated by common types of dress. Representations of Arsacid dignitaries and kings on coins, Elymaean reliefs, and in sculpture at Susa, Hatra, and Palmyra show embroidered, knee-length tunics or short jackets with belts, trousers, and shoes. While these garments rarely survive in the archaeological record, comparable belt buckles are known from graves ascribed to Sarmatians or Sakas (Treister 2003) and in Kushan territory (Bactria), for example at Tillya Tepe (Sarianidi 1985). These attest a common mode of dress (Curtis 2001; Winkelmann 2006: 133–4). Typical Arsacid weaponry included long swords with a specific type of scabbard slide (Trousdale 1975) and daggers (with a gold-mounted hilt, as in Tillya Tepe) housed within a quadrilobe scabbard, a weapon that probably originated in Mongolia or southern Siberia (Winkelmann 2003: 94) and was worn, fixed at the thigh, by horse-riding, trouser-wearing peoples all over the Arsacid Empire and beyond. Examples are known from Saka-Sarmatian tombs, and are illustrated on the reliefs of Antiochus I of Commagene at Nemrud Dağ, on statuary at Hatra, and on Arsacid coinage (Winkelmann 2006; Peterson 2011).

This wide distribution of rather unspecific dress types and specific weaponry connected with cavalry hardly demonstrates a specific nomadic disposition within the Arsacid Empire. Rather, it points to common ways of dressing and warfare irrespective of the mode of living.

On the fringes of empire

Leaving aside any possible Arsacid nomadic tendencies, nomadism certainly played an important role in the empire. As could be expected, coordination in animal breeding and trade is reflected in coin distribution and the proliferation of Iranian and Western artifacts in nomadic burials. Confrontations also occurred. For example, Phraates II and his successor died fighting nomadic incursions. Furthermore, the empire encompassed several areas of great aridity, for example on the Iranian plateau and in eastern Iran, that are best suited to a pastoral-nomadic mode of living. Nevertheless, our evidence suggests that, in the Arsacid period, the borders of settlement and agriculture were pushed further into the steppe than at almost any time before or since. In the later Arsacid period scores of settlements existed in Parthyene and Hyrcania (Venco Ricciardi 1980; Trinkaus 1983; Kaim 2008). This period has even been called "the golden age" of Margiana, because of the extent of irrigation works and the construction of fortifications as protection against nomadic incursions (Gaibov and Koshelenko 2002: 51; Koshelenko 2007). The adjacent drainage of the Amu Darya and the Darya-e-Siah River in Bactria shows a dramatic increase in settlement density and size (Leriche 2007: 137–8). A similar development occurred in the western steppe around Hatra (Ibrahim 1986; Hauser 2000) and may also be reflected in the poorly researched area of southeastern Iran by Arsacid-period sites like Damba Koh (Basafa 2008; cf. Stein 1937; Choubak 1999).

In summary, where climatic conditions were favorable, the Arsacid rulers followed a policy of intense expansion of irrigation via *qanats* and canals nurturing sedentary lifestyles to the cost of transhumant pastoralism. Intense exchange with nomads on the borders and inside the empire had no visible bearing on the rulers who lived in urban environments.

Organization of Empire

An idea commonly encountered in literature on the Arsacid Empire is that it was internally fragmented, with weak central authority. Roman sources (especially Tacitus) report repeated struggles amongst contenders for the throne in the later first century BC and early first century AD. A bilingual Greek–Aramaic inscription on a bronze statue of Heracles from Seleucia-on-the-Tigris attests to Arsacid dynastic conflict in 150/51 (Pennachietti 1987; Invernizzi 1989). In the absence of further reports on internal affairs in the first to third centuries AD, concurrent coin issues by different kings have been interpreted as evidence of further struggles. The minting of coins by the kings of Media, Elymais, Persis, and Characene was also interpreted as a statement of independence from Arsacid rule in those regions. The erroneous assumption that the King of Kings lacked authority over troops acting under the orders of influential landowners and petty kings (Wolski 1993 versus Hauser 2006b) gave the Arsacids a reputation as weak kings or even "clowns of the millennium" (Keall 1994).

Since written evidence bearing on the internal structure and administration of the Arsacid Empire is limited, archaeological sources are particularly important. This overview first discusses the evidence of coins, followed by settlement history, trade, religion, and regionalization in material culture.

Coins and autonomy

Arsacid coinage largely followed the Seleucid system. While drachms were used in Iran, tetradrachms predominated in greater Mesopotamia and Elymais. Still, the system and its implications are not fully understood. A *Sylloge Nummorum Parthicorum* is currently in preparation to replace the present, provisional reference system, which has been criticized for its typology and dubious attributions, and for insufficient illustrations (Sellwood 1980; de Callataÿ 1994; Alram 1998). Aside from royal mints at Seleucia-on-the-Tigris and Ecbatana, drachms and tetradrachms were also struck by the local rulers of Mesene, Elymais, Persis, and the eastern Indo-Parthian areas. This has long been considered unequivocal evidence of the independence of these areas from Arsacid control, but this is far from certain. In medieval Europe, for example, the minting, issuing, and distribution of coins was often delegated by rulers to their dependent nobles as part of their fiefdom. Emissions by satraps are also known from the Achaemenid (Kolb and Tietz 2001) and Seleucid periods. Particularly the *frataraka* in Persis are seen as "lords of Persis by order of the Seleucids" in the most recent literature (Wiesehöfer 2007: 40–3; Klose and Müseler 2008). The minting of coins does not, therefore, constitute unambiguous evidence of autonomy. It all depends on the regulations that governed the emissions.

Central planning: irrigation

In trying to estimate the strength of central authority we might look again at irrigation systems. In diverse surveys across Iran it has been conclusively demonstrated that settlement and irrigation reached high levels during the Arsacid period. Several examples from the fringes of empire have already been cited. Other cases include Elymais, with its capital Susa, and the central Zagros region. Although the dating of survey pottery must be corrected (Boucharlat 1987), it is clear that settlement and agriculture, particularly in Elymais, were greatly expanded (Adams 1962; Wenke 1987). An enormous density of sites with Arsacid occupation (N = 340) was recorded in the central Zagros region (Niknami et al. 2007). Unfortunately, our knowledge of Arsacid pottery is still very uneven. While forms and chronology in Elymais (especially at Susa) and the northern provinces are fairly well known, stratigraphic excavations are lacking in other regions, especially Fars and the southern provinces of Iran. This renders the interpretation of survey material in Fars difficult (*MAPSO*: 13, 181; Boucharlat and Fazeli Nashli 2009). Likewise, few Arsacid sites have been documented in Luristan's Kuh–Giluye province (Roustaei and Azadi 2011: 200). Despite these problems a strong trend toward intensive settlement is also observable near Bushehr on the Persian Gulf coast (Carter et al. 2006). Probably many *qanats* throughout the country were dug in Arsacid times, but more systematic research is needed (cf. Boucharlat 2001; Weisgerber 2004).

In general the picture in northern, western, and southwestern Iran is comparable to the situation in Babylonia, where the size and complexity of irrigation systems reached unprecedented levels during the Arsacid period (cf. Adams 1981). While this could have been achieved to some extent by local rulers, the enormity of irrigation in the west and the overall pattern speak in favor of central planning.

State control may also be visible in border protection. Although the Gorgan wall was recently assigned a late Sasanian construction date (Omrani Rekavandi et al. 2008; Sauer et al. 2009), a number of Arsacid-period fortresses are known in the region beyond the wall and in Margiana (Bader et al. 1998; Jakubiak 2006). It remains to be seen whether the troops stationed there were in the pay and under the authority of local rulers or the Arsacid King of Kings.

Trade

Political stability also positively influences long-distance trade (for a different view see V. S. Curtis 2000: 28). The flourishing of the transcontinental caravan trade in luxury goods and spices in the Arsacid period is indicative of stability and contributed to the empire's prosperity. The first channels of commerce are the Central Asian caravan routes, the so-called Silk Road, along which merchants traded wares from China to northern Iraq via Bactria and Margiana. Within Iran the route crossed the most important Arsacid cities of Comisene and Media, Hecatompylus, Rhagae, and Ecbatana. Exchange along the Silk Road was supported by favorable climates and facilitated, in the east, by the military protection of routes by Han China, as recent research in Xinjiang has shown (Wieczorek and Lind 2007 with references). A similar level of security and protection has yet to be demonstrated in Arsacid Iran. Nevertheless, some of the fortresses in Margiana and northern Iran might have served this end.

Trade induced close contact between western Bactria and the Arsacid realm, as indicated by the enormous quantities of Arsacid coinage found there. The first century AD burials at Tillya Tepe in northwest Bactria, for example, contained more than 20,000 items, including gold plaques for clothing, jewelry, and weapons, and may serve as an example for the economic, cultural, and material influence of the Arsacid Empire on areas outside its borders (Peterson 2011). While the people buried at Tillya Tepe might have been the sedentary elites from neighboring Emshi Tepe, long-distance trade is also a typical feature in the integration of nomads (Khazanov 1994: 202–12).

Cultural exchange along the Silk Road is vividly demonstrated by the spectacular finds from Begram (Afghanistan), where Chinese lacquer work and Indian ivories were found alongside painted and millefiori glass and fine gypsum tondi representing Hellenistic gods, humans, and animals from the Mediterranean and Egypt (Hackin 1939; Ghirshman 1946; Mehendale 2005; Cambon 2007). These objects are outstanding examples of the cultural milieu created by transcontinental trade in the first and second centuries and facilitated by Han and Arsacid political stability.

The second main trade artery was the sea route between India and the Persian Gulf. Although the route along the Persian coast and across the Indian Ocean had a long history, commerce multiplied in the Arsacid period due to the growing demand for silk and spices in the Roman Mediterranean and Arsacid Babylonia. Written sources, like the *Periplus Mare Erythraeum* (Schoff 1912), Strabo's *Geography* (16.3–4), and Pliny's *Natural History* (book 6) offer abundant information (cf. Raschke 1978; Schuol 2000; Young 2001). The main port, "where the merchants of the east meet," according to the *Acts of Thomas*, was Spasinou Charax, the capital of Mesene. Trade in the Persian Gulf is reflected by finds of Roman glass, pottery from Baluchistan, India, and plenty of Babylonian glazed wares, particularly at ed-Dur on the coast of the United Arab Emirates (UAE, cf. Potts 2001b). On Kharg Island the tombs of Palmyrenes were found (Haerinck 1975; Potts 2004). Military posts were set up along the coast, for example at Thaj (Potts 1993) and on Bahrain (ancient Tylos/Thiloua; Herling and Salles 1993; Lombard and Kevran 1993), but the areas of modern Oman and UAE seem not to have been under direct Arsacid control. Further evidence comes from Fars and Mesene (cf. Potts 1990, 1996; Carter et al. 2006). On the south coast of Iran sea trade may be indicated by the distribution of Mesopotamian or Elymaean (?) green-glazed pottery and Londo ware from Pakistan at Damba Koh, an important site in the Chah Bahar district (Basafa 2008).

Regionalization in material culture

Recently the question was raised as to whether the distribution of material culture could reflect political autonomy (*MAPSO*: 12). This was prompted by the relatively clear regional distinctions between pottery inventories across Iran. In his seminal study on Parthian pottery Haerinck (1983) distinguished nine different regions with distinctive pottery productions. While these by and large match the distribution of Arsacid kingdoms (and modern provinces), the divisions reflect natural geographic boundaries as well.

Generally speaking, while pottery was mostly locally made, Arsacid Iran was "divided into two large zones, the southern and central regions characterized by painted pottery, the northern ones by burnished wares" (Boucharlat and Haerinck 1991: 306). Green- to blue-glazed ceramic, a trademark of western Arsacid pottery, was restricted to southwestern and western Persia. The latter regions thus show strong connections to Mesopotamian production, also in the often Hellenistic shapes, like "fish plates," two-handled amphorae, and "pilgrim flasks," and the thin-walled eggshell ware. In Sistan connections to Bactria and the Kushan areas in modern Pakistan are visible in the fine wares.

This distribution does not reflect political borders, but rather different contacts and cultural zones, which probably resemble in large measure the distribution patterns of minor art objects. Unfortunately, our knowledge of everyday objects like glass, seals (Gaibov 1996, 2007; Bivar 1982), and even terracotta (Martinez-Sève 2002) is very rudimentary.

Burial patterns

A growing interest in Arsacid-period burials is clear in the recent archaeological literature. A number of cemeteries in ancient Media Atropatene around Garmi (Kambakhsh

Fard 1998) and Gilan (Egami et al. 1966; Sono and Fukai 1968; Fukai and Matsutani 1980) were excavated in the 1960s. Larger cemeteries are known at Kangavar and Sang-e Shir near Hamadan (Azarnoush 1975). An impressive addition is Damba Koh in ancient Carmania (mod. Kerman province), where 2500 to 3000 Arsacid and Sasanian cairn and pit-graves were found (Basafa 2008). Important new finds include tomb chambers at Cheram in the southwestern Zagros with a rich collection of pottery, bronze bowls and weapons (Roustaei and Azadi 2011), and the family hypogeum of Veliran near Tehran, consisting of several rooms, housing couples of the same or different generations as well as pits for older bones. The burials of the first century BC to first century AD were richly furnished, for example with silver objects and clay rhyta (Nemati et al. 2011).

While simple pit-graves and pithos- or jar-graves are known all over Iran (cf. Mohammadifar and Sarraf 2006), more complex tombs have different distributions. Huge, probably specifically produced burial pithoi were used in the first century BC to second century AD burials at Germi (Kambakhsh Fard 1998; Curtis and Simpson 2000). Cairns were typical in southern and southeastern Iran (Choubak 1999; Khosrowzadeh 2007), and have also been found in Fars and along the Persian Gulf coast (Boucharlat 1989). Cist graves were favored at Kangavar. Clay coffins were found in Media (at Kangavar and Hamadan) and most often in the lowlands of Elymais. Aside from glazed coffins, underground burial chambers in Elamite tradition are attested at several sites in Elymais (Nemati et al. 2011: 90). Of the hundreds of Arsacid burials discovered at Susa, six burial vaults with rich inventories of glass vessels, figurines, metal objects, and pottery with obvious connections to Babylonia were recently published (Boucharlat and Haerinck 2011). None of the burials show obvious religious affinities. Zoroastrian *astodans* are difficult to identify and date.

Decentralization and weakness?

The material culture of the Arsacid period shows obvious regional tendencies, especially in mass-produced pottery and inherited burial customs within Iran and outside it. Nevertheless, these patterns bear only a coincidental relationship to political organization. The political situation is better inferred by archaeological correlates of economy and security: the characteristic, massive intensification of irrigation and settlement not only in the lowlands of Elymais, but all along minor rivers across Iran. Local rulers might have been responsible for individual canals or *qanats*. Facilitation of these infrastructural measures as well as the vast projects in Elymais and Babylonia required a well-functioning imperial administration. Also, the unprecedented amount of long-distance trade within and across Arsacid Iran, via the Silk Road and along the Iranian coast, would have been inconceivable without political control and stability supported by military installations and the integration of nomadic groups. In contrast to older views, this stability seems a hallmark of much of the Arsacid period. As argued elsewhere, for about the last two centuries of Arsacid rule the important provinces were most probably ruled by Arsacid family members bearing the title "king" (Hauser 2006b). Precisely the same system was continued by the Sasanians. Neither the title king nor the right or duty to mint coins necessarily implies autonomy. On the contrary, the submission of these local kings finds its expression in the Arsacid title King of Kings (Hauser 2005: 185–99).

HELLENIZATION AND "PARTHIAN ART"

Ever since Herzfeld (1941: 275) stated that there was "no archaeological object produced after [Alexander's conquest] that does not bear its stamp," only the intensity of Arsacid Hellenization, not the fact of it, has been questioned. Hellenization has been seen in the adaptation of Greek coinage, language, and iconography, and in the realm of religious syncretism (Callieri 2007). Arsacid sculpture and minor arts have been viewed as provincial offshoots of Greco-Roman art, relying on a constant or repeated influx of Western inspiration (Mathiesen 1992: 13; Pfrommer 1993). The idea of a Hellenized interlude between the "true" Iranian Achaemenids and Sasanians needs a critical reevaluation, especially with respect to Iran. The use of Greek, for example, seems to have been limited to certain communities with a minority of Greco-Macedonian settlers. But while the latest Greek inscription from Susa dates to 21 AD, a Greek version was nonetheless produced of Šābuhr's I's inscription on the Ka'ba-ye Zardosht 240 years later (Huyse 1999).

Architecture

Herzfeld's view was influenced by the "Hellenistic temple" with Ionic columns at Khorheh. But Hellenistic contributions to Arsacid architecture in Iran are difficult to identify. While the Macedonian foundation Aï Khanoum in Bactria, which was destroyed in the mid-second century BC, displays the impact of Greek settlers with its theater and gymnasium, the Hellenistic sculpture at Nisa was found in an architectural context that is typically Central Asian. Even Aï Khanoum's temples and palace are local or Achaemenid in style (Bernard 2007 with references).

Later examples of Western architectural forms in Iran are rare. The manor house at Khorheh, which displays Ionic capitals, is the only clear example (Hakemi 1990; Rahbar 1999). Western architectural complexes like private houses with interior courtyards and flat tiles were found in three successive levels of Ville Royale A in Susa but, in contrast to Babylon and Seleucia-on-the-Tigris in Mesopotamia or Aï Khanoum in Bactria, no Greek temple or theater was unearthed there. Even at Susa the Hellenistic style of the houses in Ville Royale A might not be representative of the entire city. Temples in Elymais and Central Asia, such as Takht-e Sangin, seem to follow local traditions.

Later Arsacid architecture introduced three new features. As a new form the *iwan* appeared for the first time in the early first century AD. While popular in Mesopotamia, in Arsacid Persia this hallmark of later Iranian architecture is attested only at Khorheh (Wright 1991; Lecuyot 1993) and Qal'eh Zohak (Kleiss 1973). As a new technique the generous use of fast-setting mortar, which allowed the construction of large vaults, became popular. The third new feature was the lavish use of stucco in private residences, which transformed an idea of earlier Hellenistic architecture. Outstanding evidence of later Arsacid visual culture is provided at Qal'eh Yazdegerd, a 40 ha stronghold overlooking the main route from Babylonia to the Iranian plateau (Keall 1977). The well-preserved walls and columns of its palace complex were covered with more than 300 stucco panels, reliefs, and figurative capitals dating to the later second to third century AD. While ornamental bands of interlocking meanders and some figures interpreted as Dionysus, Aphrodite, and their followers relate to Hellenistic ideas, others show standing males in "Parthian" costume, naked dancers, and mythological creatures like *sēn-murw*s (Keall et al. 1980; Keall 1982, 2002). The rendering of forms and motifs is local, late Arsacid in style and foreshadows Sasanian art in medium, subject, and style.

Minor arts

Hellenistic influence is less visible in everyday objects than in sculpture and luxury products. For the late third and early second centuries BC direct contact with the Mediterranean is witnessed by some Rhodian amphorae found at Susa (Monsieur et al. 2011). Into the late Arsacid period green-glazed pottery from Susa and the vicinity continued to display some "typical Hellenistic" forms, known throughout (Arsacid) Mesopotamia and Syria. But the important question is whether we should appraise these Hellenistic cultural traits as evidence of foreign impact or rather as part of the constantly evolving regional culture that already produced its own class of artifacts integrating various influences handed down locally.

Greek influence in the visual arts was particularly strong in the early Arsacid period at Nisa. This is vividly illustrated by marble statues of Aphrodite (possibly identified with Anahita), Artemis, and Dionysus in purely Mediterranean style, as well as life-sized clay heads found in the palace (Invernizzi 2009). But Greek and Central Asian elements are also found side by side in gilded silver or bronze figurines including Athena, Eros, griffins, and eagles (Invernizzi 1999). This truly non-Greek but Hellenistic blend of influences finds supreme expression in the splendid collection of ivory rhyta found in the monumental Square House (Invernizzi and Lippolis 2007).

The use of rhyta with mostly zoomorphic protomes for serving and pouring liquids seems an Iranian invention. In the fifth to fourth century BC rhyta were widespread in the steppe and the Greek world and later very popular in Arsacid Iran, as illustrated by several groups of long, slender silver rhyta with zoomorphic protomes (Gunter and Jett 1992; Pfrommer 1993; O'Neill 1996). Sold on the art market together with richly decorated silver bowls and horse trappings, they may have originated in elite burials in northern Iran. Clay rhyta are widely dispersed in Iranian Azerbaijan (Kambakhsh Fard 1998) and Media (Nemati and Sadraie 2010).

The ivory rhyta from Nisa partly display Greek mythological scenes and deities on the body. But often their execution and the recurring presence of typically eastern subjects demonstrate a perfect blend of both local and Western traditions (Masson and Pugačenkova 1982; Pappalardo 2010).

Sculpture

Outside of Nisa our understanding of representational arts in Arsacid Iran is still limited. Among the more than thirty statues found at Susa some appear to be imported marble statues of Greek deities. Others, such as the city *tyche* (Amiet 2001: 173, fig. 9), seem to have been locally produced, according to Western norms. Alongside Hellenic male statues are others showing men clad in long tunics, coats, trousers, and shoes. These are rendered less naturalistically and look straight at the beholder. This "frontality" is considered the most typical formal aspect of "Parthian art" as defined by Rostovtzeff (1938). According to Amiet (2001), these three groups of sculpture represent three periods of direct Seleucid control, strongly Hellenized art under early Arsacid rule, and the decline of Greek influence after the mid-first century AD (in connection with a period of assumed, but unlikely [see above] Elymaean autonomy). While the general trend outlined by Amiet may be correct, we should allow for the coexistence of various styles at the same time, as demonstrated also by the celebrated "prince" from Shami and the other sculptures found there (Godard 1937).

The diminishing impact of Greek ideas of proportion in figures and portraits is also evidenced on Arsacid coins. While early central and regional Arsacid coins followed Seleucid models in their obverse portraits, from the first century AD onward these became less detailed. In Iranian issues from Ecbatana and Persis the traditional Greek legend was replaced by Parthian Middle Persian (cf. Le Rider 1965; van't Haaff 2007).

Dwindling Greek influence is not necessarily the same as a loss of quality, but rather indicative of a different set of values. This is illustrated by life-sized statues of rulers of the second and third centuries excavated at Masjed-e Solayman which appear rigid, but demonstrate a certain virtuosity in their finely embroidered tunics, trousers, and shoes. The steadfast quality and frontality is found even in scenes of communicative acts between persons, which still gaze out of the reliefs toward the beholder. This produces immediacy, a direct contact between the person depicted and the observer, and was obviously considered more important than a naturalistic rendering. This non-Hellenistic way of representation is, nevertheless, neither ethnically "Parthian art" nor official "Arsacid art," simply the most commonly used form of visual communication within the empire and in its vicinity.

Religion

Hellenistic influence is also seen in syncretic deities. Syncretism between local and Western deities is already attested in the Seleucid period, especially in the case of Heracles who was venerated as Nergal or Verethragna. Gods in Greek attire and style are depicted, for example at the Arsacid court of Nisa, in sculpture and on rhyta. The best documented among the syncretic goddesses is Nanaya, who became prominent from about the second century BC in many parts of the Arsacid realm. Her cult is attested in Bactria, where she was associated with Kushan kingship; at Nisa und Susa as Artemis; on coins at Elymais as a huntress; in Adiabene; and even in Greece and Egypt (Potts 2001a; Ambos 2003; Invernizzi 2005). Although not originally a moon goddess and identified with Artemis, Nanaya was transformed via syncretism into a lunar deity equal to Roman Selene.

It is often presumed that the Arsacids were Zoroastrians. The first collection of all testimonies of the *Avesta* and *Zand* was probably ordered by Vologases I (Hintze 1998). But the impact of Zoroastrism in Iranian religious life is barely traceable archaeologically. *Frataraka* coins from Fars show possible fire temples already in the first half of the second century BC. Later ones may represent fire altars, but their interpretation is disputed (Haerinck and Overlaet 2008; Potts 2007). On rock reliefs at Tang-e Sarvak rulers worship at fire altars (Mathiesen 1992: 119–51). Kuh-e Khwaja (Chapter 46) is possibly the earliest known fire temple dated to the second to first century BC, followed by Mele Hairam, the earliest level of which has been dated tentatively to the second century AD (Kaim 2004).

The number of excavated Arsacid-period temples is small. A four-pillared building at Bard-e Neshanda has been identified as an Anahita temple of the first to second century AD. The god revered in the centrally placed "great temple" on the 2 ha large stone terrace at Masjed-e Solayman, probably of second century AD date, is unknown. A smaller temple there was possibly dedicated to Heracles (Ghirshman 1976; Augé et al. 1979). While Judaism and Christianity gained ground in Mesopotamia, Buddhism found followers in the eastern part of the Arsacid realm. Our limited knowledge of these various cults suggests neither alignment between religions and specific regions or administrative units nor extensive Hellenic impact in the realm of religion.

Hellenized Iran?

The above survey of the impact of Hellenism on Arsacid Iran suggests that, aside from Nisa and Susa, Hellenic influence appears to have been limited throughout Iran and should be treated with care. Only in and around Susa did Hellenistic culture become part of the local heritage attested in terracotta and pottery. The idea that Arsacid Iran shared the visual culture of the Hellenistic world confines it to the role of a dependent, nonproductive backwater. This limits our understanding of domestic artistic expression within the Arsacid realm, which combined elements of Mediterranean, Mesopotamian, and Iranian material culture.

Arsacid Iran, a reevaluation

One hopes that the discussion here has contributed in various ways to a reevaluation of the Arsacid Empire. Three explanatory concepts for the empire—nomadic heritage, political fragmentation, and Hellenic culture—have been discussed and challenged. Already in the founding phase of the empire the Arsacids displayed no specific nomadic attitudes. Instead, expansion of the agricultural base through canalization and the digging of *qanats*, as well as incentives for sedentarization, seems to be a hallmark of this period. The organization and maintenance of the huge irrigation systems in Elymais and elsewhere indicate comprehensive, abstract planning. This contradicts the traditional idea of a weak central government and internal fragmentation. The intensification of trade also supports this view as it both required and expressed stability and security.

The various regions of Arsacid Iran offer no uniform picture of material culture. Local traditions are clearly present in burial practices and pottery. The local economies remain largely unexplored. The finds of mummified workmen in the salt mine at Chehrabad near Zanjan and the silver mines at Nakhlak (Stöllner et al. 2004) offer some opportunities to examine questions of economic organization.

Differences between the strongly Hellenized city centers such as Susa and sites in the countryside are marked. Western influence in material culture and visual representation diminished with time through the Arsacid period. Regional differences appear to have been expressions of fundamental geographical rather than political divisions.

These results offer a new research paradigm. Because of the evidence of agricultural intensification, expansion of long-distance trade, and cultural exchange, as well as the multiplicity of religions, languages, and material expressions found in Iran, the Arsacid period is a most intriguing field of research. Archaeology is particularly useful in attempting to arrive at a more nuanced picture of one of the most successful empires in Iranian history.

Further reading

There is no single up-to-date book on Arsacid (Parthian) archaeology in Iran. Useful introductions include volume 271 of *Dossiers d'archéologie* (March 2002) and Herrmann (1977). Potts (1999) provides an excellent overview on Elymais. The written sources are collected and translated in three volumes (*QGP*). Important resources on the web include the *EnIr* online edition, though the entries there are sometimes outdated. For coins and bibliographic information see E. C. D Hopkins' www.parthia.com.

Historical summaries are often controversial in their approach to Arsacid rule. The classic summary is Debevoise (1938), which appears less dated than Schippmann (1980). The nomadic heritage is augmented by Koshelenko and Pilipko (1994) and Olbrycht (2003). For a critical approach, see Hauser (2005, 2006). Excellent summaries are those sections in *QGP* 1, chap. 2, which were written by B. Jacobs.

REFERENCES

Adams, R. McC. 1962. Agriculture and urban life in early southwestern Iran. *Science* 136: 109–22.

———. 1981. *Heartland of cities: Surveys of ancient settlement and land use on the central floodplain of the Euphrates.* Chicago: University of Chicago Press.

Alram, M. 1998. Stand und Aufgaben der arsakidischen Numismatik. *PSZ*: 365–87.

Ambos, C. 2003. Nanaja: Eine ikonographische Studie zur Darstellung einer altorientalischen Göttin in hellenistisch-parthischer Zeit. *ZA* 93: 231–72.

Amiet, P. 2001. La sculpture susienne à l'époque de l'Empire parthe. *IrAnt* 36: 239–91.

Augé, C., R. Curiel, and G. Le Rider. 1979. *Terrasses sacrées de Bard-è Néchandeh et Masjid-e Solaiman. Les trouvailles monétaires.* Paris: MDAI 44.

Azarnoush, M. 1975. Kāvoša-ye gurestān-e mohavvate-ye Sang-e Šir. *PASARI* 3: 51–72.

———. 2007. Gozāreš-e maqadamāti-ye kāvoša-ye lāyešenākhti-ye Tepe-ye Hegmatāneh Hamedān. In *Archaeological Reports, 7. On the occasion of the 9th Annual Symposium on Iranian Archaeology*, vol. 1, ed. H. Fazeli Nashli, 19–60. Tehran: ICAR.

Bader, A., P. Callieri, and T. Khodzhaniyazov. 1998. Survey of the "Antiochus Wall": Preliminary report on the 1993–1994 campaigns. *AMMD*: 159–86.

Baimatowa, N. S. 2008. *5000 Jahre Architektur in Mittelasien: Lehmziegelgewölbe vom 4./3. Jt. v. Chr. bis zum Ende des 8. Jhs. n. Chr.* Mainz: AIT 7.

Barnard, H., and W. Wendrich. 2008. *The archaeology of mobility: Old World and New World nomadism.* Los Angeles: Cotsen Advanced Seminars 4.

Basafa, H. 2008. A new perspective on Dambakoh site in southeast Iran. *IrAnt* 43: 185–206.

Bernard, P. 2007. La colonie grecque d'Aï Khanoum et l'hellénisme en Asie centrale. In *Afghanistan: les trésors retrouvés. Collections du Musée National de Kaboul*, ed. P. Cambon, 55–68. Paris: Réunion des Musées Nationaux (English version in *Afghanistan: Hidden Treasures from the National Museum, Kabul*, ed. F. Hiebert and P. Cambon, 81–130. Washington, DC: National Geographic Society, 2008).

Beyer, K. 1998. *Die aramäischen Inschriften aus Assur, Hatra und dem übrigen Ostmesopotamien (datiert 44 v.Chr. bis 238 n.Chr.).* Göttingen: Vandenhoeck & Ruprecht.

Bivar, A. D. H. 1982. Seal-impressions of Parthian Qūmis. *Iran* 20: 161–76.

Böck, B. 2010. Keilschriftliche Texte. *QGP* 3: 1–174.

Boucharlat, R. 1987. Les niveaux post-achéménides à Suse, secteur nord. Fouilles de l'Apadana-Est et de la Ville Royale-Ouest (1973–1978). *CDAFI* 15: 145–312.

———. 1989. Cairns et pseudo-cairns du Fars: L'utilisation des tombes de surface au 1er millénaire de notre ère. *AIO*: 675–712.

———. 2001. Les galeries de captage dans la péninsule d'Oman au premier millénaire avant J.-C.: Question sur leurs relations avec les galeries du plateau iranien. In *Irrigation et drainage dans l'antiquité, qanāts et canalisations souterraines en Iran, en Égypte et en Grèce*, ed. P. Briant, 157–83. Paris: Persica 2.

———. 2008. L'archéologie de la Perse éternelle dans la République islamique d'Iran. In *Patrimoines culturels en Méditerranée orientale: recherche scientifique et enjeux identitaires. 2e atelier (27 novembre 2008): Identités nationales et recherche archéologique: les aléas du processus de patrimonialisation (Levant, pays du Golfe, Iran)*, ed. J.-C. David and S. Müller-Celka. Lyon: Rencontres scientifiques en ligne de la Maison de l'Orient et de la Méditerranée. http://www.mom.fr/2eme-atelier.html.

Boucharlat, R., and H. Fazeli. 2009. The Achaemenid/Post Achaemenid remains in Tang-i Bulaghi near Pasargadae: A report on the salvage excavations conducted by five joint teams in 2004–2007. *ARTA* 2009.001.

Boucharlat, R., and E. Haerinck 1991. Ceramics xii. The Parthian and Sasanian periods. *EnIr* 5: 304–7.

———. 2011. *Tombes d'époque parthe. Chantiers de la Ville des Artisans*. Leiden : MDAI 35.

Callataÿ, F. de. 1994. *Les tétradrachmes d'Orodès II et de Phraate IV: étude du rythme de leur production monétaire à la lumière d'une grande trouvaille*. Paris: Cahiers de *StIr* 14.

Callieri, P. 2007. *L'archéologie du Fārs à l'époque hellénistique*. Paris: Persika 11.

Cambon, P. 2007. Begram, ancienne Alexandrie du Caucase ou capitale kouchane. In *Afghanistan: les trésors retrouvés. Collections du Musée National de Kaboul*, ed. P. Cambon, 81–112. Paris: Réunion des Musées Nationaux (English version in *Afghanistan: Hidden Treasures from the National Museum, Kabul*, ed. F. Hiebert and P. Cambon, 131–210. Washington, DC: National Geographic Society, 2008).

Carter, R. A., K. Challis, S. M. N. Priestman, and H. Tofighian 2006. The Bushehr hinterland: Results of the first season of the Iranian-British Archaeological Survey of Bushehr Province, November—December 2004. *Iran* 44: 63–103.

Chaumont M.-L. 1973. Etudes d'histoire parthe. *Syria* 50: 197–222.

Choubak, H. 1999. Une étonnante céramique dans une necropole parthe dans la région de Kerman. *DA* 243: 94–5.

Cribb, R. 1991. *Nomads in archaeology*. Cambridge: Cambridge University Press.

Curtis, V. S. 2000. Parthian costume and culture. In *Mesopotamia and Iran in the Parthian and Sasanian periods: Rejection and Revival c. 238 BC–AD 642*, ed. J. Curtis, 23–43. London: British Museum Press.

———. 2001. Parthian belts and belt plaques. *IrAnt* 36: 299–320.

Curtis, V. S., and St.-J. Simpson 2000. Archaeological news from Iran and Central Asia Third Report: Germi. *Iran* 38: 151–60.

Debevoise, N. C. 1938. *A political history of Parthia*. Chicago: University of Chicago Press.

Egami, N., S. Fukai, and S. Masuda. 1966. *Dailaman II: The excavations at Noruzmahleh and Khoramrud, 1960*. Tokyo: Tokyo University Iraq-Iran Archaeological Expedition Report 7.

Flandin, E., and P. Coste. 1851–4. *Voyage en Perse*, 6 vols. Paris: Gide and J. Beaudry.

Fukai, S., and T. Matsutani. 1980. *Halimehjan I. The Excavation at Shahpir 1976*. Tokyo: Tokyo University Iraq-Iran Archaeological Expedition Report 16.

Gaibov, V. 1996. Bullae from Göbekly-depe (Margiana): Bronze Age traditions in Parthian sphragistics. In *Archives et sceaux du monde hellénistique*, ed. M.-F. Boussac and A. Invernizzi, 385–93. Paris: *Bulletin de Correspondance Hellénique* Supplement 29.

Gaibov, V., and G.A. Koshelenko 2002. La Margiane—Asie Centrale. *DA* 271: 46–53.

Gaibov, V. 2007. The bullae of *Gobekly*-depe. *AACA*: 285–94.

Ghirshman, R. 1946. *Bégram. Recherches archéologiques et historiques sur les Kouchans*. Cairo: MDAFA 12.

———. 1976. *Terrasses sacrées de Bard-è Néchandeh et Masjid-i Solaiman. L'Iran du Sud-Ouest du VIIIe s. av. n. ère au Ve s. de n. ère*. Paris: *MDAI* 45.
Godard, A. 1937. Les statues parthes de *Shami*. *Athār-é Īrān* 2: 285–305.
Golze, U., and K. Storm 2010. Chinesische Texte. *QGP* 3: 482–512.
Gunter, A. C., and P. Jett 1992. *Ancient Iranian metalwork in the Arthur M. Sackler Gallery and the Freer Gallery of Art*. Washington, DC: Arthur M. Sackler Gallery and Freer Gallery of Art.
Haaff, P. A. van't. 2007. *Catalogue of Elymaean coinage: Ca. 147 B.C.–A.D. 228*. Lancaster: Classical Numismatic Group.
Hackin, J. 1939. *Recherches archéologiques à Begram, chantier no. 2 (1937)*. Paris: MDAFA 9.
Haerinck, E. 1975. Quelques monuments funéraires de l'île de Kharg dans le Golfe persique. *IrAnt* 11: 134–67.
———. 1983. *La céramique en Iran pendant la période parthe (ca. 250 av. J.C. à ca. 225 après J.C.): Typologie, chronologie et distribution*. Gent: *IrAnt* Supplement 2.
Haerinck, E., and B. Overlaet 2008. Altar shrines and fire altars? Architectural representations on *frataraka* coinage. *IrAnt* 43: 207–33.
Hakemi, A. 1990. The excavation at Khurha. *EW* 40: 11–41.
Harmatta, J. 1996. *History of civilizations of Central Asia, vol. 2, The development of sedentary and nomadic civilizations: 700 B.C. to A.D. 250*. Paris: UNESCO.
Hauser, S. R. 2000. Ecological borders and political frontiers: The Eastern Jazirah in the later Preislamic period. In *Landscapes: Territories, frontiers and horizons in the Ancient Near East: Papers presented to the XLIV Rencontre Assyriologique Internationale, Venezia, 7–11 July 1997, part II*, ed. L. Milano, S. de Martino, F. M. Fales, and G. B. Lanfranchi, 187–201. Padua: Sargon srl.
———. 2005. Die ewigen Nomaden? Bemerkungen zu Herkunft, Militär, Staatsaufbau und nomadischen Traditionen der Arsakiden. In *Krieg—Gesellschaft—Institutionen: Beiträge zu einer vergleichenden Kriegsgeschichte*, ed. B. Meissner, O. Schmitt, and M. Sommer, 163–208. Berlin: Akademie Verlag.
———. 2006a. *Die Sichtbarkeit von Nomaden und saisonaler Besiedlung in der Archäologie: Multidisziplinäre Annäherungen an ein methodisches Problem*. Halle (Saale): Orientwissenschaftliche Hefte 21.
———. 2006b. Was there no paid standing army? A fresh look on military and political institutions in the Arsacid Empire. In *Arms and armour as indicators of cultural transfer: The steppes and the Ancient World from Hellenistic times to the early Middle Ages*, ed. M. Mode and J. Tubach, 295–319. Wiesbaden: Nomaden und Sesshafte 4.
———. 2012. The Arsacid (Parthian) Empire. In *A companion to the archaeology of the Ancient Near East*, ed. D. T. Potts, 1001–20. Malden/Oxford: Wiley-Blackwell.
———. Forthcoming. *The visibility of nomads and seasonal occupation in the archaeological record: Multi-disciplinary approaches to a methodological problem*. Wiesbaden: Nomaden und Sesshafte 17.
Herling, A., and J.-F. Salles 1993. Hellenistic Cemeteries in Bahrain. *MASP*: 161–82.
Herrmann, G. 1977. *The Iranian revival*. Oxford: Elsevier-Phaidon.
Herzfeld, E. 1941. *Iran in the Ancient East*. London/New York: Oxford University Press.
Hintze, A. 1998. The Avesta in the Parthian period. *PSZ*: 147–61.
Huyse, P. 1999. *Die dreisprachige Inschrift Šābuhrs I. an der Ka'ba-i Zardušt (ŠKZ)*. 2 vols. London: CII 3/1/1.
Ibrahim, J. K. 1986. *Pre-islamic settlement in Jazirah*. Baghdad: State Organization of Antiquities and Heritage.

Invernizzi, A. 1989. Héraclès à Séleucie du Tigre. *Revue Archéologique*: 65–113.
———. 1999. *Sculture di metallo da Nisa*. Louvain: Acta Iranica 35.
———. 2001. Arsacid dynastic art. *Parthica* 3: 133–57.
———. 2005. Representations of gods in Parthian Nisa. *Parthica* 7: 71–9.
———. 2007. The culture of Parthian Nisa, between steppes and empire. *AACA*: 163–77.
———. 2009. *Nisa Partica: Le sculture ellenistiche*. Florence: Monografie di *Mesopotamia* 11.
Invernizzi, A., and C. Lippolis. 2007. *Nisa Partica: Ricerche nel complesso monumentale arsacide 1990–2006*. Florence: Monografie di *Mesopotamia* 9.
Jakubiak, K. 2006. The origin and development of military architecture in the province of Parthava in the Arsacid period. *IrAnt* 41: 127–50.
Kaim, B. 2004. Ancient fire temples in the light of the discovery at Mele Hairam. *IrAnt* 39: 323–37.
———. 2008. The Parthian settlements in the Serakhs Oasis. *Parthica* 10: 129–34.
Kambakhsh Fard, S. 1998. *Gurkhomrekha-ye ashkani/Parthian pithos burials at Germi (Azarbaijan)*. Tehran: Markaze Nashre Daneshgahi.
Kawami, T. S. 2005. Ernst Herzfeld, Kuh-e Khwaja, and the study of Parthian art. In *Ernst Herzfeld and the Development of Near Eastern Studies, 1900–1950*, ed. A. C. Gunter and S. R. Hauser, 181–214. Leiden: Brill.
Keall, E. J. 1977. Qaĺeh-i Yazdigird: The question of its date. *Iran* 15: 1–9.
———. 1982. Qaĺeh-i Yazdigird: An overview of the monumental architecture. *Iran* 20: 51–72.
———. 1994. How many kings did the Parthian King of Kings rule? *IrAnt* 29: 253–72.
———. 2002. Qaĺeh-i Yazdigird. *DA* 271: 64–71
Keall, E. J, M. A. Leveque, and N. Willson. 1980. Qaĺeh-i Yazdigird: Its architectural decorations. *Iran* 18: 1–41.
Khazanov, A. M. 1994. *Nomads and the outside world*, 2nd ed. Madison: University of Wisconsin Press.
Khosrowzadeh, A. 2007. A review on cairn burial of southeastern Iran. *Nāme-ye Pažuhešgah-e Miras-e Farhangi* 20/21: 89–104 (in Persian, with an English summary).
Kiani, M. Y. 1982. *Parthian sites in Hyrcania: The Gurgan plain*. Berlin: *AMI* Ergänzungsband 9.
Kleiss, W. 1973. Qaĺeh Zohak in Azerbajdjan. *AMI* 6: 163–88.
Klose, D. O. A., and W. Müseler. 2008. *Statthalter, Rebellen, Könige: Die Münzen aus Persepolis von Alexander dem Großen zu den Sasaniden*. Munich: Staatliche Münzsammlung.
Kolb, F., and W. Tietz. 2001. Zagaba: Münzprägung und politische Geographie in Zentrallykien. *Chiron* 31: 347–416.
Koshelenko, G. A., and V. N. Pilipko 1994. Parthia. In *History of civilizations of Central Asia, vol. 2, The development of sedentary and nomadic civilizations: 700 B.C. to A.D. 250*, ed. J. Harmatta, 131–50. Paris: UNESCO.
Koshelenko, G. A. 2007. The fortifications at Gobekly-depe. *AACA*: 269–83.
Lecuyot, G. 1993. Résidences hellénistiques en Bactriane, résidences parthes en Iran et en Mésopotamie: Diffusion ou communauté d'origine. *Northern Akkad Project Reports* 8: 31–45.
Leriche, P. 2007. Bactria, land of a thousand cities. *AACA*: 121–54.
Le Rider, G. 1965. *Suse sous les Séleucides et les Parthes. Les trouvailles monétaires et l'histoire de la ville*. Paris: MMAI 38.
Lerner, J. D. 1999. *The impact of Seleucid decline on the eastern Iranian plateau: The foundations of Arsacid Parthia and Graeco-Bactria*. Stuttgart: Historia-Einzelschriften 123.

Lombard, P., and M. Kevran 1993. Les niveaux "hellénistique" du Tell de Qal`at al-Bahrain. Données préliminaires. *MASP*: 127–60.

Martinez-Sève, L 2002. *Les figurines de Suse. De l'époque néo-élamite à l'époque sassanide.* Paris: Réunion des Musées Nationaux.

Masson, M. E., and G. A. Pugačenkova 1982. *The Parthians rhytons of Nisa.* Florence: Monografie di *Mesopotamia* 1.

Mathiesen, H. E. 1992. *Sculpture in the Parthian Empire: A study in chronology*, 2 vols. Aarhus: Aarhus University Press.

Mehendale, S. 2005. Begram: New perspectives on the ivory and bone carvings. Los Angeles. http://ecai.org/begramweb/.

Miroschedji, P. de. 1987. Fouilles du chantier Ville Royale II à Suse (1975–1977). II. Niveaux d'époques achéménide, séleucide, parthe et islamique. *CDAFI* 15: 11–144.

Mohammadifar, Y., and M. R. Sarraf. 2006. A glance at burial rites in pithos of Arsacid era located in western region of central Zagros (Mariwan). *Journal of Humanities* 13: 51–62.

Monsieur, R., R. Boucharlat, and E. Haerinck 2011. Amphores grecques timbrées découvertes à Suse (SO-Iran). *IrAnt* 46: 161–92.

Nehru, L. 1999/2000. Khalchayan revisited. *SRAA* 6: 217–39.

Nemati, M., F. H. Nadooshan, M. M. Kohpar, and A. R. H. Nobari. 2011. Parthian burial traditions at Veliran, north-central Iran. *Parthica* 13: 87–106.

Nemati, M., and A. Sadraie 2010. Parthian rhytons from Veliran. *IrAnt* 45: 305–319.

Niknami, K. A. D., Y. Mohammadifar, and M. R. Sarraf. 2007. An analytical approach to the study of Parthian archaeological materials from the central Zagros, western Iran. *Journal of the Faculty of Letters and Humanities* 180: 93–110 (in Persian).

Olbrycht, M. J. 1998. *Parthia et ulteriores gentes. Die politischen Beziehungen zwischen dem arsakidischen Iran und den Nomaden der eurasischen Steppen.* Munich: Quellen und Forschungen zur antiken Welt 30.

———. 2003. Parthia and nomads of Central Asia: Elements of steppe origin in the social and military developments of Arsacid Iran. *Orientwissenschaftliche Hefte* 12: 69–109.

Omrani Rekavandi, H., et al. 2008. Sasanian walls, hinterland fortresses and abandoned ancient irrigated landscapes: The 2007 season on the Great Wall of Gorgan and the Wall of Tammishe. *Iran* 46: 151–78.

O'Neill, J. P. 1996. *Ancient art from the Shumei Family Collection.* New York: Metropolitan Museum of Art.

Pappalardo, E. 2010. *Nisa Partica: I rhyta ellenistichi.* Florence: Monografie di *Mesopotamia* 12.

Pennachietti, F. A. 1987. L'iscrizione bilingue greco-partica dell`Eracle di Seleucia. *Mesopotamia* 22: 169–85.

Peterson, S. 2011. Parthian aspects of objects from Grave IV, Tillya Tepe. http://soas.academia.edu/SaraPeterson/Papers/1540774/Parthian_Aspects_of_Objects_from_Grave_IV_Tillya_Tepe.

Pfrommer, M. 1993. *Metalwork from the Hellenized East: Catalogue of the Collection.* Malibu: J. Paul Getty Museum.

Pilipko, V. N. 2008. The central ensemble of the fortress Mihrdatkirt: Layout and chronology. *Parthica* 10: 33–51.

Potts, D. T. 1990. *The Arabian Gulf in antiquity*, vol. 2, *From Alexander the Great to the coming of Islam.* Oxford: Clarendon Press.

———. 1993. The sequence and chronology of Thaj. *MASP*: 87–110.

———. 1996. The Parthian presence in the Arabian Gulf. In *The Indian Ocean in antiquity*, ed. J. Reade, 269–85. London: Kegan Paul International.

———. 1999. *The archaeology of Elam: Formation and transformation of an ancient Iranian state.* Cambridge: Cambridge University Press.

———. 2001a. Nana in Bactria. *SRAA* 7: 23–35.

———. 2001b. Before the Emirates: An archaeological and historical account of developments in the region c. 5000 BC to 676 AD. In *United Arab Emirates: A new perspective*, ed. I. al-Abed and P. Hellyer, 28–69. London: Trident.

———. 2004. Kharg Island. *EnIr* online edition.

———. 2007. Foundation houses, fire altars and the *frataraka*: Interpreting the iconography of some post-Achaemenid Persian coins. *IrAnt* 42: 271–300.

Pugačenkova, G. A. 1971. *Skulp'tura Khalchayana.* Moscow: Iskusstvo.

Rahbar, M. 1999. Khorheh, une résidence parthe sur le Plateau iranien. *DA* 243: 44–6.

Rante, R. 2008. The Iranian city of Rayy: Urban model and military architecture. *Iran* 46: 189–211.

———. 2010. Ray i. Archeology. *EnIr* online edition.

Raschke, M. G. 1978. New studies in Roman commerce with the East. In *Aufstieg und Niedergang der Römischen Welt*, part 2, vol. 9/2, ed. H. Temporini and W. Haase, 604–1361. Berlin: De Gruyter.

Rawlinson, G. 1873. *The sixth great Oriental monarchy; or the geography, history, & antiquities of Parthia.* London: John Murray.

Rostovtzeff, M. 1938. *Dura Europos and its art.* Oxford: Clarendon Press.

Roustaei, K., and A. Azadi. 2011. Discovery of a Parthian tomb chamber in Cheram, Kohgiluye, SW Iran. *IrAnt* 46: 193–206.

Sarianidi, V. 1985 *The golden hoard of Bactria from the Tillya-Tepe excavations in Northern Afghanistan.* Leningrad: Aurora.

Sarraf, M. R. 2003. Archaeological excavations in Tepe Ekbatana (Hamadan) by the Iranian Archaeological Mission between 1983 and 1993. *CE*: 269–79.

Sauer, E. W., H. Omrani Rekavandi, J. Nokandeh, and T. J. Wilkinson 2009. Die sasanidischen Grenzwälle im Nord-Iran. In *Mauern als Grenzen*, ed. A. Nunn, 127–43. Mainz: von Zabern.

Schippmann, K. 1980. *Grundzüge der parthischen Geschichte.* Darmstadt: Wissenschaftliche Buchgesellschaft.

———. 1986. Arsacid ii. The Arsacid dynasty. *EnIr* online edition.

Schmidt, E. F. 1940. *Flights over ancient cities of Iran.* Chicago: University of Chicago Press.

Schoff, W. 1912. *The Periplus of the Erythraean Sea: Travel and trade in the Indian Ocean by a merchant of the first century.* London/Bombay/Calcutta: Longmans, Green, and Co.

Schubert, G. 2010. Arabische Texte. *QGP* 3: 455–81.

Schuol, M. 2000. *Die Charakene: Ein mesopotamisches Königreich in hellenistisch-parthischer Zeit.* Stuttgart: Oriens et Occidens 1.

Sellwood, D. 1980. *An introduction to the coinage of Parthia.* 2nd ed. London: Spink.

Shahbazi, A. S. 1986. Arsacids vi. Arsacid chronology in traditional history. *EnIr* 2: 541–3.

Sono, T., and S. Fukai 1968. *Dailaman III: Excavations at Hassani Mahale and Ghalekuti, 1964.* Tokyo: Tokyo University Iraq-Iran Archaeological Expedition Report 8.

Stein, Sir M. A. 1937. *Archaeological reconnaissances in north-western India and south-eastern Īrān.* London: Macmillan.

Stöllner, T., G. Weisgerber, M. Momenzadeh, and E. Pernicka 2004. Die Bedeutung der Blei-/Silbergruben von Nakhlak im Altertum. *PAP*: 478–93.

Thommen, L. 2010. Griechische und lateinische Texte. *QGP* 2: 1–491.

Traina, G. 2010. Armenische Quellen. *QGP* 3: 402–54.

Treister, M. 2003. Further thoughts about Parthian and related belt and belt plaques. *IrAnt* 38: 247–57.
Trinkaus, K. M. 1983. Pre-Islamic settlement and land use in Damghan, northeast Iran. *IrAnt* 18: 119–44.
Trousdale, W. 1975. *The long sword and scabbard slide in Asia*. Washington, DC: Smithsonian Contributions to Anthropology 17.
Vanden Berghe, L., and K. Schippmann. 1985. *Les reliefs rupestres d'Elymaïde (Irān) de l'époque parthe*. Gent: IrAnt Supplement 3.
Venco Ricciardi, R. 1980. Archaeological survey in the Upper Atrek valley (Khorasan, Iran): Preliminary report. *Mesopotamia* 15: 51–72.
Weber, D. 2010. Parthische Texte. *QGP* 2: 492–588.
Weisgerber, G. 2004. Bergbau auf Wasser—Käris und Qanat. *PAP*: 532–43.
Wenke, R. J. 1975-6. Imperial investments and agricultural developments in Parthian and Sasanian Khuzistan: 150 B.C. to A.D. 640. *Mesopotamia* 10–11: 31–221.
———. 1987. Western Iran in the Partho-Sasanian period: The imperial transformation. *AWI*: 251–81.
Wieczorek, A., and C. Lind. 2007. *Ursprünge der Seidenstrasse*. Stuttgart: Theiss.
Wiesehöfer, J. 2007. Fars under Seleucid and Parthian rule. In *The Age of the Parthians*, ed. V. S. Curtis and S. Stewart, 37–49. London: I. B. Tauris.
Winkelmann, S. 2003. Eurasisches in Hatra? Ergebnisse und Probleme bei der Analyse partherzeitlicher Bildquellen. *Orientwissenschaftliche Hefte* 9: 21–140.
———. 2006. Waffen und Waffenträger auf parthischen Münzen. *Parthica* 8: 131–52.
Wolski, J. 1993. *L'empire des Arsacides*. Leuven: Acta Iranica 32.
Wright, G. R. H. 1991. Abu Qubur. The "Parthian Building" and its affinities. *Northern Akkad Project Reports* 7: 75–91.
Young, G. K. 2001. *Rome's eastern trade: International commerce and imperial policy, 31BC–AD 305*. London/New York: Routledge.
Zehnder, M. 2010. Aramäische Texte. *QGP* 3: 175–401.

CHAPTER 38

PARTHIAN AND ELYMAEAN ROCK RELIEFS

TRUDY S. KAWAMI

Introduction

Rock reliefs are sculptures on living rock in which the background is cut back leaving the desired images in relief. They are distinguished from petroglyphs, which are produced by pecking a smoothly weathered, often shiny, surface to produce flat images with a contrasting, matte finish. Rock reliefs are also distinguished from large-scale sculpture on stelae or other (once) portable stone surfaces in that they cannot leave their original location. Not surprisingly the Parthian-period reliefs occur in areas where rock reliefs were also cut in earlier times. The carving of rock reliefs was a specialized skill, and the production of rock reliefs on any scale presupposes a patron capable of housing and feeding the craftsmen needed for such a project. As artistic undertakings meant to be visible, reliefs presented in some way a public statement by the patron. They were not a document of reality but a statement of what the patron intended to be real.

The identity of the patrons is known in some cases because of accompanying inscriptions. Unfortunately, inscriptions can be added to a relief well after its completion, and the practice of coopting a predecessor's relief by a later inscription is documented in western Iran (Potts 1999: 254). Adding to our difficulty in understanding the reliefs is the lack of information regarding the details of internal politics in western Iran in the Parthian period. If one believes Arsacid propaganda, the Parthian King of Kings, *basileus basileôn* on the coinage, controlled the entire plateau and the southwestern lowlands. However the existence of local rulers producing their own coinage and calling themselves "great king" shows that central authority was not exercised with any consistency (Bivar 1983; Nadooshan et al. 2005). Only one Parthian relief can be directly attributed to an Arsacid, that is, paramount, ruler. The rest appear to have been sponsored by local lords who may or may not have been Arsacid vassals.

Geographically speaking, the rock reliefs considered here form two groups. The first group includes reliefs along the Baghdad–Khorasan Road in the vicinity of Kermanshah. The second group comprises three subclusters in the mountains of Khuzestan, ancient Elymais.

Kermanshah region

The Baghdad–Khorasan Road is the name given to the ancient track through the central Zagros Mountains that connects the Baghdad region in what is now modern Iraq with the Iranian plateau and points to the east. It was, and still is, the main road through the mountains and has been enhanced since at least the late third millennium BC with reliefs and inscriptions of the rulers from both the lowlands and the plateau who controlled the route at various times.

Bisotun

The so-called Mithradates panel (Fig. 38.1) carved on the southern face of the mountain of Bisotun well below the Darius relief and above a natural spring, is in fact two adjacent panels of different depths. Both panels were substantially marred by a centrally placed third panel with an inscription dated to 1684–5 AD. The two Parthian sections were

FIGURE 38.1 Bisotun. Parthian reliefs (courtesy of the Ernst Herzfeld Archive, Freer Gallery of Art, Smithsonian Institution, neg. # 1909).

cut into a single, long, rectangular, smoothed surface of probable Achaemenid date. The western segment depicts two half-length male figures in profile to the viewer's right. Vertical clefts in the stone beneath suggest the lower portions of the bodies. However, in 1976 a careful examination of the stone and the ledge beneath it revealed that these clefts are natural fissures in the rock. Furthermore, the stone surface in this area is in higher relief than the figures themselves, indicating that the lower portion of the rock face was never smoothed, let alone carved. The vertical shadows at the base of the panel suggesting legs and feet are created by deep cuts for the reception of the scaffolding needed to support the workers of the original Achaemenid panel and its subsequent recutting. Above the two half-figures, but outside their sunken panel, is a two-line Greek inscription utilizing four-bar sigmas that reads "Kophasates, Mithrates ..." and below that "satrap of satraps ... " The name Mithradates is not found in the inscription, having been supplied by Ernst Herzfeld (1920: 39, 1935: 54–5) in a creative reconstruction. Given the lack of royal Arsacid titulary and iconography, as well as the flat surface and simple linear detail of the two figures, a suggested date between 138 and 123 BC, when Arsacid control of the region waned, seems likely (Kawami 1987: 34–7, 155–7). The eastern section, cut at a deeper level, contains no images at all, only the terminal fragments of a two-line Greek inscription using lunate sigmas, a letter form that postdates the four-bar sigma of the Kophasates inscription. This eastern fragment includes only the name "Gotarzes" in the upper line and three letters in the lower. There is no evidence for any figure in the space below, merely the channels and holes for the scaffolding.

Directly adjacent to the east is a 6 m long panel with a sharp upper edge and vague lower register that fills the eastern portion of the presumed Achaemenid surface (Fig. 38.2). This relief features three small horsemen and a single riderless horse. The

FIGURE 38.2 . Bisotun. "Gotarzes" relief. Photo courtesy of Hubertus von Gall. Note four scaffolding holes on the left.

central rider charges with a horizontal lance while crowned by a wreath-bearing Nike. The rider on the right-hand side, upended by the lance, falls from his horse, which also crumples from the blow. A third rider, also armed with a lance, follows the central rider from the left. Above this scene is the hybrid Greek–Persian phrase "Gotarzes, son of Gew(Gev)" in small, irregularly placed letters. The spacious composition and naturalistic figures are rendered with a classical sense of action and movement, recalling Hellenistic parallels. While the relief is usually dated to the reign of the Arsacid king Gotarzes II (40–51 AD), the inscription makes no claim to royal identity. The small size of the inscription, its shallow depth, and limited legibility raise the possibility that the relief was taken over by a later, local ruler using Gotarzes as a dynastic name. Gotarzes, son (or sometimes companion) of Gev, is a heroic, nonroyal figure in the *Šāhnāme*, the Iranian epic dated a little before 1000 AD, which retains vestiges of pre-Sasanian history in romanticized form (Kawami 1987: 37–43, 157–9). The name Gotarzes also appears on another Parthian relief near Sar-e Pol-e Zohab (see below).

The only Arsacid, that is royal, rock relief is the so-called Parthian Stone (*Partherstein*), a natural boulder on the rock-strewn broad slope (*Partherhang*) east of the two reliefs discussed above. The main face of the rock bears the life-size image of a frontal, standing male wearing the Arsacid royal headgear who is shown making an offering over an altar (Fig. 38.3). On the central shaft of the altar is a damaged inscription "… Vologases, king of kings, son of (…), great king, grandson of P (…)," identifying this figure as an Arsacid ruler. To the king's left is a figure that may be an Elymaean priest or priest-ruler

FIGURE 38.3 Bisotun. "Parthian stone," sides A—B. Photo by David Kawami.

FIGURE 38.4 Bisotun. "Parthian stone," side C. Photo by David Kawami.

to judge from his dress, and to his right, on a less visible face of the boulder, is what may be a subject vassal presenting an untied filet to the ruler (Fig. 38.4). Six Arsacid kings from the first to the early third century AD took the throne name Vologases and various aspects of the imagery on this relief can be found on Arsacid coinage. The general style, however, suggests Vologases III (105–147 AD) or IV (147–191 AD) as the most likely candidates (Vanden Berghe 1983: no. 22, pl. 11; Kawami 1987: 43–5, 160–2)

Sar-e Pol-e Zohab

Like the Bisotun reliefs, the shallow, rectangular relief panel at Sar-e Pol-e Zohab occupies a highly visible place, in this case a cliff just east of the Zagros Gates, a narrow and easily defended pass on the Baghdad–Khorasan Road that leads to the Iranian plateau. In its immediate vicinity are four rock reliefs of the early second millennium BC and across the stream from it are two more small reliefs. The Parthian panel depicts a mounted male figure and a frontal standing one in a simple, flat style (Fig. 38.5). Two inscriptions, one to the left (Inscription A), the other to right (Inscription B), identify the figures. A: "This is Gotarzes' own picture, the great king, son of Gev, the great king"; B: "This is the image of ... šrwn, lord/commander of (placename of uncertain reading)." Inscription A indicates that the patron was a local dynast using Gotarzes, son of Gev, as

FIGURE 38.5 Sar-e Pol-e Zohab. "Gotarzes" relief. Photo by David Kawami.

a throne name. The squat proportions and awkward forms reinforce the probable provincial patronage, and suggest a date in the second half of the Parthian period (Kawami 1987: 45–8, 162–4).

The mountains of Khuzestan (ancient Elymais)

In contrast to the reliefs in the Kermanshah region, the rock reliefs of Khuzestan are dispersed. Centering on three different mountainous areas, they are not associated with well-known or easily traversed routes. The reliefs are more diverse iconographically and appear to have more religious content than those of the Kermanshah region. Like the inscriptions of the Kermanshah area reliefs, those of the Khuzestan reliefs are at times enigmatic and incomplete, often raising more questions of meaning, date, and patronage than they answer. The southernmost cluster will be discussed first, followed by the other two clusters, moving northward.

Tang-e Sarvak

The dramatic cleft of Tang-e Sarvak in the mountains on the edge of the Behbehan plain in eastern Khuzestan is easily visible at a distance. The steep, stony path up the southeastern side of the gorge passes four huge boulders bearing a total of fourteen large reliefs. Here numbered I through IV, the numbers reflect the order in which one encounters

FIGURE 38.6 Tang-e Sarvak, Rock II, north and west faces showing multiple panels cut one into the other at increasing depths especially on north (left) face. Photo courtesy of Hubertus von Gall.

the boulders ascending the gorge. The difficulty of the narrow track, with its numerous switchbacks, the spacious view to the southwest from the mid-portion of the climb, and the unexpected open bowl near the top of the trail make the ascent physically and visually memorable.

The reliefs of Tang-e Sarvak are important for the number and variety of the images. They are also significant as they demonstrate the adoption and adaptation of motifs new to the Iranian plateau in the Parthian period. They cover a long span of time, ranging probably from the late second century BC to the early third century AD (Vanden Berghe and Schippmann 1985: 59–88; Kawami 1987: 88–110, pls. 35–48; Matthiesen 1992 2: nos. 9–22). Panels were cut and recut, especially on Rock II (Fig. 38.6), creating a virtual palimpsest of Parthian rock reliefs and adding to the difficulty of establishing a chronology. The earliest reliefs show Achaemenid and/or Hellenistic influences in both imagery and style. The row of eight standing figures with what appear to be barsom bundles on the west side of Rock II (Fig. 38.7) suggests Zoroastrian ritual in an open-air shrine. The relief of Herakles *soter* with the apples of the Hesperides on Rock I (Fig. 38.8), the only image of this aspect of Herakles known from Iran, is strikingly Hellenistic in theme and style despite its battered state. It is also unique among the Tang-e Sarvak sculptures in utilizing the bulges in the rock to enhance the naturalistic modeling of the figure.

The remaining dozen reliefs are more decidedly Parthian in their flat forms, frontal orientation, dress of long tunics and full trousers, and splay-footed stance of some

FIGURE 38.7 Tang-e Sarvak, Rock II, west side. Photo by David Kawami.

FIGURE 38.8 Tang-e Sarvak, Rock I, north side. Photo by David Kawami.

figures. Indeed some images look Kushan in style (Fig. 38.9), suggesting the possibility of connections via an overland, Gulf-oriented trade route between Khuzestan and the Indus regions (Kawami 1987: 93). Other elements, like the tall Arsacid-style helmet or miter with fillet and the textile roll worn over the shoulder, are local Elymaid elements that are also found on the independent coinage of the region. The equestrian bear (?) hunter and the lion conqueror on Rock II (Colledge 1986: 15, pl. 11b), present imagery best known from later Sasanian art. The relief of the mounted warrior on Rock III

FIGURE 38.9 Tang-e Sarvak, Rock IV, north side. Photo by David Kawami.

(Fig. 38.10) retains sufficient ancillary figures to show that it was once a large-scale battle scene that included archers and other combatants. Its linear style and richly incised surface details mark a change in style at the site, and its apparently secular subject matter may reflect a change in patronage as well (Kawami 1987: 105–9, 201–4).

The imagery of other reliefs links them to northern Mesopotamia and Syria (Vanden Berghe and Schippmann 1985: 108–11). The two reclining figures on Rocks II (Fig. 38.11) and IV evoke the heroized dead of Kharg's South Tomb (Haerinck 1975; Potts 2004) as well as Palmyrene funerary reliefs. Indeed the elaborate *kline* on Rock II and the adjacent seated and standing figures follows the basic Palmyrene funerary composition. However, there is nothing overtly funereal about the open-air setting, and the reclining figure holds a ring or wreath instead of a wine bowl. The image of a living ruler relaxing on a *kline* is well known in the Sasanian period (e.g., Ghirshman 1962: fig. 259) and the Tang-e Sarvak reliefs may be the point where the significance of the pose shifted from the heroized dead to the heroic living.

The *betyl*, a vertical stone that serves as a nonanthropomorphic image of divinity, is known as early as the Bronze Age in Syria and is documented in the Parthian period on the funerary reliefs at Edessa (Drijvers 1980: 126, 135–7, pl. 33). The *betyl* shown on Rocks I (Vanden Berghe and Schippmann 1985: 65, pls. 24–5) and II (Fig. 38.11) at Tang-e Sarvak have no parallels in Iranian art. The closest example dated to the late second or early third century AD is a *betyl* crowned by a Nike at Gali Zerdak in Iraqi Kurdistan (Mathiesen 1992 1: 67–8; 1992 2: 183, no. 136). The appearance of *betyl*s in

FIGURE 38.10 Tang-e Sarvak, Rock III. Battle scene. Drawing by the author.

the mountains of Khuzestan are a clear indication of the transfer of both concepts and imagery from Syria and northern Mesopotamia, probably via trade. The beribboned fillet ornamenting the *betyl* on Rock II is a standard Parthian indicator of kingship. Why it is applied to a *betyl,* rather than worn by a human being, may reflect some short-lived local belief or practice of Syrian or Palmyrene origin.

The radiate halo or nimbus of the outermost seated figure on Rock II (Vanden Berghe and Schippmann 1985: pls. 31–2), also unusual in Iran, is worn by both male and female deities in northern Mesopotamia and Syria during the Parthian period. It is best documented at Palmyra (Colledge 1976: 38, 41–3, 47, 212) and Hatra (Colledge 1977: 107; Ghirshman 1962: figs. 1–2) and appears later in Sasanian art (Ghirshman 1962: fig. 233). Its appearance at Tang-e Sarvak, along with the *betyl* and the reclining heroic figure, demonstrates the penetration of non-Iranian motifs well into the mountains of Khuzestan during the later Parthian period.

The language and orthography of the six Tang-e Sarvak inscriptions, some of which are fragmentary and others repetitive, show strong influence from Aramaic (Hennning 1952). Even the personal names include both Iranian (Orodes/Werod)

FIGURE 38.11 Tang-e Sarvak, Rock II, northwest corner. Photo courtesy of Hubertus von Gall.

and Semitic (Beldusha) examples. The minimal content of the inscriptions casts little light on the meaning of the reliefs. There is no evidence that the inscriptions and the various reliefs were executed together; the inscriptions may even postdate the reliefs with which they are associated (this was the case, for example, in the Izeh valley where the Neo-Elamite official Hanni added his name to earlier reliefs; see Potts 1999: 254). However, an intriguing connection has been noted with an inscription on the *betyl* relief at Edessa using similar phrases and terms (Drijvers 1980: 135). The Syriac inscriptions from the late Parthian period on Kharg Island, just off the coast of Khuzestan, add to the cultural context in which the Tang-e Sarvak inscriptions should be placed (Steve 2003: 45–68).

Why was this difficult but picturesque route ornamented with so many reliefs? W. B. Henning suggested that Tang-e Sarvak was a shrine to kingship (Henning 1952), but this concept is without parallel in ancient Iran. It is more probable that Tang-e Sarvak was an open-air sanctuary, along the lines of the Elamite sites in the Izeh valley to the north (Potts 1999: 253–6). The reliefs and their adjacent inscriptions have few parallels with contemporaneous Iranian works and are difficult to date, let alone interpret. The accompanying inscriptions often repeat themselves, and some seem to have no relationship to the nearby scenes.

The blossoming of relief sculpture at Tang-e Sarvak reflected the autonomy of the region in the later Parthian period with local strongmen or perhaps merchant princes exercising the patronage practices of earlier rulers. The Syrian or Palmyrene elements in the reliefs and inscriptions of the site reflected ideas and practices probably brought into southwestern Iran by merchants.

Izeh

Another cluster of reliefs occurs in the Izeh valley (El. Ayapir) which lies intermediate between lowland Khuzestan and Fars, the seat of Achaemenid power. The well-watered and easily defended valley has numerous Late (or Neo-) Elamite rock reliefs associated with open-air sanctuaries (Potts 1999: 253–6; Waters 2000: 82–5, 116). The reliefs of the Parthian period suggest a renewal or continuation of this practice. In contrast to the reliefs at Tang-e Sarvak, the Izeh reliefs were not oriented to the approaching traveler, but are on the sides or backs of boulders not visible on approach (Kawami 1987: 118–19).

The most unusual relief (Fig. 38.12) is the equestrian composition at Hung-e Azhdar (erroneously called Hung-e Nowruzi), which is carved on the back of a huge boulder facing the rocky jumble of a small cul-de-sac. The relief is directly opposite a cave and traces of at least two rows or terraces of worked stone lie between the relief and the cave. The horizontal panel depicts a classical rider on a prancing horse in profile with an attendant facing four flat frontal figures in Parthian tunics and trousers. The stylistic disjuncture between the profile figures and the frontal ones has no parallel in Iranian art of the Parthian period. The unusual orientation and peculiar combination of styles and images in the relief panel itself have given rise to various interpretations of the relief, such as that it was cut in stages over a period of time. Visual inspection of the relief in 1976 found that the entire panel shares the same height of relief and the same depth of

FIGURE 38.12 Hung-e Azhdar, Izeh Valley. Photo courtesy of Louis Vanden Berghe.

background. The edges of the panel also do not reveal any differences in depth of finish, unlike the reliefs at Bisotun. Most likely the relief represents an Elymaid ruler, the large central figure, claiming association with or descent from an earlier heroic figure with Hellenistic attributes. One possible reference may be to Kamnaskires Nikephoros, a ruler who achieved Elymaid independence from the Seleucids and established a dynasty that controlled at least parts of Elymais in the second and first centuries BC (Vanden Berghe 1983: no. 23, pl. 12; Vanden Berghe and Schippmann 1985: 32–7, pls. 1–6; Kawami 1987: 5, 124, 209–13; Curtis 2007: 19–20). A nearly life-size figure in long tunic, trousers, and boots, carved on a low flat rock lying at the base of the equestrian relief, displays a different, more linear style. Its presence suggests that the small Hung-e Azhdar cul-de-sac was once a more complex installation than it now appears (Kawami 1987: 174).

About 1 km north of Hung-e Azhdar in a box canyon at the north end of the Izeh valley called Hung-e Kamalvand is a shallow relief featuring a frontal male on a small-headed horse together with a frontal standing figure. Above both figures is a clear Pahlavi inscription "[Phr]aates the priest, son of Kabnaskir." The inscription, dated to about 100 AD on paleographic grounds, gives an approximate date for the relief as well. A third, badly damaged relief showing two standing figures grasping a ring or wreath (?) is located nearby at Hung-e Yar Alivand (Vanden Berghe 1983: no. 25, fig. 5; Kawami 1987: 177–8, 214–15).

Shimbar and environs

The rock reliefs in and around Tang-e Butan, north of the Izeh valley near Shimbar, form the third and most provincial cluster in Khuzestan. Situated along the side of a gorge, the main relief comprises at least five adjacent panels (Fig. 38.13), each featuring two or three frontal figures. In four of the panels the figure to the viewer's left appears to be a Herakles-like male nude, sometimes carrying a club, addressed or attended by a figure clothed in long tunic and loose trousers with raised right hand (Vanden Berghe and Schippmann 1985: 46–53, pls. 11–17). A series of similar inscriptions provide personal names and titles, but these cannot yet be linked with any other historical data. There appears to be no genealogical link between the individuals mentioned in each inscription, so one may assume that the reliefs were executed over more than a few generations. The orthography of the inscriptions also suggests that they, and the reliefs, were produced over a span of time in the second and early third centuries AD (Bivar and Shaked 1964; Colledge 1986: 22, pl. 8c; Kawami 1987: 73–4, 181, n. 8 for a revision by Shaked). A single, frontal figure in a long tunic and trousers is carved elsewhere in the gorge.

Two roughly cut reliefs at Kuh-e Tina and Kuh-e Taraz provide evidence for additional rock relief production in the area. The Kuh-e Tina relief depicts a reclining figure with attendant and that at Kuh-e Taraz seems to show three frontal figures, one seated and two standing (Vanden Berghe 1983: no. 27, fig. 6; Vanden Berghe and Schippmann 1985: 54–8, pls. 18–20; Kawami 1987: 109–110, 204–5). Their simplistic execution and poor state of preservation preclude further analysis at this point. Additional reliefs in the region have been reported and assigned a second century CE date (Curtis 2007: 20).

FIGURE 38.13 Tang-e Butan, Shimbar. White patches mark location of inscriptions. Photo courtesy of A.D.H. Bivar.

FURTHER READING

In addition to the survey of Parthian rock reliefs provided in Kawami (1987), two of the best publications for the Parthian and Elymaean reliefs, with extensive prior bibliography, remain Vanden Berghe (1983) and Vanden Berghe and Schippmann (1985). On chronology see especially Mathiesen (1992). For the history of Elymais generally see Potts (1999). Several remote and poorly preserved reliefs, generally unattributable, have been discovered in recent years by J. Mehr Kian (Mehr Kian 1997, 2000, 2001). Results of recent Iranian-Italian investigations are reported in Messina and Mehr Kian (2010, 2011). For the inscriptions on these reliefs see Chapter 40 and Haruta (2006).

REFERENCES

Bivar, A. D. H. 1983. The political history of Iran under the Arsacids. *CHI* 3/1: 21–99.
Bivar, A. D. H., and S. Shaked. 1964. The inscriptions at Shīmbār. *BSOAS* 27: 265–90.
Colledge, M. A. R. 1976. *The art of Palmyra*. Boulder: Westview Press.
——. 1977. *Parthian art*. Ithaca: Cornell University Press.
——. 1986. *The Parthian period*. Leiden: Iconography of Religions 14/3.
Curtis, V. S. 2007. The Iranian revival in the Parthian period. In *The age of the Parthians*, ed. V. S. Curtis and S. Stewart, 7–25. London: I. B. Tauris.
Drijvers, H. J. W. 1980. *Cults and beliefs at Edessa*. Leiden: Brill.
Ghirshman, R. 1962. *Persian Art: The Parthian and Sassanian dynasties, 249 BC–AD 651*. New York: Golden Press.

Haerinck, E. 1975. Quelques monuments funéraires de l'île de Kharg dans le Golfe persique. *IrAnt* 11: 134–67.

Haruta, S. 2006. Elymaean and Parthian inscriptions from Khūzestān: A survey. In *Proceedings of the 5th Conference of the Societas Iranologica Europaea held in Ravenna, 6–11 October 2003*, vol. 1, *Ancient & Middle Iranian Studies*, ed. A. Panaino and A. Piras, 471–78. Milan: Mimesis.

Henning, W. B. 1952. The monuments and inscriptions of Tang-i Sarvak. *Asia Major* 2: 151–78.

Herzfeld, E. E. 1920. *Am Tor von Asien: Felsdenkmale aus Irans Heldenzeit*. Berlin: D. Reimer.

———. 1935. *Archaeological history of Iran*. London: Oxford University Press

Kawami, T.S. 1987. *Monumental art of the Parthian period in Iran*. Leiden: Acta Iranica 26.

Mathiesen, H. E. 1992. *Sculpture in the Parthian Empire: A study in chronology*, 2 vols. Aarhus: Aarhus University Press.

Mehr Kian, J. 1997. The Elymaian rock-carving of Shavand, Izeh. *Iran* 35: 67–72.

———. 2000. Un nouveau bas-relief d'Élymaïde à "Shirinow," sur un passage de la migration des Baxtiyaris. *IrAnt* 35: 57–68.

———. 2001. Trois bas-reliefs parthes dans les monts Bakhtiaris. *IrAnt* 36: 293–8.

Messina, V., and J. Mehr Kian. 2010. The Iranian-Italian joint expedition in Khuzistan. Hung-e Azdhar: 1st campaign (2008). *Parthica* 12: 31–45.

———. 2011. Ricognizione dei rilievi partici d'Elimaide. La piana di Izeh-Malamir. *Vicino & Medio Oriente* 15: 215–31.

Nadooshan, F. K, S. S. Moosavi, and F. Jafarzadeh Pour. 2005. The politics of Parthian coinage in Media. *NEA* 68/3: 123–7.

Potts, D. T. 1999. *The archaeology of Elam: Formation and transformation of an ancient Iranian state*. Cambridge: Cambridge University Press.

———. 2004. Kharg Island. *EnIr* online edition.

Steve, M.-J. 2003. *L'île de Khārg*. Neuchâtel: Civilisations du Proche-Orient, série I, Archéologie et Environnement 1.

Vanden Berghe, L. 1983. *Reliefs rupestres de l'Iran ancien*. Brussels: KMKG-MRAH.

Vanden Berghe. L. and K. Schippmann. 1985. *Les Reliefs rupestres d'Elymaïde (Irān) de l'époque parthe*. Gent: *IrAnt* Supplement 3.

Waters, M. W. 2000. *A survey of Neo-Elamite history*. Helsinki: SAAS 12.

CHAPTER 39

ARSACID, ELYMAEAN, AND PERSID COINAGE

KHODADAD REZAKHANI

Introduction

The particular nature of the Arsacid dynasty (c.238 BC–AD 224) provided the basis for the presence of multiple minting authorities in the territories of their empire. From the beginning of the Arsacid state in the late third century BC, the mint centers were established either anew or on the site of older Seleucid mints. However, by the time the Arsacids had effectively taken over the former territories of the Seleucids, independent minting centers and authorities had been established all around the Iranian plateau in the core territories of the Arsacids. Since the Arsacids often sought not to establish exclusive central authority over mints, and additionally tolerated the existence of subordinate, but autonomous, polities in their territories, mints producing the coinage of these autonomous states also existed in the Arsacid territories. Among these, the most significant ones were the mints of the client kingdoms of Persis (centered on Istakhr, in the heart of the old Achaemenid homeland) and Elymais (the polity formed around the ancient Elamite, lowland city of Susa), as well as Characene/Mesene.

The Arsacid Empire

Stylistically, Arsacid coinage has its roots in Seleucid and Achaemenid satrapal coinage (Curtis 2007: 415–17). The weight, based originally on the Athenian drachm (Alram 1986b), was standardized and adopted for subsequent Arsacid and even Sasanian coinage in a debased form, weighing on average 3.7–8 g and using silver, bronze, and occasionally, copper (Sellwood 1980). The coins of Arsaces I, the eponymous founder of the dynasty (c.238–211 BC), produced in both silver and bronze (Sellwood 1980: 20–1), essentially provided the prototype for all subsequent Arsacid coinage, although itself undergoing a few changes. Probably initially only produced in Nisa/Mithradatkert, the "capital" of the Arsacids (Sellwood 1980: 23), later coins were also minted in Hecatompylus (near modern Damghan), showing the extension of the power of the new dynasty to the west and south of their original territories. The coins initially portrayed the Arsacid ruler's profile on the obverse—facing right in the Seleucid manner—with the head covered in a soft cap, a borrowing from Achaemenid satrapal issues (e.g., Tiribazos of Lydia/Taros, Alram 1986a: Type 324). The reverse shows a seated figure, again wearing the satrapal soft cap, holding, and seemingly stringing, a bow. This again is a borrowing from an Achaemenid satrapal issue, namely that of Datames/Tarkumuwa, the late Achaemenid satrap of Cilicia (Alram 1986a: Type 340). Unlike the satrapal coins, however, Arsacid coinage bears few Aramaic inscriptions, the reverse being dominated by standard Greek legends, including the title ΒΑΣΙΛΕΩΣ (king/ruler: only after Arsaces III/Priapatius) and the generic name of Arsaces in genitive form (ΑΡΣΑΚΟΥ). Although all Arsacid kings had their own personal names, attested in Greco-Roman sources and occasionally in the Babylonian astronomical diaries, they universally used the title Arsaces as their regnal name, supposedly in honor of Arsaces I, although even that dynastic founder might have had the personal name Tiridates (Parth. *trd't), making Arsaces a clan name of the dynasty (Rezakhani 2004: 200). In fact, in the absence of narrative sources for Arsacid history and the prominence often given to numismatic evidence for reconstructing Arsacid history, the universal use of the title Arsaces poses a particular hindrance to our understanding of the history of the dynasty.

Apart from the Greek title ΒΑΣΙΛΕΩΣ and the name Arsaces, later Arsacids made use of other titles, such as ΕΥΕΡΓΕΤΟΥ (munificent) and ΦΙΛΑΔΕΛΦΟΥ (brother-loving), as well as the more grandiose title of ΒΑΣΙΛΕΩΣ ΜΕΓΑΛΟΥ (the Great King; e.g., Mithridates I, Sellwood 1980: no. 13.2). The most controversial title is of course ΦΙΛΕΛΛΗΝΟΣ (lover of Greeks/Hellenes) which seems to have begun appearing following the conquest of the former Seleucid territories in Media, Mesopotamia, and Susiana/Khuzestan by Mithridates II (c.120 BC). An early title, used only on the earliest coins of Arsaces I, was ΑΥΤΟΚΡΑΤΟΡΟΣ which might suggest an initial submission to Seleucid suzerainty, as the title suggests that Arsaces I thought of himself as the appointed military governor of Parthia, a fact that might also show his self-understanding as the successor of Andragoras, the rebellious Seleucid satrap of Parthia (Justin 41.4.7). Along these lines, some issues from Nisa, in addition to including the name of Arsaces in Greek, bear Aramaic krny, an Achaemenid military title for Arsaces, replacing any Greek titles.

Already on the coins of Arsaces I, changes had occurred that differentiated them from those of Seleucid and earlier Achaemenid satrapal issues. The most significant of these was the change of direction for the profile of the king on the obverse, this time looking left, which then became standard on all Arsacid coins. On the reverse, too, the bow-holding archer, initially seated right on a throne (Curtis 2007: 418), and looking left, was turned to face right, a position which became more or less standard as well. The coins of the immediate successors of Arsaces I, namely Arsaces II (whose name may have been Parth. 'rt'bn, "Artabanus"; Rezakhani 2004: 197–200) and Arsaces III/Priapatius, are variations of the coinage of the dynastic founder. The most significant change occurred on the coins of Phriapitos who, for the first time, used and thus standardized the Greek title ΒΑΣΙΛΕΩΣ and even added the title ΜΕΓΑΛΟΥ (Great) to it. The use of these titles was probably related to the reconquest of the territories lost to Antiochus III, the Seleucid king who, beginning in 210 BC, had launched a major campaign to conquer the territories in the east, including Hyrcania (Chapter 34; Schippmann 1986), and might have forced Arsaces II to give up his right to mint coins independently. The weakness of the Seleucids after this point allowed Arsaces II and Phriapitos to again start issuing coins, this time bearing the title of the Great King, and claiming divine right. The coins, however, kept the same beardless portrait of the king in profile wearing a soft hat and looking left, on the obverse, while the reverse has the full bust of a king, holding a bow, seated on a throne and surrounded by the titles and name of the authority (Alram 1986b: Typology).

The coins of Phraates I, the successor of Phriapitos, and the early issues of his brother and successor, Mithridates I, also bear a close resemblance to the previous series. Phraates I, who defeated the Seleucid Antiochus IV around 165 BC (Schippmann 1986), reestablished Arsacid control over Hyrcania, an important province, and opened the way to both the southern Caspian provinces and the central parts of the Iranian plateau. Mithridates I can be called the real founder of Arsacid power, in an imperial sense, since his brilliant conquests effectively made the Arsacids the strongest power on the Iranian plateau. Between 164 and 135 BC Mithridates I attacked and conquered territories belonging to the Greco-Bactrian kingdom, immediately east of Parthia proper, as well as large parts of the Seleucid possessions east of the Euphrates, including Media and Mesopotamia. Although Demetrius II tried in 138 to recover the Seleucid territories in Mesopotamia, his army and that of his allies were defeated (Shayegan 2011: 68–77). A by-product of the removal of Seleucid suzerainty from these regions might have been the emergence of local dynasties in Characene, Elymais, and Persis, each of which began minting coinage around this time.

The coinage of Mithridates I almost completely changed the subsequent output of coins in the Arsacid territories. Although his initial issues followed the types of his predecessors, and were issued in drachm and obol denominations of silver or copper, the conquest of Mesopotamia and the Seleucid capital of Seleucia-on-the-Tigris required a fundamental change. The obverse of the coins now showed a bearded man, with a diadem, looking again right in the Seleucid fashion, while the reverse alternated between the standard Arsacid seated man with a bow, or a standing Hercules holding a club and the lion skin, or even a seated Zeus (Alram 1986b: Typology). The influence of Hellenistic types on these coins is obvious, not only from the iconography, but also from the appearance of the title *Philhellene*, as well as *Theopator* ("of a divine father"), suggesting that Mithridates' father was now deified in a Greek manner (Daryaee 2006). Subsequently, although its iconographic innovations were modified by subsequent rulers, the coinage of Mithridates I became the inspiration for later Arsacid productions, and the obverse type of the beardless king with the soft hat was completely abandoned. The direction of the obverse bust, initially looking right, but changed back to looking left on the coins minted at Hecatompylus and other older Arsacid mints, was continued until the reign of Mithridates II. Another important feature of the coinage of the Arsacids, established during the reign of Mithridates I, was the limitation of the issuing of tetradrachms to the mint of Seleucia-on-the-Tigris, while other mints, including the important ones of Ecbatana and Susa, emitted only drachms and smaller fractions (Alram 1986b: Metals, Denominations, Mints).

Mithridates' successors, his son Phraates II and his brother Artabanus II, were both killed in an unexpected series of invasions by the Sakas who attacked Parthia from the east between 130 and 124 BC (Schippmann 1986). The coinage of these two kings followed that of their illustrious predecessor, occasionally revealing personal allegiances with the use of titles such as *Philadelphos* by Artabanus. Mithridates II (123–88 BC), an energetic ruler like his namesake, managed to appease the Sakas in the east and settle them to the south of Parthia, in what became Sakastan (modern Sistan). In the west, he defeated the insurgent rulers of Characene and Elymais (Shayegan 2011: 110–25; Potts 1999: 391) and reestablished Arsacid control over Media and Mesopotamia. In northern Media, he reached an agreement with the rising Armenian power of Tigranes I and received an area known as the Seventy Valleys as a concession from that ruler (Schippmann 1986). His coinage established the standard of all later Arsacid issues, with a bearded portrait of the king, facing left, and probably partly reflecting the actual likeness of the king, on the obverse, as well as the seated archer surrounded by legends on the reverse. The seat of the archer, however, was changed from a full throne to a Greek-style *omphalos* under Mithridates I (Curtis 2007: 408), which might be an indication of the more Hellenized culture of Mithridates' reign. The legends, since at least the time of Mithridates I, also carried a date according to the Seleucid era (Alram 1986b: Metals, Denominations, Mints), although this was not consistently applied, as well as several monograms and minor iconographic features. The exclusive production of tetradrachms by the mint of Seleucia allows us to partly disentangle the subsequent confused succession and political infighting among multiple Arsacid claimants to the throne.

The immediate consequence of Mithridates' death was the beginning of a divided monarchy among his direct descendants, in the form of his son Gotarzes I, as well as a possible brother of Mithridates, named Sinatruces, who must have been quite an old man, judging by the portraits on his coins (see Assar 2000: 8ff. for some discussion of this period). Gotarzes' position as heir of Mithridates II is established not only by his coinage, but also by evidence in the Babylonian astronomical diaries (Sachs and Hunger 1996: no. 87; Shayegan 2011: 192–7), as well as a badly eroded relief at Bisotun in Media, identifying him as "Satrap of the Satraps" during the reign of his father (Chapter 38; Herzfeld 1920: 35–9). The competition between Gotarzes and Sinatruces, however, allowed the Armenian king Tigranes I (the Great) to temporarily capture large tracts of Arsacid, as well as Roman, territory and to expand his power all the way to the Mediterranean (Sherwin-White 1984: 109–110). In the meantime, Sinatruces was in charge of areas in the east, including the mints of Ecbatana and Rhagae (Rayy), while Gotarzes controlled Seleucia-on-the-Tigris and occasionally minted coins in Rhagae and Ecbatana as well (Assar 2000). Among the successors of these two kings is a certain Orodes I, who appears to have initially reigned without any opposition, but who was later challenged by an unnamed claimant from the east who eventually removed him from the throne, even in Babylonia (*c.*78 BC). Phraates III (*c.*70–58 BC), who may have been the son of Sinatruces (Shayegan 2011: 227), was the most successful king of this period, controlling both Parthia and Babylonia, and appeasing rebellious rulers such as the Kamnaskirids of Elymais. However, he had a challenger by the name of Darius of Media who controlled Media Atropatene, and was an Arsacid prince of a cadet branch. The coins of Phraates III, issued at Seleucia, Ecbatana, Rhagae, Hecatompylus, Margiana, Traxiana, Nisa, and Areia, were also supplemented by an itinerant mint which probably accompanied the king while on campaign (Alram 1986b)

Phraates was killed by his two sons, the subsequent Mithridates III/IV (58–55 BC) and Orodes II (58–38 BC). The former, although largely an insignificant ruler, was important numismatically because he standardized the reverse legend of ΒΑΣΙΛΕΩΣ ΒΑΣΙΛΕΩΝ ΑΡΣΑΚΟΥ ΕΥΕΡΓΕΤΟΥ ΔΙΚΑΙΟΥ ΕΠΙΦΑΝΟΣ ΦΙΛΕΛΛΕΝΟΣ (the King of Kings, Arsaces, the munificent, the just, the illustrious, the Philhellene), which continued more or less unchanged so long as Arsacid coinage continued to be produced, or Greek legends can actually be discerned. One issue, largely overstruck by his brother Orodes II, gives his personal name (ΜΙΘΡΑΔΑΤΟΥ), though this proved to be an unstable feature of later Arsacid coin legends (Alram 1986a: Type 394).

The coins of Mithridates III/IV and Orodes II show minor stylistic changes, in both silver and bronze issues, mainly consisting of a new type of portrait which shows the ruler, still facing left, with short, well-trimmed hair and short beard and a visible moustache, possibly actual portraits of these kings (Sellwood 1980: Types 40 and later). The full bust of a man, sitting on the *omphalos*, wearing a soft cap and holding a bow, was left unchanged on the reverse, save for some tetradrachms of Orodes II from Seleucia, on which the king replaces the sitting figure with a kneeling Tyche in front of him, shown presenting him with a scepter (Sellwood 1980: Type 46). These innovations, in addition to the increasingly elaborate titles of the king on the reverse, might have been a result of Orodes' increasing power following the Battle of Carrhae in 53 BC, which caused the destruction of several Roman regions and the death of Crassus, the ill-fated Roman politician (Bivar 1983: 48–58).

Orodes' successors largely preserved his coin type, including the portraiture, and occasionally even the alternative reverse just described. Two features of the obverse, the addition of a mole-like "royal wart" to the forehead of the king and a star and crescent behind his head, are the most significant features of the coins of Phraates IV (*c.*38–7 BC) (Tanabe 1998: 365–84). The son of Phraates IV, known as Phraataces, most significantly had an obverse portrait of himself on his coins, but a reverse portrait of his mother, Queen Musa (Sellwood 1980: Type 58), along with a circular inscription identifying Queen Musa as "heavenly," in contrast to the square inscriptions that had been common until that time on Arsacid coinage (Sellwood 1980: Type 58.4; Strugnell 2008).

The coins of Vonones I, the Romanized son of Phraates IV who was placed on the Arsacid throne as a candidate of Rome, show, on the reverse, an image of the Nike, possibly denoting "victory" against his enemies. They are particularly distinguished by the fact that they bear inscriptions in Greek on the obverse, in a circular design possibly influenced by both Roman coins and those of Phraataces.

The period after Phraates IV is generally one of uncertain succession to the Arsacid throne (or what might be called Arsacid high kingship). Due to this, the iconography of the coins tended to stabilize, reflecting the claims of various contenders to the crown. The kings who ruled in the first half of the first century AD, from Artabanus III to Vardanes II, tended to model their coins roughly on those of Orodes II and Phraates IV, with variations reflecting different mints. Silver tetradrachms continued to be minted exclusively at Seleucia-on-the-Tirgris (Alram 1986b), while Ecbatana appears to have been the second most productive, and probably important, mint of the realm. On the coins of this period, the obverse type of Orodes II or Phraates IV seems to have become almost canonical, while the reverses show either the bow-holding king or Tyche in front of a seated king (and occasionally alone). The Greek inscriptions on the obverse, generally following the pattern of Phraates IV, slowly became more debased and harder to read, particularly on the reverse of drachms, while the legends on the tetradrachms continued to be legible (Alram 1986b: Legends).

With Vologases I, the reforming Arsacid emperor of the first century AD, the coinage also followed the ambitions of the crown. With more stable iconography, higher-standard metal, and more careful stylistic considerations, quality appears to have returned to the currency of the empire (Simonetta 1949: 237–9). Vologases' diplomatic and military successes, particularly against Rome in the case of Armenia, appear to have increased his prestige and brought more mints into production (Millar 1995: 29–34). It was also under Vologases I that the use of Greek dates, based on the Seleucid era, became more common on Arsacid coins, with more examples appearing on the coinage of Vologases II (Alram 1986b).

The most important successor of Vologases I, Pakores (Pacorus) I, followed the established iconography of Vologases, although from this period, for almost a century (up to Vologases III), the appearance of Tyche instead of the seated king with a bow became more common on Arsacid coinage, particularly issues from Ecbatana. Vologases V, the last strong Arsacid king, presented himself on the reverse of his coins seated on a throne, facing left, with an increasingly Iranian-looking Nike (in a shape in a bearded man in a three-pronged crown) presenting him with a diadem (Sellwood 1980: no. 88.10). In fact, Iranian influences seem to have increased in tandem with a decrease in the quality of the Greek inscriptions. As early as the reign of Vologases I, the appearance of the personal name of the king, or an abbreviated version of it, had become common on Arsacid coinage. By the time of Vologases V, this was indeed quite common, with the reverse inscription increasingly depicting illegible Greek, and more commonly letters that spell words in Aramaic script, used for the Parthian language (Alram 1986b: Legends).

Vologases V was famously succeeded by his two sons, Vologases VI and Artabanus V/IV. While the former was in charge of Seleucia, and thus issued tetradrachms, he was only occasionally in charge of Ecbatana, where his brother Artabanus held sway. In fact, Artabanus appears to have been in charge on the Iranian plateau. He is depicted giving a crown to a certain Khwasak, possibly a local governor of Khuzistan or an Elymaean king, at Tang-e Sarvak (Henning 1952), as well as checking the advances of the rebellious Persid prince, Ardašīr. However, Ardašīr, having together with his father removed the Persid kings from their throne, defeated the Elymaean vassals of Artabanus, as well as the Arsacid himself. Another victory against Vologases VI guaranteed the ascendance of the Sasanian Ardašīr I in 224 and the final fall of the Arsacids from power. The last Arsacid coin, of either Vologases VI in exile or the last claimant to the Arsacid throne (Tiridates III?), was issued in 226 at Ecbatana (Sellwood 1990: 157), after which the minting of Arsacid coins ceased completely and all mints converted to the production of Ardašīr's coinage.

The kingdom of Elymais

Elymais, the Hellenized kingdom formed to the east of the ancient city of Susa, was among the minor powers that appeared at the twilight of Seleucid imperial power and was eventually absorbed into the larger Arsacid Empire. Elymais, however, enjoyed a great deal of autonomy, and occasionally even independence, one of the indications of which was the minting of coinage. With their territory consisting largely of the lowland domains of the ancient Elamite kingdom (hence the name Elymais, a Greek rendering of Elam; see Potts 1999: 375), the Elymaean kings controlled access to the head of the Persian Gulf (Hansman 1998). Additionally, their economy probably relied on the fertile Susiana plain, where much of their later coinage has been found, which had a history of intensive cultivation and high agricultural yields, a factor that further strengthened the Elymaean coin issues.

The political history of Elymais dates from the refoundation of Susa, one of the Achaemenid "capitals," as a Hellenistic *polis* under Seleucid rule, where Seleucid rulers minted coins (Le Rider 1965; Kritt 1997). While the city was ruled by a council, in the style of a Greek *polis* (Chapter 35), the region was a Seleucid satrapy itself, known as Susiana. It may have been following the defeat of the Seleucids by the Romans at Apamea, in 188 BC, that a local rebel, possibly a former Seleucid satrap, by the name of Okkanapsos, took temporary control of the region and started issuing coinage in Seleucid style, the obverse of which shows a right-facing portrait of the king wearing a diadem, and the reverse Apollo sitting on an *omphalos* holding a bow and arrow in his hands, with a variant of the legend on Seleucid coins that named the issuer ΒΑΣΗΛΕΩΣ ΟΚΚΑΝΑΨΟΥ ΣΩΤΕΡΟΣ (Alram 1986a: pl. 14.445–6). Issued in debased tetradrachm and drachm denominations, as well as copper varieties down to obols, these coins probably reflect their issuer's claim to independent rule, rather than genuine kingship.

Following his defeat by the Romans at Apamea, Antiochus III entered Susa in 187 BC and attempted to seize the treasury of the local god, Bel, for himself (Diodorus Siculus

28.3/20.15; Potts 1999: 382). Based on the evidence of Justin (32.2), he was then killed by the local people for this insult (although II Maccabees assigns this death to Antiochus IV, who later attempted a similar robbery of a sanctuary at Susa, before dying at Gabae). This incident demonstrates both the power and the independence of Susa, and its Elymaean kings, as well as Seleucid attitudes toward that independence.

Numismatically, the coins of the subsequent kings of Elymais, the Kamnaskirids, betray influences from the coinage of Demetrius II and Alexander Balas, suggesting that their coming to power postdated these two Seleucid rulers (Hansman 1998). Consequently, a date between 147 and 145 BC seems likely for the beginning of the reign of Kamnaskires I, the founder of the Kamnaskirid dynasty of Elymais (for alternative arguments and the existence of two Kamnaskires, see Shayegan 2011: 88–100). At the time the Elymaeans probably controlled the eastern and southeastern parts of Khuzestan, with their capital at Seleucia-on-the-Hedyphon (unlocated but possibly near modern Behbahan; Hansman 1998). They don't, however, appear to have controlled Susa, and historical accounts show a clear understanding that Elymais, a rugged and mountainous region, was different than and separate from Susa and the Susiana plain (Hansman 1998; see Potts 1999: 391–3 for Susa during the Elymaean period).

Probably because of their support of Demetrius II, the Elymaeans' territory was invaded by Mithridates I in 140–139 BC, but a few decades later, the Elymaeans regained most of their territory and established a mint in Seleucia-on-the-Hedyphon. Silver tetradrachms and drachms issued under the authority of Kamnaskires II and dated to around 82 BC, show an obverse portrait similar to that of Kamnaskires I, with a right-facing, clean-shaven king wearing a diadem, and Apollo sitting on the *omphalos*, surrounded by Greek legends, on the reverse. Kamnaskires II was followed by another Kamnaskires (III) who also minted silver tetradrachms and drachms until 39 BC. These coins all follow the basic Seleucid type, with some coins of Kamnaskires III also including a portrait of Queen Anzaze alongside (and behind) his bust (Alram 1986a: pl. 15.454–5). These latter types, however, show a shift in style, with the king shown bearded, wearing a flat cap, and facing left, on the obverse. The reverse shows a left-facing, seated Zeus holding a scepter, in a gesture that suggests he is crowning the king on the obverse. The obverse also shows an anchor symbol behind the king's bust. This symbol, which first appeared on the reverse of the coins of Kamnaskires II (Alram 1986a: Type 434), became the identifying marker of the Elymaean kings.

The fact that an Elymaean envoy was sent to the Roman general Pompey seems to suggest an effort by the Elymaeans to attract Roman support against the Arsacid Phraates III, who also minted bronze coins at Susa (Hansman 1998). From this point on, two more Kamnaskirid kings, Kamnaskires IV and V, ruled the kingdom until the middle of the first century AD. In fact, after 45 AD (in the reign of the Arsacid king Vardanes), there does not seem to have been any Arsacid minting activity at Susa, suggesting that the Elymaeans may have taken effective control of the city, turning its active mint to their own use (although on the earlier Elymaean issues from Susa, see Potts 1999: 384). Elymaean coins after Kamnaskires III show a remarkable consistency, with an obverse portrait of a bearded king, facing left, often wearing a diadem and occasionally a flat cap, and an anchor behind the king's bust, as well as the old Achaemenid satrapal star and crescent signs. The reverse, initially depicting a seated Zeus, surrounded by Greek legends, quickly deteriorated into meaningless Greek and occasional, Aramaic-looking legends, with unidentifiable figures. These coins were issued in tetradrachms, drachms, and hemidrachms of both silver and copper, as well as occasional bronze and billon, up to the end of the rule of the Kamnaskirid dynasty sometime in the late first century AD (Hansman 1998).

Around the end of the first century AD, a cadet branch of the Arsacid dynasty, starting with Orodes I, began minting coins in the style of the Kamnaskirids in Elymais, at both Seleucia and Susa (Le Rider 1965: 428). This seems to have been the starting point of a second line of Elymaean rulers, the so-called "Arsacid" line, although this is purely based on the onomastic logic of the use of Parthian names, while the coinage itself was unchanged and closely resembled that of the so-called "Kamnaskirids." However, while the Kamnaskirid coins used Greek for their inscriptions, the Arsacid dynasty used both Greek and Aramaic, the number of coins bearing Greek legends higher among issues from the Susa mint, while those bearing Aramaic ones were more commonly issued at Seleucia, although both mints produced coins with legends in both languages (Hansman 1990: 5–10). Additionally, although the obverse of the "Arsacid" types remained largely faithful to the Kamnaskirid issues, the reverse became more varied, occasionally repeating the anchor symbol, while at other times showing birds, female portraits, an archer, or even simple leaf-like designs.

Orodes II, known as Kamnaskires-Orodes, was followed by a certain Phraates, then another king known as Osroes, who could have been the same as Osroes I, the Arsacid Emperor known to have temporarily used the Susa mint to issue bronze coinage for the payment of his army (Hansman 1998; Le Rider 1965: 431). Coins of Osroes, depicting the frontal portrait of the king, were probably copies of, or identical to, coins of the Arsacid king by the same name, some of whose influence can be seen on the coins of some later Elymaean rulers. Another king, Orodes III, was accompanied on the reverse of some of his coins by the bust of a woman, identified with a proto-Pahlavi legend as Ulfan, possibly a queen. The inscriptions of Tang-e Sarvak identify a king called Abar-Basi, and another as Orodes, who may be the same as the king identified on his coins as Orodes (IV) who ruled c.165–170 AD. A relief discovered at Susa shows a governor of Susa named Khwasak who ruled under the suzerainty of Artabanus IV and is shown receiving his crown from the latter (Henning 1952: 166–76). The accounts of the rise of Ardašīr I, founder of the Sasanian dynasty, mention another Orodes, the "king of Khuzestan," who was instructed by Artabanus IV to check the advances of Ardašīr I around 222 AD. The operation was unsuccessful, forcing Artabanus IV himself to get involved. His defeat ceded control of Khuzestan, and eventually all of Iran, to the Persid king who went on to found the Sasanian dynasty (224 AD). Elymais, including Susiana, capitulated to the Sasanian state, which largely abolished the Arsacid style of local, autonomous polities, and consequently the right to issue coinage.

KINGDOM OF PERSIS

The coinage of Persis provides an interesting example of Hellenistic influence on coin production during the suzerainty of the Arsacid dynasty. Containing much Achaemenid-influenced iconography, the coins of the Persid dynasty also changed in response to Seleucid, Arsacid, and unknown local political, and of course economic, challenges. There were, in general, three periods of coin production in Persis, each characterized either by a stylistic shift or by a major disruption in production.

The beginnings of Persid coin production are quite obscure. Reigning in the heartland of the once great Achaemenid kings, the rulers who issued the earliest Persid coins are thought to have been local commanders or satraps (Chapter 36). This is in fact evidenced by the title they used, *frataraka*, an Achaemenid military rank, which also distinguished the first period of Persid coin production (Curtis 2010: 380). Additionally, Achaemenid or local Persid influence is noticeable in the use of imperial Aramaic as the preferred script for the coin legends, marking a departure from Seleucid and Arsacid issues, as well as those of other Hellenistic kingdoms around them, most importantly Elymais. It is commonly believed that the earliest coins were produced by a certain Baydad (Aramaic *bgd't*), who is shown clean shaven, apart from a moustache, on the obverse wearing an elaborate, soft hat with turned-up ear flaps (Alram 1986a: pl. 17.511–19). Some of the early reverses show Baydad sitting on a crown with a standard behind him, an image copied from Seleucid satrapal coins. He soon switched to an image that became more or less canonical in the first two stages of Persis coin production, that of a large, square building, with an image of *frauahr* (either Ahuramazda or the Glory of the King) above it (Klose and Müseler 2008: 24–5). On the left, the king is shown standing, wearing a soft cap with a chin-piece, resembling the garb of a priest from post-Achaemenid tomb reliefs, holding a barsom bundle and facing the central structure in a respectful manner. On the right of the structure is a standard, sometimes with an eagle on top of it, and the whole image is surrounded by an inscription, varying in its placement, identifying the king as "Baydad, the *frataraka* of the Lord" (Klose and Müseler 2008: 18).

Nevertheless, scholars disagree on the date of the beginning of Persid coin production. An early date—as early is 295 BC—has been suggested by some scholars (e.g., Klose and Müseler 2008: 16–18; Hoover 2008; Curtis 2010: 386), while others prefer to put the beginning of Persid emissions at the same time as those of Elymais and Characene, namely the period of the declining Seleucid influence and the rise of Arsacid power (*c*.180 BC). The former rely on iconographic similarities between the early Seleucid and Persis coinage, as well as the evidence of overstrikes that would allow a possible sequence, and relative dating, for these coins. The supporters of a later dating of the Persid coinage (Alram 1986a) point out the stylistic continuity within the coinage and the fact that there does not seem to be any break in coin production in Persis, something that is necessary if one favors the earlier dating (cf. Chapter 36).

The normal divisions of Persid history rely both on stylistic information as well as coin legends that show a shift in the ideology of the ruling authorities. While stylistically the coinage from the beginning to the rule of Darev I remained rather faithful to its predecessors, the legend changed significantly, marking a new era in the political history of Hellenistic Persis. The first series of coins have obverses and reverses like those described above, while those after Darev II, including some issues of Darev himself, abandoned the image of the large building on the reverse and opted for a more minimalistic representation of a standing man/king, worshiping before a simple fire altar (Alram 1986a: Type 564ff.). Although the reverses went through several design changes, the major change affecting the obverse was the adoption of Arsacid models (e.g., in case of Vadfradad III, Alram Type 561), mostly of Mithridates II, as well as a change in the direction of the profile from the right to the left, which became standard on Persid coinage after Darev II.

Following changes to the obverse portrait on Arsacid coins, those of Pakor I (Alram 1986a: Type 588) adopted the same sort of "wavy" hairstyle present on the obverse of the coins of Phraates III (*c*.73–58 BC). On the reverse, beginning with Pakor I, the coins sometimes show a second, left-facing portrait in profile, wearing a diadem, which might represent the father of the ruler shown on the obverse. This interpretation would be supported by the fact that, as in the reign of Darev II, the coins of some rulers include a reverse legend naming the father of the king (in case of Darev, Vadfradad IV). Additionally, the coins of rulers such as Pakor II (Alram 1986a: Type 597/598) or Nambed show symbols, including a three-pronged "star," on their reverse, the significance of which is unclear.

The coin legends, as mentioned, are important for determining the sequence of Persid coin production. While the earliest rulers, specifically Baydad, Ardaxshir I, Vahbarz, and Vadfradad I, used the title "*frataraka* of the Gods" (written in cursive Aramaic as *prtrk' ZY ALHYA*) on the reverse of their coins, the rulers after Darev I identified themselves as Aramaic *MLKA* ("king"), thus making a more significant claim to rulership (Klose and Müseler 2008: 43). This may have been preceded by the earlier title *krny*, a higher military rank than *frataraka*, which is found on some earlier coins of the *frataraka* series (Alram 1987b; Klose and Müseler 2008: 36). It thus seems that, after Darev I, the rulers of Persis felt secure enough to claim a royal title for themselves, and despite political challenges did not abandon the claim and the title until the end of their rule. Stylistically, legends remained confined to the reverse of Persid coinage well into the history of the kingdom, with Pakor II being the first ruler to display his name on the obverse of his coins. Thereafter, the normal pattern was to include the name of the ruler on the obverse, while the reverse was reserved for a legend identifying his descent, occasionally including names that are not known from other coins (e.g., Mithras on the reverse of the coinage of Mančihr I or Artaxšir III; Alram 1986a: pl. 21.628–31).

Alram (1986a) identified three "unknown kings" within the Persid sequence. These preceded Darev I, Vadfradad IV, and Mančihr III, respectively, and are classified as "unknown" due to the illegibility of the legends on these coins, making it difficult to identify them. The sequential numbers given to these kings are thus a result of modern numismatic research and may have to be revised when and if legible specimens are discovered.

After the major change under Vadfradad III and Darev II, Persid coinage remained largely consistent. Minor changes in reverse and obverse style, nonetheless, kept the style recognizable and distinct. Otherwise, the issue of tertradrachms was abandoned after the *fratarakā* Dynasty, possibly under Arsacid pressure, and Persid issues were limited to drachms and fractions of silver, bronze, and copper (Klose and Müseler 2008: 24–44). The mint is assumed to have been located at Istakhr/Stakhr—attested as the capital of Persis in the written sources—although this is never mentioned on the coins. The whole series is also completely devoid of any sort of dating, thus forcing us to rely on conjectural evidence, as well as comparisons with Arsacid coinage, for dating both the coins and the reigns of the rulers who minted them.

The consistency of Persid coinage, however, came to a dramatic end sometime in the early third century. According to later sources, such as Tabari I, 814 (Bosworth 1999), a rebellion against the ruling family of Persis ("the Bazrangids"), led by Babak (MP *Pabag*), a supposed local strongman, toppled Ardašir IV. Pabag and his son, Šābuhr, then ruled the region, the coins of the latter showing his father's bust on the reverse in a completely new style which included visibly larger flans, although the denomination was still a drachm; a portrait of Šābuhr in frontal pose, while that of Pabag was shown in profile, facing left; and a much more elaborate design and pearl circle surrounding the entire scene (Alram 1986a: pl. 22.653–5). Most astonishing, and significant, is the script used for the legends on the obverse and the reverse of the coins. While cursive Aramaic had undergone significant changes during the Persid period, the script that appears on the coins of Šābuhr is fully "Pahlavi," of the kind associated with and visibly legible on Sasanian coins. This should probably cause little surprise, at least politically, since the next ruler of this new line was none other than Ardašīr (V of Persis) who, shortly after defeating Artabanus IV/V, would become Ardašīr I, King of Kings and founder of the Sasanian dynasty (Daryaee 2007: 2–5). The coinage sequence of Persis thus came to an abrupt end, as Sasanian imperial coinage completely replaced all local issues, including those of Elymais and Persis.

FURTHER READING

Arsacid, Elymaean, and Persid coinage (as well as that of Characene) is often classified as part of the general category of Hellenistic coinage, due to the initial stylistic influence of Seleucid emissions. The major work on Parthian coins is still Sellwood's compact, but informative, handbook (1980). The most comprehensive catalog of Persid coinage is now Klose and Museler (2008). The coins of Elymais were cataloged by van't Haaff (2007), although his typology and categorizations are not widely accepted and the whole series is in need of a reevaluation. Alram's monumental work (1986a) is overall the most comprehensive catalog of all of these various series and still one of the most useful sources.

REFERENCES

Alram, M. 1986a. *Nomina propria iranica in nummis. Materialgrundlagen zu den iranischen Personennamen auf antiken Münzen.* Vienna: Iranisches Personennamenbuch 4.

———. 1986b. Arsacid iii. Arsacid coinage. *EnIr* online edition.
———. 1987a. Die Vorbildwirkung der arsakidischen Münzprägung. *LNV* 3: 116–47.
———. 1987b. Eine neue Drachme des Vahbarz (Oborzos) aus der Persis? *LNV* 3: 147–55.
Assar, G.R.F. 2000. Recent studies in Parthian history: Part I. *The Celator* 14/12: 6–22.
Bivar, A. D. H. 1983. The political history of Iran under the Arsacids. *CHI* 3/1: 21–99.
Bosworth, C. E. 1999. *The history of al-Ṭabarī (Taʾrīkh al-rusul waʾl-mulūk)*, vol. 5, *The Sāsānids, the Byzantines, the Lakhmids, and Yemen*. Albany: State University of New York Press.
Curtis, V. S. 2007. Religious iconography on ancient Iranian coins. In *After Alexander: Central Asia before Islam*, ed. J. Cribb and G. Herrmann, 413–34. Oxford: Proceedings of the British Academy 133.
———. 2010. The Frataraka coins of Persis: Bridging the gap between Achaemenid and Sasanian Persia. *WAP*: 379–94.
Daryaee, T. 2006. The importance of Seleucid kingship on Iranian imperial ideology. *Bulletin of Ancient Iranian History* 1. www.iranancienthistory.com.
———. 2009. *Sasanian Persia: The rise and fall of an empire*. London: I. B. Tauris.
Haaff, P. A. van't. 2007. *Catalogue of Elymaean coinage: ca. 147 B.C.–A.D. 228*. Lancaster: Classical Numismatic Group.
Hansman, J. 1990. Coins and mints of ancient Elymais. *Iran* 28: 1–11.
———. 1998. Elymais. *EnIr* online edition.
Henning, W. B. 1952. The monuments and inscriptions of Tang-i Sarvak. *Asia Major* 2: 151–78.
Herzfeld, E. 1920. *Am Tor von Asien. Felsdenkmale aus Irans Heldenzeit*. Berlin: D. Reimer.
Hoover, O. D. 2008. Overstruck Seleucid coins. In *Seleucid coins: A comprehensive catalogue*, vol. 2/1, ed. A. Houghton and C. Lorber, 209–30. New York: American Numismatic Society.
Klose, D. O. A., and W. Müseler. 2008. *Statthalter, Rebellen, Könige: Die Münzen aus Persepolis von Alexander dem Großen zu den Sasaniden*. Munich: Staatliche Münzsammlung.
Kritt, B. 1997. *The Seleucid mint at Susa*. Lancaster: Classical Numismatic Studies 2.
Le Rider, G. 1965. *Suse sous les Séleucides et les Parthes: Les trouvailles monétaires et l'histoire de la ville*. Paris: MMAI 38.
Millar, F. 1995. *The Roman Near East: 31 BC–AD 337*. Cambridge: Harvard University Press.
Potts, D. T. 1999. *The archaeology of Elam: Formation and transformation of an ancient Iranian state*. Cambridge: Cambridge University Press.
Rezakhani, K. 2004. Tirdad and Ardavan: A new look at the genealogy of the early Arsacids. *Farhang* 17/1: 195–201.
Sachs, A. J., and H. Hunger. 1996. *Astronomical diaries and related texts from Babylonia*, vol. 3. Vienna: Denkschriften der Österreichischen Akademie der Wissenschaften 247.
Schippmann, K. 1986. Arsacid ii. The Arsacid dynasty. *EnIr* online edition.
Sellwood, D. 1980. *An introduction to the coinage of Parthia*, 2nd ed. London: Spink.
———. 1990. The end of the Parthian Dynasty. *Spink Numismatic Circular* 98/5: 157.
Shayegan, M. R. 2011. *Arsacids and Sasanians: Political ideology in post-Hellenistic and Late Antique Persia*. Cambridge: Cambridge University Press.
Sherwin-White, A. N. 1984. *Roman foreign policy in the East, 168 B.C. to A.D. 1*. Norman: University of Oklahoma Press.
Simonetta, A. 1949. The drachms of Vologases I. and Artabanus IV. *NC* 9: 237–9.
Strugnell, E. 2008. Thea Musa, Roman Queen of Parthia. *IrAnt* 43: 275–98.
Tanabe, K. 1998. Iranian Xvarnah and the treasure of Shosoin at Nara in Japan. *IrAnt* 23: 365–84.
Wolski, J. 1993. *L'empire des Arsacides*. Leuven: Textes et Memoires 18.

CHAPTER 40

ARAMAIC, PARTHIAN, AND MIDDLE PERSIAN

SEIRO HARUTA

INTRODUCTION

This chapter deals with sources written in the Aramaic language or scripts derived from the Aramaic script within the area ruled by Iranian dynasties before Islamic times, that is, it deals with sources in Aramaic under the Achaemenid Empire; those in Aramaic dialects, Parthian, and Early Middle Persian during Parthian times; and those in Middle Persian (and Parthian) under the Sasanian dynasty. Aramaic is a Northwest Semitic language, while both Parthian and Middle Persian are Middle West Iranian languages. Aramaic scripts were originally consonantal alphabetic scripts written from right to left.

Texts written on archaeological objects, such as lapidary inscriptions, ostraca, and papyri, are treated here; sources in manuscripts such as Old Testament texts or Pahlavi literature are excluded for lack of space. Areas covered in this chapter vary considerably according to period. The area covered corresponds to the territory of the Islamic Republic of Iran when sources before the Achaemenids are discussed; to the vast area of the whole Persian Empire during Achaemenid times; to the area of the Arsacid dynasty and its neighboring, so-called "vassal" states during Parthian times; and to the area of the Sasanian Empire under the Sasanids.

The length of each section in this chapter bears no relation to the quantity and quality of sources available. The section on the Parthian period occupies a large part of this chapter only because that era encompassed many languages and dialects. Dates of texts follow previous studies; note that the year may increase or decrease by one (or more) depending on which calendars are applied to these texts; this is of particular importance in studying sources during the Parthian period.

Before and under the Achaemenids

During the Neo-Assyrian period Aramaic became a main chancellery language alongside Assyrian. Its use was widespread within the Assyrian Empire and in some neighboring regions. An Aramaic inscription of this period was found near Bukan (West Azerbaijan), attesting to a West Semitic god, Hadad, as well as an Urartian god, Haldi (Fales 2003). Several metal objects said to be from Luristan (now Lorestan and Ilam) bear short Aramaic inscriptions naming their owners (Dupont-Sommer 1964).

Under the Achaemenid dynasty, or to be precise, from the reign of Darius I onward, Aramaic was adopted as the principal language for official written communication. Thus, within the vast Old Persian Empire, the Aramaic language and script were used for letters, administrative texts, memorial inscriptions, and so on. This language or its script is sometimes referred to as Official Aramaic or Imperial Aramaic (Ger. Reichsaramäisch). Various texts have been found (cf. also Beyer 1984: 28–33; Fitzmyer and Kaufman 1992: 11–188; Weber and Wiesehöfer 1996: 78–84, 129–46; Beyer 2004: 16–18).

Several types of Aramaic texts, with dates ranging from the end of the sixth to the fifth century BC, have been excavated at Persepolis in Fars. Only a very small number of the several hundred Aramaic texts written on clay tablets from the site, which are far fewer than those in Elamite, have been published so far, while the remainder are being prepared for publication (Azzoni 2008). Many of the Aramaic and Elamite tablets bear seal inscriptions with legends written in those languages. Among the Aramaic seal inscriptions from Persepolis, one identifying a high official belonging to the royal family, Parnaka, son of Arshama, is noteworthy (Garrison and Root 2001). About 200 published Aramaic texts on mortars, pestles, and other utensils indicate that the objects, with their inscriptions, were made in Arachosia. Although these texts are undoubtedly important for studying rituals, probably of the Zoroastrians, the first edition of them (Bowman 1970) has been criticized in many respects (Naveh and Shaked 1973; Delaunay 1974).

Thanks to the dry conditions that favor the preservation of perishable materials and to the use of papyri, ostraca, and leathers before the Achaemenids, Egypt has yielded more than 600 Aramaic texts of Achaemenid date. These come from various sites, including Elephantine Island at Aswan, Hermopolis, and Saqqara (Yardani and Porten 1986–99). From these texts, we learn that soldiers from the eastern or northeastern border of the empire (Arachosia or Choresmia) worked in Aswan and that the Jewish community there was in contact with the governor of Judaea. Correspondence on papyri between Arshama, governor of Egypt, and a member of the royal family also yields clues about the management of estates by high officials.

Papyri and ostraca were also found in Syro-Palestine, for example, in Wadi el-Daliyeh, near Jericho (Dušek 2007) and in Idumaea (Eph'al and Naveh 1996). A few Aramaic inscriptions from Anatolia (Folmer 1995: 796), including a bilingual funerary inscription in Aramaic and Lydian from Sardis (348 BC) (Lipiński 1975: 153–61) and a trilingual commemorative stele in Aramaic, Lycian, and Greek from Xanthos (337 BC, first year of

Artaxerxes IV Arses) (Dupont-Sommer 1979), are invaluable for studying local administration and acculturation in Anatolia just before Alexander's conquest. Local languages (Lycian, Lydian) appear, as do the regional lingua franca (Greek) and the language of the empire (Aramaic). It should also be noted that the editor of the Xanthos inscription reported numerous errors in the Aramaic script used (Dupont-Sommer 1979: 148, 152), showing that the engravers were ignorant of and unfamiliar with Aramaic letters. A lapidary inscription in Aramaic (Lipiński 1975: 150–3) as well as twelve seal inscriptions on bullae (Röllig 2002) were found at Daskyleion in Phrygia. Some legends on local coins issued in the western provinces were also written in Aramaic (Alram 1986: 101–21).

A total of forty-eight parchments and wooden plates with Aramaic inscriptions have been reported from Bactria (Shaked 2004; Naveh and Shaked 2012). All but one text are dated by Shaked to 354–324 BC, that is, from the end of the Achaemenid Empire and the reign of Alexander. These texts are very important for understanding the history of the empire's collapse. For example, the year formulae of the texts include "1st year of Artaxerxes V (Bessos)."

Hellenistic and Parthian times

After the fall of the Achaemenid Empire, the realm of Alexander and the Seleucid dynasty that succeeded in the eastern parts of territory conquered by Alexander adopted Greek as their official language. Only a few Aramaic inscriptions dating from 330 to around 200 BC have come to light so far. The use of Aramaic, however, did not cease in the eastern provinces of the Seleucids. Beginning around 200 BC, two major changes gradually occurred. One was that the divergence between dialects grew in both grammars and scripts; thus, in the Middle Aramaic periods (*c.*200 BC–200 AD), we can identify not one but several Middle Aramaic languages, such as Parmyrene, Hatran, Old Syriac, and Elymaean. The other change was that several Middle Iranian languages, such as Parthian, Middle Persian, Sogdian, and Choresmian, began to be written in scripts derived from the Aramaic script used under the Achaemenids.

Those unfamiliar with Middle Iranian studies should be aware of certain conventions in regard to these Iranian materials. First, there are two ways of transliterating Parthian and (Early) Middle Persian texts during the Parthian period. One is to follow Aramaic; the other is to adopt that of Sasanian Middle Persian. Second, these different methods are also applied to the transcription of words in these languages. The proper name *wrtrgn* was transcribed as *Warhragn*, in its early form, by some scholars, whereas other scholars rendered it as *Warhrān*, in its third-century AD form. Third and last, these Middle Iranian Languages, including Sogdian and Choresmian, were written with "heterograms" ("logograms," "Aramaeograms"). Scribes wrote Aramaic words to be read as corresponding Iranian words. For example, ZNH/ZNE, "this," should be read /im/ in Parthian texts and /ēn/ in Middle Persian ones. Scholars usually transliterate these heterograms with capital letters. It is extremely difficult to determine the language of the texts, whether

Aramaic or Middle Iranian, when they are very short or full of standard expressions such as greeting formulae. In particular, this has caused continuing disagreement among scholars about early sources belonging to the second century BC or a little later. Several studies discuss how the heterographic writing systems in Middle Iranian developed (e.g., Henning 1958: 24–40; Kutscher 1970: 393–9; Skjærvø 1995; Shaked 2003: 129–33), but these remain hypothetical, mainly due to the paucity of sources in this period.

Many texts are known from the northeastern provinces of Iran, namely Semnan, Golestan, North Khorasan and Razavi Khorasan, and the southern districts of Turkmenistan, though most of them are brief and do not contain much information. A hoard found near Bojnurd, in North Khorasan, has yielded a number of coins issued by Arsaces I (r. c.238–211 BC), the first Arsacid ruler, all bearing Greek legends, but some also bearing a legend written in Aramaic script (Weber 2010b). The legend reads *krny*, thought to mean "leader of army/people," perhaps a synonym of *autokrator* in the Greek legend. These coins are, however, unique and the successors of Arsaces I did not employ Aramaic for the legends on their coins. In excavations at Old Nisa, near Ashgabat (Turkmenistan), more than 2700 texts written on ostraca were found, many bearing a date in the Arsacid era (Diakonoff and Livshits 1976–2001; Bader 1996; Morano 2008; Weber 2010a: 494–561). The vast majority of these texts date from the very end of the second century BC to c.19–10 BC, although one or two texts are thought to be earlier (mid-second century BC). Over 90 percent of the texts concern the delivery or preservation of wine brought to Old Nisa, called Mihrdatkirt at that time. Texts on the genealogy of a newly enthroned king are also known. Despite the high frequency of heterograms in the texts the language of the Nisa ostraca is generally thought to be Parthian, not Aramaic. Indeed, one would be unlikely to find a phrase such as *HŠKḤW B ḤWT' ZNH W ptšyḥt 'L 'ḤRN ḤWT'* ("discovered in this jar and poured into another jar") (Diakonoff and Livshits 1976–2001: no. 194) in Aramaic. Some legible inscriptions on seals are also known from Old Nisa (Nikitin 1993–4), while ostraca with Parthian inscriptions are reported from several sites in southern Turkmenistan such as Igdi Kala and Kosha Depe (Livshits 1977, 1984). Within the territory of the Islamic Republic of Iran, excavations at Shahr-e Qumis, southwest of Damghan in Semnan province, which has been identified as ancient Hecatompylus, yielded three ostraca written in Parthian. Another Parthian ostracon was also excavated at Tureng Tepe in Golestan (Bivar 1981).

In 1909, three parchments, two in Greek, dated to 88 BC and 22/1 BC, and one in Parthian, dated to 53 AD, were found at Avroman (Weber 2010a: 566–7) in Kurdistan and brought to London. All three documents are contracts for the sale of vineyards. Judging by the geographical names mentioned in them, the original place(s) where the contracts were made may now be in the more western parts of Iraqi Kurdistan (Edmonds 1952). On a rock at Bisotun and on the Parthian relief at Sar-e Pol-e Zohab, both in Kermanshah province, short Parthian inscriptions are incised (Gropp 1968). Although they contain the names of the Arsacid rulers, Vologases and Gotarzes, the readings and interpretations of them are not firmly established.

During the first half of the first century AD the Greek legends on Arsacid coins issued in the Iranian plateau region became almost illegible. Parthian abbreviations such as *wl*, for *wlgšy*, that is, Vologases, appear on coins issued after the reign of Vologases I (r. *c*.51–78 AD). Some coins also have proper legends in Parthian (Weber 2010b). Several Parthian inscriptions on metal objects have been reported, including one excavated at a site in southern Siberia (Livshits 2003: 165–9).

Persis, now Fars and Bushehr, was the homeland of the Achaemenids and the Sasanians. From the second century BC, a local dynasty existed (see Chapters 36 and 39) that issued coins with legends in Aramaic script (Alram 1986: 162–86) and later gave rise to the Sasanians (Wiesehöfer 1994). The first rulers called themselves *prtrk' dy 'lhy'* ("deputy of the gods"). It is virtually impossible to determine the language of these legends: it may be Aramaic or Early Middle Persian. Later rulers of the Persid dynasty, beginning in the first century BC, called themselves *šāh*, written with the heterogram *MLK'*. Several silver dishes incised with Early Middle Persian inscriptions are known; many of them mention only their weights, but one has a longer inscription from which we can say that it was written not in Aramaic but in Early Middle Persian and that the reading of the name of the rulers *D'ryn* /Dārayān/ or /Dārēn/ is preferable to the previously accepted reading *D'ryw* (Skjærvø 2000). Moreover, an inscription in Aramaic script has long been known on the tomb of Darius the Great at Naqš-e Rustam, but the condition of the letters deteriorated during the twentieth century, making the inscription difficult to interpret (Boyce and Grenet 1991: 118–20).

During the Parthian period, Susiana and Elymais, now Khuzestan and part of Kohgiluye va Boyer Ahmad, were governed by two dynasties, the Arsacids and a local Elymaean dynasty, the Kamnaskirids. In addition to the Greek inscriptions written under the Seleucids and Arsacids at Susa (see Chapter 41), there are several inscriptions and coin legends from these areas in Aramaic scripts (Alram 1986: 137–53). These Aramaic scripts are divided into two scripts and languages, Parthian and Elymaean Aramaic (Henning 1952). The letters of an inscription at Ḫong-e Azhdar (Ḫong-e Nouruzi), Izeh, Khuzestan, may belong to the Parthian script, but the inscription has deteriorated so much that it is almost illegible (Haruta 2006). Thus, the reading proposed by some scholars, which includes the phrase "King of Kings," is highly dubious. Inscriptions on the stele of Artabanus IV (r. 214–224 AD) from Susa, dating to 215 AD, were written in Parthian (Henning 1952) and identify him as "king of kings." Elymaean Aramaic inscriptions on rock reliefs are known at Ḫong-e Kamalvand, Tang-e Butan (both in Khuzestan) and Tang-e Sarvak (in Kohgiluye va Boyer Ahmad) (Bivar and Shaked 1964; Henning 1952; Gzella 2008: 112–22). Although the reliefs are thought to depict religious scenes, the interpretation of the inscriptions is quite difficult. A very unusual cylinder seal with an Elymaean Aramaic inscription has also been reported (Bivar 1992: 192–5). The paleographical study of the Elymaean Aramaic inscriptions strongly supports Augé's (1979) relative, numismatic chronology of the Elymaean dynasty during the first and second centuries AD (Haruta 2006).

In the southernmost part of Mesopotamia, known as Mesene, a small local dynasty called Characene emerged in the second half of the second century BC. Coin legends were written in Greek until the second century AD, when the script changed to the local Aramaic (Alram 1986: 154–61; Schuol 2000: 235–7). Materials written in Characenean script are so rare that even the readings of the legends are not entirely confirmed. Several Aramaic inscriptions have also been found on the southern side of the Persian Gulf (Healey and Bin Seray 1999–2000; Gzella 2008: 123–6).

Several Aramaic texts are also known from Babylonia (Oelsner 1986: 245–50). Those in cuneiform are dated to about the first half of the second century BC. Ostraca written in Parthian and Aramaic script were found at Nippur (Livshits 1984: 34–40; Shaked 1994b; Weber 2010a: 564–5). The most important source from Babylonia in Parthian times is the Greco-Parthian bilingual inscription incised on the thighs of a Heracles statue found at Tell ʿUmar, ancient Seleucia-on-the-Tigris. Dated to 151 AD, the inscription identifies the statue as booty from Mesene (Characene) when Vologases IV (r. 147–191 AD) defeated Mithridates, king of Mesene. The inscription reveals religious syncretism in that Heracles in the Greek version corresponds to Varhragn (Varhrān) in the Parthian version, and Apollon to Tīr (Morano 1990; Weber 2010a: 569–71).

Over 400 inscriptions have been published from the excavations at Hatra, west of Assur, in northern Mesopotamia. The Hatran language is a dialect of Aramaic and the Hatran script is a local variation of Aramaic script. The Hatra texts shed light on the various phases of an autonomous city under the Arsacids; local laws displayed on the walls are especially interesting. Both Aramaic and Arabic gods were popular there. Slightly fewer than 100 texts found at Assur are similar in both language and script to Hatran. From the theophoric names in these texts we see that the people of Assur continued to worship the city god Assur, even though the Assyrian empire had fallen centuries earlier (Aggoula 1985, 1991; Beyer 1998; Zehnder 2010: 289–343).

Edessa (modern Şanlıurfa, Turkey) was the capital of the small kingdom of Osrhoene during Parthian times. About ninety Aramaic inscriptions on stones and mosaics from Edessa and surrounding areas, both in Turkey and in Syria, have been published (Drijvers and Healey 1999; Zehnder 2010: 343–64). Both the language and script are called Old Syriac. These sources (Fig. 40.1) are important for understanding the emergence and development of Syriac culture. Although Christianity had already spread to Edessa during the second century AD, the religion attested in these texts is pagan. A few inscriptions in Parthian script have also been reported from northern Syria and Nineveh (Fuller and Bivar 1998).

Dura Europos, in eastern Syria, was controlled successively by the Seleucids, the Arsacids, and the Romans, and several texts have been found there in Hatran, Syriac, and Palmyrene, as well as in Greek, Latin, and Safaitic (a North Arabian dialect) (Zehnder 2010: 365–74). Palmyra, in central Syria, was not governed by the Arsacids, but some texts in Palmyrene refer to commercial traffic between Palmyra and the eastern provinces such as Characene (Hillers and Cussini 1996; Schuol 2000: 47–89).

Inscriptions written under the Artaxiad dynasty on border stones dating to the early second century BC have been found in Armenia (Périkhanian 1971). These were written in Aramaic using a local form of the Aramaic script. Some of the sealings and bullae from Artashat (Artaxata), related to the Artaxiads, also bear Aramaic inscriptions (Khachatrian 1996). An Aramaic inscription of second century AD date is also known from Garni.

FIGURE 40.1 Old Syriac inscriptions on the top of the central hill at Soğmatar, east of Şanlıurfa, Turkey.

Several inscriptions written in Aramaic script(s), one of which is in Parthian, have been reported from Georgia (Tsereteli 1998). The most famous inscription from Georgia is the Greco-Aramaic inscription found at Mtskheta. The Aramaic of the inscription is so corrupt that there are arguments over whether the language is Aramaic or not (Henning 1958: 37–40).

An Aramaic inscription of Hellenistic date was found at Aï Khanoum in Bactria (Afghanistan). The Hellenistic inscription at Arebsun, in Cappadocia, written in Aramaic, is important for the history of Zoroastrianism in Anatolia (Lemaire 2003). East of the territory controlled by the Seleucids, some of the inscriptions of the Mauryan king Aśoka, dating to the 280s BC, were written in Aramaic; some scholars have pointed to Iranian elements in these inscriptions (Humbach 1974).

SASANIAN TIMES

In this section, Classic Syriac sources and Jewish Babylonian literature such as Talmud are excluded except Babylonian incantation bowls; also excluded are Pahlavi (Zoroastrian) literature in books (cf. Tafazzoli 1997: 111–330; Cereti 2001; Macuch 2009) and Manichaean texts from Chinese Turkestan (cf. Sundermann 2009). Thus, only Middle Persian and Parthian inscriptions are dealt with here. Transcription of Middle Persian is based on MacKenzie's (1971) dictionary; scholars have been gradually following MacKenzie's method with some modification by Humbach and Skjærvø (1983) for purposes of transliteration (Skjærvø 1996: 518–20). It should also be noted that the term "Pahlavi" has three meanings: (1) Middle Persian in Zoroastrian literature contained in books; (2) Middle Persian written in a late cursive script, the so-called Pahlavi script; (3) Middle Persian written in Middle Persian script.

The royal inscriptions of Ardašīr I, Šābuhr I, and Narseh are valuable sources for the study of early Sasanian history and society. Two inscriptions of Ardašīr I at Naqš-e Rustam (ANRm-a, ANRm-b) and two of Šābuhr I at Naqš-e Rajab (ŠNRb) and on the wall of Ka'ba-ye Zardosht at Naqš-e Rustam (ŠKZ) were written in three languages: Middle Persian, Parthian, and Greek. Three inscriptions of Šābuhr I at Hajjiabad (ŠH), Tang-e Boraq (ŠTBq), and Bishapur (ŠVŠ) and one of Narseh at Paikuli were written in Middle Persian and Parthian (Back 1978). With the exception of Paikuli in Iraqi Kurdistan, all of these sites are in Fars. One of the two longest inscriptions, Šābuhr I's inscription on the Ka'ba-ye Zardosht (ŠKZ) (Huyse 1999), tells about his victories over three Roman emperors, enumerating the areas conquered; the other, Narseh's Paikuli inscription (NPi) (Humbach and Skjærvø 1978–83), narrates his accession and acceptance by the dignitaries of the Sasanian Empire. Among the nonroyal inscriptions from the third century AD, four commissioned by the high Zoroastrian priest Kerdīr at Naqš-e Rajab (KNRb, Fig. 40.2), Naqš-e Rustam (KNRm), Ka'ba-ye Zardosht (KKZ), and Sar Mashhad (KSM) are in Middle Persian. These give us precious information about both the spiritual and political dimensions of Zoroastrianism at that time (MacKenzie 1989; Gignoux 1991). Abnun's inscription (ABD) at Barm-e Delak, in Fars (Skjærvø 1992; MacKenzie 1994), and an inscription on a silver bowl in Middle Persian (Skjærvø and Harper 1994) reflect the royal ideology vis-à-vis the Sasanian rulers' subjects (Huyse 2009: 90–101).

In the course of excavations at Dura Europos, several ostraca, papyri, and parchments in Middle Persian and Parthian were unearthed (Harmatta 1958; Frye 1968; Weber 2010a: 562–4, 567–9). These are supposed to have been written some decades after the capture of the city by the Sasanians around 255 AD (Grenet 1988). After the reign of Narseh, Parthian disappeared in inscriptions, whether royal or not, except in some

FIGURE 40.2 Kirdīr's inscription at Naqš-e Rajab (KNRb).

eastern regions such as southern Turkmenistan. Parthian inscriptions at Kal-e Jangal (Weber 2010a: 588; Livshits and Nikitin 1991: 117–19) and Lakh Mazar (Livshits 2002), both in South Khorasan, were probably written in the early Sasanian period. About 700 rock graffiti in Middle Iranian have been found and published from the Upper Indus Valley in Pakistan. Most of these are in Sogdian, but two are in Middle Persian and two in Parthian (Sims-Williams 1989–92: nos. 232, 233, 410, and 487). Even in these areas, the use of the Parthian script seems to have ceased during the fourth century.

Middle Persian lapidary inscriptions of the fourth and fifth centuries are known not only in Fars (Persepolis and Firuzabad) but also in Kermanshah (Taq-e Bustan), Ardabil (Meshkinshahr) (Frye and Skjærvø 1998), and Razavi Khorasan (Bandiyan) (Gignoux 1998b). A number of lapidary inscriptions of late Sasanian and early Islamic date have been reported; most of them are the funerary inscriptions of Zoroastrians (Akbarzadeh and Tavoosi 2006; Huyse 2009: 101–2; Tafazzoli 1997: 81–110). Such inscriptions have been found in various places, though many of them are in Fars at sites such as Iqlid, Tang-e Jilu, and Kazerun. Middle Persian has also been reported from very remote places, for example, on a sarcophagus in Constantinople (Blois 1990). A bilingual funerary inscription in Middle Persian and Chinese was found at Xian in China (Humbach 1989).

There are numerous Middle Persian documents on papyri. Most of these were written for economic and administrative purposes during the decade-long Persian occupation of Egypt, from 619 to 629 (Weber 1992, 2003). Recently, a number of economic documents on leather and linen of early Islamic date were found in Iran and brought to Berkeley, California, and Berlin (Gignoux 1998a, 2009, 2010; Azarpay et al. 2007; Weber 2008).

The legends of Sasanian coins (Alram 1986: 186–214) and Arab-Sasanian coins are in Middle Persian. Some coins bear mint signatures (beginning in the late fourth century) and dates (beginning in the mid-fifth century). The publication of comprehensive catalogs of the Sasanian coins in Paris, Berlin, and Vienna is in progress (Alram and Gyselen 2003; Schindel 2004). It should also be noted that there are some coins with ink inscriptions written during early Islamic times (Gignoux 1978). For several decades now sigillographical works have been leading the way in the study of the administration systems of the late Sasanian period (Gyselen 1989). Seal inscriptions of the late period often include geographical names as well as names of offices; thus, they are very useful for the reconstruction of the Sasanian administrative system (Gyselen 2001, 2002, 2007; cf. Frye 1973a; Gignoux 1974, 1985; Gubaev et al. 1996; Akbarzadeh et al. 2009).

Publications of the inscriptions on silver vessels have appeared in scattered catalogs and articles (e.g., Frye 1973b; Brunner 1974; Harmatta 1974; Gignoux 1975; Livshits et al. 1987; Skjærvø and Harper 1994; Akbarzadeh et al. 2005). Other objects bearing Middle Persian inscriptions have also been published, three of which are particularly notable. One is a processional cross from Herat (Afghanistan) with an inscription in Pahlavi Psalter script (Gignoux 2001), a script attested in Chinese Turkestan. The other two are pieces of sandalwood which were long kept at Nara but are now in Tokyo; each bears an incised, one-word inscription with a Sogdian brand (Tōno 1987).

Several magical amulets in Middle Persian are also known (Harper et al. 1993; Shaked 1994a; cf. Callieri 2001: 22–31). Far more important for the study of magic in the late Sasanian and early Islamic periods, however, are Babylonian incantation bowls from Mesopotamia and southwestern Iran (e.g., Montgomery 1913; Naveh and Shaked 1985: 124–214; Segal 2000; Hunter 2004; Callieri 2001: 20–21; Bohak 2008: 183–93). Magic spells were written on the inside of these clay bowls, often accompanied by drawings of demons. Various scripts are attested, including rectangular Aramaic (Jewish Aramaic), Syriac, Mandaic, Pahlavi (not yet deciphered, cf. Shaked 1992: 83–5), and pseudo-scripts. Scholars believe that spells in Syriac were used by both pagans and Christians. Many Iranian and Semitic names of clients and their parents (usually their mother's names are mentioned) appear in spells written in Jewish Aramaic, Syriac, and Mandaic. Incantation bowls provide invaluable evidence of popular religious practices and of interrelations among different religions in the late Sasanian Mesopotamia. Mandaic amulets from these periods are also known (cf. Müller-Kessler 1999).

Conclusions

Sources belonging to the periods "between tablets and paper" from areas under Iranian dynastic control have been considered here. For a variety of reasons, however, these are few in number. First, many texts written on perishable materials such as parchment must have been lost because of environmental conditions. Second, there does not seem to have been a strong habit amongst common people to write epitaphs or other commemorative inscriptions, except in Syria during the Hellenistic and Parthian periods and in Iran after the late Sasanian period. Third, the number of sites excavated so far remains small and many archaeological sites await scientific excavation. That not only Old Nisa but also small sites in south Turkmenistan have yielded Parthian ostraca suggests that there must be a vast number of texts still underground.

Further reading

For the descriptive grammar of Aramaic, see, for example, Muraoka and Porten (1998), Muraoka (2011). For the descriptive grammar of Middle Persian and Parthian, see Skjærvø (2009). For sources in other Middle Iranian Languages, see Huyse (2009: 105–15). Iranian personal names in sources in various languages have been collected in the *Iranisches Personennamenbuch* series and in Tavernier (2007). Modern forgeries present a serious problem in the study of ancient inscriptions. On forgeries, particularly in Aramaic scripts, Shaked (1992) is the most important study; cf. Folmer (1995: 781–2), Skjærvø (1992), and Sims-Williams (2003: 119–21).

REFERENCES

Aggoula, B. 1985. *Inscriptions et graffites araméenes d'Assour*. Naples: *AION* Supplement 43.
——. 1991. *Inventaire des inscriptions hatréennes*. Paris: Institut français d'archéologie du Proche-Orient.
Akbarzadeh, D., C. G. Cereti, and F. Sinisi. 2009. *Glyptic antiquities from the Museum of Khoy*. Rome: IsIAO.
Akbarzadeh, D., T. Daryaee, and J. A. Lerner. 2005. Two recently discovered inscribed Sasanian silver bowls. *BAI* 15: 71–5.
Akbarzadeh, D., and M. Tavoosi. 2006. *Pahalvi Inscriptions (Katībehā-ye fārsī-ye miyāne)*. Tehran: Khane-ye Farhikhtegan-e Honarhaye Sonati Publication (in Persian).
Alram, M. 1986. *Nomina propria iranica in nummis. Materialgrundlagen zu den iranischen Personennamen auf antiken Münzen*. Vienna: Iranisches Personennamenbuch 4.
Alram, M., and M. Gyselen. 2003. *Sylloge nummorum sasanidarum–Paris–Berlin–Wien*, vol 1. *Ardashir I.–Shapur I.* Vienna: Verlag der Österreichischen Akademie der Wissenschaften.
Augé, C. 1979. Monnaies d'Élymaïde, de Bard-è Néchandeh et Masjid-i Solaiman. In *Terrasses sacrées de Bard-è Néchandeh et Masjid-i Solaiman: Les trouvailles monétaires*, ed. C. Augé, R. Curiel and G. Le Rider, 35–162. Paris: MDAI 44.
Azarpay, G., K. Martin, M. Schwartz, and D. Weber. 2007. New information on the date and function of the Berkley MP Archive. *BAI* 17: 17–29.
Azzoni, A. 2008. The Bowman MS and the Aramaic tablets. *AFP*: 253–74.
Back, M. 1978. *Die sassanidischen Staatsinschriften: Studien zur Orthographie und Phonologie des Mittelpersischen der Inschriften zusammen mit einem etymologischen Wortgutes und einem Textcorpus der behandelten Inschriften*. Leiden: Acta Iranica 18.
Bader, A. 1996. Parthian ostraca from Nisa: Some historical data. In *La Persia e l'Asia Centale da Alessandro al X secolo*, 251–76. Roma: Accademia Nazionale del Lincei.
Beyer, K. 1984. *Die aramäischen Texte vom Toten Meer*. Göttingen: Vandenhoeck & Ruprecht.
——. 1998. *Die aramäischen Inschriften aus Assur, Hatra und dem übrigen Ostmesopotamien (datiert 44 v.Chr. bis 238 n.Chr.)*. Göttingen: Vandenhoeck & Ruprecht.
——. 2004. *Die aramäischen Texte vom Toten Meer*, vol. 2. Göttingen: Vandenhoeck & Ruprecht.
Bivar, A. D. H. 1981. The second Parthian ostracon from Qūmis (Qūmis Commentaries No. 3). *Iran* 19: 81–5.
——. 1992. Glyptica Iranica. *BAI* 4: 191–9.
Bivar, A. D. H., and S. Shaked. 1964. The inscriptions at Shīmbār. *BSOAS* 27: 265–90.
Blois, F. de. 1990. The Middle-Persian inscription from Constantinople: Sasanian or post-Sasanian? *StIr* 19: 209–18.
Bohak, G. 2008. *Ancient Jewish magic: A history*. Cambridge: Cambridge University Press.
Bowman, R. A. 1970. *Aramaic ritual texts from Persepolis*. Chicago: OIP 91.
Boyce, M., and F. Grenet. 1991. *A history of Zoroastrianism*, vol. 3. *Zoroastrianism under Macedonian and Roman rule*. Leiden/New York: HdO 1/8/1/2/2/3.
Brunner, C. J. 1974. Middle Persian inscriptions on Sasanian silverware. *MMJ* 9: 109–21.
Callieri, P. 2001. In the land of the Magi: Demons and magic in the everyday life of pre-Islamic Iran. In *Démons et merveilles d'Orient*, ed. R. Gyselen, 11–36. Bures-sur-Yvette: RO 13.
Cereti, C. G. 2001. *La letteratura Pahlavi*. Milan: Mimesis.
Delaunay, J. A. 1974. A propos des *Aramaic ritual texts from Persepolis* de R. A. Bowman. In *Hommage Universel II*, 193–217. Leiden: Acta Iranica 2.

Diakonoff, I. M., and V. A. Livshits. 1976–2001. *Parthian economic documents from Nisa*. London: CII 2–3/1.

Drijvers, H. J. W., and J. F. Healey. 1999. *The Old Syriac inscriptions of Edessa and Osrhoene: Texts, translations and commentary*. Leiden: HdO 1/42.

Dupont-Sommer, A. 1964. Trois inscriptions araméennes inédites sur des bronzes du Luristan. *IrAnt* 4: 108–18.

———. 1979. L'inscription araméenne. In *Fouilles de Xanthos, VI: La stèle trilingue du Létôon*, ed. H. Metzger, 129–78. Paris: Klincksiek.

Dušek, J. 2007. *Les manuscrits araméens du Wadi Daliyeh et la Samarie vers 450–332 av. J.-C.* Leiden: Brill.

Edmonds, C. J. 1952. The place-names of the Avroman parchments. *BSOAS* 14: 478–82.

Eph'al, I., and J. Naveh. 1996. *Aramaic ostraca of the fourth century BC from Idumaea*. Jerusalem: Magnes Press.

Fales, F. M. 2003. Evidence for west-east contacts in the 8th century BC: The Bukān stele. *CE*: 131–48.

Fitzmyer, J. A., and S. A. Kaufman. 1992. *An Aramaic bibliography, Part I: Old, Official, and Biblical Aramaic*. Baltimore: John Hopkins University Press.

Folmer, M. L. 1995. *The Aramaic language in the Achaemenid period: A study in linguisitic variation*. Leuven: OLA 69.

Frye, R. N. 1968. *The Parthian and Middle Persian inscriptions of Dura-Europos*. London: CII 3/3/1.

———. 1973a. Inscriptions and monograms on the sealings. In *Sasanian remains from Qasr-i Abu Nasr: Seals, sealings, and coins*, ed. R. N. Frye, 47–65. Cambridge: Harvard University Press.

———. 1973b. Sasanian numbers and silver weights. *JRAS*: 2–11.

Frye, R. N., and P. O. Skjærvø. 1998. The Middle Persian inscription from Meshkinshahr. *BAI* 10: 53–61.

Fuller, M., and A. D. H. Bivar. 1998. Parthian ostraca from the Syrian Jazira. *BAI* 10: 25–31.

Garrison, M. B., and M. C. Root. 2001. *Seals on the Persepolis Fortification Tablets*, vol. 1, *Images of heroic encounter*. Chicago: OIP 117.

Gignoux, P. 1974. Les bulles sassanides de Qasr-i Abu Nasr. In *Mémorial Jean de Menasce*, ed. P. Gignoux and A. Tafazzoli, 169–87. Leuven: Imprimerie Orientaliste.

———. 1975. Coupes inscrites de la collection Mohsen Foroughi. In *Monumentum H. S. Nyberg*, vol. 1, 269–76. Leiden: Acta Iranica 4.

———. 1978. Les inscriptions en surcharge sur les monnaies de trésor sasanide de Suse. *CDAFI* 8: 137–53.

———. 1985. Les bulles sassanides de Qasr-i Abu Nasr (Collection du Metropolitan Museum of Art). In *Papers in Honour of Professor Mary Boyce*, pt. 1, ed. A. D. H. Bivar and J. R. Hinnels, 195–206. Leiden: Acta Iranica 24.

———. 1991. *Les quatre inscriptions du mage Kirdīr*. Paris: Cahiers de *StIr* 9.

———. 1998a. Six documents pehlevis sur cuir du California Museum of Ancient Art, Los Angeles. *BAI* 10: 63–72.

———. 1998b. Les inscriptions en moyen-perse de Bandiān. *StIr* 27: 251–8.

———. 2001. Une croix de procession de Hérat inscrite en pehlevi. *Le Muséon* 114: 291–304.

———. 2009. Les comptes de monsieur Friyag: Quelques documents économiques en pehlevi. In *Sources pour l'histoire et la géographie du monde iranien (224–710)*, ed. R. Gyselen, 115–42. Bures-sur-Yvette: RO 18.

———. 2010. La collection de textes attribuables à Dādēn-vindād dans l'Archive pehlevie de Berkeley. In *Sources for the history of Sasanian and post-Sasanian Iran*, ed. R. Gyselen, 11–134. Bures-sur-Yvette: RO 19.

Grenet, F. 1988. Les sassanides a Doura-Europos (253 ap. J.-C.): Réexamen du matériel épigraphique iranien du site. In *Géographie historique au Proche-Orient (Syrie, Phénicie, Arabie, grecques, romaines, byzantines)*, ed. P.-L. Gatier, B. Helly and J.-P. Rey-Coquais, 133–58. Paris: CNRS.

Gropp, G. 1968. Die parthische Inschrift von Sar-Pol-e Ẓohāb. *ZDMG* 118: 315–19.

Gubaev, A. G., S. D. Loginov, and A. B. Nikitin. 1996. Sasanian bullae from the excavations of Ak-Depe by the Station of Artyk. *Iran* 34: 55–9.

Gyselen, R. 1989. *La géographie administrative de l'empire sassanide: Les témoignages sigillographiques*. Paris: RO 1.

———. 2001. *The four generals of the Sasanian Empire: Some sigillographic evidence*. Rome: IsIAO.

———. 2002. *Nouveaux matériaux pour la géographie historique de l'empire Sassanide: Sceaux administratifs de la collection Ahmad Saeedi*. Paris: Cahiers de *StIr* 24.

———. 2007. *Sasanian seals and sealings in the A. Saeedi Collection*. Leuven: Acta Iranica 44.

Gzella, H. 2008. Aramaic in the Parthian period: The Arsacid inscriptions. In *Aramaic in its historical and linguistic setting*, ed. H. Gzella and M. L. Folmer, 107–30. Wiesbaden: Harrassowitz.

Harmatta, J. 1958. Die parthischen Ostraka aus Dura-Europos. *AAASH* 6: 87–175.

———. 1974. Remarques sur les inscriptions des vaisselles sassanides. In *Mémorial Jean de Menasce*, ed. P. Gignoux and A. Tafazzoli, 189–98. Leuven: Imprimerie Orientaliste.

Harper, P. O., P. O. Skjærvø, L. Gorelick, and A. J. Gwinnett. 1993. A seal-amulet of the Sasanian era: Imagery and typology, the inscription and technical comments. *BAI* 6: 43–58.

Haruta, S. 2006. Elymaean and Parthian inscriptions from Khūzestān: A survey. In *Proceedings of the 5th Conference of the Societas Iranologica Europaea held in Ravenna, 6–11 October 2003*, vol. 1, *Ancient & Middle Iranian Studies*, ed. A. Panaino and A. Piras, 471–8. Milan: Mimesis.

Healey, J. H., and H. Bin Seray. 1999–2000. Aramaic in the Gulf: Towards a corpus. *ARAM* 11–12: 1–14.

Henning, W. B. 1952. The monuments and inscriptions of Tang-i Sarvak. *Asia Major* 2: 151–78.

———. 1958. Mitteliranisch. In *Iranistik 1: Linguistik*, ed. B. Spuler, 20–130. Leiden: HdO 1/4/1.

Hillers, D. R., and E. Cussini. 1996. *Palmyrene Aramaic texts*. Baltimore: John Hopkins University Press.

Humbach, H. 1974. Aramaeo-Iranian and Pahlavi. In *Hommage Universelle I*, 237–43. Leiden: Acta Iranica 2.

———. 1989. Die pahlavi-chinesische Bilingue von Xi'an. In *A green leaf: Papers in honour of Professor Jes P. Asmussen*, ed. J. Duchesne-Guillemin, W. Sundermann, and F. Vahman, 73–82. Leiden: Acta Iranica 28.

Humbach, H., and P. O. Skjærvø. 1978–83. *The Sassanian inscriptions of Paikuli*, 3 vols. Wiesbaden: L. Reichert.

Hunter, E. C. 2004. Nippur and Aramaic incantation texts. In *Verbum et calamus: Semitic and related studies in honour of the sixtieth birthday of Professor Tapani Harviainen*, ed. H. Juusola, J. Laulainen, and H. Palva, 69–82. Helsinki: StOr 99.

Huyse, P. 1999. *Die dreisprachige Inschrift Šābuhrs I. an der Ka'ba-i Zardušt (ŠKZ)*, 2 vols. London: CII 3/1/1.

———. 2009. Inscriptional literature in Old and Middle Iranian languages. *LPII*: 72–115.
Khachatrian, Z. 1996. The archives of sealings found at Artashat (Artaxata). In *Archives et sceaux du monde hellénistique*, ed. M.-F. Boussac and A. Invernizzi, 365–70. Paris: *Bulletin de Correspondance Hellénique* Supplement 29.
Kutscher, E. Y. 1970. Aramaic. In *Current trends in linguistics VI. Linguistics in South West Asia and North Africa*, ed. T. A. Sebeok, 347–412. The Hague: Mouton.
Lemaire, A. 2003. Les pierres et inscriptions araméennes d'Arebsun, nouvel examen. In *Irano-Judaica V*, ed. S. Shaked and A. Netzer, 137–64. Jerusalem: Ben-Zvi Institute.
Lipiński, E. 1975. *Studies in Aramaic inscriptions and onomastics*. Leuven: OLA 1.
Livshits, V. A. 1977. New Parthian documents from South Turkmenistan. *AAASH* 25: 157–85.
———. 1984. Novye parfyanskie nadpisi iz Turkmenii i Iraka. *Épigrafika Vostoka* 22: 18–40.
———. 2002. Parthian joking. *Manuscripta Orientalia* 8: 27–35.
———. 2003. Three silver bowls from the Isakovka Burial-Ground No. 1 with Khwarezmian and Parthian inscriptions. *ACSS* 9/1–2: 147–72.
Livshits, V. A., V. G. Lukonin, and P. Gignoux. 1987. Nadpisi. In *Sasanidskoe serebro*, ed. K. V. Trever and V. G. Lukonin, 121. Moscow: Iskusstvo.
Livshits, V. A., and A. B. Nikitin. 1991. The Parthian epigraphic remains from Göbekli-depe and some other Parthian inscriptions. In *Corolla Iranica: Papers in honour of Prof. Dr. David Neil MacKenzie on the occasion of his 65th Birthday on April 8th, 1991*, ed. R. E. Emmerick and D. Weber, 109–26. Frankfurt: Peter Lang.
MacKenzie, D. N. 1971. *A concise Pahlavi dictionary*. London: Oxford University Press.
———. 1989. Kerdir's inscriptions: Synoptic text in transliteration, transcription and commentary. In *The Sasanian rock reliefs at Naqsh-i Rustam. Naqsh-i Rustam 6: The triumph of Shapur I (together with an account of the representations of Kerdir)*, ed. G. Herrmann and D. N. MacKenzie, 35–72. Berlin: Iranische Denkmäler 13.
———. 1994. The fire altar of happy *Frayosh. *BAI* 7: 105–9.
Macuch, M. 2009. Pahlavi Literature. *LPII*: 116–96.
Montgomery, J. A. 1913. *Aramaic incantation texts from Nippur*. Philadelphia: University Museum.
Morano, E. 1990. Contributi all'interpretazione della bilingue greco-partica, dell'Eracle di Seleucia. In *Proceedings of the First European Conference of Iranian Studies held in Turin, September 7th–11th, 1987 by the Societas Iranologica Europaea*, vol. 1, ed. G. Gnoli and A. Panaino, 229–38. Rome: IsMEO.
———. 2008. Iscrizioni partice da Nisa Vecchia su ostraka e intonaco. In *Nisa Partica: Ricerche nel complesso monumentale arsacide 1990–2006*, ed. A. Invernizzi and C. Lippolis, 344–50. Florence: Le Lettere.
Muraoka, T. 2011. *A grammar of Qumran Aramaic*. Leuven: ANES Supplement 38.
Muraoka, T., and B. Porten. 1998. *A grammar of Egyptian Aramaic*. Leiden: HdO 1/32.
Müller-Kessler, C. 1999. Interrelations between Mandaic lead rolls and incantaion bowls. In *Mesopotamian magic: Textual, historical, and interpretative perspectives*, ed. T. Abusch and K. van der Toorn, 197–209. Groningen: Styx.
Naveh, J., and S. Shaked. 1973. Ritual texts or treasury documents? *Or* 42: 445–57.
———. 1985. *Amulets and magic bowls*. Jerusalem: Magnes Press.
———. 2012. *Ancient Aramaic documents from Bactria (fourth century B.C.E.)*. London: CII 1/5/2.
Nikitin, A. B. 1993–94. Parthian bullae from Nisa. *SRAA* 3: 71–9.
Oelsner, J. 1986. *Materialien zur babylonischen Gesellschaft und Kultur in hellenistischer Zeit*. Budapest: Eötvös Loránd Tudományegyetem.

Périkhanian, A. 1971. Les inscriptions araméennes du roi Artachès. *Revue des études arméniennes* 8: 169–74.
Porten, B., and A. Yardeni. 1986–99. *Textbook of Aramaic documents from Ancient Egypt*, 4 vols. Jerusalem: Hebrew University.
Röllig, W. 2002. Appendix II. Aramaic inscriptions. In *The Daskyleion bullae: Seal images from the western Achaemenid Empire*, ed. D. Kaptan, 198–210. Leiden: AchHist 13.
Schindel, N. 2004. *Sylloge Nummorum Sasanidarum, Paris—Berlin—Wien*, vol. 3/1–2, *Shapur II—Kavad I/2 Regierung*. Vienna: Verlag der Österreichischen Akademie der Wissenschaften.
Schuol, M. 2000. *Die Charakene: Ein mesopotamisches Königreich in hellenistisch-parthischer Zeit*. Stuttgart: Oriens et Occidens 1.
Segal, J. B. 2000. *Aramaic and Mandaic incantation bowls in the British Museum*. London: British Museum Press.
Shaked, S. 1992. Spurious epigraphy. *BAI* 4: 267–88.
———. 1994a. Notes on the Pahlavi amulet and Sasanian courts of law. *BAI* 7: 165–72.
———. 1994b. Two Parthian ostraca from Nippur. *BSOAS* 57: 208–12.
———. 2003. Between Iranian and Aramaic: Iranian words concerning food in Jewish Babylonian Aramaic, with some notes on the Aramaic heterograms in Iranian. In *Irano-Judaica V*, ed. S. Shaked and A. Netzer, 120–37. Jerusalem: Ben-Zvi Institute.
———. 2004. *Le satrape de Bactriane et son gouverneur: Documents araméens du IVe s. avant notre ère provenant de Bactriane*. Paris: Persika 4.
Sims-Williams, N. 1989–92. *Sogdian and other Iranian inscriptions of the Upper Indus*, 2 vols. London: CII 2/3/2.
Sims-Williams, U. 2003. Forgeries from Chinese Turkestan in the British Library's Hoernle and Stein Collection. *BAI* 14: 111–29.
Skjærvø, P. O. 1992. A copy of the Hajiabad inscription in the Babylonian Collection, Yale. *BAI* 4: 289–93.
———. 1992. L'inscription d'Abnūn et l'imparfait en moyen-perse. *StIr* 21: 153–60.
———. 1995. Aramaic in Iran. *ARAM* 7: 283–318.
———. 1996. Aramaic scripts for Iranian languages. In *The world's writing systems*, ed. P. T. Daniels and W. Bright, 515–35. Oxford: Oxford University Press.
———. 2000. The joy of the cup: A pre-Sasanian Middle Persian inscription on a silver bowl. *BAI* 11: 93–104.
———. 2009. Middle West Iranian. In *The Iranian languages*, ed. G. Windfuhr, 196–278. London: Routledge.
Skjærvø, P. O., and P. O. Harper. 1994. The earliest datable inscription on a Sasanian bowl: Two silver bowls in the J. Paul Getty Museum. *BAI* 7: 181–92.
Sundermann, W. 2009. Manichaean literature in Iranian languages. *LPII*: 197–265.
Tafazzoli, A. 1997. *Tarix-e adabiyāt-e Irān piš az Islām*. Tehran: Čāpxāne-ye Mahārat.
Tavernier, J. 2007. *Iranica in the Achaemenid period (ca. 550–330 B.C.): Lexicon of Old Iranian proper names and loanwords, attested in non-Iranian texts*. Leuven: OLA 158.
Tōno, H. 1987. Hōryūji Kennō Hōmotsu: Kōboku no meibun to kodai no kōryō bōeki (Inscriptions on the sandalwoods in the Horyuji Treasures and ancient incense trade: With special reference to Pahlavi inscription and Sogdian brand, with Appendices by H. Kumamoto and Y. Yoshida). *Museum [Bimonthly Magazine of the Tokyo National Museum]* 433: 4–18 (in Japanese).

Tsereteli, K. 1998. Les inscriptions araméennnes de Géorgie. *Semitica* 48: 75–88.
Weber, D. 1992. *Ostraca, papyri und pergamente: Textband*. London: CII 3/4/5/1.
——. 2003. *Berliner Papyri, Pergamente und Leinenfragmente in Mittelpersischer Sprache*. London: CII 3/4/5/2.
——. 2008. *Berliner Pahlavi-Dokumente: Zeugnisse spätsassanidischer Brief- und Rechtskultur aus frühislamischer Zeit*. Wiesbaden: Iranica 15.
——. 2010a. Parthische Texte. *QGP* 2: 492–588.
——. 2010b. Iranica auf arsakidischen Münzen. *QGP* 2: 633–9.
Weber, U., and J. Wiesehöfer, J. 1996. *Das Reich der Achaimeniden: Eine Bibliographie*. Berlin: AMI Ergänzungsband 15.
Wiesehöfer, J. 1994. *Die "dunklen Jahrhunderte" der Persis*. Munich: Zetemata 90.
Zehnder, M. 2010. Aramäische Texte. *QGP* 3: 175–401.

CHAPTER 41

THE USE OF GREEK IN PRE-SASANIAN IRAN

GEORGES ROUGEMONT

Greek domination over Iran lasted less than two centuries. Iran was never Hellenized as were Anatolia or even the Near East. However, the Greek language was used before Alexander, in the Achaemenid Empire, and remained in use after the Seleucids, under the Arsacid Empire; a handful of Greek documents are even dated to the beginning of the Sasanid period. Previously, the use of Greek in Iran has been dealt with by P. Huyse (Huyse 1995, 1996) and R. Schmitt (Schmitt 1990). Since these studies were published, progress has been made in the establishment and interpretation of some texts (*IGIAC*), but the overall conclusions have not changed radically.

AVAILABLE SOURCES

Ancient writers—at least those whose works have reached us—say very little about Iran. Therefore, in order to study the use of the Greek language in Iran, we must rely mainly on Greek documents found in Iranian territory. These comprise about eighty inscriptions on stone, pottery, or metal objects (I exclude here texts on objects that are by definition mobile, such as coins and stamped amphora handles). This is of course a provisional number and one will never find as many Greek inscriptions in Iran as in Anatolia, but there will be more finds; those already discovered provide us with a sample that is certainly not representative. Although fifty of the eighty documents were found at Susa (*IGIAC* 1–50bis), this does not mean that the Greek community there was much more important than others, rather that Susa is the only site where systematic excavations have explored not only the Hellenistic and Parthian levels, but also, it seems, the very place where the Greek community displayed its written documents (*IGIAC* 7, n. 107). Particularly in Persis and Media future discoveries may increase markedly the number of texts (at present: fifteen in Persis [*IGIAC* 51–65]; ten in Media [*IGIAC* 66–75]); important documents might also appear in regions that are presently almost devoid of texts (*IGIAC* 80bis).

THE ACHAEMENID PERIOD

It is well known that already in Achaemenid times there were Greeks in Iran—at the king's court (Briant 1996: 276–7), among his mercenaries (whose role was certainly exaggerated by Greek authors, cf. Briant 1996: 803–810, 1062–5), and at building sites. We also know that Greek communities were deported to Persia (Briant 1996: 447, 980–81; Knoepfler 2004). But these Greeks are attested mainly in literary sources (Hofstetter 1978). Inscriptions documenting their presence are relatively scarce. There is an isolated account document from Persepolis (*IGIAC* 54), found among the Fortification tablets (see Chapter 27), as well as a few graffiti in a quarry. Susa has yielded an epitaph (*IGIAC* 2), the style of which might indicate that it was made prior to Alexander's conquest. In fact, prior to the fourth century, inscriptions are rare everywhere in the Greek world, except in Athens. The heavy bronze astragalus unearthed in Susa, with an archaic dedication to Apollo (*IGIAC* 1), is in fact a piece of loot brought from Ionia at the beginning of the fifth century, whether from Didyma or another sanctuary.

THE SELEUCID PERIOD

From the conquest of Alexander (331–325 BC) to the second quarter of the second century BC, when the Seleucids lost control over Iran (see Chapters 34, 36), Greek was the language of the dominant political power. It was the language of the monarch and his high officials, of the Greek settlers gathered in cities (*poleis*) founded or protected by the kings, and of the culture shared by the kings and settlers.

The Greek inscriptions from Iran include no fewer than four Seleucid royal letters (*IGIAC* 51, 52, 66 = 68, 80bis): two from Antiochus III (one of those in two copies); one from his eldest son, the crown prince Antiochus; and one from a "King Seleucus" who is probably Seleucus II. Inscribed and displayed in different provinces, ranging from Media (*IGIAC* 66–8) to Drangiana (*IGIAC* 80bis?), these letters are sometimes preserved along with the "cover letter" of the governor to whom they were sent and who in turn passed it on to his subordinates (*IGIAC* 66–8). The curious document *IGIAC* 76 might have been produced also by a royal administrator. At Susa, honorific inscriptions (*IGIAC* 6–9, 28[?], 67, 70) document high officials of the kingdom, governors of provinces, high-ranking officers, "high priests" (*archiereus*), and people bearing aulic titles. From the early Hellenistic period, Greek milestones found near Persepolis (*IGIAC* 64) and at Pasargadae (*IGIAC* 65, a document which might be a Greek–Aramaic bilingual) reflect efforts made to mark out and signpost roads (at least some of them). These might have resulted from the work of the *bematistai*, whom Alexander charged with measuring road distances throughout the empire. At Persepolis, five small marble slabs from one or more altars (*IGIAC* 59–63), engraved carefully and obviously at the same time and dating to the early Hellenistic period (see Chapters 34–36), attest to the existence of a joint cult to five Greek divinities (the evidence has also been interpreted, without sufficient proof, as an *interpretatio graeca* of Iranian divinities). The question is whether the introduction of these cults at Persepolis happened at the behest of the central Greco-Macedonian power or one of its officials.

The lives of Greek settlers in Iran and of their cities are not very well known. Laodikeia (Laodicea) in Media (Nehavand), where many archaeological discoveries dating to the Hellenistic period have been made, is securely identified thanks to the heading of the royal letter *IGIAC* 66, which was found there. However, this letter provides us with no other information on the city. It is only possible to note that the writing on the stele, which is elegant and even a bit affected, does not suffer from comparison with the most carefully executed epigraphic documents from the ancient Greek world. We know only the patronym of the citizen from Laodikeia who honored the governor of the province (*IGIAC* 67). At a site near Kermanshah, the epitaph of an individual called Eumenes (*IGIAC* 69) proves that there was a Greek community there (with at least one letter-cutter and Greek-speaking readers able to understand the inscription, which is partly metrical), but we know neither the status of this community nor its name. We can say nothing of the Greek Hyakinthos, son of Pantauchos, whose patronym is typically Macedonian and who, in the mid-second century, dedicated at Bisotun, in the sanctuary of an Iranian divinity, a carved representation of Herakles banqueting "for the preservation (*soteria*)" of a governor (*IGIAC* 70). In Karafto Cave, on the border between Media and Media *Atropatene*, one wonders who the inhabitants of the cave rooms were whose entrance was guarded against evil by a Greek apotropaic formula, written in letters characteristic of the early Hellenistic period (*IGIAC* 75), a formula also attested in the same form at Thasos, Mylasa, Side, and even Pompeii.

Only two Greek cities are slightly better known in Seleucid Iran: Antioch-in-Persis (*IGIAC* 51–3), founded or refounded by Antiochus I on a site that is unlocated (Reshahr near Bushehr being only a likely guess), and Seleucia-on-the-Eulaeus, founded on the site of Susa at an uncertain date, sometime prior to 205 BC (*IGIAC* 11–12, n. 153). On Antioch-in-Persis we have only one source, but it yields a considerable amount of information: the long decree (*IGIAC* 53), found at Magnesia in Ionia (modern western Turkey), voted by Antioch in 205 in order to recognize officially the panhellenic character of a competition created by the city of Magnesia-on-the-Meander in Ionia, a city which, at the request of Antiochus I, had sent settlers to Antioch-in-Persis a few decades earlier. This decree provides a great number of details concerning the history and life of Antioch-in-Persis. Subject to the authority of the Seleucids, like many Anatolian and Aegean Greek cities, the city was organized and functioned just like any city in the ancient Greek world. The fact that an Ionian city officially appealed to Antioch—as well as to many other Greek cities in Susiana, Persis, and Mesopotamia, including

Seleucia-on-the-Eulaeus (*IGIAC* 53, ll. 101ff.)—proves that the Greek settlers in Iran were considered full members of the Greek world. As to Seleucia-on-the-Eulaeus, we get a glimpse of life in this city thanks to a small group of inscriptions (*IGIAC* 4–10, 13–27) discovered there and dated, for the most part, to the first half of the second century: dedications to the gods (sometimes metric), honorific inscriptions, and, most of all, manumission inscriptions. The procedure of manumission (via consecration of the slave to a divinity who hence became the guarantor of his freedom) is a purely Greek one and is abundantly documented in Aegean Greece. At Susa, the only non-Greek elements in these manumission documents is the divinity to whom the slave was consecrated—in this case Nanaya (*IGIAC* 15, 17, 18, 20, 23)—and one of the slaveholders who, to judge by her name, was Babylonian (*IGIAC* 18).

In general, in those Greek documents from the Seleucid period, non-Greek personal names are rare, and signs of bilingualism, of contacts between Greeks and non-Greeks, of cultural intermingling, are even rarer. Yet we do not know if this is a fair reflection of reality. Greek documents discovered in Iran indicate the cultural identity displayed by the Greek settlers there, but nothing else; this identity was Greek, flawlessly Greek. In Iran, more than in any other region, the Greek culture displayed was a literary culture, relying in particular, as expected, on an acquaintance with poets, the practice of poetry, and the knowledge of mythology. On the eighty Greek inscriptions from Iran known to date, we have no fewer than five poems: a dedication (*IGIAC* 5), honorific inscriptions (*IGIAC* 11–12), epitaphs (*IGIAC* 32 [?], 69), and hymns to the gods (*IGIAC* 32 [?], 33). Among the personal names attested—besides a significant number of Macedonian names, which is not surprising—an important group of rare names were borrowed from legendary figures: Asios (*IGIAC* 3), Clio (*IGIAC* 5), Arètè, the name of Alkinoos' wife (*IGIAC* 7), Dryas (*IGIAC* 30), Thoas (*IGIAC* 68), Hyakinthos (*IGIAC* 70). In Iran perhaps more than anywhere else, the Greeks, who were numerically few, isolated, and far from their country of origin, might have felt the need to display the characteristic (or supposedly characteristic) features of the Hellenism. This trend was as strong in the Arsacid period as it was during the Seleucid period, making it difficult, for example, to date a dedication from Susa (*IGIAC* 5) in which Chaireas, father of a child named Clio, prides himself, in elegiac distichs, not only for having made with his own hands the statue standing over the inscription, but also for having himself written the poem in which he dedicated the statue to Apollo.

The Arsacid Period

At the time when the Seleucids, in the third quarter of the second century, lost control of Iran to the Arsacids, the few extant Greek documents, all of which come from Media and Susiana, give an impression of continuity rather than discontinuity.

At Susa, where local, poorly known rulers minted coins (Le Rider 1965: 379–80; Will 1982: 410), manumission acts still dated according to the Seleucid era from 142/1 BC

(*IGIAC* 15) and 131 BC (*IGIAC* 16) are identical in both formula and procedure to acts dated to 183/2 and 177/6 (*IGIAC* 13 and 14), when the city was still under Seleucid control. The only change, in the text from 131 BC, is the use of a double dating system, according to both the Seleucid and Arsacid eras (although in this case the Arsacid ruler's name is not preserved). Only in the late second and early first century did Greek documents become rare at Susa and more difficult to date. We do not know why this happened. Around 30 BC the city was renamed and probably refounded under an Arsacid dynastic name, Phraata, a name attested both in coin legends, which remained Greek, and inscriptions. At the very beginning of the Christian era, two well-dated sets of inscriptions illustrate clearly that Phraata was still a Greek city, like Seleucia-on-the-Eulaeus. In 9/8 BC, or most probably (the reading is uncertain) in 1/2 AD, two Greek poems (*IGIAC* 11–12) celebrate one and the same governor of Susa (or Susiana), appointed by the Arsacid king. This governor had ordered hydraulic works that benefited the local agriculture. One of the poems expresses the gratitude of the citizens of Phraata, the other, the gratitude of the soldiers of the garrison, who benefited from plots of land in the countryside. On the other hand, an official letter (*IGIAC* 3) sent by the Parthian king Artabanus II, precisely dated to the year 21 BC, exposes the following facts. The city of Phraata had broken its own laws by appointing an individual named Hestiaios as treasurer of the city twice within a period of three years. The second appointment was probably questioned; in any case, the matter was laid before the king, who confirmed the city's decision and prohibited any future legal action against Hestiaios. In the first set of documents, two successive governors of Susa (or Susiana) were called Tiridates and Zamaspes, respectively, both of which are Iranian names; but in the second set of documents, the right-hand man of Artabanus II at Susa (the governor? the *epistates*?) was one Antiochus, and about the same time, Tacitus mentions two governors of provinces, respectively named Hieron and Phraates. The royal letter was dated according to the Arsacid era, but the city recorded it with both Arsacid and Seleucid dates. For internal matters, the city obviously continued to use the Seleucid era. All of these documents were written in flawless Greek, a perfect example of the Hellenistic *koine*. In the appointment of the magistrates, as well as in its civic values, the city of Phraata looked exactly like an Anatolian or Aegean city: it was effectively a Greek city with an Arsacid dynastic name, just as Seleucia-on-the-Eulaeus was a Greek city with a Seleucid dynastic name.

In Media, Greek documents from Parthian times, at least as known at present, were not produced in Greek cities and are therefore all the more significant. At the beginning of the first century AD a rock relief commemorating Gotarzes, "satrap of the satraps", was carved at the foot of the Bisotun Mountain (see Chapter 38). Gotarzes was represented at the head of several of his colleagues, before the "great king Mithridates" (Mithridates II). The relief belongs to a purely Iranian tradition, but the inscription identifying the king and the satraps is in Greek (*IGIAC* 71). Yet it is clearly an "official" inscription, displayed on one of the busiest roads in the Middle East. A very different discovery was made a century ago, about 150 km from Bisotun, but still in Media, in the mountains of modern Kurdistan, near the border between Iran and Iraq. A single jar, which was found sealed, contained at least three private documents written in ink on parchment. Two sale documents (*IGIAC* 73 and 74), dated to 88/7 and 22/1 BC, deal with plots of land where grapevines were cultivated. The contracting parties, the witnesses, and the place names are all Iranian, but both contracts are written in Greek. The third document written in Parthian (see Chapter 40) dates to 52/3 AD.

Thus, judging by the documents currently available—and let us recall that they are still very rare, and that they almost all (seventy-six of eighty) come from Media, Susiana, and Persis—the use of Greek, the language of the dominant power and the Greek colonists during the Seleucid period, did not wane under the first Arsacid rulers. It was only in the middle of the first century AD that Greek texts disappeared almost completely.

The Sasanian period

Near Persepolis, however, monuments of the third century AD, erected by the first Sasanian kings, used Greek (*IEO*: nos. 257–60) to identify the kings and a divinity. More importantly, the great trilingual inscription of Naqsh-e Rustam, known to all historians of the Greco-Roman world by the name of *Res gestae divi Saporis*, was translated and engraved also in Greek, in seventy long lines (Huyse 1999). This, however, lies outside the scope of the present chapter.

Further reading

New editions of all of the original Greek inscriptions discussed here from sites in Iran can be found in *IGIAC*. For the broader political context see, in addition to Chapters 34 and 36 in this volume, Le Rider (1965), and Will (1982). Other important studies of the use of Greek in ancient Iran include Huyse (1995, 1996).

References

Briant, P. 1996. *Histoire de l'Empire perse*. Paris: Fayard.
Hofstetter, J. 1978. *Die Griechen in Persien: Prosopographie der Griechen im persischen Reich vor Alexander*. Berlin: *AMI* Ergänzungsband 5.
Huyse, P. 1995. Die Begegnung zwischen Hellenen und Iraniern: Griechische epigraphische Zeugnisse von Griechenland bis Pakistan. In *Iran und Turan. Beiträge Berliner Wissenschaftler, Werner Sundermann zum 60. Geburtstag gewidmet*, ed. C. Reck and P. Zieme, 99–126. Wiesbaden: Harrassowitz.
———. 1996. Die Rolle des Griechischen im "hellenistischen" Iran. In *Hellenismus: Beiträge zur Erforschung von Akkulturation und politischer Ordnung in den Staaten des hellenistischen Zeitalters*, ed. B. Funck, 57–76. Tübingen: J.C. Mohr Siebeck.

———. 1999. *Die dreisprachige Inschrift Šābuhrs I. an der Ka'ba-i Zardušt (ŠKZ)*, 2 vols. London: CII 3/1/1.

Knoepfler, D. 2004. Les Érétriens d'Arderrika. In *Érétrie. Guide de la cité antique*, ed. P. Ducrey, S. Fachard, D. Knoepfler and T. Theurillat, 32. Gollion: Infolio Editions.

Le Rider, G. 1965. *Suse sous les Séleucides et les Parthes. Les trouvailles monétaires et l'histoire de la ville*. Paris: MMAI 38.

Schmitt, R. 1990. *EX OCCIDENTE LUX*. Griechen und griechische Sprache im hellenistischen Fernen Osten. In *Beiträge zur hellenistischen Literatur und ihrer Rezeption in Rom*, ed. P. Steinmetz, 41–58. Stuttgart: Palingenesia 28.

Will, É. 1982. *Histoire politique du monde hellénistique*, 2nd ed., vol. 2. Nancy: Annales de l'Est, Mémoir 32.

PART VII

THE SASANIAN PERIOD

CHAPTER 42

SASANIAN POLITICAL IDEOLOGY

M. RAHIM SHAYEGAN

INTRODUCTION

Sasanian political ideology underwent numerous changes during the four centuries in which the house of Sasan ruled in the East. The numismatic evidence exhibits four radical departures in the royal titulature, which may be indicative of vicissitudes within ideological and political conceptions of kingship (Shayegan 2003).

From the establishment of the empire by Ardašīr I up to the reign of Yazdgerd II (224–439), the title of the Sasanian sovereigns, despite minor alterations, remained *mazdēsn bay* [name of the sovereign] *šāhān šāh Ērān (ud An-ērān) kē čihr az yazdān*, "His Mazdayasnian Majesty [*name of the sovereign*] king of kings of Iran(ians) (and non-Iran[ians]) whose seed is from the gods." The title "king of kings of Iran," which was established by Ardašīr, augmented by the important element *ud An-ērān* "and non-Iran(ians)," under Šābuhr I, with ephemeral omission of the selfsame under Narseh (Huyse 2006: 183–4), thus represented *mutatis mutandis* the core of the Sasanian titulature during this period.

Under Yazdgerd II and up to and including Kawād I, the titulature changed considerably. The main constant of the titulary, *šāhān šāh Ērān*, disappeared entirely and was replaced by the title *kay*, which referred to a mythical and heroic sovereign (Huyse 2006: 186; Daryaee 2006a: 500–501). The titulature—except under Walāxš and Jāmasp—included the title *kay* after the king's name: *mazdēsn bay (rāmšahr) kay* [name of the sovereign], and later only [name of the sovereign] *kay*.

It was during the reign of Kawād I that the next change in the titulature took place. Under Xosrow I, the king was called neither *šāhān šāh* nor *kay*. Only the king's name occurred and, beginning with his sixth year, it was followed by the term *abzōn* "increase": [name of the sovereign] *abzōn*.

The next change in Sasanian titulature occurred under Xosrow II, when the name of the sovereign was followed by the expression *xwarrah abzūd*: [name of the sovereign] *xwarrah abzūd* "increased is the (royal/epic) glory of/by [name of the sovereign]." However, Xosrow II also occasionally used the term *abzōn*, as well as, for the first time after the early period, the element *šāhān šāh* (*Xosrow šāhān šāh xwarrah abzūd*), which was undoubtedly a consequence of his Byzantine policy, and may have been a conscious reference to the political program of his victorious predecessors, notably, Šābuhr II.

Royal ideologies throughout the ages

The age of political realism

The political ideology of the Sasanian Empire in the first period under review was strongly impacted by the consuming wars against Rome. This period may further be divided into two distinct subperiods: the aggressive campaigns led by Ardašīr and Šābuhr I, which despite spectacular but ephemeral successes did not lead to any substantial transformation of the Sasanian and Roman conflict (Mosig-Walburg 2009: 19–89); and the dogged wars conducted by Šābuhr II over several decades, during the reigns of Constantine, Constantius II, Julian, and Jovian (Mosig-Walburg 2009: 193–266; 283–324; Frendo 2012). Although opinions differ as to the rationale behind the offensives of Ardašīr and Šābuhr I, it seems unlikely that they were motivated by the desire to revive Achaemenid traditions, and Roman accounts to that effect ought to be viewed with skepticism (Shayegan 2011: 1–38; 2008). Indeed, this interpretation may have been caused by the effects of a contemporaneous Alexander imitation in Rome, which, by equating Rome with Macedon, could have resuscitated Alexander's former adversaries, the Achaemenids, and portrayed the Sasanians as their heirs. However, beginning at the latest with Šābuhr I, the neo-Persian empire seems to have made known its universalist claim to (co)regency, if we are to interpret the addition of the element *ud An-ērān* "and non-Iran(ians)" in the royal title as the manifestation of such an all-encompassing projection of might. Indeed, it can probably be assumed that the concept of *Ērān ud An-ērān* was meant to be understood as an ideological riposte to Rome's view of the Roman Empire as an *imperium sine fines* (Börm 2008: 426–7). The impetus for Šābuhr II's large-scale Roman campaigns in the second half of the fourth century, however, undoubtedly lies in the inherent inequity of the peace treaty of Nisibis, concluded in 298 between the Sasanian king Narseh and Diocletian's Caesar in the East, Galerius. Following the battle of Satala in Armenia, consequent upon which the fate of the entire imperial train (his wife and children) hung in the balance, Narseh acquiesced to the unfavorable terms of the treaty. These were not destined to generate lasting peace with Persia but instead prepared the ground for future hostilities (Blockley 1984: 28–34; 1992: 5–7; Mosig-Walburg 2009: 91–155). Accordingly, once his rule had been consolidated,

Šābuhr II's aim was to reclaim (and eventually obtain) the territories stripped from his grandfather Narseh in the wake of the treaty of Nisibis, which had resulted in Armenia becoming a Roman vassal state and Mesopotamia being lost to the Sasanians, as the transtigritane territories were yielded to Rome in Upper Mesopotamia and the Tigris was established as the frontier between the two states in Lower Mesopotamia.

The heroic (Kayānid) age

The reign of Yazdgerd II represented an age in which the political perspective of the Sasanian Empire, previously inclined toward the West, completed its shift toward the East. This shift, which had already begun under Yazdgerd I and Warahrān V and reached its climax under Yazdgerd II and his successor Pērōz, may have been caused by the arrival of belligerent Hunnic tribes on the empire's eastern borders. The mobilization of the empire's resources in the East may have given rise to a more accelerated and sustained reception of eastern mytho-epic (oral) traditions. What is more, the warfare against the Hunnic tribes may have evoked the mythical antagonism prevailing between the Iranian Kayanian (Av. *kauuaiia-*) rulers and their Turanian (Av. *tūiriia-*) foes, exemplified in the Younger *Avesta*. This antagonism between Iran and its eastern foe must have prompted the adoption of the title *kay*, descendent of the title (Av. *kauui-*) borne in the *Avesta* by the mythical kings of the Iranians in their fight against the eastern Turanians. Similarly, the fully developed myth of the Iranian hero-king Frēdōn/Fereydūn dividing the world among his three sons as known to us through recensions transmitted in the Pahlavi literature and the *Šāhnāme*—according to which Frēdōn's/Fereydūn's eldest son Sarm/Salm was allotted the empire of the West, Hrōm/Rūm; the *puîné* Tōz/Tūr was given the empire of the East, Tūrān/Turkestān; and the youngest Ēriz/Ēraǰ received the heartland of the empire, Ērānšahr—ought as well to be dated to this period, when the concerted collection of legendary and epic material under the late Sasanians took place (Huyse 2009: 151–2; Wiesehöfer 2005a: 139, n. 240, and 145, n. 254). Consequently, influenced by Kayānid reception, the Sasanians under Yazdgerd II, possibly considering themselves heirs to Frēdōn (and Ēriz/Ēraǰ), could have regarded not only Roman possessions in the West but also Turanian lands disputed by the Hephthalites in the East, as belonging to Frēdōn's empire, and may have sought, through the adoption of the Kayānid title *kay*, symbolically to lay claim to them (Daryaee 2006b: 389–93; Wiesehöfer 2005a: 144–5; 2005b: 114–16).

The significance of introducing the title *kay* may also be measured in religious matters. The radical departure in Sasanian religious policy initiated by Yazdgerd I at the turn of the fifth century while dealing with the Christians of Iran may have prompted a reaction, to which Yazdgerd II's persecutions were testimony, and of which the title *kay* might have been a symbolic token. At least since Constantine's moral embrace of the Christians of the Sasanian Empire, this community was perceived as a political threat to the stability of the Iranian state. Indeed, before the Synod of Seleucia in 410—which was convened upon Yazdgerd I's authorization and led to the creation of the Persian Church, as well as the recognition of the doctrinal canons of the Council of Nicaea (Jullien and Jullien 2002: 189–200, 206–15, 224–5)—and the later Synod of 424, in which the independence of the Persian Church from Rome was declared, the Christians of Persia had experienced sundry state persecutions. Under Yazdgerd I the empire underwent a dramatic shift in its religious policy and sought to maintain political cohesion among its disparate religious communities by domesticizing their structures of governance and partially acculturating their constituents to the Iranian element (Bakhos and Shayegan 2010: xiv–xv). Thus, both the Jewish institution of the Exilarchate, which may well have been a Sasanian creation (Herman 2012), and the institutionalization of the Persian Church, may be seen as attempts to integrate these different religious forces into the confines of the Sasanian state, which, despite the Mazdean character of its culture and dominant ethno-class, had found no means of pacification other than the promotion of confessional coexistence (Bakhos and Shayegan 2010: xiv–xv). In fact, this strategy may be reflected in Yazdgerd I's title *rāmšahr* "(who) pacifies the empire" (Huyse 2006: 185).

Under Yazdgerd II, however, we may observe a reaction to the concept of a nascent "multiconfessional" empire, and the very sources of this legitimacy may be found in the *Avesta*-inspired, mytho-epic reception of the Iranian past. The adoption of the title *kay* simultaneously denounced both its transcendental or cosmic nature, whence Sasanian kingship perceived itself to derive (in contrast to the *realpolitical* dimension of the term *šāhān šāh*), and its indubitably Mazdean quality. The new *kay*'s attempt to reintroduce Mazdeism in Armenia and renew the persecution of Christians in Iran are testimony to the religious quality inherent in the title. Similarly, the war waged against Rome under Yazdgerd II is significant. The devastating struggle against the Hephthalites and the dire financial condition of the empire did not prevent Sasanian sovereigns from waging war against Rome in order to obtain subsidies for an even more devastating struggle against the Hephthalites. Indeed, in their endeavor to contain the Hephthalite threat, Yazdgerd II and Pērōz turned for subsidies to Rome, with whom, since the peace treaty of 384–9, they were bound by an agreement of common defense against nomadic incursions from the Caucasus. Rome's refusal to provide financial assistance triggered the brief war of 441–2 between Yazdgerd II and Theodosius II at a time when the latter was engaged in a campaign against the Vandals in the West (Blockley 1992: 56–61; Greatrex 1993; Rubin 2001: 641). The financial burden of the preparations for the war against the Hephthalites also caused the crisis of 464, as Pērōz issued a request for financial support from Rome, which included not only the annual subsidies but, additionally, a substantial advance payment with which to conduct his eastern campaign against the Hephthalites. It is likely that Sasanian propaganda perceived and represented Roman contributions toward their common defenses as tribute, just as Šābuhr I had done in his *res gestae* in the third century, when alluding to war reparations disbursed by Phillipus Arabus (*Filipōs Kaysar amāh ō *nemastīg āyad ud gyān guxan dēnār 500 hazār ō amāh dād pad bāž aweštād* "Philippus came to us in homage, paid 500,000 *dēnār* blood money, and became tributary"). Seen in this light, the Roman payments that had begun with the emergence of the Hephthalite threat in the East may have inadvertently lent credence to

Sasanian ideological designs to depict Rome as a vassal state which could thus be seen as a renegade province of *Ērānšahr* dating back to the very division of the world by the Iranian mythical hero-king Frēdōn, a claim that the adoption of the title of *kay* surely helped to uphold.

Turmoil and recovery

The next change in titulature, announced already under the reign of Kawād I, was completed under Xosrow I, when the titles *šāhān šāh* and *kay* disappeared and only the king's name, followed by the term *abzōn* "increase," became the norm. This age, which would be dominated by the reigns of Kawād I and his son Xosrow I, is intimately associated with the "Mazdakite" movement, the emergence and containment of which shaped royal ideology at the dawn of the late empire (Gnoli 2004: 439–56; Wiesehöfer 2009; Börm 2007: 230–3). This movement, which was attributed by later sources to a certain Mazdak, may have originated in royal quarters with the intention of achieving or at least paving the way for a centralized state. Indeed, contemporary sources, such as Procopius and Joshua the Stylite, make Kawād I solely responsible for enabling, or consenting to, the communal possession of women, whereas reference to the persona of Mazdak (e.g., *Mazdak ahlomōy* or *gizistag Mazdak ī Bāmdādān*) appears only in the later Middle Persian Zoroastrian writings, such as the *Bundahišn*, the *Dēnkard*, and the *Zand ī Wahman Yašt*, and in the Muslim chronicles, notably, Ṭabarī's history. These later sources may have been contaminated by Iranian oral traditions, since blaming Mazdak for the redistribution of nobiliary estates and possessions to the populace— aside from having sought communal access to women (*zan ud frazend ud xwāstag pad hamīh ud hambāyīh abāyēd dāštan framūd* "He [Mazdak] ordered that wives, children, and belongings should be held [by men] in common [*pad hamīh*] and in copartnership [*hambāyīh*]")—is a recurrent theme of Iranian oral traditions, upon which the royal epigraphic material drew. Other evil-doers, such as Gaumāta in Darius' Bisotun inscription and Wahnām son of Tadrōs in the Paikuli inscription, are often accused of comparable crimes (Shayegan 2012). Thus, there are grounds for considering Mazdak a literary fiction displaying some of the same misdeeds as the prototypical evil-doers of the oral and epigraphic traditions (Gaube 1982). What is more, the character of a fictitious Mazdak could have served as a means whereby Kawād I or Xosrow I were able to cover up the former's involvement in the movement he may have instigated, by ascribing to the fictitious character misdeeds Kawād I himself may have perpetrated against nobiliary women. By the same token, the fictitious Mazdak could also have inherited the usual crimes attributed to prototypical evil-doers in (oral) epic traditions, namely, the material dispossession of the nobility, a crime which, having served for decades as the basis of the thesis of "Mazdakite communism," may be deemed void of historical merit. The policy of forced communal access to women by the "Mazdakite" movement may have been aimed at eroding the ideological foundation of the nobility's political entitlements, namely, the "mystique of blood" (Gaube 1982). Unable to subdue the nobility on the political battlefield, the sovereignty may have been tempted to dilute its ranks by taking control over its progeny, in order to compromise the purity of noble lineages. The manipulation of Zoroastrian law may have provided the legal and religious underpinning for this collective abuse. The law provided for a man to hand over his spouse to another member of the community in a temporary marriage (*stūrīh*), as an act of religious piety, albeit the "permanent" husband (*xwadāy*) retained any children born in the transient period. Thus, the Mazdakites coerced noblemen into acquiescing in the temporary marriages of their consorts, with the result that the ensuing offspring legally belonged to the nobility but were ideologically unfit to assure the continuity of aristocratic lineages. Once the continuity of noble lineages was threatened and the nobility's political prerogatives jeopardized, Kawād I dissolved and annihilated the instrument of his policy, the Mazdakite movement, thus paving the way for his successor Xosrow I to create a new social order. Xosrow I achieved the transmutation of the nobility into a *noblesse de robe* by reestablishing the landed nobility and integrating it into an invigorated Sasanian state apparatus. Furthermore, Kawād I and Xosrow I laid the foundation for a knighthood that, loyal to the royal authority, was partially recruited from among the selfsame offspring the "Mazdakite" revolt had generated, the landed nobility had rejected, and Xosrow I had collectively adopted as his foster children (Nöldeke 1879: 164).

The last age

The *Xwarrah Abzūd* period was marked from the outset by the steady decline of Sasanian royal authority, heralded by the uprising of the commander Warahrān Čōbīn against his rightful sovereign Ōhrmazd IV. The legitimacy of the Sasanian royal house was grounded in the belief that the nimbus of kingship, the *xwarrah*, was bestowed upon the house of Ardašīr and his progeny following the latter's triumph over the Arsacids and the establishment of a new Iranian empire. The seizure of power by Warahrān Čōbīn was the first attempt by a grandee to challenge the nimbus of the Sasanian dynasty and, thus, openly to contest the inherited right of its members to rulership. Several factors contributed to friction between the crown and the nobility. Xosrow I's social and economic reforms paved the way for Xosrow II's policy of expansion, but they may have also sown the seeds of dissent between the king and his subjects. The devastation consequent upon the "Mazdakite" revolution appears to have enabled the Sasanian state to make the landed nobility subservient to greater state control, allowing it to levy regularly imposts and taxes, not only on royal demesnes, but on the totality of the empire's cultivated surface (Wiesehöfer 2010: 138, 141; Gariboldi 2006). The establishment by the crown of a potent military nobility, whose members were not only equipped, but also endowed with fiefs in return for military service, created a formidable, uniform force accountable only to the sovereign. The dramatic increase of state income, further enhanced by poll tax and Byzantine indemnities under Xosrow I, had created an economically powerful state that would have possessed the means as well as the military capacity to sustain a large-scale campaign aimed at overpowering Byzantium, when the ideological underpinning for such an enterprise was put in place under Xosrow II (Greatrex 2007: 123). These reforms, albeit salutary for the fortunes of the state, may have also led to the deterioration of the traditional bonds between the nobility and the king under Ōhrmazd IV and Xosrow II, to the extent that members of the high nobility (*wuzurg*)—such as Warahrān Čōbīn of the Mihrān family, and later Farrōxān Šahrwarāz of the Warāz family—dared to challenge the legitimacy of the Sasanian dynasty and reach for the throne. The promotion of the lower nobility (*āzād*) and the enfeoffment of the knighthood (*dēhgān*), undertaken with the intent of establishing a military class that, once economically secure, would provide a counterweight to the potency of the high nobility, did not yield the intended results. Increased affluence may have prompted the rapprochement of the military class with the high aristocracy—from among whose ranks such military leaders as Warahrān Čōbīn and Farrōxān Šahrwarāz hailed—with whom, beyond economic interests, it shared a common ethos. Thus, the military class originally created as a bulwark against the aspirations of the high nobility may have, *nolens volens*, contributed to the erosion of royal power due to its increasing affinity with the selfsame nobility. In order to prevent the accession of Warahrān Čōbīn, whose victorious campaigns had elevated him to an exalted position, whence he could defy royal legitimacy, Xosrow II was forced to overthrow his father Ōhrmazd IV, the principal object of Warahrān's enmity, and possibly to acquiesce in his assassination. However, his regicide falling short of preventing Warahrān Čōbīn from seeking the throne, Xosrow II was forced to take refuge in Byzantium, whence he set out to retake his empire with Byzantine troops in return for territorial concessions (Rubin 2001: 643–4; Whitby 1988: 250–304). The rebellion of Warahrān having already diminished the prestige of the Sasanian house, Xosrow II's act of regicide (or acquiescence thereto), as well as Byzantine intervention in Persia's internal affairs at Xosrow's instigation, followed by territorial concessions, decisively shattered the nimbus of Sasanian rule, as illustrated by a further, long-lasting, mutiny, this time initiated by Xosrow II's uncle Wistāhm. The war of conquest waged against Byzantium by Xosrow II could have aimed at increasing the Sasanian dynastic fortune, and by the same token, resuscitating the Achaemenid Empire, historical knowledge of which (through Roman intermediaries), interwoven with epic elaboration, seems to have been commonplace in Sasanian Iran since the reign of Šābuhr II. One should not underestimate the importance of Byzantium suspending the payment of subsidies to Persia toward the defense of their common borders against foreign intruders, and Justin II's negotiating with the newly emerging Turcic power to form an alliance against the Sasanian state, which led to a new chapter in Roman–Persian relations (Whitby 2001: 91–4). With the discontinuation of these subsidies, both empires adopted a confrontational attitude, which led first to Justin II's thwarted campaign against the Sasanian Empire in 572–3; eventually to the first Roman intervention in Persia's internal affairs by Maurice; and finally to the ill-advised attempt by Xosrow II to overpower Byzantium (Whitby 2001: 102–4; Howard-Johnston 2006: 93–113; Shahîd 2004). Thus, the elimination of subsidies, which up to Justin II warranted the interdependence of Rome and Persia, may have ultimately brought forth an attitude that sanctioned the opponent's downfall. By conquering, albeit ephemerally, all of Byzantium's eastern possessions, Xosrow II seems to have implemented this logic to the letter. Indeed, Xosrow II's territorial expansion, to an extent never experienced since the Achaemenids, may be regarded as the instauration of a new empire that, surpassing in glory even Ardašīr's founding act, invested the Sasanian house with new legitimacy. The legend on Xosrow II's coinage, *Xosrow xwarrah abzūd* "Xosrow whose *xwarrah* is increased/Xosrow, by whom the *xwarrah* is increased," seems to indicate the king's political agenda of Sasanian renewal subsequent to his seizure of power in Persia, inasmuch as the later reintroduction of the old Sasanian title *šāhān šāh* "king of kings," this time with possible allusions to the Persians of old, was indicative of an Achaemenid revival.

References

Bakhos, C., and M. Rahim Shayegan. 2010. *The Talmud in its Iranian context*. Tübingen: Texts and Studies in Ancient Judaism 135.

Blockley, R. C. 1984. The Romano-Persian peace treaties of A.D. 299 and 363. *Florilegium* 6: 28–49.

———. 1992. *East Roman foreign policy: Formation and conduct from Diolectian to Anastasius*. Leeds: Classical and Medieval Texts, Papers, and Monographs 30.

Börm, H. 2007. *Prokop und die Perser: Untersuchungen zu den römisch-sasanidischen Kontakten in der ausgehenden Spätantike*. Stuttgart: Oriens et Occidens 16.

———. 2008. Das Königtum der Sasaniden: Strukturen und Probleme. Bemerkungen aus althistorischer Sicht. *Klio* 90/2: 423–43.

Daryaee, T. 2006a. The construction of the past in Late Antique Persia. *Historia* 55/4: 493–503.

———. 2006b. Sasanians and their ancestors. In *Proceedings of the 5th Conference of the Societas Iranologica Europæa Held in Ravenna, 6–11 October 2003*, vol. 1, *Ancient & Middle Iranian Studies*, ed. A. Panaino and A. Piras, 387–93. Milan: Mimesis.

Frendo, D. 2012. Dangerous ideas: Julian's Persian campaign, its historical background, motivation, and objectives. *BAI* 21: 79–96.

Gariboldi, A. 2006. *Il regno di Xusraw dall'anima immortale: Riforme econimiche e rivolte sociali nell'Iran sasanide del VI secolo*. Milan: Mimesis.

Gaube, H. 1982. Mazdak: Historical reality or invention. *StIr* 11: 111–22.

Gnoli, G. 2004. Nuovi studi sul Mazdakismo. In *La Persia e Bisanzio*, ed. G. Gnoli and A. Panaino, 439–56. Roma: Accademia Nazionale dei Lincei.

Greatrex, G. 1993. Two fifth-century wars between Rome and Persia. *Florilegium* 12: 1–14.

———. 2007. Roman frontiers and Roman foreign policy in the East. In *Aspects of the Roman Near East: Papers in honour of Professor Fergus Millar FBA*, ed. R. Alston and S. N. C. Lieu, 103–73. Turnhout: Studia Antiqua Australiensia 3.

Herman, G. 2012. *A prince without a kingdom: The Babylonian Exilarch in the Sasanian era*. Tübingen: J.C. Mohr Siebeck.

Howard-Johnston, J. D. 2006. *East Rome, Sasanian Persia and the end of Antiquity: Historiographical and historical studies*. Aldershot/Burlington: Ashgate/Variorum.

Huyse, P. 2006. Die sasanidische Königstitulatur: Eine Gegenüberstellung der Quellen. In *Ērān ud Anērān: Studien zu den Beziehungen zwischen dem Sasanidenreich und der Mittelmeerwelt*, ed. J. Wiesehöfer and P. Huyse, 181–201. Stuttgart: Oriens et Occidens 13.

———. 2009. Die königliche Erbfolge bei den Sasaniden. In *Trésors d'Orient: Mélanges offerts à Rika Gyselen*, ed. P. Gignoux, C. Jullien, and F. Jullien, 145–57. Paris/Leuven: Cahiers de StIr 42.

Jullien, C., and F. Jullien. 2002. *Apôtres des confins: Processus missionnaires chrétiens dans l'empire iranien*. Leuven: RO 15.

Mosig-Walburg, K. 2009. *Römer und Perser: Vom 3. Jahrhundert bis zum Jahr 363 n. Chr.* Gutenberg: Computus Druck Satz & Verlag.

Nöldeke, T. 1879. *Geschichte der Perser und Araber zur Zeit der Sasaniden, aus der arabischen Chronik des Tabari übersetzt und mit ausführlichen Erläuterungen und Ergänzungen versehn.* Leiden: Brill.

Rubin, Z. 2001. The Sasanid monarchy. *CAH* 14: 638–61.

Shahîd, I. 2004. The last Sasanid-Byzantine conflict in the seventh century: The causes of its outbreak. In *La Persia e Bisanzio*, ed. G. Gnoli and A. Panaino, 223–44. Roma: Accademia Nazionale dei Lincei,.

Shayegan, M. R. 2003. Approaches to the study of Sasanian history. In *Paitimāna: Essays in Iranian, Indo-European, and Indian studies in honor of Hanns-Peter Schmidt*, 2 vols., ed. S. Adhami, 363–84. Costa Mesa: Mazda Publishers.

———. 2008. On the rationale behind the Roman wars of Šābuhr II the Great. *BAI* 18: 111–33.

———. 2011. *Arsacids and Sasanians: Political ideology in post-Hellenistic and Late Antique Persia*. Cambridge: Cambridge University Press.

———. 2012. *Aspects of epic and history in Ancient Iran: From Gaumāta to Wahnām*. Washington, DC/Cambridge: Hellenic Studies Series.

Whitby, M. 1988. *The Emperor Maurice and his historian: Theophylact Simocatta on Persian and Balkan warfare*. Oxford: Clarendon Press.

———. 2001. The successors of Justinian. *CAH* 14: 86–111.

Wiesehöfer, J. 2005a. *Iraniens, Grecs et Romains*. Paris: Cahiers de StIr 32.

———. 2005b. Rūm as enemy of Iran. In *Cultural borrowings and ethnic appropriations in Antiquity*, ed. E. S. Gruen, 105–20. Stuttgart: Oriens et Occidens 8.

———. 2009. Kawad, Khusro I and the Mazdakites: A new proposal. In *Trésors d'Orient: Mélanges offerts à Rika Gyselen*, ed. P. Gignoux, C. Jullien, and F. Jullien, 391–409. Paris/Leuven: Cahiers de StIr 42.

———. 2010. King and kingship in the Sasanian Empire. *CKA*: 135–52.

CHAPTER 43

SASANIAN COINAGE

NIKOLAUS SCHINDEL

Introduction

It is difficult to overestimate the importance of Sasanian coinage as an historical and archaeological source. Coinage is the major resource for the political, religious, and propagandistic identities and messages the royal administration wanted to transport to a wide audience throughout the Sasanian realm. It is of utmost importance for the archaeologist in several respects: first and foremost, coins offer an uninterrupted picture gallery of all Sasanian rulers, from the first Sasanian King of Kings, Ardašīr I (224–240), to the last, Yazdgerd III (632–651). Since every king wore a crown specific to himself, at least up to the sixth century, only the combination of names and crowns as attested in the numismatic sequence enables us to identify rulers in other media, such as rock reliefs and silver vessels. The development of other features in the king's appearance is also best studied through coins. Although most Sasanian coins available for study today do not come from secure archaeological contexts, their occurrence in excavation provides an important chronological marker, even if one must bear in mind that in a stratigraphic context, coins offer only a *terminus post quem*.

In an attempt to keep references to a minimum, no citations are given for the volumes of the *Sylloge Nummorum Sasanidarum* (hereafter *SNS*) published so far (Alram and Gyselen 2003, 2011; Schindel 2004, 2009; Baratova and Schindel 2012), since anyone with a deeper interest in Sasanian coins will have to consult these volumes (as well as Göbl 1971). In addition, reference to the older literature, which can easily be traced through these publications, has been omitted here due to space considerations.

Rulers

In order to construct a chronological framework within which the most relevant features of Sasanian coinage can be discussed, the first step naturally is to draw up a list of the Sasanian rulers attested on coins (Table 43.1). Problematic cases are discussed below. The individual date ranges are indicated and the regnal years as attested on the coins, as well as the figure number(s) of the coin for each ruler.

Three persons are said to have ruled as Kings of Kings of whom no coins are extant. Warahrān III was a son of Warahrān II and, in 293, was an unsuccessful rival of his uncle

Table 43.1 Key to Figs. 43.1–4 with regnal years of the Sasanian kings.

Name	Duration of reign	Regal years on coins	Fig. reference
Ardašīr I	224–240	n/a	43.1.1–2
Šābuhr I	240–272	n/a	43.1.3
Ōhrmazd I	272–273	n/a	43.1.4
Warahrān I	273–276	n/a	43.1.5
Warahrān II	276–293	n/a	43.1.6–7
Narseh	293–302/3	n/a	43.1.8
Ōhrmazd II	302/3–309/10	n/a	43.1.9–10
Šābuhr II	309/10–379	n/a	43.1.11–12
Ardašīr II	379–383	n/a	43.2.1
Šābuhr III	383–388	n/a	43.2.2
Warahrān IV	388–399	n/a	43.2.3
Yazdgerd I	399–420	n/a	43.2.4–5
Warahrān V	420–438	n/a	43.2.6
Yazdgerd II	438–457	n/a	43.2.7
Pērōz	457–484	2–7	43.2.8
Walāxš	484–488	n/a	43.2.9
Kawād I (first reign)	488–496	n/a	43.2.10
Jāmāsp	496–499	1–3	43.2.11
Kawād I (second reign)	499–531	11–43	43.3.1–2
Xosrow I	531–578	1–48	43.3.3
Ōhrmazd IV	578–590	1–13	43.3.4
Xosrow II (first reign)	590	1	43.3.5
Warahrān VI	590–591	1–2	43.3.6
Wistām	591/92–c.597	2–7	43.3.7
Ōhrmazd V	590s	1	43.3.8
Xosrow II (second reign)	591–628	2–38	43.3.9–11
Kawād II	628	2	43.4.1
Ardašīr III	628–630	1–2	43.4.2
Bōrānduxt	630–631	1–3	43.4.3
Xosrow III	around 630	2–3	43.4.4
Ōhrmazd VI	around 630	1–3	43.4.5
Ādarmīgduxt	around 630	1	43.4.6
Yazdgerd III	632–651	1–20	43.4.7

Narseh. Although some coins have been attributed to him in several older numismatic treatises, the internal logic of the sequence of Narseh's coinage proves that these coins belong to the latest phase of this king's reign, and thus their attribution to Warahrān has to be disregarded. A certain Adur-Narseh is attested in some Greek sources as a short-lived successor to Ōhrmazd II. The oriental tradition is unaware of him, and no coins can be attributed to this shadowy person who, in all probability, was never King of Kings. The same seems to be true of Ōhrmazd III, brother and rival of Pērōz. Although he allegedly ruled Iran for two years (457–459), there are no genuine coins of him. Two specimens published recently (Amini 2006: 314, nos. 564 and 564-2) appear to be modern forgeries. Moreover, the most reliable Oriental chronicles give Pērōz a reign of twenty-seven years. Since we know that he died in 484, there is simply no room for a King of Kings Ōhrmazd III, who seems instead to have been no more than an unsuccessful pretender to the throne. The identification of the king(s) named Xosrow after 628 with persons known from Tabari or other later chronicles is highly problematic. Whereas the beardless issues featuring the name Xosrow (Fig. 43.4.3) certainly belong to a distinct king, namely Xosrow III in the current numbering system (Malek 1993), the existence of Xosrow IV is much less certain, and therefore he is not included in Table 43.1.

In addition to the kings known from historical sources, there are also persons attested on coins of which we otherwise hear nothing. The clearest case concerns a certain Ōhrmazd, whose issues were first published in Mochiri (1977), and who is nowadays numbered as Ōhrmazd V (Fig. 43.3.8). Rare issues from the mint WYHC (i.e., Ctesiphon), invariably dated to regnal year 1, are known. From a stylistic and typological point of view, they must belong to the first years of the second reign of Xosrow II, that is, the 590s. Since it seems unlikely that Xosrow's father Ōhrmazd IV, murdered in Ctesiphon in 590, is meant, we are apparently faced with a short-lived usurper who managed to control the mint in the Sasanian capital for a short while, but who failed not only to gain broader acceptance, but also to attract the attention of historiographical sources. Another even more enigmatic issue, apparently from the east of the Sasanian realm, follows a type of the second reign of Kawād I, but clearly bears the name Šābuhr instead of Kawād. Finally, an enigmatic coin from APL, dated year 4, bearing the name Xosrow, but apparently belonging neither to Xosrow I nor to Xosrow II, should be mentioned (Mochiri 1977: 221ff., fig. 539). Since the historical sources do not offer the slightest clue as to his identity, we can only hope for excavated coin finds to add to our understanding of these enigmatic series. The latter two have been not been included in Table 43.1 since it is not certain if they were claiming to rule as King of Kings.

In summary, we have at least thirty-one different persons who issued coins during the Sasanian period, a period of 427 years. Among them are two women: Bōrānduxt (Fig. 43.4.3) and Ādarmīgduxt (Fig. 43.4.6) (Mochiri 1972: 12), even if the latter's issues almost always show a bearded portrait modeled after that of Xosrow II (the few unbearded obverses seem to originate from recut obverse dies of Xosrow III). The alternative reading of the name, Ādarmīg-dōst or "friend of Azarmi" (Alram 1986: 213), has failed to gain general acceptance.

Coinage technique, administrative basis

As is to be expected with premodern coinage, all Sasanian coins were hand struck. The obverse side, the lower or anvil die, bore the portrait of the king, while the reverse or upper die, normally featuring a fire altar with attendants and administrative data, was held in the craftsman's hand and then struck with a hammer to simultaneously impress the images of the two dies onto the flan placed between them. The most typical and distinct technical feature of Sasanian coins is their thinness. They were the first thin coins in numismatic history, and their model spread to Byzantium and Central Asia and ultimately to many medieval European coinages. Drastically enlarging the diameters in comparison with earlier Parthian drachms, for example, had the advantage of offering the craftsmen more space for the depictions on the obverse and reverse. The disadvantage of the thinness, especially in the sixth century, was the so-called "dead spot." Parts of the die image remain obscure since the flans were too thin (e.g. Fig. 43.3.8). Two actual coin dies made of iron have survived from the second reign of Xosrow II.

As in Imperial Rome and Byzantium, issuing coins was a royal prerogative. Planning, organization, and execution of coin production was conducted according to procedures that are now lost but that can be reconstructed to some extent from the coins themselves. This reconstruction of the coinage system is the main aim of the "Vienna school" of numismatics. As proven by the uniformity of coin designs, especially from the fifth century onward, royal power over mint administration was maintained even in periods when the weakness of the king vis-à-vis the nobility is attested in the historiographical sources, for example, under Walāxš or in the first reign of Kawād I. The mint organization, which, apart from an inscribed stamp seal (Göbl 1973: pls. 1, 2, 2a), has left no trace in Sasanian administrative sigillography (at least at the present stage of research), can be reconstructed only on the basis of actual coins. From Ardašīr I to the late fourth century, the number of mints was not very large and never seems to have exceeded twelve. As stylistic and typological analysis shows, the dies in this period were mostly produced locally. With rare exceptions, mostly in eastern Iran (Marw, Herat, Sakastan), the names of the mints are not present on the coins and therefore their attribution to specific mints must remain hypothetical until more archaeological data become available. Under Šābuhr III and Warahrān IV, the organizational scheme was drastically changed. The number of mints increased, and in several cases, dies were produced for several individual mints in one administrative area (e.g., Fars, Khuzestan) at the same workshop, as style analysis shows. From Pērōz onward, dies seem to have been produced centrally (in all probability in the capital, Ctesiphon) and then distributed to mints throughout the entire realm. This is a level of centralization that not even the Roman or Byzantine Empire achieved. Compared with their issues, the Sasanian series are much more uniform as regards denominations and typology; the same main denomination—the silver drachm—and the same types were used in mints from the Caucasus to Central Asia. Amazingly, the great administrative reform of the Sasanian state carried out by Kawād I and finalized under his successor, Xosrow I, does not appear to have left any trace in Sasanian coinage, apart from a few mint signatures which might possibly be connected with it (GNCKL, DYNAN, DYNAS, DYNAT, all attested for only a few years under Kawād I).

Mints and mint signatures

For the numismatic, historical, and archaeological interpretation of coins, especially those found in known stratigraphic contexts, establishing where they were actually minted is vital. An indication of the place of minting, mostly in an abbreviated form, is quite common on various ancient coinages, such as the Parthian or the Roman series from the mid-third century onward. Already under Šābuhr I, the first Sasanian coin bearing a mint name—MLWY, Marw—is attested and some other place names, such as Sakastan, Herat, and Ray, occur on late third- and fourth-century issues. Until Warahrān IV, however, most drachms did not bear a mint signature and for their location we have to rely on stylistic comparisons with signed pieces and, to some extent, on conjectures. Under Warahrān IV, things changed and the use of mint signatures became common, even if it was only from Pērōz onward that all drachms (with the exception of rare, special issues of Xosrow II, Fig. 43.3.11) canonically bear a mint signature, from Warahrān V onward always on the reverse at 3 o'clock. At the same time as mint abbreviations were introduced, the number of mints was greatly enlarged, and from that point on at least twenty-five mints striking drachms are attested per reign. These patterns are totally different than what prevailed in Rome and Byzantium. At present it is not possible to provide a list of all known Sasanian mint signatures with their varieties, but their number exceeds 100, many of which are only rarely attested (especially in the late fourth and early fifth centuries).

It is thus evident that mint abbreviations are an extremely important feature of Sasanian coinage. For various reasons, however, making sense of them is not easy. First, the mint name is normally given in an abbreviated form consisting typically of the first two or three letters of the name. Longer variants—especially in early Sasanian times and later on Arab-Sasanian coins—also exist. The correct reading of the Pahlavi letters that make up these signatures is essential: several incorrect identifications rested on faulty readings of the letters, most notably the misinterpretation of BBA (= the court, i.e., Ctesiphon) (Fig. 43.2.3) as BHL (Balkh in Khorasan). Thus, a sound methodological approach, especially where numismatic data are concerned, must be followed. Considering not only the signatures as such, but also the evidence of style and typology, greatly enhances the credibility of the interpretations. Two typical examples are AS and WH (discussed below). However, this method works only until the introduction of central die production from Pērōz onward, which by and large put an end to the existence of

FIGURE 43.1 Sasanian coinage from Ardašīr I through Šābuhr II (see Table 43.1 for details).

FIGURE 43.2 Sasanian coinage from Ardašīr II through Jāmāsp (see Table 43.1 for details).

FIGURE 43.3 Sasanian coinage from Kawād I (second reign) through Xosrow II (see Table 43.1 for details).

FIGURE 43.4 Sasanian coinage from Kawād II through Yazdgerd III (see Table 43.1 for details).

local styles. Thus, for signatures introduced after Pērōz, the certainty of mint attribution is generally less.

The names of the most common and most important Sasanian mint signatures and their locations are shown in Table 43.2 (for administrative geography, see Gyselen 1989, 2002). This is far from complete and does not represent the present writer's opinion. I have tried to indicate—according to the criteria listed in the caption—the varying degrees of certainty of the respective locations. In dubious cases, I have used a question mark rather than suggest an identification that I do not consider reliable enough to be of real use for further research.

Table 43.2 Principal Sasanian mint signatures and their locations.

Signature	Pahlevi form	Province	Region	Probability
AH		Ahmadān	Media	C
AHM		Ahmadān	Media	C
ALM		Armenia	Armenia	E
AM		Amul	Tabaristan	C
AP		Abarshahr	Khorasan	B, C
APL		Abarshahr	Khorasan	B, C
ART		Ardašīr-Xvarrah	Fars	A, C
AS		Asuristān (Ctesiphon)	Asuristan	B, C
AT		Azerbaijān	Azerbaijan	B, C
AW		Ōhrmazd-Ardašīr	Khuzestan	B, C
AWH		Ōhrmazd-Ardašīr	Khuzestan	B, C
AY		Ērān-xvarrah-Šābuhr	Khuzestan	B, D
AYL		?	?	?
AYLAN		?	?	?
BBA		Mobile court mint	-	B
BN		?	Kirman	B
BYŠ		Bīšabuhr	Fars	A, C
DA		Dārābgerd	Fars	A, C
DYWAN		?	?	?
GD		Jay	Media	C
GW		Gurgan	Gurgan	B, C
HL		Herat	Khorasan	B, C
HW		Xosrow-Šad-Kawād	Asuristan	C
HWC		Khuzestan	Khuzestan	C
KA		Karzi	Fars	A
KL		Kirman	Kirman	C
LAM		Ram-Ōhrmazd	Khuzestan	C
LD		Ray	Media	A, C
LDY		Ray	Media	A, C
LYW		Rew-Ardašīr	Khuzestan	A, C
MA		Media	Media	C
ML		Marw	Khorasan	A, C
MY		Meshan	Meshan	B, C
NAL/WAL		?	?	?
NY		Nihawand	Media	D
PL		Furat-Meshan	Meshan	D
SK		Sakastan	Sakastan	A, C
ST		Stakhr	Fars	A, C
ŠY		Shiraz	Fars	A, C
WH		Weh-Andiok-Šābuhr	Khuzestan	B
WYH		Weh-Kawād	Asuristan	D
WYHC		Weh-az-Andiok-Xosrow	Asuristan	B
YZ		Yazd	Fars	C

1. A = location certain because of numismatic evidence (combination of short and full form on the same coin); B = location probable because of numismatic evidence (numismatic evidence in favour of location, but not totally conclusive); C = location probable because of seal evidence (seal evidence strongly in favour of location); D = location likely because of seal evidence (seal evidence in favour of location, but not conclusive); E = location possible, but only because place names sound similar; ? = reliable location not yet possible.

2. *Notes on some signatures.* AS: Even if it has been repeated several times in the literature, AS certainly does not represent Isfahan, because the city's name in Pahlavi is SPHAN. In reality, AS denotes the Sasanian capital Ctesiphon under the name of the province in which it is situated, viz. Asuristan. As Mochiri correctly observed, the latest known date for AS is regnal year 22 of Xosrow I (Mochiri 1977: 258–61). From year 23 onward, WYHC emerged as one of the most important Sasanian mint signatures, and this clear numismatic sequence provides further proof for the equation of AS with Ctesiphon. AW/AY: These two signatures are quite often mistaken for each other; the length of the last letter, however, normally makes a distinction in all but some very poorly struck cases possible. AYL: Style analysis makes it certain that AYL was just a longer variant of AY under Wahram IV and Yazdgerd I. The use of

Table 43.2 (Continued)

AYL was then discontinued until the second reign of Kawad I, under whom it certainly referred to a different location than AY, that also began with "Eran," and most probably to a city that he founded, e.g. Eran–asan–kerd–Kawad or Eran–win(n)ard–Kawad. BBA: Leaving the misreading as BHL (Balkh) aside, BBA (*dār* = the court) refers to a mobile mint that travelled with the king. It was discontinued after Peroz, probably because it fell into the hands of the Hephthalites after the king's death in battle against them in 484. In its early period of use, it normally shared the style of AS and thus was located at the Sasanian capital Ctesiphon. Under Xosrow II, when BBA re-emerged, and for the Arab–Sasanian series, an eastern location is certain, but the equation with Balkh rests on too little actual evidence. GW: Under Yazdgerd I, two stylistically different mints used the abbreviation GW: Juwaym (fully rendered GWDMY), and Gurgan, identified by its markedly eastern style. After Yazdgerd I, GW always meant Gurgan. Proof of this is offered by a drachm of Wahram V of the same style with the longer variant GWL. HL: From Peroz onward, this signature certainly referred to Herat in Khorasan. Under Wahram IV and Yazdgerd I, however, because of style it does not mean Herat, but an unknown location, probably in Fars, while the Herat issues of these two kings bear the full mint name HLYDY. KL: A spelling variant which seems to read DL, but with the letters unconnected, certainly also has to be read KL and thus belongs to Kirman. ML/MY: These two signatures are often mistaken for each other (e.g. in the coin trade), even if the form of the second letter is normally distinct enough for a reliable identification. NAL/WAL: Due to the ambiguity of the later Pahlavi script, both readings are equally possible. Even if Nahr–Tira has been suggested, no reliable location seems to be possible. WH: The traditional equation with Weh–Ardašīr, a part of the city complex of Ctesiphon, has to be rejected. Under Wahram IV, Yazdgerd I, and Wahram V, WH always displays the same stylistic criteria as AW and AY, two signatures which can be safely attributed to mints in Khuzistan province. At the same time, WH is totally different in style from AS. It follows that WH has to be equated with Weh–Andiok–Šābuhr(Jundy-Shapur) in Khuzestan, one of the most important cities in Sasanian Iran which otherwise would lack a mint altogether. WYHC: This signature was used under Kawad I and in the early years of Xosrow I for Kawad's new foundation Weh–az–Amid–Kawad in Fars. From Xosrow's regnal year 23 onward, however, the signature WYHC denoted Weh–az–Andiok–Xosrow, a part of the city complex of Ctesiphon. WYHC is the only mint signature attested for some of the short-lived rulers after Xosrow II who are known to have been crowned in Ctesiphon, another proof of the location.

DENOMINATIONS

General remarks

The origins of Sasanian coinage can be traced back to two different sources, both of which ultimately originated in the Greek monetary system introduced by Alexander the Great. On the one hand Fars, the home region of Ardašīr I, had a local tradition of issuing silver drachms, half-drachms, and sixth-drachms. The Parthian Kings of Kings, on the other hand, refrained from issuing gold coins, but struck vast quantities of silver drachms, originally according to the Athenian weight standard, with an ideal weight of $c.4.25$ g and a high silver content of $c.95$ percent. By the early third century, the weights had decreased to $c.3.70$ g, and the silver content to $c.70$ percent. Apart from the fact that the drachm was the main denomination, produced in late Parthian times exclusively in the Ecbatana (Hamadan) mint, billon tetradrachms with a silver content of only $c.20$ percent (the remaining 80 percent being copper) were issued in Seleucia-on-the-Tigris (near the city complex of Ctesiphon), as well as tiny bronze coins. Ardašīr I combined these two elements into a new, distinctively Sasanian coinage. The only source at our disposal for reconstructing the denominational standards are the coins themselves; in Pahlavi literature we find only the Middle Persian terms *drahm*, *dēnār* and *dang* (one-sixth drachm).

The main denomination: The drachm

While the earliest drachms struck by Ardašīr I after his victory over the Parthians in 224 show the same weight and fineness as the latest Parthian issues (viz. *c*.3.70 g or *c*.70 percent silver), in his latest coinage he raised the drachm weight to *c*.4.20 g and at the same time increased the silver content to *c*.95 percent, the highest quality common in ancient coinage. Even if the weight of the drachm was very close to that of the Attic drachm, the reckoning system according to which this weight was attained seems to have been different. Minor weight reductions under Pērōz, as well as the evidence of fourth- and fifth-century gold coinage, imply that rather than reckoning the drachm as a fraction of a larger unit, that is, the Athenian mina, the Sasanian drachm represented a multiple of minor units. As in the Late Roman, Byzantine, and Early Arabic systems this was most probably the seed of the carob tree (Lat. *siliqua*, Gr. *keration*, hence English "carat"; Ar. *kharubah*). It appears that a different *siliqua* weight was used than in the Classical world, namely one with a basic weight of 0.212 g per unit. A Sasanian drachm consisted of twenty such units from the early third to the mid-fifth century. It is certainly not mere chance that the ideal weight of the Umayyad post-reform dinar—which we know for certain to have been 4.25 g—is the same as that of the Sasanian drachm, and also a Sasanian gold denomination struck from the reign of Šābuhr II onward. Under Pērōz, the ideal weight of the drachm seems to have been decreased by half a *siliqua* to 4.15 g. While drachm hoards before Pērōz show a peak of weights around 4.20 g, from his reign onward the most common weight range was 4.10–4.14 g. At the same time, weight fluctuations decreased markedly. The striking of coinage thus now took place *al pezzo* (where weight was controlled individually) rather than *al marco* (in which, from a certain amount of metal, a fixed number of coins had to be struck, but individual weights might vary considerably). This standard weight remained in use until the end of Arab-Sasanian coinage; the post-reform silver dirham established by the Umayyad caliph 'Abd al-Malik in 78 AH (697/8) at a rate of seven-tenths of the Sasanian drachm had a safely established weight of 2.97 g, exactly seven-tenths of 4.25 g.

The drachm was the main denomination of the Sasanian realm; it was perceived as such also in antiquity (for the testimony of Cosmas Indicopleustes, see McCrindle 1897: 323ff.). Most museum collections, as well as nonspecialized private holdings, tend to contain 95 percent or more drachms; in *SNS* 3, for example, the percentage of drachms compared with all other denominations is over 90 percent. However, gold might have played a fairly important role for royal propaganda and donative purposes in the uppermost social stratum, and copper coins were important for transactions in every day life.

Silver fractions (half drachm, sixth drachm)

While the Arsacids had not minted any silver fractions since the mid-first century BC, half drachms (Fig. 43.1.12) and sixth drachms (Fig. 43.2.5) (hemidrachms and obols, respectively, in Greek numismatic terminology) were a common feature in Persis, where Ardašīr I originated. There can be no doubt that the striking of these silver fractions in Ardašīr's series as King of Kings represents a takeover. Following the practice in Fars, we can safely assume that they were intended to serve practical purposes in monetary circulation. However, this three-denominational set did not survive long; the fractions apparently could not exist alongside the drachms. Hemidrachms were struck for the last time under Ōhrmazd II; their sudden reappearance in eighth-century Tabaristan—first under local princes of Iranian stock, then under Abbasid governors—is certainly unrelated to the long-defunct denomination.

The sixth drachm had a different fate. It was not issued in quantity after Šābuhr II, but it survived until approximately regnal year 30 of Kawād I. From Šābuhr III to Yazdgerd I, the reverses often show special types not found on any other denominations. At the same time, the weights became quite erratic and basically tended to decline. It is obvious that the sixth drachm was no longer intended to serve as an interim denomination between drachms and copper coins, but rather functioned as a donative coin on festive occasions. The erratic weights of these coins have parallels in Late Roman and Early Byzantine donative issues; postulating the existence of various different denominational standards is methodologically unsound. Let us have a look at the sixth drachms of Jāmāsp. Although new material might change the picture, in our present state of knowledge, all known examples with a legible mint name, with one exception, are dated to regnal year 1, and were struck at the mint of DA (Dārābgerd). It is a fair guess that these silver fractions were issued to celebrate the king's accession to the throne. Later sixth drachms, however, show the same types as the drachms, and are thus no longer marked by their typology as something special.

Gold coinage ("old" dinar, "new" dinar, fractions)

No Arsacid gold coins exist that are universally accepted to be genuine. In a marked deviation from his Parthian predecessors, Ardašīr I issued dinars already very early in his career as King of Kings. Gold coins were issued by every Sasanian ruler with the exception of Jāmāsp, Ōhrmazd IV, and the successors of Xosrow II (except Bōrānduxt). Thus, issuing dinars and their fractions was a fairly common and continuous phenomenon. But apart from Šābuhr II and Pērōz, gold coins are generally very rare, and hardly reach a two-digit number of specimens known per individual reign. In the case of Šābuhr II, his engagements in the east of the Sasanian realm and the Kushano-Sasanian kingdom may have been the reason for their minting, and most of Šābuhr II's dinars were struck in eastern mints such as Marw. Under Pērōz, the dinar mints were invariably situated in western Iran, but since almost all of them employ one single type (*SNS* IIIb/1c) and thus belong to the same, rather limited time span, there might have been a special reason for their issue. In the present writer's opinion, it is possible that Pērōz distributed them as donatives to safeguard the loyalty of the Persian nobility after his first defeat and capture by the Hephthalites. By and large, one might conclude that gold coins did not primarily serve the purpose of large payments in everyday life, but represented a donative coinage presented by the king to high-ranking members of the Iranian elite, presumably often on festive occasions. From Šābuhr II onward, special types on the obverses can be observed; from Kawād I's second reign onward, all undoubtedly genuine gold coins feature special types on both sides not attested in the drachm coinage. Quite a large number of modern forgeries of Sasanian gold coins exist.

Due to the paucity of surviving specimens, reconstructing their ideal weights is not very easy. While the earliest known, so far unique dinar of Ardašīr I weighs 8.47 g and thus comes remarkably close to the stater in the coinage system of Alexander the Great, with only one attested coin, this might be mere chance, particularly as later dinars have a weight peak around 7.20 g. Interestingly enough, this weight does not fit into the two established contemporary gold coinages. It is lighter than contemporary Kushan dinars ($c.8.00$ g), but heavier than Roman denarii aurei ($c.6.50$ g under Alexander Severus, 222–235). No changes in weight can be observed until Šābuhr II who, rather late in his reign, to judge from a stylistic point of view, introduced a "new" dinar with an ideal weight of $c.4.25$ g. There is no obvious relationship between the "old" dinar of 7.20 g and this new denomination, which at the same time is slightly, but consistently, lighter than the Late Roman and Byzantine solidus of 4.55 g. What is important to note is that the ideal weight of the "new" dinar and the drachm was exactly the same, and that the Umayyad post-reform dinar, while generally modeled after the Byzantine solidus, also had exactly the same weight (4.25 g) as the Sasanian "new" dinar. Under Šābuhr II, the "new" dinars were marked by a special obverse type without the usual mural crown. Under his successors, both weight standards can be observed alongside each other. The "old," heavier dinar is attested until Warahrān V. Pērōz uses two different dinar weights alongside each other: the "new" dinar of $c.4.25$ g and a typologically identical variant, the weight of which clustered around 3.70 g. This apparently represents a dinar of 18 rather than 20 *siliquae*. Under Xosrow II, yet another weight standard of $c.6.50$ g, apparently representing one and a half "new" dinars, was used (Fig. 43.3.10).

Dinar fractions are even rarer than dinars. Most commonly, they aim at one-sixth of the dinar—either the "old" one, of which the ideal weight is a little bit more than 1.00 g, or the light "new" one, with an ideal weight around 0.70 g. Even if individual weights vary considerably, the coins more often than not are lighter than they should be. A rare category of coins—attested so far for Warahrān IV, Yazdgerd I, and Pērōz—appears to be third dinars, modeled after the Late Roman tremissis or third solidus (1.50 g).

Base-metal coinage (copper, lead)

Sasanian base-metal issues are still quite poorly known. It seems that the soil in Iraq and Iran tends to lead to heavy corrosion of copper coins. The majority of thin, small coins seem to have suffered so badly that the pieces were of no market value and therefore were utterly disregarded. Thus, they did not enter most museum collections during their formative periods in large numbers (late nineteenth and early twentieth centuries). Archaeological excavations tend to correct the image of a silver-only currency in favor of one in which copper played an important role in daily monetary transactions. However, our understanding of Sasanian small change is still far from complete; we only can hope that in the coming years archaeological finds will enlarge both the material basis and our understanding of Sasanian copper coinage, the importance of which is demonstrated by the fact that almost all Sasanian kings, except for some of the short-lived successors of Xosrow II, minted in copper. Even Bōrānduxt and Yazdgerd III are attested on copper coins. In contrast to drachms, hoards of copper coins are quite rare (Schindel 2009).

For Ardašīr I, a complex system consisting of four different denominations has been reconstructed, but this cannot be applied to later periods. It must be emphasized that this system was a new creation. For quite a long time, the Parthians had issued only tiny copper coins similar to Ardašīr's smallest denomination. Large copper coins weighing around 10 g seem to have been a peculiarity of eastern mints, especially Sakastan (Fig. 43.1.10), to which a series of large bronzes of Ardašīr (as well as some rare drachms) may be attributed. It is possible that these large issues were ultimately inspired by the thick, heavy Kushan copper coins. In western Iran, smaller and rather thin coins seem to have been the norm by the reign of Šābuhr II at latest. Special types or type variants are attested from Šābuhr I to the second reign of Kawād I, the most interesting of which were minted at Marw. Only rarely do we have enough coins to establish individual weight standards. Among the finds from Marw, the weight peak for Kawād I's copper coins lies around 1.50 g, but for Xosrow I it is only around 0.60 g. This proves how complex weight standards may have been, and represents a caveat against any solution that tends to oversimplify a complex situation. From the mid-fifth century onward, the copper coins basically followed the drachm typology. Due to their tiny lettering, poor-quality striking and corrosion, more often than not mint and regnal years are illegible. Since style or typology do not normally assist attribution much in the late period, it is a sad fact that many copper coins from excavations cannot be attributed and it is unlikely that this situation will improve much in the future.

Rarer and even more obscure than copper coins are lead issues, which are attested from the later third to the mid-fifth century (Fig. 43.1.12). Their typology follows that of the copper coins and basically no drachm-size issues are known, so the pieces cannot be trial strikes. In all probability they represent local petty currency. Very little archaeological data exist on these lead coins. One should bear in mind that in Umayyad and early Abbasid times lead coins were issued in sizable quantities on both sides of the Persian Gulf (Siraf, Bahrain). Even if the Sasanian lead coins did not originate in these regions, the later evidence conclusively proves that lead coins were used locally in Iran and nearby regions.

Typology

General remarks

The typology of Sasanian coinage basically follows that of Hellenistic coinage. The obverse features the bust of the ruler while the reverse shows the most important religious symbol of the dynasty—in the Sasanian case a fire altar, normally flanked by two attendants. If one compares Roman coins from the 220s (Severus Alexander), contemporary with the reign of Ardašīr I, with issues of Heraclius (610–641), contemporary with the last Sasanian kings, one can easily see that in Roman coinage basically all features have changed—denominations, obverse images, reverse images, artistic conventions, religious allegiances, methods of time reckoning. In contrast, an early and a late Sasanian drachm, while displaying considerable stylistic changes and variations in typological details, deploy the same basic types on both sides, and display much more continuity. This is proof that the basic political and religious concepts of the dynasty and its imperial propaganda did not drastically change during the nearly four and a half centuries of its existence (but see Chapter 42).

Sasanian coinage normally does not allude directly to actual political or military events. The only clear exception is a double dinar of Šābuhr I (Alram et al. 2007; I am not convinced this is genuine, however). Sasanian coins rather celebrate the majesty and victoriousness of the king in a more general fashion. According to the traditional interpretation, the wings attached to the crown (Warahrān II, Warahrān IV, third crown of Pērōz, second crown of Xosrow II, second crown of Ardašīr II, Xosrow III, Ōhrmazd VI, Ādarmīgduxt, Yazdgerd III) allude to Verethragna, god of victory, to whom the falcon is sacred, as does the almost full depiction of a bird of prey in the crown of Ōhrmazd II. Apart from the theophoric name Warahrān—together with that of the supreme god of Zoroastrianism, in the form Ōhrmazd, the most common one in the list of Sasanian rulers—two kings use the epithet *pylwcy*, "victorious," in their obverse legends: Wistām and Kawād II. The mural elements (Ardašīr I, Šābuhr I, Šābuhr II, and all rulers after Warahrān IV except Burān) are usually taken to refer to Ahura Mazda, the rays in the crown of Warahrān I to Mithra. Up to the reign of Šābuhr III, only theophoric elements alluding to a single deity were employed in the crowns. Warahrān IV was the first ruler who combined two markedly different theophoric elements, namely, the mural element of Ahura Mazda and the wing(s) of Verethragna. Thereafter, such composite crowns become common. The crescent above the forehead (which in reality was placed parallel to it and only as a numismatic convention turned 90° so as to be fully visible) was introduced by Yazdgerd I; its connection with a specific deity is not as obvious as is the case with the above mentioned elements. Save for those of Warahrān V, Yazdgerd II Jāmāsp, Ardašīr III, and Bōrānduxt, all crowns in the fifth to seventh centuries show this crescent. After Jāmāsp, only two crown forms are commonly used, and thus the principle of individual crowns was dropped. The first corresponds to the second crown of Pērōz; it was worn by Kawād I, Xosrow I, Ōhrmazd IV, Xosrow II (first reign), Warahrān VI, and Kawād II. The only development concerns the height of the crown cap. The second crown adds two wings to the same basic form and was introduced by Xosrow II at the beginning of his second reign to demonstrate his victory over Warahrān VI—hence the allusion to Verethragna. This crown was also used by Ōhrmazd V, Ardašīr III (second crown), Xosrow III, Ōhrmazd VI, and Ādarmīgduxt. Until the reign of Pērōz, attempts to depict the most important elements of the crown were also made in the representations of the attendants on the reverses. This clearly demonstrates how important crowns were as a means of identifying the respective king, also to the ancient Sasanians and others who used this coinage.

A typical and at the same time remarkable feature of Sasanian coins is their use of multiple rims and astral symbols outside the outermost rim. Multiple rims—two or three—occur for the first time on rare copper coins from a western mint (probably Ctesiphon) of Šābuhr II. The double rim seems to have been used also on rare base-metal issues of Yazdgerd I (of doubtful authenticity) and of Yazdgerd II (rather obscure). Walāxš invariably used two obverse rims, and on two coins double rims appear on the reverse. Late in the reign of Kawād I coinage with an unusually wide gap between the first and second rims appeared; in this isolated case, one might wonder whether the second rim was intended to make clipping easier to detect, even if the outer rim is almost never fully visible due to the small size of the flan. On his later copper coins, Kawād I employed three rims on the reverse and two on the obverse. Then, the use of multiple rims was dropped until Xosrow II's first reign. What was to be the basically canonical distribution—two on the obverse, three on the reverse—can already be observed, even if the astral symbols were changed, in his second reign. Only Kawād II and Ardašīr III, the two immediate successors of Xosrow II, refrained from using multiple rims in their drachm coinage, as did Yazdgerd III on his early obverses. On gold coins, multiple rims were never used, in all probability due to the influence of Roman and Byzantine gold coinage.

Šābuhr II was also the first to employ astral symbols outside the obverse rim on some scarce copper coins from the same western mint. Copper issues of Kawād I with a single rim, but a *frawahr* symbol at similar locations as the crescents under Šābuhr II, suggest that this king's issues served as a model in the early sixth century. In regnal year 13, Kawād introduced the canonical use of astral symbols on the obverse, a combination of crescent and star placed at 3, 6, and 9 o'clock, respectively. Ōhrmazd IV used the same combination; Xosrow I and—following his model—Warahrān VI also had crescents only on the obverses, while Wistām used a symbol resembling two crescents with a dot. From the second reign of Xosrow II onward astral symbols—if employed at all—invariably consist of the combination of crescent and star.

Obverses

The obverses of Sasanian coins always depict the bust of the ruling Sasanian King of Kings. In some rather rare cases, one or two additional busts are added, either jugate, or opposite the king's bust, or both at the same time (Fig. 43.1.7). As there is no information in the legends as to the identity of these additional figures, it is not very easy to identify them. In the case of Ardašīr I, a local ruler of Sakastan is probably depicted. Under Warahrān II, his queen, one or more different crown princes, and possibly the goddess Anahita are shown. A thus far unique copper coin of Šābuhr III displays an unidentified bust facing the king's; since this type is not attested on silver drachms, it cannot have had great importance. Under Jāmāsp, it was probably the god Ahura Mazda who was depicted. The Roman practice of issuing imperial coins in the name and with the image of another, living or dead, member of the royal family, without showing the emperor, was totally alien to Sasanian coinage.

In contrast to Parthian coinage, the majority of which shows a head in profile facing left, most Sasanian issues feature the royal head turned to the right, as in Roman coinage contemporary with Ardašīr I. After Ardašīr I became King of Kings, depictions of frontal heads are rare and are attested only on ceremonial issues, never on regular coins struck in large quantities. These are attested on gold issues of Warahrān IV, Pērōz, Walāxš, Kawād I (second reign), Xosrow I, Xosrow II (second reign) (Fig. 43.3.10), and Bōrānduxt, as well as on rare drachms of Xosrow II's second reign (Fig. 43.3.11). Frontal portraits (in three-quarter and, after 538, in fully frontal view) became the rule for Late Roman and Early Byzantine gold solidi, beginning in the late fourth century, and for larger copper issues in the sixth century. Since the earliest frontal Sasanian dinar was struck by Warahrān IV shortly after the introduction of three-quarter front portraits on regular eastern Roman coinage, it seems quite probable that this feature was taken over by the Persians from their western neighbors. Some large copper coins of Ōhrmazd II (Fig. 43.1.10) and Šābuhr II from Sakastan show left-facing portraits, which are certainly intentional, all other examples being due to die cutters' mistakes.

When we talk about these directions, it is important to bear in mind that only the heads are turned to the right; the shoulders are always (save for a few issues of Ardašīr I) shown fully frontal, an artistic convention also encountered on rock reliefs and silver vessels.

The fabric of the king's tunic was shown in a rather naturalistic fashion in the third century, but then it became more stylized. Under Kawād and Jāmāsp, varying combinations of dots, circles, and stars can be observed on the shoulders and on the breast. From Xosrow I onward, a star and a crescent on the shoulders and two dots on the breast (with a third one being incorporated into the pearl row at the neck cut-out) became canonical. Ardašīr III and sometimes Yazdgerd III were shown wearing a necklace with three large pendants in the middle of the breast. The neck cut-out was mostly adorned with a row of pearls which might represent an embellishment of the tunic. Alternatively, we might take this to represent a necklace. On the breast, two straps holding the breast ornament, well known on rock reliefs and silver vessels, are visible, normally in the form of two parallel rows of pearl. Sometimes the upper part of the breast ornament appears as a semicircle.

Apart from Ardašīr III and Xosrow III, all kings were shown wearing a beard, though Kawād I in his first reign normally had only whiskers, without a moustache. The depiction of the beard varied; the most common convention was to depict the whiskers with many small circles and the moustache with a wavy line. As with the hair bundle at the back of the neck, the beard was bound below the chin in globular form with a ribbon that can normally be distinguished by two small strands running to the left. This convention disappeared in the middle of the fifth century. Bōrānduxt was always shown without a beard, while—amazingly enough—Ādarmīgduxt was mostly bearded. The few drachms with unbearded busts seem to have been struck from altered dies of Xosrow III.

A typical feature of Sasanian royal dress was the earring. Under Ardašīr I, it is not visible due to the cheek protection he is shown wearing. Similarly, most of Šābuhr I's issue with the prominent cheek protector does not show it, and this is true of Warahrān I as well. From Warahrān II onward, all rulers were depicted wearing earrings. Until the reign of Yazdgerd II, the earring normally consisted of one smaller element attached to the earlap, and a larger round element; under Pērōz, the depiction was changed to a triplet. Thereafter, only Ardašīr III and Bōrānduxt, who was shown wearing no earring at all because of her pendilia, deviated from this convention.

The diadem, placed around the ruler's forehead and bound together on the neck with a burl, was the most important royal emblem. Its depiction changed through time. From Ardašīr I to the early years of Šābuhr II, it took the form of a plain ribbon, the ends of which normally floated upward. The diadem was thus depicted as if it were a Hellenistic cloth diadem, even though, as an element of the crown, we have to assume that in fact it consisted of a golden circlet. When Šābuhr II ascended the throne, the depiction was changed and a row of pearls (sometimes waves) was placed above the diadem; later in his reign this became so prominent that, from then on, the diadem consisted of a row of dots and from Walāxš onward a second row of pearls was added. When one considers that there are (admittedly rare) special obverse-type coins which depict the ruler without crown and korymbos and with uncovered hair only, but still with a diadem (Šābuhr II, Šābuhr III, Warahrān IV), then it becomes clear that the diadem was the single most important element among the royal insignia. Very similar issues of Warahrān IV and Yazdgerd I followed these patterns, but they used the most important element of the crowns, namely wings or a crescent. A special type, distantly similar, was struck by Šābuhr I; it also lacks the mural elements but features the korymbos and covered hair (Schindel 2009: 13; 2010).

The diadem ribbons are a typical feature of Sasanian art in general. On coins, they are shown hanging down on many issues of Ardašīr I, even if the more common variant pointing upward can be observed on his coinage. During a middle phase the horizontally ribbed rendering of the ribbons appeared for the first time. Until the reign of Šābuhr II the ribbons invariably commenced above the bundle of hair on the neck, and were thus clearly attached to the back of the diadem. Beginning with Ardašīr II, the ribbons were increasingly shown commencing below the bundle of hair, a convention that became canonical under Yazdgerd I. Even if, from this point onward, a small dot, triangle, or triplet was shown at the back end of the diadem, there can be no doubt that the main ribbons still belonged to it. Starting with the last obverse type of Pērōz, both ribbons were depicted in a very prominent fashion in the left and right field, commencing behind the shoulder.

The king's hair was normally shown in two bundles due to the convention of the right-facing head. As the frontal variants show (Fig. 43.3.10–11), there were in reality three bundles, two at the neck and one above the head. The hair at the neck was always uncovered. Apart from Ardašīr I, Warahrān I, and Narseh, in whose reigns the hair was arranged in the form of pearl rows, all other kings had globular bundles. The depiction of the individual curls became more and more stylized until the late sixth century, when Xosrow II returned to a more naturalistic rendering.

The bundle of hair above the head—the korymbos—was almost always covered by a piece of cloth; its texture is indicated by semicircular lines representing wrinkles and it was often adorned with several triplets. With time, the depiction became increasingly stylized. From the second reign of Xosrow II onward, the astral symbols—star and crescent—replaced the korymbos on drachms. However, this was done only for the sake of symmetry; rare gold coins of Xosrow II (Fig. 43.3.10), as well as the issues of his son Kawād II, prove that the rendering of the korymbos itself was not changed. Under Warahrān V a crescent was added between crown and korymbos. This feature immediately became canonical and serves as a reliable marker for the attribution of Sasanian coins, especially for worn copper issues.

The piece of cloth covering the korymbos was bound together with a ribbon, the ends of which are depicted inconsistently. They were prominent on rare early coins of Yazdgerd I and in the later reign of Kawād I (Fig. 43.3.1). Their use became canonical from Yazdgerd II onward, with the important exception of those crowns that also comprise wings (third crown of Pērōz, second reign of Xosrow II and many of his successors).

The treatment of these elements shows that even if the basic typology of Sasanian coins seems to be quite uniform, development was taking place all the time. However, yet another development remains to be addressed. From the fifth century onward, astral symbols became increasingly common, both outside the rim(s) and in the fields. Kawād I introduced a star in the left obverse field when he came to power and in his 19th regnal year added a second star in the right field. From Xosrow I onward, the star in the right field was invariably placed above the crescent which belongs properly to the crown. These two elements—despite having totally different origins, the star being a symbol and thus a numismatic convention, the crescent an actual element of the royal crown—were combined and from Xosrow II onward were placed quite randomly in the right field. More often than not, the crescent was no longer attached to the crown above the diadem on the forehead, where in principle it still belonged, as depictions in other forms of Sasanian art prove.

Reverses

There are two groups of Sasanian coin reverses. The first and by far largest one depicts the Zoroastrian fire altar, almost always with a standing figure to the left and right of it from Ardašīr I onward. The second shows other images and symbols, and is attested only on rare festive or local issues. The depiction of one figure standing in front of a lit fire altar was common in Persid (*fratarakā*) coinage, even though this was discontinued after Ardašīr II (first century BC).

Let us start with the fire altar. This consists of five main elements: the altar base, shaft, ribbons, table, and flames. From Ardašīr I to Yazdgerd II, the altar base consisted mainly of two elements. Beginning with reverse type *SNS* 3a of Šābuhr II (Fig. 43.1.11), these two elements were shown much more clearly separated from the altar shaft than before. With the introduction of type *SNS* 1 of Yazdgerd II (on which the attendants raise their hands toward the altar, rather than holding a barsom bundle), three elements were shown, a convention that remained in use until the end of Sasanian coinage.

From Šābuhr I to Šābuhr II the altar shaft was broad and prominent. Under Šābuhr II this changed, and the shaft was thenceforward thinner than the elements below and above it. Moreover, it was also almost invariably round, whereas previously both round and square versions had occurred alongside each other. Under Xosrow I, the shaft was reduced to a thin line and this convention persisted until the end of Sasanian-type coinage.

A diadem ribbon bound round the altar shaft with its ribbed ends hanging down appeared for the first time under Warahrān II and become canonical late in the reign of Narseh. When Šābuhr II placed the legend *l'st* (*rāst*, "just") on the altar shaft, the part of the ribbon connecting the two ends to the left and the right disappeared, since there was no longer room for them, and did not reappear until the legend was dropped in the mid-fifth century. As with many other typological elements, the treatment of the altar ribbons became increasingly stylized with time. The most important change took place when the reverse type *SNS* 2 of Xosrow I was introduced and from then onward the ribbons appeared upright and more prominent. The three dots that marked the place where the ribbons joined the altar also disappeared at this time. With the exception of Ardašīr III, all subsequent kings followed Xosrow I's model.

The altar table consisted of four sections when only the altar flames were depicted, and of three when—from Ōhrmazd II onward—a bust was added in the flames. The third section was the broadest, with a dotted outline. From Warahrān IV until early in the reign of Xosrow I, three elements were visible. Later, Xosrow I radically altered the depiction of the fire altar with the addition of a fourth section.

From the beginning of Sasanian coinage the treatment of the altar flames varied considerably, even within the same mint. Initially, several parallel, generally slightly curved lines were shown. Under Warahrān IV, the flames were shown for the first time as small strokes arranged in several rows, one above the other. From Pērōz onward, the flames were invariably arranged in four rows of four, three, two, and single strokes, respectively.

As noted above, the representation of attendants flanking the altar originated in the *fratarakā* coinage of Persis, yet interestingly the imperial issues of the first Sasanian King of Kings, Ardašīr I, did not depict them at all. Rather, Ardašīr's coinage depicted a fire altar with pillars resting on mushroom-shaped objects, with a depiction of the imperial Achaemenid throne incorporated into this type as well. From Šābuhr II to Yazdgerd I, the fire altar without attendants was used for festive issues, mainly on gold coins and silver fractions.

The first Sasanian king to make use of attendants was Šābuhr I, on whose coinage both figures were shown wearing a mural crown, almost always without korymbos. These face away from the altar and hold scepters. In all probability, both figures were meant to represent the king. Under Ōhrmazd I, the attendants invariably faced the altar and wore different crowns. In the case of Šābuhr I's coinage, the conventional interpretation was that the sun god Mithra (distinguishable by his crown with several short strokes representing rays) is shown holding a diadem, toward which Ōhrmazd raises his hand. According to conventional wisdom, a similar scene, depicting Anahita instead of Mithra, appeared under Warahrān II. From Narseh onward, the attendants invariably faced the altar and, starting with Šābuhr II, both figures were invariably shown wearing the same crown, the great king's. After Yazdgerd II the main theophoric elements in the crowns were no longer recognizable as the depiction became more and more stylized. Yazdgerd II was also the first king to use a new type on which the attendants raise one hand toward the altar in a gesture of veneration, a variant which was to become canonical until the accession of Xosrow I. On his early coins, the mural elements of the royal crown were very prominent, but these disappeared with the introduction of type *SNS* 2. From this variant onward, the crown cap was increasingly prominent and tall. This development continued until regnal year 10 of Xosrow II. Thereafter, the crown cap was no longer depicted at all. Instead, the crescent above the forehead on the obverse crown was shown. On the early issues of Xosrow I the attendants hold a lance or scepter in one hand, while the other rests on a scabbard. From regnal year 5 onward, the attendants were shown holding a sword, point downward, in both hands. This iconography remained unchanged until the end of Sasanian-type coinage.

Apart from these basic outlines of the Sasanian main type, two further features deserve mention. The first is the bare-headed bust with diadem in the flames first employed by Ōhrmazd II. The lack of a crown makes its identification difficult, but it must be emphasized that the same depiction can be observed on rare, special-type obverses from Šābuhr II to Yazdgerd I. My suggestion is that this depicts the King of Kings and might allude to his military role, but this is merely a conjecture. It is last attested under Yazdgerd I. The other feature is a bust in front of the altar table used by Warahrān V and, following his model, Walāxš. Here, the clearly recognizable crown proves beyond doubt that the king himself was meant.

Generally speaking, different reverse coin types were rare, used either for special or local issues. The most conspicuous group depicted the standing king, either holding a ribbon under Kawād I and Xosrow I or resting his hands on a sword in a gesture very similar to the attendants' from type *SNS* 2 of Xosrow I onward. The latter variant is attested for Xosrow I (Schindel 2006), Xosrow II (Fig. 43.3.10), and Bōrānduxt (Göbl 1983). These special types were always accompanied by special legends. Under Xosrow, a deity in a nimbus of flames was used on dinars and drachms (Gyselen 2000; Fig. 43.3.11). In the late fourth and early fifth century, special reverses appeared on sixth drachms and copper coins. On the silver fractions, a diadem ribbon under Šābuhr III, a cock's head under Warahrān IV, and the mint name under Yazdgerd I are attested. Special-type copper coins, struck mainly at Marw, depicted the king on horseback under Šābuhr I (Schindel 2010); an altar type with a bust following a Kushano-Sasanian model under Šābuhr II; an unidentifiable, *tamga*-like object under Warahrān IV; a cross with diadem ribbons under Yazdgerd I; and a diadem ribbon under Yazdgerd II. Drachm-size copper coins of Kawād depict a bust, probably representing *shahrewar*, "best rule," on the reverse.

Legends

In a marked deviation from Parthian coinage, but continuing the traditional practices of *fratarakā* coinage in Fars, Ardašīr I did not use Greek on his coins, but only Middle Persian, written in the Pahlavi script. Admittedly, later Parthian drachms featured legends in Parthian, which in the latest decades were more legible than the debased Greek inscriptions on the drachms, but the tetradrachms from Seleucia-on-the-Tigris displayed only Greek legends until the very end of the Arsacid period. Minor details of the rendering of the legends, and paleographic variants, need not detain us here; let us concentrate on the main features. It must be emphasized that the legends discussed below represent reconstructed, ideal forms; more often than not, they were abbreviated and, especially in the third century, the lettering was often defective. In most cases, however, no intentional deviation from the ideal form can be observed.

Ardašīr I's obverse legend as King of Kings reads as follows:

Transliteration: mzdysn bgy 'rthštr MLKAn MLKA 'yr'n MNW ctr NMW yzd'n
Transcription: mazdēsn bay Ardašir šāhān šāh Ērān kē čihr az yazdān
Translation: the Mazda-worshiping, divine Ardašīr, King of Kings of the Iranians, whose image/brilliance is from the gods

Under Ōhrmazd I, the phrase *W 'nyr'n* "(King of Kings of the Iranians) and the non-Iranians" was added and the legend thus read *mazdēsn bay Ōhrmazd šāhān šāh Ērān ud Anērān kē čihr az yazdān*. This ideal form remained in use until the fifth century. Yazdgerd I added the title *l'mštly, rāmšahr*, "joy of the empire," before his name. Warahrān V followed him in this respect; on some rare drachms from Fars, the title *kirbakkar*, "beneficent," was employed (Fig. 43.2.6). Yazdgerd II placed the mythical royal title *kdy, kay*, "king," before his name, but the second part of the titulature (*šāhān šāh Ērān kē čihr az yazdān*) was mostly missing. Under Pērōz, only the two elements *kdy pylwcy, kay Pērōz*, "King Pērōz," are clearly legible. A large seal, however, proves that the traditional elements were still used, which is to say that coins do not necessarily provide us with the full official titulature. Walāxš was styled *hwkd*, "the good king," while Kawād I, up to his 15th regnal year, and Jāmāsp put only their names, without any title, on their coins, abbreviated *g'm* in the latter case because the small bust to the left did not leave enough space for a longer form. From regnal year 16 of Kawād I onward, the phrase *'pzwn, abzōn*, "may he increase," was added to the legends, and this remained in use until the beginning of the second reign of Xosrow I. After defeating Warahrān VI and reclaiming the throne, Xosrow added the ideogram *GDH*, for *xwarrah*, "royal splendor," in combination with the word *abzōt*, "he has increased." The canonical form on Late Sasanian and Arab-Sasanian drachms thus reads:

Transliteration: *hwslwb GDH'pzwty*
Transcription: *Khūsrō khwarrah abzōt*
Translation: Xosrow, he has increased the royal splendor

On rare special-type issues in gold and silver of Xosrow II, the ideogram *MLKAn MLKA*, *šāhān šāh*, "King of Kings," reappeared (Fig. 43.3.10–11). Apparently wishing to set themselves apart from Xosrow II, his immediate successors, Kawād II and Ardašīr III, departed from this practice: Kawād II's obverse legend reads *Kawād pērōz*, "Kawād the victorious," while Ardašīr III reverted to the form with *abzōn* used before Xosrow II's reign. All later kings and queens, however, followed Xosrow II's model, as did most Arab-Sasanian drachms. On some drachms of Xosrow II, at 4 o'clock on the obverse, the word *'pd/afīd*, "wonderful," was added. Its meaning is unclear. Since religious phrases like *bism Allah*, "In the name of God," appear in the same place on Arab-Sasanian coins, one may assume a religio-propagandistic meaning for *afīd* (Gariboldi 2003) as well. Most fourth- and fifth-century fractional silver and copper issues have no legends at all, but in their place display various symbols (Fig. 43.2.5).

From Ardašīr I until Warahrān V, the reverse legends provide the ruler's name and an expression for "fire"—the ideogram *NWRA* from Ardašīr I to Ardašīr II, and from Šābuhr III onward the Pahlavi word *ādur*, in both cases accompanied by the particle *ZY*, *ī*, "of," to denote the genitive case of the king's name. One half of the legend is placed at 3 o'clock, the other at 9 o'clock. The legend thus reads:

Transliteration: NWRA ZY or 'twly ZY wlhl'n
Transcription: *ādur-ī Wahrām*
Translation: the fire of Warahrān

Eastern issues, particularly those of the fourth century, often had anepigraphic reverses. Since the mint signature was often placed at 3 o'clock, beginning with the reign of Warahrān IV, the inscriptions were shortened, giving only the royal name at 9 o'clock. Other variants contain the word *'twly* or *l'st*, *rāst*, "just," as on the altar shafts. The concrete meaning of this is obscure, but in all probability it has to be understood in the context of royal propaganda. Placing the royal name at 9 o'clock became the rule when Warahrān V moved the mint signature to its now canonical place at 3 o'clock. Most intriguing is the word *nwky*, *nōk*, "new" at 3 o'clock, used instead of a mint indication on many issues of Yazdgerd II (Fig. 43.2.7). A monogram formed apparently by the letters M and P for *pylwcy MLKA*, *Pērōz šāh*, "king Pērōz," at 9 o'clock is attested only on some of this ruler's issues (Fig. 43.2.8). From Jāmāsp onward, the indication of the regnal year at 9 o'clock became canonical, thus the reverse legends are limited to administrative data, providing the place and date of issue. From Kawād I to Bōrānduxt special legends can be observed on rare gold and silver issues featuring special types.

Further reading

The major ongoing research project in the field of Sasanian numismatics is the *Sylloge Nummorum Sasanidarum* (*SNS*). The main series presents the holdings of the coin collections of the Cabinet des Médailles, Bibliothèque Nationale de France (Paris); the Bode Museum (Berlin); and the Münzkabinett of the Kunsthistorisches Museum (Vienna), as well as additional material, and is intended to offer a detailed numismatic overview of the coinage of each Sasanian king. So far the volumes on Ardašīr I and Šābuhr I (Alram and Gyselen 2003), Ōhrmazd I to Ōhrmazd II (Alram and Gyselen 2011), and Šābuhr II to Kawād I (Schindel 2004) have been published. Apart from these, two additional volumes have come out, presenting Sasanian coins from collections in Israel (Schindel 2009) and Uzbekistan (Baratova and Schindel 2012). Further volumes on collections in Tübingen and Syria, as well as an American private collection (Schaaf) are in preparation, as are the remaining volumes of the main Paris–Berlin–Vienna series. Another published collection is that of the Iran Bastan Museum in Tehran (Curtis et al. 2010). The Prague collection has been published on a CD (Novak and Militky 2000). An important private collection was published by Gyselen (2004). The only scientifically sound overview on Sasanian coinage in its entirety is Göbl (1971: an updated version of Göbl 1954 and 1962). Apart from the *SNS* volumes mentioned above, detailed studies of the coinage of single kings exist for Šābuhr II (Göbl 1984), Pērōz (Szaivert 1987), Kawād II (Malek 1995), Buran (Malek and Curtis 1998), and Yazdgerd III (Tyler-Smith 2000). Mochiri (1977) offers a large amount of material, even if some of his conclusions are to be treated with caution. The bibliographic survey by Malek (1993), though not absolutely complete, is useful for the period up to 1993; for the following years, the relevant chapters in the series entitled *Survey of Numismatic Research* which appears every six years in association with the International Numismatic Congress should be consulted.

References

Alram, M. 1986. *Nomina propria iranica in nummis. Materialgrundlagen zu den iranischen Personennamen auf antiken Münzen*. Vienna: Iranisches Personennamenbuch 4.
Alram, M., M. Blet-Lemarquand, and P. O. Skjærvø. 2007. Shapur, King of Kings of Iranians and Non-Iranians. In *Des Indo-Grecs aux Sassanides: Données pour l'histoire et la géographie historique*, ed. R. Gyselen, 11–40. Leuven: RO 17.
Alram, M., and R. Gyselen. 2003. *Sylloge nummorum sasanidarum Paris–Berlin–Wien*, vol. 1, *Ardashir I.–Shapur I*. Vienna: Verlag der Österreichischen Akademie der Wissenschaften.
Alram, M., and R. Gyselen. 2011. *Sylloge nummorum sasanidarum Paris–Berlin–Wien*, vol. 2, *Ohrmazd I.–Ohrmazd II*. Vienna: Verlag der Österreichischen Akademie der Wissenschaften.
Amini, A. 2006. *Sikkah'ha-yi Sasani*. Yazd: private publication.
Baratova, L., and N. Schindel. 2012. *Sylloge Nummorum Sasanidarum Usbekistan*. Vienna: Verlag der Österreichischen Akademie der Wissenschaften.

Curtis, V. S., M. E. Askari, E. Pendleton, R. Hodges, and A.-A. Safi. 2010. *A Sylloge of the Sasanian coins in the National Museum of Iran, Tehran (Muzeh Melli Iran)*, vol. 1, *Ardashir I – Hormizd IV*. London: Royal Numismatic Society Special Publication 47.

Gariboldi, A. 2003. *La monetazione sasanide nelle civiche raccolte numismatiche di Milano*. Milan: Civica biblioteca archeologica e numismatic.

Göbl, R. 1954. Aufbau der Münzprägung. In *Ein asiatischer Staat. Feudalismus unter den Sasaniden und ihren Nachbarn*, ed. F. Altheim and R. Stiehl, 51–128. Wiesbaden: Limes-Verlag.

———. 1962. *Die Münzen der Sasaniden im Königlichen Münzkabinett*. The Hague: Koninklijk Penningkabinet.

———. 1971. *Sasanian Numismatics*. Braunschweig: Klinkhart & Biermann.

———. 1973. *Der sāsānidische Siegelkanon*. Braunschweig: Handbücher der Mittelasiatischen Numismatik 4.

———. 1983. Supplementa Orientalia I. *LNV* 2: 97–112.

———. 1984. *System und Chronologie der Münzprägung des Kušānreiches*. Vienna: Veröffentlichungen der Numismatischen Kommission, Sonderband.

Gyselen, R. 1989. *La géographie administrative de l'empire Sassanide. Les témoignages sigillographiques*. Paris: RO 1.

———. 2000. Un dieu nimbé de flammes d'époque sassanide. *IrAnt* 35: 291–314.

———. 2002. *Nouveaux matériaux pour la géographie historique de l'empire Sassanide: Sceaux administratifs de la collection Ahmad Saeedi*. Paris: Cahiers de *StIr* 24.

———. 2004. New evidence for Sasanian numismatics: The collection of Ahmad Saeedi. In *Contributions à l'histoire et la géographie historique de l'Empire sassanide*, ed. R. Gyselen, 49–140. Bures-sur-Yvette: RO 16.

Malek, H. M. 1993. A survey of research on Sasanian numismatics. *NC* 1993: 227–69.

———. 1995. The coinage of the Sasanian King Kawad II (AD 628). *NC* 1995: 120–9.

Malek, H. M., and V. S. Curtis. 1998. History and coinage of the Sasanian Queen Buran. *NC* 1998: 113–29.

McCrindle, J. W. 1897. *The Christian topography of Cosmas, an Egyptian monk*. London: Hakluyt Society.

Mochiri, M. I. 1972. *Études de numismatique Iranienne sous les Sassanides*, vol. 1. Tehran: Bank Melli Iran Press.

———. 1977. *Études de numismatique Iranienne sous les Sassanides et Arabe-Sassanides*, vol. 2. Tehran: Bank Melli Iran Press.

Novak, V., and J. Militky. 2000. *Orientalia Regni Bohemiae: Corpus Sasanicus*. Prague: National Museum (CD-ROM).

Schindel, N. F. 2004. *Sylloge Nummorum Sasanidarum, Paris—Berlin—Wien*, vol. 3, *Shapur II—Kawad I/2 Regierung*. Vienna: Verlag der Österreichischen Akademie der Wissenschaften.

———. 2006. Khusro I. oder Khusro II.? *Mitteilungen der Österreichischen Numismatischen Gesellschaft* 46/1: 16–29.

———. 2009. *Sylloge Nummorum Sasanidarum Israel*. Vienna: Verlag der Österreichischen Akademie der Wissenschaften.

———. 2010. The 3rd century "Marw Shah" bronze coins reconsidered. In *Commutatio et Contentio. Studies in the Late Roman, Sasanian and Early Islamic Middle East in memory of Zeev Rubin*, ed. H. Börm and J. Wiesehöfer, 23–32. Düsseldorf: Wellem Verlag.

Szaivert, W. 1987. Die Münzprägung des Sāsānidenkönigs Pērōz. Versuch einer historischen Interpretation. *LNV* 3: 157–68.

Tyler-Smith, S. 2000. Coinage in the name of Yazdgerd III (AD 632–651) and the Arab Conquest of Iran. *NC* 160: 135–70.

CHAPTER 44

SASANIAN INTERACTIONS WITH ROME AND BYZANTIUM

PETER EDWELL

Introduction

The relationship between Sasanian Iran and Rome spanned four centuries and contributed in important ways to the destiny of each empire. The key elements in relations between the two powers were established by the beginning of the fourth century and owed much to the outcomes of military campaigns led by Šābuhr I and Galerius. The Sasanians were capable of mounting far-reaching and successful campaigns against Rome but retaining territory in the face of Roman power in the Near East was mostly an unrealistic proposition. Roman emperors in the third and fourth centuries were unable to prosecute successful invasions of Iran as their second-century predecessors had against the Parthians, but they were able to mount a spirited defense of their holdings in Cappadocia, Armenia, and northern Mesopotamia. Religion, a new element injected into the relationship between Iran and Rome, came to play an increasingly important role in the relationship between the two powers as the centuries unfolded, and there were times when it played a role in cooperation between Sasanian and Roman rulers. From the fourth century onward, Sasanians and Romans accepted the existence of each other and there were times when they took action jointly against differently constituted common threats, perhaps preferring a known and predictable enemy to one which was not. As a general rule conflict, mistrust, and competition ruled the day until the extinction of the Sasanians in the seventh century and the transformation of what was left of the Roman Empire into a markedly different entity.

Sources

The extraordinary inroads of the Sasanians into the Roman eastern provinces in the third century were celebrated in Iran on rock reliefs and in epigraphy by Šābuhr I. This followed a tradition revived by his father Ardašīr I in probable emulation of the Achaemenid Persians. Rock reliefs commissioned by Šābuhr I depicting victory over Rome complemented the victorious claims on his inscription at Naqš-e Rustam (ŠKZ), but for the most part they were not repeated by later Sasanian rulers. Sasanian coins provide virtually no evidence for conflict with Rome (Gariboldi 2010: 20) with the notable exception of a gold double dinar of Šābuhr I depicting and naming Philip and the Romans in tribute and servitude (Alram 2008: 23–4). The rock reliefs and epigraphy shed light on interactions between the two powers for a period in which contemporary and later Roman literary sources are paltry. Consequently, the Iranian sources afford the Sasanian perspective a greater voice on the mid-third century conflict with Rome (see Edwell 2010).

The limited nature of Roman literary sources on conflict with the Sasanians in the third century is partly explained by a general lack of Greco-Roman historical writing in the third century after the conclusion of Dio *c*.230. Only Dexippus is known to have written in any contemporary detail about Rome's wars with Šābuhr but none of his work on this topic survives. Greek and Latin works of the fourth century relied on Dexippus extensively, however, most of these were epitomes. The Armenian historians Agathangelos, Moses Khorenatsi and Faustus Buzandatsi (*Epic Histories*) also provide information on conflict between Rome and Sasanian Iran in the third and fourth centuries, however, their chronology is questionable as is their tendency to exaggerate Armenia's role in the conflicts.

A lost Sasanian tradition, especially for events in the sixth and seventh centuries, survives in a number of Persian and Arabic works including the *Šāhnāme* of Firdausī (977–1019), the *History* of Ṭabarī (839–923) and the *Chronicle of Seʿert* (*c*.850–1050). These works, and a number of others, draw on the *Khwadāy-nāmag* (*Book of Kings*) thought to have been written during the reign of the last Sasanian King, Yazdgerd III. This work focused on historical events during the entire Sasanian dynasty (Yarshater 1983: 360). The most important of these is the universal history of Ṭabarī which focused especially on conflict between the Sasanians and Rome in its coverage of Iranian history under the Sasanians. Ṭabarī's chronology is confused in places, and the version of the *Khwadāy-nāmag* that reached him is thought to have contained distortion and invention (Howard-Johnston 1995: 170–2). While Ṭabarī provides important insights into late Sasanian perspectives on the history of conflict with Rome, the Roman sources often take precedence due to problems with Ṭabarī's sources and his tendency to focus on legendary tales. Similar criticisms, however, can be leveled at the Roman sources.

The problems with the Iranian sources after the third century result in considerable reliance on the Roman literary sources to illuminate conflict and interaction from the fourth to the seventh centuries. The significance of Ammianus Marcellinus on the conflicts of the mid-fourth century is difficult to overstate, while the *Chronicle of Pseudo-Joshua the Stylite*, covering events in Mesopotamia at the turn of the sixth century, provides invaluable insights into the war between Kawād and Anastasius (Trombley and Watt 2000). Procopius of Caesarea, John Malalas, and Evagrius provide considerable detail on events in the sixth century, especially the wars between Xosrow I and Justinian. For the momentous conflict between Xosrow II and the Byzantine Empire in the first three decades of the seventh century, the *Chronicon Paschale* (*c*.630) together with the *Chronicle of Theophanes* (*c*.815) provide important detail, as does the Armenian historian Pseudo-Sebeos, who wrote a work titled *The History of Xosrow* around 650.

Ardašīr's wars with Rome

The Sasanian overthrow of the Parthians around 224 AD was a watershed for relations between Rome and Iran. However, the event became significant for Rome only once the Sasanians took a more bellicose approach to Roman encroachment on Mesopotamia and the Tigris. Within a few years of defeating the Parthians, Ardašīr attacked Hatra, Roman Mesopotamia, and Armenia (Dio 80.3.2–3, 4.1–2; Herodian 6.2.1–2; Agathangelos 1.18–23) which signaled the priority of halting of Roman expansion further east. The extent to which Ardašīr sought to go further and regain territory lost by the Achaemenids to Alexander the Great centuries earlier has long been a source of debate. Dio (80.4.1) and Herodian (6.2.1–2) claimed Ardašīr sought to regain territory once under Achaemenid rule all the way to the coast of Asia Minor. A similar claim made by Šābuhr II (Ammianus 17.5.5; Zonaras 13.98.25–31) over a century later suggests this was an ongoing Sasanian aim. Some argue that such claims were placed in Ardašīr's mouth by Greek and Latin writers drawing on their own knowledge of the past and that much of this knowledge in the Iranian world was lost in the Parthian period (Yarshater 1971: 517–31; Rubin 1998: 179–80; Potter 1990: 371–6). The emphasis in the *Shāh-nāma*, for example, is on the semimythical Kayanids of eastern Iran as dynastic precursors of Sasanian kingship rather than the Achaemenids (Davis 1996), and there is no indication of dynastic links to the Achaemenids on the ŠKZ. Others argue that the development of Naqš-e Rustam near Persepolis as a site of Sasanian dynastic significance demonstrates attempts to link to the Achaemenid past and that reports in Dio, Herodian, and Ammianus are reflected in Sasanian historical traditions drawn upon by Ṭabarī (I, 813–14) (Fowden 1993: 28–36; Dignas and Winter 2007: 53–62; see Edwell 2008: 156–60 and Canepa 2009: 49–51, whose balanced position on this question is the most sensible).

Severus Alexander responded to Ardašīr's attacks by invading Sasanian Iran in 231/2. The war was a failure in the Greek tradition following Herodian (6.5.1–6.6.6) but a victory in the Latin tradition probably following the *Kaisergeschichte* (Edwell 2008: 160–67). Whatever the outcome, the situation remained quiet until 237/8 when Ardašīr attacked Roman Mesopotamia and Syria. A graffito of April 239 from Dura Europos indicates a Sasanian attack on the city, in which the tribune of *Cohors XX Palmyrenorum* probably died (Baur et al. 1933: 112–14; Welles 1941; Edwell 2008: 257). Syncellus (*Chronographia*, p. 443, 3–9) claimed that Nisibis and Carrhae were captured by Ardašīr during the reign of Maximinus Thrax (235–238) and this is supported by numismatic evidence (Kettenhofen 1982: 31). The successful Sasanian siege of Hatra in 240, for which there is archaeological evidence, was part of this overall offensive, as Hatra received a Roman military garrison by 235 on the basis of epigraphic evidence (Gawlikowski 1994 for archaeological evidence; Oates 1955 for the inscriptions). The remains of a Roman ballista at the base of a tower at Hatra further indicate that the city had Roman military assistance at the time of the siege (Baatz 1978). The Roman fortifications of Kifrin and Bijan on the lower Euphrates, together with Ain Sinu/Zagurae, 30 km east of Singara, may have been captured by the Sasanians in this period, however, the archaeological and numismatic evidence is problematic (Edwell 2008: 175–8).

Gordian III responded with a large army, which departed Antioch in spring 243. The army advanced to Carrhae via Zeugma before winning a battle against Ardašīr's son and coregent, Šābuhr I, at Rhesaina (Ammianus 23.5.17; Kettenhofen 1982: 23–5). From this point Šābuhr I's trilingual inscription on the Ka'ba-ye Zardošt (ŠKZ) at Naqš-e Rustam is of seminal importance to our knowledge of Šābuhr's momentous conflicts with the Romans (Huyse 1999; Edwell 2010: 166–71). The rock reliefs at Naqš-e Rustam, Bishapur, and Darabgerd celebrating Šābuhr's victories over the Romans are also important. In 244, the ŠKZ (Gk. ll. 6–9) claims Gordian was killed in battle on the lower Euphrates at Meshike, which was subsequently renamed Pērōz-Šābuhr (Victorious is Šābuhr). The Roman army had probably made its way down the Khabur and Euphrates Rivers after the victory at Rhesaina. In 363 Ammianus Marcellinus (23.5.7) saw Gordian's tomb at Zaitha on the Euphrates, approximately 30 km upstream from Dura Europos. Numerous attempts have been made to locate it but none have succeeded (Geyer and Monchambert 2003: 156–61). Gordian is shown trampled under Šābuhr's horse in the rock reliefs at Bishapur and Darabgerd, which also depict Gordian's successor Philip in prostration before the Sasanian king, together with Valerian who was captured sixteen years later (Herrmann and Howell 1980, 1981). There is debate regarding the Darabgerd relief, as the king's crown is that of Ardašīr rather than Šābuhr. However, the identities of the Roman emperors are secure (Huff 2008: 40–1). The death of Gordian III, in battle according to the ŠKZ or due to Philip's treachery in the Greek and Latin sources, left his successor in a precarious position. The ŠKZ details financial obligations and alludes to a clause prohibiting Roman involvement in the affairs of Armenia as the concessions extracted from Philip (ŠKZ Gk. ll. 8–9; Edwell 2008: 173–81). The newly published gold double dinar of Šābuhr I also depicts and names *firipōs kēzar ud hrōmāy pad bāz ud bandag<īh> estād hēn*, "Philippos Caesar and the Romans in tribute and servitude" (Alram 2008: 23).

Roman interference in Armenia was the pretext for a series of campaigns by Šābuhr deep into Roman territory in the 250s (ŠKZ Gk. l. 10). The first began in 252/3 and saw the capture of thirty-seven cities, including Antioch, and the destruction of a large

Roman army at Barbalissos (ŠKZ Gk. ll. 11 and 19). The campaign was actually a series of campaigns but they are differentiated on the ŠKZ from the campaign of 259/60 in which Valerian was captured. The order of the captured cities listed in the two campaigns allows partial reconstruction of the invasion route and Šābuhr's overall strategy (see especially Kettenhofen 1982; also Edwell 2008: 186–98). The first campaign was directed up the Euphrates and at the important cities of Syria, whereas the second was directed further north at Mesopotamia, Osrhoene, and into Cilicia.

The second campaign is best known for the capture of Valerian in AD 260 (ŠKZ Gk. ll. 24–5). He was captured along with the Praetorian Prefect, senators, and army commanders following the defeat of an army of 70,000 men between Edessa and Carrhae. The event was celebrated on rock reliefs at Bishapur, Naqš-e Rustam, and Darabgerd, and on the Paris Cameo (Ghirshman 1962: fig. 195). It was recounted vividly in Roman texts for centuries to come (see especially Lactantius, *De mortibus persecutorum* 5) and Valerian's son, Gallienus, was forced to rely on Odenathus of Palmyra to finally halt Šābuhr's invasions around 262 (*Oracula Sibyllina* XIII.163–70; Zosimus I.39.1–2).

THE IMPACT OF ŠĀBUHR I'S INVASIONS

Šābuhr's invasions did not result in the retention of territory but there were deportations of Roman captives to purpose-built cities throughout Sasanian Iran. The ŠKZ (ll. 34–5) reports that Roman captives were settled in Persis, Parthia, Susiana, and Āsōristān, while the ninth-century Arabic *Chronicle of Seʿert* (pp. 220–1) claimed Šābuhr settled captives in Šād–Šābuhr in Meshan, Bishapur in Fārs, and Okbara on the Tigris. According to Ṭabarī (I, 826–7), Šābuhr rebuilt Gundēshāpūr for the Roman captives and renamed it Wēh Antiōk Šābuhr. Ṭabarī (I, 827) also claimed that Valerian worked on the construction of a dam at Shushtar and the ruins of the Band-e Kaisar Bridge, still visible at Shushtar, bear Roman architectural attributes. Mosaics unearthed at Šābuhr's palace at Bishapur in the 1930s display Syrian styles and were probably executed by Roman captives (Ghirshman 1956).

One of the cities captured by Šābuhr in the campaign beginning in 252/3 was Dura Europos on the middle Euphrates and excavations have returned extraordinary evidence for the Sasanian siege. Dura is listed on the ŠKZ (Gk. l. 17) considerably after Anatha and Antioch, which were captured in 252/3, and numismatic evidence dating the siege to 256/7 confirms this. It is likely, however, that, despite being listed only once on the ŠKZ, Dura was captured twice (James 2004: 22–5). Overall, there is good evidence to suggest that Dura was captured briefly in 252/3 before reoccupation by Roman troops followed by a second and final Sasanian siege in 256/7.

The archaeological evidence for the final siege of Dura Europos reveals that the desert wall of the city was surrounded by embankments by the Roman defenders to limit the effectiveness of siege machinery and tunneling. James (2011) provides a comprehensive and up-to-date analysis of the siege and earlier interpretations of the evidence for it. The buildings adjacent to the rampart pathway inside the city were reclaimed and partially filled with earth during the construction of the internal embankment. This preserved portions of temples, a synagogue, a Christian house, and numerous other buildings. The Sasanian besiegers dug a tunnel directed at tower 19 and hollowed out a gallery under the southwest corner of the tower and part of the adjacent curtain wall. The Roman defenders dug a countermine to gain control of the tunnels but the Sasanian attackers possibly used a brazier emitting noxious fumes which overcame the Roman counterminers (James 2011: 93–7). The Sasanians piled up the bodies of the suffocated Romans close to the entrance of the countermine before firing the countermine, causing its collapse. Some of these bodies contained coins from the Antioch mint dating to 256/7. These are the latest coins found at Dura and represent a *terminus post quem* for its final capture (Bellinger 1949; Carson 1968). The partially charred body of a soldier, whose helmet and jade sword pommel lay close by, was found near the Roman body pile. Based on the style of the helmet and the Central Asian origin of the jade sword pommel, the body has been identified as that of a Persian soldier (James 2004: 104–6, 151; James 1986a). The gallery underneath tower 19 and the curtain was fired but the embankments stopped them from toppling outwards.

An attack was also directed at the southwest corner of the city (tower 14) where the foundations of the tower were hollowed out to form a gallery supported by timber props which were then fired. The tower was disabled as a platform from which to fire projectiles at the besieging Sasanians allowing the construction of a siege ramp adjacent to tower 15. The ramp included paving to allow access for siege machines. Tunnels were dug under the ramp to allow access to the city and a Roman countermine aimed at taking control of the tunnels and destabilizing the siege ramp eventually failed. It is likely that the attack on this part of the city was one of the ways the Sasanians gained entry to Dura. The remarkable evidence for the siege of Dura is a reminder of the sophisticated techniques employed by the forces of Šābuhr I and of the fact that considerable resources were invested in capturing the dozens of Roman cities named in the ŠKZ.

Šābuhr's invasions did not result in the acquisition of territory but they proved the military capability of the Sasanians and provided skilled manpower in the form of thousands of captives. The invasions had long-term ramifications for the future relationship between Sasanian Iran and Rome and the ŠKZ is central to understanding this. Šābuhr claimed in the first line of the inscription that he was "the Mazda-worshiping divine Šābuhr, King of Kings of Ērān ud Anērān." Anērān is generally interpreted as the lands conquered by Šābuhr outside of Iran including Roman territory and suggests a claim of universal sovereignty by the Sasanian king (Canepa 2009: 54–5). At the same time, the term Anērān suggests a concession on Šābuhr's part to the impossibility of incorporating this territory into Iran and that advertising Roman emperors in tribute, servitude, and captivity implies an acceptance of the Roman Empire, by far the most detailed component of Anērān on the inscription, as a subordinate but insoluble foe.

The death of Šābuhr around 272 was followed by instability in Sasanian leadership but conflict and suspicion between the two powers remained. Aurelius Victor (38.2–4) claimed Carus' invasion of Iran in 283 was a response to regular threats to Mesopotamia by the Sasanians. He captured Ctesiphon before a bolt of lightning brought the venture to an abrupt end. In 296, Narseh II defeated Galerius in northern Mesopotamia (Eutropius IX.24.5) but in the following year the *Shāhanshāh* was overwhelmingly defeated by Galerius in Armenia. The treaty imposed in 298 saw Roman power in Armenia extended further east, the king of Iberia (modern Georgia) became a Roman client and all commercial transactions between Roman and Persian merchants were to be conducted in Nisibis (Petrus Patricius, Frag. 14, FGrH 4.189). The treaty also placed the *Regiones Transtigritanae* under formal Roman control, extending Roman power to the eastern banks of the upper Tigris. This represented the high point of Roman power on the eastern frontier during the Sasanian period. Galerius celebrated the victory on an arch in Thessaloniki, which is an important visual source for his campaign (Leadbetter 2009: 89–96; Canepa 2009: 83–99). Rhetorical messages produced by both powers in celebration of victory over the other in the third century contained implicit messages of mutual acceptance of the opposing power's existence. In an important recent study, Canepa (2009: 34ff.) emphasizes the development between the two powers of a "shared visual, ritual and discursive language of legitimacy to conceptualise their co-existence" and how this was negotiated in the momentous conflicts of the third century (Canepa 2009: 122ff.).

Šābuhr II and Rome

Conflict between Sasanian Iran and Rome was at a relatively low level until the middle of the fourth century, although interaction and communication between the two powers increased during this period. In Rome a long series of civil wars following the abdication of Diocletian in 305 was not finally resolved until Constantine emerged as sole ruler twenty years later. Political instability in Iran was reflected in the defection of Šābuhr II's brother Ōhrmazd to the Romans about 324 (Zosimus 2.27.1–4). With the emergence of Šābuhr II as a strong ruler in adulthood about 330 and Constantine's establishment of sole power a few years earlier, greater conflict between the two appeared inevitable. Constantine was in the organizational stages of a campaign against Iran when he died in May 337 (Eusebius *Vita Constantini*, 4.46), and Šābuhr had earlier harassed the Roman *limes* in Arabia.

Constantine's reign is often marked by religious factors as an element in the relationship between Sasanian Iran and Rome, but there is evidence to indicate that this was emerging earlier. During Šābuhr I's invasions in the 250s, both Mani and Kerdīr, the Zoroastrian *Mobadān Mobad*, accompanied the *Shāhanshāh* (Alexander Lycopolitanus *contra Manichaei opiniones disputatio* 2; KKZ, ll. 11–13). The KKZ, an inscription put up by Kerdīr about 280, names Zoroastrian communities in Syria, Cilicia, Cappadocia, and Pontus, which he protected from harm and brought under his authority (see especially Boyce and Grenet 1991). Some of the Roman captives taken to Iran were Christians and according to the *Chronicle of Se'ert* (pp. 221–2) they built churches and monasteries in Gundēshāpūr and Rev-Ardašīr. Candida, daughter of captive Roman Christians, became the favorite wife of Bahrām II but suffered martyrdom along with Mani during the period when Kerdīr's power reached its zenith (Brock 1978; Ṭabarī I, 834; Daryaee 2009: 75–81). Suspicions about the loyalty of subjects on the basis of religion emerged during the reign of Diocletian, who issued an edict against the Manichaeans in 302 because they represented a covert threat due to the Persian origins of the religion (*Collatio Mosaicarum* 15.3).

In 324, Constantine wrote to Šābuhr II in his own hand making strong overtures on behalf of Christian populations in Iran. This appears to have increased Šābuhr's already wary attitude and sparked a series of persecutions (Eusebius, *Vita Con.* 4.8–13; Aphrahat, *Demonstrationes* 5. 1.24, 25). The hope in a Roman victory in Constantine's impending Persian war expressed by Aphrahat, Bishop of Mar Mattai on the Tigris, indicates that the *Shāhanshāh* had something to worry about (Barnes 1985). Soon after Constantine's death in May 337, Šābuhr besieged Nisibis and strengthened his hand in Armenia (Theodoret, *Historia Ecclesiastica* II 30.1–14). The new Augustus in the east, Constantius II, was in a difficult position, with only one-third of the empire's military forces and a Persian enemy primed for war. Even after he became sole ruler in 353, however, there is no evidence he sought to prosecute the war. Constantius was heavily criticized for this defensive approach in antiquity but his policy was part of conceding the reality of ongoing Sasanian power in practical, military terms. This stood in stark contrast to his successor Julian's outmoded approach, which ended in disaster.

In 358, having recently dealt with problems on his eastern frontier, Šābuhr increased the rhetoric of war, writing to Constantius demanding the return of territory once in Achaemenid possession (Ammianus 17.5.5). His claims rebuffed, Šābuhr mounted an invasion of Roman Mesopotamia in 359 which is covered in detail by Ammianus who was a participant in the conflict. Šābuhr's forces bypassed Nisibis and attempted a surprise advance on Syria but were diverted north to Amida when the Euphrates proved impossible to cross due to serious flooding. The siege of Amida took ten weeks and the Sasanians were so worn down by it that they could advance no further west. Ammianus' narrative of the siege of Amida bears comparison with the graphic archaeological evidence for the Sasanian siege of Dura Europos a century earlier (Ammianus 19.1.1ff.). In 360, the Sasanians returned to Mesopotamia and captured the legionary fortresses of Singara and Bezabde (Ammianus 20.6.1–7.18). Throughout the campaign of 359/60 they also captured numerous smaller Roman fortifications. Only Bezabde was retained by the Persians and the strong defensive system on the upper Tigris, which Constantius II's defensive strategy was based on, succeeded in halting the Sasanian advance further west.

The invasion of Iran by Julian in 363 emulated those of the second-century emperors who invaded the Parthian Empire and demonstrated that this approach was now badly outmoded as the Sasanians were much stronger in military and organizational terms. Unlike any other Roman invasion of Iran, literary evidence for Julian's invasion is considerable and includes an eyewitness description by Ammianus, and Zosimus who used the now-lost history of Eunapius and the memoirs of Julian's physician, Oribasius. The details of the campaign have been fleshed out in modern scholarship many times (see, e.g., Matthews 1989:

140–61; Barnes 1998: 162–5) but some points are worth emphasizing. Julian was accompanied by the fugitive Sasanian prince Ōhrmazd, who had been a favourite of Constantius II, accompanying him on his only state visit to Rome in 357 (Ammianus 16.10.16). Ōhrmazd was still recognized by inhabitants of Persian fortifications on the lower Euphrates as Julian's army progressed toward Ctesiphon. There were also reminders of earlier conflicts including the tomb of Gordian III at Zaitha (Ammianus 23.5.7; Zosimus 3.14) and a tribunal of the emperor Trajan at Ozogardana (Ammianus 24.2.3). At Anatha, an old captive Roman soldier was discovered, who had been there since the days of Galerius' wars with Narseh II in 296/7 (Ammianus 24.1.10), and the ruins of a city destroyed by Carus during his invasion in 283 were encountered near Ctesiphon (Ammianus 24.5.3).

The disastrous decision taken by Julian to burn the fleet once the army crossed the Tigris just south of Ctesiphon, together with the failure of a second force to arrive under the command of Procopius, left Julian in a precarious position. The extent of the disaster was underlined by his death on June 26, 363 (Ammianus 25.3.23). Julian's hapless successor Jovian had little choice but to strike a humiliating peace, which gave Persia the Mesopotamian metropolis of Nisibis and saw the permanent relegation of Roman influence in Armenia to its western portions (Greatrex and Lieu 2002: 1–9; Dignas and Winter 2007: 131–4). Šābuhr's victory over Julian brought the conflict with Rome since the late reign of Constantine to a close, and either Šābuhr II or Ardašīr II commissioned a rock relief at Taq-e Bustan showing the dead Roman emperor lying at his feet (Herrmann and Curtis 2002; Canepa 2009: 109–110).

Conflict between the Sasanians and Rome immediately after 363 was confined to Armenia. The western portion had increasingly looked to the Roman world since the early fourth century due to the influence of Christianity, and by the middle of the fourth century it had become tradition for the Armenian Catholicos to be invested at Caesarea in Cappadocia (Baynes 1955). In the eastern portion of Armenia Zoroastrianism remained more dominant and this part of Armenia looked to Sasanian Iran. The accession of Šābuhr III in 383 marked the beginning of a period of détente between the two powers, and in 387, a deal was struck to partition Armenia between Rome and Iran (*Epic Histories* 6.1; Chaumont 1986).

After Šābuhr II: Cooperation and détente?

The end of the reign of Šābuhr II, the settlement in Armenia, and the return of much of northern Mesopotamia to Sasanian control removed significant elements in the conflict between Sasanian Iran and Rome. Conflict and competition over the previous 150 years had effectively negotiated recognized territorial limits of each other's power. There is also evidence for increasing direct contact between the Sasanian and Roman courts, which Canepa emphasizes resulted in each court orienting itself more to the other from the fifth century onward (Canepa 2009: 127–30). In the fifth century there were moments that suggested even an amicable relationship between the two. This was partly due to an overall reduction in persecution of Christians by the Sasanians. According to Socrates of Constantinople (*Historia Ecclesiastica* 7.8.1–20), Yazdgerd I favorably received Marutha, the Bishop of Silvan in Roman Armenia, and was so impressed by him that he almost became a Christian. Yazdgerd's favorable disposition toward the Christians allowed the first synod of the Persian church to be held in Ctesiphon in 410 (Socrates, *Hist. Eccles.* 8.7.9; Asmussen 1983: 940).

Perhaps as a result of the more favorable treatment of Christians in Iran, Arcadius approached Yazdgerd to help ensure the succession of his young son Theodosius. The report is found only in Procopius (*De Bello Persico* 1.2.6–10) and even in antiquity it was doubted by Agathias (4.26.3–7), who questioned its omission from more contemporary accounts. Yazdgerd agreed to Arcadius' request and wrote to the senate in Constantinople indicating so. By the end of Yazdgerd's reign, however, the situation had deteriorated as the Zoroastrian clergy and sections of the Iranian nobility opposed the king's favorable disposition toward the Christians and the Romans. A newly powerful *Mobadān Mobad*, Mihr Narseh, persecuted Christians once again, and on Yazdgerd's death in 420, his son Warahrān V came to power with a distinctly different attitude to Christians and Romans (Theodoret, *Hist. Eccles.* 5.39.1–6). War broke out but was quickly concluded with diplomacy, and persecution of Christians came to an end (Procopius, *Bello Pers.* 1.2.11–15; Socrates, *Hist. Eccles.* 8.20).

Some important developments in the fifth century contributed to less conflict between Iran and Rome than earlier or later centuries. First, the Christian church in Persia, which often looked to the church in the Roman Empire for theological inspiration, adopted the position of Nestorius on the nature of Christ. In the Roman Empire, Nestorius' position was condemned at the Councils of Ephesus (431) and Chalcedon (451) and at a popular level was mostly rejected in favor of Monophysitism, which was itself condemned but increasingly supported in the cities and towns of Syria. Monophysitism was eventually embraced by Anastasius who came to power in 491. The final rejection of Nestorianism in the Roman church was reflected in the closure in 489 of its last bastion, the School of the Persians at Edessa, where the doctrines of Nestorius were still taught (Brock 1994). Monophysitism also gained a following in Persia but Nestorianism was formally endorsed at a council in 486 (Brock 1992). The dominant Nestorians in Iran attempted to expose their weaker Monophysite opponents as supporters of Rome due to the adoption of the Monophysite position by Anastasius and at Kawād's direction they were persecuted (John of Ephesus, *Lives*, 17.142). The recognized church in Persia, however, had formally broken away from the Roman church due to its adoption of Nestorianism and this reduced the concern of Iranian rulers that the loyalty of the bulk of their Christian subjects may be suspect.

The Sasanians also faced the growing threat of the Hephthalites on their eastern frontier and fought many battles against them which were not always successful (Procopius, *Bello Pers.* 13.1–5). The low points came in 469 when Kawād, son of Pērōz and his ultimate successor, was taken captive by the Hephthalites and in 484 Pērōz was killed fighting against them (*Pseudo-Joshua the Stylite*, 11; Dignas and Winter 2007: 97-8). During the same period the Romans faced serious threats from the Goths, Huns, and Vandals, which saw the loss of the western provinces, represented figuratively in the abdication of the last Western emperor, Romulus Augustulus, in 476. Also of importance was an agreement by the Romans to contribute funds to assist the Sasanians in defending the Caucasus passes. This was aimed at stopping tribal groups, especially the Huns, entering the territory of both empires (Greatrex and Lieu 2002: 56-9). On a number of occasions—in 421, 441, and especially on the death of Pērōz in 484—these funds were withheld, leading to friction (Dignas and Winter 2007: 188-95; *Pseudo-Joshua the Stylite*, 18).

INCREASED CONFLICT UNDER KAWĀD AND XOSROW I

After the death of Pērōz a serious struggle emerged in Iran between the dynasty and the increasingly powerful nobility. Kawād I, who came to power in 488, embraced a religio-political movement known as Mazdakism and the nobility and Zoroastrian clergy reacted violently against the move, deposing him in 497 (Daryaee 2009: 26-8). Kawād fled to the Hephthalites who supported his return in 499 when he regained the throne and ruled until 531. An important element of Kawād's restoration of Sasanian dynastic power was the subordination of Rome, Iran's legitimate western rival. A dispute in 502 over financial and territorial claims saw Kawād invade Roman Mesopotamia. Amida was captured in 503, and the Sasanians were in the ascendancy until 506, when the Hephthalites again became a problem forcing Kawād to strike a truce with Anastasius (*Pseudo-Joshua the Stylite* 49-101; Procopius, *Bello Pers.* 1.9.1-25; Greatrex and Lieu 2002: 62-77).

Anastasius took advantage of a period of peace to strengthen the frontier in Armenia and Mesopotamia, represented most starkly in the construction of a fortress at Dara only 28 stades from the agreed border. There were also disputes over Iberia and Lazika on the southeastern shores of the Black Sea, and in 525 Justin I refused a request from Kawād to adopt his son Xosrow and ensure his succession (Procopius, *Bello Pers.* 1.11.23-30). These issues led to open conflict in 526 resulting in battles and sieges along the middle Euphrates and in Armenia over the next five years. During this period Justinian became emperor and Xosrow I succeeded to power in Iran. In 529, the closure of the Academy at Athens by Justinian resulted in six philosophers seeking refuge in Ctesiphon, where Xosrow welcomed them with open arms (Malalas 451.16-18). In 532, the "eternal peace" was struck which lasted only eight years but gave Justinian time to reconquer much of the West (Procopius, *Bello Pers.* 1.26.2).

The reigns of Justinian and Xosrow witnessed the apogee of diplomatic exchange between the two courts and the military confrontations during their reigns demonstrated clearly the well-entrenched notion of competition for universal sovereignty (Canepa 2009: 127ff.). In 540, Xosrow launched an attack whose crowning achievement was the capture of Antioch. In similar fashion to its capture in 252/3, large numbers of captives were taken from the city back to Iran (Procopius, *Bello Pers.* 2.10.4–9; 14.1–4; Ṭabarī I, 898). Jacob of Edessa (Brooks 1905–7: 300–301 [text], 320–21 [trans.]) referred to deportations from other Syrian cities including Sura, Beroea, Apamea, and Callinicum. The captives were taken to Wēh Antīōk Xosrow/Rūmagān, a purpose-built city not far from Ctesiphon. It is possible that parts of a circumvallation wall associated with the city still exist (Huff 1987: 336). Ṭabarī (I, 898, 959–60) claimed that the city replicated Antioch in its layout and urban features and it is possible that the partially surviving palace at Ctesiphon constructed by Xosrow I was designed to celebrate the Sasanian capture of Antioch (Kröger 1993). In the ninth century, the Arabic poet al-Buhturi (821–897) referred to a mosaic still visible at the palace which depicted Xosrow's capture of Antioch, and in the twelfth century, Ibn Balkhi's *Fārsnāma* (97) referred to Xosrow's placement of three chairs adjacent to his own throne in the palace's reception hall. Each chair represented the kings of China, Rome, and the Khazars. The obvious rhetorical inference is that all three kings were subordinate but it also implies a concession to the ongoing existence of Rome and the other powers. This was a visual representation of *Ērān ud Anērān* first conceptualized in Šābuhr I's ŠKZ inscription almost three centuries earlier.

Despite attempts at a truce (Procopius, *Bello Pers.* 2.28.7–11), conflict became an annual event over the following two decades and included a Sasanian siege of Edessa in 544 and serious losses for the Persians in Lazika in the 550s. In similar fashion to the defection of Ōhrmazd to Constantine, a Persian prince named Kawād defected to Justinian in 543 (Procopius, *Bello Pers.* 1.23.23–4). Neither side scored lasting victories and in 562 a peace agreement was concluded, which brought the conflict to a formal end (Greatrex and Lieu 2002: 115–34; Dignas and Winter 2007: 138–48). Only ten years later war broke out again over an alliance between Justin II and the new eastern enemy of the Sasanians, the Western Turks (Dignas and Winter 2007: 109–15). The irritant on the Byzantine side was Sasanian expansion into the Arabian Peninsula as far as Yemen. This war lasted until 591 and saw the Sasanians capture Dara and prosecute invasions into Syria (Greatrex and Lieu 2002: 151–75).

Xosrow II's conflicts with Rome and the end of the Sasanian dynasty

Internal turmoil toward the end of Ōhrmazd IV's reign resulted in profound changes in the relationship between Sasanian Iran and Rome/Byzantium. Ōhrmazd's general, Warahrān Čōbīn, suffered a humiliating defeat against the Byzantines in 590 and was removed by the king (Theophylact Simocatta 3.8.1). Warahrān rebelled with the support of large sections of the army and Ōhrmazd was overthrown. His son Xosrow II was backed by some sections of the nobility but Warahrān became king soon after. Both Warahrān and Xosrow appealed to the emperor Maurice for support, offering substantial territorial and financial inducements. Maurice supported Xosrow and sent an army to assist him (Dignas and Winter 2007: 43). Xosrow defeated Warahrān in 591 at Ganzak and established a peace treaty with Byzantium soon after (Theophylact Simocatta 5.II-2). Xosrow sent golden crosses to the sanctuary of St. Sergius at Resafe/ Sergiopolis in Syria in thanks to the martyr for his elevation to the Iranian throne (Evagrius, *Historia Ecclesiastica* 6.21). Theophylact provides interesting detail on the phenomenon of Byzantine and Persian troops fighting side by side, while the *Strategikon* of Maurice (11.1) provides a Byzantine perspective on the composition and tactics of the late Sasanian army.

The overthrow of Maurice by Phocas in 602 saw Xosrow intervene to bring down the usurper on behalf of Maurice's son, Theodosius (Ṭabarī I, 1002; Theophylact Simocatta 8.15.2-7). Xosrow's invasions over the next seventeen years saw most of the Byzantine Empire come under Persian authority (see Greatrex and Lieu 2002: 182-97). By 610, the year of Phocas' death, Xosrow's armies were in full control of Mesopotamia, Armenia, and Cappadocia together with large parts of Asia Minor. Phocas' successor, Heraclius, sought a settlement with Xosrow but the king was in such a strong position that he continued the war. In 611, Sasanian troops marched into northern Syria and captured Antioch and in 613 took Damascus and Jerusalem. In 615, the Sasanians occupied Chalcedon, placing Constantinople itself under threat. The senate in Constantinople wrote to Xosrow in desperation requesting him to recognize Heraclius as his adopted son (*Chronicon Paschale* a. 615) but Xosrow refused the request and continued to threaten the Byzantine capital. From 616 to 619 Xosrow's forces attacked Egypt and Alexandria fell in 619. Xosrow's monumental rock relief and grotto at Taq-e Bustan is thought to have been commissioned as a result of these successes, although there are no direct references to victories over Heraclius on either (Herrmann 1978: 131-4).

Heraclius made a last desperate attempt to regain the lost territories, setting out in 622 to confront Xosrow. In 623/4 Heraclius attacked Media from Armenia while the Iranian general Šahrwarāz scored further victories in Asia Minor (Theophanes, *Chron.* A.M. 6114 [307.19-308.25]). Heraclius met with some success in Media but in 626, Šahrwarāz advanced to Chalcedon while the Avars advanced on Constantinople from the north. The city was surrounded, but a Byzantine victory against the Avars saw the Iranian attack fall apart (Theophanes, *Chron.* A.M. 6116 [312.19-314.23]). Meanwhile Heraclius had established alliances with tribes in the Caucasus and in 627 this alliance scored a major victory over Sasanian forces in the southern Caucasus (Theophanes, *Chron.* A.M. 6116 [315.26-316.16]). Heraclius invaded Persian territory soon after and won a victory at Nineveh. Xosrow fled to his palace at Dastagerd and was overthrown in 628 (Theophanes, *Chron.* A.M. 6118 [317.11-26; 317.32-323.22, 324.16-325.10]; *Chronicon Paschale* 727.15-734.17). His son, Kawād II, struck a treaty with Heraclius which saw Armenia, western Mesopotamia, Syria, Palestine, and Egypt returned to the Byzantines (*Chronicon Paschale* 724, 147.18-24; Dignas and Winter 2007: 148-51).

Heraclius celebrated the recovery of territory with the ceremonial return of the True Cross to Jerusalem in March 628. The conflict of the previous twenty-five years had significantly weakened both sides and the Byzantines did not have long to celebrate, losing virtually all of the regained territory within a decade to the Muslim Arabs. The Sasanians were even more devastated by these wars, unable to withstand the Islamic Caliphates and ceasing to exist as a dynasty by 651, when Yazdgerd III was deposed and killed.

Conclusion

The relationship between the Sasanians and Rome/Byzantium contributed importantly to the destiny of each empire from the third to the seventh century. Šābuhr I's successes stood as one of the great triumphs of the Sasanian dynasty and at the same time represented one of the worst losses experienced by the Romans in their two-thousand-year history. Šābuhr's rock reliefs, the ŠKZ, the ruined palace at Bishapur, and the evidence for the siege of Dura Europos still tell the story vividly. The victory of Galerius in 297 and the ensuing treaty, however, indicated that the rulers of both empires knew they had a worthy rival in each other by the end of the third century. This seems not to have been questioned in later centuries, even when conflict assumed the heightened levels of the fourth, sixth, and seventh centuries. Conflict and suspicion were punctuated by periods of peace, cooperation, and even goodwill, especially in the fifth century. Yazdgerd I's favorable treatment of Christians for at least part of his reign is one example, while the common defense of the Caucasus passes was an admission, at times grudging, that a less familiar enemy represented an unpredictable threat to both powers. Requests for assistance against dynastic rivals in the cases of Arcadius, Xosrow II, and Maurice's son, Theodosius, were recognitions that sometimes internal enemies are more destructive than external ones. Ultimately, conflict between Sasanian Iran and Byzantium in the seventh century, which was shaped by conflict in preceding centuries, was fundamental to the destinies of both empires and also those of the triumphant Islamic Caliphates.

References

Alram, M. 2008. Early Sasanian coinage. In *The Sasanian era*, ed. V. S. Curtis and S. Stewart, 17–30. London: I. B. Tauris.
Asmussen, J. P. 1983. Christians in Iran. *CHI* 3: 924–48.
Baatz, D. 1978. Recent finds of ancient artillery. *Britannia* 9: 1–17.
Barnes, T. D. 1985. Constantine and the Christians of Persia. *Journal of Roman Studies* 75: 126–36.
———. 1998. *Ammianus Marcellinus and the representation of historical reality*. Ithaca: Cornell University Press.
Baur, P. V. C., M. I. Rostovtzeff, and A. R. Bellinger. 1933. *The excavations at Dura Europos: Preliminary report of the fourth season: 1930–31*. New Haven: Yale University Press.

Baynes, N. H. 1955. *Byzantium and other essays*, London: Athlone Press [186–208 reprinted from Rome and Armenia in the fourth century. *English Historical Review* 25 {1910}: 625–43].

Bellinger, A. R. 1949. *The excavations at Dura Europos: Final report VI—The coins*. New Haven: Yale University Press.

Boyce, M., and F. Grenet 1991. *A history of Zoroastrianism*, vol. 3, *Zoroastrianism under Macedonian and Roman rule*. Leiden: HdO 8/1/2/2/3.

Brock, S. P. 1978. A martyr at the Sasanid court under Vahran II: Candida. *Analecta Bollandiana* 96: 167–81.

———. 1992. *Studies in Syriac Christianity*. Aldershot: Variorum Collected Studies Series 357.

———. 1994. The Church of the East in the Sasanian Empire up to the sixth century and its absence from the councils in the Roman Empire. In *Syriac Dialogue*, vol. 1, ed. A. Stirnemann and G. Wilflinger, 69–85. Vienna: Pro Oriente.

Brooks, E. W. 1905–7. *Jacob of Edessa, Chronicon*. Paris: Corpus Scriptorum Christianorum Orientalium 5/5 and 6/6.

Canepa, M. 2009. *The two eyes of the Earth: Art and ritual of kingship between Rome and Sasanian Iran*. Berkeley: University of California Press.

Carson, R. A. G. 1968. The Hama Hoard and the eastern mints of Valerian and Gallienus. *Berytus* 17: 123–42.

Chaumont, M.-L. 1986. Armenia and Iran II. *EnIr* 2: 418–38.

Davis, D. 1996. The problem of Firdausī's sources. *JAOS* 116: 48–57.

Daryaee, T. 2009. *Sasanian Persia: The rise and fall of an empire*. London: I. B. Tauris.

Dignas, B., and E. Winter. 2007. *Rome and Persia in Late Antiquity: Neighbours and rivals*. Cambridge: Cambridge University Press.

Dodgeon, M. H., and S. N. C. Lieu.1994. *The Roman eastern frontier and the Persian Wars*. London/New York: Routledge.

Edwell, P. M. 2008. *Between Rome and Persia: The Middle Euphrates, Mesopotamia and Palmyra under Roman control*. London/New York: Routledge.

———. 2010. The sources for Rome's wars with Shāpūr I: Eurocentric and eastern perspectives. *AWE* 9: 155–80.

Fowden, G. 1993. *Empire to Commonwealth*. Princeton: Princeton University Press.

Gariboldi, A. 2010. *Sasanian coinage and history*. Costa Mesa: Mazda.

Gawlikowski, M. 1994. Fortress Hatra: New evidence on the ramparts and their history. *Mesopotamia* 29: 147–84.

Geyer, B., and J.-Y. Monchambert. 2003. *La basse vallée de l'Euphrate syrien du Néolithique à l'avenement de l'Islam*, 2 vols. Beirut: Institut Français du Proche-Orient.

Ghirshman, R. 1956. *Bîchâpour Vol. II: Les Mosaïques Sassanides*. Paris: Geuthner.

———. 1962. *Iran, Parthians and Sassanians*. London: Thames and Hudson.

Greatrex, G., and S. N. C. Lieu. 2002. *The Roman eastern frontier and the Persian Wars: Part II AD 363–630*. London/New York: Routledge.

Herrmann, G. 1977. *The Iranian revival*. Oxford: Phaidon.

Herrmann, G., and V. S. Curtis. 2002. Sasanian rock reliefs. *EnIr* online edition.

Herrmann, G., and R. Howell. 1980. *The Sasanian rock reliefs at Bīshāpūr 1, Bīshāpūr III, Triumph attributed to Shāpūr I*. Berlin: Iranische Denkmäler 9.

———. 1981. *The Sasanian rock reliefs at Bīshāpūr 2, Bīshāpūr IV, Bahrām II receiving a delegation, Bīshāpūr V, The investiture of Bahrām I, Bīshāpūr VI, The enthroned king*. Berlin: Iranische Denkmäler 10.

Howard-Johnston, J. 1995. The two great powers in Late Antiquity: A comparison. In *The Byzantine and Islamic Near East*, vol. 3, *States, resources and armies*, ed. A. Cameron, 157–226. Princeton: Darwin Press.

Huff, D. 1987. Archaeology iv: Sasanian. *EnIr* 2: 302–8.

———. 2008. Formation and ideology of the Sasanian state in the context of archaeological evidence. In *The Sasanian era*, ed. V. S. Curtis and S. Stewart, 31–59. London: I. B. Tauris.

Huyse, P. 1999. *Die dreisprachige Inschrift Šābuhrs I. an der Ka'ba-ye Zardušt (ŠKZ)*, 2 vols. London: CII 3/1/1.

James, S. 1986a. Evidence from Dura Europos for the origins of late Roman helmets. *Syria* 63: 107–34.

———. 2004. *The Excavations at Dura Europos: Final Report VII: The arms and armour and other military equipment.* London: British Museum Press.

———. 2011. Stratagems, combat, and "chemical warfare" in the siege mines of Dura-Europos. *AJA* 115: 69–101.

Kettenhofen, E. 1982. *Die römisch-persischen Kriege des 3. Jahrhunderts n. Chr. nach der Inschrift Sāhpuhrs I. an der Ka'be-ye Zartošt (ŠKZ)*, Wiesbaden: TAVO Beiheft B 55.

Kröger, J. 1993. Ctesiphon. *EnIr* 6: 446–8.

Leadbetter, W. 2009. *Galerius and the will of Diocletian*. London/New York: Routledge.

Matthews, J. F. 1989. *The Roman Empire of Ammianus*. London: Duckworth.

Oates, D. 1955. A note on three Latin inscriptions from Hatra. *Sumer* 11: 39–43.

Potter, D. S. 1990. *Prophecy and history in the crisis of the Roman Empire: A historical commentary on the Thirteenth Sibylline Oracle*. Oxford: Clarendon Press.

Rubin, Z. 1998. The Roman Empire in the *Res Gestae Divi Saporis*. In *Ancient Iran and the Mediterranean world*, ed. E. Dabrowa, 177–85. Krakow: Jagiellonian University Press.

Trombley, F. R., and J. W. Watt. 2000. *The chronicle of Pseudo-Joshua the Stylite*. Liverpool: Liverpool University Press.

Welles, C. B. 1941. The epitaph of Julius Terentius. *Harvard Theological Review* 34: 79–102.

Yarshater, E. 1971. Were the Sasanians heirs to the Achaemenids? In *La Persia nel Medioevo*, 517–31. Rome: Accademia Nazionale dei Lincei.

———. 1983. Iranian national history. *CHI* 3/1: 359–477.

CHAPTER 45

SASANIAN ROCK RELIEFS

MATTHEW P. CANEPA

INTRODUCTION

The Sasanian Empire (224–651) was the last major Western Asian empire ruled by an Iranian-speaking dynasty before the coming of Islam. After consolidating power in their home province of Pārs (Old Persian, Pārsa, New Persian Fārs) in the early third century, the Sasanian dynasty overthrew the Arsacids to build an empire that stretched from upper Mesopotamia to Northern India. The Sasanians spoke a Middle Iranian dialect, a descendant of Old Persian, shared some of the names of the Achaemenid kings, and generally understood themselves to be the ancestors of a long line of Iranian kings stretching back through the Achaemenids to the mythological Kayānid dynasty. While they certainly did not set out to rebuild the Achaemenid Empire, the Sasanian kings understood themselves to be continuators and reinvigoraters of ancient and august traditions of Iranian kingship (Canepa 2010).

Monumental rock reliefs played a unique role in the formation of early Sasanian kingship. By the time the Sasanians took power, monumental reliefs rock reliefs had long been an important artistic genre and royal practice in ancient Iran and the wider ancient Western Asian world. At the rise of the Sasanian dynasty, the landscape of Iran bore several millennia of relief sculptures carved into the living rock. This rupestrian heritage challenged and stimulated the Sasanians' own practices in a variety of ways. The Sasanians responded to the recent iconographic and ideological precedents of the overthrown Arsacid dynasty and appropriated many artistic and architectural forms from Achaemenid sculpture. In one case, the Sasanian King of Kings Warahrān II integrated an Elamite relief into the composition of his new relief. The early Sasanians found the sculptural forms of the Achaemenid dynasty to be especially inspiring as they created visual and architectural forms worthy of a renewed Persian kingship. Within Pārs, the Sasanians held the surviving reliefs of the Achaemenid tombs in particularly high regard. In the remains of the Achaemenid palaces at Persepolis the late antique dynasty carved small-scale incised figural scenes in structures that had been rebuilt, providing important precedents as the dynasty began to carve monumental rock reliefs near the Achaemenid tombs (Callieri 2003).

The early Sasanians' experience of their home province's landscape, marked with the reliefs of their predecessors, likely inspired them to engage new sites within Pārs and shape the wider topography of their empire with rock reliefs. By the fall of their empire, the Sasanians were among the most prolific patrons of monumental relief sculpture in ancient Iran and Western Asia. The sheer number of reliefs they carved, as well as the jealousy with which the dynasty guarded relief carving as the exclusive preserve of the court, ensured that in late antiquity, monumental relief carving became an exclusively royal and quintessentially Iranian practice.

Overview

With a dearth of contemporary textual sources, rock reliefs join inscriptions, coins, seals, and objects derived from a secure archaeological context as the only unquestionably authentic primary sources for the study of Sasanian Iran (Canepa 2009: xvii–xx). Scholarship knows of thirty-four Sasanian rock reliefs that the dynasty brought to some level of completion on the Iranian plateau, or thirty-nine if one counts multiple panels within single reliefs separately (Table 45.1). An additional nine or ten unfinished reliefs were possibly carved in the Sasanian era, given their shape, wear, and location (Table 45.2). It is entirely likely that the dynasty carved others that were completely destroyed, especially in areas outside their home province. Scholarship refers to reliefs by their New Persian toponym and a number that corresponds to their relative location at the site, not the order in which they were created. Although one will encounter alternative numbering schemes in earlier scholarship, the designations reflected in this chapter have now become the accepted and conventional ones (Vanden Berghe 1983).

The Sasanians carved most of their rock reliefs within their home province of Pārs, which was slightly larger than the modern province of Fārs. Within Pārs, the majority cluster in the vicinity of Persepolis. Outside of Pārs, the Sasanians carved six reliefs at a number of sites stretching across the northern Iranian plateau. The dynasty carved the majority of these northern reliefs in the Sasanian province of Ādurbāyagān (Azerbaijan), with one carved in northern Ādurbāyagān near the modern town of Salmās by Lake Urmia and a cluster of three in southern Ādurbāyagān (modern Kurdistan). The other two appear in the Sasanian provinces of Gēlān and Kushān on sites related to major trade routes. The relief in Gēlān was located near the city of Rayy, and the relief in Kushān was carved in territory the Sasanians conquered from the Kushān Empire, in the present-day province of Baghlān, Afghanistan.

The majority of Sasanian rock reliefs were carved in the first 175 years of the empire, between the reigns of Ardašīr I (224–240) and Šābuhr III (383–388), with a final, brief, florescence of the genre before the fall of the empire in the seventh century. Three kings,

Table 45.1 Table of Sasanian rock reliefs.

Relief	Patron	Location	Size in m (l × h)	Subject Matter	Site Features
Firuzabad 1	Ardašīr I	Fars	19.80 × 4	equestrian triumph	river gorge, near city
Firuzabad 2	Ardašīr I	Fars	4.90 × 3.90	divine investiture	river gorge, near city
Naqsh-e Rajab 3	Ardašīr I	Fars	4.90 × 3.04	divine investiture	spring, near city
Salmās	Ardašīr I	Azerbaijan	10.0 × 3.50	investiture of governors	cliffside, near city by Lake Urmia
Naqsh-e Rustam 1	Ardašīr I	Fars	6.75 × 4.28	divine investiture and triumph	major Sasanian cult site; cliffside near Achaemenid tombs and tower and tower
Naqsh-e Rajab 1	Šābuhr I	Fars	7 × 4.17	support of nobles	spring, near city
Naqsh-e Rajab 4	Šābuhr I	Fars	6.40 × 2.9	divine investiture	spring, near city
Naqsh-e Rustam 6	Šābuhr I	Fars	7 × 4.17	triumph	see Naqsh-e Rustam 1
Bishapur 1	Šābuhr I	Fars	9.20 × ?	divine investiture and triumph	river gorge, near city
Bishapur 2	Šābuhr I	Fars	12.46 × 4.52	triumph and support of nobles	river gorge, near city
Bishapur 3	Šābuhr I	Fars	9.20 × 6.80	triumph and support of nobles	river gorge, near city
Rag-e Bibi	Šābuhr I	Baghlan (Afgh.)	6.50 × 5.90	hunting	cliffside, near major north south route from Bactria to India
Bishapur 5	Warahrān I (recut by Narseh)	Fars	9.40 × 5.04 /4.90	divine investiture and triumph	river gorge, near city
Naqsh-e Rustam 2	Warahrān II	Fars	4.58 × 2.1–2.3	support of family and nobles	see Naqsh-e Rustam 1
Sarab-e Bahram	Warahrān II	Fars	4 × 2.60	support of family and nobles	spring
Tang-e (or Sarab-e) Qandil	Warahrān II	Fars	2.75 × 2.23	divine investiture (king receiving flower from Anahita)	river
Barm-e Delak 1	Warahrān II	Fars	2.1–2.6 × 1.80	courtly scene, king giving flower to queen	spring
Barm-e Delak 2	Warahrān II	Fars	left panel 1.25 × 2.75 right panel 1.25 × 2.08	king making gesture of reverence, courtier offering diadem	spring
Guyum	Warahrān II	Fars	1.6 × 2.60	king making gesture of reverence	spring
Bishapur 4	Warahrān II	Fars	7.45 × 3.40	triumph	river gorge, near city
Sar Mashhad	Warahrān II	Fars	4.65 × 2.14	hunting	cliffside, near city
Naqsh-e Rustam 3	Warahrān II	Fars	9.35 × 3.52–3.90	equestrian triumph	see Naqsh-e Rustam 1

Site	King	Province	Dimensions (m)	Subject	Setting
Naqsh-e Rustam 7	Warahrān II	Fars	upper panel: 6.85 × 5.80;	equestrian triumph	see Naqsh-e Rustam 1
Naqsh-e Rajab 2	Kerdīr	Fars	1.64 × .87	bust portrait with gesture of respect with inscription	spring, near city
Naqsh-e Rustam 6	Kerdīr	Fars	6.40 × 1.9	bust portrait making gesture of respect with inscription	see Naqsh-e Rustam 1
Naqsh-e Rustam 8	Narseh	Fars	5.65 × 3.50	divine investiture	see Naqsh-e Rustam 1
Naqsh-e Rustam 4	Ōhrmazd II	Fars	7.97 × 3.52	equestrian triumph	see Naqsh-e Rustam 1
Naqsh-e Rustam 5	Šābuhr II	Fars	c.1 × 3.5	king enthroned	see Naqsh-e Rustam 1
Bishapur 6	Šābuhr II	Fars	11 × 4.40–4.60	king enthroned, triumph	river gorge, near city
Taq-e Bustan 1	Ardašīr II	Kermanshah	4.60 × 3.44	divine investiture and triumph	spring, mountain, and hunting paradise
Taq-e Bustan 2	Šābuhr III	Kermanshah	5.75 × 5.50, 3.80 deep	dynastic continuity	spring, mountain, and hunting paradise
Taq-e Bustan 3 (Great Ayvan)	Xosrow II	Kermanshah	vault: 7.5 × 8.90–9.2, 6.78 deep; left side panel 5.95 × 4.30, relief 5.74 × 3.85 right side panel 5.74 × 4.30, relief 5.74 × 3.85	divine investiture, military prowess, hunting	spring, mountain, and hunting paradise
Sorsoreh, Ray	Šābuhr II?	Tehran	c.1.8	equestrian triumph, now destroyed	

Table 45.2 Additional Sasanian reliefs, either entirely unfinished and/or with unidentified patrons.

Site	Location	Description	Patron
Cave of Šābuhr I	Fars	Panels prepared for relief carving within the cave; accompanied by colossal statue in the round	Shapur I
Naqsh-e Rustam	Fars	Unfinished Rectangular surface above cistern	
Naqsh-e Rustam	Fars	Small unfinished figure of a male figure with raised right hand to the left of Narseh's relief	
Naqsh-e Rustam	Fars	Small unfinished figure of a lion to the left of Narseh's relief	
Naqsh-e Rustam	Fars	Unifinished Rectangular frame, deep relief, to right of Narseh's relief	Khosrow II?
Naqsh-e Rustam	Fars	Unifinished rectangular panel between the cistern and Warahrān II's Relief 2	
Naqsh-e Rustam	Fars	Unifinished square panel to the lower left of Šābuhr I's relief	
Dārābgerd	Fars	Small panel of female figure	
Terash-e Farhad	Kermanshah	Enormous unfinished rectangular panel, 20 × 30 m	Khosrow II?
Boşat	Diyarbakir (Turkey)	Horseman and standing figure	

Ardašīr I, his son, Šābuhr I (240–272), and great-grandson, Warahrān II (276–293), carved over half of all known reliefs, although, with a few exceptions, most kings in the early empire created at least one relief. Of the early Sasanian kings, Warahrān II was the most prolific patron of rock reliefs (Weber 2009). Warahrān II carved rock reliefs at sites that had already begun to accumulate reliefs, such as Naqsh-e Rustam and Bishapur, and at new sites throughout the province of Pārs, often with a natural feature, such as a spring or river (Callieri 2006). While Warahrān II sponsored scenes of equestrian duels and the submission of foreign envoys, the most common theme or subsidiary theme of his reliefs was the King of Kings receiving the respect of his family or courtiers.

For most of Sasanian history, sponsoring a rock relief remained exclusively a royal privilege. The Zoroastrian priest Kerdīr, who achieved the office of chief priest of the empire (*mowbedān mowbed*) under Warahrān II, took advantage of the relative weakness of this King of Kings to usurp a number of royal prerogatives including this privilege. Kerdīr's rock reliefs are very simple, consisting only of a profile bust portrait carved adjacent to more extensive royal reliefs, and no other than the royal family carved a rock relief thereafter. Between the late fourth and early seventh centuries, no Sasanian king carved a rock relief as the practice, for whatever reason, fell out of favor. The last great Sasanian King of Kings, Xosrow II (591–628), reinvigorated the practice in the second half of his reign. He began a series of grand reliefs, which his abrupt fall from power left in various states of completion.

Most Sasanian rock reliefs consist of recessed, rectangular panels framing low-relief sculpture. While Achaemenid rock reliefs served as tombs, the early Sasanian reliefs, much like Parthian reliefs, simply contained figural imagery, albeit often in connection with a sacred site. The last two reliefs of the dynasty, Taq-e Bustan 2 and 3, expand on this tradition and create rock-cut architecture whose interior serves as a support for reliefs. They evoke the forms of Sasanian palatial architecture, excavating out of the living rock an *ayvan* (*iwan*), the barrel-vaulted entranceway of Sasanian palaces. It is likely that these two rock-cut *ayvans* hosted activities relating to the courtly environment. It is likely that the rock reliefs were painted and some have suggested that later reliefs were finished with stucco (Herrmann and Curtis 2002).

Many reliefs have suffered some measure of natural or man-made damage throughout the centuries. After the fall of the Sasanians, iconoclasts damaged the faces of most figures, particularly those of gods and kings. The relief in Afghanistan is almost completely destroyed, although enough details survive to allow its patron and general subject matter to be identified (Grenet 2005; Grenet et al. 2007). The most extreme case is the relief at Sorsoreh, Rayy, which the Qājārs deliberately effaced in the nineteenth century to make way for a relief of their own. Under the Pahlavi dynasty in the late 1960s, the rock on which the relief was carved was completely demolished to accommodate the construction of a cement factory. In this regard, the scholarship of Sasanian rock reliefs owes a debt to the documentation of early explorers, diplomats, and entrepreneurs. The drawings of Sir Robert Ker Porter (1777–1842) and Sir William Ouseley (1767–1842), in particular, preserve a record of a number of reliefs that were subsequently damaged or totally destroyed before more systematic photographic documentation in the twentieth century (Ker Porter 1821–2; Errington and Curtis 2007: 166–78). Many of the Sasanian rock reliefs in Fārs were documented as a part of the University of Chicago's Persepolis expedition (Schmidt 1970). These and several others in Fārs were later documented as a part of the *Iranische Denkmäler* series (Trümpelmann 1975a, 1975b; Herrmann and Howell 1977, 1980–83; Herrmann et al. 1989). A Japanese expedition documented the reliefs of Taq-e Bustan in great detail (Fukai et al. 1969–84). L. Vanden Berghe's exhibition catalog provides the most accessible single-volume overview of the reliefs (Vanden Berghe 1983).

Every Sasanian King of Kings adopted a distinct, personal crown upon taking the throne. Because Sasanian coinage provides a relatively complete record of the Sasanian crowns, comparisons between numismatic portraits and rock reliefs have enabled scholarship to identify the patron of most rock reliefs. Ker Porter was the first to compare Sasanian rock reliefs to coin portraits and in this way succeeded in correctly identifying a number of them (Errington and Curtis 2007: 171). This methodology has guided much of later scholarship's attribution of rock reliefs as well as representations of kings in other media, such as sliver plate or gems. In several cases ambiguous or damaged representations of figures' headgear frustrate easy attribution. Context, comparisons with the style or subject matter of other reliefs, or internal iconographic clues and conventions in most cases provide enough evidence to identify the figures. Nevertheless, a handful of cases, including Dārābgerd, Taq-e Bustan 1, and several of the equestrian reliefs, are ambiguous enough to elude scholarly consensus and ensure that an alternative theory is always circulating.

IMPORTANT THEMES AND IMPORTANT PATRONS

From the early days of the empire, the two most important and commonly occurring subjects of Sasanian rock reliefs were triumph and divine investiture (De Waele 1989). The reliefs of Ardašīr I established iconographic forms and compositions that greatly influenced his successors. Ardašīr I's first rock relief at Firuzabad (ancient Ardašīr-Xwarrah) was carved on a cliff in the river gorge that controlled access to the city from the north. It contained three figural groupings from right to left (Fig. 45.1). On the right, the King of Kings unhorses the last Arsacid sovereign, Ardawān IV, with his lance. In the center, Šābuhr I unhorses another Arsacid warrior and on the left a beardless page defeats stabs a third enemy with his sword. This composition and subject matter responded to Arsacid precedents, such as the equestrian victory of Gotarzes Geopothros at Bisotun, but executed it on a much larger scale.

Ardašīr I's second relief at Firuzabad portrays a scene of divine investiture where the god Ōhrmazd (Ahura Mazda), portrayed as a royal figure, offers the King of Kings a diadem, similar to those both he and the King of Kings wear. This relief establishes a compositional precedent for Ardašīr I's later relief at Naqsh-e Rajab. Just as importantly,

FIGURE 45.1 Firuzabad 1: Equestrian triumph of Ardašīr I over Ardawān IV on the cliff to the right at the end of the Tang-e Ab with the plain of Ardašīr-Xwarrah (modern Firuzabad) opening to the left.

this relief establishes an important precedent in directly portraying Ōhrmazd in human form offering a diadem directly to the open hand of the King of Kings, who appears in this manner only under the Sasanians. In this and later reliefs the primary symbol of power and authority is a diadem, often erroneously referred to as a "ring of power." The Sasanian diadem clearly descends from the Arsacid, and thence, Hellenistic diadem, though the Sasanian diadem ties became increasingly long and developed a characteristic pleated pattern. The Sasanian reliefs no doubt responded to early Western Asian investiture scenes wherein a deity presents a circular object to a king, as seen on the Stele of Hammurapi or, more proximately, in the relief of Anubanini at Sar-e Pol-e Zohāb in Kermanshah. In those early cases, deities often presented a coil of rope, along with a measuring rod. The Sasanian reliefs replaced that motif, which no longer had any meaning, with the contemporary iconographic feature of royal headgear. In most Sasanian reliefs, the craftsmen took care to conform the style of the diadem to the one that the King of Kings is shown wearing.

Sasanian reliefs often portrayed triumph and divine investiture in some sort of combination with each other. Here too, Ardašīr I established important and influential compositional and iconographic precedents. Relief 1 at Naqsh-e Rustam was likely the last relief that Ardašīr I carved and it presents a highly innovative and powerful composition that elegantly and forcefully proclaims the early, developing Sasanian ideology of divinely inspired kingship and irresistible victory (Figs. 45.2–3). The relief, located on

FIGURE 45.2 Naqsh-e Rustam 1 and 2: Triumph and investiture of Ardašīr I (left) and Warahrān II with family and court (right, carved over Elamite reliefs).

FIGURE 45.3 Naqsh-e Rustam 1: Equestrian triumph and investiture of Ardašīr I (left) by the god Ōhrmazd (right) with Ardawān IV (left) and Ahriman (right) under hoof.

a spur of Hosayn Kuh, the site of the Achaemenid tombs, portrays the King of Kings as a nearly symmetrical reflection of the god Ōhrmazd, who is the same size as the King of Kings. Portraying them in profile, both king and god are mounted and their horses each trample enemies under their hooves. The prone figure under Ardašīr I's horse is the last Arsacid King of Kings, Ardawan (Artabanus) IV, identified by his royal headgear and a dynastic symbol. Snakes writhe in the place of hair on the male figure under Ōhrmazd's horse marking him as none other than Ahriman, the demon of demons in Zoroastranism. Ōhrmazd extends the diadem to Ardašīr I with his right hand and blesses him with barsom, a bundle of sacred twigs used in Zoroastrian ritual, held in his left hand. A beardless attendant stands behind Ardašīr I holding a fly whisk behind his head, but only the eyes of the King of Kings meet those of Ōhrmazd.

The relief very efficiently demonstrates that Ōhrmazd brought Ardašīr I to power. The symmetrical composition, set up a cosmological and qualitative equivalency between Ardašīr I's recent defeat of the last Arsacid King of Kings, Ardawān IV and Ōhrmazd's future, yet inevitable, defeat of Ahriman at the end of days. Ardašīr I wears his normal regnal crown, while Ōhrmazd wears a crown that evokes certain Achaemenid mural crowns, including Darius I's relief at Bisotun and certain issues of darics. The sculptural forms of the relief appropriate many formal and figural aspects of Achaemenid relief sculpture. Features such as eyes, the beard of Ōhrmazd, the horses, and the figures' hands show that the craftsmen had carefully studied the sculptures still visible in the ruins of Perseopolis, about 10 km away. Ardašīr I's reliefs were quite influential. His early equestrian victory inspired those of several later kings. His standing divine investitures provide a basic template that his successors followed. All later kings who did so portrayed the god Ōhrmazd in human form, as Ardašīr I had done. In addition, Ardašīr's relief at Naqsh-e Rustam directly informed the compositions and subject matter of the early reliefs of his son, Šābuhr I, and grandson, Warahrān I, who both experimented with this composition for their equestrian investitures and triumphs.

Šābuhr I was a prolific patron of rock reliefs, carving them at sites that his father also had chosen, such as Naqsh-e Rustam and Naqsh-e Rajab, as well as entirely new sites, such as Bishapur and Dārābgerd, and even within what was the heartland of the former conquered Kushan Empire. Although Šābuhr I had featured prominently in a number of his father's reliefs, appearing even as coruler in the relief investing local rulers in Salmās, Šābuhr I's early reliefs were all located at Naqsh-e Rajab. These two reliefs sought to underscore divine sanction or the support that he enjoyed from the realm's nobles. Naqsh-e Rajab 1 portrays the nobles of the realm standing respectfully behind the King of Kings, who is seated on his horse, and Naqsh-e Rajab 4 adapts the equestrian investiture composition of Ardašīr I at Naqsh-e Rustam, though omits the defeated adversaries below the hooves of the horses.

Šābuhr I's succession of campaigns in Rome's eastern provinces and his string of victories over armies led by the Roman emperors transformed the visual culture of his court and figure prominently in the majority of his later reliefs (Canepa 2009: 55). Šābuhr I took credit for the death of Gordian III (238–244) and portrayed the negotiated settlement of Gordian III's battlefield successor, Philip (244–249), as a submission.

After turning back a subsequent invading force and sacking many cities in Syria and Cappadocia, he captured the emperor Valerian (253–260), deporting him and the remains of his defeated army. Šābuhr I experimented with a number of iconographic and compositional means of expressing his Roman victories. His first experiment with portraying his victory over Gordian and submission of Philip drew from Ardašīr I's classic symmetrical victory and investiture relief at Naqsh-e Rustam I. Bishapur I, which is highly damaged, now portrayed the King of Kings receiving a diadem from Ōhrmazd, whose horse tramples the body of Ahriman. In the place of Ardawān IV, Šābuhr I's horse tramples Gordian III. In a departure from the Ardašīr I's composition, Bishapur I incorporates the figure of Philip performing kneeling before Šābuhr I's with his arms outstretched to clutch the legs of the King of Kings' horse. Šābuhr I's capture of Valerian and his army impacted almost all of his later reliefs. It is the sole subject of Dārābgerd, which reflects an early way of portraying the event that was not repeated. Here the King of Kings grabs Valerian's head as his army stands around him. Behind Šābuhr stand the grandees of the Persian Empire. Šābuhr modified these basic themes, laying hands on Valerian and the grandees, and incorporated them with elements from Bishapur 1 to produce a composition that he repeated twice at Bishapur. The central panels of Bishapur II and Bishapur III are nearly identical and portray Valerian standing next to Šābuhr with the King of Kings grasping the emperor's wrists, Gordian prone underneath his horse, and Philip kneeling. Rows of mounted Persian nobles stand in panels behind Šābuhr I in both reliefs. Šābuhr I's relief at Naqsh-e Rustam presents a simplified version, portraying only Valerian and Philip and omitting Gordian III and any other figures (Fig. 45.4). These rock reliefs reflect a wider propaganda campaign and these themes appear smaller luxury objects such as cameos or medallions (Canepa 2009: 53–78).

While Šābuhr I's Roman victories have received the greatest attention, his conquest of the Kushan Empire also makes its presence felt in his later reliefs' subject matter. In Bishapur II and III, figures in Iranian dress with hairstyles paralleling contemporary Kushan sculpture figure prominently. In Bishapur III, Kushan and Roman armies both bring gifts to the King of Kings while their sovereigns submit to the King of Kings in the central panel. In Bishapur II, the Romans and Kushans are joined by other subject peoples. In addition to his relief at Bishapur, Šābuhr I carved a colossal statue in the round in a cave high above the Tang-e Chowgan gorge. The 8 m tall statue stood in the center of the cave and likely transformed a natural rock feature connecting the top and bottom of the cave. It portrayed the King of Kings standing wearing his normal crown and reflects the sculptural style of his later reliefs. The cave's side walls were prepared for bas-reliefs, though relief work was never started (Ghirshman 1971: 179–85). Šābuhr I marked the conquest of the core of the Kushan Empire by carving a rock relief in the heart of what was Kushan Bactria. Portraying the King of Kings hunting South Asian quarry, rhinoceros, it expressed the King of Kings' victorious power symbolically rather than in the brutally direct mode of the reliefs in the homeland of the dynasty (Grenet et al. 2007).

The themes and compositions that Ardašīr I and Šābuhr I established influenced the rock reliefs of their successors for the next century. The theme of the submission

FIGURE 45.4 Naqsh-e Rustam 6: Triumph of Šābuhr I over the Roman emperors Valerian (standing) and Philip the Arab. Bust and inscription of Kerdīr to the right.

of defeated rulers and peoples appears as the sole subject of reliefs of Warahrān II and Šābuhr II. Central to Sasanian triumphal imagery since Ardašīr I, the theme of equestrian combat continued to be a popular and effective mode of expressing victory. Although Šābuhr I did not carve a relief with this theme, the equestrian duel was current under his reign and appears on the sardonyx cameo in the Cabinet des Médailles, Paris (Göbl 1974). Valerian and the King of Kings charge at each other and Šābuhr I grabs the emperor's wrist as he does in every rock relief incorporating Valerian. Three reliefs at Naqsh-e Rustam deal with this theme. Directly underneath the tomb of Darius I, Warahrān II carved two reliefs portraying equestrian triumphs. Ōhrmazd II (302–309) carved an equestrian triumph under the tomb traditionally associated with Artaxerxes I (Fig. 45.5). A third, attributed to Warahrān II appears under the Achaemenid tomb traditionally associated with Darius II. The double equestrian relief and the relief single relief attributed to Warahrān II contain many of the same compositional elements. In the upper relief of the double combat, the king charges his adversary with a lance while his adversary's horse rears up and falters. The lower relief, which could portray the king again or the victory of the crown prince, portrays the adversary with a striding horse yet a raised and broken lance. Under the hooves of both of the protagonists' horses lie fallen armored adversaries, no doubt adapting what was now a familiar motif to a scene of active equestrian combat. The relief attributed to Ōhrmazd II portrays the King of Kings turning his adversary on his head, as well as his horse. Behind the King of Kings stands a page who holds a battle standard.

FIGURE 45.5 View of Naqsh-e Rustam: Achaemenid tombs (above) Sasanian reliefs (below).

Sir William Ouseley's 1811 sketch of the rock relief at Sorsoreh near Rayy depicts an armored, mounted king charging with a lance. It is likely that this relief originally portrayed an equestrian battle, since Sasanian Kings of Kings do not appear anywhere else hunting in armor. The lower central panel of the relief of Xosrow II portrays the nimbated King of Kings in full armor, mounted and holding a lance, which alludes to this theme, though the relief does not portray any adversary. While not matching the popularity and frequency of the theme in Sasanian silver, Šābuhr I, Warahrān II, and Xosrow II sponsored reliefs portraying the King of Kings hunting. The game could vary: rhinoceros in the case of Šābuhr I, lions in the relief of Warahrān II, and boar and deer in the case of Xosrow II. Battle and hunting scenes appear in different artistic media and contexts. For example, Ammianus Marcellinus alludes to the popularity of scenes of battle and hunting in the Persian aristocratic houses he saw during Julian's invasion and the fragments of stucco carving from the fire temple of Bandiyan in eastern Iran portray a scene of a King of Kings unhorsing an adversary as well as hunting scenes.

The themes of dynastic continuity and nobles, the royal family, or vassal kings paying respect to the King of Kings take their place as some of the most important subsidiary concerns in early Sasanian reliefs. Support for the King of Kings appears as the main theme in a handful of reliefs, such as Šābuhr I's Naqsh-e Rajab 1, where the nobles stand behind the mounted king, or Warahrān II's reliefs at Sarab-e Bahram and Naqsh-e Rustam 2, where his family and court turn toward the King of Kings, who is enthroned or stands at the centre of the composition. Several other rock reliefs integrate this theme into scenes of submission or triumph, including Šābuhr I's relief at Dārābgerd, and Bishapur 2 and 3, where the nobles appear behind the King of Kings in overlapping rows, standing or on horseback. Dynastic continuity is one of the subsidiary themes in the relief at Salmās, where Ardašīr I and Šābuhr are portrayed identically and performing an identical act of investiture. This theme forms of the sole focus of Taq-e Bustan 2, which portrays two nearly identical Kings of Kings standing side by side. Others integrate this theme into scenes of divine investiture, although in these cases only the royal family and highest courtiers would appear. Ardašīr I's investiture by Ōhrmazd in Firuzabad 2 and Naqsh-e Rajab 3 and Narseh's investure by Anahid in Naqsh-e Rustam 8 portray the crown prince among the figures standing behind the king.

Marking a shift from the traditional importance of the Sasanian's home province, the last two rock reliefs of the early empire appear at the site of Taq-e Bustan, located in southern Ādurbāyagān (ancient Media, modern Kurdistan), near present-day Kermanshah. Two successors of Šābuhr II carved these reliefs: Taq-e Bustan 1 and 2. Šābuhr II's brother, Ardašīr II, carved Taq-e Bustan 1, a rectangular relief slab that celebrates the part he played in the Persians' success in defending the empire against Julian's invasion by showing him receiving a diadem from a figure who wears the crown of Šābuhr II (Fig. 45.6). The god Mihr, who makes an unprecedented appearance in this relief, blesses the King of Kings with a barsom and this likely alludes to Julian's support of Roman Mithraism and his assertion of the god's true worship in Zoroastrianism (Hollard 2010). Carved in the form of an *ayvan*, Taq-e Bustan II's subject matter is relatively simple, in the upper register of the rear wall of the *ayvan* (Fig. 45.7). The relief

FIGURE 45.6 Taq-e Bustan 1: Investiture and triumph over Julian the Apostate, Kermanshah, Iran.

FIGURE 45.7 Taq-e Bustan 2 and 3: Rock cut ayvan with Šābuhr II and III (right) and the "Great Ayvan" of Xosrow II (left), Kermanshah, Iran.

portrays two Kings of Kings standing next to each other with their heads slightly turned to each other. Inscriptions flank each of the kings and identify the figures as Šābuhr III and his father, Šābuhr II. The king on the viewer's right clearly wears the crown of Šābuhr II. The king on the viewer's left wears a crown that does not accurately replicate the crown of Šābuhr III. It has been suggested the crown of the king on the left originally was that of Ardašīr II, who sponsored the relief, and that Šābuhr III reworked the residual features of the crown to match his own (Overlaet 2011). However, the crown does not match the crown of Ardašīr II either, as the relief contains a single crescent at the king's brow, which does not appear on his coins, indicating this might be yet another instance of a King of Kings changing his crown after taking power.

After the fourth century no King of Kings carved a rock relief until Xosrow II (590–628). Xosrow II began several reliefs between defeating the usurper Warahrān Čōbīn and the invasion of Heraclius, which hastened his fall. An especially large, unfinished relief panel at Naqsh-e Rustam, may have been the work of Xosrow II given its size and relative wear, but this is only speculation without further evidence. Two other reliefs are located in southern Ādurbāyagān (ancient Media, modern Kurdistan) along the main east-west route across the north of Iran and were created in conjunction with other building projects. The Terash-e Farhad is a colossal, unfinished 20 × 30 m relief panel carved into the cliff about half a kilometer along the cliff face from Bisotun (Luschey 1996). An equally colossal terrace of earthworks and rough-hewn stone blocks was fashioned before the huge relief panel. A number of column capitals, which carried images of gods and Xosrow II in the same sculptural style as Taq-e Bustan, were discovered in association with the terrace.

The "Great *Ayvan*" at Taq-e Bustan (relief 3) was the only relief that Xosrow II brought anywhere near to completion (Fig. 45.8). There he carved a colossal *ayvan* with reliefs on all three of its walls (Movassat 2005). This relief no doubt responded to the smaller and much simpler late fourth-century rock-cut *ayvan* as well the site's role as a royal retreat and hunting paradise under Xosrow II. More importantly, it replicates in stone the sculptural themes that graced the stucco decoration of in the late Sasanian audience hall, as attested in late Roman and early Islamic sources (Canepa 2009: 139–49). The themes that the *ayvan*'s figural sculpture dealt with reflect those of the third- and fourth-century reliefs: divine investiture, hunting, and military triumph. However, it deals with these all-important themes differently than previous reliefs, choosing to portray the King of Kings multiple times in the same panel. The relief also presents sculptural styles and compositions that differ markedly from earlier reliefs, indicating that the relief was the product of a separate artistic florescence.

FIGURE 45.8 Taq-e Bustan 3, the "Great *Ayvan*," rear of *ayvan*. Above: Xosrow II invested by the goddess Anahid (left) and the god Ohrmazd (right). Below: Xosrow II portrayed with a nimbus behind his head, in full armour mounted on his famous black stallion, Shabdiz.

The central wall opposite the entrance was the *ayvan*'s main focus. Divided into an upper and lower register, it presents two sculptural groups achieved in very high relief. In the centre of the upper group, the King of Kings stands on a short, bejeweled plinth or cushion while the god Ōhrmazd stands to the King of Kings' left and the goddess Anāhīd stands to his right, also on such plinths. Though facing frontally, Xosrow II reaches his right arm across his chest to grasp a diadem that Ōhrmazd offers with his right hand. Anahid mimics this gesture, reaching across her chest with her right arm and holding a diadem in her hand and offering it to the King of Kings. In contrast to every previous investiture, the King of Kings is actually taller than the gods. In the lower register, and framed by several rock architectural elements such as architraves and pilasters decorated with vegetal ornament, stands the great figure of the King of Kings astride his horse, both in full chain mail. The King of Kings holds a lance and shield, and a giant concave disk is hollowed out around his head, finding an ingenious solution for portraying in high-relief sculpture the disk nimbus, now part of the standard Persian royal iconography. In contrast to the two high-relief sculptural groups in the rear of the *ayvan*, which are over life-size, the left and right side panels carry small, low-relief hunting vignettes (Fig. 45.9). Both portray the King of Kings twice, in the process of hunting and at rest after a successful hunt and, in the case of the left wall, with the royal nimbus shining around his head.

FIGURE 45.9 Taq-e Bustan 3 the "Great *Ayvan*," left side panel. Xosrow II portrayed twice standing in a boat hunting wild boar with a bow in a marshy hunting enclosure. Elephants (left and below) drive the quarry into range while courtiers applaud and musicians play.

The sculptural forms of the Sasanian rock reliefs indicate a wide arc of development, with several offshoots and regional variations. Firuzabad 1 presents sculptural forms that are quite different from later reliefs. Very flat and with an interest in representing surface textures such as chain mail or curly hair with repeated stylized forms, the relief nonetheless presents a very dynamic composition with a great deal of movement. In many ways, its length and interest in portraying linear details hint at a burgeoning workshop that descended from the elaborate early preimperial Sasanian graffiti etched into the window frames at Persepolis (Canepa 2010; Callieri 2003) With their massive figures, expressionistic limbs, multiple figures, and similar basic composition, Ardašīr I's relief at Firuzabad 2 and Naqsh-e Rajab appear to have come from the same workshop. While these reliefs describe the main lines of development, the relief of Salmās shows the work of a less experienced hand and adheres closely to a two-dimensional model, slightly recessing all material around the figures.

Ardašīr I's relief at Naqsh-e Rustam, marks a turning point, where the sculptural forms themselves become more measured and refined and the composition more carefully thought out. Ardašīr I's relief at Naqsh-e Rustam took formal cues from Achaemenid sculpture visible at Persepolis and in the tombs and produces the beginnings of what one might term the "classical style" of the early Sasanian Empire. In addition, the figures themselves were finished to a polish. Šābuhr I's early reliefs at Naqsh-e Rajab, his relief at Naqsh-e Rustam, and his first relief at Bishapur, as far as we can tell, both reflect and depart from the forms portrayed in Ardašīr I's last relief. As has often been noted, Šābuhr I's last two reliefs at Bishapur (II and III) as well as his colossal statue in the round show some influence of Roman sculptural and compositional elements on the early Sasanian style.

The reliefs of Warahrān I, Warahrān II, Narseh, and Ōhrmazd II develop and refine this classical style, but do not depart from its forms too dramatically. The relief ascribed to Šābuhr II at Bishapur presents a noticeable break with the sculptural forms of his predecessors, though the composition reflects earlier developments. The forms are heavier and the figures, especially those in the background, appear to float in space. The workshop did not depart too far from the precedents in front of them in their design of musculature and hair. However in achieving them, the workshop tended toward incising details rather than modeling them. This is a tendency that we see taken to a new extreme in the first two reliefs at Taq-e Bustan. The treatment of the hair and beard as well as drapery relates to the forms of the earlier classical style; however, those details are incised into the surface of the major sculptural forms instead of modeled. The figures' diadem ties and their capes and in some cases their limbs all appear as flat, raised sections that carry undulating lines, indicating drapery folds.

The sculptural forms of Xosrow II's reliefs at Taq-e Bustan and column capitals at Bisotun mark a clear break from the traditions of the past. The reliefs themselves and the forms of the column capitals reflect several Roman features. The column capitals were the standard "basket shape," as one would expect to find on late Roman impost capitals in post-Justinian Constantinople. The exterior of the façade presents a low relief of two winged victories in the space over the *ayvan* that would correspond to the spandrel of a triumphal arch, and the forms of their drapery easily find parallels in late Roman ivory work, such as the Barberini Ivory in the Louvre. Nevertheless the sculptural forms of the elephants parallel cotemporal South Asian representations of the animal. This suggests, though surely does not prove, that the court amalgamated multiple influences and craftsmen to produce this final brilliant florescence of Sasanian sculpture.

Controversies

The majority of the Sasanian kings used the same crown throughout their reigns, with some slight variations in representation, depending on mint or media. In a few exceptional cases a king would adopt a new crown entirely after suffering a major military defeat, as befell Narseh and Pērōz, or temporary usurpation, in the case of Xosrow II. Questions and controversies have arisen when reliefs were left unfinished, such as Bishapur VI, or damaged, like Guyum (Haerinck and Overlaet 2009) or Rayy. Other controversies have emerged when the relief portrays a king in something other than his official crown, such as in hunting clothing or in armor. Controversies have also arisen when the sculptural representation does not exactly match the numismatic portraits or when it provides more information than the numismatic portraits. In general, these stem from scholarly interpretations that assume that Sasanian rock reliefs adhere to crown identifications as an inflexible and unvarying system or privilege one peripheral detail as their interpretative key (Herrmann and Curtis 2002). A certain amount of controversy circulated about the identification of the Roman emperors in Šābuhr I's reliefs in the last century, although B. C. McDermot's identifications and reasoning, put forth in 1954, remains the most cogent reading (McDermot 1954; Canepa 2009: 261, n. 27).

The first two Sasanian Kings of Kings both wore a number of crowns in the early days of their reigns. We know from the coinage that Ardašīr I experimented with a variety of royal headgear early in his reign and Šābuhr I was depicted with his father's crown in two reliefs. Dārābgerd portrays a King of Kings wearing the crown that recalls that of Ardašīr I, with a high globe and no mural crown. However, the kings' hair and horse trappings match representations of Šābuhr I. The sculptural style and subject matter present a scene that closely matches Šābuhr I's other reliefs. The consensus is that the relief portrays Šābuhr I, who appears wearing the crown of Ardašīr I alongside his father in a relief at Salmās and whose military headgear as portrayed on the Paris Cameo (Göbl 1974) also lacks the mural crown of his official headgear. A number of reliefs portray the king in armor or hunting without his normal crown. Such is the case in reliefs of Ardašīr I at Firuzabad (relief 1), Warahrān II (reliefs 3 and 7), and Ōhrmazd II (relief 4) at Naqsh-e Rustam, which portray the king in armor unhorsing an enemy in an equestrian combat. While the subject matter of the relief at Firuzabad is clear from its location and information from the other figures, alternative attributions have been put forward for several of the equestrian reliefs at Naqsh-e Rustam and Rayy.

While the crowns of both royal figures are easily identifiable, Taq-e Bustan 1 generated a great deal of controversy in the past, although the consensus in both past and recent scholarship is solidly that the relief was the work of Ardašīr II. The relief portrays two figures who wear crowns of two different Kings of Kings, Ardašīr II and Šābuhr II and a figure representing the god Mihr. The figure wearing the crown of Šābuhr II wears the same archaic clothing as the figure of Mihr, who is identified by a rayed diadem and who blesses the figure with the crown of Ardašīr II. This figure wears a tunic with a rounded front, a style of clothing that came into vogue in the late fourth century. More indicative of who is doing the investing and who is being invested, the figure wearing the crown of Šābuhr II grasps the diadem with his right hand, while the figure wearing the crown of Ardašīr II holds out his right hand open in anticipation of the diadem. Every other previous Sasanian divine investiture relief portrays the god with the diadem and the king with an open hand. It is entirely possible that the relief was intended to portray Ardašīr II invested by Šābuhr II. Both kings were involved in countering the invasion of Julian, who lies defeated beneath their feet, and such slippage between divine and royal iconographies and investitures would not have been discouraged. In the last century, a handful of scholars argued that Taq-e Bustan 3 should be attributed to Ardašīr III because of certain minor details in the king's crown or jewelry, ignoring the larger weight of the evidence pointing to Xosrow II. Beyond these ambiguous cases, attempts to read very specific or anachronistic religious interpretations into all aspects of the reliefs' subject matter have generated many outright fallacies. Most often these have arisen when scholars privilege textual evidence from a much earlier or later period of Iranian history over other primary sources or the internal features and context of reliefs themselves.

Conclusions

Beyond simply communicating visual information, Sasanian rock reliefs actively shaped the cultural topography of the Iranian plateau. The majority of Sasanian rock reliefs were created next to a spring or river, or a mountain, or both. In carving rock reliefs next to these natural features, considered holy in Iranian culture, the Sasanian kings appropriated the significance for themselves. The Sasanian kings thus used rock reliefs to manipulate their subjects' understanding of the past and shape their experience of the landscape. Because of the durability of the medium and the fact that they modified the very landscape of the empire, rock reliefs implied that whatever they portrayed was as ancient and immutable as the living rock. Sasanian kings used rock reliefs to connect themselves to the remnants of the Achaemenid dynasty at Naqsh-e Rustam, weaving the entire site into a larger meaningful whole that blurred the temporal and political discontinuities that separated the two dynasties.

In addition to marking out individual natural features as culturally and politically significant, rock reliefs could define a wider symbolic topography, either of a region or even of an empire. Rock reliefs proliferated around newly created cities such as Firuzabad and Bishapur, as well as at sites, such as Naqsh-e Rustam or Taq-e Bustan, that held a ritual or courtly significance. Rock reliefs could serve as colonizing tools to establish the imperial presence in subjected regions, such as the case of the relief of Ardašīr I and Šābuhr I at Salmās and Šābuhr I's relief in the heart of Bactria. Long after the fall of the Sasanian Empire, rock reliefs drew the attention of the succeeding Islamic regimes. The topographies of power of the Sasanian rock reliefs defined and affected Iran's later inhabitants' perception of the landscape and often inspired their own activities. Either effaced in attempts to sever ties with the pre-Islamic past, or used to manufacture new connections with the ancient kings, Sasanian rock reliefs shaped, and arguably continue to shape, the experience of the landscape of Iran.

FURTHER READING

The most accessible and comprehensive survey of ancient Iranian rock reliefs remains Vanden Berghe (1983). Herrmann and Curtis (2002) provide a basic overview of the Sasanian material and entry into the older literature. Additional high-quality images or line drawings of most major Sasanian rock reliefs can be found in the third volume of the University of Chicago's Persepolis excavation report (Schmidt 1970) and within the subsection "Iranische Felsreliefs" in the *Iranische Denkmäler* series published by Dietrich Reimer Verlag. Fukai et al. (1969–84) present unparalleled photographic documentation of Taq-e Bustan. As the present chapter has stressed, many of the publications from the last century present conflicting attributions of the reliefs.

REFERENCES

Callieri, P. 2003. At the roots of the Sasanian royal imagery: The Persepolis graffiti. www.transoxiana.org/Eran/Articles/callieri.html [accessed December 18, 2012].

———. 2006. Water in the art and architecture of the Sasanians. In *Proceedings of the 5th Conference of the Societas Iranologica Europaea*, vol. 1, ed. A. Panaino and A. Piras, 339–49. Milan: Mimesis.

Canepa, M. P. 2009. *The two eyes of the earth: Art and ritual of kingship between Rome and Sasanian Iran*. Berkeley: University of California Press.

———. 2010. Technologies of memory in early Sasanian Iran: Achaemenid sites and Sasanian identity. *AJA* 114/4: 563–96.

De Waele, E. 1989. L'Investiture et le triomphe dans la thématique de la sculpture rupestre sassanide. *AIO*: 811–29.

Errington, E., and V. S. Curtis. 2007. *From Persepolis to the Punjab: Exploring Ancient Iran, Afghanistan, and Pakistan*. London: British Museum.

Fukai, S., K. Horiuchi, K. Tanabe, and M. Domyo. 1969–84. *Taq-i Bustan I–IV*. Tokyo: Tokyo University Iraq-Iran Archaeological Expedition.

Ghirshman, R. 1971. *Fouilles de Châpour: Bîchâpour*, vol. 1. Paris: Geuthner.

Göbl, R. 1974. *Der Triumph des Sāsāniden Šahpuhr über Gordian, Philippus und Valerianus*. Vienna: Denkschriften der Österreichische Akad. d. Wiss., phil.-hist. Kl. 116.

Grenet, F. 2005. Découverte d'un relief sassanide dans le nord de l'Afghanistan. *CRAIBL* 149/1: 115–34.

Grenet, F., J. Lee, P. Martinez, and F. Ory. 2007. The Sasanian relief at Rag-i Bibi (Northern Afghanistan). In *After Alexander: Central Asia before Islam*, ed. J. Cribb and G. Herrmann, 243–67. London/Oxford: British Academy.

Haerinck, E., and B. Overlaet. 2009. The Sasanian rock reliefs of Bahram II at Guyum (Fars, Iran). *IrAnt* 44: 531–58.

Herrmann, G., and V. S. Curtis. 2002. Sasanian rock reliefs. *EnIr* online edition.

Herrmann, G., and R. Howell. 1977. *Naqsh-i Rustam 5 and 8: Sasanian reliefs attributed to Hormuzd II and Narseh*. Berlin: Iranische Denkmäler 8.

———. 1980–83. *The Sasanian rock reliefs at Bīshāpūr*. Berlin: Iranische Denkmäler 9 and 11.

Herrmann, G., D. N. MacKenzie, and R. Howell. 1989. *The Sasanian rock reliefs at Naqsh-i Rustam: Naqsh-i Rustam 6, the triumph of Shapur I, representation of Kerdir and inscription*. Berlin: Iranische Denkmäler 13.

Hollard, D. 2010. Julien et Mithrā sur le relief de Tāq-e Bostān. In *Sources for the history of Sasanian and post-Sasanian Iran*, ed. R. Gyselen, 147–63. Bures-sur-Yvette: RO 19.

Ker Porter, R. 1821–2. *Travels in Georgia, Persia, Armenia, ancient Babylonia, &c. &c. during the years 1817, 1818, 1819, and 1820*. London: Longman, Hurst, Rees, Orme, and Brown.

Luschey, H. 1996. Die Felsabarbeitung des Farhad ("Tarrash-e Farhad"). In *Bisutun: Ausgrabungen and Forschungen in den Jahren 1963–1967*, ed. W. Kleiss and P. Calmeyer, 117–20. Berlin: Gebr. Mann.

McDermot, B. C. 1954. Roman emperors in the Sasanian reliefs. *Journal of Roman Studies* 44: 76–80.

Movassat, J. D. 2005. *The large vault at Taq-i Bustan: A study in Late Sasanian royal art*. Lewiston/Queenston/Lampeter: Mellen Studies in Archaeology 3.

Overlaet, B. 2011. Ardashir II or Shapur III? Reflections on the identity of a king in the smaller grotto at Taq-i Bustan. *IrAnt* 46: 235–50.

Schmidt, E. 1970. *Persepolis III. The royal tombs and other monuments*. Chicago: OIP 70.

Trümpelmann, L. 1975a. *Das sasanidische Felsrelief von Dārāb*. Berlin: Iranische Denkmäler 6

———. 1975b. *Das sasanidische Felsrelief von Sar Mašhad*. Berlin: Iranische Denkmäler 5.

Vanden Berghe, L. 1983. *Reliefs rupestres de l'Iran ancien*. Brussels: KMKG-MRAH.

Weber, U. 2009. Wahrām II König der Könige von Ērān und Anērān. *IrAnt* 44: 559–643.

CHAPTER 46

KUH-E KHWAJA AND THE RELIGIOUS ARCHITECTURE OF SASANIAN IRAN

SOROOR GHANIMATI

Kuh-e Khwaja is a large and a well-preserved archaeological site of mainly Sasanian date that takes its name from an isolated basalt extrusion situated in the delta of the Helmand River, in the Iranian province of Sistan, 35 km southwest of the city of Zabol. Kuh-e Khwaja, or the "mountain of the Lord," is first attested in the variant form, Kuh-e Khoda, in a Zoroastrian text of early Islamic date (Boyce and Grenet 1991: 151, n. 139).

Setting

Over 2 km in length, the desolate mountain, in the form of a truncated cone, rises abruptly from the flat plain of the Helmand basin at an altitude of 600 m (Stein 1928: 909; Gullini 1964: 89; Afshar (Sistani) 1984: 86; Mousavi 1999: 81; Sajjadi 1995: 201; Landor 1902: 236ff.). It is surrounded by a large body of shallow water, fed by the terminal streams of the Helmand River, forming a seasonal lake, a sheet of water that constantly varies in size and is known as the Hamun Lake (or, in ancient times, as Lake Kasaoya). Although it is nowhere more than 12 m deep, this lake is the largest single expanse of fresh water on the Iranian Plateau (Fisher 1968: 76–81). The site consists of a walled settlement that lies on the southeastern side of Kuh-e Khwaja, on the lower slopes of a rock promontory, at a point protected from the effects of the notorious "winds of 120 days" by the mass of the mountain. Today this part is known as Qal'a-ye Kafaran ("fort of the Infidels") or sometimes as Qal'a-ye Sam. The site is bounded by a slender, angular, fortified wall that encloses an area with maximum dimensions of 153 m from north to south and 177 m from east to west. Remains of a once densely populated town are represented by a labyrinth of cells, chambers, and courts in the

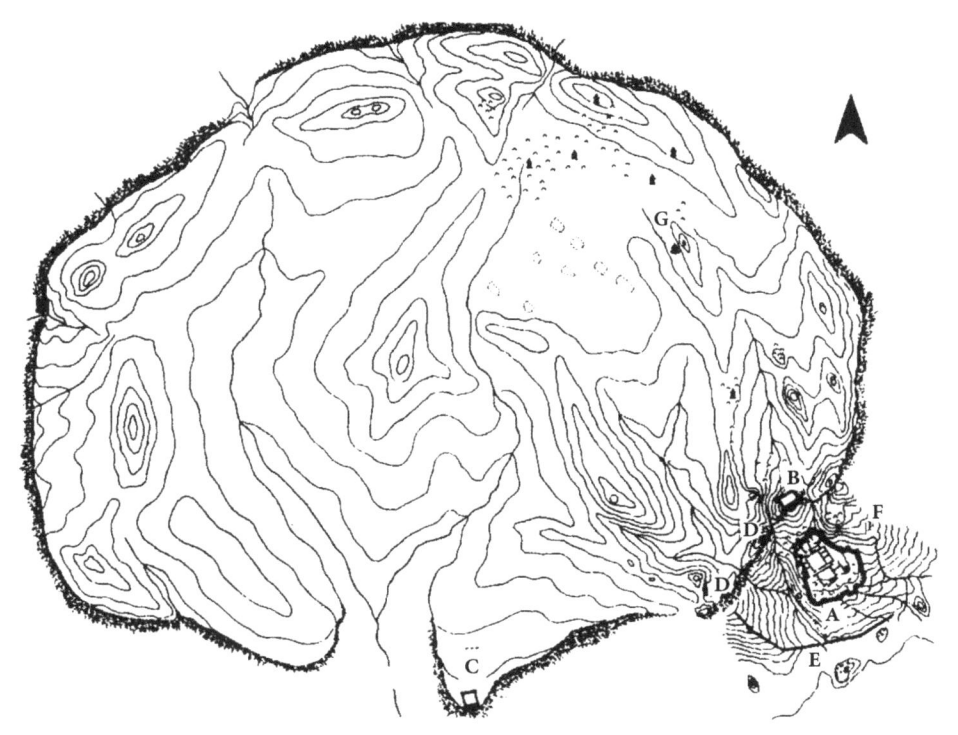

FIGURE 46.1 Topographic map of Kuh-e Khwaja. A. Ghagha Shahr and the Sacred Precinct; B. Kok-e Zal; C. Chehel Dokhtaran; D. Watch Towers; E. Ruined Wall; F. Cisterns; G. Tomb of Khwaja (after Ghanimati 2001).

lower portion of the settlement that, in the early twentieth century, was locally known as Ghagha Shahr (Fig. 46.1; Stein 1928: 909).

History of research

Sistan has been visited by many European travelers in the course of the last centuries but only a handful mentioned Kuh-e Khwaja (Fig. 46.2). The first general description of the site was written by B. Lovett, who explored it in March 1872 (Lovett 1874: 145–50). This was followed in 1902 by H. Savage Landor's detailed account and a fairly accurate map of the summit of the mountain which noted, among other things, two reservoirs on top of the mountain (reference kindly supplied by K. Lofstrom). Savage Landor called the ancient ruins the city of "Qah-qaha," or "roar of laughter" (Savage Landor 1902). However, many of the most important details were first noted several years later by G. P. Tate (Tate 1910: 265–8).

Sir Aurel Stein was the first scholar to make a thorough examination of the mudbrick buildings on Kuh-e Khwaja when he visited the site in December 1915. Stein mapped

FIGURE 46.2 Kuh-e Khwaja, looking westwards. The ancient ruins are visible on the left-hand side of the mountain (photo S. Ghanimati, 1997).

the entire mountain and transferred twelve painted panels from the site to the National Museum in Delhi where, regrettably, only two survive (Faccenna 1981: 87, n. 6). Stein subsequently identified the mountain as Mount Ushidam, of *Yasht* 19 in the *Avesta*, yet still speculated—despite such vivid Avestan/Zoroastrian associations—that the Sacred Precinct may have been a Buddhist monastery.

The next archaeologist to inspect the ruins was E. Herzfeld, who visited the site in February 1925 and again in the winter of 1929 (Herzfeld 1931–2; 1941: 291–7). Herzfeld concerned himself only with the Sacred Precinct, which he defined as a "palace with a fire-temple" in part, no doubt, because his excavations revealed the overturned stone Fire Holder on the floor of the of the Sanctuary (Herzfeld 1941: 292–301), the whereabouts of which is unknown (Mousavi 1999: 84). While the Sacred Precinct is often referred to as a "Palace-Temple" following Herzfeld (e.g., Erdmann 1941: 22), the validity of this label has seldom been questioned (Ghanimati 2000: 141–4). Like Stein, Herzfeld removed a significant number of wall paintings. These were sent to Berlin, where they are believed to have been destroyed during World War II. At the same time, however, two images from Kuh-e Khwaja (Herzfeld 1941: pl. 103, top two) eventually came to be acquired by the Metropolitan Museum of Art, New York, from Herzfeld's own collection (MMA accession nos. 45.99.1, 45.99.2). Importantly, Herzfeld also recorded the presence of stucco reliefs.

Herzfeld not only followed Stein in identifying Kuh-e Khwaja with Mount Ushidam, he also suggested that it could represent the *Mons Victorialis* where, in a legend pertaining to the birth of Christ, the Magi are said to have maintained their vigil (Herzfeld 1941: 291–2). In addition, he speculated that the Sacred Precinct had once been the seat of the Indo-Parthian ruler Gondophares (c.19–46 AD) and he speculated that Gondophares and Rostam were one and the same person (cf. Bailey 1937: 1154–5; Duchesne-Guillemin 1973: 167–8; Bivar 1983: 197; Boyce and Grenet 1991: 451–5, n. 447; Bernard 1996: 518ff.).

In 1961 Kuh-e Khwaja was reexamined by G. Gullini, who sank a series of trenches on the south side of the Central Court and who claimed to have distinguished six occupation levels (Gullini 1964: 65, 105, 224, 263, 283, 354, figs. 53–6). Eight years later, in response to Herzfeld's earlier claim that the art and architecture of Kuh-e Khwaja could be regarded as half-Greek and half-Eastern, D. Schlumberger suggested that the buildings and arts of Kuh-e Khwaja belonged to a new Eastern culture, "primarily a Greco-Iranian syncretic culture with the three elements of Greece, nomadic Iran, and the Ancient Near Eastern legacy of the Achaemenids fused" (Schlumberger 1969: 40, 55; 1983: 1052–5).

In the winter of 1974–5 a further fragment of wall painting was accidentally discovered in the Inner Domed Chamber of the South Gate by a restoration team led by D. Faccenna who suggested that there could be a direct link between the content of the scenes and the ceremonies that once took place in the South Gate (Faccenna 1981: 84, 92–3).

The Iranian Cultural Heritage and Tourism Organization conducted several seasons of fieldwork at Kuh-e Khwaja, beginning in 1995 (Mousavi 1999). Two wall paintings were discovered in the immediate vicinity of the North Gate as well as part of a stone staircase on the east side of the Painted Gallery (and which may have predated it).

THE SACRED PRECINCT

The monumental upper (northern) portion of the site has unavoidably attracted considerable attention. This area, the Sacred Precinct, could be approached only from the south by way of a narrow path that still winds its way through the ruins of Ghagha Shahr. An Entry Court gave access from this direction, leading to an Entry Terrace, with a single impressive portal, the so-called South Gate, consisting of a vestibule and an Inner Domed Chamber (Fig. 46.3).

Following the natural contours of the mountain, the buildings of the Sacred Precinct are arranged on and around a well-ordered axial plan, on a split-level elevation that ascends from south to north (for convenience this account follows earlier commentators in treating the site's long southeast-northwest axis as a north-south line). The lower level includes the South Gate with a vestibule and a main Inner Domed Chamber; the Entry Terrace; and the capacious Central Court. In its original state the mudbrick north façade of the Court was distinguished by a series of engaged columns of Classical inspiration (Herzfeld 1941: 98; Kleiss 1990: 774–80, 1993: 50–4). The north side of

882 THE SASANIAN PERIOD

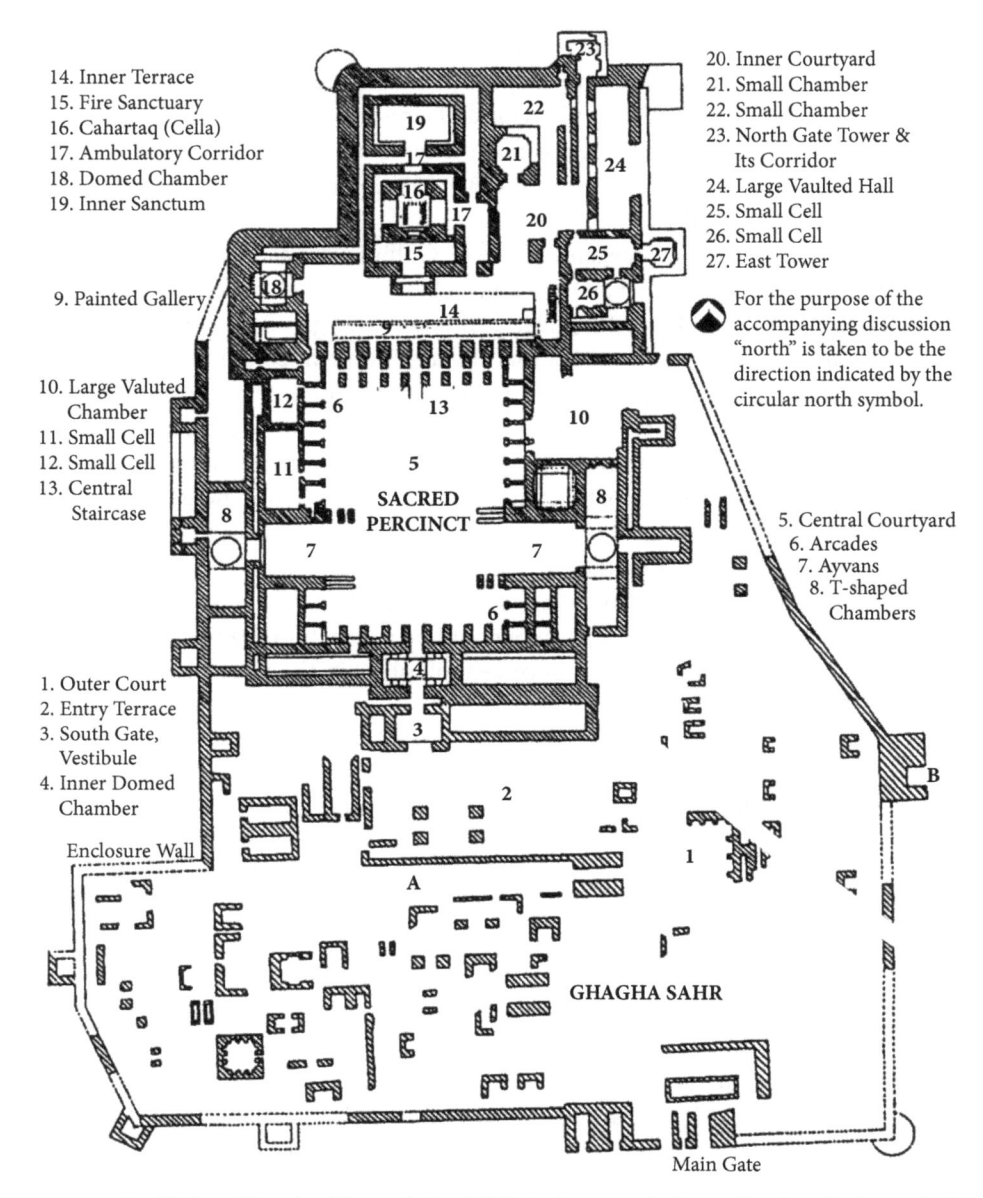

14. Inner Terrace
15. Fire Sanctuary
16. Cahartaq (Cella)
17. Ambulatory Corridor
18. Domed Chamber
19. Inner Sanctum

20. Inner Courtyard
21. Small Chamber
22. Small Chamber
23. North Gate Tower &
    Its Corridor
24. Large Vaulted Hall
25. Small Cell
26. Small Cell
27. East Tower

9. Painted Gallery

For the purpose of the accompanying discussion "north" is taken to be the direction indicated by the circular north symbol.

10. Large Valuted Chamber
11. Small Cell
12. Small Cell
13. Central Staircase

5. Central Courtyard
6. Arcades
7. Ayvans
8. T-shaped Chambers

SACRED PERCINCT

1. Outer Court
2. Entry Terrace
3. South Gate, Vestibule
4. Inner Domed Chamber

Enclosure Wall

GHAGHA SAHR

Main Gate

FIGURE 46.3 Kuh-e Khwaja. Plan of the Walled Area, including Ghagha Shahr and the Sacred Precinct (after Ghanimati 2001).

the Court was flanked by the now celebrated Painted Gallery, with its tall windows originally opening southwards onto the Court (Kawami 1987: 18). At some point the entire Court underwent a major program of reconstruction, when the Painted Gallery was blocked off; two lateral, nonaxial *ayvans* were added (each of which led to an elongated "back room" with a north-south axis, together creating a T-shaped plan); and tall arcades were erected on each side of the Court. In addition, a staircase was built in the midpoint of the north wall of the Court, directly in line with the entrance to the all-important Fire Sanctuary on the far side of the Inner Terrace above the staircase (Fig. 46.4).

The Fire Sanctuary consisted of a *chahartaq* (literally "four arches," a square, domed chamber), in which the ring of the dome was originally supported by squinches springing from four corner piers. The side walls of the *chahartaq* were open, but the Sanctuary was nonetheless closed off by the creation of an immediately adjoining, Ambulatory Corridor. In the center of the domed chamber Herzfeld found an overturned, stone "fire holder" which presumably had once rested on a square, plastered plinth. As the "three-step" shape of the Fire Holder at Kuh-e Khwaja closely corresponds to the shape of those from earlier times, it is possible that it dates to an earlier phase of occupation at the site (Boyce 1989b). If so, then this form, which has three outsteps at the top and three more toward the base (Herzfeld 1941: fig. 397, pl. 99) was already established by the early Sasanian period. On its north side, the *chahartaq* was connected to a smaller room or inner cella which presumably functioned as a storeroom and which was surrounded by the Ambulatory corridor. In addition, the western end of the Inner Terrace led to a smaller domed chamber, probably used for keeping the perpetual embers. There are several other, unidentified spaces on the north and east side of the Sacred Precinct, and apparently also an Eastern Gate Tower. The northwestern and northern sectors of the Sacred Precinct's outer wall were strengthened and thickened, from a point a little to the south of the smaller domed chamber to a point directly east of the North Gate.

FIGURE 46.4 Sacred Precinct. A bird's eye view from NE to SW (photo S. Ghanimati, 1997).

Construction techniques

Many of the mudbrick masons who worked at Kuh-e Khwaja must have been masters of their craft, for not only do a number of the extant walls still stand to a height of 15 m or more, they also bear witness to an intriguing variety of building procedures. Specifically, a number of the mudbrick walls exhibit not only standard layers of mortar, but also a band of stones near the foundation, as well as layers of reed, cow dung, or a mixture of the two toward the top (Ghanimati 2000: 144–5). Such bands of stone served to strengthen the lower portion of tall walls, while the introduction of light materials at a higher elevation lightened the overall weight of construction (Fig. 46.5).

The use of stone bands is not attested in other Sasanian mudbrick construction, and since the work of "Roman" prisoners of war is thought to be discernible at various sites in Sasanian Iran (Frye 1983a: 296; 1983b: 126–38; Bosworth 1968: 2; Garsoïan 1983: 581; Matthews 1989: 133–40), it may be that Kuh-e Khwaja's banded walls—and perhaps its multiple external cisterns (cf. Tate 1910: 266; Shahbazi 1990: 588–99)—provide proof of the presence of a nonlocal labor force. Indeed, it is striking that Roman and Byzantine walls of concrete were often faced with small limestone blocks that were leveled or reinforced at varying intervals by bands of thin baked bricks in mortar beds of equal thickness (Krautheimer 1965: 49; Talbot Rice 1958: 53–7, pls. 9D, 18).

FIGURE 46.5 Sacred Precinct. The Inner Terrace, showing the remains of two squinches in the Western Chamber (photo S. Ghanimati, 1995).

As illustrated by the main chamber in the South Gate; the major rooms that opened off the center-rear of the two *ayvans*; the cella of the Fire Sanctuary; and some of the units associated with the Inner Terrace, domes served as the main method of roofing in all of the principal chambers associated with the Sacred Precinct. All of the domes appear to have been constructed with the aid of cone-shaped squinches (Persian *sehkonj*, *filpush*, and *gushvara*)—an architectural device which originated in Sasanian times and which ultimately gave birth to the more complex *moqarnas* of the Islamic period, which have persisted to the present day (Fig. 46.6; Huff 1990: 634–8; Ghanimati 2001: 86–7).

Elsewhere, barrel vaults or *taq-ahang* were usually used to roof corridors or galleries. In such cases (in order to obviate the need for wooden centering) the builders customarily resorted to pitched brick vaults composed of sundried bricks set in gypsum mortar. On the other hand, arches and arcades were constructed with the aid of long, reed-reinforced, molded mudbrick struts. Such prefabricated mudbrick elements began to be used in Media during the seventh century BC (Roaf and Stronach 1973: 129–41; cf. Hansman and Stronach 1974: 11–22) and can still be found in use in parts of Iran today (Huff 1990: 150–60). Last but not least, almost all surfaces were given a generous coat of gypsum plaster as a standard protective measure.

FIGURE 46.6 Ghagha Shahr. A typical wall construction, showing string courses of stone and/or broken backed bricks (photo S. Ghanimati, 1995).

Ornamentation

The importance of the Sacred Precinct is confirmed by the wealth of luxurious decoration in this part of the site (Kawami 1987: 18, 25; Schlumberger 1969: 53–9). This included stucco moldings, stucco colonnettes, stucco panels with geometric design, mud and plaster figurative reliefs, and of course the celebrated wall paintings. The high quality of the stucco ornamentation at Kuh-e Khwaja has elicited extensive commentary (e.g., Stein 1928: 909–21; Faccenna 1981: fig. 11; Herzfeld 1941: 293–4, pls. 96 bottom and 99; Schlumberger 1969: 53–9; Kröger 1982: 35, 74, 133, 185, 226–7, 247, 257, 267, pls. 103–4; Kawami 1987: 17–18, 24).

Reliefs

The reliefs were discovered by the two original excavators, Stein and Herzfeld. Those on the north wall of the Central Courtyard, on either side of the Central Staircase, and on the south façade of the Fire Sanctuary, were made of mud and coated with gypsum plaster, which was then painted. Tamarisk pegs or *qova*, about 15 cm long, were used to fix the reliefs to the walls.

In the Central Courtyard

On the north wall of the Central Courtyard Herzfeld discovered a pair of life-size male figures molded in high relief, above the arch of the middle doorway, which he suggested had originally held a wreath. Only fragments of the drapery of the westernmost figure still survived (Herzfeld 1941: 292, pl. 96 bottom; Kröger 1982: 210–11, pl. 104; Kawami 1987: 18). The better-preserved, opposing image retained some portions of the left shoulder, arm, torso, and leg, as well as a mass of curly hair and a few flying ribbons. This frieze was still visible in 1961 (Gullini 1964: 389, fig. 219). J. Kröger considered the various decoration elements in this part of the site to be early Sasanian (Kröger 1982: 35, 74, 133, 185, 226–7, 247, 267), while T. Kawami identified this particular figure as that of a Sasanian king. Stein noted that a section of wall just east of these figures had originally been painted, and he also observed traces of rippling ribbons and a ring or circle (Stein 1928: 913).

At the Fire Sanctuary

Remnants of a stucco relief portraying combat between a horseman and a lion were discovered on the imposing south façade of the Fire Sanctuary. An adjacent wall to the west had an equally worn equestrian scene in "mud-stucco" executed in low relief (Ghanimati 2001: pls. SD-5–7). The scene shows three figures on horseback, all facing right, taking part in a procession, according to Stein. Although the equestrian figures are now almost completely destroyed, the bodies and heads of the horses have survived and were still visible in 2007. Stein suggested a Sasanian date for this relief (Stein 1928: 909–12; cf. Ghirshman 1954: pl. 35.1–3; Kawami 1987: 19).

Paintings

Copious murals or wall paintings were discovered by both Stein and Herzfeld within and near the South and the North Gates, as well as in the Painted Gallery. Later, D. Faccenna reported the discovery of a further painting in the Sacred Precinct. In addition, two new pieces were recently recovered by an Iranian team near the North Gate. These paintings have given rise to a wide range of interpretations and chronological attributions. Although much has been destroyed, these constitute the largest collection of pre-Islamic paintings in Iran.

At the South Gate

Stein uncovered a large number of paintings in passage *i*, near the western façade of the South Gate, most of which were on walls that had been sealed off by later additions (Stein 1928: 915–21). One painting showed a standing, nearly life-sized, robed figure. The faintly preserved colors, together with the overall contours of the figure and the style of the dress, evoked Central Asian Buddhist parallels in Stein's mind, and as a result he identified the figure as a Bodhisattva (Stein 1928: 917–18). A second painting on a later, adjacent wall showed two registers of standing figures in belted tunics and trousers with out-turned feet and heads turned slightly to the viewer's right. The fabrics and their ornaments varied from figure to figure. In the lower register, a partly obliterated, seated figure faced several standing ones. Elsewhere in passage *i*, Stein observed a three-headed creature and an ox-headed mace held by a seated figure. He subsequently identified the seated figure with Rostam and took the weapon to be his mace.

In 1974 Faccenna discovered a fragmentary painting in the Inner Domed Chamber of the South Gate. The new fragment was detached from its original setting and, after restoration in Italy, presented to the Archaeological Museum in Tehran (Faccenna 1981: 83). This painting is a cityscape that depicts people in procession. It shows two overlapping male heads in profile, facing left, and below them, to the right, four male heads compressed into an equivalent area. These males are bareheaded with large eyes; large, sharp nose-profiles; and a compact mass of hair. The heads appear against a light background in a setting of light-colored walls, battlements, and two towers, between which are two more heads, facing left (Faccenna 1981: 85–97; cf. Kawami 1987: 26–52). The head in front is bearded and the other, partly hidden behind the first, wears a low, red, hemispherical helmet with a jutting visor and a side-flap from which a white cheekpiece reaches down under the chin. This side-flap and other similar devices have generally been identified as a *padam*, a mouthpiece or mask which is now worn by Zoroastrian priests primarily during various rituals in order not to pollute pure objects, but in the past was worn on occasion by royal attendants and others as well.

In the Painted Gallery

The paintings discovered here were distributed over two zones: on the vaulted ceiling, and on its supporting walls.

On the Ceiling

The barrel vault bore a pattern of painted coffers arranged in three rows. The painted squares ascended from the cornice (at the springing of the vault) to the apex of the vault and thus created a three-dimensional representation of a coffered ceiling. In addition, alternating squares were filled with floral rosettes of varying designs and styles. Some rosettes had a solid circular form much like a dense sunflower or lotus, while others had long, curling leaves that unfurled into the corners of the square; a few of the leaves folded back on themselves. The remainder of the squares contained single human figures varying in character and compositional style. A few of these are defined by a relatively heavy, dark outline and are depicted with musical instruments in postures of repose, some as dancers, others as acrobats. A small winged Eros riding a horse or a feline is also depicted (Herzfeld 1941: 294–5). It should be noted that while Herzfeld assigned a Hellenistic origin to the paintings on the ceiling, Kawami suggested a date in the first century AD or later (Kawami 1987: 28).

On the Window Wall

An elaborate painted frieze ran the length of the "window" or south wall of the Painted Gallery, just next to the crown molding. The first element at the top of the frieze consisted of a row of red and white dentils, framed top and bottom by a painted red band. A pale, two-step molding was installed below this, followed by a frieze of laurel leaves wrapped in a dark red ribbon. This was bordered itself at the bottom by a wide, dark red band with a floral pattern in red and green. Kawami noted this was based on the Greek Lesbian *cyma*, and speculated that the purpose of the frieze was to set off a series of painted, over life-sized figures arranged in groups of two or three between the eight windows which pierced the south wall at regular intervals (Kawami 1987: 30). These figures appeared to be proceeding westward from the eastern end of the Gallery. The first painting in the series shows a pair of beardless figures. On the left is a male with short, curly brown hair who is shown in three-quarter view. He holds an upright trident in his left hand and wears a long, yellow tunic decorated with a red band with yellow and green roundels about the neck (Kawami 1987: 30–52). A mantle is wrapped around his waist and falls over his left shoulder in a triangular fold. Standing to the right of the trident bearer is a female who holds a long rod with a rounded head against her left shoulder; Herzfeld referred to this as a mace. Apparently, she wears a yellow, sleeveless gown that is gathered above her right breast by a roundel or brooch whose center seems to have held a mounted stone. The mace-bearer has her right hand raised, and her left elbow virtually leans against the upper arch of the window, while the head of the beardless trident-bearer protruded slightly into the painted cornice at the top of the wall. The identity of these two figures has not been established. Herzfeld saw the figures as deities, but Kawami has strongly opposed this (Herzfeld 1941: 296; Kawami 1987: 32–52). The identity of the mace bearer is also problematic (for the image of Saoshyant with a mace, see Ghanimati 2001: 171–4).

The stretch of wall between the second and third windows was decorated with three standing figures, each of which seems to have been male. Like all other figures in the

Gallery, these were visible only from the waist upward. They stand in three-quarter view, turned to the viewer's left, and are grouped very closely. Their heads are small, necks thick, and shoulders broad and sloping. The two on the left wore tunics and mantles over the left shoulder, like the mace-carrier, and both had dark hair and rounded beards. The third figure is beardless and wears a type of round headgear with a thin rim and a wing-like feature that rises at each side. This third figure wears a white tunic and carries a reddish-brown and yellow shield (Kawami 1987: 32–3). These figures have not been identified.

Although the painting occupying the space between the third and fourth windows was already destroyed by the time of Herzfeld's visit, Stein found a painted mural in this position which showed life-size, seated, youthful (beardless) figures in a Classical style in profile, facing each other and holding long lances. They were nude to the waist, with white drapery at the waist interpreted by Stein as a loincloth (Stein 1928: 920). Evidently, the left-hand figure was shown bent forward and grasping with both hands a leveled lance aimed at the figure on the right, who leaned back as if anticipating the thrust. The latter's upright weapon was held in his left hand. Kawami observed that above this mural were remnants of a painted cornice, showing dentils, beribboned laurels, and dark red bands. She concluded from this that the panel was one of those described by Herzfeld, and hence was located somewhere near the center of the Gallery. She also noted that the Stein panel portrayed a type of combat that was intended to be witnessed by the row of standing figures painted between the other windows and that, most probably, the contestants would have been riding elephants (Kawami 1987: 36–8; Matthews 1989: 63–6). Kawami observed that only Šābuhr I (240–272) and Xosrow II (591–628) had elephants in their armies, although Šābuhr II (309/10–79) did as well (Frye 1983b: 132–40).

The spaces between windows four, five, and six in the western half of the Gallery had no paintings. Herzfeld recorded "two heads" between the sixth and seventh windows, but Kawami indicated that the notation in Herzfeld's notebook for the space between the seventh and eighth windows was illegible. The painting between the eighth window and the western end of the Painted Gallery was severely damaged. Herzfeld's drawing of it shows a beardless male figure framed by a yellow nimbus, whom he identified as a moon god (Kawami 1987: 37–9, for other representations of "moon," see Samadi Rijali 1988: 49–51).

On the Window Recesses

The walls and vaults of the window recesses were also painted, and evidently two windows retained some of their paintings. In his sketch book Herzfeld described the paintings of the second window from the east end of Gallery as having "coffers and pictures." He also made an annotated sketch of a row of five standing figures on the wall of the second window recess in the eastern half of the Painted Gallery. All five figures were shown frontally, their heads in profile facing toward the viewer's right. Each figure has the right hand flexed at chest level, while the left arm is bent and held to the side and across the waist. All have short hair and wear sleeved tunics. The five figures are depicted in procession, with the figure at the head of the procession, on the right, shown at half the size of the others. It is unclear if the figure at the head of the procession is a child or an adult male. This small figure carries a vertical object in his raised right hand. The figure behind him holds an almost white, tulip-like flower with two green leaves in his right hand and a reddish, ball-like object, interpreted as the pommel of a sword hilt (Kawami 1987: 39), in his left.

Another figure behind the flower-bearer carried in his right hand an oval ring, and above his head were two small flowers, one with four petals and the other with five. Behind these flowers rose a pale yellow, leafy branch resembling a stylized laurel. This figure was distinguished from the rest by his belt and inverted sword, held by the hilt in the left hand. Behind the ring-bearer stood a man whose upper garment was decorated with yellow circles; other details were obscure (Herzfeld 1941: 294–303).

On the Back Wall

The north or back wall of the Painted Gallery was windowless and preserved remnants of the same painted cornice noted on the south wall. Only one section of the wall painting itself had survived in the eastern half of the Gallery, located directly opposite the trident-bearer. This showed three standing figures, one overlapping pair, and a single figure to the left that was barely visible (Stein 1928: 921; Herzfeld 1941: 295–303, pl. 104 top; Kawami 1987: 42–4). The pair consisted of a male and a female, each wearing a long-sleeved, V-necked tunic, facing toward the viewer's right. A sword hung from a thin belt worn low over the hips of the male. The left arm of the other, presumably female, figure hung down by her side while her right arm was obscured by the male figure. This composition, which Herzfeld took to represent a "King and Queen," was set within a frame of light and dark vertical bands. Kawami dated this painting to the late third or early fourth century.

At the North Gate

The North Gate, presumably a two-story vaulted structure, included a Tower, the upper room of which retained traces of wall paintings, two fragments of which are now in the Metropolitan Museum of Art. These are the only surviving paintings from this context recorded by Herzfeld (Stein 1928: 912–13, pl. 53). Each of the fragments in the Metropolitan depicts a single head. According to Herzfeld, the larger one depicts a beardless male in profile, facing left, with short, black, curly hair, while the other shows a beardless head in profile, facing right, which Herzfeld identified originally as a female and later as "a flute player" (Herzfeld 1941: pl. 103 top left caption). Nevertheless, Kawami considered the first description uncertain and the second incorrect. In her view, the second head wears a *padam*, that is, a thin band tied across the mouth and fastened at the top of the head. However, she suggested that the *padam* cannot be taken as a definite sign of religious activity, for it could have belonged to a secular servant or attendant (Kawami 1987: 45–50; cf. Harper 1981: 117, n. 86). However, it should be noted that, if a servant wore a *padam*, this could indicate that his master was a Zoroastrian priest who was required to observe purity laws. Kawami dated this painting to the late Sasanian period (Kawami 1987: 48–50).

A further painted panel was recovered from a small chamber in the vicinity of the North Gate by the Iranian team, showing a classical Iranian contest between man and beast. In addition to the paintings discussed above, it seems that the Eastern Tower of the Inner Terrace also retained traces of painting. These were noticed by Herzfeld on his 1925 visit; by 1929, however, all traces of these paintings had disappeared. In summary, as Kawami has noted, "the murals of Kuh-e Khwaja provide an unexpectedly complex picture of artistic activity in Sistān and form the largest corpus of painting in ancient Iran" (Kawami 1987: 50).

CHRONOLOGY

Stein initially speculated, at least in his correspondence, that Kuh-e Khwaja was Parthian but later ascribed the site to both the Parthian and Sasanian periods (Stein 1928: 909–25; Mirsky 1977: 390–91; Kawami 1987: 15, n. 12.). Herzfeld's view of the date of Kuh-e Khwaja was also subject to modification. Initially, he placed an early phase of construction in the Sasanian period and a later one in the early Islamic period. In later years, however, he recognized a Parthian building phase dated to the first century and a subsequent Sasanian phase represented by alterations of third century date (Herzfeld 1941: 291–7).

Gullini dated his six occupation levels from Achaemenid to Islamic times (Gullini 1964: 65, 105, 224, 263, 283, 354). This was immediately challenged by G. Tucci (Tucci 1966: 143–7). Schlumberger dated Kuh-e Khwaja to the early Sasanian era (Schlumberger 1969: 40, 55; 1983: 1052–5) and K. Schippmann concluded that a Sasanian date was most likely (Schippmann 1971: 55–70; cf. Boucharlat 1984: 129–30; Besenval 1984: 137–8). In 1981 Faccenna put forward the suggestion that Kuh-e Khwaja could be late Parthian (Faccenna 1981). In a comprehensive survey of Sasanian stucco published in 1982, J. Kröger attributed all of the stucco at Kuh-e Khwaja to the Sasanian era and the majority to early Sasanian times (Kröger 1982: 35, 74, 133, 185, 226–7, 247, 257, 267). Similarly, basing herself on Herzfeld's field records in the Freer Gallery of Art, Kawami ascribed the paintings in the South Gate and the Painted Gallery to the Sasanian rather than the Parthian period (Kawami 1987: 13–52). She noted that the style, proportions, dress, and coiffure of the stucco figures are distinctly Sasanian; that one figure is likely to represent a king; and that the equestrian reliefs on the entrance façade of the Fire Sanctuary accord with Sasanian taste. With reference to specific and stylistic elements in the Sacred Precinct that recall classical architecture, Kawami stressed that classical influences in Iranian architecture were not restricted to the Parthian period but persisted well into Sasanian times (Kawami 1987: 154; cf. Schlumberger 1983: 1052–5). On the other hand, neither her suggestion that the second phase of construction in the Sacred Precinct dates to the early Islamic period (Kawami 1987: 19, 24, 47; cf. Faccenna 1981: 93, n. 18) nor her further proposal—echoing Stein's early speculation—that the site first functioned as a Buddhist shrine (cf. Kawami 2005: 181–214) is particularly convincing. Based on the recent work of the Iranian team,

S. M. Mousavi suggested that the Sacred Precinct underwent two periods of construction, one in the late Parthian period and one of Sasanian date (Mousavi 1999: 84).

More recently, radiocarbon samples from two chronologically distinct contexts within the Sacred Precinct were dated at the Lawrence Berkeley National Laboratory. The first C14 sample, which derived from organic materials used in the construction of the ceiling of the Painted Gallery, yielded a date of 80–240 ± 50, while the second sample, taken from tamarisk pegs that had been used in the construction of the stucco reliefs on the entrance façade of the Fire Sanctuary, provided a date of 540–650 ± 50 (Ghanimati 2000: 145).

Apart from the chronological testimony of the paintings, the stucco elements, and the above-mentioned C14 results, the vaulted mudbrick architecture of Kuh-e Khwaja is itself consistent with Sasanian construction techniques and elements of design. Indeed, it is not improbable that the first Sasanian building plan was initiated by Ardašīr I (224–240) and completed by Šābuhr I (241–272/3) (Ghanimati 2000: 144–5). The testimony of the architectural details that are associated with the site's subsequently remodeled areas are consistent with a date in the late Sasanian period (Schippmann 1971: 67; Duchesne-Guillemin 1973: 67; Kröger 1982: 257; Kawami 1987: 38, 40; Boucharlat and Lecomte 1987: 51–7, 64–72), suggesting that the architectural development and formation of the Sacred Precinct was a gradual process that took place under the patronage of several pious kings. This view is supported by two newly found coins in the vicinity of Painted Gallery (Ghanimati 2015). The more legible coin appears, from the available photographs, to be a silver drachm of Šābuhr II (309–379). Unfortunately, the peripheral legends on the obverse are not clear enough to be read with confidence. The crown worn by the king is Göbl's Type b (Göbl 1983: 322–9; Frye 1983b: 135).

Finally, the collapse, in the spring of 1998, of part of the floor of the Entry Terrace chanced to reveal the existence of a still older mudbrick structure that had been wholly covered by the first phase of monumental construction. Consequently, on this evidence alone, Kuh-e Khwaja appears to have belonged to at least to three separate phases of construction: a relatively modest, late Parthian building level; the all-important first phase of Sasanian construction; and an almost equally significant phase of late Sasanian building activity that included the introduction of the stucco reliefs on the facade of the Fire Sanctuary, as well as still other substantial architectural changes, especially in the immediate vicinity of the Central Court.

Pre-Islamic religious architecture of Iran

Fire Temples

Before considering the place of Kuh-e Khwaja in the history of Sasanian religious architecture, it may be helpful to say a few words about this subject more broadly. In early

Zoroastrianism divine beings were offered worship without the aid of temples or statues, and all that was needed for a place to perform the high rituals was a clean, flat piece of ground, marked off by a ritually drawn furrow and then consecrated. Offerings were consecrated there and made to the invisible deities, including the spirits of fire and water (1975b: 455, n. 3). It is known that "the fire was placed in a low container within the ritual precinct because the celebrating priest himself sat cross-legged upon the ground" (Boyce 1975a: 166ff.). This fire was regularly tended with care and received a threefold offering of dry wood, incense, and fat from a sacrificial animal.

It has been suggested that a Zoroastrian temple cult of fire was first instituted in Iran in the later Achaemenid period, during or after the reign of Artaxerxes II (405–359 BC) (Boyce 1982: 221ff.; 1989c: 9ff.; Boyce and Grenet 1991: 270.). Thereafter it seems that, from having had no "temples"—that is, enclosed, consecrated buildings—Zoroastrians began to have sanctuaries of two different types, one that contained a cult statue of a divine being, the other kind housing an ever-burning fire. Each was known by various names in the Middle Iranian languages; for instance in Parthian, the former was called a *bagin*, "place of the god," or *ayazan*, "place of worship," while the latter was named an *ataroshan*, "place of burning fire," or simply a "house of fire" (Boyce 1989c: 9ff.). It has been observed that the use of images among Zoroastrians increased because of Hellenistic influence in the Seleucid period, but there was also a growth in the temple cult of fire. The Sasanians initiated an iconoclastic campaign, and though evidently the old image shrines continued to exist, these either contained a sacred fire, which was put there to replace the former image, or were left empty (Ghanimati 2001).

Schippmann suggested that, since the Zoroastrians had no tradition of temple building, the image shrine provided an architectural model for the fire temple (1971: 197, 266ff.; for other types of religious monuments, see Duchesne-Guillemin 1973: 64ff.). He recorded eleven "fire temples" of Seleucid and Parthian date but several of these have nothing to do with fire, and include, for example, the temple at Khorheh and what is now identified as a Sasanian palace at Kangavar.

The study of Sasanian fire temples has long been a contentious subject. Many scholars have assumed both that the temple cult of fire belonged to primitive Zoroastrianism and that it provided its one form of public worship at all times. S. Wikander was the first to question these matters, arguing that the temple cult of fire was unknown to the early Zoroastrians (Wikander 1946: 58ff., 101ff.). This argument has been strengthened by more recent scholarly work highlighting similarities between Zoroastrian cult and ancient Brahmanic observance, in which temples were unknown (Boyce 1975b: 455; 1989c: 9ff.). Moreover, many early identifications of fire temples have been challenged during the past few decades, most notably by K. Schippmann (1972) who recorded fifty Sasanian temple ruins, the majority of which are in Fars, the homeland of the Sasanians (twenty-one in Fars; seven in Kerman; three in Khuzestan; one on Kharg Island; fourteen in Iraq-e Ajami; one each in Azerbaijan, Kurdistan, and Sistan). In addition, no longer extant fire temples once stood in Ray and at Tureng Tepe in Gorgan (present-day Golestan). Oddly enough, in spite of importance of the Zoroastrianism in Sistan, only the fire sanctuary of Kuh-e Khwaja was listed by Schippman in the east. This is perhaps due to the destruction of fire temples by the Arabs and later by the Mongols. Whatever the case may be, the archaeological evidence suggests that a wide variety of fire temples existed in the Sasanian period when religious buildings included both large and small fire temples and shrines to individual divinities.

No set architectural standards for the construction of fire temples appear to have existed in Parthian or Sasanian times, but certain common architectural features appear in most of the known temple complexes. Furthermore, it is clear that various structural components evolved from the older architectural vocabulary of the Iranian plateau, as well as from local traditions in each area. The most characteristic architectural element of Sasanian temples, and often the only part to survive, is the so-called *chahartaq*. This type of construction and spatial arrangement was very simply referred to in the Pahlavi books as *gombad* or "dome." It was beneath the *gombad* that the perpetual fire was enthroned. The "fire temple" as a whole was called *atashkada* or "house of fire" (Boyce 1989c: 9ff.).

E. Herzfeld, U. Monneret de Villard, and O. Reuther were the first to maintain that fire temples were always closed buildings, more complex than a simple open canopy; and D. Huff argues that "the Chahartaq, with or without ambulatory but always surrounded by walls or adjoining rooms, served as the sanctuary where the fire altar was kept and worship took place" (Huff 1990: 637) and that the same architectural unit also appeared in various secular contexts. In all cases, the term *chahartaq* describes an equilateral architectural unit consisting of four arches, or short barrel vaults between four corner piers, which is roofed by a dome on squinches over a central square (Huff 1990: 634ff.). This square, together with the lateral bays under the arches, or barrel vaults, provides a room of cruciform (Pers. *chalipa*) ground plan. The origin of the *chahartaq* remains a matter of debate (Monneret de Villard 1935–6: 176ff.). Reuther and Herzfeld suggested that the dome on squinches originated in the mudbrick architecture of eastern Iran, where it developed from the simple, pitched-brick dome or squinch vault (Reuther 1938: 501–4; Herzfeld 1941: 17–18). However, the earliest evidence of pitched-brick vaulting comes from the early second millennium BC in Mesopotamia, in the corbeled vaulting at Ur (Huff 1990: 634ff.). Although this can be regarded as a forerunner, in Iran itself there is no evidence of the *chahartaq* proper before the beginning of the Sasanian period. Therefore, it has been suggested that perhaps the first step in the development of the *chahartaq* was taken at Takht Neshin in Firuzabad in the third century AD, in the buildings erected by Ardašīr before he became king in 224/6 (Huff 1990; cf. Schippmann 1971: 104). Eventually, as Huff observed, the structural and aesthetic properties of the *chahartaq* led to it becoming the most prominent element in traditional Iranian architecture after the *ayvan*. Indeed, the *chahartaq* seems to have been widely adopted in Iranian architecture of the Islamic period when it was used in the mosque, the mausoleum, the palace and the garden pavilion (for earlier literature, cf. Huff 1990; Erdmann 1941: 35ff.; Godard 1951: 7ff.).

Schippmann divided the known *chahartaqs* into two groups, those that were surrounded by a roofed ambulatory which protected the inner chamber, and those that apparently stood open to the wind and were thus unsuitable as permanent sanctuaries for fire. However, Huff later reexamined several of the "open" *chahartaqs* and traces of the roofing of an outer passage, which led him to conclude that, while it is relatively easy to demolish a low passageway, it is treacherous to try to bring down a dome. Thus, it now seems that *chahartaqs* were normally surrounded by a roofed ambulatory. Various views exist on the exact purpose of the ambulatory. Thus, Herzfeld suggested it had a ceremonial function (Herzfeld 1941: 302). P. Bernard supported this theory noting that ambulatories are found in Greek and Indian (Buddhist and Hindu) temples, where they enabled ritual circumambulation around the sanctuary (Bernard 1996: 510; cf. Stronach 1985: 618ff.). It would appear that in view of the Zoroastrian requirement that a sacred fire be kept in both actual and ritual purity, a second barrier in the form of an ambulatory was one way of achieving this.

Other architectural units attested in the remains of many fire temples include a central courtyard; arcades and passageways; various chambers for storing firewood, incense, and utensils; a "place of worship" (Pers. *yazishn-gah*) for officiating priests; one or two ash-rooms; a large hall presumably for congressional purposes and the celebration of feasts (Pers. *gahambar-khana*); and perhaps a residence for priests (cf. Boyce 1989c). No rituals were performed under the *gombad* itself, where only veneration offered directly to the fire itself occurred. It has also been postulated that a treasury might have existed in some temple complexes, such as at Takht-e Soleyman (Schippmann 1971: 331). It is clear that the Sacred Precinct at Kuh-e Khwaja also included other structures, including secondary shrines, courtyards, domed chambers, passageways, and perhaps even a dormitory for the learning priests, as well as other unidentified units. The original function of such features may never be known, but their incorporation in the plan of the Sacred Precinct may one day permit a reasonably full architectural analysis of the buildings of a major Zoroastrian temple complex.

Architectural Comparisons

The uniqueness of Kuh-e Khwaja makes architectural comparison difficult. In the few architectural studies available on the Sacred Precinct, scholars have compared it with monuments from various periods scattered all over the region extending from Central Asia and India to the Mediterranean. Such studies have adduced both secular and religious architecture in these areas. Thus, the Sacred Precinct at Kuh-e Khwaja, which is clearly a Zoroastrian establishment, has been compared with Greco-Roman temples in the West and with Buddhist shrines in the East. The complex as a whole has also been compared with palatial buildings and/or dynastic shrines in and adjacent to the Iranian plateau. Consequently, while many antecedents have been sought and numerous parallels have been proposed, no convincing interpretation of the architecture of the Sacred Precinct at Kuh-e Khwaja has been articulated.

It would seem desirable, however, for architectural comparisons to be made solely with buildings and complexes that are both functionally and chronologically related, that is, in the religious architecture of Parthian and especially Sasanian Iran. Yet the problem is that many of the relevant Parthian and the Sasanian remains are only partially preserved, often consisting of no more than one or two rooms. Moreover, the few Zoroastrian complexes that have yielded a coherent plan consist of private residences incorporating a temple, while few represent exclusively religious complexes.

In her valuable architectural studies, Kawami compared the first phase of the Sacred Precinct at Kuh-e Khwaja broadly with the "sanctuaries of Central Asia," and the second phase with the Buddhist shrine at Kara Tepe in Bactria, dated between the second and fourth centuries AD; the Sasanian palaces at Firuzabad, Sarvestan, and Qasr-e Shirin (Taq-e Xosrow); and the early Islamic complexes at Qasral-Kharanah and Khirbat Minyah in Jordan, and Tulul al-Ukhaidir in Iraq (Kawami 1987: 20ff.). Kawami argued that the off-center alignment of the two great *ayvans* in the Central Courtyard could not be Sasanian. On the other hand, since *ayvans* represent a fundamental form in Iranian architecture (Grabar 2011), it is possible that the symmetrical, yet off-centered, positioning of the *ayvans* ending in T-shaped rooms reflects a stage in the architectural evolution of Iranian religious complexes that occurred during the late Sasanian era (or even earlier). Moreover, this particular configuration is likely to have served as a source of inspiration for later Islamic builders, not the other way around, as previously suggested by Kawami and others (Kawami 1987: 24).

The Sasanian fire temple at Tureng Tepe stood within a large, fortified complex, but only traces of a *chahartaq* remain (Boucharlat 1987: 15ff., 43ff., 51ff.), making a detailed architectural comparison with Kuh-e Khwaja impossible. Other fire temples of this period, such as that at Panjikent in Sogdiana (Tajikistan; Gropp 1969: 168ff.; Azarpay 1981: 181; 1983: 1145ff.; 1987: 595ff.; Duchesne-Guillemin 1973: 66; Boyce and Grenet 1991: 168, 178) and the dynastic shrine at Bandian in Khorasan (Rahbar 1998: 213ff.; 1999: 62ff.), will not be considered for the same reason. Thus, aside from Kuh-e Khwaja itself, the few temple complexes with a relatively complete plan are those at Bishapur, Hajiabad, and Kunar Siah, all in Fars, as well as Takht-e Soleyman in Azerbaijan. The temples at both Bishapur and Hajiabad are thought to have been private sanctuaries devoted to the worship of the Iranian *yazata Anahita*, while those at Kunar Siah and Takht-e Soleyman were dedicated to the worship of fire.

The principal complex at Bishapur, the new capital built by Šābuhr I, has been identified as a palace-temple (Ghirshman 1962: 149; Schippmann 1971: 151ff.; Shepherd 1983: 1075; Keall 1989: 287ff.). It includes, among various features, a court and an *ayvan*. The complex is built of ashlar masonry, possibly of Roman derivation. The centrally placed Great Hall has an enormous, stepped, cruciform plan (cf. the temple at Nush-e Jan near Hamadan, Stronach and Roaf 2007: fig. 2.2), for which Ghirshman proposed a vault that would have spanned over 22 m (Keall 1989: 288). Although this latter hypothesis has remained a matter of debate, it has been argued that this was the first *chahartaq* to be surrounded by an ambulatory. This ambulatory separated the central cruciform unit from all other spaces in the complex. Apparently, sixty-four painted niches decorated the walls around the room (Ghirshman 1971: 9ff.; Schippmann 1971: 142ff.).

Behind the Great Hall is a semisubterranean building with a square main room (originally roofed with beams), the walls of which were built of rubble masonry faced with cut stone. This was originally roofed with beams, supported by stone capitals in the shape of bull protomes (Ghirshman 1971: 9ff.; Keall 1989). This building is now generally identified as a temple. A. A. Sarfaraz found a water channel which led to the building from the nearby river (Sarfaraz 1975). In addition, an elaborate arrangement of pipes and conduits built in the subfloor area and within the building's two-layer stone pavement suggested that the whole edifice could have been flooded. These considerations lend support to the notion that this was a temple devoted to Anahita (M. Boyce, pers. comm., expressed doubt as to whether this building was a temple; it is certainly unlike the Anahita temples known in Asia Minor, see Boyce and Grenet 1991: index s.v. "Anāhīt"). Other features in this complex include a court with elaborate floor mosaics which show reclining nobles and musicians (Ghirshman 1971; Keall 1989).

Thus, apart from their often secular decorative elements, the complexes at Kuh-e Khwaja and Bishapur share several architectural features, including a cruciform plan with an ambulatory; a court with an *ayvan*; and perhaps a *chahartaq*. However, the layout of the complex at Bishapur clearly reflects its mixed, secular and religious, function. Its nonaxial architectural arrangement points to a fundamentally different usage and it can be concluded, therefore, that the two complexes served different purposes. One was used privately, while the other was also used by the public. Whereas construction details in the two monuments differ greatly, the use of various Greco-Roman elements in both buildings is apparent.

Another alleged temple complex is located at Hajiabad (Fars), in what the excavator M. Azarnoush termed a manor house dated to the reign of Šābuhr II (309–379) according to the iconographic identification of one of the stucco busts discovered there (Azarnoush 1994: 158ff.). Azarnoush thought it contained a private sanctuary devoted to the worship of Anahita (Azarnoush 1987, 1994). Its association with the *yazata* Anahita is based on the fact that statues identified as being of her and other representations attributed to her adorned the walls of the "chapel" (Azarnoush 1994: 81ff., 163). Azarnoush's restored plan shows that the entire construction was based on several intermingling axes (Azarnoush 1994: 55ff., 91ff.). The complex presumably consisted of a large section dedicated to receiving the public, which was connected through a number of *ayvans* and a central courtyard to the chapel; the living quarters or *shabestan*; and a service area. The temple (if it was one) occupies the central portion of the complex, and although almost nothing remains of the building and its roof, it has been suggested that it may have been partially open (Azarnoush 1994: 66ff., 88ff.). This elite "manor house" has also yielded a great number of stucco sculptures, panels, and other architectural ornaments and a few painted murals.

In sum, the complexes at Kuh-e Khwaja and Hajiabad differ in their organizational layout but share certain architectural features. Hajiabad, like Bishapur, seems to have had mixed, secular and religious, functions. Special attention was given at both sites to decoration that included a wealth of stucco ornamentation. Greco-Roman architectural elements are also present at Hajiabad.

The large religious monument at Kunar Siah, south of Firuzabad in Fars, was identified as a fire temple complex by L. Vanden Berghe (1961; cf. Schippmann 1971: 97–9). The monument is laid out around the sides of two parallel but intersecting rectangles placed on two parallel axes and is constructed of the usual Sasanian rough rubble and mortar. The exterior façade was decorated with blind stucco niches. Entrance to the complex was through a domed gatehouse at the northern corner of the site, which led to a long, vaulted corridor situated to the southeast of the gateway. This corridor gave access, through two other narrower corridors, to a central *chahartaq* with a vaulted ambulatory, pierced by four central openings (cf. Duchesne-Guillemin 1973: 68). To the south and southeast of this central *chahartaq* were several parallel chambers, while to its east were clusters of apartments. Vanden Berghe identified these as the residences of priests, but Schippmann questioned this (Schippmann 1971: 98). In addition, it seems that the fire temple at Kunar Siah also contained a large courtyard located on the northwest of the complex, which was bordered on its long side by a corridor (Shepherd 1983: 1074ff.).

Individual architectural features at Kuh-e Khwaja and Kunar Siah are more or less identical. Both were used by the general public, but their overall plan arrangements and construction methods are completely different.

One of the most impressive Sasanian religious sites in Iran is Takht-e Soleyman in Azerbaijan. This architectural complex has been identified as an important place of Zoroastrian pilgrimage, the "house" of the ancient sacred fire, *Adur Gushnasp* (Naumann 1967: 3050ff.; 1975: 188ff.; Schippmann 1971: 329ff.; Boyce 2011). This is proven by a hoard of clay *bullae* with stamp seal impressions bearing the Fire's name that was discovered at the site. Takht-e Soleyman occupies an oval, flat-topped hill, the limits of which are defined by a fortified wall with semicircular towers that were once considerably taller than the intervening stretches of wall. But for all its impressive scale, the massive circumference wall built of quarried stone and faced with cut ashlars, seems more like a *temenos* enclosure than a true fortification. These walls encompass a sacred precinct, within which the temple complex stood beside a natural lake. Based on the construction method of the walls and the row of seven niches which appear above the southern gateway, inspired by similar niches on late Roman city gates (Naumann 1977: 37), as well as numismatic finds, the first phase of construction probably dates to the reign of Pērōz I (mid-fifth century), while the main phase dates to the sixth century, when Xosrow I moved the Fire Adur Gushnasp from Shiz to the site (Naumann 1977: 69). Takht-e Soleyman was destroyed in 624 by Heraclius (for the sources, see Howard-Johnston 1994; 2010: 124, 245).

The complex was laid out along several parallel axes, and excavation has revealed about thirty rooms which include several *chahartaqs*, corridors, *ayvans*, courtyards, porticos, and arcades, all of which were organized within a roughly square area (Naumann 1977; cf. Schippmann 1971: 329ff.). Access to the complex was controlled by two vaulted gateways which stood on the opposed, northern and southern, sides, which apparently had no trace of the ancient door fastenings. The approach to the temple itself on the north side was through a small domed room which led to a large central courtyard surrounded by large halls on three sides. Through an axial *ayvan*, the courtyard gave access to a very large central *chahartaq* with an ambulatory. The center of this *chahartaq* was marked by a square cavity sunk into the floor, with several built-in pedestal fire holders placed around the room. This large *chahartaq* was connected on its south side to a further axial *ayvan* that opened onto the lake.

The eastern flank of this group of buildings was occupied by various structures. In the southeastern section, to the east of the central *chahartaq*, a small cruciform room was connected to the central *chahartaq* by a narrow vaulted doorway. This room was in turn bordered on its eastern side by two other chambers with double cruciform plan (Schippmann 1971: 331). It seems that the small cruciform room, too, had a sunken cavity in the floor. It has been suggested, furthermore, that this cruciform room may have been covered with a canopy-type roof. In should be noted that these latter chambers, together with the central *chahartaq*, were constructed entirely of mudbrick, the domes included. The rest of the complex, however, was built generally of well-cut limestone. A couple of small courtyards, situated to the south of these rooms, were bordered by an arcade.

Another group of buildings occupies the northeastern corner of the temple complex. At the center of the design stands a once arcaded courtyard flanked by long pillar-rooms on all four sides and behind these on each side are long corridors. The western room, or corridor, offers a direct link with a small cruciform chamber which stands near the northwest corner of courtyard. This chamber has been considered as a secondary fire sanctuary, since the base of a large fire holder of limestone was discovered there (Schippmann 1971: 331). Thus, it has been suggested that, since the long rooms or corridors stand close to the large central *chahartaq* and other parts of the complex in the southeastern corner, they may have been used to store firewood or fuel.

The south façade of the temple complex was once composed of arcades that extended to the east and the west of a large central *ayvan*. Indeed, the main way to reach a third set of buildings situated on the western side of the central *chahartaq* may have been *via* the west arcade. This third set of buildings consists of a series of pillared halls and antechambers running from south to north and parallel to the main axis. At the extreme north end of these latter spaces was another, quite small, *chahartaq*, evidently with a stone dome. At its center was a three-stepped pedestal, presumably belonging to a fire holder. Finally, the west arcade gave access to a large *ayvan*, presumably reserved for high officials, which opened onto the lake and was located at the extreme southwestern corner of the complex as a whole.

The original functions of these rooms have been interpreted in various ways. Some scholars have proposed that the central *chahartaq* housed a perpetual fire and was the sanctuary of *Adur Gushnasp* itself (Naumann 1967: 3050ff.). At the same time a water conduit existed in the cross-shaped room with sunken basin, east of the central *chahartaq*. According to Naumann, a vaulted outlet in the middle of the south side of the basin showed that water could be drained from the basin. Based on this evidence, Naumann suggested that the cross-shaped room might be regarded as a secondary shrine within the complex, possibly a sanctuary of Anahita. Furthermore, he proposed that the double cruciform chambers could have functioned as a treasury for gifts sent by Sasanian kings (Naumann 1975: 188ff.; Schippmann 1971: 329ff.). On the other hand, it has also been suggested that the large *chahartaq* and the adjoining cruciform room, both of which had sunken cavities in their floors, were halls where pilgrims performed prayers and ritual ablutions, at the sunken basin, before proceeding in a state of purity to the small *chahartaq* with a stone dome at the extreme north end of the pillared halls, which was the *Adur Gushnasp*, "enthroned in deep security at the remotest part of the temple" (Boyce 1975b: 465).

At all events, the important point is that in the temple complexes at both Kuh-e Khwaja and Takht-e Soleyman included rooms of a very varied character, arranged in a carefully organized way to accommodate different activities, presumably of both priests and pilgrims, and that, regardless of the exact location of various rooms and other vagaries in their overall plans, the overarching conception corresponds relatively closely in function and setting at both sites. Each complex was placed within a protective enclosure wall, and each possessed monumental gateways. Their main architectural features are more or less identical. Most importantly, even disregarding the fact that nothing remains of the decoration at Takht-e Soleyman, it is clear that both complexes were very rich and offer clear testimony to the wealth and power of the patronage that called them into being.

Summation

The main objective here has been to give a brief survey of Kuh-e Khwaja and contemporary pre-Islamic Iranian religious architecture. As we have seen, scholarly opinion about its function has been divided. Since the mountain on which it is located is physically isolated, rising out of the Hamun Lake, Stein concluded that the choice was made for defensive reasons. Herzfeld, who relied on the artistic style of the paintings and the architectural style of the columns, assigned a secular, royal function to the Sacred Precinct. As noted above, Schlumberger assigned the buildings and arts of Kuh-e Khwaja to "a Greco-Iranian syncretic culture" and concluded that vaults and domes, united with Hellenized decoration, as well as the adaptation of stucco to mask walls under a "sculpted tapestry," were previously unrecognized characteristics of Sasanian architecture (Schlumberger 1969: 55). Kawami noted that "the wall paintings of Kuh-e Khwaja, like the architecture of the site, do not form one contemporaneous whole, but reflect changes, additions, and perhaps repairs made over a span of time" (Kawami 1987: 50). She considered "the architecture of Kuh-e Khwaja … a specific response to a unique location" and followed Stein in thinking that the site was originally a Buddhist monastery.

Importantly, it should be noted that various types of Zoroastrian temple complexes, with a wide range of architectural plans, existed during the Sasanian period and that, in contrast to Greek temples, which are usually uniform in their plans and functional purposes, no two Iranian temple complexes were alike in their layout. Each establishment satisfied a specific local set of requirements, while meeting the general demands of the practices and rituals of Zoroastrianism, all within the strictures of Sasanian architecture. Wall paintings, reliefs and stucco panels were among the media of decoration and, with the exception of Takht-e Soleyman, a variety of Iranian and classical architectural elements were used in the structure and decoration of temple complexes. Hence, it would appear that the characteristics of Iranian religious architecture evolved throughout the Sasanian period.

A NEW INTERPRETATION

Veneration of the Creations

Zoroastrian concepts about the physical world were based on very ancient speculations that it had been made in seven stages, each stage adding another "creation" (Boyce 1975a: 293ff.). The first creation was the Sky, the second Water, the third Earth, followed by Plants, Animals, and Man. The seventh creation was Fire, the vital force giving warmth and life to all the others, whose greatest manifestation is the sun. Boyce noted that, originally, "There was no temple or altar, statue or other artificial icon. The direct objects of veneration were natural things, and the major acts of worship thus fixed people's thoughts on the world about them, both its tangible forms and apprehended inner forces. Zoroastrians still believed that caring for and cherishing the seven creations were part of man's duty, and part of man's struggle against Angra Mainyu, the 'Evil Spirit'" (Boyce 1975a: 203ff.). Boyce also noted that Zoroaster gave the ancient doctrine deeper spiritual significance by associating with each creation one of seven great divinities, the Zoroastrian *Heptad*. These could be venerated and served through their creations, which were in a way their icons. In her view, Kuh-e Khwaja would "have been superbly satisfying to the needs of orthodoxy, since … few better places could be found to venerate the natural 'creations' of fire and water, sky and earth" (Boyce 1975b: 461). It is in light of these beliefs, and in the coming of the *Saošyant*, that an understanding of the architectural complexes on Kuh-e Khwaja must be sought.

Function

As far as the overall function of Kuh-e Khwaja is concerned, a number of previously mentioned hypotheses can be ruled out. For example, it is inconceivable that a site of such importance to the Zoroastrian faith could ever have been the location of a Buddhist monastery (cf. Bulliet 1976: 140–5; Boyce and Grenet 1991: 148–52; Duchesne-Guillemin 1973: 165–9; Emmerick 1983: 949–64; 1990; Ghanimati 2000:

140–1; Gnoli 1980: 183–4). In addition, the plan of the Sacred Precinct appears to lack the range of appointments that would have been expected of the residence of a royal ruler of substance. Together with new chronological considerations, these points argue against Herzfeld's proposal that Gondophares once had his seat at Kuh-e Khwaja and it also undermines his more general claim that the Sacred Precinct represented a "Palace-Temple." Rather, the true function of the buildings on Kuh-e Khwaja was related to the site's natural holiness over the centuries. Unfortunately, while no written records suggest any direct affirmative explanation of the various ways in which the island was used, the surviving archaeological remains and their excavation history do little to illuminate the situation.

Specifically, the most sanctified part of the Sacred Precinct shelters the square, domed Cella where the Fire Holder was discovered and where the sacred fire was enthroned (Huff 1990: 634–8; Boyce 1975b: 457–65; Boyce 1989a: 1–5, 1989c: 9–10; cf. Erdmann 1941: 22–37; Gropp 1969: 150–70; Monneret de Villard 1935–1936: 176–84; Wikander 1946: 58, 101). The Cella was surrounded, moreover, by a roofed (likely vaulted) ambulatory, presumably for ritual circumambulation and other ceremonial functions (Herzfeld 1941: 302; Bernard 1996: 510; Stronach 1985: 618–27). In addition, the Sacred Precinct includes another domed chamber immediately adjacent to a reinforced portion of the outer wall (perhaps a second unit associated with the safe-keeping of the sacred fire), open courts, and covered galleries and passageways. While such a plan cannot be exactly compared to that of any other extant Zoroastrian temple, it is now well known that these boasted a wide range of architectural plans fulfilling the demands of Zoroastrian rituals and devotional life (cf. Marshall 1960: 85–90; Duchesne-Guillemin 1973: 64–9, 159–70; Boyce 1975b: 461–5; Boyce and Grenet 1991: 287–9).

In the case of the Sacred Precinct it has been suggested, in fact, that the design was partly intended to meet the requirements of an *Erbedestan*, or Zoroastrian "priestly college" (Ghanimati 2000: 142–4). Moreover, the lower, southeastern section of the Sacred Precinct may have functioned as a dormitory for the *Erbeds*. In addition, the whole built environment at Kuh-e Khwaja is strongly suggestive of a place in which pilgrimage played a key role. The still-visible physical arrangements would have obliged pilgrims to pass through the tightly packed residential area of the "lower town" along an ancient pathway before entering the well-ordered upper religious precinct. Pilgrims may then have assembled in the Central Court (or in the large *ayvans*, in case of cold, rain, or sandstorm) for various rituals before they proceeded past the Fire Sanctuary and through the monumental North Gate toward the summit of the mountain (for Zoroastrian processions see Boyce 1975a: 166–77; Boyce 1968: 52–3; Ghanimati 2001: 183–93).

Significance

The most impressive aspect of Kuh-e Khwaja is its enduring sanctity. Although nothing is known of the fame of the mountain and the Hamun Lake in pre-Zoroastrian times (Gnoli 1980: 71, n. 80), the significance of these features in Zoroastrian lore is well documented. The mountain is mentioned several times in the *Avesta*, and the area of the Hamun Lake is named in other Zoroastrian texts, such as the first *fargerd* or chapter of *Vendidad*, as being among the lands which were created excellent by Ahura Mazda (Boyce 1975a: 249–93; Ghanimati 2001: 167–95). Kuh-e Khwaja is also identified with Mount Ushidam (Ushidam Ushidarena in the *Kasaoya* or Ushendava in the *Vourukasha*) (Gnoli 1980: 68–70, 129–38). Thus, the waters of the Hamun Lake were considered sacred, the natural seat of royal *xwarnah*, and were believed to guard the divinely preserved seed of Zoroaster from which the future Saoshyant, or World Savior, would be born (Boyce 1975a: 274; Gnoli 1980: 63ff.). The Zoroastrian apocalyptic belief pertaining the legend of Saoshyant is narrated in the *Zamyad Yasht* (*Yasht* 19), and the coming of the Saoshyant, who regularly has the epithet *verethragan* or "victorious," also involves the Resurrection of the Dead and the Last Judgment (Duchesne-Guillemin 1973: 229–35; Boyce and Grenet 1991: 451–6). Consequently, scholars have suggested that the Zoroastrian priests of Sistan played an important role in the development of Zoroastrian eschatology and in the transmission of the *Avesta*, and presumably there were respected scholar-priests in this area as well (Boyce 1975a: 78, 274; 1982: 128–31; 1992: 4–10, n. 35; Gnoli, 1977: 309–20; 1980: 59–65, 129–38; Gershevitch 1995). In such circumstances the isolated rock of Kuh-e Khwaja, emerging from this same body of water, was clearly endowed with exceptional religious significance (Gnoli 1980: 135; Boyce 1975a: 277–85; 1984: 39).

Once the eschatological myth pertaining to the Lake Hamun and the Saoshyant had been widely accepted, it is suggested, Zoroastrians each year would have made their way on pilgrimage to this holy site, a custom which continued through the Achaemenid, Parthian, and Sasanian periods (Boyce 1982: 278–9; 1992: 4–10, 182; Boyce and Grenet 1991: 149–51). Most likely, for a long time these pilgrims went up to the summit of the bare mountain for worship and prayers, and to watch over the holy lake, and it appears from a Zoroastrian text of early Islamic date, "the Zoroastrians who lived round about sent their virgin daughters each year, at the holy days of Nowruz and Mihragan, to bathe in the lake there, in the hope that the time had come for the Saoshyant to be conceived" (Boyce and Grenet 1991: 151; for other religious and mythological significance attached to the site, such as its association with the god Zhun, see e.g., Marquart and de Groot 1915; Bosworth 1968: 34, 91; Scarcia 1973; Boyce 1975a: 145, 274, 282; Frye 1975: 45–77; Gnoli 1980: 70, 129, 149; Sajjadi 1995: 243; Yarshater 1983; Utas 1983).

The repute of Kuh-e Khwaja seems to have reached lands beyond Iran, if it is correct to identify it with the "victorious mountain" (*Mons Victorialis*) mentioned in a "book in the name of Seth" cited in the *Opus imperfectum in Matthaeum*, which was translated from a Greek original dating to *c*.400. Although some scholars have rejected the identification of Kuh-e Khwaja with *Mons Victorialis*, the identification has its adherents. Although the *Opus imperfectum* says only that *Mons Victorialis* was in "Persia," Boyce suggested that Saoshyant's epithet *verethragan*, "victorious," may have been applied to Kuh-e Khwaja itself (cf. Duchesne-Guillemin 1973: 17, 167–8, 229; Boyce and Grenet 1991: 447–56, n. 447) and that Zoroastrian priests kept watch on Kuh-e Khwaja for the coming of the Saoshyant (Boyce 1975a: 234, 282–93). Today, Kuh-e Khwaja draws large numbers of Muslim pilgrims, both at Nowruz and at other holiday times. Indeed, the present inhabitants of the region continue to cherish many stories of saints and heroes associated with Kuh-e Khwaja over the long centuries past. In this context it is interesting to note that the summit of the mountain is marked by a solitary block of stone, $c.1$ m tall, that stands but a short distance from the reputed tomb of the Khwaja where pilgrims regularly leave offerings.

To conclude, the sanctity of the solitary mountain rising out of the Hamun Lake is the essential factor of legendary and religious importance attached to the site from the earliest times to the present. The immense lake lent its importance to the site through its association with the myth of the coming Saoshyant and the birth legend of Jesus. Thus, a major Zoroastrian temple complex was created, dedicated to Fire as a symbol of Truth, in the perfect setting of the mountain in the heart of the sacred waters of the Lake, where the elements of creation could be seen and venerated. The magnificent buildings at Kuh-e Khwaja were designed for both processional and devotional purposes, while the focus of the monuments can always be seen to have been the holy Hamun Lake. Over the centuries as a continuously used Zoroastrian religious center, the basic function of the building complexes was always to give access to the mountaintop, via the Sacred Precinct, to worshipers and pilgrims. Thus, the natural geography, architectural siting, building forms, and their decoration together formed a remarkable composition for worship and adoration. The site's important wall paintings and its distinctive stucco reliefs were intended, in a large part, for the eyes of pilgrims as they passed through the Sacred Precinct. As such, these striking decorations may have served to accentuate both a rhythmic sense of progression and an awareness of the degree of royal patronage that had been attached to this uniquely sanctified location.

FURTHER READING

For a comprehensive overview of religious architecture in the Sasanian period, see Schippmann (1971), Herrmann (1989), and Nauman (1975). Later studies of fire-temples include Yamamoto (1981), and Boucharlat (1999). Broad overviews of Sasanian architecture, both secular and religious, can be found in Ettinghausen (1972), Duchesne-Guillemin (1974), and Huff (1987). For some early references to Kuh-e Khwaja see also Le Strange (1905: 334–51).

REFERENCES

Afshar (Sistani), I. 1984. *Negahi beh Sistan va Baluchistan*. Tehran: A. Khazraei Publication.
Azarnoush, M. 1987. Fire temple and Anahita temple: A discussion on some Iranian places of worship. *Mesopotamia* 22: 391–401.

———. 1994. *The Sasanian manor house at Hajiabad, Iran*. Florence: Monografie di *Mesopotamia* 3.
Azarpay, G. 1981. *Sogdian painting: The pictorial epic in Oriental art*. Berkeley: University of California Press.
———. 1983. The development of the arts in Transoxiana. *CHI* 3/2: 1130–51.
———. 1987. Art in Iran vi. Pre-Islamic Eastern Iran and Central Asia. *EnIr* 2: 595–603.
Bailey, H. W. 1937. review of E. Herzfeld, *Archaeological history of Iran*. *BSOS* 8/4: 1154–5.
Bernard, B. 1996. L'Aornos bactrien et l'Aornos Indien: Philostrate et Taxila: géographie, mythe, et réalité. *Topoi* 6/2: 475–519.
Besenval, R. 1984. *Technologie de la voute dans l'Orient ancien*, 2 vols. Paris: Éditions Recherche sur les Civilisations.
Bivar, A. D. H. 1983. The history of eastern Iran. *CHI* 3/1: 181–232.
Bosworth, C. E. 1968. *Sīstān under the Arabs, from the Islamic conquest to the rise of the Ṣaffārids (30–250/651–864)*. Rome: IsMEO Reports and Memoirs 11.
Boucharlat, R. 1984. Monuments religieux de la Perse achéménide: État des questions. In *Temples et sanctuaires*, ed. G. Roux, 119–35. Lyon: TMO 7.
Boucharlat, R., and O. Lecomte. 1987. *Fouilles de Tureng Tepe 1: Les périodes sassanides et islamiques*. Paris: Éditions Recherche sur les Civilisations.
Boyce, M. 1968. On the sacred fires of the Zoroastrians. *BSOAS* 31: 52–68.
———. 1975a. *A history of Zoroastrianism*, vol. 1: *The early period*. Leiden/New York: HdO 1/8/1/2/2A.
———. 1975b. On the Zoroastrian temple cult of fire. *JAOS* 95/3: 454–65.
———. 1982. *A history of Zoroastrianism*, vol. 2: *Under the Achaemenians*. Leiden/New York: Brill.
———. 1984. *Textual Sources for the Study of Zoroastrianism*. Chicago: University of Chicago Press.
———. 1989a. Ātaš. *EnIr* 3: 1–5.
———. 1989b. Ātašdān. *EnIr* 3: 7–9.
———. 1989c. Ātaškada. *EnIr* 3: 9–10.
———. 1992. *Zoroastrianism, its antiquity and constant vigour*. Costa Mesa: Mazda.
———. 2011. Ādur Gušnasp. *EnIr* online edition.
Boyce, M., and F. Grenet. 1991. *A history of Zoroastrianism*, vol. 3: *Under Macedonian and Roman rule*. Leiden/New York: HdO 1/8/1/2/2/3.
Bulliet, R. 1976. Naw Bahar and the survival of Iranian Buddhism. *Iran* 14: 140–5.
Duchesne-Guillemin, J. 1973. *The religion of Ancient Iran*. Bombay: Tata Press.
Emmerick, R. E. 1983. Buddhism among Iranian peoples. *CHI* 3/2: 949–64.
———. 1990. Buddhism i. In pre-Islamic times. *EnIr* 4: 492–6.
Erdmann, K. 1941. *Das iranische Feuerheiligtum*. Leipzig: Sendschrift der Deutschen Orient-Gesellschaft 11.
Faccenna, D. 1981. A new fragment of wall painting from Ghaga Sahr (Kuh-i Hvaga–Sistan, Iran). *EW* 31: 83–97.
Fisher, W. B. 1968. Physical geography. *CHI* 1: 3–110.
Frye, R. 1975. *The Golden Age of Persia: The Arabs in the East*. New York: Barnes & Noble.
———. 1983a. *The history of Ancient Iran*. Munich: Beck.
———. 1983b. The political history of Iran under the Sasanians. *CHI* 3/1: 116–81.
Garsoïan, N. 1983. Byzantium and the Sasanians. *CHI* 3/1: 568–93.
Gershevitch, I. 1995. Approaches to Zoroaster's Gathas. *Iran* 33: 1–29.
Ghanimati, S. 2000. New perspectives on the chronological and functional horizons of Kuh-e Khwaja in Sistan. *Iran* 38: 137–50.

———. 2001. Kuh-e Khwaja: A major Zoroastrian temple complex in Sistan. Unpublished PhD diss., University of California Berkeley.

———. 2015. Kuh-e Kvāja. *EnIr* online edition.

Ghirshman, R. 1954. *Iran: From the earliest times to the Islamic conquest*. Harmondsworth: Penguin.

———. 1962. *Persian Art: The Parthian and Sassanian dynasties, 249 BC–AD 651*. New York: Golden Press.

———. 1971. *Bichâpour I*. Paris: Geuthner.

Gnoli, G. 1977. More on the Sistanic hypothesis. *EW* 27: 309–20.

———. 1980. *Zoroaster's time and homeland: A study on the origins of Mazdeism and related problems*. Naples: Istituto Universitario Orientale Seminario di Studi Asiatici Series Minor 7.

Göbl, R. 1983. Sasanian coins. *CHI* 3/1: 322–39.

Godard, A. 1951. L'origine de la madrasa, de la mosquée et du caravansérail à quatre iwans. *Ars Islamica* 15/16: 1–9.

Grabar, O. 2011. Ayvān. *EnIr* online edition.

Gropp, G. 1969. Die Funktion des Feuertempels der Zoroastrier. *AMI* 2: 147–75.

Gullini, G. 1964. *Architettura Iranica dagli achemenidi ai sasanidi: Il "palazzo" di Kuh-i Khwaja (Seistan)*. Turin: Einaudi.

Hansman, J., and D. Stronach. 1974. Excavations at Shahr-i Qūmis, 1971. *JRAS*: 8–22.

Harper, P. O. 1978. *The royal hunter: Art of the Sasanian Empire*. New York: Asia Society.

Herzfeld, E. 1931–2. Sakastān: Geschichtliche Untersuchungen zu den Ausgrabungen am Kūh i Khwādja. *AMI* 4/1–2: 1–116.

———. 1941. *Iran in the Ancient East*. New York: Oxford University Press.

Howard-Johnston, J. 1994. The official history of Heraclius' Persian campaigns. In *The Roman and Byzantine army in the East*, ed. E. Dąbrowa, 57–87. Krakow: Drukarnia Uniwersytetu Jagiellońskiego.

———. 2010. *Witnesses to a world crisis: Historians and histories of the Middle East in the seventh century*. Oxford: Oxford University Press.

Huff, D. 1990. Čahārtāq i. In pre-Islamic Iran. *EnIr* 4: 634–8.

Kawami, T. S. 1987. Kuh-e Khwaja, Iran, and its wall paintings: The records of Ernst Herzfeld. *MMJ* 22: 13–52.

———. 2005. Ernst Herzfeld, Kuh-e Khwaja, and the study of Parthian art. In *Ernst Herzfeld and the development of Near Eastern studies*, ed. A. C. Gunter and S. R. Hauser, 181–214. Leiden: Brill.

Keall, E. J. 1989. Bīšāpūr. *EnIr* 4/3: 287–9.

Kleiss, W. 1990. Capitals. *EnIr* 4: 774–80.

———. 1993. Columns. *EnIr* 6: 50–4.

Krautheimer, R. 1965. *Early Christian and Byzantine architecture*. New Haven/London: Yale University Press.

Kröger, J. 1982. *Sasanidischer Stuckdekor: Ein Beitrag zum Reliefdekor aus Stuck in sasanidischer und frühislamischer Zeit nach den Ausgrabungen von 1928/9 und 1931/2 in der sasanidischen Metropole Ktesiphon (Iraq) und unter besonderer Berücksichtigung der Stuckfunde vom Taḫt-i Sulaimān, aus Niẓāmābād (Iran) sowie zahlreiche anderer Fundorte*. Mainz: Baghdader Forschungen 5.

Landor, A. H. S. 1902. *Across coveted lands*, vol. 2. London: Macmillan.

Le Strange, G. 1905. *Lands of the eastern Caliphate*. Cambridge: Cambridge University Press.

Lovett, B. 1874. Narrative of a visit to the Kuh-i-Khwajah in Sistan. *JRAS* 44: 145–52.

Marquart, J., and J. J. M. de Groot. 1915. Das Reich Zābul und der Gott Žūn vom 6.–9. Jahrhundert. In *Festschrift Eduard Sachau zum siebzigsten Geburtstage gewidmet von Freunden und Schülern*, ed. G. Weil, 248–92. Berlin: Georg Reimer.

Marshall, Sir J. 1960. *A guide to Taxila*, 4th ed. Cambridge: Cambridge University Press.

Matthews, J. F. 1989. *The Roman Empire of Ammianus*. London: Duckworth.

Mirsky, J. 1977. *Sir Aurel Stein, archaeological explorer*. Chicago/London: University of Chicago Press.

Monneret de Villard, U. 1935–6. The fire temples. *Bulletin of the American Institute for Persian Art and Archaeology* 4: 175–84.

Mousavi, S. M. 1999. Kuh-e Khadjeh: Un complexe religieux de l'est iranien. *DA* 243: 81–4.

Naumann, R. 1967. Takht-i Suleiman. *SPA* 16: 3050–60.

———. 1975. Takht-i Suleiman, excavation report. *Iran* 13: 188–90.

———. 1977. *Die Ruinen von Tacht-e Suleiman und Zendan-e Suleiman und Umgebung*. Berlin: Führer zu archäologischen Plätzen in Iran 2.

Rahbar, M. 1998. Découverte d'un monument d'Époque sassanide à Bandian, Dargaz (Nord Khorassan), fouilles 1994 et 1995. *StIr* 27/2: 213–50.

———. 1999. À Dargaz (Khorasan): Découverte de panneaux de stucs sassanides. *DA* 243: 62–5.

Reuther, O. 1938. Sāsānian architecture. *SPA* 1: 493–578.

Sajjadi, S. M. S. 1995. *Bāstānšenāsī va Tārīkh-e Baluchestān*. Tehran: Sazman-e Miras-e Farhangi-e Kishvar.

Samadi Rijali, M. 1988. *Mah dar Irān*. Tehran: Sherkat-e Entesharart-e Elmi va Farhangi.

Sarfaraz, A. A. 1975. Anāhītā: Ma'bad-e 'azm-e Bīšāpūr. *PASARI*, 91–110.

Scarcia, G. 1973. Kūh-e Khwāgè: Forme Attuali del Mahdismo Iranico. *Oriente Moderno* 53/9: 755–64.

Schippmann, K. 1971. *Die iranischen Feuerheiligtümer*. Berlin/New York: De Gruyter.

Schlumberger, D. 1969. *L'orient hellenisé: L'art grec et ses héritiers dans l'Asie non méditerranéenne*. Paris: Albin Michel.

———. 1983. Parthian art. *CHI* 3/2: 1027–54.

Shahbazi, A. S. 1990. Byzantine-Iranian relations. *EnIr* 4: 588–99.

Shepherd, D. 1983. Sasanian art. *CHI* 3/2: 1055–112.

Stein, M. A. 1928. *Innermost Asia: Detailed report of explorations in Central Asia, Kan-Su, and eastern Iran, carried out and described under the orders of H.M. Indian Government*, 4 vols. Oxford: Oxford University Press.

Stronach, D. 1985. On the evolution of the early Iranian fire temple. In *Papers in honour of Professor Mary Boyce*, vol. 2, ed. J. Duchesne-Guillemin and J. R. Hinnells, 605–27. Leiden: Acta Iranica 25.

Stronach, D., and M. Roaf. 2007. *Nush-i Jan I: The major buildings of the Median settlement*. Leuven/Paris/Dudley: British Institute of Persian Studies and Peeters.

Talbot Rice, D. 1958. *The Great Palace of the Byzantine emperors*. Edinburgh: Edinburgh University Press.

Tate, G. P. 1910. *Seistan: A memoir on the history, topography, ruins, and people of the country*. Quetta: Nisa Traders (repr. 1977).

Tucci, G. 1966. review of G. Gullini, *Architettura Iranica dagli achemenidi ai sasanidi: Il "palazzo" di Kuh-i Kwagia, Seistan*. *EW* 16: 143–7.

Utas, B. 1983. The Pahlavi treatise Avdēh u Sahīkēh ī Sakistān or "Wonders and Magnificence of Sistan." *AAASH* 28: 259–67.

Vanden Berghe, L. 1961. Neuentdeckte archäologische Denkmäler in Süd-Iran. *ZDMG* 111: 410–12.

Wikander, S. 1946. *Feuerpriester in Kleinasien und Iran*. Lund: Acta Regiae Societatis Humaniorum Litterarum Lundensis 11.

Yarshater, E. 1983. Iranian National History. *CHI* 3/1: 359–477.

CHAPTER 47

SASANIAN ADMINISTRATION AND SEALING PRACTICES

NEGIN MIRI

SEALS AND SEALINGS

According to J. M. Upton, "most of the Sasanian seals so far published seem to have served either a religious or magical purpose, protecting the owner as an amulet, serving as a substitute for a signature, and possibly identifying his position or occupation" (Upton 1973: 23). Seals of office, on the other hand, confirmed the identity of an administrative authority. After a seal was impressed in clay or bitumen, the resultant sealing, often shaped like a ball (Lat. *bulla*, pl. *bullae*) was attached to documents and parcels, often with string. The primary function of such sealings was to confirm the identity of the author or witness(es) of the document or the ownership of merchandise (Frye 1989). Sasanian clay sealings both were larger than their Seleucid or Arsacid counterparts and have survived in greater number (Huff 1987a: 307). The Middle Persian word for bulla, *gil muhrag*, is known to us from the Iranian loanword *glmhrg* attested in Middle Aramaic in the Babylonian Talmud (*mwhrq'* < MP *muhrag* "seal"; *glmhrg*, cf. NP *gel-mohra*) (Shaked 1986).

Major collections of Sasanian clay bullae are known from Takht-e Soleyman (Göbl 1976; Huff 1987b; Naumann 1965), Qasr-e Abu Nasr (Harper 1973; Frye 1973a; Wilkinson 1936), Aq Tepe (Gubayev and Lelekov 1970; Gubayev et al. 1996; Lukonin 1971), the Armenian town of Dvin (Lukonin 1983: 742–3; cf. Kalantarian 1996), Susa (Ghirshman 1950: 233ff.; 1952: 1ff.; Göbl 1960: 39ff.), Tell Abu Sha'af (Al-Kassar 1979), and Tureng Tepe (Gyselen 1987). Other important collections of seals and bullae of unknown provenance exist in private collections and museums (Akbarzadeh and Daryaee 2012; Akbarzadeh et al. 2010; Bivar 1969; Brunner 1978; Daryaee and Safdari 2009, 2010; Frye 1968, 1970; Gignoux 1978; Gignoux and Gyselen 1982, 1987; Gyselen 1993; Lerner and Skjærvø 1997); the Pahlavi Archive of the University of California, Berkeley, which contains 390 bullae and 260 manuscripts dated to 600–888 AD (Azarpay 2003); the Freie

Universtät Berlin (Weber 1992; the Berlin collection awaits publication by Weber in a forthcoming volume of *CII*); and the California Museum of Ancient Art, which holds seventy-one bullae and a number of manuscripts (Gignoux 1996).

The extant Sasanian administrative seals and sealings date from the fifth to the seventh centuries. They contain the personal name and title of an official, as well as the name of the larger province or district under his jurisdiction. Thus, they provide us with only indirect information regarding government offices, religious positions, and administrative units. As Wiesehöfer noted, "by mentioning the owner and his title and functions, seals and bullae acquaint us with state and religious officials both from the prosopographic and onomastic point of view, and as regards their political, administrative and religious competences" (Wiesehöfer 1996: 163). Gyselen has conducted a study of the administrative geography of the Sasanian Empire on the basis of seals and sealings (Gyselen 1989), while Frye has published 505 clay sealings, found at Qasr-e Abu Nasr, and elaborated two categories of personal and official seals and their applications (Frye 1973a, 1973b: 47–58).

Sasanian administration

Numismatic evidence from the reign of Ardašīr I shows the king using the word *Ērān* for the first time on his coins, identifying himself as King of the Kings of *Ērān* in order to identify his domain (Alram 2003: 25; Göbl 1983: 330). Later this word stood in contrast to the word *Anērān* or non-Iran. According to Šābuhr I's ŠKZ inscription, in which he introduces himself as the king of *Ērān* and *Anērān*, *Ērān* consisted of the following provinces or *šahr*s listed in a form of geographical order (ŠKZ, ll. 1–3; KNR, l. 14) (Back 1978: 420–2, 286–7; Brunner 1974; Gignoux 1971; Gnoli 1991; Henning 1939, 1954, 1963; Honigmann and Maricq 1953; Huyse 1999: 22–4; MacKenzie 1989; Maricq 1958; Sprengling 1940): Pārs, Partaw (Pahlaw), Ḫūzistān, Mēšān, Āsūrestān, Nōdšīragān (Adiabene), Arabestān, Ādurbādagān (Āzarbāyejān), Armen (Armenia), Wiržān (Iberia), Sagān, Ardān (Albania), Balāsagān up to the Kāf (Caucasus) Mountains and to the Alānān Gate and all of the Parišxwār (Alborz) mountains, Māh (Media), Gurgān, Marγ, Harēw, Abaršahr, Kirmān, Sagestān (Sīstān), Tūrestān, Makurān, Pāradān, Hindestān, (India), Kušānšahr up to Paškabur (Pēšāwar?) and Kaš, Suγd, Čāč (Tashkent), and the lands of Mazūn ('Omān) on the other side of the sea. This list is repeated in a slightly different order by Kerdīr (KKZ) as well. The *Bundahišn* (Bd 31) and Pahlavi *Widēwdād* (PhlVd 1) also list the provinces of the late Sasanian Iran (Shapira 2001: 321–2). Yaqut attributed a further definition of *Ērān* to Ardašīr I: "it was told of Ardašīr that he said that the Earth is divided into four parts ... one part is the land which belongs to Persia: what is between the River of Balx up to the outskirts of Āzarbāyejān and Persarmenia, then up to the Euphrates, the Arab desert up to 'Omān and Makrān (also Mokrān), then up to Kābul and Taxāristān" (Yaq. I: 18; Shapira 2001: 327).

The provinces located in *Ērān* or *Ērānšahr* were grouped into quadrants based on four geographical directions (Brunner 1983: 750; Christensen 1944: 364; Daryaee 2002: 11–13; Frye 1983: 154). This division is documented in the Armenian geography of Ananias of Širak (Brunner 1983: 750; Hewsen 1992) and in the Pahlavi *Šahrestānīhā ī Ērānšahr* (completed in the eighth century; Brunner 1983: 750; Daryaee 2002: 2) and *Mādayān ī Hazār Dādestān*. The latter is believed to have been written about 620, during the reign of Xosrow II (591–628), and refers to the *Kustag ī Xwarāsān* (MHD A31.4; Perikhanian 1997: 12, 302–3). Literary references to four *spāhbeds* of the *kusts* can also be found in the *Bundahišn* (Brunner 1983: 750; Gignoux 1990: 8), *Letter of Tansar* (Minovi 1975–6; Boyce 1968) and *Sūr Saxwan*. The latter only mentions *spāhbeds* of *Xwarāsān*, *Xwarbarān*, and *Nēmrōz* as a result of a mistake made by a copyist, or a choice made by the author (Tavadia 1935: 44–5, 65). References to this quadripartition can be also found in Armenian sources (Greenwood 2012)

The quadripartition of *Ērān* is mentioned both in the Islamic historical sources (Tab. ed. Bosworth 1999: 149; Tha'alibi, ed. Bosworth 1968: 609) and in Firdawsī's *Šāhnāme* (Firdawsī 1990 6: 83). There are some contradictions in the Islamic sources pertaining to the quadripartition of Iran during the Sasanian period. Some like Gardizi attribute it to the reign of Ardašīr: "From Afridun to Ardašīr the whole world was under one *spāh-sālār*'s command. When Ardašīr came [to power] he divided the world into four quarters: Xwarāsān, west, Nēmrōz and Āzarbāyejān," while others name Husraw as the author of this system (Tabari, ed. Bosworth 1999: 149; on the nature and chronology of the quadripartition see Daryaee 2003: 193–5).

A similar geographical order can also be recognized in ŠKZ and may reflect Zoroastrian mythological perceptions of the world. Literary sources date the division of the empire into four military commands (or *kusts*) to the reigns of Kawād I (488–531) and Xosrow I (531–578 AD), who undertook a series of administrative reforms (Tabari, ed. Bosworth 1999: 149). Although criticism has been voiced as to the existence of this quadripartition, numismatic and sigillographic evidence offers strong support for it. The coins of Kawād I, and the seals of generals or *spāhbeds* of the four "sides" of the Sasanian Empire, provide clear evidence of this quadripartition, at least during the later Sasanian period (Daryaee 1381Š: 38–42, 2002: 13–4; Gnoli, 1985; Gyselen, 2001; Gignoux 1984 proposed that this was a symbolic division rather than a real division), with literary sources mentioning the office of *Ērān-Spāhbed* in the early Sasanian period (Asha 1999: 48–9). The *spāhbed* sealings display a central, mounted figure in armor, surrounded by a series of inscriptions. These data confirm the existence of a military division of the empire, if not necessarily an administrative one. The four *kusts* included *Kust ī Xwarāsān* in the east-northeast (Xwarāsān, Sīstān, and Kirmān; Kirmān being recorded in *Kust ī Nēmrōz* as well), *Kust ī Xwarārān* in the west-southwest (including Mesopotamia), *Kustī Nēmrōz* in the south-southeast (including Pārs and Hūzistān), and *Kust ī Ādurbādagān* in the north-northwest (including Mād and Āzarbāyejān) (Brunner 1983: 750; Christensen 1944: 364; Daryaee 2003: 194; Gyselen 2001). Some of the provinces like Kirmān were included in different *kusts* according to different sources.

The term *kust* has been translated as "region" or "quarter" (Marquart 1901), although it can also be translated as "side" or "direction" in an administrative context. This is shown in *Mād-kust-ī-Hamedān, Hamedān-kust-ī-šahristān, Māh-kust-ī-Nēmāwand, Māh-kust-ī-Vastān* and *Māh-kust-ī-Vēmānōy*, recorded on Sasanian administrative sealings (Akbarzadeh and Daryaee 2012: 15; Daryaee 2002: 40; Gyselen 1989: 53–4, 2001: 13–14, 2002: 149, 157), and in references to *kust* in the *Kārnāmag ī Ardašīr ī Pābgān*, where it is used for "region" (I.2, V.12, VII.4) or "side" (e.g., the two *sides* engaged in a battle) (VII.13). These regions were further divided into provinces or *šahr*.

Šābuhr I's ŠKZ and Narseh's inscription at Paikuli (NPi) (Frye 1957; Herzfeld 1924; Skjærvø 1983) point to some of the administrative units of the early Sasanian period, while the Syrian *Acts of the Persian Martyrs* (early fifth century) and the Sasanian book of laws or *Mādayān ī Hazār Dādestān*, believed to have survived in its original form, provide information regarding the late empire. No other Sasanian epigraphic or literary evidence exists that sheds light on the provincial divisions of the empire, and Islamic writers from later centuries offer the only other source of information on the subject.

According to ŠKZ, the word *šahr* (MP. *štly* or *štry*, Parth. *ḫštr* and Gr. ἔθνος) pertains to a province under the command of a *šahrab* (ŠKZ, l. 50). These terms are also used to refer to provinces in the NPi (ll. 13–15, 32). ŠKZ also records a certain Ardašīr as *šahrab* of Neyrīz (ŠKZ, l. 50). The term *šahr* was thus used to describe both major provinces of the Sasanian Empire as well as smaller divisions within each province during the early period (Daryaee 2002: 37; Frye 1975: 10; Wiesehöfer 1996: 185; cf. Huyse 1999: 22–30). The *Acts of the Persian Martyrs* provides further evidence of the application of this terminology, recording Bišābuhr as a town (*mdynt'*) in Fārs province ('*tr'*), while also referring to, for example, Staxr (Istakhr) as a province ('*tr'*) (Jullien 2004: 142, 156, 165). Natural features such as rivers, ridges, deserts, climate, soil, and so on, as well as cultural dynamics, were major factors that helped determine provincial boundaries.

The term *šahrestān* was used in reference to the center or capital of a province, and also a city with its surrounding region (cf. *Šahrestānīhā ī Ērānšahr*). Xwarrah was the term used in Fārs during the Sasanian period to refer to a provincial division or *šahr*. The terms *tasūg* (or *tasūk*), *rōstāg* (*rustāq*), and *deh* were used to describe smaller administrative units (Frye 1975: 10). In *Mādayān ī Hazār Dādestān* there are references to the following administrative divisions of the late Sasanian era, presented here in hierarchical order: *kustag* (MHD 78.3), *šahr* (MHD 48.7–8; 100.5; A34.17; A35.2, 4, 6, 8, 10; A38.17), *tasūg* (MHD 100.6; 100.15), *rōdastāg* (MHD 78.3), and *deh* (MHD 78. 14; A29.13). Two other terms, although less common, are used in this text, namely *nahang* (MHD 78.3; 78.13) and *gyāg* (MHD A35.4). *Nahang* appears twice in *Mādayān ī Hazār Dādestān* in relation to Ardašīr Xwarrah in Fars. *Nahang* also appeared as *nsngy* in reference to the provinces of the Sasanian Empire in Kerdīr's inscription (KKZ ll. 4–5) below ŠKZ. Frye has suggested that *nahang* may have originally meant "the Seleucid subdivision of a province, the eparchy" (Frye 1975: 248, n. 8), and that it may have been used as a substitute for *xwarrah* during the Sasanian period. *Gyāk* appears to describe a "place," a usage which is echoed in *Kārnāmag ī Ardašīr ī Pābgān* (e.g., IV.8, V.5, VII.10; Asha

1999: 22–3, 26–7, 32–3). Furthermore, the *Acts of the Persian Martyrs* provide evidence of the use of the word *rustāq* for district (Jullien 2004: 142).

This hierarchy appears in later literary sources as well. A Middle Persian inscription, discovered in Istanbul, names the birthplace of Hōrdād, son of Ōhrmazd-Āfrīd, a Christian Iranian, as Xešt village (*deh*) in *rōstāg* of Čālakān in Iran (Blois 1990; Menasce 1967). This inscription was initially dated to a period before 430 by Menasce (Menasce 1967: 59), and to the sixth to seventh centuries by the excavator of the site in which the inscription was discovered (Blois 1990: 210). Blois has dated it to the ninth to tenth century (Blois 1990). References to *šahr*, *šahrestān*, *rōstāg*, and *deh* can be found in a number of other pre-Islamic literary sources, including the *Kārnāmag ī Ardašīr ī Pābgān* (KAP. V. 8, 13; VI. 6; VII. 10–11; VIII. 7, IX. 13; Asha 1999: 26–35, 42–3), *Wizīdagīhā ī Zādsparam* (XXIII.5) (Anklesaria 1964: xcvii; Frye 1973b: 50, n. 15), *Ayādgār ī Jāmaspīg* (XVI.19), *Wahman Yašt* (II. 27), *Ardāy-Wīrāz Nāmag* (XV.10), and in various passages of the *Dēnkard* (Piacentini 1994: 97–8). Islamic sources complement those of the Sasanians, with Tabari recording the birthplace of Ardašīr as Ṭirūdeh village (*deh* in *rōstāg* of Xīr, of Staxr-Xwarrah (or province), in Fārs (Tabari, ed. Bosworth 1999: 3–4).

Thus, many Sasanian provinces (*šahr*) were divided into smaller administrative units, namely *xwarrah* (MP *xwarrah*, "glory/fortune," hence Ardašīr Xwarrah is "Glory of Ardašīr"; and/or Greek *chora*, introduced during the Seleucid period; see Daryaee 2003: 195), *rōstāg* or *tasūg* (districts), and *dehs* (villages). These divisions were not, however, applied consistently throughout the empire, with references to other units occurring in some instances, such as an *awestām* under the command of an *awestāmdār*. Until recently it was perceived that this term was applied only to frontier regions, such as Armenia, during the fifth to seventh centuries, when a number of territories were divided into *awestām*s and then into *gawar*s (Daryaee 2004: 128–30; Gyselen 1989: 94). The discovery of a sealing of the *awestāmdār* of Dārābgerd has since altered this perception, and an *awestām* was seemingly a provincial division similar to a *šahr* (Gyselen 2002: 30, 106–9). It has also been suggested that a *tasūg* may have been a region approximately one-quarter the size of a *rōstāg*. Yaqut noted that the term *rōstāg* was more commonly used in Iran, while *ṭsūj* was used in Iraq (Yaq. 1: 38). A reference in *Mādayān ī Hazār Dādestān* (MHD 78.3; 100.15) to these divisions, however, indicates that both existed in areas such as Ardašīr-Xwarrah. It is possible that, during the Islamic period, the term *rustāq* was confined to Iran, while in Iraq *ṭsūj* was the more prevalent expression.

An analysis of the administrative officials and organization of the Sasanian Empire can help increase our understanding of its administrative units. As with the different administrative division outlined above, administrative positions were not uniform geographically or chronologically throughout the Sasanian period. The *Mādayān ī Hezār Dādīstān* has an extensive chapter on the jurisdictions of officials (MHD A25.15–A30.5; Perikhanian 1997: 293–301). Based on literary and sigillographic evidence, Gyselen has outlined the hierarchy of officials within the Sasanian administration and their spheres of influence during the late Sasanian period (sixth and seventh centuries). A revised version of her chart is presented in Table 47.1 (*handarzbed*, *dādwar*, *dehqān*, and *darīg* are not included in Gyselen 2002: 91).

Table 47.1. Hierarchical list of Sasanian officials and their level of jurisdiction.

Administrative division	Administrative official
Region comprising several provinces	zarrbed
	wāspuhragan-framādār
	āmārgar
Province	šahrab
	ōstāndār
	mogbed
	driyōšān-jādaggōw ud dādwar
	gund-ī-kadag-xwadāygān-framādār
	framādār
	darīgbed
	āmārgar
	andarzbed
Part of province or district	maguh
	dātwar
Village	dehqān
	darīg

Until the mid sixth century the *marzbān* was the military governor of the frontiers in the four quadrants of the empire. During the late Sasanian period, however, the functions of the *marzbān* appear to have been changed and the term became applied to a provincial governor, replacing the previous title *šahrab* (Christensen 1944: 148; Frye 1975: 9). The *wispuhragān-framādār*, lower down in the Sasanian administrative hierarchy, probably acted as supervisor of the domains of the princes. The *āmārgar* acted at both the provincial and regional levels and was in charge of fiscal and financial issues such as taxes, revenues and property rights. Sigillographic and literary evidence highlights a link between the administration of the *āmārgar* and that of the *šahrab* or *awestāmdār* (Daryaee 2003: 195; Gyselen 1989: 29, 36; 2002: 122; Lukonin 1983: 726; Wiesehöfer 1996: 186–7). A *šahrdār* (or *šahrab*) was, as mentioned above, the provincial governor in charge of the civil affairs of a *šahr* or province (Daryaee 2003: 195; Gyselen 1989: 29, 36; 2002: 122; Lukonin 1983: 726; Wiesehöfer 1996: 186–7). Recent studies and sigillographic finds suggest that the *awestāmdār* operated within an area commensurate with that controlled by a *šahrab*, not merely on royal lands or frontier territories as the example of *awestāmdār* of Dārābgerd demonstrates (Gyselen 2002: 30, 106–9).

The *mowbed*s acted as the chief religious officials at the provincial level. Apart from their supervision of legal affairs and the application of property rights within the provinces, *mowbed*s were involved in "the administration of the domains of the clergy," temple treasury and its landed property (Daryaee 2003: 195; Frye 1975: 17; Gyselen 1989: 29; Lukonin 1983: 733; Wiesehöfer 1996: 187). The *driyōšān-jādaggōw ud dādwar* (or advocate of the poor, judge) also performed religious and legal functions, acting as the official representative of the poor during trials at a provincial level (Gyselen 1989:

31; Wiesehöfer 1996: 188). Little is known of the tasks and administrative jurisdiction of a *framādār* or commander-in-chief (Gyselen 1989: 37; Wiesehöfer 1996: 187). A *handarzbed* (or councilor) operated at a provincial level, also within the court apparatus, and was involved with advisory functions and moral issues (Daryaee 2003: 200; Gyselen 1989: 33; Wiesehöfer 1996: 187). A *dādwar* (judge), under the authority of a *mowbed*, acted as a judge in civil cases at a district level (MHD 100.11–15; Daryaee 2003: 197, 201; Frye 1975: 17; Wiesehöfer 1996: 187). The *mow* was likely involved in solving local disputes, as a mediating authority to the *mowbed* or *driyōšān-jādaggōw ud dādwar*, who worked at the provincial level (Gyselen 1989: 30, 39–40; Wiesehöfer 1996: 188). *Dehs* were under the control of *dehqān*s, who were the chiefs and owners of farmlands and village(s?), acting as local government agents among the lower class of Sasanian society, farmers and villagers, within the territory of the *deh* (Christensen 1944: 124; Daryaee 2003: 197).

The office of *argbed* has been variously interpreted as that of a castellan, castle lord, tax collector, or commander of a fortress. Whatever the function of this office, it occupied an important position within the organization of the state, similar to that of a commander-in-chief of the army (Tabari, ed. Bosworth 1999: 6, nn. 15 and 104). At present, little information exists on the functions of the *darīgbed* and *zarrbed*. Two Pahlavi documents from the late Sasanian period show that a *darīg* operated at the village level (Gignoux 2004: 41).

Regarding the chronology of the development of the administrative organization of the empire, only some offices, such as those of *framādār*, *handarzbed*, *šahrab*, and *dādwar*, are known to have existed in the early Sasanian period (ŠKZ, NPi), although no indication exists as to the origins of the other Sasanian offices, recorded on the sixth- to seventh-century seals and sealings. The absence of these offices in the third-century inscriptions, however, does not necessarily imply their nonexistence during the early Sasanian period, especially considering that these inscriptions were tools of royal propaganda, not records of administration of the Sasanian Empire (Gyselen 2002: 180–1).

Further reading

There is a considerable literature on Sasanian seals and sealing practice. In addition to the works cited in the text, the standard classification of Sasanian seals is Göbl (1973) and a classification according to form is given in Gyselen (1976). For further information on Sasanian clay bullae see, for example, Gropp (1974) and Huff (1987c).

References

Akbarzadeh, D., and T. Daryaee. 2012. Inscribed Sasanian bullae at the National Museum of Iran. e-*Sasanika Series* 19: 1–27. http://www.humanities.uci.edu/sasanika/pdf/e-sasanika-1 9-Akbarzadeh-Daryaee.pdf.

Akbarzadeh, D., C. G. Cereti, and F. Sinisi. 2010. Notes on the collection of Sasanian bullae held in Khoy. In *Iranian identity in the course of history: Proceedings of the conference held in Rome, 21–24 September 2005*, ed. C. G. Cereti, 11–22. Rome: SOR 105.

Alram, M. 2003. Numismatics and history: An outline, a. Ardashir I. In *Sylloge Nummorum Sasanidarum: Paris–Berlin–Wien. Band I: Ardashir I – Shapur I*, ed. M. Alram and R. Gyselen, 21–31. Vienna: Verlag der Österreichischen Akademie der Wissenschaften.

Anklesaria, B. T. 1964 *Vichitakiha-i Zatsparam with text and introduction*. Bombay: Trustees of the Parsi Punchayet Funds and Properties.

Asha, R. 1999. *The Book of the Acts of Ardašir son of Pābag (Kārnāmag ī Ardašīr ī Pābgān), text, transliteration and translation*. Paris: Institute of Eric Studies.

Azarpay, G. 2003. Bullae from the Pahlavi Archive at the University of California, Berkeley. In *Ērān ud Anērān: Studies presented to Boris Ilich Marshak on the occasion of his 70th birthday*, ed. M. Compareti, P. Raffetta, and G. Scarcia. Buenos Aires: Transoxiana Webfestschrift. http://www.transoxiana.org/Eran/Articles/azarpay.html.

Back, M. 1978. *Die sassanidischen Staatsinchriften: Studien zur Orthographie und Phonologie des Mittelpersischen der Inschriften zusammen mit einem etymologischen Wortgutes und einem Textcorpus der behandelten Inschriften*. Leiden: Acta Iranica, 18.

Bivar, A. D. H. 1969. *Catalogue of the Western Asiatic seals in the British Museum. Stamp seals II: The Sassanian dynasty*. London: British Museum.

Blois, F. de. 1990. The Middle Persian inscription from Constantinople: Sasanian or post-Sasanian? *StIr* 19: 209–18.

Bosworth, C. E. 1968. *The Book of Curious and Entertaining Information, the Latā'if al-Ma'ārif of Ta'ālibī*. Edinburgh: Edinburgh University Press.

——. 1999. *The history of al-Ṭabarī (Ta'rīkh al-rusul wa'l-mulūk)*, vol. 5, *The Sāsānids, the Byzantines, the Lakhmids, and Yemen*. Albany: State University of New York Press.

Boyce, M. 1968. Middle Persian literature. In *Iranistik, Literatur*, ed. B. Spuler, 31–66. Leiden/Cologne: HdO 1.4.2.1.

Brunner, C. 1974. The Middle Persian inscriptions of the priest Kardir at Naqsh-i Rustam. In *Near Eastern numismatics, iconography, epigraphy and history: Studies in honor of George C. Miles*, ed. D. Kouymjian, 97–114. Beirut: American University of Beirut.

——. 1978. *Sasanian seals in the Metropolitan Museum of Art*. New York: Metropolitan Museum of Art.

——. 1983. Geographical and administrative divisions: Settlement and economy. *CHI* 3/2: 747–7.

Christensen. A. 1944. *L'Iran sous les Sassanides*, tr. R. Yasemi, Tehran: Negah Publications (in Persian).

Daryaee, T. 2002. *Šahrestānīhā ī Ērānšahr. A Middle Persian text on Late Antique geography, epic, and history*. Costa Mesa: Mazda.

——. 1381Š/2002-3. Espahbodan-e Sasani. *Bokhara* 24: 38–42 (In Persian)

——. 2003. The effect of the Arab Muslim conquest on the administrative division of Sasanian Persis/Fars. *Iran* 41: 193–204

——. 1383Š/2004. *Shahanshahi-ye Sasania (Sasanian Empire)*. Tehran: Qoqnoos Publishing (in Persian).

Daryaee, T., and K. Safdari. 2009. A bulla of the Ērān-Spāhbed of Nēmrōz. *e-Sasanika Series 8*: 1–4. http://www.humanities.uci.edu/sasanika/pdf/e-sasanika8-dar-saf.pdf.

——. 2010. Spāhbed bullae: The Barakat Collection. *e-Sasanika Series* 12: 1–15. http://www.humanities.uci.edu/sasanika/pdf/e-sasanika12-Barkat%20Collection%20Final.pdf

Firdawsī, Abū al-Qāsim. 1990. *Šāh Nāma*. Tehran: Sherkat-e Sahami-e Ketabha-ye Jibi (in Persian).
Frye, R. N. 1957. Remarks on the Paikuli and Sar Mašhad inscriptions. *Harvard Journal of Asiatic Studies* 20/3–4: 702–8.
———. 1968. Sasanian clay sealings in the collection of Mohsen Foroughi. *IrAnt* 7: 118–32.
———. 1970. Sasanian clay sealings in the Baghdad Museum. *Sumer* 26: 237–40.
———. 1973a. *Sasanian remains from Qasr-i Abu Nasr: Seals, sealings, and coins*. Cambridge: Harvard University Press.
———. 1973b. Inscriptions and monograms on the sealings. In *Sasanian remains from Qasr-i Abu Nasr: Seals, sealings, and coins*, ed. R. N. Frye, 47–65. Cambridge, MA: Harvard University Press.
———. 1975. *The golden age of Persia: The Arabs in the East*. London: Weidenfeld and Nicolson.
———. 1983. The political history of Iran under the Sasanians. *CHI* 3/2: 116–80.
———. 1989. Bullae. *EnIr* 4/5: 545–6.
Ghirshman, R. 1950. Notes iraniennes III: A propos des bas-reliefs rupestres sassanides. *Artibus Asiae* 13: 86–98.
———. 1952. Cinq campagnes de fouilles à Suse, 1946–1951. *RA* 46: 1–18.
Gignoux, P. 1971. Le liste des provinces de l'Ērān dans les inscriptions de Šābuhr et de Kirdīr. *AAASH* 19: 83–94.
———. 1978. *Catalogue des sceaux, camées et bulles sasanides de la Bibliothèque Nationale et du Musée du Louvre*, vol. 2. *Les sceaux et bulles inscrits*. Paris: Bibliothèque Nationale.
———. 1984. Les quatres régions adminstratives de l'Iran sassanide et la symbolique des nombres trois et quatres. *AION* 44: 555–72.
———. 1990. Le *spāhbed* des Sassanides à l'Islam. *JSAI* 13: 1–14.
———. 1998. Six documents pehlevis sur cuir du California Museum of Ancient Art, Los Angeles. *BAI* 10: 63–72.
———. 2004. Aspects de la vie administrative et sociale en Iran du 7ème siècle. In *Contributions à l'histoire et la géographie historique de l'Empire sassanide*, ed. R. Gyselen, 37–48. Bures-sur-Yvette: RO 16.
Gignoux, P., and R. Gyselen. 1982. *Sceaux sasanides de diverses collections privées*. Leuven: Cahiers de *StIr* 1.
———. 1987. *Bulles et sceaux sassanides de diverses collections*. Paris: Cahiers de *StIr* 4.
Gnoli, G. 1985. The quadripartition of the Sasanian empire. *EW* 35: 265–70.
———. 1991. L'inscription de Šābuhr à le Ka'be-ye Zardošt et la propagande sassanide. In *Histoire et cultes de l'Asie centrale préislamique: Sources écrites et documents archéologiques*, ed. P. Bernard and F. Grenet, 57–63. Paris: Éditions du CNRS.
Göbl, R. 1960. Monnaies sassanides de Suse. In *Numismatique susienne: Monnaies trouvées à Suse de 1946 à 1956*, ed. R. Göbl, G. Le Rider, G. C. Miles, and J. Walker, 41–8. Paris: MDAI 37.
———. 1973. *Der sāsānische Siegelkanon*. Braunschweig: Handbücher der Mittelasiatischen Numismatik 4.
———. 1976. *Die Tonbullen vom Tacht-e Suleiman: Ein Beitrag zur spätsasanidischen Sphragistik*. Berlin: Dietrich Reimer.
———. 1983. Sasanian coins. *CHI* 3/1: 322–39.
Greenwood, T. 2012. *Sasanian reflections in Armenian sources*. Irvine: Sasanika Occasional Papers 2.
Gropp, G. 1974. Some Sasanian clay bullae and seal stones. *American Numismatic Society Museum Notes* 19: 119–44.

Gubayev, A. G. and L. Lelekov. 1970. *Bullae of the Sasanian period from Ak-depe*. Ashgabat: Antiquities from the Karakum 3 (in Russian).

Gubayev, A. G., S. D. Loginov, and A. B. Nikitin. 1996. Sasanian bullae from the excavations of Ak-Depe by the Station of Artyk. *Iran* 34: 55–9.

Gyselen, R. 1976. Une classification des cachets sasanides selon la forme. *StIr* 5: 139–46.

———. 1987. Bulles et sceaux sassanides. In *Fouilles de Tureng Tepe I. Les périodes sassanides et islamiques*, ed. R. Boucharlat and O. Lecomte, 187–90. Paris: Éditions Recherche sur les Civilisations.

———. 1989. *La géographie administrative de l'empire sassanide. Les témoignages sigillographiques*. Paris: RO 1.

———. 1993. *Catalogue des sceaux, camées et bulles sassanides de la Bibliothèque Nationale et du Musée du Louvre*, vol. 1, *Collection générale*. Paris: Bibliothèque Nationale.

———. 2001. *The four generals of the Sasanian Empire: Some sigillographic evidence*. Rome: IsIAO.

———. 2002. *Nouveaux materiaux pour la géographie historique de l'empire Sassanide: Sceaux administratifs de la collection Ahmad Saeedi*. Paris: Cahiers de *StIr* 24.

Harper, P. O. 1973. Seals and finger rings. In *Sasanian remains from Qasr-i Abu Nasr: Seals, sealings, and coins*, ed. R. N. Frye, 37–41. Cambridge, MA: Harvard University Press.

Henning, W. B. 1939. The Great Inscription of Shapur I. *BSOS* 9: 823–50.

———. 1954. Notes on the Great Inscription of Šāpūr I. In *Professor Jackson Memorial Volume: Papers on Iranian subjects*, 40–54. Bombay: K. R. Cama Oriental Institute.

———. 1963. *Minor inscriptions of Kartir together with the end of Naqš-i Rustam*. London: CII 3/2.

Herzfeld, E. 1924. *Paikuli: Monuments and inscriptions of the early history of the Sasanian Empire*. Berlin: Dietrich Reimer.

Hewsen, R. H. 1992. *The geography of Ananias of Širak (AŠXARHACʿOYCʿ). The long and the short recensions. Introduction, translation and commentary*. Wiesbaden: TAVO Beiheft B 77.

Honigmann, E., and A. Maricq. 1953. *Recherches sur les Res Gestae Divi Saporis*. Brussels: Académie Royale de Belgique, Classe des lettres et des sciences morales et politiques, Mémoires 47.4.

Huff, D. 1987a. Archaeology iv. Sasanian. *EnIr* 2: 302–8.

———. 1987b. Architecture iii. Sasanian. *EnIr* 2: 329–34.

———. 1987c. Technological observations on clay bullae from Takht-i Suleiman. *Mesopotamia* 22: 367–90.

Huyse, P. 1999. *Die dreisprachige Inschrift Šābuhrs I. an der Kaʿba-i Zardušt (ŠKZ)*. 2 vols. London: CII 3/1/1.

Jullien, C. 2004. Contribution des Actes des Martyres perses et à la géographie historique à l'administration de l'empire sassanide. In *Contributions à l'histoire et la géographie historique de l'Empire sassanide*, ed. R. Gyselen, 141–69. Bures-sur-Yvette: RO 16.

Kalantarian, A. A. 1996. *Dvin. Histoire et archéologie de la ville médiévale*. Neuchâtel/Paris: Civilisations du Proche-Orient, Hors Série 2, Recherches et Publications.

Al-Kassar, A. 1979. Tanqibat Tell Abfi Shaʾaf. *Sumer* 35: 468–71.

Lerner J., and P. O. Skjærvø. 1997. Some uses of clay bullae in Sasanian Iran: Bullae in the Rosen and Museum of Fine Arts Collections. In *Sceaux d'Orient et leur emploi*, ed. R. Gyselen, 67–78. Bures-sur-Yvette: RO 10.

Lukonin, V. G. 1971. Po povodu bulli iz Aq-Tepe (About the bullae at Aq-Tepe). *Epigrafika Vostoka* 20: 50–2.

———. 1983. Political, social and administrative institutions: Taxes and trade. *CHI* 3/2: 681–743.
Maricq, A. 1958. Res Gestae Divi Saporis. *Syria* 35: 295–360.
MacKenzie, D. N. 1989. Kerdir's inscription. In *The Sasanian rock reliefs at Naqsh-i Rustam 6*, ed. G. Herrmann, 35–72. Berlin: Iranische Denkmäler 13/2/1.
Marquart [Markwart], J. 1901. *Ērānšahr nach der Geographie des Ps. Moses Xorenacʻi, mit historisch-kritischen Kommentar und historischen und topographischen Excursen*. Berlin: Abhandlungen der Königlichen Gesellschaft der Wissenschaften zu Göttingen, phil-hist. Kl. NF 3/2.
Menasce, J. P. de. 1967. L'inscription funéraire pehlevie d'Istanbul. *IrAnt* 7: 59–71.
Minovi, M. 1975–6. *Name-ye Tansar be Goshnasp*. Tehran (in Persian).
Naumann, R. 1965. Takht-i-Suleiman und Zendan-i-Suleiman: Vorläufiger Bericht über die Ausgrabungen im Jahren 1963 und 1964. *AA* 80: 619–65.
Perikhanian, A. 1997 *Mādigān ī Hezār Dādīstān. The book of a thousand judgments: A Sasanian law book*. Costa Mesa: Mazda.
Piacentini, V. F. 1994. MADINA/SHAHR, QARYA/DEH, NAHIYA/RUSTAQ. The city as political-adminstrative institution: the continuity of a Sasanian model. *JSAI* 17: 85–107
Shaked, S. 1986. Aramaic iii. Iranian loanwords in Middle Aramaic. *EnIr* online edition.
Shapira, D. 2001. Was there geographical science in Sassanian Iran? *AOASH* 54/2–3: 319–38.
Skjærvø, P. O. 1983. *The Sasanian inscription of Paikuli*, Part 3.1–2. Wiesbaden: L. Reichert.
Sprengling, M. 1940. Shahpur I, the Great, on the Kaabah of Zoroaster (KZ). *AJSL* 57/4: 341–429.
Tavadia, J. C. 1935. Sūr saxwan, a dinner speech in Middle Persian. *Journal of the K. R. Cama Oriental Institute* 29: 40–99.
Upton, J. M. 1973. The site of Qasr-i Abu Nasr and a description of the sealings. In *Sasanian remains from Qasr-i Abu Nasr: Seals, sealings, and coins*, ed. R. N. Frye, 6–25. Cambridge, MA: Harvard University Press.
Weber, D. 1992. *Ostraca, papyri und pergamente*. London: CII 3/4–5.
Wiesehöfer, J. 1996. *Ancient Persia from 550 BC to 650 AD*. London/New York: I. B. Tauris.
Wilkinson, C. K. 1936. Notes on the Sassanian seals found at Kasr-i Abu Nasr. *Metropolitan Museum of Art Bulletin* 31/9: 180–2.
Yāqūt al-Ḥamawī. 1956. *Mu'jam al-Buldān*. Beirut: Dar Sadir-Dar Beyrut.

CHAPTER 48

LUXURY SILVER VESSELS OF THE SASANIAN PERIOD

KATE MASIA-RADFORD

INTRODUCTION

Discussion, debate, and controversy regarding silver attributed to the Sasanian period has been an ongoing issue since collections were initially assembled in the nineteenth and twentieth centuries (Harper 1983: 1113, n. 1 and bibliography for early references). The formation of early collections, consisting of objects found by chance in areas such as northern Russia, Armenia, the Ukraine, India, Asia Minor, and Iran, or purchased in markets in India and Afghanistan, helped facilitate an interest in the study of Sasanian silver. In the twentieth century, an increase in the number of objects coming from clandestine excavations, particularly in Iran, added to the corpus of Sasanian silver, albeit with little information regarding provenance, place of manufacture, or chronology.

More recently, controlled excavations in Iran, Central Asia, Mesopotamia, and China have brought to light metalwork of or connected to Sasanian tradition. Due to the scientific nature of this work, including datable contexts and advances in technical analysis, new evidence has enhanced our knowledge of Sasanian silverware, its manufacture, production, consumption, chronology, and range of influence. A detailed analysis by Harper and Meyers (1981: 124, 150–2) has demonstrated that there existed both a central, royal Sasanian production of silver plate, subject to royal controls, and an independent, provincial industry that was the source of a related class of vessels of variable style. Vessels described as "post-Sasanian" continued Sasanian traditions but were manufactured after the fall of the Sasanian Empire (Harper and Meyers 1981: 141; Ward 1993: 43; Carter 2003: 191).

Two significant problems that arise when researching Sasanian silver concern chronology and authenticity. While comparisons with more firmly dated objects, such as coins and reliefs, are useful in dating silverware, the chronology of Sasanian silver and even the term "Sasanian" are areas of investigation that have engendered much debate (Grabar 1967: 19–83; Carter 1974: 171; Harper and Meyers 1981: 5–8; 2006: 163ff.). The vessels included in this chapter have all been attributed to the Sasanian Empire and, as Carter suggested in relation to silver plates, at the very least represent visual expressions of elements of Iranian culture within the Sasanian orbit of influence (Carter 1974: 171).

The majority of Sasanian vessels do not come from reliable archaeological contexts and there is little or no information available regarding their provenance. Sasanian themes were copied or used as inspiration by Islamic artisans, making it difficult to judge authenticity based on stylistic features alone. While modern forgeries are to be found in both private and public collections, a number of organizations and individuals have distinguished between forgeries and authentic items based on stylistic and technical analysis (Grabar 1967: 27; Moorey 1981: 119–25; Harper and Meyers 1981: 148; Gunter and Jett 1992: 230ff.; Muscarella 2000: 203ff.). Although it is almost impossible to authenticate items without extensive research, there has been considerable progress in establishing a corpus of authentic works through typological, stylistic, scientific, technical, and other criteria (e.g., Gunter and Jett 1992: 106ff.; Meyers 1981: 145–83; 1996a–d; 1997: 313–20).

Silverware attributed to the Sasanian period is suggestive of a carefully regulated production. Types and designs were limited at the beginning of the period, with early examples such as animal-shaped rhyta and deep, hemispherical bowls reflecting earlier Iranian traditions, while the picture-plate demonstrates an influence from the Greco-Roman world (Harper 1988a: 153; 1992: 148; 2006: 78ff.). The silver used was derived from a single ore source (Harper and Meyers 1981: 144–83; Harper 1992: 148) and under Šābuhr II in the fourth century restrictions were placed on the manufacture of silver plate (Harper 1978: 66).

Stylistic development in the fifth century, when both natural and human causes weakened the empire, is somewhat obscure (Harper 1983: 1118; Frye 1983: 147ff.). Prosperity increased in the later fifth or sixth century due to social and political reform (Göbl 1971: 68ff.; Frye 1983: 153ff.) and it is only during the sixth and seventh centuries that Sasanian forms, iconography, and style can be defined on the basis of a larger corpus of material. The growth of a strong, central power appears to have led to expanded production and while earlier styles and designs, such as the royal hunter motif, continued to appear on silver plates, new vessel types and a wider range of designs entered the Sasanian repertoire (Harper 2006: 82–3). The introduction of such vessels and their designs reflects the political events of this region. In the middle of the sixth century, following the collapse of Hephthalite rule in western Central Asia, contacts between Iran, Central Asia, and China increased and a period of political and cultural expansion and change ensued (Harper 1991a: 78). New types of silverware derived from eastern models entered the Sasanian repertoire, including polylobed and elliptical bowls that reflect eastern Iranian and western Central Asian influence (Harper 1992: 148; 2006: 82–3). Vases, ewers, and high-footed bowls reflect the continuing influence of eastern Mediterranean styles, while areas such as Bactria, where Hellenized forms and motifs had persisted, may also have played a role (Harper 2006: 83).

At this time a larger segment of society owned silver plate, and metallurgical analysis has shown that different sources of silver were utilized (Harper 1992: 148). The form of the vessels and their decorative motifs were, however, still standardized, indicating the continued existence of some form of state control (Harper 1992: 148). While some are classified as central Sasanian vessels, others appear to have been manufactured in provincial workshops. Those attributed to this latter category do, however, display stylistic features inspired by Sasanian traditions and as such are often included amongst vessels attributed to the Sasanian Empire.

BOWLS

Hemispherical bowls, ranging in size from approximately 18 cm to just over 23 cm in diameter and 6–8 cm high, are amongst the earliest examples of Sasanian silverware. Four examples, allegedly found together in western Iran near Kermanshah, are decorated on the interior with a central medallion enclosing a bust, in partial relief, above a stylized leaf base. Three are decorated with male busts (Fig. 48.1 and Freer Gallery of Art, 57.20: Gunter and Jett 1992: 157–60, no. 24; Cincinnati Art Museum, 1955.71: Harper and Meyers 1981: 204, pl. 3; Metropolitan Museum of Art, 55.57: Harper and Meyers 1981: 207, pl. 6), while the fourth depicts the bust of a female holding a flower to her nose, a gesture symbolic of attendees at court or indicative of rank or courtly status (Iran Bastan Museum, Tehran, 1385: Harper and Meyers 1981: pl. 7). Flowers were also associated with banqueting and wine drinking, as well as the act of inhaling the fragrance

FIGURE 48.1 Hemispherical bowl (Freer Gallery of Art, 57.20).

of the flower, its scent being reminiscent of wine (Melikian-Chirvani 1996: 122–3).The bowls share a number of design features linking them as a group. These include their method of manufacture (Harper and Meyers 1981: 24–40, 152), as well as motifs indicating a connection to the Sasanian elite, such as diadems, a hairstyle incorporating the ball of curls, a beaded halter, jewelry, and fluttering ribbons. The right to wear the diadem was a royal or divine privilege indicative of rank or position well established by the Sasanian period and recorded by Kerdīr in his inscription on the Ka'be-ye Zardosht (MacKenzie 1970: 264; Rose 2012 for additional references).

In addition to bowls with a single medallion is one example, allegedly of Iranian provenance, decorated on the exterior with five medallions, each enclosing a female bust above an acanthus leaf (Metropolitan Museum of Art, 1970.5: Harper and Meyers 1981: pl. 5). An additional portrait appears on the base of the vessel. Features indicative of rank or nobility include the hairstyle with a ball of curls at the top, the beaded diadem, and fluttering ribbons, jewelry, and clothing.

It is likely that vessels decorated with the portrait medallion date from the late third to the early fourth century (Harper and Meyers 1981: 181; Gunter and Jett 1992: 158; Loukonine and Ivanov 1996: 91–3). Such images, demonstrating Parthian influence and a selection of elements of Roman design (Harper and Meyers 1981: 28 and Gunter and Jett 1992: 158 for comparisons), reflect the beginning of new designs incorporating earlier and contemporary influences within a distinct Sasanian framework. This was a form of portraiture used by people of consequence before silverware became dominated by royal imagery and is reminiscent of the royal image on Sasanian coins (Gunter and Jett 1992: 159). The careful choice of motifs asserts the importance of the figures represented, reinforcing their link to an increasingly dominant Sasanian court. A unique two-handled cup decorated with images of Warahrān II and his family is related to this form of portraiture (see below).

Smaller hemispherical bowls, c.12–14 cm in diameter and just over 5 cm high, with designs on the exterior, are attributed to the later part of the Sasanian period and may reflect an eastern influence (Harper 1988: 156; examples include Cleveland Museum of Art, 66.369: Harper 1978: 53–4, no. 14; Collection of Elie Borowski: Harper 1978: 54–5, no. 15, and an unpublished example in the Metropolitan Museum of Art: 1970.7). Vessels of this type were probably manufactured for a broader class of social elite (Harper 2006: 82). Their decoration includes plant or floral motifs, wine-making scenes, figural scenes linked to themes of wine-drinking, and courtly entertainments such as hunting, wrestling, and music, sometimes incorporating the medallion motif. The combination of wine drinking, music, and courtly entertainments is made explicit on a bowl in the Arthur M. Sackler Gallery that probably belongs to the post-Sasanian tradition (Arthur M. Sackler Gallery, s1987.105: Gunter and Jett 1992: 161–5, no. 25; Rosen-Ayalon 1984; Melikian-Chirvani 1992).

A number of shallow bowls exhibiting Sasanian stylistic features and Hellenistic designs have been attributed to this period, although they were probably manufactured in Bactria (Freer Gallery of Art, 45.33: Gunter and Jett 1992: 148–56, no. 23, with further references), an area in which Hellenized forms and motifs persisted long after they had disappeared in

Iran (Harper 2006: 83). Such vessels continued decorative traditions of Greek iconography and style and in this way are related to other, later Sasanian vessel types decorated with imagery clearly indebted to Classical Greek forms and styles (see below). According to Gunter, vessels decorated in this way may have a Central Asian provenance and provide evidence of the continuity of Greek artistic forms in this area (1992: 154).

A variation of the small hemispherical bowl includes a type with a small loop for suspension from a belt or harness strap. Examples with motifs executed in the Sasanian style have been found in Iran and appear to indicate an influence from eastern nomads, such as the Turks or Avars (Harper 1988a: 156–7; 2006: 89–90). Such vessels indicate the way in which the Sasanians incorporated new designs into their repertoire, reflecting the contact between cultures that existed at this time.

High-footed bowls

The high-footed bowl with fluted exterior is a shape represented in silver (Arthur M. Sackler Gallery, s1987.106: Gunter and Jett 1992: 166–9, no. 26; Royal Museum of Art and History, Brussels, inv. IS.57: Overlaet 1993: 253, no. 101), bronze (Moorey 1981: 121, no. 707) and pewter (Harper 1978: 86, fig. D). *Niello* is present on some examples, suggestive of a date later in the Sasanian period (Arthur M. Sackler Gallery: Gunter and Jett 1992: 166–9, no. 26) and vessels may be decorated on the interior with designs including birds such as guinea fowl within a medallion. These bowls are represented in the archaeological record, although they lack a clear stratigraphic association (Gunter and Jett 1992: 170, n. 2), and were themselves depicted on Sasanian silver where they are shown being used as serving vessels, sometimes in festive ceremonies (for example, a vase in the Hermitage Museum, s6: Trever and Lukonin 1987: pls. 37–41; a ewer in the Arthur M. Sackler Gallery (Fig. 48.4), s1987.118: Gunter and Jett 1992: 198–201, no. 36; a wine bowl in the Arthur M. Sackler Gallery, s1987.105: Gunter and Jett 1992: 161–5, no. 25). While prototypes for the high-footed bowl may be found in the West and it appears this was a type derived from fourth-century products (Strong 1966: 204, pl. 66A), they are found throughout a wide geographical range, with examples documented from India (Harper 1988a: 156), China (Harper 1988a: 156), and later Islamic periods (Melikian-Chirvani 1982: 63, fig. 27, and 64, fig. 28). The carved, fluted exterior decoration is a feature derived from Hellenistic and Roman ceramics, also seen on polylobed bowls and plates dated toward the end of the Sasanian period (Harper 2002: 116).

A silver cup

A unique silver-gilt, two-handled cup from a site in Sargveshi, western Georgia, depicts the busts of Warahrān II (276–293), his wife, Šābuhrduxtak, and son, and has been dated to the reign of this king (Art Museum of Georgia, Tbilisi, R134: Loukonine and Ivanov 1996: 91–5, no. 63). This vessel continues the motif of a portrait within a medallion seen on bowls attributed to the earlier part of the empire and is the only example with an identifiable royal figure. An inhabited grapevine scroll is placed beneath the rim of the vessel, a precursor to the much wider use of this design in later Sasanian silverware. While there is a similarity with Greco-Roman designs and the shape of the cup is Western in origin, details of the clothing and figures, the position of the bust with the head in profile, the extended forefinger of the king in a gesture of reverence often used when the king or members of his court were before a deity or fire altar (Choksy 1990b: 205), the flower held by the queen to her nose, and the ring held by the prince are significant and recurring features in Sasanian art. Such motifs represent an early example of the visual expression of Sasanian kingship and the use of symbols representing the right to rule.

PLATES

Plates with a low foot-ring represent a shape documented from the early Sasanian period with Parthian predecessors and Hellenistic and Roman antecedents (Gunter 1992: 26). Such vessels, found within Iran and in more distant areas, were exported and later used as objects of barter or trade (Frye 1971: 260; Harper 1988a: 154). One of the earliest examples depicts a male bust within a central medallion, a style reminiscent of and current with the portrait medallion bowls described above (Janashia Museum of Georgia, Tbilisi, 18:55:53: Loukonine and Ivanov 1996: 95, no. 64). Found in an early fourth-century grave at Mtskheta, eastern Georgia, in a tomb of Georgian nobles with stylistic features linking it to the third century, it appears this plate arrived in Georgia almost immediately after its manufacture (Harper and Meyers 1981: 28–9; Loukonine and Ivanov 1996: 95).

An inscription beneath the exterior rim of the vessel, in a style suggestive of a date around 300 AD, identifies the high rank of "Papak" the "*pitiakhsh*," one of the highest offices in the Sasanian court (Brunner 1974: 110; Loukonine and Ivanov 1996: 95). His beaded necklace and diadem with small ribbons indicates his position and he holds a flower to his nose, a meaningful and much-repeated gesture in Sasanian art. Two plates decorated with a bust wearing a crown attributed to Xosrow II, one in the Los Angeles County Museum of Art (AC1993.140.1) and the second in the Miho Museum (Harper 1997b; Meyers 1996a), indicate a reappearance of the medallion style of portraiture much later in the period.

At the same time as the medallion bust was in fashion, the well-known hunting plate imagery developed. This soon became the prominent theme on Sasanian silver plates and while the earliest silver plates depict individuals other than the king, only royal images appear on works from the third, fourth, and fifth centuries (Harper and Meyers 1981: 126–7). The hunter motif, imagery with a history in Persian art (see Shahbazi 2004 for references to the hunt in pre-Islamic Iran), was used as an allegory for war and as a symbol of power, kingship, and invincibility (Harper and Meyers 1981: 142; 1991a: 96) and may also have been closely related to the idea of supernatural valor and heroism (Garsoïan 1981: 50–4; 1997: 24).

Studies of plates decorated with the royal hunter motif have often been controversial (Haskins 1952: 249–52 for a history of this controversy prior to 1952 and Harper and Meyers 1981: 40 and n. 1 for later theories). A detailed examination by Harper and Meyers helped distinguish Sasanian vessels produced by royal and non-royal workshops on the basis of drapery styles, composition, manufacture, decorative detail, and technical and metallurgical analysis. Central Sasanian vessels are believed to have been manufactured under the direction of ruling members of the dynasty between 226 and 651 (Harper and Meyers 1981: 5). These works have been isolated from provincial ones produced in workshops outside official Sasanian control or from post-Sasanian contexts. The metal used for central Sasanian vessels often differs from that used in vessels classed as provincial works (Harper and Meyers 1981: 144–86). Stylistic details comparable to those on more firmly dated reliefs and coins and identifiable crowns provide some evidence for a chronological sequence. Evidence from crowns is somewhat limited as there was repetition in types and it is possible the intention was to represent an "ideal" rather than an individual monarch (Harper and Meyers 1981: 139 and pls. 15–17 for examples with identifiable crowns).

In the mid- to late third century the hunters depicted appear to have been members of the Sasanian nobility (Museum of the History of Azerbaijan: Harper and Meyers 1981: pl. 8), possibly princes (Abkhazian State Museum, Abkhaz Autonomous Soviet Socialist Republic, acc. no. 47.71: Harper and Meyers 1981: pl. 9), or rulers of provinces connected to the Sasanian Empire (Iran Bastan Museum, Tehran: Harper and Meyers 1981: pl. 10). The plates dated to this earlier period were larger in diameter than later examples (28–9 cm versus 23–4 cm) and share stylistic features with early Sasanian rock reliefs (Harper and Meyers 1981: 56–7).

Beginning in the fourth century individuals other than the king ceased to appear on silver plates for over a century. Compositionally speaking, the convention of vertically and horizontally balanced figures fitting carefully within the plate was followed over the centuries with only minor variations in iconography and design (Harper 2006: 121). Significant changes include the rendering of drapery as a series of short, paired lines sometime in the fourth century, possibly due to an influence from newly conquered Kushan lands (Harper and Meyers 1981: 127). The way in which gilding was applied changed sometime in the late fifth century, possibly due to the discovery of an easier technique of application (Harper 1988a: 159). There appears to have been an increase in the complexity of compositions over time although the figural imagery, composition and stylistic features became standardized and may indicate a dynastic monopoly on this type of vessel and its production (Harper and Meyers 1981: 127).

Related to this core group of central Sasanian silver plates are "provincial" works that differ in style, iconography, and technique. They may have a deep, bowl-like form and/or they may depict crown types unknown in the Sasanian period. Additional differences include the rendering of the drapery in parallel lines and a triangular design in which certain elements do not fit (Harper and Meyers 1981: 134; 2006: 120). Designs may be rendered by simply chasing and engraving on the surface following a dotted pattern, a technique not used in any vessel classified as central Sasanian. While some vessels are stylistically close to central Sasanian vessels (Harper and Meyers 1981: pls. 20, 24, 27), the composition of the metal suggests they are provincial works. It is possible some vessels were manufactured by craftsmen at the periphery of the empire as they reflect developments in court style (Harper and Meyers 1981: 138).

While the royal hunter motif continued to decorate silver plates throughout the period, a wider range of designs may be noted from the sixth century. A small number of vessels with enthronement scenes have been attributed to the Sasanian period and while a number are more likely to represent post-Sasanian vessels (e.g., Harper and Meyers 1981: pls. 19, 33-6), true Sasanian examples may include a gold, glass, and rock crystal bowl in the Bibliothèque Nationale (Harper and Meyers 1981: 234, pl. 33; Harper 2006: 139-40) and a plate in the State Hermitage Museum (Hermitage Museum, s250: Harper and Meyers 1981: pl. 19; Overlaet 1993: 206-7, no. 61). The latter appears to have been made in a Sasanian workshop, as indicated by comparisons with central Sasanian vessels and silver composition (Harper and Meyers 1981: 114, 129), and the crowns have been linked to types employed from Pērōz to Xosrow II (Marshak 1993: 206). This vessel is decorated with both a hunting vignette and what has been described as an enthronement (Harper and Meyers 1981: 67) or banquet scene (Garsoïan 1997: 13), in which the king is surrounded by attendants, possibly rulers of the four Sasanian districts (Marshak 1993: 206).

A number of plates and bowls attributed to the Sasanian period may represent the *bazm* ritual, an early Islamic term describing wine drinking to music at courtly entertainments, after meals lasting for hours or even days in royal receptions during late Sasanian and early Islamic Iran (Melikian-Chirvani 1992: 95). Such events may have been organized for specific occasions that arose in daily life, as well as for great celebrations, such as the *Nowruz* festival (Melikian-Chirvani 1992: 96). The scenes on such vessels revolve around a seated, drinking male and contain imagery related to courtly and/or banqueting scenes with aspects of New Year celebrations, symbols of honor/investiture, and the ritual of filtering *hom* and/or wine in a ceremonial and/or celebratory context (Walters Art Gallery, Baltimore, 57.709: Overlaet 1993: 211, no. 65; Arthur M. Sackler Gallery, s1987.113: Gunter and Jett 1992: 131-5, no. 18; Hermitage Museum, s-47: Overlaet 1993: 210, no. 64; British Museum, 1953-12-10-3: Duchesne-Guillemin 1993: fig. 11).

Additional motifs include animals, both real (plate with a horse, Arthur M Sackler Gallery, s1987.123: Gunter and Jett 1992: 139, no. 20; plate with a feline, Miho Museum: Harper 1997a: 108) and fantastic (Hermitage Museum, inv. s-26: Trever and Lukonin 1987: no. 36, pl. 106 and Overlaet 1993: 223, no. 73), ceremonial scenes (Bibliothèque Nationale, Paris: Harper 2000: 87, fig. 18), nude females (Cleveland Museum of Art, 62.295: Overlaet 1993: 225, no. 75) and scrolling grapevines (Arthur M. Sackler Gallery, s1987.124: Gunter and Jett 1992: 128-9, no. 17). Images reflecting Iranian literary traditions include depictions of Warahrān V and Azada (Guennol

Collection: Harper 1978: 48–50, no. 12; Hermitage Museum, s-252: Overlaet 1993: 192, no. 51, and Loukonine and Ivanov 1996: 100, no. 71). The mythical *senmurw* appears at the end of the Sasanian period, an image closely associated with the monarchy (British Museum, London, BM.124095: Overlaet 1993: 220-1, no. 71*)*.

Plates decorated with a ram wearing fluttering ribbons (Arthur M. Sackler Gallery, s1987.115: Gunter and Jett 1992: 136–8, no. 19) and a bird (Hermitage Museum, s-18: Overlaet 1993: 217, no. 69) with both ribbons and a necklace in its beak may reflect the concept of royal fortune or *xvarrh*, recounted in a number of texts and in a number of guises, where it has been described as taking the form of both the ram (Duchesne-Guillemin 1966: 24; Ettinghausen 1972: 43) and the bird (*Yašt* 14.18–21; Darmesteter 1882: 236). The most appropriate translation of the word appears to be "glory" (Gnoli 1999), corresponding to the concept of royal fortune as well as fortune in a more general sense (Schmidt 1980: 21), possibly explaining the popular use of such motifs in both royal and nonroyal depictions.

A Greco-Roman influence in iconography may also be noted with the appearance of the Dioscuri, Castor and Pollux (Arnold 1996: 63.152: Harper 1978: 42–3, no. 8), and Dionysiac themes (Freer Gallery of Art, 64.10: Gunter and Jett 1992: 121–7, no. 16; History Museum, Moscow, 84845: Loukonine and Ivanov 1996: 98, no. 68.). A plate depicting an eagle seizing a woman reflects a theme originating in Gandharan sources and may have been produced in an eastern Iranian workshop (Hermitage Museum, s-217: Trever and Lukonin 1987: no. 22, pls. 57–8; Overlaet 1993: 224, no. 74; Azarpay 1997: 99–125). While the imagery on such vessels is derived from other cultural milieux, artisans working within the Sasanian sphere of influence made changes that clearly distinguished the scenes from their original source. Such plates indicate the way in which influences from non-Sasanian contexts were adopted, altered, and possibly took on new meanings relevant to a Sasanian audience.

Rhyta

Rhyta of various types have been attributed to the Sasanian period and include a unique early example in the form of a recumbent horse (Cleveland Museum of Art, 64.41: Shepherd 1966: 291ff.; Harper 1978: 28–30, n. 1), a style also represented in terracotta (e.g., Harper 1978: 166, no. 86). The rhyton had a long history in Iran going back to the Iron Age, although it is difficult to know how long the shape persisted. Medallions on the shoulders of the horse depict the busts of two bearded male figures and, while they lack a headdress or crown indicating rank or nobility, they may be connected to early medallion portraiture. Although the identity of the figures is unclear, their importance is suggested by the presence of a proffered ring and hand gestures of reverence reserved for deities, altars, and icons of the Zoroastrian faith (Choksy 1990a: 35 regarding this gesture and its symbolism in the Sasanian period). A related example may include a recumbent oryx (private collection: Grabar 1967: 132, no. 49), and silver rhyta in the form of horse protomes should also be noted (Louvre, MAO 132: David-Weill 1954: 157; Cincinnati Art Museum: Grabar 1967: 130, no. 47).

A silver-gilt horn rhyton terminating in the neck and head of a gazelle or oryx with a frieze of animals placed above the fluting of the horn section of the vessel has been dated to the third or fourth century (Fig. 48.2; Arthur M. Sackler Gallery, s1987.33: Gunter and Jett 1992: 205–10, no. 38.). Wine horns terminating in the head of an animal appear to have been a type of vessel manufactured throughout the period, as indicated by fragments of a similar example in a grave (Harper 1988a: 157); depictions on other forms of Sasanian silverware (a lobed bowl in the Cleveland Museum of Art: Melikian-Chirvani 1996: 87, fig. 1; a small bowl or cup in the Arthur M. Sackler Gallery, s1987.105: Gunter and Jett 1992: 161–5, no. 25); and possibly on a seal with a banqueting scene (Bivar 1969: 65, CF1 and pl. 8, CF1; Harper 1978: 148, no. 73), all of which postdate the fifth century. This style appears to have had a fairly wide distribution in Central Asia and China from the fifth to the seventh centuries (Harper 1988a: 157–8). A silver cup depicting a courtly wine banquet shows a vessel of this type and suggests that rhyta were used in wine-drinking ceremonies (Arthur M. Sackler Gallery, s1987.105: Gunter and Jett 1992: 161–5; Melikian-Chirvani 1996: 115ff. for an analysis of the ceremony shown on this vessel).

Wine horns terminating in the foreparts of an animal are well documented in the Achaemenid and Parthian periods, and the tradition continued in the Sasanian period. Later Persian texts refer to rhyta in the form of a complete animal as well as examples terminating in the foreparts of an animal (Melikian-Chirvani 1982: 263–92). Gazelles and caprids were depicted as the quarry of the king in depictions of the hunt on silver plates and on the relief at Taq-w Bustan and such vessels of this type may represent a

FIGURE 48.2 Silver-gilt horn rhyton (Arthur M. Sackler Gallery, S1987.33).

link to courtly pursuits. Later examples include a form of rhyton depicting the head of a female, sometimes with that of an animal, a type documented in both silver (Cleveland Museum of Art, 64.96: Harper 1978: 68–71, no. 23) and pottery (University Museum, Philadelphia, B9471: Harper 1978: 162–4; no. 84). Silver-gilt rhyta in the form of caprids have also been attributed to the Sasanian period, although such vessels may be of Central Asian origin (Harper 2006: 138, 158–9, figs. 85–6). When vessels of this type are shown on Sasanian silver or seals they are clearly being used in a banqueting setting, a social and religious activity bound by ritual and religious doctrine and closely connected to the Sasanian court.

Single and twin-spouted vessels, also known as amphora-rhyta or rhyton-vases, have also been attributed to the Sasanian period. They continue a tradition dating back to the fifth century BC and comparanda occur in Parthian contexts as well (Fukai 1977: pl. 24; Haerinck 1980: 198). A single-spouted rhyton-vase with a pear-shaped body rests on a pierced, circular, decorated base and dates from the mid to late Sasanian period (Cleveland Museum, 1962.294: Shepherd 1964: figs. 20–2). It is decorated with four female figures holding attributes linking it to vases and ewers decorated with this motif (see below). Additional examples include a vase with a flat, sieve-like base with a number of holes (British Museum, WAA 124094: Collon 1995: 207, fig. 173). Glass versions have been dated between the fourth and sixth centuries (Fukai 1977: 54, pl. 30, fig. 59; Whitehouse 2005: 54–6, no. 65 with additional references). A twin-spouted vase decorated with female figures has also been attributed to the late Sasanian/early Islamic period (Tehran National Museum, 2500: Stierlen 2006: 243). While it is certainly inspired by and closely linked to Sasanian silverware, it is more likely to belong to the post-Sasanian tradition.

Vases and ewers

The characteristic Sasanian vase has a pear-shaped body; a low, flat, circular foot; a narrow, tapering neck; and an offset rim, and stands $c.16$–19 cm tall, weighing $c.400$–600 g (Fig. 48.3). Decorative molding in relief separates the neck from the body. Ceramic versions are known from the fifth century (Harper 1992: 148, n. 6 for references). Examples deviating from this style may have been made in peripheral regions or may postdate the Sasanian period (Hermitage Museum, s256: Trever and Lukonin 1987: pls 48–52; Museum of Fine Arts, Boston, 58.94: Overlaet 1993: 242, no. 91; Hermitage Museum, s 37: Overlaet 1993: 241, no. 90).

Typologically speaking, the Sasanian ewer belongs to a category of silver vessels of Central Asian or east Iranian rather than central Sasanian origin, although such vessels may have their antecedents in Western styles (Fig. 48.4; Harper 1991b: 78; Carter 2003: 188). Ewers are characterized by a pear-shaped body with a high, hollow, flaring foot, and are, on average, 32–35 cm tall, weighing $c.1039$–1542 g. The elongated neck has a horizontal, wedge-shaped spout, sometimes with a lid. Moldings are placed at the shoulder

FIGURE 48.3 Silver-gilt vase (Freer Gallery of Art, 1966.1).

and high on the foot. The handle is topped by a spherical thumb guard and its ends terminate in animal heads. The ewers have been dated predominantly to the sixth or seventh centuries (Harper 1978: 25; 1992: 149; Gunter and Jett 1992: 198; Carter 2003: 185). Variations, including jug-like vases (Hermitage Museum, S60: Overlaet 1993: 246–7, no. 95; Cleveland Museum of Art, 61.200: Shepherd 1964: 80, fig. B, and 89–92, 90, fig. 30) and other forms show significant differences in style, and may be of provincial manufacture or belong to the post-Sasanian tradition (e.g., Fig. 48.3: Cincinnati Art Museum, 1966.1091: Grabar 1967: 106–7, no. 19; Nasli and Alice Heeramaneck Collection, New York: Grabar 1967: 108, 110, no. 21).

Pairs of vases and ewers indicate that identically decorated vessels were created (a pair of vases decorated with birds, Miho Museum: Harper 1997c: 110; a pair of vases with a geometric pattern, Freer Gallery of Art, 64.3: Gunter and Jett 1992: 185; Metropolitan Museum of Art, Rogers Fund, 62.78.2: Overlaet 1993: 245; a pair of ewers with fluted decoration, Arthur M. Sackler Gallery and the collection of Noriyoshi Horiuchin, Gunter and Jett 1992: 202–4, no. 37 and n. 4 for references). Technological analyses suggest the vases and ewers were a relatively homogenous group with a composition similar to that of Sasanian plates on which royal figures are represented (Harper 1992: 149). As with other vessel types, vases and ewers are divided into groups based on their decoration, although shared motifs suggest such groups are linked.

Two silver-gilt vases are decorated with an uninterrupted vine scroll motif inhabited by animals, birds, and small, nude males busily engaged in various activities including wine production (National Collection, Tehran, 578: Harper 1978: 71–3, no. 24; British Museum, WAA 124094: Overlaet 1993: 240, no. 89). While inhabited scroll motifs and the vine arbor were well established in Near Eastern iconography, the imagery appears to have been inspired in part by Dionysiac traditions and its themes of eternal life and fruitfulness (Carter 1978: 72).

Although the grapevine may have symbolized abundance and prosperity, supported by seals that depict an abbreviated version of the vine with the word *abzōn*, "prosperity" or "increase" (Harper 2006: 87), the vintaging motifs relate to the production of wine, appropriate imagery for vessels most likely used in this context. Wine-drinking parties were a ritual event with both religious and social significance and the imagery may have had a deeper religious or ritual symbolism. The ritual drinking of *hom* and/or wine occurred during festivities such as *Nowruz* and it has been suggested that the vine motif may have come to embody the Zoroastrian *hom* tree, the tree of immortality (Shepherd 1966: 302). Wine may have been equated with or confused with *hom*, and thus seen as the liquor of immortality (Melikian-Chirvani 1990–91: 52–3). If so, then scenes of vintaging may be more relevant to Sasanian ritual and belief than might have been thought the case at first glance.

While the grapevine may represent eternal life and the paradisiacal and fruitful nature of the Sasanian Empire under the just rule of the Sasanian king, it may also have become representative of the *hom* tree, the source of immortality that played such an important role in Zoroastrian religion, ritual, and thought.

Female figures with associated attributes belong to a class of design found predominantly on the vases and ewers, although examples may be seen on bowls of varying forms (Fig. 48.4; Shepherd 1980: fig. 25a: nos. 17–19). The women surround the body of the vessel and are shown most commonly in groups of four in a position of movement. They are associated with attributes including animals, birds, plants, fruit, vessels, and small figures, most commonly held in their hands but sometimes placed within the decorative field of the vessel. Some of the figures are framed by arches while others show decorative elements that forge a connection to this motif.

While Roman representations of the seasons and depictions of the maenads had an influence in the positioning of the female figures (Harper 1971: 508), the Sasanians created a simplified design framework with less variation. Some of the figures appear to have an Eastern influence as seen by the use of the *urna* and by the curvaceous form of the body and the emphasis on the breasts and hips (for comparisons to female figures in Gandharan art, see Hallade 1968: pls. 28–9, 46–7).

The curvaceous bodies of the women, their lack of clothing or the sheer nature of their dresses, the hairstyle reserved for dancers, musicians, attribute-bearers, and those involved in mythological or narrative scenes, and the contrast in their depiction when

FIGURE 48.4 Silver-gilt ewer (Arthur M. Sackler Gallery, S1987.118).

compared to royal or religious figures, set these women apart. Motifs symbolic of investiture and/or *xvarrh* including the beaded, diadem-like headband, sometimes with ribbons, the necklace, halo, and the topknots that may take the form of a ball of curls, indicate a link to the Sasanian king or royal court and suggest these vessels played a role in activities connected to the royal domain.

The identification of the female figures and what or whom they may have represented has been a topic of some discussion. Dionysiac elements have been noted (Ettinghausen 1967–8: 41; 1972: 5) and they have been connected to Anahita (Trever 1967: 121ff.; Shepherd 1980: 49), the seasons or seasonal festivals (Harper 1971: 508; Carter 1974: 200ff.; 2003: 186), as symbols of royal banquets and princely pastimes (Ghirshman 1953: 56ff.; Grabar 1967: 63), as women of the Sasanian court or king's harem (Duchesne-Guillemin 1971: 379), and connected to the *daena*, the female associated with the reward the faithful will receive in the afterlife (Gnoli 1993: 82–3; Choksy 2002: 71). It is possible they are a reminder that the worthy man can expect to enjoy happiness and the good things of life on this earth and be rewarded thereafter. While it is difficult to form an opinion without entering the realm of speculation, it is clear that a generic female form representing an idealized female, discussed in both secular (for Tabari, 1025, see Bosworth 1999: 352; "King Xosrow and his Boy," see Unvala 1936: 35–6; Ferdowsi, see Levy 1967: 402–3) and religious (*Avesta*, as in Darmesteter 1882: 273; *Hādōxt Nask, Yašt* 22, see Darmesteter 1882: 315–6) literature, came to be depicted on Sasanian silverware rather than a specific person.

The female figures are closely associated with the attributes they present. Motifs indicative of banqueting and ritual wine drinking include flowers, fruit, musical instruments, incense burners, cups, trays, drinking vessels, the wreath or *pasāk*, and possibly the wine bucket. Images of prosperity and paradise are represented by motifs such as the bird pecking at grapes, the panther drinking from a vessel, the child-like figures and the peacock, closely linked to vases decorated with inhabited vine scrolls and Dionysiac themes that had come to be associated with celebrations and drinking ceremonies. Motifs indicative of the Sasanian court and kingship include the necklace, halo, and ring. Symbols suggestive of Zoroastrianism and its worldview are identifiable and include the bird and dog, two animals closely associated with this religion as identified in the textual evidence. Symbols of *xvarrh* indicate that such vessels were linked with the notion of royal fortune.

While we cannot confidently associate the attributes with a particular festival or individual, they do incorporate symbols relevant to both the social and religious aspects of banqueting and festivities of the Sasanian world. Religious iconography was combined with motifs relevant to celebration and feasting, a combination reflective of a culture where the two were closely entwined. Such events would have taken place in architectural settings, indicated by the arches depicted on some of the vases and ewers. Their style is reflective of structures used in the Sasanian period and their decorative detail is indicative of stucco.

A number of vases and ewers depict female dancers, jugglers, and musicians playing instruments including panpipes, castanets, clappers, and horns, sometimes with small, child-like figures and birds at their feet in a format related to those with attributes (Fig. 48.3; Freer Gallery of Art, 66.1: Brunner 1974: 114, no. 16; Gunter and Jett 1992: 191–3, no. 34; Musée d'Art et d'histoire de Genève: Duchesne-Guillemin 1993: 93–6, figs. 32a–c; collection of Bernard Barnett, Louisville, Kentucky: Ettinghausen 1967–8: 40, figs. 18–20; Duchesne-Guillemin 1993: 99–100, fig. 35; Arthur M. Sackler Gallery, s1987.117: Gunter and Jett 1992: 194–7, no. 35). This link is made clear by a vase that incorporates a musical instrument amongst the attributes (Museo Nazionale d'Arte Orientale, Rome, 8542: Duchesne-Guillemin 1993: 98, fig. 34). As indicated by Sasanian reliefs (Taq-e Bustan: Duchesne-Guillemin 1993: 29, figs. B31, C32, D, and E33), stucco (Overlaet 1993: 151, no. 10), and mosaics (Overlaet 1993: 162–3, no. 21), female minstrels and singers were part of the court. Depictions of musicians on silver plates with *bazm* scenes (Hermitage Museum, s47: Overlaet 1993: 210, no. 64), as well as literary evidence (Unvala 1936: 29; Ferdowsi, XXVII, ii: Levy 1967: 298–9; Tabari, 1041: Bosworth 1999: 376–7; Melikian-Chirvani 1992: 97ff.), suggest music accompanied wine-drinking ceremonies and religious rituals, and females were employed as servants for music making and singing and as companions of the king. Female musicians on vases, ewers, and silver wine-bowls (Azarpay 1976; Duchesne-Guillemin 1993: 88, fig. 29 for wine bowls), classes of silverware used to hold wine, make the link between music and wine drinking explicit, and vases and ewers depicting Dionysiac imagery (see below), dancers, and musicians reflect more explicit celebratory themes.

Vases with figural scenes include hunting vignettes in a mountainous landscape (National Collection, Tehran, 577: Harper 1978: 65–7, no. 22). Figures dressed as Sasanian courtiers hunt animals in what may be a *paradeisos* or private game park, a popular activity associated with the king. Such paradisiacal landscapes may suggest themes of abundance and harmony. A vase with four youthful males overpowering animals within a series of arches (National Collection, Tehran, 579: Harper 1978: 51–2, no. 13) and two jug-like vases with similar scenes (Hermitage Museum, S60: Overlaet 1993: 246–7, no. 95; Cleveland Museum of Art, 61.200: Shepherd 1964: 80, fig. B, and 89–92, 90 fig. 30) may have represented an idealized hero and/or concepts pertaining to supernatural valor, courage, and honor, attributes connected to the Sasanian court (Marshak 1993: 246).

Additional Dionysiac motifs associated with celebrations and drinking ceremonies may be connected to vases with both female figures and grapevine scrolls (Freer Gallery of Art, 65.20: Gunter and Jett 1992: 188–90, no. 33). Geometric designs may also be noted (Freer Gallery of Art, 64.3: Gunter and Jett 1992: 185, no. 32; Metropolitan Museum of Art, 62.78.2: Overlaet 1993: 245, no. 94).

Bird motifs were a popular form of decoration on all forms of silverware and the vases are no exception. Examples include birds of prey (Museum of Fine Arts Boston, 58.94: Overlaet 1993: 241, no. 90; Hermitage Museum, S70: Overlaet 1993: 243, no. 92), unadorned birds (Miho Museum: Brunner 1974: 112, no. 5; Harper 1997c: 110; Hermitage Museum, s38: Trever and Lukonin 1987: pl. 98.), as well as a bird with a necklace (Museum of Fine Arts Boston, 58.94: Overlaet 1993: 242, no. 91). Birds played an important role in both textual and archaeological evidence and their multifaceted religious and royal significance made them an important symbol in the Sasanian period. Passages from the *Bundahishn* suggest birds "were given an *Avesta* with its tongue" and demons were repelled (*Bundahishn* 19.19–20; West 1880: 71). The bird's role as guardian of the *Avesta* imbues it with a religious symbolism and suggests it may represent the *Avesta* or the knowledge that may be gained from it, a theme echoed in later Persian poetry (Melikian-Chirvani 1992: 114ff. for Persian references). As a benevolent creation of Ahura Mazda, the bird had the power to oppose the spirit of evil.

Elliptical bowls

Elliptical bowls, also referred to as boat-shaped bowls or wine-boats, represent a large group of Sasanian silverware and are one of the few types represented in the archaeological record. These drinking vessels may be classified based on their form, the presence or lack of a foot, and the location of the decoration. While boat-shaped vessels have a history in Iran going back to the third and second millennia BC, there are no similar vessels from the Achaemenid, Seleucid, or Parthian periods (Melikian-Chirvani 1990–91: 11ff.; Harper 2006: 88).

Boat-shaped bowls without a foot or handles, symmetrical in form with a slightly crescentic longitudinal profile, are one type of elliptical bowl (Harper 1988b: 333, n. 8 for a list of vessels in collections; Gunter and Jett 1992: 171–3, no. 27 and 174–6, no. 28 for examples in the Arthur M. Sackler Gallery and the Freer Gallery of Art; an example in the Miho Museum with technical details: Meyers 1996c). Predominantly dated to the sixth and seventh centuries and represented in the archaeological record, they are on average 22 cm long and 11 cm wide, with the height being roughly one-fifth of the length, and a weight of 200–500 g (Harper 1988b: 334–5). Some are gilded and decoration may be on the interior, exterior, or both. Designs are in relief on better examples and chased on those with simpler patterns. A number of examples have inscriptions, usually dotted onto the exterior beneath the rim (Harper 1988b: 335), one of which indicates they were referred to as a "boat" (Gignoux 1984: no. 39; Melikian-Chirvani 1990–91: 13 and 61, n. 62).

The compressed elliptical bowl is a variation of the boat-shaped vessel (Harper 1988b: 338–41, 338 n. 20 for a list of examples). The width-to-length ratio increases and a proportionately larger number are inscribed, usually with their weight and the name of the owner. Examples in silver and alloy may be noted, and a bronze bowl of this shape was excavated at Susa in association with material of late Sasanian or early Islamic date (Harper 1988b: 341). While many are decorated in a similar manner to the boat-shaped vessels, with scrolling grapevines and rippling lines (Los Angeles County Museum of Art, M.76.174.5: Moorey et al. 1981: 122–3, no. 711; Overlaet 1993: 230, no. 81), female figures (private collection of M. Foroughi: Azarpay 1976: 45–6, pl. 1.2), figural (Arthur M. Sackler Gallery, s1987.143: Gunter and Jett 1992: 177–9, no. 29), and animal (Los Angeles County Museum of Art, M.76.174.265: Moorey et al. 1981: 123, no. 712a [monkey playing a pipe]; Los Angeles County Museum of Art, M.76.174.14: Moorey et al 1981: 123, no. 712b [boar's head]) motifs, a number of examples depict Christian motifs with a cross in the interior (Richard Ettinghausen Collection: Grabar 1967: 135, no. 53). This is the only type of Sasanian silverware decorated in this manner and examples are never of a very high quality (Harper 1988b: 340). Such vessels may have been owned by and symbolically relevant to the Christian population in the Sasanian realm. Gignoux has noted the concept of Jesus as the "pilot of the boat" in Manichaean and Christian texts, and such literary symbolism may explain why this type of vessel was adopted by the Christian population (Gignoux 1993: 68).

References in Persian literature suggest such boat-shaped bowls were precious objects, referred to in connection with the kings of Sasanian Iran (Melikian-Chirvani 1990–91: 4ff.). References to the king drinking wine from a wine-boat in a paradisiacal garden may suggest a link between vessels of this type and a certain type of banquet in a royal garden (Melikian-Chirvani 1990–91: 6). This may be suggested by two examples decorated with scrolling grapevines, nude female musicians and dancers, and vintaging figures reflective of a garden of paradise (collection of M. Foroughi: Azarpay 1976: 46, pl. 2.3; Cleveland Museum of Art, 63.478: Shepherd 1964: 86, fig. 25).

A small number of shallow wine-boats tapering at the ends with the addition of a low, oval foot-ring have also been attributed to the Sasanian period, although it is probable such vessels belong to the post-Sasanian tradition (Harper 1988b: 341ff. and nn. 27–9; Melikian-Chirvani 1990–1: 15ff.). Motifs include a seated king, flanked by two attendants with two dancers appearing on either end in what appears to be a *bazm* scene (Walters Art Gallery, acc. no. 57.625: Harper and Meyers 1981: 102, 119–20, pl. 36; 1988a: 341ff.), leaping tigers with stylized vine motifs (Norbert Schimmel Collection: Harper 1988b: 341ff., pl. IIb–c; Melikian-Chirvani 1990–1: 15ff.), elaborate *grylli*-like creatures (History Museum, Moscow, inv. no. 83746: Loukonine and Ivanov 1996: 99, cat. 70.), and a geometric pattern of hexagons enclosing shallow hemispherical cavities (private collection: Melikian-Chirvani 1990–1: 16ff. and 82, figs. 16–17).

Related to these groups are lobed elliptical bowls with a low foot-ring, referred to in later Persian texts as a *rikāb* and classed as wine-boats (Melikian-Chirvani 1990–91:17ff. and 74, n. 242, where the lobed *rikāb* is referred to as a crescent-shaped wine-boat in Persian texts; Melikian-Chirvani 1995; Harper 2006: 84ff.). There are three subsets of this type, although the original place of manufacture and development of these bowls is unclear. Available evidence indicates that cultural influences between Iran and areas to the east may have played a role. A type with both elongated lobes and smaller lateral lobes treated as individual elements has been found in Iran, and their decoration suggests they may be attributed to Sasanian workshops (including examples in the Abegg-Stiftung Bern, 8.123.65: Vollenweider et al. 1966: no. 77, Cat. 681; Arthur M. Sackler Gallery, s1987.137: Gunter and Jett 1992: 182–4, no. 31; Metropolitan Museum of Art, 1992.233: Harper 1992: figs. 1–3). The example in the Metropolitan Museum has a stamp, the only known example in Sasanian art (Harper 1992: 113ff.). The smaller lobes are fluted on the exterior and the alternate larger ones are left plain (Arthur M. Sackler Gallery, s1987.137) or decorated with geometric (Abegg-Stiftung Bern, 8.123.65) or floral and geometric motifs, with guinea fowl within medallions (Metropolitan Museum of Art, 1992.233). Designs on the interior of the vessels include a running boar, a tiger, or a fish, and the use of *niello* and gilding may be noted. Vessels of this type are similar in form to a bowl excavated in Datong, northern China, believed to have been buried in 493 AD but probably manufactured in Central Asia (Gunter 1992: 182–3; Harper 1988a: 157; 2002: 122). It is possible that the Datong bowl represents a prototype for Sasanian vessels of this form (Harper 2006: 86–7). With the shape probably originating east of Iran and aspects of the decoration reflecting patterns familiar in the eastern Mediterranean world, vessels of this type reflect interactions between people and exchanges of ideas between lands from the eastern Mediterranean to the borders of China (Harper 2002: 116ff.).

Other types of polylobed bowls include examples with four separate and two conjoined lobes (Cleveland Museum of Art, 63.478: Shepherd 1964: 86–7, fig. 25) and examples having three or more conjoined lobes and only two separate lateral lobes, with or without a foot (Hermitage Museum, s525: Overlaet 1993: 232, no. 83; a variant of this form with a greater width than other types may be seen in the Arthur M. Sackler Gallery, s1987.116: Gunter and Jett 1992: 180–1, no. 30 [no foot], and the Seattle Art

Museum, pls. 6.28: Grabar 1967: 124, No 40). Designs include figural scenes, such as scrolling grapevines and female musicians or swimmers, and animals, and undecorated examples. Parallels for polylobed bowls may be seen on wall paintings from Panjikent from the seventh to eighth centuries (Shepherd 1964: 86, fig. 24; Azarpay 1976: 111, fig. 48) and they continued to be made in the Islamic period (Melikian-Chirvani 1995).

ARTISANS AND VESSEL MANUFACTURE

Although little information is available regarding the artisans of this period, various royal workshops and gold and silversmiths are mentioned, though their low status is reflected in the literature (Harper 1992: 151; Simpson 2000: 64). According to the *Avesta*, they belonged to the fourth and lowest class of the citizenry and were grouped together with peasants (Simpson 2000: 64). Syriac sources, notably in the *Acta Martyrum et Sanctorum* and the Acts of the Nestorian Councils, suggest the organization of urban crafts into guilds (Harper 1992: 151, n. 39), each with its own "chief of the artisans" appointed by the king, and there is some information regarding individual artisans (Christensen 1944: 451; Harper 1992: 151; Tabari, see Bosworth 1999: 255). The presence and influence of foreign artisans may be noted, particularly as a result of the transfer of prisoner populations from the eastern Mediterranean, especially Antioch and Edessa (Ettinghausen 1972: 8).

Techniques used in the manufacture of Sasanian silver were relatively consistent throughout the empire and radiographic, metallographic, and microscopic studies by Meyers (Harper and Meyers 1981; Meyers 1996a–d, 1997) and Jett (Gunter and Jett 1992) have increased our knowledge significantly. The single shell of vessels such as plates and bowls was hammered into shape. The bodies of vases and ewers consist of one sheet of metal formed by hammering, and the feet, lids, and handles were made separately and probably hammered. Chasing, repoussé, and carving techniques were used to form designs, and in the later period incised designs largely replaced chasing (Harper 1988a: 158). Areas of high relief were achieved by adding separate pieces of worked metal, which were then worked and gilded, a technique that may reflect an influence from eastern Mediterranean craftsmen (Harper 1992: 150). Fire gilding with an amalgam of gold and mercury replaced the foil or leaf gilding of the Achaemenid and Parthian periods, a practice that may have come from China (Harper 2006: 30). *Niello*, a method of coloristic decoration adopted from the West, was used to enliven the surface of the vessel and is a feature suggestive of a later date (Harper 1988a: 156; Gunter and Jett 1992: 170, n. 9).

A number of vessels were inscribed and while some inscriptions were later additions, many appear to be of the same or of a similar date to the vessels manufacture. Often in Middle Persian or Sogdian, these may record the type of vessel, the name of its owner, their social position, and/or the weight of the vessel, possibly relating to its value (Gignoux 1984 for references). A Sasanian law book indicates that a vessel was a symbol of moveable property as against immoveable wealth and could serve as a deposit or loan (Perikhanian 1997: 404). The relationship between the weight measurement and true value is, however, somewhat unclear (Harper 1992: 150).

Conclusion

From the very beginning of the period, the Sasanians created a range of vessels displaying motifs related to nobility and kingship, reflecting notions of prestige and power in a modern, original way. As new vessel types and designs entered the repertoire, demonstrating both internal developments and a willingness to incorporate designs and motifs from other cultures and regions, we may see these vessels not only as objects of prestige but as symbols reflective of Sasanian notions of power, propaganda, banqueting and festivities, court ritual, and their own unique worldview. The iconography on such vessels combines elements from different sources, both past and present, as well as Sasanian innovations, creating a new and distinct artistic framework and subject matter that had meaning and relevance to a Sasanian audience.

Further reading

For orientation on silver vessels attributed to the Sasanian period see Grabar (1967), Harper (1978, 1983, 1988a, 1993, 1997a–c, 2006); Gunter and Jett (1992); Duchesne-Guillemin (1993); Overlaet (1993); Metropolitan Museum of Art (1996); Loukonine and Ivanov (1996); and Trever and Lukonin (1987). Most vessel types are represented within these texts. More specifically, see Harper and Meyers (1981) for a comprehensive study of silver plates with the royal hunter theme. Harper (1971), Shepherd (1980), Gunter and Jett (1992), and Carter (2003) are informative on vases and ewers, and for elliptical bowls, see Harper (1988b) and Melikian-Chirvani (1990–91, 1995). For technical studies, see Moorey (1981), Meyers (1981, 1996a–d, 1997), and Gunter and Jett (1992), Harper (1992) and Simpson (2000) for information regarding artisans of the period.

References

Arnold, D. 1996. *Ancient Art from the Shumei Family Collection*. New York: Metropolitan Museum of Art.
Azarpay, G. 1976. The allegory of dēn in Persian art. *Artibus Asiae* 38: 37–48.
———. 1997. A Jataka tale on a Sasanian silver plate. *BAI* 11: 99–125.
Bivar, A. D. H. 1969. *Catalogue of the Western Asiatic seals in the British Museum. Stamp seals II: The Sasanian dynasty*. London: British Museum.
Bosworth, C. E. 1999. *The history of al-Ṭabarī (Ta'rīkh al-rusul wa'l-mulūk)*, vol. 5, *The Sāsānids, the Byzantines, the Lakhmids, and Yemen*. Albany: State University of New York Press.
Brunner, C. J. 1974. Middle Persian inscriptions on Sasanian silverware. *MMJ* 9: 109–21.
Carter, M. 1974. Royal festal themes in Sasanian silverwork and their Central Asian parallels. In *Commémoration Cyrus: Actes du Congrès de Shiraz 1971 et d'autres etudes rédigées à l'occasion du 2500e anniversaire de la foundation de l'empire perse*, vol. 1, 171–202. Leiden: Acta Iranica 1.

———. 1978. Silver bowl with female musicians. In *The royal hunter: Art of the Sasanian Empire*, ed. P. O. Harper, 77–8. New York: Asia House Gallery.

———. 2003. Preliminary notes on a silver-gilt ewer with bird medallions in a private collection. *SRAA* 9: 185–211.

Choksy, J. K. 1990a. Gesture in ancient Iran and Central Asia I: The raised hand. In *Iranica varia: Papers in honor of Ehsan Yarshater*, 30–7. Leiden: Acta Iranica 30.

———. 1990b. Gesture in ancient Iran and Central Asia II: Proskynesis and the bent forefinger. *BAI* 4: 201–7.

———. 2002. *Evil, good, and gender: Facets of the feminine in Zoroastrian religious history.* New York: Peter Lang.

Christensen, A. 1944. *L'Iran sous les Sassanides.* Copenhagen: Levin and Munksgaard.

Collon, D. 1995. *Ancient Near Eastern art.* London: British Museum Press.

Darmesteter, J. 1882. *The Zend Avesta, Part II.* London: Sacred Books of the East 4.

David-Weill, J. 1954. Têtes de chevaux sassanides. *Revue des Arts* 4: 157–64.

Duchesne-Guillemin, J. 1966. *Symbols and values in Zoroastrianism: Their survival and renewal.* New York: Harper and Row.

———. 1971. Art et religion sous les Sassanides. In *La Persia nel Medioevo*, 377–88. Rome: Accademia Nazionale dei Lincei.

Duchesne-Guillemin, M. 1993. *Les instruments de musique dans l'art Sassanide.* Gent: IrAnt Supplement 6.

Ettinghausen, R. 1967–8. A Persian treasure. *Arts in Virginia* 8: 28–41.

———. 1972. *From Byzantium to Sasanian Iran and the Islamic world.* Leiden: Brill.

Frye, R. N. 1971. History and Sasanian inscriptions. In *La Persia nel Medioevo*, 215–23. Rome: Accademia Nazionale dei Lincei.

———. 1983. The political history of Iran under the Sasanians. *CHI* 3/2: 116–80.

Fukai, S. 1977. *Persian glass.* New York/Tokyo/Kyoto: Weatherhill/Tankosha.

Garsoïan, N. 1981. The locus of the death of kings: Iranian Armenia: The inverted image. In *The Armenian image in history and literature*, ed. R. G. Hovanissian, 27–64. Malibu: Undena.

———. 1997. Les éléments iraniens dans l'Arménie paléochrétienne. In *Des Parthes au califat: Quatre leçons sur la formation de l'identité arménienne*, N. Garsoian and J.-P. Mahé, 9–37. Paris: Travaux et Mémoires du Centre de Recherche d'Histoire et Civilisation de Byzance, Collège de France, Monographies 10.

Ghirshman, R. 1953. Notes iraniennes V. Scènes de banquet sur l'argenterie sassanide. *Artibus Asiae* 16: 51–71.

Gignoux, P. 1984. Éléments de prosopographie: II. Les possesseurs de coupes sasanides. *StIr* 13: 19–40.

———. 1993. Contacts culturels entre Manichéisme et Mazdéisme: Quelques exemples significatifs. *StOr* 70: 65–73.

Gnoli, G. 1993. A Sasanian iconography of the *Dēn*. *BAI* 7: 79–85.

———. 1999. Farr(ah). *EnIr* online edition.

Göbl, R. 1971. *Sasanian numismatics.* New York: Sanford J. Durst Numismatic Publications.

Grabar, O. 1967. *Sasanian Silver: Late antique and early medieval works of luxury from Iran.* Michigan: University of Michigan Museum of Art.

Gunter, A.C., and P. Jett. 1992. *Ancient Iranian metalwork in the Arthur M. Sackler Gallery and the Freer Gallery of Art.* Washington, DC: Arthur M. Sackler Gallery and Freer Gallery of Art.

Haerinck, E. 1980. Twin-spouted vessels and their distribution in the Near East from the Achaemenian to the Sasanian periods. *Iran* 18: 43–54.

Hallade, M. 1968. *The Gandhara style and the evolution of Buddhist art*. London: Thames and Hudson.

Harper, P. O. 1971. Sources of certain female representations in Sasanian art. In *La Persia nel Medioevo*, 503–15. Rome: Accademia Nazionale dei Lincei.

———. 1978. *The royal hunter: Art of the Sasanian Empire*. New York: Asia House Gallery Publication.

———. 1983. Sasanian silver. *CHI* 3: 1113–29.

———. 1988a. Sasanian silver: Internal developments and foreign influences. In *Argenterie romaine et byzantine, De l'archéologie à l'histoire*, ed. F. Baratte and N. Duval, 153–61. Paris: De Boccard.

———. 1988b. Boat shaped bowls of the Sasanian period. *IrAnt* 23: 332–45.

———. 1991a. Luxury vessels as symbolic images: Parthian and Sasanian Iran and Central Asia. In *Histoire et cultes de l'Asie Centrale préislamique. Sources écrites et documents archéologiques*, ed. P. Bernard and F. Grenet, 95–100. Paris: Éditions du CNRS.

———. 1991b. The Sasanian ewer: Questions of origin and influence. In *Near Eastern Studies Dedicated to H. I. H. Prince Takahito Mikasa on the occasion of his seventy-fifth birthday*, ed. M. Mori, H. Ogawa and M. Yoshikawa, 67–84. Wiesbaden: Bulletin of the Middle Eastern Culture Centre in Japan 5.

———. 1992. State controls in the production of Sasanian silver vessels. In *Ecclesiastical silver plate in sixth century Byzantium*, ed. S. A. Boyd and M. M. Mango, 147–54. Washington: Dumbarton Oaks Research Library and Collection.

———. 1993. Metalen vaatwerk. In *Hofkunst van de Sassanieden*, ed. B. Overlaet, 95–108. Brussels: KMKG-MRAH.

———. 1997a. Plate decorated with a feline. In *Miho Museum catalogue: South wing*, 104–5. Shiga: Miho Museum.

———. 1997b. Plate with the bust of a king. In *Miho Museum catalogue: South wing*, 106–7. Shiga: Miho Museum.

———. 1997c. Vase with dancing female figures. In *Miho Museum catalogue: South wing*, 108–9. Shiga: Miho Museum.

———. 2000. Sasanian silver vessels: the formation and study of early museum collections. In *Mesopotamia and Iran in the Parthian and Sasanian periods: Rejection and revival c. 238 BC–AD 642*, ed. J. Curtis, 46–56. London: British Museum Press.

———. 2002. A gilded silver vessel: Iran and Byzantium in the sixth and seventh centuries. In *Of pots and plans: Papers on the archaeology and history of Mesopotamia and Syria presented to David Oates in honour of his 75th Birthday*, ed. L. Al-Gailani Werr, J. Curtis, H. Martin, A. McMahon, J. Oates, and J. Reade, 113–27. London: Nabu Publications.

———. 2006. *In search of a cultural identity: Monuments and artifacts of the Sasanian Near East, 3rd to 7th Century A.D.* New York: Bibliotheca Persica.

Harper, P. O., and P. Meyers. 1981. *Silver vessels of the Sasanian period*, vol. 1, *Royal imagery*. New York/Princeton: Metropolitan Museum of Art and Princeton University Press.

Haskins, J. F. 1952. Northern origins of "Sasanian" metalwork II. *Artibus Asiae* 15/2: 324–47.

Levy, R. 1967. *The epic of the kings: Shah-Nama, the national epic of Persia by Ferdowsi*. London: Routledge and Kegan Paul.

Loukonine [Lukonin], V. G., and A. Ivanov. 1996. *Persian Art*. London: Parkstone.

MacKenzie, D. N. 1970. A Zoroastrian master of ceremonies. In *W. B. Henning Memorial Volume*, ed. M. Boyce and I. Gershevitch, 264–71. London: Lund Humphries.

Marshak, B.I. 1993. Catalogue. In *Hofkunst van de Sassanieden*, ed. B. Overlaet. Brussels: KMKG-MRAH.

Melikian-Chirvani, A. S. 1982. *Islamic metalwork from the Iranian world: 8th–18th centuries*. London: Victoria and Albert Museum.
———. 1990–91. From the royal boat to the beggars bowl. *Islamic Art* 4: 3–113.
———. 1992. The Iranian *Bazm* in early Persian sources. *RO* 4: 95–120.
———. 1995. *Rekāb*: The polylobed wine boat from Sasanian to Saljuq times. In *Banquets d'Orient*, ed. R. Gyselen, 187–204. Leuven: RO 7.
———. 1996. The Iranian wine horn from pre-Achaemenid antiquity to the Safavid age. *BAI* 10: 85–139.
Meyers, P. 1996a. Plate decorated with the bust of a king; Vase decorated with dancing figures. *AASFC*: 191.
———. 1996b. Two vases decorated with medallions enclosing birds. *AASFC*: 192.
———. 1996c. Eliptical bowl decorated with a vine scroll; Ewer decorated with a plant design. *AASFC*: 193.
———. 1996d. Plate. *AASFC*: 194.
———. 1997. Acquisition, technical study and examination. In *Miho Museum Catalogue: South Wing*, 313–20. Shiga: Miho Museum.
Moorey, P. R. S. 1981. The art of ancient Iran. In *Ancient bronzes, ceramics and seals*, ed. P. R. S. Moorey, E. Bunker, E. Porada, and G. Markoe, 119–25. California: Los Angeles County Museum of Art.
Muscarella, O. 2000. *The lie became great: The forgery of Ancient Near Eastern cultures*. Groningen: Styx Publications.
Overlaet, B. 1993. *Hofkunst van de Sassanieden*. Brussels: KMKG-MRAH.
Perikhanian, A.1997. *Mādigān ī Hezār Dādīstān. The book of a thousand judgements: A Sasanian law book*. New York: Bibliotheca Persica.
Rose, J. 2012. Investiture iii. Sasanian period. *EnIr* online edition.
Rosen-Ayalon, M. 1984. Themes of Sasanian origin in Islamic metalwork. *JSAI* 4: 69–80.
Schmidt, H. 1980. The *Sēnmurw*: Of birds and dogs and bats. *Persica* 9: 1–85.
Shahbazi, A. S. 2004. Hunting in Iran. *EnIr* online edition.
Shepherd, D. 1964. Sasanian art in Cleveland. *BCMA* 51/4: 66–93.
———. 1966. Two silver rhyta. *BCMA* 53: 289–311.
———. 1980. The iconography of Anāhitā. *Berytus* 28: 47–86.
Simpson, St.J. 2000. Mesopotamia in the Sasanian period: Settlement patterns, arts and crafts. In *Mesopotamia and Iran in the Parthian and Sasanian periods: Rejection and revival c. 238 BC–AD 642*, ed. J. Curtis, 57–66. London: British Museum Press.
Stierlen, H. 2006. *Splendours of ancient Persia*. Vercelli: Whitestar.
Strong, D. E. 1966. *Greek and Roman gold and silver plate*. London: Methuen.
Trever, C. 1967. A propos des temples de la déesse Anahita en Iran sassanide. *IrAnt* 7: 121–32.
Trever, K. V., and V. G. Lukonin. 1987. *Sasanidskoe serebro*. Moscow: Iskusstvo.
Unvala, J. M. 1936. *King Khusro and his boy*. Paris: Paul Geuthner.
Vollenweider, M.-L., F. Brüschweiler, and R. A. Stucky. 1966. *Trésors de l'ancien Iran*. Geneva: Musée Rath.
Ward, R. 1993. *Islamic metalwork*. London: Thames and Hudson.
West, E. W. 1880. *The sacred books of the East*, vol. 5, *Bundahishn*. Oxford: Clarendon Press.
Whitehouse, D. 2005. *Sasanian and post-Sasanian glass in the Corning Museum of Glass*. New York/Manchester: Corning Museum of Glass.

CHAPTER 49

SASANIAN TEXTILES

CAROL BIER

The category "Sasanian textiles," is complicated by the fact that Sasanian attributions of figural patterned silks and related textiles advanced in the late nineteenth and twentieth centuries rest upon speculative hypotheses, many of which were critically questioned in the late twentieth century (Jeroussalemskaja 1972; Bier 1978). Sasanian attributions have been reexamined in the light of new archaeological evidence from the Caucasus, Central Asia, and western China (Otavsky 1998; Compareti 2004; Schorta 2006). In general, there seems to be an emerging consensus that many of the early attributions might now be shifted to Sogdian production or elsewhere in Central Asia rather than Iran, but Sasanian attributions persist in the nonspecialist literature. Archaeologically, textiles of the Sasanian period have been found only at Shahr-e Qumis in northeastern Iran, and those are not silk nor do they bear figural images (Hansman and Stronach 1970; Bier 1978; Kawami 1992). Nonetheless, during the late nineteenth and twentieth centuries, more than 100 pattern-woven silk textiles and fragments from diverse locations in Europe and Asia received Sasanian attributions based upon their representation of Sasanian royal imagery and their visual relationship to textile patterns represented in carved stone reliefs in the larger of two rock-carved *iwans* at Taq-e Bustan in western Iran (Ackerman 1938; Geijer 1963; Holmes 1965; among others). The imagery represented in the textiles includes the mythical *senmurv*, winged horses with fluttering ribbons, rams with diadems, boar's heads, birds with necklaces and jewels, ducks and other water birds, and the occasional lion or elephant, as well as stars and crescents, royal jewels and pearls, all of which find parallels represented on Sasanian coins, seals, silver vessels, stucco panels, and rock reliefs (Harper 1978, 1981; Kröger 1982; Bivar 2006). The broad body of pattern-woven silks includes tailored garments and large fragmentary textiles, as well as smaller pieces—found in locations as disparate as wrapping the relics of saints in European church treasuries and grave-sites in the northern Caucasus and Egypt—and textiles with related imagery found in Japanese temple repositories (Bier 1978). More recently, numerous garments tailored using pattern-woven silk textiles, and textile fragments, have emerged from excavations of burial sites in Central Asia and western China, that bear similar imagery, potentially affirming early critical speculation that the advanced weaving technology of patterned silks attributed to Sasanian Iran may represent Sogdian manufacture with a reliance upon Sasanian royal iconography in post-Sasanian periods (Bier 1978; Compareti 2004; Zhao 2006). Indeed, representations of tailored garments showing similar patterns appear in wall paintings of palaces excavated at several Sogdian sites of the seventh to ninth centuries, such as Afrasiyab, Panjikent, and Varaksha (Azarpay 1981; Marshak 2006; Raspopova 2006), in which the same motifs appear arranged according to the same systems of repeat and with similar colors and identical stylization of anatomical details. At Afrasiyab and at Qizil the tailored garments illustrated show fabrics with facings, edges, and hems of different textiles, suggestive of pieces sewn together, the orientations of which are intentionally not consistent—that is to say, warp direction is not always vertical, and a fabric's pattern, even if depicting animals or birds, is not always shown "right side up." The consistency of this type of illustration suggests that this is an aesthetic choice rather than an artistic conceit. But by this visual rendering, the viewer is assured that the fabrics represent pattern-woven textiles, the repetition of the motifs being cut off at folds and seams. A similar arrangement in the sewn seams of surviving textiles may be seen in the complete silk caftan excavated at Moshchevaya Balka in the north Caucasus (Riboud 1976; Jerusalimskaya 1978), and a man's leggings and caftan, tailored of linen with silk facings and edges, that are thought to be from the same site, acquired by the Metropolitan Museum on the market in 1996 (Harper 2001; Kajitani 2001; Knauer 2001).

The recent excavations of textiles and fragments in Central Asia and western China affirm both technological and aesthetic relationships between the West (i.e. Iran) and China (i.e., Xinjiang), but the nature and flow of these relationships have not been conclusively established (Xu 2006; Li 2006; Wu 2006). In the 1990s the Abegg-Stiftung acquired a number of silk textiles representative of this broad group that were radiocarbon dated to the period between 650 and 900; the textiles, mainly fragments, have been intensively studied by an international group of scholars from different disciplinary perspectives (Schorta 2006). This investigative process has led to the publication of nine volumes of the *Riggisberger Berichte*, offering substantive documentation and a breadth of analyses of designs, patterns, weave structure, dyes, and technology. But there is still no conclusive understanding of the origins and development of the elaborate patterns of these silk textiles, the compound weaves of which all are agreed must have been woven using a drawloom. By reorienting textile fragments in the warp direction (sometimes based on the presence of a selvedge), some scholars interpret certain patterns as warp-faced, arguing that warp-patterned weaves using silk emerged from Chinese traditions (Xu 2006; Wu 2006), and weft-patterned weaves from Iran or Central Asia, where the weaving of wool was paramount and silk-weaving had been introduced from the East (Li 2006), but these assumptions need further corroboration and elaboration. Attributions to local manufacture and delineation of trade patterns continue to be based on speculative historical reconstructions of production and commerce, despite the advancement of several new plausible hypotheses regarding technological developments in the East and in the West (Jain 1998; Sheng 1998; Zhao 2006; Xu 2006; Wu

2006). Meanwhile, textiles with related imagery, but made of wool and cotton, produced on a drawloom or by means of other technologies, namely tapestry techniques and embroidery, augment the body of materials attributed to Sasanian manufacture or to production after the fall of the Sasanian Empire (Lamm 1937; Bier 1978; El-Homossani 1988; Li 2006).

As industrial weaving developed in Europe in the nineteenth century, the advanced weaving technology represented by these textiles fostered the establishment of museums for *Kunstgewerbe* (Lessing 1900) and efforts to reproduce both weave structures and patterns at weaving schools in Germany and Italy, among other places. This, in turn, led to the acquisition of textile fragments in the United States and abroad, which in some instances has further complicated the processes of attribution. Even more troubling are the results of radiocarbon dating of several textiles purported to be from Rayy and Bibi Shahr Banu in Iran, reputedly of Buyid or Seljuk date, suggesting that fakes were introduced to the market in the middle of the twentieth century (Blair et al. 1993).

Museums with collections acquired in the late nineteenth and early twentieth centuries in the United Kingdom and Europe include the Victoria & Albert Museum (London), Musée des Tissus (Lyon), and Musée des Arts Decoratifs and the Louvre (Paris). Key holdings in the United States are in the Museum of Fine Arts (Boston), the Metropolitan Museum and Cooper-Hewitt (New York), the Textile Museum and Dumbarton Oaks (Washington, DC), and the Cleveland Museum of Art.

As for excavated materials, an archaeological team from Yale University excavated Dura Europos, Syria, in the early twentieth century, the textile finds from which are today in the Yale Gallery of Art. The textiles are representative of Parthian traditions and relate to the representation of small repeat patterns on garments scratched in graffiti at Persepolis of early Sasanian date and on wall paintings at Kuh-e Khwaja in Iran (Kawami 1992). The excavated remains from Moshchevaya Balka are housed in the Oriental Department of the Hermitage in St. Petersburg. A share of the finds from Shahr-e Qumis, Iran, is held by the Ancient Near East Department at the Metropolitan Museum of Art in New York. Textiles from Antinoë, once in the care of the Musée Guimet in Paris, are now in the Louvre. The textiles excavated by Sir Aurel Stein at Astana in the Turfan oasis of northwestern China are housed in the National Museum of New Delhi and at the British Museum in London, and those more recently excavated are in Urumqi at the Museum of the Xinjiang Autonomous Region. Materials from Dulan are in Xining, Qinghai Cultural Relics and Archaeological Institute, and those from Dunhuang are at the British Museum in London and the Musée Guimet in Paris.

The core body of material related to the appearance of Sasanian royal imagery from these diverse locations is distinguished not only by the use of silk, but also by bright, vibrant colors that are sometimes preserved and by the formal arrangement of pattern in the plane according to an underlying square or rectangular grid (Bier 1977). These distinct formats, comprising tessellations in which a single visual unit (no matter how complex) is repeated to cover the plane with no gaps and no overlaps, are intimately related to an advanced weaving technology, in which the pattern warps and structural warps are manipulated separately in groups controlled by one set of harnesses to control the weave structure, and a second set of harnesses to control the pattern. As in all woven textiles, longitudinal warp elements interlace at right angles with the transverse weft elements. But using this technology, these textiles exhibit complicated weave structures that encompass more than one set of warps and wefts, which serve separate functions to allow for the manipulation of the pattern using different colors, which interact simultaneously within the structure of the weave such that the pattern is integral with the weave structure (Becker 1987; Bier 1995a, 2005, 2007). In contrast, the designs and patterns of printed textiles or embroidery are ontologically distinct from the fabric of the textile and represent entirely different technological processes, which take place after weaving is complete. Generally these textiles exhibit one of two weave structures—a compound weft-faced plain weave (*taqeté*) or a compound weft-faced twill weave (*samit*). Note that the terminology in different publications is not always consistent. The complexity of these weave structures implies the use of a drawloom, a loom outfitted with a mechanism that allows the weaver with the assistance of a drawboy to separately control the interaction of pattern and weave by the use of a double set of harnesses. One set controls the pattern warps according to the particular tie-up of the pattern warps in sequence, while the other controls the structural set of warps to control the ground weave (Jain 1994; Bier 1995a; Zhao 2006).

The patterns of these textiles often show curvilinear designs and various grids or networks, which frame individual motifs that are repeated from selvedge to selvedge. The most characteristic repeat system is referred to as a pearl roundel framework (Meister 1970; Bier 1978; Carmel 1990). It is composed of tangential circles, each of which contains a circlet of circles, the so-called pearl roundel that is related to the depiction of actual pearls worn by Sasanian royalty and illustrated in stylized form to represent royal diadems and necklaces as well as edges and borders. That this rectilinear pattern of circles within circles is achieved in the woven medium indicates a profound understanding of weaving in relation to geometry and design and full control of the gauge and density of materials, in order to be able to achieve the visual appearance of circles that counters the rational, orderly orthogonal interlacing of warp and weft. These textiles indeed represent an unusually advanced level of understanding of loom technology, in this case drawloom weaving, for which the origins and early development remain unclear. Later, at some as yet undetermined date, the term *naqsh* designated the tie-up mechanism that was used to create the pattern and *naqshbandi* referred to the person responsible for the tying up of the warps. This esteemed craft tradition may, in fact, be related to the subsequent emergence of the *Naqshbandi* Sufi order, a relationship that is not yet historically established.

A subset of this group of textiles is sometimes referred to as "Zandanījī" and attributed to Zandane, a town in the neighborhood of Bukhara identified as a weaving center in Islamic sources (Shepherd and Henning 1959; Shepherd 1981; Otavsky 1998; Frye 2006). This smaller group of textiles exhibits similar motifs, for the most part also dependent on (or derivative of) Sasanian royal imagery. The silk is more coarse and the weaving less fine than textiles attributed to Sogdiana or Sasanian Iran, and the motifs of the Zandanījī group tend to have stepped outlines (rather than appearing to be curvilinear), a feature that renders the figural designs more angular in appearance, and this has led to their being called "more geometric," in addition to which the motifs are often paired in confronted or addorsed poses, with the animals or birds sometimes flanking a central plant or tree (Marshak 2006). The Zandanījī attribution is based on a single silk fragment that was found in the cathedral of Huy in Belgium and on which there is an inscription in ink suggestive of this name, as read by Henning (Shepherd and Henning 1959). Islamic textual sources, however, use the term Zandanījī to refer to coarse textiles woven of cotton. Among the animals that are illustrated on extant textiles are stylized birds and lions; curiously, none of the findspots of silk textiles attributed to Zandanījī were located in Sogd, but rather in the Caucasus to the west or at Dunhuang to the east (Jerusalimskaya 1972).

The finer silk textiles that have in the past received Sasanian attributions are widely dispersed, having emerged in vastly differing geographic contexts—from European church treasuries and museums to temple repositories in Japan—and having been found in archaeological sites (mainly burials) in Egypt, the Caucasus, Central Asia, northern India, and the Turfan oasis in western China. None, as far as we know, was found at its point of origin (although this possibility has on occasion been put forward, if not argued forcefully (Kitzinger 1946)), and none is definitively linked to an original context. Notice the distinct absence, however, of Iran in this list of findspots. Each of the objects seems to represent trade or transport and import for a particular end use, often funerary or commemorative, although these uses may have been secondary in intent. The burial contexts seem to suggest a contemporary appreciation for their treatment as luxury goods, consistent with their original colors, figural designs, and layout, as well as their exhibiting evidence for advanced technological developments in the weaving of patterns at the loom.

Textiles, besides being easily transported, are also phenomenally fragile. Made using organic materials, they are subject to deterioration from use and wear as well as from fluctuations in humidity and temperature. They are thus best preserved in areas of climatic extremes, extremely dry regions with little or no rainfall or areas so cold there is permafrost. This is borne out by preservation in archaeological contexts in Egypt, Central Asia, and western China. The textile finds from Moshchevaya Balka, which were found in shallow graves on rock terraces protected by an overhanging cliff face above a mountain river valley in the northern Caucasus (Harper 2001), are an exception. Despite these rare survivals in secondary locations, we do not know where, when, why, or for whom these textiles were originally made, except by the hypothetical reconstruction of historical contexts.

What we do know is that textiles with Sasanian imagery have survived in exceptional circumstances where they were treated as luxury goods, that they represent a pinnacle of weaving technology long before the advent of industrial production in Europe, and that the imagery is integral with the fabric of the textile. That is to say, the pattern of a pattern-woven textile is ontologically inseparable from the weave, a direct result of the careful planning and full utilization of the weaving technology. The tie-up mechanism (*naqsh*) at the loom effectively allows for the production of repetitions of designs that exhibit what crystallographers in the nineteenth century have identified as the four basic symmetries of reflection (point repeat), glide reflection (drop repeat and/or half-drop repeat), translation (repeat), and rotation. With respect to weaving, in which the orthogonal grid of warp and weft interlacing underlies any pattern, the symmetry operation of rotation is a special instance, effected through the use of color symmetry. The presence of rotational symmetry is rare within the broad category of "Sasanian textiles," whereas translation is paramount (yielding rows of motifs in horizontal and vertical alignment), and reflection and glide reflection are both quite typical, each having a central axis across which the motif (or half a motif) is repeated in reverse. As a body of material, these textiles represent an intimate understanding of this advanced technology and they exhibit brilliant applications of the possibilities for pattern formation—repeats, point repeats, drop repeats, half-drop repeats, reversals, doubling, and quadrupling design elements to create pattern units and overall repeat patterns that cover the plane, with neither gaps nor overlaps.

The pictorial representation of male figures wearing garments that are carefully depicted as having been tailored of such patterned textiles offers intriguing parallels to extant textiles and textile fragments (Peck 1969). Of particular importance are the reliefs of the great *iwan* at Taq-e Bustan in western Iran (Movassat 2005), attributed to Xosrow II (r. 590–628) on the basis of the appearance of the crown worn by the king at his investiture, sculpted in nearly full three dimensionality on the rear wall, discussed in more detail below. But perhaps equally important is the persistent absence of such patterned textiles fashioned into tailored garments on all other Sasanian royal rock reliefs, where the textiles depicted are more often shown with drapery folds that seem to suggest more expressive movement and a diaphanous quality. Also significant is the fact that in the wall paintings at Afrasiyab, those garments constructed of solid-color textiles show drapery, whereas those tailored with patterned textiles are shown flat (Bier 1978). This contrast also appears in the reliefs of the great *iwan* at Taq-e Bustan, and may suggest a particular aesthetic choice both for clothing and its representation. The sidewalls of the *iwan* show two low bas-reliefs, each of which depicts a pictorial scene in a royal hunting preserve (Fukai et al. 1972, 1984; Movassat 2005). One shows the king hunting boar from a boat in reed marshes (left side); the other shows a stag hunt (right side), which was blocked out but left unfinished. In the Boar Hunt the textile patterns illustrated on the garments of the king and his courtiers (mounted on elephants) and musicians (seated in boats) have usually been taken as the basis for many Sasanian textile attributions. But the parallels are not as precise as one might expect. First, although the textile patterns are represented to show individual motifs repeated in rows (birds, ducks, boar's head, crescents) none is arranged as a pair, confronted or addorsed (Bier 1977). Two *senmurvs* face each other, but the front seam of the king's garment separates them, and they appear to be appliquéd over a pattern-woven textile. Disks or circles enclose some of the motifs, but none is set within a framework. The only pattern framework that appears at Taq-e Bustan is at the back of the *iwan* beneath the investiture of the king, where a mounted horseman outfitted with helmet, armor, and spear is seated on his steed. The pattern coming out from under his armor shows a stylized floral framework enclosing the mythical *senmurv* set within a roundel of trilobate leaves. Here the framework forms a grid in which a *senmurv* is repeated in each square cell. The two side relief panels are generally given a date consistent with the nearly three-dimensional royal sculpture of the rear wall, with which they show no obvious physical connection but for proximity to indicate date. If we remove this presumed chronological link, we position ourselves to consider new hypotheses regarding the transmission of ideas and the arts in relation to patterns of trade and conquest along the routes that came to be known as the Silk Road.

Traditionally the basis for all Sasanian textile attributions, the side-panel reliefs at Taq-e Bustan illustrate the king and courtiers wearing garments that are recognized to be Central Asian styles and cut (Holmes 1965; Peck 1969) with patterns that may allude to Sasanian royalty. That they represent a Sasanian king, or kings, and Sasanian styles has yet to be proved rather than asserted. The king is shown twice in the Boar Hunt relief and three times in the Stag Hunt, the multiple depictions interpreted as representing pictorial narration within the scene, showing the passage of time and space. Again, there is nothing to suggest, beyond assumption, that it is the same king depicted on both reliefs. The Stag Hunt remains unfinished in a blocked-out state of carving and its unique combination of frontal and profile views of the king may argue for separate chronological placement. The Boar Hunt and Stag Hunt are unique scenes, not otherwise treated as subjects in monumental Sasanian art. Likewise, to judge from numismatic evidence, the broad facial features of the kings in each of the hunt scenes are not familiar among Sasanian royal images prior to the very end of the Sasanian era, but they assume familiarity in the art of later periods.

The immensely complex cultural interplay that surrounds textiles on which Sasanian royal imagery is evident reflects a fashion for tailored garments and an aesthetic preference for luxury materials, including silk textiles characterized by figural imagery; technological sophistication, marked by the use of the drawloom in the production of pattern-woven textiles; and artistic influences from many directions reflecting the ethnic diversity and extensive trade networks of the routes that connected the Sasanian world with distant points to the east and west.

In conclusion, the category, "Sasanian textiles," is ripe for thorough review and reinvestigation (Bier 1977, 1978; Compareti 2009). Early assumptions should be articulated and questioned, and original attributions must be cast aside. Expanded archaeological resources from the Caucasus, Central Asia, and western China, greater access to local histories in translation for Iran, Turkmenistan, and Uzbekistan, new analyses of dyes and recent finds of early evidence for cotton in Arabia and Bahrain (Bouchard et al. 2011), and the availability of many resources online, may all contribute to the reevaluation of earlier sources for the study of Sasanian textiles and their prospective relationship to textiles of Byzantium, China, and points in between, and to the acknowledgment of Sasanian royal imagery and art as key purveyors of influence upon later Islamic textiles in the centuries following the end of Sasanian rule. Separate but parallel is the need for continued reconsideration of Sasanian royal imagery and its survival or revival in post-Sasanian contexts, and more critical understanding of its thoughtful utilization by subsequent local rulers in Iran and beyond. There is still a need for further research into the origins and early technological development of the drawloom to understand its impact on patterns of production, trade, and influence between China and the West. Careful, critical scrutiny of the existing body of materials, considering fabrics, weave structure, fiber preparation and dyes, material attributes, garments, imagery, design, and pattern arrangements, as well as the history of collecting in Europe and the United States, may contribute to these broader endeavors. Finally, the integration of various branches of knowledge may contribute to a better understanding of these complex patterns as design algorithms and of how these relate to both the history of mathematics and the history of art (Bier 2000, 2007, 2009).

Further reading

Apart from the now very outdated study by Ackerman (1938), there is no synoptic study of Sasanian textiles per se. Bier (1978) provides a concise overview of the topic while Bivar (2006) discusses the iconography of Sasanian textile decoration. As the references below attest, more and more discoveries in Inner Asia are shedding light on Sasanian textiles.

References

Ackerman, P. 1938. Textiles through the Sasanian period. *SPA* 2: 681–715.
Azarpay, G. 1981. *Sogdian painting: The pictorial epic in Oriental art*. Berkeley: University of California Press.
Becker, J. 1987. *Pattern and loom: A practical study of the development of weaving techniques in China, Western Asia, and Europe*. Copenhagen: Rhodos International.
Bier, C. 1977. Sasanian textiles: A critical review. Unpublished MA thesis, New York University.
———. 1978. Textiles. In *The royal hunter: Art of the Sasanian Empire*, ed. P. O. Harper, 119–40. New York: Asia Society.
———. 1995a. Textile arts in ancient Western Asia. In *Civilizations of the Ancient Near East*, ed. J. Sasson, 1567–88. New York: Charles Scribner's Sons.
———. 1995b. *The Persian velvets at Rosenborg*. Copenhagen: Rosenborg Palace.
———. 2000. Choices and constraints: Pattern formation in Oriental carpets. *Forma (Journal of the Society for Science on Form, Japan)* 15/2: 127–32.
———. 2005. Pattern power: Textiles and the transmission of mathematical knowledge. In *Appropriation, acculturation, transformation: Proceedings of the 9th Biennial Symposium of the Textile Society of America*, ed. C. Bier, 144–53. Madison: Textile Society of America.
———. 2007. Patterns in time and space: Technologies of transfer and the cultural transmission of mathematical knowledge across the Indian Ocean. *Ars Orientalis* 34: 174–96.
———. 2009. Number, shape, and the nature of space: Thinking through Islamic art. In *Oxford Handbook of the History of Mathematics*, ed. E. Robson and J. Stedall, 827–51. Oxford: Oxford University Press.
Bivar, A. D. H. 2006. Sasanian iconography on textiles and seals. In *Central Asian textiles and their contexts in the Early Middle Ages*, ed. R. Schorta, 5–22. Riggisberg: Riggisberger Berichte 9.

Blair, S. S., J. M. Bloom, and A. E. Wardwell. 1993. Reevaluating the date of the "Buyid silks" by epigraphic and radiocarbon analysis. *Ars Orientalis* 22: 1–41.

Bouchard, C., M. Tengberg, and P. Dal Prá. 2011. Cotton cultivation and textile production in the Arabian Peninsula during antiquity: The evidence from Madâ'in Salih (Saudi Arabia) and Qal'at al-Bahrain (Bahrain). *VHA* 20/5: 405–17.

Carmel, L. 1990. An exploration of a textile pattern: Pearl roundels joined by smaller pearl discs. Unpublished MA thesis, University of Maryland, College Park.

Compareti, M. 2004. The Sasanian and the Sogdian "pearl roundel" design: Remarks on an Iranian decorative pattern. *Study of Art History* 6: 259–72.

———. 2009. Sasanian textiles. *EnIr* online edition.

Frye, R. N. 2006. Bukhara and Zandanījī. In *Central Asian textiles and their contexts in the Early Middle Ages*, ed. R. Schorta, 75–80. Riggisberg: Riggisberger Berichte 9.

Fukai, S., K. Horiuchi, K. Tanabe, and M. Domyo. 1972. *Taq-i Bustan*, II. Tokyo: Tokyo University Iran-Iraq Archaeological Expedition. Report 13.

———. 1984. *Taq-i Bustan*, IV. Tokyo: Tokyo University Iran-Iraq Archaeological Expedition. Report 20.

Geijer, A. 1963. A silk from Antinoë and the Sasanian textile art. *Orientalia Suecana* 12: 2–36.

Hansman, J., and D. Stronach. 1970. A Sasanian repository at Shahr-i Qumis. *JRAS*: 142–55.

Harper, P. O. 1978. *The royal hunter: Art of the Sasanian Empire*. New York: Asia Society.

———. 2001. A man's caftan and leggings from the north Caucasus of the eighth to tenth century: Introduction. *MMJ* 36: 83–4.

Harper, P. O., and P. Meyers. 1981. *Silver vessels of the Sasanian period*. New York: Metropolitan Museum of Art.

Holmes, E. J. 1965. Form and decoration of late Sasanian textiles: A study of the costumes and selected textile motifs on the Sasanian reliefs of Taq-i Bustan. Unpublished MA thesis, New York University.

El-Homossani, M. M. 1988. Creating a protocol for reconstructing weaving technologies: Early compound non-silk fabrics found in Egypt. In *Textiles as primary sources: Proceedings of the First Symposium of the Textile Society of America*, ed. J. E. Vollmer, 26–9. Minneapolis: Minneapolis Institute of Art.

Jacoby, D. 2004. Silk economics and cross-cultural artistic interaction: Byzantium, the Muslim world, and the Christian West. *DOP* 58: 197–240.

Jain, R. 1994. The Indian drawloom and its products. *Textile Museum Journal* 32–3: 50–81.

———. 1998. The samit and lampas silks: The case for an Indian provenance. In *Samit & lampas: Motifs indiens. Indian Motifs*, ed. K. R. Riboud, 27–37. Paris: Association pour l'Étude et la Documentation des Textiles d'Asie.

Jeroussalemskaja [Ierusalimskaja], A. A. 1975. Nouvelles excavations des sépulcres des VII–IX siècles au Caucase septentrional et le problème de datation de quelques groupes de soieries anciennes. In *Preprints of the contributions to the Stockholm Congress 2–6 June, 1975*, 27–32. London: International Institute for Conservation of Historic and Artistic Works.

———. 1978. Le cafetan aux simourghs du tombeau de Mochtchevaja Balka (Caucase Septentrional). *StIr* 7: 183–211.

Kajitani, N. 2001. A man's caftan and leggings from the north Caucasus of the eighth to tenth Century: A conservator's report. *MMJ* 36: 85–124.

Kawami, T. S. 1992. Archaeological evidence for textiles in pre-Islamic Iran. *IrSt* 25/1–2: 7–18.

Kitzinger, E. 1946. The horse and lion tapestry at Dumbarton Oaks: A study in Coptic and Sasanian textile design. *DOP* 3: 3–72.

Knauer, E. R. 2001. A man's caftan and leggings from the north Caucasus of the eighth to tenth century: A genealogical study. *MMJ* 36: 125–54.

Kröger, J. 1982. *Sasanidischer Stückdekor: Ein Beitrag zum Reliefdekor aus Stuck in sasanidischer und frühislamischer Zeit nach den Ausgrabungen von 1928/9 und 1931/2 in der sasanidische Metropole Ktesiphon (Iraq) und unter besonderer Berücksichtigung der Stuckfunde vom Taḫt-i Sulaimān, aus Niẓāmābād (Iran) sowie zahlreiche anderer Fundorte*. Mainz: Baghdader Forschungen 5.

Lamm, C. J. 1937. *Cotton in mediaeval textiles of the Near East*. Paris: Geuthner.

Lessing, J. 1900. *Die Gewebe-Sammlung des Königlichen Kunstgewerbe-Museums*. Berlin: Wasmuth.

Li, W. 2006. Textiles of the second to fifth century unearthed from Yingpan cemetery. In *Central Asian textiles and their contexts in the Early Middle Ages*, ed. R. Schorta, 242–64. Riggisberg: Riggisberger Berichte 9.

Marshak, B. 2006. The so-called Zandanījī silks: Comparisons with the art of Sogdia. In *Central Asian textiles and their contexts in the Early Middle Ages*, ed. R. Schorta, 49–60. Riggisberg: Riggisberger Berichte 9.

Meister, M. 1970. The pearl roundel in Chinese textile design. *Ars Orientalis* 8: 255–67.

Movassat, J. D. 2005. *The large vault at Taq-i Bustan: A study in Late Sasanian Royal Art*. Lewiston/Queenston/Lampeter: Mellen Studies in Archaeology 3.

Otavsky, K. 1998. Zur Kunsthistorische Einordnung der Stoffe. In *Entlang der Seidenstrasse: Frühmittelalterliche Kunst zwischen Persien und China in der Abegg-Stiftung*, 119–214. Riggisberg: Riggisberger Berichte 6.

Peck, E. H. 1969. The representation of costumes in the reliefs of Taq-i Bustan. *Artibus Asiae* 31/2–3: 101–25.

Raspopova, V. I. 2006. Textiles represented in Sogdian murals. In *Central Asian textiles and their contexts in the Early Middle Ages*, ed. R. Schorta, 61–73. Riggisberg: Riggisberger Berichte 9.

Riboud, K. R. 1976. A newly excavated caftan from the northern Caucasus. *Textile Museum Journal* 4/3: 21–42.

———. 1998. *Samit & lampas: Motifs indiens. Indian Motifs*. Paris: Association pour l'Étude et la Documentation des Textiles d'Asie.

Schorta, R., ed. 2006. *Central Asian textiles and their contexts in the Early Middle Ages*. Riggisberg: Riggisberger Berichte 9.

Sheng, A. 1998. Innovations in textile techniques on China's northwest frontier, 500–700 AD. *Asia Major*, 3rd Ser. 11/2: 117–60.

Shepherd, D., and W. B. Henning. 1959. Zandanījī Identified? In *Aus der Welt des islamischen Kunst: Festschrift für Ernst Kühnel*, ed. R. Ettinghausen, 15–40. Berlin: Gebr. Mann.

Wu, M. 2006. The exchange of weaving technologies between China and Central and Western Asia from the third to the eighth century based on new textile finds in Xinjiang. In *Central Asian textiles and their contexts in the Early Middle Ages,* ed. R. Schorta, 211–42. Riggisberg: Riggisberger Berichte 9.

Xu, X. 2006. The discovery, excavation, and study of Tubo (Tibetan) tombs in Dulan County, Qinghai. In *Central Asian textiles and their contexts in the Early Middle Ages*, ed. R. Schorta, 265–90. Riggisberg: Riggisberger Berichte 9.

Zhao, F. 2006. Weaving methods for Western-style *Samit*. In *Central Asian textiles and their contexts in the Early Middle Ages*, ed. R. Schorta, 189–210. Riggisberg: Riggisberger Berichte 9.

CHAPTER 50

PRE-ISLAMIC IRANIAN CALENDRICAL SYSTEMS IN THE CONTEXT OF IRANIAN RELIGIOUS AND SCIENTIFIC HISTORY

ANTONIO C. D. PANAINO

Astral sciences and celestial lore in Ancient Iran

A discussion of the origin of the ancient Iranian calendars requires a presentation of the fundamental patterns that framed their elaboration as well as a discussion of the nature of science in Iran, particularly mathematics and astronomy, but including religious astral speculation and myth as well. As far as we know, the pre-Islamic cultures of Iran did not generate any advances of their own in the astral sciences, at least compared to the Mesopotamian world, which exerted profound influence on Iran, producing a clear development in the field of astronomy already under the Achaemenid Empire. This does not mean that Iranian people did not possess their own astral mythology or empirical calendrical systems, but the sources strictly related to this domain are unfortunately limited. We may summarize some basic data: apart from the simple distinction between heaven (above) and earth (below it)—very common in the Old Persian inscriptions—heaven in the Avestan framework was divided into three levels, the lowest belonging to the stars, the middle to the Moon, and the third to the Sun, while above them was the Paradise of Ahura Mazdā. This uppermost level was connected with a special category of stars, the "lights without beginning," which probably represented the Milky Way and the highest part of the galactic sphere not infected by the presence of the Evil Spirit. It is possible that the tripartite division of heaven reflected earlier Mesopotamian speculations, while its influence on the doctrines of some pre-Socratic philosophers is a matter of debate (Panaino 1995b). The stars, in any case, were considered divine beings that manifested the cosmic order in opposition to falling stars (called *stārō.kərəmā*—"starred worms") that were considered demons (*pairikā-* "witches") responsible for drought and famine (Panaino 1995a, 2005). The Sun and the Moon were also divine beings, to whom two Avestan hymns were dedicated. The Zodiac and the planets were unknown, at least before the direct influence of the Mesopotamian tradition. For instance, following current usage in the Assyrian and Babylonian traditions, the Persians, and other later Iranian peoples, used names of Akkadian origin, such as Saturn (Pahl. *Kēwān* < *kaiav/mānu*; MacKenzie 1964: 520, n. 46), for the five visible planets. Jupiter, the planet of Marduk, was associated in Greece with Zeus and in Iran with Ahura Mazdā, while Venus, that is Ištar, became Aphrodite in the West and Anāhitā in Iran (Panaino 1995a).

The extant Avestan sources do not indicate the presence of a developed practice of astral divination, only of astral myths. For this reason, in the context of this chapter, it is necessary to stress that "astral divination" and "astrology" are different matters, although historically related. The latter was based on a number of speculations combined with real knowledge of astral phenomena underpinned by a system of geometrical and philosophical patterns, mostly of Aristotelian derivation. It is clear that the celestial observations of Mesopotamian diviners provided an enormous impulse toward the birth of the exact sciences, although this knowledge was used for the determination of astral reports. The legacy of the Mesopotamia astral sciences directly influenced the evolution of Greek astronomy and astrology. Hellenistic astrology, in particular, probably emerged only in the second century BC at Alexandria (Egypt), thanks to a mixture of different traditions (Pingree 1997: 21–9). Greek astronomy and astrology entered Iran in Late Antiquity, perhaps already in Parthian times or before, but the results of these "arts" are only known thanks to a significant number of sources from the Sasanian period. Thus, while we cannot speak of astrology for the Avestan tradition, the astral elements of which lie on the borders of astral mythology, it was in Sasanian times that many interpretations patently based on a number of astrological doctrines appeared (Panaino 1996b, 1998, 2009a). It is worth noting that Sasanian astronomy and astrology were directly influenced not only by Hellenistic culture but also by Indian traditions as Pahlavi and other Iranian sources contain concepts absent in Greek astrological literature, but clearly developed in the Hindu framework (Raffaelli 2001). Cosmological and religious speculations had, of course, a direct impact on calendrical systems, their adaptations and reforms, and on the creation of large calendrical periods (or cosmic years) in which theological and astrological speculations were mixed (Panaino 1998). Persian astrologers, in particular, invented patterns that attained an impressive level of notoriety in Islamic astrology, as well as in Byzantine and Latin Mediaeval astrological literature. These included doctrines concerning the planetary conjunctions of Jupiter and Saturn (Pingree 1963, 1989; Kennedy 1964; Panaino 1998, 2009a; Yamamoto and Burnett 2000). Notwithstanding the limited number of sources of astral relevance for the earliest Iranian periods, it would be incorrect to presume that the Iranian peoples, particularly the Persians and the Medes, were primitive and completely uninterested in these matters. In fact, Achaemenid cultural elites were surely attracted by some of these astronomical problems, as calendrical reforms introduced during the Achaemenid period clearly attest. Thus, it would be far-fetched to suggest that Persians, in particular among the priestly circles of the Magi, who were concerned not only with sacrifice but also with administration and other secular (and political) activities, had no interest in astral divination and calendrics (based on mathematics and astronomy as well), and that the principal centers of "astral investigation" in Mesopotamia remained completely outside the control of the leading political authorities. For instance, the earlier Babylonian ritual of the king's substitution was surely known in Achaemenid times (Panaino 2000; Hunger 1997: 15–17; Lloyd 2002: 27), while the existence of an Old Persian calendar, harmonized with its Babylonian and Elamite counterparts, clearly reveals an interest in this scientific domain (Hartner 1985; Blois 1996, 2002; Panaino 1990b, 1999a, 2002). Furthermore, the assumption that only Greeks and Indians had the opportunity to become acquainted with many aspects of the scientific development generated by the Mesopotamian astronomical schools, while Iranians, Persians in particular, remained unaffected by these doctrines, is unfounded. On the contrary, the remarkable progress of the Babylonian astral sciences between the fifth and second centuries BC (Neugebauer 1969: 102; 1975 1: 128–9) seems to support the conclusion that these cultural centers were not only tolerated, but, if not openly protected, at least accorded the intellectual freedom needed to continue their research.

The few notions that we possess about ancient Iranian astral culture come from Avestan literature, which, because of its mainly religious purpose, does not contain relevant data of a mathematical and scientific nature. About two-thirds of the material traditionally attributed to the so-called "Avestan canon" of the Sasanian period, did not survive the Islamic invasion. These lacunae can be partly filled by Pahlavi and other Middle Iranian sources, while external astronomical and astrological documents belonging to Late Antiquity and the Middle Ages preserve some materials of genuine Iranian derivation. In addition, a good number of Mesopotamian and Greek sources concerning the Iranian world offer additional statements that must be taken into consideration. The Iranian region was open to external influences but, in turn, favored the circulation of foreign doctrines between East and West or, conversely, exported traditions that were previously adapted to its cultural and religious patterns. For example, the sexagesimal numerical system, fundamental in astronomy, was derived, as in Greece, from Mesopotamia and was also used in Iran for astronomical purposes, while the later diffusion of spherical models was a cultural acquisition from a Greek source. A similar situation can be postulated for the elaboration of the Zodiac, which became standard in Babylonian astronomy around the fifth century BC (Panaino 1999b; 2009b). On the other hand, we have no direct references to the idea of a celestial sphere or *mundus* (very different from that of circularity or circumference) in the earliest Mesopotamian and Indo-Iranian sources. Thus, it may be presumed that the spherical model was an original Greek invention that spread widely in the Orient, where it gradually became standard. Its Western origin is clearly attested, for instance, in Pahlavi, where the word meaning "sphere" (*spihr*) is, as Henning demonstrated (1942: 239–40), a loanword from Gr. σφαῖρα (*sphaîra*).

THE IRANIAN CALENDARS IN THE PRE-ISLAMIC CONTEXT

The Old Persian calendar

The creation of an empire compelled the royal Achaemenid dynasty to elaborate an official calendrical system, synchronized with the most important ones of that time, and led to the adoption of regnal years, beginning with the first month of the new year after the enthronement of each king (Parker and Dubberstein 1956). As in other cases, the Persians found inspiration for the determination of their own calendar in Mesopotamia, particularly in the Babylonian and Elamite calendars (Gnoli 1974, 1988; Oppenheim 1985). The great trilingual inscription of Bisotun (*c.*519 BC), commissioned by Darius I (521–486 BC), is the main source for the reconstruction of the Achaemenid calendar. In the Old Persian (OP) recension only eight month names are attested, while a ninth, **Vr̥kazana-*, or, perhaps, **(H)uvarkajana-* (Gershevitch 1951: 142), was reconstructed thanks to the parallel Elamite version (DB III 88, *Mar-qa-za-na-iš*; Weissbach 1911: 56–7; Schmitt 1991: 67; 2003: 18, 44–7, with a discussion of possible interpretations). The complete absence of three-month names (V, VI, XI) in the OP and El. versions of this inscription initially raised a number of questions concerning the exact sequence of the menology (Ginzel 1906: 276), which was finally determined by A. Poebel (1938a, 1938b, 1939a, 1939b). Essential assistance was provided by the Persepolis tablets in Elamite (Cameron 1948: 44–5: Schmitt 2003: 18–24), in which "Persian" month names were preserved (although with an Elamite adaptation in their spelling; thus, they are distinguished by * in Table 50.1). Etymological discussions of the names of the months are ongoing (Kent 1953; Gershevitch 1951; Bandenstein-Mayrhofer 1964; Hinz 1973: 64–70; 1975; Schmitt 1981, 2003; Panaino 1990b: 658). It is impossible to establish the exact date of the introduction of this calendar and to determine its technical rules under the first kings of the Achaemenid dynasty, but it is probable that it followed the Babylonian calendar with twelve months of twenty-nine or thirty days each (Hartner 1979: 146; 1985: 747 assumes that it was already lunisolar, with twelve months of thirty days each, but this radical departure from contemporary systems is difficult to accept). The missing days were recovered by means of empirical intercalations of one whole month. The days were numbered but not denominated, except the last one, which was distinguished by

Table 50.1 The Old Persian calendar.

Old Persian	O.P. in Elamite texts	Elamite	Akkadian	English
Ddukan(a)iša-	Hadukannaš	Zikli	Nīsannu	March–April
Θūravāhara	Turmar	Zarpakim	Ayyāru	April–May
Θāigr(a)ci-	Sākurriziš	Hadar	Sīmannu	May–June
Garmapada-	Karmabataš	Hallime	Du'ūzu	June–July
*Dṛnabāji(ya)	Turnabaziš	Zillatam	Ābu	July–August
*K/Xārapaθiya	Karbašiyaš	Belilit	Ulūlū	August–September
Bāgayādi-	Bagiyatiš	Manšarki	Tašrītu	September–October
*Vṛkazana-	Markašanaš	Lankelli	Ara'samna	October–November
Āçiyādiya-	Hašiyatiš	Šibari	Kisilīmu	November–December
Anāmaka-	Hanamakaš	Šermi	Ṭebētu	December–January
*Θwayauvā	Samiyamaš	Kutmama	Šabāṭu	January–February
Viyax(a)na-	Miyakannaš	Aššetukpi	Addāru	February–March

the expression *jiyamnam patiy* "the decreasing (day?) of" (where, *jiyamna-m*, a middle participle neuter from *ji-*, means "the growing old, decreasing one [?]," DB II 62 [Kent 1953: 122, 124; Schmitt 1991: 59], although it is possible that this formula simply concerns the end of the lunar phase of the month).

A dearth of sources has unfortunately produced different opinions about the rules adopted for intercalation. Whereas Hallock (1969: 74–5) assumed that the OP calendar followed the patterns of the Babylonian and Elamite ones, Hartner (1979: 1–3; 1985: 741–9, 786) noted some discrepancies in the years 503–499 BC. These he attributed to problems connected with an alleged reform of the Babylonian calendar in the 19th regnal year of Darius I (503 BC). Originally, the Babylonian calendar (Neugebauer 1969: 106–9; Hunger 1976–80: 297–9; Rochberg 1995: 1931–2) was based on the synodic lunar cycle, with twelve months of twenty-nine or thirty days (beginning with the first sighting of the moon), to which empirical intercalations of the VI and XII months, Ulūlū II and Addāru II (Table 50.1), that is, just before the vernal and autumnal equinoxes, were added at least every three years. For practical purposes it used a conventional month of thirty days, which eliminated the inconvenience caused by the different length of the synodic lunation (Swerdlow 1998: 37). Bickerman (1967: 206, n. 49) suggested that such a formal pattern was also followed by the Persian administration at Persepolis. According to Hartner (1985: 738–9), a new system, conventionally called *octaëteris* (eight years with three intercalations; $8 \times 12 + 3 = 99$ synodic months), was introduced in the 3rd regnal year of Cambyses (527 BC) while, from 503 BC onward, a more precise cycle of nineteen years with seven intercalations ($19 \times 12 + 7 = 235$ months) was used. This system corresponded to the famous "Metonic cycle," adopted at Athens only in 430 BC. Hartner emphasized that, while the Babylonian calendar intercalated the month of Ulūlū (VI) in the year 503–502 BC, in the OP calendar it was the tenth month that seems to have been doubled (for other cases, see Hartner 1985: 747–8, 786). Recently Blois has proposed a good explanation for this apparent difference, showing that El. *beptika* (OP *hamiçiya*) does not denote an "intercalated" month but simply one "displaced by intercalation" (Blois 2006: 44, 49–51). Aramaic glosses in some Persepolis Fortification texts attest to a good number of correspondences between OP and Babylonian month names, which are compatible with those of Bisotun. As Basello also suggested, the intercalation systems were quite similar, if not identical (Basello 2002: 15). It should also be noted that some scholars postulate a later introduction (early fifth century BC) of the nineteen-year cycle, while the origin of the *octaëteris* is much more disputed (Bowen and Goldstein 1988).

The Elamite treasury tablets from Persepolis (Cameron 1948: 34, 44–5; 1965: 167; Gershevitch 1951: 133) confirm the practical use of the Persian calendar until 459 BC (on the Elamite calendar and its historical evolution, also with regard to its intercalatory systems, see Basello 2002, 2006), while the Aramaic texts from Elephantine (Cowley 1923; Kraeling 1953; Horn and Wood 1954; Bickerman 1967: 205), belonging to the Persian administration in the years 471–401 BC, show that the system in use there was the Babylonian one. This practice, followed also by Macedonians in Iran (Bickerman 1967: 205), lasted not only throughout the entire Achaemenid period, but also found expression in Parthian and Sasanian times (Hartner 1985: 757). Important, but perhaps concerning another calendrical system (basically similar to that attested in the Avestan sources), is a statement of Quintus Curtius Rufus (3.3.10) implying that the Persians were also familiar with a solar year of 365 days (Bickerman 1967: 205, n. 41; Panaino 1990b: 659). As noted above, the year began in March (vernal equinox), but other traditional periods were important as well, such as the summer solstice. The assumption that Persepolis was used for the New Year's Festival in March presupposes that the court was there in a period when it was still cold, but no positive proof of this tradition is attested and certainly living conditions at the site would have been more comfortable in summer (Wiesehöfer 2009).

THE ORIGIN AND BACKGROUND OF THE ZOROASTRIAN CALENDAR

It is clear that the ancient Iranian peoples had one or more calendrical systems of an empirical nature. Avestan sources, for instance, attest to a knowledge of the lunar phases (*Yašt* 7), whose cycle was already divided into two round periods of fifteen days (increasing and decreasing), and (at least) three subperiods, the importance of which has been emphasized by Blois (2006). The religious festivals known as *Gāhānbār*s had a remarkable importance and various hypotheses concern the beginning of the year (Bielmeier 1992). The observation of the rising and setting of some asterisms may have been relevant as well (as assumed by Hartner 1985), but it is difficult to reconstruct a calendrical model from such ambiguous evidence. A different situation, although problematic, is presented by the so-called Zoroastrian calendar, historically attested both in religious and in secular sources. Apparently, the first reference to a month

Table 50.2 The names of the months in the Zoroastrian calendar.

Avestan	Pahlavi	New Persian
1. Frauuašinąm (Y. I, 11)	Frawardīn	Farvardīn
2. Ašahe Vahištahe (Ā. III, 7)	Ardwahišt	Ordībehešt
3. Hauruuatātō	Hordād	Kordād
4. Tištriiehe (Ā. III, 8)	Tīr	Tīr
5. Amərətātō	Amurdād	Mordād
6. Xšaθrahe Vairiiehe (Ā. III, 9)	Šahrewar	Šahrīvar
7. Miθrahe (Ā. III, 10)	Mihr	Mehr
8. Āpąm	Ābān	Ābān
9. Āθrō	Ādur	Āḏar
10. Daθušō (Ā. III, 11)	Day	Dey
11. Vaŋhəuš Manaŋhō	Wahman	Bahman
12. Spəntayå Ārmatōiš (Vd. 21)	Spandarmad	Esfand

name (Spandarmad) according to this calendar appears in a badly damaged Aramaic inscription on Darius' tomb (Frye 1982; cf. Bickerman 1967: 204, n. 30). This has been ascribed to an unidentified Seleucid king, The latest who could come into consideration is Antiochus I (r. 281–261 BC). This means that the new menology was *surely* current in western Iran during the third century BC, although its introduction was much earlier, probably during the reign of Xerxes (486–465 BC), as suggested by Blois (1996: 49).

Its basic structure is very simple: twelve months (Table 50.2), each of thirty days (Table 50.3), to which five extra days or *epagomenæ* were added. The Old Avestan sources contain no calendrical information, while in the Younger *Avesta* some details are preserved: two litanies, entitled (in Pahlavi) *Sīh rōzag ī xwurdag* "The Little Thirty Days" and *Sīh rōzag ī wuzurg* "The Great Thirty Days" (Geldner 1889: 260–7; Hartman 1957; Dhabhar 1927: 175–81, 223–59; 1963: 307–41), preserve two lists of the thirty days, each one dedicated to a Mazdean divine being. The theological rationale behind the disposition of the days has often been investigated, but it remains unclear (it was thought to be divided into four subperiods by Nyberg [1931: 128–34] and into two by Lewy [1941: 64, n. 2], while Belardi stressed the centrality of Miθra [1977: 59–139]). A full list of the twelve months is missing in the *Avesta*, where only seven names (Table 50.2) are mentioned (*Āfrīnagān*; Belardi 1977: 77), but its full reconstruction is certain thanks to the consensus of later Iranian, classical and Arabic sources (Lagarde 1866: 229–32; Gray 1904: 175; 1910: 128). The five *epagomenæ* were also denominated as "Gāθic" epact (Pahl. *gāhānīg*), because each was named after one of the five Avestan *Gāθā*s. Attested in the Pahlavi-Avestan *Āfrīnagān ī Gāhān*, these names have been transmitted in a large number of variants (Belardi 1977: 77–81), and al-Bīrūnī knew six different lists of them (Sachau 1878: 43–5; 1879: 53–4).

The five *gāhānīg* days plus the last five days of the month *Spandarmad* were connected with the important celebration of the *Frawardīgān* (Belardi 1977: 81), dedicated to the souls of the dead. Furthermore, every day was divided into four parts (five in summer), denominated *Gāh*s (Panaino 1990b: 42; Boyce 2001a), beginning with the rising of the

Table 50.3 The names of the thirty days in the Zoroastrian calendar.

Avestan	Pahlavi	New Persian
1. Ahurahe Mazdå	Ohrmazd	Hormoz
2. Vaŋhāuš Manaŋhō	Wahman	Bahman
3. Ašahe Vahištahe	Ardwahišt	Ordībehešt
4. Xšaθrahe Vairiiehe	Šahrewar	Šahrīvar
5. Spəntaiiå Ārmatōiš	Spandarmad	Esfand(ārmo_d_)
6. Hauruuatātō	Hordād	_K_ordād
7. Amərətātō	Amurdād	Mordād
8. Daθušō Ahurahe Mazdå	Day pad Ādur	Dey be Ād°ar
9. Āθrō	Ādur	Ād°ar
10. Apąm	Ābān	Ābān
11. Huuarəxšaētahe	Xwar	K√or/_K_ūr
12. Måŋhahe	Māh	Māh
13. Tištriiehe	Tīr	Tīr
14. Gəūš	Gōš	Gūš
15. Daθušō Ahurahe Mazdå	Day pad Mihr	Dey be Mehr
16. Miθrahe	Mihr	Mehr
17. Sraošahe	Srōš	Sorūš
18. Rašnaoš	Rašn	Rašn
19. Frauuašinąm	Frawardīn	Farvardīn
20. Vərəθraγnahe	Wahrām	Bahrām
21. Rāmanō	Rām	Rām
22. Vātahe	Wād	Bā_d_
23. Daθušō Ahurahe Mazdå	Day pad Dēn	Dey be Dīn
24. Daēnaiiå	Dēn	Dīn
25. Ašōiš	Ard (Ahrišwang)	Ard
26. Arštātō	Aštād	Aštā_d_
27. Ašnō	Asmān	Āsmān
28. Zəmō hudåŋhō	Zamyād	Zamya_d_
29. Mąθrahe spəntahe	Māraspand	Māraspand
30. Anaγranąm	Anagrān	Anīrān

sun. According to the *Widēwdād*, I, 3, the year was divided into ten winter and only two summer months, but already in the Pahlavi commentary to this passage the number of the summer months increased to seven (Anklesaria 1949: 3–4). Such a subdivision is attested also in the *Bundahišn* (*Ir.Bd.*, XXV, 9; *Ind.Bd.*, XXV, 7; Anklesaria 1956: 206–7; Pakzad 2005: 286–91), although there it is stated (*Ir.Bd.*, XXV, 21–27; *Ind.Bd.* XXV, 20; Justi 1868: 33–5; West 1880: 91–7; Anklesaria 1956: 208–11; Pakzad 2005: 290–1) that, according to another calendrical system, termed *wihēzagīg* or "intercalary(?)" (see below), there are four seasons of three months each. A remarkable function was attributed to the *Gāhānbār*s (Roth 1880; Taqizadeh 1938; Bielmeier 1992; Boyce 2001b), attested both in the Younger *Avesta* (*Āfrīnagān Gāhānbār*; Geldner 1889: 270–5; Darmesteter 1892/2: 729–35; Wolff 1910: 309–12) and in Pahlavi sources, but their existence was well known to al-Bīrūnī (Sachau 1878: 215–33; 1879: 119–219). These periods have usually been considered seasonal festivals (for their chronological disposition see Panaino 1990b) but, according to Hartner, they represent a survival of an earlier "Old Avestan Calendar," later embedded in the Younger Avestan one, where they served to mark the cosmical setting of some asterisms visible from Persepolis (Lentz and Schlosser 1969). In this way, the *Gāhānbār*s would constitute a sort of skeleton for the lunisolar (later sidereal) year, by means of which empirical intercalations would have been introduced. On the other hand, this theory suffers from the fact that none of the asterisms identified by Hartner is attested in the extant Avestan literature, while the suggestion that Persepolis was the chief place of observation for an ancestral Iranian calendar of Avestan origin (Eastern Iranian) is historically questionable. *Nowrūz*, "the new day," on the first day of the month *Frawardīn*, originally occurring in March at the vernal equinox, marked the beginning of the year (for other feasts, e.g., *Tīragān*, *Mihragān*, *Ābānagān*, *Frawardigān*, etc. see Gray 1912; Markwart 1930; Taqizadeh 1937, 1938, 2010: 75–8; Boyce 1968, 1970, 1983; Hartner 1985: 779–81).

Regarding the prototype of the Zoroastrian calendar, we must note that a wandering year of 365 days without intercalations of any day was essentially discovered and fixed in Egypt (Depuydt 1997). Thus, it is reasonable to assume that this pattern was known and then adopted by some Persians only after the occupation of Egypt by Cambyses. Kellens (1998: 488–516) has plausibly suggested that the oral redaction of the Old Avestan texts was followed by the fixing and canonization of two ritual texts, called Proto-*Yasna* A and Proto-*Yasna* B, and then by the reorganization of the Canon of the *Yašt*s, that is, the Avestan hymns, which was, at least in part, linked with the Mazdean calendrical system. With regard to calendrical problems, Kellens' chronology presumes that the location of the second canonization of the Proto-*Yasna* B took place in western Iran. But the assumption that this process was connected with the introduction of the new calendar, whose origin is probably Western, and ultimately Egyptian, does not prove that the Avestan oral text was actually rearranged at the same time and in the same place. This work of reassessment could have been easily done in eastern Iran, because the calendrical hemeronymy was fixed according to an "Avestan" theological pattern (e.g., with the inclusion of divinities like Tištrya instead of Tīriya, the planet Mercury), while the new month names were probably established, we can presume, in Eastern Iran, in to the original Western calendar, which was older, and that used different nomenclature. The earlier names of the months, in fact, are still attested, in their Western forms, in many other calendrical systems following the same solar pattern, such as the Armenian, Sogdian, Choresmian, among others (Panaino 1990b, with the lists of month and days; 2002: 226–9). For example, the name of the first month of the Armenian calendar, *nawasard-i* (< Ir. **naua-sarda-* "the new year"), corresponds to that of the first month of the Choresmian (al-Bīrūnī: *n'wsr'jy*), Sogdian (*n'wsrδyc*), and Bactrian (ναγοσαρδο) calendars; the name of the fourth Armenian month, *trē* < **tīria-*, corresponds to the Cappadocian month name τειρε, τιρι, or τιριχ, Choresmian *tyry* or *jyry* [= *cyry*], and *tyr ky'nw'* in the Sīstānic calendar. These clearly come from OP **tīriya-* (cf. Pahl. *tīr*), rather than Av. *tištriia-* (Pahl. *tištar*), which, in contrast, is attested in the proper "Zoroastrian" calendar (Panaino 2002: 228–9). The presence in both Western and Eastern countries of the same month names, which differ from those attested in the standard Avestan calendar, demonstrates the existence of an earlier tradition, which was theologically different than the "Avestan" one, and which was propagated in the Persian Empire at a time in which different, often distant countries were brought into closer contact via a shared political administration. The Zoroastrian clergy presumably did not modify the essential structure of that calendar, but introduced the names of the thirty days (which are generally similar in all Middle Iranian calendars and reflect a common Zoroastrian background) and when possible or necessary changed the names of some months. This, perhaps, may explain why the first month was not attributed to Ahura Mazdā, whereas the day of the highest god is the first of the hemerology (repeated three times under the denomination of *dāy* "creator" in the list).

The Sasanian "Civil" Calendar and the Problem of the Religious Intercalatory Calendrical System

While the existence of a so-called Zoroastrian "civil" calendar (Pahl. *ošmurdīg*, "calculated") is historically attested and indisputable, scholarship, particularly in recent times (Blois 1996: 42–5), has seriously questioned the existence of a second (and contemporary) "religious" calendrical system (Pahl. *wihēzagīg*, lit. "mobile, wandering"). The essential difference between these two systems would have resulted in the fact that the "civil" one did not use intercalations in order to recover the approximately six hours lost every solar year. Consequently, this calendar would have suffered a difference of one day every four years (or one whole month every 120 years) via-à-vis the solar one. Thus, it was a vague year, comparable to the Egyptian calendrical system, incorrectly termed "Sothiac" (Neugebauer 1938). The Zoroastrian civil and the Egyptian calendars maintained a certain synchronism, so that, for example, June 16, 632 AD (JD 1952063), corresponding to the 1st of *Frawardīn*, coincided with the 1st of *Thoth* (Hartner 1985: 764–9). In the religious calendar the difference with the seasonal periods would have been avoided by an intercalation of one month every 120 years. But the ancient sources offer contradictory statements and also make reference to another, more complex, system. In fact, Abu'l Ḥasan Kūšyār bin Labbān al-Jīlī (c.971–1029) stated in his astrological compendium *az-Zīju l-jāmi* (Ideler 1826: 547–8 [German trans.], 624–5 [Arabic text]; Ginzel 1906: 291; Hartner 1985: 757–8; cf. Blois 1996: 41–2), that since remotest times the Persians intercalated one month every 120 years. Furthermore, he noted that at the time of Kisrā ben Qubād Anūširwān (i.e., Xosrow I) the sun reached Aries in the month of *Ādhārmāh*. Al-Bīrūnī in turn stated that an intercalation of one month took place every 120 years in order to regain the six hours lost every year (Sachau 1878: 44; 1879: 54–6; Hartner 1985: 758–9; cf. also *Tafhīm*, Wright 1934: 271) and this is repeated by other Islamic authors like Šāh Kholjī and Quṭb al-Dīn al-Šīrāzī (Hyde 1770: 203–5;

Ideler 1826: 540–51, 623–9; Ginzel 1906: 290–3). Just to make things more complicated, al-Bīrūnī himself, in a different chapter of his *Chronology* (Sachau 1878: 11; 1879: 12–13; Hartner 1985: 762), affirmed that the intercalary month was introduced every 116 years in order to compute not only the lost fraction of one-quarter of a day (six hours), but also an additional fraction of one-fifth of an hour (twelve minutes). A passage in the third book of the *Dēnkard* confirms the existence of both calculations (Madan 1911 1: 402–5; Dresden 1966: 516–19; Nyberg 1934: 30–3; Boyce *apud* de Menasce 1973: 374–9). Setting aside the question of their coexistence, the main difference between the "civil" and the "religious" calendars would appear to be the progressive retrogradation of the former with respect to the latter. In other words, if the first intercalary month was inserted, as assumed, after 120 years (or 116 in the alternative cycle), by a duplication of *Frawardīn* (first month), with the location of the epact after the second *Frawardīn*, then from that moment until the next intercalation (years 121–240 or 117–232), the first month of the religious calendar would correspond to the second of the civil system (*Ardwahišt*), with an additional difference of five days for the following months until this gap was resolved by the presence of the (standard) epact traditionally fixed at the end of the twelfth month in the civil system. With the next intercalation (year 240 or 232 of the cycle), it was the second month, *Ardwahišt*, that was doubled, and the epact moved after the repeated month, so that the first month of the religious calendar (*Frawardīn*) would correspond to the third month of the civil calendar (*Xordād*), and so on, until the last attested intercalation. It is unclear from the sources how and/or if such an intercalary month was actually named. Abu'l Ḥasan Kūšyār (Ideler 1826: 547–8 [German trans.], 624–5 [Arabic text]) affirms that the first month of the year was computed twice, once at the beginning and once at the end of the same year, stating that the Persians "attached the epagomenæ to the intercalary month." Conversely, according to al-Bīrūnī (Sachau 1878: 55), the Persians "did not call the intercalary month by a special name, nor did they repeat the name of another month, but they kept it simply in memory from one turn to another" (but cf. al-Bīrūnī's *Tafhīm*, Wright, 1934: 271, where the intercalary month is called *bīhtarak* "the best"). Furthermore, al-Bīrūnī remarked that the Persians, "being, however, afraid that might arise uncertainty as to the place where the intercalatory month would have again to be inserted, transferred the five epagomenæ and put them at the end of that month, to which the turn of intercalation had proceeded on the last occasion of intercalating" (Sachau 1878: 55). Thus, according to these sources the intercalatory system was regularly used for centuries without interruption. On the base of this assumption many scholars have tried to fix the exact date for the introduction of the first intercalation and, consequently, that of the calendar itself. This determination can be theoretically obtained by means of a backward calculation, by multiplying 120 (or 116) the number of supposed intercalations that should have taken place since the last one. In the absence of explicit sources, this number was deduced from the crude inference that the position of the *epagomenæ* in the last known intercalation must show how many cycles had previously occurred. Unfortunately, the sources are ambiguous on this point: in fact, Abu'l Ḥasan Kūšyār stated that in the reign of Xosrow I (531–578) the Sun entered in Aries in the month of *Ādar* and the epact was moved after *Ābān* (VIII month). Then, because of the collapse of the Sasanian Empire, no intercalation was introduced until a new correction was ordered in the year 375 Yezdegerdī (= 1006 AD; Hartner 1985: 770–2; Blois 1996: 42). On the other hand, al-Bīrūnī (Sachau 1878: 45) says that at the time of Yezdegerd b. Šābuhr (= Yazdgerd I, 399–420, the Persians "anticipated intercalating the year at once by two months," in the first case probably in order to correct the calendar, while the latter was added "for no other motive but precaution." In any case, al-Bīrūnī also noted that at that time the *epagomenæ* were added after the month *Ābān* (cf. *Tafhīm*, Wright 1934: 168). But again al-Bīrūnī, in his later work *Qānūn al-Masʿūdī* (Baranī 1954 1: 132; Marshak 1992: 146–7), made a correction to his previous statement, and dated the last intercalation to the reign of Pērōz (457–484). Recently, Blois has reviewed the problem, rejecting as a pseudo-historical "legend" the existence of such an intercalatory system (1996). He suggests instead that the civil calendar, surely of Achaemenid origin, was simply modified in later Sasanian times by means of a radical change, which moved the beginning of the year from the first month to the ninth one, with the contemporary location of the *epagomenæ* at the end of the eighth month. Following Blois, it is historically improbable that any intercalatory pattern, implying a regular cycle of intercalations performed every 120 years since the Achaemenid period, could have been established so early and actually respected without interruption during the course of so many centuries. Furthermore, Blois emphasized another striking negative argument for the existence of an intercalatory pattern: we know that the Armenian, Choresmian, and Sogdian calendars preserved the epact after the twelfth month, making it likely that they maintained an earlier scheme, which was modified only in the Persian system (Blois 1996: 46–9). If one or more months were actually intercalated, we should find a difference of thirty days (or multiples of thirty by as many as were the intercalations) between the reformed calendar and the others, while the divergence is only five days. This means that no month was intercalated, while the difference of these five days can easily be explained as a mistake (Blois 1996: 47–8; Panaino 2002: 230 suggested that such a mistake could have occurred in the third century, on the occasion of the first reform). Although Blois was probably correct in rejecting the historicity of such an ancestral intercalatory cycle, it is still possible that the references to the introduction of a Sasanian intercalation do not reflect a completely false tradition (Blois 1996: 46ff.). In fact, we cannot exclude the possibility that the sources referring to the introduction of a double intercalation simply attest the occurrence of a real adjustment of the Mazdean calendar based on astronomical data (Panaino 1999a: 114–23; 2002: 222–5, 229–30). We know that the Sasanians developed an astronomical school which produced at least three different versions of "Astronomical Tables," termed *Zīg*, and that meetings of astronomers, the most important of which was held in 556, were patronized by Xosrow I (Panaino 1998, 2010a). This calendrical change did not imply any real intercalation of one or more months, but a simple shift of the starting point of the year to coincide with the vernal equinox. Only later was that reform interpreted and presented as the fruit of a systematic rule based on a secular tradition. Some data support the suggestion that another calendar reform occurred during the reign of Ardašīr I (as Lewy 1941: 22–45 supposed) with the direct shift of the *epagomenæ* after the sixth month (*Šahrewar*), so that the beginning of the year was synchronized with the contemporary entrance of the Sun in the first degree of Aries (the so called "vernal" point). The introduction of an earlier calendrical reform under Ardašīr I or Šābuhr I, moreover, is supported by two important ancient statements. First, a Manichaean Middle Persian manuscript confirms that the month of *Mihr*, in the (civil) calendar, coincided before the year 240 AD with March–April and the constellation of Aries (*warrag*), as noted also by Henning (1934: 33). Second, according to al-Bīrūnī (Sachau 1879: 37), the poet al-Buḥturī said that, "The day of Naurûz has returned to the time which was fixed by Ardashîr." Furthermore, in the *Kitāb al-Tanbīh*, Mas'ūdī stated that Ardašīr had modified the earlier royal chronologies (Carra de Vaux 1986: 141). All of these independent references support the view that a reform might have already taken place at the beginning of the Sasanian period. M. Boyce, on the other hand, assumed, although in the context of a particular reconstruction of the Persian calendar, that a radical reassessment of the calendar had taken place under Ardašīr I (Boyce 1970: 518). Thus, the reform realized during the reign of Pērōz with the location of the five epagomenal days after *Ābān* and with the *Nōgrōz* (Pers. *Nawrōz*) in *Ādur* (the new first month of the calendar, but originally the ninth one), would have been the result of a second correction, probably stimulated by the Sasanian redactors of the *Zīg*. Whereas Blois (1996: 48) assumed only one radical modification of the calendrical pattern directly established about the year 500, "when the religious New Year, and with it all the other festivals, were shifted at one go by eight months," another possibility can be suggested. It may be that the mathematical and astronomical reasons behind the second reform (i.e., the one probably introduced under Pērōz) were derived from real knowledge of the fact that the standard calendar suffered a loss of one-quarter of a day every year, a phenomenon which produced, after 120 years, a difference of one month. The essential knowledge of this crude parameter was later transformed into the legendary existence of a secular cycle of intercalations ("pseudo-intercalations"). The fact that the Sasanians, already between the reign of Yazdgerd II and Pērōz, had developed a new set of *Zīg* should have actually favoured the acquisition of important astronomical and mathematical competence, both practical and theoretical. In fact, however, although earlier astronomical tables of Greek derivation were probably known in Persia (Pingree 1973: 35), the definitive redaction of the first Sasanian set of astronomical tables (*Zīg ī Šahriyārān*) was established only around 450, as shown by a remark made by Ibn Yūnis (Pingree 1965), that is, during the kingdom of Yazdgerd II (438–457) or at the beginning of that of Pērōz while there is no reason to postulate such a redaction during the brief reign of Ōhrmazd III (457–459). Pērōz ascended the Sasanian throne in 459, and al-Bīrūnī's (second) attribution to him of the postposition of the epact after *Ābān* is probably the correct one, because such a reform should reasonably follow in time a more careful mathematical treatment of the astronomical problems connected with the calendar, a competence that was obtained thanks to the *Zīg*s only lately edited during the last years of Yazdgerd II or in the first years of Pērōz. The later conference of the astronomers, convened under Xosrow I, simply confirmed the efficacy of the previous reform (Table 50.4).

Table 50.4 The Zoroastrian calendar in its historical evolution (two reconstructions).

First Hypothesis		Second alternative Hypothesis	
Original scheme (Achaemenid period)	First Reform (c. 240 A.D.) (Ardašīr's reign)	Second Reform (c. 460/480) (Pērōz's reign)	Only one shift about year 500
1. Frawardīn 2. Ardwahišt 3. Hordād 4. Tīr 5. Amurdād 6. Šahrewar			
	--------- Epagomenæ* ---------		
7. Mihr 8. Ābān	Mihr (New first month)	(Pseudo-intercalation of 2 months: Mihr and Ābān)	
		--------- Epagomenæ ---------	
9. Ādur 10. Day 11. Wahman 12. Spandarmad		Ādur (New first month)	
--------- Epagomenæ			

*The epagomenal days were not computed at the end of the last yera before the reform and removed before the 7th month. In this way the difference of five days with respect to the earlier "civil" calendar was produced. The second alternative hypothesis follows the interpretation given by F. de Blois, who puts the same transfer of the epact directly after the eight month without its computation at the end of the previous year. In any case, the two solutions agree on the main visbile results.

An interesting final warning concerns the evidence that the reform(s) introduced in the Persian calendar did not satisfy everybody and that a certain resistance endured, as we can observe in the duplication or triplication of religious festivals in Sasanian Iran (Boyce 1970), although some attempts to reconcile their dates seem to have been attempted (Blois 1996: 47–8).

Later developments

Although a number of problems still remain and cannot be discussed in detail here, it is clear that the Zoroastrian calendar with the epagomenal days placed after *Ābān* endured for centuries. The so called "era of Yazdgerd," computed from June 16, 632, has been in use up to the present day (Ginzel 1906: 299–300; Birashk 1992: 25). Another era, that of the Magi, beginning with the year of Yazdgerd's death (June 11, 652), is also attested (Blois 1996). The

Arab invaders, too, made use of an administrative Sasanian calendar, named *kārājī* ("tax on the earth"), for tax purposes (Abdollahy 1990: 669–70; Blois 2000). The epact was probably moved to the end of the month *Esfendārmod* (as noted by Abu'l Ḥasan Kūšyār) only on March 15, 1006. The Zoroastrians living in India were acquainted with this reform. The later reforms and adaptations of the Mazdean calendar that occurred amongst the various Zoroastrian communities of the diaspora go beyond the limits of this presentation (Panaino 1990b). In chapter XXV, 27 (Nyberg 1934: 18–21, 62–3) and XXVI, 21–2 (Anklesaria 1956: 210–11; 214–15; Pakzad 2005: 291, 296–7) of the *Ir.Bd.* another calendrical pattern, based on the lunar cycle, was described. According to different Middle Persian sources it had 355, 353, or 360 days (but 365 in the *Ind.Bd.*; Belardi 1977: 117–20). Perhaps, a basic scheme of 360 days could be connected with the so-called Pēšdādic calendar, described by al-Bīrūnī (Sachau 1878: 11; 1879: 13), with twelve months of thirty days each, to which an intercalatory month was added every six years (in order to recoup the *epagomenæ* which were not calculated before; $6 \times 5 = 30$) and another month every 120 years (for the computation of the quarter of a day still missing). The historicity of such a complex system is, however, doubtful (Hartner 1985: 750, n. 2; Belardi 1977: 82). Recently, Blois (2006) suggested that the origin of this calendrical pattern might be ascribed to an ancient lunar cycle, which already finds already some perhaps fitting antecedents in Avestan literature.

OTHER CALENDRICAL SYSTEMS

Many calendrical systems are attested throughout the Iranian lands after the fall of the Achaemenid Empire. As noted above, the Babylonian calendar, although sometimes mimicked, was never completely forgotten, and its use endured until the Sasanian period (Bickerman 1967, 1980; Hartner 1985). The pattern of a solar vague year, similar to the Zoroastrian one, but probably earlier, entered different Iranian (Parthia, Sogdiana, Choresmia, Bactria, etc.) and Iranized countries, in particular Armenia (Markwart 1905: 199–215; Schmitt 1985; Gippert 1987) and Cappadocia (Panaino 2010b). In Armenia, Cappadocia, Sogdiana, and Choresmia the position of the epact remained fixed after the twelfth month, while only the calendar of Sīstān followed the "Persian" change, with the five *epagomenæ* placed after *Ābān*. It is worth noting that a certain Iranian influence is visible not only in the month names, but also on the list of the thirty days of the Armenian calendar (Gray 1910: 130; Abramjan 1973: 100–101; Tumanian 1974: 93). Some aspects of the Sogdian calendar were already known thanks to al-Bīrūnī (Sachau 1878: 45–7; 1879: 56–7), but direct access to original sources has enormously increased our knowledge (Müller 1907; Frejman 1962: 27–60; Henning 1939, 1945; for the lists of months and days, see Panaino 1990b). Other remarkable improvements have been gained in the case of Bactrian chronology and its calendrical systems; for instance, the tentative list of the Bactrian months, established by Harmatta (1969: 369–70), has been greatly revised following the discovering and decipherment of a number of new documents by N. Sims-Williams and the identification of another list of month names, made by Blois, in the context of al-Bīrūnī's *Chronology* (Sachau 1878: 69; 1879: 82). In the second case, it is clear that the month name attributed to Bukhara must be interpreted as Tokharian "Bactrian" (cf. Sims-Williams and Blois 1998 with an updated list of the month names).

Although Sasanian influence was very strong in the eastern Iranian areas, such as Khotan (Bailey 1936: 575; 1982: 29–30; Panaino 1990b: 666), other, completely different calendrical systems were adopted there under Hindu or Central Asian influence, as in the case of the "duodecennial" (or animalistic) calendar (Bazin 1973: 355; 1991: 545–54). The diffusion of the planetary week, also to eastern Iranian countries and China (Chavannes and Pelliot 1913: 161–77), mostly via Christian and Manichaean communities, is, on the other hand, a Western influence, although Sogdian mediation was important (Sims-Williams 1985: 106; cf. al-Bīrūnī, Sachau 1878: 48–9; 1879: 58; Panaino 1995a: 69).

In the Indian context, among the Maga Brāhmaṇas we find a calendrical system which clearly imitates a Zoroastrian pattern in the denomination of the thirty days of the month by means of substitution and syncretistic associations with Hindu divinities (Panaino 1996b).

Further reading

A basic and general description of the calendrical systems and their complexity can be found in the fundamental works of Ginzel (1906, 1911, 1914) which need some integration with newer material because of their age. In the case of the different Mesopotamian and Egyptian calendars, which are most relevant for an understanding of the Old Persian and Mazdean calendrical systems (and their prototypes and variants) it is worth reading the fundamental contributions of Neugebauer, Parker, Dupuyt, Pingree, and Hunger listed in the references list. With regard to the Iranian area, a detailed history of the exact sciences is still lacking, but the astronomical and astrological subjects have been covered in contributions by Blois, Henning, MacKenzie, Pingree, Panaino, Raffaelli, and others (see references). A critical collection of sources and data concerning the astronomical and astrological traditions of Iranian origin in Arabic sources has been published by Sezgin (1978, 1979), to which one may add many contributions by Kennedy, Kunitzsch (1975, 1993), Pingree, Burnett, and others. Calendrical problems have been the subject of a tremendous number of studies, beginning in the seventeenth century with Josephus J. Scaligerus (Scaliger). General articles like those by Hartner (1985), Blois (1996, 2006), and Panaino (1990b, 1999a, 2002) offer a conspectus of the history of research in these fields. In all cases, entries in the *Encyclopædia Iranica* can be very helpful. Similarly, the *Encylopedia of ancient natural scientists* (Keyser and Irby-Massie 2008) contains some articles regarding the Iranian world. It is worth noting that many important contributions have appeared not only in the "traditional" periodicals dedicated to ancient or Oriental studies, but also in journals dedicated to the history of science, in particular astronomy and mathematics. An interdisciplinary field necessarily compels the scholar to venture into other "foreign" realms. The bibliography here should be considered a starting point for further investigations, and makes no pretention to completeness on such a large and complex subject.

References

Abdollahy, R. 1990. Calendars ii. Islamic period. *EnIr* 5: 668–74.
Abramjan, A. G. 1973. *Armjanskoe pis'mo i pis'mennost.'* Erevan: Izdatel'stvo Erevanskogo Universiteta.
Anklesaria, B. T. 1949. *Pahlavi Vendidâd.* Bombay: K. R. Cama Oriental Institute and Library.
———. 1956. *Zand-Ākāsīh.* Bombay: Published for the Rahnumae Mazdayasnan Sabha by its Honorary Secretary Dastur Framroze A. Bode.
Bailey, H. W. 1936. Handschriften aus Chotan und Tunhuang. *ZDMG* 90/3: 573–8.
———. 1982. *The culture of the Sakas in Ancient Iranian Khotan.* New York: Bibliotheca Persica 1.
Baranī, S. H. 1954–6. *Kitāb al-Qānūn al-Mas'ūdī fi'l-hay'a wa'l-nojūm,* 3 vols. Hyderabad: Osmania Oriental Publications Bureau.
Basello, G. P. 2002. Elam and Babylonia: The evidence of the calendars. In *Ideologies as intercultural phenomena,* ed. A. Panaino and G. Pettinato, 13–36. Milan/Rome: Università di Bologna and IsIAO.
———. 2006. Persia and Elam: The evidence of the calendars. The spellings of Old Persian month-names in Achaemenid Elamite. In *Proceedings of the 5th Conference of the Societas Iranologica Europæa held in Ravenna, 6–11 October 2003,* vol. 1. *Ancient & Middle Iranian Studies,* ed. A. C. D. Panaino and A. Piras, 19–38. Milan: Mimesis.
Bazin, L. 1973. Histoire et philologie turque. *Annuaire de l'École pratique des hautes études,* 4th section: 353–6.
———. 1991. *Les systemes chronologiques dans le monde turc ancien.* Budapest: Bibliotheca orientalis Hungarica 34.
Belardi, W. 1977. *Studi Mithraici e Mazdei.* Roma: Biblioteca di ricerche linguistiche e filologiche 6.
Bickerman, E. J. 1967. The "Zoroastrian" calendar. *Archív Orientální* 35: 197–207.
———. 1980. *Chronology of the ancient world,* 2nd rev. ed. Southampton: Camelot Press.
Bielmeier, R. 1992. Zur Konzeption des avestischen Kalenders. *Münchener Studien zur Sprachwissenschaft* 53: 15–74.
Birashk, A. 1992. *A comparative calendar of the Iranian, Muslim lunar, and Christian eras for three thousand years (1200 B.H.–2000 A.H./639 B.C.–2621 A.D.).* Costa Mesa: Mazda.
Blois, F. de. 1996. The Persian calendar. *Iran* 24: 39–54.
———. 2000. Ta'rikh. *EI*² 10: 260–303.
———. 2002. Ta'rikh I: Dates et ères dans le monde islamique. *EI*² 10: 277–90.
———. 2006. Lunisolar calendars in ancient Iran. In *Proceedings of the 5th Conference of the Societas Iranologica Europæa held in Ravenna, 6–11 October 2003,* vol. 1. *Ancient & Middle Iranian Studies,* ed. A. C. D. Panaino and A. Piras, 39–52. Milan: Mimesis.
Bowen, A. C. and B. R. Goldstein. 1988. Meton of Athens and astronomy in the late fifth century B.C. In *A scientific humanist: Studies in memory of Abraham Sachs,* ed. E. Leichty, M. de J. Ellis, and P. Gerardi, 39–81. Philadelphia: Occasional Publications of the Samuel Noah Kramer Fund 9.
Boyce, M. 1968. Rapithwin, Nō Rūz, and the Feast of Sade. In *Pratidānam: Indian, Iranian and Indo-European studies presented to Franciscus Bernardus Jacobus Kuiper on his Sixtieth*

Birthday, ed. J. C. Heesterman, G. H. Schokker, and V. I. Subramoniam, 201–15. The Hague: Mouton.

———. 1970. On the calendar of the Zoroastrian Feasts. *BSOAS* 33: 513–39.

———. 1983. Iranian Festivals. *CHI* 3/2: 778–91.

———. 2001a. Gāh. *EnIr* 10: 253–4.

———. 2001b. Gāhānbār. *EnIr* 10: 254–6.

Cameron, G. C. 1948. *Persepolis Treasury Tablets*. Chicago: OIP 65.

———. 1965. New tablets from the Persepolis Treasury. *JNES* 24: 167–92.

Carra de Vaux, B. 1986[1896]. *Le livre de l'avertissement et de la révision. Übersetzung des Kitāb al-Tanbīh wa'l-išrāf von al-Mas'ūdī (gest. ca. 956 n. Chr.). Nachdruck der Ausgabe Paris 1896*. ed. F. Sezgin. Frankfurt: Veröffentlichungen des Institutes für Geschichte der Arabisch-Islamischen Wissenschaften B 2.

Chavannes, É., and P Pelliot. 1911–13. Un traité manichéen retrouvé en Chine. *JA* 10th ser. 18 (1911): 191–201 and 11th ser. 1 (1913): 99–199, 261–394.

Cowley, A. E. 1923. *Aramaic Papyri of the Fifth Century B.C*. Oxford: Clarendon Press.

Darmesteter, J. 1960 [1892–3]. *Le Zend-Avesta*, 3 vols. Paris: Annales du Musée Guimet 21, 22 and 24.

Depuydt, L. 1997. *Civil calendar and lunar calendar in Ancient Egypt*. Louvain: OLA 77.

Dhabhar, B. N. 1927. *Zand i Khūrtak Avistāk*. Bombay: K. R. Cama Oriental Institute and Publishers.

———. 1963. *Translation of Zand-i Khūrtak Avistak*. Bombay: K. R. Cama Oriental Institute and Publishers.

Dresden, M. J. 1966. *Dēnkart: A Pahlavi text. Facsimile edition of the ms. B of the K.R. Cama Oriental Institute Bombay*. Wiesbaden: Harrassowitz.

Frejman, A. A. 1962. *Sogdijskie dokumenty s gory Mug. I: Opisanie, publikatsij i issledovanie dokumentov s gory Mug*. Moscow: Institut narodov Azii.

Frye, R. N. 1982. The "Aramaic" inscription on the tomb of Darius. *IrAnt* 17: 85–90.

Geldner, K. F. 1886–1889–1896. *Avesta, the Sacred Books of the Parsis*, 3 vols. Stuttgart: Kohlhammer.

Gershevitch, I. 1951. Review of Cameron 1948. *Asia Major N.S.* 2: 132–44.

Ginzel, F. K. 1906. *Handbuch der mathematischen und technischen Chronologie. Das Zeitrechnungswesen der Völker*, vol. 1, *Zeitrechnung der Babylonier, Ägypter, Mohammedaner, Perser, Inder, Südostasiaten, Chinesen, Japaner und Zentralamerikaner*. Leipzig: J. C. Hinrichs.

———. 1911. *Handbuch der mathematischen und technischen Chronologie. Das Zeitrechnungswesen der Völker*, vol. 2, *Zeitrechnung der Juden, der Naturvölker, der Römer und Griechen sowie Nachträge zum I. Bande*. Leipzig: J.C. Hinrichs.

———. 1914. *Handbuch der mathematischen und technischen Chronologie. Das Zeitrechnungswesen der Völker*, vol. 3, *Zeitrechnung der Makedonier, Kleinasier und Syrer, der Germanen und Kelten, des Mittelalters, der Byzantiner (und Russen), Armenier, Kopten, Abessinier, Zeitrechnung der Neueren Zeit, sowie Nachträge zu den drei Bänden*. Leipzig: J. C. Hinrichs.

Gippert, J. 1987. Old Armenian and Caucasian Calendar Systems. *Annual of Armenian Linguistics* 8: 63–72.

Gnoli, G. 1974. Politica religiosa e concezione della regalità sotto gli Achemenidi. In *Gururājamañjarikā. Studi in Onore di Giuseppe Tucci*, vol. 1, ed. G. Gnoli, 23–88. Naples: Istituto Universitario Orientale Seminario di Studi Asiatici Series Minor 1.

———. 1988. Babylonia ii. Babylonian influences on Iran. *EnIr* 3: 334–6.

Gray, L. H. 1904. Medieval Greek references to the Avestan calendar. In *Avesta, Pahlavi and Ancient Persian studies in honour of the late Shams-Ul-Ulama Dastur Peshotanji Behramji Sanjana*, 167–75. Strassburg/Leipzig: K. J. Trübner and Harrassowitz.

———. 1910. Calendar (Persian). In *Encyclopædia of Religion and Ethics*, vol. 3, ed. J. Hastings, 128–31. Edinburgh: T. & T. Clark.

———. 1912. Festival and Fasts (Iranian). In *Encyclopædia of Religion and Ethics*, vol. 5, ed. J. Hastings, 872–5. Edinburgh: T. & T. Clark.

Hallock, R. T. 1969. *Persepolis Fortification Tablets*. Chicago: OIP 92.

Harmatta, J. 1969. Late Bactrian inscriptions. *AAASH* 17: 297–432.

Hartner, W. 1979. The Young Avestan and Babylonian calendars and the antecedents of precession. *Journal for the History of Astronomy* 10: 1–22.

———. 1985. Old Iranian calendars. *CHI* 2: 714–91.

Hartman, S. S. 1957. La disposition de l'Avesta. *Orientalia Suecana* 5: 30–78.

Henning. W. B. 1934. Ein manichäisches Henochbuch. *Sitzungsberichte der Preussischen Akademie der Wissenschafte, phil.-hist. Kl.* 5: 27–35.

———. 1939. Zum soghdischen Kalender. *Orientalia* 8: 87–95.

———. 1942. An Astronomical Chapter of the *Bundahishn*. *JRAS*: 229–48.

———. 1945. The Manichaean Fasts. *JRAS*: 146–64.

Hinz, W. 1973. *Neue Wege im Altpersischen*. Wiesbaden: Göttinger Orientforschungen III/1.

———. 1975. *Altiranisches Sprachgut der Nebenüberlieferungen*. Wiesbaden: Göttinger Orientforschungen III/3.

Horn, S.-H., and L. H. Wood. 1954. The fifth-century Jewish calendar at Elephantine. *JNES* 13: 1–20.

Hunger, H. 1976–80. Kalender. *RlA* 5: 297–303.

———. 1997. *Astrology and other predictions in Mesopotamia: Mesopotamian Astronomy in the Achaemenid and Hellenistic Periods*. Rome: Conferenze IsIAO.

Hyde, T. 1770. *Veterum Persarum et Parthorum et Medorum religionis historia*. Oxford: Clarendon Press.

Ideler, L. 1826. *Handbuch der mathematischen und technischen Chronologie*, vol. 2. Berlin: A. Rücker.

Justi, F. 1868. *Der Bundehesh*. Leipzig: F. C. Vogel.

Kellens, J. 1998. Considérations sur l'histoire de l'Avesta. *JA* 286/2: 451–519.

Kennedy, E. S. 1964. Ramifications of the world-year concept in Islamic astronomy. In *Actes du dixième Congrès International d'Histoire des Sciences, Ithaca 26 VIII 1962–2 IX 1962*, 23–43. Paris: Hermann.

Kent, R. G. 1953. *Old Persian: Grammar, texts, lexicon*, 2nd ed. New Haven: AOS 33.

Keyser, P., and G. L. Irby-Massie. 2008. The Greek tradition and its many heirs. In *Encyclopedia of ancient natural scientists*, ed. P. Keyser and G. L. Irby-Massie, 203–4. London/New York: Routledge.

Kraeling, E. G. 1953. *The Brooklyn Museum Aramaic papyri: New documents of the fifth century B.C. from the Jewish colony at Elephantine*. New Haven: Yale University Press.

Kunitzsch, P. 1975. Über das Frühstadium der arabischen Aneignung antiken Gutes. *Saeculum* 26: 273–82.

———. 1993. The chapter of the fixed stars in Zarādusht's *Kitāb al-mawālīd*. *Zeitschrift für Geschichte der arabisch-islamischen Wissenschaften* 8: 241–9.

Lagarde, P.-A. de. 1866. *Gesammelte Abhandlungen*. Leipzig: Brockhaus.

Lentz, W., and W. Schlosser. 1969. Persepolis: Ein Beitrag zur Funktionsbestimmung. In *XVII Deutscher Orientalistentag vom 21. bis 27. Juli 1968. Vorträge*, ed. Wolfgang Voigt, 957–83. Wiesbaden: *ZDMG* Supplement 1/3.

Lewy, H. 1941. Le calendrier perse. *Or* 10/1–2: 1–64.
Lloyd, G. E. R. 2002. *The ambitions of curiosity: Understanding the world in Ancient Greece and China*. Cambridge: Cambridge University Press.
MacKenzie, D. N. 1964. Zoroastrian astrology in the *Bundahišn*. *BSOAS* 27/3: 511–29.
Madan, M. D. 1911. *The complete text of the Pahlavi Dinkard*, vols. 1 (Books 3–4) and 2 (Books 6–9). Bombay: Society for the Promotion of Researches into the Zoroastrian Religion.
Markwart, J. (= Marquart). 1905. *Untersuchungen zur Geschichte von Ērān*. Leipzig: *Philologus* Supplement 10/2.
———. 1930. Das Naurōz, seine Geschichte und seine Bedeutung. In *Dr. Modi Memorial Volume: Papers on Indo-Iranian and other subjects*, ed. Dr. Modi Memorial Volume Editorial Board, 721–3. Bombay: Fort Printing Press.
Marshak, B. I. 1992. The historico-cultural significance of the Sogdian calendar. *Iran* 30: 145–54.
Menasce, J. de. 1973. *Le troisième livre du Dēnkart*. Paris: Klincksieck.
Müller, F. W. K. 1907. Die "persischen" Kalenderausdrücke im chinesischen Tripiṭaka. *Sitzungsberichte der Königlich Preussischen Akademie der Wissenschaften* 1907/1: 458–65.
Neugebauer, O. 1938. Die Bedeutungslosigkeit der "Sothisperiode" für die älteste ägyptische Chronologie. *Acta Orientalia* 17: 169–95.
———. 1969. *The exact sciences in antiquity*, 2nd ed. New York: Dover.
———. 1975. *A history of ancient mathematical astronomy*. 3 vols. New York/Berlin: Springer.
———. 1983. *Astronomy and history: Selected essays*. New York/London: Springer.
Nyberg, H. S. 1931. Questions de de cosmogonie et cosmologie mazdéennes. *JA*: 1/134, 193–244.
———. 1934. *Texte zum mazdayanischen Kalender*. Uppsala: Uppsala Universitets Årsskrift.
———. 1938. *Die Religionen des alten Iran*. Leipzig: Mitteilungen der Vorderasiatischen-Ægyptischen Gesellschaft 43.
Oppenheim, A. L. 1985. The Babylonian evidence of Achaemenian rule in Mesopotamia. *CHI* 2: 529–87.
Pakzad, F. 2005. *Bundahišn: Zoroastrische Kosmogonie und Kosmologie*. Tehran: Centre for the Great Islamic Encyclopaedia Ancient Iranian Studies Series.
Panaino, A. 1990a. *Tištrya. Part I. The Avestan Hymn to Sirius*. Rome: SOR 68/1.
———. 1990b. Calendars. i. Pre-Islamic calendars. *EnIr* 4: 658–68.
———. 1990c. Calendars. iv. Other modern calendars. *EnIr* 4: 675–7.
———. 1995a. *Tištrya. Part II. The Iranian Myth of the star Sirius*. Rome: SOR 68/2.
———. 1995b. Uranographia Iranica I. The Three Heavens in the Zoroastrian tradition and the Mesopotamian background. In *Au carrefour des religions. Mélanges offerts à Philippe Gignoux*, ed. R. Gyselen, 205–25. Bures-sur-Yvette: RO 7.
———. 1996a. The Year of the Maga Brāhmaṇas. In *La Persia e l'Asia Centrale. Da Alessandro al X secolo*, 569–87. Rome: Accademia Nazionale dei Lincei.
———. 1996b. Saturn, the lord of the seventh millennium. *EW* 46/3–4: 235–50 (with a contribution by D. Pingree).
———. 1998. *Tessere il cielo. Considerazioni sulle Tavole astronomiche, gli Oroscopi e la Dottrina dei Legamenti tra Induismo, Zoroastrismo e Mandeismo*. Rome: SOR 79.
———. 1999a. G. Schiaparelli e la storia dei più antichi sistemi calendariali iranici. In *Giovanni Schiaparelli: Storico della astronomia e uomo di cultura*, ed. A. Panaino and G. Pellegrini, 99–148. Milan: Mimesis.
———. 1999b. Le développement de l'uranographie iranienne. *Annuaire EPHE, Section sciences religieuses* 106: 211–16.
———. 2000. The Mesopotamian heritage of Achaemenian kingship. In *The heirs of Assyria*, ed. S. Aro and R. M. Whiting, 35–49. Helsinki: Melammu Symposia 1.

———. 2002. Quelques réflexions sur le calendrier zoroastrien. In *Iran. Questions at Connaissances. Quatrième Conférence européenne d'Études Iraniennes. Paris, 6–10 septembre 1999*, vol. 1, *La période ancienne*, ed. P. Huyse, 221–32. Paris: Cahiers de StIr 25.

———. 2005. Yt. 8, 8: stārō kərəmā? "Stelle infuocate" o "Stelle-verme"? In *Indogermanica: Festschrift Gert Klingenschmidt*, ed. G. Schweiger, 455–63. Taimering: Schweiger VWT-Verlag.

———. 2009a. Sasanian astronomy and astrology in the contribution of David Pingree. In *Kaid: Studies in history of mathematics, astronomy and astrology in memory of David Pingree*, ed. Gh. Gnoli and A. Panaino, 71–99. Rome: SOR 102.

———. 2009b. Zodiac. *EnIr* online edition.

———. 2010a. The astronomical conference of the year 556 and the Politics of Xusraw Anōšag-ruwān. In *Commutatio et contentio. Studies in the Late Roman, Sasanian, and Early Islamic Near East in memory of Zeev Rubin*, ed. by H. Börm and J. Wiesehöfer, 293–306. Düsseldorf: Wellem Verlag.

———. 2010b. Nuove considerazioni sul Calendario Cappadoce. Persistenze e adattamenti dell'eredità achemenide nella storia di un piccolo regno tra mondo macedone, seleucide, attalide, partico e romano. *Electrum* 18: 158–73.

Parker, R. A., and W. H. Dubberstein. 1956. *Babylonian chronology 628 B.C.–A.D. 75*. Providence: Brown University Press.

Pingree, D. 1963. Astronomy and astrology in India and Iran. *Isis* 54/2: 229–46.

———. 1965. The Persian "observation" of the solar apogee in ca. A.D. 450. *JNES* 24/4: 334–6.

———. 1973. The Greek influence on early Islamic mathematical astronomy. *JAOS* 93/1: 32–43.

———. 1989. Classical and Byzantine astrology in Sassanian Persia. *DOP* 43: 227–39.

———. 1997. *From astral omens to astrology: From Babylon to Bīkāner*. Rome: SOR 78.

Poebel, A. 1938a. The names and the order of the Old Persian and Elamite months during the Achaemenid period. *AJSL* 55/2: 130–41.

———. 1938b. Chronology of Darius' first year of reign. *AJSL* 55/3: 142–65, 285–314.

———. 1939a. The duration of the reign of Smerdis, the Magian, and the reigns of Nebuchadnezzar III and Nebuchadnezzar IV. *AJSL* 56/2: 121–45.

———. 1939b. Critical note. The king of the Persepolis tablets: The nineteenth year of Artaxerxes I. *AJSL* 56/3: 301–4.

Raffaelli, E. G. 2001. *L'oroscopo del mondo: Il tema di nascita del mondo e del primo uomo secondo l'astrologia Zoroastriana*. Milan: Mimesis.

Rochberg, F. 1995. Astronomy and calendars in Ancient Mesopotamia. In *Civilizations of the Ancient Near East*, vol. 3, ed. J. M. Sasson, J. Baines, G. Beckman, and K. S. Rubinson, 1925–40. New York: Scribner.

Roth, R. 1880. Der Kalender des Avesta und die sogenannten Gahanbār. *ZDMG* 34: 698–720.

Sachau, E. 1878. *Chronologie orientalischer Völker, al-Bīrūnī*. Leipzig: Harrassowitz.

———. 1879. *The chronology of ancient nations: An English version of the Arabic text of the Athâr-ul-Bâkiya of AlBîrûnî or "Vestiges of the Past," collected and reduced to writing by the author in A.H. 390–1, A.D. 1000*. London: W. H. Allen.

Schmitt, R. 1981. Forschungsbericht. Altpersisch-Forschung in den Siebzigerjahren. *Kratylos* 25: 1–66.

———. 1985. Zu den alten armenischer Monatsnamen. *Annual of Armenian Linguistics* 6: 91–100.

———. 1991. *The Bisitun inscriptions of Darius the Great: Old Persian text*. London: CII 1/1/1.

———. 2003. *Meno-Logium Bagistano-Persepolitanum. Studien zu den altpersischen Monatsnamen und ihren elamischen Wiedergaben*. Vienna: Sitzungsberichte der Österreichischen Akademie der Wissenschaften, phil.-hist. Kl. 705.

Sezgin, F. 1978. *Geschichte des arabischen Schrifttums. Bd. VI. Astronomie bis ca. 430 H.* Leiden: Brill.

———. 1979. *Geschichte des arabischen Schrifttums. Bd. VII. Astrologie—Meteorologie und Verwandtes bis ca. 430 H.* Leiden: Brill.

Sims-Williams, N. 1985. *The Christian Sogdian Manuscript C2.* Berlin: Akademie-Verlag.

———. 2007. *Bactrian documents from northern Afghanistan II. Letters and Buddhist texts.* London: Studies in the Khalili Collection 3 and CII 2/3.

Sims-Williams, N., and F. de Blois. 1998. The Bactrian calendar. *BAI* 10: 149–65.

Swerdlow, N. M. 1998. *The Babylonian theory of the planets.* Princeton: Princeton University Press.

Taqizadeh, S. H. 1937. *Gāh-šomārī dar Īrān-e qadīm.* Tehran.

———. 1938. *Old Iranian calendars.* London: Royal Asiatic Society.

———. 2010. *Il computo del tempo nell'Iran antico.* Rome: Il Nuovo Ramusio 2.

Tumanian, B. E. 1974. Measurement of time in ancient and mediaeval Armenia. *Journal for the History of Astronomy* 5: 91–8.

Weissbach, F. H. 1911. *Die Keilinschriften der Achämeniden.* Leipzig: Vorderasiatische Bibliothek 3.

West, E. W. 1880. *Pahlavi Texts, Part I.* Oxford: Sacred Books of the East 5.

Wiesehöfer, J. 2009. Nouruz in Persepolis? Eine Residenz, das Neujahrsfest und eine Theorie. *Electrum* 15: 12–25.

Wolff, F. 1910. *Avesta, die heiligen Bücher der Parsen übersetzt.* Strassburg: K. J. Trübner.

Wright, R. R. 1934. *The Book of instruction in the elements of the art of astrology by Abu'l-Rayhan Muḥammad ibn Aḥmad al-Bīrūnī, written in Ghaznah, 1029 A.D.* London: Luzac.

Yamamoto, K., and C. Burnett. 2000. *Abū Maʿšar on Historical Astrology: The Book of Religions and Dynasties (On the Great Conjunctions)*, 2 vols. Leiden/Boston/Cologne: Brill.

CHAPTER 51

THE ISLAMIC CONQUEST OF SASANIAN IRAN

MICHAEL G. MORONY

Introduction

There is almost no archaeological evidence for the Islamic conquest of Sasanian Iran. This is partly because of the accidents of excavation, partly because of the difficulty of distinguishing late Sasanian from early Islamic pottery, and partly because, according to the literary accounts, most places in Iran surrendered on terms, so there is unlikely to be evidence of destruction in the material record. There has also been a lack of communication in the past between the fields of ancient and Islamic archaeology in western Asia. When the top, Islamic, levels of a site have not simply been ignored, they usually occur as a tag at the end of site publications. Although the trend in recent decades has been toward more attention to and integration of Islamic archaeology, this Handbook does not have a chapter on the Islamic archaeology of Iran.

Nevertheless, in earlier archaeological publications there was a tendency to identify ceramic types as Sasanian or early Islamic and to assume that the change occurred at the moment of the Muslim conquest and was perhaps "caused" by the conquest. It is now recognized that distinctive Islamic-period pottery emerged only in the early eighth century, so it cannot be used to date the conquest except perhaps in Central Asia, which was conquered only in the early eighth century. According to Vanden Berge and Tourovets (1992: 12) it is both arbitrary and difficult to separate the Sasanian period from the following one because of the uninterrupted use of sites and buildings. Sumner and Whitcomb (1999: 317) speak of an inability to separate the Sasanian period in terms of pottery from the mid-seventh-century events associated with the rise of Islam because of the continuity of Sasanian ceramic traditions.

It is also the case that conquest archaeology as such has been subject to criticism for at least two decades. This has taken the form of minimizing the material effects of the

Sasanian conquest of the Levant in 613–14, of the Byzantine destruction of Ganzak in 624, and of the Muslim conquest of Syria–Palestine in 635–40, based on the lack of archaeological evidence (Shboul and Walmsley 1998). Magness (1992) questioned some of the archaeological evidence for destruction associated with the Sasanian conquest of Palestine, while, according to Maeir (2000: 176–7), "it is in fact difficult to explicitly pinpoint a wide body of archaeological evidence relating to the Persian conquest and to the subsequent occupation," except for coin hoards. Johns (2003: 433) found no material evidence for the presence of Islam before 690 and Walmsley reinforces the dominant opinion that both the Sasanian occupation of the Levant from 613 to 628 and the Islamic conquest left virtually no archaeological record; indeed, the Muslim conquest of Syria–Palestine is "indiscernible in the archaeological record," and extensive excavation at Baysan, Pella, Jarash, Bayt Ras, Amman, and Apamea "has failed to turn up one shred of evidence in favour of destruction to churches, houses and civic utilities" (Walmsley 2007: 47). These views are repeated by Milwright (2010), along with an appeal to conservatism to explain continuity in the ceramics of seventh-century Jordan and Palestine and why "it is only in the eighth century that significant new forms evolve in the ceramic repertoire" (Milwright 2010: 29). Stoyanov has recently revisited and thoroughly analyzed the disconnection between literary accounts of Persian destruction in Jerusalem in 614 and the general absence of any archaeological evidence for it and concluded that archaeology shows "patterns of continuous use throughout the seventh century and into the early Islamic period, without any evident major disruptions" (Stoyanov 2011: 20–1).

The case is similar with the Byzantine sack of the Adur Gushnasp fire temple of the Zoroastrians at Ganzak/Shīz (Takht-e Soleyman) in 624 during the Byzantine–Sasanian war. This site was excavated in the 1960s and 1970s and there was some evidence of destruction. Fragments of broken stucco reliefs from the wall decoration were found buried under the latest pavement of stone slabs in the second temple (Huff 2008: 5). But the fire temple was apparently restored; the fire was reinstalled and burned there into Islamic times alongside a neighboring Zoroastrian village (Naumann et al. 1975: 135, 166; Huff 2000: 108; 2008: 1). It was still functioning in the tenth century, according to Abu Dulaf (Schippmann 1971: 321), and was only destroyed in the tenth or eleventh century (Huff 1977: 786). It is worth noting that when Schnyder (Naumann et al. 1975) analyzed the ceramics and glass from Takht-e Soleyman he made the late Sasanian and early Islamic pottery a single category.

Any discussion of archaeology relative to the Muslim conquest of Iran thus needs to occur in the larger context of these trends in the discipline. In what follows, excavations at individual sites will be treated first and then regional surveys will be considered.

Individual sites

In spite of the precedent of Jerusalem, it seems logical to suppose that one might be likely to find physical evidence of conquest in places where the literary accounts speak of destruction. There are at least four candidates. We are told that at Rayy the Muslims destroyed the Sasanian city and built a new town with a *masjid* next to it for the Arab garrison. At Isfahan the Sasanian urban center at Qih was destroyed in the caliphate of 'Uthman (644–56) and an Arab garrison and *masjid* were established at Jayy. 'Abdullah ibn 'Amr ibn Kurayz, the governor of Basra (649–55) is said to have destroyed the walls of Istakhr with mangonels after it rebelled and left it in ruins. Paikand, in Central Asia, was razed by Qutayba ibn Muslim during the conquest in the early eighth century, but it was quickly rebuilt (Semenov 1998: 111).

There does not appear to have been any relevant archaeology at Isfahan, but at Rayy the Islamic site was excavated by Schmidt between 1934 and 1936. This was not a stratigraphic excavation, but Umayyad to Seljuq pottery was found in trash pits. No Sasanian material was found beneath the Islamic site (Schmidt 1935; Keall 1979). Information on the stratigraphy of the pits was collected but still remained to be analyzed in 2007 (Treptow 2007: 32). The terminal Sasanian site of Rayy nearby was never excavated, and, because of damage caused by modern urbanization, industrialization, and agriculture, both Sasanian and Islamic Rayy are now beyond recovering (Rante 2007). However, there are a pair of late Sasanian palaces at Chal Tarkhan, which would have been on the outskirts of Rayy, that apparently continued to be occupied and received some rebuilding and redecoration probably in the Umayyad period (Thompson 1976). The significance of this lies in the fact that these buildings are evidence for continuity from the late Sasanian into the early Islamic period. They appear to have been maintained with only minor changes to their material fabric.

Istakhr was excavated by Herzfeld in 1932 and 1934 and by Schmidt in 1935 and 1937. Sasanian Istakhr was laid out in a grid pattern and occupied the western part of the mound. Early Islamic Istakhr was laid out on the eastern part of the mound in a square pattern next to the older Sasanian city, but with a different orientation and overlapping part of it. Whitcomb attributes the *masjid*, with its reused Achaemenid columns, to Ziyad ibn Abihi, who was governor of Istakhr from 659 to 662. Schmidt limited his excavations in 1935 to the area of the *masjid* and large soundings in various parts of the city, with the predictable result that most of the material was Islamic and very little was Sasanian (Schmidt 1939: 119–21; Whitcomb 1979; 1985a: 22). According to Whitcomb (1979) the shift in the direction of Istakhr's growth left the Sasanian city visible and partly abandoned. It was later covered by a prosperous Abbasid-period city during the ninth and tenth centuries. In theory it ought to be possible to excavate the walls of Sasanian Istakhr to see if there is any evidence of seventh-century destruction. With regard to the hinterland of Istakhr, Whitcomb (1979) finds it difficult to see any changes introduced with the Islamic conquest, based on archaeological evidence.

Excavations at Paikand have revealed that the citadel began to be built in the fourth century and remained in use until it was abandoned in the eighth century. A burnt chamber east of the palace, possibly a treasury, which was looted following a fire, is not said to be related to the conquest. The last major building on the city wall dates from the eighth century and may have been a response to the threat of Arab attack. It was never rebuilt (Semenov 1998: 114–16). Otherwise, according to Semenov (1998: 121), "excavations have failed to bring to light any evidence for the destruction of the city in the eighth century or for a break in habitation." A stronger case for conquest destruction can be made for the fate of the seventh- to early eighth-century palace of the *ikhshids* of Samarqand that was abandoned after the Arab conquest of Samarqand in 712. The upper parts of its walls were destroyed and the remains of the rooms were filled with debris to create a platform for a new building (Fedorov 2006).

Tureng Tepe, in Gorgan, is an even better example of a site with a transitional Sasanian-Islamic period. Located 18 km northeast of the modern city of Gorgan (ancient Astarabad), occupied from the third to the fourteenth century, and conquered by Muslims in 716–17, it was excavated between 1960 and 1977. A Sasanian fort that was on this site from the third to the fifth century was reshaped in the sixth century (period VI B) and was then replaced by a Zoroastrian fire temple in the seventh and eighth centuries (period VII A/B) that was still in use at the beginning of the Islamic period (Boucharlat and Lecomte 1987). According to Boucharlat (1987a: 18–20), the two phases of period VII A and VII B are so close to each other that it is difficult to distinguish them. Period VII A/B followed period VI B very quickly, corresponded to the abandonment of the fort, and changed the nature of the site. A fire temple, house, and walls were built directly on top of the ruins of the fort with no trace of an abandonment level. This replaced the defensive function of the site with a religious purpose (Boucharlat 1987b: 51–2).

There is also the case of the Long Wall at Tammishe, built of large bricks typical of Sasanian fortifications and said to have been built by Xosrow I Anoshirvan (531–579). The building of this wall and the Gorgan Wall is now securely dated to the fifth century (Nokandeh et al. 2006: 124, 161–2; Omrani Rekavandi et al. 2010: 601). But the bricks of the Tammishe wall were not found in their original position. Signs of disturbance indicated that the fortifications had been reworked in the Islamic period. The foundation of a rounded tower was on top, with a secondary construction built of smaller bricks made in the Islamic period by cutting down the original Sasanian bricks (Bivar and Fehervari 1972). On the face of it, this only means that these changes occurred at some point after the Muslim conquest, not necessarily that they happened at the time of the conquest.

The same applies to Salles' (1941: 519) assumption that the covering of the mosaic panels on the floor of the central hall at Bishapur with a coat of mortar probably occurred following the Arab conquest. The city itself survived for five centuries after it fell to the Muslims in 637, although by the tenth century it seems to have been in decline (Salles and Ghirshman 1936).

Another example of a transitional site is Qasr-e Abu Nasr, also in Fars, where the fortress and town were excavated from January 1933 to the fall of 1934. Hauser, one of the excavators, originally thought that the fortress had been in use for a while in the Parthian period and during the entire Sasanian period and that the "absence of any objects which can be assigned to the Arab period other than a few coins seems conclusive evidence that it fell into complete decay after the Arab conquest" (Hauser 1934: 13). By the 1970s Qasr-e Abu Nasr was recognized as a true transitional site that had flourished mainly from the sixth to the eighth century because of the presence of both authentic Sasanian coins and Arab–Sasanian copper and silver coins. There were no postreform Islamic coins (Upton in Frye 1973: 25; Wilkinson 1973: xxvi). According to Upton, who was one of the original excavators, most of the clay sealings found at Qasr-e Abu Nasr came from two rooms in the fortress that had been destroyed by fire, where the floors were covered by a layer of ash from the ceiling beams (Upton in Frye 1973: 15, 19). But he does not say that this occurred at the time of the conquest.

There is no real stratigraphy at Qasr-e Abu Nasr; periodization has been based on coins and ceramic style. The ceramics from the fortress range chronologically from 100 to 800, but occupation was in discrete periods rather than continuous. A late Sasanian date for most of the buildings in the Western Area is based on ceramics with parallels to Siraf. Phases in the Islamic period are based on the architecture and include a Buyid period in the ninth and tenth centuries (Whitcomb 1985a: 41–7, 111). A settlement history based on coins posits a major expansion of the fortress during the late Sasanian period, when the occupants were relatively wealthy compared to the people of the town. According to Whitcomb "the concentration of a monetized settlement on the fortress continued with little or no interruption during the early Islamic period" (1985a: 21). There were, however, two important changes. First, the late Sasanian coins (650–750) are all silver, while the Arab-Sasanian coins are bronze or copper, perhaps reflecting a need for small change and the greater use of coins in daily transactions. Second, most of the late Sasanian coins were struck outside of Fars at places like Susa or Rayy, possibly indicating economic interaction with other parts of Iran. Following the Muslim conquest most of the coins at Qasr-e Abu Nasr were struck at other places in Fars, possibly reflecting a more provincial economic horizon (Whitcomb 1985a: 20, 24–5).

There was a different sort of transition at Siraf, a major Islamic urban commercial site on the Gulf coast of Fars that was excavated in the 1970s. A Sasanian fort was found there beneath the Islamic city. But the fort had fallen into ruin and its gate house had been eroded by some time in the eighth century before the congregational *masjid* was built over part of it and with a different orientation. It is not certain that the ruin of the fort had anything to do with the Muslim conquest of Siraf. Its outer enclosure had a long history of continuous settlement, being "occupied without a break from the Sasanian period until shortly before the construction of the mosque" near the end of the eighth century (Whitehouse 1971; 2009: 9, 12, 101).

The two most important examples of urban continuity are at Susa and Merv. Kervran (1977: 88) identifies the Sasanian–Islamic transition period at Susa as the second and third quarters of the seventh century. A hoard of over 1000 silver coins found near a house makes it possible to date the house to the end of the Sasanian period, a time of insecurity corresponding to the Arab invasion. Susa was not very important in the late Sasanian period, in the defense of the province of Ahwaz during the Arab conquest or in the early Islamic period. The Sasanian occupation on the western tells of the Apadana and the Ville Royale simply continued during the first three centuries under Islam without any sudden change in the material culture. Portable objects testify to the continuing coexistence of Zoroastrians, Christians, and Jews there. The earliest buildings of the Islamic period there were superimposed on the Sasanian remains. Following this earliest Islamic settlement a New City (Ville des Artisans) was constituted around the *masjid* in an unoccupied part of the eastern hill at the site in the second half of the seventh century. From the end of the ninth to the end of the tenth century the old quarters on the western hills were progressively abandoned, to the advantage of the settlement on the eastern hill. (Whitcomb 1985b; Kervran 1985, 1987).

In the wake of Soviet archaeology, Merv was subject to a major excavation for nine seasons from 1992 to 2000. The earliest of the settlements, the polygonal, walled Erk Kala, was established in the Achaemenid period and served as the citadel for the rectilinear Seleucid walled city of Antiochia Margiana (modern Gyaur-Kala), founded by Antiochus I (281–261 BC), from the Seleucid into the early Islamic period. The standing monuments are mainly Islamic, and early archaeological work at Erk Kala includes the plan of a Late Sasanian to Early Islamic monumental building that once occupied the summit of the citadel. This building had been removed in order to get at the underlying Achaemenid levels. The Late Sasanian period, from the sixth to the early seventh century, was seen as the last significant occupation phase over large areas of Erk Kala and Gyaur-Kala, with archaeological evidence for the presence of Buddhists, Christians, Jews, and Zoroastrians (Hermann et al. 1993). By the second season it was evident that there had been considerably greater Islamic occupation of both Erk Kala and Gyaur-Kala than had previously been thought. Excavation at an extensive mudbrick house at Erk Kala showed that it belonged to the transition from the Late Sasanian to the post-Sasanian (i.e., Arab-Sasanian) periods without any indication of a break in sequence. The final, Arab-Sasanian phase at Erk Kala may have been contemporary with the monumental structure that stood on the citadel mound (Hermann et al. 1994).

REGIONAL SURVEYS

Regional surveys are based on the collection of diagnostic potsherds from the surface of the ground, normally without excavation, in order to map settlement patterns and population density over time. Surveys are usually chronologically inclusive, ranging from the earliest prehistoric to sometimes fairly recent historic times. There is a useful list of earlier surveys in Wenke (1987: 252) and a discussion of theory in Wilkinson (2003). The questions that are usually addressed for the Late Sasanian to Early Islamic transition have to do with land-use patterns, the evidence for extensive irrigation systems, for imperial investment in the latter in the late Sasanian period (up to 651), and whether or not there was a major change in settlement patterns in early Islamic times (Abdi 1999: 38).

There have been more regional surveys in southwestern Iran, in Khuzestan and Fars, than anywhere else. In spite of, or perhaps because of, the poorly defined differentiation between Late Sasanian and Early Islamic pottery the settlement pattern of Early Islamic sites on the Susiana plain in Khuzestan is essentially the same as during the Sasanian period. The population in the early Islamic period was slightly larger (Wenke 1975–6:

137–9). Neely (1974: 27–35) presented the Sasanian and early Islamic sites, datable from about 226 to 800, in the Deh Luran plain of Khuzestan together because of the difficulty of distinguishing Sasanian from Early Islamic ceramics there, and because most of the 249 sites were occupied continuously through both periods. According to Wenke (1987: 257), population densities in the Deh Luran plain rose to about seventy-five persons per square kilometer in the Sasanian and Early Islamic periods, close to the maximum for traditional farming. Investment in underground channels (*qanats*) and drop towers occurred during both periods, but the peak of agricultural development and intensive exploitation was in the Umayyad period. However, there is no evidence of similar growth in the early Islamic period on the Izeh plain in northwestern Khuzestan, where settlements had been reoriented along a northwest-southeast axis, coinciding with the building of several Sasanian bridges across the Karun. Eqbal (1979: 116) speculates that the use of irrigation might have enabled the population to grow to a point that threatened natural resources, or that there might have been problems with nomads because campsites increased in number during Partho-Sasanian times. Wright remarks on the need for further stratified samples because of the complexity of Islamic ceramics and suggests that some Sasanian sites on the Izeh plain probably continued a few centuries into the Islamic period (1979: 124). This contrasts with the evidence for demographic growth in the Mianab plain below Shushtar, where fifty-four Sasanian sites were succeeded by seventy-four early Islamic sites (seventh to eleventh century) that were more concentrated in the northern part of the plain (Moghaddam and Miri 2003: 104–5). In the region southeast of Sushtar and east of the Karun, where there is little evidence of Sasanian occupation, there was a major expansion across the southern part of the plain in the Islamic period accompanied by the spread of *qanat* irrigation and the foundation of Askar Mukarram. Moghaddam and Miri (2007: 48–51) see this as a postconquest development and appear to assume that new sites were settled by Arabs.

A regional survey of the hinterland of Bushehr, in Fars, has been related to much larger issues by Carter et al. (2006). Settlement on the Bushehr peninsula had peaked by the late Sasanian to Early Islamic period. There were thirty-six Sasanian sites, the largest number of any period, several of which were large. The extensive spread of Sasanian pottery indicates the existence of an agricultural economy that supported urban settlements for which Bushehr was both port and entrepôt. A Sasanian town near Deh Qa'ed may have coordinated supplies to Bushehr and the redistribution of goods from the port. It was probably during the late eighth and/or early ninth centuries that a major retraction in settlement occurred across the peninsula. There was a dramatic reduction in the number of sites (nine Islamic sites from c.700 to 1000), although Carter cautions that "pottery from the earliest century of Islam cannot be readily distinguished from Sasanian, and a small number of sites of this period may be included in the Sasanian horizon" (Carter 2006: 100). There may have been a connection between the decline of Bushehr after a long period of growth and the abandonment of the town near Deh Qa'ed at the same time. The entire regional infrastructure collapsed, after which there was a major reoccupation of Tawwaj. This site had not been occupied in the Sasanian period; Tawwaj was founded after the Arab conquest. It was probably no earlier than the eighth century that settlement spread across the entire site simultaneously, and Carter suggests that a substantial proportion of the population from the abandoned Sasanian town may have moved to the new site. Although the foundation of Tawwaj and the decline of the Bushehr ports have traditionally been attributed to the Arab conquest, Carter remarks that "more recently the processes involved in the spread of Islam to Persia have been viewed in a less destructive way" and offers an alternative explanation that relates the decline of the Bushehr ports to the growth of the new port of Siraf at the same time (Carter 2006: 98).

There have been regional surveys in other parts of Iran. The growth of population and the number of sites in Sistan in the Sasanian period was followed by a growth of cities and a shift of population away from villages in the early Islamic period (Fairservis 1961). At Damghan the settlement was clustered round the area irrigated by the river in the alluvial fan during the Parthian and Sasanian periods. The late Sasanian settlement pattern involved a retraction of the central settlement and a slightly expanded settlement at the entrance to the river valley (Trinkaus 1983). The main settled area remained on the alluvial plain until the mid-seventh century, about the time of the Islamic conquest. There were two important changes during a single, long period from about the mid-seventh to the mid-eleventh century. One was reduced settlement on the alluvial fan; the other was extensive settlement on both banks of the river in the mountain valley. These changes signified a shift from lowland agricultural resources to highland resources (orchards and sheep) and the export of apples and woolens. The changes in settlement may go back to conditions associated with the Islamic conquest, but they need not have happened immediately. They could have happened gradually or rapidly at some time during those 400 years. At any rate, according to Trinkaus (1985), these changes are unlikely to have been caused by Islamic military conquest.

More recently, the conquest explanation has been revived by Alizadeh and Ur (2007) with regard to the Mughan Steppe in northwestern Iran. Their method includes the use of CORONA satellite photography, taken in the 1960s, to identify what they call a "signature landscape" of nucleated settlements associated with irrigation canals, intended to maximize agricultural production, in turn associated with urban settlement patterns and high population densities. They attribute the earliest such landscape in the Mughan Steppe to the Sasanian period (224–642) because of a series of rectangular sites surrounded by extensive settlements. This, in itself, does not prove these sites were Sasanian, and they offer no concrete evidence for dating these sites to the Sasanian period. They seem to argue by analogy based on the similarity to Sasanian settlement patterns and irrigation systems in southern Iraq and southwestern Iran. They then assert that these settlements and irrigation systems were abandoned sometime after the seventh century. They use the absence of Islamic sherds on the fortified settlements along the canals near the foothills to support the possibility "that abandonment coincided with the Islamic conquest and collapse of the Sasanian state in the mid-seventh century" (Alizadeh and Ur 2007: 154). This could just as easily mean the opposite. We have learned by now that if these really were Sasanian sites, the absence of "Islamic" sherds is more likely to mean that they survived for a while into the Islamic period. But this leaves us without an explanation for their abandonment and the chronology is sketchy. The settlement at Ultan Qalasi continued to function as an urban center into the tenth century, and a few villages may have survived during the Islamic period.

Thus, apart from widespread evidence for continuity, it is impossible to generalize about the Islamic conquest of Sasanian Iran based on the current state of the archaeological evidence. Different places had different experiences; populations increased, remained stable, or decreased. Some of the most important changes occurred decades afterward and were not directly related to the conquest itself.

FURTHER READING

For general background on the early Islamic period in Iran see Morony (1987, 2004, 2012). For the redating of the change in pottery see Morony (1995). For the situation in Sistan see also Bosworth (1968) and for an overview of the period, see Frye (1975).

REFERENCES

Abdi, K. 1999. Archaeological research in the Islamabad plain, central western Zagros Mountains: Preliminary results from the first season, summer 1998. *Iran* 37: 33–43.

Alizadeh, K., and J. A. Ur. 2007. Formation and destruction of pastoral and irrigation landscapes on the Mughan Steppe, north-western Iran. *Antiquity* 81: 148–60.

Bivar, A. D. H., and G. Fehervari. 1972. Tammisha. In *Excavations in Iran: The British contribution*, ed. P. R. S. Moorey, 18–20. Oxford: Organizing Committee of the 6th International Congress of Iranian Art and Archaeology.

Bosworth, C. E. 1968. *Sīstān under the Arabs, from the Islamic Conquest to the Rise of the Ṣaffārids (30–250/651–864)*. Rome: IsMEO.

Boucharlat, R. 1987a. Tureng Tepe, les niveaux supérieurs du grand tepe. Périods VI, VII, VIII, et IX. In *Fouilles de Tureng Tepe 1. Les périodes sassanides et islamiques*, ed. R. Boucharlat and O. Lecomte, 13–23. Paris: Editions Recherche sur les Civilisations.

———. 1987b. La périod VII A/B. In *Fouilles de Tureng Tepe 1. Les périodes sassanides et islamiques*, ed. R. Boucharlat and O. Lecomte, 51–75. Paris: Éditions Recherche sur les civilizations.

Boucharlat, R., and O. Lecomte. 1987. *Fouilles de Tureng Tepe 1. Les périodes sassanides et islamiques*. Paris: Éditions Recherche sur les Civilisations.

Carter, R. A., K. Challis, S. M. N. Priestman, and H. Tofighian. 2006. The Bushehr Hinterland: results of the first season of the Iranian-British Archaeological Survey of Bushehr Province, November–December, 2004. *Iran* 44: 63–103.

Eqbal, H. 1979. The Seleucid, Parthian, and Sasanian periods on the Izeh Plain. *AINX*: 114–23.

Fairservis, W. A., Jr. 1961. *Archaeological studies in the Seistan basin of southwestern Afghanistan and eastern Iran*. New York: Anthropological Papers of the American Museum of Natural History 48/1.

Fedorov, M. 2006. Returning to the Sogdian incense-burner of the late VII–early VIII c. AD: A portrait of Ikhshid Varkhuman? *IrAnt* 41: 221–31.

Frye, R. N. 1973. *Sasanian remains from Qasr-i Abu Nasr: Seals, sealings, and coins.* Cambridge, MA: Harvard University Press.

———. 1975. *The golden age of Persia: The Arabs in the East.* London: Weidenfeld and Nicholson.

Hauser, W. 1934. The Persian Expedition 1933–1934. The Excavations. *Bulletin of the Metropolitan Museum of Art* 29/12, section 2: 3–14.

Herrmann, G., K. Kurbansakhatov et al. 1994. The International Merv Project: Preliminary Report on the Second Season (1993). *Iran* 32: 53–75.

Herrmann, G., V. M. Masson, K. Kurbansakhatov et al. 1993. The International Merv Project: Preliminary Report on the First Season (1992). *Iran* 31: 39–62.

Huff, D. 1977. Recherches archéologiques à Takht-i Suleiman, centre religieux royal sassanide. *CRAIBL*: 774–89.

———. 2000. Takht-i Sulaiman, Tempel des sassanidischen Reichsfeuers Atur Gushnasp. In *Archäologische Entdeckungen: Die Forschungen des Deutschen Archäologischen Instituts im 20. Jahrhundert*, 103–9. Mainz: von Zabern.

———. 2008. The functional layout of the fire sanctuary at Takht-i Sulaimān. In *Current research in Sasanian archaeology, art and history*, ed. D. Kennet and P. Luft, 1–13. Oxford: Archaeopress.

Johns, J. 2003. Archaeology and the history of early Islam: The first seventy years. *JESHO* 46/3: 411–36.

Keall, E. J. 1979. The topography and architecture of mediaeval Rayy. In *Akten des VII. Internationalen Kongresses für Iranische Kunst und Archäologie, München 7.–10. September 1976*, ed. W. Kleiss, 537–44. Berlin: D. Reimer Verlag.

Kervran, M. 1977. Les niveaux islamiques du secteur oriental du tépé de l'Apadana. II. Le matériel céramique. *CDAFI* 7: 75–161.

———. 1985. Transformations de la ville de Suse et de son économie de l'époque sasanide à l'époque abbaside. *Paléorient* 11/2: 91–100.

———. 1987. Niveau I (époque islamique). In Fouilles du Chantier Ville Royale II à Suse (1975–1977). *CDAFI* 15: 53–5.

Maeir, A. M. 2000. Sassanica Varia Palaestiniensa: A Sasanian seal from T. Isaba, Israel, and other Sasanian objects from the southern Levant. *IrAnt* 34: 159–83.

Magness, J. 1992. A reexamination of the archaeological evidence for the Sasanian Persian destruction of the Tyropoeon valley. *BASOR* 287: 67–74.

Milwright, M. 2010. *An introduction to Islamic archaeology.* Edinburgh: Edinburgh University Press.

Moghaddam, A. and Miri, N. 2003. Archaeological research in the Mianab Plain of lowland Susiana, south-western Iran. *Iran* 41: 99–137.

———. 2007. Archaeological surveys in the "Eastern Corridor," south-western Iran. *Iran* 45: 23–55.

Morony, M. 1987. Arab ii. Arab conquest of Iran. *EnIr* 2: 203–10.

———. 1995. Material culture and urban identities: The evidence of pottery from the Early Islamic period. In *Identity and material culture in the Early Islamic world*, ed. I. A. Bierman, 1–48. Los Angeles: UCLA Near East Center Colloquium Series.

———. 2004, Social elites in Iraq and Iran: After the conquest. In *The Byzantine and Early Islamic Near East VI. Elites old and new in the Byzantine and Early Islamic Near East*, ed. J. Haldon and L. I. Conrad, 275–84. Princeton: Darwin Press.

———. 2012. Iran in the Early Islamic period. In *The Oxford handbook of Iranian history*, ed. T. Daryaee, 208–26. New York: Oxford University Press.

Naumann, R., D. Huff, and R. Schnyder. 1975. Takht-i Suleiman: Bericht über die Ausgrabungen 1965–1973. *AA* 1975: 109–204.

Neely, J. A. 1974. Sasanian and early Islamic water-control and irrigation systems on the Deh Luran Plain, Iran. In *Irrigation's impact on society*, ed. T. E. Downing and M. Gibson, 21–42. Tucson: Anthropological Papers of the University of Arizona 25.

Nokandeh, J., E. W. Sauer, H. O. Rekavandi, T. J. Wilkinson, G. A. Abbasi, J.-L. Schwenninger, M. Mahmoudi. 2006. Linear barriers of northern Iran: The great wall of Gorgan and the wall of Tammishe. *Iran* 45: 121–73.

Omrani Rekavandi, H., E. W. Sauer, J. Nokandeh, and T. J. Wilkinson. 2010. At the frontiers of the Sasanian Empire: The Gorgan and Tammishe walls in northern Iran. In *Proceedings of the 6th International Congress on the Archaeology of the Ancient Near East, May, 5th–10th 2008, "Sapienza": Università di Roma*, vol. 2, ed. P. Matthiae, F. Pinnock, L. Nigro, and N. Marchetti, 599–611. Wiesbaden: Harrassowitz.

Rante, R. 2007. The topography of Rayy during the early Islamic period. *Iran* 45: 161–80.

Salles, G. 1941. Les fouilles de Chapour. *CRAIBL*: 507–22.

Salles, G., and R. Ghirshman. 1936. Chapour, rapport préliminaire de la première campagne de fouilles (automne 1935–printemps 1936). *Revue des Arts Asiatiques* 10: 117–22.

Schippmann, K. 1971. *Die iranischen Feuerheiligtümer*. Berlin/New York: De Gruyter.

Schmidt, E. 1935. Excavations at Rayy. *Ars Islamica* 2: 139–41.

———. 1939. *The Treasury of Persepolis and other discoveries in the homeland of the Achaemenians*. Chicago: OIC 21.

Semenov, G. L. 1998. Excavations at Paikend. In *The art and archaeology of Ancient Persia: New light on the Parthian and Sasanian Empires*, ed. V. S. Curtis, R. Hillenbrand, and J. M. Rogers, 111–21. London: I. B. Tauris.

Shboul, A. M. H., and A. G. Walmsley. 1998. Identity and self-image in Syria-Palestine in the transition from Byzantine to Early Islamic rule: Christians and Muslims. In *Identities in the Eastern Mediterranean in Antiquity*, ed. G. Clarke and D. Harrison, 255–87. Sydney: Meditarch 11.

Stoyanov, Y. 2011. *Defenders and enemies of the True Cross: The Sasanian conquest of Jerusalem in 614 and Byzantine ideology of anti-Persian warfare*. Vienna: Sitzungsberichte der Österreichischen Akad. d. Wiss., phil.-hist. Kl. 819.

Sumner, W. M., and D. S. Whitcomb. 1999. Islamic settlement and chronology in Fars: An archaeological perspective. *IrAnt* 34: 309–24.

Thompson, D. 1976. *Stucco from Chal Tarkhan-Eshqabad near Rayy*. Warminster: Aris & Phillips.

Treptow, T. 2007. *Daily life ornamented: The medieval Persian city of Rayy*. Chicago: Oriental Institute Museum Publications 26.

Trinkaus, K. M. 1983. Pre-Islamic settlement and land use in Damghan. *IrAnt* 18: 119–44.

———. 1985. Settlement of highlands and lowlands in early Islamic Dāmghān. *Iran* 23: 129–40.

Vanden Berge, L., and A. Tourovets. 1992. Prospections archéologiques dans le district de Shīrwān-Chardawal (PUSHT-i KŪH, LURISTĀN). *IrAnt* 27: 1–73.

Walmsley, A. 2007. *Early Islamic Syria: An archaeological assessment*. London: Duckworth.

Wenke, R. J. 1975–6. Imperial investment and agricultural development in Parthian and Sasanian Khuzestan: 150 B.C. to A.D. 640. *Mesopotamia* 10–11: 31–221.

———. 1987. Western Iran in the Partho-Sasanian period: The imperial transformation. *AWI*: 251–81.

Whitcomb, D. S. 1979. The city of Istakhr and the Marvdasht Plain. In *Akten des VII. Internationalen Kongresses für iranische Kunst und Archäologie, München 7.–10. September 1976*, ed. W. Kleiss, 363–70. Berlin: Dietrich Reimer Verlag.

———. 1985a. *Before the roses and nightingales: Excavations at Qasr-i Abu Nasr, Old Shiraz*. New York: Metropolitan Museum of Art.

———. 1985b. Islamic archaeology at Susa. *Paléorient* 11/2: 85–90.

Whitehouse, D. 1971. Siraf: A Sasanian port. *Antiquity* 45: 262–7.

———. 2009. *Siraf: History, topography and environment*. London: British Institute of Persian Studies.

Wilkinson, C. K. 1973. *Nishapur: Pottery of the Early Islamic Period*. New York: Metropolitan Museum of Art.

Wilkinson, T. J. 2003. Archaeological surveys and long-term population trends in Upper Mesopotamia and Iran. *YBYN*: 39–51.

Wright, H. T. 1979. *Archaeological investigations in northeastern Xuzestan, 1976*. Ann Arbor: University of Michigan Museum of Anthropology Technical Report 10.

Index

Ābān 964ff.
Ābānagān 961
Abar-Basi 774
Abaršahr 910
Abbas, Shah 642
'Abd al-Malik 825
Abdanan 205
Ab–e Dez/Diz, *see* Dez River
Abkhaz 429
Abu Burda 234
Abul' Hasan Kusyar 967
Abulites 674
abzōn 805ff., 809, 932
Achaemenes 566
Achaemenid, empire 424, 503ff., 528ff.
Acheulean 33
Āçi-yādiya 553
Acropole, *see* Susa
Acta Martyrum et Sanctorum 938
Adab 415
Adad 553
Adad-nerari I 353, 401, 413, 452, 471, 548
Adamshah 408
Ādar 963
Ādarmīg-dōst 816
Ādarmīgduxt 816, 829, 830, 832
Ādhārmāh 962
Adiabene 742, 910
Ādu-kanaisha 553
ādur (fire) 837; Burzēnmihr 556; Farrōbag (Farnbag) 556; Gushnasp 556, 898ff., 976
Ādur (month) 965
Ādurbād/yagān 91; *see also* Azerbaijan
Adur-Narseh 816
Aegilops 59
Aeschylus 658
Afghanistan 423, 427, 430, 434, 497, 625, 627ff., 736, 857

Afrasiyab 944, 948
Afridun 911
Āfrīnagān ī Gāhān 959ff.
Agathangelos 841
Agathias 849
Agrab Tepe 330, 368
Ahrimen 550ff., 557ff.
Ahura Mazdā (Ahuramazda) 425, 434, 517, 547, 550ff., 552ff., 554ff., 557, 559ff., 563, 577, 586, 604, 644, 647, 677, 722, 775, 829ff., 863, 865ff., 869, 872, 903, 953ff.
Ahwaz 979; anticline 106
Aï Khanoum 627, 631, 703, 739, 785
Ain Sinu 843
Ainaira 555
Aivan, region 207; valley 380
Ajrak 628
Akaufachiyans 419
Akhur-e Rustam 705
akinakes 631
Akkadian, language 234, 263ff., 269, 272, 407ff., 412, 447, 534, 549, 647; period 207; style 209
Akra 432
Al Untash–Napirisha, *see* Choga Zanbil
alabaster 60, 312, 315
Alaçahöyük 167
Alalakh 410
Alānān Gate 910
Alashia 411
Albania 910
Alborz mountains 31, 35, 80, 183, 188, 328, 392ff., 624, 732
Alexander I Balas 773; III, of Macedon 629, 660, 671ff., 680, 718ff., 796ff., 806, 824, 827; IV 676; sarcophagus 599
Alexandria 852
Alhagi maurorum 106

Ali Kosh, phase 54, 109; *see also* Tepe Ali Kosh
Ali Tappeh 31, 185, 189
Aliabad 306; period 147, 148
Alishtar 95
Alkinoos 798
Allabria 411, 415
Almalou, Lake 26
almond 50, 52
altar, fire 581, 722, 742, 834ff., 925
Altyn-Dilyar 631
Alvand, Mt. 548
āmārgar 914
Amarna 411
Amar–Sin 221
amber 359
Amel-Marduk 278
Amestris 661
Ammianus Marcellinus 842, 847, 868
Amorite 272
amphorae, Rhodian 740, 795
Amu Darya 734
amulets 788
Amurdad 552
Anāhīd 557ff., 869, 872; *see also* Anahita
Anahita 522, 551ff., 677, 685, 693, 740, 742, 896ff., 899, 933
Ānāmaka 553
Ananias, of Širak 911
Anastasius 842, 849ff.
Anatha 848
Anau 191ff.
andarzbed 914
Andia 415
andirons 166
Andjireh 207
Andragoras 685, 767
Andronovo 428ff; Andronovo-Sintashta culture 426
An-ērān 805ff., 845, 910
Anglo-Afghan War, First 643
Angra Manyu 550, 552
Anjoman-e Āthār-e Melli 7
Anshan (Anšan) 221ff., 225, 228, 269, 276, 278, 285, 408, 416, 418ff., 431, 433, 457, 470ff., 478ff., 504, 506, 548, 566, 568ff., 572ff., 638; *see also* Tal–e Malyan
Anshanites 233, 285, 297

Antigonus Monophthalmus 676ff., 720
Antinoë 945
Antioch(ia), in-Margiana 980; in-Persis 681, 683ff., 699, 721, 797; on-the-Orontes 843, 851ff.
Antiochus I 680, 682, 797, 959; I, of Commagene 556, 733; II 682; III 678, 680, 682, 685ff., 692ff., 721ff., 725, 768, 772, 796; IV 680, 685ff., 723, 768, 773; VII 680, 686, 721, 723; son of Dryas 696; Wall of 628
Anubanini 269, 414, 575, 863
Anzan, *see* Anshan
Anzaria 450
Anzaze 773
Apadana, *see* Persepolis, Susa
Apām Napāt 552
Apame 678, 681, 772, 851
Aparytae, *see* Pargyetae
Aphrahat 847
Aphrodite 707, 740, 954
Apilkin 415
Apollo 556, 667, 677, 796, 798
Apollodotus 667
Apollon 719, 784
Apollonos 699
Appalaya 487
Appian 730
apple 528
Aq Tappeh 82, 192
Aq Tepe 909
Ar(r)ame 352
Arabestān 910
Arabia 851, 949
Arabians 419
Arabs 853, 893
Arachosia 425, 548, 623, 629, 679, 780
Arachosians 419
Arachoti/Arachotus 629
Aram(a)eans 471, 482
Aramaeograms 781
Aramaic 280, 408, 531ff.; epigraphs 532, 549, 553, 627, 648ff., 651ff., 666, 679, 684, 693, 696, 704, 723, 729, 760, 774, 776, 779ff., 788, 958ff.
Aranzešu 452
Aras river 418

Araškun 352
Arattas 630
Aravali Depe 628
Araziaš 452
Arbinas (Erbbina) 666
Arcadius 849
archer, royal 583
arches 885, 894
archives 530ff.
Ard/takhshahr, see Ardašīr I
Ardabil 163, 787
Ardakhshir, of Persis 720, 722, 724
Ardān 910
Ardašīr I 556ff., 560, 691, 700, 702, 704, 708, 728, 730, 772, 774, 777, 786, 805ff., 810, 814, 817, 824, 825, 826ff., 827, 832ff., 833, 835, 836, 837, 838, 841ff., 857, 861ff., 865ff., 869, 873ff., 892, 910ff., 964ff.; II 829, 834, 837, 848, 869ff., 875; III 829ff., 830; IV 777; V of Persis (= Ardašīr I) 772, 774, 777
Ardašīr-Xwarrah 862, 913; see also Firuzabad
Ardawān IV 704, 862, 865; see also Artabanus IV/V
Ardaxšahr II, of Armenia 560, 704
Ardāy-Wīrāz Nāmag 913
Ardwahisht (Ardwahišt) 552, 963
Ardwī Surā Anāhitā, see Anahita
Arebsun 785
Areia 435, 623, 628ff., 679, 770
Areians 628
Areimanios 551
Ares 556
Arete (Arètè) 683, 798
Arg-e Dasht B 62
Ariaramna, see Ariaramnes
Ariaramnes 549, 566, 640
Aries 965
Arin 428
Ariobarzanes 673
Arisman 35, 57, 80, 87
Aristoboulos 640
Aristos, of Salamis 641
Arjan 23, 419, 457, 462, 468, 472, 486, 505ff.
Arkavaz 208
Arkesimas 667
Ārma(n)ti-dāta 553

Ārmaiti 552
Armen, see Armenia
Armenia 328, 613, 679, 685, 771, 784, 806ff., 840, 843, 846ff., 852, 910
Armenians 420
armor 359
army 915
Aroras 630
Arrajan, see Arjan
Arrian 665ff.
Arsaces I 730ff., 766ff., 782; II 768; III 767ff.
Arsacids 690, 728ff., 766, 825
Arsakia 732
Aršāma/es (Arshama) 279, 534, 549, 566, 640, 780
Artabanus (Arsaces II?) 768; II 731, 769, 799; III 771; IV/V 690, 696, 771, 774, 777, 783
Artana 553
Artaphernes 659
Artashat (Artaxata) 784
Artaxerxes I 534, 550, 578; II 520, 527ff., 549, 551ff., 665ff., 696, 703, 893; III 517, 552, 578, 609, 639, 666, 674, 701, 724; IV 781
Artaxiads 685, 784
Artaxšir III 776
Artaxwant 553
Artemidos 699
Artemis 677, 719, 740, 742; Leucophryene 682
Artemisia 18
Arya 427, 434, 436, 626
Aryaman 430
Aryans 427ff., 567
Arzizu 414
Arzuhina 450
Asadabad 444
Ašbazana 581
Asclepiades 682
Ashgabat 782
Asia Minor 678, 920
Asios 798
Askar Mukarram 981
Aśoka 785
Āsōristān (Āsūrestān) 844, 910
Aspabara (Ašpabarra) 435, 548
Aspathines (Aspacanā) 581, 608, 662
Aspianus 681
Assur 448ff., 451, 729, 784

Assurbanipal 443, 451, 472, 481, 483ff., 576
Aššur-da'nanni 443
Assur-nadin-shumi 471
Assurnasirpal II 414, 443, 471, 570
Assyria 328, 363, 364, 442ff., 573
Assyrians 417, 419
Astana 945
Astara 392
astodan 724, 738
Astrabad, treasure 184
astragalus, bronze 796
Astragalus 54
astrology 954ff.
astronomers 964
astronomy 953ff.
Astyages 661
Aśvins 433
Atabegs 203
Atamrum 223
ataroshan 893
atashkada 894
At-Chapa 631
Athamaita 465
Athena Basileia 677, 699, 719;
  Hyppia 697
Atheno 683
atlantids 587
Atrek River 732; valley 63, 185, 192, 624ff.
Ātr-farna 553
ātrwakhsha 559
Atta-hamiti-Inshushinak 462
Atta-hušu 270
Attar-kitah 276
Auramazda, *see* Ahura Mazda
Aurelius Victor 845
Aurignacian 39, 45
aurochs 51, 54, 59, 61, 62, 65
autokrator 782
Avars 852, 924
Avesta 430, 433, 547ff., 563, 742, 807ff., 880, 903, 935, 953, 955, 959ff.
Avestan 423, 425, 427, 429, 434, 549, 638, 643, 959
Avroman 729, 782
Awafi, Lake 495
Awan 219ff., 234, 266ff., 269
awestādār 913ff.

awestām 913
āyadana 556
Ayādgār ī Jāmaspīg 913
Ayapir 466, 762
āyazan 556, 893
ayvan 861, 869ff., 872ff., 882, 885, 896ff., 902;
  see also iwan
Azada 927
Azarnoush, Massoud 11, 12, 897
Azerbaijan 60, 163, 327ff., 363, 411, 741, 857, 869, 893, 896;
  Republic of 328

Baba Guri 33
Baba Mohammad 97
Babite 414
Babylon 226, 330, 411, 481, 504, 506, 555, 672ff., 729
Babylonia 410ff., 720, 735, 738
Babylonian 408
Babylonians 471
Bactria (Bactriana) 316, 425, 430, 432, 534ff., 548, 623, 627, 628, 630ff., 679, 685, 707, 733ff., 736, 739, 742, 781, 785, 866, 921, 923
Bactria–Margiana Archaeological Complex (BMAC) 196ff., 222, 311, 429, 431, 433, 436
Bactrian 423, 437
Bactrians 419, 436, 628, 678
Badawar, valley 205
Bādgīš gap 437
Badr, region 207, 210
Badra 481
Baga-farna 553
Bagastana, *see* Bisotun
Bāga-yādi 553
Baga-zushta 553
Bagh Kahreh Sarab 206
Baghan 700
Baghlān 857
bagin 893
Bahrain 411, 721, 737, 949
Bakhtiyari, mountains 35, 64, 203
Bakr Awa 443
Bakun, period 124ff.; pottery 137ff.; *see also* Tal-e Bakun

Balāsagān 910
Balkh 630, 818
Balloy, René de 6
Baluchi 423, 437
Baluchistan 313, 423, 497, 626; Pakistani 145
Bampur 9, 305ff., 308, 313ff., 316, 493; basin 134; oasis 626; River 305; valley 132, 146
Ban Chaliah 210
Bandar Abbas 305
Bandar Bushehr 124, 408, 682, 735, 783, 797
Band-e Kaisar 844
Bandiyan 787, 868, 896
Bandykhan Saj 630
Banesh, period 137ff., 147ff., 208, 283ff., 289; see also Tal-e Malyan
Bangani 432
Bangui 631
Bani Sol 208
Bani Surmah 205, 209
Bannu 432
Baradostian 31, 38, 40ff., 45
Barbalissos 844
Barbaro, Josephat 642
Bard Sir 65, 131, 133, 145, 494, 496
Bard Spid 31
Barda Balka 33
Bard-e But 698
Bard-e Neshanda 697, 730, 742
Bardiya 566, 662; see also Gaumata, Smerdis
Barlekin Tepe 394
barley 110, 138, 169
barley 49ff., 69, 534; six-row 63, 64; six-row hulled 59; six-row naked 59; two-row 64; two-row hulled (*Hordeum distichum*) 51, 54; wild (*H. spontaneum*) 52
Barm-e Delak 786
Barsa, see Parsa
barsom 702ff., 834, 865
Baryaxes 673
Bashime 221ff.
Basileus Kaunios 667
Bastam 368
Batrakataš 506
Bavanat 125
Bāxtriš 629; see also Bactria
Bayat, phase 110ff.; see also Tepe Sabz
al-Bayda' 700

Baydad 720, 722ff., 775
Bayza' 700, 708
Bazian 414
bazm 927, 934, 937
Bazrangids 777
beads 52, 317, 349
beards 831, 832
beer 535
bees 428; beeswax 428
Begram 736
Behbahan 12, 505, 773; plain 110
Behesht-e Zahra 394
Bel 695, 772
Belgian Archaeological Mission to Iran 205
Bēl-ibni 485
Bēl-iqīša 484ff.
Belt Cave 10, 30. 38, 57, 63, 181, 185, 189
bematistai 797
Benjamin, of Tudela 234
Beroea 851
Beshkent 432
Bessus (Bessos) 672, 674, 781
betyl 759ff.
bevel-rim bowls 139, 143, 150ff., 171ff., 235
Bezabde 847
Bibi Shahr Banu 945
Bidzard 698
Bikni, Mt. 443, 548
Bilalama 222, 270
al-Bīrūnī 960ff.
Bishapur (Bišābuhr) 9, 843ff., 861, 865ff., 869, 873ff., 896, 912, 978
Bisotun 4, 12, 30, 34, 35, 457, 510, 512, 522, 566ff., 573ff., 624ff., 627, 630, 639, 643, 649, 662, 684, 693, 752ff., 763, 769, 782, 797, 809, 863, 870, 956
Bit-Abdadani 444
Bit-Bagaia 450
Bit-Barua 384
Bit-Bunaki 548
Bit-Hamban 411, 417, 443ff., 446
Bit-Sagbat 444, 483
Bit-Sangibuti 444
bītu 520
bitumen 106, 113
Black Sea 850
blue, Egyptian 359, 597, 612

boar 51, 52, 54, 61, 66, 868, 948
Bode, Baron Clement Augustus de 184
Bojnurd 782
bone, pins 385; plaques 385
bookkeeping 233, 537
Bōrānduxt 816, 826ff., 829, 832, 835, 837
Borazjan (Borāzğān) 511, 531, 535, 539, 708
Bouluran 205
Bowman, Raymond A. 532
Boyce, Mary 897, 965
bracelets 60
Brāhmaṇas, Maga 968
Braidwood, Robert J. 31, 95
Bramans 558
brands 787
Britt-Tilia, Ann 605
bronze 208, 382, 824; casting 384 ; Luristan 205, 377ff.; processing 315
Bruin (Bruijn), Cornelis (Cornelius) de 4, 642
Buckingham, James S. 602
Buddhism 742, 880, 889, 895ff., 901, 980
Buddhists 558
Buff Ware, Late 331
al-Buḥturī 965
Bukan 415ff., 443, 780
Bukhara 946, 968
bullae 241ff., 784, 909ff.
Bundahišn 809, 910ff., 935, 960, 967
Buran 829
burials 52, 59, 61, 205ff., 207, 209, 219ff., 226, 311, 316ff., 339, 356, 380ff., 402, 696, 730, 737
Burna–Buriash (Burna-Buriaš) II 211, 226
Burnished Ware, Monochrome 331
Burnouf, Eugène 643
Burton–Brown, Theodore 164, 176ff., 394
Burujird 95, 203
Burushaski 433
Burusho 423
Bus Mordeh, phase 54; *see also* Ali Kosh
Bushehr, peninsula 529, 708, 981; *see also* Bandar Bushehr
butter, clarified 255
Buyids 945
Byzantium 810ff., 817, 949

Čāč 910
Cadusians 681
Čālakān 913
calendar, Armenian 961, 964; Avestan 962; Cappadocian 961; Choresmian 961, 964; Egyptian 962; Mazdean 964, 967; reform 864; Sistanic 961; Sogdian 961, 964; Zoroastrian 961ff.
calendrics 553ff., 953ff.
Callinicum 851
Calliope 681
Calmeyer, Peter 605ff.
Cambyses I 639; II 436, 511, 523, 537, 555, 566ff., 573, 650, 652, 961
camel, Bactrian 313
Cameron, George G. 531
Candida 847
capacity 253
Cappadocia 553, 840, 852, 866
Cappadocians 419ff.
Carians 420
Carmania 419, 613, 623, 679, 738
Carmanians 681
Carrhae, Battle of 770, 843ff.
Carus 845ff., 848
Caspian, Gates 418; Sea 21ff., 67, 80, 183, 188ff., 328, 396, 433, 443, 679, 684, 728, 731
Caspians 624
Cassius Dio 729, 841
casting 384; lost wax 428; *see also cire perdue*
Castor 928
cattle 49, 52, 55, 59, 63, 65, 66, 110, 138, 169, 255
Caucasian 433
Caucasus 329, 400, 417ff., 428, 430, 432, 436, 808, 817, 850, 852, 910, 943, 947, 949
cavalry 733
cemeteries 114; *see also* burials
Central Asia 627, 681, 817, 920ff., 929ff., 937, 943, 947, 949
Chagha Sefid 52, 54, 59ff., 105
Chaghar Bazar 410
Chah Hussaini 134
Chahar Boneh 62, 81
chahār-tāq (chahartaq) 560, 883, 894ff., 896ff., 898ff.

Chahbahar 737
Chaireas 798
Chakhmaq Li 35
Chal Tarkhan 977
Chalcedon, Council of 849, 852
chalcedony 317
Chalcolithic 62, 79ff., 121ff.
Chaldeans 471, 483, 485
chalipa 894
Chaman 205; B, C 211
Chandragupta Maurya 678ff.
Characene 721, 723, 734, 768ff., 775, 783; *see also* Mesene
Charax, *see* Spasinou Charax
Chardin, Jean 4, 602, 642
chariot 219, 402, 428, 432; driver 428
Charis 681
Charon, of Lampsacus 649
chasing 927, 938
Chavar 208
Chechen 428, 430
Chedor-Laomer 223
cheese 255
Chehrabad 743
Chendar 394
Cheram 738
Cheraq-Ali Tepe 396
Cherkes 428
chert 61
Cheshmeh Ali 63, 80ff., 181, 392, 403, 732
Cheshmeh Kahreh 34
Cheshmeh-e Takht-e Khan 208
Chia Sabz (Saimarreh) 97ff.
Chia Zargaran 96
Chigha Pahn 95
Chigha Sabz (Rumishgan) 205, 211, 464, 468
Childe, V. Gordon 400
China 851, 920, 929, 938, 943ff., 947, 949
chineh 50, 53, 58, 64, 65, 127, 138
Chitral 434
chlorite 66; carved 309ff.; série ancienne 309
Chogha Bonut 54, 55, 59, 105
Chogha Do Sar 110, 115
Chogha Gavaneh 272, 447
Chogha Khulaman 54
Chogha Mami 60

Chogha Mish (Čōḡā Miš) 59, 97, 105, 108, 109, 110ff., 218, 241ff., 539
Chogha Zanbil 224, 226ff., 276, 408, 459ff.
chora 913
Choresmia 623, 780
Choresmian 781
Choresmians 548, 628
chreophylax 683
Christian 968
Christianity 742
Christians 558, 788
Chronicle, Babylonian 454, 465, 483ff., 486
Churchill, Henry 5
Cilicia 767, 844
Cimmerians 418, 451
Circassian 429
cire perdue 384, 428
Čišpiš 566; *see also* Teispes
Cissians 681
clams 54
Clazomenae 666
Cleomenes 684
climate 106, 122, 181ff., 204, 285, 382, 494ff.
Clio 798
clover 59
club-rush, sea 61
coiffure 832, 923
coinage 577, 741, 766; Achaemenid 571, 574, 577, 583ff.; Arsacid 690, 733ff., 736, 751, 755, 766ff.; Byzantine 831; distributed by Alexander III 674; eastern Roman 831; Elymaean 758, 772ff.; Kushano-Sasanian 836; Persid (*fratarakā*) 691, 701, 703ff., 720, 723, 725, 775ff.; Sasanian 556, 787, 812, 814ff., 862, 874, 978
colonies 681ff.
colonization 681
color 596ff.
columned hall 453
columns, Ionic 739
combat, animal 588
Comisene 736
Commagene 556, 685
Concobar 693; *see also* Kangavar
Constantine 806ff., 846ff., 851
Constantinople 787
Constantius II 806, 847

Contenau, Georges 8, 94, 205
Coon, Carleton 10, 30, 34, 38, 185
Cophen 629
copper 85, 136, 208, 312, 613, 824, 837; arsenical 86; crucibles 86, 137, 613; processing 315; slag 311; smelting 311
core, bullet 55, 56, 59
Cosmas Indicopleustes 825
cosmology 954ff.
Coste, Pascal 5, 603
cotton 949
courts (law) 915
cow 429
Crassus 770
Crawford, Vaughn 185
Croesus 506
crown, Achaemenid 578; Sasanian 814ff., 830, 835ff.
Ctesias, of Cnidus 512, 626, 640ff., 662, 664
Ctesiphon 733, 816, 818, 824, 830, 846, 848ff., 851
Cumans 434
Cunaxa 664
cups, conical 150ff.
Cyaxares 435, 449, 451
cyma 888
Cyprians 420
Cyropaedia 658
Cyrus I 566, 639; II (the Great) 279, 415, 454, 472, 486, 498, 504, 506ff., 523, 549, 566ff., 573, 627, 630, 638, 640, 648ff., 660ff., 673ff.; Cylinder 504, 566

Da o Dokhtar 470, 706
Dadabad 204
Dâdarši 627
dādwar 915
daena 933
Dagara 414
Daghestan 436
Dāha 436
Dahan-e Ghulaman 494, 625ff.
Dahlich 204
daiva 555, 558, 563
Dalbergia sissoo 626
Dalma Tepe (Tappeh) 84, 97, 336ff.; phase 81; pottery 97

Dalta (Daltâ) 483, 548
Damascus 852
Damavand 392, 443
Damba Koh 734, 737ff.
Damerow, Peter 240
Damghan 9, 80, 185, 732, 767, 782, 982
Damin 305, 313ff.
dams 539; *see also* irrigation
dang 824
Daniel 234
Daphne 681
Dar Tanha 210
Dara 850
Darab 125, 288, 290
Darabgerd (Dārābgerd) 707, 826, 843ff., 862, 865ff., 868, 913
Dārāyān 556, 783; I 720
Dardic-Nuristani 416
Dārēn 783
Darestan 56
Darev I 776; II 776
Dārēw, *see* Dārāyān
Dargaz, *see* Darreh Gaz
Dari 434
darīg 914ff.
darīgbed 914ff.
Darius I 279, 457, 504, 512ff., 516, 518, 522, 531, 534, 537, 548ff., 551ff., 554ff., 563, 573, 582, 601, 607ff., 613, 624, 626, 629ff., 639, 643, 648, 662, 667, 684, 693ff., 705, 724, 780, 809, 865, 956, 959; II 639, 641, 867; III 607, 630, 663, 672ff., 718; of Media 770
Darreh Gaz 57, 64, 185, 192, 625
Darre-ye Bolaghi 129; *see also* Tang-e Bolaghi
Darvand A 210
Darvazeh Tepe 285, 287ff., 293
Darwand 205
Darya-e-Siah River 734
Dasht-e Kavir 79, 304, 451
Dasht-e Lut 121, 304
Dasht-e Rostam 35, 42, 45
Dasht-i Qala 631
Dashtiari 497
Daskyleion 534, 579, 582
Dastagerd 852
Dastova 696

Datames 767
dates 528
Datis 659
Datong 937
dātwar 914
Daulier-Deslandes, André 602
dāy 962
decimal, system 254
decipherment 4, 640
deer 868; fallow 51; red 51, 61
deh 912ff., 915
Deh Hosein 206, 208
Deh Kheir Tepe 63
Deh Luran 54, 59, 60, 97, 105, 107, 109ff., 114, 203, 217, 220, 981
Deh Qa'ed 981
Deh-e Now 227, 276
Dehistan 624
dehqān 914ff.
Della Valle, Pietro 4, 642
Demetrius I 677, 685; II 680, 686, 721, 723, 768, 773
Demodamas 679
demons 954
Demosthenes 665
dēnār 824
Denavar 694
Dēnkard 559, 809, 913, 963
denominations, coin 825ff.; *see also* drachm, hemidrachm, tetradrachm
denticulates 41
deportation 448, 538, 938
Der 471, 481ff.
Deshayes, Jean 9, 185
Dexendrusi 630
Deylaman 396, 398
Dez River 106, 203, 227, 377
Dezful 203ff., 377; anticline 106
diadem 768, 832, 863, 875, 923, 925; *see also* tiara
Diadochs 676
dialects 408
diaries, Babylonian astronomical 769
Dieulafoy, Jane 6; Marcel-Auguste 6, 234
dinar 825, 826ff., 831
Dinkha Tepe 330ff., 335ff., 339ff., 348ff., 352, 356, 361, 367

Diocletian 806, 846ff.
Diodorus Siculus 641, 663ff., 672
Diodotus 685
Dionysus 694, 740; imagery 933ff.
Dios Megistou 699
Dioscuri (Dioskuroi) 433, 928
dispersals, Neolithic 67
divination 954
diviners 954
Diyala River 207, 272, 410, 443
Djeitun 63; Culture 189
DNA, ancient 66, 69, 426
dog 61
Dokkan-e Dawud 703
dolmens 402
dome 885, 894
Dorudzan 140
Do-Tolan 9
drachm 82, 734, 766, 768, 771, 817, 824ff., 835, 836, 892
drahm 824
Drangiana 418, 548, 623, 625, 629, 796
Drangianians 419
driyōšān-jādaggōw ud dādwar 914
Druvā 553, 559
Druwāspā 553
Dryas 696, 798
dualism 550ff., 561
Duga 415
Dulan 945
Dum Gar Parchineh 114
Dum'avize 205, 211
Dum-e Mil 707
Dunhuang 945, 947
Dura Europos 784, 786, 843ff., 847, 945
Dur-Aššur 443
Dur-Papsukkal 471, 481
Durrah-i Bust 498
Dūr-Šarrukin 435, 445ff.
Dur-Untash (Dūr-Untaš) 276, 408
Dvin 909
dyes 949
dynastic cult, Seleucid 683

Early Transcaucasian Culture (ETC) 164ff., 206ff.
earthquakes 25, 296

Eastern Corridor, Khuzestan 111
Ebarat (Ebarti) 222, 224, 270; II 270ff.
Ecbatana 444, 504, 529, 531, 572ff., 600, 673, 681, 685ff., 693, 732, 736, 741, 769ff., 771ff., 824
ed-Dur 737
Edessa 759, 761, 784, 844, 849, 851
Egigi 265
Egypt 518, 534, 569, 574, 577, 611, 661ff., 672, 722, 780, 787, 852, 943, 947, 961
Egyptian 411, 652
Egyptians 419, 448
ēhrbed 558
einkorn, *see* wheat
Ekikuanna 225, 270
El'ken 624
Elam 6, 220ff., 234, 265, 418ff., 457ff., 478, 483, 506, 548, 573, 695ff., 772
Elamite 218, 233ff., 273ff., 277, 279ff., 408ff., 419, 431, 530ff., 549ff., 553, 639, 644ff., 649, 651ff.; linear 219, 236ff., 257ff., 267
Elamites 264, 407, 433, 480, 486
Elenzaš 450
Elephantine 780, 958
elephants 678, 889
Ellipi 384, 411, 416, 471, 483, 548
Elul-dan 265
Elymaean 781
Elymais 681ff., 684ff., 690, 698, 721, 723, 730, 732, 734ff., 738ff., 742, 756ff., 763, 768ff., 772ff., 775, 783
Emir Grey ware 306, 308, 315, 317
emmer, *see* wheat
Emshi Tepe 736
Emuq-Aššur 450
encounter, heroic 587
engraving 927
environment 18ff.
Eoritae 630
epact 963, 967
epagomenæ 959, 96ff., 967
Ephesus, Council of 849
Ephorus 665
Epipaleolithic 34, 38, 53
Epirmupi 265
epistatēs 683
equids 63, 255

equinox, vernal 958, 964
era, Seleucid 771
Ēraĵ 807
Ērānšahr 807, 809, 911
Ērān-Spāhbed 911
Erbbina, *see* Arbinas
Erbedestan 902
Eridu 111
Ēriz 807
Erk Kala 628, 980
Eros 888
Erridu-pizir 414
Ertana Fraverti 553
Erythraean Sea 679
Esarhaddon 414, 448, 451, 453, 471, 484
Esfahān, *see* Isfahan
Esfendārmod 967
Eshkaft-e Gavi 41
Eshkaft-e Ghad-e Barm-e Shur Cave 34ff., 40
Eshkevar 396
Eshnunna (Ešnunna) 222ff., 270, 274, 409; *see also* Tell Asmar
Esmailabad 403
Ešpum 265
Esther 601
Etana 272
ethics 561
ethnicity 425
ethnogenesis 567
euergetism 683
Eumenes, of Cardia 676, 719, 797
Evagrius 842
Evetts, Basil Thomas Alfred 366
ewer 931ff.
Exilarch 808
Eyvan-e Karkha 12

Fahliyan 42, 469, 535
faience 383
Failaka 721
Fara 209
Farrōxān Šahrwarāz 811
Fars 41, 283ff., 423, 504, 535, 556, 559, 638ff., 691, 718ff., 742, 787, 844, 856ff., 893, 896, 913, 980
Farukh, phase 113ff.; *see also* Tepe Farukhabad
Fasa 125, 287ff., 290, 707

Fasil 54
Faustus Buzandatsi 841
favissae 383
feasts 895
Ferdowsi (Firdawsī) 729, 911, 934
Fereydūn 807
Ferghana 423, 429
festivals 960
Field, Henry 30
fields 253
Figueroa, Don Garcia de Silva y 4, 642
figurines 55, 57, 59, 459; animal 52, 316; human 52, 398
filpush 885
Fin 392
Finno-Ugric 428
fire 837; sacred 558; *see also ādur*
firewood 895
Firuzabad 125, 707, 787, 862, 869, 873ff., 894, 896, 898; *see also* Ardašīr-Xwarrah
fish 54
Flandin, Eugène 5, 603
flax 110
flint 61
Flower, Samuel 642
flowers 922, 925
foragers 68
forgeries, Sasanian 921
fortifications 345, 539, 736, 844ff., 898; Urartian 368
fowl, guinea 924
fox 51, 52
Frâda 627
framādār 914ff.
fratadarā 720
fratakara 720
fratarakā 550, 556ff., 685, 691, 699, 701, 704, 708, 718, 735, 742, 775ff., 834ff.,
Frauahr 775
frawahr, symbol 830
Frawardīgān 553, 959, 961
Frawardīn 961ff.
frawashis 552ff.
Frēdōn 807ff.
frit 358, 359, 460
frontality 741
fruit 106, 528, 535; trees 529

Gaba/e 535, 773
Gabiene 676
Gachsaran, anticline 106
Gadar Çay 332
Gadatas 666ff.
Gāh 959
gahambar-khana 895
Gāhānbār 958, 960ff.
Galehdar 124, 708
Galerius 806, 840, 846
Gali Zerdak 759
Gallienus 844
Gambulu 484
Gandhara 432, 623, 626, 679, 928
Gandharians 419, 624
Gandharva 431
Ganj Dareh Tepe 50ff., 52, 57ff., 66, 93
Ganj Par 33
Ganj Tepe 394
Ganzak 852, 976
Gar Arjeneh 34, 38
Gardizi 911
Garma-pada 553
Garmi 737
garmsir 378
Garni 784
Garrod, Dorothy 30ff.
Garru 204
Gathas 425, 434, 547, 549
Gaubaruva 581; *see also* Gobryas
Gaugamela 672
Gaumata 511, 522, 555ff., 566, 627, 809; *see also* Bardiya, Smerdis
gawar 913
gazelle 51, 54, 55, 59, 62, 65, 66; winged 385
Gedrosia 623, 626, 629, 679
Gelalak 696
Gēlān, *see* Gilan
Gemelli-Carreri, Giovanni-Francesco 642
genetics 426
genre Luristan 383
Georgia 607, 785, 846, 924ff.
Geoy Tepe 164ff., 171, 176ff., 331, 335ff., 347, 353, 367
Gerd-e Hassan ʿAli 169
Gergis (Kheriga) 666
Gershevitch, Ilya 409

Gew (Gev) 754
Ghagha Shahr 879, 881
Ghaleh Gusheh 45
Ghalekuti 398, 402
Ghamari Cave 34
Ghar Huchi 34
Ghar Sefid 34
Ghar Villa 34
Ghar-e Boof 42ff.
Ghirshman, Roman ff., 94, 205, 400, 611, 692, 695
gil muhrag 909
Gilan 11, 62, 396, 425, 738
gilding 596ff., 926, 938
Giljar 171, 177
Gilviran 205, 210
Ginguhtu 411
Girairan 379
Girsu 221
Gizilbunda 411, 417
glass 358, 359
glyptic, *see* seals
goat 49ff., 52, 54, 55, 59, 61, 63, 65, 66, 110, 138, 169, 255, 295, 428, 538
goblet, Elamite 459ff.
Gobryas 581, 608
Godard, André 7
Godin Tepe 95, 96, 140, 166, 172ff., 206ff., 210ff., 220, 242, 287ff., 332, 396, 451ff.
Gohar Tepe 194
gold 359, 397, 598, 606, 613, 631, 736, 824, 825, 826, 837
Golestan 187, 782, 893; *see also* Gorgan
gombad 894
Gonbad-e Qavus 188, 624
Gondophares 881, 902
Gonur Tepe 257
Gordian III 557, 843, 865; tomb of 848
Gordon, Robert 5
Gorgan 9, 63, 80, 82, 183, 185, 194, 396, 418, 425, 624, 730, 893, 978; wall 753ff., 978
Gotarzes 693, 753ff.; I 769ff.; II 754; (Geopothros) at Bisotun 782, 799
Goths 850
Gouvea, Antonio de 642
governor, military 914
Gowar-Rud 396

Grande Tranchée, *see* Susa
Granicus River 672
graves 397, 505; *see also* burials
gray ware, incised 313
Greek 280, 666, 771, 774, 781, 795ff.
Greeks 420; in Iran 796ff.; in the Persian Empire 640
Grey Ware, Early Western 328, 331; Late Western 331
griffin 468
Grotefend, Georg Friedrich 4, 643
Gudea 266
Gul Khanan Murdah 386
Gulgul 207
Gullini, Giorgio 881
Gululal-e Galbi 205, 210
Gundēshāpūr 844, 847
gund-ī-kadag-xwadāygān-framādār 914
Gungunum 222
Guran, Tepe 51
Guraz 204
Gurgān 910; *see also* Gorgan
Gur-i Dukhtar 470
gushvara 885
Gutians 414ff.
Gutium 223, 409, 412ff.
Guyum 874
gyāg 912
Gyaur-Kala 628, 980
gypsum 106, 226

Hablum 415
Habruri 413
Habuba Kabira 140, 149
Hadad 780
hadiš 520
Haft Tepe 11, 225ff., 275ff., 408; anticline 106
Haftad Pahlu 204
Haftavan Tepe 165ff., 176ff., 331ff., 356
Hajiabad 703, 708, 896ff.
Hajji Firuz Tepe 336ff.
Hajjiabad 786
Hakalan 114
Hakemi, Ali 10, 310ff., 394, 694
Hakhaimaniš 566
Halab (Aleppo) 223
Halaf 96

Haldi 415, 647, 780
Halil Rud 131, 145ff., 304ff., 308, 310
hall, columned 365
Hallock, Richard T. 531
Halluŝu 481, 487
Hallutash-Inshushinak (Hallutaš-Inšušinak) 462, 464, 481, 488ff.
halo 760; *see also* nimbus
Halule 482ff.
Hamadan 93, 96, 444, 452, 504, 529, 640, 692ff., 738, 824
Hammurab/pi 222, 223, 272, 274ff., 409, 863; law code of 228, 257
Hamrin, basin 106, 207, 380
Hamun, Lake 625, 878, 902ff.
Hanaŝiruka 444
handarz-bed 915
handaxe 33
Hanni 466, 468, 761
haoma 430, 559; *see also* hom
Haraiva 628
Harakhwatī 548
hare 51ff.
Harēw 910
Harhar 444ff., 448ff., 452
Hari Rud 628
harp 253, 467
Harsin 203, 205
Hasanlu 10, 11, 81, 165ff., 169, 178, 330ff., 398
Hassuna 61
Hatra 729, 760, 784, 842ff.
Hatran 781
Hattians 420
hearths 54, 58, 166
Hecataeus 682
Hecatompylus 681, 732, 736, 767, 769ff., 782; *see also* Shahr-e Qumis
Hedyphon River 681
heirlooms 389
Hekatomnos 666
Helbaek, Hans 109
Helios 677, 719
Heliou 699
Hellanicus 649
Hellenism 798
Hellenization 690, 739, 742ff., 900
Helmand, basin 878; River 314, 625; *see also* Hamun, Lake

hemidrachm 825, 826
Henning, Walter Bruno 704
Hephthalites 807ff., 826, 849ff.
Heptad 901
Herac/kles 694, 734, 757, 763, 784, 797; Artagnes 556; Callinicus (Kallinikos) 684, 693
Heraclea 681
Heraclitus 682
Heraclius 829, 852ff., 870, 898
Herat 437, 628, 787, 817; River 435
Herbert, Thomas 601, 642
herding 56
Hermes 556
Hermopolis 780
hero, royal 582
Herodian 842
Herodotus 425, 435, 453ff., 503, 522, 549, 561, 567, 572, 582, 600, 624ff., 628, 630, 641, 658, 660
heron 61
Herzfeld, Ernst 7, 8, 185, 205, 530, 550, 604ff., 608, 694, 699, 730, 880, 886ff., 894, 902, 977
Hesperides 757
Hestiaios 799
heterograms 781, 783
Heydarabad-e Mishkhas 384, 451
Hidalu 472, 481, 483, 485
hieroglyphs, Egyptian 533
Hieron 667, 799
Hieronymus, of Cardia 676, 678
Hincks, Edward 644
Hindestān 910; *see also* India
Hindu Kush 431, 437, 630
Hindu 968
Hinduism 895
Hindus 558
Hinduš 623
Hissar, Tepe 9
Hittite 411, 430, 645
hoard, silver 453
hoes, stone 109
Holabad 38
Holmes Expedition to Luristan 95, 206
Holocene 18ff.; optimum 66
hom/homa 927, 932
Hōm-dāta 553

Hong-/Khong-e Yar-e Alivand 698
Hong-e Azhdar (Hung/Khong-e Azhdar) 698, 762, 783
Hong-e Kamalvand (Hung/Khong-e Kamalvand) 698, 763, 783
Hong-e Nouruzi (Hung-e Nowruzi) 762, 783
Hordad (Hōrdād) 552, 913
Hormuz, Straits of 686, 721
Hormuzgan, province 131, 305, 493, 497, 625
horns, as architectural elements 50
Horomasdes 551
horse 429, 432ff., 442, 449ff.; bits 385; trappings 359, 377ff., 385
Hosayn Kuh 580, 865
hostages 449
Hoti Cave 24
Hotu Cave 10, 30, 38, 63, 181, 185, 189
Houmian 31
Houssay, Frédéric 603
Houtum Schindler, Albert 185
Howe, Bruce 31, 34
Hrōm 807
Hsuan Tsang 629
Hu'urti 409
Huban-habua 486
Huban-haltaš 481; I, II 483ff.; III 486
Huban-immena 480
Huban-kitin 468
Huban-mena II 480
Huban-menanu 481, 483
Huban-nikaš I 480ff.; II 484ff., 489
Huban-tahra 480, 487
Hubushkia 411
Huhnur(i) 408, 464, 472
Hulailan, valley 34, 40, 93, 95, 97, 205
Humadešu 511
Humban 553
Humban-Numena 226, 276, 471
Humban–shimti 222
Hundir 448
Hungarians 434
Hungary 423
Huns 429, 434, 807, 850
hunter, Sasanian royal 926
Hunters' Cave 30
hunting 51, 868, 872

Hurrian 409, 416, 645
Hurrians 416
Hurro-Urartians 416ff.
Hutelutush–Inshushinak 228
Hūzistān 910; see also Khuzestan
Hyacinthus (Hyakinthos) 684, 693, 797ff.
Hyctanis 613
hyparchy 679
Hyphasis 672
Hyrcania 425, 624, 679, 683, 728, 734, 768
Hyrcanian Ocean 624
Hyspaosines 685
Hystaspes 523, 537, 566

Iabrat 408; see also Ebarat
Ianzi-buriash 411
Ianzu 411
Ibate 415
Ibbi-Sin 221
Iberia 846, 850, 910
Ibn Abu al-Dunya 234
Ibn Balkhi 851
Ibn Hawqal 641
Ibn Kathir 234
Ibni-Adad 270
Ibranum 415
ICAR (Iranian Center for Archaeological Research) 11, 12, 13, 126, 181
ICHO (Iranian Cultural Heritage Organization) 12
iconography, Achaemenid 566ff.
Idattu 270; II 270
Iddin-Dagan 222
Idu 414
Idumaea 780
Igdi Kala 782
Igeshaush 415
Igi-halki 225ff., 276
Igihalkids 225, 276
Ikkipšaḫmat 269
Ilam 54, 207, 377
Ilišmani 265
Imazu 222
Inanna 270
incantation bowls 788
incense 895
Indabibi 486

Indada 468
Indaššu 414
India 535, 678, 920, 947, 954
Indo-Aryan 411, 416, 424, 430ff., 434
Indo-Aryans 410, 433ff., 436, 548
Indo-European 426, 431
Indo-Europeans 9
Indo-Iranian 424, 427, 431
Indo-Iranians 416, 426, 547ff., 567
Indus River 630
Inimabakesh 415
Inkishush 415
inlay 600
Inshushinak (Inšušinak) 225, 227, 267, 270, 272
Inšušinak-šar-ilani 275
intercalation 957ff., 964
Intercultural Style, *see* chlorite
interglacial 18
investiture 875
Ionia 797
Ionian Revolt 659
Ipiq-Adad I 274
Ipsus, Battle of 678
Iqlid 787
Iranian 424, 434; Prehistoric Project 95
Iranians 423ff., 548ff.
Iraq-e Ajami 893
Irarum 415
Irdabama 537
iron 329ff., 382, 613
irrigation 50, 60, 110, 295, 496, 539, 734ff., 738, 743, 799, 980ff.
Isfahan (Esfahān) 37, 531, 535, 642, 676, 977
Isfareyan 197
Ishbi-Erra 222
Ishme-Dagan 223
Ishpuini 352ff., 363, 368
Isidore, of Charax 625ff., 629, 693ff., 730
Isin 222
Islam 975ff.
Islamabad-e Gharb 272, 447
Išme-Karab 271
Isocrates 665
Ispandāramaiti 553
Ispid Kuh 204
Issus 672

Istakhr 8, 9, 703ff., 777, 912, 977
Istakhri 396
Istanbul 913
Ištar (Ishtar) 954
Ištarnandi 481, 485
ivory 630; Barberini 873
iwan 740, 943; *see also* ayvan
Izeh 217, 228, 465, 467, 471ff., 535, 761ff., 783, 981; *see also* Malamir

J Ware 96
Jacob, of Edessa 851
jade 845
Jajarm 64, 197, 392
Jamasp (Jāmāsp) 826ff., 829ff., 836ff.
Jamdat Nasr, period 140
Jam-o-Riz 35
Jamshēd 554
Japan 943, 947
Jari, phase 126
Jarrahi river 467
Jayy 977
Jaz Murian 305ff., 313ff.
Jebel Aruda 140, 240
Jebel Hamrin 106
Jerusalem 852ff., 976
jewelry 389, 831, 832
Jews 558, 980
Jeyran Tepe 84
al-Jīlī, Abu'l–Ḥasan Kūšyār bin Labbān 962ff.
Jinjun, *see* Qaleh Kali
Jiroft 433
John Malalas 842
Josephus, Flavius 730
Joshua, the Stylite 809, 842, 850
Jovian 806, 848
Judaism 742
judges 914ff.
Juglans 298
Julian, the Apostate 558, 806, 847, 869, 875
juniper 18
Jupiter 954
Justin I 850; II 811, 851
Justinian 842
Justin-Trogus 721, 729, 773

JuTAKE (Južno-Turkmenistanskoj
    arheologičeskoj kompleksnoj
    ekspedici) 627

Kaʿba-ye Zardosht 8, 557, 739, 786, 843, 846,
    910, 912, 923
Kab(b)aš 535
Kabardian 429
Kabir Kuh 93, 203ff., 377
Kabnak 225ff., 275
Kabnaskir 763
Kabul 910
kadag-xwadāy 729
Kaempfer, Engelbert 4, 602
Kāf mountains 910
Kafiri 427
Kaftari, period 283ff., 288, 292; *see also* Tal-e
    Malyan
Kahrizak 394
Kalasha 427, 434
Kalate Khan 63
Kal-e Jangal 787
Kalleh Nisar 205, 207ff., 209, 211
Kalmakarra 487, 504, 506
Kaluraz 10, 396ff., 398, 401ff.
Kamarband 10; *see also* Belt Cave
Kambarma 581
Kamboja 423, 434, 436ff.
Kamfiruz 535
Kamnaskires I 697, 773; II (Nikephoros) 763,
    773; III 773; IV 773; V 773
Kamnaskires-Orodes, *see* Orodes II
Kamnaskirids 685, 690, 698, 770, 773ff.
Kampa(n)da 279
Kampsax 205
Kamtarlan 95, 205, 209ff., 211
Kandahar 497, 627, 629ff.
kandys 629
Kangavar 164, 220, 380, 451, 693, 738, 893;
    plain 93, 95ff.
Kanishba 413
Kapnak 408; *see also* Kabnak
Kar-Adad 450
Kar(a)har 446
Kar(an)duniash 411
Karafto Cave 694, 797
Karahöyük 640

kārājī 967
Karakum 627
Kara Tepe 896
Karen, treasure 693
kāren 723
Kar-Issar 450
Karkheh River 105ff., 112, 204
Karmanā 613
Karmania 626; *see also* Carmania
Karmánioi 626
Karmir Blur 368
Kar-Nabû 450
Kārnāmag ī Ardašīr ī Pābgān 912
Kar-Nergal 444ff., 447, 452
Kar-Šarrukin 446ff., 452
Kar-Sin 450
Kar-Sin-ahhe-eriba 450
karsup 600
Kartvelian 429
Karun River 106, 981
Karvandar mountains 305
Kaš 910
Kasaoya, Lake 878
Kashafrud 33
Kashan 8, 35, 38, 62, 63, 79, 328, 392ff.
Kashgan River 204
Kashmiri 427
Kassites 226ff., 352, 380, 407, 410ff., 417, 435;
    inscriptions 212
Kaštaritu 435
katoikoi 721ff.
Kavar 700
Kawād I 805, 809, 816ff., 826ff., 830ff.,
    836ff., 837, 842, 849, 911; II 829ff., 830,
    833, 852; prince 851
kay 805ff., 807ff., 836
Kayanians 807
Kazabad 95
Kazakhstan 429, 627
Kazerun 41, 787
Kedor-Laomer 223
Kelardasht 401
Kel-e Dawud 703
Kel-i Shin 329, 353
Ker Porter, Sir Robert 5, 861ff.
Kerdīr 550, 558, 562, 786, 846ff., 861,
    910, 923

Kerman 56, 65, 132, 304ff., 311, 493, 531, 559, 613, 625ff., 893
Kermanshah 10, 34, 39, 45, 49, 93, 203, 272, 443, 446, 451, 681, 694, 782, 797, 869, 921
Ket 428
Kēwān 954
Keyaram Cave 31, 35
Khabur Ware 212, 332, 335
Khafajah 209
Khalchyan 732
Khana Mirza, plain 64
Khaneh 329
Kharg Island 737, 759, 761, 893
Khargoar-e Robat 96
Khatunban 385ff.
Khaweh 95, 97, 98
Khazars 434, 851
Khazineh, phase 110; pottery 97; *see also* Tepe Sabz
Kheriga, *see* Gergis
Khinaman 9, 310
Khirbat Minyah 898
Khorasan 64, 184, 187ff., 392, 418, 625, 782, 787, 818, 896; Road, Great 93, 329, 377, 380, 442ff., 575, 698
Khorheh 6, 694ff., 739ff., 893
Khorramabad 34, 35, 38, 93, 96, 98, 204, 207, 383
Khorrambid 125
Khorsabad 435, 573, 606, 611
Khorvin 10, 394, 398, 400, 402ff.
Khosrowshah 174
Khotan 968
Khotanese 548
Khowrabad 402
Khoy 328, 368
Khunik Cave 30
Khurab 305, 313ff.
Khuzestan 54, 105ff., 203, 217ff., 225, 283, 286, 408, 419, 478, 535, 603, 691ff., 767, 783, 817, 893, 980
khvarnah 722, 724
Khwadāy-nāmag 841
khwarrah 554; *see also* xwarrah
Khwasak 696, 772, 774
KI 553
Kibaba 445

Kidin-Hutran 505
kidinnu 409
Kidinu 225
Kidinuids 225, 275
Kikkuli 430
kilns, ceramic 84, 394
Kimash 409
Kindattu 221ff., 270
King List, Sumerian 220, 414ff.
Kirmān 910; *see also* Carmania, Karmania, Kerman
Kišešlu 450
Kišessim 444, 446, 449ff., 452
Kish 220
Kiṣirtu 414
Kisrā ben Qubād Anūširwān 962; *see also* Xosrow I
Kiyalan 204
Kizylvank 335
Kleomenes 693
klēroi 683
kline 759
Kobeh Cave 34
Kohgiluye va Boyer Ahmad 783
Konar Sandal North 305, 310; South 305, 307ff.
Kopet Dagh 183, 188, 623ff.
Kophasates 753
Kordan Rud 394
Kordlar Tepe 335ff., 347ff., 353, 367
Korea 423
korymbos 832, 833, 835
Kosha Depe 782
Kossaioi 410
Kot Diji 315
Kott 428
Krefter, Friedrich 7, 8, 605ff.
krny 767, 782
Kuban 432
Kudar-Lagar(mar) 223
kudurrus 6, 228, 274
Kuh Astan 204
Kuh Biab 204
Kuh-e Dasht 31, 205, 383
Kuh-e Garin 93, 377
Kuh-e Ghazal 204
Kuh-e Gird 204

Kuh-e Khoda 878
Kuh-e Khwaja 730, 742, 878ff., 945
Kuh–e Maleh 204
Kuh-e Paru 694
Kuh-e Pataweh 469
Kuh-e Rahmat 703
Kuh-e Sahend 174
Kuh-e Sefid 93, 377
Kuh-e Taraz 698, 763
Kuh-e Tina 698, 763
Kuh-Giluye 203
Kuhistan 624
Kuk-kirwaš 271
Kuk-našur 272
Kuk-simut 271
kukunnum 227
Kul Tarike 367
Kul-e Farah 465ff., 573, 603
Kullar, Mt. 414
Kunar Siah 896, 898
Kunji Cave 30, 34, 207
Kupal, anticline 106
Kur River Basin 41, 64, 68, 124, 126, 137ff., 283, 285, 287, 297, 699
Kura River 418
Kura-Araxes; *see also* Early Transcaucasian Culture
Kurangun 286, 469, 471, 521, 573
Kuraš, king of Parsuwa 638
Kurayz, 'Abdullah ibn 'Amr ibn 977
Kurdish 423, 437
Kurdistan 328, 352, 363, 412, 415, 417, 694, 782, 799, 893
Kurigalzu 211ff.; I 226; II 211
Kurluš 505
kurtaš 537ff.
Kurum 415
Kušānšahr 910
Kushan 429, 857; coinage 827ff.; empire 865ff.
Kushano-Sasanians 826
Kushans 733, 742, 758, 926
kust 911ff; *ī Ādurbādagān* 911; *ī Nēmrōz* 911; *ī Xwarāsān* 911
kustag 913
Kutal-e Gulgul 380ff.
Kutik-Inšušinak 267; *see also* Puzur-Inshushinak

Kutir-Lakamar 223
Kutir-Nahhunte 228, 277
Kutium, *see* Gutium
Kutlug-Tepe 631
Kuzeh Garan 95
Kyzyl Tepe 631

lacquer, Chinese 736
Ladizian 33
Laerabum 415
Lagamaru 223
Lakh Mazar 787
Lalehzar River 494ff.
Lameh Zamin 397, 402
lan 559ff.
Langsdorff, Alexander 8
Laodice 692
Laodicea (Laodikeia) 681, 683ff., 693, 797; in-Media 682; in-Persis 699
lapis lazuli 194, 315, 317, 598
Lapui, period 137ff., 284, 289; pottery 135, 138, 140; *see also* Tal-e Malyan
Larsa 222
Lassen, Christian 643
Lasulkan 402
law 561ff., 938; antiquities 7
Lazika 850ff.
Le Breton, Louis 108
lead 208, 827, 828
legends, Sasanian coin 836ff.
legumes 52, 59, 63
lentil (*Lens culinaris*) 50ff., 55, 59, 63, 110, 138
Leon 683
letters 799; Seleucid royal 796ff.
Levallois, flaking technique 35ff., 38
Libur-nirum 222
limestone 612
linen 944
lion 389, 868; sculpture 692
lion-and-bull 585, 587ff.
Livy 721
Liyan 271, 408
loanwords 408ff., 428; Akkadian 278
Loftus, William Kennett 234
logograms 781
Lolium 59
Londo, ware 737

looms 946
Laval, Lottin de 603
Louvre Museum 9, 108, 238, 240
Lovett, Beresford 879
Lullu, *see* Lullubum 432
Lullubi 269, 407, 412, 435
Lullubum 269, 409, 412ff., 432
Lur-e Buzurg 203; Kuchek 203
Luristan 49, 95, 203ff., 265, 377ff., 412, 453, 460ff., 468, 504, 735, 780; bronzes 205, 377ff.
Lurs 412
Lycia 666ff.
Lycian 666, 780ff.
Lycians 420
Lydian 780ff.
Lydians 420, 506, 538

Ma'murin 396
Ma 684
maceheads 359
Macro-Caucasian 429, 433
Madaktu 483
Mādayān ī Hazār Dādestān 911ff.
Madga 413
Maeander, valley 684
Maenad 694
Magi 558ff., 560, 881, 955
magic 788
Magnesia-on-the-Maeander 680, 682, 685, 797
maguh 914
Māh 910; *see also* Media
Mahabad 328, 353
Mahabharata 630
Maharlou, Lake 25, 296, 700
Mahidasht 93, 95, 96
Mahtoutabad 131, 146, 148, 151, 306
Maikop 167
Maka 623, 625ff.
Makdags 558
Maketa 626
Makran 305, 626
Maku 177, 328
Makurān 910; *see also* Makran
malachite 613
Malamir 107, 217, 228, 275, 465, 467, 471ff.; texts 273; *see also* Izeh

Malayer 96, 203, 446, 452
Malgium 409
mallard 61
Mamasani 65, 125ff., 137ff., 286ff., 292, 298, 706
Mančihr I 776; III 776
Mandaic 788
Manichaean 968
Manichaeans 551, 558, 785,
Manishtushu (Maništušu) 265, 297
Manjil 396
Mann(a)ea 368, 411, 415ff., 443ff.
Mann(a)eans 352ff., 363, 415ff.
manumission 798ff.
Mānushchihr 559
Manzat-Ištar 276
mar bīti 652
Mar Gurgalan Sarab 206
Mar Mattai 847
Mar Ruz 206
Mar Tarik 35
Marand 328
Marathon 659
Marduk 443, 954
Marduk-balassu-iqbi 471, 482
Margiana 197, 316, 409, 430, 623, 627ff., 734, 736, 770
Marhashi 221, 409, 431
Mari 223, 410
Marivan 329
Marlik Tepe 11, 385, 396ff., 402
marriage, diplomatic 221, 226; next-of-kin 558; tempoorary 810
Marsyas 684, 708
Martyrs, Acts of the Persian 912ff.
Marutha, Bishop of Silvan 849
Marv Dasht 8ff., 35, 65, 700
Marw 817ff., 826ff., 836, 910; *see also* Merv
marzbān 914
Mary 910
Mas'ūdī 966
Masileh Basin 392
Masjed-e Kabud 356
Masjed-e Solayman 684, 697, 730, 741
Massagetae/i 434, 627
Masson, M.E. 627
Matezziš 511

mathematics 953
Matum-niattum 222
Maurice 852
Mauryans 678
Mausolus 666
Mazamua 443, 446, 450
Mazandaran 30, 185, 187, 194, 396, 624
Mazar-e Sharif 630
Mazda/eism 547, 808
Mazdak 809
Mazdakites 809
Mazdayasnianism 547
Mazdayasnians 547, 557ff.
Mazda-yazna 553
Mazūn 910
McBurney, Charles 31
McCown, Donald E. 8, 10
mead 431
Mebaragesi (Enmebaragesi) 220
Mecquenem, Roland de 219, 235, 252, 272
Medes 328, 330, 366, 368, 400, 403, 416, 419, 423, 425, 435ff., 442ff., 449, 451, 486, 504, 506, 547ff., 681
Media 411, 417ff., 434ff., 627, 677, 679ff., 684, 686, 690ff., 694, 703, 707, 732ff., 738, 741, 767, 768ff., 795ff., 797, 799, 852, 869, 910; Atropatene 679, 694, 737, 770, 797
Median 279, 437, 638, 649
megaliths 402
Mehi 305
Mehmeh, phase 110; *see also* Tepe Sabz
Mehr War Kabud 208ff.
Mehran, plain 54, 110
Meiduk 613
Me-Kubi 222, 270
Meldgaard, Jørgen 205
Mele Hairam 742
Meluhha 409
Memphis 448
Menedemus 682
Menua 352ff., 363, 368
Mercury 961
Meriggi, Piero 240
Merodach-baladan 483
Merv 623, 628, 979ff.; *see also* Marw
Mesambria 529
Mēšān (Mēshān) 560, 910; *see also* Mesene

Mesene 556, 560, 685, 708, 732, 735, 737, 784, 844; *see also* Characene
Meshike 843
Meshkinshahr 165, 787
Mesopotamia 767, 840, 842, 844, 847, 850, 852, 920
metallurgy 81, 206; *see also* bronze, copper, gold, lead, mining, silver, tin
Metsamor-Lchashen 1–2 344
Mianab, plain 696, 981
Middle Persian 779ff., 781, 785, 836, 938
migration, Iranian 418ff., 423, 478; Neolithic 66ff.
Mihr Narseh 849
Mihr 557, 869, 875, 965
Mihragān 553, 961
Mihrān, family 811
Mihrdatkirt 782
Miles, George C. 205
milestones 796
milk 61ff., 255
milking 84
mining 613; salt 743
mints 777, 817ff.; signatures 822ff.
Mir Khair 207ff.
Mir Vali 205, 210
Mir Zakah 2 631
Mirabad, Lake 19ff., 25
Mirak 35ff.
Miri Qalat 131, 145ff., 305, 315
Mirshade 630
Mirza, Iraj 7
Mitanni 226, 411, 430, 432, 435ff.
Mitanni-Indo-Aryan 424, 432
Mithra 430, 522, 551ff., 557, 677, 829, 959; Helios 556
Mithra-dāta 553
Mithradates, at Bisotun 743
Mithradatkert 731, 767
Mithraism 869
Mithrates 753
Mithra-yazna 553
Mithridates 698, 721, 723; I 731ff., 767ff., 772; II 692ff., 728, 767, 769, 776, 799; III/IV 770; of Mesene 784
Mitridates 556
Miyandoab 328, 353

Mizhdushi 553
mogbed 914
Moghak 35
Mohammad Jaffar, phase 54, 109; *see also* Tepe Ali Kosh
Mokhrablur 175
Molali 432
al-Molk, Momtaz 7
Molon 680, 685, 702, 721
Mongolia 733
Mongols 378, 894
Monneret de Villard, Ugo 894
Monophysitism 849
Mons Victorialis 880ff., 903
monsoon 24, 495; *see also* climate
months 956ff.; *see also* calendrics
moqarnas 885
Mordvin 428
Morgan, Jean-Jacques Marie de 6, 30, 94, 204, 234, 237, 252, 272, 402
Morier, James Justinian 5
mortar 885
Mortensen, Peder 33ff., 40
mosaics 844, 934
Moses Khorenatsi 841
Moshchevaya Balka 944ff., 947
Mousterian 34ff., 37, 40
mowbed 914
Mtskheta 785, 925
mudbrick 50, 64, 83, 175
Mughan, steppe 982
Mūja 423, 434
Mūjavant, Mt. 430, 434
mulberry 528
mules 537
multilingualism 532
Mundigak 305, 314ff., 433
Münter, Friedrich 643
Murghab, plain 9
Murteza Gerd 181
Musa 696, 770
Musasir 481
Mushki, phase 126; *see also* Tal-e Mushki
Muslim, Qutayba ibn 977
Mustafavi, Muhammad Taqi 10
Mutba 204
Muža 423

Mycii 625; *see also* Maka
Mylasa 666
mythology 431

Nabopolassar 451, 472, 486
Nabû-bēl-šumāti 483, 485ff.
Nad-e Ali 497, 626
nahang 912
Najafehabad 444ff., 452
Nakhichevan 328
Nakhlak 743
Nal 314
Namazga 188, 192, 196, 315ff., 418
Nambed 773
Namri 411, 444
Nanaya 685, 742, 798
Nanna 222
Napir irshara 553
Napir-Asu 6, 227ff.
Napirisha 227
Naqarreh-Khaneh 394
naqsh 946ff.
Naqshbandi 946
Naqsh-e Rajab 562, 786, 863, 865, 868ff., 873
Naqsh-e Rustam 3, 286, 470, 472, 516ff., 523, 539, 550, 557, 560, 577ff., 580, 602, 607ff., 614, 629, 639, 673, 703ff., 724, 783, 786, 800, 841ff., 861, 863, 868, 873
Naram-Sin 6, 220, 228, 264ff., 271, 274, 278, 413; Victory Stele of 257
Narēča 535
Narezzaš 511, 523, 535; *see also* Neyriz
Narseh 550, 553, 557, 786, 805ff., 816, 833ff., 846, 869, 873; II 846, 848; king of Hind, Sagestān and Tūrestān 560
Narundi 265
Narunte 267
Naryasanga 553
Naser al-Din Shah 6, 234
Nāṣrā 558
Natanz 80
National Heritage, Society for 7
Nausud 329
Nazarabad 453
Nazarenes 558
Nebuchadnezzar (Nebuchadrezzar) I 228, 466; II 278; son of Nabonidus 555

Negahban, Ezattolah 11, 395
Nehavand 8, 96, 203, 205, 331, 446, 684, 692, 797
Nēmrōz 911
Nemrud Dağ 556, 733
Neo-Assyrian 408; empire 531; palaces 598
Neo-Babylonian, empire 531; kings and court 573
Neo-Elamite 12, 278ff., 383, 457ff., 478ff., 504ff., 508, 538, 572ff., 761
Neolithic 10, 49ff.; Pre-Pottery 54
Nergal 742
Neriglissar 278
Nestorianism 849; *see also* Monophysitism
Nestorius 849
New Year, *see* Nowruz
Neyriz, Lake 35, 912; *see also* Niriz
Nicaea, Council of 808
Nicolaus, of Damascus 662
Nidintu-Bēl 555
Niebuhr, Carsten 4, 643
niello 924, 937ff.
Nike 759, 771
Nikkur 443
nimbus 760, 810, 835, 872, 889
Nimrud 573, 611
Nimušis, Mt. 412
NIN.GAL 224
Nineveh 408, 451, 487, 573, 852; letters 465, 488ff.
Ninhursag 227; temple of, at Susa 221
dNIN.KIŠ.UNU 265
Nippur 218, 415, 784
Niqdime 414
Niqdira 414
Niriz (Nīrīz) 511, 535
Nisa 556, 729, 731, 739ff., 767, 770, 782
Nishapur 12, 188
Nisibis 843, 846, 848; treaty of 806ff.
nobility 810ff.
Nōdšīragān 910
nomadism 114, 212, 378, 470, 732ff., 743
nomads 287, 295
Nowruz 904, 927, 932, 958, 961, 965
Numenius 685, 721, 723
Nurabad-e Mamasani 469
Nuristani 424, 427, 434

Nusku 227
Nuzi 242, 410, 412ff.

oak (*Quercus* sp.) 18
obol 768
Oborzus 720, 722ff.
obsidian 55, 61
ocher 54, 61
octaëteris 957ff.
Odenathus, of Palmyra 844
Odoricus 641
offerings 559
Ōhrmazd 557ff.; I 836; II 816, 826, 831, 867, 873ff.; III 816, 965; IV 810ff., 826, 830ff., 851ff.; V 826, 830; VI 829; for the deity, *see* Ahura Mazda; prince 846, 848
Ōhrmazd-Āfrīd 913
Okbara 844
Okkanapsos 772
Old Avestan 554
Old Indian 643
Old Iranian 432, 434, 638, 652
Old Median 424
Old Persian 4, 279, 408, 419, 424, 427, 434, 437, 554, 638ff.; titulature 647; word-dividers 646
Old Syriac 768, 781
olive (*Olea* sp.) 298, 528
Olympia 611
Oman 24, 737, 910
omphalos 769, 770
onager (*Equus hemionus*) 54, 59, 65, 66, 429
Onesicritus 640ff.
Oppert, Jules 644
Opus imperfectum in Matthaeum 903
ordeal, river 410
Oribasius 847
Oriental Institute (Chicago) 8, 530, 550
Orodes 760; I 774; II 770ff., 774; III 774; IV 774; king of Khuzestan 774
Orontids 685
Orxines 673
oryx 928ff.
ošmurdīg 962
Osrhoene 784, 844
Osroes I 774
Ossete 423

Ossetes 432
ōstāndār 914
Otchounak 35
Ouseley, Sir Gore 5; Sir William 5, 861, 868
ovens 54
oxen 169
Oxus Civilization, see Bactria-Margiana Archaeological Complex
Oxus River 631; treasure 631
Ozogardana 848

Pa Sangar 38
Pa'e 486
Pābag 556ff., 560, 777
Pacorus I 771
padam 887, 889
Pahir-ishshan 226
Pahlavi 550, 561, 563, 777, 785, 788, 835; dynasty 861; Psalter script 787
Pahlaw 910
Paikand 977
Paikuli 550, 553, 786, 809
painters 600, 611
painting, wall 140, 598, 881, 886ff.
pairikā 954
Pakistan 625, 737, 787
Pakor I 776; II 776
Pakores I, see Pacorus I
Paktha 436
Pal Barik 33
paleoenvironment 17ff.; see also climate
Paleolithic 29ff.; Lower 33ff.; Middle 34ff., 37, 38; Upper 38ff.
Palestine 852
Pali 427
palmettes 584, 589
palms, date 589
Palmyra 760
Palmyrene 781, 784
Palmyrenes 737
Pamirs 423, 430, 434, 437
Panjab 432
Panjikent 896, 944
Pantauchus (Pantauchos) 684, 693, 797
Papak 925; see also Pābag
Pāradān 910

paradise (Gr. paradeisos) 509, 513, 528ff., 539, 935
Paraetacene 676
Pardameh 30
Pargyetae 630
Paric/kanians 419, 624
Parišxwār 910; see also Alborz
Parkhai II 194
Parmenion 673
Parna 436
Parnaka 780
Parni (Parnoi) 418, 731
Paropamisadae 679
Pārs 856ff., 910; see also Fars
Parsa (Pārsa) 418, 512, 528, 548, 638
Parsis 547
Parsu/wa (Paršua/s) 352, 416ff., 435, 443, 446, 471, 638
Parsumash (Parsuw/maš) 548, 638
Parsyetae, see Pargyetae
Partaw 910
Parthava 623ff., 629
Partherhang 693, 754; see also Bisotun
Partherstein 754; see also Bisotun
Parthia 418, 629, 679, 684, 844
Parthian Stations 625, 694; see also Isidore of Charax
Parthian 691, 693, 779ff., 781
Parthians 419, 556, 628, 728ff.; see also Arsacids
Parthyene 731, 734
Parysatis 673
pasāk 934
Pasargadae 4, 5, 7, 9, 12, 503, 506ff., 512ff., 528ff., 567, 569ff., 604, 614, 624, 641, 648ff., 673ff., 699, 705ff., 720, 723; inscriptions 570
Pašeru 471
Pashime 408; see also Bashime
Pashto 423, 437
Paškabur 910
pastoralism 538; nomadic 122; see also nomadism
pastoralists 56, 295
patikarā 599ff.
Patischorian 581
Patrocles 679

pavilion, Achaemenid 529, 539
Pazyryk 427ff., 631
pea 59; grass 110
pear 528
pebble tools 33, 41
Pechenegs 434
Peithon 676, 678, 680
Periplus Mare Erythraeum 736
Pērōz 807ff., 816ff., 822, 825ff., 827, 829, 830ff., 833ff., 836, 849ff., 898, 927, 964ff.
Pērōz-Šābuhr 843
persecution, of Christians 849
Persepolis 257
Persepolis 3, 4, 5, 13, 257, 409, 419, 503, 505, 511ff., 523, 559, 577ff., 631, 639, 641, 643, 673, 677, 681, 699, 701, 721, 723, 780, 787, 856ff., 865, 958; Apadana 514ff., 554, 578ff., 598ff., 610ff., 614; Central Building 579, 585; Council Hall (Tripylon) 579, 599; doorjambs 580, 604; Fortification archive 469, 513ff., 530ff., 567, 626, 630, 651; *frātadāra* temple 677; Hall of 100 Columns 599, 604, 614; Harem 580, 604; Mountain Fortification 534ff.; Palace of Darius 580; Palace of Xerxes 580; reliefs 580; stairways 580; Treasury 604; Treasury archive 534ff., 958; trilingual inscriptions 589ff.
Persian, Gulf 106, 121, 297, 304ff., 411, 423, 680ff.; coast 124; Wars 659
Persian 424
Persians 328, 400, 403, 416, 423, 436, 486, 547ff.
Persica 664ff.
Persis 418ff., 433ff., 626, 638, 673, 676, 679, 681, 691ff., 719ff., 734ff., 741, 768, 775ff., 795ff., 797, 844; see also *fratarakā*
Pesce, Luigi 5
Peshawar 910
Petra 611
Peucestas 676ff., 719ff.
Peutinger Table, see *Tabula Peutingeriana*
Philadelphos 769
Philhellene 768
Philip, II, of Macedon 671; III Arrhidaeus 676; the Arab 557, 808, 841, 843, 865
Phocas 852

Phraata 798ff.
Phraataces 770ff.
Phraates 763, 799; I 768; II 732ff.; III 770, 776; IV 770ff.
Phragmites 55
Phrygia 534, 692; Hellespontine 534
Phrygian 280, 533, 651
Phrynichus 658
Piedmont Style 207; *see also* seals, cylinder
pig (*Sus* sp.) 49, 55, 59, 61, 63, 138
pigment 59, 307, 596ff.; analysis 597; bowls 610ff.
pilgrimage 898, 903
Pilla Qaleh 398
Pindar 658
Pisdeli, phase 81, 178; *see also* Hajji Firuz Tepe, Hasanlu
pisé 83; *see also* chineh
Pish-e Kuh 95ff., 203ff., 378ff.
Pishva 396, 402
pistachio 50, 52, 59
pitiakhsh 925
Pixodaros 666
planets 954
Plantago 59
plaster 51, 886
Platanus 298
platforms, mudbrick 497ff.
Plato 665
Pliny, the Elder 730, 736
plow 169, 253
Plutarch 551, 641, 665
Poaceae 18
polis 683, 772, 796
pollen 18, 25, 296
pollution 425, 561
Pollux 928
polos 577
Polyaenus (Polyainos) 666, 721ff.
polychrome, Jamdat Nasr-related 207
polychromy 597ff.
pomegranate 528
Pompey 773
porphyry 613
portraiture, on Sasanian coinage 831ff.
Potratz, J.H. 378
poultry 535

precipitation 21
Priapatius 768; *see also* Arsaces III
Prickett, Martha E. 133
Procopius 809, 842, 848ff.
proskynesis 675
Proto-Dravidian 407
proto-Elamite 88, 145, 147, 149, 151, 218, 233ff., 266, 283, 306
proto-Elamites 194
Proto-Indo-Iranian 430
Proto-Iranian 432
Proto-Nuristani 431
protowriting 240
provinces, Sasanian 911ff.
Ptolemy, Claudius 629, 730
Pulvar, valley 510
Pumpelly, Raphael 627
Pumpokol 428
Puneh 204
purity 561, 895
purple 601
Pusht-e Kuh 95, 203ff., 220, 378ff.; Qaleh-e Abdanan 209
Puzur-Inshushinak (Puzur-Inšušinak) 219ff., 234, 258, 265ff.
Puzur-Suen 415

Qabr Nahi 209
Qadar River, valley 165
Qah-qaha 879
Qajars 861
Qal'a-ye Dokhtar 707
Qal'a-ye Kafaran 878
Qal'a-ye Now 700
Qal'a-ye Sam 878
Qal'e Bardine 367
Qal'eh Yazdegerd 730, 740
Qal'eh Zohak 740
Qala Khandan 624
Qalaichi Tepe 365ff., 443
Qalatgah 353, 368
Qaleh Bozi 35, 37
Qaleh Gusheh 38
Qaleh Ismail Agha 367
Qaleh Kali (Qalēh-ye Kalī) 469, 521, 539ff., 706
Qaleh Khan 192

Qaleh Mortezagird 393
Qaleh Rostam 64
Qaleh Tul 107
Qaleh, pottery 283ff., 288ff., 293, 298; *see also* Tal-e Malyan
qanats 26, 183, 392, 496, 734ff., 738, 743, 981; *see also* irrigation
Qara Su 204
Qara Tepe 80, 394
Qasr al-Kharanah 896
Qasr-e Abu Nasr 700, 909ff., 978ff.
Qasr-e Shirin 12, 896
Qatna 223ff.
Qazvin 11, 57, 62, 80, 83, 328, 395ff., 398, 403
Qeytariyeh 392, 394, 398ff., 400, 402ff.
Qih 977
Qindau 450
Qir-Karzin 125, 708
Qizil 944
Qobeira 494
Qolhak 392
Qoli Darvish 396, 398ff., 402ff.
Qom 396, 402ff.
Qom-Rud 392
Qomrud 80
quadripartition, of Iran 911
quarrying 612
Quetta 315
quince 528
Qumish 205
Quri Gol 33
Qutium, *see* Gutium

Rabat Tepe 367
Rad, Mahmoud 10, 394
Rafsanjan 310
rainfall 21, 49, 106, 204, 295
Ram Hormuz 107, 110, 218, 460ff., 464, 467ff., 521, 535; burials 457
rāmšahr 808, 836
rank, social 86
Raphia 680
Rashnu 552
Rask, Rasmus 643
rations 247, 529, 536ff.
Ravaz 165ff., 177

Rawlinson, George 730; Sir Henry C. 4, 204, 643
Rayy 9, 12, 181, 392ff., 403, 730, 732, 769, 857, 861, 868, 874, 945, 977ff.
reeds 55
Regiones Transtigritanae 846
reliefs, Elymaean 729, 751ff.; Palmyrene funerary 759; Parthian 751ff.; Sasanian 856ff.; stucco 886
repoussé 938
reptiles 51
Res gestae divi Saporis 800; *see also* Kaʻba-ye Zardosht, Šābuhr I
Resafe 852
Reshahr 708, 797
Reuther, Oskar 894
Rev-Ardašir 708, 847; *see also* Reshahr, Bandar Bushehr
Revolt, Satraps' 666
Revolution, Islamic 11
Reza Shah 212
Ṛgveda 430, 433, 435
Rhagae 681, 732, 736, 769; *see also* Rayy
Rhesaina 843
rhinoceros 866
Rhodogoune 640
Rhoplutae 630
Rhoxane 676
rhyta 928ff.
rikāb 937
Rizaʾiyyah, Lake 164; *see also* Urmia, Lake
roads 539
Robat 98
robes 578
rōdastāg 912
Romania 423
Romans 557
Rome 808, 840ff., 851
Romulus Augustulus 850
rosettes 589
rōstāg 912ff.
Rostam 881
Rostamian bladelets 43
Rouhani, M. Darvish 187
Rowanduz Gorge 329
Royal Ontario Museum 95
Royal Road 521

Rudbar 396
Rud-e Biyaban 2, 314, 316
Rud-e Gushk 133, 148
Rudra 431
Rufus, Quintus Curtius 672, 958
ruhu šak 224
Rūm 807
Rūmagān 851
Rumishgan 95, 97, 205, 210ff., 504
Russia 920
rustāq, see rōstāg
rye grass 61

S(h)iruktuh 271
Šābuhr I 550, 557ff., 701, 739, 786, 805, 808, 817ff., 828ff., 834, 836, 840ff., 843ff., 862, 865ff., 868ff., 873ff., 892, 896, 910, 912, 965; II 557, 806ff., 811, 825ff., 829ff., 830, 835, 836, 842, 846ff., 848, 867, 869ff., 873, 875, 892, 897, 921; III 817, 829ff., 832, 835, 848, 857, 870; cameo of 867; king of Mēšān 560; of Persis 777; statue of 866
Šābuhrduxtak 924
Sabum 409
Sabz, phase 109; pottery 97; *see also* Tepe Sabz
Sabzevar 188
sacrifice 537, 559ff., 563
Sadeghabadi 63
Šād-Šābuhr 844
Safavids 4
Sagān 910
Sagartians 625
Sagbita 444, 452; *see also* Bit-Sagbat
Sagdodonacus 723
Sagestān 910; *see also* Sakastan, Sistan
Sagzabad 11, 398ff.
Šāh Kholjī 961
šāh, see shah
Sahand, Mt. 18, 328
Šāhnāme 729, 754, 807, 911
šahr 910, 912ff.
šahrab 912, 914
šahrdār 914
šahrestan 912ff.
Šahrestānīhā ī Ērānšahr 911ff.
Šahrewar 965
Saimarreh river 93, 204; sites 34

Saka 418, 423, 425, 434, 436ff., 548, 723, 769;
    Haumavarga 430; see also Scythians
Sakasene 418
Sakastan 418, 769, 817, 828, 831
Sal/rm 807
Salamis 658
Salihabad 208
Šalla 275
Salmas 176, 328, 332, 857, 869, 873
salt 743
salt-cedar tree (konar) 107
Samarqand 978
Samarran 96
Šamaš-belu-uṣur 450
Samati 384, 487, 504
Sambulos, Mt. 693
Sami, Ali 10
samit 946
Samos 577
Sanandaj 329, 443
sanctuaries 383
Sang-e Chakhmaq 56, 63, 181, 185, 189; East
    82, 84
Sang-e Shir 692, 738
Sangtarashan 383, 386
Sankhast 197
Sanskrit 427ff., 433
Saoshyant (Saošyant) 888, 901, 903ff.
Ša-pī-bēl 484
Saqqara 780
Sar Cheshmeh 613
Sar Sarab 34
Sar(-e) Mashhad 558, 786
Sarab Bagh 211
Sarab-e Bahram 868
Sarangians 625, 630
Sarasvati 434ff.
Sarayu 435
Sardant 205, 210ff.
Sardasht 329
Sardis 780
sardsir 378
Sar-e Pol-e Zohab 269, 575, 755ff.,
    782, 863
Sargon, of Akkad 264, 661; II 368, 414, 435,
    444ff., 451, 481, 483, 548, 576, 606;
    Geography 412

Sargveshi 924
Sari 185, 188ff., 624
Sariqoli 423
Šar-kali-šarri 265
Sarm 403
Sarmatians 434, 732
Sarvestan 125, 896
Sasanians 3, 4, 556ff., 774, 803–986
Satala 806
Sātu Qala 414
Saturn 954
Savage Landor, Arnold Henry 879
Savajbulaq 395, 403
Saveh 396
scabbard 733; slide 733
Scarlet Ware 210
scepter 722
Scheil, Vincent 235ff., 239, 252
Schippmann, Klaus 893
Schlumberger, Daniel 881
Schmidt, Erich F. 8, 9, 83, 95, 164, 185, 205,
    393, 730, 977
scribes 265
sculptors 611
Scythia 577, 661
Scythians 328, 418, 423, 425, 435, 437, 451,
    548, 575, 723, 731; Amyrgian 630; see also
    Saka
Scythic 638
Seʿert, Chronicle of 841, 844
seal, cylinder 87, 140, 149, 209, 211ff., 235,
    246, 315, 330, 359, 401, 533, 539,
    631; Early Dynastic 209; legends 265;
    Piedmont style 209; royal-name 585;
    stamp 87, 130, 313, 316, 401, 533, 909ff.
Sealand 410, 483ff.
sealing, cylinder 146, 149, 207, 226, 307,
    464ff.; jar 111; practices 536; Sasanian
    909ff.; stamp 315, 913
Sebeos 842
secondary products 84
sedentarization 743
sedentism 212
Sefid Rud 396ff.
Sefid, phase 54; see also Chagha Sefid
sehkonj 885
Selene 742

Seleuc(e)ia, on-the-Erythraean Sea (Persian Gulf) 681, 699; on-the-Eulaeus 681ff., 695, 798ff.; on-the-Hedyphon 681, 695, 773; on-the-Tigris 681ff., 686, 691, 693, 733ff., 768ff., 771, 774, 784, 836; Synod of 807
Seleucids 690, 718ff., 767ff., 772, 781ff., 784ff., 795ff.
Seleucus I Nicator 677ff., 682ff., 704, 720ff.; II 680, 686, 796; IV 723
Seljuks 945
Semitic 409
semitization 263ff., 273ff.
Semnan 187, 782
sēn-murw 740, 928, 943, 948
Sennacherib 411, 450, 471, 481, 483, 548
Serakhs 732
Sercey, Count de 5
Sergiopolis 852
Sergius, St. 852
Šešpeš 504; *see also* Teispes, Čišpiš
Severus Alexander, Marcus Aurelius 827, 829, 842
sexagesimal, numerical system 247
Seyitömer Höyük 534
shabestan 897
shah (*šāh*) 783, 836
Shah Abad 93
Shah Maran-Daulatabad valley 65ff., 131, 133ff., 146, 148, 150
Shah Rokh 393
Shah Tepe 9, 185
Shahabad 447
Shahdad 10, 12, 131ff., 146, 149, 258, 304ff., 308ff., 312, 316, 431, 493
Shahi-Tump 131, 146, 305, 315
Shahnishin 204
Shahr-e Daqyanus 9
Shahr-e Kord plain 64
Shahr-e Qumis 730, 782, 943, 945
Shahr-e Sokhta 219, 239, 247, 305, 308, 310, 312ff., 493ff.
Shahrewar (Khshahrewar) 552
shahrewar 836
Shahrizor 443
Shahrud 56, 63, 181, 185
Shahryar 394

Shalmaneser III 352, 414, 452, 471, 548, 638; Fort 611
shamans 558
Shami 9, 697, 730, 741
Shamsabad, period 64, 126ff.; *see* Tal-e Bakun, Tal-e Jari, Tal-e Mushki
Shamshi-Adad (Šamši-Adad V) 222ff., 352, 444, 452, 471, 481, 548
Shamshirgah 396, 402
Shanidar 10, 31
Shapur, *see* Šābuhr
Shatt-i Siah Safalaki 208
Shaur, anticline 106
sheep 49ff., 52, 55, 59, 61, 62, 65, 66, 110, 138, 169, 255, 295, 538
Shehrizor 412
Sheikh-e Abad 50, 66
Shekaft-e Salman 228, 464, 466
shell 359
Sheplarpak, *see* Siwepalarhuppak
Sherabad Darya 630
Shikaft-e Gulgul 384, 451
Shilhaha 222
Shilhak-Inshushinak 228, 277
Shimashki (Šimaški) 219ff., 221ff., 266, 269ff., 271, 409, 431
Shimbar 698, 763ff.
Shimbishuk-Inshushinak 221
Shiraz 203, 535, 707
Shir-e Shian 82, 181
Shiruk-tuh 223
Shiwatoo 33
Shiz (Shīz) 898, 976; *see also* Takht-e Soleyman
Shogha-Teimuran 283, 285, 289
Shugu, temple of 221
Shu-ilishu 221
Shulgi 221
Shulistan 203
Shulme 415
Shur River 304
Shushan 5; *see also* Susa
Shusharra 410, 413
Shushtar 12, 107, 844, 981
Shu-Sin 221
Shutrukids 225, 228, 277ff.

Shutruk-Nahhunte (Šutruk-Nahhunte) 226ff., 274, 277, 380, 483, 489; II 278, 462, 480ff., 487
Siah Cheshme 177
Siberia 607, 733, 783
sickle 111; blades 63
Sidari 266
Sidon 599
Sidri 630
Sigrish 409
Sīh rōzag ī wuzurg 959; *xwurdag* 959
Silenus 694
Šilhaha 270ff., 274
Šilhak-Inšušinak 271, 487ff.
Silhazi 443
silk 943ff.; Road 736, 949
Silulu 415
Silulumesh 415
silver 194, 312, 397, 534, 598, 743, 824, 825, 837ff.; Sasanian vessels 787, 920ff.
Silvestre de Sacy, Antoine Isaac 643
Simias 667
Simineh Rud 329, 332
Šimpi-išhuk 266ff.
Simurrum 413
Simut-wartaš 271
Sinatruces 769ff.
Singara 843, 847
Sintashta 430
Sintashta-Petrovka-Arkhaim culture 429
Sipirmena 412
Sippar 228, 410, 415, 484
Siraf 9, 828, 978
al-Šīrāzī, Qutb al-Dīn 962
Sirius 551
Sirynx 681
Sistan 9, 18, 122, 131, 146, 418, 629, 769, 878, 893, 903; and Baluchistan, province 131, 304ff., 493
Si-um 415
Sivand, dam 12
Ṣiwepalarhuppak 223, 271, 274
Skudrians 420, 538
Skunkha 575
sluices 53
smelting 86, 137; *see also* copper, metallurgy
Smerdis 511, 566; *see also* Bardiya
snails, land 51
Socrates, of Constantinople 849
sodalities 429
soft ware 57, 134, 189
softstone 311; *see also* chlorite
Sogd 947
Sogdia/na 429, 623, 896, 946
Sogdian 423, 437, 781, 939, 968
Sogdians 548, 628
Soghun valley 65ff., 306, 497
Solduz, plain 169, 368
solstice, summer 958
soma 430ff., 559; *see also* haoma, hom
Sorsoreh 861, 868
Sos Höyük 164, 172, 173
Soteira 681
spāhbed 911
spāh-sālār 911
Spandārmad 552, 959
Sparta 663
Spasinou Charax 737; *see also* Characene, Mesene
specialization 84ff.
Spentā Ārmaiti 552ff.
Spenta-dāta 553
sphere, celestial 955ff.
spihr 956
spindle whorls 84
Spitamenes 678
Sraosha 551
stag 948
Stakhr, *see* Istakhr
Starij Kishman 628
Stark, Freya 205
stārō.karəmā 954
Stateira 674
Staxr 704, 912; *see also* Istakhr
Stein, Sir Marc Aurel 9, 95, 124, 165, 169, 205, 305, 307, 700, 705, 730, 879, 900, 945
Stephen, of Byzantium 629
storage 84
Strabo 640ff., 722, 730, 736
stucco 861, 868, 886, 901, 934
Suaš-takal 265
Subartu 223, 409
substrate languages 434
Sufis 946

ᵈŠU.GU 267
sukkal 224
sukkalmah 221ff., 224; Dynasty 269
Sumbar Valley 194
Sumbi 414
Sumerian 234, 255, 269, 274, 407ff., 412
Sumu-abum 274
Sungun 613
Su-people 222
Sūr Saxwan 911
Sura 851
Surk Dum-e Luri 205, 209, 211, 383, 386, 389, 464
Surkh, phase 54; *see also* Chagha Sefid
Surkhan Darya 630ff.
Susa 3, 5, 6, 9, 10, 12, 108, 114, 207ff., 225, 227, 236, 247, 249, 251, 255, 264, 267, 269, 274, 276ff., 280, 283, 314, 329, 408, 458ff., 460ff., 465, 471ff., 478ff., 481, 483, 486ff., 489, 503, 505, 512ff., 517ff., 520ff., 535, 572ff., 577ff., 601, 629ff., 640, 673ff., 681, 686, 690, 695ff., 730, 738, 740, 742, 772ff., 795ff., 797ff., 909, 978; I, period 112, 217ff.; II, period 139, 218, 283; III, period 145, 147, 218, 283ff., 289, 296; IV, period 219ff., 288; A 96, 112; Acropole 6, 112, 218ff., 233, 236ff., 272, 462; Acropole texts 488; Apadana 6, 228, 458ff., 462, 696, 518ff., 979; D 219; Donjon 218; Grande Tranchée 6; Shaur palace 696; Ville des Artisans 6, 980; Ville Royale 218ff., 221, 224ff., 268, 276ff., 458ff., 520, 695, 739, 979;
Susiana 56, 59, 97, 110, 408, 431, 433, 458, 486, 673ff., 679, 695ff., 721, 767, 783, 844, 980; a, phase 109; b, phase 109; c, phase 109, 111; d–e 111ff.
Susians 409
Šutruk-Nahhunte, *see* Shutruk-Nahhunte
Šutruru 467
Šutur-Nahhunte 466, 468, 481
Šū-turul 265
Suyd 910; *see also* Sogd, Sogdia/na
symbols, anchor 774; astral 774, 776, 830, 832ff.; *frawahr* 830; winged 586
Syncellus 843

syncretism 742
Syria 866, 945

Tabalians 419
Tabari (Ṭabarī) 809, 841
Tabaristan 826
Table, Royal 537
tables, astronomical 964ff.; anepigraphic 533; numerical 241ff.
tablets, Susa II 140, 146, 149, 151; Susa III 218
Tabriz 163, 356
Tabula Peutingeriana 625
tačara 520
Tacitus 641, 729, 734, 799
Tadrōs 809
Tahhi 466
Tahmaka 511
Taiga 428ff.
Taip 628
Tajik 434
Tajikistan 432, 434, 678, 896
Takab 328, 360
Takhirbaj 628; period 197
Takht Neshin 894
Takht-e Khan 205, 208ff.
Takht-e Rustam 511
Takht-e Sangin 631, 739
Takht-e Solayman 35, 556, 895ff., 898ff., 909, 976
Talashkan Tepe I 631
Tal-e Bakun 96, 113, 124ff., 127ff., 137ff., 255
Tal-e Gap 124ff., 127
Tal-e Gawd-e Rahim 707
Tal-e Ghazir 218, 219, 251, 467
Tal-e Iblis 65, 131ff., 306ff., 493ff.
Tal-e Jari 64ff., 124ff.
Tal-e Kureh 138, 140, 144, 287
Tal-e Malyan 10, 137ff., 208, 219, 239, 249, 255, 269, 272, 285ff., 287, 291ff., 297, 314, 408, 457, 470, 504, 700, 708
Tal-e Mushki 64
Tal-e Nokhodi 286
Tal-e Qarib 139ff.
Tal-e Shogha 10
Tal-e Teimuran 10, 470
Tal-e Vakilabad 286
Tal-e Zohak 286, 707

Talesh 396, 402
Tall Lelan 410
Tall Shemshara 410, 414
Tall-e Abu Chizan 111
Tall-e Zohar 470
Tall-i Takht, *see* Pasargadae
Taloqan 631
tamarisk (*Tamarix*) 52, 106
Tammaritu 481, 485ff., 489
Tammishe, wall 978
Tamukkan 535; *see also* Taokê, Tawwaj
Tangavan 204
Tang-e Bolaghi (Tang-e Bolāḡi) 68, 125, 523, 539ff., 705
Tang-e Boraq 786
Tang-e Butan 698, 763, 783
Tang-e Chowgan 866
Tang-e Hamamlan 205
Tang-e Jilu 787
Tang-e Sarvak 698, 742, 756ff., 772, 774, 783
Tang-e Shimbar 684
Tang-e sin Kazab 205
Tan-ruhurater 222, 270; II 275
Tansar, Letter of 911
Taokê 511, 535
Tappeh Asiab, *see* Tepe Asiab
Tappeh Mehr Ali, *see* Tepe Mehr Ali
Tappeh Rahmatabad, *see* Tepe Rahmatabad
Tappeh Sarab, *see* Tepe Sarab
taq-ahang 886
Taq-e Bustan (Tāq-e Bustān) 557, 694, 787, 848, 852, 862, 869ff., 873, 875, 929, 948ff.
Taq-e Mani 204
Taq-e Xosrow 896
taqeté 946
Tarditu-Aššur 450
Tarhan 95, 205
Tarkumuwa 767
Tashkent 910
tasūg/k 912
Tate, G.P. 879
Tattulban 386
taumā 567
Tauq Chai 414
Tavalli, Fereydoun 10
Tawarsa 209
Tawwaj 981ff.

tax 536, 967; poll 810
Taxāristān 910
Tazekand 174
Te'umman 481, 484, 487
Tedzhen river 437
Tehran 62, 80, 392, 396, 403, 423, 451, 738; plain 57; University of 10; Institute of Archaeology 11
Teispes 472, 504, 566, 639; *see also* Čišpiš, Šešpeš
Teispids 567, 569
Tell 'Umar, *see* Seleucia-on-the-Tigris
Tell Abraq 308, 313
Tell Abu Fanduweh 112
Tell Abu Salabikh 209
Tell Abu Sha'af 909
Tell Agrab 207
Tell Ahmad al-Hattu 207ff.
Tell al-Hiba 210
Tell Aqar 481
Tell Asmar 207, 270
Tell el-'Oueili 109, 113
Tell es-Sotto 61
Tell Gubba 207
Tell Razuk 207
Tell-e Atashi 56
Telloh 221
Telul eth–Thalathat 61
Telyab 205
temple, fire 560, 626, 868, 883, 892ff., 901ff., 978
Temti-Agun 271, 274
Temti-halki 272, 275
Tepe Abdul Hosein 51, 52, 66, 93
Tepe Ali Kosh 52, 54, 55, 59ff., 105
Tepe Aliabad 207, 209
Tepe Arastu 63
Tepe Asiab 10, 93
Tepe Baba Jan 210, 212, 365, 379, 382ff., 453
Tepe Bandebal 108
Tepe Bandykhan 631
Tepe Bazgir 197
Tepe Bormi 464, 467; *see also* Tol-e Bormi
Tepe Chalow 197
Tepe Chena A 97
Tepe Damghani 188
Tepe Djamshidi 379

Tepe Ebrahimabad 62, 81
Tepe Faisala 206
Tepe Farukhabad 110, 113, 207ff., 218
Tepe Gaz Tavila (R37) 65
Tepe Ghabrestan 81, 86, 87
Tepe Ghenil 50, 52
Tepe Giljar 165
Tepe Giyan 8, 10, 94, 96, 206ff., 211, 329, 332, 384, 446, 452, 454
Tepe Guran 50, 51, 52, 53, 58, 93, 205, 211ff., 380
Tepe Hissar 80ff., 87, 181ff., 185, 187, 189, 192, 194, 196, 312, 329, 393, 395, 403
Tepe Hoseynabad 185
Tepe Jaffarabad 108ff., 111
Tepe Jalaliyeh 398
Tepe Jalyan 287ff., 291
Tepe Jamshidabad 397
Tepe Jamshidi 205, 211ff.
Tepe Jarali 207
Tepe Jowi 108
Tepe Kazabad, A, B and C 206
Tepe Khargush 185
Tepe Ma'murin 398
Tepe Mehr Ali 125, 126, 138, 140, 143
Tepe Mohammadabad 395
Tepe Mushalan 395
Tepe Musiyan 110, 114
Tepe Nurabad (Luristan) 206
Tepe Nush-e Jan 365, 396, 418, 451ff., 896
Tepe Ozbaki 219, 239, 247, 395, 418, 453
Tepe Pahlavan 64
Tepe Pardis 63, 84
Tepe Qazemi 50
Tepe Rahmatabad 56, 69, 129
Tepe Sabz 110ff.
Tepe Sagzabad 81, 395
Tepe Sarab 10, 93
Tepe Siah 96
Tepe Sialk 8, 10, 11, 62, 63, 80ff., 87, 140, 238, 242, 247, 329, 393ff., 398ff., 402ff.
Tepe Sofalin 219, 239, 241ff., 247, 249
Tepe Tula'i 56, 59, 105
Tepe Yahya 65ff., 131ff., 219, 239, 241, 249, 304, 306, 308ff., 312, 314, 316, 431, 493ff.
Tepe Zagheh 11, 62, 81, 83

Tepe-ye Hegmataneh 692; *see also* Hamadan
Tepti-ahar 2225, 75
Tepti-Huban-Inšušinak 484, 487ff.
Terash-e Farhad 870
Terqa 410
tetradrachms 722, 734
Texier, Charles 602ff.
textiles 359, 534, 598; Sasanian 943ff.
Thaj 737
Thebes 448
themes, Dionysiac 928
Themistocles, 21st Letter of 648
Theodosius II 808, 852
Theopator 768
Theophylact Simocatta 852
Thespius 677
Thevenot, Jean 4
Thiloua 737
Thoas 681, 683, 798
Thrace 577, 678
Thracians 420
Thūra-vāhara 553
Thwāsha 551
tiara, satrap's 724ff.; upright 724ff.
Tien Shan 430
Tierkampfszene, see combat, animal
Tiglath-pileser I 401, 413, 449, 453; III 435, 443ff., 451, 482, 548
Tigranes I 769
Tikunani 410
Til-Aššuri 443
Til Tuba 481, 484
Tilia, Giuseppe 605
Tillya Tepe 733, 736
Tilmun 411
Timarchus 680, 685
Timon 683
tin 208
Tīr 784
Tīragān 553, 961
Tirazziš 535
Tīri 556
Tiribazos, of Lydia/Taros 767
Tiridates 767, 799; III 772
Tirigan 414
Tīrī-pāta 553
Tīriya 961

Ṭīrūdeh 913
Tishtriya (Tištrya) 551, 553, 961
titulature 568, 722, 728, 767, 805ff., 845
Toc/kharian 415, 428, 433, 968
Tocharians 432
tokens 59, 240ff.
Tol-e Bashi 64, 65, 124
Tol-e Bormi 472; *see also* Tepe Bormi
Tol-e Khandaq 708
Tol-e Nurabad 124ff., 138ff., 286, 469, 706
Tol-e Peytul 297, 408
Tol-e Pir 124
Tol-e Rahmatabad 125; *see also* Tepe Rahmatabad
Tol-e Spid 125ff., 137ff., 286, 288, 469, 523, 706
Tomb-e Bot 700
tombs 209ff.; royal 227; *see also* burials
tools, bone 52
tortoise 66
Tōz 807
Trajan 848
Transcaucasus 175
Transeuphrates 506
Transpotamians 419
Traxiana 770
trays, low-sided 150ff., 171
Triangle Ware 368
trident 888
Trigonella 54
Tugrya 435
Tukrish (Tukriš) 415, 431, 435
Tukulti-Ninurta II 413
Tulul al-Ukhaidir 896
Tum-e Podu 708
Tupliaš 277
Tūr 807
Tūrān 807
Turanians 807
Tureng Tepe 9, 63, 181, 185, 189, 194, 196ff., 624, 782, 893, 909, 978
Tūrestān 910
Turfan 945, 947
Turkestan, Chinese 415, 785, 787, 807
Turkmen, Yomut 184
Turkmenistan 188, 194, 257, 315, 430, 556, 623ff., 627, 782, 787, 949
Turks 924; Western 851

turtles 54
Turukku 413
Tus 12
Tuttul 410
Tyche 696, 770
Tychsen, Olav Gerhard 643
Tylos 679, 737

Ubaid, period 96, 113; pottery 109
Uč-Depe 628
Ukraine 423, 429, 920
Ulai (Karkheh, Eulaeus) river 228
Ulanbulak Saj 630
Ulfan 774
Ultan Qalasi 983
Ulug Depe 418, 624
Umm Dabaghiyah 61
Ummanunu 488
Unknown King, Persid 720
Untash-Napirisha (Untaš-napiriša) 226ff., 277
Upper Satrapies 678, 680ff., 684, 691, 693
Ur 208, 221, 308, 462; Seal Impression Strata 308; Third Dynasty of 220ff., 268ff., 414
Ural mountains 429
Uralic 428
Urartian 407, 647, 649
Urartians 368
Urartu 352ff., 363, 415, 442, 444
Urmia, Lake 9, 18, 34, 57, 80, 163ff., 177, 328, 332, 352, 360, 407, 415, 443, 638, 857; Ware 331
Ur-Namma/u 266, 414
Ur-Ningišzida 274
Ursi 411
Urtak 471ff., 484
Uruk 114, 206, 218, 233, 240, 242ff., 247; Late, period 140, 283; Late, pottery 171
Urumqi 945
Ururu, bronze 465
Ushidam, Mt. 880, 903
Ushnu-Solduz, valley 57, 60, 165, 328, 330, 368
'Uthman 977
Utians 625
Utu-hengal 414
Uxians 673
Uzbekistan 627, 732, 949

Vadfradad I, III, IV 776
Vahyazdāta 569
Valerian 557, 843ff., 866ff.
Van, Lake 329, 640
Vandals 850
Vanden Berghe, Louis 10, 95, 124, 212, 394, 708
Vani 607
Varaksha 944
Varamin 396
Vardanes I 773; II 771
Varhragn (Varhrān) 784
Varizard 204
Varuṇa 430
vaults, barrel 885, 888, 894
Vedic, texts 424ff., 432ff.
Veliran 738
Vendidad 903
verethragan 903
Verethragna 684, 742, 829, 830
vessels, silver 920
vetch 110; milk 59
vetchling 110
Vīdēvdād 425, 434, 549, 554, 628, 910
Ville des Artisans, *see* Susa
Visai Bagā 553, 559
Vištāspa 279, 566
Vitis 298
Vivana 630
Viyaxana 553
Vologases (Bisotun) 556, 754, 782; I 742, 771, 783; II 693; III 755; IV 784; V 771; VI 772; king of kings 693
Vonones I 770

Wadfradad I 720, 722ff.; II 720; III 720; IV 720
Wadi el-Daliyeh 780
Wahbarz 720, 722ff.; *see also* Oborzus
Wahīxšahr 704
Wahman Yašt 913
Wahnām 809
Wahuman 552
Wahunām 557
Walāxš 817, 830ff., 832, 835ff; *see also* Vologases
Warahrān I 558, 832ff., 873; II 558, 815, 829ff., 834, 861, 867ff., 923ff.; III 557, 815; IV 817ff., 829ff., 832, 834ff., 873ff.; V 807, 818, 827, 829, 836ff., 849, 927; VI 836; Čōbīn 810ff., 851, 870
Warāz, family 811
Warhragn 781
Warhrān 781
Warthragn 556; *see also* Verethragna
Warwasi 34, 39, 45
wāspuhragan-framādār 914
waterfowl 51, 61
weaponry 87, 359, 387, 400, 467
weaving 946ff.
Wēh Antiōk Šābuhr 844
Wēh Antiōk Xosrow 851
weights 824ff., 825, 938
Werod 760; *see also* Orodes
wheat (*Triticum* aestivum) 49ff., 59, 110, 138, 169; bread 61, 65; einkorn (*Triticum monococcum*) 55, 64; emmer (*Triticum dicoccum*) 51, 54, 61, 63, 64; free-threshing 63; hard (*Triticum durum*) 55
wheels, wooden 219
Widēwdād 960; *see also* Vīdēvdād
wihēzagīg 960
Wikander, Stig 893
willow 52
wine 932, 935ff.
Wiržān 910
wispuhragān-framādār 914
Wistāhm 811, 829ff.
Wizīdagīhā ī Zādsparam 913
wood 106, 528
wool 84, 106
worms, starred 954
wreath 934

Xanthos (Xanthos) 666, 780
Xenophon 658, 660, 663
Xerxes I 512, 514, 518, 520, 537, 549, 552, 555, 558, 560, 578, 582, 630, 639, 658, 660ff., 671ff., 673, 701, 718, 959
Xešt 913
Xinjiang 423, 427, 437, 944
Xīr 913
Xosrow I 805, 809ff., 818, 828ff., 850ff., 898, 911, 962ff., 978; II 558, 694, 806, 810ff., 818, 826ff., 829ff., 830, 833ff., 835ff., 842, 851ff., 861, 868, 870ff., 873ff., 911, 925, 927, 948; III 816, 829, 830, 831, 832; IV 816

INDEX 1021

Xosrow-Ādur-Anāhīd 560
Xosrow-Šābuhr 560
xvarrh 928, 933
Xwarāsān 911; *see also* Khorasan
Xwarbarān 911
xwarnah 903
xwarrah 812, 836, 912ff.

Yafteh Cave 38ff., 45
Yaghnobi 423
Yam Tepe 188
Yan Tepe 83
Yanik Tepe 60, 165ff., 174ff., 336ff.
Yaqut 396
Yarim Tepe 63, 185, 624
Yarla 415
Yarlaganda 415
Yarlagash 415
Yarlan/gab 415
yasna 559, 961; *Haptanghāiti* 549
Yašt 549, 961
Yaz Depe 625; tradition 630
yazd 557
Yazdgerd I 807ff., 827, 829, 830, 832, 833, 849; II 805, 807ff., 833ff., 849, 965; III 814, 828, 829, 831, 841, 852, 964; III, era of 966ff.
yazishn-gah 895
Yemen 851
Yenesei, plains 429
Yeneseian 428, 433
Yezdegerd b. Šābuhr 964; *see also* Yazdgerd I
Yima 554
Young, T. Cuyler, Jr. 3, 330, 400
Younger Dryas 19
Yüechi (Yueji) 429, 732
yurt 419

Z'tr 415
Zab, Lower 413; Upper 329
Zabol 878ff.
Zadracarta 624
Zagheh, *see* Tepe Zagheh
Zagros, mountains 24, 25, 30, 32, 34, 49, 106, 121, 204, 272, 286, 304, 407, 411, 417ff., 442ff.
Zagurae 843

Zaitha 848
Zamaspes 799; *see also* Zhāmāspa
Zamua 412ff., 417; Sea of Inner 414
Zamyad Yasht 903
Zand 742
Zandane 946
Zandanījī 946ff.
Zandīgs 558
Zanjan 62, 743
Zapshali (Zabshali) 409
Zaranj 625
Zarathus/htra, *see* Zoroaster
Zarde Savar 211
Zarians 487
Zarin 625ff.
Zarineh Rud 329, 332
Zarlagab 415
zarrbed 914ff.
Zarzi 30
Zarzian 30, 38, 40ff., 45
Zavyeh 37
zebu (*Bos indicus*) 316
Zendan-e Suleiman 353ff.
Zeribar (Zeribor), Lake 18ff., 25, 329, 412, 414
Zeus 768, 954; Megistos 677, 719; Oromasdes 556
Zhāmāspa 553; *see also* Zamaspes
Zhob 629
Zig/k/qirtu 415
Zīg 964ff.; *ī Šahriyārān* 965
ziggurat 227, 276
Zimaga 415
Zimri-Lim, of Mari 223
Zivya (Ziwiye/h) 10, 366ff., 415
Zodiac 954ff.
Zoes 682
Zohreh, plain 110
Zoroaster 425, 434, 547ff., 554, 562ff., 903
Zoroastrianism 424ff., 547ff., 626, 630, 719, 724, 742, 785, 786, 809ff., 829, 848, 865, 869, 878ff., 887, 893ff., 895, 901ff., 928
Zoroastrians 780, 787, 980
Zosimus 847
Zranka 548, 629
Zruwā 553
Zurwan 551

Lightning Source UK Ltd.
Milton Keynes UK
UKHW032013170519
342860UK00005B/188/P